P9-CRF-020

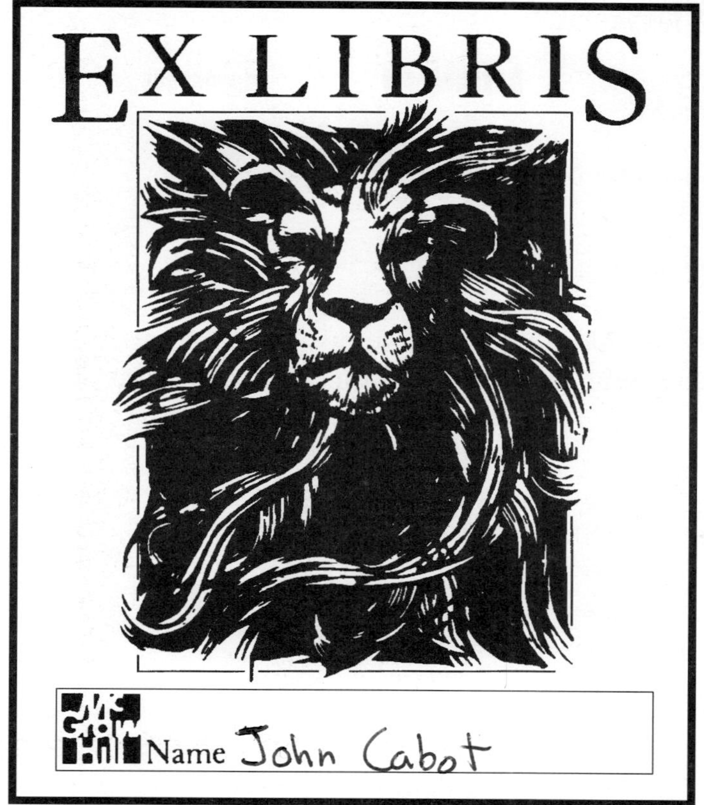
EX LIBRIS
McGraw Hill
Name John Cabot

NOTE TO STUDENTS

STUDY GUIDE
for use with
FUNDAMENTALS OF MARKETING
by R. David Nowell

ISBN 0-07-560436-1

Make studying a breeze! Use this Study Guide as a supplement to the text to ensure that you have a full understanding of marketing theory and its application. This new edition of the *Study Guide for use with Fundamentals of Marketing*, Eighth Canadian Edition, is tailored to meet your study needs.

Get your copy from your campus bookstore or ask them to order one for you and make your study time worthwhile!

Fundamentals of MARKETING

Eighth Canadian Edition

CANADIAN SUPPLEMENTARY TITLES AVAILABLE

Study Guide for use with Fundamentals of Marketing 0-07-560436-1

Marketing in Motion: Fundamentals of Marketing Interactive
(Network Version) 0-07-560367-5
(CD-ROM) 0-07-560368-3

Understanding Consumer Behaviour (Peter, Olson, & Rosenblatt) 0-256-17048-7

Canadian Retailing (Mason et al.) 0-256-19521-8

Canadian Marketing Cases (McDougall & Weinberg) 0-07-551370-6

Editor's Choice (McDougall & Weinberg) 0-390-14706-0

Fundamentals of

Eighth Canadian Edition

MONTROSE S. SOMMERS
Ryerson Polytechnic University

JAMES G. BARNES
Memorial University of Newfoundland

WILLIAM J. STANTON
University of Colorado – Boulder

MICHAEL J. ETZEL
University of Notre Dame

BRUCE J. WALKER
University of Missouri – Columbia

Toronto New York Burr Ridge Bangkok Bogotá Caracas
Lisbon London Madrid Mexico City Milan New Delhi
Seoul Singapore Sydney Taipei

McGraw-Hill Ryerson Limited
A Subsidiary of The **McGraw-Hill** *Companies*

FUNDAMENTALS OF MARKETING
Eighth Canadian Edition
Sommers Barnes Stanton Etzel Walker

ISBN: 0-07-560067-6

1 2 3 4 5 6 7 8 9 10 GTC 7 6 5 4 3 2 1 0 9 8

Care has been taken to trace ownership of copyright material contained in this text; however, the publisher will welcome any information that enables them to rectify any reference or credit for subsequent editions.

Senior Sponsoring Editor: Evelyn Veitch
Associate Editor: Elke Price/Lenore Gray Spence
Production Editor: Geraldine Kikuta
Copy Editor: John Eerkes
Production Co-ordinator: Nicla Dattolico
Designer: David Murphy/ArtPlus Design Consultants Limited
Cover Design: ArtPlus Design Consultants Limited
Cover Illustration/Photo: Superstock
Page Make-up: Heather Brunton/ArtPlus Design Consultants Limited
Typeface(s): Bembo, Frutiger
Printer: Transcontinental Group

Canadian Cataloguing in Publication Data

Main entry under title:

Fundamentals of marketing

8th Canadian ed.
Includes index.
ISBN 0-07-560067-6

1. Marketing. 2. Marketing — Canada. I. Sommers, Montrose S.

HF5415.S745 1998 658.8 C97-932656-7

Printed and bound in Canada

DEDICATED TO

Jessie, Annie, and Michael

Jennifer, Stephanie, and Karen

ABOUT THE AUTHORS

Montrose Sommers is Adjunct Professor in the School of Business Management of Ryerson Polytechnic University. He received his B. Comm. from the University of British Columbia, his M.B.A. from Northwestern University and his D.B.A. from the University of Colorado. Dr. Sommers has been a consultant to private- and public-sector organizations involved in petroleum marketing, financial services, telecommunications, various retailing specializations, marketing research, and advertising. His teaching background is extensive; he has worked with Bachelor, Master, and Ph.D. students at the Universities of British Columbia, Texas, Hawaii, Toronto, York, Nairobi in Kenya, Witwatersrand in South Africa, Huazhong and Tianjin in China, and the LSE in Great Britain. Dr. Sommers has also served on the editorial boards of the *Journal of Marketing*, the *Journal of International Management and Organizations*, and the *Journal of the Service Industries*.

Jim Barnes is Professor of Marketing at Memorial University of Newfoundland. Dr. Barnes received his B. Comm. and B.A. degrees from Memorial, his M.B.A. from Harvard Business School, and his Ph.D. in Marketing from the University of Toronto. He has been a member of the faculty at Memorial since 1968 and served as Dean from 1978 to 1988. He has held visiting positions at Queen's University and the University of Bath in England. Dr. Barnes has served as a consultant in Marketing and Service Quality to numerous companies in North America and Europe. He is co-founder and Chairman of the Board of Omnifacts Research Limited, the largest full-service marketing and survey research company in Atlantic Canada. He has served on the boards of directors of a number of national organizations, including the Institute of Canadian Bankers. He is currently a director of several Canadian firms, including NewTel Enterprises, the Bristol Group of Companies, and McGraw-Hill Ryerson.

William J. Stanton is Professor Emeritus of Marketing at the University of Colorado — Boulder. He received his Ph.D. in Marketing from Northwestern University, where he was elected to Beta Gamma Sigma. He has worked in business and has taught in several management development programs for marketing executives. He has served as a consultant for various business organizations and has engaged in research projects for the U.S. federal government. Professor Stanton also has lectured at universities in Europe, Asia, Mexico, and New Zealand.

A co-author of the leading text in sales management, Professor Stanton has also published several journal articles and monographs. *Fundamentals of Marketing* has been translated into Spanish, and separate editions have been adapted (with co-authors) for Canada, Italy, Australia, and South Africa. In a survey of marketing educators, Professor Stanton was voted one of the leaders in marketing thought, and he is listed in *Who's Who in America* and *Who's Who in the World*.

Michael J. Etzel received his Ph.D. in Marketing from the University of Colorado in 1970. Since 1980, he has been a Professor of Marketing at the University of Notre Dame. He also has been on the faculties at Utah State University and the University of Kentucky. He has held visiting faculty positions at the University of South Carolina and the University of Hawaii. In 1990, he was a Fulbright Fellow at the University of Innsbruck, Austria, and in 1994 he directed and taught in the University of Notre Dame overseas program in Fremantle, Australia.

Professor Etzel has taught marketing courses from the introductory through the doctoral level. He is also a frequent presenter in executive training programs.

His research, primarily in marketing management and buyer behaviour, has appeared in the *Journal of Marketing*, *Journal of Marketing Research*, *Journal of Consumer Research*, and other publications. He is the co-author of another college-level text, *Retailing Today*.

He has been active in many aspects of the American Marketing Association at the local and national levels, most notably serving as Chairman of the Board in 1996–1997.

Bruce J. Walker is Professor of Marketing and Dean of the College of Business and Public Administration at the University of Missouri — Columbia. Professor Walker received his undergraduate degree in economics from Seattle University and his master's and Ph.D. degrees in business from the University of Colorado.

Professor Walker was a member of the marketing faculties at the University of Kentucky and then at Arizona State University. He moved to the University of Missouri in 1990.

Dr. Walker has taught a variety of courses, including principles of marketing. His research, focussing primarily on franchising, marketing channels, and survey-research methods, has been published in the *Journal of Marketing, California Management Review, Journal of Marketing Research*, and other periodicals. He has also co-edited or co-authored conference proceedings and books, including *Retailing Today*.

Dr. Walker has been involved with both the American Marketing Association and the Western marketing Educators Association. He served as vice president of AMA's Education Division and president of WMEA. Currently, he is a trustee for the International Franchise Association's Education Foundation.

Contents in Brief

Contents

List of Cases

Preface

TO THE STUDENT

Ask yourself the question: "What does marketing have to do with me?" We think the answer is: "A lot more than you would think!" When you finish reading this book, we know you will agree.

Marketing is an integral part of all of our lives. A surprising amount of time is taken up by our efforts to market something — our ideas, our skills, our experiences, ourselves — to others. And, of course, others spend a lot of time marketing to us. Whether you are a student, a small business owner, a lawyer, a professor, or an accountant doesn't make any difference, you are engaged in marketing. The challenge is to do it well and that requires an understanding of what marketing is and how to perform it.

But there is more to modern marketing than learning what it involves. Much of the excitement of marketing is created by the context in which it occurs. Take the field of communications as an example. Consider how the recent developments in electronic mail, fibre optics, the Internet, cellular phones, and fax machines are changing our lives. Then multiply that impact by the changes in other areas, such as in manufacturing, transportation, entertainment, financial services, and agriculture. Add to this the globalization that the new communication technology enables. Evidence of the rate of technological change and the shrinking of distances is all around us. We are faced with new challenges, large and small, domestic and international, and they seem to come at us almost daily. But every change, every challenge, from whatever the source, creates new marketing opportunities.

What does this mean for marketers? In some respects their jobs won't change. They will still decide what products and services to offer, set prices they think customers will consider to be good value for their money, provide products where customers can conveniently find them, and design promotional information to inform and persuade buyers. At the same time, in today's highly dynamic environment, marketing and other managers will be faced with more new situations than ever before. They will have access to more information than did their predecessors, and they will have to learn how to separate the essential from the interesting and how to use it effectively. They will have more strategic alternatives from which to select, but the cost of selecting the wrong one will be greater. They will be pursuing smaller market segments with products that have shorter lives. They will face a changing mix of competitors. In short, marketers will be operating in a faster-paced, higher-risk environment.

What does this mean for you? Your career is beginning during a time of unprecedented challenge and change. You could translate this into success. To make the most of this opportunity, you need an understanding of contemporary marketing and how it works in the dynamic world of today. The objective of this new edition of *Fundamentals of Marketing* is to help you gain that understanding.

SPECIAL FEATURES OF FUNDAMENTALS OF MARKETING

Since 1971, when it was first published, *Fundamentals of Marketing* has been a leader — easy and enjoyable to read, practical and comprehensive in its content and orientation, full of current topical information, and examples and illustrations of marketing as it is "best practiced" in Canada and around the world by leading Canadian and Canadian-based global firms, large and small. This eighth edition not only continues this tradition, but also meets the challenges we face in our ever-changing environment.

We present marketing as a total system of business actions carried out by managers in individual organizations in the context of the larger economy and society as a whole. Regardless of whether managers are employed by a business or nonprofit organization, are providers of goods or services, or are doing business domestically or globally, they need to understand certain fundamentals of marketing.

We share those fundamentals with you through the framework of the marketing management process. An organization first sets objectives, taking into consideration the environmental forces and competitors that influence its efforts. The managers then select target markets and build a marketing program to achieve those objectives. The four elements integrated by managers in designing a marketing program — product, price, distribution, and promotion — are at the heart of marketing as is working through people for successful implementation of marketing programs. Finally, an organization evaluates its performance and makes adjustments to its marketing strategy.

To help you understand and appreciate this process, we have provided explanations that are accompanied by many current, real-life examples of large and small Canadian firms and a variety of interesting boxed inserts, we call Marketing At Work Files, that illustrate how firms actually implement the ideas you are studying in the Canadian and the global marketplace. We have highlighted the importance of people and their contribution to the development and delivery of marketing programs.

Now, turn to Chapter 1 and start discovering that marketing is much more than you thought!

TO THE INSTRUCTOR

Revising a successful book is a delicate process. It is essential that new developments and material be incorporated into a revised edition and the presentation be lively and engaging. At the same time, many of the features that have been eminently successful over time should be retained. We have worked hard to maintain this balance by updating and revising the book while preserving the organization. This book has always been noted by students as an enjoyable "fun" book to read compared with others. It has been noted by instructors as being well structured, comprehensive, and containing more Canadian perspectives, information, illustrations and examples than others.

The book is divided into seven parts to reflect the marketing management process.

Part One: The Field of Marketing and Its Dynamic Environment Serves as an introduction and includes chapters on the marketing environment and strategic marketing planning.

Part Two: Target Markets Devoted to the analysis and selection of target markets (both consumer and business-to-business markets. It also includes a detailed treatment of the very important strategic concepts of market segmentation and positioning, and the collection and use of market information.

Part Three: Products and Services Topics related to the product are discussed with separate chapters on product planning and development, product mix strategies, and branding and packaging. There is also a special chapter on the marketing and delivery of services.

Part Four: Price The choice of a price and the adjustments made are handled in a price determination and a pricing policies and strategies chapter.

Part Five: Distribution The nature of channels of distribution and their management, the wholesaling and logistics operations, and retailing institutions and their dynamics and management are discussed in separate chapters.

Part Six: Marketing Communications Chapters in this part cover effective communication to markets with a focus on the nature of promotional programs, personal selling and its management, and the management of advertising, sales promotion, and public relations.

Part Seven: Managing the Marketing Effort This concluding part presents specialized discussions on international marketing and global issues in marketing management, marketing in not-for-profit organizations, and the issues associated with successful marketing implementation. The concluding chapter looks at the performance of marketing and presents our view of future developments.

Three cases follow each of the seven parts, for a total of twenty-one cases. Of these, eleven are new, three have been up-dated and revised, and six have been retained in their original form owing to their effectiveness, timeliness, and popularity.

WHAT'S NEW AND IMPROVED IN THIS EDITION

Throughout the text, developments that reflect a strong information age orientation consistent with the rapid changes in communications technology that are increasingly affecting Canadian and global marketing have been explored in an integrated fashion.

Coverage emphasizes the increased role of marketing personnel in developing consumer trust and confidence to achieve the successful implementation of marketing programs that deliver quality products and services.

A significant new addition to the text is *Marketing Math: An Interactive Tutorial* by R. David Nowell. Contained on a disk found in the back of each text, this interactive tutorial will guide students through the mathematics involved in marketing.

This eighth edition maintains the strengths of the past with every chapter having been updated to include:

- New developments and emphases such as marketing on the Internet, value pricing, power centres, market fragmentation, market response systems, mass customization, Quality ISO 9000 standards, and other evolving topics.
- All new examples, illustrations, and features of marketing today and for the near future.
- New chapter opening topical vignette.
- New Marketing At Work Files to illustrate new developments and successful implementations.
- Web site addresses for companies and organizations mentioned in the chapter to enable students to follow up, either for their own interest or as part of an assignment.

TEACHING AND LEARNING SUPPORT

Each chapter ends with

- A chapter summary.
- A list of key terms and concepts with chapter page references.
- Questions and Problems designed to help students discover how to analyze issues and make applications based on the chapter discussion.

- Hands-on Marketing assignments that require the student to get out of the classroom and interact with customers or marketers.

TEACHING AND LEARNING SUPPLEMENTS

For the Instructor

Instructor's Resource CD-ROM The new Instructor's Resource CD-ROM for *Fundamentals of Marketing* contains the Instructor's Manual, PowerPoint® Overheads, Test Bank, and Lecture Launchers.

Instructor's Manual The instructor's manual uses a fresh approach that is based on the practical needs of instructors who want to help the students learn in the way that works best for the students. The goal is to help students learn more effectively by providing instructor's with strategy suggestions (such as World Wide Web activities, group work, and case studies) to encourage learning in the context of an Introductory Marketing course. Case solutions for the text cases are also provided.

PowerPoint® New to this edition, this software includes a set of over 300 slides. The slides include point-form summaries of key concepts discussed in the text.

Test Bank The test bank comprises multiple choice and true/false questions, as well as caselettes — short, current case descriptions with accompanying multiple choice questions. The 2,200 questions in the testbank are coded to identify the type — concept, definition, or application.

Lecture Launchers The lecture launchers, which are also in PowerPoint® format, provide an overview of the key points in the chapters.

Marketing in Motion: Fundamentals of Marketing Interactive This new CD-ROM gives students an exciting way to explore Introductory Marketing. It is referenced directly to the Eighth edition of *Fundamentals of Marketing*. Complete with animation, sound, and video, the interactive student tutorial segment presents review material, quizzes, and feedback to promote independent study, freeing class time for discussion and analysis. Combined with an easy-to-use navigation bar and built-in glossary, the student has full control in this learning environment.

For the instructor, the comprehensive class management system can be used for any size class. Marketing in Motion allows the instructor to "level the playing field" for all students, bringing them up to speed on essential marketing principles. Instructors can effortlessly track student progress and grades, generate reports, monitor lab hours, and assign and mark quizzes automatically. Network version also available.

Video Cases and Video Guide This collection of video cases correspond with selected companies profiled in the Case sections of the text. They feature a variety of organizations and marketing topics. Sugggestions for their use are provided in the video guide.

Transparency Acetates A comprehensive colour transparency program is available to enhance lectures and class discussions.

For the Students

Study Guide by R. David Nowell. This useful study guide provides guidelines for analyzing marketing cases, chapter goals, chapter summaries, key terms and concepts, self-test questions (true-false, multiple choice, matching, and sentence completion), problems and applications questions, and interesting real world cases and articles related to chapter concepts. There is a new focus on applied, hands-on marketing exercises. A new feature is the emphasis on the World Wide Web as it relates to Marketing in the student's world.

***Fundamentals of Marketing* Web Site** Students and instructors can visit this web site to gain access to a variety of aides and support, including cases and Marketing at Work Files.

ACKNOWLEDGEMENTS

Through eight editions of this book, many people have made important contributions. These include students, colleagues, clients, marketing managers in Canadian firms, and instructors at many universities and colleges. All have provided insights and commentary on the Canadian marketing scene and the teaching and learning of marketing. We sincerely thank them for their insight and aid.

We wish to acknowledge in particular those research and editorial assistants who contributed to the essential research and material preparation process necessary for this revision. Editorial and material preparation assistance was provide in a most able fashion by Jan Dicks in St. John's and Judith Coates in Toronto. Special research assistance was provided by Jill Cavanagh. Judy Cumby of Memorial University authored several of the cases in this edition, and John Pippy, also of Memorial, assisted in identifying relevant web sites. We are also indebted to the business and other executives who allowed us to write cases on their companies or organizations.

Another group that was instrumental in the preparation of this book was the group of reviewers used by our publisher. These include the following colleagues: May Aung, *University of Guelph*, Neil Beattie and Barbara Eddy, *Sheridan College*, Angus N. (Gus) Cameron, *Fanshawe College*, Malcolm Howe, *Niagara College*, Bob Jershy, *St. Clair College*, Lea Katsanis, *Concordia University*, Stephen Lee, *Algonquin College*, Morie Shacker, *BCIT*, Donald Shiner, *Mount Saint Vincent University*, and Brock Smith, *University of Victoria*.

One colleague in particular requires special mention. David Nowell of Sheridan College. In addition to reviewing the manuscript, David made a significant contribution in the preparation of the supplementary materials for this edition of the text.

Finally, we would like to acknowledge with much appreciation the support and cooperation we receive from the staff of McGraw-Hill Ryerson. We are particularly grateful to Evelyn Veitch, our Senior Sponsoring Editor, who kept both her team and us focussed on the task. We owe special thanks to Lenore Gray, Elke Price, and Geraldine Kikuta who provided important assistance and information and helped us ensure that this edition will meet the goals and objectives of all those involved.

Montrose S. Sommers
James G. Barnes

Part One

The Field of Marketing and Its Dynamic Environment

An overview of the new marketing, the rapidly changing marketing environment, and the essentials of strategic planning in marketing

Marketing is dynamic, challenging, and rewarding. Sometimes it may be frustrating. But it is never dull! Welcome to the part of the business or organization where everything comes together and finally happens — the place where ideas, planning, and execution get the acid test of market acceptance or rejection.

Chapter 1 explains what the new view of marketing is, how it continues to develop, and its importance to society and you personally. Chapter 2 discusses the environmental forces that shape a marketing program. Then, Chapter 3 discusses the management process in marketing and introduces the basic elements of strategic marketing planning.

CHAPTER 1 GOALS

"What is marketing?" Chapter 1 answers this question — and the answer may surprise you. After studying this chapter, you should have an understanding of:

- The relationship between exchange and marketing.
- How marketing applies to business and nonbusiness situations.
- The evolution of marketing.
- Services and relationship marketing.
- An understanding of the factors that drive customer satisfaction.
- The difference between selling and marketing.
- The marketing concept.
- The impact of quality, service, and ethics in modern marketing.
- Marketing's role in the global economy, in Canada's economy, in an individual organization, and in your life.

R O Y A L B A N K F I N A N C I A L G R O U P

NEWS

BEYOND THE TRADITIONAL BANK

How we've changed to meet your growing needs. See Page 2.

HELPING YOU UNDERSTAND HOW YOUR BANK WORKS • ISSUE 4, VOLUME IV, MAY 23, 1997

How you measure leadership

We used to be Canada's leading bank. But thanks to you, now we're Canada's leading financial institution

Over the past 15 years, the financial needs and expectations of Canadians have grown dramatically. And so have our capabilities to meet them. We've grown from a traditional bank offering primarily loans and deposits, to a full-service financial group providing mutual funds, investment management, brokerage, trust, insurance, custody, and much more.

How many people invested in mutual funds 25 years ago?

Before the 1980s, most Canadians had never heard of mutual funds, had never bought stocks, and rarely used investment management. But as Canada began to deregulate financial services and allow banks into these once exclusive domains, consumers were able to access these types of products more conveniently and cost-effectively than ever before.

One good thing leads to another

This "democratization" of financial services changed the face of Canadian banking. In order to meet consumer demand for these new services, banks reinvented themselves as full-service financial providers with more products and more knowledgeable staff than they previously offered as "traditional" banks.

	RBFG		Top Competitor	
Leading in overall performance*	**$ millions**	**Industry Ranking**	**$ millions**	**Name**
Market capitalization (April '97)	**16,517**	#1	13,051	CIBC
Net income	**399**	#1	375	CIBC
Revenues	**2,238**	#1	2,080	CIBC
Return on equity	**18.9%**	#1	17.9%	CIBC
Leading in traditional businesses	**Market Share**	**Industry Ranking**	**Market Share**	**Name**
Residential mortgages	**14.1%**	#1	12.0%	CIBC
Consumer loans	**17.0%**	#1	14.6%	CIBC
Business loans	**15.0%**	#1	11.7%	CIBC
Personal deposits	**17.1%**	#1	12.2%	CIBC
Leading in non-traditional businesses[1]				
Mutual Funds (assets)	**9%**	#3 (1)	11%	Investors Group
Full-service brokerage (earnings)	**21%**	#1 (1)	n/a	n/a
Discount Brokerage[2] (accounts)	**16%**	#2 (2)	55%	TD GreenLine
Securities custody (assets)	**43%**	#1 (1)	24%	CIBC
Insurance				
Life insurance (new premiums)	**2%**	#14 (1)	18%	London Life
Travel insurance[2] (premiums)	**24%**	#1	11%	Blue Cross
Creditors insurance (premiums)	**27%**	#1	n/a	CIBC

[1] Measured against all industry competitors (ranking among banks in parenthesis)
[2] Market share is estimated
* In quarter ended Jan. 31 1997

At a glance

THE ISSUE: Leadership

THE FACTS

1. The financial needs and expectations of consumers keep growing.
2. Traditional banks have responded by becoming financial services institutions.
3. Royal Bank has grown from Canada's leading bank to Canada's leading financial institution.
4. Our current success is now measured by leadership in a wide variety of measures.
5. Our future success will come from being the leading financial institution for employees, customers and shareholders.

From bank to financial partner

Royal Bank embraced this philosophy of financial partnership by rapidly expanding its capabilities through acquisition and internal growth. For example, we acquired Canada's leading full-service broker Dominion Securities in 1988, opened Canada's fastest growing discount broker Royal Bank Action Direct in 1990, and merged with Canada's premier trust company Royal Trust in 1993. And consumers responded in droves, giving us an industry-leading 10 million customers and making us the leader in almost every single financial measure used to gauge the size and success of today's financial services institutions.

Staying a leader in the next millennium

We're grateful for your support in helping us move from being Canada's leading bank to Canada's leading financial institution as measured by our financial performance. But we've learned that strong financial performance doesn't happen by accident — it comes from employee commitment and customer satisfaction. That's why our corporate strategy places equal emphasis on being the leader for shareholders, employees and customers. And that's why we measure our performance in all three of these categories and reward our employees accordingly. We believe it's the only way you'll keep us the industry leader in the 21st century.

• The eighth in a series for employees and clients •

Chapter One

The Field of Marketing

www.royalbank.com

INFORMATION TECHNOLOGY

The new marketing of today is based on information technology, on the ways it is being put to work in more and more spheres of life, and on how it is beginning to change the ways we all behave. Consider, for example, the Royal Bank of Canada — Canada's biggest bank — which already has one-third of Canadians as its customers.

The Royal has just invested $15 million in database technology so that it can serve each customer uniquely, by becoming nine million individual banks instead of one monolithic big-brother bank. The result of much investment and four years of work at the bank is the Marketing Information File, which provides, for the first time, a detailed profile of each of the bank's nine million customers. According to Charlie Millbury, senior vice-president of marketing, "We don't have any more information than we did ten years ago." But now, the Royal can focus its marketing efforts very closely to pinpoint the needs and interests of customers. Instead of putting ads in newspapers or undertaking mass mailings with account statements yielding a 4 percent response rate to a direct product offering, the Royal can now direct well-targeted product offerings that result in 60 percent positive-response rates. Since these offerings are much more relevant to those who receive them, new relationships have been developed. Focus-group research indicates that customers, rather than resenting the Royal's use of customer information, are pleased that this information is being used and that their individual needs are being recognized.[1]

NATURE AND SCOPE OF MARKETING

The Royal Bank's use of new information technology to "mass customize" products and services and build better relationships with its existing clients is an example of the new marketing. Of course, the Royal isn't the only bank to reorient its marketing this way, nor is it rare for companies to do so. The intelligent use of information technology and the growing and systematic focus on creating better relationships between buyers and sellers are the hallmarks of the new marketing.

Let's step back and look at marketing in more general terms. Marketing exists in many forms — we participate in various aspects of the marketing process every time we buy goods and services. You probably have had a job that included dealing with customers. But did you realize that you also engage in a form of marketing when you vote in a provincial election, donate to the Salvation Army, and prepare your résumé? At the heart of each of these forms of marketing is the concept of exchange.

Exchange as the Focus

Marketing occurs any time one social unit (person or organization) strives to exchange something of value with another social unit. In this broad sense, marketing consists of activities designed to generate and facilitate exchanges intended to satisfy human needs or wants.

Exchange is one of three ways in which a person can satisfy a want. If you want some clothes, you can sew them, borrow them, or use some form of coercion to get them. Or you can offer something of value (money, service, other products) to another person who will voluntarily exchange the clothes for what you offer. It is only the third approach that we call an exchange, in the sense that marketing is taking place.

The following conditions must exist for a marketing exchange to take place:

- Two or more social units — people or organizations — must be involved, and each must have wants to be satisfied. If you are totally self-sufficient in some area, there is no need for an exchange.
- The parties must be involved voluntarily (although some argue that a situation in which consumers deal with monopolies, such as electric utilities or public transit systems, violates this condition).
- Each party must have something of value to contribute in the exchange, and each must believe that it will benefit from the exchange. In the case of an election, for example, the things of value are the votes of the electorate and the representation of the voters by the candidate.
- The parties must communicate with each other. The communication can take many forms and may even be through a third party, but without communication there can be no exchange.

These exchange conditions introduce a number of terms that deserve some elaboration. First, there are the parties involved in the exchange. On one side of the exchange is the marketer. **Marketers** take the initiative in trying to stimulate and facilitate exchanges. They develop marketing plans and programs and implement them in hopes of creating an exchange that can be repeated over time. A college or university recruiting students, the United Way soliciting donors, and Canadian Airlines International seeking passengers are all marketers.

On the other side of the exchange is the **market**, made up of people or organizations to whom marketing programs are directed and who will play a key role in the acceptance or rejection of a marketer's offer. Markets are made up of *customers* — any person or group with whom an individual or organizational marketer has an existing or potential exchange relationship.

The people who constitute a market play a number of roles. First, there is the *decision-maker*, the individual or organizational unit that has the authority to commit to an exchange. Then there is the *consumer*, the one who actually uses or consumes the product. Another role is that of *purchaser*, the party who actually carries out the exchange. Finally, there are *influencers*, who affect the decisions of others because of their expertise, position, or power. These definitions are not simply semantic distinctions. The makers of the Worth baseball, a new safer baseball for children's leagues, discovered that the different roles affected marketing decisions. Concerned parents (influencers) were pleased with the ball, and the kids (consumers) were more comfortable playing with it.

Yet, despite the fact that the Worth baseball had the weight, feel, and bounce of a regular ball, many coaches and youth league officials (decision-makers) rejected it as nontraditional. The marketing problem for Worth's marketing managers was: What should the marketing effort look like, and how should it be directed at the various role players?[2]

An organization's markets include more than the customers for its primary product. For example, in addition to soliciting the students who consume an education and the parents who frequently pay for all or a good deal of it, a university or college directs its marketing to local and provincial officials in order to secure resources, to people living near the university who are affected by its activities, and to graduates who support various university programs. A firm's markets include government regulatory agencies, environmentalists, and its shareholders.

Marketers, while keeping in mind the various roles in the marketplace, are obligated to offer a product or service that will produce satisfaction. Marketing is the process of satisfying customer needs and wants through an exchange process. In describing exchanges, we use the terms *needs* and *wants* interchangeably because marketing is relevant to both. Technically, needs can be viewed in a strict physiological sense (food, clothing, and shelter), and everything else can be defined as a want. However, from a customer's perspective, the distinction is not clear. For example, many people consider a television set or a computer to be a necessity.

Finally, the objective of the exchange or what is being marketed is referred to generically as the **product**. It can be a tangible, physical product, a service, an idea, a person, or a place. A box of corn flakes is a tangible product; accounting advice is an example of a service; an advertising slogan sold by an ad agency represents an idea; an individual who applies for a job is marketing a person; and a provincial government trying to attract tourism is an example of marketing a place as the product. All of these products can and are marketed, as we shall see. Beyond the obvious examples of products, some exchanges involve less obvious things, such as an individual providing a service showing a strong interest in the customer's well-being. The expression of interest can add an element to the process that takes it beyond the simple product being purchased. The exchange then includes more *affective* components, or emotional dimensions.

The Concept of Relationship in Exchange

When two people or organizations are voluntarily involved in an exchange situation, are communicating with each other, and are contributing something of value to the exchange and thereby mutually satisfying needs or wants, a **relationship** can develop. Some people refer to transient interactions as relationships. Generally, however, relationships are of a more long-term nature and involve many exchanges and interactions over a number of years. At the level of relationships between customers and suppliers, more affective exchanges occur. The longer the exchange relationship lasts, the more likely it is to be of special value to those taking part in it. Buyers and sellers understand each other better; they better understand the value of what they are exchanging and how their needs are being satisfied, and they are able to communicate more easily. The Royal Bank of Canada, in this chapter's opening example, invested in the capability to develop better client relationships. Clients responded by appreciating the increased value of the relationship and by providing the bank with more exchange opportunities.

APPLICATIONS OF MARKETING

This book focuses on the activities carried out by individuals and organizations to facilitate mutually beneficial exchanges and develop marketing relationships. The organizations may be business firms in the conventional sense of the word, or they may be nonbusiness, or not-for-profit, organizations, such as a hospital, a university, a Big Brothers/Big Sisters organization, a church, a police department, or a museum. Both groups — business and nonbusiness — face the same basic marketing problems and can make use of the same marketing ideas. And it is the people in organizations, in their own businesses and even in their personal lives, who apply marketing ideas not only inside and outside their firms but also in their daily lives. As you study this text, keep in mind that you can use marketing principles for your job search as well as for the development of your career.

Our definition of marketing — applicable in businesses, not-for-profit organizations, and personal situations — is as follows:

Marketing is a total system of business activities designed to plan, price, promote, and distribute want-satisfying products, services, and ideas to target markets in order to achieve the objectives of both the consumer and the organization.

Marketing is:

a system:	for business activities
designed to:	plan, price, promote, and distribute
something of value:	want-satisfying products, services, and ideas in the context of a valuable relationship
for the benefit of:	the target market — present and potential household consumers or business users
to achieve:	satisfaction of the needs and objectives of both consumers and the firm or organization.

This definition has some significant implications when marketing is properly applied:

- It is a systems definition, which means that it should be understood and applied by everyone in an organization.
- The entire system of business or organizational activities must be customer-oriented and focus on the quality of the customer relationship — customers' needs and wants must be recognized and satisfied effectively.
- The marketing program starts with an idea for a product or service and does not end until the customer's wants are completely satisfied, which may be some time after an exchange is made.
- An organization's marketing program, generally termed the *marketing mix*, usually consists of four co-ordinated elements:

  1. a product or service assortment,
  2. a pricing structure,
  3. distribution systems and channels, and
  4. promotional activities.

Marketers have recently begun to express the view that although getting the components of the marketing mix right is important or even necessary, this may not be sufficient to guarantee customer satisfaction. In other words, as marketers have begun to pay more attention to the application of the marketing concept to marketing in service organizations and to the development of long-term customer relationships, they have realized that other factors, such as the ways in which customers are treated, are important in influencing customer satisfaction.

EVOLUTION OF MARKETING

The foundations of marketing in Canada were laid in pioneer times, when French-speaking and then English-speaking settlers developed marketing relationships and traded among themselves and with various groups of Native peoples. Some settlers became retailers, wholesalers, and itinerant peddlers. Since then, marketing has evolved through three successive stages of development: production orientation, sales orientation, and marketing orientation. Following from the last stage, marketing is now focusing more on the processes involved in providing service and developing marketing relationships.

The three stages of marketing reflect not only development over time, but also states of mind. Although many firms have progressed to the third stage and beyond, the orientation of some firms and some individuals is still in the second or even the first stage, as shown in Figure 1-1.

Production-Orientation Stage

Firms in the **production-orientation stage**, typically manufacturers, focused on increasing output while assuming that customers would seek out and buy reasonably priced and well-made products. Executives in production and engineering shaped the firm's planning. The function of the sales department was simply to sell the company's output at a price set by production and finance executives. The primary focus in business at this stage was to produce

MARKETING AT WORK FILE 1–1

MONTREAL MARKETS ART

Canada's oldest museum, founded in 1860, is the Montreal Museum of Fine Arts — famous for its daring and innovative programming. The MMFA presents its product in the form of thematic blockbuster exhibitions, including "The 1920s: Age of the Metropolis"; great names such as Marc Chagall; events that draw big crowds and get critics talking, such as "Snoopy," featuring Peanuts; and "Moving Beauty," featuring auto design. The museum advertises and promotes these shows with billboards, ads on buses and bus shelters, trailers for movie houses, and even placemats for downtown restaurants and cafés. It takes every opportunity to increase its market share with discounts, coupons, sweepstakes, door prizes, and open days. It targets schools, ethnic groups, families with small children, and business organizations, and for each it mounts special thematic events.

The museum has built a network of relationships that it is able to call upon time and time again: with other museums, with whom it shares events; with corporations that make use of the museum for product launches and other business events; and even with families, for birthday parties. The MMFA wants to be a "destination" every bit as attractive as a fashionable ski resort or shopping mall, and it prizes its relationships because they provide support today and help with developing the museum's market for the future.

Source: Adapted from Daniele Sauvage, "The Art of Marketing Art," *Marketing Magazine*, June 3, 1996, p. 13.

FIGURE 1-1

The Three Stages of Marketing Evolution

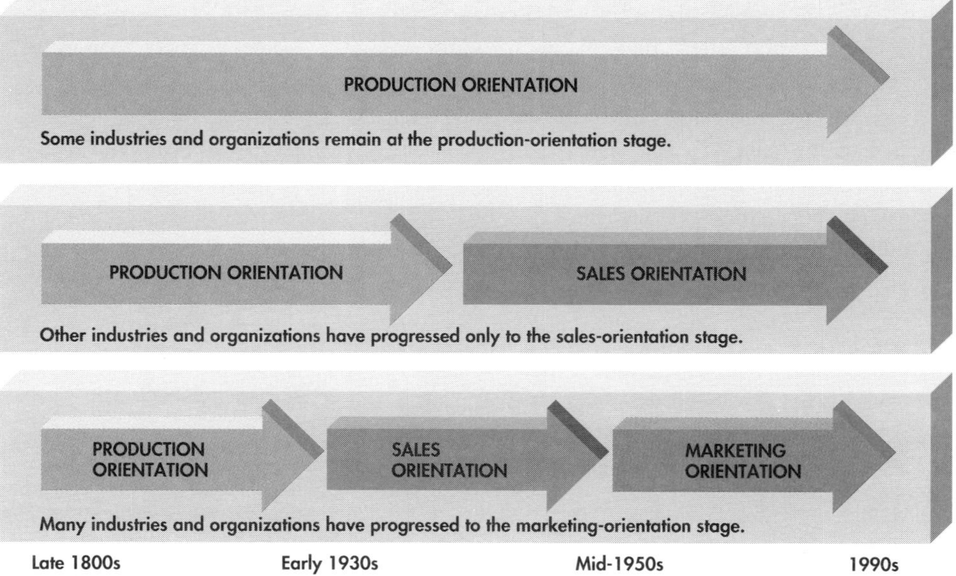

large quantities of goods and produce them efficiently. Finding customers was viewed as a relatively minor function.

During this stage, the term *marketing* was not yet used. Instead, producers had sales departments headed by executives whose sole job was to manage a sales force. This stage was dominant until the early 1930s, although some firms in resource industries and some small business owners/managers still think like this today.

Sales-Orientation Stage

The Great Depression of the 1930s made it clear that the main problem in the economy no longer was to produce or grow enough, but rather was to sell the output. Just making a better product brought no assurance of market success. Firms started to realize that the sale of products required substantial promotional effort. Thus began a period — the **sales-orientation stage** — when selling activities and sales executives gained new respect and responsibility from company management. It was also during this period that selling acquired much of its bad reputation, as "hard sell" approaches and shady sales tactics evolved. The sales stage was common until the 1950s, when the marketing era began to emerge.

Marketing-Orientation Stage

At the end of World War II and as a result of the war, there was an enormous pent-up demand for consumer goods. Manufacturers produced large quantities of goods that were quickly purchased. However, the postwar surge in consumer spending slowed down as supply caught up with demand, and many firms found they had excess production capacity. In an attempt to stimulate sales, firms reverted to the aggressive promotional and sales activities of the sales-orientation era. However, this time consumers were less willing to be persuaded. Because of their experiences, gained through travel and the expanding scope of the mass media, consumers had become more knowledgeable, less naive, and less easily influenced. In addition, they had more choices. Advancing technology made it possible to produce a much greater variety of goods.

Thus the evolution of marketing continued. Many companies recognized that to put idle capacity to work they had to produce what consumers wanted. In the **marketing-orientation stage**, companies identify what customers want and tailor all the activities of the firm to satisfy those needs as efficiently as possible. The objective of marketing-oriented companies became to satisfy the customer.

In this third stage, firms are marketing rather than merely selling. Tasks that were once associated with other business functions become the responsibility of the top marketing executive, typically the marketing manager or vice-president of marketing. For instance, inventory control, warehousing, and some aspects of product planning are turned over to the head of marketing as a way of serving customers better. For a firm to be most effective, the top marketing executive must be involved at the beginning of a production cycle as well as at the end. In addition, marketing must be included in both short-term and long-term company planning.

For a firm's marketing to be effective, its top executive must have a favourable attitude toward marketing. Philip Knight, chairman and CEO of Nike, makes this point: "For years we thought of ourselves as a production-oriented company, meaning we put all our emphasis on designing and manufacturing the product. But now we understand that the most important thing we do is market the product."[3]

TABLE 1-1 What Business Are You In?

Company	Production-Oriented Answer	Marketing-Oriented Answer
Bell Canada	We operate a telephone company.	We provide multiple forms of reliable, efficient, and inexpensive communications services.
Esso	We produce oil and gasoline products.	We provide various types of safe and cost-effective energy.
Visa Canada	We provide credit cards.	We facilitate the purchase of products and services and the transfer of funds.
Canadian National	We run a railway.	We offer a transportation and materials-handling system.
Levi Strauss	We make blue jeans.	We offer comfort, fashion, and durability in wearing apparel.
Kodak	We make cameras and film.	We help preserve beautiful memories.

It is not necessary for marketing executives to hold the top positions in a company or for the president of a firm to have come up through the marketing department. But it is necessary for the CEO to understand the importance of marketing, that is, to be *marketing-oriented* and to focus on putting in place programs and systems that will contribute to satisfying the customer in the long term.

Many business firms and not-for-profit organizations are in this third stage in the evolution of marketing. Others may recognize the importance of a marketing orientation but have difficulty implementing it, for at least two reasons. First, implementation requires accepting the notion that the wants and needs of customers, not the desires of management, direct the organization. A leading business publication puts it this way: "Instead of choosing from what you have to offer, the new consumer tells you what he wants."[4]

Placing customers first affects the way an organization describes what it does. Table 1-1 shows how some well-known organizations might define their businesses under a production orientation and how differently the business would be defined using a marketing orientation.

In some situations, an organization may be viewed as not needing to be marketing-oriented to prosper. A monopoly service provider, such as a provincial power utility, is virtually guaranteed to have customers. In such a situation, management is often more concerned with low-cost, efficient production. Nevertheless, the customer's satisfaction should remain the primary concern. In some cases, notably the telecommunications industry, former monopolies such as Bell Canada are now facing competition from companies such as AT&T Canada and Sprint Canada and, potentially, from cable television operators. Firms that have not focused on customers may be in danger of losing them to new competitors.

In some instances, potential customers consider a product or service to be so superior or so desirable that they will seek it out. In such situations, the need for marketing may not be obvious, especially if one considers marketing to imply the need to *sell* the product or service. This may be the case when you line up for hours to buy tickets to a rock concert. But, even in these cases, if a company does not get its customer service right, customers will not continue to buy. An important lesson at this stage is that a great product and an attractive price are not enough to guarantee long-term customer satisfaction and long-term success for the firm or organization.

Differences Between Marketing and Selling Orientations

As marketing has evolved from a sales orientation to a market orientation, the terms *marketing* and *selling* are often used interchangeably. Some people think they are synonymous, but there are vast differences between the two activities. The basic difference is that selling is oriented to what is available and to the organization's needs, while marketing is oriented to the customer's needs and to how a product and service mix can satisfy them.

Selling Orientation	Marketing Orientation
Emphasis is on the product.	Emphasis is on satisfying customers' needs.
Company first makes the product and then figures out how to sell it.	Company first determines customers' wants and then figures out how to make and deliver a product to satisfy those wants and needs.
Management is sales-volume oriented.	Management is profit oriented.
Focus is short-term: sell the product, meet the sales quota.	Focus is longer-term: create long-term customer value and repeat business.
Planning is short-run oriented, in terms of today's products and markets.	Planning is long-run oriented, in terms of new products, tomorrow's markets, and future growth.
Stresses needs of seller.	Stresses needs and wants of buyers.

www.bce.ca/bce • www.attcanada.ca • www.sprintcanada.ca

Services

The Canadian economy, like that of most of the developed world, has experienced a major shift from goods production to service production over the last twenty years. The growth of service industries has resulted in an increased focus on the requirement to meet customers' needs through providing efficient, effective, and high-quality service. We can think of services as falling into two categories: first, as a non-tangible product to be sold, such as a cleaning service; second, as the service accompanying the sale of most tangible products. For example, a consumer who buys a refrigerator may require it to be delivered; the delivery of the product is a service provided by the retailer.

Marketers have become very conscious of the fact that consumers are demanding more and better services. To meet the requirements for customer satisfaction, marketers must think about how services are provided and what component parts make up a service. It is useful to distinguish between *core* elements and *noncore* features. For example, a traveller who checks into a hotel is purchasing a room for the night — that is the core product. However, the purchaser expects that certain things will be included with the purchase of the room that go beyond the provision of a place to spend the night. The hotel usually will be expected to allow the customer to reserve the room. Upon arrival, the customer will check in. There are certain processes involved in completing the check-in which the customer expects will run smoothly and efficiently. Once the guest is shown to the room, there is an expectation of cleanliness, pleasant decor, and amenities such as bath supplies, water glasses, and laundry bags. The temperature of the room must allow the guest to be comfortable. If the individual calls for room service or valet service, there is an expectation that it will be provided in a timely, competent, and courteous manner. In interactions with hotel staff, the customer has certain expectations about the appropriate way for staff to respond. The employees involved in the exchange must be able to interact so that the customer receives the right amount of service to meet his or her needs and wants. This interaction may lead to relationship development between the customer and the employees or the business. If the interaction is not handled satisfactorily, the customer may have negative feelings about it. Often these feelings arise from brief comments made by unthinking or inappropriately trained staff.

FIGURE 1-2 Factors That Drive Customer Satisfaction

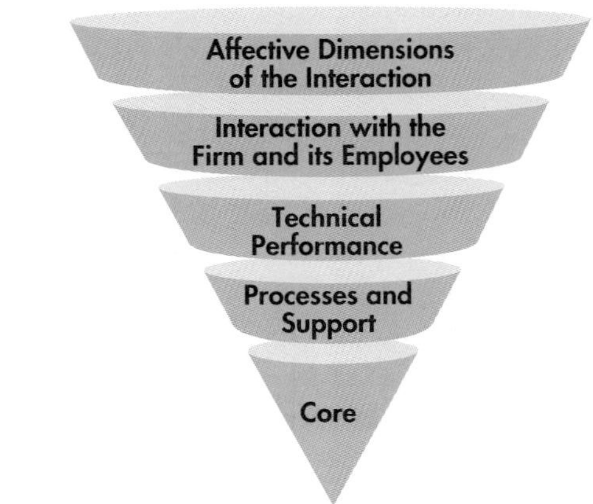

The above example includes five levels of customer satisfaction,which we can call **drivers of customer satisfaction**.[5] Figure 1-2 illustrates these five levels. The core is the basic product or service provided by the organization. Generally, we tend to think of tangible products as the core because they are easy to visualize, but a service may be the core offering. In the hotel example, the core product is the room, the bed, and the bathroom. These aspects of the product are the most basic things being offered to the customer. When customers evaluate service, they require that the hotel gets at least the core product right.

The second level in the drivers of customer satisfaction model is that of support services and systems. It includes such things, in our example, as reservation services, billing systems, convenience of hotel location, and room service menu. Failing to provide satisfactory support services can cause customers to be unsatisfied and not return.

Moving further up the model, the third level is technical performance, which determines whether the service provider gets the core product and support services right. The emphasis is on meeting the expectations of the customer. Is the hotel room clean and ready when the guest arrives? Customer dissatisfaction will result from a failure to meet customer expectations that things will go smoothly and as promised.

The fourth level of the model concerns the customer's interaction with the organization and its employees. This level can involve both face-to-face interaction and the interaction that occurs through technology-based contact over the telephone or through e-mail or the Internet. Satisfaction, at this level, is determined by whether or not the service provider makes it easy for customers to do business with it. Are customers treated with respect? Are the staff efficient, pleasant, helpful, and courteous? Understanding this level of customer satisfaction indicates that a firm has thought beyond the provision of the core product and service and is focused on the delivery of service at the point where the company meets the customer.

Finally, service marketers must think beyond the basic elements of the interaction with customers to consider the sometimes subtle messages that firms send to customers. These messages may create either positive or negative feelings toward the company. Essentially, this level is concerned with affective considerations. Often a customer's satisfaction or dissatisfaction has nothing to do with the quality of the core product or service or with how it is provided to the customer. Business may be lost because of some comment from a staff member or some other "little thing" that goes wrong and that may not even be noticed by staff.

Relationship Marketing

As marketers began to think about the elements of satisfaction involved in the provision of services to consumers, a new awareness of the value of relationships in marketing began to emerge. The concept of **relationship marketing** embodies building personal, long-term bonds with customers. Many of the factors discussed in relation to the fourth and fifth levels of the drivers of customer satisfaction in Figure 1-2 contribute to the development of relationships in marketing exchanges. This new emphasis on relations and relationship marketing is a further step in the development of the market orientation. Identifying the needs of customers and satisfying them can be profitable, but establishing a connection with customers so that the organization is regularly relied on for products and services is much more valuable — as demonstrated by both the Royal Bank of Canada and the Montreal Museum of Fine Arts. Such a relationship, which involves being more like a partner than simply a participant in an exchange, only occurs if a sense of closeness, trust, and commitment is established between buyer and seller. While many factors affect the development of a strong relationship marketing program, two major factors are (1) the provision of quality products and services, and (2) the conducting of marketing relationships within a trusting and ethical framework.

THE MARKETING CONCEPT

The evolution of marketing thinking from an emphasis on production to a focus on relationships has led to successive steps in the development of a philosophy of doing business. Called the **marketing concept**, this philosophy emphasizes customer orientation and the co-ordination of marketing activities to achieve the mutual long-term objectives of both the customer and the organization. Although customer satisfaction is important, this focus will work only if it is accomplished at the same time that the organization's objectives are being met. The needs of both parties in the marketing exchange must be met simultaneously.

Long-term customer satisfaction leads to the retention of customers and generates substantial profits.[6] It is more profitable for firms to keep customers than to be constantly seeking new ones.[7] Developing satisfied customers is therefore an important way to meet the organization's performance objectives.

Nature and Rationale

The marketing concept is based on three beliefs that are illustrated in Figure 1-3:

- All planning and operations should be *customer oriented*. Every department and employee should be focused on contributing to the satisfaction of customers' needs. At potato-chip producer Frito-Lay, engineers developed a simulated human mouth to measure the jaw effort needed to crunch a chip. By comparing taste-preference results with test results from the simulated mouth, researchers found that four pounds per square inch (2 kg per 2.5 cm) of oral pressure is the ideal

FIGURE 1-3

Components and Outcomes of the Marketing Concept

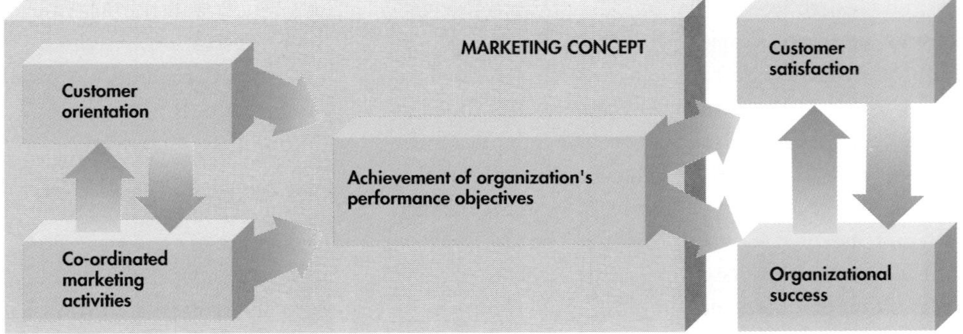

level of crunchiness. Now all chips are tested to meet this standard. As a company executive pointed out, "We have to be perfect; after all, no one really needs a potato chip."[8]

- All marketing activities in an organization should be *co-ordinated*. Marketing efforts (product and service planning, pricing, distribution, promotion, and customer service) should be designed and combined in a coherent, consistent way, and one executive should have overall authority and responsibility for the complete set of marketing activities. Other employees who work in different organizational functions should be made aware of their roles in supporting a marketing orientation for the organization.
- Customer-oriented, co-ordinated marketing is essential to achieve the *organization's performance objectives* while at the same time meeting the customer's needs. The primary objective for a business is typically a profitable sales volume. In not-for-profit organizations, the objective might be increasing the number of people served or the variety of services offered. Hotel chains across North America are becoming very conscious of the requirement for customer oriented, co-ordinated approaches to marketing. To better meet the needs of the business traveller, Delta Hotels has introduced a centralized concierge service for members of its frequent-guest program. Staff have access to a database that allows them to quickly find the service or product a guest requires anywhere in Canada, the United States, Cuba, and Asia. "We want to do anything we can to take away the hassle of business travel," said Scott Allison, Delta's vice-president of marketing.[9]

www.delta.com

New Focal Points in the Marketing Concept

All ideas and concepts evolve and become more refined, and the marketing concept is no exception.

The Societal Marketing Concept As the marketing concept has become widely accepted by many organizations, it has also come under fire. Critics have charged that it ignores social responsibility — although it may lead to an organization achieving its goals, it may at the same time encourage actions that conflict with society's best interests.

From one point of view, these charges are true. A firm may totally satisfy its customers (and in the process achieve a hefty profit), while also adversely affecting society. To illustrate, a pulp and paper mill in British Columbia may be supplying its customers in Alberta and Saskatchewan with the right product at a reasonable price, but in doing so may be polluting the air and water near Vancouver.

However, this need not be the case. A firm's social responsibility can be quite compatible with the marketing concept. Compatibility depends on two things: how broadly a firm perceives its marketing goals, and how long it is willing to wait to achieve those goals. A firm that sufficiently extends the breadth and time dimensions of its marketing goals to fulfil its social responsibility is practising the **societal marketing concept**.

When a company extends the marketing concept's *breadth*, it recognizes that its market includes not only the buyers of its products but also anyone directly affected by its operations. In our example, the pulp and paper mill has several "customer" groups to satisfy (1) the buyers of the pulp and paper, (2) the consumers of the air and water that contain impurities given off by the mill, and (3) the recreational users of the local river and bay where the mill releases its waste matter.

Extending the *time* dimension of its marketing goals means that a firm should take a long-term view of customer satisfaction and performance objectives, rather than concentrating only on tomorrow. For a company to prosper in the long run, it must satisfy its customers' social needs as well as their economic needs.

The marketing concept and a company's social responsibility are compatible if management strives over the long run to (1) satisfy the wants of its product-buying customers, (2) meet the societal needs of others affected by the firm's activities, and (3) achieve the company's performance objectives. The challenges of balancing these three often-conflicting goals frequently places marketers in ethical predicaments. The issue of ethics deserves our consideration.

TRUST, ETHICS, AND MARKETING RELATIONSHIPS

The task of marketers is to "deliver a standard of living" to customers. To accomplish this goal, marketers have a variety of tools at their disposal. Broadly speaking, these tools include the design of a product or service, the price at which it is offered, the message used to describe it, the channel through which it is made available, and the level of service provided to customers. And, of course, what is of utmost importance is the manner in which these tools are used.

Marketers are also responsible to a variety of groups. Certainly their customers depend on them to provide good products and services at reasonable prices. Their employers expect them to generate sales and profits; suppliers and distributors look to them for their continued business, and society expects them to be responsible citizens. The potential for the misuse of marketing tools and the frequently divergent interests of the groups dependent on the marketer create a wide variety of ethical challenges.

What Is Ethical Behaviour?

The professional association for North American marketers, the American Marketing Association, has formulated the code of ethics presented in Table 1-2.

A discussion of the philosophical underpinnings of ethics is beyond the scope of this book.[10] However, it is safe to say that there is considerable disagreement about what constitutes ethical conduct. Ethics vary from society to society. For example, bribery, though repugnant in many societies, is an accepted and even necessary aspect of business behaviour in some parts of the world. For our purposes, it is sufficient to say that **ethics** are the rules we play by, the standards of behaviour generally accepted by a society. Some of these standards are found in the various provincial and company consumer and human rights codes. One is more likely to find them in company ethics codes, but most likely of all to find them in individual codes of conduct.

TABLE 1-2 Code of Ethics for Members of the American Marketing Association

As a member of the American Marketing Association, I recognize the significance of my professional conduct and my responsibility to society and the other members of my profession:

1. By acknowledging my accountability to the organization for which I work.
2. By pledging my efforts to assure that all presentations of goods, services, and concepts be made honestly and clearly.
3. By striving to improve marketing knowledge and practice in order to better serve society.
4. By supporting free consumer choice in circumstances that are legal and consistent with generally accepted community standards.
5. By pledging to use the highest professional standards in my work and in my competitive activity.
6. By acknowledging the right of the American Marketing Association, through established procedure, to withdraw my membership if I am found to be in violation of ethical standards of professional conduct.

Source: American Marketing Association.

www.ama.org

www.newtel.com
www.xerox.com
www.canadiantire.com
www.bankofmontreal.com
www.maytag.com

Many organizations have discovered that employees do not necessarily develop a strong sense of ethical standards on their own. Embarrassing scandals and legal proceedings are frequent reminders that ethical behaviour cannot be taken for granted. The results can be costly as well; a survey sponsored by the Canadian Public Relations Society in 1997 yielded the following opinions concerning when it is acceptable to lie:

- A small white lie to prevent someone's embarrassment: 59 percent agree.
- For the good of the organization: 24 percent agree.
- To help negotiate a deal for the organization: 13 percent agree.[11]

Just as telling is the finding that employees think that only 57 percent of top management were completely honest or mostly honest with customers — clearly not the stuff to instil consumer confidence and loyalty. Much remains to be done.

Instilling an Ethical Orientation

Organizations are not ignoring ethical issues. A growing number are holding ethics workshops and setting up ethics committees. However, as long as there are conflicting goals and opportunities for people to make judgments, ethical failures will occur. To relieve some of the pressure on employees faced with ethical challenges and perhaps reduce the frequency and severity of ethical problems, organizations have taken several steps.

One dimension of creating an ethical environment is to make sure that the performance demands on employees are reasonable. People faced with unrealistic quotas and deadlines are much more likely to cut corners to accomplish their objectives.

Another important facet of an ethical orientation is communicating clearly the organization's standards. Hewlett-Packard, for example, makes sure that all employees are completely familiar with its extensive code of conduct. To remind employees of the importance of ethical behaviour, Texas Instruments includes a weekly column on ethics in its international electronic news service. Included in the column are answers to specific issues raised by employees.

To help employees deal with ethical issues, some companies employ a full-time ethics officer or ombudsman. This high-level executive gives advice to senior management and responds to the complaints and questions of employees at all levels.

Organizations are also taking greater care to reward ethical performance. It is important for employees to see that success is the result of admirable behaviour, not questionable practices.

www.hp.com

The Benefits of Ethical Behaviour: Consumer Trust

One could argue that ethical behaviour should in itself be rewarding. However, there are tangible benefits as well. Successful long-term businesses are built on successful relationships with suppliers, customers, employees, and other groups. The strength of a relationship is largely a function of the amount of trust the parties have in each other. Unethical behaviour undermines trust and destroys closeness in a relationship. The Social Investment Organization recently quantified the social performance of the top three hundred companies on the Toronto Stock Exchange. Through a process that looked at nine issues of ethical and social behaviour — including community relations, corporate governance, the status of women in the workplace, environmental practices, and employee relations — this organization rated the top fifty social performers. Among those companies listed in the top fifty are Alcan Aluminium Ltd., Canadian Airlines International, NewTel Enterprises, Xerox Canada, Canadian Tire, Trans Canada Pipe Lines, and the Bank of Montreal. Ethics is a highly significant issue in business today, and the building of trust results in profitable marketing relationships.[12]

QUALITY AND THE MARKETING RELATIONSHIP

Quality has always been important to consumers. The success of Maytag's long-running "lonely repairman" television commercials is a good indication of this. The campaign, which communicates the dependability of Maytag service and appliances, started on Canadian radio in the 1960s and ran for more than twenty-five years. Rather than focusing on quality, many businesses chose in the past to maximize output through mass production and

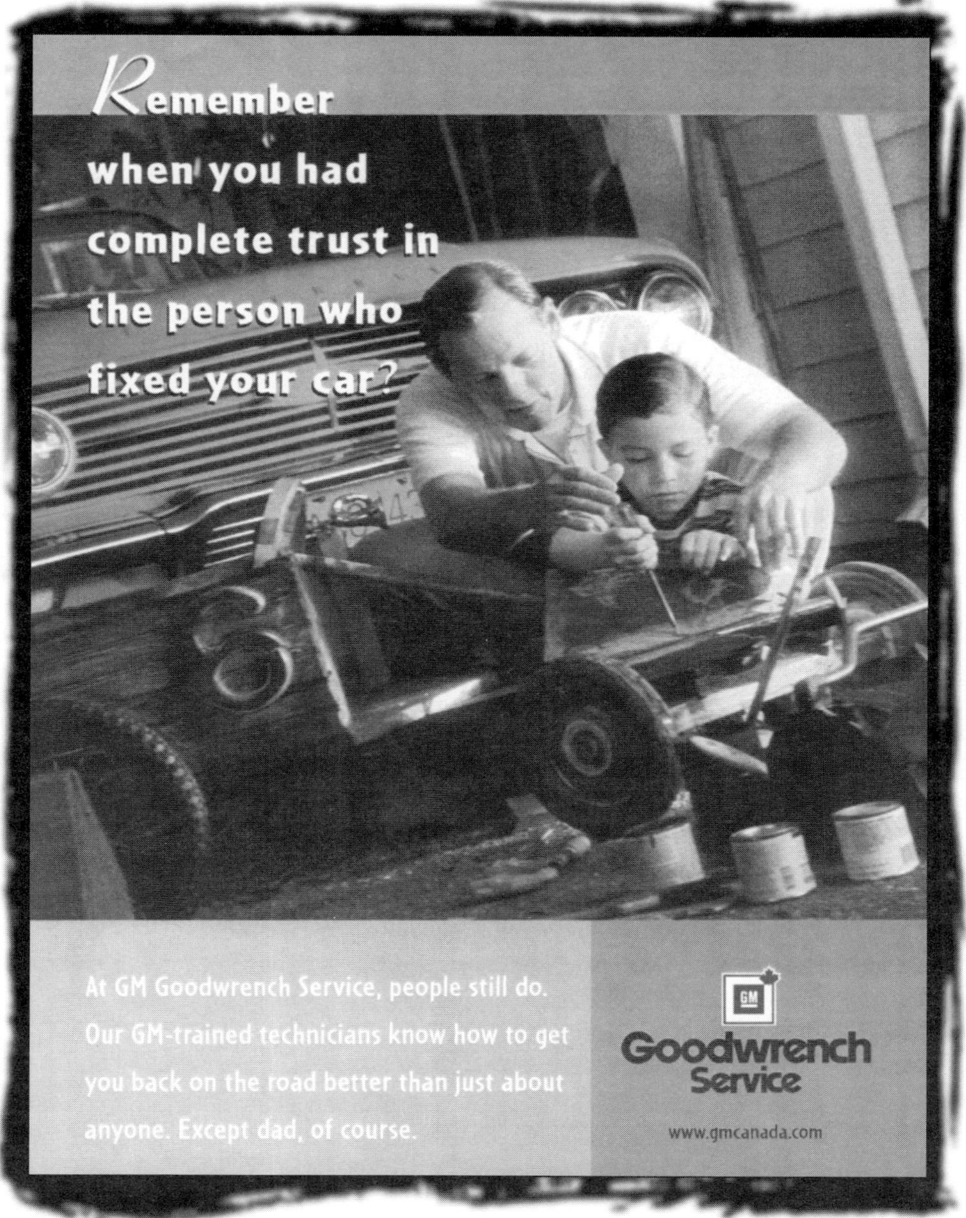

GM Goodwrench now focuses on trust in the process of developing long-term relationships with dealers.

minimize prices through cost controls. The objective was to have an "acceptable" level of quality, which meant being as good as the competition. This strategy was successful as long as quality remained fairly constant across competitors.

Some would argue that some North American managers allowed themselves to become complacent about quality, convincing themselves that even minor product and service improvements would raise costs dramatically and thus make a firm uncompetitive. Meanwhile, new state-of-the-art manufacturing techniques were adopted by overseas firms who then added quality as a key ingredient of their strategies. We know from the success of foreign firms in automobiles, electronics, and computer hardware that a commitment to quality has many benefits. Thus, improving quality became a high priority for many North American and European organizations in the 1980s.

What Is Quality?

One definition of quality is the absence of variation in products and services. That doesn't mean that a Chevrolet should perform as well as a Lexus, or that the service at a Holiday Inn should be the same as the service at a Four Seasons hotel or resort. What it does mean is that a product or service should consistently deliver what it was designed to deliver, without variation from one experience to another. Thus, every Chevrolet model or every Holiday Inn service category should provide consumers with an identical experience. A series of "quality experiences" is a foundation for a quality relationship.

The most obvious application of variance control is in manufacturing. Variance control in service provision, while possible, is more difficult to achieve. Most manufacturers have had quality control departments for many years. However, the title "quality control" was misleading because it was limited to inspecting finished products in order to prevent defective ones from leaving the plant. But meeting specifications in production did not ensure quality if the product was poorly designed or if it was improperly serviced after it was sold. Thus, the real indication of **quality** is how well a product meets both the product and service expectations of the customer, not of the production department.

Organizations also learned that quality control cannot be delegated to one department — it must permeate the organization and be every employee's responsibility. This is known as **total quality management**, which has as its goals:

- Better, more appealing, and less variable product and service quality.
- Quicker and less variable responses from design all the way to delivery.
- Greater flexibility in responding to customers' needs, both before and after the sale.
- Lower costs as a result of quality improvements, reductions in reworking, proper service performance, and waste elimination.[13]

For marketers, the best measure of quality is repeated customer satisfaction. In a competitive environment, the ultimate indication of satisfaction is whether the customer returns to buy the product or service a second, third, or fourth time and forms a long-term relationship with the provider. However, a firm can't assume that its marketing decisions are correct and wait for repeat purchases to confirm or reject those judgments. Instead, managers realize that satisfaction is determined by the extent to which a product or service meets or exceeds a customer's expectations. Therefore, marketers must do two things:

1. Ensure that all marketing activities, such as the price of a product, the claims made for it in advertising, and the places in which it is sold, contribute to creating reasonable customer expectations.
2. Eliminate variations in customers' experiences in purchasing and consuming the product. For example, not only should every new Honda Civic or Compaq notebook computer provide the same level of performance, but every customer interaction with a dealer or service person should be appropriately consistent, without surprises, and aid in creating trust.

Instilling Quality As managers have become more concerned about quality, a variety of quality-improvement programs have been developed. Though the programs have some differences, they typically involve:

- Studying competitors and noncompetitors to identify the highest standards of performance in such areas as delivery delays, eliminating defects, and training for product operations. This process is called *benchmarking*.
- Management and employees working closely together in an atmosphere of trust and co-operation to improve production and customer contact performance.
- All employees making a commitment to constantly search for better ways of performing their functions and improving their relationships with customers.
- Forming partnerships with suppliers and customers so that their inputs for improvement can be incorporated into the firm's internal operations and external contacts.
- Measuring product and service quality and the resulting customer satisfaction.

MARKETING AT WORK FILE 1-2

MAINTAINING THE RELATIONSHIPS YOU WANT

Holding on to customers, in addition to generating new ones, is tricky but terribly profitable. Angus Reid, president of the Angus Reid Group of Winnipeg and a leading marketing researcher, says that "customer retention is the number one issue for corporate winners." Research shows that customers question why they should show loyalty to any company or brand that they do not perceive as delivering a valuable service or incentive to purchase. Since 50 percent of all grocery purchases involve a brand switch, the need to communicate on the basis of individual needs for quality, service, and value causes grocery-product manufacturers and others to look for ways to strengthen the customer relationships they want.

Sears Canada learned to mine its database in order to force a corporate culture shift from a sales mindset to a profit mindset. It learned to link customer behaviour with contribution to profit so that it could develop better relationships with profitable customers. Canadian Tire adopted a similar approach and now knows that for every dollar invested in maintaining a good customer relationship, $2.25 in sales resulted.

Source: Adapted from James Pollock, "Marketers Boost Customer Retention Efforts," *Marketing Magazine*, May 20, 1996, p. 4.

IMPORTANCE OF MARKETING

Coca-Cola is sold in virtually every country in the world. Japanese autos continue to be popular in North America, more so in Canada than in the United States. Consumers choose from numerous brands of personal computers and foods. Some students at your school obtained good jobs following graduation last year. Effective marketing is the common denominator in these diverse situations. And, as these examples suggest, marketing plays a major role in the global economy, in Canada, and in any individual organization. It also has significance for you personally — in business, in your personal life, and certainly in your role as a consumer.

In the Global Economy

In the early 1980s, the competition facing Canadian firms came primarily from American, Western European, and Japanese companies. Later, firms in the four "Asian tigers" (Hong Kong, Korea, Taiwan, and Singapore) added to the competitive pressures. In the not too distant future there will be new challenges from the countries of Eastern Europe, the growth of capitalism in China, the change of pace in Russia, and the new dynamism of Chile, Brazil, and Argentina. Canadians have become accustomed to more global brands, as well as to well-known brands originating in and manufactured in many other countries. We live in a global economy where products, services, and marketing ideas in one part of the world influence people and businesses in many other parts.

The increases in global competition and international marketing opportunities are enhanced by the developments in global and regional trading agreements. New world-trading arrangements and the establishment of the World Trade Organization are increasing marketing activity, both domestic and international. The European Union (EU), the North American Free Trade Agreement (NAFTA), the Asia Pacific Economic Co-operation (APEC) organization, and Mercosur (an expanding group of South American countries) continue to reduce barriers and liberalize trade between members.

Although we don't yet know all the results of these developments, one thing is certain: We live in a global economy. Most nations today — regardless of their degree of economic development or political philosophy — recognize the importance of marketing beyond their own borders. Indeed, economic growth in the less developed nations of the world depends greatly on their ability to design effective marketing systems that will produce global customers for their raw materials and industrial output.

In the Canadian System

Aggressive, effective marketing practices have contributed to the high standard of living in Canada. Today we have the continued efficiency of mass marketing — extensive and rapid communication with customers through a wide variety of media and a distribution system that makes products readily available — combined with mass production that makes more products available with increased value. At the same time, we have growing mass customization, combined with more personally focused databases and innovative personal media, providing products that are continually becoming closely tailored to individual needs. As a result, we enjoy things that once were considered luxuries and in many countries are still available only to people earning high incomes.

Since about 1920 (except during World War II), the supply of products in Canada has far surpassed total demand. Making most products has been relatively easy; the real challenge has been marketing them.

Employment and Costs We can get an idea of the significance of marketing in the Canadian economy by looking at how many of us are employed in some way in marketing and at how much of what we spend covers the cost of marketing. Between one-fourth and one-third of the Canadian labour force is engaged in marketing activities. This figure includes employees in retailing, wholesaling, transportation, warehousing, and communications industries, as well as people who work in marketing departments in manufacturing, agriculture, mining, and service industries. Furthermore, over the past century, jobs in marketing have increased at a much more rapid rate than have jobs in production, reflecting marketing's expanded role in the economy.

On average, about fifty cents of each dollar consumers spend goes to cover marketing costs. The money pays for designing the products to meet our needs, making them readily available when and where we want them, and informing us about their benefits and features. These activities add want-satisfying ability, or what is called utility, to products.

Creating Customer Value A customer purchases a product or service because it provides satisfaction. The quality that makes a product capable of satisfying wants is its **value** or **utility**. Marketing creates much of a product's value or utility. The concept of value is an important one in marketing because marketers must be aware of what will be *valued* by customers. The addition of value to what marketers offer to customers and the ways in which marketers treat customers through the purchase and postpurchase processes add value to the customer's experience, thereby contributing to the creation of satisfaction. "Marketing at Work" File 1–3 illustrates how firms and organizations are able to add value for their customers.

In Organizations

Marketing considerations should be an integral part of all short-range and long-range planning in any company. Here's why:

- The success of any business comes from satisfying the needs and wants of its customers, which is the social and economic basis for the existence of all organizations.
- Although many activities are essential to a company's growth, **marketing is the only activity that produces revenue directly**. (This is sometimes overlooked by the production managers who use these revenues and the finance executives who manage them.) When managers are internally focused, products are designed by designers, manufactured by manufacturing people, priced by accounting staff, and then given to sales managers to sell. This approach generally won't work in today's environment of intense competition and constant change. Just building a good product will not result in sales.

A Statistics Canada 1997 report on how over three thousand small business startups fared over ten years underscores the importance of marketing. Only one in five new small ventures make it past their tenth birthday. The study shows that to become ten years old, businesses must focus on the basics of

MARKETING AT WORK FILE 1-3

ROLLERBLADE MARKETING CREATES SIX TYPES OF VALUE OR UTILITY

Consider this example. A marketer came up with the idea for a new product that combined the concept of a single blade from ice skates and the wheels of roller skates: the in-line skate. To produce the product, a company called Rollerblade Ltd. was established in Montreal. But Rollerblades in Montreal in April are of little value to a person in Vancouver who wants to buy a pair for a Christmas present. So the in-line skates must be transported to the West Coast (and hundreds of other places) and placed in stores near potential customers. Then, potential buyers must be informed about the product's existence and benefits through various forms of promotion. Let's see what kinds of value or utility have been created in this process:

- **Form utility** is associated primarily with production — the physical or chemical changes that make a product more valuable. When lumber is made into furniture, form utility is created. This is production, not marketing. However, marketing research may aid in decisions about product design, colour, quantities produced, or some other aspect of a product. For in-line skates, as with most other products, marketing is involved in developing the concept, designing the appearance, and selecting the materials and colours. All these things contribute to the product's form utility.
- **Place utility** exists when a product is readily accessible to potential customers. Rollerblades in Montreal are of little value to customers in Vancouver or other parts of the country, so moving the product to a store near the customer adds to its value.
- **Time utility** means having a product available when you want it. In the case of Rollerblades, customers like having a selection of skates in stores so that they can shop at their convenience. Having a product available when we want it is very convenient, but it means that the retailer must anticipate our desires and maintain an inventory. Thus, there are costs involved in providing time utility.
- **Information utility** is created by informing prospective buyers that a product exists. Unless you know a product exists and where you can get it, the product has no value. Advertising that describes in-line skates, or a sales person answering a customer's questions about the durability of Rollerblades, creates information utility. **Image utility** is a special type of information utility. It is the emotional or psychological value that a person attaches to a product or brand because of its reputation or social standing. Image utility ordinarily is associated with prestige or high-status products such as designer clothes, expensive foreign automobiles, and certain residential neighbourhoods.
- **Possession utility** is created when ownership is transferred to the buyer. Rollerblades in a store's window or on a shelf don't provide customers with any satisfaction. To consume and enjoy the product, a transaction must take place. This occurs when you exchange your money for a pair of the skates.
- **Satisfaction utility** is created when the customer is pleased with the product or service and it meets the individual's expectations. If the customer is satisfied, value is created in the organization. The customer is more likely to repurchase from that organization, promote the products offered by Rollerblades Ltd. through word of mouth, and generate increased revenue for the firm.

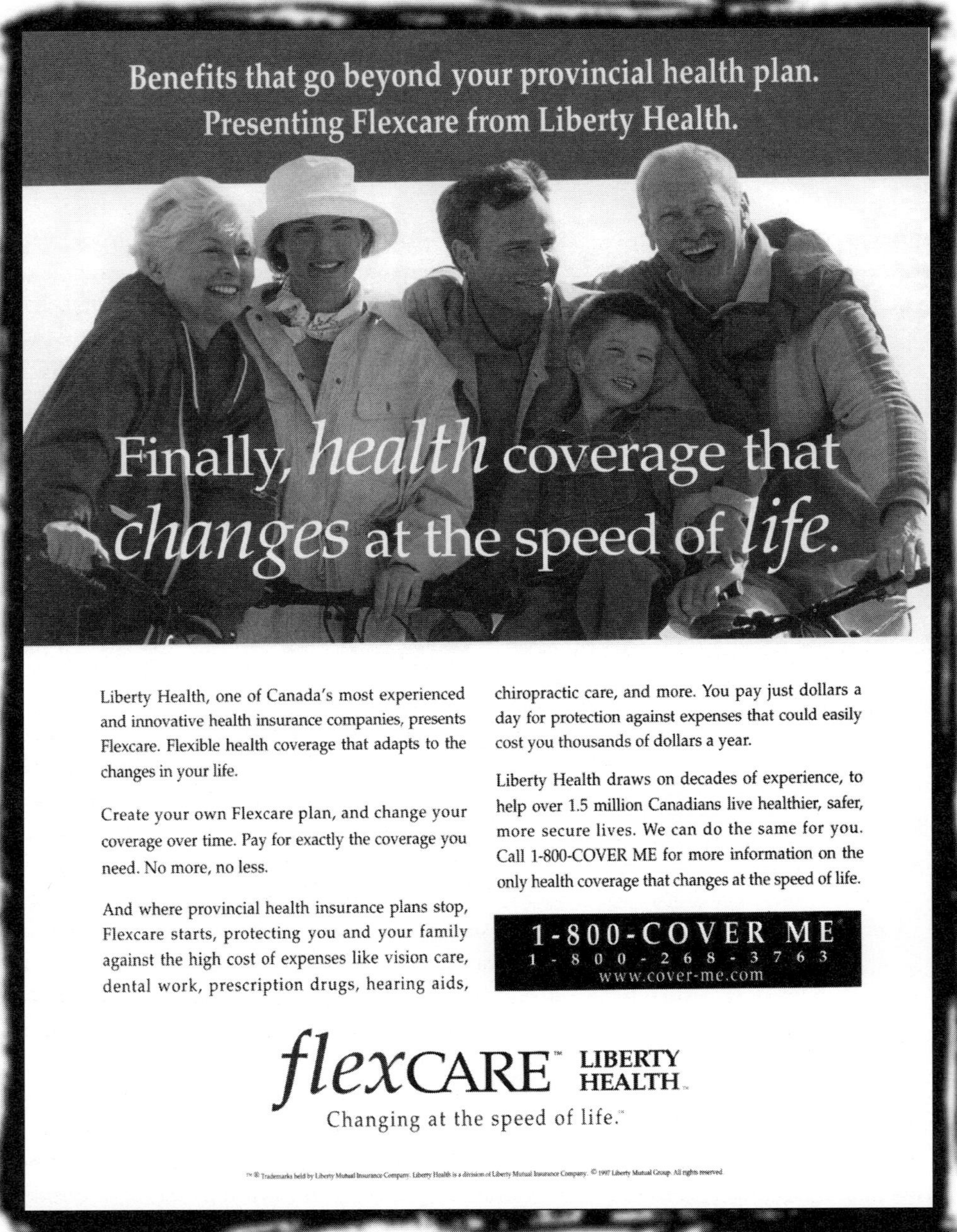

Liberty Health produces intangible but important services for an aging population.

product quality and customer satisfaction. Once the business moves beyond the basics, innovation and employee training appear to add greatly to business growth. Technological innovation without the basics does not guarantee survival.[14]

Service Marketers Canada has gone from being primarily a manufacturing economy to becoming a more service-oriented economy. Services are now much more important than goods as the object of a transaction; examples are transportation, tourism, communications, entertainment, education, financial services, health care, and a host of professional services. Services probably will be even more important in the economy in the early part of the next century than they now are.

Not-for-Profit Marketers During the late 1980s and early 1990s, many not-for-profit organizations realized that they needed effective marketing programs to counteract difficult economic times, shrinking government subsidies, and a decrease in charitable contributions. Charities with falling donations, service clubs with declining memberships, and symphony orchestras playing to vacant seats all began to understand that marketing was essential to help them turn their situations around.

Today political organizations, museums, and even churches — all organizations that formerly rejected any thought of marketing — are embracing it as a means of growth and, for some, survival. This trend is likely to accelerate during the remainder of the 1990s, for two reasons:

- Increasing competition among not-for-profit organizations. For example, the competition among colleges and universities for students interested in specialized programs is intensifying as the number of young people of college age declines, and the search for donors has become more intense as the number of charities has increased.
- Not-for-profit organizations need to improve their images and gain greater acceptance among donors, government agencies, news media, and, of course, consumers, all of which collectively determine an organization's success.

In Your Life

Okay, so marketing is important globally, in our economy, and in an individual organization. But what's in it for you? Why should you study marketing? There are a number of reasons:

- Marketing pervades our daily activities. Consider how many marketers view you as part of their market. With people like you in mind, firms such as Nike, Loblaws, Air Canada, MuchMusic, and Tim Hortons have designed their products and services, set prices, created advertisements, and chosen the best methods of making their products and services available to you. They have devised customer service strategies and developed programs to ensure that you come back to do business with them in the future. In response, you watch television commercials, buy various items from different retail stores or through the Internet, and sometimes complain about prices or the quality of service you receive. Marketing occupies a large part of your daily life. If you doubt this, just imagine for a moment what it would be like if there were no marketing institutions — no retail stores to buy from and no advertising to give you information, for example.
- Studying marketing will make you a better-informed consumer. You'll understand more about what underlies a seller's pricing and how brand names are selected, as well as the role of promotion and distribution.
- Lastly, marketing probably relates, directly or indirectly, to your career aspirations. If you are thinking about studying more marketing courses and considering employment in a marketing position, you can develop a feel for what marketing managers do. If you're planning a career in accounting, finance, or an other business field, you can learn how marketing affects managerial decision-making in these areas. Finally, if you are thinking about a career in a nonbusiness field such as health care, government, music, theatre, or education, you will learn how to use marketing in these organizations. When you become serious about a job search, all the marketing ideas and tools will be of great help to you in defining potential employer groups and their interests and clarifying how you can present yourself to them.

www.loblaws.com
www.muchmusic.com
www.timhortons.com

Summary

The foundation of marketing is exchange within the context of a successful marketing relationship. One party provides to another party something of value in return for something else of value. In a broad sense, marketing consists of all activities designed to generate or facilitate an exchange intended to satisfy human needs.

Business firms and not-for-profit organizations engage in marketing. Products marketed include goods as well as services, ideas, people, and places. Marketing activities are targeted at markets, consisting of product purchasers as well as the individuals and groups that influence the success of an organization.

In a business context, marketing is a total system of business activities designed to plan, price, promote, and distribute want-satisfying products to target markets in order to achieve consumer and organizational objectives. The main difference between marketing and selling is that, in selling, the emphasis is on the product; in marketing, the emphasis is on meeting customers' wants and needs.

Marketing's evolution in Canada has gone through three stages. It began with a production orientation, passed through a sales orientation, and is now in the marketing orientation. In this third stage, a company's efforts are focused on identifying and satisfying customers' needs in order to establish effective marketing relationships.

Some organizations remain at the first or second stage, not progressing to the marketing-orientation stage, because they have monopoly power or because their products are in such great demand. Other firms have difficulty implementing a marketing orientation.

The service industries have provided opportunities for marketers to explore in depth the process of interaction that occurs between the buyer and the seller. To meet customer needs, it is usually necessary to go beyond providing core products. Customers demand a great deal more that can be considered as the five levels of the factors that drive customer satisfaction. Failure to provide satisfaction at any one of these levels can lead to lost customers and lost revenue.

A business philosophy called the marketing concept has evolved in marketing. According to the marketing concept, a firm is best able to achieve its performance objectives by adopting a customer orientation and co-ordinating all its marketing activities. Relationship marketing helps to build long-term customer relationships based on getting to know customers and understanding their needs in order to provide quality and service within a trusting and ethical framework.

Marketing is practised today in all modern nations, regardless of their political philosophy. As international competition has heated up, increasing attention has been paid to marketing. Between one-fourth and one-third of the work force is involved in marketing, and about one-half of consumer spending covers the cost of marketing. Marketing creates form, information, place, time, and possession utilities.

Depending on circumstances, marketing can be vital to an organization's success. In recent years numerous service firms and not-for-profit organizations have found marketing to be necessary and worthwhile. Marketing also can be useful to individual students, particularly in reference to career opportunities.

Key Terms and Concepts

Exchange (4)
Marketers (4)
Market (4)
Product (5)
Relationship (5)
Marketing (6)
Production-orientation stage (6)
Sales-orientation stage (8)
Marketing-orientation stage (8)
Drivers of customer satisfaction (10)
Relationship marketing (11)
Marketing concept (11)
Societal marketing concept (12)
Ethics (13)
Quality (16)
Total quality management (16)
Value/utility (18)
Form utility (19)
Place utility (19)
Time utility (19)
Information utility (19)
Image utility (19)
Possession utility (19)
Satisfaction utility (19)

Questions and Problems

1. Explain the concept of an exchange, including the conditions that must exist for an exchange to occur, and give an example of an exchange that does not involve money.
2. Name some companies that are still in the production or sales stage in the evolution of marketing. Explain why you chose each of them.
3. Explain the five levels in the model of the drivers of customer satisfaction. Discuss how each level can influence the customer and generate satisfaction or dissatisfaction.
4. "The marketing concept does not imply that marketing executives will run the firm. The concept requires only that whoever is in top management be marketing-oriented." Give examples of how a production manager, company treasurer, or personnel manager can be marketing-oriented.
5. For each of the following organizations, describe what is being marketed.
   - **a.** Calgary Stampeders professional football team.
   - **b.** Canadian Airline Pilots Association labour union.
   - **c.** Professor teaching a first-year chemistry course.
   - **d.** Police department in your city.
6. One way of explaining the value or utility provided by marketing is to consider how we would live if there were no marketing facilities. Describe some of the ways in which your daily activities would be affected if there were no retail stores or advertising.
7. Name two service firms that, in your opinion, do a good marketing job. Then name some that do a poor marketing job. Explain your reasoning in each case.

Hands-On Marketing

1. Select an organizational unit at your school (e.g., food service, placement office, intramural sports, library), observe the operation, and interview an administrator and some customers to identify: (a) what is being exchanged; and (b) whether the unit is production-, sales-, or marketing-oriented.
2. Find out from a retailer in your community what changes or additions it has made during the last year to better retain customers. Categorize the changes by the six types of utilities discussed in this chapter. Based on your conversation, what value or utility dimension has the greatest potential for improving customer relationships in the future?

CHAPTER 2 GOALS

After studying this chapter, you should have an understanding of:

- The concept of environmental monitoring (environmental scanning).
- How external environmental forces such as demography, economic and competitive conditions, social and cultural forces, technology, and political and legal systems can influence a company's marketing program.
- How external forces such as suppliers and intermediaries that are specific to a firm can influence its marketing program.
- How the nonmarketing resources and departments within a firm can influence the ways in which it practises marketing.

Chapter Two

The Changing Marketing Environment

www.mcdonalds.com

McDONALD'S: RESPONDING TO A CHANGING WORLD

McDonald's has been selling hamburgers in the United States since 1955 and in Canada for over thirty years. It is undisputed as the global fast-food king, operating more than twenty thousand restaurants in over one hundred countries. From its early beginnings and simple menus of hamburgers, French fries, milkshakes, and soft drinks, McDonald's has added a variety of products, including eggs and sausage for breakfast, pizza, crispy chicken, and salads, and regional product variations including McLobster sandwiches and poutine.

Around the world the company has opened outlets in unusual locations, including zoos, sports facilities, and Wal-Mart stores. The familiar golden arches, seen in Hong Kong, Warsaw, Moscow, London, and Sydney, Australia, among hundreds of other locations, symbolize, for many, a product that is well-known and loved. To maintain its position as product leader, this company has made continuous changes in response to changes in its external environment.

www.redlobster.com
www.wendys.com
www.aw.ca

Over the years, McDonald's has directed its promotional activity toward a number of market segments, including young couples with children. In fact, a theme of one of the company's early advertising campaigns was "You deserve a break today." McDonald's continues its emphasis on children and families, from Happy Meals toys to PlayPlaces and McDonaldland fun characters, a focus that is not likley to change in the foreseeable future. In fact, McDonald's has recently entered into a marketing alliance with the Walt Disney Company to become its promotional partner and to link McDonald's restaurants to Disney theatrical releases, theme parks, and home video releases.[1] Despite these efforts to ensure that it meets the needs of its traditional market base, a change in the demographics of the Canadian population has created a shift in the external environment of this company — a factor that McDonald's must address. The early McDonald's advocates have now grown up. Their tastes in food products are being influenced by middle age and by a well-established trend toward fat-free and cholesterol-conscious diets.

In 1996, the company developed a specific campaign to introduce the Arch Deluxe, a hamburger designed with "grown-up taste" in mind. To capitalize on the sale of this product in Ontario, the company began a limited-time supplementary promotion that mirrored the kids' Happy Meal by offering Arch Deluxe Happy Meals for adults.[2] This promotion included, in addition to the Arch Deluxe burger, fries, drink, a Nestlé Coffee Crisp chocolate bar, and a coupon that could be redeemed for a $1 Lotto 6/49 ticket. This promotion was designed to create more value for McDonald's customers in Ontario.

Other efforts to link the McDonald's product with an adult target group include the high-profile sponsorship of Olympic events and NBA basketball in the United States. To establish itself as a socially responsible corporation, McDonald's also is involved in rain forest preservation, environmental education and community programs, and waste reduction efforts. All these efforts, some more successful than others, are designed to reflect things that are happening outside the four walls of a McDonald's outlet — the values, opinions, and demographics of the societies in which it operates.

At the same time that all of these changes have been taking place, competition in the family restaurant market has grown fiercer. Chains such as The Keg, Swiss Chalet, Red Lobster, and Mother Tucker's offer more extensive menus, all-you-can-eat salad bars, and a casual family atmosphere. Long-established fast-food outlets such as Burger King, Wendy's, and A&W compete directly with McDonald's on price, fast service, and menu offerings. In an effort to fight its direct competition and solidify its position as fast-food leader, McDonald's introduced a short-term price promotion in the United States in early 1997. "Campaign 55" cut the price of breakfast sandwiches and Big Macs to fifty-five cents for a limited time.[3]

The strategic changes being considered by McDonald's and others are the result of environmental monitoring, a practice that many companies are adopting in order to stay on top of the changing world in which they operate. Environmental forces influence the way in which a company does its marketing. Some of these forces are external to the company, while others come from within. There isn't much that management can do about controlling the external forces; at most, it can monitor them and respond in a manner to capitalize on opportunities and reduce threats. Generally, management can control internal forces. McDonald's, like any other organization, must manage its marketing program within its combined external and internal environments.

ENVIRONMENTAL MONITORING

Environmental monitoring, also called environmental scanning, is the process of (1) gathering information regarding a company's external environment, (2) analyzing it, and (3) forecasting the impact of the trends suggested by the analysis.

Today, much environmental discussion concerns the state of the *physical* environment — air quality, water pollution, the disposal of solid waste, and the conservation of natural resources. However, the term environment is used in a much broader sense in this chapter.

An organization operates within an external environment that it generally cannot control. At the same time, there are marketing and nonmarketing resources within the organization that generally can be controlled by its management group.

www.disney.com

There are two levels of external forces:

- Macro influences (so called because they affect all firms) include demographics, economic conditions, technological development, culture, and laws.
- Micro influences (so called because they affect a particular firm) consist of suppliers, marketing intermediaries, and customers. Micro influences, while external, are closely related to a specific company and are part of its total marketing system.

Successful marketing depends largely on a company's ability to manage its marketing programs within its environment. To do this, a firm's marketing executives must determine what makes up the firm's environment and then monitor it in a systematic, ongoing fashion. These marketing managers must be alert to spot trends in the firm's environment that could be opportunities or problems for their organization. And they must be able to respond to these trends with the resources they can control.

EXTERNAL MACROENVIRONMENT

The following six interrelated macroenvironmental forces have a considerable effect on any organization's marketing system. Yet they are largely not controllable by management (see Figure 2-1).

- Demography.
- Economic conditions.
- Competition.
- Social and cultural forces.
- Technology.
- Political and legal forces.

Note that these forces are *largely*, but not *totally*, uncontrollable by management. A company must be able to manage its external environment to some extent. For example, through company and industry lobbying in Ottawa or provincial capitals, a company may have some influence on the political and legal forces in its environment. In addition, new-product research and development that is on the technological frontier can influence a firm's competitive position. In fact, one company's technology may be the external environmental force of technology that is affecting other organizations.

If there is one similarity in the six environmental factors, it is that they are all subject to considerable change, and at different rates. Also, an important point from a marketing perspective is that not all markets or all consumers are affected by these changes in the same way. For example, some consumers cope with difficult economic times better than others do; some people are more adept at using the latest technological innovations; some accept new ideas and new ways of doing things much more readily than others do. The result is an extremely complex marketplace that is influenced by external factors that the marketer cannot influence but must understand and appreciate. The following section examines each of the six major environmental forces.

FIGURE 2-1 External Macroenvironment of a Company's Marketing Program

Six largely uncontrollable external forces influence an organization's marketing activities.

Demography

Demography is the statistical study of human population and its distribution. It is especially important to marketing executives, because people constitute markets. Demography will be discussed in greater detail in the section on markets; at this point, we shall mention just a couple of examples of how demographic factors influence marketing systems.

One of the most significant demographic factors that Canadian marketers are addressing today is the phenomenon of the baby boomers — that segment of the population born between 1946 and 1966, the twenty years following World War II.[4] What is special about this population segment is the fact that there are so many of them. Canada produced more than 400,000 new Canadians in each year of the baby boom, and the number peaked in 1959 at 479,000. In the first of the baby boom years, 1946, 19 percent more babies were born than was the case a year earlier. During several of these years the birthrate reached 120 per thousand women, compared with 67.2 per thousand women in 1988.[5] Canada's demographics are unique because that segment of the population is larger in Canada than anywhere else. Because this segment is so large, some marketers feel that buying patterns can be significantly influenced by it. The existence of so many people in a particular age range is an important factor for anyone interested in the demographic patterns of the population to consider.

The baby boom segment is passing through its middle years. The aging of the baby boom generation is beginning to bring changes in middle-aged values, tastes, and concerns. When their children have grown, they will indulge themselves with well-earned vacations and luxury cars instead of a family minivan. Their expanding waistlines will bring a boom in larger-sized jeans and more conservative casual clothes. As they forsake their city and suburban residences for cottage country, the price of recreational property will rise. Their interest in healthy living will continue into their fifties and sixties, resulting in a renewed emphasis on sensible eating and less active sports such as curling, golf, and bowling.

But it is not just the baby boomers who represent a lucrative and challenging target segment. Their children, now in their late teens and early twenties — a group often referred to as Generation X — also constitute an attractive age segment. Because there were so many babies born between 1946 and 1966, they produced lots of children, even though they had fewer children per family. This generation, which is facing the challenge of entering the work force in circumstances less attractive than those their parents faced, tends to react differently to conventional approaches to marketing.[6]

Another population segment undergoing major change is the seniors market. In the mid-1980s, for the first time in history, the number of people aged sixty-five and older surpassed the number of teenagers — and this gap is widening considerably. The seniors market includes an aging population and a seniors population. Prominent Canadian demographer David Foot breaks this market down into three groups: young seniors (65–74), mid-seniors (75–84), and senior seniors (85 and up). The most senior of the groups is the segment that is growing the most rapidly because these individuals were born in a time of strong population growth.

During the early part of this century Canada welcomed its greatest influx of immigrants, so it would be incorrect to assume that all seniors have the same interests and wants from the marketplace. They come from many backgrounds and span a wide range of age categories. Many new products and services are being offered and developed for seniors in all categories. The cruise ship industry, for instance, has benefited greatly from the young seniors group, and upscale retirement homes are of interest to the mid-seniors. The oldest age group is the group of lowest affluence, and many in this category tend to be interested in affordable retirement services and products.[7]

A further demographic change relates to the growing market segment consisting of single people. Today, well over 20 percent of Canadian households are made up of people who live alone. An increasing percentage of these single-person households contain older people, mostly women, who have been widowed. Many of these single, older consumers are healthy and lead active lives, and they represent an attractive target market for travel and tour companies.

The marketing implications of this demographic segment are almost limitless. The frozen-food industry caters to this market with high-quality frozen entrées in a wide variety of menu offerings, many of which involve single servings. Automobile manufacturers and banks recognize the increased buying power of single women and have developed marketing programs and services specifically for this segment. Homebuilders are designing homes, condominium units, and housing developments with older singles in mind, while tour companies regularly offer bus tour vacations and cruises for this increasingly affluent group.

Some researchers feel that demographics, as an explanation of economic forces, is vastly overrated. A Royal Bank of Canada study, conducted in 1997, reported that there is no evidence to support focusing on demographics to the exclusion of other factors. The authors of the report stated that demographics can assist in determining where demand is going to be, but the information should not be considered the sole determining factor.[8]

Economic Conditions

People alone do not make a market. They must have money to spend and be willing to spend it. Consequently, the **economic environment** is a significant force that affects the marketing system of just about any organization. A marketing system is affected especially by such economic considerations as the current stage of the business cycle, inflation, and interest rates.

Stage of the Business Cycle Marketing executives should understand what stage of the business cycle the economy currently is in, because this cycle has a large impact on a company's marketing system. The traditional business cycle goes through four stages: prosperity, recession, depression, and recovery. However, various economic strategies have been adopted by the federal government; these strategies have averted the depression stage in Canada and other developed countries for more than sixty years. Consequently, today we think of a three-stage **business cycle**: prosperity, recession, and recovery.

A company usually operates its marketing system quite differently during each stage. Prosperity is characterized typically as a period of economic growth. During this stage, organizations tend to expand their marketing programs as they add new products and enter new markets. A recession, on the other hand, involves higher rates of unemployment and reduced consumer spending and typically is a period of retrenchment for consumers and businesses. People can become discouraged, scared, and angry. These feelings affect their buying behaviour, which, in turn, has major implications for the marketing programs in countless firms.

Recovery finds the economy moving from recession to prosperity: The marketers' challenge is determining how quickly prosperity will return and to what level. As the unemployment rate declines and disposable income increases, companies expand their marketing efforts to improve sales and profits.

Inflation **Inflation** is a rise in price levels. When prices rise at a faster rate than personal income, there is a decline in consumer buying power. During the late 1970s and early 1980s, Canada experienced a relatively high inflation rate of 10 to 15 percent. Although inflation rates declined during the 1990s to less than 3 percent, economic growth has been accompanied by a fear that higher rates may return. This spectre continues to influence government policies, consumer psychology, and business marketing programs.

Inflation presents some real challenges in the management of a marketing program, especially in the area of pricing and cost control. Consumers are adversely affected as their buying power declines. At the same time, they may overspend today for fear that prices will be higher tomorrow.

Interest Rates **Interest rates** are another external economic factor influencing marketing programs. When interest rates are high, for example, consumers tend to hold back on long-term purchases such as housing. Consumer purchases also are affected by whether consumers think that interest rates will increase or decline. Marketers sometimes offer below-market interest rates (a form of price cut) as a promotional device to increase business. Auto manufacturers have used this tactic extensively in recent years.

Unemployment Rates One of the most important indicators of the strength of an economy is the percentage of people who are employed and the percentage looking for work. During a strong economic growth period, unemployment rates are generally lower. At other times, and in certain parts of Canada, unemployment is higher. This affects greatly the amount of disposable income that consumers have to spend on products and services and is of considerable interest to marketers.

A marketer must pay considerable attention to the condition of the economy in which his or her company is operating. Purchasers of certain products and services may react quickly to changes or expected changes in economic conditions. The marketer must be ready to respond with changes in the marketing program.

Competition

A company's competitive environment is a major influence in shaping its marketing system. Any executives worth their salt should be constantly gathering intelligence and otherwise monitoring all aspects of their competitors' marketing activities. Expanded trade with other countries means that Canadian firms will have to pay greater attention to foreign competition and, with the movement toward global free trade, increasingly find opportunities for Canadian products and services in foreign markets. The North American Free Trade Agreement (NAFTA), for example, is expanding the Canadian business environment to include the United States and Mexico. In some cases this shift in the environment has resulted in Canadian businesses having to deal with significantly increased competition. One such situation occurred with the entry into Canada of large American retailers such as Home Depot and Wal-Mart, which prompted Canadian retailers to mount a defensive strategy. Two aspects of competition we shall consider briefly here are the types of competition and the competitive market structure in which the companies may be operating.

A firm generally faces competition from three sources:

- *Direct brand competition and store competition* from marketers of similar and directly competing products and services. Air Canada competes with Canadian Airlines International on many domestic routes and with KLM, British Airways, United Airlines, Cathay Pacific, and other foreign carriers on international routes. Bauer competes with Micron, Lange, and CCM in the skate business. Cooper competes with overseas companies such as Karhu and Koho for the Canadian hockey stick business. Domestic retailers face competition from international retailers such as Wal-Mart, Ikea, and Marks and Spencer. Even charitable organizations such as the Canadian Cancer Society, the Heart and Stroke Foundation of Canada, and the Salvation Army compete for donations and for the time of canvassers and volunteers.
- *Substitute products* that satisfy the same basic need. For example, vinyl records have disappeared in the face of competition first from tape cassettes and then from compact discs. Local courier companies and Canada Post have seen a portion of their business taken away by the business use of facsimile (fax) machines and increasingly by electronic mail. Many conventional delivery services are threatened by the use of electronic delivery systems. The use of mail services and long-distance telephone calling is being challenged by electronic mail, and even business air travel may be under threat from the teleconferencing and video conferencing services offered by telephone companies. Many department stores and clothing retailers are realizing that their competition is coming not only from other stores down the street or in the same town, but from catalogue companies such as Sears and Tilley Endurables, some of which, including L. L. Bean and Land's End, are in other countries.
- In the third type of competition — more general in nature — *every company or organization* is competing for the consumer's limited buying power. In this regard, the competition faced by a marketer of tennis racquets may come from other companies that are marketing slacks or shoes, or from a car repair bill, or a weekend ski holiday.

On the international scene, two major competitive environmental developments in the 1990s have created important challenges for Canadian marketers. One is the creation of blocs of nations around the world that have combined into free-trade zones, thereby allowing a less restricted flow of products and services across international borders. The unification

www.ikea.com
www.marks-and-spencer.com
www.cancer.ca
www.hss.ca
www.sally.net.org
www.mailposte.ca
www.sears.com
www.tilley.com
www.llbean.com
www.landsend.com

www.homedepot.com • www.wal-mart.com • www.aircanada.com • www.klm.nl • www.british-airways.com • www.ual.com • www.cathay-usa.com

of the European Community has created one such bloc, while NAFTA has linked Canada, the United States, and Mexico in an economic union. The second development involves the radical change from a government-controlled system to a relatively free market economy in many countries, particularly in Eastern Europe and the countries of the former Soviet Union. Prices have been decontrolled and government subsidies removed on many products in Poland, Russia, and Estonia, for example. In addition, some major companies and industries, formerly 100 percent government-owned, have been sold to private interests. We will discuss some of these developments in greater detail in the chapter on international marketing.

Social and Cultural Forces

The task facing marketing executives is becoming more complex because cultural patterns — lifestyles, social values, and beliefs — are changing much more quickly than they used to. Here are a few changes in **social and cultural forces** that have significant marketing implications.

Changing Values — Emphasis on Quality of Life Our emphasis today is increasingly on the quality of life rather than merely on the quality of goods and services. The theme is "Not more — but better." We seek value, durability, comfort, and safety in the products and services we buy. Looking ahead, we will worry more about education, health, and the environment, and less about keeping up with the neighbours in automobiles, clothing, and homes. Our growing concern for the physical environment and our discontent with pollution and resource waste are leading to significant changes in our lifestyles. And when our lifestyles change, marketing is affected.

This change in values among Canadians is evident in a number of areas, as consumers reject the accumulation of assets that characterized the 1980s in favour of a return to products that reflect the values of the past. An important influence on the changing values of which Canadian marketers should be aware is the effect of the large number of recent immigrants on shaping values in certain parts of the country. Each immigrant group brings with it a unique set of values shaped by the culture of its home country. One group of authors has identified the following as characteristic of many of the immigrant groups who have recently made Canada their home:

- A high degree of control by family elders over purchasing power and buying decisions.
- A suspicion of government and government-sponsored programs.
- An aversion to the use of credit cards and to the accumulation of debt.
- A focus on household and family goals, including securing a job, home ownership, and education for the children.

Such values lead to recurrent patterns of behaviour among these consumers, which marketers must consider when plotting marketing strategy to appeal to them.[9]

Role of Men and Women One of the most dramatic shifts in our culture has been the changing role of women. What is especially significant is the erosion of stereotypes regarding male–female roles in families, jobs, recreation, and product use.

The evolving roles of women have many implications for marketers. Well over one-half of the women in Canada are working outside the home today. This has changed some traditional buying patterns in households. Long gone are the days when women were the sole buyers of groceries and household items and men were the purchasers of hardware and car maintenance. The entry of women into the work force on a mass scale has increased the requirement for day-care facilities and the usage of time-saving appliances and food products. Women working outside the home buy different clothing than do women working at home. The sharing of family responsibility is a characteristic of most modern Canadian families, to the point where many employers have begun to extend programs to men that had been available only for women, including paternity leave, pregnancy-education programs, and parenting seminars.

Attitudes Toward Physical Fitness and Eating In recent years, an increased interest in health and physical fitness seems generally to have cut across most demographic and economic segments of our society. Participation in physical fitness activities from aerobics to yoga is on the increase. Stores supplying activity products and service organizations catering to this trend have multiplied. Public facilities (bicycle paths, hiking trails, jogging paths, and playgrounds) have been improved.

Paralleling the physical fitness phenomenon, significant changes are occurring in the eating patterns of Canadians. We are becoming more sensitive to the relationship between our diet and major killing diseases such as heart disease and cancer. Consequently, there is a growing interest in weight-control eating, in foods low in salt, food additives, and cholesterol, and in foods high in vitamins, minerals, and fibre content. Health foods now occupy large sections in many supermarkets. Over the past twenty years, per capita consumption of chicken in Canada has increased by more than 35 percent, while the consumption of fish has increased by almost 50 percent. School cafeterias, once considered havens of junk food, have dramatically changed their menus to meet the needs of ethnic groups and the many teenagers who have become vegetarians. According to the Toronto Board of Education, there has been a shift to pasta and salads. Sales of hamburgers have dropped off dramatically.[10]

Emphasis on Service Quality As consumers have become more confident of their rights and the power they wield in the marketplace, they have become increasingly demanding about the manner in which they are treated by business. Although companies have long appreciated that they must produce quality products to compete effectively for the consumer's loyalty, most are now beginning to realize that quality is equally important in service delivery.

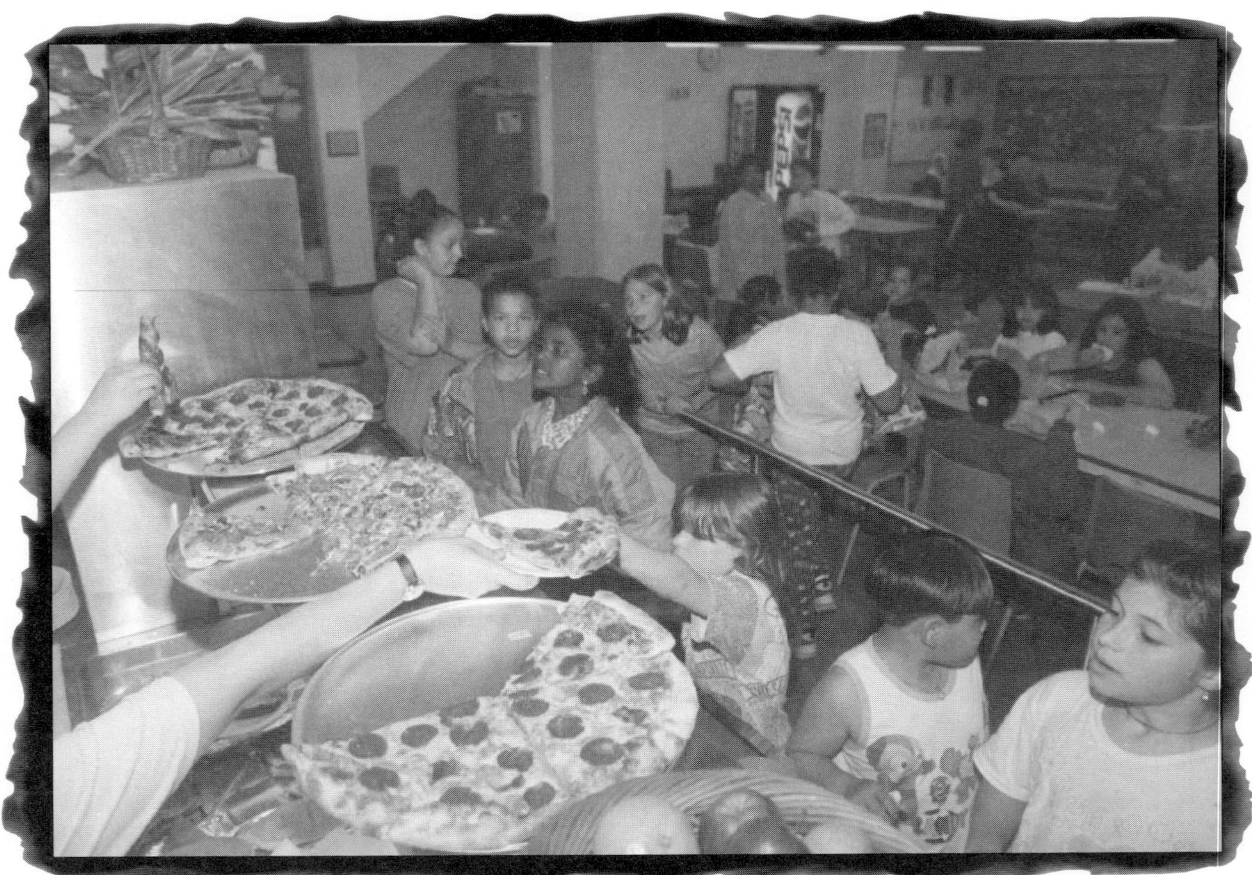

School meals change with the times.

MARKETING AT WORK FILE 2–1

MULTICULTURALISM — A GROWTH MARKET

Canada's growing multicultural population offers an environment of opportunity for marketers. According to James Pollock, writing in *Marketing Magazine*, this opportunity is being recognized and seized upon by Canadian companies. This is particularly true within the Chinese community. Statistics Canada figures indicate that in December 1996, an estimated 915,000 Chinese people were living in Canada. That figure is expected to grow to 2.1 million by the year 2001. Products such as Campbell's soup are being sold with labels written in Chinese characters; Clairol offers cosmeticians a chart suggesting colours to use for Asian customers' hair. Both of these companies are reflecting the cultural forces that are affecting the Canadian marketplace.

The growth of ethnic-minority populations has resulted not only in stronger and more varied cultural voices demanding to be satisfied with products, but in a mainstream population whose tastes have broadened. This expansion of tastes offers companies the opportunity to, in turn, expand their available products to meet the varied interests and needs as well as the opportunity to introduce other Canadians to product choices developed for the "ethnic market." For example, Knorr Chicken Broth, a product of Best Foods Canada Inc. of Toronto, is made from a Chinese formula obtained from Hong Kong.

The marketing industry is also using multilingual advertisements in both electronic and print formats to reach immigrants who do not speak English or French. Clairol is airing Chinese-only TV commercials on Toronto's multicultural station CFMT. The spots invite viewers to call a toll-free number to receive the brochure, coupons-for-trial, and a chance to win a makeover. The company received more than one thousand calls in four weeks. Companies are also hiring models from a variety of cultural backgrounds to use in product advertisements.

All of these approaches are aimed at reaching these new residents by reflecting and satisfying their needs and wants. As stated by Martin Seto, vice-president of accounts at Access Advertising: "With 25 percent of the population in certain areas being Chinese, for example, you'd be crazy not to be there."

Source: Adapted from James Pollock, "Testing the Multicultural Waters," *Marketing Magazine*, November 18, 1996.

Quality in services is not easily defined because it depends on the expectations of the customer. Each individual brings to a service encounter his or her own concept of what constitutes quality. The concept is based on personal experiences and individual likes and dislikes. Much work has been done by marketers on how to measure quality in service industries. Unlike manufacturing, where standards can be objectively set on the basis of stress factors, safety features, and size, among others, services cannot be as easily standarized.

With the growth in the service economy, the quality of service delivery and the level of customer expectations is becoming more of an issue. More people are spending money on services, and more services are available to them. Consumers are also more sophisticated than ever before, they travel more, and they are more able to discern quality and dictate what they want and don't want.

Decisions to purchase at certain stores or stay at specific hotels are made not only on the basis of tangible products, the decor of the room, or the quality of food in the restaurant (although these are important), but on the much more intangible factor of the level and quality of the service provided. Customers now regularly tell businesses that they want to be treated as though their business is welcomed and appreciated. The best companies have responded with sophisticated programs to measure the satisfaction of customers and with other programs designed to deliver a higher level of service quality.

Concern for the Environment Possibly one of the most important forces that will influence Canadian business and marketing in the coming years is Canadians' concern for the physical environment. As we have seen the damage done to the quality of water, air, and the land during this century, there has been a collective outpouring of support for programs and products that allow us to take action to protect the environment.

Consequently, governments have moved to control the emissions of automobiles and factories; food manufacturers package products in less wasteful and more biodegradable packages; and municipalities across the country have established recycling programs in which many householders and most businesses participate. Supermarket chains stock many products labelled "environmentally friendly," meaning that their packages and ingredients are not harmful to the environment. The result is a major movement driven by the changing values of consumers, who are concerned about air and water pollution, acid rain, holes in the ozone layer, the destruction of forests, overfishing, and the disposal of chemicals and solid waste. The environmental movement is a global concern, as consumers in most countries of the world have adopted similar attitudes.

Within Canada, concern for the environment is a major factor. In a global survey conducted in twenty-four countries, three-quarters of Canadians felt that protecting the environment was more important than promoting economic growth. In this regard, Canada was tied for second place among all the countries surveyed.[11]

This has several implications for business:

- As many as 50 percent of consumers in the future are expected to make purchases on the basis of environmental factors.
- McDonald's and other fast-food retailers have replaced their polystyrene containers with cardboard and paper containers.
- Companies such as The Body Shop have successfully positioned themselves on the basis of their concern for the environment and other social issues.
- A number of cosmetics manufacturers have begun to offer products packaged in recyclable containers and developed without testing on animals.
- Many consumers are altering their purchase behaviour significantly as they look for products that do not contain harsh or unnecessary chemicals.

Desire for Convenience As an outgrowth of the increase in discretionary purchasing power and the importance of time, there has been a continuing increase in consumers' desire for convenience. We want products ready and easy to use, and convenient credit plans to pay for them. We want these products packaged in a variety of sizes, quantities, and forms. We want stores located close by and open at virtually all hours.

Every major phase of a company's marketing program is affected by this craving for convenience. Product planning is influenced by the need for customer convenience in packaging, quantity, and selection. Pricing policies must be established in conformity with the demand for credit and with the costs of providing the various kinds of convenience. Distribution policies must provide for convenient locations and hours of business. As a result, Canada's banks have placed thousands of automated banking machines in various locations in cities and towns across Canada, so that their customers now have access to banking services in off-premise locations and at any time of the day or night. Banks also offer telephone banking and banking by personal computer where bills can be paid by phone or on line, transfers can be made, and account information can be obtained. With new advances in the development of "smart cards," banks will soon offer customers access to cash without their ever having to enter a bank.

Another example of business responding to the consumer's desire for convenience is the increasing use of catalogues to order products. Even people who live in major cities and who have access to a wide variety of retail stores find it less time-consuming and more convenient to shop from catalogues. These catalogue retailers make shopping from home as easy as possible through the use of toll-free 1-800/888 telephone numbers, their acceptance of major credit cards, and relatively risk-free shopping through generous exchange and refund policies.

www.thebodyshopo.ca

The advances in the availability and efficiency of the Internet are a major change that is creating considerable convenience for the consumer. Information on product and service quality and availability can be easily accessed through the World Wide Web. Companies are also making it increasingly easy for products to be purchased directly on the Internet.

Impulse Buying Partly as a result of attractive in-store displays, much retail purchasing involves impulse buying — purchasing done without much advance planning. A shopper may go to the grocery store with a mental note to buy meat and bread. In the store, he may also select some fresh peaches because they look appealing or are priced attractively. Another shopper, seeing facial tissues on the shelf, may be reminded that she is running low and may buy two boxes. These are impulse purchases.

A key point to understand is that some impulse buying is done on a very rational basis. Self-service, open-display selling has brought about a marketing situation wherein planning may be postponed until the buyer reaches the retail outlet. Because of the trend toward impulse buying, emphasis must be placed on promotional programs designed to get people into a store. Displays must be appealing because the manufacturer's package must serve as a silent sales person.

Even the new breed of nonstore retailers, those who sell their products through vending machines, catalogues, and home demonstration parties, must be mindful of the phenomenon of impulse shopping. Again they make their offerings as attractive as possible and facilitate the process by offering free delivery, free catalogues, credit, and toll-free telephone numbers.

TECHNOLOGY

Technology has a tremendous impact on our lifestyles, consumption patterns, and economic well-being. Just think of the effect of major technological developments such as the airplane, plastics, television, computers, antibiotics, lasers, and compact discs. Except perhaps for the airplane, all these technologies reached the large-scale marketing stage only in your lifetime or your parents' lifetime. Think about how your life in the future might be affected by cures for the common cold, the development of energy sources to replace fossil fuels, low-cost methods for making ocean water drinkable, or even commercial travel to outer space.

Consider for a moment some of the dramatic technological breakthroughs that are expanding our horizons as we move into the new millennium. The role of robotics undoubtedly will expand considerably. Robots are now used extensively in manufacturing, space exploration, and satellite maintenance. At the heart of a robot's operating mechanism is a miniature electronic computer system, which leads us into another technological breakthrough area — miniature electronic products. It's hard to grasp the fantastic possibilities in this field. Then there is the awesome potential of the superconductor, a means of transmitting electrical energy with virtually no resistance. Further developments in fibre optics, the Internet, high-definition television, digital transmission, and CD-ROM technology will open vistas of communication that were not possible even five years ago.

The advancement of CD-ROM technology is changing the way we buy books, videos, and records. New developments in digitizing have led to the creation of the digital versatile disc (DVD), which enables the storage of multimedia formats. DVDs have established a technology that will enable us to buy recordings that combine text, graphics, sound, video, and music on a single disc that is available for use when the individual consumer wants it. Such digital technology will establish a new high standard in home entertainment and information storage and retrieval.

The Internet has seen rapid development in the last few years. Virtually every home and office in Canada is becoming linked through interactive telephone lines, thereby allowing families to shop and do their banking from their living room and to order video movies from a catalogue for instant viewing. In Canada a number of direct-to-home satellite services have been approved by the CRTC. These innovative approaches to TV viewing are bypassing earlier technologies and offering consumers opportunities not previously considered. In another area, travel plans to practically any location can now be made by directly accessing airline Internet home pages and destination marketing sites.

Technology allows people to stay in touch.

Technological development is not only changing the lives of consumers, it is also changing the way companies do business. Any firm in today's marketplace must be able to integrate electronic communications and marketing with other forms of customer contact. Though Internet commerce is still experiencing some drawbacks (such as guaranteed security for credit card users), more and more companies are marketing through this interactive medium. Internally, companies are engaging in projects that are undertaken by "virtual" teams — groups formed through electronic mail communications who may never meet face to face. Linking the core technologies of the Internet with the company's own needs, intranets, or private corporate networks is resulting in more effective internal communications, distribution, and retrieval and updating of information.[12]

Major technological breakthroughs have a threefold impact on marketing:

- To start entirely new industries, such as computers, robots, lasers, facsimile machines, and microwave ovens have done, and as the Internet, CD-ROM and its heir-apparent the DVD-ROM, as well as other digital technologies, will do in the future.

MARKETING AT WORK FILE 2-2

DIAL A CARD — THE SMART WAY TO BANK

In the changing marketplace of today an age-old institution, banking, is dramatically changing the way it does business. According to Justin Smallbridge, writing in *Marketing Magazine*, banks are telling us that branches will soon start to disappear. People will be banking virtually via computer. Banking by personal computer through any number of home banking software packages is just the latest step in an evolutionary process that began with the introduction of automated banking machines and has progressed to the "smart card" with embedded chips that can store transferable electronic cash.

David Livingston, senior vice-president for card and direct services at Toronto Dominion Bank, says that access to banking through the personal computer may not be the most basic and widely used approach in the future. The device now being extensively explored for banking services is the telephone. Using embedded chips on smart cards allows the potential for accessing money over a telephone line. "It's a technology that everyone has, that everyone is comfortable with, and the service that you can offer over it is increasing," says Livingston. Soon people will not have to go to a branch or a banking machine; a simple phone call to their account will enable them to apply cash to their smart card. The introduction of technology is on the way.

Mondex International Limited, an independent global payments company owned by MasterCard International and twenty-six other major companies on four continents, is introducing the first version of the smart card. The participants in Mondex are the major financial institutions who are working in conjunction with retailers and telecommunications companies around the world.

Banks are heavily advertising the electronic services that personal computer access has made possible. The strategy is to ensure that as many people as possible become involved with electronic banking. Smallbridge suggests that "the more advances in technology you can sell to your customers, the likelier they'll be to try the next innovation." To facilitate the conversion from face-to-face banking to "virtual" banking, the institutions are pushing to tie in the familiar technology of the telephone. Adjusting to new environments can involve ensuring that customers retain some of the familiar while learning to use the new.

Sources: Adapted from Justin Smallbridge, "Banking on the Future," *Marketing Magazine*, December 16, 1996, p. 8; "Mondex International Company Profile," 1997, http:///www.mondex.com/mondex/cg...pl?english&company.html.

- To alter radically or virtually destroy existing industries. Television had a significant impact on movies and radio when it was introduced in the 1950s. Compact discs have eliminated vinyl records and threaten cassette tapes. Facsimile (fax) machines have cut into the conventional mail business of Canada Post, which now offers its own courier and electronic mail services. Sensors imbedded in toll highways, such as the 407 north of Toronto, record cars as they pass over them and bill their owners for the tolls they have used, thereby eliminating toll booths and speeding up traffic.[13] Movie companies in the United States are sending movies to theatres directly from the studio through digital transmission over the telephone lines, thereby eliminating traditional distribution channels and companies.
- To stimulate other markets and industries not related to the new technology. New home appliances and entertainment products have certainly altered the pattern of time use within the home and outside. Cable television, the VCR, CD players,

video games, computer games, and microwave ovens have revolutionized the ways consumers use their time. This development has also led to new industries providing entertainment products and food products that are used with these new devices and that were not available a few years ago.

There is virtually no aspect of our lives that is not being affected in a significant way by new technology. By early 1997, 8 percent of Canadians, or about two million people, were accessing the World Wide Web on a weekly basis. This number is increasing rapidly.[14] Banks are offering their customers the use of debit cards, PC banking, and smart cards, which allow shoppers to pay bills or buy products by a direct debit to their bank accounts, thereby eliminating the use of cheques and the incurring of interest charges, although some financial institutions may charge a fee to customers each time they use these services. Interactive technology is the tone of the new age. The Internet allows consumers not only to receive messages, as the old media did, but to respond to them. According to Sympatico, a Canadian Internet service, Internet marketing and shopping is the direction for the future. Marketers can provide customers with as much information as they feel is necessary, or they can give customers an opportunity to provide information about themselves. The medium makes one-to-one communication possible.[15] With new advances in multimedia such as in-home shopping that uses cable, telephone, and Internet connections, technology is opening up whole new vistas for marketers.

Despite the advances that have been made, technology is often a mixed blessing. A new technology may improve our lives in one area while creating environmental and social problems in other areas. The automobile makes life great in some ways, but it also creates traffic jams and air pollution. Television provides a built-in baby-sitter, but it also can have an adverse effect on family discussions and on children's reading habits. The Internet provides virtually unlimited access to information, but that material must be organized and catalogued to be useful. It is ironic that technology is strongly criticized for creating problems (air pollution, for example), but at the same time it is expected to solve these problems.

POLITICAL AND LEGAL FORCES

To an increasing extent, every company's conduct is influenced by **political and legal forces** in society. Legislation at all levels exercises more influence on the marketing activities of an organization than on any other phase of its operations. The political–legal influences on marketing can be grouped into six categories. In each, the influence stems both from legislation and from policies established by the maze of government agencies.

1. *General monetary and fiscal policies.* Marketing systems obviously are affected by the level of government spending, the money supply, and tax legislation.

2. *Our legislative framework and codes and policies set by government agencies.* Human rights codes and programs to reduce unemployment fall into this category. Also included is legislation controlling the environment. For example, marketers in the direct-mail business are coming under increasing attack for what some consumers feel is the waste involved in flyers and mailing pieces that arrive unsolicited in their mailboxes, much of which ends up in the garbage unread. Legislators are being pressured by environmental groups to pass legislation regulating the sending of such mail.

3. *Social legislation.* Governments often pass legislation that is intended to protect members of society. A ban on smoking in airplanes, mandatory seat belt use, and the prohibition of cigarette advertising are examples of this type of legislation.

4. *Government relationships with individual industries.* Here we find subsidies in agriculture, shipbuilding, passenger rail transportation, culture, and other industries. Tariffs and import quotas also affect specific industries. Throughout the 1990s, governments in Canada and in many other countries have moved to reduce the extent to which they are involved in the operation of businesses. Many have sold government-owned corporations to the private sector. There has been a major move toward deregulation, as industries such as banking, airlines, trucking, telecommunications, and broadcasting have been freed to a greater extent from regulations imposed by government.

Through subsidies and tariff protection, Canadian governments have been involved in such traditional industries as the production of agricultural products. Some of these industries have been threatened with the removal of that protection as industries are deregulated throughout the world and as tariff barriers are removed. Such barriers will continue to fall as the movement toward freedom in international trade expands and as such government involvement in industry is seen to be an impediment to free trade.

5. *Legislation specifically related to marketing*. Marketing executives do not have to be lawyers. But they should know something about these laws, especially the major ones — why they were passed, what their main provisions are, and the current ground rules set by the courts and government agencies for administering these laws.

   The federal department Industry Canada, through its Consumer Products, Marketing Practices, and Competition Policy divisions, administers much of the legislation included in categories 3 and 4 above. Table 2-1 contains examples of the legislation administered by that department that are relevant for marketers. In addition, many other pieces of legislation relating to such topics as food products and advertising are administered by other departments of the federal government. We shall discuss these laws and regulations at the appropriate places throughout this book.

6. *The provision of information and the purchase of products*. This sixth area of government influence in marketing is quite different from the other five. Instead of telling marketing executives what they must do or cannot do — instead of legislation and regulations — the government is clearly helping them. The federal government, through Statistics Canada, is the largest source of secondary marketing information in the country, and the government is the largest single buyer of products and services in the country.

TABLE 2-1 Marketing-Related Legislation Administered by Industry Canada

• Bankruptcy and Insolvency Act	• National Research Council Act
• Boards of Trade Act	• Natural Sciences and Engineering Research Council Act
• Business Development Bank of Canada Act	• Patent Act
• Canada Business Corporations Act	• Precious Metals Marketing Act
• Canada Co-operative Associations Act	• Public Servants Inventions Act
• Canada Corporations Act	• Radiocommunication Act
• Canadian Space Agency Act	• Small Business Investment Grants Act
• Companies' Creditors Arrangement Act	• Small Business Loans Act
• Competition Act	• Social Sciences and Humanities Research Council Act
• Competition Tribunal Act	• Standards Council of Canada Act
• Consumer Packaging and Labelling Act	• Statistics Act
• Copyright Act	• Telecommunications Act
• Department of Industry Act	• Textile Labelling Act
• Electricity and Gas Inspection Act	• Timber Marketing Act
• Industrial Design Act	• Trademarks Act
• Integrated Circuit Topography Act	• Weights and Measures Act
• Investment Canada Act	• Winding-up Act
• Lobbyists Registration Act	

EXTERNAL MICROENVIRONMENT

Three environmental forces that are external, but are a part of a company's marketing system, are that firm's market, its suppliers, and its marketing intermediaries. Although they are generally uncontrollable, these external forces can be influenced more than the macro forces can. A marketing organization, for example, may be able to exert pressure on its suppliers or intermediaries. And, through its advertising, a firm should have some influence on its market (see Figure 2-2).

The Market

The market really is what marketing is all about — how to reach it and serve it profitably and in a socially responsible manner. The market should be the focus of all marketing decisions in an organization. But just what is a market? A market may be defined as a place where buyers and sellers meet, goods or services are offered for sale, and transfers of ownership occur. A market may also be defined as the demand made by a certain group of potential buyers for a good or service. For instance, there is a farm market for petroleum products.

These definitions are not sufficiently precise to be useful to us here. For business purposes we define a **market** as people or organizations with wants (needs) to satisfy, money to spend, and the willingness to spend it. Thus, in the market demand for any given product or service, there are three factors to consider:

- People or organizations with wants (needs).
- Their purchasing power.
- Their buying behaviour.

When we say "needs," we mean what the dictionary says it means: the lack of anything that is required, desired, or useful. We do not limit needs to the physiological requirements of food, clothing, and shelter essential for survival. In our discussions about marketing, the words *needs* and *wants* are used synonymously and interchangeably.

Suppliers

You can't sell a product if you can't first make it or buy it. That's why the people or firms who supply the goods or services that we need to produce what we sell are critical to our marketing success. And that's why we consider a firm's **suppliers** as part of its marketing system. Marketing executives often are not concerned enough with the supply side of the marketing system. But they do become very concerned when shortages occur. Shortages make clear the need for co-operative relationships with suppliers.

Marketing Intermediaries

Marketing intermediaries are independent business organizations that directly aid in the flow of goods and services between a marketing organization and its markets. There are two types of intermediaries: (1) the firms we call *middlemen* or *intermediaries*[16] — wholesalers and retailers; and (2) various *facilitating organizations* that provide such services as transportation, warehousing, and financing that are needed to complete exchanges between buyers and sellers. These intermediaries operate between a company and its markets and between a company and its suppliers. Thus they are part of what we call *channels of distribution*.

In some cases it may be more efficient for a company to take a "do-it-yourself" approach and not use marketing intermediaries. A producer can deal directly with its suppliers or sell directly to its customers and do its own shipping, financing, and so on. But marketing intermediaries are specialists in their respective fields. They often do a better job at a lower cost than the marketing organization can do by itself.

FIGURE 2-2

External Microenvironment of a Company's Marketing Program

ORGANIZATION'S INTERNAL ENVIRONMENT

An organization's marketing system is also shaped by internal forces that are controllable by management (see Figure 2-3). These internal influences include a firm's production, financial, and personnel activities. If Procter & Gamble is considering the manufacture of a new brand of soap, for example, it must determine whether existing production facilities and expertise can be used. If the new product requires a new plant or machinery, financial capability enters the picture.

Other nonmarketing forces are the company's location, its research and development (R&D) strength, and the overall image the firm projects to the public. Plant location often determines the geographic limits of a company's market, particularly if transportation costs are high or its products are perishable. The R&D factor may determine whether a company will lead or follow in its industry.

Another thing to consider in a firm's internal environment is the need to co-ordinate its marketing and nonmarketing activities. Sometimes this can be difficult because of conflicts in goals and executive personalities. Production people, for example, like to see long production runs of standardized items. However, marketing executives may want a variety of models, sizes, and colours to satisfy different market segments. Financial executives typically want tighter credit and expense limits than the marketing people feel are necessary to be competitive.

To wrap up this discussion of the marketing environment, Figure 2-4 shows how all environmental forces combine to shape an organization's marketing program. Within the framework of these constraints, management should develop a marketing program to provide want-satisfaction to its markets. The strategic planning of marketing programs is the topic of the next chapter. Permeating the planning and operation of a marketing program is a company's marketing information system — a key marketing subsystem intended to aid management in solving its problems and making decisions. Chapter 8 is devoted to the subjects of marketing research and a company's flow of information.

FIGURE 2-3

Internal Environment Affecting a Company's Marketing Activities

A company's internal nonmarketing resources influence and support its marketing program.

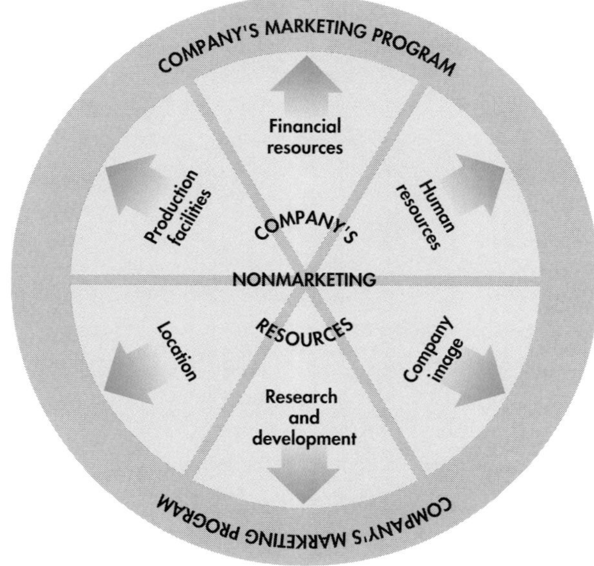

FIGURE 2-4 A Company's Complete Marketing Environment
A framework of internal resources operate within a set of external forces.

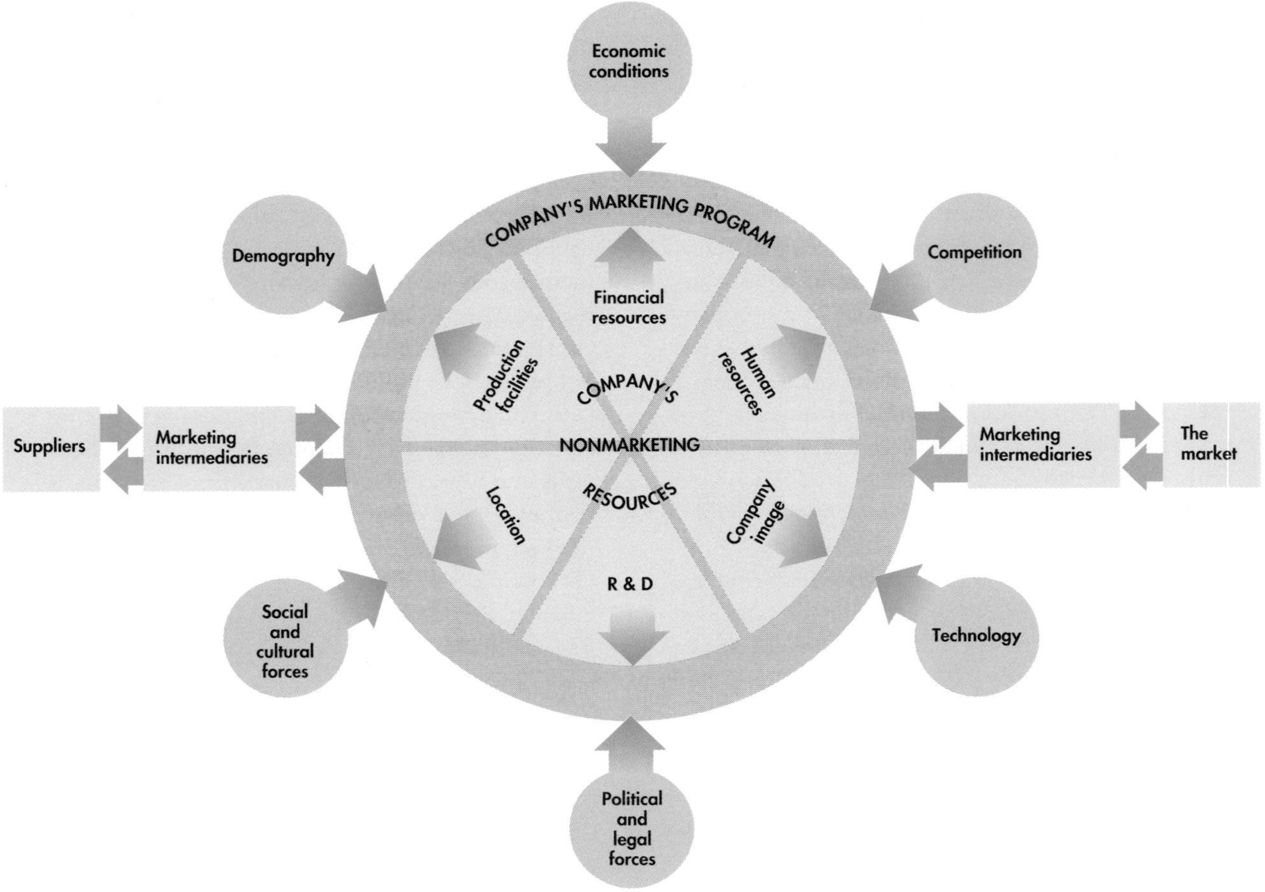

Summary

Various environmental forces influence an organization's marketing activities. Some are external to the firm and are largely uncontrollable by the organization. Other forces are within the firm and are generally controllable by management. A company manages its marketing system within this external and internal environment. To start with, management should set up a system for environmental monitoring — the process of gathering and evaluating environmental information.

Six broad variables constitute the external environment that generally cannot be controlled by an organization. Demographic conditions are one of these macro influences. Another is economic conditions such as the business cycle, inflation, and interest rates. Management must be aware of the various types of competition and the competitive structure within which a given firm operates. Social and cultural forces, including cultural changes, are another factor with which to contend. Technology and political and legal forces round out the group of external macroenvironmental influences.

Another set of environmental factors — suppliers, marketing intermediaries, and the market itself — is also external to the firm. But these elements are part of the firm's marketing system and can be controlled to some extent by the firm. At the same time, a set of nonmarketing resources within the firm — production facilities, personnel, finances, location, research and development, and company image — influences its marketing system. These variables generally are controllable by management.

Key Terms and Concepts

Environmental monitoring (26)
Demography (27)
Economic environment (29)
Business cycle (29)
Inflation (29)
Interest rates (29)
Social and cultural forces (31)
Technology (35)
Political and legal forces (38)
Market (40)
Suppliers (40)
Marketing intermediaries (40)

Questions and Problems

1. It is predicted that university and college enrolments will decline during the next several years. What marketing measures should your school take to adjust to this forecast?
2. For each of the following companies, give some examples of how its marketing program is likely to differ during periods of prosperity as contrasted with periods of recession.
   a. McCain's orange juice.
   b. CCM skates.
   c. Adidas athletic shoes.
   d. Sony Walkman.
3. If interest rates are high, how is the situation likely to affect the market for the following products?
   a. Roots sweatshirts.
   b. Building materials.
   c. Videocassette recorders.
   d. Day-care programs.
4. Explain the three types of competition faced by a company. What marketing strategies or programs would you recommend to meet each type?
5. Give some examples of how the changing attitudes of Canadians toward the environment and their changing food consumption patterns have been reflected in the marketing programs of various companies.
6. What are some of the marketing implications of the increasing public interest in health and physical fitness?
7. What should be the role of marketing in treating the following major social problems?
   a. Air pollution.
   b. The depletion of irreplaceable resources.
   c. Seasonal unemployment.
8. Using examples other than those in this chapter, explain how a firm's marketing system can be influenced by the environmental factor of technology and particularly by the Internet.
9. Give some examples of the effects of marketing legislation in your own buying, recreation, and other everyday activities. Do you believe these laws are effective? If not, what changes would you recommend?
10. Explain how each of the following resources within a company might influence that company's marketing program.
    a. Plant location.
    b. Company image.
    c. Financial resources.
    d. Personnel capability.
11. Specify some internal environmental forces affecting the marketing program of:
    a. Shoppers Drug Mart.
    b. Your school.
    c. A local restaurant.
    d. Air Canada.
12. Explain how or under what conditions a company might exert some control over its suppliers and intermediaries in its marketing program.

Hands-On Marketing

1. Identify two controversial social-cultural issues in the community where your school is located, and explain their impact on firms that market in the community.
2. After interviewing some consumers and/or business people in your community, identify two products or companies (national or local) that you think are doing very well regarding the physical environment. Identify two that you think are doing a poor job.

CHAPTER 3 GOALS

In this chapter we'll examine how a company plans its total marketing program. After studying this chapter, you should have an understanding of:

- The nature and scope of planning and how it fits within the management process.
- Similarities and differences among mission, objectives, strategies, and tactics.
- The essential difference between strategic company planning and strategic marketing planning.
- The steps involved in strategic marketing planning.
- The purpose and contents of an annual marketing plan.
- Similarities and differences as well as weaknesses and strengths across several models used in strategic planning.

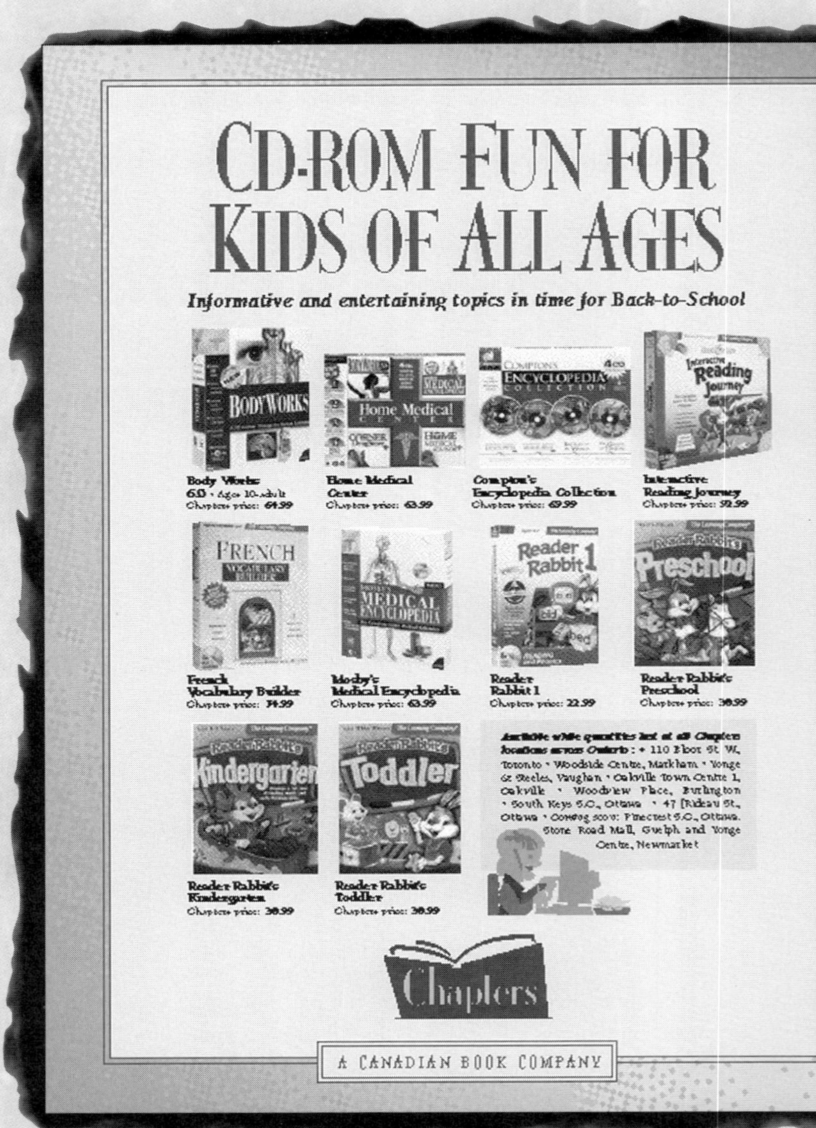

Chapter Three

Strategic Marketing Planning

TURNING THE PAGE

When was the last time you were in a bookstore? A real bookstore, not a textbook store? For more and more people, young and old, the answer is not too long ago. And they had more fun, got more value, had more service, and even developed a favourite place when they didn't have one before. A few years ago, it wasn't like this at all. Bookselling had been a pretty staid and established business. But then came new forms of competition, the CD-ROM, and the superstore.

It was thought that the CD-ROM was going to kill the book, never mind the book business. A few years ago, publishers rushed to create CD-ROM divisions; these days they are rushing to close them down. Not that the CD-ROM has disappeared; it fits into all kinds of niche markets, but, to the relief of booksellers and publishers, the end of the world is not in sight, and now CD-ROMs are often companions or supplements to books. And, of course, quite a few are sold in bookshops.

Many people believed that the superstore was going to kill the book business even as the book survived the CD-ROM. When Coles and Smithbooks merged to create Chapters and announced the launching of superstores, large and small independents and chains shuddered and quickly began to rethink the business they were in. Many have done quite a good job of this, with the result that at a time when retailing in general was not growing, the book business was. Chapters, the superstore chain, reported a 125 percent increase in its sales from $13 million to $29.5 million as a result of the success of its eleven new stores. At the same time, many independents are doing quite well. For consumers, it is quite pleasant being courted by powerful, spacious, and well-stocked superstores as well as high-service, comfortable, and nicely specialized independents. As one book browser said of superstores, "Amazing. Rows of gleaming computer books, titles packed in the business section," and of independents, "I can shop for price and selection or I can shop for service. Or just for the pleasure of shopping in beautiful stores."

What have been the stores' new missions, goals, objectives, strategies, and tactics? Superstores have basically sought to increase the total book market by bringing "big-box" store strategies and tactics to the business. They have concentrated consumer buying by introducing lots of high-visibility titles, low prices, sophisticated computerized buying, inventory and customer-operated book search systems, heavy promotion, consistent discounting, and reading space and facilities. And, of course, they have got publishers to reduce prices based on volume, obtained better return policies than in the past, and sold display space in the stores for special promotions.

Independents have taken a number of approaches. Most are distinctly and distinctively service oriented. Paragraph Books in Montreal has had a 10 percent sales increase since a Chapters superstore opened nearby. Owner Richard King says, "Your staff has to talk to every customer; here if you spend more than $75, you get a Paragraph mug. This forces our staff to talk to customers even if it's only to say 'this receipt is good for a cup of coffee in our café.'" Toronto's Nicholas Hoare bookstore attracts customers with a cozy reading area, overstuffed chairs, and a fireplace with a blazing fire. Victoria's Bolen Books has presented itself as a "destination" store, a place to go. It is styled after a turn-of-the-century stage set: The walls are covered with thirty oil paintings, chandeliers hang from the ceiling, and old plush theatre seats are scattered about. Manager Samantha Bolen says, "It's almost like a library atmosphere. People spend more money because they are comfortable that they can spend three hours here." Bolen presents various social events, such as a singles party, and is awaiting its first wedding.

Clearly, bookstores large and small have revised their missions, clarified their objectives, and developed a host of new strategies and tactics. They will continue to do this as the competition increases and consumers make their interests, demands, and choices known with their patronage. For the time being, business is pretty good for those who have taken up the challenge.[1]

The shake-up in the book business is a good illustration of how competition causes firms to work through all aspects of their business. It is also clear that the development of strategies, tactics, and plans and their implementation is what large and small organizations, chains and independents alike, can and do become involved with. In Chapter 1 we discussed the marketing component of marketing management; now we discuss the management component.

PLANNING AS PART OF MANAGEMENT

The **management** process, as applied to marketing, consists basically of (1) planning a marketing program, (2) implementing it, and (3) evaluating its performance. This process is illustrated in Figure 3-1.

The planning stage includes setting goals and designing strategies and tactics to reach these goals. The implementation stage entails forming and staffing the marketing organization and directing the actual operation of the organization according to the plan. The evaluation stage consists of analyzing past performance in relation to organizational goals. This third stage indicates the interrelated, continuing nature of the management process. That is, the results of this stage of the management process are used in planning goals and strategies for future periods. And the cycle continues.

db.paragraphbooks.com

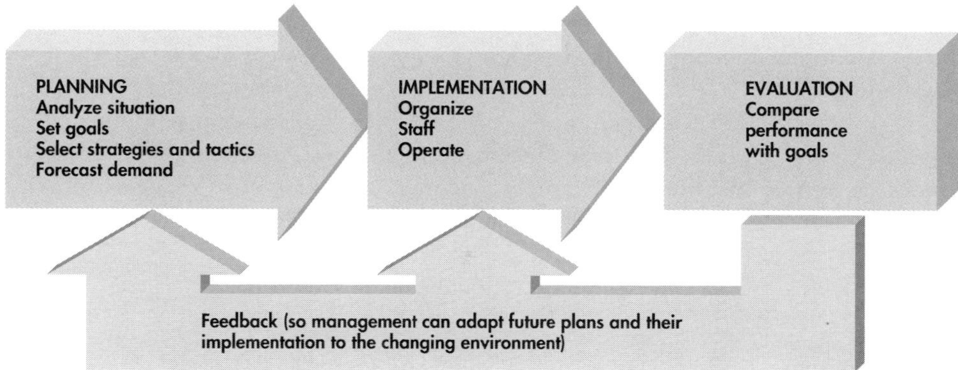

FIGURE 3-1
The Management Process in Marketing

The Nature of Planning

"If you don't know where you're going, any road will get you there." The point of this axiom is that all organizations need both general and specific plans to be successful. Management first should decide what it intends to accomplish as a total organization and then develop a strategic plan to achieve these results. On the basis of this overall plan, each division of the organization should determine what its own plans will be. Of course, the role of marketing in these plans needs to be considered.

If planning is so important, exactly what is it? Quite simply, **planning** is deciding now what we are going to do later, including how and when we are going to do it. Without a plan, we cannot get things done effectively and efficiently, because we don't know what needs to be done or how to do it. In **strategic planning**, managers match an organization's resources with its market opportunities over the long run.

The fact that strategic planning has a long-run perspective does not mean that plans can be developed or executed in a casual manner. Many years ago the term **strategic window** was suggested to describe the limited amount of time in which a firm's resources can actually be made available to take advantage of a particular market opportunity.[2] Typically, the window is open only temporarily. Thus a firm must be able to move rapidly and decisively when a strategic window opens. Netscape Communications did just that when the World Wide Web part of the Internet grew explosively. Almost overnight, there were thousands of Web sites — locations on the Internet that provide information and/or sell products. Internet users were faced with the task of having to sort through many sites in the Web in order to find the specific material they were looking for. Netscape quickly developed its Navigator browser software and continues to upgrade it to make "surfing" and searching more efficient.

Key Planning Concepts

We'll begin by becoming familiar with the basic terms used in discussing marketing management, especially the planning phase.

Mission An organization's **mission** states what customers it serves, what needs it satisfies, and what types of products it offers. A mission statement indicates in general terms the boundaries of an organization's activities.

A mission statement should be neither too broad and vague nor too narrow and specific. To say that a firm's mission is "to benefit Canadian consumers" is too vague; to state that its purpose is "to make tennis balls" is too narrow. Neither statement outlines meaningful benefits for customers or provides much guidance to management. Unless the firm's purpose is clear to executives, strategic planning will likely result in disagreement and confusion.

Traditionally, companies stated their missions in production-oriented terms, such as "We make furnaces" (or telephones or tennis racquets). Today, firms following the marketing concept express their mission in customer-oriented terms. Executives should think about the wants they are satisfying and the benefits they are providing. Thus, instead of "We make furnaces," Lennox Company's statement of mission should be "We provide home climate control" or "We make you comfortable." Recall that Table 1-1 illustrated different ways of stating a company's mission.

Objectives and Goals We treat objectives and goals as synonyms. An **objective** is simply a desired outcome. Effective planning must begin with a set of objectives that are to be achieved by carrying out plans. To be worthwhile and workable, objectives should be:

- Clear and specific.
- Stated in writing.
- Ambitious, but realistic.
- Consistent with one another.
- Quantitatively measurable wherever possible.
- Tied to a particular time period.

Consider these examples:

Weak (too general)	Workable
Increase our market share.	Increase our market share to 25 percent next year from its present 20 percent level.
Improve our company's public image.	Receive favourable recognition awards next year from at least three consumer or environmental groups.

Strategies and Tactics The term *strategy* originally applied to the art of military leadership. In business, a **strategy** is a broad plan of action by which an organization intends to reach its objectives. In marketing, the relationship between objectives and strategies may be illustrated as follows:

Objectives	Possible Strategies
Increase sales next year by 8 percent over this year's figure.	1. Intensify marketing efforts in domestic markets.
	2. Expand into foreign markets.
	3. Increase customer retention by reducing account closings by 10 percent.

Two organizations might have the same objective but use different strategies to reach it. For example, two firms both might aim to increase their market shares by 20 percent over the next three years. To do that, one firm might intensify its efforts in household markets, while the other might concentrate on expanding into institutional markets (e.g., food-service organizations). Conversely, two organizations might have different objectives but select the same strategy to reach them.

A **tactic** is a means by which a strategy is implemented. A tactic is a more specific, detailed course of action than is a strategy. Also, tactics generally cover shorter time periods than strategies. Here's an illustration:

Strategy	Tactics
Direct our promotion to males aged 25–40.	1. Advertise in magazines read by this group of people.
	2. Advertise on television programs watched by this group.
Increase revenue from existing customers.	3. Redesign the customer information system.
	4. Create a loyalty program for light and medium users.
	5. Retrain account analysts and service personnel.

I have been a customer of mbanx since November 1996. (When) I experienced (Internet) software difficulties...one of your Portfolio Managers went out of his way to make sure that... I stayed as a customer. His name is Rob Rae. I literally talked to Rob more than I talked to my family. He followed up and followed through every time.

This guy cares about his job and his customer and it showed up big-time with his actions. You should be proud to know that you have front line people like Rob Rae. mbanx has my loyalty and you can thank Rob for this.

Sincerely,
W.J. Moloney

No one ever wrote anything like this about a micro-chip.

Banking on the internet. Technology makes it easy for any bank to offer it these days. But only mbanx has Rob Rae and people like him behind the software and hardware that makes banking this way possible. Which means if you ever have any questions or problems, you can access someone like Rob for a fast, simple, real-time, human answer. That's the kind of service mbanx makes available to personal and SOHO customers, 24 hours a day, along with cash rewards, one low monthly service charge, and immediate access via phone, fax, ABM or PC.

You make us proud, Rob. Now go dazzle someone else.

mbanx™
1-888-mbanx-11

™ Trade mark of Bank of Montreal

The mbanx goal is to increase the internet banking business; the strategy is to emphasize superior service; the tactic is to use a customer testimonial approach.

To be effective, a tactic must coincide with and support the strategy to which it is related.

Scope of Planning

Planning may cover long or short periods. Strategic planning is usually long-range, covering 3, 5, 10, or (infrequently) 25 years. It requires the participation of top management and often involves a planning staff.

Long-range planning deals with company-wide issues such as expanding or contracting production, markets, and product lines. For example, all firms in the North American auto industry must look ahead to, say, 2005 to identify key markets, plan new products, and update production technologies.

Short-range planning typically covers one year or less and is the responsibility of middle and lower-level managers. It focuses on such issues as determining which target markets will receive special attention and what the marketing mix will be. Looking again at the auto industry, Chrysler annually decides which target markets it will concentrate on and whether its marketing mixes for each of these markets should be changed. Naturally, short-range plans must be compatible with the organization's long-range plans.

Planning the marketing strategies in a firm should be conducted on three different levels:

- *Strategic company planning.* At this level, management defines an organization's mission, sets long-range goals, and formulates broad strategies to achieve these goals. These company-wide goals and strategies then become the framework for planning in the firm's different functional areas, such as production, finance, human resources, research and development, and marketing.

www.chrysler.com

MARKETING AT WORK FILE 3-1

BURGER KING CANADA ANSWERS KEY QUESTIONS

Concept	Question	Burger King Answers
Mission	What business are we in?	Convenience food: Whoppers and fries.
Objectives	What do we want to accomplish?	Growth through expansion.
Strategies	In general terms, how are we going to get the job done?	Increase outlets from 240 to 500 in five years by targeting underdeveloped markets.
Tactics	In specific terms, how are we going to get the job done?	Acquire new sites in Alberta and the Maritimes; campuses, hospitals, partnerships with retailers, gas stations.

George Michel, president of Burger King Canada, adds: "You can have all the strategies and the best marketing plan in the world, but if the execution at the restaurant level is not there, then you're going to miss."

Source: Adapted in part from Mikala Folb, "BK Targets West, Maritimes for Growth," *Marketing Magazine*, January 27, 1997, p. 3. Reprinted with permission.

- *Strategic marketing planning.* The top marketing executives set goals and strategies for an organization's marketing effort. Strategic marketing planning should be co-ordinated with company-wide planning.
- *Annual marketing planning.* Short-term plans should be prepared for a firm's major functions. Covering a specific period, usually one year, the annual marketing plan is based on the firm's strategic marketing planning.

STRATEGIC COMPANY PLANNING

Strategic company planning consists of four essential steps:

1. Defining the organizational mission.
2. Analyzing the situation.
3. Setting organizational objectives.
4. Selecting strategies to achieve these objectives.

The process is shown in the top part of Figure 3-2.

The first step, defining the organizational mission, influences all subsequent planning. For some firms, this step requires only reviewing the existing mission statement and confirming that it is still suitable. Still, this straightforward step is too often ignored.

The second step, conducting a situation analysis, is vital because strategic planning is influenced by many factors beyond and within an organization. By **situation analysis**, we simply mean gathering and studying information pertaining to one or more specified aspects of an organization. We'll talk more about conducting a situation analysis in an upcoming section.

The third step in strategic company planning requires management to decide on a set of objectives to guide the organization in fulfilling its mission. Objectives also provide standards for evaluating an organization's performance.

By this point in its strategic planning, the organization has determined where it wants to go. The fourth step, selecting appropriate strategies, indicates how the firm is going to get there. **Organizational strategies** represent broad plans of action by which an organization intends to achieve its goals and fulfil its mission. Strategies are selected either for the entire company, if it is small and has only a single product, or for each division, if the company is large and has multiple products or units.

FIGURE 3-2
Three Levels of Organizational Planning

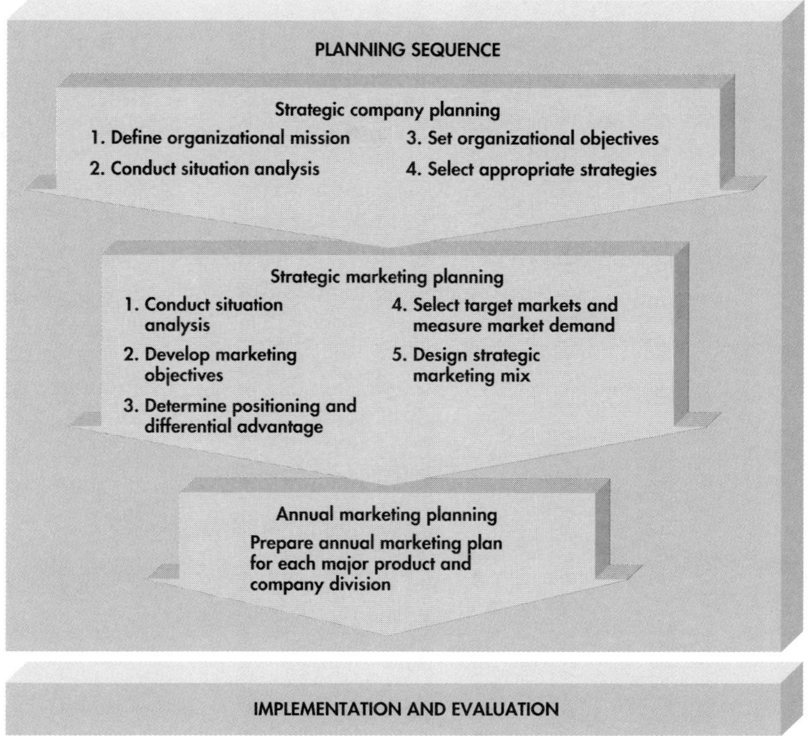

Do companies actually engage in this kind of planning and then prepare a written plan? According to one survey, almost 70 percent of firms have strategic plans in place; among them, nearly 90 percent believe their strategic plans have been effective.[3] Interestingly, a larger proportion of younger firms (one to ten years old) than older firms have formal strategic plans.

STRATEGIC MARKETING PLANNING

After conducting strategic planning for the organization as a whole, management needs to lay plans for each major functional area, such as marketing or production. Of course, planning for each function should be guided by the organization-wide mission and objectives.

Strategic marketing planning is a five-step process:

1. Conduct a situation analysis.
2. Develop marketing objectives.
3. Determine positioning and differential advantage.
4. Select target markets and measure market demand.
5. Design a strategic marketing mix.

These five steps are shown in the middle of Figure 3-2, indicating how they relate to the four steps of strategic company planning. Each step is discussed below.

Situation Analysis

The first step in strategic marketing planning, situation analysis, involves analyzing where the company's marketing program has been, how it has been doing, and what it is likely to face in the years ahead. Doing this enables management to determine if it's necessary to revise the old plans or devise new ones to achieve the company's objectives.

Situation analysis normally covers external environmental forces[4] and internal nonmarketing resources, discussed in Chapter 2. A situation analysis also considers the groups of consumers served by the company, the strategies used to satisfy them, and key measures of marketing performance.

www.travelcuts.com www.eatons.com www.wal-mart.com www.hbc.com www.canadiantire.com

MARKETING AT WORK FILE 3-2

TRAVEL CUTS PLANS FOR THE INTERNET

Travel Cuts is a twenty-three year-old chain with forty-six travel shops across Canada. Like all other travel companies, the chain has been hit by technological change, deregulation of the airline industry, travel agency consolidation, and the growth of boutique travel agencies. And it is taking the Internet very seriously. The Internet and its largely untapped commercial potential is a worry for travel operators of all stripes because it gives travellers the capacity to book a trip from their desktop, thus bypassing the agency. But for Travel Cuts there is more urgency, since its target market is students and youths, and these students and youths are the Internet's biggest users. Heather Crosbie, general manager of Travel Cuts, believed that scenario planning, about which she had read in *Wired*, was an ideal approach to developing the alternative futures that the firm could face. Such alternatives could then be used for developing a series of strategies and plans. Developing alternative futures seemed essential, since "in our environment, you may lead yourself down the garden path if you focus on one strategy."

Ms. Crosbie hired Arden Brummel, a strategist from Calgary's Global Business Network Canada, to work with managers to develop their thinking on futures. By November 1996, Mr. Brummel had started working with fifteen Travel Cuts managers in the process of "imagineering." After four months, the group decided on four potential futures. Of course, the Internet was a major ingredient in the futures. The group examined best- and worst-case scenarios. First, the Internet is a real threat and could bury conventional travel agencies. Second, the Internet is simply another innovation in a long line, like television or the telephone, that can be worked with or around. The Travel Cuts team examined every scenario from all possible perspectives and then developed strategies based on the invasion as well as the non-invasion of the Internet into their business. What are the strategies? Ms. Crosbie's response was, "I don't want to show my hand to my competitors."

Source: Adapted from Gayle MacDonald, "Cutting-edge Companies Cover All the Angles," *The Globe and Mail*, May 23, 1997, p. B11.

As the basis for planning decisions, situation analysis is critical. But it can be costly, time-consuming, and frustrating. For example, it's usually difficult to extract timely, accurate information from the "mountains" of data compiled during a situation analysis. Moreover, some valuable information, such as sales or market-share figures for competitors, is often unavailable.

As part of a situation analysis, many organizations perform a **SWOT assessment**. In this activity, a firm identifies and evaluates its most significant strengths, weaknesses, opportunities, and threats. To fulfil its mission, an organization needs to capitalize on its key strengths, overcome or alleviate its major weaknesses, avoid significant threats, and take advantage of the most promising opportunities.

We're referring to strengths and weaknesses in an organization's own capabilities. For example, prior to the Eaton's reorganization, the company's strength was its large size, which gave it — among other things — clout in dealing with suppliers. However, a weakness was its frequent merchandising changes and its comparatively high operating expenses.

Opportunities and threats often originate outside the organization. For example, an opportunity identified by Wal-Mart when expanding into Canada was the large number of metropolitan areas in which it could open stores. But an unknown threat was the competition that could come from such firms as Zellers and Canadian Tire.

Marketing Objectives

The next step in strategic marketing planning is to determine marketing objectives. Marketing goals should be closely related to company-wide goals and strategies. In fact, a company strategy often translates into a marketing goal. For example, to reach an organizational objective of a 20 percent return on investment next year, one organizational strategy might be to reduce marketing costs by 15 percent. This company strategy would become a marketing goal. In turn, converting all sales people from salaried compensation to a commission basis might be one of the marketing strategies adopted to achieve this marketing goal.

We already know that strategic planning involves matching an organization's resources with its market opportunities. With this in mind, each objective should be assigned a priority based on its urgency and potential impact on the marketing area and, in turn, the organization. Then resources should be allocated in line with these priorities.[5]

Positioning and Differential Advantage

The third step in strategic marketing planning actually involves two complementary decisions: how to position a product in the marketplace, and how to distinguish it from competitors. **Positioning** refers to a product's image in relation to directly competitive products as well as other products marketed by the same company.[6] For example, given rising health consciousness among many consumers, manufacturers of mayonnaise, corn oil, and other food products recognized the need to introduce products that would be perceived as more wholesome.[7] CPC International is trying to position its Hellmann's Dijonnaise, which combines no-fat mustard with mayonnaise ingredients (but no egg yolks), as a healthful and tasty product.

After the product is positioned, a viable differential advantage has to be identified. **Differential advantage** refers to any feature of an organization or brand perceived by customers to be desirable and different from those of the competition.[8] At the same time, a company has to avoid a differential disadvantage for its product. Consider Apple Computers: For many years, the Macintosh's user friendliness (based on its unique operating system) represented a strong differential for the brand and allowed Apple to sell the computer at a premium price. Then, when Microsoft introduced its Windows 95 operating system, which provided a very similar form of user friendliness, this advantage disappeared and Apple was faced with **differential disadvantages** stemming from both its operating system and its pricing strategies. Apple has since been forced into many product and marketing changes in the search for new differential advantages.[9]

Target Markets and Market Demand

Selecting target markets is the fourth step in marketing planning. A **market** consists of people or organizations with needs to satisfy, money to spend, and the willingness to spend it. For example, many people need transportation and are willing to pay for it. However, this large group is made up of a number of segments (that is, parts of markets) with various transportation needs. One segment may want low-cost, efficient transportation, while another may prefer luxury and privacy. Air Canada and Canadian Airlines International segment the air travel market by offering economy, business, and first-class travel, with each class offering a different service bundle ranging from checking-in privileges to different seat widths, and, of course, at very different prices.

Ordinarily it is impractical for a firm to satisfy all segments that have different needs. Instead, a company targets its efforts at one or more of these segments. Thus a **target market** refers to a group of people or organizations at which a firm directs a marketing program.

Target markets must be selected on the basis of opportunities. In a new company, management should analyze markets in detail to identify potential target markets. In an existing firm, management should routinely examine any changes in the characteristics of its target markets and alternative markets. A firm must forecast demand, that is, sales, in each market. The results of sales or demand forecasting will determine whether the firm's targets are worth pursuing or whether alternatives need to be identified. We'll consider demand forecasting in Chapter 5.

Marketing Mix

Next, management must design a **marketing mix** — the combination of a product or service, how it is distributed and promoted, and its price. Traditionally, the marketing mix has been considered in terms of four elements that together must satisfy the needs of the organization's target markets and, at the same time, achieve its marketing objectives. In recent years, as marketers have turned their thinking more toward marketing in service organizations and to the service elements that must accompany the sale and marketing of any product or service, some have expanded their view of the marketing mix to include the essential element of customer service, or the way in which the customer is treated not only by marketing personnel but by all employees and by the company itself. Let's consider the elements of the expanded marketing mix and some of the concepts and strategies you'll learn about in later chapters:

- *Product.* Strategies are needed for managing existing products over time, adding new ones, and dropping failed products. Strategic decisions must also be made regarding service levels, branding, packaging, and other product features such as warranties.
- *Price.* Necessary strategies pertain to the locations of customers, price flexibility, related items within a product line, and terms of sale. Also, pricing strategies for entering a market, especially with a new product, must be designed.
- *Distribution.* Here, strategies involve the management of the channel(s) by which ownership of products is transferred from producer to customer and, in many cases, the system(s) by which goods are moved from the place where they are produced to the place where they are purchased by the final customer. Strategies applicable to intermediaries, such as wholesalers and retailers, must be designed.
- *Marketing communications.* Strategies are needed to combine individual methods such as advertising, personal selling, and sales promotion into a coordinated campaign. In addition, these strategies must be adjusted as a product moves from the early stages to the later stages of its life. Strategic decisions must also be made regarding each individual method of marketing communications.
- *Customer Service.* This component of the marketing mix deals with how the customer is handled as he or she deals with the firm or organization. Marketers must develop strategies concerning how customer service is to be delivered, what level of service is needed to allow the company to compete, and what level of service it can afford to provide to customers.

The elements of the marketing mix are interrelated; decisions in one area often affect actions in another. To illustrate the design of a marketing mix is certainly affected by whether a firm chooses to compete on the basis of price, service, or on one or more other elements. When a firm relies on price as its primary competitive tool, the other elements must be designed to support aggressive pricing. For example, the promotional campaign likely will be built around a theme of "low, low prices." In nonprice competition, however, product, distribution, customer and service strategies, and/or promotion strategies come to the forefront. For instance, the product and supporting services must have features worthy of a higher price, and marketing communications must create a high-quality image for the product.

Each marketing-mix element contains countless variables. An organization may market one product or many, and these products may be related or unrelated to each other. The product may be distributed through wholesalers, to retailers without the benefit of wholesalers, or even directly to final customers. Ultimately, from the multitude of variables, management must select a combination of elements that will satisfy target markets and achieve organizational and marketing goals.

ANNUAL MARKETING PLAN

Besides strategic planning for several years into the future, more specific, shorter-term planning is also vital. Thus, strategic marketing planning in an organization leads to the preparation of an annual marketing plan, as shown in the bottom part of Figure 3-2. An **annual marketing plan** is the master blueprint for a year's marketing activity for a specified organizational division or major product. Note that it is a written document.

A separate plan normally should be prepared for each major product and company division. Sometimes, depending on a company's circumstances, separate plans are developed for key brands and important target markets.[10] As the name implies, an annual marketing plan usually covers one year. However, there are exceptions. For instance, because of the seasonal nature of some products or markets, it is advisable to prepare plans for shorter time periods. In the fashionable-clothing industry, plans are made for each season, lasting just several months.

Purposes and Responsibilities

An annual marketing plan serves several purposes:

- It summarizes the marketing strategies and tactics that will be used to achieve specified objectives in the upcoming year. Thus it becomes the "what-to-do" document that guides executives and other employees involved in marketing.
- The plan also focuses on "how to do it," pointing to what needs to be done with respect to the other steps in the management process, primarily implementation. The detail of implementation provides important basic information that gives direction to the evaluation of the marketing program.
- Moreover, the plan outlines who is responsible for which activities, when the activities are to be carried out, and how much time and money can be spent.

The executive responsible for the division or product covered by the plan typically prepares it. All or part of the task may be delegated to subordinates.

Preparation of an annual marketing plan may begin nine months or more before the start of the period covered by the plan. Early work includes necessary research and arranging other information sources. The bulk of the work occurs one to three months prior to the plan's starting date. The last steps are to have the plan reviewed and approved by upper management. Some revision may be necessary before final approval is granted. The final version of the plan, or relevant parts of it, should be shared with all employees who will be involved in implementing the agreed-upon strategies and tactics. The failure to have a plan understood and accepted by those implementing it both within and outside of the organization threatens both service quality and the quality of the market relationships ultimately established. Since an annual plan contains confidential information, it should not be distributed too widely.

Recommended Contents

The exact contents of an annual marketing plan should be determined by an organization's circumstances. For example, a firm in an intensely competitive industry would assess its competitors in a separate section. A firm in another industry would present this assessment as part of the situation analysis. Similarly, some organizations include alternative (or contingency) plans; others don't. An example of a contingency plan is the set of steps the firm will take if a competitor introduces a new product, as is rumoured.

Annual marketing planning follows a sequence similar to strategic marketing planning. However, annual planning has a shorter time frame and is more specific, both with respect to the issues addressed and to the plans laid. Still, as shown in Table 3-1, the major sections of an annual marketing plan are similar to the steps in strategic marketing planning.

In an annual marketing plan, more attention can be devoted to tactical details than is feasible in other levels of planning. As an example, strategic marketing planning might stress personal selling within the marketing mix. If so, the annual plan might recommend increased college or university recruiting as a source of additional sales people.

Also note that an annual marketing plan relates to all three steps of the management process, not just planning. That is, sections 5 through 7 in Table 3–1 deal with implementation, and section 8 is concerned with evaluation. We will return to implementation when we discuss the various components of the marketing mix in the chapters that follow.

SELECTED PLANNING MODELS

A number of frameworks or tools — we'll call them *models* — have been designed to assist with strategic planning. Most of these models can be used with both strategic company planning and strategic marketing planning. In this section, we briefly discuss several planning models that have received ample

TABLE 3-1 Contents of an Annual Marketing Plan

1. *Executive Summary.* In this one- or two-page section, the thrust of the plan is described and explained. It is intended for executives who desire an overview of the plan but need not be knowledgeable about the details.
2. *Situation Analysis.* Essentially, the marketing program for the strategic business unit (SBU) or product covered by the plan is examined within the context of pertinent past, present, and future conditions. It is vital that a reliable assessment of human resource needs and capabilities be part of the analysis. Much of this section might be derived from the results of strategic marketing planning. Additional information of particular relevance to a one-year planning period may be included in this section.
3. *Objectives.* The objectives in an annual plan are more specific than those produced by strategic marketing planning. However, annual objectives must help achieve organizational goals and strategic marketing goals.
4. *Strategies.* As in strategic marketing planning, the strategies in an annual plan should indicate which target markets are going to be satisfied through a combination of product, price, distribution, and promotion.
5. *Tactics.* Specific activities, sometimes called action plans, are devised for carrying out each major strategy included in the preceding section. For ease of understanding, strategies and tactics may be covered together. Tactics specifically answer the question of what is to be done, who will do it, and how the tasks will be accomplished. The who and the how tend to show that a plan is actually implementable, given the finances in item 6.
6. *Financial Schedules.* This section normally includes two kinds of financial information: projected sales, expenses, and profits in what's called a pro-forma financial statement; and the amounts of resources dedicated to different activities in one or more budgets.
7. *Timetable.* This section, often including a diagram, answers the question of when various marketing activities will be carried out during the upcoming year.
8. *Evaluation Procedures.* This section addresses the questions of what, who, how, and when connected with measuring performance against goals, both during and at the end of the year. The results of evaluations during the year may lead to adjustments in the plan's strategies and/or tactics or even in the objectives to be achieved.

attention in recent years. First, however, you need to be familiar with a form of organization, the strategic business unit, that pertains to these planning models.

Strategic Business Units

Most large and medium-sized companies, and even some smaller firms, consist of multiple units and produce numerous products. In such diversified firms, company-wide planning cannot serve as an effective guide for executives who oversee the organization's various divisions. Bombardier Inc., a company probably best known to most Canadians as the manufacturer of Ski-Doo snowmobiles, provides a good example. The mission, objectives, and strategies of the divisions within the motorized consumer products group (which includes the Sea-Doo/Ski-Doo Division) are — and must be — quite different from those that guide marketing and other activities in its aerospace group (where the strategic business units include Canadair and De Havilland, manufacturers of airplanes) and its transportation equipment group, where the strategic business units are involved in the manufacture of subway and railway cars, shuttle-train cars for the tunnel under the English Channel, and PeopleMover Transportation systems.

Consequently, for more effective planning and operations, a multibusiness or multiproduct organization should be divided according to its major markets or products. Each such entity is called a **strategic business unit (SBU)**. Each SBU may be a major division in an organization, a group of related products, or even a single major product or brand.

To be identified as an SBU, an entity should:

- Be a separately identifiable business.
- Have a distinct mission.
- Have its own competitors.
- Have its own executive group with profit responsibility.

The trick in setting up SBUs in an organization is to arrive at the optimum number. Too many can bog down the top management in details associated with planning, operating, and reporting. Too few

www.bombardier.com • www.canadair.ca

MARKETING AT WORK FILE 3-3

THE UNSPOKEN FIFTH ELEMENT IN THE MARKETING MIX — PEOPLE

Four Seasons Hotels of Toronto is one of six Canadian entries among 238 world wide that Morgan Stanley & Co. has identified as having a "competitive edge" in their industries. Morgan Stanley says market-beating companies generally have low cost structures, differentiated products and brands, strong management, access to capital, sound distribution, and strong product development. But Isadore Sharp, president and CEO, adds one basic explanation for the renowned front-line service of Four Seasons. "If candidates possess the right personality, you can train them to do any job."

Finding employees with the right attitudinal edge is not easy. To staff a New York hotel, Four Seasons looked at 17,000 candidates before arriving at the 400 it needed. "This was in a New York market where people are not, by nature, pleasant." In Hawaii, much more laid back than New York, 2,000 applicants were chosen to develop a short list of 400. Obviously, if you know the kind of service you need to provide in order to protect and project your differential advantage, you need people who can implement, you need people with the right attitude, and then you can train them.

The right people, with the right training and the right attitude, make it work. Otherwise, nothing gets off the paper. (See item 5 in Table 3-1.)

Source: Adapted in part from Gordon Pitts, "Hotel Chain Hires for Attitude," *The Globe and Mail*, June 3, 1997, p. B13. Reprinted with permission from *The Globe and Mail*.

SBUs can result in each one covering too broad an area for managerial planning. Of course, most companies have fewer SBUs than Bombardier.

Let's now consider two of many different planning models: the Boston Consulting Group matrix and the product-market growth matrix.

The Boston Consulting Group Matrix

Developed by a management consulting firm, the **Boston Consulting Group (BCG) matrix** dates back at least twenty-five years.[11] Using this model, an organization classifies each of its SBUs (and, sometimes, its major products) according to two factors: its market share relative to competitors, and the growth rate of the industry in which the SBU operates. When the factors are divided simply into high and low categories, a 2 × 2 grid is created, as displayed in Figure 3-3.

In turn, the four quadrants in the grid represent distinct categories of SBUs or major products. The categories differ with respect not only to market share and industry growth rate but also to cash needs and appropriate strategies.

FIGURE 3-3 The Boston Consulting Group (BCG) Matrix

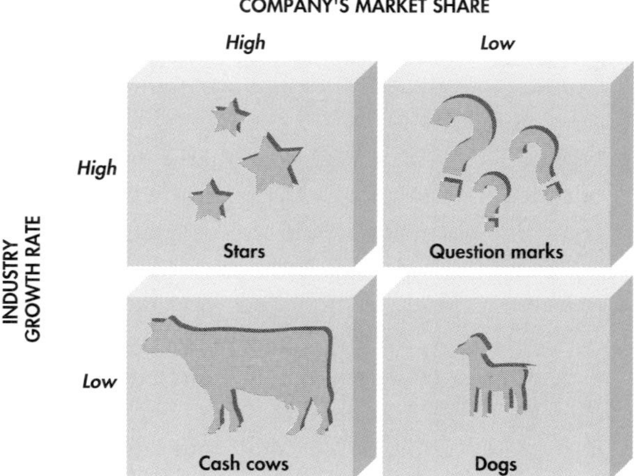

- **Stars.** High market shares and high industry growth rates typify SBUs in this category. However, an SBU that falls into this category poses a challenge for companies because it requires lots of cash to remain competitive in growing markets. Aggressive marketing strategies are imperative for stars to maintain or even build market share.

- **Cash cows.** These SBUs have high market shares and do business in mature industries (those with low growth rates). When an industry's growth diminishes, stars move into this category. Because most of their customers have been with them for some time and are still loyal, a cash cow's marketing costs are not high. Consequently, it generates more cash than can be reinvested profitably in its own operations. As a result, cash cows can be "milked" to support the firm's other SBUs that need more resources. Marketing strategies for cash cows seek to defend market share, largely by reinforcing customer loyalty.
- **Question marks** (sometimes called *problem children*). SBUs characterized by low market shares but high industry growth rates fit in this category. A question mark has not achieved a strong foothold in an expanding but highly competitive market. The question surrounding this type of SBU is whether it can gain adequate market share and be profitable. If management answers "no," then the SBU should be divested or liquidated. If management instead answers "yes," the firm must come up with the cash to build market share — more cash than the typical question mark generates from its own profits. Appropriate marketing strategies for question marks focus on creating an impact in the market by displaying a strong differential advantage and, thereby, building customer support.
- **Dogs.** These SBUs have low market shares and operate in industries with low growth rates. A company normally would be unwise to invest substantial funds in SBUs in this category. Marketing strategies for dogs are intended to maximize any potential profits by minimizing expenditures or to promote a differential advantage to build market share. The company can instead say "Enough's enough!" and divest or liquidate an SBU that's a dog.

Ordinarily, one firm cannot affect the growth rate for an entire industry. An exception might be the leading firm in a fairly new industry. If growth rate cannot be influenced, companies must turn their attention to the other factor in the BCG matrix, market share. Hence, marketing strategies based on the BCG matrix tend to concentrate on building or maintaining market share, depending on which of the four SBU categories is involved. Various strategies require differing amounts of cash, which means that management must continually allocate the firm's limited resources (notably cash) to separate marketing endeavours.

In the financial arena, an investor needs a balanced portfolio with respect to risks and potential returns. Similarly, a company should seek a balanced portfolio of SBUs. Certainly, cash cows are indispensable. Stars and question marks are integral to a balanced portfolio, because products in growing markets determine a firm's long-term performance. While dogs are undesirable, it is rare that a company doesn't have at least one. Thus, the portfolios of most organizations with numerous SBUs or major products include a mix of stars, cash cows, question marks, and dogs.

Product-Market Growth Matrix

Most organizations' statements of mission and objectives focus on growth — that is, a desire to increase revenues and profits. In seeking growth, a company must consider both its markets and its products. Then it has to decide whether to continue doing what it is now doing — only do it better — or establish new ventures. The **product-market growth matrix**, first proposed by Igor Ansoff, depicts these options. Essentially, as shown in Figure 3-4, there are four product-market growth strategies:[12]

- **Market penetration.** A company tries to sell more of its present products to its present markets. Supporting tactics might include greater spending on advertising, targeted mailings, or telemarketing. A company can try to become a single source of supply by offering preferential treatment to customers who will concentrate all their purchases with it. Retail patronage cards such as Dominion's are an example of this strategy.
- **Market development.** A firm continues to sell its present products, but to a new market. For example, ski resort operators' efforts to attract families and tourists represent market development.
- **Product development.** This strategy calls for a company to develop new products to sell to its existing markets. To remain competitive, Kodak

Chrysler emphasizes how customers' ideas and opinions have allowed the firm to develop the market with a stream of product innovation for over thirteen years.

has to develop and introduce new products continuously. This company's recent product releases include digital imaging cameras such as the DC120 zoom camera, an affordably priced point-and-shoot camera with 1.2 million pixels per image — an extremely high-quality product for the home consumer market.[13]

- **Diversification.** A company develops new products to sell to new markets. This strategy is risky because it doesn't rely on either the company's successful products or its position in established markets. Sometimes it works, but sometimes it doesn't.

As market conditions change over time, a company may shift product-market growth strategies. For example, when its present market is fully saturated, a company may have no choice other than to pursue new markets.

FIGURE 3-4 **Product-Market Growth Matrix**

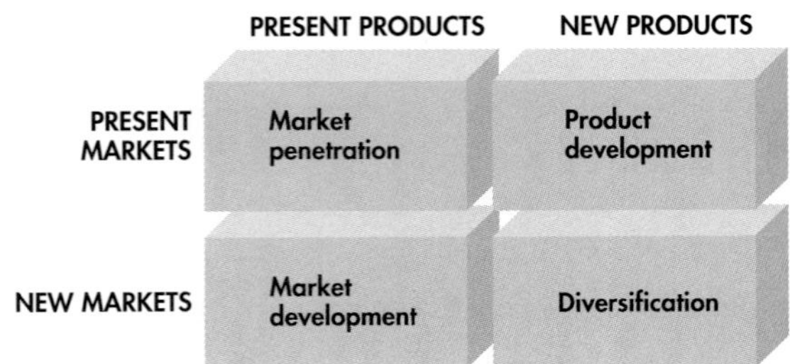

Assessment of the Planning Models

Each of these planning models has been praised and criticized. While each is somewhat distinctive, all share some common weaknesses and strengths.

The primary weakness is probably oversimplification. Each model bases its assessment of market opportunities and subsequent decisions on only two or three key factors. Another weakness is the possibility of placing an SBU on a grid or choosing a strategy without relevant, reliable information. For example, the extent to which market share is critical to a product's profitability is still debated. A third possible weakness is that the results from one of the models might be used to contradict or substitute for the critical business judgments made by line managers (such as a marketing vice-president).

However, these models also possess noteworthy strengths. Most notable is straightforward classification. That is, each model permits an organization to examine its entire portfolio of SBUs or major products in relation to criteria that influence business performance. A second strength is that the models can pinpoint attractive business opportunities and suggest ventures to avoid. They encourage the careful, consistent assessment of opportunities, allocation of resources, and formulation of strategies. Without planning models, these activities might be haphazard — for example, using one set of criteria this month and, with no good reason, another set next month.

Overall, these and other planning models can help management in allocating resources and in developing sound business and marketing strategies. Of course, any planning model should supplement, rather than substitute for, managers' judgments and decisions.

Summary

The management process consists of planning, implementation, and evaluation. Planning is deciding now what we are going to do later, including when and how we are going to do it. Planning provides direction to an organization. Strategic planning is intended to match an organization's resources with its market opportunities over the long run.

In any organization, there should be three levels of planning: strategic company planning, strategic marketing planning, and annual marketing planning. In strategic company planning, management defines the organization's mission, assesses its operating environment, sets long-range goals, and formulates broad strategies to achieve the goals. This level of planning guides planning in different functional areas, including marketing.

Strategic marketing planning entails five steps: conduct a situation analysis; develop objectives; determine positioning and differential advantage; select target markets and measure market demand; and design a marketing mix. Based on strategic marketing plans, an annual marketing plan lays out a year's marketing activities for each major product and division of an organization. An annual plan includes tactics as well as strategies and should be specific about the people involved — the who and how of implementation. It is typically prepared by the executive responsible for the division or product.

Management can rely on either or both of the models discussed for assistance with strategic planning: the Boston Consulting Group matrix and Ansoff's product-market growth matrix. A planning model helps management see how best to allocate its resources and to select effective marketing strategies.

Key Terms and Concepts

Management (46)
Planning (47)
Strategic planning (47)
Strategic window (47)
Mission (47)
Objective (48)
Strategy (48)
Tactic (48)
Strategic company planning (50)
Situation analysis (50)
Organizational strategies (50)
Strategic marketing planning (57)
SWOT assessment (52)
Positioning (53)
Differential advantage (53)
Differential disadvantage (53)
Market (53)
Target market (53)
Marketing mix (54)
Annual marketing plan (54)
Strategic business unit (SBU) (56)
Boston Consulting Group (BCG) matrix (57)
Stars (57)
Cash cows (58)
Question marks (58)
Dogs (58)
Product-market growth matrix (58)
Market penetration (58)
Market development (58)
Product development (58)
Diversification (59)

Questions and Problems

1. Should a small firm (either a manufacturer or a retailer) engage in formal strategic planning? Why or why not?
2. Using a customer-oriented approach (benefits provided or wants satisfied), answer the question "What business are we in?" for each of the following companies:
   a. Holiday Inn.
   b. Tim Hortons
   c. Dell computers.
3. In the situation-analysis step of strategic marketing planning, what specific external environmental factors should be analyzed by a manufacturer of equipment used for backpacking in the wilderness?
4. If you were the vice-president of marketing for a large airline, which of the planning models would you find most useful? Why?
5. "The economic unification of the European Community means absolute chaos for firms trying to market to consumers in these countries. For a number of years, the situation will be so dynamic that executives should not waste their time on formal strategic planning related to European markets." Do you agree with this statement? Support your position.
6. Use an example to explain the concept of a strategic business unit.
7. What market factors might you logically use in estimating the market potential for each of the following products?
   a. Central home air conditioners.
   b. Electric milking machines.
   c. Luxury airline travel.
   d. Sterling silver flatware.
   e. Personal computer repair services.

Hands-On Marketing

1. Go to your school's library and obtain a copy of an annual report for a major corporation. Based on your examination of the year-end review, which of the following product-market growth strategies is being used by this company: market penetration, market development, product development, and/or diversification?
2. Talk with a marketing executive at a local firm. Which of the various methods of forecasting demand does this company employ, and why?

Case 1-1

THE SALVATION ARMY RED SHIELD APPEAL (A)

When Lt. Col. Melvyn Bond, territorial public relations secretary of The Salvation Army, met with Julian Elwes, senior vice-president of BBDO Canada,[1] to discuss the 1994 Salvation Army Red Shield advertising program, there were a number of things on his mind. Col. Bond knew that the 1993 Red Shield Appeal had raised more than $30 million to support the work of the Salvation Army in Canada, but he also knew that the demands being placed on the Army were greater than ever and that even more funds were needed.

Col. Bond was aware that the expectations for support and assistance from the Salvation Army were almost greater than the Army was able to provide, because of the many social and economic problems facing a Canadian population dealing with a recession and the resulting effects on families and individuals. But Col. Bond also had other objectives for The Salvation Army's advertising. He wanted to make sure that the advertising communicated a message to Canadians about The Salvation Army and its work, that it not simply be an appeal for funds. He felt it was not enough to have a successful fund-raising campaign; the advertising should also tell Canadians something about "who we are and why we do what we do."

The Salvation Army is an internationally respected religious and charitable organization that is represented in more than one hundred countries. The Army originated in England, where, in 1865, a Methodist minister, William Booth, and his wife, Catherine, began to preach to residents of East London who they believed were not being reached by the established churches. The Booths directed their ministry to the working class, the sick, and the poor. The evangelists realized that, to help these people, they would need to combine practical support and material assistance with their Christian teachings. Social programs for the betterment of all members of society have been an integral part of The Salvation Army's work since its establishment.

The Salvation Army was originally referred to as the Christian Revival Association and later was named the Christian Mission. It was not until 1878 that the name, The Salvation Army, was adopted. With this name also came the adoption of a quasi-military command structure that was derived from a combination of the military traditions of nineteenth-century Europe and biblical reference to spiritual warfare. The Army uses military ranks and terminology, and all officers, or ordained clergy, are required to wear its uniform.

The Salvation Army in Canada

The work of The Salvation Army spread rapidly after its establishment in London; adherents were working in Wales by 1874 and in Scotland by 1879. During 1880, the Army began its work in Ireland, the United States, and Australia, and operations were begun in France in 1881. Canadian operations of The Salvation Army were established in 1882 in London, Ontario.

For organizational purposes, Canada and Bermuda are combined into a single "territory" or geographical area of administration. Worldwide, there are more than fifty such territories covering more than one hundred countries. The Salvation Army's international headquarters are in London, England, while the administrative headquarters for the Canada and Bermuda territory are in Toronto, where plans for the Army's religious, health, social services, and fund-raising programs are prepared. Regional administration of approximately four hundred local "corps" or church congregations and of

---

[1] BBDO Canada has been the advertising agency of The Salvation Army in Canada and Bermuda for more than forty years. The agency began as McKim Advertising, changed its name to McKim Baker Lovick/BBDO in 1992, and became BBDO Canada in 1994.

 The authors wish to thank Lt. Col. Mel Bond of The Salvation Army and Julian Elwes of BBDO Canada for their support and assistance in the preparation of this case.

community service programs is handled by the fifteen divisional headquarters, located in major cities across Canada and in Bermuda.

The Salvation Army's mission today is a reflection of the original objectives of its founders William and Catherine Booth — to preach the gospel and to improve social conditions so as to enhance the physical and spiritual well-being of all people. For this reason, members express their faith not only through religious activity, but also through participation in a wide variety of community service activities. However, in translating religious conviction into acts of practical, philanthropic assistance, The Salvation Army requires both the active and financial support of many individuals from all faiths and all walks of life. Thousands of individuals willingly contribute their time and skills as volunteers and advisers for The Salvation Army.

Community Activities and Social Programs

The Salvation Army is world-renowned for its multifaceted community services programs, which involve many types of social service. A list of many of the activities, programs, and organizations supported by The Salvation Army in Canada is presented at the end of this case.

Understanding the public's concern that its programs and services are operated using sound financial principles and integrity, The Salvation Army consistently ensures that it ranks among the most efficient and cost-effective charities. In addition to continuous internal audits, the accounts of all programs that receive government assistance are subject to audit by external professional accountants, and all financial records are available for public inspection on request. Less than 10 percent of funds received from its members and the Canadian public is directed to fund-raising and administration expenses.

The Public Relations Department

It is the responsibility of The Salvation Army's public relations department to ensure that fund raising and media relations are professionally organized and conducted. The Salvation Army in Canada operates a national public relations department and communications services unit centralized in Toronto, headed by the territorial public relations secretary. This national office is supported by twenty regional offices throughout the territory of Canada and Bermuda. Each office is managed by a Salvation Army officer, assisted by skilled professionals who may or may not be Salvationists or hold Salvation Army rank. Each regional office is operated by a public relations director, with the support of a public relations officer.

The responsibilities of the regional public relations offices include not only ensuring and collecting financial support, but also enlisting the practical support of the thousands of volunteers who organize and canvass for the annual Red Shield Blitz, held across Canada at the community level each May. Each local public relations office is supplied with brochures and materials on Salvation Army programs and activities for members of the media and anyone else interested in learning about the Army. The offices also provide speakers, films, and videos on many aspects of The Salvation Army to church groups, service clubs, and other community organizations.

The territorial public relations department, through its advertising agency, purchases and solicits complementary or public service media coverage, such as newspaper or magazine space or radio and television time. All such marketing activities, including the development of campaign themes and slogans and the printing of promotional material, are carried out at the national level. A major factor that contributes to The Salvation Army's economic efficiency is this national direction policy. The result is less expenditure on marketing and administration and more on social services. In addition to initiating large, and usually cheaper, contracts with national companies, this technique establishes strong relationships with companies that are then motivated to complete some services for the Army free of charge. This system of centralized, top-down direction also avoids expensive repetition of efforts.

The Fund-raising Program

The public relations department is responsible for fund-raising aimed at corporations and the general public. Most of the contributions received each year by the Salvation Army are the result of the National

Red Shield Appeal, which consists of a door-to-door collection blitz in May, as well as postal donation requests sent to selected households in both May and December, and the traditional Christmas Appeal with the Army's famous "red kettles," which are seen on street corners and in shopping centres across the country. Additional income is received from "offerings" during Sunday religious services and the ongoing Planned Giving program, which encourages arrangements such as bequests from wills or gift annuities. In addition, since 1985, The Salvation Army has held an annual World Services Appeal, which raises money to assist the needy in Third World countries and in areas subject to natural disasters.

The History of the Red Shield Appeal

In 1993, The Salvation Army marked the seventy-fifth anniversary of the Red Shield Appeal and the use of the Red Shield as the official symbol for the Army's social services. The use of the Red Shield originated in Canada and has since spread worldwide. In the early 1900s, a silver metal shield carrying The Salvation Army's name was worn by uniformed Salvationists or converts who did not have the resources to purchase a full uniform. This lapel badge or pin was worn on street-corner or door-to-door collecting missions. Use of the shield evolved when British Salvationists serving or helping during World War I began to use shields to identify their Naval and Military League rest huts.

Although Canadian Salvation Army workers were not required to serve in Europe during World War I, at the end of the war, the Canadian government asked the Army to set up military hostels for returning soldiers and a visiting program for wives, widows, and orphaned children. The fourth military hostel, opened in Winnipeg in 1918, was the first to receive "Red Shield" designation. The significant increase in the need for Salvation Army services required more than local funding, and plans for a national "Red Shield" Appeal were prepared in late 1918. Calgary became the first place in the world to use the reputation of the Red Shield to create a link between The Salvation Army's social services and public funding. Calgary Army workers, in 1918, began campaigning for funds using the Red Shield with white lettering to stimulate donations from the public. The world's first official Red Shield Appeal, which was not formally undertaken until January 1919, raised $4.5 million.

The Red Shield Appeal, in the form it is known today, began in the late 1940s. Since its inception, Salvation Army officers and others from across the globe have adopted the principles and methods of the Canada and Bermuda territory's Red Shield Appeal. Today, the Red Shield is one of the most widely recognized and universally respected symbols in the world, communicating a practical expression of hope to the countless people who turn to The Salvation Army for help. A summary of the fund-raising objective for the Red Shield appeal and the amounts actually raised for selected years since 1965 are presented in Exhibit 1.

EXHIBIT 1

Red Shield Campaign Objectives and Amounts Collected (Selected Years, 1965–1993)

Year	Objective	Amount Collected
1965	$ 3,257,568	$ 3,458,738
1970	3,712,968	4,189,726
1971	3,819,961	4,380,271
1972	4,002,641	4,720,227
1976	5,204,937	6,772,710
1977	5,875,903	7,509,148
1978	7,408,462	8,237,814
1979	7,916,526	9,001,730
1980	8,741,000	9,997,957
1981	10,101,136	11,430,564
1982	12,000,000	13,590,380
1983	14,000,000	15,908,129
1984	15,450,000	17,160,795
1985	18,100,000	20,937,652
1986	20,000,000	23,082,280
1987	22,150,000	25,873,394
1988	26,427,906	28,858,655
1989	29,000,000	31,345,944
1990	31,045,523	32,905,890
1991	32,693,534	34,321,975
1992	34,096,724	34,861,490
1993	36,255,949	34,692,243

Red Shield Advertising

The annual Red Shield Appeal of The Salvation Army has been supported for many years by a national advertising campaign, which has been co-ordinated for more than forty years by the Army's advertising agency, BBDO Canada. While most of the advertising appears in mass media across Canada in a six-week period leading up to the May door-to-door blitz, some advertising exposure is obtained throughout the year, largely in the form of public service announcements and billboard placements.

In keeping with The Salvation Army's objective of ensuring that the largest possible percentage of funds donated reaches people in need, the budget for the annual advertising campaign is necessarily small. Placing advertisements in local newspapers, radio stations, magazines, billboards, television, and on public transit systems across the country is co-ordinated by BBDO Canada. Each year, the agency solicits input from the Army's regional public relations directors, concerning which media they feel should be used in their regions. BBDO Canada is also successful in getting air time and advertising space donated by the various media. In 1993, the Salvation Army spent approximately $300,000 on paid advertising, but received additional advertising worth three times that amount as public service announcements and donated space.

Again, in order to keep the costs of advertising to a manageable level, BBDO Canada has been preparing new advertising materials for the Red Shield Campaign in four- to five-year cycles. Each campaign contains a simple message captured in a slogan that represents the focal point of all advertising materials. The slogans used in recent years have included:

"Who says you can't buy happiness? Please give." (1973-76)

"If you don't need our help, we need yours." (1977-79)

"All you need is love. Please give." (1980-83)

"For the love of God, give." (1984-88)

"God knows, you can make a difference." (1989-93)

Examples of recent advertising for the Red Shield Appeal are presented on pages 66 and 67.

The 1993 Decision

While there was little information available to The Salvation Army and its advertising agency concerning how successful past advertising campaigns for the Red Shield Appeal had been, apart from the fact that actual amounts raised had exceeded annual objectives in every year up to 1993, Lt. Col. Bond and Julian Elwes were familiar with a research study that had been conducted in 1987 by Decima Research. It indicated that The Salvation Army was extremely well regarded by Canadians, but not necessarily as a religious organization. There appeared to be some confusion about whether the Army is a charity or a religious denomination. There was also evidence from the Decima study that the Army's message might not be getting through to younger Canadians.

Partly as a result of the conclusions drawn from the Decima study, a decision was made to reposition The Salvation Army slightly in the Red Shield advertising campaign that was introduced in 1989 and that continued to run through 1993. In that campaign, it was decided to reinforce the image of The Salvation Army as a religious denomination, but to do so softly, through the slogan "God knows, you can make a difference."

In planning the 1994 Red Shield advertising program, Col. Bond and Elwes considered the increasing demands being placed on The Salvation Army's programs across Canada and the fact that the competition for charitable donations had become fierce in an economy where many people could not afford to donate as much as they had in the past. They were facing the question of whether the appeal embodied in the slogan for the 1994 campaign should be much more blunt than that used for the past four years and whether the advertising should make the religious side of the Salvation Army more obvious.

FOR THE LOVE OF GOD. GIVE.

The uniform is like a beacon on the street. It signals help. Compassion. Caring.

But not many people know how much it takes to be a soldier in the Salvation Army. The inhuman hours. The incredible patience. The brutal situations.

Taking responsibility for those whom society is unable to take responsibility for.

Providing help, and then hope, for the people who need it most.

But they know.

Anyone whose life the Salvation Army has touched knows.

And we ask for them, that you give.

As much as you can.

For the love of God.

For more information, please contact:

Friday night is Red Shield Appeal Night

Your generosity can shed light into someone's life.
The lonely heart crying out for comfort. The lost soul searching for a haven.
The child crying for compassion. These are the people for whom the Salvation Army
provides help, and then hope, the people who need it most.
We ask for them that you give. As much as you can.

THE NATIONAL RED SHIELD APPEAL

God knows
you can make a difference

Activities of the Salvation Army in Canada

- Emergency services, which offer material and emotional support in emergency situations and at times of natural disaster.
- Suicide prevention services to counsel individuals in distress.
- Senior citizens' residences.
- "Fresh Air" camps for less privileged children from low-income families, for the physically and mentally challenged, and for single mothers and their children.
- Public hospitals, including maternity hospitals and palliative care centres.
- Addiction and rehabilitation services for victims of alcohol and drug abuse; hostels, rehabilitation centres, and industrial units, where recovering victims are provided with a place where they can receive guidance as well as material assistance.
- Emergency shelters for the homeless and for arriving immigrants.
- Family thrift stores, where people can purchase refurbished clothing, furniture, and household items at affordable prices.
- Many programs of social services for women: maternity homes for prenatal and postnatal single mothers and their infants; facilities for developmentally handicapped women, battered women, postpsychiatric women, and women with alcohol and substance addiction problems, emergency shelters, and day-care centres.
- Correctional and justice-related social services, such as parole supervision, legal aid assistance, victim witness assistance, bail verification and supervision, shoplifter programs, and employment assistance.
- Visiting the sick, shut-in, elderly, hospitalized, and imprisoned; dedicated volunteers visit individuals in institutions such as convalescent or children's homes, and also visit private homes.
- Material aid to overseas countries in need; the Army provides food products, accommodations, and training to many developing countries.
- Sheltered workshops, where physically and mentally challenged adults are given work assignments and the ability to earn an income.
- Family services, which provide counselling and support groups, pastoral care, and material assistance for a variety of individuals such as teen mothers, single parents, seniors, and those in search of employment or homes. In addition, food and toy hampers are distributed during the Christmas season.
- Youth camps, where children can receive training in music or drama and learn about the Bible; Guide and Scout camps are also available at Salvation Army camp grounds.
- Social and educational groups for men, women, seniors, and children, which offer character-building programs and activities that assist in the social and spiritual development of members and promote the sanctity of the family.

Pertinent Web Sites

http://www.salvationarmy.org
http://www.sallynet.org

Questions

1. What are the factors that influence a person's decision to donate to a charitable organization? What do you feel is the image of The Salvation Army among prospective donors in Canada? Is it perceived to be a religious organization or a charity?
2. How are the attitudes of Canadians toward charitable donations affected by the changing environment in which they live? What are the implications for The Salvation Army?
3. How do your answers to questions 1 and 2 influence the decision The Salvation Army and its advertising agency have to make concerning the direction of the advertising campaign to support the 1994 Red Shield Appeal?

Case 1-2

GREEN MARKETING: IS IT REAL?

Concern for and protection of the environment is in vogue. While concern for the environment has always been socially acceptable, in recent years it has become a priority for many consumers and business entities. Some businesses have attempted to capitalize on the green movement by waving a banner advocating that they too are environmentally friendly. The result has been a proliferation of new and improved products and services designed to help save the planet. However, any such claims made without support have usually been met with a backlash of responses. The task for marketers has become one of convincing consumers of the legitimacy of their concerns for the environment. This must be done in a manner that does not alienate the customer.

It has been estimated that nearly 10 percent of all products introduced in the early 1990s were touted as being "green" or "environmentally friendly." The time was ripe for combining the consumerism of the 1980s with the shift in personal values of the 1990s. People were said to be taking more control of their future, including protection of the environment. The result has been a lot of green marketing, some of which is best described as dealing in half-truths, lies, and broken promises.

Mobil Chemical Company's claim that its garbage bag would break down is technically correct; however, the process is extremely slow and occurs only when the bag is exposed to direct sunlight, not when it is buried in a landfill site. Controversy surrounding the claims associated with green products has motivated the development of federal guidelines on environmental advertising. Mobil's promotion of its "biodegradable" trash bag is a notorious example of a claim that, despite being scientifically correct, has met with considerable controversy.

The lesson learned was that the negative fallout can be tremendous if the customer feels that his or her genuine interest in the environment is being exploited. Any manufacturer making such ill-supported claims can find itself the subject of intense scrutiny and negative publicity. For years, C.E. Jamieson had been quietly producing all-natural products such as vitamins and food supplements. When management sensed that the aggressive green approach was losing credibility with consumers, it decided that it did not want to be accused of jumping on the environmentally friendly bandwagon. It altered the packaging of its product to tone down the "greenness." However, it has stood by its tradition of recycling, reusing, and reducing throughout the production process. Television advertisements, set in a pleasant outdoors scene, emphasize the all-natural ingredients of the company's products.

The great debate between the use of cloth or disposable diapers is as yet unresolved in terms of the impact on the environment. Issues include the use of water and energy in the cleaning process in one instance, and the contribution to landfill problems in the other. One of the dominant players in this controversy over disposable diapers was Procter & Gamble, which later educated its customers regarding the benefits of buying recyclable plastic pouches of its detergents and household cleansers. Given that these pouches use 70 percent less plastic by weight than equivalent-sized bottles, the environmental benefits are obvious. The task for marketers was to convey the merits of the product in a way that would convince customers of their ability to make a difference to the protection of the environment. Such initiatives are challenging, as the message deals with the customer's values and beliefs.

However, not everyone has proven to be as quick a study of the risks associated with not delivering what has been promised in the name of green marketing. McDonald's replaced its paperboard packaging with polystyrene plastic packaging because of the superiority of the latter when consideration is given to all aspects from manufacturing to disposal. Despite its research into the issue, McDonald's had failed to

---

This case was prepared by Judith A. Cumby, assistant professor, Faculty of Business Administration, Memorial University of Newfoundland, as a basis for class discussion and is not intended to reflect either an effective or an ineffective handling of management problems.

convince the customer of the merits of polystyrene packaging and elected to return to paper packaging. The company's realization of the importance of public education *prior* to the introduction of any new product has led to the incorporation of environmental education into the curriculum at Hamburger University, its franchisee training facility.

Although there are benefits to both the customer and the manufacturer in engaging in environmentally responsible activities, the fact is that for some customers it is imperative that the companies with which they do business be socially proactive. Since its inception in 1976, The Body Shop has promoted the fact that its cosmetics are produced in such a way as to not harm animals. In recent years the company's founder, Anita Roddick, has been a spokesperson on human rights issues. She has aligned The Body Shop alongside human rights groups such as Friends of the Earth and Amnesty International. While some people view such activities with a degree of cynicism, others have considerable respect for both the company and its owner.

The reality, however, is that many companies are judged more by their immediate financial results than by their long-term investments in environmental and other socially responsible matters. For some, the environment is taken up as a cause when it is a means by which to boost profits. This is particularly true in the area of services. Hotels regularly encourage guests to reuse their towels and linens and to turn down their thermostats in an effort to help the environment, not to mention the facility's operating costs. After years of walking over abandoned print-outs from banking machines, customers are now asked whether they would like a printed receipt of their ATM transactions. This choice enables the customer to cut down on paper wastage and, at the same time, to pass along a cost saving to the banks.

Ecotourism, which involves trips with some nature or wilderness component, seems to be the fastest-growing segment of the tourism industry. In ... countries, the premium fees charged for ...tures permit the purchase of supplies ...cal market, preservation of the ...bitat, and a monetary return to ... like its manufacturing counter- ... faces a problem of labelling: Going on an ecotour is no guarantee of good ecology. In this industry, as in the whole field of green marketing, there is a wide gamut of participants, from the money grabbers to the purists.

Another problem with environmental marketing is that some hold on to the notion that the concepts of genuine concern for the environment and operation of a profitable enterprise cannot coexist. One goal is bound to dominate the other. The argument is made that these green products and services do not deal with the problem of overconsumption. Rather, they deal with ways to ease environmental pressures in the preconsumption (production and packaging) phase and in the postconsumption phase.

How then will marketers deal with the dilemma of distinguishing the good from the bad in the field of environmental marketing? Some are advocating that a set of international standards might help. In response to customer reactions and the 1992 United Nations Conference on Environment and Development held in Rio de Janeiro, new ISO standards are emerging: the International Standards Organization (ISO) 14000 series, which are supposed to help any company in any country to meet the goals of "sustainable development" and environmental friendliness. Back in the 1980s, when many were jumping on the quality bandwagon, there emerged a set of ISO 9000 standards that specified minimum levels of quality. Some companies specified that they would deal only with suppliers that had an ISO rating; consequently, many companies became involved in the accreditation procedure. However, the experience with the ISO 9000 process was that a company had to clear so many hurdles to obtain the rating that it often lost sight of what it was that the customer really wanted. Will those marketers who pursue an ISO 14000 rating be caught with the same short-sightedness as their colleagues in the quality sector? Can such regulations realistically deal with the concerns that have plagued the marketing of environmental products and services? How should marketers deal with customer concerns about the sincerity of their offerings?

Pertinent Web Sites

http://www.thebodyshop.ca
http://www.isogroup.iserv.net/index.html

Questions

1. What macroenvironmental trends affect the marketing of environmentally friendly products?
2. What problems have marketers encountered in the past when attempting to promote environmentally friendly products and services? What problems are they likely to face in the future?
3. Identify the factors that influence consumer buying behaviour for environmentally friendly products.
4. Make some recommendations for packaging and labelling that may enhance the environmentally friendly aspect of products.
5. How can a company stimulate publicity for its environmentally friendly products and services? How should a company deal with related negative publicity?

Sources: Michael Adams, *Sex in the Snow* (Toronto: Penguin Books Canada Ltd.,1997); Harry P. Cleghorn and Renka Gesing, "Marketing Green Products: A Canadian Perspective," *Environmental Manager*, September 1995, pp. 13–21; "Consumers Confused by Green Marketing Ploys," *The Calgary Herald*, July 22, 1991, p. B11; Joel J. Davis, "A Blueprint for Green Marketing," *The Journal of Business Strategy*, July/August 1991, pp. 14–17;"Ecotourism: A Good Trip?" *The Economist*, August 30, 1997, pp. 48, 49; Stephen J. Grove, Raymond P. Fisk, Gregory M. Pickett, and Norman Kangum, "Going Green in the Service Sector: Social Responsibility Issues, Implications and Implementation," *European Journal of Marketing*, vol. 30, no. 5, pp. 56–66; M. Mauti and K. Slater, "The Ethical Marketing of Green Products," *Canadian Home Economics Journal*, Spring 1997, pp. 66–70; Molly Miller, "The Color of Money," *Mother Earth News*, February/March 1996, pp. 78–80; Pat Morden, "Why Green Isn't Always Great," *Profit*, June/July 1991, pp. 30, 31; Diana Swift, "The De-Greening of a Company," *Metropolitan Toronto Business Journal*, July/August 1992, p. 9.

Case 1-3

SERVICE DEVELOPMENT STRATEGY

Julian and Corby had been good friends since elementary school. They had gone to college together, and both graduated with degrees in information technology and business. Both had worked part-time in electronics shops while in school and knew their way around computers, the Internet, and a whole host of new microchip-based communications products and appliances. Both were expected, by their parents as well as their girlfriends and other friends, to get pretty good jobs when they finished their studies in a few months. Both had another idea that had been brewing ever since they had worked together on a software-development course project last term. They wanted to start a consumer telecommunication consulting and service business.

Their experience with their course project convinced them that they had at least two good ideas; that the time was right for their kind of services, and that they had the programming knowledge to design the necessary software and the general business background to be able to operate a small business. Their instructor not only gave them a top grade for their software ideas but also encouraged them to think seriously about either starting a business and operating it themselves or putting the whole service concept, in detail, on paper and selling it to an existing telecommunications consulting

---

This case is prepared, in part, from material provided by Mary Gooderham, "Consumers Face Bills, Bills and More Bills," *The Globe and Mail*, September 2, 1997, pp. C1, C14.

firm or some other buyer. Of course, they were both in debt to the provincial government as well as to their parents and didn't have an immediate source of working capital. But they had ideas that they thought were worthwhile, and, after all, there were a lot of software-development millionaires.

Their idea for one new service originally came directly out of their experience with their parents, friends, and neighbours of their parents. It seemed to them that for years they were continuously being asked for advice about telecommunications and computer-based products and services: "Is it useful to have a pager these days? How can you tell which cell phone is technically a good buy? What's the difference between the service offered by a Mobility Canada company, say Bell Mobility, and Rogers Cantel Mobile Communications? I think I could use the Internet but I'm not sure, and how do you find out what you need and what it costs?" They felt they could easily develop the software to make comparisons and recommendations based on a householder's "specifications," which they could develop from conversations or by designing a questionnaire and having it completed. They saw this approach as similar to what communications consultants would do for large and medium-sized businesses.

Their second idea had to do with the multiple billings that householders receive from various communications companies. Right now, a person could receive a bill from the local telephone service supplier, the long-distance supplier, the cell phone service provider, and maybe a monthly cell phone rental charge; there could be other bills for a high-speed data line, an Internet access service charge, and perhaps a pager service charge. And then there was the cable-TV bill. While working on their software-development project, they noted that many people who had begun using new communications products and services complained not only about all the bills they were getting but also their complexity. It was not always easy to know what was costing what! And then, many of these bills had to be paid separately. Here again, Julian and Corby felt they could easily develop software to create, from all the various suppliers' information, a single straightforward bill. They believed that the software needed to deal with both ideas would have many elements in common.

While Julian and Corby liked both ideas, they were concerned about the sense of working on both, either at the same time or at all. They wondered if they could answer the standard questions: What business are we in or should we be in? What are or could our goals be? What product and market strategy should we start with? They knew that whatever else they did, they would have to approach a bank or their provincial business-startup office for potential financing, and they had to be able to present a business plan that answered basic questions and showed how they were going to operate.

Questions

1. What business do you think Julian and Corby are interested in? Do you think both ideas are part of this business, or are they separate businesses?
2. Write a set of mission goals and objectives statements that make sense for Julian and Corby as well as a potential financial supporter.
3. Using the product-market growth matrix, suggest a basic strategy for Julian and Corby.

Part Two

Target Markets

An analysis of the people and organizations who buy, why they buy, and how they buy

In Part Two, we discuss the selection of an organization's intended customers — its target market. Chapter 4 examines the concept of market segmentation as it relates to the selection of target markets, and we discuss several approaches to the segmentation of markets. In Chapter 5, we explore the strategic concept of positioning as a means to ensure that a company's offerings appeal to its target segments. We also discuss the important topic of forecasting. Chapter 6 is devoted to consumer buying behaviour and the buying process involved in the purchase of products and services. In Chapter 7, we examine in detail the business-to-business market, thereby reminding ourselves that there is a massive market that many end consumers rarely see — the one that involves businesses marketing to businesses and other organizations. Finally, Chapter 8 covers marketing research and marketing information systems, the means whereby marketers learn about their markets and the target consumers and customers who comprise them.

CHAPTER 4 GOALS

After studying this chapter, you should have an understanding of:

- The fundamental principles behind target market identification and selection.
- The concept of market segmentation — its meaning, benefits, limitations, and situations where it finds greatest use.
- The difference between ultimate consumer markets and business markets.
- The principal bases for segmenting consumer markets.
- Segmentation of the market through examination of the distribution and composition of the population of Canada.
- Segmentation of the market through examination of consumer groups on the basis of income distribution and spending patterns.

Chapter Four

Foundations for Market Segmentation

http://ymca.sask.com

WHO IS THE TARGET SEGMENT FOR YMCA DAY CAMPS?

When you think of the YMCA, what comes to your mind? Perhaps it's where you have gone to play basketball. Maybe you are enrolled there for an aerobics course. The YMCA is well known to most Canadians for offering a variety of programs and services in the communities in which its associations are located. These programs are geared to many age groups, from seniors to adults to children. In some locations, the YMCA offers pre-school programs. For example, the YMCA of Regina offers "Mini Moves," a program for children who are walking but under the age of two.[1] The program promises to provide an exciting, creative environment for toddlers to learn more about body awareness and motor skills.

This service represents a good example of an organization targeting a specific market segment and positioning its product to appeal to that segment. On the surface, it may appear that this is a program targeted at children under age two. But there may be more to this program than meets the eye. In order to gain a more complete understanding of why the YMCA is offering this service, we need to think a little more about the concept of target segments as discussed in this chapter. We also need to have some understanding of why parents enrol their children in programs of this type. It may help us to consider some questions such as: Who buys pre-school programs? Who makes the purchase decision? What factors are taken into consideration?

Once we deal with such questions, it should be obvious that the target market is, in fact, the parents of these young children and that the YMCA of Regina is trying to appeal to certain motives and needs of these parents. Members of the specific segment of the population who will purchase programs of this nature for their toddlers are probably conscious of the need for motor skill development in small children and the importance of exposing small children to new things. This example serves to introduce a number of very important topics in marketing: the selection of a target market segment; the fact that the target segment should be characterized on the basis of a number of factors, only some of which may be demographic; and the need to position a product so that it appeals to the target segment.

The YMCA's pre-school program — Mini Moves — provides an example that is relevant for the next three chapters. We will discuss in this chapter the factors that a company takes into account in selecting a target segment for its product or service. In Chapter 5, we will deal with the positioning of that product so it has greatest appeal for the target segment. In Chapter 6, we will gain a better understanding of the consumer psychology and behaviour that guide the marketer in making strategic decisions about segmentation and positioning.

SELECTING A TARGET MARKET

In Chapter 1 we defined a **market** as people or organizations with (1) wants (needs) to satisfy, (2) money to spend, and (3) the willingness to spend it. A **target market** is a group of customers (people or firms) at whom the seller specifically aims its marketing efforts. The careful selection and accurate definition (identification) of target markets are essential for the development of an effective marketing program. One of the fundamental principles underlying the practice of market segmentation is that most companies and brands can no longer aspire to be "all things to all people." With the fragmentation of the Canadian marketplace and the increased level of competition from local, domestic, and international competitors, most marketers practise a strategy of carving out of the mass market a manageable target group of consumers upon which they will concentrate.

Guidelines in Market Selection

Four general guidelines govern the selection of target markets. The first one is that target markets should be compatible with the organization's goals and image. A firm marketing high-priced personal computers should not sell through discount chain stores in an effort to reach a mass market.

A second guideline — consistent with our definition of strategic planning — is to match the market opportunity with the company's resources. In many ways, the YM-YWCA of Regina did this when it introduced its pre-school program, Mini Moves. The organization has a long history in Canada and in many other countries of offering programs and services to the public in the communities it serves. When the YMCA of Regina introduced this pre-school program it was a logical extension of other family-oriented programs offered by the organization. However, there was also an obvious appreciation for the fact that a viable segment existed for the introduction of a program directed at parents who believe very young children benefit from learning environments outside the home. Consequently, the YMCA matched its considerable expertise and positive image with the recently identified emerging market segment.

Over the long run, a business must generate a profit if it is to survive. This rather obvious third guideline translates into what is perhaps an obvious market selection guideline. That is, an organization should consciously seek markets that will generate sufficient sales volume at a low enough cost to result in a profit. Surprisingly, companies often have overlooked the profit factor in their quest for high-volume markets. The goal was sales volume alone, not *profitable* sales volume.

Finally, a company ordinarily should seek a market wherein the number of competitors and their size are such that the new entrant is able to compete effectively. An organization should not enter a market that is already saturated with competition unless it has some overriding competitive advantage that will enable it to take customers from existing firms.

Market Opportunity Analysis

Theoretically a market opportunity exists at any time and at any place where there is a person or an organization with an unfilled need or want. Realistically, of course, a company's market opportunity is much more restricted. Thus, selecting a target market requires an appraisal of market opportunities available to the organization. A market opportunity analysis begins with a study of the environmental forces (as discussed in Chapter 2) that affect a firm's marketing program. Then the organization must analyze the three components of a market — people or organizations, their buying power, and their willingness to spend. Analysis of the "people" component involves a study of the geographic distribution and demographic composition of the population. The second component is analyzed through the distribution of consumer income and consumer expenditure patterns. Finally, to determine consumers' "willingness to spend," management must study consumer buying behaviour. Population and buying power are discussed more fully later in this chapter. Buying behaviour is covered in Chapter 6.

Target-Market Strategy: Aggregation or Segmentation

In defining the market or markets it will sell to, an organization has its choice of two approaches. In one, the total market is viewed as a single unit — as one mass, aggregate market. This approach leads to the strategy of market aggregation. In the other approach, the total market is seen as many smaller, homogeneous segments. This approach leads to the strategy of market segmentation, in which one or more segments are selected as the top target market(s). Deciding which **target-market strategy** to adopt is a key in selecting target markets. We shall discuss market aggregation and segmentation in more detail in Chapter 5.

Measuring Selected Markets

When selecting target markets, a company should make quantitative estimates of the potential sales volume of the market for its product or service. This process requires estimating, first, the total industry potential for the company's product in the target market or among the target segment and, second, the share of this total market that can be achieved. It is essential that management also prepare a sales forecast, usually for a one-year period. A sales forecast is the foundation of all budgeting and short-term operational planning in all departments — marketing, production, and finance. Sales forecasting will be discussed in more detail in Chapter 5, after we build a better knowledge of market segmentation.

NATURE OF MARKET SEGMENTATION

The total market for most types of products is too varied — too heterogeneous — to be considered a single, uniform entity. To speak of the market for vitamin pills or electric razors or education is to ignore the fact that the total market for each product or service consists of submarkets that differ significantly from one another. This lack of uniformity may be traced to differences in buying habits, in ways in which the product or service is used, in motives for buying, or in other factors. Market segmentation takes these differences into account.

Not all consumers want to wear the same type of clothing, use the same shampoo, or participate in the same recreational activities. Nor do all business firms want to buy the same kind of computers or delivery trucks. At the same time, a marketer usually cannot afford to tailor-make a different product or service for every single customer. Consequently market segmentation is the strategy that most marketers adopt as a compromise between the extremes of one product or service for all and a different one for each customer. A major element in a company's success is its ability to select the most effective location on this segmentation spectrum between the two extremes.

What Is Market Segmentation?

Market segmentation is the process of dividing the total heterogeneous market for a product or service into several segments, each of which tends to be homogeneous in all significant aspects. Management selects one or more of these market segments as the organization's target market. A separate marketing program and approach is developed for each segment or group of segments in this target market.

Benefits of Market Segmentation

Market segmentation is a customer-oriented philosophy and thus is consistent with the marketing concept. We first identify the needs of customers within a submarket (segment) and then develop an approach to marketing that will satisfy those needs.

By tailoring marketing programs to individual market segments, management can do a better marketing job and make more efficient use of marketing resources. A small firm with limited resources might compete very effectively in one or two market segments, whereas the same firm would be buried if it aimed for the total market. By employing the strategy of market segmentation, a company can design products and services that really match market demands. Advertising media can be used more effectively because promotional messages — and the media chosen to present them — can be aimed specifically toward each segment of the market.

Some of the most successful marketers are small or medium-sized firms that have decided to concentrate on a small number of market segments and to gain a strong market position and disproportionate market share in these segments. This relates to the principle of niche marketing, which will be discussed in greater detail in Chapter 5.

Even very large companies with the resources to engage in mass marketing supported by expensive national advertising campaigns are now abandoning mass marketing strategies. Instead, these companies have accepted market segmentation as a more effective strategy to reach the fractured fragments that once constituted a mass, homogeneous market. Procter & Gamble's marketing program nicely illustrates these changing conditions. Once the epitome of a mass marketer with innovative but utilitarian products, P&G advertised heavily on network television. But today it's a different ball game. Fewer people are at home during the day to watch television. Those who spend time in front of the television may be watching programs, viewing videos or a film or program that was taped a day or two earlier, or playing video games. Even if they are watching TV, viewers may be tuned to any one of up to one hundred channels. With such a variety of programming to choose from, many viewers spend much of their time "flicking" from channel to channel, using their remote-control devices.

www.pg.com

Faced with this fragmentation of the television audience, Procter & Gamble has developed a variety of marketing campaigns, each designed to appeal to a different target market segment. The company now offers six varieties of its market-leading Tide detergent, each targeted to consumers with different needs and reasons for buying laundry detergent. Within its line of hand and bath soaps, P&G offers Ivory, Zest, Coast, Safeguard, Camay, and Oil of Olay. Many of these brands come in different sizes for sink and tub, various colours to match bathroom decor, and different forms — bar soaps, body wash, and liquid soap in pump dispensers. Procter & Gamble, by offering such a wide range of options to the consumer, is competing in a soap market that is segmented by skin type (oily versus dry; normal versus sensitive), fragrance, aesthetics, the desire for convenience, and the primary benefit sought (clean hands or a pleasant, deodorized fragrance). It is clear that all consumers buy soap for cleansing, but they also expect other benefits from the soap they use. Hence, many segments exist.

Advances in technology have made market segmentation easier for companies in many industries as they have created efficiencies by permitting the targeting of specific segments. For example, many companies regularly collect data on their customers and their purchasing patterns. Data can be collected that offer specific information on individuals or groups of individuals. Telephone companies, for example, can identify the types of services used by individuals or groups of people, and can assess that information in relation to demographics or other individual characteristics. When companies maintain data bases on purchasing behaviour, it is possible to target products and brands to customers who have certain characteristics and needs. Such targeting of products and services to specific segments or even to specific customers through the use of databases makes marketing much more cost-effective than was ever possible in the past.

Limitations of Market Segmentation

Although market segmentation can provide a lot of marketing benefits to an organization, this strategy also has some drawbacks with respect to costs and market coverage. In the first place, market segmentation can be an expensive proposition in both the production and marketing of products and services. In production, it obviously is less expensive to produce mass quantities of one model and one colour than to produce a variety of models, colours, and sizes. Similarly, offering a variety of services costs more than providing only one.

Segmentation increases marketing expenses in several ways. Total inventory costs go up because adequate inventories of each style, colour, and the like must be maintained. Advertising costs go up because different ads may be required for each market segment. Or some segments may be too small for the seller to make effective use of television or another advertising medium. Administrative expenses go up when management must plan and implement several different programs.

Conditions for Effective Segmentation

Ideally, management's goal should be to segment markets in such a way that each segment responds in a homogeneous fashion to a given marketing program. Three **conditions for effective segmentation** will help management move toward this goal.

- The basis for segmenting — that is, the characteristics used to categorize customers — must be measurable, and the data must be accessible. The "desire for ecologically compatible products" may be a characteristic that is useful in segmenting the market for a given product, but data on this characteristic may not be readily accessible or easily quantified.
- The market segment itself should be accessible through existing marketing institutions — distribution channels, advertising media, company sales force — with a minimum of cost and waste. To aid marketers in this regard some national magazines, such as *Maclean's* and *Chatelaine*, publish separate geographical editions. This allows an advertiser to run an ad aimed at, say, a Western segment of the market, without having to pay for exposure in other, nontarget areas.
- Each segment should be large enough to be profitable. In concept, management could treat each single customer as a separate segment. (This situation may be normal in business markets, as when Canadair markets passenger airplanes to commercial airlines or when the Royal Bank of Canada makes a loan to a company planning to export to Europe.) But in segmenting a consumer market, a firm must not develop too broad an array of styles, colours, sizes, and prices. Usually the diseconomies of scale in production and inventory will put reasonable limits on this type of oversegmentation.

From a customer-oriented perspective, the ideal method for segmenting a market is on the basis of customers' desired benefits. Certainly, using benefits to segment a market is consistent with the idea that a company should be marketing benefits and not simply the physical characteristics of a product. After all, a carpenter wants a smooth surface (benefit), not sandpaper (the product). However, in many cases the benefits desired by customers do not meet the first condition described above. That is, they are not easily measured, because customers are unwilling or unable to reveal them. For example, what benefits do people derive from clothing that has the label on the outside? Conversely, why do others refuse to wear such clothing?

Even when benefits are identified, possibly in focus-group studies, it is difficult to determine how widely they exist in the market. As a result, a variety of indirect indicators of benefits are often used to describe segments. These indicators, such as age, are not the reason customers buy, but they are easily measured characteristics that people seeking the same benefit frequently have in common. For example, middle-aged people are more likely to read *Canadian Business* than are teenagers, not because they are middle aged but because the content of the magazine is more directly relevant to their lives. Marketers of *Canadian Business* find it easier to measure age than relevance, so age becomes a segmentation variable for them. Several of these commonly used, indirect bases for segmentation are discussed next.

BASES FOR MARKET SEGMENTATION — ULTIMATE CONSUMERS AND BUSINESS USERS

A company can segment its market in many different ways, and the bases for segmentation vary from one product category to another. At the top of the list, however, is the division of the entire potential

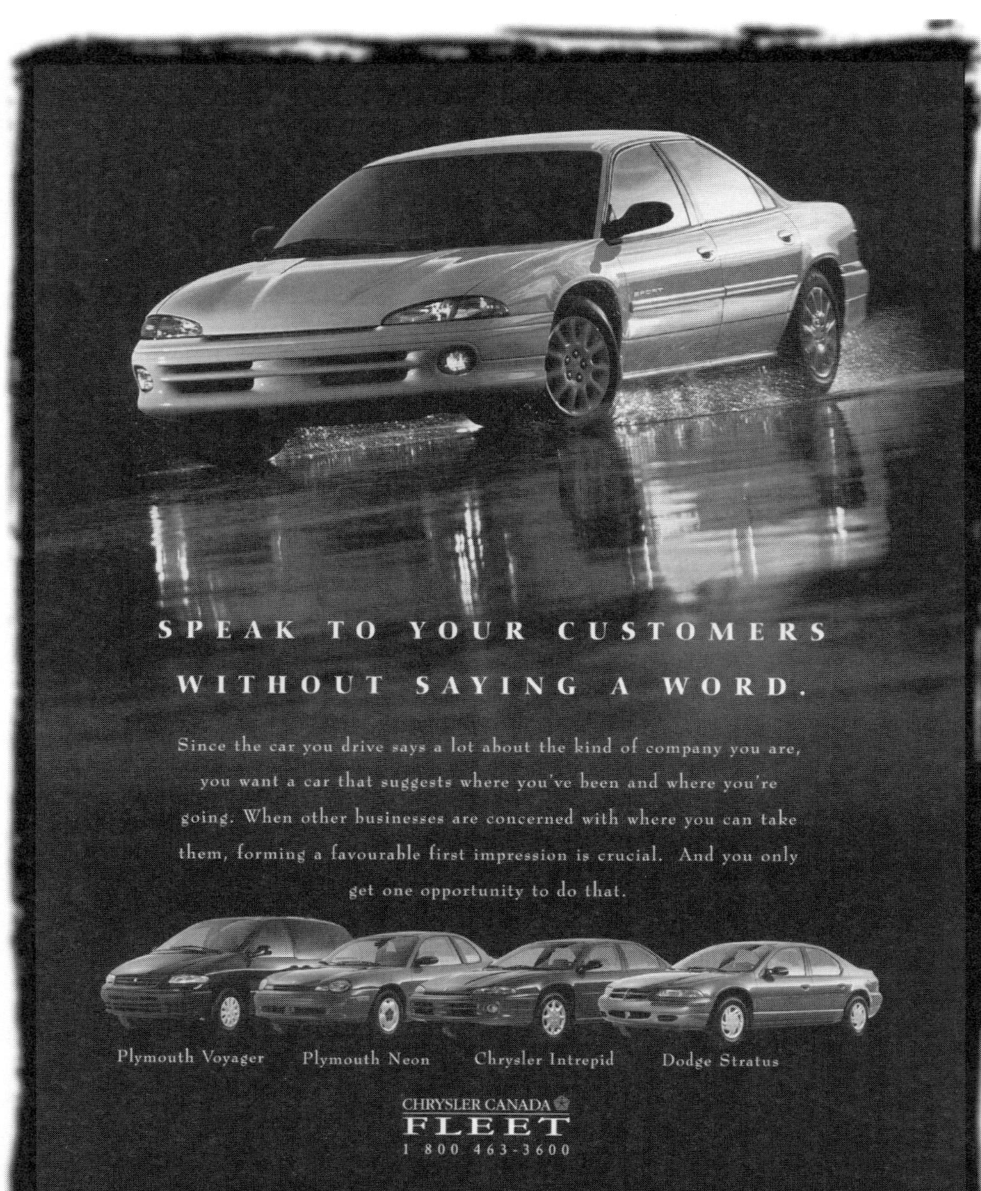

Image is also important in the business market.

market into two broad categories: ultimate consumers and business users.

The sole criterion for placement in one of these categories is the customer's reason for buying. **Ultimate consumers** buy goods or services for their own personal or household use. They are satisfying strictly nonbusiness wants, and they constitute the "consumer market."

Business users are business, industrial, or institutional organizations that buy goods or services to use in their own businesses or to make other products. A manufacturer that buys chemicals with which to make fertilizer is a business user of these chemicals. Farmers who buy the fertilizer to use in commercial farming are business users of the fertilizer. (If homeowners buy fertilizer to use on their yards, they are ultimate consumers because they buy it for personal, nonbusiness use.) Supermarkets, museums, and paper manufacturers that buy the service of a chartered accountant are business users of this service. Business users constitute the "business market," which is discussed in greater detail in Chapter 7.

The segmentation of all markets into two groups — consumer and business — is extremely significant from a marketing point of view because the two markets buy differently. Consequently the composition of a seller's marketing mix — products and services, distribution, pricing, and promotion — will depend on whether it is directed toward the consumer market or the business market.

BASES FOR CONSUMER MARKET SEGMENTATION

Dividing the total market into consumer and business segments is a worthwhile start toward useful segmentation, but it still leaves too broad and heterogeneous a grouping for most products. We need to identify some of the bases commonly used to segment these two markets further. As shown in Table 4-1, the following characteristics may provide **bases for segmenting the consumer market**:

- Geographic.
- Demographic.
- Psychographic.
- Behaviour toward product or service (product/service-related bases).

Marketing managers should be particularly aware of trends taking place in the demographic, psychographic, and behavioural characteristics of the markets in which they are operating. For example, if the population of Victoria is increasing because of a large number of people moving there to retire, this has obvious implications for businesses that operate in and around Victoria. Similarly, a company should be interested in knowing if the customers it has been serving are gradually reducing their usage of its product and using more of an indirectly competing product. This is precisely what has been happening in the beer market in Canada in recent years, as per capita consumption of the product has been declining gradually and as consumers have switched to consuming more wine and nonalcoholic drinks. The key word that marketers should keep in mind when examining such trends or changes in consumption and other segmentation variables is *implications*. The marketer should always look into the implications of such change and should be seeking information to guide an appropriate response to the market.

In using the bases outlined in Table 4-1 to segment markets, we should bear in mind two points. First, buying behaviour is rarely traceable to only one segmentation factor. Useful segmentation is developed by including variables from several bases. To illustrate, the market for a product rarely consists of all people living in British Columbia or all people over age sixty-five. Instead, the segment is more likely to be described with a few of these variables. Thus a market segment for notebook computers might be travelling business persons, earning above average income, who are well educated and over thirty. As another example, one clothing manufacturer's target market might be affluent young women (income, age, gender).

The other point to observe is the interrelationships among these factors, especially among the demographic factors. For instance, age and life-cycle stage typically are related. Income depends to some degree on age, life-cycle stage, education, and occupation.

We shall discuss the two most commonly used bases for segmentation — geographic and demographic — in this chapter, leaving to Chapter 5 a detailed discussion of the more complex bases for market segmentation.

Geographic Segmentation

Subdivisions in the geographical distribution and demographic composition of the population are widely used bases for segmenting consumer markets. The reason for this is simply that consumers' wants and product usage often are related to one or more of these subcategories. Geographic and demographic groupings also meet the conditions for effective segmentation — they are measurable, accessible, and large enough. Let's consider how the geographic distribution of population may serve as a segmentation basis.

TABLE 4-1 Segmentation Bases for Consumer Markets

Segmentation Basis	Examples of Typical Market Segments
Geographic	
Region	Atlantic provinces; Quebec; Ontario; Prairie provinces; British Columbia: census regions.
City or CMA size	Under 25,000; 25,000 to 100,000; 100,000 to 250,000; 250,000 to 500,000; 500,000 to 1,000,000; over 1,000,000.
Urban–rural	Urban; rural; suburban; farm.
Climate and topography	Mountainous; seacoast; rainy; cold and snowy; etc.
Demographic	
Age	Under 6, 6–12, 13–19, 20–34, 35–49, 50–64, 65 and over.
Gender	Male, female.
Family life cycle	Young single; young married; no children; etc.
Education	Grade school only, high school graduate, college graduate.
Occupation	Professional, manager, clerical worker, skilled worker, sales person, student, homemaker, unemployed.
Religion	Protestant, Catholic, Jewish, other.
Ethnic background	White; black; Asian. British; French; Chinese; German; Ukrainian, Italian; Indian; etc.
Income	Under $10,000; $10,000–$25,000; $25,000–$35,000; $35,000–$50,000; over $50,000.
Psychographic	
Social class	Upper class, upper middle, lower middle, upper lower, etc.
Personality	Ambitious, self-confident, aggressive, introverted, extroverted, sociable, etc.
Lifestyle	Conservative, liberal, health and fitness oriented, adventuresome.
Behaviour Toward Product or Service (or Product/Service-Related Bases)	
Benefits desired	Examples vary widely, depending upon product or service: appliance: cost, quality, life, repairs. aerobics class: fitness, appearance, health, fellowship. toothpaste: no cavities, plaque control, bright teeth. hairdressing: image, style, price, self-confidence.
Usage rate	Nonuser, light user, heavy user.

Total Population

A logical place to start is with an analysis of total population, and here the existence of a "population explosion" that has fizzled becomes evident. The population of Canada did not reach ten million until about 1930. However, it took only another thirty-five years to double, and by 1966 the total population of the country stood at just over twenty million. But then the rapid growth in population that had been experienced during the baby boom years from 1945 to the early 1960s began to slow down, and by 1996 the Canadian population had reached only 28.8 million. The current low birth rate is expected to continue, so projections are that the total population will not go much beyond 32 million by 2011. Unless the federal government relaxes restrictions on immigration, Canada could face a situation of *declining* population early in the twenty-first century. The result of a decline in the birth rate (from 15.5 per thousand people in 1976 to 12.7 per thousand people in 1996) and reduced immigration levels is a static, aging population.

The total market is so large and diverse that it must be analyzed in segments. Significant shifts are occurring in regional and urban–rural population distribution patterns. Market differences traceable to differences in age, gender, household arrangements, lifestyles, and ethnic backgrounds pose real challenges for marketing executives.

Regional Distribution

Figure 4-1 shows the distribution of the Canadian population in 1996 and its projected growth to 2016 by province. The biggest markets and the largest urban areas are located in Central Canada, where Ontario and Quebec together account for 62 percent of the Canadian population. However, the greatest rate of population growth since the early 1990s has occurred in Ontario and Western Canada, particularly in British Columbia, where the population increased by 13.5 percent from 1991 to 1996.

The **regional distribution of population** is important to marketers, because people within a particular geographic region broadly tend to share the same values, attitudes, and style preferences. However, significant differences do exist among the various regions, because of differences in climate, social customs, and other factors. Ontario is a more urbanized province and represents the greatest concentration of people in Canada, especially in the corridor between Oshawa and Niagara Falls. This market is attractive to many marketers because of its sheer size and the diversity of consumers living there. On the other hand, the Atlantic region and the Prairie provinces are characterized by a much more relaxed and rural lifestyle, which suggests a demand for different types of products and services. People in the West appear to be more relaxed and less formal than Eastern Canadians, and they spend more time outdoors. As this Western Canadian market grows, there will be a growth in demand for products associated with an outdoors lifestyle.

Urban, Rural, and Suburban Distribution

For many years in Canada there has been both a relative and an absolute decline in the farm population, and this decline in the rural market is expected to continue. The declining farm population has led some people to underestimate the importance of rural markets. However, both as an industrial market for farm machinery and other resource industry equipment and supplies, and as a consumer market with increased buying power and more urban sophistication, the rural market is still a major one. Sociological patterns (such as average family size and local customs) among rural people differ significantly from those of city dwellers. These patterns, affected by the **urban–suburban-rural distribution** of populations, have considerable influence on buying behaviour. Per capita consumption of cosmetics and other beauty aids, for example, is much lower in farm and rural markets than in city markets.

Census Metropolitan Areas

As the rural population has shrunk, the urban and suburban population has expanded. In recognition of the growing urbanization of the Canadian market, some years ago the federal government established the concept of a **census metropolitan area (CMA)** as a geographic market-data measurement unit. A CMA is defined by Statistics Canada as the main labour market of a continuous built-up area having a population of 100,000 or more. Table 4-2 indicates the growth in the population of the twenty-five CMAs in Canada from 1986 to 1996. By 1996, these twenty-five areas accounted for nearly 62 percent of the total population of Canada, and this percentage is expected to continue to increase. This is especially so as immigration to Canada increases and as most immigrants settle in urban areas. Obviously, these census metropolitan areas represent attractive, geographically concentrated market targets with considerable sales potential.

In several places in Canada, the metropolitan areas have expanded to the point where there is no rural space between them. This joining of metropolitan areas has been called "interurbia." Where two or more city markets once existed, today there is a single market. For example, there is virtually no

FIGURE 4-1 **Provincial Distribution of Canadian Population, 1996, and Projected Growth to 2016 (thousands)**

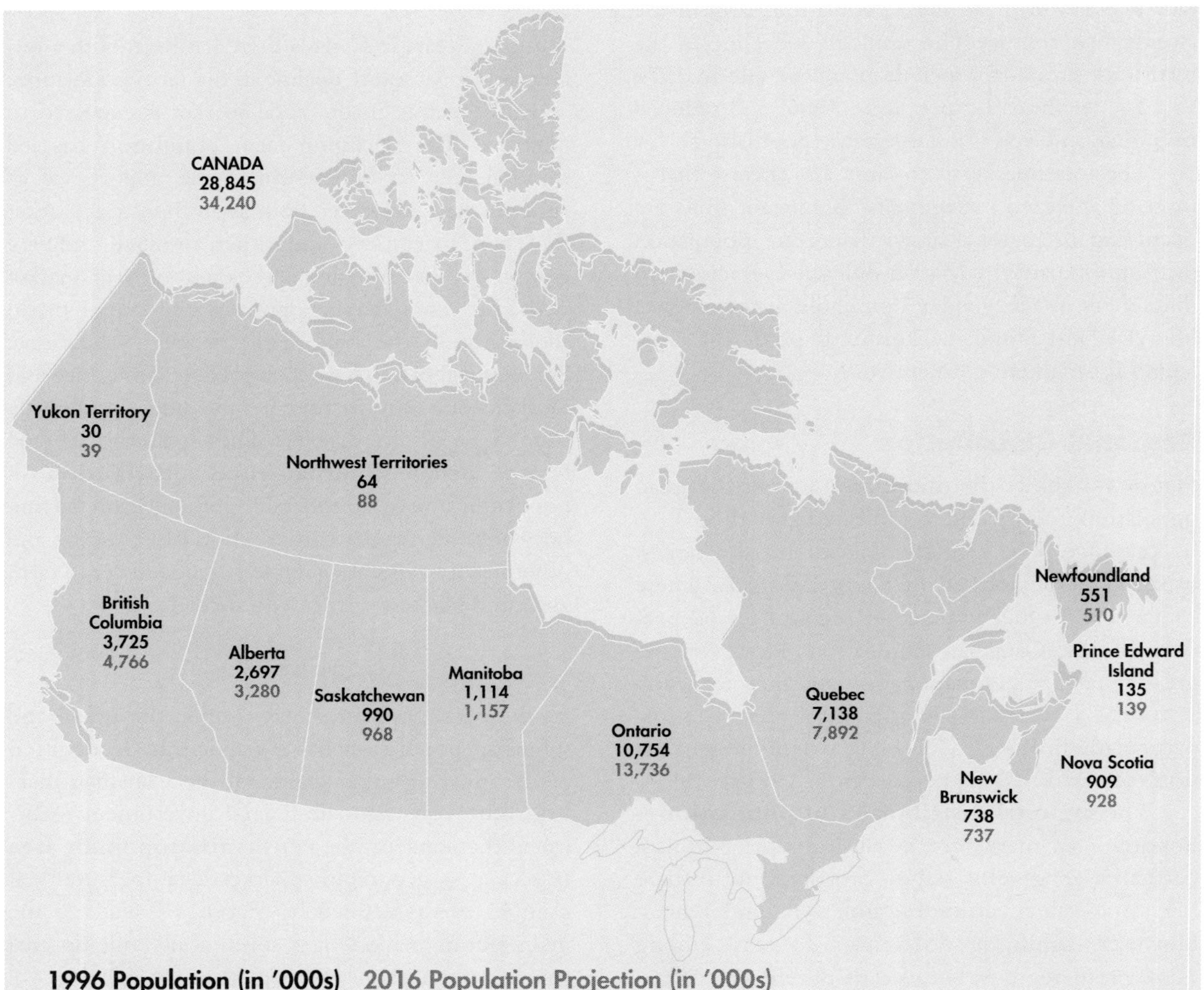

Source for 1996 Data: Statistics Canada, *1996 Census of Canada, Population and Dwelling Counts*, cat. no. 93-357, 1997. Source for projected figures: *Market Research Handbook, 1995*, cat. no. 63-224, pp. 576–77. The projections of provincial population figures to 2016 are based on a series of assumptions: that the birth rate continues at approximately the level that pertained at the end of the 1980s (approximately 1.67 births per woman), and that the level of immigration is approximately 200,000 per year. Life expectancy is expected to increase to 77.2 years for men and 84.0 years for women by 2016.

space between Quebec City and Niagara Falls that is not part of a major urban area.

Suburban Growth

As the metropolitan areas have been growing, something else has been going on within them. The central cities are growing very slowly, and in some cases the older established parts of the cities are actually losing population. The real growth is occurring in the fringe areas of the central cities or in the suburbs outside these cities. For the past forty years, one of the most significant social and economic trends in Canada has been the shift of population to the suburbs. As middle-income families have moved to the suburbs, the economic, racial, and ethnic composition of many central cities (especially their core areas) has changed considerably, thus changing the nature of the markets in these areas.

TABLE 4-2 Census Metropolitan Areas Population, 1986, 1991, and 1996 (thousands)

	1986	1991	1996
Calgary, Alberta	671.3	754.0	821.6
Chicoutimi-Jonquière, Quebec	158.5	160.9	160.4
Edmonton, Alberta	785.5	839.9	862.5
Halifax, Nova Scotia	296.0	320.5	332.5
Hamilton, Ontario	557.0	599.7	624.3
Kitchener, Ontario	311.2	356.4	382.9
London, Ontario	342.3	381.5	398.6
Montreal, Quebec	2,921.4	3,127.2	3,326.5
Oshawa, Ontario	203.5	250.1	268.7
Ottawa–Hull, Ontario–Quebec	819.3	920.8	1,010.4
Quebec City, Quebec	603.3	645.5	671.8
Regina, Saskatchewan	186.5	191.6	193.6
St. Catharines–Niagara Falls, Ontario	343.3	364.5	372.4
St. John's, Newfoundland	161.9	171.8	174.0
Saint John, New Brunswick	121.3	124.9	125.7
Saskatoon, Saskatchewan	200.7	210.0	219.0
Sherbrooke, Quebec	130.0	139.1	147.3
Sudbury, Ontario	148.9	157.6	160.4
Thunder Bay, Ontario	122.2	124.4	125.5
Toronto, Ontario	3,427.2	3,893.0	4,263.7
Trois-Rivières, Quebec	128.9	136.3	139.9
Vancouver, British Columbia	1,380.7	1,602.5	1,831.6
Victoria, British Columbia	255.5	287.8	304.2
Windsor, Ontario	254.0	262.0	278.6
Winnipeg, Manitoba	625.3	652.3	667.2

Source: Statistics Canada, *1996 Census of Canada, Population and Dwelling Counts*, cat. no. 93-357-XPB, 1997.

The growth of the suburban population has some striking marketing implications. Since a great percentage of suburban people live in single-family residences, there is a vastly expanded market for lawn mowers, lawn furniture, home furnishings, and home repair supplies and equipment. Suburbanites are more likely to want two cars than are city dwellers. They are inclined to spend more leisure time at home, so there is a bigger market for home entertainment and recreation items.

As we near the end of the century, marketing people are watching two possible countertrends. One is the movement from the suburbs back to the central cities by older people whose children are grown. Rather than contend with commuting, home maintenance, and other suburban challenges, older people are moving to new apartments located nearer to downtown facilities. And it is not just older people who are returning to the downtown areas. In many Canadian cities, young professional families

MARKETING AT WORK FILE 4-1

TARGETING CHILDREN ON THE INTERNET

Children are considered by some to be the ultimate consumers. They crave everything they see, at some ages, and are forever in search of the new and the different. Television has proven to be an excellent medium for reaching children; so much so, in fact, that advertisers have been and continue to be heavily criticized for exploitation of that market. Legislation has been invoked in some jurisdictions to prevent marketing that is directed explicitly at children. But what of the Internet? That new medium offers many opportunities to reach the children's market. But is it an easy segment to target by this medium?

Children's usage of the Internet is growing in great numbers each year. In 1997 it was estimated that at least one million children in North America were regularly on the Web, and that number was expected to grow particularly through the increased usage of the Internet in the school system. Some marketers feel they cannot afford not to be on-line to reach this current children's market and future adult market. Scott Irwin, senior vice-president of Irwin Toy Ltd. of Toronto, feels that the Internet is probably at the stage of early television. Not everyone is set up to interact and use the technology most effectively, but marketers must be there to participate when the marketplace is ready.

Many international companies such as Kelloggs have already been criticized for children's advertising on the Web. At Kelloggs, children were being enticed to play with "Tony the Tiger" and other commercial characters. Critics felt that this was an inappropriate weaving of advertising and content. They felt that marketers using product characters as spokespersons are essentially creating on-line infomercials for kids. Kelloggs has now changed its site.

Other problems facing marketers trying to reach kids on Internet sites include the sometimes painfully slow response rate of the Web. Children today grow up on what some have described as a fingertip culture. Weaned on gadgets like television remote controls, VCRs, and computers, they are used to accessing and controlling information quickly. While this makes the Internet market a seemingly good match for kids, it also creates difficulties with accomplishing the marketing objective. Kids just click past the ads.

At Kraft Canada Inc.'s Web page, children are invited to play an adventure-safari game and save the critter from poachers. The Web site for this game is www.post-mystery.com. Other companies use puzzles, quizzes, and chatting via e-mail. Sega Online (www.sega.com) is one of the busiest sites for kids. Kerry Bradford, general manager of Sega Online, says "Kids gravitate to those areas where the content is entertaining."

As the Internet expands and the World Wide Web becomes more a part of the life of all children, it will be interesting to see how marketers use it to reach this very important and all-demanding segment.

Source: Deborah Stokes, "Cashing in on Cybertots," *Marketing Magazine*, September 23, 1996, p. 18. Reprinted with permission.

are locating close to their downtown places of work, preferring to renovate an older home rather than contend with commuting and other perceived shortcomings of suburban living.

The other reversal is that there has been an increase in the rural population near larger cities. Although the rural population of Canada has increased very little in recent years, most of that growth occurred in close proximity to the large census metropolitan areas. This growth has been brought about, not only because some people wish to live in a more rural setting, but also because of rising real estate prices in and near many Canadian cities. Some of the growth that has been experienced in the population of census metropolitan areas as shown in Table 4-2 has occurred because some of the areas around these CMAs have been incorporated into the cities.

In recent years, geographic segmentation has become much more refined through the use of **geodemographic clustering**, a process that uses census and other statistical data to cluster postal code areas into similar groups or segments. By examining such data, a marketer can identify groups of postal code areas that have similar patterns of education, income, household size, age, housing, occupation, and other factors. Thus, companies can make their direct marketing efforts much more efficient by targeting their advertising to homes located in postal code areas that best reflect the characteristics of the target markets they wish to reach. Such an approach is also useful for making efficient decisions on new store locations, to determine the best products and brands to offer in specific stores, and to direct mail-order catalogues with appropriate merchandise featured.[2]

Demographic Segmentation

The most common basis for the **demographic segmentation** of consumer markets is some demographic category such as age, gender, family life-cycle stage, income distribution, education, occupation, or ethnic origin.

Age Groups

Analyzing the consumer market by age groups is a useful exercise in the marketing of many products and services. Age is one of the most fundamental bases for demographically segmenting markets, as we can see from the large number of products and services directed at seniors, children, teens, young adults, and so on. But marketers must be aware of the changing nature of the age mix of the Canadian population. Looking ahead again to the year 2016, we see an aging population that is not growing very quickly. In 1993, for example, there were 3.9 million people in Canada aged between 10 and 19. By 2011, this age group will have become slightly larger at 4.0 million; but by 2016, there will be only 3.7 million Canadians in this age bracket, assuming the birth rate remains at the present level. On the other hand, in 1986, there were only 2.7 million Canadians aged 65 and older. By 1993, this age bracket contained 3.3 million; by 2011, this group will increase in number to 4.8 million and to 5.6 million by 2016.[3] The youth market (roughly aged 5 to 13) carries a three-way market impact. First, these children can influence parental purchases. Second, millions of dollars are spent on this group by their parents. Third, these children make purchases of goods and services for their own use and satisfaction, and the volume of these purchases increases as the children get older. Promotional programs are often geared to this market segment. Manufacturers of breakfast cereals, snack foods, and toys often advertise on television programs that are directed at children — except on the CBC television network, which prohibits advertising on children's programs.[4]

In an attempt to lure more of the family leisure-travel market, Air Canada introduced a special children's menu, board games, books, colouring materials, cockpit visits, and play areas at major Canadian airports. This company states that it believes children have a great influence on their parents when decisions are being made as to which airline to use. Air Canada management call it "pester power." Keeping children entertained, they hope, will also create "relax power" for parents and for other passengers. This represents a good example of marketing to children by an organization whose target market is principally adults, but which is clearly interested in meeting family needs in the short term and in building brand loyalty to expand its market in the future.[5]

The teenage market is also recognized as an important one, yet many companies find it difficult to reach. The mistake might be in attempting to lump all teenagers together. Certainly, the 13–16 age group is very different from the 17–20 age bracket. Yet marketers must understand the teenage market because of the size of the segment and because its members have a great deal of money to spend.

Among young adults, postsecondary students are an excellent example of a segment that spends money. One author estimates that the amount is between $2 billion and $5 billion. Because this group is hard to reach, Campus Fest — a kind of travelling carnival — brings loud music, games, and a lot of interactive activities to more than twenty universities across the country. Through this venue, products are sold. The company sees the value of this population segment as an entry-level market for most products and brands. Attracting students offers good promise for future purchases.[6] Because the size of this young-adult segment will decline in coming years, Canada's universities are aggressively competing for students by taking new strategic approaches to recruiting and introducing advertising and marketing campaigns, new scholarships, integrated student services, and enrolment management systems.[7]

In the 1990s the early-middle-age population segment (35 to 50) was an especially large and lucrative market. These people are the products of the post–World War II baby boom and were the rebels of the 1960s and 1970s. They also were a very big and profitable teenage and young-adult market for many companies during those years. Now, as they move into middle age in the late 1990s, they are reaching their high-earning years. Typically, their values and lifestyles are far different from those of the people of the same age category in previous generations. Already, companies are adjusting to these changing demographics. While toothpaste manufacturers like Procter & Gamble and Colgate-Palmolive capitalized on concern about cavity prevention in children's teeth in the 1950s and 1960s, thirty-five or more years later they are producing toothpaste to fight tartar — an adult dental problem. This generation, with more dual-income families and fewer children, have more money to spend on themselves. As a result, they are a prime market for products that promise convenience and for home and garden services.

The aging baby-boom generation makes an attractive market segment for a number of other reasons. Many are seeing their children graduate from college and university and have likely paid off the mortgage on the family home. Suddenly, they have a lot more disposable money to spend on themselves and on indulging their new grandchildren. Coupled with the fact that this age group has reached this stage in their family life cycle is the fact that, as a result of the recession that gripped Canada in the early 1990s, many have opted to take early retirement from their jobs. As a result, many have a lot of leisure time on their hands. Consequently, this age group makes an attractive target for vacation travel, smaller homes and condominiums, and long-term investments intended to finance a long retirement.

At the older end of the age spectrum are two market segments that should not be overlooked. One is the group of people in their fifties and early sixties. This mature market is large and financially well off. Its members are at the peak of their earning power and typically no longer have financial responsibility for their children. Thus, this segment is a good target for marketers of high-priced, high-quality products and services.

The other older age group is made up of people over 65 — a segment that is growing both absolutely and as a percentage of the total population. Manufacturers and intermediaries alike are beginning to recognize that people in this age group are logical prospects for small, low-cost housing units, cruises and foreign tours, health products, and cosmetics developed especially for older people. Many firms are also developing promotional programs to appeal to this group because their purchasing power is surprisingly high. Also, the shopping behaviour of the over-65 market typically is different from that found in other age segments. On a per capita basis, seniors are increasing their spending faster than average in areas such as health care, entertainment, recreation, gifts, and contributions. In this latter category, seniors give more dollars than the average Canadian, making them an attractive market segment for charities and religious groups.

This is a rapidly growing market segment that is spanning new products and presenting opportunities for marketers. One food company, Dinner Date Inc., of Scarborough, Ontario, specializes in meals for the elderly. The company partners with a number of organizations in local areas providing services to this target group. Sage and Co. operates a mail-order business providing gadgets for seniors. Items such as special gardening tools, leisure clothing, jar openers for arthritic hands, and other specially designed kitchen aids are made available to this population segment.[8]

We should not fall into the trap, however, of assuming that all seniors are inactive or financially disadvantaged. Research shows that Canadians aged 75 and older are generally in good health, and an increasing percentage are living alone and enjoying an active life.

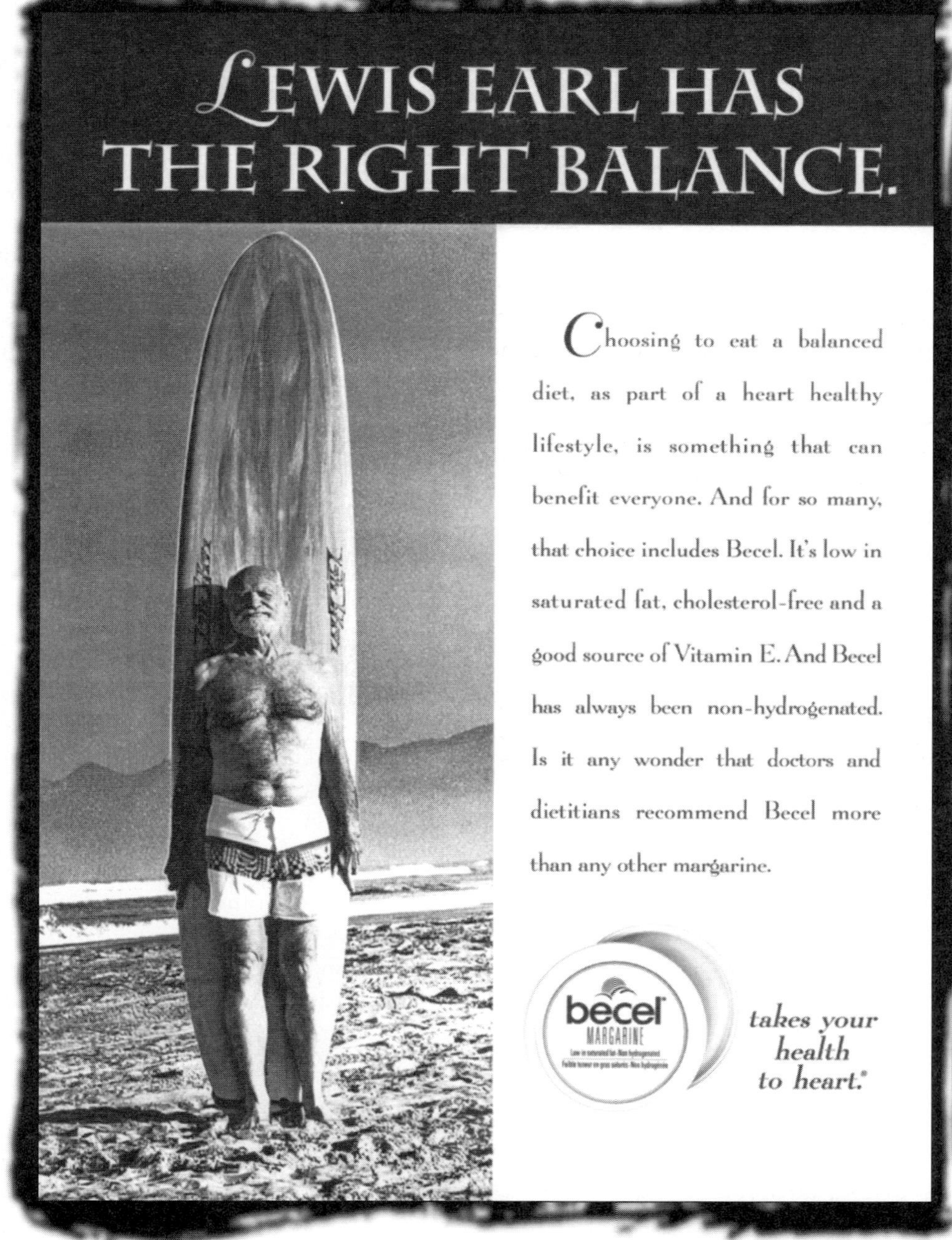

Healthy eating targets all ages.

Gender

Gender is an obvious basis for consumer market analysis. Many products are made for use by members of one gender, not both. In many product categories — automobiles, for example — women and men typically look for different product benefits. **Market segmentation by gender** is also useful because many products have traditionally been purchased by either men only or women only.

However, some of these traditional buying patterns are breaking down, and marketers certainly should be alert to changes involving their products and services. Almost 60 percent of women in Canada are employed outside the home. The entry of women into the work force has occurred in great numbers since the 1970s. Though participation rates have levelled off in recent years, women now account for almost 47 percent of the Canadian work force in the 15-to-44 age bracket. These facts are significant for marketers. Working women share more values with working men than they do with housewives, and young women share more values with young men than with older women. Not only are the lifestyle and buying behaviour of women in the labour force quite different from those of women who do not work outside their homes, but many of those women are members of households where their spouses also are employed, thereby producing Canadian households with considerable buying power.[9]

Family Life Cycle

Frequently the main factor accounting for differences in consumption patterns between two people of the same age and sex is that they are in different life-cycle stages. The concept of the **family life cycle** implies that there are several distinct stages in the life of an ordinary family. The traditional six-stage family cycle is shown in Figure 4-2, along with three alternative stages that reflect significant changes from traditional patterns. In addition to the family configurations represented in Figure 4-2, numerous other examples exist, from same-sex marriages to families with shared child custody to co-habitation arrangements between mixed-sex groups. Lifestyles that do not reflect the traditional norm are often more the rule than the exception. We can think of life-cycle position, in any of its various patterns, as a major determinant of buyer behaviour and thus it can be a useful basis for segmenting consumer markets.[10]

A young couple with two children (the full-nest stage) has quite different needs from those of a couple in their mid-fifties whose children no longer live at home (the empty-nest stage). A single-parent family (divorced, widowed, or never married) with dependent children faces social and economic problems quite different from those of a two-parent family. Young married couples with no children typically devote large shares of their income to clothing, autos, and recreation. When children start arriving, expenditure patterns shift as many young families buy and furnish a home. Families with teenagers find larger portions of the budget going for food, clothing, and educational needs.[11]

One of the most rapidly growing segments among the Canadian population is the singles. In 1961, only 9.3 percent of Canadian households consisted of just one person — a **single**. By 1991, just thirty years later, almost 23 percent of Canadian homes had only a single occupant, although the percentage of people living alone differs considerably from province to province. In Manitoba, for example, 25.6 percent of the households have only a single occupant, while the corresponding percentage in Newfoundland is only 12.6 percent. The total number of one-person households is increasing at a much faster rate than that of family units. Among the reasons for this increase in the number of one-person households are:

- The growing number of working women.
- People marrying at a later age.
- The reduced tendency for single people to live with their parents.
- A rising divorce rate.

The impact that single people of both sexes have on the market is demonstrated by such things as apartments for singles, social clubs for singles, and special tours, cruises, and eating places seeking the patronage of singles. Even in the mundane field of grocery products the growing singles market (including the divorced and widowed) is causing changes by retailers and food manufacturers.

Singles in the 25-to-39 age bracket are especially attractive to marketers because they are such a large group. Compared with the population as a whole, this singles group is:

- More affluent.
- More mobile.
- More experimental and less conventional.
- More fashion- and appearance-conscious.
- More active in leisure pursuits.
- More sensitive to social status.

FIGURE 4-2
The Family Life Cycle

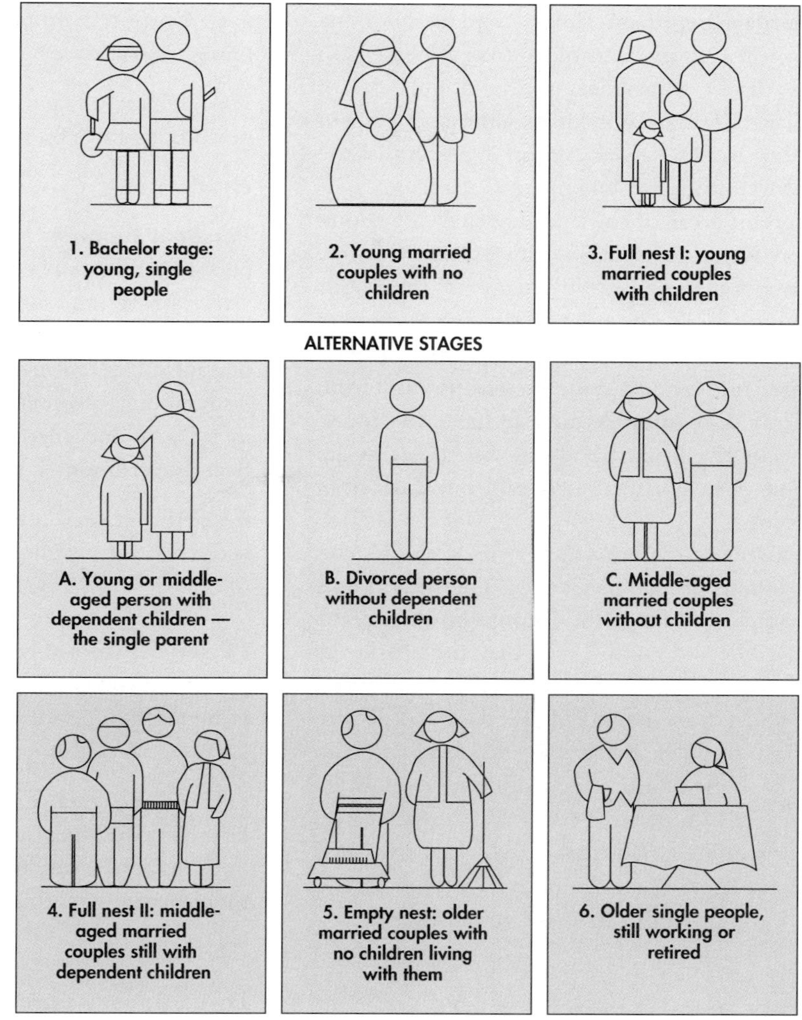

Other Demographic Bases for Segmentation

The market for some consumer products is influenced by such factors as education, occupation, religion, and ethnic origin. With an increasing number of people attaining higher levels of **education**, for example, we can expect to see (1) changes in product preferences and (2) buyers with more discriminating taste and higher incomes. **Occupation** may be a more meaningful criterion than income in segmenting some markets. Truck drivers or auto mechanics may earn as much as young retailing executives or college professors. But the buying patterns of the first two are different from those of the second two because of attitudes, interests, and other lifestyle factors.

For some products, it is useful to analyze the population on the basis of **religion** or **ethnic origin**. The most important distinction in Canada is between the two founding races. French-English differences are fundamental to doing business in Canada and will be dealt with in much greater detail in Chapter 6. Marketers have known for some time that certain products such as instant coffee and tomato juice sell much better in Quebec.

In larger Canadian cities, the cultural diversity of the population creates an increasing marketing opportunity for companies that specialize in products and services directed toward a particular ethnic community. In Toronto, for example, almost half the population was born outside Canada. Persons of

Italian heritage represent almost 5 percent of the population in Ontario and more than 8 percent in Toronto. Almost 8 percent of the population of Alberta have German roots, as do almost 13 percent of people in Saskatchewan. Almost 7 percent of the people of Manitoba are Ukrainian Canadians.

In certain areas of the country, such as around Kitchener–Waterloo, Ontario, with its large German Canadian population, and in many of the larger cities, ethnic groups represent a viable target market segment for certain specialty products and services. The large number of recent immigrants from Hong Kong and other Asian countries has transformed some neighbourhoods in some cities, as did immigrants from Portugal, Italy, and the Caribbean before them.

The Chinese community is one of the fastest-growing ethnic groups in Canada. The importance of this market segment to the Toronto business community is reflected in the fact that the market is served by three Chinese-language daily newspapers, two of which have been published since the late 1970s. Two popular magazines — *Maclean's* and *Toronto Life* — have also launched Chinese-language editions.[12] T&T Supermarkets, in Vancouver, caters to the burgeoning Asian market, which is estimated to make up more than 25 percent of the Lower Mainland population in British Columbia.[13]

CONSUMER INCOME AND ITS DISTRIBUTION

People alone do not make a market; they must have money to spend. Consequently, **consumer income**, its distribution, and how it is spent are essential factors in any quantitative market analysis.

Nature and Scope of Income

What is income? There are so many different concepts of income that it is good to review some definitions. The following outline is actually a "word equation" that shows how the several concepts are related.

National income: Total income from all sources, including employee compensation, corporate profits, and other income.

Less: Corporate profits, and pension and social program contributions.

Plus: Dividends, government transfer payments to persons, and net interest paid by government.

Equals:

Personal income: All forms of income received by persons and unincorporated businesses; including wages, salaries, and supplementary labour income; military pay and allowances; net income of nonfarm business including rent; net income of farm operators from farm production; interest, dividends, and miscellaneous investment income; and transfer payment income from government, corporations, and nonresidents.

Less: All personal federal, provincial, and municipal taxes.

Equals:

Personal disposable income: Personal income less personal direct taxes and other current transfers to government from persons; represents the amount available for personal consumption expenditure and savings.

Less: (1) Essential expenditures for food, clothing, household utilities, and local transportation and (2) fixed expenditures for rent, house mortgage payments, insurance, and instalment debt payments.

Equals:

Discretionary purchasing power: The amount of disposable personal income that is available after fixed commitments (debt repayments, rent) and essential household needs are taken care of. Compared with disposable personal income, discretionary purchasing power is a better (more sensitive) indicator of consumers' ability to spend for nonessentials.

In addition, we hear the terms "money income," "real income," and "psychic income." **Money income** is the amount a person receives in actual cash or cheques for wages, salaries, rent, interest, and dividends. **Real income** is what the money income will buy in goods and services; it is purchasing power. If a person's money income rises 5 percent in one year but the cost of purchases increases 2 percent on average, then real income increases by only 3 percent. **Psychic income** is an intangible, but highly important, income factor related to comfortable climate, a satisfying neighbourhood, enjoyment of one's job, and so on. Some people prefer to take less real income so they can live in a part of the country that features a fine climate — greater psychic income.

As measured by income, the Canadian economy has grown dramatically in recent years. With the exception of recessions in the early 1980s and early 1990s, the economy has enjoyed almost uninterrupted growth since the end of World War II. Personal disposable income, which stood at $159 billion in 1978 and at $237 billion in 1981, had jumped to $466 billion by 1991 and $511 billion by 1995. In the fifteen years from 1980 to 1995, per capita personal disposable income increased from $9,545 to $17,262. Discretionary purchasing power has, therefore, increased considerably during the past fifteen years or so. In light of the fact that inflation has been at very low levels in Canada in recent years, the improvement in consumer buying power is impressive.

Income Distribution

To get full value from an analysis of income, we should study the variations and trends in the distribution of income among regions and among population segments. Regional income data are especially helpful in pinpointing the particular market to which a firm wishes to appeal. Income data on cities and even on areas within cities may indicate the best locations for shopping centres and suburban branches of downtown stores.

A genuine income revolution has occurred in Canada over the past thirty years or so. During the second half of the twentieth century, the pattern of **income distribution** has been dramatically altered (see Table 4-3). There has been a tremendous growth in the middle- and upper-income segments, and a corresponding decrease in the percentage of low-income groups.

The purchasing power of the average Canadian family is expected to continue to increase over the next ten years. We will see the effects of higher personal incomes and higher participation rates in the labour force. It is very likely that more than half of all Canadian families will have a total annual income in excess of $55,000 by the year 2016. This anticipated increase in the number of affluent households is the result of several factors. These include (1) the large growth in the number of people in the prime earning years 25 to 45, (2) the increase in dual-income families, and (3) the wider distribution of inherited wealth. We will still have low-income families. However, there will be fewer below the poverty line, even though that level (by government definition) is moving up, in recognition of both inflation and a society that is generally better able to provide its members with a reasonable income.

TABLE 4-3

Percentage Distribution of Families by Income Groups in Canada, Annual Income 1985, 1990, and 1995

Income Group	1985	1990	1995
Less than $10,000	5.5	2.7	1.9
$10,000 to $14,999	8.4	4.3	4.1
$15,000 to $19,999	9.3	6.8	5.6
$20,000 to $24,999	8.8	7.0	7.6
$25,000 to $29,999	9.3	6.5	6.1
$30,000 to $34,999	9.7	7.2	6.9
$35,000 to $39,999	9.3	7.1	7.1
$40,000 to $44,999	8.0	7.5	6.6
$45,000 to $49,999	6.8	6.9	6.8
$50,000 to $59,999	10.2	11.2	11.4
$60,000 to $69,999	6.1	8.4	9.9
$70,000 and over	8.5	17.7	26.3

Source: Statistics Canada, *Income Distribution by Size in Canada*, cat. no. 13-207, 1995, p. 92.

Marketing Significance of Income Data

The declining percentage of families in the poverty bracket, coupled with the sharp increases in the upper-income groups, presages an explosive growth in discretionary purchasing power. And, as discretionary income increases, so too does the demand for items that once were considered luxuries.

The middle-income market is a big and growing market, and it has forced many changes in marketing

www.pantone.com
www.thebrick.com

MARKETING AT WORK FILE 4-2

SEGMENTING BY COLOUR PREFERENCE?

The last time you bought an article of clothing or a school binder or knapsack, did you spend a great deal of time choosing the colour? When it comes to things such as clothes, most people are very particular about colour. Psychologists tell us that colour can produce physiological reactions such as increased blood pressure and heart rate changes. Red can make people very assertive, while purple can calm and settle people down.

The significance of colour is not lost on marketers. They are very interested in how colour influences your buying behaviour. The Cooper Marketing Group of Oak Park, Ill., working in conjunction with Market Facts of Arlington Heights, Ill., has developed colour or lifestyle segmentation, which is a system to segment customers according to the importance of colour in their buying decisions. They have identified three colour personalities:

Colour-Forward Consumers — like to be the first to try a new or daring colour and are willing to pay more for a product in a fashionable colour. They tend to be women under 30 or over 50, or men under 30, city dwellers, impulse buyers, and people who make less than $35,000 per year.

Colour-Prudent Consumers — wait for a colour to gain acceptance before they adopt it. They put quality ahead of colour when choosing products. They tend to be women aged 30 to 50, careful shoppers, and people who make more than $50,000 per year.

Colour-Loyal Consumers — prefer safe colours such as blue or grey rather than fashionable colours. They tend to be men over 60, suburban or rural, dislike shopping, and fall anywhere on the income spectrum.

In the fashion business a season's colours are worked out two years in advance. A new colour usually appears first in fashion and then moves into home furnishings and home decor. In a study of colour preferences conducted by the Pantone Color Institute of New Jersey, blue was found to be a preferred colour, with green on the rise in popularity. Young adults favoured bright and deep colours, while those over 45 favoured pastels and candy colours.

Source: Adapted from Jo Marney, "Coloring Consumer Purchasing Patterns," *Marketing Magazine*, September 16, 1996, p. 24.

strategy. Many stores that once appealed to low-income groups have traded up to the huge middle-income market. These stores are upgrading the quality of the products they carry and are offering additional services.

In spite of the considerable increase in disposable income in the past thirty years, many households are still in the low-income bracket or find their higher incomes inadequate to fulfil all their wants. Furthermore, many customers are willing to forgo services in order to get lower prices. One consequence of this market feature has been the development of self-service retail outlets, discount houses, and the more recent superstores, such as those operated by furniture and appliance retailers like The Brick Warehouse in Ontario and Western Canada and by specialists in electronic sound equipment such as Majestic Electronic Stores.

Earlier in this chapter we noted the dramatic increase in the number of working women. This demographic factor also has had a tremendous impact on family income levels. The increase in two-income families has significant marketing and sociological implications. Dual incomes generally enable a family to offset the effects of inflation. But, more than that, two incomes often enable a family to buy within a short time the things their parents worked for years to acquire.

CONSUMER EXPENDITURE PATTERNS

How consumers' income is spent is a major market determinant for most products and services. Consequently, marketers need to study **consumer spending patterns** as well as the distribution of consumer income. Marketers also should be aware of the significant shifts in family spending patterns that have occurred over the past two or three decades. Energy costs, inflation, and heavy consumer debt loads have had a major impact on our spending patterns. As examples, let's consider just a few of the changes in spending patterns that have occurred between the 1960s and the 1990s. Over that time span, families have increased the percentage of their total expenditures going for housing, health, and utilities. Spending (as a percentage of total) has decreased for food, beverage, clothing, and home expenses (except utilities).

But expenditure patterns are not the same for all families. These patterns vary considerably, depending on family income, life-cycle stage, and other factors.

Relation to Stage of Family Life Cycle

Consumer expenditure patterns are influenced by the consumer's stage in the life cycle. There are striking contrasts in spending patterns between, say, people in the full-nest stage, with very young children, and people in the empty-nest stage. Table 4-4 summarizes the behavioural influences and the spending patterns for families in each stage of the cycle. (This table expands the number of stages shown earlier in Figure 4-2.) Young married couples with no children typically devote large shares of their income to clothing, automobiles, and recreation. When children start arriving, expenditure patterns shift as many young families buy and furnish a home. Families with teenagers find larger portions of the budget going for food, clothing, and educational needs. Families in the empty-nest stage, especially when the head of the family is still in the labour force, are attractive to marketers. Typically, these families have more discretionary buying power.

Relation to Income Distribution

The pattern of consumer expenditures is influenced significantly by the income level of the household. For example, as we can see in Table 4-5, families with incomes in the range of $15,000 to $19,999 spend an average of 18.1 percent of their expenditures on food. This percentage drops to 13.8 percent for those with annual incomes between $35,000 and $39,999, and to 11.1 percent for those with incomes above $60,000 per annum. These and other findings from the analysis of Statistics Canada data suggest the type of information that marketers might obtain from analyzing spending patterns by income groups. Some additional generalizations from such data are summarized below.

- There is a high degree of uniformity in the expenditure patterns of middle-class spending units. As we shall note in Chapter 6, however, social-class structure is often a more meaningful criterion for determining expenditure patterns.
- For each product category, there is a considerable absolute increase in dollars spent as income rises (or, more correctly, as we compare one income group with a higher income group). In other words, people in a given income bracket spend significantly more dollars in each product category than do those in lower brackets. However, the lower-income households devote a larger percentage of their total expenditures to some product categories, such as food. Marketers are probably more concerned with the total dollars available from each income group than with the percentage share of total expenditures.
- In each successively higher income group, the amount spent for food declines as a percentage of total expenditures.
- The percentage of expenditures devoted to housing, household operation, and utilities totals approximately 22 percent. This varies from more than 33 percent for consumers with incomes between $15,000 and $20,000 to 20 percent for those whose family incomes are more than $60,000 annually.
- Dramatic differences are observed across income groups in their actual dollar expenditures on recreation. Whereas a family in the lower-income bracket may spend as little as $483 annually, the higher-income family will spend as much as $5,000.

TABLE 4-4 Behavioural Influences and Buying Patterns, by Family Life-Cycle Stage

Bachelor stage: young single people not living at home	Newly married couples; young, no children	Full nest I; youngest child under 6	Full nest II; youngest child 6 or over	Full nest III; older married couples with dependent children
Few financial burdens. Fashion opinion leader. Recreation-oriented. Buy: basic kitchen equipment, basic furniture, cars, equipment for the mating game, vacations.	Better off financially than they will be in near future. Highest purchase rate and highest average purchase of durables. Buy: cars, refrigerators, stoves, sensible and durable furniture, vacations.	Home purchasing at peak. Liquid assets low. In some cases, both spouses work outside the home. Dissatisfied with financial position and amount of money saved. Interested in new products. Like advertised products. Buy: washers, dryers, TV sets, baby food, chest rubs and cough medicine, vitamins, dolls, wagons, sleds, skates.	Financial position better. In many cases, both spouses work outside the home. Less influenced by advertising. Buy larger-sized packages, multiple-unit deals. Buy: many foods, cleaning materials, bicycles, music lessons, pianos.	Financial position still better. In many cases, both spouses work outside the home. Some children get jobs. Hard to influence with advertising. High average purchase of durables. Buy: new, more tasteful furniture, auto travel, non-necessary appliances, boats, dental services, magazines.

Empty nest I; older married couples, no children living with them, head in labour force	Empty nest II; older married couples, no children living at home, head retired	Solitary survivor, in labour force	Solitary survivor, retired
Home ownership at peak. Most satisfied with financial position and money saved. Interested in travel, recreation, self-education. Make gifts and contributions. Not interested in new products. Buy: vacations, luxuries, home improvements.	Drastic cut in income Keep home. Buy: medical appliances, medical care, products that aid health, sleep, and digestion.	Income still good but likely to sell home.	Same medical and product needs as other retired group; drastic cut in income. Special need for attention, affection, and security.

Source: William D. Wells and George Gubar, "Life Cycle Concept in Marketing Research," *Journal of Marketing Research*, November 1966, p. 362. Reprinted with permission from the American Marketing Association.

TABLE 4-5

Detailed Family Expenditure by Selected Family Income Categories, All Families and Unattached Individuals, 1992

Expenditure Category	Family Income		
	$15,000–$19,999	$35,000–$39,999	$60,000 and over
Food	18.1%	13.8%	11.1%
Shelter	27.8	19.1	16.3
Household operation	5.9	4.7	4.1
Household furnishings and equipment	3.4	3.2	2.9
Clothing	4.6	4.6	5.0
Transportation	2.2	13.7	12.0
Health care	2.6	2.3	1.7
Personal care	2.5	2.0	1.7
Recreation	4.3	4.9	5.6
Reading materials and other printed matter	0.7	0.5	0.5
Education	0.7	0.7	1.1
Tobacco products and alcoholic beverages	4.5	3.5	2.7
Miscellaneous	2.6	2.9	2.7
Security	1.5	4.7	6.3
Gifts and contributions	3.9	3.8	2.7

Source: Statistics Canada, *Market Research Handbook*, cat. no. 63-224, 1995, pp. 204–205.

- The percentage spent on clothing remains fairly constant across income groups, ranging from 4 percent to 5 percent. Dollar expenditures, however, range from $530 to more than $5,000 annually.
- A major difference between low-income and higher-income Canadian families lies in the percentage of their total income that goes to government in the form of taxes. Whereas a family whose total income is in the top 20 percent in Canada may pay 35 percent or more of total personal income in taxes, lower-income families may pay no tax at all.
- Major differences in expenditure patterns are also found when the Canadian population is examined across geographic regions. This is related in part to income differences, but also is caused to a degree by the differences in the cost of certain items in different areas of the country. For example, the average family in Montreal spends 13.0 percent of total expenditures on food, while a family in Halifax spends only 11.3 percent. On the other hand, a family in Victoria will spend 18.2 percent of its total expenditures on housing, as compared with only 16.0 percent in St. John's, Newfoundland.

Generalizations such as these provide a broad background against which marketing executives can analyze the market for their particular product or service. People with needs to satisfy and money to spend, however, must be willing to spend before a market can be said to exist. Consequently, Chapter 6 looks into consumer motivation and buying behaviour — the "willingness-to-buy" factor in our definition of a market.

Summary

A sound marketing program starts with the identification and analysis of target markets for whatever an organization is selling. A market consists of people or organizations with needs or wants, money to spend, and the willingness to spend it. There are some general guidelines to follow when selecting target markets.

Some form of market segmentation is the strategy that most marketers adopt as a compromise between the extremes of an aggregate, undifferentiated market and a different product tailor-made for each customer. Market segmentation is the process of dividing the total heterogeneous market into several homogeneous segments. A separate marketing program is developed for each segment that the seller selects as a target market. Market segmentation is a customer-oriented philosophy that is consistent with the marketing concept.

Market segmentation enables a company to make more efficient use of its marketing resources. Also, this strategy allows a small company to compete effectively in one or two segments. The main drawback of market segmentation is that it requires higher production and marketing costs than does a one-product, mass-market strategy. The requirements for effective segmentation are that (1) the bases for segmentation be measurable with accessible data; (2) the segments themselves be accessible to existing marketing institutions; and (3) the segments be large enough to be potentially profitable.

The total market may be divided into two broad segments: ultimate consumers and business users. The four major bases that may be used for further segmenting the consumer market are: (1) geographic — the distribution of population; (2) demographic — the composition of population such as age, gender, and income distribution; (3) psychographic — personality traits and lifestyles; and (4) product-related — product benefits desired and product usage rates.

In the consumer market, the makeup of the population — its distribution and composition — has a major effect on target-market selection. For some products it is useful to analyze population on a regional basis. Another useful division is by urban, suburban, and rural segments. In this context, the bulk of the population is concentrated in metropolitan areas. Moreover, these areas are expanding and joining together in several parts of the country.

The major age groups of the population make up another significant basis for market analysis — young adults, teenagers, the over-65 group, and so on. The stage of the family life cycle influences the market for many products. Other demographic bases for market analysis include education, occupation, religion, and ethnic origin.

Consumer income — especially disposable income and discretionary income — is a meaningful measure of buying power and market potential. The distribution of income affects the markets for many products. Income distribution has shifted considerably during the past twenty-five years. Today, a much greater percentage of families are in the over $60,000 bracket and a much smaller percentage earn under $10,000. A family's income level and life cycle are, in part, determinants of its spending patterns.

Key Terms and Concepts

Market (76)
Target market (76)
Target-market strategy (77)
Market segmentation (77)
Conditions for effective segmentation (79)
Ultimate consumers (80)
Business users (80)
Bases for segmenting the consumer market (81)
Regional distribution of population (83)
Urban–suburban–rural distribution (83)
Census Metropolitan Area (CMA) (83)
Geodemographic clustering (87)
Demographic segmentation (87)
Market segmentation by gender (89)
Family life cycle (90)
Single (90)
Education (91)
Occupation (91)
Religion (91)
Ethnic origin (91)
Consumer income (92)
National income (92)
Personal income (92)
Personal disposable income (92)
Discretionary purchasing power (92)
Money income (92)
Real income (92)
Psychic income (92)
Income distribution (93)
Consumer spending patterns (95)

Questions and Problems

1. Outline some reasons why a company might adopt a strategy of market segmentation.
2. What benefits can a company expect to gain from segmenting its market?
3. Cite some regional differences in product preferences caused by factors other than climate.
4. Give several examples of products whose market demand would be particularly affected by each of the following population factors:
   a. Regional distribution.
   b. Marital status.
   c. Gender.

  d. Age.
  e. Urban–suburban–rural distribution.
5. List three of the major population trends noted in this chapter (for instance, a growing segment of the population is over 65 years of age). Then carefully explain how each of the following types of retail stores might be affected by each of the trends.
  a. Supermarket.
  b. Sporting goods store.
  c. Drugstore.
  d. Restaurant.
6. In which stage of the life cycle are families likely to be the best prospects for each of the following products or services?
  a. Braces on teeth.
  b. Suntan lotion.
  c. Second car in the family.
  d. Vitamin pills.
  e. Refrigerators.
  f. Life insurance.
  g. Aerobics classes.
  h. Fourteen-day Caribbean cruise.
7. In what ways has the rise in disposable personal income since 1960 influenced the marketing programs of a typical department store? A supermarket?
8. Give examples of products whose demand is substantially influenced by changes in discretionary purchasing power.
9. Using the demographic and income segmentation bases discussed in this chapter, describe the segment likely to be the best market for:
  a. Skis.
  b. Good French wines.
  c. Power hand tools.
  d. Birthday cards.
  e. Gas barbecues.
10. Describe what you believe to be the demographic characteristics of heavy users of:
  a. Dog food.
  b. Ready-to-eat cereal.
  c. CD players.
  d. Electronic mail.
11. Suppose you are marketing automobiles. How is your marketing mix likely to differ when marketing to each of the following market segments?
  a. High school students.
  b. Husbands.
  c. Blue-collar workers.
  d. Homemakers.
  e. Young single adults.
12. Why should a marketer of children's clothing be interested in expenditure patterns on this product category across income levels and across provinces and cities? Consult Statistics Canada data to identify whether major differences exist in expenditures on children's clothing by these categories of consumers.

Hands-On Marketing

1. Interview three friends or acquaintances who all own running shoes, but who are from different demographic groups (for example, different education, age, or gender). Using demographic characteristics only, describe in as much detail as possible the market segment each of your friends represents. Is yours a very complete segment picture? Why?
2. Consider three retailers or three restaurants in your home town or the town or city in which your university or college is located, and describe in as much detail as possible the target market segment each of the stores or restaurants is serving.

CHAPTER 5 GOALS

In this chapter, we continue our discussion of market segmentation and introduce the important strategic concept of positioning. Positioning involves occupying a position in the minds of consumers by creating an image that distinguishes a brand or store or company from the competition.

We conclude the chapter with a detailed discussion of forecasting, the last stage in the marketer's quest for target markets. To do an effective job of targeting, the marketer must not only know the characteristics of the segments, but also must be aware of their buying potential. After studying this chapter, you should have an understanding of:

- How to approach the segmentation of markets from a lifestyle or product-related perspective.
- How to deal with a number of different segments.
- The importance of positioning a brand or company to appeal to target market segments.
- Niche marketing and other positioning strategies to appeal to different consumers or segments.
- The importance of being able to forecast market demand and the market potential of each target segment.

Chapter Five

Segmentation, Positioning, and Forecasting

www.gm.com

MUCH MORE THAN A CAR

This chapter brings together two of the most important concepts in marketing: segmentation and positioning. Most successful marketing organizations, whether in the private, public, or not-for-profit sectors, have effectively combined segmentation with positioning to ensure that they appeal to a particular target segment of their market and occupy a position in the minds of target customers that sets them apart from their competitors.

The Saturn vehicle, which General Motors began producing to respond to the fierce competition from the Asian car manufacturers, has generated a following of loyal customers since it first appeared in 1991. This product has been positioned as a high-quality, reasonably priced vehicle with sporty styling. In addition to marketing these features, the manufacturer has established a reputation of quality service. Ads depict employees on production lines taking a strong interest in the product they are assembling, dealerships providing extra service and attention, and current owners meeting at reunions to share the "experience of Saturn." Phrases such as "The Saturn Family" and "Customer Enthusiasm" are sprinkled liberally throughout the company's promotional materials and advertising. Saturn dealerships are famous for their low-pressure, low-hassle sales environment. The response to these strategies has been extremely positive. Sales have been steadily increasing, and positive feedback abounds from those who purchase the automobiles. Customer ratings, such as those published by J.D. Power & Associates and *Consumer Reports*, have consistently been very high.[1]

Through the production of Saturn, GM has targeted the car buyer who is discriminating on the basis of quality, service, and style. The manufacturer is defying the common apprehension that North American products cannot compete with Japanese and Korean vehicles. Owners of the vehicle are shown as family people and identified as being members of the Saturn Family. The company is going after the medium-income earner who sees value in good service and is interested in investing in a vehicle that has a strong reputation. These people don't want the high-impact sales pitches usually associated with car dealerships. They feel confident about making their own decisions when making purchases of this nature. Through the creation of these associations in the minds of the car buyer, the product is being set apart from other subcompact vehicles.

This example reflects the principal topics of Chapter 5. We see how Saturn has segmented the market for cars, not merely on demographics, but on the lifestyles and psychological makeup of prospective buyers. The result is an effective positioning of Saturn in the minds of consumers. The positioning ensures that the brand appeals to certain types of consumers and is distinct from other brands of vehicles available at the medium price range.

Psychological Segmentation

Demographic data are used to segment markets because these data are related to behaviour and are relatively easy to gather. However, demographics are not in themselves the causes of behaviour. Consumers don't buy windsurfing equipment because they are young. They buy it because they enjoy an active, outdoor lifestyle, and it so happens that such people are also typically younger. Thus, demographics often correlate with behaviour, but they do not explain it.

Marketers have gone beyond demographic attributes in an effort to better understand why consumers behave as they do. They now engage in **psychological segmentation**, which involves examining attributes such as personality and lifestyles. When demographics and psychological attributes are combined, richer descriptions of segments are produced.

Personality Characteristics An individual's **personality characteristics** are usually described in terms of traits that influence behaviour. Theoretically, they would seem to be a good basis for segmenting markets. Experience tells us that compulsive people buy differently from cautious consumers, and quiet introverts do not buy the same things nor in the same way as gregarious, outgoing people. However, personality characteristics pose problems that limit their usefulness in practical market segmentation. First, the presence and strength of these characteristics in the population are virtually impossible to measure. For example, how many people in Canada could be classified as aggressive? Another problem is associated with the accessibility condition of segmentation. There is no advertising medium that provides unique access to a particular personality type. That is, television reaches introverts as well as extroverts, aggressive people as well as timid people. So one of the major goals of segmentation, to avoid wasted marketing effort, is not likely to be accomplished using personality as a basis for market segmentation.

Nevertheless, many firms tailor their advertising messages to appeal to certain personality traits. Even though the importance of the personality dimension in a particular decision may be unmeasurable, the seller believes that it does play an influential role. Thus we see products and services advertised to consumers who are "on the way up," or are "people with taste," or who "want to break away from the crowd."

Lifestyles The term **lifestyle** is a broad concept that sometimes overlaps personality characteristics. Being cautious, sceptical, ambitious, a workaholic, a copycat — are these personality or lifestyle traits? Lifestyles relate to your activities, interests, and opinions. They reflect how you spend your time, what books you read, which television programs you watch, where you take vacations, and what your beliefs are on various social, economic, and political issues.

There is no commonly accepted terminology of lifestyle categories for segmenting markets. Nevertheless, people's lifestyles undoubtedly affect their choice of products and their brand preferences. Marketers are well aware of this and often attempt to segment their markets on a lifestyle basis.

As consumer tastes and lifestyles have changed in recent years, most companies have had to make adjustments in their products and services to ensure that they remained attractive to their target customers. One company that has taken an aggressive approach in the retail industry is Nike. Back in the 1980s, the advertising of this company set out to define the meaning of "cool" for millions of teenagers. Today, Nike is continuing to capture lifestyle images with the introduction of Nike Towns — single-brand stores — set up to reflect and represent the brand's desire to appear action-oriented and "with it." These stores are decorated in cyber-age video glyphs with screens showing athletes continuously in motion. This chain of shops is directly targeted at the young, athletic consumer who responds positively to the electronic age.[2]

Labatt, owner and producer of Kokanee beer in British Columbia, has developed this brand to reflect the lifestyle of that province. Its advertising agency describes the image it is trying to create as "work to live." The B.C. attitude and lifestyle are assisting the company to market this product in Ontario, a province that has been associated with a high-paced, aggressive business way of life. The company feels it reflects how "people would like to live."[3]

Although it is a valuable marketing tool, lifestyle segmentation has some of the same serious limitations ascribed to segmentation based on personality characteristics. It is very difficult to measure accurately the size of lifestyle segments in order to determine their viability. Another problem that may affect the marketer's ability to deal with specific lifestyle segments relates to their accessibility. Although certain of the mass media (particularly magazines and television) offer options that appeal to particular lifestyle groups, such options for advertising may be out of the cost range of many smaller companies, making it difficult for them to reach their lifestyle targets in a cost-effective manner.

Psychographics The term **psychographics** was coined to describe a wide variety of psychological and behavioural descriptions of a market. The development of psychographics evolved from attempts by marketers to find measures more directly related to purchase and consumption than demographics.

Values are one such descriptor. According to psychologists, values are a reflection of our needs adjusted for the realities of the world in which we live. Research at the Survey Research Center at the University of Michigan has identified nine basic values that relate to purchase behaviour.[4] The nine, which they call the **List of Values (LOV)**, are:

- Self-respect.
- Self-fulfilment.
- Security.
- Sense of belonging.
- Excitement.
- Sense of accomplishment.
- Fun and enjoyment in life.
- Being well-respected.
- Having warm relationships.

While most people view all these values as desirable, their relative importance differs among people and their importance changes over a person's life. For example, people who value fun and enjoyment especially like skiing, dancing, bicycling, and backpacking, and people who value warm relationships give gifts for no particular reason. Thus, the relative strength of values could be the basis for segmenting a market.

Probably the best-known psychographic segmentation tool is **VALS**, developed in 1978 by the research firm SRI International and redesigned in 1990 as **VALS2**.[5] The VALS system was developed from a large study that divided adults into nine segments based on similarities in their values (beliefs, desires, and prejudices) and their lifestyles — hence, the VALS acronym. The VALS2 version reflects changes in how we live and make decisions.[6] The two primary dimensions in the new version are an individual's resources and self-orientation. Resources are broadly defined to include not only income but other factors such as health, education, and self-confidence. Based on a representative sample of the population, and using resources and self-orientation, eight consumer segments of approximately equal size have been identified.

Several organizations have used VALS2 to develop or refine their marketing strategies. For example, Transport Canada, the agency that managed major Canadian airports, used VALS2 to study the flying public passing through Vancouver. Though "actualizers" make up about 12 percent of the general population, the study found that 37 percent of the travellers belonged to this group. Since actualizers are a good market for quality arts and crafts, the results suggest that stores such as Sharper Image or Nature Company could do well at the airport.

Behavioural Segmentation

Some marketers regularly attempt to segment their markets on the basis of product-related behaviour — they utilize **behavioural segmentation**. This section briefly considers two of these segments: the benefits desired from a product, and the rate at which the consumer uses the product.

Benefits Desired Russell Haley is credited with drawing attention to the notion of benefit segmentation when he described a hypothetical division of the toothpaste market based on the **benefits desired**. The segment names, the benefits sought by each segment, and the likely preferred brands were:

- Sensories: flavour and appearance — Colgate or Stripe.
- Sociables: brightness of teeth — Macleans or Ultra Brite.
- Worriers: decay prevention — Crest.
- Independents: low price — any brand on sale.[7]

If Haley were to prepare a similar division today, he might include "plaque control" as a fifth benefit segment.

Two things determine the effectiveness of benefit segmentation. First, the specific benefits consumers are seeking must be identified. This typically involves several research steps, beginning with the identification of all possible benefits related to a particular product or behaviour through brainstorming, observing consumers, and listening to focus groups. Then, more focus groups are conducted to screen out unlikely or unrealistic benefits and to amplify and clarify the remaining possibilities. Finally, large-scale surveys are conducted to determine how important the benefits are and how many consumers seek each one.

To illustrate, Mobil Corporation conducted a market segmentation study of gasoline buyers to determine how to design its gasoline stations. The study identified five primary segments. Contrary to conventional wisdom, only one, accounting for about 20 percent of the buyers, consisted of price shoppers. To attract the four more profitable non-price segments, Mobil has begun offering things that appeal to them — nicer snack foods, quick service, a personal touch, privileges for regular customers and cleaner facilities.[8]

A second task, once the marketer has identified the various benefits that are to be used to segment the overall market, is to develop detailed **profiles** of each of the market segments that have been identified. The purpose of the profiling exercise is to develop as detailed an overview as possible of the consumers who make up each of the segments of interest, in terms of their demographic, psychographic, and lifestyle characteristics. The main premise behind this profiling is, the better we know the customers in each of the segments that we plan to target, the more likely it is that we can put together an integrated marketing program that they will find attractive, will lead them to buy our products or services, and will keep them coming back to do business with us in the future. We indicated earlier that "accessibility" is a requirement for successful segmentation. Only by knowing as much as we can about our target customers can we possibly know how to reach them with our marketing messages.

Another approach to benefit segmentation that has become popular in the last twenty years is segmenting the market based on the occasions that customers would associate with the use of the product or service. There are numerous examples of this type of segmentation. The rental of a limousine for graduation or a wedding is familiar to most of us. Many restaurants and hotels cater to special occasions by offering special entertainment and all-inclusive rates. Some companies have grown up around meeting special-occasion needs. One such example is The Artful Cookie in St. Catharines, Ontario. This company specializes in preparing floral-like cookie arrangements, wrapped and presented as flower arrangements. It offers a variety of "bouquets" specifically designed for holidays, anniversaries, and special occasions.[9]

Usage Rate Another product-related basis for market segmentation is **usage rate** — the rate at which people use or consume a product. Thus we can have categories for nonusers, light users, medium users, and heavy users. Normally a company is most interested in the heavy users of its product. The 50 percent of the people who are the "heavy half" of the users of a product typically account for 80 to 90 percent of the total purchases of a given product or service.

That is not to say that this percentage applies precisely in all product or service categories. Rather, it is the principle that is important. Typically, a company can identify a number of different segments among its target customers. Among these segments, there are usually one or two that contain disproportionately heavier consumers of the product or service. For example, one segment may contain only 15 percent of customers, but these customers may account for 24 percent of all purchases of the company's product. Another segment may have a comparatively small number of consumers, accounting possibly for only 8 percent of potential customers, but their consumption patterns may be such that they account for 20 percent of all sales of the product or service. These segments, because they include such heavy consumers, represent important target segments. In such circumstances, most companies would prefer to be the market leader among the heavy users, rather than targeting their marketing efforts at customers who use relatively little of the product.

The remarkable feature of usage patterns is that they seem to be fairly constant across industries and over time. In most of the situations a marketer might encounter, there are bound to be heavy-user and light-user segments. Thus this segmentation base becomes an effective predictor of future buying behaviour.

Sometimes the target market is the nonuser or light user, and the objective is to woo this customer into a higher-use category. Or light users may constitute an attractive niche for a marketer simply because they are being ignored by other firms that are targeting heavy users. Once the characteristics of these light users have been identified, management can go to them directly with an introductory low-price offer. Or a marketer might increase usage rates by promoting (1) new uses for a product (baking soda as a deodorant); (2) new times for uses (off-season vacations); or (3) multiple packaging (a 12-pack of soft drinks).

TARGET-MARKET STRATEGIES

Let's assume that a company has segmented the total market for its product. Now management is in a position to select one or more segments as its target markets. The company can follow one of three **target-market strategies**: market aggregation, single-segment concentration, or multiple-segment targeting, as illustrated in Figure 5-1. To evaluate the strategies, management must determine the market potential of each segment it has identified. But before a strategy is chosen, the potential of the identified segments must be determined. This calls for establishing some guidelines for target-market selection.

Guidelines in Selecting a Target Market

Four guidelines govern how to determine which segments should be the target markets. The first is that target markets should be compatible with the organization's goals and image. One business keenly aware of this guideline is The Bay in Richmond, B.C. It has recently undergone a $14 million facelift in an effort to appeal to the upscale tastes of the Asian customer. The store focuses on high-end fashions, cosmetics, and housewares. The Bay has set up elegant boutiques and offers smaller sizes in an effort to customize to the market goal of attracting Asian women.[10]

A second guideline — consistent with our definition of strategic planning — is to match the market opportunity represented in the target markets with the company's resources. In examining new product opportunities, 3M considered many options but chose the do-it-yourself home improvement market because of the marketing economies that could be achieved. The firm's name was already well known to consumers, and the products could be sold through many of the retail outlets already selling 3M products. Thus, entering this market was much less expensive than entering a market in which 3M was inexperienced.

www.3m.com

MARKETING AT WORK FILE 5–1

NEW STRATEGIES FOR MARKETING IN THE NEW MILLENNIUM

As we have noted throughout this chapter, the ability to forecast demand is a major asset in targeting market segments. As the new millennium approaches, marketers are trying to determine what strategies will be required to reach consumers and what impact the 1990s have had on changing consumer demand.

One company that is trying hard to forecast consumer demands is Bozell Worldwide, an international advertising agency with offices in Toronto. Bozell states that the consumer of the new millennium will have different values. The first decade will be characterized by a major withdrawal from the traditional retail marketplace by consumers who will desperately be trying to save enough money to ensure their quality of life as they head toward retirement. They call this new decade "The Decade of Solitude."

At the retail division of Bozell, the company is adopting a new strategic approach with its clients — passing the control of the message to the consumer. It refers to this approach as transactional advertising. To accomplish it, the firm seeks to stimulate a purchase, not make a sale. In other words, the marketer needs to pick the right merchandise assortments for its customers. To do that, Bozell recommends that efforts go into prioritizing the markets that the business wishes to focus on. The advertising budget needs to maintain and hold market share. Targeting is very important in this situation. Critical to the success of surviving in the new market environment will be attracting the right kind of consumer through the front door. This will mean placing a lot of emphasis on market segmentation.

Bozell believes that in retail, consumers buy because they want products, not because they need them. Wants are contracting with changing consumer values, and therefore psychographic systems that can differentiate target segments are very important. The agency believes that advertising will be bought on the basis of its being able to drive quality traffic through the door. In other words, advertising must reach the consumer that is most valuable to the firm. The information age, begun in this decade and anticipated to grow more rapidly in the next, has reduced the effectiveness of advertising messages. Therefore, efforts must make sure the features of the product or service are clearly transmitted to the interested consumer. This strategy is designed to address a new kind of consumer with a very different motivation and a strong new set of priorities.

Source: Elliotte Ettenberg, "Time to Toss Out the Old Rule Book," *Marketing Magazine*, May 19, 1997, p. 22. Reprinted with permission.

Over the long run, a business must generate a profit to survive. This rather obvious statement translates into our third market-selection guideline. That is, an organization should seek markets that will generate sufficient sales volume at a low enough cost to result in a profit. Surprisingly, companies often have overlooked profit in their quest for high-volume markets. Their mistake is going after sales volume, not profitable sales volume. Companies that target the higher-yield customer must offer products or services that are perceived by the customer to have value. The Camera Shop, in Calgary, is an example of such a company. This business caters to customers willing to pay up to four-digit prices for photographic supplies. The proprietor of this establishment is a technical adviser to his customers and "does not underestimate the art involved in crafting strong images." Through this approach, and by providing equipment of superior quality, The Camera Shop can sell a sufficient volume of merchandise to be profitable.[11]

Fourth, a company ordinarily should seek a market where there are the fewest and smallest competitors. A seller should not enter a market that is already saturated with competition unless it has some over-

www.bozell.com

FIGURE 5-1
The Three Target-Market Strategies

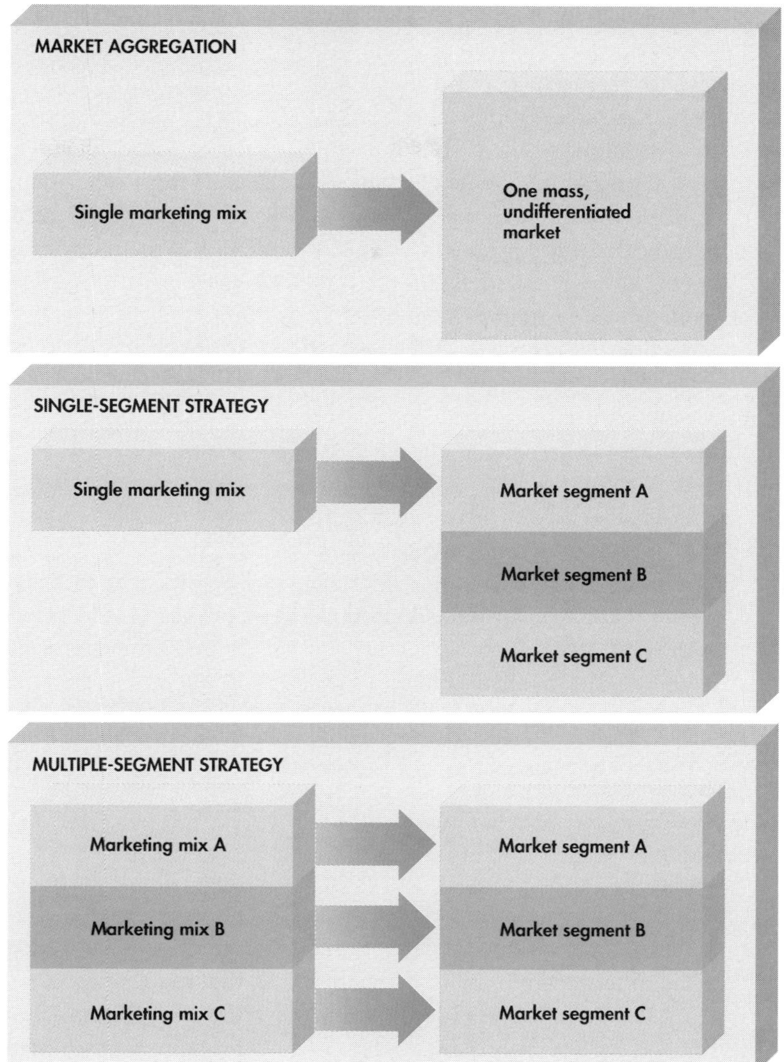

riding differential advantage that will enable it to take customers from existing firms. When Häagen-Dazs, a brand of premium ice cream, entered Europe and Asia in the late 1980s, it had little competition at the high end of the market. Because per capita ice cream consumption on these continents is well below that of North America, many viewed the prospects of a high-price brand in a low-usage market as not very attractive. However, Häagen-Dazs, now with sales well over $500 million, proved the doubters wrong. It wasn't that consumers disliked ice cream; rather, many simply had not been exposed to a high-quality version. By getting to the market first, Häagen-Dazs now has a significant advantage over later entrants.[12]

These are only guidelines. A marketer still has to decide how many segments to pursue as its target market, as we will see next.

Market Aggregation

By adopting a strategy of **market aggregation**, also known as a mass-market or an undifferentiated-market strategy, an organization treats its total market as a single unit. This unit is one mass, aggregate market whose parts are considered to be alike in all major respects. Management then develops a single marketing program to reach as many customers as possible in this aggregate market. That is, the company

http://207.93.234.201/sunoco/
www.irvingoil.com
www.chevron.com
www.imperial oil.ca

develops a single product or service for this mass audience; it develops one pricing structure and one distribution system for its product; and it uses a single promotional program aimed at the entire market.

When is an organization likely to adopt the strategy of market aggregation? Generally when a large group of customers in the total market tends to have the same perception of the product's want-satisfying benefits. This strategy often is adopted by firms that are marketing a nondifferentiated, staple product such as gasoline, salt, or sugar. In the eyes of many people, sugar is sugar, regardless of the brand. All brands of table salt are pretty much alike, and one unleaded gasoline is about the same as another.

Basically, market aggregation is a production-oriented strategy. It enables a company to maximize its economies of scale in production, physical distribution, and promotion. Producing and marketing one product for one market means longer production runs at lower unit costs. Inventory costs are minimized when there is no (or a very limited) variety of colours and sizes of products. Warehousing and transportation efforts are most efficient when one product is going to one market.

Market aggregation will work only as long as the seller's single marketing mix continues to satisfy enough customers to meet the company's sales and profit expectations. The strategy of market aggregation typically is accompanied by the strategy of product or service differentiation in a company's marketing program. **Product or service differentiation** is the strategy by which one firm attempts to distinguish its product from competitive brands offered to the same aggregate market. By differentiating its product or service, an organization hopes to create the impression that what it offers is better than the competitors' brands. The seller also hopes to engage in nonprice competition and thus avoid or minimize the threat of price competition.

A seller implements this strategy either (1) by changing some feature of the product (for example, packaging, colour, or label design, or, in the case of a service, staff image, decor of the establishment, or amount of attention); (2) by using a promotional appeal that features a differentiating benefit; or (3) by using advertising and other promotional strategies to create a differentiating image for the brand, product, or service. Oral-B has differentiated its toothbrushes by introducing a band of blue bristles on each toothbrush that indicates the extent of wear and, therefore, shows when the toothbrush should be replaced. Diet Pepsi has sought to differentiate itself from other brands of soft drinks by indicating a "best before" date on the bottom of its cans. AT&T, the telecommunications company, offers online translation services to its customers as a differentiating service. Individuals who wish to phone parties who speak other languages can do so through the operator at their AT&T exchange.

We know, for example, that oil companies do not practise market aggregation. Although the gasoline and many other products that each of them sells are virtually indistinguishable across brands, the major oil companies engage in a number of marketing practices that are intended to attract customers and dispel the impression that they are all alike. Sunoco, for example, stresses the high octane levels of its premium gasoline, indicating that it offers the highest octane rating in the industry, thereby positioning its brands squarely for owners of performance cars. In Western Canada, Mohawk positions itself as an environmentally friendly oil company, while in the East, Irving Oil portrays itself as a local, down-home firm. In British Columbia, Chevron positions itself as a technologically advanced retailer, offering its customers access to instant payment at the pumps via credit cards. On the other hand, Imperial Oil has chosen in recent years to compete for customers on the basis of the service offered at its retail outlets. Reflecting on the factors that affect customer satisfaction that were presented in Chapter 1, we realize that Sunoco is concentrating on differentiating its core product, gasoline, Chevron is differentiating itself by making payment more convenient for its customers, while the others are differentiating their entire company, or their brands, by appealing to customers' higher-order needs.

Differentiation is an important strategy in any situation where there is little difference across the offerings of various companies, or where the consumer is unable to understand or appreciate the differences that do exist. Increasingly, companies are turning to service to differentiate their products and even their companies. With so many products now being perceived by consumers to be quite similar, companies that can offer the best service to their customers are getting the business. In many industries, the highly competitive marketplace brought about by the recession of the early 1990s has forced companies to compete on the basis of service, thereby attempting to set themselves apart from their competitors.[13] British Airways has used this strategy successfully over the past few years. Despite the stiff competition in the airline business, British Airways has consistently outperformed its competitors. According to the CEO of British Airways, Sir Colin Marshall, an element of the travelling public is willing to pay a slight premium for superior service. One of the things offered by this company is free lounge services to Concorde, First Class, Club World, and Club Europe customers. In addition, it seeks to make all customers feel that they are special by treating them individually in a caring manner. The company uses the phrase "Nothing too small, nothing too big" to let customers know it is looking after their individual needs while simultaneously providing a global service.[14]

Single-Segment Strategy

A **single-segment concentration strategy** involves selecting as the target market one homogeneous segment from within the total market. One marketing mix is then developed to reach this single segment. A small company may want to concentrate on a single market segment rather than to take on many competitors in a broad market. One example of this is Lavender Expressions, a Calgary-based greeting card manufacturer. This company is differentiated from other such manufacturers because it develops cards for the gay and lesbian community. The company focuses its products to meet the needs and interests of people who are differentiated by lifestyle. The cards are distributed through specialty shops in forty-eight cities throughout North America.[15]

When manufacturers of foreign automobiles first entered the North American market, they typically targeted a single-market segment. The Volkswagen Beetle was intended for the low-priced, small-car market. Honda originally sold only lower-powered motorcycles, and Mercedes-Benz targeted the high-income market. Today, of course, most of the original foreign car marketers have moved into a multisegment strategy. Only a few, such as Jaguar and Ferrari, continue with a concentration strategy.

This strategy enables a company to penetrate one small market in depth and to acquire a reputation as a specialist or an expert in this limited market. A company can enter such a market with limited resources, and as long as the single segment remains a small market, large competitors are likely to leave the single-segment specialist alone. However, if the small market shows signs of becoming a large market, bigger companies may well jump in. This is exactly what happened in the market for herbal and specialty teas.

Prior to the 1980s, rose-hip, camomile, Earl Grey, and similar specialty teas were sold primarily in health-food stores and specialty shops and were available from only a small number of manufacturers and importers. With changing consumer tastes and preferences during the past ten years or so, specialty teas have become more popular. The growth of the herbal and specialty segment was such that new tea companies entered this expanding corner of the market, including some major competitors such as Tetley and Lipton.

The big risk and limitation to a single-segment strategy is that the marketing firm has all its eggs in one basket. If that single segment declines in market potential, the seller can suffer considerably. Also, a seller with a strong name and reputation in one segment may find it difficult to expand into another segment.

The strategy of not concentrating the entire marketing effort on a single segment is also reflected in other industries. Both Volkswagen and Honda have traded their lines up to compete with the higher-priced models of BMW and Mercedes: VW with its Audi line, and Honda with its Acura. Nestlé has successfully marketed its instant coffees Nescafé and Taster's Choice for many years and later entered the ground coffee segment with its Taster's Choice ground.

Multiple-Segment Strategy

Under a **multiple-segment strategy**, two or more different groups of potential customers are identified as target markets. A separate marketing mix is developed to reach each segment. A marketer of personal computers, for example, may identify three distinct market segments — university and college students, small businesses, and a home market — and then design a different marketing mix to reach each segment. Apple Computer Inc. has followed this approach in its recent release of the Emate 300. This computer is designed for students and sells for under $1,000 U.S. It is a stripped-down portable machine, easy to use, with few of the features needed in the corporate or consumer markets.[16] In segmenting the automobile market, General Motors originally developed separate marketing programs for each of its five brands of passenger cars — the company had different marketing programs for its Chevrolet and GMC trucks. The five divisions — Chevrolet, Buick, Pontiac, Oldsmobile, and Cadillac — essentially tried to reach the total market for automobiles on a segmented basis. This segmentation has been further enhanced with the addition of the Geo and Saturn brands, each of which is targeted at a different segment than are the five established brands or makes offered by General Motors. The distinction across the various GM brands has diminished over the years, however, as models offered by Chevrolet, Buick, and the others overlap in price, appearance, and features. As a result, the target markets for the brands are no longer clearly defined, and GM brands find themselves competing with one another.

In a multiple-segment strategy, a seller frequently develops a different version of the basic product for each segment. However, market segmentation can also be accomplished with no change in the product, but rather with separate distribution channels or promotional appeals, each tailored to a given market segment. Wrigley's, for example, targets smokers by promoting chewing gum as an alternative in situations where smoking is unwelcome. Air Wair, the company that markets and distributes Doc Martens footwear, is starting to target an older market segment. To do so it is first making sure that the retailers are aware of how its products can be sold to this segment and encouraging them to carry a broader line. The company is also developing a travelling shoeshine booth to feature at charity events across the country. Along with a shine, visitors can view a range of Doc Martens products.[17]

POSITIONING

The concept of market **positioning** is closely related to segmentation; a marketer must determine how the company's brands or stores or image are perceived by the public in general and more particularly by the segment of the market that has been selected as the principal target. As part of a company's marketing strategy, decisions must be made concerning how the company and its brands are to be portrayed to convey the correct image to the target segment. Positioning, therefore, relates to the use of various marketing techniques and marketing-mix variables to create the image or perception that will best fit with what the company wishes to be known for.

A company may develop a positioning strategy for a particular brand or group of brands, for a retail store or chain, or for the company itself. The process involves answering questions such as: Who are the target-market segments for this brand or store or company? On what basis do we wish to appeal to this segment? What do we want people to think of when they hear our name? How do we wish to be seen to be different from our competitors or from other brands or companies in the market? In dealing with questions such as these, the company is really asking: What position do we wish to occupy in this market?

The company's positioning strategy may be applied at the brand level, at the level of the retail store, or for entire companies. Sun-Rype Products, the largest fruit-products maker in Western Canada, positions its brand as healthy, fresh products produced in Canada from Canadian fruit. The company has a line of snack foods, chilled juices and drinks, fortified juices, and 100 percent juices. When this company recently entered the competitive juice market it did so by building on its healthy approach already established in snack foods.[18]

Another food company that has successfully positioned itself to compete is New York Fries. This product is sold as a premium fry product. Some people even refer to the product as "designer fries." This company is marketing quality fries described as "with the potato skins on to ensure protein is retained." Though the fries are higher priced, they are purchased because the product is perceived to be distinctive. The extra value created by this positioning seems to work, as avid buyers of New York Fries are prepared to pay more.[19]

MARKETING AT WORK FILE 5-2

CREATING NICHES IN THE SNOW

Many of the students reading this text have experienced the thrill of coming down a ski slope on a snowboard. The snowboard has become almost as common in some ski lodges as traditional ski equipment. This sport is rapidly expanding, and its popularity is growing across Canada in every resort. To date it has largely been the choice of a young group who are possibly looking for a new form of downhill adventure. Many of you who fit that market segment may also be in the segment targeted by Revelation snowboards, a product manufactured in Vancouver by Pure Form Design Corporation. These boards are being created for serious snowboarders who are concerned with high-quality materials and performance. Sold at premium prices, this product is aimed at the high end of the snowboard market.

Though the market niche for snowboarding has been largely dominated by the Generation X segment of the skiing market, their parents, also known as "greys on trays," are taking to the sport in greater numbers in recent years. The growth in popularity of the sport has augered well for the introduction of the premium product, the Revelation.

The Revelation was developed by three snowboard enthusiasts in Vancouver. David Partridge, a New Zealander well known in snowboard racing circles, had a reputation for custom designing his own boards. Partridge joined with two brothers, Darrell and Floyd Ryan, to produce the Revelation. The company has been in existence since 1993 and has experimented with ways of making the product most attractive to the target group. It capitalizes on the fact that the product is locally designed and manufactured and made from B.C. wood and Kevlar strips. The company has found that colour, logos, and graphic design are features valued by the purchasers of this product.

Source: Wendy Stueck, "Snowboard Maker Carves Niche," *The Globe and Mail*, October 14, 1996, p. B3. Wendy Stueck is a freelance writer in Vancouver. Reprinted with permission.

Positioning, therefore, is a strategy for locating a brand or store in the consumer's mind, with respect to its rating on certain dimensions or attributes that the consumer considers important. It involves staking out a place in the collective perception of consumers in which the brand or store or company can establish an image that will be appropriate for certain segments of the market. This image is created through the effective use of marketing-mix variables, including advertising, product design, pricing, packaging, store decor, and level of service.

The creation of the appropriate image may be approached in a combination of ways. In the first place, a firm may wish to occupy a position in a market in relation to that occupied by competitors. It may choose a position that is distinct from that occupied by a competitor or may choose to challenge a competitor directly, thereby trying to occupy roughly the same position.

On the other hand, the positioning strategy may be developed so as to position the brand or firm through the creation of an image tailored to the characteristics, preferences, attitudes, and feelings of a particular segment of the market. This approach is dependent on the company having selected certain target segments. The image of the product, brand, or store is then tailored to appeal to those segments.

Finally, a brand or company may be positioned on the basis of its inherent characteristics. In other words, the marketing staff of the company would have to decide what the brand or retailer is to be known for and set about creating the appropriate image. Such an approach deals implicitly with positioning against competition and meeting the needs of particular segments, but is often undertaken in response to the identification of a market gap, where no company has established a dominant position. Bell Canada and the other long-established telephone

There has never been any doubt about where this brand is positioned.

companies in Canada have chosen to position themselves to some extent on the basis of their inherent characteristics. In competing against their major long-distance competitors, AT&T Canada and Sprint Canada, both of whom are subsidiaries of American companies, the Canadian firms compete as full-service telecommunications providers and "local" companies, both of which are claims that should be important to their customers and which cannot be made by the competition.

Positioning Maps

One of the easiest ways to get a feel for the concept of positioning is to examine products, brands, or stores as they are arrayed on a **positioning map**. Such maps

FIGURE 5-2

Perceptual Space Solution Based on Data in Table 5-1

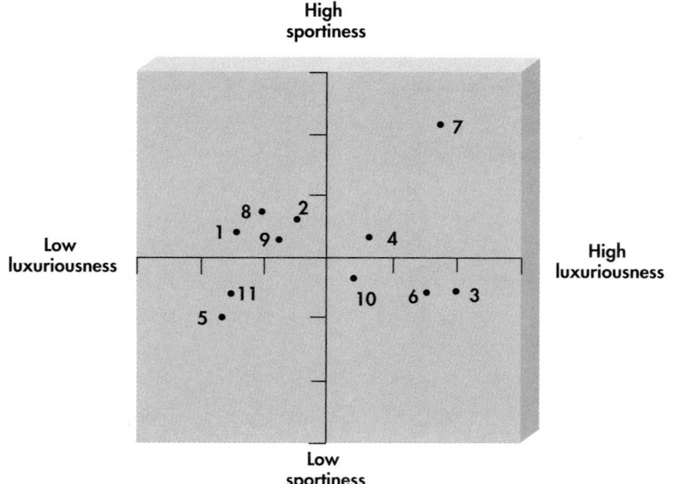

1994 Car Models

1. Ford Taurus
2. Mercury Sable
3. Lincoln Continental
4. Ford Thunderbird
5. Ford Escort
6. Cadillac Eldorado
7. Jaguar XJ Sedan
8. Mazda 626
9. Dodge Intrepid
10. Buick Le Sabre
11. Chevrolet Cavalier

TABLE 5-1 Rank Order of Similarities Between Pairs of Car Models

Stimuli	1	2	3	4	5	6	7	8	9	10	11
1	—	8	50	31	12	48	36	2	5	39	10
2		—	38	9	33	37	22	6	4	14	32
3			—	11	55	1	23	46	41	17	52
4				—	44	13	16	19	25	18	42
5					—	54	53	30	28	45	7
6						—	26	47	40	24	51
7							—	29	35	34	49
8								—	3	27	15
9									—	20	21
10										—	43
11											—

The rank number "1" represents the most similar pair.

Source: Thomas C. Kinnear and James R. Taylor, *Marketing Research: An Applied Approach*, 5th ed. (New York: McGraw-Hill Inc., 1996), pp. 637–638. Reprinted with permission of The McGraw-Hill Companies.

are developed through marketing research, which explores the image that consumers have of the various brands or stores in the market and rates each competing brand or store on a series of attributes. In such research, consumers are typically asked to identify the elements of the purchase situation and the product or store attributes that are important in influencing the purchase decision. Once these attributes and elements have been identified, research is undertaken to determine which are most important in influencing the consumer to select one brand over another. Finally, consumers are asked to rate the competing brands or stores in the market on each of the important dimensions or attributes. Such research data allow the researcher to present the brands or stores of interest in a map similar to that shown in Figure 5-2.

Positioning maps allow the marketer to see where its brand is perceived to lie in the market in comparison with competing brands, how the brand is rated on various attributes, and where the brand lies in relation to the various identified segments. Typically, a number of brands that are perceived to have similar characteristics are clustered together in close proximity to those large segments of the market that have considerable buying power. Other brands occupy positions in the market where they

www.selkirk-tangiers.com
www.marriott.com/marriott/BKKTH/
www.marriott.com

are seen to appeal to different segments and to display different characteristics.

One benefit of examining perceptual market maps is that the marketer can identify how its brand or store is perceived by consumers in comparison with competitors. Such examination often leads to a decision to reposition a brand, a topic covered later in this chapter. Also, the examination of market maps may lead to the identification of market gaps — positions in the market that are not now filled by existing brands or stores and where untapped market demand may be said to exist. One of the most interesting industries for which to prepare a market map is the restaurant business in any medium-sized to large city. There are usually enough restaurants and residents are sufficiently familiar with many of them that they can rate them on various dimensions, such as price, atmosphere, menu selection, value for money, speed of service, target-market group, and so on. Once such data are collected, a positioning map may be prepared that will identify those restaurants perceived by consumers to be located close to one another and that, therefore, are competing directly with one another. At the same time, it is likely that certain parts of the map will be "empty," suggesting that no restaurants occupy those positions and, therefore, reflecting a gap in the local restaurant market.

Niche Marketing

Some marketers may stake out "niche" positions for their brands; they create an image that is quite distinct and intended to appeal to a fairly narrow segment of the market. Within the Canadian beer market, for example, brands such as Schooner and Celtique, import beers such as Heineken, Guinness, and Corona, and the "handmade" brands are considered to be "niche" brands, while mainstream brands such as Molson Canadian and Labatt's Blue are positioned to appeal to much larger segments. Niche brands generally are not positioned to meet major competitors head-on, but rather to be leaders in a very narrow area of the market. Smaller companies often successfully carve out a niche for themselves. To continue with our beer examples, successful microbrewers such as Upper Canada Brewing, McAuslan Brewing, Sleeman's, Red Rock, and Granville Island Brewery are really niche marketers; they are satisfied with occupying a relatively small position in a very large market by catering to the tastes and preferences of consumers who want something different.

www.mcauslan.com

Niche marketing is generally a successful strategy for smaller companies that do not have the financial and other resources generally available to large companies. In the travel business, for example, many travel agencies are seeking ways to set themselves apart from their competitors by specializing in narrow parts of the market. As travel has become more complex and travellers more demanding, some travel agencies have found it impossible to serve all segments equally well. Consequently, some become niche players, specializing in cruises, business travel, the ethnic market, or adventure travel. Bestway Tours and Safaris sells tours of South Asia, Central Asia, and the Middle East. It concentrates on providing tours to the least-visited locations on the globe and specializes in ecology and generally soft-adventure experiences. Tourism operators also choose to specialize in the products they provide. For example, Selkirk Tangiers is a company located in the interior of British Columbia that offers only helicopter skiing. The Royal Garden Riverside in Bangkok, Thailand, is owned by the Marriott chain. This hotel is designed to serve the upscale business traveller who wishes to entertain and develop business connections in that country.[20]

Large organizations often target small market niches. For example, the Toronto Dominion Bank has developed a service it calls "TD Aboriginal Banking Services." The service's outlets are located across Canada and are set up to serve clients of the First Nations.[21] To be successful in positioning itself as a niche player in the market, a company or the managers of a niche brand must have identified a segment of the market that is not now being served adequately by the brands and companies that are in the market; that segment must have sufficient potential buying power to warrant the development of a marketing program; it must be sufficiently small that larger companies are unlikely to retaliate if the niche brand is successful; and the niche marketer must have detailed knowledge of the characteristics of the members of the segment and their needs and preferences.

Some beers stand out from the crowd.

One author has suggested that a company should follow four steps in implementing a successful niche marketing strategy.[22]

1. *Identify an appropriate niche* through marketing research that will identify segments of the market that are not being well served by existing brands or where competition is not intense.
2. *Exploit the niche* by determining the likelihood of competitive retaliation and the length of time the company will enjoy a competitive advantage.
3. *Expand the niche* by meeting changing needs of the market segment, expanding the customer base, and making more effective use of marketing variables.

www.nortel.com

4. *Defend the niche* by continuing to meet the needs of segment members through improving the product and offering better service or lower prices.

Positioning Strategies

Once a company has determined its market segmentation objectives and has identified the segments toward which its brands are to be targeted, it may adopt a number of **positioning strategies** to accomplish its objectives.

1. *Take on the competition head-on:* By deciding to challenge the market leader or to target large segments of the market with a broad appeal, a marketer is saying, "Our brand is as good as or better than the leader." Such a strategy is exemplified in the so-called "cola wars," in which Pepsi-Cola and Coca-Cola have been fighting for market leadership by attempting to create the widest appeal to attract as many consumers as possible.
2. *Occupy a gap in the market:* A number of companies have moved to fill a gap in a market by positioning a brand to appeal to a certain segment of consumers or to take advantage of the disappearance of a competitor. For example, Michelin differentiates its tires from those of competitors by emphasizing safety.
3. *Set a brand apart from the competition:* Often a company will decide to employ a strategy that says, "Our brand is not like all the others; this is why you should buy ours." This involves positioning a brand or store so as to avoid head-to-head competition with market leaders or with brands that have an established image or reputation and a secure market share. Small communications companies in the technology sector operating in Canada are avoiding competing with the large giants such as Bell Canada and AT&T. CBCI Telecom in Montreal is concentrating on serving the needs of universities and health-care organizations. It is developing a specialization in these areas rather than fighting with the large companies for overall market share.[23]
4. *Occupy position of leadership:* Some companies that are clearly market leaders are not particularly interested in positioning themselves against the competition, but rather are likely to stake out a position as clear market leader, known to be ahead of the pack and leader in such areas as product quality, service to customers, profitability, innovations, or technology. Companies such as Loblaws, Northern Telecom, and the Royal Bank of Canada tend to be regarded by many consumers as market leaders whose market franchise is so large and well established that competitors often try to emulate them and to position themselves against them.
5. *Position to appeal to life-style segments:* Often a company will position itself to appeal to certain segments of the market that are defined not only by demographic characteristics but also by their lifestyles. For example, there are two equally large segments of Porsche buyers with quite different lifestyles and reasons for buying the car. One group is driven by power and control. Called "top guns" at Porsche, they buy the car to be noticed. Another group, the "proud patrons," view a Porsche as a reward for hard work. To them, owning the car is an end in itself. They don't need the achnowledgment of others to derive satisfaction from a Porsche. Clearly, an ad that would appeal to the top guns could easily alienate the proud patrons.[24]

Repositioning

Repositioning is a variation of a positioning strategy that involves changing the market position of a brand or store in response to changes taking place in the broader market environment. The need to reposition a brand or retail store may result from one of three market conditions. First, management may identify a gap in the market that may be filled by altering the image of the store or brand — that is, changing the position it occupies in the minds of consumers. For example, a retailer in a local market may realize that the average age of its customer base is increasing and may decide to reposition the store to have greater appeal to a younger market segment.

www.michelin.com • www.canvasvisual.com

Second, repositioning may be required by an increase in competitive activity. For example, Canada's retail industry has suffered considerable upheaval with the entry of new U.S. competitors. Birks, of Montreal, has repositioned itself to include in its target market more mid-range shoppers. Its price/value positioning will include a broader range of prices, greater selection in specific goods, and more everyday prices.[25] Pharma Plus, a Toronto-based drug store, is undergoing a makeover involving a new store image. This company is positioning itself as a store that focuses on the core product categories of pharmacy, over-the-counter drugs, health and beauty aids, and baby care. This firm is finding it difficult to compete in nonpharmacy items because of the increased number of low-priced chains, such as Wal-Mart, who can undercut drugstores in these product categories.[26]

Third, it may be necessary to reposition a brand or store in response to a change in the demographic characteristics or attitudes or values of the target consumer market. The packaged-food industry has dealt with this situation a great deal in recent years as a result of significant changes in eating habits. High-fat foods are no longer appealing to mass markets. This is becoming particularly evident now that labels must carry information on package contents, and customers can easily determine the contents in the supermarket. Heinz, RJR Nabisco, Kraft, and other major packaged-food suppliers are creating new products such as Life-Savers Delites, Budget Gourmet, and Snack Wells to respond to these changing consumer values.[27]

FORECASTING MARKET DEMAND

As the final step in selecting its target markets, a company should forecast the market demand for its product or service. **Forecasting market demand** is estimating the sale of a product during some defined future period. Forecasting is done to make various kinds of predictions. For example, a forecast can refer to an entire industry (such as apparel), to one firm's product line (Levi casual wear), or to an individual brand (Levi 501 jeans). Thus, for a forecast to be understood, it is important to make very clear what it describes.

Basic Forecasting Terms

This section defines some terms so that the discussion will be easier to follow.

Market Factor and Market Index A **market factor** is an item or element that (1) exists in a market, (2) is measurable, and (3) is related to the demand for a product in a known way. To illustrate, the "number of cars three years old and older" is a market factor related to the demand for replacement tires that can be sold. A **market index** is simply a market factor expressed as a percentage or some other quantitative form. To illustrate, one market factor is "households owning appliance X"; in 1997, the market index for this factor was 132 (relative to 1980 equals 100). An index may also be composed on multiple market factors, such as the number of cars three years old and older, population, and disposable personal income.

Market Potential and Sales Potential **Market potential** is the total sales volume that all organizations selling a product during a stated period of time in a specific market could expect to achieve under ideal conditions. **Sales potential** (synonymous with market share) is the portion of market potential that a specific company could expect to achieve under ideal circumstances. For example, market potential applies to all refrigerators, but sales potential refers only to a single brand of refrigerators (such as Whirlpool).

With either of these measures of potential, the market may encompass whatever group or area interests the forecaster. It could be the world, one country, or a smaller market defined by income or some other basis. For example, we may speak of the market potential for refrigerators in the Atlantic provinces, or the sales potential for Whirlpool refrigerators in homes with annual incomes of $50,000 to $75,000. The market potential and sales potential are the same when a firm has a monopoly in its market, as in the case of some public utilities.

Sales Forecast A **sales forecast** is an estimate of probable sales for one company's brand of a product during a stated period in a specific market, assuming a defined marketing plan is used. Like measures of

MARKETING AT WORK FILE 5-3

SEARS REPOSITIONS TO STAY AHEAD

In 1994, Sears Canada faced an increasingly competitive retail industry in which it competed with Zellers, The Bay, K mart, and Eaton's. At that time the retail sector was also dealing with a new threat from Wal-Mart, which was taking over the 122 Woolco stores in Canada. To meet this challenge, Sears undertook to reposition itself in the marketplace. The revamping of the company included creating a more upscale product line and image, offering value rather than price alone, and putting its name behind specific brands where it had the potential to dominate a product category. In so doing, Sears undertook to segment its market on psychographic rather than demographic grounds, thereby creating an image for the chain that would appeal to two major lifestyle segments of Canadian consumers.

Sears adopted the segmentation approach that had been developed by Goldfarb Consultants of Toronto, who had identified six psychographic groups among Canadian consumers. The retail chain decided to target two of these segments: the "day-to-day watchers," fairly conservative people who tend to conform to popular trends; and the "joiner-activists," less conservative and prepared to embrace new ideas.

Beyond the use of psychographics to better target Sears' marketing efforts, the company initiated a number of other activities to strengthen its position in the new retail environment. These included:

- Increasing direct marketing efforts by sending specific advertising messages to its database of more than seven million Canadian households.
- Undertaking store renovations in twenty-one locations where it shares a mall with new Wal-Mart (former Woolco) stores.
- Increasing focus on customer service through employee training.
- Adding more brand names in categories where Sears' brands, such as Kenmore and Craftsman, have traditionally been prominent in Sears stores.
- Meeting competition, including Wal-Mart, on price.
- Developing distinctive catalogues to reach urban and rural markets.
- Developing direct-response television advertising campaigns, so that consumers watching a Sears ad on television can telephone the company's call centre in Belleville on a toll-free number to place an order.

The repositioning strategy has shown a large payoff. Between 1994 and 1997, retail sales for Sears showed a steady increase. Correspondingly, stock prices rose dramatically by 90 percent in 1997. Sears' growth was possibly aided by the troubled times Eaton's experienced in 1996–97, an environmental advantage it could not have predicted. However, the company is committed to its repositioning strategy. Sears is continuing to move in the direction of a new image and is striving to develop itself as a brand consumers will favour.

Source: James Pollock, "Sears' New Tack," *Marketing*, March 14, 1994, pp. 9–10; Lara Mills, "Sears Planning to 'Think Like a Brand'," *Marketing Magazine*, June 30, 1997; and Zena Olijnyk, "Retailers Get Boost from Confident Consumers," *Canadian NewsWire*, June 20, 1997, http://paddle4.canoe.ca/.

market potential, a sales forecast can be expressed in dollars or product units. However, whereas market potential and sales potential are estimates based on general factors and market assumptions, a sales forecast is based on a specific marketing plan for the product.

The Sales Forecast and the Marketing Plan
The marketing goals and broad strategies — the core of a marketing plan — must be established before a sales forecast is made. That is, the sales forecast depends on these predetermined goals and strategies.

Certainly, different sales forecasts will result, depending on whether the marketing goal is (1) to liquidate an excess inventory of product A or (2) to expand the firm's market share by aggressive advertising.

However, once the sales forecast is prepared, it does become the key controlling factor in all operational planning throughout the company. The forecast is the basis of sound budgeting. Financial planning for working-capital requirements, plant utilization, and other needs is based on anticipated sales. The scheduling of all production resources and facilities, such as setting labour needs and purchasing supplies and materials, depends on the sales forecast.

Sales-Forecasting Periods Sales forecasts typically cover a one-year period, although many firms review and revise their forecasts quarterly or even monthly. Forecasts of less than a year may be desirable when activity in the firm's industry is so volatile that it is not feasible to look ahead an entire year. As a case in point, many retailers and producers in the fashion industry prepare forecasts for only one fashion season at a time. Hence they prepare three or four forecasts a year.

Methods of Forecasting Demand

Following are some commonly used **methods of forecasting demand**.

Market-Factor Analysis In many situations, future demand for a product is related to the behaviour of certain market factors. When this is true, we can forecast future sales by studying the behaviour of these market factors. Basically, **market-factor analysis** entails determining what these factors are and then measuring their relationship to sales activity.

Using market-factor analysis successfully requires (1) selecting the right market factors and (2) minimizing the number of market factors. The greater the number of factors, the greater the chance for erroneous estimates and the more difficult it is to determine how much each factor influences demand.

Direct Derivation Let's illustrate the use of this method to estimate market potential. Suppose that a manufacturer of automobile tires wants to know the market potential for replacement tires in Canada in 1999. The primary market factor is the number of automobiles on the road. The first step is to estimate how many cars are likely prospects for new tires. Assume (1) that the seller's studies show that the average car is driven about 16,000 km a year and (2) that the average driver gets about 45,000 km from a set of four tires. This means that all cars that become three years old during 1999 can be considered a part of the potential market for replacement tires during that year. The seller can obtain a reasonably accurate count of the number of cars sold in 1996. (These are the cars that will become three years old in 1999.) The information sources are provincial vehicle licensing offices or private organizations. In addition, the seller can determine how many cars will become six, nine, or twelve years old in 1999. (These ages are multiples of three. That is, in 1999, a six-year-old car presumably would be ready for its second set of replacement tires.) The number of cars in these age brackets times four (tires per car) should give a fair approximation of the market potential for replacement tires in 1999. We are, of course, dealing in averages. Not all drivers will get 45,000 km from a set of tires, and not all cars will be driven exactly 16,000 km per year.

The direct-derivation method has much to recommend it. It is relatively simple and inexpensive to use, and it requires little statistical analysis. It is reasonably easy to understand, so that executives who are not statistics-oriented can follow the method and interpret the results.

Correlation Analysis This technique is a mathematical refinement of the direct-derivation method. When correlation analysis is used, the degree of association between potential sales of the product and the market factor is taken into account. In effect, a correlation analysis measures, on a scale of 0 to 1, the variations between two series of data. Consequently, this method can be used only when a lengthy sales history of the industry or firm is available, as well as a history of the market factor. For example, the data series might be the number of dogs registered in Penticton, B.C., each year from 1976 to 1996, and the sales of canned dog food in Penticton in the corresponding years.

Correlation analysis gives a more exact estimate of market demand, provided that the method is applied correctly. In direct derivation, the correlation measure is implicitly assumed to be 1.00. But rarely does this perfect association exist between a market factor and the sales of a product. Correlation analysis therefore takes the past history into account in predicting the future. It also allows a researcher to incorporate more than one factor into the formula.

There are at least two major limitations to this method. First, as suggested above, a lengthy sales history must be available. To do a really good job, researchers need about twenty periods of sales records. Also, they must assume that approximately the same relationship has existed between the sales and the market factors during this entire period. Furthermore, they must assume that this relationship will continue in the next sales period. These can be highly unrealistic assumptions. The other major drawback is that the use of correlation analysis requires some fairly sophisticated data analysis. Thus support of statistical staff may be necessary.

Surveys of Buyer Intentions Another commonly used method of forecasting is to survey a sample of potential customers. These people are asked how much of the stated product or service they would buy or use at a given price during a specified future time period. Some firms maintain consumer panels on a continuing basis to act as a sounding board for new-product ideas, prices, and other features.

A major problem is that of selecting the sample of potential buyers. For many consumer products, a very large, and thus very costly, sample would be needed. Aside from the extremely high cost and large amount of time this method often entails, there is another very serious limitation. It is one thing for consumers to intend to buy a product, but quite another for them to actually buy it. Surveys of buying intentions inevitably show an inflated measure of market potential.

Surveys of buyer intentions are probably most effective when (1) there are relatively few buyers; (2) these buyers are willing to express their buying intentions; and (3) their past record shows that their follow-up actions are consistent with their stated intentions.

Test Marketing In using this technique, firms market their products in a limited geographic area. Then, from this sample the companies project sales potential (market share) over a larger area. **Test marketing** is frequently used in deciding whether sufficient sales potential exists for a new product. The technique also serves as a basis for evaluating various product features and alternative marketing strategies. The outstanding benefit of test marketing is that it can identify how many people actually buy the product, instead of only how many say they intend to buy. If a company can afford the time and money for this method and can run a valid test, this is the best way of measuring the potential for its product.

These are big "ifs," however. Test marketing is expensive in time and money. Great care is needed to control the test-marketing experiment. A competitor, learning that a company is test marketing, is usually adept at "jamming" the experiment. That is, by unusual promotional or other marketing efforts, a competitor can create an artificial situation that distorts test results. To avoid such test-market "wars," some companies use simulations of test markets. In effect, these marketers are conducting a test market in a laboratory, rather than in the field.[28]

Past Sales and Trend Analysis A favourite method of forecasting is to base the estimate entirely on **past sales**. This technique is used frequently by retailers whose main goal is to "beat last year's figures." The method consists simply of applying a flat percentage increase to the volume achieved last year or to the average volume of the past few years.

This technique is simple, inexpensive, and easy to apply. For a firm operating in a stable market, where its market share has remained constant for a period of years, past sales alone might be used to predict future volume. On balance, however, the method is highly unreliable. **Trend analysis** is a variation of forecasting based on past sales, but it is a bit more complicated. It involves either (1) a long-run projection of the sales trend, usually computed by statistical techniques, or (2) a short-run projection (forecasting for only a few months ahead) based upon a seasonal index of sales. The statistical sophistication of long-run trend analysis does not really remove the inherent weakness of basing future estimates only on past sales activity. Short-run trend analysis may be acceptable if the firm's sales follow a reliable seasonal pattern. For example, assume that sales reach 10,000 units in the first quarter (January–March) and, historically, the second quarter is always about 50 percent better. Then we can reasonably forecast sales of 15,000 units in the April–June period.

Sales-Force Composite This is a buildup method that may be used to forecast sales or to estimate market potential. As used in sales forecasting, the **sales-force composite** method consists of collecting from all sales people and intermediaries an estimate of sales in their territories during the forecasting period. The total (the composite) of these separate estimates is the company's sales forecast. This method can be used advantageously if the firm has competent, high-calibre sales people. It is also useful for firms selling to a market composed of relatively few, but large, customers. Thus, this method would be more applicable to sales of large electrical generators than small general-use motors.

The sales-force composite method takes advantage of the sales people's specialized knowledge of their own market. Also, it should make them more willing to accept their assigned sales quotas. On the other hand, the sales force usually does not have the time or the experience to do the research needed in forecasting future sales.

Executive Judgment This method covers a wide range of possibilities. Basically, it consists of obtaining opinions regarding future sales volume from one or more executives. If these are really informed opinions, based on valid measures such as market-factor analysis, then the **executive judgment** is useful and desirable. Certainly all the previously discussed forecasting methods should be tempered with sound executive judgment. On the other hand, forecasting by executive opinion alone is risky. In some instances, such opinions are simply intuition or guesswork.

Summary

One of the most important lessons to be learned concerning the use of market segmentation as a marketing strategy is to get beyond the rather simplistic geographic and demographic bases for segmenting a market. Many marketers today are successful in segmenting markets on psychographic and product-usage bases, which involve targeting products and services at groups of consumers based on their personality and lifestyle characteristics and on why they select a product, how much of it they use, or how often they buy it.

A marketer can choose from three alternative segmentation strategies when selecting a target market: market aggregation, single-segment concentration, or multiple segmentation. Market aggregation involves using one marketing mix to reach a mass, undifferentiated market. In single-segment concentration, a company still uses only one marketing mix, but it is directed at only one segment of the total market. The third alternative involves selecting two or more segments and then developing a separate marketing mix to reach each one.

The concept of market positioning involves developing a position for a product, brand, retail store, or company in the minds of the members of the target segment or even in the minds of the general public. In essence, it involves management asking what they want the brand or store to be known for, as compared with the customer's image of the competition; what do they want consumers to think of when they hear the brand or store name? The task of creating the right position or image for a brand or store is accomplished through strategic use of the marketing mix variables.

One of the most effective ways to determine the current position that a brand or store occupies in the consumer's mind is to develop a positioning map based on research into consumer perceptions of the various competitors in the market. Such maps may be used to identify gaps in the market, to determine whether there exists a niche toward which a brand may be directed, and to identify a need to reposition a brand for some other reason.

A company may take a number of approaches to position a brand, a retail store, or the company itself in the minds of target consumers: (1) it may decide to meet competitors head on; (2) it may reposition a brand to occupy a gap in the market; (3) it may decide to distance a brand from its main competitors; (4) it may stake out a position as the market leader; or (5) it may position a brand to appeal to certain lifestyle segments. Often a decision is made to reposition a brand or store because of changes that have taken place within the market environment. Decisions to reposition may result from the identification of a market gap, an increase in competitive activity, or a decision to respond to changing consumer demographics, attitudes, and values.

Before deciding on a target market, the company should forecast the demand in the total market and in each segment under consideration. Demand forecasting involves measuring the industry's market potential, then determining the company's sales potential (market share), and finally preparing a sales forecast. The sales forecast is the foundation of all budgeting and operational planning in all major departments of a company. There are several major methods available for forecasting market demand.

Key Terms and Concepts

Psychological segmentation (102)
Personality characteristics (102)
Lifestyle (102)
Psychographics (103)
List of Values (LOV) (103)
VALS (103)
VALS2 (103)
Behavioural segmentation (104)
Benefits desired (104)
Profiles (104)
Usage rate (105)
Target-market strategies (105)
Market aggregation (107)
Product or service differentiation (108)
Single-segment concentration strategy (109)
Multiple-segment strategy (109)
Positioning (110)
Positioning map (112)
Niche marketing (114)
Positioning strategies (116)
Repositioning (116)
Forecasting market demand (117)
Market factor and market index (117)
Market potential and sales potential (117)
Sales forecast (117)
Methods of forecasting demand (119)
Market-factor analysis (119)
Surveys of buyer intentions (120)
Test marketing (120)
Past sales and trend analysis (120)
Sales-force composite (121)
Executive judgment (121)

Questions and Problems

1. Consult back issues of your local newspaper and a number of consumer magazines to identify examples of companies that are positioning their brands to appeal to target lifestyle segments of the consumer market. Identify examples of other brands that are targeted at consumers on the basis of product usage.
2. Explain the similarities and differences between a single-segment and a multiple-segment target-market strategy.
3. How might the following organizations implement the strategy of market segmentation?
   a. Manufacturer of personal computers.
   b. Canadian Red Cross.
   c. Vancouver Aquarium.
   d. Upper Canada Brewing Company.
4. Assume that a company has developed a new type of portable headphone-type cassette player in the general product category of a Sony Walkman. Which of the three target-market strategies should this company adopt?
5. What positioning strategy has each of the following marketers chosen?
   a. Mark's Work Wearhouse.
   b. Your provincial liquor board or corporation.
   c. Ikea furniture stores.
   d. Colgate toothpaste.
   e. Toronto Dominion Bank.
   f. Mr. Big chocolate bar.
6. Identify a number of brands, retailers, or restaurants with which you are familiar that have chosen to occupy a niche in the market. How would you

describe the niche each occupies? Why do you feel each has chosen this niche?

7. Why would a company decide that one of its brands needs to be repositioned? What market conditions are likely to lead to a decision to reposition a brand or company? Can you think of any brands or stores with which you are familiar that have recently been repositioned? What were their original positions? How would you describe the new position each occupies in the market? How was the repositioning accomplished in each case?
8. Carefully distinguish between market potential and a sales forecast, using examples of consumer or industrial products.
9. What are some logical market factors that you might use in estimating the market potential for each of the following products?
   a. Central home air conditioners.
   b. Symphony tickets.
   c. Golf clubs.
   d. A visit to Canada's Wonderland.
   e. Safety goggles.
10. How would you determine the market potential for a textbook written for the introductory course in marketing?
11. Explain the direct-derivation method of sales forecasting, using a product example other than automobile tires. How does this forecasting method differ from the correlation-analysis method?
12. What are some of the problems a researcher faces when using the test-market method for determining market potential or sales potential?

Hands-On Marketing

1. Identify a number of brands of breakfast cereal (both hot and cold) available in supermarkets in your town or city, and indicate how each of the brands is differentiated and how each is positioned to appeal to a specific segment of the market.
2. Prepare a positioning map of the restaurants in the area around your college or university. On what dimensions should the restaurants be positioned? What gaps in the market have you identified?

CHAPTER 6 GOALS

In Chapters 4 and 5, our discussions of market segmentation, positioning, and forecasting focused on the target market. In this chapter, we consider the consumer's willingness to buy as determined by information sources, social environment, psychological forces, and situational factors.

After studying this chapter, you should have an understanding of:

- The process consumers go through in making purchasing decisions.
- The importance of commercial and social information sources in buying decisions.
- The influence of culture, subcultures, and social class characteristics on buying behaviour.
- The direct impact of reference groups on buying behaviour.
- Family and household buying behaviour.
- The roles of motivation, perception, learning, personality, and attitudes in shaping consumer behaviour.
- The importance of situational factors in buying.

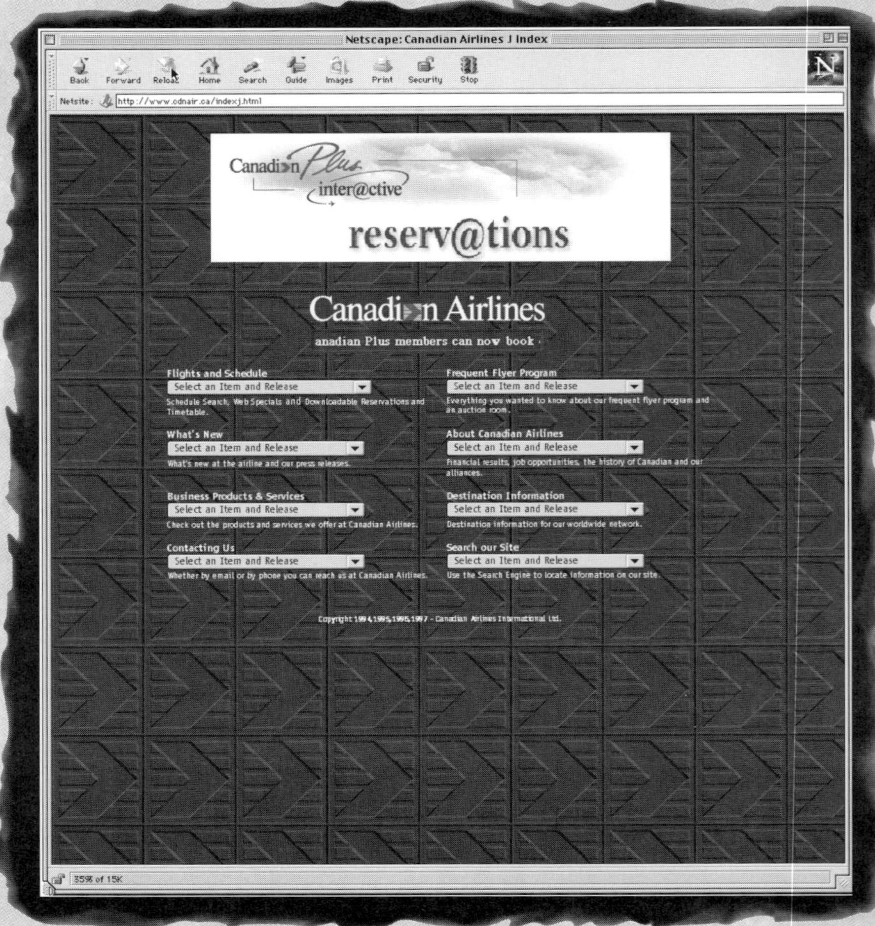

Chapter Six

Social and Psychological Influences on Buyer Behaviour

ON-LINE SHOPPING: WILL YOU BUY IT?

For the past few years, the cry has gone up: "Is this the year for Internet commerce?" And the answer has come back resoundingly — from some — "Yes! Get ready for explosive growth as consumers change the way they shop." Just as resoundingly the response from others has been, "No! It will take years, not months, for consumers to adopt a new way of shopping."

Mark Greene, the IBM vice-president of electronic payment and certification of the Internet Division, stood in front of his Toronto audience and forecast explosive growth in Internet commerce in the next decade. Imagine, $2 billion U.S. in 1997, $200 billion by 2000. But if in 1996, Internet sales were $900 million — is this kind of increase possible? Jim Carroll, co-author of *The Canadian Internet Handbook*, says, "I just don't think we're all prepared to drop our lives and rush to the terminal and become dweeb-geek cybershoppers... I look at the guys at IBM and think it's a lot of wishful thinking... If I'm going to buy a new suit, I'm going to want to step in front of a mirror and try it on... Just because the technology can do it, doesn't mean that it is going to happen." Carroll believes that assuming flashy new technology will transform consumer behaviour is a cardinal sin. Such views are supported by industry consultant Erina DuBois, who says that most technologically savvy consumers are already on the Internet and many of those are already using it for electronic purchases. These consumers represent a small part of the total market potential, and to get the mass market involved in on-line shopping requires "a huge educational process." There is consumer apathy, perceived payment and information security problems, and the notion that using the Internet is, for many, more complicated than operating a VCR. Besides, why should you trust an Internet site?

At present, consumers prepared to engage in on-line shopping seem to be quite comfortable with shopping, gathering information, and making decisions for such products and services as computers from Dell Computer Corporation, music on CDs from BigNote, books from Amazon.com, and airline ticket specials from Canadian Airlines International. For these kinds of goods and services, on-line shopping is seen as a value-added service. But in addition to wanting to make fast and relatively routine purchase decisions, today's on-line consumers want to make better-informed complex purchase decisions quickly and not just purchase at the lowest price.

The more tiresome or onerous a purchase is in the physical world, as opposed to the electronic world, the more likely consumers will try an on-line alternative. For example, shopping for autos or mortgages is tedious, difficult, and time consuming, and it requires a lot of information and consumer information processing. Internet sites offering straightforward mortgage terms and rates and easy-to-understand comparisons are doing better and better. Automobile-purchase Internet sites allow a consumer to set specifications and request firm bids from dealers and, as more consumers who hate the auto-buying process turn to on-line shopping, auto producers have begun to wonder about the need for their own Web sites, and perhaps they may need fewer dealers.

No question about it, Internet commerce is here in about ten different forms. But how consumers will operate is not very clear. Right now, cyberspace retailers are having troubles, and this includes IBM and Amazon Books. Consumers, but not enough of them, shop around at lot — each one visits a lot of sites. They gather a lot of information, but not enough of them actually buy on-line — they frequently buy in a physical retail outlet. They zap a lot, since it's as easy to do as with TV, and besides, waiting for graphics to download is boring. After the novelty has worn off, consumers tend to be loyal to approximately seven sites rather than spend endless hours searching for something interesting or entertaining.

Some experts now believe that electronic sites must be linked to physical ones, that they must be complementary because many consumers will not give up on being in a physical environment for many purchases, nor will they give up the benefits of good personal service and satisfactory face-to-face relationships in the marketplace. What is the technology doing to consumer behaviour? What is consumer behaviour doing to the technology?[1]

As this discussion of Internet consumer behaviour illustrates, marketing to consumers has become more complicated. The reason is simple. The domestic and international marketplaces have become more competitive and more technologically complex, and our understanding of consumer buying behaviour is constantly improving. But there is still much more to learn. And because marketing success largely depends on the ability to anticipate what buyers will do, in this chapter we examine the challenging topic of consumer buying behaviour. First we develop an overview by describing the buying-decision process. Next we consider the sources of information used by consumers — without information there are no decisions. We then describe the various social and group forces in society that influence decision-making and the psychological characteristics of the individual that affect the decision process in buying. In the final section, our focus shifts to the significant role that situational factors play in buying decisions.

Figure 6-1 brings all the dimensions of buying behaviour together in a model that provides the structure for our discussion. The model features a six-stage **buying-decision process** influenced by four primary forces.

THE BUYING-DECISION PROCESS

To deal with the marketing environment and to make purchases, consumers engage in a decision process. The process, which divides nicely into six stages, can be thought of as a problem-solving approach. When faced with a buying problem ("I'm bored. How do I satisfy my need for entertainment?"), the consumer goes through a series of logical stages to arrive at a decision. As shown in the centre of Figure 6-1, the stages are:

1. **Need recognition:** The consumer is moved to action by a need.

FIGURE 6–1

The Consumer Buying-Decision Process and the Factors That Influence It

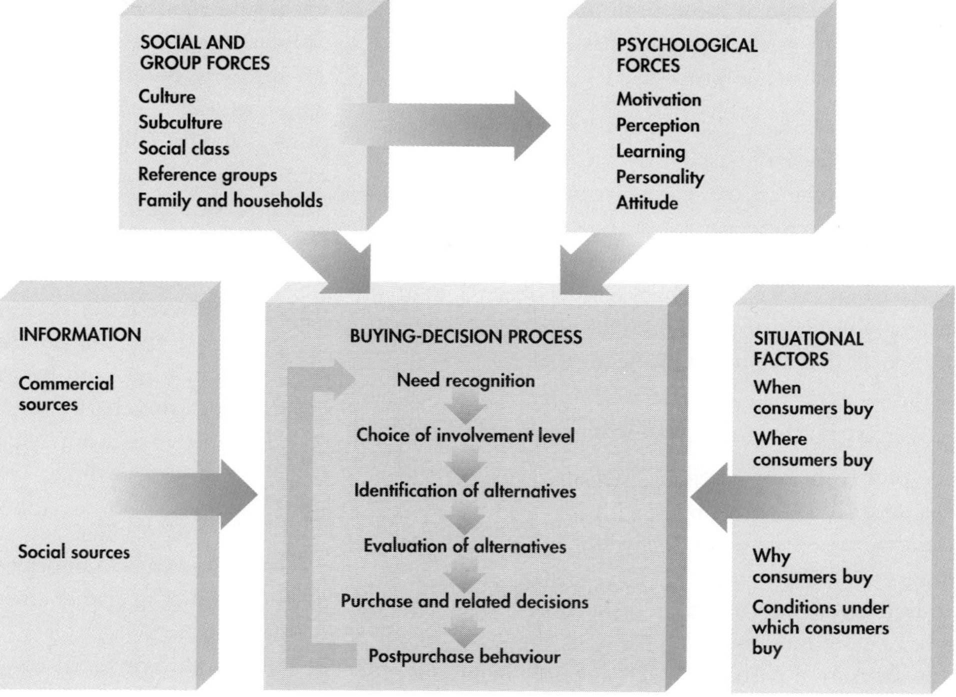

2. **Choice of an involvement level:** The consumer decides how much time and effort to invest in satisfying the need and thus the energy devoted to the remaining stages of the problem solving process.
3. **Identification of alternatives:** The consumer collects information about products, services, and brands.
4. **Evaluation of alternatives:** The consumer weighs the pros and cons of the alternatives identified.
5. **Purchase and related decisions:** The consumer decides to buy or not to buy.
6. **Postpurchase behaviour:** The consumer seeks reassurance that the choice made was the correct one, experiences the product or service in use, and, the marketer hopes, becomes satisfied and is prepared to engage in the process again as the need arises.

Though this model is a useful starting point for examining purchase decisions, the process is not always as straightforward as it may appear. Consider these possible variations:

- The consumer can withdraw from the purchase process at any stage prior to the actual purchase. If, for example, the need diminishes, or no satisfactory alternatives are available, or the search is not worth the effort, the process will come to an abrupt end.
- It is not uncommon for some stages to be skipped. All six stages are likely to be followed only in certain buying situations — for instance, when buying high-priced, infrequently purchased items. However, for frequently purchased, familiar products, purchasing is usually routine. The aroused need is often satisfied by repurchasing a familiar brand, and the third and fourth stages are bypassed.
- The stages are not generally of the same length. When a mechanic tells you that your car's engine needs an overhaul, it may take only a moment to recognize the need for a new car. However, the identification and evaluation of alternative models may go on for weeks.
- Some stages may be performed consciously in certain purchase situations and subconsciously in others. For example, we don't consciously calculate for every purchase the amount of time and effort we will put into reaching a decision. Yet the

fact that we spend more time on some purchases and less on others indicates that level of involvement is part of the process.

In the following discussion we use this six-stage process. However, the stages may have to be adjusted to fit the circumstances of a particular purchase situation. Also, what a consumer wants at the end of the process is satisfaction, and that doesn't necessarily mean a simple exchange. As we have observed in Chapter 1, there are many aspects of the interaction between buyers and sellers that can affect satisfaction levels.

1. Recognition of an Unsatisfied Need

The process begins when an unsatisfied need creates tension or discomfort for the consumer. This condition may arise internally (for example, a person feels hungry). Or the need may be dormant until it is aroused by an external stimulus, such as an ad or the sight of a product. Another possible source of tension is dissatisfaction with a product currently being used.

Once the need has been recognized, consumers often become aware of conflicting or competing uses for their scarce resources of time and money. Let's say a student wants to purchase a personal computer for school, but for the same amount of money she could buy a stereo. Or she may be concerned that if she doesn't buy the computer she may not be able to access a lot of information she needs for her courses. She must resolve these conflicts before proceeding. Otherwise the buying process stops.

2. Choice of an Involvement Level

Very early in the process the consumer consciously or subconsciously decides how much effort to exert in satisfying a need. Sometimes when a need arises, a consumer is dissatisfied with the quantity or quality of information about the purchase situation and decides to actively collect and evaluate more. These are **high-involvement** purchases that entail all six stages of the buying-decision process. If, on the other hand, a consumer is comfortable with the information and alternatives readily available, the purchase situation is viewed as **low involvement**. In such a case, the buyer will likely skip directly from need recognition to purchase, ignoring the stages in-between.

Some of the major differences in consumer behaviour in high- and low-involvement situations are shown in the chart below.

Though it is somewhat risky to generalize because consumers differ, involvement tends to be greater under any of the following conditions:

- The consumer lacks information about the purchase.
- The product or its benefits are viewed as important.
- The practical or social consequence of making a bad decision is perceived as high.
- The quality of the interaction is high.

Thus most buying decisions for relatively low-priced products that have close substitutes would be low-involvement. Typical examples are the majority of items sold in supermarkets, variety stores, and hardware stores. However, for a wealthy person the purchase of a car could be a low-involvement experience, while for a person with a high need for social acceptance, purchasing toothpaste might be highly involving. Thus it is important to remember that involvement must be viewed from the perspective of the consumer, not the product.

Impulse buying, or purchasing with little or no advance planning, is an important form of low-involvement decision-making. A shopper who goes

Behaviour	High Involvement	Low Involvement
Time invested	Large amount	Small amount
Information search	Active	Little or none
Response to information	Critically evaluate	Ignore or accept without evaluation
Brand evaluations	Clear and distinct	Vague and general
Likelihood of brand loyalty developing	High	Low
Interaction with sales/service persons	Committed and demanding	Nominal but sensitive

IBM suggests a solution of maintaining and enhancing the involvement level of hockey fans.

SOLUTIONS

Hockey's popularity is on a power play. The coolest game on earth is also the fastest growing. So how does the National Hockey League® keep this momentum up with fans around the world?

Give them hockey, hockey, and yet more hockey at www.nhl.com – a Website that wires together fans and players. Thanks to an assist from IBM.

Fans get detailed write-ups on every game, daily news and the chance to interview their favourite players online. They can also share their opinions, something every hockey fan has plenty of.

Official NHL merchandise will soon be just a click away, too. You will be able to buy jerseys, T-shirts and other hockey memorabilia, safely and securely, from anywhere on the planet. The desktop-Zamboni® is a must.

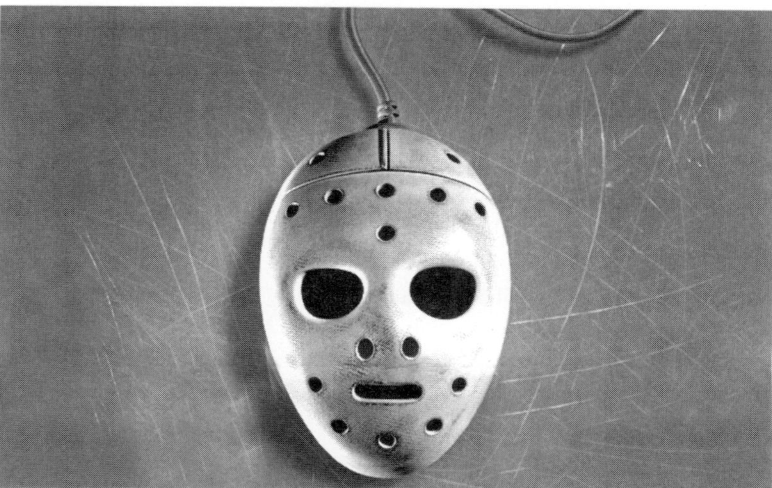

Hockey fans should visit www.nhl.com. CEOs should visit www.internet.ibm.com/secureway/commercepoint.html or call 1-800-IBM-CALL, ext. G228.*

The Net-net: The Internet can help create a community of your customers, keep them involved, up-to-date, and increase their loyalty to your brand.

Solutions for a small planet™ IBM®

*1-800-426-2255. NHL and the NHL Shield are registered trade-marks of the National Hockey League. Zamboni is a registered trade-mark of Frank J. Zamboni Co., Inc. IBM is a registered trade-mark and Solutions for a small planet is a trade-mark of International Business Machines Corporation and are used under licence by IBM Canada © 1996 IBM Corporation.

to the grocery store with the intention of buying vegetables and bread and on noticing a display of peaches at an attractive price decides to buy some engages in impulse buying.

Self-service, open-display retailing has conditioned shoppers to postpone planning and engage in more impulse buying. Because of the growth of this type of low-involvement purchasing, greater emphasis must be placed on promotional programs to get shoppers into a store or to visit a virtual mall site. Also, displays and packages must be made appealing because they serve as silent sales people.

3. Identification of Alternatives

Once a need has been recognized and the level of involvement is determined, the consumer must next identify the alternatives capable of satisfying the need. First, alternative products and then alternative brands are identified. Product and brand identification may range from a simple memory scan of previous experiences to an extensive external search. Consider this example. Suppose a couple decides not to cook but to have an already-prepared item for their evening meal. Identifying alternatives might entail checking the freezer to see if any frozen dinners are on hand, examining the newspaper for specials or discount coupons, and recalling a radio advertisement that described a new restaurant.

The search for alternatives is influenced by:

- How much information the consumer already has from past experiences and other sources.
- The consumer's confidence in that information.
- The expected benefit or value of additional information or, put another way, what the additional information is worth in terms of the effort, time, or money required to obtain it.

4. Evaluation of Alternatives

Once all the reasonable alternatives have been identified, the consumer must evaluate them before making a decision. The evaluation involves establishing some criteria against which each alternative is compared. In the preceding meal example, the decision maker may have a single criterion ("How quickly can we sit down to eat?") or several criteria (speed, taste, nutrition, and price). When multiple criteria are involved, they typically do not carry equal weight. For example, preparation time might be more important than nutrition.

The criteria that consumers use in the evaluation result from their past experience and feelings toward various brands, as well as the opinions of family members, friends, or even experts. Differences in the criteria applied or in the relative importance that different consumers place on them are what determine market segments.

Because experience is often limited or dated and information from sources such as advertising or friends can be biased, evaluations can be factually incorrect. That is, a consumer may believe that the price of brand A is higher than that of brand B, when in fact the opposite is true. Marketers monitor consumers to determine what choice criteria they use, to identify any changes that may be taking place in their criteria, and to correct any damaging misperceptions.

5. Purchase and Related Decisions

After searching and evaluating, the consumer must decide whether to buy. Thus the first outcome is the decision to purchase or not to purchase the alternative evaluated as most desirable. If the decision is to buy, a series of related decisions must be made regarding features, where and when to make the actual purchase, how to take delivery or possession, the method of payment, and other issues. So the decision to make a purchase is really the beginning of an entirely new series of decisions that may be as time-consuming and difficult as the initial one. Alert marketers recognize that the outcome of these additional decisions affects satisfaction, so they find ways to help consumers make them as efficiently as possible. For example, car dealers have speeded up loan approval, streamlined the process of tracking down a car that meets the buyer's exact specifications, and made delivery of the car a "mini-ceremony" to make the customer feel important.

Selecting a source from which to make a purchase is one of the buying decisions. Sources can be as varied as Internet sites or manufacturers' outlets. The most common source is a retail store, and the reasons a consumer chooses to shop at a retail store or a cyberspace or electronic store are called **patronage buying motives**. People want to feel comfortable when they shop. This may mean that they want the assurance of being around people like themselves and in an environment that reflects their values or that they can trust, or that they want the convenience, lack of pressure, and anonymity of an electronic store.

Patronage motives can range from something as simple as convenience when you want a soft drink, to something more complex, such as the atmosphere of a restaurant.

Some common patronage motives are:

- Location or access convenience.
- Merchandise assortment.
- Service speed.
- Services offered.
- Merchandise accessibility.
- Appearance of the premises.
- Confidence in the firm or supplier.
- Quality of staff.
- Prices.
- Mix of other customers.

Like the criteria consumers use to choose products and brands, their patronage motives will vary depending on the purchase situation. Successful retailers evaluate their target customers carefully and design their stores accordingly. A manufacturer, in turn, selects physical or electronic retailers with the patronage characteristics that complement its product and appeal to the desired target market. Tourist destinations market their attraction based on the factors that target segments want in a vacation.

Postpurchase Behaviour

What a consumer learns from going through the buying process has an influence on how he or she will behave the next time the same need arises. If the consumer's expectations for all aspects of the decision-making process are met, consumer satisfaction results. The consumer will feel that he or she has received fair value. If the consumer's expectations have been more than met, then satisfaction is even greater and the consumer feels that superior value has been received. From the marketer's viewpoint, for both these cases, and in varying degrees, the foundation for a long-term customer relationship has been established.

By completing the buying process, by having gathered information, evaluated alternatives, and arrived at a decision, the consumer has acquired additional knowledge about the product and various brands. Furthermore, new opinions and beliefs have been formed and old ones have been revised. The appreciation of product benefits, the service that was provided, the quality of the interaction between the buyer and seller or service person — all of these can then be fed back, as is indicated by an arrow in Figure 6-1, from the **postpurchase behaviour** stage of the buying-decision process model to the next need-recognition stage. In other words, a consumer who has experienced a high degree of satisfaction in a purchase situation will be prepared to repeat the process with the same marketer for the same product or service.

Something else often occurs following a purchase. Have you ever gone through a careful decision process for a major purchase (say, a set of tires for your car or an expensive item of clothing), selected what you thought was the best alternative, but then had doubts about your choice after the purchase? What you were experiencing is postpurchase **cognitive dissonance** — a state of anxiety brought on by the difficulty of choosing from among several alternatives. Unfortunately for marketers, dissonance is quite common; and, if the anxiety is not relieved, the consumer may be unhappy with the chosen product even if it performs adequately!

Postpurchase cognitive dissonance occurs when each of the alternatives seriously considered by the consumer has both attractive and unattractive features. For example, in purchasing tires, the set selected may be the most expensive (unattractive), but they provide better traction on wet roads (attractive). The brand not chosen was recommended by a friend (attractive), but came with a very limited warranty (unattractive). After the purchase is made, the unattractive features of the product purchased grow in importance in the consumer's mind, as do the attractive features offered by the rejected alternatives. As a result, we begin to doubt the wisdom of the choice and experience anxiety over the decision.

Dissonance typically increases: (1) the higher the dollar value or perceived risk of the purchase; (2) the greater the similarity between the item selected and item(s) rejected; and (3) the greater the importance of the purchase decision to the consumer. Thus buying a house or car creates more dissonance than buying paper for your printer.

The Pro Plan advertisement challenges consumers to think about the leading ingredient of Pro Plan compared with those of two competitors and offers a 1-800 number to answer customer inquiries.

Consumers try to reduce their postpurchase anxieties. They avoid information (such as ads for the rejected products) that is likely to increase the dissonance. And they seek out information that supports their decision, even to the extreme of reading ads for a product after it has been purchased. Also, prior to the purchase, putting more effort into evaluating alternatives can increase a consumer's confidence and reduce dissonance.

Some useful generalizations can be developed from the theory of cognitive dissonance. For example, anything sellers can do in their advertising or personal

MARKETING AT WORK FILE 6-1

GETTING INFORMATION, NEGOTIATING, AND DECISION-MAKING BECOMES JOB ONE

Most people hate having to go out and buy a car; they don't do it very often (every five or six years), so they lack experience in handling the transaction and worry about making a mistake. Also, technology changes a lot in five or six years, and many people know they don't have enough information to make a good decision.

Might it have something to do with all the confusion, haggling, and pressure they know they're doomed to confront on the showroom floor? Might it have something to do with not knowing what you think you ought to know to make a good decision? To boot, if you're a woman, you probably find — as did 66 percent of women in a *Chatelaine* magazine survey — that you don't get taken very seriously by sales staff.

All in all, recent consumer studies show that frustration with the retail end of the automobile industry is high. The new president of Ford of Canada, Bobbie Gaunt, happens to be a marketer — not a production person. It also happens that she is a woman — the first woman to head up the company since its inception in 1904. She intends making marketing Ford's job one. Today, 50 percent of cars are bought by women and they exert "significant" influence on another 25 percent of purchases. In the past, Ms. Gaunt has set up a woman's marketing committee within Ford that was to provide the woman's market perspective to engineers, designers, and production and marketing people. Today, as president, her major concern is the auto dealership; the sales experience, the price negotiation, the downstream service — the whole basis of the customer relationship.

Today, auto dealers are facing competition from a growing number of auto superstores who provide sharper pricing, but lots of negotiation. They are also facing competition from at least one manufacturer, Daiwoo, and a number of dealers who have changed by adopting "no-dicker" pricing — a strategy in which the dealer attaches a non-negotiable price tag to every car and thus simplifies the negotiation process for the consumer immeasurably. Of course, a buyer must have a lot of trust in the buyer–seller relationship for this approach to work — and the seller must work to achieve this with valid and reliable information and quality customer service.

A further form of competition is the growing Internet selling of cars. A buyer, having collected all the information he or she needs, whether from Web sites, dealerships, or "expert" publications, can enter its purchase specifications with either auto cyber shops or an auto manufacturer. Bids are requested for the vehicle as specified. Lots of dealers are making sharp bids, and vehicles are being sold without confusion and haggling. The buyer can make a decision in comfort without having to see the sales manager three or four times before there is a deal.

And then there is Car$mart, the car consulting service. For a $100 fee, Jim Davidson, a former car salesman who founded the Toronto-based car-buying consulting service, recommends car makes and models that suit his customers' needs before leading clients through a step-by-step method of how to negotiate a purchase. If you want, he'll even go a few steps further — accompany you on a test drive or even shop the market for a good price and set up a dealer appointment for you. "Originally I thought my service would mainly appeal to women, senior citizens, or first-time car buyers," says Davidson. "But a lot of my customers have been professionals who just don't have the time and detest the whole process. It's almost impossible to get accurate, unbiased information in this industry and when you're only in the market once every six years, it's really hard to become an overnight expert." Bobbie Gaunt, Ford's new CEO, has to overcome all this.

Source: Adapted from Laura Fowlie, "Easing the Car-Buying Hassle," *Financial Post*, March 13, 1993, p. 18; John Greenwood, "Job One," *The Financial Post Magazine*, June 1997, pp. 19–22.

selling to reassure buyers — say, by stressing the number of satisfied owners — will reduce dissonance. Also, the quality of a seller's follow-up and postsale service programs can be significant factors in reducing dissonance.

With this background on the buying-decision process, we can examine what influences buying behaviour. We'll begin with the sources and types of information used by consumers.

INFORMATION AND PURCHASE DECISIONS

Consumers must find out what products and services are available, what brands offer what features and benefits, what services are available to support the purchase, who sells them at what prices, where they can be purchased, and what kind of follow-up is likely. Without this market information there wouldn't be a decision process because there would not be any decisions to make.

What are some of the sources and types of information that exist in the buying environment? As shown in Figure 6-1, two information sources, the commercial environment and the social environment, influence the buying-decision process. The **commercial information** environment consists of all marketing organizations and individuals that attempt to communicate with consumers. It includes manufacturers, retailers, advertisers, and sales people whenever any of them are engaged in efforts to inform or persuade. The other source is the **social information** environment, made up of family, friends, and acquaintances who directly or indirectly provide information about products. If you think for a moment about how often your conversation with friends or family deals with purchases you are considering or those you have made, you will begin to appreciate the marketing significance of these social sources.

Advertising is the most common type of commercial information. Other commercial sources are direct sales efforts by store clerks, telemarketing, and direct mail to consumers' homes, as well as consumers' physical involvement with products (examining packages, trial product use, and sampling). Increasingly, consumers are obtaining the information they need about products and services through the Internet. In business-to-business marketing, one of the first sources of information on prospective suppliers is their Web pages.

The normal kind of social information is word-of-mouth communication, in which two or more people simply have a conversation about a product or service. Other social sources include the observations of others using products and exposure to products in the homes of others.

When all the different types of information are taken into consideration, it becomes apparent that there is enormous competition for the consumer's attention. It has been estimated that the typical adult is exposed to about three hundred ad messages a day, or almost ten thousand per month.[2] Coincidentally, the consumer's mind has to be a marvelously efficient machine to sort and process this barrage of information. To understand how the consumer functions, we will begin by examining the social and group forces that influence the individual's psychological makeup and also play a role in specific buying decisions.

SOCIAL AND GROUP FORCES

The way we think, believe, and act is determined to a great extent by social forces and groups. In addition, our individual buying decisions — including our needs, the alternatives we consider, and the way in which we evaluate them — are affected by the social forces that surround us. To reflect this dual impact, the arrows in Figure 6-1 extend from the social and group forces in two directions: to the psychological makeup of the individual and to the buying-decision process. Our description begins with culture, the force with the most indirect impact, and moves to the force with the most direct impact, the household.

Definition of Culture and Cultural Influence

A **culture** is the complex of symbols and artifacts created by a given society and handed down from generation to generation as determinants and regulators of human behaviour. The symbols may be intangible (attitudes, beliefs, values, languages, religions) or tangible (tools, housing, products, works of art). A culture implies a totally learned and "handed-down" way of life. It does not include instinctive acts. However, standards for performing instinctive biological acts (eating, eliminating body wastes, and sexual relationships) can be culturally established. Thus everybody gets hungry, but what people eat and how they act to satisfy the hunger drive will vary among cultures.

Actually, much of our behaviour is culturally determined. Our sociocultural institutions (family, schools, churches, and languages) provide behavioural guidelines. Years ago, Clyde Kluckhohn observed: "Culture . . . regulates our lives at every turn. From the moment we are born until we die there is constant conscious and unconscious pressure upon us to follow certain types of behaviour that other men have created for us."[3] People living in a culture share a whole set of similarities — and these can be different from those in or from another culture.

When a culture is relatively homogeneous, as in Japan, using cultural factors in analyzing for marketing purposes can be very effective. As well, within a given culture, say Canada, for those goods and services where the cultural characteristics of consumers have no effect, it is appropriate to use this criterion. For example, if all Canadians, regardless of where they live and whatever their ethnicity, believe equally in the need for efficiency, goods and services that are presented with efficiency claims would be equally acceptable. But if there is less homogeneity in terms of values and way of life or lifestyle, culture is not as effective a guide for marketing managers as is subculture.

Canadian Subcultures

Compared with many other countries, Canada is a culturally complex society. Marketers need to understand the concept of **subcultures** and analyze them as potentially profitable market segments. Any time there is a culture as heterogeneous as ours, there are bound to be significant subcultures based upon factors such as race, nationality, religion, geographic location, age, and urban–rural distribution. Some of these were recognized in Chapter 4, when we analyzed the demographic market factors. Ethnicity, for example, is a cultural factor that has significant marketing implications. Concentrations of Middle or Eastern Europeans in the Prairies provide a market for some products that would go unnoticed in Italian or Chinese sections of Toronto, Montreal, or Vancouver.

The cultural diversity of the Canadian market has taken on increased importance for some companies in recent years. Not too long ago, most companies ignored ethnic and linguistically based segmentation. Then English and French linguistic segmentation was accepted. Today, there is rapidly growing ethnic segmentation within the French and English linguistic communities or subcultures.

The most obvious marketing efforts to reach ethnic market segments are found in major markets such as Toronto, Vancouver, and Montreal. In Toronto, for example, MTV, the multicultural television channel, broadcasts in a number of languages and carries substantial programming directed to ethnic markets. Television and newspapers are available to the Chinese communities in Vancouver, Toronto, Montreal, and elsewhere. Toronto's Spanish-language *El Popular* is targeted at the area's 250,000 Spanish speakers and is distributed from Quebec to British Columbia. These and similar media represent attractive advertising outlets for companies who wish to reach growing subcultural and linguistic market segments.

The sharpest subcultural differences of concern to marketers are portrayed in the attitudinal and behavioural differences between English- and French-speaking communities on a country-wide basis. As indicated in Chapter 4, marketing to French-speaking Canada involves considerably more than a cursory acknowledgment of ethnic and linguistic differences.

The Changing Nature of the Québécois Market

While French Canada is technically, and politically for some, a subculture, its sheer size, homogeneity, main geographic location, purchasing power, and social and political orientation makes it a cultural rather than a subcultural market. No other ethnic or non-English-speaking linguistic group comes close to comprising 24 percent of the Canadian population, relatively highly concentrated in one geographic area, and with a long-established and fully developed set of social and legal institutions. Quebec consumers con-

www.mtv.com

MARKETING AT WORK FILE 6-2

THE QUEBEC MARKET: A CULTURE OR SEVERAL SUBCULTURES?

Segmentation of populations on the basis of social and psychological buying behaviour is not always as straightforward as it may seem. Sometimes we think of people who live in one province of Canada as being all the same and therefore may make the assumption that they all have the same buying behaviour. Such may not be the case. Take Quebec, for example. We are all aware that there are major differences between the culture of that province and huge parts of the rest of Canada. These differences exist because of the history and background of the people who live there. Marketers tell us that Quebecers make the fewest long-distance phone calls, give the least to charity, buy more lottery tickets, eat more pasta, use more laxatives, and drink more gin. They also possess that ever intangible but undeniable *joie de vivre* — a combination of passion, impulsiveness, open sexuality, and provocative humour that sets them apart from English-speaking Canada and allows for BMW ads to be run in which breasts are bared, while in the rest of Canada one sees only bras.

But we should not assume that all Quebecers are the same in every aspect of buying behaviour. In the first instance, we would probably expect to find some consumption differences between anglophones and franchophones in Quebec. Yet it would be a mistake to write off the Quebec phenomenon as a simple language issue, for that would be ignoring the English-speaking Quebecers who, culturally, if not linguistically, share the habits and characteristics, not of English Canadians, but of French Quebecers. It would also be ignoring the fact that Montreal constitutes the third-largest anglophone market in Canada.

Pollster Jean-Marc Léger writes about the differences between francophones in the Montreal region and the rest of Quebec. He says that people who live in, and around, Montreal present tastes and behaviours that differ from Quebec consumers in general. Léger tells us that Montrealers do much more shopping by credit card than anywhere else in Quebec — 19 percent of francophone Montrealers own four or more credit cards, while in the rest of the province only 10 percent own this many. In another area of purchase, 40 percent of Montreal francophones opt for compact or sub-compact Japanese-style cars; this percentage drops to 33% in the rest of the province. Perhaps, as Léger suggests, it may be because of the presence of an anglophone community in Montreal that is much stronger than in the rest of Quebec. Maybe there are other factors at play.

These differences in the Quebec market can serve to highlight a significant fact about using culture to segment targets. It should be done carefully and with a thorough understanding of what subcultures may be included.

Source: Adapted from Pauline Couture, "Vive la Difference," *Report on Business Magazine*, November 1993, pp. 104–112; Jean-Marc Léger, "Montreal as a Distinct Society," *Marketing Magazine*, February 17, 1996, p. 11.

sistently exhibit consumption patterns unlike those in the rest of Canada. A number of studies have found that when demographics are either matched or controlled for, consumption differences exist between Quebecers and other Canadians and that these differences are attributable to cultural factors — values and lifestyle preferences.[4] Common examples of such consumption differences are:

- A better acceptance in Quebec of premium-priced products such as premium-grade gasoline and liquors.

- A greater per capita expenditure in Quebec on clothing, personal care items, tobacco, and alcoholic beverages.
- A greater per capita consumption of soft drinks, maple sugar, molasses, and candy in Quebec than in the rest of Canada.
- Much higher consumption rates for instant and decaffeinated coffee in Quebec.
- More time spent with television and radio in Quebec than in the rest of the country.
- A greater popularity in Quebec of coupons and premiums.[5]

The Impact of Cultural Differences on Marketing

The fact that French Canada as well as the various ethnic minority communities in Canada represent distinctively different markets requires marketers who wish to be successful in, say, the Quebec market, to develop unique marketing programs for the segment. There must be an appreciation of the fact that certain products will not be successful in French Canada simply because they are not appropriate to the French Canadian culture and lifestyle. In other cases, products that are successful in English Canada must be marketed differently in French Canada because French Canadians have a different perception of these products and the way in which they are used. It may be necessary for companies to develop new products or appropriate variations of existing products specifically for the Quebec market. Similarly, the retail buying behaviour of residents of that province may necessitate the use of different channels of distribution.

A similar, but not the same, case can be made for the various ethnic-minority and linguistically based markets in our country. Because most of these communities are so much smaller in both scale and purchasing power than Quebec, the scope for and amount of marketing program adaptation that is feasible for firms to engage in is frequently limited to advertising in the appropriate language and using, where possible, culturally acceptable themes.

There is an indication, however, that the significance of ethnic markets in some parts of Canada is growing, and marketers are placing more emphasis in this area. The Asian communities in Toronto and Vancouver, for example, are becoming prominent targets. The Bay recently redesigned its outlet in Richmond, B.C., to attract Asian shoppers.[6] *Maclean's* and *Toronto Life* are now offering Chinese-language editions, and these publications are providing opportunities for advertisers to reach that population. Some companies exploring this market through magazine advertising include General Motors, Visa, Cathay Pacific, Toronto Dominion Bank, and Canon. White Spot restaurants, many Vancouver financial institutions, jewellers, and clothiers are advertising in *Mehfil*, an English-language publication aimed at the South Asian market.[7]

Entrepreneurs in these communities have catered specifically to ethnic needs. We have numerous examples of ethnic foods such as Italian, Ukrainian, Chinese, or Indian, which were originally imported or produced and distributed exclusively for ethnic communities but which have become staples in other communities or the Canadian market at large. Every supermarket has them on display, and Loblaws makes a practice of continually adding more prepared ethnic foods to their offerings.

REFERENCE GROUP INFLUENCES

Consumers' perceptions and buying behaviour are also influenced by the reference groups to which they belong. These groups include the large social classes and smaller reference groups. The smallest, yet usually the strongest, social-group influence is a person's family.

Influence of Social Class

People's buying behaviour is often influenced by the class to which they belong, or to which they aspire, simply because they have values, beliefs, and lifestyles that are characteristic of a **social class**. This occurs whether they are conscious of class notions or not. The idea of a social-class structure and the terms upper, middle, and lower class may be repugnant to many Canadians. However, using class concepts does provide a useful way to look at a market. We can consider social class as another useful basis for segmenting consumer markets.[8]

www.visa.com • www.cathay-usa.com • www.tdbank.ca • www.canon.com

A social-class structure currently useful to marketing managers is one developed by Richard Coleman and Lee Rainwater, two respected researchers in social-class theory. The placement of people in this structure is determined primarily by such variables as education, occupation, and type of neighbourhood of residence.[9]

Note that "amount of income" is not one of the placement criteria. There may be a general relationship between amount of income and social class — people in the upper classes usually have higher incomes than people in the lower classes. But within each social class there typically is a wide range of incomes. Also, the same amount of income may be earned by families in different social classes.

For purposes of marketing planning and analysis, marketing executives and researchers often divide the total consumer market into five social classes. These classes and their characteristics are summarized below. The percentages are only approximations and may vary from one city or region to another.

Social Classes and Their Characteristics The **upper class**, about 2 percent of the population, includes two groups: (1) the socially prominent "old families" of inherited wealth and (2) the "new rich" of the corporate executives, owners of large businesses, and wealthy professionals. They live in large homes in the best neighbourhoods and display a sense of social responsibility. They buy expensive products and services, but they do not conspicuously display their purchases. They patronize exclusive shops.

The **upper-middle class**, about 12 percent of the population, is composed of moderately successful business and professional people and owners of medium-sized companies. They are well educated, have a strong drive for success, and want their children to do well. Their purchases are more conspicuous than those in the upper class. This class buys status symbols that show their success, yet are socially acceptable. They live well, belong to private clubs, and support the arts and various social causes.

The **lower-middle class**, about 32 percent of the population, consists of the white-collar workers — office workers, most sales people, teachers, technicians, and small-business owners. The **upper-lower class**, about 38 percent of the population, is the blue-collar "working class" of factory workers, semi-skilled workers, and service people. Because these two groups together represent the mass market and thus are so important to most marketers, the attitudes, beliefs, and lifestyles they exhibit are the focus for much marketing research.

The **lower-lower class**, about 16 percent of the population, is composed of unskilled workers, the chronically unemployed, unassimilated immigrants, and people frequently on welfare. They typically are poorly educated, with low incomes, and live in substandard houses and neighbourhoods. They tend to live for the present and often do not purchase wisely. The public tends to differentiate (within this class) between the "working poor" and the "welfare poor."

Marketing Significance of Social Classes Now let's summarize the basic conclusions from social-class research that are highly significant for marketing:

- A social-class system can be observed whether people are aware of it or not. Such systems can be found in every society. There are substantial differences between classes regarding their buying behaviour.
- Differences in beliefs, attitudes, and orientations exist among the classes. Thus the classes respond differently to a seller's marketing program.
- For many products, class membership is a better predictor of buyer behaviour than is income.

This last point — the relative importance of income versus social class — has generated considerable controversy. There is an old saying that "a rich man is just a poor man with money — and that, given the same amount of money, a poor man would behave exactly like a rich man." Studies of social-class structure have proved that this statement simply is not true. Two people, each earning the same income but belonging to different social classes, will have quite different buying patterns. They will shop at different stores, expect different treatment from sales and service people, and buy different products and even different brands. Also, when a family's income increases because more family members get a job, this increase almost never results in a change in the family's social class.

Influence of Small Reference Groups

Consumer behaviour is influenced by the small groups to which consumers belong or aspire to belong. These groups may include family, sports clubs or teams, church groups, or a circle of close friends from school, work, or the neighbourhood. Each of these groups has its own standards of behaviour that serve as guides or "frames of reference" for actual or aspiring members. A person may agree with all the ideas of the group or only some of them. Also, a person does not have to belong to a group to be influenced by it. Actual and potential **reference groups** operate to influence a person's attitudes, values, and behaviour.

Studies have shown that personal advice in face-to-face reference groups is much more effective in influencing buying behaviour than is advertising in newspapers, television, or other mass media. That is, in selecting products or changing brands, we are more likely to be influenced by advice, comments, or word-of-mouth from satisfied (or dissatisfied) customers in our reference group. This is true especially when we consider the speaker to be knowledgeable regarding the particular product or service or concerning the problem a product or service is designed to address.

Advertisers are relying on reference group influence when they use celebrity spokespersons. Professional athletes, musicians, models, and actors can influence people who would like to be associated with them in some way or who admire them — for example, Michael Jordan for Nike shoes and Elizabeth Hurley for Estee Lauder. Bauer Inc., for example, as part of its parent company Nike's sponsorship deal with the International Ice Hockey Federation, dressed the Canada Hockey team in Bauer uniforms and equipment.[10]

Reference-group influence in marketing is not limited to well-known personalities. Any group whose qualities a person admires can act as a reference. The physically fit, the environmentally conscious, and the professionally successful have all served as reference groups in advertisements. Another useful reference group factor pertains to the flow of information between and within groups — it tends be flow horizontally from group to group on a similar social level rather than trickle down from high-status to lower-status groups.[11]

The proven role of small groups as behaviour determinants, plus the concept of horizontal information flow, suggests that a marketer is faced with two key problems. The first is to identify the relevant reference group likely to influence a consumer in a given buying situation. The second is to identify and communicate with two key people in the group — the **innovator** (early buyer) and the influential person (**opinion leader**). Every group has a leader — a taste-maker, or opinion leader — who influences the decision-making of others in the group. The key is for marketers to convince that person of the value of their products or services. The opinion leader in one group may be an opinion follower in another. A person who is influential in matters concerning food, because of a special interest or skill in that area, may follow the opinions of another when it comes to buying gardening equipment.

Family and Household Influence

A **family** is a group of two or more people related by blood, marriage, or adoption living together in a household. During their lives many people will belong to at least two families — the one into which they are born and the one they form at marriage. The birth family primarily determines core values and attitudes. The marriage family, in contrast, has a more direct influence on specific purchases. For example, family size is important in the purchase of a car.

A **household** is a broader concept than a family. It consists of a single person, a family, or any group of unrelated persons who occupy a housing unit. Thus an unmarried homeowner, college students sharing an off-campus apartment, and cohabiting couples are examples of households.

Since households are not necessarily comprised of a couple with children, sensitivity to household structure is important in designing marketing strategy. It affects such dimensions as product type and form (semi-processed or prepared gourmet meals for singles or busy working couples), product size (how large a serving for older couples, how large a refrigerator or microwave oven), and the design of advertising (Who shall be depicted in a TV ad: a traditional family or a couple? What kind of couple?).

In addition to the direct, immediate impact households have on the purchasing behaviour of members, it is also interesting to consider the buying behaviour of the household as a unit. Who does the buying for a household? Marketers should treat this question as four separate ones, because each may call for different strategies:

- Who influences the buying decision?
- Who makes the buying decision?
- Who makes the actual purchase?
- Who uses the product or service?

Different household members may assume these various roles, or one individual may play several roles in a particular purchase. In families, for many years the female household head did most of the day-to-day buying. However, this behaviour has changed as more women have entered the work force, and men assumed greater household responsibility.

Teenagers and young children are important decision-makers in family buying, as well as actual shoppers. Canadian teenagers could represent a $10 billion market by the year 2000. According to a study by YTV, the 2.3 million Canadian "tweens" who are between kids and teenagers have $1.1 billion in disposable income to spend.[12] This certainly is enough to warrant the attention of many manufacturers. Even very young children influence buying decisions today because they watch TV advertising and ask for products when they shop with their parents. Cadbury's Chocolate Canada, for example, created *The Tale of the Great Bunny* to market Easter candy directly to children.[13] Purchasing decisions are often made jointly by husband and wife. Young couples are much more likely to make buying decisions on a joint basis than older couples are. Apparently the longer a couple live together, the more they feel they can trust each other's judgment.

Knowing which family member is likely to make the purchase decision will influence a firm's entire marketing mix. If children are the key decision-makers, as is often the case with breakfast cereals, then a manufacturer will produce something that tastes good to children, design the package with youngsters in mind, and advertise on Saturday morning cartoon shows. This would be done regardless of who actually makes the purchase and who else (besides the children) in the household might eat cereal.

PSYCHOLOGICAL FACTORS

In discussing the psychological component of consumer behaviour, we continue to use the model in Figure 6-1. One or more motives within a person activates goal-oriented behaviour. One such behaviour is perception — the collection and processing of information. Other important psychological activities are learning and attitude formation. We then consider the roles that personality and self-concept play in buying decisions. These psychological variables help to shape a person's lifestyle and values. The term **psychographics** is used in marketing as a synonym for those variables that include lifestyle and values.

Motivation — The Starting Point

To understand why consumers behave as they do, we must first ask why a person acts at all. The answer is, "Because he or she experiences a need." All behaviour starts with a recognized need. Security, social acceptance, and prestige are examples of needs. Thus, a **motive** is a need sufficiently stimulated to move an individual to seek satisfaction.

We have many dormant needs that do not activate behaviour because they are not sufficiently intense. Hunger strong enough to cause us to search for food and fear great enough to motivate a search for security are examples of aroused needs that become motives for behaviour.

Identifying the motive(s) for behaviour can range from simple to unexplainable. To illustrate, buying motives may be grouped in three different levels, depending on consumers' awareness of them and their willingness to divulge them. At one level, buyers recognize, and are quite willing to talk about, their motives for buying certain products or services. At a second level, they are aware of their reasons for buying but will not admit them to others. A man may buy a luxury car because he feels it adds to his social position in the neighbourhood. Or a woman may buy expensive golf clubs to keep up with her peer group. But when questioned about their motives, they offer other reasons that they think will be more socially acceptable. The most difficult motives to uncover are those at the third level, where even the buyers themselves cannot explain the real factors motivating their buying actions.

www.ytv.com • www.cadbury.co.uk

Sunlight is sensitive to the effect of a new addition on family life.

To further complicate our understanding, a purchase is often the result of multiple motives. Moreover, various motives may conflict with one another. In buying a jacket, a young man may want to (1) please himself, (2) please his girlfriend, (3) be considered fashion savvy among his friends, and (4) strive for value. To accomplish all these objectives in one purchase is truly a difficult assignment. Also a person's buying behaviour changes because of changes in income, lifestyle, and other factors. Finally, identical behaviour by several people may result from quite different motives, and different behaviour by the same person at various times may result from the same motive.

Classification of Motives Psychologists generally agree that motives can be grouped in two broad categories:

- Needs aroused from physiological states of tension (such as the need for sleep).
- Needs aroused from psychological states of tension (such as the needs for affection and self-respect).

A refinement of these two sets is Maslow's hierarchy of five levels of needs, arrayed in the order in which people appear to seek to gratify them.[14] **Maslow's hierarchy of needs**, shown in Figure 6-2, recognizes that a normal person is most likely to be working toward need satisfaction on several levels at the same time and that rarely are all needs on a given level fully satisfied. However, the hierarchy indicates that the majority of needs on a particular level must be reasonably well satisfied before a person is motivated at the next higher level.

In their attempts to market products or communicate with particular segments, marketers often must go beyond a general classification like Maslow's to understand the specific motives underlying behaviour. For example, to observe that a consumer on a shopping trip may be satisfying physiological and social needs because he or she purchases food and talks to friends in the store may be useful, but often more detail is required. Addressing this issue, Edward Tauber described thirteen specific motives reported by shoppers, including recreation, self-gratification, sensory stimulation, peer group attraction, and status.[15] Using these motives, marketers are better prepared to design appealing products and services. Much more needs to be done, however, to identify marketing-specific motives and to measure their strengths.

FIGURE 6-2 Maslow's Hierarchy of Needs

Perception

A motive is an aroused need. It, in turn, activates behaviour intended to satisfy the aroused need. One form that behaviour takes is collecting and processing information from the environment, a process known as **perception**. We constantly receive, organize, and assign meaning to stimuli detected by our five senses. In this way, we interpret or give meaning to the world around us. Perception plays a major role in the alternative-identification stage of the buying-decision process.

What we perceive — the meaning we give something sensed — depends on the object and our experiences. In an instant, the mind is capable of receiving information, comparing it with a huge store of images in memory, and providing an interpretation.

Though important, visual stimuli are just one factor in perception. Consumers make use of all five senses. Scents, for example, are powerful behaviour triggers. Who can resist the aroma of popcorn in a theatre or of fresh cookies in a bakery? As with all perception, memory plays a large part with aromas. A recent study of common odours that evoke pleasant childhood memories found that older consumers identified natural smells of horses, flowers, and hay. However, younger subjects associated pleasant recollections with the scent of Play-Doh and even jet fuel! Marketers are using this type of information to associate odours with products and shopping environments to create positive perceptions.

Every day we come in contact with an enormous number of marketing stimuli. However, a process of selectivity limits our perceptions. As an illustration, consider that:

- We pay attention by exception. That is, of all the marketing stimuli our senses are exposed to, only those with the power to capture and hold our attention have the potential of being perceived. This phenomenon is called **selective attention**.
- We may alter information that is inconsistent with our beliefs and attitudes. Thus someone may say, "Despite the evidence, I don't believe smoking will be hazardous to my health." This is **selective distortion**.
- We retain only part of what we have selectively perceived. We may read an ad but later forget it. This is known as **selective retention**.

There are many communication implications in this selectivity process. For example, to grasp and hold attention, an ad must be involving enough to stimulate the consumer to seek more information. If the ad is too familiar, it will be ignored. On the other hand, if it is too complex, the ad will be judged not worth the time and effort to understand it. Thus, the goal is a mildly ambiguous first impression that heightens the consumer's interest.

Selective distortion tells us that marketers cannot assume that a message, even if it is factually correct, will necessarily be accepted as fact by consumers. In designing a message, the distance between the audience's current belief and the position proposed by the message must be considered. If the distance is large, a moderate claim may be more believable than a dramatic claim and therefore more effective in moving consumers in the desired direction.

Even messages received undistorted are still subject to selective retention. Consequently ads are repeated many times. The hope is that numerous exposures will etch the message into the recipient's memory. This partially explains why a firm with very familiar products, such as Wrigley's, spends over $100 million a year in Canada and the United States to reinforce its brand name.

Learning

Learning may be defined as changes in behaviour resulting from previous experiences. Thus it excludes behaviour that is attributable to instinct, such as breathing, or temporary states, such as hunger or fatigue. The ability to interpret and predict the consumer's learning process enhances our understanding of buying behaviour, since learning plays a role at every stage of the buying-decision process. No simple learning theory has emerged as universally workable and acceptable. However, the one with the most direct application to marketing strategy is the stimulus-response theory.[16]

According to **stimulus-response theory**, learning occurs as a person (1) responds to some stimulus and (2) is rewarded with need satisfaction for a correct response or penalized for an incorrect one. When the same correct response is repeated in reaction to the same stimulus, a behaviour pattern or learning is established.

Once a habitual behaviour pattern has been established, it replaces conscious, wilful behaviour. This is the same as saying that a consumer, having been satisfied or more than satisfied, continues a relationship with the seller. The task for competitors is to find a way, by arousing need in a different way or once need has been aroused, to break into the process and cause the consumer to pay attention to other information.

Marketers have taught consumers to respond to certain cues:

- End-of-aisle displays in supermarkets suggest that an item is on sale.
- Sale signs in store windows suggest that bargains can be found inside.
- Large type in newspaper grocery ads suggests that featured items are particularly good bargains.

But the sad fact for marketers is that what is learned can be unlearned, and effective competitors search the decision-making process and the detail of each stage to find ways of disrupting habitual learned behaviour. Of course, the consumer adds to a marketer's frustration by seeking variety, by finding oneself short of time or money and thus prepared to behave differently, or by facing an empty shelf where one expects to find a favorite brand.

Personality

The study of human personality has given rise to many, sometimes widely divergent, schools of psychological thought. As a result, attempts to inventory and classify personality traits have produced a variety of different structures. In this discussion, **personality** is defined broadly as an individual's pattern of traits that influence behavioural responses. We speak of people as being self-confident, aggressive, shy, domineering, dynamic, secure, introverted, flexible, or friendly and as being influenced (but not controlled) by these personality traits in their responses to situations.

It is generally agreed that personality traits do influence consumers' perceptions and buying behaviour. However, there is considerable disagreement about the nature of this relationship, that is, about how personality influences behaviour. Although we know that people's personalities often are reflected in the clothes they wear, the cars they drive (or whether they use a bike or motorcycle instead of a car), and the restaurants they eat in, we have not been successful in predicting behaviour from particular personality traits. The reason is simple: Many things besides personality enter into the consumer buying-decision process.

The Self-Concept Your **self-concept**, or self-image, is the way you see yourself. At the same time, it is the picture you think others have of you. Social psychologists distinguish between (1) the **actual self-concept** (the way you really see yourself) and (2) the **ideal self-concept** (the way you want to be seen or would like to see yourself). To some extent, the self-concept theory is a reflection of other psychological and sociological dimensions already discussed. A person's self-concept is influenced, for instance, by innate and learned physiological and psychological needs. It is conditioned also by economic factors, demographic factors, and social-group influences.

Studies of purchases show that people generally prefer brands and products that are compatible with their self-concept. There are mixed reports concerning the degree of influence of the actual and ideal self-concepts on brand and product preferences. Some researchers contend that consumption preferences correspond to a person's actual self-concept. Others hold that the ideal self-concept is dominant in consumers' choices.

Perhaps there is no consensus here because in real life we often switch back and forth between our actual and our ideal self-concepts. A middle-aged man may buy some comfortable, but not fashionable, clothing to wear at home on a weekend, where he is reflecting his actual self-concept. Then later he buys some expensive, high-fashion exercise clothing, envisioning himself (ideal self-concept) as a young, active, upwardly mobile guy. This same fellow may drive a beat-up pickup truck for his weekend errands (actual self-concept). But he'll drive his new foreign sports car to work, where he wants to project a different (ideal) self-concept.[17]

The various self-concept frames of reference can be used to design marketing research projects as well as help to organize approaches to interviewing consumers and analyzing research results. The self- and/or ideal self-concept frames of reference can be used in advertisements as a before-and-after approach as well as by sales and service personnel in determining customer problems, needs, and aspirations.

Attitudes

A classic definition of **attitude** is: a learned predisposition to respond to an object or class of objects in a consistently favourable or unfavourable way.[18] In our model of the buying-decision process, attitudes play a major role in the evaluation of alternatives. Numerous studies have reported a relationship between consumers' attitudes and their buying behaviour regarding both types of products and services selected and brands chosen. Surely, then, it is in a marketer's best interest to understand how attitudes are formed, the functions they perform, and how they can be changed.

All attitudes have the following characteristics in common:

- Attitudes are learned. The information individuals acquire through their direct experiences with a product or an idea, indirect experiences (such as reading about a product in *Canadian Living* or on the Internet), and interactions with individuals in their social groups all contribute to the formation of attitudes. For example, the opinions expressed by a good friend about diet foods plus the consumer's favourable or unfavourable experience as a result of using diet foods will contribute to an attitude toward diet foods in general.
- Attitudes have an object. By definition, we can hold attitudes only toward something. The object can be general (professional sports) or specific (Toronto Blue Jays); it can be abstract (campus life) or concrete (the computer lab). In attempting to determine consumers' attitudes it is very important to define carefully the object of the attitude because a person might have a favourable attitude toward the general concept (exercise) but a negative attitude toward a specific dimension (jogging).
- Attitudes have direction and intensity. Our attitudes are either favourable or unfavourable toward the object. They cannot be neutral. In addition, they have a strength. For example, you may mildly like this textbook or you may like it very much (we hope!). This factor is important for marketers because strongly held attitudes are difficult to change.
- Finally, attitudes are arranged in structures that tend to be stable and generalizable. Once formed, attitudes usually endure, and the longer they are held, the more resistant to change they become. People also have a tendency to generalize attitudes. For instance, if a person is treated well by a sales person in a particular store, there is a tendency to form a favourable attitude toward the entire store.

A consumer's attitudes do not always predict purchase behaviour. A person may hold very favourable attitudes toward a product but not buy it because of some inhibiting factor. Typical inhibitors are not having enough money or discovering your preferred product or brand has been replaced by a new model or is out of stock when the purchase must be made. Under such circumstances, purchase behaviour may even contradict attitudes.

As the preceding discussion suggests, it is extremely difficult to change strongly held attitudes. Moderately held or weakly held attitudes are much more amenable to change. Marketers need to know what consumer attitudes are to many aspects of their products, services, personnel, and advertisements, as well as the strength of such attitudes. Only then can they determine the bases for either satisfaction or dissatisfaction and where their relationships with consumers are vulnerable. When a marketer is faced with strongly held negative or unfavourable attitudes, it has two options. The first is to try to change the attitude to be compatible with the product. The second is to change the product, or more likely its image, to match attitudes. Ordinarily it is much easier to change the product image than to change consumers' strongly held attitudes.

Nevertheless, in many situations, attitudes have been changed. Consider how negative attitudes have changed in favour of small cars or seat belts, how positive attitudes have changed about tobacco products, how yellow tennis balls or off-season vacations have been accepted.

Values and Lifestyles

One of the most valuable ways of looking at a market and its potential involves consideration of consumer **lifestyles and values**. Marketers now develop marketing programs based not only on how old their customers are or where they live, but also on how they spend their leisure time, what type of movies they like to watch, and what things they consider important in their lives. This is an integral part of the concept of market segmentation, which we discussed in Chapters 4 and 5. Essentially, the Canadian market is made up of many types of people. Once we can identify how these various groups think and live, we can do a better job of developing products, services, advertising, and other marketing techniques to appeal to them.

The field of psychographic research was developed in the 1960s and initially examined consumer activities, interests, and opinions. Further developments of this approach have been the use of a program known as VALS (Values, Attitudes, and Lifestyle), which was developed at the Stanford Research Institute and is discussed in Chapter 5. VALS research involved the study of thousands of consumers and measures their opinions, interests, attitudes, values, beliefs, and activities in a variety of different areas. Today, psychographic research is considered by many in marketing to have transcended the demographic categories of age, gender, religion, social class, and ethnicity. Michael Adams, president of Environics Research Ltd., has produced the social-value "tribes" of Canada (see the accompanying box), which presents the three major generational divisions that exist in Canada: the elders, the boomers, and the GenXers. Everyone in the country fits into one of these three on the basis of age alone. Each of these generational groups is further subdivided pyschographically, resulting in thumbnail sketches for the twelve social value tribes of Canada. Each sketch provides a quick review of the group size, age distribution, geographic location, common motivation factors, social values, catchphrases, and, finally, heroes or icons. Locate yourself, your parents, friends, employers, or potential employers in these groups. The social-value tribes classification provides marketers with a quick, comprehensive, and integrated multivariate view of the basic segmentation of the country. This kind of information signals who is interested in what kinds of products and services, their location, their preferred information themes, their orientations to product claims, and the kinds of information contexts they would likely attend.

The Social-Value "Tribes" of Canada

In the book *Sex in the Snow*, author and pollster Michael Adams proposes that Canadians can be segmented into one of twelve social-value tribes. Initially, Adams divides the Canadian population into three sections: Elders, Boomers, and GenXers. Each of these three categories can be further divided by distinguishing the fundamental motivators, key values, words of advice, and icons of each of the twelve groups. Take a look at the categories below to determine where you fall in Michael Adams's social tribes!

The Elders (aged 50+)

Rational Traditionalists
(54% of Elders: 3.5 million Canadians)
Financial independence, stability, and security are the fundamental motivators of this population group.

Some of their key values include primacy of reason, deferred gratification, duty, and guilt. A rational traditionalist could be heard saying "Better safe than sorry," "A woman's place is in the home," or "A bird in the hand is worth two in the bush." These Canadians would idolize individuals such as Sir Winston Churchill, Ward Cleaver, and Franklin D. Roosevelt.

Extroverted Traditionalists
(26% of Elders: 1.7 million Canadians)
This category includes a higher than average proportion of women and individuals from the Maritimes and Quebec. Their fundamental motivators include social status, institutions, and traditional communities. Religion, family, fear, and respect for tradition and institutions are highly valued, and words of wisdom would include epitaphs such as "Duty above all else," "A woman's work is never done," and "A penny saved is a penny earned." Icons of the Extroverted Traditionalists would include Mother Teresa and Jesus Christ.

Cosmopolitan Modernists
(20% of Elders: 1.4 million Canadians)
The category of Cosmopolitan Modernists includes a higher than average proportion of individuals who are from British Columbia, are over fifty, and possess postsecondary education. Traditional institutions and experience seeking are the fundamental motivators of this group, and they place high value on things such as education, innovation, and a global perspective. Cosmopolitan Modernists believe that people should "take time to smell the roses" and that "the world is their oyster." Icons of this group include Pierre Berton and Pierre Trudeau.

The Boomers (aged 30–49)

Autonomous Rebels
(25% of Boomers: 2.5 million Canadians)
This category of the boomers have fundamental motivators that include personal autonomy and self-fulfilment. They place a high value on freedom and individuality and are sceptical about traditional institutions. Words of advice from an individual in the autonomous rebel category could be: "To each his own," "Knowledge is power," or "I did it my way." Icons include Bill and Hillary Clinton, John Lennon, and Scully and Mulder from *The X-Files*.

Anxious Communicators
(20% of Boomers: 2.1 million Canadians)
Traditional communities, institutions, and social status are considered the fundamental motivators of this social tribe. They value family, community, respect, and fear. The anxious communicators believe that "wisdom comes with age" and "the children are our future." The icons of this category would include individuals such as Oprah Winfrey, Martha Stewart, and Ann Landers.

Disengaged Darwinists
(41% of Boomers: 4.3 million Canadians)
This is the largest group within the Boomers category. It includes a higher proportion of men and blue-collar workers who are motivated by financial independence, stability, and security. Key values of the Disengaged Darwinists are fear and nostalgia for the past. Advice from this group would include "Look out for number one" and "Every man for himself." Icons include Chuck Norris and David Frum.

GenXers (aged 15–29)

Aimless Dependents
(27% of GenXers: 1.9 million Canadians)
This section of GenXers crave the financial independence, security, and stability that their parents, members of the boomers, possessed. Their key values include a desire for independence and fear. Words of wisdom from this group would include: "What's the point," "I couldn't care less," and "What's the system going to do for me?" The icons for this group include Eric Lindros, Courtney Love, and the Smashing Pumpkins.

Thrill-Seeking Materialists
(25% of GenXers: 1.7 million Canadians)
The fundamental motivators of Thrill-Seeking Materialists include traditional communities, social status, and experience seeking. Their key values include the desire for money, material possessions, respect, and admiration. Words of advice from this group would be "Live dangerously" and "Money is power." Icons of the Thrill-Seeking Materialists are Pamela Anderson Lee and Calvin Klein.

New Aquarians
(13% of GenXers: 900,000 Canadians)
This group is characterized by their desire for new experiences and new communities. They believe in hedonism, ecologism, and egalitarianism. Advice from the New Aquarians could include "There is no being, only becoming" and "Unity is diversity." Their icons include Tori Amos, Sarah McLachlan, and William Gibson.

Autonomous Post-Materialists
(20% of GenXers: 1.4 million Canadians)
The fundamental motivators of this group of GenXers are personal autonomy and self-fulfilment, and their key values include freedom and respect for human rights. In the mind of an Autonomous Post-Materialist, words to live by would include "It's my life," "Image is nothing," and "There is more to life than money." Icons of this group include Dennis Rodman, Bart Simpson, and Ashley MacIsaac.

Social Hedonists
(15% of GenXers: 900,000 Canadians)
This group of GenXers seeks new experiences and new communications. They value immediate gratification, sexual permissiveness, and hedonism. They advise people, "Party hard," "If you look good you feel good," and "Don't worry, be happy." The icons of this group include Janet Jackson and Chris Shepard.

Source: Adapted from Michael Adams, "The Demise of Demography," *The Globe and Mail*, January 18, 1997, p. D5, and based on *Sex in the Snow: Canadian Social Values at the End of the Millennium* (Toronto: Penguin Canada, 1997).

SITUATIONAL INFLUENCES

After all is said and done, the situations in which we find ourselves play a large part in determining how we actually behave. Students, for example, act differently in a classroom than they do in their favorite coffee shop. The same holds true of buying behaviour. You might get your hair cut because of an upcoming job interview. On vacation you might buy a souvenir that seems very strange when you get home. For a close friend's wedding gift, you might buy a fancier brand of small appliance than you would buy for yourself. These are all examples of **situational influences**, temporary forces associated with the immediate purchase environment that affect behaviour. Situational influence tends to be less significant when the consumer is very loyal to a brand and when the consumer is highly involved in the purchase. However, it often plays a major role in buying decisions. The five categories of situational influences are explained next.

When Consumers Buy — The Time Dimension

Marketers should be able to answer at least two time-related questions about consumer buying: Is it influenced by the season, week, day, or hour? What impact do past and present events have on the purchase decision?

The time dimension of buying has implications for promotion scheduling. Promotional messages must reach consumers when they are in a decision-making frame of mind. Marketers also adjust prices in an attempt to even out demand. For instance, supermarkets may offer double coupons on Wednesdays, usually a slow business day. If seasonal buying patterns exist, marketers can sometimes extend the buying season. There is obviously little opportunity to extend the buying season for Easter bunnies or Christmas ornaments, although some "Christmas" stores operate year round. But the season for vacations has been shifted to such an extent that winter and other "off-season" or "shoulder-season" vacations are now quite popular.

The second question concerns the impact of past or future events. For example, the length of time since you last went out to dinner at a nice restaurant may influence a decision on where to go tonight. Or the significance of an upcoming event, such as a vacation trip to a resort area, could result in a greater than normal amount of clothing purchases. Marketers need to know enough about the targeted consumers to anticipate the effects of these past and future events.

Dual-income baby boomers are finding it difficult to make time in their busy schedules to prepare meals at home, yet they can afford to take the family out to eat at a restaurant that offers something more in terms of quality than do the mainstream fast-food outlets such as McDonald's, Burger King, and Harvey's. Rather than standing in long lines for burgers and fries, these families are heading for restaurants that offer a wider menu selection, table service, and a family atmosphere. As a result, there is currently considerable growth in the sector of the restaurant business labelled family restaurants, which include Swiss Chalet, White Spot, and Golden Griddle, and in the slightly more pricey casual-dining sector, where we find East Side Mario's, Jack Astor's, and such regional chains as Milestone's.[19]

The growth and popularity of fast-food restaurants, quick-oil-change outlets, and catalogue retailers are marketers' responses to consumers' time pressures. Dual-income households, job activity (including business trips and travel time to and from work), and mandatory leisure-time activities (such as car pooling children to social and sports events) leave little time for relaxed shopping. The results are measurable. In 1988 the average consumer spent 90 minutes on a mall shopping trip. The figure today is 68 minutes. To help consumers conserve time, marketers are making large and small changes. For example, some photoprocessing operations return the developed prints by mail to eliminate the customer's second trip to pick up the pictures.

Where Consumers Buy — The Physical and Social Surroundings

Physical surroundings are the features of a situation that are apparent to the senses, such as lighting, smells, weather, and sounds. Think of the importance of atmosphere in a restaurant or the sense of excitement and action created by the sights and sounds in a gambling casino. Music can be an important element in a store's strategy.

The social surroundings are the number, mix, and actions of other people at the purchase site. You probably would not go into a strange restaurant that has an empty parking lot. And in a crowded store with other customers waiting, you will probably ask the clerk fewer questions and spend less time comparing products.

How Consumers Buy — The Terms and Conditions of the Purchase

How consumers buy refers to the terms and conditions of sale as well as the transaction-related activities that buyers are willing to perform. Many more retailers sell on credit today than just a few years ago. Not only do consumers use credit for instalment purchases (to buy things today with future income), but many now use credit for convenience. The ability to use Visa or MasterCard to make a wide variety of purchases while not carrying cash is an attractive option to many consumers. Another recent development is the increase in purchases made by mail and phone. The growth of catalogue distribution and telephone shopping services has enabled consumers to buy everything from jewellery to food without setting foot in a store. This trend is developing further with the use of the Internet. Many firms now make products and services available through this network. Maple Square, Sympatico's Canadian Internet directory, for example, offers a listing of hundreds of companies in all areas ranging from private investigative services to accounting services to kitchen appliances.[20] Finally, the trend toward one-stop shopping has encouraged retailers to add even unrelated items to their basic mix of products. Consider, for example, the wide variety of goods found in what we call a drugstore.

Marketers have also experimented with transferring functions or activities to consumers. What were once called "service stations" are now called "gas stations" because you pump your own gas and wash your own windshield. Consumers have shown a willingness to assemble products, bag their own groceries, and buy in case quantities — all in exchange for lower prices. Banks have succeeded in getting customers to complete many of their own transactions through ATMs and telephone and PC banking.

Why Consumers Buy — The Objective of the Purchase

The intent of or reason for a purchase affects the choices made. We are likely to behave very differently if we are buying a product for a gift rather than buying the same product for our personal use. When purchasing a wristwatch, a consumer may be most interested in one that will provide accurate time at a reasonable price. However, the appearance of a watch bought as a graduation present can be very important. Occasions often represent reasons why consumers make purchases and can influence the type of purchase made. Commemorating wedding anniversaries, for example, can be the objective for jewellery purchases and dinner arrangements.

A marketer must understand the consumer's objective in buying the product or service in order to design an effective marketing mix. For example, the failure of most watchmakers to appeal to the functional, nongift watch market is what allowed Timex to be so successful with its reasonably priced product.

Conditions Under Which Consumers Buy — States and Moods

Sometimes consumers are in a temporary state that influences their buying decisions. When you are ill or rushed, you may be unwilling to wait in line or to take the time or care that a particular purchase deserves. Moods can also influence purchases. Feelings such as anger or excitement can result in purchases that otherwise would not have been made. In the exciting atmosphere of a rock concert, for example, you might pay more for a commemorative T-shirt than you would under normal circumstances. Sales people must be trained to recognize consumers' moods and adjust their presentations accordingly.

Marketers must also monitor long-term situational influences. The optimistic consumers of the 1980s were free-spending and apparently carefree. Household debt grew 50 percent faster than disposable income during the decade as the baby boom generation acquired cars, homes, and household possessions. However, the recession that rocked the economy at the end of the 1980s produced many changes. It created more conservative buyers who save more, avoid debt, and purchase more carefully. Though it is difficult to predict if changes such as these in consumer psychology are temporary or permanent, they have important implications for virtually all marketers.

When a particular situational influence becomes widely accepted and strongly embedded (such as shopping on particular days of the week), overcoming it can be difficult. The marketer may have to carry out an extensive campaign with no guarantee of success.

Summary

The buying behaviour of ultimate consumers can be examined using a five-part model: the buying-decision process, information, social and group forces, psychological forces, and situational factors.

The buying-decision process is composed of six stages consumers go through in making purchases. The stages are need recognition, choice of an involvement level, identification of alternatives, evaluation of alternatives, purchase and related decisions, and postpurchase behaviour.

Information fuels the buying-decision process. Without it, there would be no decisions. There are two categories of information sources: commercial and social. Commercial sources include advertising, personal selling, selling by phone or Internet, and personal involvement with a product. Word of mouth, observation, and experience with a product owned by someone else are social sources.

Social and group forces are composed of culture, subculture, social class, reference groups, family, and households. Culture has the broadest and most general influence on buying behaviour, while a person's household has the most immediate impact. Social and group forces have a direct impact on individual purchase decisions as well as a person's psychological makeup.

Psychological forces that affect buying decisions are motivation, perception, learning, personality, and attitudes. All behaviour is motivated by some aroused need. Perception is the way we interpret the world around us and is subject to three types of selectivity: attention, distortion, and retention. Learning is a change in behaviour as a result of experience. Continued reinforcement leads to habitual buying and brand loyalty.

Personality is the sum of an individual's traits that influence behavioural responses. Personality patterns predispose consumers to certain types of information, product features, and interactions. The self-concept is related to personality. Because purchasing and consumption are very expressive actions, they communicate to the world our actual and ideal self-concepts.

Attitudes are learned predispositions to respond to an object or class of objects in a consistent fashion. Besides being learned, all attitudes are directed toward an object, have direction and intensity, and tend to be stable and generalizable. Strongly held attitudes are difficult to change.

Situational influences deal with when, where, how, and why consumers buy, and with the consumer's personal condition at the time of purchase. Situational influences are often so powerful that they can override all of the other forces in the buying-decision process.

Key Terms and Concepts

Buying-decision process (126)
Need recognition (126)
High involvement (128)
Low involvement (128)
Impulse buying (128)
Patronage buying motives (130)
Postpurchase behaviour (131)
Cognitive dissonance (131)
Commercial information (134)
Social information (134)
Culture (134)
Subculture (135)
Social class (137)
Upper class (138)
Upper-middle class (138)
Lower-middle class (138)
Upper-lower class (138)
Lower-lower class (138)
Reference groups (139)
Innovator (139)
Opinion leader (139)
Family and household (139)
Psychographics (140)
Motive (140)
Maslow's hierarchy of needs (141)
Perception (142)
Selective attention (142)
Selective distortion (142)
Selective retention (142)
Learning (143)
Stimulus-response theory (143)
Personality (143)
Self-concept (143)
Actual self-concept (143)
Ideal self-concept (143)
Attitude (144)
Lifestyles and values (145)
Situational influence (147)

Questions and Problems

1. When might the purchase of a colour television be a low-involvement decision?
2. When a consumer's experience with a product equals her or his expectations for the product, the person is satisfied. Is there any disadvantage to a marketer whose product causes consumers' experience to greatly exceed expectations?
3. From a consumer-behaviour perspective, why is it incorrect to view the European Union or the countries of Asia as single markets?
4. Explain why reference-group influence would affect the choice of the product, the brand, or neither for the following items:
   a. Bath soap.
   b. Auto tune-up.
   c. Haircut.
   d. Laptop computer.
5. What roles would you expect a couple and their young child to play in the purchase of the following items?
   a. Nintendo.
   b. Choice of a fast-food outlet for dinner.
   c. Personal computer.
   d. Lawn-care service.
6. Explain how self-concept might come into play in the purchase of the following products:
   a. Eyeglasses.
   b. New suit.
   c. Eye-shadow.
   d. College education.
7. What situational influences might affect a family's choice of a motel in a strange town while on a vacation?

Hands-On Marketing

1. Interview the manager of a store that sells big-ticket items (furniture, appliances, electronic equipment) about what methods, if any, the store uses to reinforce purchase decisions and reduce the cognitive dissonance of its customers. What additional methods can you suggest?

2. Have a friend describe a high-involvement purchase that he or she recently made. Show how each of the six stages described in this chapter are reflected in the description. Identify the primary social influences that played a part in the decision.

CHAPTER 7 GOALS

In many ways business markets are similar to the consumer markets we have been examining, but there are also important differences. After studying this chapter, in addition to being able to describe how business markets differ from consumer markets, you should have an understanding of:

- The nature and scope of the business market.
- The components of the business market.
- The characteristics of business market demand.
- The determinants of business market demand.
- The buying motives, buying processes, and buying patterns in business markets.

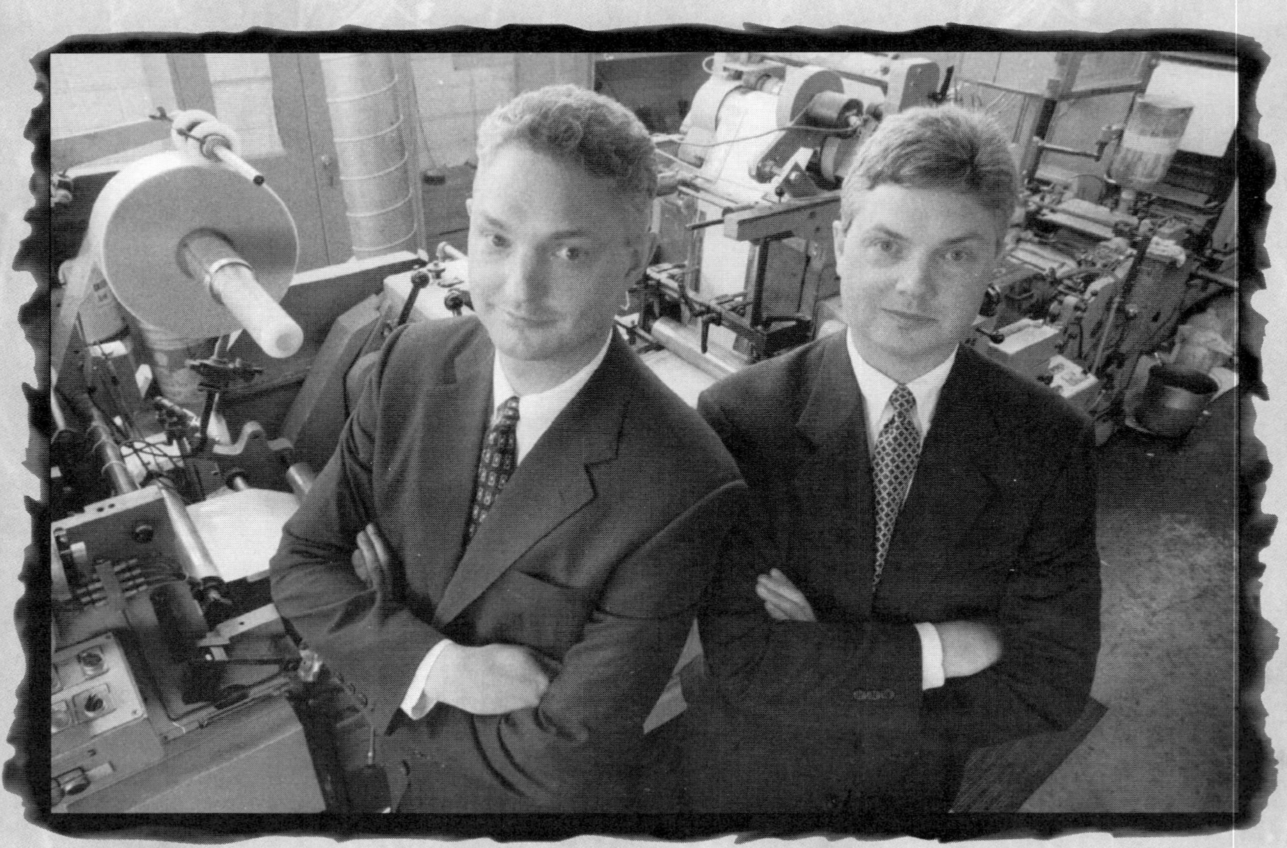

Chapter Seven

The Business Market

www.supremex.com

DAVID CANADA vs. GOLIATH AMERICA: AND THE WINNER IS... THE BUSINESS MARKET!

The last few years have seen lots of high-profile mergers, acquisitions, new market entries, and invasions of Canadian markets by U.S. firms. So how does a medium-sized Canadian family company operating in a mature business market deal with the entrance of a very big U.S. competitor? Easy — just like many other Davids battling their Goliaths, whether they are American or Canadian, one of the best ways for the smaller business to survive is to carve out a market niche at the top of the particular market, emphasize service, and make sure the quality of the business-to-business relationship is solid and sustainable.

The names of the firms involved here are not well known: giant Supremex Inc. is the Montreal-based subsidiary of U.S.-based Mail-Well Inc.; National Paper Goods is a family company operating from Hamilton, Ontario, since 1904. Both are manufacturers competing in the Canadian envelope market. Supremex produces and markets its products to the business market using its own name and those of the firms it has acquired under such brand names as Innova, Supreme Envelope, Unique, and PNG Global. David Bennett, National Paper's director of sales, thinks that many business customers believe they are either dealing with different firms or getting bids from different suppliers when they are actually dealing with different units of the same company.

Brothers Chip and Lindsay Holton see the Supremex approach to the market as offering them an opportunity: "We have to stress where we can differentiate ourselves. We have to be better than they are." To differentiate, National Paper has gone up-market from its high-volume competitors by targeting three segments of the market, each sensitive to value-added products and customer service: (1) large-scale users of envelopes, such as the billing centres of credit card companies; (2) direct-mail organizations, who are trying to get customer attention with distinctively designed envelopes; and (3) users of special packaging envelopes, such as photography shops. National has improved its plant technology and its staff training.

When dealing with potential customers, National is able to make the point that if a buyer does not want to place all its business with one supplier, or believes it is getting different bids from competing firms, the buyer should know which brands belong to the same owner. If National can start by becoming a second supplier, it believes that superior performance and service will allow it to become a number one supplier.

National has been able to increase its production by 35 percent in the past two years and its market share to about 10–12 percent. Can David hold on to his niche? The competition is fierce.[1]

THE NATURE AND SCOPE OF THE BUSINESS MARKET

The **business market** consists of all **business users** — organizations that buy goods and services for one of the following purposes:

- *To make other goods and services.* Campbell's buys fresh vegetables to make soup, and Bombardier buys a variety of metal products to make Ski-Doos as well as regional jets.
- *To resell to other business users or to consumers.* Loblaws buys canned tuna fish to sell to consumers, and Western Pipe Supply Company buys lawn sprinkler equipment and supplies from manufacturers and resells them to sprinkler contractors.
- *To conduct the organization's operations.* The University of Calgary buys office supplies and electronic office equipment for use in the registrar's office, and Winnipeg's St. Boniface General Hospital buys supplies to use in its operating rooms.

In the business market we deal with both consumer products and business products. **Business marketing**, then, is the marketing of goods and services to business users, in constrast to ultimate consumers.

Because the business market is largely unknown to the average consumer, we are apt to underrate its significance. It is huge when measured by total sales volume and the number of firms involved. About 50 percent of all manufactured products are sold to the business market. In addition, about 80 percent of all farm products and virtually all mineral, forest, and sea products are business goods. These are sold to firms for further processing.

The magnitude and complexity of the business market are also evident from the many transactions required to produce and market a product. Consider, for example, the business marketing transactions and total sales volume involved in getting leather workboots to their end users. First, cattle are sold through one or two intermediaries before reaching a meatpacker. Then the hides are sold to a tanner, who in turn sells the leather to a shoe manufacturer. The shoe manufacturer may sell the finished boots to a wholesaler, who markets them to retail stores, or to factories that supply footware to their workers. Each sale is a business marketing transaction.

In addition, the shoe manufacturer buys metal eyelets, laces, thread, glue, steel safety toe plates, heels and soles, and shoe polish. Consider something as simple as the shoelaces. Other industrial firms must first buy the raw cotton and then spin, weave, dye, and cut it so that it becomes shoestring material. All the manufacturers involved have factories and offices with furniture, machinery, furnaces, lights, and maintenance equipment and supplies required to run them — and these also are business goods that have to be produced and marketed. In short, thousands of business products and business marketing activities come into play before almost any product — consumer good or business good — reaches its final destination.

The magnitude and complexity of the business market loom even larger when we consider all the business services involved throughout our workboot example. Each firm engaged in any stage of the production process probably uses outside accountants, computer systems designers, and law firms. Several of the producers may use advertising agencies. All the companies will use the services of various financial institutions.

Every retail store and wholesaling establishment is a business user. Every bus company, airline, and railway is part of this market. So is every hotel, restaurant, bank, insurance company, hospital, theatre, and school. In all, there are close to half a million business users in Canada. While this is far short of the approximately thirty million consumers, the total sales volume in the business market far surpasses total sales to consumers. This difference is due to the very many business marketing transactions that take place before a product is sold to a single ultimate user.

COMPONENTS OF THE BUSINESS MARKET

Traditionally, business markets were referred to as industrial markets. This caused many people to think that the term referred only to approximately forty thousand Canadian manufacturing firms. But as you can see from what we just explained, the business market is a lot more than that. Certainly manufacturers constitute a major portion of the business market, but there are also six other components: agriculture, resellers, government agencies, service companies, and not-for-profit organizations. Although they are often underrated or overlooked because of the heavy attention devoted to manufacturing, each is a significant part of the business market. Keep in mind that some of Canada's most important business markets are outside Canada — in the United States and many other countries.

The Agriculture Market

The worldwide income from the sale of Canadian agricultural products gives farmers, as a group, the purchasing power that makes them a highly attractive market. Moreover, world population forecasts and food shortages in many countries undoubtedly will keep pressure on farmers to increase their output. Companies hoping to sell to the farm market must analyze it carefully and be aware of significant trends. For example, both the proportion of farmers in the total population and the number of farms have been decreasing and probably will continue to decline. Counterbalancing this has been an increase in large corporate or "business" types of farms. Even the remaining "family farms" are expanding in order to survive. Farming is becoming more automated and mechanized. This means, of course, that capital investment in farming is increasing. **Agribusiness** — farming, food processing, and other large-scale farming-related businesses — is big business in every sense of the word.

Agriculture is a modern industry. Like other business executives, farmers are looking for better ways to increase their productivity, cut their expenses, and manage their cash flows. Technology is an important part of the process. For example, one large business farmer has developed a sensor and remote steering system that guides a tractor between the rows in a field to avoid destroying any crops. And, as farmers become fewer and larger, marketing to them effectively requires carefully designed strategies. For example, some large fertilizer producers have sales people who visit individual farms. There, working with the farmer, the sales rep analyzes the soil and crops to determine exactly what fertilizer mix is best for the particular farm. Based on the analysis, the manufacturer prepares the appropriate blend of ingredients as a special order.

The Reseller Market

Intermediaries in the Canadian marketing system — approximately half a million wholesalers, retailers, and other organizations — constitute the **reseller market**. The basic activity of resellers — unlike that of any other business market segment — is buying products from supplier organizations and reselling these items in essentially the same form to the resellers' customers. In economic terms, resellers create time, place, and possession utilities, rather than form utility.

Resellers also buy many goods and services for use in operating their businesses — items such as office supplies and information and communication equipment, warehouses, materials-handling equipment, legal services, computer-system design services, electrical services, and janitorial supplies. In these buying activities, resellers are essentially no different from manufacturers, financial institutions, or any other segment of the business market.

www.debbs.ndhq.dnd.ca
www.spar.ca
www.gov.nb.ca/supply

It is their role as buyers for resale that differentiates resellers and attracts special marketing attention from their suppliers. To resell an item, you must please your customer. Usually it is more difficult to determine what will please an outside customer than to find out what will satisfy someone within your own organization. For example, an airline that decides to redesign the uniforms of its flight crews can carefully study the conditions under which the uniforms will be worn and work closely with the people who will be wearing the uniforms to get their views. As a result, the airline should be able to select a design that will be both functional and acceptable. Contrast that with a retailer trying to anticipate what clothing fashions will be popular next spring. In both cases, clothing is being purchased, but the opportunity for interaction with the users and the greater interest by those likely to be affected by the purchase make buying for internal use less difficult and less risky than buying for resale.

Buying for resale, especially in a large reseller's organization, can be a complex procedure. For a supermarket chain such as Sobey's, Loblaw's, or Safeway, buying is frequently done by a buying committee made up of experts on market demand, trends, supply, and prices. Department stores may retain resident buyers — independent buying agencies — located in Toronto, London, Hong Kong, or other major market centres to be in constant touch with the latest fashion developments.

The Government Market

The large government market includes federal, provincial and municipal governments, as well as various Crown agencies and corporations that spend millions of dollars worth each year buying for institutions such as schools, offices, hospitals, and military bases. At the federal level, Public Works and Government Services Canada purchases billions of dollars' worth of goods and services annually for other government units. Provincial and local governments taken together are more important markets than the federal government.

Government procurement processes are different from those in the private sector of the business market. A unique feature of government buying is the competitive bidding system. Much government procurement is done on a bid basis. That is, the government agency advertises for bids using a format that states specifications for the intended purchase. Then it must accept the lowest bid that meets these specifications.

In other buying situations, the government may negotiate a purchase contract with an individual supplier. This marketing practice might be used, for instance, when the Department of National Defence wants someone to develop and build a new aircraft tracking system and there are no comparable products on which to base bidding specifications.

A glance at an issue of the *Weekly Bulletin of Business Opportunities*, a government publication that lists business opportunities with the government, provides some idea of the size of this market. The potential is sufficiently attractive that some firms concentrate almost exclusively on government markets.

Despite the opportunities, many companies make no effort to sell to the government, because they are intimidated by the red tape. There is no question that dealing with the government to any significant extent usually requires specialized marketing techniques and information. Some firms, such as Spar Aerospace and Bombardier, have established special departments to deal with government markets. Also, information and guidelines are available from Supply and Services Canada on the proper procedures for doing business with the government.

The Services Market

Currently, firms that produce services greatly outnumber firms that produce goods. That is, there are more service firms than the total of all manufacturers, mining companies, construction firms, and enterprises engaged in farming, forestry, and fishing. The **services market** includes all transportation carriers and public utilities, communications firms, and the many financial, insurance, legal, and real estate firms. This market also includes organizations that produce and sell such diverse services as rental housing, recreation and entertainment, repairs, health care, personal care, and business services.

Service firms constitute a huge market that buys goods and other services. Four Seasons Hotels, for

www.sobeysweb.com • www.safeway.com • http://w3.pwgsc.gc.ca

example, buy blankets and sheets from textile manufacturers. Hospitals in Canada and abroad buy supplies from Baxter Healthcare. These and other service firms buy legal, advertising, accounting, information systems, and consulting advice from other service marketers. The importance to Canadian marketers of the services market is dealt with in greater detail in Chapter 12.

The "Nonbusiness" Business Market

In recent years, we have been giving some long-overdue marketing attention to the multi-million-dollar market made up of so-called nonbusiness or not-for-profit organizations. The **nonbusiness market** includes such diverse institutions as churches, colleges and universities, museums, hospitals and other health institutions, political parties, labour unions, and charitable organizations. Actually, each of these so-called nonbusiness organizations is a business organization. However, our society (and the institutions themselves) in the past did not perceive a museum or a hospital as being a business. Many people today still feel uncomfortable thinking of their church, school, or political party as a business organization. Nevertheless, these organizations do virtually all the things that businesses do — offer a product or service, collect money, make investments, hire employees — and therefore require professional management.

Not-for-profit organizations also conduct marketing campaigns — albeit under a different name — in an effort to attract millions of dollars in contributions. In turn, they spend millions of dollars buying goods and services to run their operations.

The International Market

Since Canada exports over $180 billion or 25 percent of its gross domestic product, and since a major portion of this export trade is conducted on a business-to-business basis, the international market is an important business market. Although international marketing is discussed in greater detail in Chapter 21, we wish to underscore here that marketing to businesses based abroad, whether in the United States, Japan, the United Kingdom, or the Gulf states, requires even more work on developing relationships than one would expect. This is the case because, whether one is dealing with a foreign subsidiary of a Canadian firm or with foreign firms, the cross-cultural dynamics of negotiation and relationship building cannot be taken for granted. Canadian marketers doing business abroad must become familiar with the values, customs, symbols, and standard practices and expectations of their foreign-based buyers, who include the individuals with whom one must negotiate as well as the firms that they represent. "Marketing at Work" File 7-1 provides a sample of what marketers doing business abroad can expect.

CHARACTERISTICS OF BUSINESS MARKET DEMAND

Four demand characteristics differentiate the business market from the consumer market: Demand is derived, demand tends to be inelastic, demand is widely fluctuating, and the market is well informed.

Demand Is Derived

The demand for a business product is derived from the demand for the consumer products in which that business product is used. Thus the demand for steel depends partially on consumer demand for automobiles and refrigerators, but it also depends on the demand for butter, hockey pads and equipment, and CD players. This is because the tools, machines, and other equipment needed to make these items are made of steel. Consequently, as the demand for hockey equipment increases, Bauer Sporting Goods may buy more steel sewing machines or filing cabinets.

There are two significant marketing implications of the fact that business market demand is a derived demand. First, to estimate the demand for a product, a business marketer must be very familiar with how it is used. This is fairly easy for a company like Pratt & Whitney, a maker of jet engines. But what about the manufacturer of rubber O-rings (doughnut-shaped rings of all sizes that are used to seal connections)? Considerable research may be necessary to identify uses and users.

MARKETING AT WORK FILE 7-1

NEGOTIATING INTERNATIONALLY IN BUSINESS MARKETS

In doing business around the world, executives have found that economic and political environments are major factors in determining success or failure. But what have they learned about the styles of their international business counterparts? Consider these tips on what marketers going abroad can expect:

- In Germany, executives are thorough, systematic, well prepared, and quite rigid. They tend to be assertive, even intimidating, and not very willing to compromise. They are punctual and prize efficiency and directness.
- In France, managers may insist that negotiations be conducted in French. Because they consider speaking to be an art, the French dislike being interrupted. Lengthy lunches with lots of wine are more likely to affect the negotiating skills of Americans than French executives, who are more used to such meals.
- In England, the style is friendly and easygoing. Executives are more likely to be underprepared than overprepared. They are flexible and open to initiatives. However, their kindly posture can be misleading, and they can become very stubborn if they sense a lack of respect.
- In Mexico, personal relationships are very important, so face-to-face contact is a must. Unlike in Canada, the rule is to socialize first and work later. Mexicans are very ego-involved in business decisions, so concessions that make the decision-maker look good are important. They are quite flexible when it comes to trade-offs, but it is often best to negotiate with them in private, one-on-one conversations rather than in front of others.
- In China, small courtesies and follow-up gifts are important in establishing friendship. Being meticulous in preparation and consistent in presentations is crucial, because the Chinese are very thorough. Decision-making cannot be rushed, so business deals often take a long time.
- In Japan, executives often consider the long-term relationship with a business contact to be as important as the immediate negotiations, so negotiators should keep the future as well as the present in mind. Because decisions often involve more people and more levels of management than in Canada, meetings tend to be large. The Japanese avoid saying no directly. As a result, any answer other than a definite yes may, in fact, be a no. If circumstances change after an agreement is reached, the Japanese assume the right to renegotiate.
- In Russia, the tone of negotiations will be very bureaucratic and the red tape will be extensive. Decision-makers must be prepared for many delays. It is likely that managers will be unfamiliar with many free-market concepts and will require detailed explanations of costs and pricing strategies. The price of a mistake is very large, so a manager's job or even career may be at stake in the negotiations.

Source: Sergy Frank, "Global Negotiating: Vive Les Differences!" *Sales & Marketing Management*, May 1992, pp. 65–69. Reprinted with permission of *Sales & Marketing Management*.

Second, the producer of a business product may engage in marketing efforts to encourage the sale of its buyers' products. For example, Intel advertises to consumers, urging them when buying computers to ask specifically for products made with an Intel processor. Similarly, the NutraSweet Company ran a consumer advertising campaign designed to build consumer loyalty for products sweetened with NutraSweet. The idea, of course, is that increases in consumer demand will, in turn, trigger increases in derived demand for these business products.

www.nutrasweet.com

Demand Is Inelastic

Another characteristic of the business market is demand elasticity of business products. Elasticity of demand refers to how responsive demand is to a change in the price of a product. (To review some economics, demand elasticity is explained early in Chapter 13.)

The demand for many business products is relatively inelastic, which means that the demand for a product responds very little to changes in its price. If the price of buttons for men's jackets should suddenly rise or fall considerably, how much effect would it have on the price of jackets? Because the buttons are such a small part of the jacket, the price increase would not likely change the price of jackets. As a result, demand for jackets would remain the same, so there would be no appreciable change in the demand for buttons either.

The demand for business products is inelastic because ordinarily the cost of a single part or material is a small portion of the total cost of the finished product. The cost of the chemicals in paint is a small part of the price a consumer pays for paint. The cost of the enamel on a refrigerator is a small part of its retail price. Even the cost of expensive capital equipment, such as a robot used in assembling automobiles, when spread over the thousands of units it helps produce, becomes a very small part of the final price of each one. As a result, when the price of the business product changes, there is very little change in the price of the related consumer products. Since there is no appreciable shift in the demand for the consumer goods, then — by virtue of the derived-demand feature — there is no change in the demand for the business product.

From a marketing point of view, there are three factors that can moderate inelasticity of business demand.

- Price changes must occur throughout an entire industry, not in a single firm. An industry-wide cut in the price of steel belts used in tires will have little effect on the price of tires and therefore little effect on the demand for automobile tires. Consequently, it will cause little shift in the total demand for steel belts. The pricing policy of an individual firm, however, can substantially alter the demand for its products. If one supplier cuts the price of its steel belts significantly, the drop in price may draw a great deal of business away from competitors. Thus, in the short run, the demand curve faced by a single firm may be quite elastic. However, any advantage will likely be temporary, because competitors will almost certainly retaliate in some way to recapture their lost business.
- The second marketing factor that can affect the inelasticity of demand is time. Much of our discussion here applies to short-term situations. Over the long run, the demand for a given industrial product is more elastic. If the price of cloth for women's suits rises, there probably will be no immediate change in the price of the finished garment. However, the increase in the cost of materials could very well be reflected in a rise in suit prices for next year. This rise could then influence the demand for suits, and thus for cloth, a year or more hence.
- The third factor is the relative importance of a specific business product in the cost of the finished good. We may generalize to this extent:

The greater the cost of a business product as a percentage of the total price of the finished good, the greater the elasticity of demand for this business product.

Demand Is Widely Fluctuating

Although the demand for business goods does not change much in response to price changes, it does respond to other factors. In fact, market demand for most classes of business goods fluctuates considerably more than the demand for consumer products. The demand for installations — major plant equipment, factories, and so on — is especially subject to change. Substantial fluctuations also exist in the market for accessory equipment — office furniture and machinery, delivery trucks, and similar products. These tend to accentuate the swings in the demand for business raw materials and fabricating parts. We can see this very clearly when declines in demand in the construction and auto industries affect suppliers of lumber, steel, plastics and other materials and parts.

A major reason for these fluctuations is that individual businesses are very concerned about having a shortage of inventory when consumer demand increases or being caught with excess inventory if consumer demand declines. Thus they tend to overreact to signals from the economy, building inventories when they see signs of growth in the economy and working inventories down when the signs suggest a slowdown. When the actions of all the individual firms are combined, the effect on their suppliers is widely fluctuating demand. This is known as the acceleration principle. One exception to this generalization is found in agricultural products intended for processing. Because people have to eat, there is a reasonably consistent demand for animals intended for meat products, for fruits and vegetables that will be canned or frozen, and for grains and dairy products used in cereals and baked goods.

Fluctuations in the demand for business products can influence all aspects of a marketing program. In product planning, fluctuations in demand may stimulate a firm to diversify into other products to ease production and marketing problems. For example, IBM has moved from concentrating on large, mainframe computers to personal computers, software, microcomputer chips, and consulting. Distribution strategies may be affected. When demand declines, a manufacturer may discover that selling to some resellers is unprofitable, so they are dropped as customers. In its pricing, management may attempt to stem a decline in sales by cutting prices, hoping to attract customers away from competing firms.

Buyers Are Well Informed

Typically, business buyers are better informed about what they are buying than are ultimate consumers. They know more about the relative merits of alternative sources of supply and competitive products for three reasons. First, there are relatively few alternatives for a business buyer to consider. Consumers typically have many more brands and sellers from which to choose than do business buyers. Consider, for example, how many options you would have in purchasing a TV set. However, in most business situations a buyer has only a few firms that offer the particular combination of product features and service desired. Second, the responsibility of a buyer in an organization is ordinarily limited to a few products. Unlike a consumer who buys many different things, a purchasing agent's job is to be very knowledgeable about a narrowly defined set of products. Third, for most consumer purchases, an error is only a minor inconvenience. However, in business buying, the cost of a mistake may be thousands of dollars or even the decision-maker's job!

This need for a large amount of up-to-date information has significant marketing implications. Manufacturers and marketers of business products place a much greater emphasis on product information and personal contact to communicate than do firms that market consumer products. Business sales and service people must be carefully selected, properly trained, and adequately compensated. They must give informative and effective presentations and furnish satisfactory service to potential buyers both before and after a sale is made. Sales executives are devoting increased effort to the assignment of specialized sales people to key accounts to ensure that they are compatible with business buyers.

DETERMINANTS OF BUSINESS MARKET DEMAND

To analyze a consumer market, a marketer would study the distribution of population and various demographics such as income, and then try to determine the consumers' buying motives and habits. Essentially the same type of analysis can be used by a firm selling to the business market. The factors affecting the market for business products are the number of potential business users and their purchasing power, buying motives, and buying habits. In the following discussion we'll identify several basic differences between consumer markets and business markets.

Number and Types of Business Users

The business market contains relatively few buying units compared with the consumer market. There are approximately a half million business users, with about forty thousand of these being manufacturing establishments. In contrast, there are about thirty million consumers divided among more than nine million households. The business market will seem even more limited to most companies because they sell to only a segment of the total market. A firm selling to meat-processing plants, for example, would have about forty-five potential customer plants. If you

www.ibm.com

were interested in providing services to battery manufacturers, you would find about twenty-five companies as basic prospects. Consequently, marketing executives must try to pinpoint their market carefully by type of industry and geographic location. A firm marketing hard-rock mining equipment is not interested in the total business market, nor even in all firms engaged in mining and quarrying.

One very useful source of information is the current **Standard Industrial Classification (SIC)** system (see "Marketing at Work" File 7-2), which enables a company to identify relatively small segments of its business market. All types of businesses in Canada are divided into groups, as follows:

1. Agriculture.
2. Forestry.
3. Fishing and trapping.
4. Mines, quarries, and oil wells.
5. Manufacturing industries (twenty major groups).
6. Construction industry.
7. Transportation, communication, and other utilities.
8. Trade.
9. Finance, insurance, and real estate.
10. Community, business, and personal service industries (eight major groups).
11. Public administration and defence.
12. Industry unspecified or undefined.

A separate number is assigned to each major industry within each of the above groups; then, three- and four-digit classification numbers are used to subdivide each major category into finer segments. To illustrate, in division 5 (manufacturing), major group 4 (leather) contains:

SIC code	Industrial group
172	Leather tanneries
174	Shoe factories
175	Leather-glove factories
179	Luggage, handbag, and small-leather-goods manufacturers

Size of Business Users Although the market may be limited in the total number of buyers, it is large in purchasing power. As one might expect, business users range in size from very small companies with fewer than five employees to firms with staff numbering more than a thousand. A relatively small percentage of firms account for the greatest share of the value added by a given industry. For example, Statistics Canada data on the manufacturing sector in Canada indicate that slightly more than 1 percent of manufacturing firms — those with five hundred or more employees — account for approximately 40 percent of the total value added by manufacturing and for more than 30 percent of the total employment in manufacturing. The firms with fewer than fifty employees, while accounting for more than 80 percent of all manufacturing establishments, produce less than 15 percent of the value added by manufacturing.

The marketing significance in these facts is that buying power in the business market is highly concentrated in relatively few firms. This market concentration has considerable influence on a seller's policies regarding its channels of distribution. Intermediaries are not as essential as in the consumer market.

Regional Concentration of Business Users There is substantial regional concentration in many of the major industries and among business users as a whole. A firm selling products usable in oil fields will find the bulk of its market in Alberta, the Northwest Territories, offshore Newfoundland, and the United States and abroad. Rubber-products manufacturers are located mostly in Ontario, shoes are produced chiefly in Quebec, and most of the nation's garment manufacturers are located in southern Ontario and Quebec. There is a similar regional concentration in the farm market.

Although a large part of a firm's market may be concentrated in limited geographic areas, a good portion may lie outside these areas. Consequently, a distribution policy must be developed that will enable a firm to deal directly with the concentrated market and also to employ intermediaries (or a company sales force at great expense) to reach the outlying markets.

Vertical and Horizontal Business Markets For effective marketing planning, a company should know whether the market for its products is vertical or horizontal. If a firm's product is usable by virtually

MARKETING AT WORK FILE 7-2

STATISTICS CANADA WORLD-CLASS INFORMATION SOURCE

StatsCan is considered by U.N. agencies and many national data-gathering organizations as one of the few that are the world's best — reliable, valid, current, accessible, and user-oriented. It has become an aggressive supplier of information, analysis, and services to Canadian businesses. The agency earns about $35 million a year — $12 million of which comes from selling statistics that it already produces for the public good. The rest comes from conducting special surveys.

Although Statistics Canada is not the only government agency for whom selling information for profit has become a driving force, it is in the vanguard and as such is an inspiration to other federal departments looking to hawk their wares as well. Says Denis Desjardins, director-general of the agency's marketing and information services branch, "We, as public servants, have a culture that has always been to give stuff away. . . [Now] we've become more marketing-oriented."

The agency has done this by identifying its two distinct types of clients: the general public, who obtain statistical information from the media and public libraries; and specialists, such as private economists and academics, who require highly specialized information. It is to the latter that StatsCan has been directing marketing efforts that go beyond the mere publication of figures by providing analysis, explanation, and even custom-tailored information packages that the agency offers to private-sector clients — for a fee. Not only have such initiatives proved financially profitable, but they have done much to bolster StatsCan's public image as a cutting-edge "information consultant."

In 1997, Statistics Canada, with its U.S. and Mexican counterparts, announced the creation of a new North American industry classification system (NAICS) which is to be in effect by the year 2000, if not sooner. The new system provides new common standards for the collection of economic and financial data. In Canada, the new NAICS, which groups economic activity into 20 sectors and 920 industries, will replace the existing standard industrial classification system (SIC) with its 18 sectors and 860 industries.

The sixty new industries, mainly service-producing ones, will provide details previously hidden in general categories. The biggest changes reflect:

- A new information sector covering software publishing, database and directory publishing, satellite telecommunications, on-line information services, and paging, cellular, and other wireless communications.
- A new arts, entertainment, and recreation sector with industries such as performing arts companies, arts and sports promoters, agents and managers for athletes and entertainers, and gambling.
- Professional, scientific, and technical services cover traditional providers such as lawyers, engineers, architects, interior designers, and advertising agencies, and now include custom software designers.
- The new health care and social assistance sector will include family planning centres, out-patient mental health and substance abuse centres, and continuing-care facilities for the elderly.
- Within the manufacturing sector, a new subsector will cover computer and electronic products.

The redesign will do at least one thing — provide real information on new industries where only commercial hype was available.

Source: Adapted from Alanna Mitchell, "Numbers for Sale: Call StatsCan," *The Globe and Mail*, August 18, 1993, pp. A1, A5; and Bruce Little, "StatsCan to Slice Data More Finely," *The Globe and Mail*, April 9, 1997, p. B4.

all firms in only one or two industries, it has a **vertical business market**. For example, some precision instruments are intended only for the marine market, but every boatbuilder or shipbuilder is a potential customer. If the product is usable by many industries, then it is said to have a broad or **horizontal business market**. Business supplies, such as Esso lubricating oils and greases and Canadian General Electric small motors, may be sold to a wide variety of industries.

A company's marketing program ordinarily is influenced by whether its markets are vertical or horizontal. In a vertical market, a product can be tailor-made to meet the specific needs of one industry. However, the industry must buy enough to support this specialization. In addition, advertising and personal selling and servicing can be directed more effectively in vertical markets. In a horizontal market, a product is developed as an all-purpose item, to reach a larger market. However, because of the larger potential market, the product is likely to face more competition.

Buying Power of Business Users

Another determinant of business market demand is the purchasing power of business users. This can be measured either by the expenditures of business users or by their sales volume. Many times, however, such information is not available or is very difficult to estimate. In such cases, it is more feasible to use an **activity indicator of buying power** — that is, some market factor that is related to income generation and expenditures. Sometimes an activity indicator is a combined indicator of purchasing power and the number of business users. Following are examples of activity indicators that might be used to estimate the purchasing power of business users.

Measures of Manufacturing Activity Firms selling to manufacturers might use as market indicators such factors as the number of employees, the number of plants, or the dollar value added by manufacturing. One firm selling work gloves used the number of employees in manufacturing establishments to determine the relative value of various geographic markets. Another company that sold a product that controls stream pollution used two indicators: (1) the number of firms processing wood products (paper mills, plywood mills, and so forth) and (2) the manufacturing value added by these firms.

Measures of Mining Activity The number of mines operating, the volume of their output, and the dollar value of the product as it leaves the mine all may indicate the purchasing power of mines. This information can be used by any firm marketing industrial products to mine operators.

Measures of Agricultural Activity A company marketing fertilizer or agricultural equipment can estimate the buying power of its farm market by studying such indicators as cash farm income, acreage planted, or crop yields. The chemical producer that sells to a fertilizer manufacturer might study the same indices, because the demand for chemicals in this case is derived from the demand for fertilizer.

Measures of Construction Activity If a firm is marketing building materials, such as lumber, brick, gypsum products, or builders' hardware, its market is dependent on construction activity. This may be indicated by the number and value of building permits issued or by the number of construction starts by type of housing (single-family residence, apartment, or commercial).

BUSINESS BUYING BEHAVIOUR

Business buying behaviour, like consumer buying behaviour, is initiated when an aroused need (a motive) is recognized. This leads to goal-oriented activity designed to satisfy the need. Once again, marketers must try to determine what motivates the buyer, and then understand the buying process and buying patterns of business organizations in their markets.

The Importance of Business Buying

Business buying or purchasing, formerly a relatively minor function in most firms, is now an activity that top management is very much interested in. Once viewed as an isolated activity that focused primarily on searching out low prices, purchasing has become an important part of overall strategy for at least three reasons:

PERFORMANCE. RELIABILITY. RESULTS. JUST WHAT THE ROB 1000 EXPECTS.

Canada 1Q 1997 | HIGHLIGHTS | IDC Canada Ltd.

Dell's performance within the Canadian PC Market in the first three months of 1997 mirrors its unprecedented success worldwide.

Dell placed third in both worldwide and U.S. PC markets in 1Q97. And Dell has captured third place in the overall Canadian PC market with 7.3% share, up from 4.8% share in 1Q96. Meanwhile the trials and tribulations of

Every business looks down at the bottom line. And when they look hard enough they find Dell®. The #3 computer vendor in the world. Because Dell's business model delivers a superior product. Dell computers, such as Dell's Optiplex® line featuring Intel® Pentium® and Pentium Pro Processors, provide exceptional performance. They deliver reliability across any network. And the results are as amazing as the prices. That's what the best corporations in the world expect. And that's what Dell delivers. Which is why you should call Dell for the business computers you need. Now.

intel inside pentium

DELL Canada

1-800-863-7408

www.dell.ca

Intel, the Intel Inside logo and Pentium are registered trademarks of Intel Corporation. Dell, the Dell logo and Optiplex are registered trademarks of Dell Computer Corporation.

Dell promotes its business computers to a broad horizontal market by emphasizing performance, reliability, results, and its growing market strength.

- Companies are making less and buying more. For example, 93 percent of the cost of an Apple computer is purchased content, and for all manufacturers, purchased content is over 50 percent of their final products. In 1996, Chrysler had 1,200 suppliers and, though it has been attempting to reduce that number, its efforts are to consolidate purchases rather than reduce outside buying.[2] With outside suppliers so significant, buying becomes a prime strategic issue because product planning, materials and production costs, and, ultimately, product performance and quality are all at issue and more difficult to manage unless suppliers and Chrysler work more closely.
- Firms are under intense quality and time pressures. To reduce costs and improve efficiency, firms

www.apple.com

no longer buy and hold inventories of parts and supplies. Instead, they demand that raw materials and components that meet specifications be delivered "just in time" to go into the production process. Compaq's Prolinea line of personal computers is a good example of how a firm used its purchasing to help reposition itself and become the success it currently is.[3] The firm had an established reputation for high quality and high prices, but intense competition from lower-priced clones forced a change. Compaq established a goal of developing the Prolinea in six months to sell for less than one-third of the price of its similar Deskpro model, without a cut in quality. To accomplish its goal, Compaq searched around the world for suppliers that combined the best prices with consistent quality and on-time delivery.

- To get what they need, firms are concentrating their purchases with fewer suppliers and developing long-term "partnering" relationships. This level of involvement extends beyond a purchase to include such things as working together to develop new products and providing financial support.[4]

Buying Motives of Business Users

One view of **buying motives** is that business purchases are methodical and structured. Business buying motives, for the most part, are presumed to be practical and unemotional. Business buyers are assumed to be motivated to achieve the optimal combination of price, quality, and service in the products they buy. An alternative view is that business buyers are human and thus their business decisions are influenced by their attitudes, perceptions, and values. In fact, many sales people would maintain that business buyers seem to be motivated more toward personal goals than organizational goals, and the two are often in conflict.

The truth is actually somewhere in between. Business buyers have two goals — to further their company's position (in profits, in acceptance by customers) and to protect or improve their position in their firms (self-interest). Sometimes these goals are mutually consistent. For example, the firm's highest priority may be to save money, and the buyer knows that he or she will be rewarded for negotiating a low price. Obviously the more consistent the goals are, the better for both the organization and the individual, and the easier it is to make buying decisions.

However, there are often significant areas where the buyer's goals do not coincide with those of the firm, as when the firm insists on dealing with the lowest-price supplier, but the buyer has developed a good relationship with another supplier and doesn't want to change. In these cases a seller must appeal to the buyer both on a rational "what's good for the firm" basis and on a self-interest "what's in it for me" basis. Promotional appeals directed to the buyer's self-interest are particularly useful when two or more competing sellers are offering essentially the same products, prices, and postsale services.[5]

Types of Buying Situations

In Chapter 6 we observed that consumer purchases can range from routine to complex buying decisions. Similarly, the buying situations in business organizations vary widely in their complexity, number of people involved, and time required. Researchers in organizational buying behaviour have identified three classes of business buying situations. The three **buy classes** are new-task buying, straight rebuy, and modified rebuy. The stages in the business buying-decision process and the three buy classes are illustrated in Table 7-1.

- **New-task buy.** This is the most difficult and complex buying situation because it is a first-time purchase of a major product. Typically more people are involved in new-task buying than in the other two situations because the risk is great. Information needs are high and the evaluation of alternatives is difficult because the decision-makers have little experience with the product. Sellers have the challenge of finding out the buyer's needs and communicating the product's ability to provide satisfaction. A hospital's first-time purchase of laser surgical equipment or a company buying robots for a factory (or buying the factory itself) are new-task buying conditions. In these situations, firms with established relationships can work with buyers to help them define the buying task and suggest solutions because they are trusted. Potential suppliers must provide information and aid in the buying task in

TABLE 7-1 The Buy-Grid Framework

Stages in the Business Buying Process (Buy Phases) in Relation to Buying Situations (Buy Classes)			
	Buy Classes		
Buy Phases (Stages in Buying-Decision Process)	**New Task**	**Modified Rebuy**	**Straight Rebuy**
1. Recognize the problem.	Yes	Maybe	No
2. Determine product needs.	Yes	Maybe	No
3. Describe product specifications.	Yes	Yes	Yes
4. Search for suppliers.	Yes	Maybe	No
5. Acquire supplier proposals.	Yes	Maybe	No
6. Select suppliers.	Yes	Maybe	No
7. Select an order routine.	Yes	Maybe	No
8. Evaluate product performance.	Yes	Yes	Yes

Source: Adapted from Patrick J. Robinson, Charles W. Faris, and Yoram Wind, *Industrial Buying and Creative Marketing* (Boston: Allyn and Bacon, 1967), p. 14.

a form that engenders trust and allows them to begin the task of establishing a relationship.

- **Straight rebuy.** This is a routine, low-involvement purchase with minimal information needs and no great consideration of alternatives. The buyer's extensive experience with the seller has been satisfactory, so there is no incentive to search. An example is the repeat purchase of steering wheels by Freightliner, a truck manufacturer. These buying decisions are made in the purchasing department, usually from a predetermined list of acceptable suppliers. Suppliers who are not on this list may have difficulty getting in to make a sales presentation to the buyer. But as more buyers gain experience making use of the Internet to both gather product and service information and actually buy on-line, the predetermined list is easily expanded by asking for bids from a broader base of suppliers.
- **Modified rebuy.** This buying situation is somewhere between the other two in time and people involved, information needed, and alternatives considered. In selecting diesel engines for the trucks it manufactures, Freightliner considers Cummins and Caterpillar products, among others. However, because these engine makers frequently introduce new design and performance features, Freightliner evaluates each on a regular basis. Close relationships are common in situations where modified rebuys are frequent and, of course, should work to benefit both buyer and seller.

www.cummins.com • www.cat.com

Buying-Decision Process in Business

The buying-decision process in business markets is a sequence of five stages similar to the ones followed by consumers, as discussed in the preceding chapter. Not every purchase involves all five steps. Straight-rebuy purchases usually are low-involvement situations for the buyer, so purchasers typically skip some stages. But a new-task purchase of an expensive product or service is likely to be a high-involvement, total-stage buying decision.

To illustrate the process, let's assume that Weston Bakeries is considering a fat substitute in a special line of baked goods:

- *Need recognition.* Weston's marketing executives are sensitive to the concerns of consumers about fat in their diets. The opportunity to produce a line of high-quality, good-tasting baked goods without fat is very attractive, but finding the right substitute is the challenge.
- *Identification of alternatives.* The marketing staff draws up a list of product-performance specifications for the fat-free baked goods — attractive appearance, special features, good taste, and reasonable cost. Then the purchasing department identifies the alternative brands and supply

sources of fat substitutes that generally meet these specifications.

- *Evaluation of alternatives.* The production, research, and purchasing people jointly evaluate both the alternative products and sources of supply. They discover that some brands cannot withstand high temperatures, there are differences in how well they simulate the taste and texture of fat, and some have not received final approval from federal health authorities. The complete evaluation considers such factors as product performance, appearance, and price, as well as the suppliers' abilities to meet delivery schedules and provide consistent quality.
- *Purchase decision.* Based on the evaluation, the buyer decides on a specific brand and supplier. Next, the purchasing department negotiates the contract. Since large sums are involved, the contract will likely include many details. For example, if Weston feels confident about the supplier, the contract might go beyond price and delivery schedules to include the producer of the fat substitute gaining consistent access, through electronic data interchange (EDI) to production, quality control, shelf life, and product movement data so as to be able to provide a higher degree of accuracy in product delivery and better targeted service. In such a situation, a long-term relationship appears to be in the making.
- *Postpurchase behaviour.* Weston continues to evaluate the performances of the fat substitute and the selected supplier to ensure that both meet expectations. Continued dealings will depend on this performance evaluation and on how well the supplier handles the total interaction process.

Multiple Buying Influences — The Buying Centre

One of the biggest challenges in business-to-business marketing is to determine which individuals in the organization play the various buying roles. That is, who influences the buying decision, who determines product specifications, and who makes the buying decision? In the business market, these activities typically involve several people. In other words, there are **multiple buying influences**, particularly in medium-sized and large firms. Even in small companies where the owner-managers make all major decisions, knowledgeable employees are usually consulted before certain purchases are made.

Understanding the concept of a **buying centre** is helpful in identifying the multiple buying influences and understanding the buying process in business organizations. A buying centre may be defined as all the individuals or groups involved in making a decision to purchase. Thus a buying centre includes the people who play any of the following roles:

- **Users.** The people who actually use the business product — perhaps a secretary, an executive, a production-line employee, or a truck driver.
- **Influencers.** The people who set the specifications and aspects of buying decisions because of their technical expertise, their organizational position, or even their political power in the firm.
- **Deciders.** The people who make the actual buying decision regarding the business product and the supplier. A purchasing agent may be the decider in a straight-rebuy situation. But someone in top management may make the decision regarding whether to buy an expensive computer.
- **Gatekeepers.** The people who control the flow of purchasing information within the organization as well as between the firm and potential vendors. These people may be purchasing agents, secretaries, receptionists, or technical personnel.
- **Buyers.** The people who interact with the suppliers, arrange the terms of sale, and process the actual purchase orders. Typically this is the purchasing department's role. But again, if the purchase is an expensive, complex new buy, the buyer's role may be filled by someone in top management.

Several people in an organization may play the same role: There may be several users of the product. Or the same person may occupy more than one role: A secretary may be a user, an influencer, and a gatekeeper in the purchase of office equipment.

The size and composition of a buying centre will vary among business organizations. In one study, the average size of buying centres ranged from 2.7 to 5.1 persons.[6] Within a given organization, the size and makeup of the buying centre will vary depending on the product's cost, the complexity of the decision, and the stage of the buying process. The buying centre for a straight rebuy of office supplies will be quite different from the centre handling the purchase of a building or a fleet of trucks.

The variety of people involved in any business buying situation, plus the differences among companies, present real challenges to sales people. As they try to determine "who's on first" — that is, determine who does what in a buying situation — sales reps often call on the wrong executives. Even knowing who the decision-makers are at a certain time is not enough, because these people may be very difficult to reach, and people move into and out of the buying centre as the purchase proceeds through the decision process. This, in part, explains why a sales person typically has only a few major accounts.

Certainly the challenges presented in the business buying-decision process should suggest the importance of co-ordinating the selling activities of the business marketer with the buying needs of the purchasing organization.

Buying Patterns of Business Users

Buying behaviour in the business market differs significantly from consumer behaviour in several ways. These differences stem from the products, markets, and buyer–seller relationships in business markets.

Direct Purchase In the consumer market, consumers rarely buy directly from the producer except in the case of services. In the business market, however, direct purchase by the business user from the producer is quite common, even for goods. This is true especially when the order is large and the buyer needs much technical assistance. Computer-chip makers deal directly with personal computer manufacturers because the chip technology is changing so rapidly. From a seller's point of view, direct sale in the business market is reasonable, especially when there are relatively few potential buyers, when they are big, or when they are geographically concentrated. With phone, fax, and the Internet readily available, smaller sellers can both concentrate their efforts and work to expand their reach into markets that in the past were too expensive to serve at an appropriate level.

Nature of the Relationship Many business marketers take a broad view of exchanges. Rather than focus only on the immediate customer, they approach marketing as a value chain. That is, they consider the roles of suppliers, producers, distributors, and end users to see how each adds value to the final product. This perspective leads to a recognition of the importance of all the parties involved in successfully bringing a product to market and an emphasis on building and maintaining relationships. For example, Apple Computer, which once relied exclusively on dealers, recognized that many of its larger customers needed specialized service. To satisfy this segment of the market and maintain strong ties to these key customers, the firm now has its own sales force calling directly on large accounts. However, many of the orders taken by the sales force are contracted out to dealers to ensure that they are protected.[7] A key factor in establishing and maintaining relationships is the seller working to build confidence and trust.

Frequency of Purchase In the business market, firms buy certain products very infrequently. Large installations are purchased only once in many years. Small parts and materials to be used in the manufacture of a product may be ordered on long-term contracts, so that a selling opportunity exists as seldom as once a year. Even standard operating supplies, such as office supplies or cleaning products, may be bought only once a month.

Because of this buying pattern, a great burden is placed on the personal-selling programs of business sellers. The sales force must call on potential customers often enough to provide the first-hand information that other media cannot effectively provide and to know when a customer is considering a purchase.

Size of Order The average business order is considerably larger than its counterpart in the consumer market. This fact, coupled with the infrequency of purchase, highlights the importance of each sale in the business market. A sales person losing the sale of a pair of shoes to a consumer is not nearly as devastating as Canadair losing the sale of ten airplanes.

MARKETING AT WORK FILE 7-3

BIG MONEY IN BUSINESS-TO-BUSINESS ELECTRONIC BUSINESS

While marketers of consumer goods spend more money on Web marketing than they take in, business marketers live in a different world. The most successful electronic commerce business models tend to be business-to-business ones. This should be no surprise, since business transactions are worth at least ten times as much as consumer sales. Few realized how quickly stodgy business firms would convert to electronic business, but, after all, many if not most business transactions are actually done at a distance, by fax, phone, mail, or private electronic links. Moving these processes to the Internet reduces transactions costs, speeds them up, and makes them easier to conduct.

One of the most impressive examples of business marketing and purchasing on the Internet comes from innovating and benchmark-setting General Electric. The Electric Services Information Division has established a Trading Process Network (TPN), a Web site where GE now does $1 billion worth of business with about 1400 of its suppliers — an amount greater than all consumer electronic commerce in 1997. It has designed software that lets GE's purchasers specify from whom they want bids and what sort of information a bid should include. The software manages the bids that come back, eliminates high bidders, handles further bidding rounds, and notifies the bidders of results of the process. Selected suppliers are notified and get an on-line form on which to complete necessary details.

Results: The length of the bidding process in the Lighting Division has been cut in half, from 21 days to 10; purchasing officers now approach more suppliers because it is so easy to do; the increased bidding competition has lowered the cost of goods by 5 to 20 percent; it is now much easier to include foreign suppliers in the process, and 15 percent of orders have gone abroad; GE's size results in pulling small and medium-sized suppliers into electronic commerce, where they did not operate before, and they are able to increase their efficiency, sharpen prices, and improve service at a low cost, sometimes for just the price of a Web page. These suppliers have then broadened their market reach beyond GE with a more sophisticated use of the Internet.

Source: Adapted from Christopher Anderson, "A Survey of Electronic Commerce: In Search of the Perfect Market," *The Economist*, May 10, 1997, pp. 3, 16–17.

Length of Negotiation Period The period of negotiation in a business sale is usually much longer than in a consumer transaction. General Electric, for example, negotiated over a five-year period before completing the purchase of a $9.5 million Cray supercomputer to aid in managing operations and research activities in Canada and the United States. Some reasons for extended negotiations are:

- Several executives participate in the buying decision.
- The sale involves a large amount of money.
- The business product is made to order, and considerable discussion is required to establish the specifications.

Reciprocity Arrangements A highly controversial business buying practice is reciprocity, the policy of "I'll buy from you if you'll buy from me." Reciprocity was common among firms marketing homogeneous basic business products (oil, steel, rubber, paper products, and chemicals).

There has been a significant decline in, but not an elimination of, reciprocity. This decline has occurred for two reasons, one legal and the other economic. The Competition Act applies to reciprocity when the practice is similar to price discrimination. A firm can buy from a customer, but it must be able to prove that it is not given any special privileges regarding price, quality, or service that are not made available to competing buyers.

From an economic point of view, reciprocity may not make sense because the price, quality, or service offered by the seller may not be competitive. In addition, when a firm fails to pursue objectives that maximize profits, the morale of both the sales force and the purchasing department may suffer.

Reciprocity is an area in which firms run into problems in doing business overseas. In many parts of the world, it is taken for granted that if I buy your product, you will buy mine.

Demand for Service The user's desire for excellent service is a strong business buying motive that may determine buying patterns. Frequently a firm's only differentiating feature is its service, because the product itself is so standardized that it can be purchased from any number of companies. Consider the choice of suppliers to provide elevators for a major office building or hotel. The installation of the elevators is no more important than keeping them operating safely and efficiently. Consequently, in its marketing efforts a firm such as Otis emphasizes its maintenance service as much as its products.

Sellers must be ready to furnish a continuous service program, not just before or just after a sale. For example, suppliers such as Kraft General Foods conduct a careful analysis of a supermarket's customers and sales performance and then suggest a product assortment and layout for the store's dairy department. In the case of office copiers, manufacturers train the buyers' office staffs in the use of the equipment, and after the machines have been installed, offer other services, such as repairs by specially trained technicians.

Dependability of Supply Another business buying pattern is the user's insistence on an adequate quantity of uniform-quality products. Variations in the quality of materials going into finished products can cause considerable trouble for manufacturers. They may be faced with costly disruptions in their production processes if the imperfections exceed quality control limits. The right quantities at the right time are as important as the right quality. A work stoppage caused by an insufficient supply of materials is just as costly as one caused by inferior quality of materials. In one study of problems faced by purchasing agents for smaller manufacturers, the problem most often reported was the failure of sellers to deliver on schedule.

The emphasis on total quality management (TQM) has increased the significance of dependability. Now that it has been established that firms can operate with virtually zero defects, buyers expect a very high standard of performance.

Leasing Instead of Buying A growing tendency among firms in the business market is leasing business goods instead of buying them. In the past this practice was limited to large equipment, such as mainframe computers, packaging equipment, and heavy construction equipment. Industrial firms are now expanding leasing arrangements to include delivery trucks, automobiles used by sales people, machine tools, and items such as software site licences that are generally less expensive than major installations.

Leasing has several merits for the lessor — the firm providing the equipment:

- Total net income — the income after charging off repairs and maintenance expenses — is often higher than it would be if the equipment were sold.
- The lessor's market may be expanded to include users who could not afford to buy the product, especially for large equipment.
- Leasing offers an effective method of getting users to try a new product. They may be more willing to rent a product than to buy it. If they are not satisfied, their expenditure is limited to a few monthly payments.

From the lessee's — or customer's — point of view, the benefits of leasing are:

- Leasing allows users to retain their investment capital for other purposes.
- Firms can enter a new business with less capital outlay than would be necessary if they had to buy equipment.
- Leased products are usually repaired and maintained by lessors, eliminating one headache associated with ownership.
- Leasing is particularly attractive to firms that need equipment seasonally or sporadically, such as food canning or construction.

www.otis.com • http://kraftfoods.com

BASES FOR BUSINESS MARKET SEGMENTATION

Several of the bases used to segment the consumer market can also be used to segment the broad business market. For example, we can segment business markets on a geographical basis. Several industries are geographically concentrated, so any firm selling to these industries could nicely use this segmentation basis. Sellers also can segment on product-related bases such as usage rate or benefits desired.[8]

Let's look at three of the bases that are used solely for segmenting business markets — type of customer, size of customer, and type of buying situation.[9]

Type of Customer

Any firm that sells to customers in a variety of business markets may want to segment this market on the basis of customer types. We discussed the Standard Industrial Classification (SIC) code as a very useful tool for identifying business and institutional target markets. A firm selling display cases or store fixtures to the retail market, for example, might start out with potential customers included in the two-digit code number 61 for shoe, apparel, fabric, and yarn industries — retail. Then the three-digit code 612 identifies potential customers in the retail clothing business. Finally, the four-digit code number 6121 pinpoints men's clothing specialty stores.

A firm selling janitorial supplies or small electric motors would have a broad potential market among many different industries. Management in this firm could segment its market by type of customer and then perhaps decide to sell to firms in only a limited number of these segments.

Size of Customer

In this situation, size can be measured by such factors as sales volume, number of production facilities, or number of sales offices. Many business-to-business marketers divide their potential market into large and small accounts, using separate distribution channels to reach each segment. The large-volume accounts, for example, may be sold to directly by the company's sales force. But to reach the smaller accounts, the seller may use a telemarketing or Internet approach or a manufacturers' agent or some other form of intermediary.

Type of Buying Situation

Earlier in this chapter, we discussed the three types of buying classes — new buy, modified rebuy, and straight rebuy. We also recognized in that discussion that a new buy is significantly different from a straight rebuy in several important respects. Consequently, a business seller might well segment its market into these three buy-class categories. Or the seller could at least set up two segments by combining new buy and modified rebuy into one segment. Then different marketing programs would be developed to reach each of these two or three segments.[10]

Summary

The business market consists of organizations that buy goods and services to produce other goods and services, to resell to other business users or consumers, or to conduct the organization's operations. It is an extremely large and complex market, spanning a wide variety of business users that buy a broad array of business goods and services. Besides manufacturing, the business market includes the agriculture, reseller, government, services, not-for-profit, and international markets.

Business market demand generally is derived, inelastic, and widely fluctuating. Business buyers usually are well informed about what they are buying. Business market demand is analyzed by evaluating the number and kinds of business users and their buying power.

Business buying, or purchasing, has taken on greater strategic importance because organizations are buying more and making less, under intense time and quality pressures, and developing long-term partnering relationships with suppliers.

Business buying motives are focused on achieving a firm's objectives, but the business buyer's self-interest must also be considered.

The buying-decision process in business markets may involve as many as five stages: need recognition, identification of alternatives, evaluation of alternatives, purchase decision, and postpurchase behaviour. The actual number of stages in a given purchase decision depends largely on the buying situation, whether new-task buy, straight rebuy, or modified rebuy.

The concept of a buying centre reflects the multiple buying influences in business purchasing decisions. In a typical buying centre are people playing the roles of users, influencers, deciders, gatekeepers, and buyers.

Buying patterns (habits) of business users often are quite different from patterns in the consumer market. In the business market, direct purchases (without intermediaries) are more common, purchases are made less frequently, and orders are larger. The negotiation period usually is longer, and reciprocity arrangements can exist. The demand for service is greater, and the dependability of supply is more critical. Finally, leasing (rather than product ownership) is quite common in business marketing.

Three segmentation bases that are used solely for segmenting the business market are customer type, customer size, and type of buying situation.

Key Terms and Concepts

Business market (154)
Business users (154)
Business marketing (154)
Agribusiness (155)
Reseller market (155)
Services market (156)
Nonbusiness market (157)
Standard Industrial Classification (SIC) (161)
Vertical business market (163)
Horizontal business market (163)
Activity indicator of buying power (164)
Buying motives (165)
Buy classes (166)
New-task buy (165)
Straight rebuy (166)
Modified rebuy (166)
Multiple buying influences (buying centre) (167)
Users (167)
Influencers (167)
Deciders (167)
Gatekeepers (167)
Buyers (167)

Questions and Problems

1. What are some marketing implications of the fact that the demand for business goods:
   a. fluctuates widely?
   b. is inelastic?
   c. is derived?
2. What are the marketing implications for a seller of the fact that business customers are geographically concentrated and limited in number?
3. What differences would you expect to find between the marketing strategies of a company that sells to horizontal business markets and those of a company that sells to vertical business markets?
4. A manufacturer has been selling specialized software to a large oil company in Norway. In which of the three buy classes would you place this buyer–seller relationship? Is there any aspect of the relationship that is likely to fall into the straight-rebuy category?
5. Explain how the five stages in the buying-decision process might be applied in the following buying situations:
   a. New-task buying of a conveyor belt for a soft-drink bottling plant.
   b. Straight rebuying of maintenance services for that conveyor belt.
   c. Modified rebuy of advertising agency services for a hotel chain.
6. How would you go about determining who influences the buying decisions of business users?
7. Steelcase, IBM, Xerox, and other manufacturers of office equipment make a substantial proportion of their sales directly to business users. At the same time, wholesalers of office equipment are thriving. Are these two market situations inconsistent? Explain.

Hands-On Marketing

1. Find an ad for a business product or service that is directed toward the business market and another ad for the same product that is directed toward consumers (such as an ad for leasing fleets of Chevrolets and an ad for Chevrolet aimed at consumers). Discuss the buying motives appealed to in the ads.
2. Interview a purchasing agent about buying a product that would qualify as a modified rebuy. Draw a diagram that shows the purchasing agent's perceptions of: (a) the stages of the decision process; (b) who was in the buying centre at each stage of the decision process; and (c) what role(s) each person played at each stage of the process. Comment on how this diagram might be useful to a sales person representing the product in question.

CHAPTER 8 GOALS

The management of any business or organization, whether a major automobile manufacturer, an auto dealership, or an art gallery, requires one fundamental input in order to achieve success in a competitive marketplace: accurate and timely information. To be effective, marketing managers need current information about the markets they are trying to reach, the macroenvironment that affects their particular industry, and the internal and external factors that affect their specific market. We're about to see where this information can be obtained and how to use it. After studying this chapter, you should have an understanding of:

- What marketing research is and the role it plays in improving marketing decision-making.
- The systems that have been developed to increase the usefulness of data.
- The appropriate way to conduct a marketing research project.
- Who actually does marketing research.
- The current status of marketing research.

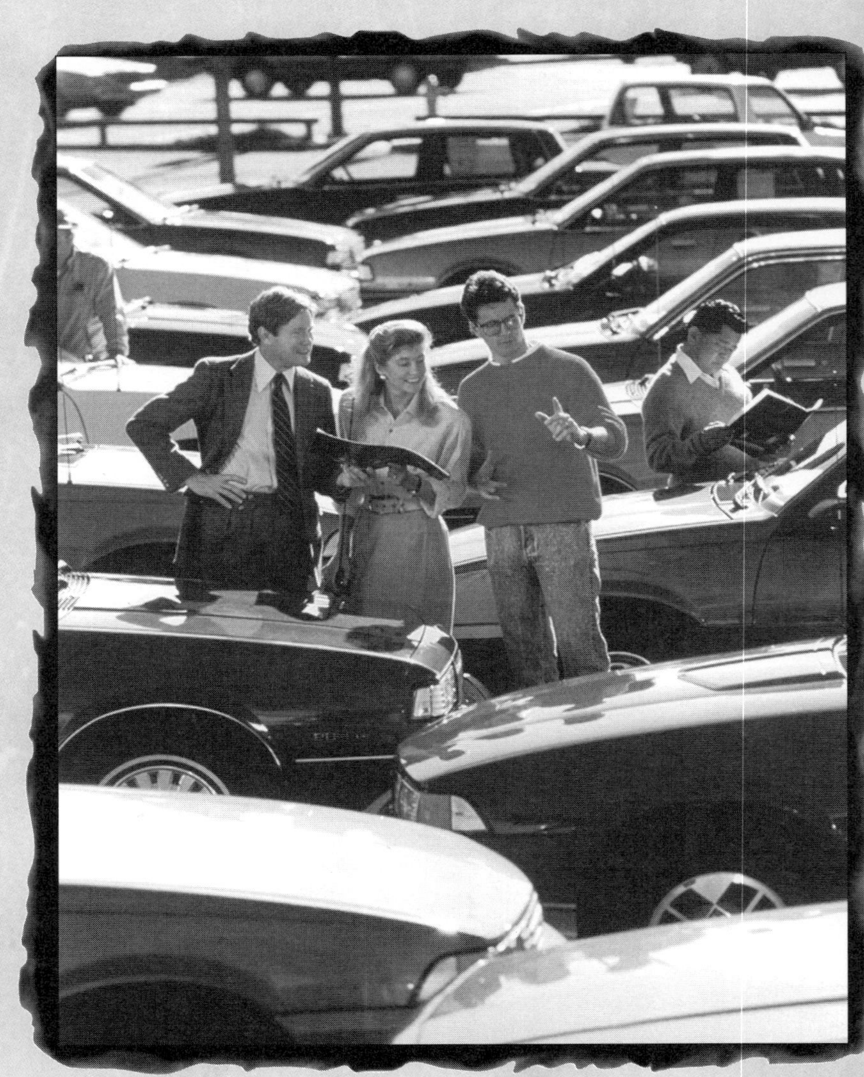

Chapter Eight

Marketing Research and Information

How do people buy cars? What is the process that they go through? What is important to them in reaching a final decision? What information do they need to be able to reach a decision that leads to their satisfaction? The answers to these questions are not obvious. While we all would have some insights into how people shop for new and used cars, those insights would, for the most part, be based upon our own personal experience and on our observations of how other people whom we know have shopped for cars.

The answer to questions such as these, which are central to a solid understanding of consumer behaviour, is usually "It depends." The answer depends on a range of factors that must be taken into consideration when marketers develop their marketing programs. How people shop for cars depends on what they want in a car: basic transportation or performance. Where they shop depends on their knowledge of and prior experience with local auto dealerships and with makes of cars. The process they go through in finally reaching a decision depends on factors such as whether it is a first car, their level of knowledge about cars, and their level of involvement in the purchase. As should be obvious from our discussion in earlier chapters of the concept of market segmentation, answers to these questions will also vary across segments of the car-buying market. Different people buy cars differently.

One aspect of auto buying that has been an important topic within the industry for many years relates to how men and women differ in their approach to the purchase of a car. Many women have been frustrated in dealing with auto sales persons when there appears to be little understanding of the role of women in the purchase decision. Although women now account for over 50 percent of all new car purchases and influence close to 80 percent of all car buying decisions, there still remains in many dealerships an apparent feeling that the man's view is most important. This appears to be particularly the case when a man and a woman go shopping for a car together. Auto manufacturers and dealers have begun to pay more attention to the differences between men and women in their tastes in automobiles. What each looks for in buying a new car couldn't be more different.

A recent study of Canadian car buyers conducted by J.D. Power and Associates revealed that women prefer more practical and economical vehicles, while men continue to be focused on image and performance. By far the majority of cars bought by women are subcompacts and economy cars, while men are much more likely to buy luxury cars and pickups. Of the top ten cars bought by men in Canada, over half are pickups — the leading car bought almost exclusively by men is the BMW 5-series, followed by Chevrolet and GMC Sierra pickups. Women, on the other hand, when they buy cars on their own, tend toward the Geo Metro, the Toyota Tercel, and the Dodge Colt. Among Metro purchasers, over 70 percent are women.

Ian Forsythe, director of marketing for Nissan Canada, explained that "women often buy less expensive cars because they tend to be more practical and want a good deal." Resale value, fuel economy, and reliability are some of the factors that are of particular interest to women car buyers. Forsythe added, "We have also found — to our surprise — that women who buy cars are often car enthusiasts. They like cars, and they are looking for good ones. If it's a two-car family, the woman often ends up with the smaller of the two cars." On the other hand, men seem to care more about the mechanical performance of the car; they want to know what's under the hood. Practicality is important to them as well, but it takes on a different form; although, according to Ian Forsythe, some men will buy a car because it's the right colour.

According to John Arnone, product information manager for Ford of Canada, women do more homework than men when it comes to buying a car. "We've found that women can spend up to six months on research before they buy. Men tend to be impulsive and will often buy for reasons of status or image."[1]

This discussion of the use of marketing research in the auto industry illustrates the importance of information about consumers and how research is used to guide the development of marketing programs. The key to appreciating the value of research is to identify the *implications* of the research results for decision-making in various areas of marketing. While the specific forms of research used may differ by product or service category and from company to company, the basic principles are the same: that a marketer can learn much about how a product or firm should be positioned and promoted by collecting relevant information from target customers before such strategic marketing decisions are made.

NEED FOR MARKETING RESEARCH

Management in any organization needs information — and lots of it — about potential markets and environmental forces in order to develop successful strategic marketing plans and to respond to changes in the marketplace. A mass of data is available both from external sources and from within a firm. The challenge is how to transform the raw data into information and how to use it effectively. To see how to do this, we will begin by briefly discussing why organizations need information and why they need to do research. Then we will focus our attention on how organizations manage their research efforts.

Today, many forces dictate that every firm have access to timely information. Consider some of these factors and their relationship to information management:

- *Competitive pressure.* To be competitive, companies must develop and market new products and services more quickly and effectively than ever before.

- *Expanding markets.* Marketing activity is becoming increasingly complex and broader in scope as more firms operate in both domestic and foreign markets.
- *Cost of a mistake.* Introducing and marketing a new product or service is enormously expensive. A failure can cause severe — even fatal — damage to a firm.
- *Growing customer expectations.* The lack of timely, adequate information about a problem with some aspect of an organization's marketing program can result in lost business.
- *Increased market complexity.* The marketplace that most companies and organizations are facing today is far more complex than it was in the past; as a result, managers must be as well informed as possible, armed with information about which they can have complete confidence.

Managers in a wide variety of organizations are called on a regular basis to make important marketing decisions. It is probably a self-evident fact that the best decisions are based upon the best available information. Before embarking upon marketing decisions relating to new product introduction, changes in the customer service program, the launch of an advertising campaign, or a program to target new customer segments, the marketing manager needs information. In most organizations, the necessary information is not generally available and must be obtained from some external sources. This is where marketing research comes in. The information obtained through research guides strategic decision-making, but it is important to realize that, in order for the marketing manager to have complete confidence in the information, the research must be conducted professionally and in accordance with certain standards that will ensure that bias is minimized and that the results accurately reflect the situation the manager is facing. Marketing research is viewed by many managers as insurance that will help them succeed.[2]

What Is Marketing Research?

Marketing research includes all the activities that enable an organization to obtain the information it needs to make decisions about its environment, its marketing mix, and its present or potential customers and consumers. More specifically, marketing research is the development, interpretation, and communication of decision-oriented information to be used in the strategic marketing process. Businesses and other organizations spend millions of dollars each year obtaining information to improve the quality of decision-making. Obviously, research is an important part of marketing!

To understand what modern marketing research is and what it does, we must keep in mind that:

- It plays a role in all three phases of the management process in marketing: planning, implementation, and evaluation.
- It is more than just collecting data.
- It recognizes the researcher's responsibility to develop information that will be useful to managers.[3]

SCOPE OF MARKETING RESEARCH ACTIVITIES

The scope of marketing research activities that are typically practised by larger companies in particular is reflected in Table 8-1. These results indicate the percentage of Canadian companies that engage in each of these types of research.[4] Some of the results are particularly interesting and reflect the activities and interests of businesses. For example, approximately 90 percent of companies indicated that they monitor market share and market trends, and close to 80 percent analyze profits and costs and perform market and sales forecasts. The relatively small percentage engaged in plant location studies and channel performance research probably reflects the fact that many companies are not engaged in the manufacture and distribution of physical products. It is encouraging to see that a very large percentage of the companies who responded to the study indicated that they are carrying out research in the areas of service quality and customer satisfaction. Possibly surprising is the fact that only 20.9 percent of respondents indicated that they are conducting export or international research.

Much of the marketing research conducted by Canadian business tends to be done on behalf of larger companies. Among companies with annual sales in excess of $5 million, 50 percent have an organized marketing research department, and an additional 28 percent have at least one person with

TABLE 8-1 **Selected Marketing Research Activities of Larger Canadian Companies**

Subject Areas Examined	% doing
Business/Economic and Corporate Research	
Industry/market characteristics and trends	91.5
Market share analyses	89.7
Corporate image research	72.3
Quality/Satisfaction Research	
Customer satisfaction research	81.6
Customer profiling and segmentation research	74.1
Service quality research	70.9
Product quality research	68.4
Pricing Research	
Profit analysis	80.9
Demand Analysis Research	
Market potential	77.0
Sales potential	74.5
Sales forecasts	77.0
Cost analysis	76.2
Product Research	
Concept development/testing	66.3
Competitive product studies	52.5
Testing existing products	50.0
Test marketing	45.4
Distribution Research	
Plant/warehouse location studies	38.7
Channel performance studies	31.6
Advertising and Promotion Research	
Copy testing	52.5
Sales force compensation studies	51.4
Media research	48.9
Public image studies	47.9
Advertising post-testing	42.9
Buyer Behaviour Research	
Market segmentation research	56.4
Brand awareness research	48.2
Brand image/attitudes	47.5
Purchase intentions research	46.5

Source: Unpublished background data from the project reported in Eva E. Kiess-Moser and James G. Barnes, "Emerging Trends in Marketing Research: The Link with Customer Satisfaction," Ottawa: The Conference Board of Canada, Report 82-92, 1992. Reproduced with permission from The Conference Board of Canada.

responsibility for marketing research. Typically in these companies, marketing research departments are quite small, averaging 3.8 employees, including researchers and support staff. The small size reflects the fact that most companies have the actual marketing research studies conducted on their behalf by outside marketing research specialists. The staff of the marketing research departments in most cases carry out studies of the economy and industry trends and will supervise the purchase of specialized research services from outside suppliers.

In addition to the research studies conducted by a company's own marketing research department or on its behalf by an external research supplier, there are two other sources that provide the marketing information needed by managers:

- The marketing information system, which provides a continuous, scheduled flow of standardized reports to managers.
- The decision support system, which permits managers to interact directly with data through personal computers to answer specific questions.

MARKETING INFORMATION SYSTEMS

As computers became common business tools over the past thirty years, firms were able to collect, store, and manipulate larger amounts of data to aid marketing decision-makers. Out of this capability developed the **marketing information system (MkIS)** — an ongoing, organized procedure to generate, analyze, disseminate, store, and retrieve information for use in making marketing decisions. Figure 8-1 illustrates the characteristics and operation of an MkIS.

The ideal MkIS:

- Analyzes data using statistical analysis and mathematical models that represent the real world.
- Generates regular reports and recurring studies as needed.
- Integrates old and new data to provide information updates and identify trends.

Designing an MkIS

To build an MkIS, marketing managers must identify what information will help them make better decisions. Working with researchers and systems analysts, managers then determine whether the data needed are available within the organization (for example, in the daily reports made by sales people or cost data from the accounting department or in customer records) or must be obtained from outside sources, how the data should be organized, the form in which they should be reported, and the schedule according to which they will be delivered. For example, the manager at Procter & Gamble who is responsible for Tide wants to know the retail sales of all detergent brands by geographic area on a monthly basis. The same manager may want quarterly reports on the prices that competitors are charging and how much advertising they are doing.

FIGURE 8-1

The Structure of a Marketing Information System

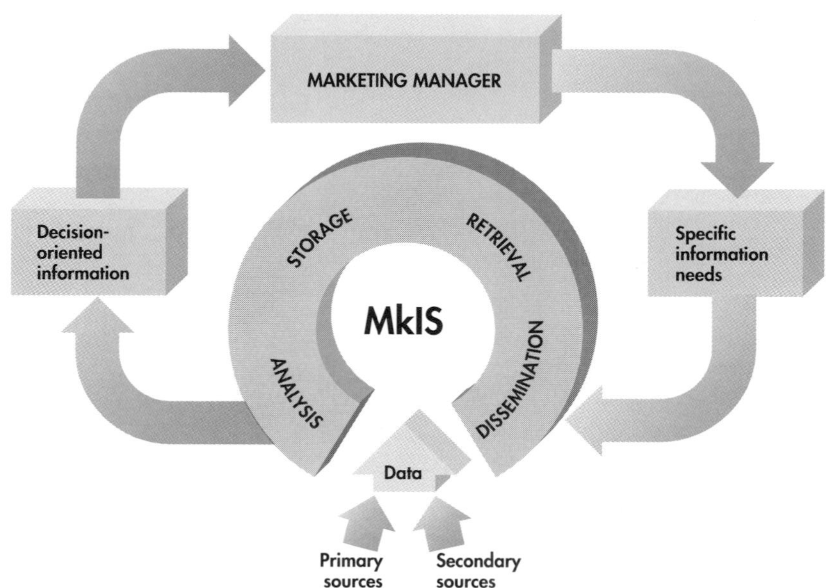

Less frequently, possibly once a year, this manager needs to know about developments in the marketplace such as demographic changes that might affect sales of Tide in the long term. In addition to these (and probably other) regular reports, the manager may periodically request special reports that can be compiled from existing data. For example, the Tide manager may want to see what share of the total market each detergent brand had by quarter over the last five years and a projection of how each is likely to perform over the next three years.

A well-designed MkIS can provide a continuous flow of this type of information to support management decision-making. The storage and retrieval capability of an MkIS allows a wide variety of data to be collected and used. With this capability, managers can continually monitor the performance of products, markets, sales people, and other marketing units.

An MkIS is of obvious value in a large company, where information for management is likely to get lost or distorted as it becomes widely dispersed. However, experience shows that even relatively simple information systems can upgrade management's decision-making in small and medium-sized firms.

How well an MkIS functions depends on three factors:

- The nature and quality of the data available.
- The ways in which the data are processed to provide usable information.
- The ability of the operators of the MkIS and the managers who use the output to work together.

MkIS Limitations

When an MkIS doesn't do what management expects it to do, there are several possible explanations:

- It is not always obvious what information is needed on a regular basis to make better decisions. Some managers are comfortable using their experience and intuition and may find that information produced by an MkIS is "interesting" but not necessarily useful. Thus, an MkIS can produce exactly what has been requested, but the results may not improve decisions because the managers have not identified what will be of greatest value to them.
- Gathering, organizing, and storing data and disseminating reports customized to the needs of many managers can be extremely expensive. Beyond the cost of operating an MkIS, there is the need to keep it updated as more sophisticated data become available and managers recognize new and different information needs.
- Possibly most important, an MkIS is not well suited to the solution of unanticipated problems. The biggest challenges managers face are situations in which a decision must be made quickly, without all the details clearly defined, nor the implications of the options known. Under these conditions, standard reports produced according to predetermined schedules are unlikely to be of much value.

The features of an MkIS — a focus on preplanned, structured reports and centralized control over the information by computer specialists — resulted from the skills required to operate computers. Organizations were forced to depend on highly trained programmers working on large computers to produce the information requested by managers from the MkIS. However, advances in computer hardware and software have reduced both problems and have led to the development of decision support systems.[5]

MARKETING DECISION SUPPORT SYSTEMS

A **decision support system (DSS)** is a sophisticated management tool that allows a manager to interact with data and methods of analysis to gather, analyze, and interpret information. Like an MkIS, the heart of a DSS is data — different types of data from a wide variety of sources. Typically, there are data describing customers, competitors, economic and social trends, and the organization's performance. Also like an MkIS, the DSS has methods for analyzing data. These methods range from simple procedures such as computing ratios or graphs to sophisticated statistical techniques and mathematical models. Where the methods differ is in the extent to which they permit managers to interact directly with the data. Through the use of personal computers and greatly simplified computer software, managers can retrieve data, examine relationships, and even produce reports to meet their specific needs. This interactive capability allows managers to react to what they see in a set of data by asking questions and getting immediate answers. Figure 8-2 depicts the relationships in a DSS.

Consider this example. Midway through the year, a manager wants to compare actual sales of a product with what was forecast. Sitting down at her computer, she calls up the monthly forecasts and the actual sales figures. Discovering that sales fell slightly below the forecast in the most recent month, she commands the system to provide similar data for the company's other products. Finding that the other products are on target, she concludes that there may be a problem with the product in question. Next, she asks the system to break down the total sales figure by geographic areas and discovers that the poor sales results occurred in only two of seven regions. Suspecting competitive activity, she then compares advertising levels and prices of her product and those of competitors in the markets where sales forecasts were achieved and where they weren't. Finding nothing out of the ordinary, she decides to examine distribution levels for the sales regions. Requesting data on the size and types of retail outlets over time, she finds that in the two regions where sales have slipped there has been a slow but steady decline in the type of small, independent retailers that account for a significant portion of the product's sales. Thus, her strategy is to investigate the use of alternative outlets for selling the product in these problem regions. Notice that, with an adequate DSS, this entire task was done in a short time by simply asking for information, analyzing it, and moving on to another question suggested by the analysis.

The DSS adds speed and flexibility to the MkIS by making the manager an active part of the research process. The increased use of desktop and laptop computers, "user-friendly" software, and the ability to link computer systems at different locations (networking) have greatly enhanced the potential of DSS. However, these systems are costly to implement and maintain. As a result, the DSS may be limited to large organizations for the time being.[6]

DATABASES

An MkIS or a DSS uses data from a variety of sources both within the organization and from outside suppliers. These data are organized, stored, and updated in a computer in what is called a **database**. Often a database will contain separate data modules on such topics as customers, competitors, industry trends, and environmental changes.

Internally, data come from the sales force, marketing, manufacturing, and accounting departments. One of the most lucrative sources of customer data, for example, already exists within customer accounts and billing files in many companies. Some organizations, such as banks and telephone companies, maintain such detailed accounts that they know precisely what a customer has purchased. Some users of databases have begun using their data for predictive modeling, which seeks to determine which customers would be interested in a particular type of product or service. For example, by scanning its data base of credit card customers for individuals who have used their gold card to purchase a computer in the past year, a bank could develop an excellent list of customers who would likely be interested in online banking and investment services.[7]

One of the most successful users of customer databases in Canada is Zellers, which operates three hundred stores across Canada and now accounts for one-quarter of all discount department store sales in the country. Zellers introduced its Club Z customer

FIGURE 8-2 The Structure of a Decision Support System

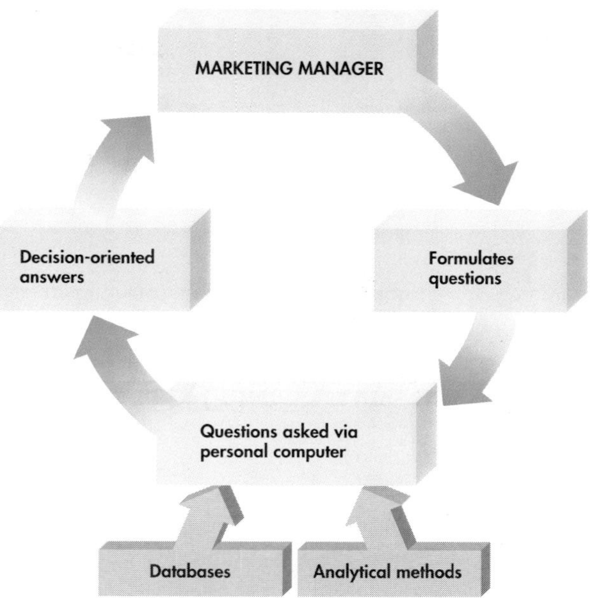

MARKETING AT WORK FILE 8-1

DATABASE MARKETING AT WORK

The practice of database marketing is flourishing. The process requires the establishment of a list of customers or potential customers by some means. That list is then segmented by appropriate characteristics and used to identify individuals to whom promotional materials, customized literature, or sample products or service offers can be sent. The company may contact the end-user directly without going through retail outlets or other distribution networks. Database marketing can make advertising and promotional programs more effective by selectively addressing the segments and groups most appropriate to your product. Reaching customers directly can also assist in establishing relationships. In the compilation of the database, information can be obtained on individuals that may suggest additional sales opportunities.

Ernie Johannson, a database marketer with B&B & Associates in Toronto, says that "without the database you can't understand what your customers are needing or wanting." Stephen Shaw of Links Database Technologies of Toronto goes further by stating that databases "will be the knowledge from which all business decisions are made." Car manufacturers, departments stores, mail-order firms, and others have begun to accumulate masses of information on households across Canada.

In addition to individual customization, marketing has also moved from focusing on the individual transaction to considering the life of the customer. In order to capture a customer for life, a firm needs information at the individual level. Ford, for example, identifies the lifetime value of a customer as $200,000. They want to ensure they are able to serve that customer over that full time period.

Results from research on the usage of database marketing in the retail sector indicate that retailers are using database systems to improve marketing efficiency through segmentation and targeting, reducing operating costs, and increasing profits. It can help firms to obtain and maintain competitive advantages, fine-tune their merchandising strategies, and improve customer service. Scanners at checkouts are now able to recognize your purchasing history. This can enable employees to identify you by name and make comments such as, "We haven't seen you in a while, Mr. Jones," which improve relationships and make the customer feel closer to the store or business.

Ethnic communities throughout Canada are being recognized as segments of the population that provide opportunities for marketers. Research is being undertaken on a regular basis to identify spending patterns of these distinct groups. A.C. Nielsen, a major marketing firm, is gathering information to create a database on the Chinese community living in Toronto. There is a similar index already complete for Vancouver. It will indicate the buying patterns and media usage of the 325,000 Chinese Canadians who make up the community in that city. The index will also help marketers pinpoint what new immigrants want compared with the patterns of those who have been in Canada for some time. For instance, when conducting research in Vancouver, Nielsen found that 90 percent of adults watch television an average of twelve hours per week and more than half of Chinese immigrants are under the age of forty.

One example of database marketing in action is Gourmet Baby Food Company. This company sells gourmet food items such as duck la orange and escargot to babies. Available in Canada and the United States, these specialty baby food products are sold directly to families by mail. Operating from Toledo, Ohio, this company has developed a strategic digital marketing program based on database marketing. It began with a test case in Toledo by sending out a questionnaire to all parents in the city with children under the age of three. If the family completed the questionnaire, they were entitled to be entered into a contest to win a university scholarship for the child. The data collected were fed into a database and analyzed, and the families were segmented into four different groups: Gourmet Lovers, Health Watchers, Knowledge Needers, and Not Interested. Each group was sent unique materials tailored to their interests. The Health Watchers, for example, received a catalogue that emphasizes the healthy ingredients of the products along with a pediatrician's report on the nutritional value of gourmet foods.

The test case was extremely successful, and the company decided to expand across North America. In this expansion, the Gourmet Baby Food Company has sent its questionnaire to more than ten million families. It further segmented the market into ten categories and continues to provide tailored information to each. From its questionnaires the company has set up a database, which is being constantly maintained by a mailing list agency. The database contains the names of all new mothers in Canada and the United States. Four months after a child is born, the parents receive a generic catalogue and the questionnaire. Once completed and mailed, it is entered into the company's database.

The Gourmet Baby Food Company has established an extremely complex and valuable database that has allowed it to market high-line baby foods through direct mail. It is an excellent example of database marketing at work.

Source: Salem Alaton, "Mountains of Data Help Marketers Make Connection," *The Globe and Mail*, April 4, 1995, p. B28; Bill Bishop, "Digital Strategies," *Marketing Magazine*, November 11, 1996, p. 12; "Nielsen Plans Toronto Chinese Media Index," *Marketing Magazine*, August 5, 1996; "What Is Database Marketing," www.ink.sramarketing.com.

loyalty program in 1986. Club Z now has almost ten million members, reaching an incredible 70 percent of all Canadian households. Club members earn one hundred points for every dollar spent at Zellers and can redeem their points for gifts from the Club Z catalogue. But the greatest value of Club Z to Zellers is the information that it provides on every item purchased by Club Z members. Douglas Ajram, general manager, loyalty and direct marketing, observed, "We use our database to paint a picture of our customers, what they like about us, and what kind of merchandise they are interested in."[8] Many companies such as Zellers are using internally generated data to establish databases on their customers. The way in which a company analyzes and combines the data from such databases will determine their usefulness in planning and implementing marketing strategy.

The development and selling of mailing lists and databases is normal business practice, and a new industry has evolved to rent computerized lists of potential customers who have certain characteristics and spending habits. A number of Canadian mailing list brokers rent more than two thousand lists to marketers wishing to target certain types of potential customers. These brokers do not sell the names and data on their lists but will rent them for one-time use to clients who wish to target direct-mail materials. Most brokers will want to approve samples of the material to be mailed before supplying the names.[9] There is growing pressure on mailing-list brokers and on users of databases generally to ensure that the information they have at their disposal is used in an ethical and responsible manner. Because of the availability of such computer-based data, there are many situations in which the privacy of consumers may be violated and information misused.[10]

Research has allowed marketers to move from undifferentiated, mass marketing to focusing on well-defined market segments. It is now suggested that through the management of databases, marketers will be able to reach the ultimate level of segmentation — the individual. For example, L.L. Bean, a mail-order catalogue marketer, uses a customer's past purchases from the catalogue to calculate a probability of future purchases for each of its merchandise lines. The firm then sends the customer only the specialized catalogues for which the likelihood of a purchase exceeds a minimum level.[11]

Scanners and Single-Source Data

An important data source for databases is scanners, the electronic devices at retail checkouts that read

Loyalty clubs build databases as well as loyalty.

the bar code on each item purchased. Scanners were originally intended to speed up checkout and reduce errors in supermarkets. By matching an item's unique code with price information stored in a computer, the scanner eliminated the need for clerks to memorize prices and reduced mistakes caused by hitting the wrong cash register key. However, retailers quickly discovered that scanners could also produce information on purchases that could be used to improve decisions about how much of a product to keep in inventory and the appropriate amount of shelf space to allocate to each product.

Knowing what customers buy is even more important if a firm knows what advertising they have been exposed to. In many countries, research companies such as A.C. Nielsen have developed consumer household panels to create databases of information on advertising exposure and retail purchases. A representative sample of households agree to have their television viewing monitored by an electronic device known as a people meter and to have their purchases recorded when they buy groceries at scanner-equipped retail stores. Demographic information is obtained from each household when its members agree to be part of the scanner panel. The result is that household demographics can be correlated to television advertising exposure and product purchases. The result is called **single-source data** because exposure to television advertising and product purchases can be traced to individual households, providing a single source for both types of data.[12]

MARKETING RESEARCH PROJECTS

Before the advent of computers and the development of marketing information systems and decision support systems, much of what was called marketing research consisted of nonrecurring projects to answer specific managerial questions. Projects, some that are nonrecurring and others that are repeated periodically, are still a major part of marketing research. The results of a project may be used to make a particular decision. They could also become part of a database to be used in an MkIS or DSS. Examples of marketing research projects are described briefly in Table 8-2. According to a recent study, the most common projects are studies of industry and market trends and market share analyses (see Table 8-1, earlier in this chapter).

TABLE 8-2 Typical Marketing Research Projects

Project	Objective
Concept test	To determine if a new product idea is attractive to potential customers, or to determine how targeted customers will respond to advertising concepts.
Copy test	To determine if the intended message in an advertisement is being communicated effectively.
Price responsiveness	To gauge the effect a price change would have on sales of a brand.
Market-share analysis	To determine a firm's proportion of the total sales of a product or service and whether that share is increasing or declining.
Segmentation studies	To identify distinct groups within the total market for a particular product or service, so that these groups may be targeted with specific marketing programs.
Customer satisfaction studies	To monitor how customers feel about an organization and its products or services, and with how they are treated by the company.

Most marketing research projects follow the procedure outlined in Figure 8-3. Let's examine what goes into conducting a marketing research project.

FIGURE 8-3 Marketing Research Procedure

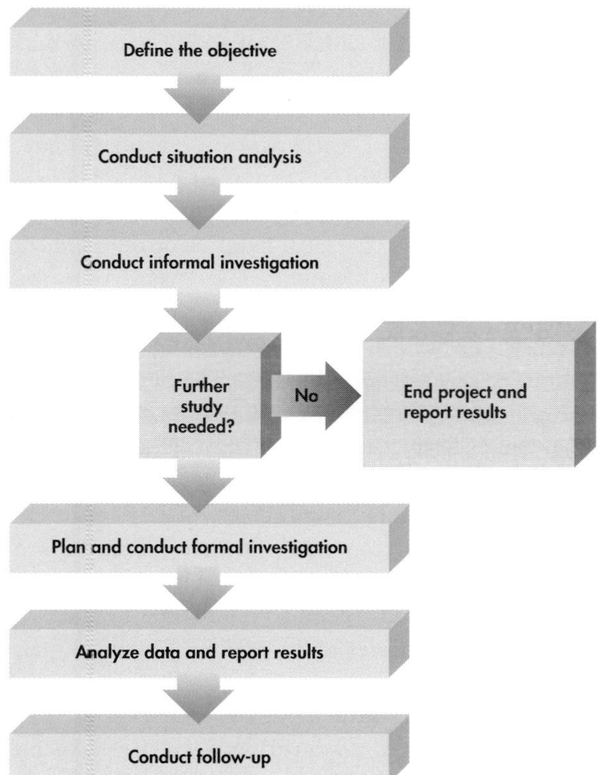

Define the Objective

Researchers need a clear idea of what they are trying to learn — the objective of the project. Usually the objective is to solve a problem, but this is not always so. Often the objective is to define the problem. Sometimes it's simply to determine if there is a problem. To illustrate, a manufacturer of commercial air-conditioning equipment had been enjoying a steady increase in sales volume over a period of years. Management decided to conduct a sales analysis. This research project uncovered the fact that, although the company's volume had been increasing, its share of the market had declined because the industry was growing even faster. In this instance, marketing research uncovered a problem that management did not know existed. After specifying the objective, the researcher is ready for the next step — the situation analysis.

Conduct a Situation Analysis

Next, the researchers try to get a "feel" for the situation surrounding the problem. They analyze the company, its market, its competition, and the industry in general. The **situation analysis** is a background investigation that helps in refining the research problem. It involves obtaining information about the company and its business environment by means of library research and extensive interviewing of company officials. This process generally relies upon the use of **secondary research**, meaning that the data already exist in some other form, often available from outside organizations such as Statistics Canada or trade associations.

In the situation analysis, researchers also try to refine the problem definition and develop hypotheses for testing. A research **hypothesis** is a tentative supposition that if proven would suggest a possible solution to a problem. Some examples of testable hypotheses are:

- Sales of grocery items are significantly greater when they are placed on display racks outside their normal aisle positions.
- Many bank customers who use automatic banking machines will be very receptive to a PC-based banking system that will allow them to do their banking from home.
- The dramatic increase in travel to Prince Edward Island is associated with the opening of the "fixed-link" causeway that connects the province to New Brunswick.
- Consumers in rural areas of Canada are more inclined to buy locally produced products and services than are those living in larger centres.

The project then turns to generating data that can be used to test the correctness of the hypotheses.

Conduct an Informal Investigation

Having gotten a feel for the problem, the researchers are now ready to collect some preliminary data from the marketplace. This **informal investigation** consists of gathering readily available information from people inside and outside the company — intermediaries, competitors, advertising agencies, and consumers.

The informal investigation is a critical step in a research project because it will determine whether further study is necessary. Decisions can frequently be made with information gathered in the informal investigation. For example, a company considering opening sales offices for its computer software support service in Western Canada might first talk with representatives of trade associations representing the personal computer industry and with officials of companies that supply computers and software. Before contacting any prospective clients for their new service, the company would be interested in getting a "feel" for the market and for the extent to which demand for software support is being satisfied. The conclusion at this stage may be that the market is large enough to warrant further investigation. The company's representatives might then meet with office managers or computer centre managers of prospective clients in cities such as Edmonton, Calgary, and Vancouver to discuss informally their needs for software support, where they are currently buying the service, and what they would look for in a new entrant into the market.

Much valuable information is obtained through an informal market investigation. The company not only will learn a great deal about the market it proposes to enter, but it will also determine whether further study is needed. A decision on the main problem can often be made with information gathered at the informal investigation stage.

Plan and Conduct a Formal Investigation

If the project warrants continued investigation, the researcher must determine what additional information is needed and how to gather it.

Select Sources of Information

Primary data, secondary data, or both can be used in an investigation. **Primary data** are original data gathered specifically for the project at hand. **Secondary data** have already been gathered for some other purpose. For example, when researchers conduct personal interviews, have individuals complete questionnaires, or answer questions on the telephone, they are collecting primary data. When they get information from Statistics Canada or from the local chamber of commerce, they are using a secondary source.

One of the biggest mistakes made in marketing research is to collect primary data before exhausting the information available in secondary sources. Ordinarily, secondary information can be gathered much faster and at far less expense than can primary data.

Syndicated data represent a third source of information that is a hybrid between primary and secondary data. Syndicated data are collected by a research supplier and may be purchased from that supplier by a number of clients, some of whom may be in direct competition with one another. The most common form of syndicated data involves the collection of data on a regular basis from an established sample or panel of consumers or retail stores. Clients subscribe to the reports, which are produced by the research company and essentially share the cost of collecting the data from the large sample. Although syndicated research does not provide privileged information to a single company, it does allow companies to obtain information on a shared-cost basis.

Sources of Secondary and Syndicated Data Several excellent sources of secondary information and syndicated data are available to marketers and marketing researchers in Canada. The following represents a summary of such sources; a much more detailed review of the main sources of secondary and syndicated data in this country may be found in a number of Canadian marketing research textbooks.

1. *Internal company records.* Information that the company already has in its files may be considered secondary data in the sense that it already exists. Companies regularly maintain orderly records of the reports of sales personnel, customer complaints, and sales by territory, product, and type of customer. When a problem must be addressed, the first place a company should go for information is its own files.

2. *Parent company records.* Many Canadian companies are subsidiaries of multinational companies. The parents and affiliates of these companies can often provide useful data on worldwide market conditions and on their experiences in foreign markets.

3. *Federal government.* The Government of Canada can furnish more marketing data than any other single source. Because of its legal powers to collect data, it has access to information that cannot be collected by private companies. Statistics Canada, as the statistical arm of government, collects much of the available information on behalf of government. Annual catalogues list the many publications of Statistics Canada and other departments and agencies of government.

4. *Provincial governments.* The provincial and territorial governments regularly produce reports and statistical summaries of broad economic interest. Many operate their own statistical offices, which produce reports of provincial statistics.

5. *Trade, professional, and business organizations.* Associations are excellent sources of information for their members. They often publish reports on surveys of members, and supply data of interest to outside groups. Some groups, such as the Conference Board of Canada and the Canadian Chamber of Commerce, which represent members with a wide variety of interests, will produce reports on an appropriately wide variety of topics. Others, such as the Canadian Bankers' Association and the Canadian Manufacturers Association, produce studies and reports specific to their industries.

6. *Advertising media.* Many magazines, newspapers, radio and television networks and stations, and outdoor advertising companies publish information that marketing researchers find useful. Such information usually relates to circulation data, station reach and coverage maps, and statistics on trading areas.

7. *University research organizations.* Some universities operate research units and publish research results that are of interest to business.

8. *Foundations.* Not-for-profit research foundations and related groups carry out many research projects of interest to business. Such groups include the Conference Board of Canada, the C.D. Howe Institute, and the Institute for Research in Public Policy.

9. *The Internet.* Increasingly, businesses and other organizations are turning to the World Wide Web for information that will be of use in addressing marketing problems or issues. In fact, the Internet now offers much information that was in the past only available in libraries and presents it in a much more accessible format.[13]

Sources of Primary Data After exhausting all the available secondary sources considered pertinent, researchers may still lack sufficient data. If so, they must turn to primary sources and gather or

www.cbserv.conferenceboard.ca • www.cdhowe.org

purchase the information. In a company's research project, for instance, a researcher may interview the firm's sales people, wholesalers or retailers, or customers to obtain the market information needed.

Determine How to Gather Primary Data There are four widely used methods of gathering primary data: survey, qualitative research, observation, and experimentation. Normally all four are not used on the same project, although more than one may be. Because each method has strengths and weaknesses, the choice of which to use depends on the nature of the problem, but it will also be influenced by how much time and money are available for the project.

Survey Method A **survey** consists of gathering data by interviewing people or by having them complete a questionnaire of some form. What distinguishes a survey from qualitative research (which will be discussed later in this chapter) is that, in a survey, the information is usually collected from a fairly large sample of customers, generally several hundred or more, and the results are entered into computer files for analysis. Consequently, the results of survey research are generally considered **quantitative** in nature because they involve statistical analysis. The advantage of a survey is that information is firsthand. In fact, it may be the only way to determine the opinions or buying intentions of a group.

Inherent in the survey method are certain limitations. There are opportunities for error in the construction of the survey questionnaire and in the data collection process. Moreover, surveys can be very expensive, and they do take some time to complete. Other possible weaknesses are that potential respondents sometimes refuse to participate, and the ones who do respond often cannot or will not give accurate answers.

Survey data collection is usually done by the researcher either in person, by telephone, or by mail. Increasingly, some marketing research companies are experimenting with alternative forms of data collection, including sending questionnaires over the Internet for completion and return by e-mail. **Personal interviews** are more flexible than the other types because interviewers can probe more deeply if an answer is incomplete. Ordinarily it is possible to obtain more information by personal interview than by telephone or mail. Also the interviewer, by observation, can obtain data regarding the respondents' socioeconomic status — their home, neighbourhood, and apparent standard of living.

Rising costs and other problems associated with door-to-door interviewing have prompted many marketing researchers to survey people in central locations, typically regional shopping centres. This technique is called the **mall intercept** method of interviewing. By interviewing people as they pass through a shopping mall, the interviewer is better able to encounter large numbers of people, as the urban mall has essentially become the "main street" of North America. Although data collection is made somewhat easier by this method, the researcher is less confident that he or she is obtaining a representative sample of the population of interest. In such a situation, the ability to access large numbers of people at relatively low cost outweighs concerns about the representativeness of the sample.[14]

In a **telephone survey**, the respondent is contacted by telephone, and the interview is completed at that time. Participants in telephone surveys are generally selected at random from telephone directories or by random dialing of telephone numbers. In the case where a company wishes to obtain information from its own customers, generally the researchers will have available a list from which those to be called may be selected at random. Telephone surveys can usually be conducted more rapidly and at less cost than either face-to-face interviews or mail surveys. Since a number of interviewers can make many calls from a few central points, this method is quite easy to administer. Computer-assisted techniques have broadened the scope of telephone interviewing. These techniques involve automated random-number dialing and a facility for the interviewer to record the respondent's answers directly into the computer as they are received. This technology speeds up the entry and processing of data and the production of reports.

A telephone survey can be timely. For instance, people may be asked whether they are watching television at the moment and, if so, the name of the program and the advertiser. One limitation of the telephone survey is that interviews cannot be too long, although telephone interviews that take up to thirty minutes to complete are not uncommon. In fact, one of the myths of telephone interviewing is that the questionnaire must be very short, because participants will not be willing to stay on the line for more than a minute or so. This is simply not so, as many Canadians appear quite co-operative in participating in telephone surveys that take five to ten minutes to complete. What is making it more difficult to conduct telephone survey research is that progressively fewer people are at home, and those who are at home are becoming more difficult to reach. Although there appears to be no dramatic increase in the frequency of unlisted numbers, more and more people are installing telephone answering machines or subscribing to services such as voice mail and call display. Many people who have such devices or services are using them to screen incoming calls, forcing callers to leave messages, or are electing not to answer the call if they do not recognize the number or name displayed. The result is that telephone interviewers are unable to reach an increasing percentage of the population, thereby making telephone interviewing more costly and resulting in more biased samples.

Telephone surveys have been used successfully with executives at work. When preceded by a letter introducing the study and a short call to make an appointment for the actual interview, these surveys can elicit a very high co-operation rate.

Collecting marketing research information through **mail surveys** involves mailing a questionnaire to potential respondents and having them return the completed form by mail. Since no interviewers are used, this type of survey is not hampered by interviewer bias or problems connected with the management of interviewers. Mailed questionnaires are more economical than personal interviews and are particularly useful in national surveys. If the respondents remain anonymous, they are more likely to give true answers because they are not biased by the presence of an interviewer.

A major problem with mail surveys is the compilation of a good mailing list, especially for a broad-scale survey. If the sample can be drawn from a limited list, such as property taxpayers in a certain province, region, or municipality, or subscribers to a certain magazine, the list presents no problem. Another significant limitation concerns the reliability of the questionnaires returned. The researchers have no control over who actually completes the questionnaire or how it is done. For example, a survey may be addressed to an adult male member of the household but because he is unavailable or not interested, his teenage daughter "helps out" by completing it. In addition, because there is no personal contact with the respondents, it is impossible to judge how much care and thought went into providing the answers.

Still another limitation is that there is usually a low response rate to a mail survey. It is not uncommon to receive completed replies from only 10 to 15 percent of those contacted. This is particularly important because if the respondents have characteristics that differentiate them from nonrespondents on certain dimensions of the survey, the results will be biased. Techniques for improving mail response rates have been the subject of hundreds of experiments.[15] Some of these include making the subject matter of the survey as interesting as possible, offering incentives to the participant to encourage involvement, and guaranteeing anonymity to encourage participation. In the case of mailed questionnaires, a higher response rate can be obtained by paying for return postage and by sending a reminder note or card, or even a second questionnaire, within a week or so of mailing the original.

Because of the lack of control over the process, increased postal rates, low response rates, and the time needed to mail out questionnaires and to receive the completed ones, most marketing researchers are using far fewer mail surveys than was the case several years ago.

Qualitative Research When research is intended to probe more deeply into the opinions and attitudes of people interviewed, different techniques are required. Qualitative research usually employs much smaller samples and interviews people in greater depth and for as long as ninety minutes or two hours. The two most widely used qualitative research techniques are the individual depth interview and the focus group interview.[16]

The **individual depth interview** is used in situations where the marketing researcher wishes to probe the consumer's thoughts concerning his or her purchase and use of a certain product or service. It is conducted in an individual rather than a group format often because the topics to be discussed are sensitive ones or because the people are difficult to reach and would be unlikely to attend a focus group session. For example, the individual depth interview is often used to interview business executives and professionals. Such interviews will generally take one hour or more to complete and range over a number of topics. The interviewer usually conducts the interview using a prepared interview guide.

In the case of the **focus group interview**, approximately eight to ten people are "recruited" to participate. They are usually selected to meet certain criteria relating to demographic characteristics, the use of a particular brand, frequent visits to certain vacation destinations, or similar criteria of interest to the researcher and client. The focus group interviewer or moderator orchestrates the discussion using a fairly loosely structured interview guide, rather than the more structured questionnaire of the typical face-to-face interview or telephone survey. Many interesting and enlightening findings are revealed through focus group interviews, which have become one of the most widely used techniques in marketing research.[17]

Because these are qualitative marketing research techniques, their results are completely nonquantifiable; typically no statistics are generated and research reports contain few if any numbers. They do produce valuable insights into how consumers feel about certain concepts and why they make decisions as they do. The principal use of the focus group interview, for example, is to allow the marketer to really understand why customers are buying one brand over another, why this bar of soap and not that one, why this locally owned fitness centre and not the national chain. The research explores what customers like and dislike about each, and what would have to happen for them to switch to the alternative.

The typical focus group interview will involve a group of eight to ten individuals who have been invited to spend ninety minutes or more discussing a certain topic with a discussion leader or moderator. Participants are invited to attend and are usually paid $25 or more. Focus groups are, by definition, loosely structured and are intended to provide marketers with insights that they simply cannot obtain through the more structured answers provided by survey research. Occasionally, marketing researchers will use the focus group technique to learn more about how consumers think about certain product or service categories or approach certain purchase decisions. They are then in a better position to design larger research surveys that may involve several hundred interviews with consumers.

It is important to realize that qualitative and quantitative approaches to marketing research are not usually competing for the researcher's attention. Rarely will a marketing researcher be in a position where he or she will have to decide whether to use a survey or a series of focus group interviews. The approaches are used for quite different purposes, and each is appropriate in certain situations. Generally, qualitative techniques such as focus group interviews will be used where the researcher wants to explore certain subjects in great depth or where he or she is carrying out exploratory research on a topic about which the client knows very little.

Observational Method In the **observational method**, the data are collected by observing some action of the respondent. No interviews are involved, although an interview may be used as a follow-up to get additional information. For example, if customers are observed buying beer in cans instead of bottles, they may be asked why they prefer that form of packaging to the other. We should not adopt a too restricted view of what constitutes observational research. We can include any form of research that involves the automatic capture of information, where the customer or consumer is being observed by a machine or by technology rather than by another person. In each case, the information is often being collected without the customer's knowledge, which may raise ethical issues concerning this form of research.

In using this approach, researchers may collect information by personal or mechanical observation. In one form of **personal observation**, the researcher may pose as a customer in a store. This

Focus groups represent an excellent way to learn what consumers really think.

technique is often referred to as "mystery shopping" and is useful in getting information about the calibre of the sales people or in determining what brands they promote. One example of **mechanical observation** that is often presented is the use of an electric cord stretched across a highway to count the number of cars that pass during a certain time period. Technology has advanced so rapidly that data are now captured by technology in many different settings. Builders of highways now imbed sensors in the surface of the road to not only count but to identify the vehicles that pass over them. Whenever we use ATMs at a bank we enable the bank to capture lots of information. The scanners that speed up the process of checking through our groceries at supermarkets also are automatically collecting information about what was purchased. If your supermarket also has a frequent-shopper club, the system uses the list of items purchased to update your personal data file. The resulting databases that most large retail firms and others now maintain on their customers are a direct result of data captured through such technology-based observation.

The observation method has several merits. It can be highly accurate. Often it removes all doubt about what the consumer does in a given situation.

MARKETING AT WORK FILE 8-2

RESEARCHING WHILE BROWSING

Qualitative research techniques are used in many ways. One method is to hold conversations with customers where they shop. This technique incorporates the shopping environment or the context of the decision-making into the shopper's mind-set in answering questions or talking about buying decisions. It is believed that recall is better when the context is provided. Five types of interviews have been proposed for this method:

- *Stream of consciousness interview:* This method is a conversation intended to elicit what the individual is experiencing at every moment while shopping, dining, travelling, and son on. For example, the technique is used with frequent travellers on long-haul flights. Passengers are encouraged to talk freely.
- *Spontaneous reaction interview:* Here the respondent is invited to spontaneously comment about the store without specific prompting. For example, the researcher asks the individual to walk around a store and then says, "Tell me about this store." One national bank discovered, through this method, that the glass walls constructed to imply that they were approachable were perceived by customers as robbing them of privacy. When customers were asked to tell the researcher about the bank, they replied that they were not comfortable in the office.
- *Directed general-response interview:* Respondents are asked general questions directed toward the research strategy. For example, "Is this restaurant friendly? Is this store easy to shop in?" In one such study, the subjects said they did not like a new restaurant because it felt threatening and too open.
- *Directed specific-response interview:* In these interviews, individuals are asked specific questions, such as "What makes this store feel modern?"
- *Prompted reaction to executive elements:* In this method, interviewees are asked about their reaction to specific elements in the environment. For example, they may be asked about the lighting levels or the decor.

These methods of obtaining qualitative data are particularly useful in analyzing impulse purchasing behaviour. Another purpose for them is constructing new products. In this case, a moderator accompanies the respondents through a store and allows them to create product concepts. They may point out that they like particular packaging types and visualize using them for other packages.

Source: David Kay, "Go Where the Consumers Are and Talk to Them," *Marketing News*, January 6, 1997, p. 14. Reprinted with permission from the American Marketing Association.

The consumers are usually unaware that they are being observed, so presumably they act in their usual fashion.

The observation technique reduces interviewer bias. However, the technique is limited in its application. Observation tells what happened, but it cannot tell why. It cannot delve into motives, attitudes, or opinions.

To overcome the biases inherent in the survey method, some firms are using sophisticated observational techniques that involve a combination of cable TV, electronic scanners in supermarkets, and computers. For example, some marketing research companies in Canada and the United States have established "scanner panels." Selected households are invited to participate in a program that involves recording electronically every TV commercial watched in participants' homes; every purchase the participants make in supermarkets equipped with checkout scanners is electronically recorded. With this observational method, researchers can measure which products members of the households are buying and determine which TV commercials they have seen. It provides an improved link between advertising and purchase that allows for more accurate measurement of the kinds of advertising that work and that don't work.

The A.C. Nielsen Company and the BBM Bureau of Measurement have installed "people meters" in more than two thousand Canadian homes. These devices record electronically the channels to which TV sets are tuned and who is watching the programs. Computers are already programmed with data on each member of the households that participate in the panel. Data are recorded continuously and fed to a central computer each night, providing the TV networks and advertisers with detailed, timely, and accurate information concerning program audiences and the exposure of TV commercials.

Experimental Method An **experiment** is a method of gathering primary data in which the researcher is able to observe the result of changing one variable in a situation while holding all others constant. Experiments are conducted in laboratory settings and in the field. In marketing research, the word laboratory is used to describe an environment over which the researcher has complete control during the experiment.

Consider the following example. A Vancouver film producer wished to determine whether Canadian films would be rented more frequently from video stores if they were identified as being Canadian. To assess this issue, he set up an experiment with ten Vancouver-area video stores in which he supplied them with a stock of Canadian videos to put on their shelves. In three stores, the tapes were mixed in with the other videos. In three stores, the Canadian films were separated on their own rack and identified as such; the remaining four stores, known as the promotional group, put the Canadian tapes in their own section, stuck little bar signs on each cassette, and promoted them with stickers and posters. Rentals were tracked over six months. The results indicated that people rented more Canadian videos when they were identified as such, and 45 percent more when they were promoted. These results, incidentally, contravene conventional wisdom that Canadians are not interested in films made in this country. As such, the information gained is of great interest to the Canadian film industry.[18]

Laboratory experiments can be used to test virtually any component of marketing strategy. However, it is important to recognize that the setting is unnatural and that consumers' responses may be biased by the situation.

An experiment carried out in the field, that is, under actual market conditions, is called **test marketing**. It is similar to a laboratory experiment but is conducted under more realistic conditions. The researcher therefore has less control. In test marketing, the researcher duplicates real market conditions in a small geographic area to measure consumers' responses to a strategy before committing itself to a major marketing effort. Test marketing may be undertaken to forecast sales or to evaluate different marketing mixes. Test marketing methodology is also used to evaluate pricing strategies, to obtain feedback on aspects of an advertisement, or to establish the effectiveness of an advertising campaign in influencing buying behaviour. Advertising testing is sometimes done by running two versions of the same advertisement and assessing changes in purchasing behaviour relative to each area.

The advantage of field experiments over laboratory experiments is their realism. However, there are several disadvantages. Test marketing is expensive (spending $500,000 or more to complete the test is not uncommon), time-consuming (nine to twelve months is normal), and impossible to keep secret from competitors (who may intentionally disrupt the test by temporarily changing their marketing programs). Another problem is the researcher's inability to control the situation. For example, a company that is test marketing a new product may encounter a certain amount of publicity while the product is in the test market, simply because of the innovativeness of the product. Although such publicity would normally be considered a good thing, when faced with it in a test market situation, the marketer is not sure about the extent to which it has distorted the sales results. In other words, what volume of sales resulted from the product and the regular marketing efforts of the company (what was actually being tested?), and what resulted from the publicity that was generated?

Because of its inherent limitations, the use of traditional test marketing declined as faster, less expensive alternatives were developed. One of these alternatives is the **simulated test market**, in which a sample of consumers is shown ads for the product being tested as well as for other products. The subjects are then allowed to "shop" in a test facility that resembles a small grocery store. Follow-up interviews may be conducted immediately and also after the products have been used to better understand the consumers' behaviour. The entire set of data goes into a statistical model, and sales for the product are forecast.

The potential benefits of simulated test marketing include:

- Lower costs than a traditional test market.
- Results in as little as eight weeks.
- A test can be kept secret.

The drawbacks are:

- Questionable accuracy for unique, new products.
- Application limited to traditional packaged goods.
- Inability to predict the response of competitors or retailers.
- Inability to test changes in marketing variables like packaging or distribution because of the simulation's short duration.[19]

Simulated test marketing has not replaced traditional test markets because of these limitations. In fact, the two methods are often used together, with the simulation results used to make marketing mix modifications before beginning the traditional test market.

Prepare Forms for Gathering Data Whether interviewing or observing subjects, or when having respondents complete questionnaires on their own, as in the case of a mail survey, researchers use a questionnaire or form on which there are instructions and spaces to record answers or responses. It is not easy to design a data-gathering form that elicits precisely the information needed. When conducting surveys, researchers use questionnaires that are fairly structured and generally provide a number of responses, asking respondents or interviewers to check the most appropriate response or to write in an answer. When conducting focus group interviews or depth interviews, researchers use interview guides that are much less structured and that ensure that the interviewer raises all of the topics that must be covered during the interview.

Depending on whether questionnaires or interview guides are being used, different considerations apply. If the researcher is to obtain qualitative information through focus groups or depth interviews, no computer-based statistical analysis can be performed. The interpretation of these results is quite subjective and will consist of conclusions drawn from the comments made by participants during the interviews. On the other hand, if the researcher chooses to obtain quantitative data, usually through survey research, such information will lend itself quite readily to statistical analysis using computers. In this latter case, care must be taken in ensuring that the questions asked will prove useful to the researcher and the marketing manager who has ordered the research.

The following represent some factors that must be considered when designing forms for the collection of research data:

- *Question wording.* If a question is misunderstood, the data it produces are worthless. Questions should be written with the potential respondent in mind. Vocabulary, reading level, and familiarity with jargon all must be considered. A common wording error is to inadvertently include two questions in one. For example, the question "How would you evaluate the speed and efficiency of our service?" followed by a rating scale that ranges from "poor" to "excellent" is likely to cause problems. Some respondents may see the service as fast, which is good, but with too many mistakes, which is bad.
- *Response format.* Questions asked in survey research are generally either designed for check-mark responses (such as yes–no, multiple choice, agree–disagree scales) or open-ended replies. Open-ended questions are more often associated with depth interviews and are easier to prepare and frequently produce richer answers, but they require more effort from the respondent and therefore lower the level of co-operation. In addition, in a mail survey it is often difficult to read and interpret open-ended responses. Open-ended questions are used most often in personal or telephone interviews, where the interviewer can probe for explanations and additional details.

- *Questionnaire layout.* The normal procedure when constructing a questionnaire for use in a survey is to begin with easier and general questions and move to the more difficult, complicated, and specific questions. To understand behaviour, researchers must sometimes ask questions about possibly sensitive topics (for example, personal hygiene) or private matters (age, income). These questions are normally placed closer to the end of a questionnaire.
- *Pretesting.* All questionnaires should be pretested on a small group of respondents who are similar to the intended sample. Pretesting is designed to identify problems in the design of the questionnaire and to allow for corrections and refinements to be made prior to the actual study.

Many books have been written on questionnaire design. Extreme care and skill are needed to produce a questionnaire that maximizes the likelihood of getting a response while minimizing bias, misunderstanding, and respondent irritation.

Plan the Sample It is, of course, not necessary to survey or observe every person who could shed light on a research problem. It is sufficient to collect data from a sample if its reactions are expected to be representative of the entire group. We all employ sampling in our everyday activities. Often we base our opinion of a person on only one or two conversations. And we taste food before taking a larger quantity. The key in these personal examples and in marketing research is whether the sample provides accurate information.

The fundamental idea underlying sampling is that a small number of items — a **sample** — if properly selected from a larger number of items — a **population** — will have the same characteristics and in about the same proportion as the larger number. Obtaining reliable data with this method requires the right technique in selecting the sample.

Improper sampling is a source of error in many studies. One firm, for example, selected a sample of calls from all the calls made to its 1-800 number and used the information to make generalizations about its customers. Would you be comfortable saying that these callers are a **representative sample** of all the firm's customers or even all the dissatisfied ones?[20]

Many hotels and restaurants use comment cards to obtain feedback from customers. The danger in generalizing from this information relates to the issue of who completes comment cards. The sample is self-selected and as such has built-in biases. Though numerous sampling techniques are used, only samples that are representative of the population of interest are appropriate for making generalizations from a sample to the population. A **random sample** is selected in such a way that every member of the population has a known probability of being included. In fact, unless the researcher has available a list of all members of the population, it is virtually impossible to select a random sample. As a result, marketing researchers will generally attempt to select a sample that is as representative of the population as possible.

Most of the samples used in survey research would be considered **convenience samples**. These are quite common in marketing research for two reasons. First, random samples are very difficult to get. Even though the researcher may select the subjects in a random fashion, there is no guarantee that all of those who are selected will participate. Some will be unavailable and others will refuse to co-operate. As a result, researchers often resort to carefully designed convenience samples that reflect the characteristics of the population as closely as possible. Second, not all research is done with the objective of generalizing to a population. Sometimes the company is interested in interviewing customers who visit a certain store or who telephone for service. In these cases, a convenience sample may be representative of the overall population. For example, if we want to assess whether regular users of a shopping centre are favourably disposed to the idea of installing lockers, then a convenience sample may be appropriate for this situation.

A common question regarding sampling is: How large should a sample be? With random sampling methods, a sample must be large enough to be truly representative of the population. Thus the size will depend on the diversity of characteristics of the population. All basic statistics books contain general formulas for calculating sample size. It is not, however, a simple matter to determine the appropriate size of a sample. The choice of sample size is normally made after consideration of a wide variety of factors. The researcher must determine whether there are natural groupings in the population, if the research objectives will require an investigation of whether one factor is associated with another, and the budget available to conduct the research.

Collect Data Collecting primary data by interviewing, observation, or distributing questionnaires through the mail is often the weakest link in the research process. Ordinarily, in all other steps, it's possible to ensure accuracy. However, the fruits of these labours may be lost if the data gatherers are inadequately trained or supervised. Data collectors need to understand the importance of maintaining the integrity of the data collection methods. In other words, if it has been decided that they need to interview every third person entering a store, and this is how the random sample is being selected, they cannot decide to interview the first twenty people because it is more convenient. Such interference with methodology can significantly bias the results. Data collectors need to be given, in their training, a basic understanding of research methodologies so that they can relate to the importance of the procedures used and why they must be observed as they are designed.

Motivating data collectors is often difficult, because they frequently are part-time workers doing what is often a monotonous task. As a result, many problems may crop up at this point. For instance, poorly trained interviewers may fail to establish rapport with respondents or may change the wording of questions. In extreme cases, there have even been instances where interviewers have attempted to fake the responses!

Analyze the Data and Present a Report

The value of research is determined by its results. Since data cannot speak for themselves, analysis and interpretation are key components of any project. Data analysis software packages have made it possible for researchers to tabulate and process masses of data quickly and inexpensively. This tool can be abused, however. Managers have little use for reams of computer output. Researchers must be able to identify pivotal relationships, spot trends, and find patterns — that's what transforms data into useful information. Proper coding of information assists in this process. Coding enables the researcher to determine how he or she wishes the data to be presented to ensure efficiency of interpretation. Qualitative data, such as the results of focus groups and depth interviews, are more time consuming and more difficult to analyze than quantitative data. It is very important to have clearly articulated the research objectives at the beginning of the project. Knowing clearly what questions the research is designed to address makes it much easier to determine what the results are saying. Sometimes trends or patterns will develop that are not expected or anticipated in the planning stages. Good researchers must be able to interpret these findings relative to the research objectives.

The end product of the investigation is the researcher's conclusions and recommendations. Most projects require a written report, often accompanied by an oral presentation to management. Here communication skill becomes a factor. Not only must researchers be able to write and speak effectively, they must adopt the perspective of the manager in presenting research results.

Conduct Follow-up

Researchers should follow up their studies to determine whether their results and recommendations are being used. Management may choose not to use a study's findings for several reasons. The problem that generated the research may have been misdefined, become less urgent, or even have disappeared. Or the research may have been completed too late to be useful. Without a follow-up, the researcher has no way of knowing if the project was on target and met management's needs or if it fell short, and an important source of information for improving research in the future would be ignored.

By this point you have probably realized that doing good research is not easy. It takes a well-designed set of objectives with a research methodology suitable to address these objectives. Unfortunately, research is not always done well. When interpreting research information, you should assess the methods used and be careful not to make generalizations that are not substantiated.

WHO DOES MARKETING RESEARCH?

Marketing research can be done by a firm's own personnel or by outside researchers. Sometimes a job is divided, with company personnel doing parts of a project and using a research specialist for such tasks as collecting data or developing approaches for the analysis of data.

Within the Company

Separate marketing research departments exist primarily in larger companies and are usually quite small. The marketing research department may consist of only a single manager or may be as large as four or five professionals in large consumer-products companies. In most such situations, the marketing research department rarely conducts research utilizing its own staff, but rather contracts the work out to suppliers outside the company. The primary role of the marketing research department, therefore, is to organize, monitor, and co-ordinate marketing research, which may be done by a number of different suppliers across the country. The manager of the marketing research department reports either to the chief marketing executive or directly to top management. The researchers who staff this department must be well versed in company procedures and know what information is already available within the company. They must also be familiar with the relative strengths and weaknesses of potential marketing research suppliers.

Outside the Company

A sign of the growth in the use of marketing research is the fact that there are now many companies across the country from which a marketing manager may seek help in marketing research problems. There exist in Canada today well over one hundred companies that operate in the field of marketing research. When a marketing manager requires information on Canadian marketing research suppliers, a number of sources exist that may be consulted in order to obtain a list of potential suppliers. One listing of such suppliers is *The Directory of Canadian Marketing Research Organizations*, produced by the Professional Marketing Research Society. This directory provides detailed information on those companies that operate in Canada in marketing research and related fields.

There are more than thirty full-service marketing research companies in Canada. These companies include such firms as the Creative Research International, Canadian Facts, Market Facts of Canada, and Thompson Lightstone. They provide a full range of marketing research services, from the design of a research study to the submission of a final report. In addition to the full-service marketing research companies, there are in Canada dozens of smaller firms that operate in various specialized areas of marketing research. These companies are usually small and may specialize by geographic region, by industry, or by service performed. Some concentrate in either consumer or industrial research or carry out studies that involve the application of specialized techniques. Other companies provide specialized marketing research services, such as the analysis of survey data. Some marketing research is also conducted in Canada by advertising agencies and management consulting firms.

STATUS OF MARKETING RESEARCH

Marketing research is a major growth area partially brought about by the new advances in technology. These advances include computer accessibility, point-of-sale data collection equipment, such as supermarket scanners, the Internet and its proliferation, and improved data-analysis software. They have enabled more efficient collection, analysis, and processing of data. The cost of computer technology has plummeted in the last decade to the point where even small businesses can collect data on their customer base. Most large companies now collect considerable amounts of data at each purchase. Frequent-buyer cards, such as those used by Zellers, A&P, and Sobeys, allow businesses to determine purchasing behaviour and patterns.

The challenge for marketers in the future will be to decide what information is needed and how it is to be integrated into decision-making. Database development and design is critical in ensuring that information is collected efficiently and meets management's need.

The role of managing databases is, therefore, a crucial one, and more emphasis is being placed on proper management. One example of this is the integration of customer files throughout business departments where previously separate data was maintained in each. Hotels, for instance, now compile data on their guests that can be accessed at check-in. The individual's file will tell the front-desk clerk that the guest may require a smoke-free room, a 6:00 A.M. wake-up call, and business services, such as access to fax or e-mail, throughout the day. In addition to providing immediate information to management, the integration of this information in research design on lifestyles or travel trend patterns can identify for marketers the areas to be explored and the types of information to be collected.

As we saw earlier, the marketing environment is changing. For example, increased competition through globalization and expanded marketing borders has sometimes made it more difficult for businesses to operated. Lifestyles and value systems are changing. Since marketing research is all about obtaining information to support marketing decision-making, the changing environment is increasing its importance. The more competently marketers can zero in on what is wanted and needed, the more effective they will be in selling their products and services.

It is still true, however, that companies are spending very large amounts on product development research, but much less on determining market opportunities for their products. Several factors account for this less-than-universal acceptance of marketing research. Unlike the results of a chemical experiment, the results of marketing research cannot always be measured quantitatively. The research director or brand manager cannot conduct a research project and then point to a certain percentage increase in sales as a result of that project. Also, if management is not convinced of the value of marketing research, it will not spend the amount of money necessary to do a good job.

Possibly a more fundamental reason for the relatively modest status of marketing research in some companies has been the failure of researchers to communicate adequately with management. Admittedly, there are poor researchers and poor research. However, researchers, like many manufacturers, are often product-oriented when they should be market-oriented. They concentrate on research methods and techniques, rather than on showing management how these methods can aid in making better marketing decisions. Executives are willing to invest heavily in technical research because they are convinced there is a payoff in this activity. Management is often not similarly convinced of a return on investment in marketing research.

Another basic problem is the apparent reluctance of management (1) to treat marketing research as a continuing process and (2) to relate marketing research and decision-making in a more systematic fashion. Too often, marketing research is viewed in a fragmented, one-project-at-a-time manner. It is used only when management realizes it has a marketing problem. One way to avoid such a view is to incorporate marketing research as one part of a marketing information system — a system that provides a continuous flow of data concerning the changing marketing environment.

Summary

Competitive pressure, expanding markets, the cost of making a mistake, and growing customer expectations all contribute to the need for marketing research. For a company to operate successfully today, management must develop a method for gathering and storing relevant data and converting it into usable information. Three tools used in research are the marketing information system, decision support systems, and the research project.

A marketing information system (MkIS) is an ongoing set of procedures designed to generate, analyze, disseminate, store, and retrieve information for use in making marketing decisions. An MkIS provides a manager with a regularly scheduled flow of information and reports. A decision support system (DSS) differs from an MkIS in that the manager, using a personal computer, can interact directly with data.

A marketing research project is undertaken to help resolve a specific marketing problem. The problem must first be clearly defined. Then a researcher conducts a situation analysis and an informal investigation. If a formal investigation is needed, the researcher decides which secondary and primary sources of information to use. To gather primary data, a survey, an observation, or an experiment may be used. The project is completed when the data are analyzed and the results reported. Follow-up provides information for improving future research.

Researchers have recently developed a stronger interest in finding out what competitors are currently doing and forecasting what they are likely to do in the future. Research is conducted internally by marketing research staff members and purchased externally from firms that specialize in doing research.

Marketing research has not yet achieved its potential because the value of research often cannot be directly measured, research does not always accurately predict the future, and researchers are too production-oriented. Further, researchers do not always communicate effectively with management, and research is frequently used in an ad hoc manner.

Key Terms and Concepts

Marketing research (177)
Marketing information system (MkIS) (179)
Decision support system (DSS) (180)
Database (181)
Single-source data (184)
Situation analysis (185)
Secondary research (186)
Hypothesis (186)
Informal investigation (186)
Primary data (186)
Secondary data (186)
Syndicated data (186)
Survey (188)
Quantitative (188)
Personal interviews (188)
Mall intercept (188)
Telephone survey (188)
Mail Surveys (189)
Individual depth interview (190)
Focus group interview (190)
Observational method (190)
Personal observation (190)
Mechanical observation (191)
Experiment (193)
Test marketing (193)
Simulated test market (194)
Sample (195)
Population (195)
Representative sample (195)
Random sample (195)
Convenience sample (195)

Questions and Problems

1. Explain how a marketing information system differs from a decision support system.
2. How involved should marketing researchers be in setting strategy for their organizations?
3. A group of wealthy business executives regularly spends some time each winter at a popular ski resort — Whistler, B.C.; Banff, Alberta; or Grey Rocks, Quebec. They were intrigued with the possibility of forming a corporation to develop and operate a large ski resort in the B.C. Rockies near the Alberta border. This would be a totally new venture and would be on federal park land. It would be a complete resort, with facilities appealing to middle- and upper-income markets. What types of information might they want to have before deciding whether to go ahead with the venture? What sources of information would be used?
4. Evaluate surveys, observation, and experimentation as methods of gathering primary data in the following projects:
   - **a.** A sporting goods retailer wants to determine college students' brand preferences for skis, tennis racquets, and golf clubs.
   - **b.** A supermarket chain wants to determine shoppers' preferences for the physical layout of fixtures and traffic patterns, particularly around checkout stands.
   - **c.** A manufacturer of conveyor belts wants to know who makes buying decisions for his product among present and prospective users.

5. Using the steps in the research process as presented in this chapter, describe how you would go about investigating the feasibility of opening a copy shop adjacent to your campus.
6. What kind of sample would you use in each of the research projects designed to answer the following questions?
   a. What brand of running shoes is most popular among the students on your campus?
   b. Should the department stores in or near your hometown be open all day on Sundays?
   c. What percentage of the business firms in the city nearest your campus have automatic sprinkler systems?
7. Would it be appropriate to interview two hundred students as they left your college hockey arena about their feelings regarding funding for athletics and then generalize the results to the student body? Why or why not?
8. If you were the research manager, what suggestions would you have for your management if they proposed that you conduct a consumer study to determine the feasibility of introducing a new laundry detergent in several Asian countries?

Hands-On Marketing

1. Assume that you work for a manufacturer of a liquid glass cleaner that competes with Windex and Glass Wax. Your manager wants to determine the amount of the product that can be sold throughout the country. To help her in this project, prepare a report that shows the following information for your home province and, if possible, your home city or region. Carefully identify the sources you use for this information.
   a. Number of households or families.
   b. Income or buying power per family or per household.
   c. Total retail sales in the most recent year for which you can find reliable data.
   d. Total annual sales of food stores, hardware stores, and drugstores.
   e. Total number of food stores.
2. Interview the manager of your campus bookstore about the marketing information system it uses (keep in mind that it may be a very informal system).
   a. What are the data sources?
   b. How are the data collected?
   c. What reports are received, and on what schedule?
   d. What problems arise with the MkIS?
   e. How could the MkIS be improved?

Case 2-1

PETER TAYLOR BUYS RUNNING SHOES

April was drawing to a close, and the signs of spring were evident throughout the nation's capital. Peter Taylor was in the process of writing the final set of examinations for his master's degree in business administration at the University of Ottawa. As a marketing major and sports enthusiast, his primary job-search objective was to find a position in sports marketing, preferably in Toronto. Peter knew that Canada's largest city contained an established base of sports and fitness organizations that could be targeted as employment prospects. In addition, Toronto contained the head offices of many large corporations that are involved in sports sponsorship. He had already made tentative plans to be in Toronto by June 1.

Peter had been involved in sports and athletics for as long as he could remember. His father, also an athlete and a soccer coach, encouraged Peter's initial involvement in hockey and baseball from the time Peter was five or six years old. Up to high school, Peter's active involvement in the local minor hockey program was maintained throughout the fall and winter, and he was active in baseball during the spring and summer seasons. The high school hockey schedule demanded early morning and evening practices, which eventually led him to decrease his hockey participation to a recreational level.

As a natural athlete, Peter enjoyed the competition offered by court sports. He became an avid competitor throughout the school year — soccer in the fall, volleyball until Christmas, basketball in the new year until Easter, and then track and field in the spring.

Peter has always felt that a physically active lifestyle enhanced his academic performance and general well-being. His parents were very outdoors-oriented and concerned about health and diet. These factors contributed to Peter's performance and drive in all his athletic endeavours. After he completed high school in Peterborough and began his undergraduate program at Trent University, a heavy course schedule prevented him from participating in team sports as actively as he had previously. For recreation and to keep the old gang together, Peter and a group of his high school friends arranged for free gym time in their old school. Every couple of weeks they would round up players for an afternoon or evening of basketball or volleyball.

Peter was also an active intramural competitor. Twenty or so of Peter's friends in his business administration class were athletically inclined. They competed in a variety of intramural sports as the nucleus of the business administration teams throughout their four years at Trent. The team performed reasonably well, although the arts and physical education teams were very competitive.

When Peter went on after graduation to the University of Ottawa for his MBA, few of his friends were surprised. They had expected for some time that Peter would try to combine his interest in marketing with his love for sports. During the often-gruelling two-year MBA program, Peter found less and less time for organized team sports. He rarely played hockey and did not compete in intramural sports. He did find time each week to swim in the university pool, and he cycled to the university regularly from his apartment in the Glebe area of the city. He also took squash more seriously, playing at least twice a week, although he had played only a little at Trent. This was a sport he felt he could continue to play after graduation.

Now that Peter was nearing the end of his MBA program, he realized that an active involvement in team sports would become difficult. He intended to continue playing squash, as he required only one partner to play. However, he wished to pursue an alternative form of exercise to balance and enhance his overall fitness. He considered weight training, but preferred more active sports. Having done quite well in middle-distance track and field competitions during high school, Peter decided to take running

---

The authors wish to acknowledge the input of Ed Ayres, editor of *Running Times*, for his comments and for permission to reproduce the exhibit in this case.

more seriously. During his two years in Ottawa, he had done a little jogging from time to time along the Rideau Canal, which runs near the university, but the cold Ottawa winters discouraged him from maintaining a year-round schedule. He realized, however, that running was one physical activity he could do according to his own schedule. He felt he might even consider competing in some of the middle- and longer-distance runs that he knew were held on a regular basis in and around Toronto.

Although Peter considered himself quite knowledgeable about most sports, he also felt there was probably more to running than just putting on a pair of sneakers and going out for a jog. He decided he should take advantage of the fact that the head office of Athletics Canada was located in Ottawa to obtain some technical information on the sport. Intuition told him that he should expand his common-sense list of "dos" and "don'ts." By placing a telephone call to the office of Athletics Canada, he was able to obtain the address of the Ontario Track and Field Association, which he was advised could provide him with a list of track and roadrunning clubs he might wish to join in the Toronto area.

As he walked through the Rideau Centre on a Saturday afternoon, following the exam in his marketing strategy course, he stopped into W.H. Smith, a bookstore that carried a wide range of magazines. He was particularly interested in buying a running magazine that might tell him something more about the right equipment for the sport. He found two such magazines in the sports and fitness section of the magazine rack, *Runner's World* and *Running Times*. He was not familiar with either magazine, but as he thumbed through them he was surprised by the number of advertisements for running shoes, and by the "high-tech" descriptions of many of the shoes. He selected *Running Times*, primarily because of the section labelled "Annual Running Shoe Guide," which seemed to be just what he needed.

Of particular concern to Peter was the financial investment he would need to make if he was to take running seriously. Although he owned an ample supply of basic sportswear such as shorts, sweatshirts, and T-shirts, he knew that top-of-the-line running shoes and a rainsuit were two necessities that together might cost him $300 or more. Peter did not yet have a salary, but he was never one to scrimp on sports equipment. He rationalized that the time he invested in such activities deserved a comparable monetary investment. His father had always taught him the value of good equipment as insurance against accidents and injuries.

Peter decided that he would wait until he moved to Toronto to join a running club and to learn more about the technique of the sport. Right now, he determined that he needed to get back to exercising regularly again, following the past few months of the MBA program, which had left him little time to work out. The more he thought about running, and stimulated by the articles in *Running Times*, the more anxious he was to begin running regularly as soon as his exams were over. He realized that he needed to know what running shoes to purchase and how best to prevent running injuries.

He was also beginning to realize that he knew very little about the engineering and technology of running shoes. Although he had bought other athletic footwear during the past few years, he had not appreciated the diversity of styles and models available. Advertisements in *Running Times* stressed materials such as Hexalite and Dynalite, cushioning based on air, fluids, gel, and foam, and glitzy colours and styles. Peter was unaware of the benefits each system offered. He read terms such as "rearfoot control," "heel counter," and "shock distribution," but felt ignorant about what shoe he should buy.

The wide variety of running shoes displayed in retail stores and featured in running magazines and the range of prices, colours, and styles made the decision even more complex. Rapidly changing technology, eye-catching innovations, and clever marketing tended to sway Peter from brand to brand without his knowing if the shoe matched his own needs and requirements. Running-shoe purchases, as Peter had learned through consumer behaviour textbooks, seemed to be determined by how the buyer wishes to be perceived, whether to be trendy or athletic. Running-shoe buyers often appeared to Peter to be very fickle, depending on what appealed to them or caught their eye at the point of purchase. He knew that serious runners often buy two or three different pairs, rotating them from day to day. He concluded that, as advanced engineering has transformed running shoes into technical and fashionable articles, their purchase had become a conspicuous activity and their wearing a "fashion statement."

Peter wanted to make sure he bought the right brand of running shoe. As he mulled over his decision, he identified criteria he felt he should consider in the selection process. Despite the wide price range of the shoes advertised in the magazine, high price was not a deterrent to Peter's purchase decision. Although he expected to pay more than $100 for a pair of quality running shoes, he preferred to keep the expense close to that level if at all possible. Comfort, availability, and protection against injury were critical to Peter. Colour was not at all important, although some shoes seemed a little too flashy. He was tending toward a lighter-weight shoe, which seemed to be preferred for longer distances, to protect against tiring. Peter felt that if each of these criteria was satisfied, he could run at his optimal capability.

To ensure that he was on the right track, he arranged a meeting with Sheila Cambridge at Athletics Canada. Sheila was a consultant with the association and held the provincial record for the 10 km distance. Peter had met Sheila at a campus party several weeks ago and knew that she was held in high regard in the local athletic community. She would also be well versed in the technical aspects of running-shoe construction, as she had graduated from the University of Ottawa a year earlier having specialized in kinesiology. Peter felt confident that she would be able to provide the expert advice he needed to pick the right pair of running shoes. "Besides," thought Peter as he walked along the canal towards Sheila's office, "it will be nice to see Sheila again."

Peter enjoyed the meeting with Sheila, as they discussed mutual friends and Sheila's training for the summer roadracing season. Peter learned that she had been training for the past four months in preparation for her first attempt at the marathon distance, to take place in mid-May in Ottawa's National Capital Marathon. Peter began to feel a little ill at ease, as he realized that Sheila was obviously far more knowledgeable about running than he was. He wondered whether he would ever reach the same level of training that she had achieved and felt a little uncomfortable at the thought of asking very basic questions about what shoes he should buy. He wondered whether he shouldn't just end the conversation.

It was too late when Sheila said, "Enough about my running. You wanted to talk about running shoes, didn't you? How much running are you planning to do?" Peter explained that he had participated in track and field in high school, but at distances from 400 to 1500 m. He now wanted to try running some longer distances, primarily to get back in shape. He also thought he might like to run some road races and even try a little cross-country. With that, Sheila pulled from a pile of magazines and books on her desk a back issue of *Running Times*. She turned to a page that contained a diagram of the various components of a running shoe (see page 204). She explained to Peter those components to which he should pay particular attention. "In selecting a running shoe," she explained, "the factor that I consider most important is fit. If the shoe doesn't fit well, you are likely to encounter problems down the road."

Sheila further suggested that one of the main criteria Peter must satisfy in his purchase of running shoes was protection against injury and overload. Research into the causes of injury has pointed to the type of running surface as one of the possible causes. She explained that common running injuries and ailments include leg fractures, muscle pulls and tears, heel spurs, shin splints, and knee injuries.

Although Peter felt he would prefer cross-country training through wooded and grassy areas, he observed that access to scenic trails would likely be limited once he moved to Toronto. "In that case," explained Sheila, "your running shoe must provide stability and protection against the high impact of pounding on the pavement. Not only do the interior components of the shoe have to protect your feet, but the exterior components such as the outsole will be important in cushioning against impact."

Other factors Sheila mentioned as contributing to injury were the type of movement, the training distance per week, and the intensity of training. She went on to explain that protection against overloading is also important. "Load is the external force acting upon a body. It results both from dynamic factors such as the type of movement, the velocity of limbs, posture, muscular activity, and the number of

Glossary of Terms

Shoe Part	Term	Explanation
	**Rearfoot Stability**	Prevents excessive lateral wobble or sag, and is important to severe pronators (see opposite page).
	Achilles Notch	Soft, padded material above heel counter cushions Achilles tendon and is sometimes notched to prevent irritation of the tendon.
	Heel Counter	Rigid cup holds heel firmly in place to prevent lateral motion.
	Heel Counter Collar	Reinforces heel counter.
	Dual-density midsole	Higher density on medial (inner) side of shoe resists compression and makes it harder for the foot to pronate (roll or sag sideways toward the inward side).
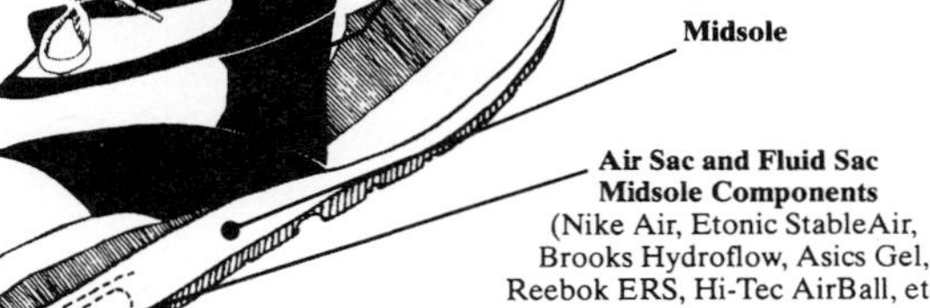	**Forefoot stability strap**	Helps to keep the upper material (usually a light nylon fabric or mesh) from sagging or bursting out; also helps to prevent excessive lateral motion of the forefoot.
	Toe Box	Should be roomy enough to let toes wiggle freely, with at least a thumb's width of space between toe and front wall of box. Foot should be snug around the heel, roomy around the toes.
	Midsole	Cushions the foot. Simplest midsoles are pieces of EVA foam. A more durable material is lightweight polyurethane (PU).
	Air Sac and Fluid Sac Midsole Components (Nike Air, Etonic StableAir, Brooks Hydroflow, Asics Gel, Reebok ERS, Hi-Tec AirBall, etc.)	Cushions impact of heel on the road, lengthens life of the shoe by preventing squashing of midsole (units are usually contained in strong PU casings) and may help stabilize ride by distributing impact.
	Flexible Plate Midsole Components (Nike Footbridge, Avia ARC, Etonic graphite plate, etc.)	Cushions impact by distributing impact over a wider area, and ARC combines this cushioning with a trampoline effect for greater energy return or "bounce."
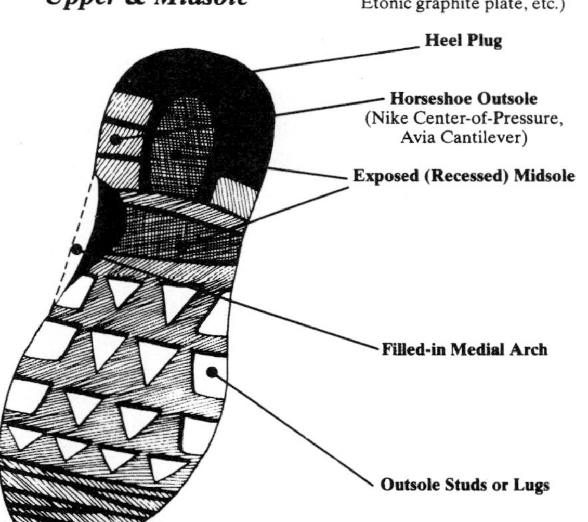	**Heel Plug**	Carbon/rubber resists abrasion, prevents wearing through prematurely at outside corner of the heel.
	Horseshoe Outsole (Nike Center-of-Pressure, Avia Cantilever)	Distributes weight to perimeter to maximize stability, while allowing center of rearfoot outsole to be scooped out (see Exposed Midsole, below).
	Exposed (Recessed) Midsole	Often in the center of the rearfoot bottom, and sometimes across the midfoot bottom, sections of dense outsole are scooped out in areas where foot contact with the ground isn't needed. This cuts down on the weight of the shoe, helps to keep the heel centered (by allowing it to sink down more in the center than on either side), and allows the foot to trampoline for better energy return.
	Filled-in Medial Arch	Resists pronation by preventing sag at instep. Similarly, **straight-lasted** shoe has straight shape suitable for stabilizing motion for hard heel-hitters and severe pronators. **Curved-lasted** models facilitate natural motion for forefoot-strikers and faster-paced runners.
	Outsole Studs or Lugs	Provide traction, especially important in the forefoot area, for both heel-strikers and forefoot-strikers. Tread patterns vary widely, but generally the smoother patterns are more effective for roads, the toothier patterns better in snow or mud or off-road.

repetitions, and also from boundary conditions such as the shoe surface, obstacles, anthropometric factors, and individual situation," she explained.

Peter found himself listening less intently as the information that Sheila was offering began to sound much more technical than he had expected. He really just wanted her to recommend a pair of running shoes and was not interested in all the technical jargon. When Sheila suggested that he attend a running clinic to check out what some of the local runners were wearing, Peter asked her what she would buy if she was in his position.

Sheila said that she really couldn't recommend a brand or model that would be best for him, as there were many acceptable shoes available. She did say that she ran in Nike shoes and that Nike was, in her opinion, the leading running shoe in the market. She suggested that he probably wouldn't be disappointed if he bought a Nike shoe, possibly an Air Stab or an Air Span. Peter wondered if her opinion might be biased by her personal choice. He thanked her, but felt a little disappointed to have left without knowing why Nike would be a good choice.

Heading home the next day, following his final exam in marketing research, Peter decided to visit Sports Experts, a sporting goods store in the Rideau Centre, to look at the selection of running shoes and to price the various brands and styles that he had seen in a recent advertising flyer from the store. He had often found the sales clerks in sporting goods stores to be knowledgeable and hoped he might get some advice concerning running shoes. Although he was familiar with a number of sporting goods stores in the Ottawa area, Peter decided to visit only three of them, all located within the downtown area. Over the next day or two, he would check the variety and prices at Sports Experts, Elgin Sports, and Sports-4.

Sports Experts had a reputation for a wide selection and good service. Generally, Peter did not appreciate being hounded by sales clerks in stores. He had never found the sales clerks in this particular store to be pushy, but rather genuinely helpful and friendly. Many seemed to be students who were working in the store part-time. After he had been given a few minutes to scan the huge wall display of running, court, squash, tennis, aerobic, basketball, cross-training, volleyball, sprinting, cycling, and windsurfing shoes, a sales clerk approached him and offered her assistance.

Peter had been looking closely at several Nike and Brooks styles, as he had worn both brands in the court and cross-training styles in the past and had been very satisfied with them. He asked the sales clerk which of the brands was considered best and what benefits each had to offer.

The Sports Experts sales clerk, Donna Williams, proceeded to explain that neither was necessarily the best brand. She suggested that Peter's decision should be based on comfort and ensuring that the width was neither too narrow nor so wide that the foot shifted from side to side. She felt that price was generally a good measure of the quality of the shoe, but not necessarily of the brand. She recommended that Peter try one style of each of the major brands, so that he could determine the fit of each of the shoes, and whether the cushioning felt right.

Donna went on to suggest that sturdiness could be tested by bending the shoe from right to left, and by ensuring that the heel components of the shoe felt firm. The lightness of the various shoes could be compared easily. Once the most comfortable brand of shoe was identified, price could be used along with a visual test of features to determine which shoe fulfilled his need. Donna suggested that generally the higher the price, the more stability and features were associated with the running shoe. She felt that gimmicks, such as endorsements by personalities, Velcro closures, and fluorescent colours, would probably inflate the price but did not necessarily enhance the shoe's quality. So the quality-conscious consumer, as compared with the socially conscious one, would need to search beyond superficial features. Donna Williams indicated that it was often very difficult to tell, having been influenced by advertising and other marketing strategies, which features were truly beneficial for a runner such as Peter and which had merely been promoted to make a shoe stand out from the competition. She felt that the consumer did not necessarily need to be a technical expert or sports engineer to perceive the difference, but should be educated as to what was most necessary given his or her running style, training schedule, desired features, and price range.

Peter proceeded to try one Nike, one Brooks, one Reebok, and one Asics running shoe, all within the same price range. Donna Williams suggested that he walk and jog down the mall corridor outside the store for a more realistic indication of comfort and stability. This comparison would give him a better basis for comparing the features offered by each brand. Peter declined the offer to jog in the mall. Instead, he tried on each pair of shoes and walked around the store. He decided that he felt most comfortable with the Nike shoes, as the air cushioning and light weight seemed to offer more spring, and he felt this would diminish some of the impact he would experience running on hard surfaces.

Peter remembered Sheila Cambridge's recommendation. Although Peter was sold on the Nike brand, the particular style he had tried, the Air Max, felt a little wide on his narrow foot. Donna Williams explained that the only shoe manufacturer who offered shoes in a full range of widths was New Balance and asked whether he would like to try a pair. Peter explained that he really liked the feel of the Nike shoe, but he wanted to find one that felt a little less wide. Donna suggested another Nike shoe, the Air Stab, which Peter proceeded to try. Feeling satisfied with the shoe, he jogged on the spot as a test of this new style. He felt that he had finally found what he had been looking for.

Peter asked Donna to hold the shoes for him until closing that night. This would provide ample time for him to ensure that the other stores were not offering the Nike Air Stab at a lower price than $129.99. Peter thanked Donna Williams for her help and left Sports Experts to see what the other stores had to offer. As he walked toward the mall exit on Laurier Street, he passed another sporting goods store and was attracted by a large wall display of athletic shoes. Athlete's World was offering Nike Air Stab at the same price he had found at Sports Experts, so Peter left the store quickly, feeling that Sports Experts deserved the sale, considering that Donna Williams had invested considerable time helping him. Peter decided to head for Bank Street, where he could see the offerings at Elgin Sports and Sports-4. Elgin Sports was an established Ottawa sporting goods store, with its original outlet on Elgin Street. A couple of years ago, the company had opened a second store on Bank Street, which offered a wide variety of sports clothing and shoes. Sports-4 was a newer store, having opened just two or three years ago. Peter felt that the Sports-4 outlet was much more of a running specialty store, as a display near the door contained notices of forthcoming road races and triathlons.

The Elgin Sports store on Bank Street also had the Air Stabs priced at $129.99, which left Peter wondering if he was needlessly running around the city when he could have purchased the pair of shoes he had seen at Sports Experts. On entering Sports-4, Peter was pleasantly surprised, as the Nike Air Stab was on a special promotion for $99.99. Peter was thrilled with this $30 savings and asked if he could try on a size 9, feeling he really couldn't buy a pair of shoes without trying them on. The sales clerk disappeared into the storage room for a few minutes only to walk out empty-handed. He looked at Peter apologetically and informed him that unfortunately a $9\frac{1}{2}$ was the smallest size they had in stock.

Peter decided to try them on anyway. Perhaps the extra half-size wouldn't make much difference to the fit. After all, he would be saving $30 in the process. However, the extra space in the toe was quite noticeable, even with the thick socks the clerk had handed him to try with the shoes. Peter wondered how this difference might affect his running performance. His past experience with athletic footwear suggested that the shoe would stretch a little with wear, especially if exposed to wet conditions. Disappointed, Peter felt he would have to forfeit the $30 savings and be satisfied with the fact that he was still fairly close to this initial price range.

Geoff Wallace, the clerk at Sports-4, suggested that he measure Peter's foot to make sure that he did indeed require a size 9. Having confirmed that this was Peter's correct size, he advised strongly against buying a half-size larger, indicating it was his opinion that fit is of critical importance when selecting a pair of running shoes. He then asked Peter to walk up and down in front of the shoe display so that he might examine how his feet struck the floor as he walked.

Geoff observed that Peter tended to strike the floor first with the outer edge of his foot, a tendency referred to as supination, and suggested that Peter might like to try a pair of Brooks GFS-105 shoes, explaining that this was a shoe that offered excellent fit and the Hydroflow cushioning system. He also explained that the GFS-105 featured a curved last, which was recommended for people who tended to supinate. Peter was impressed at the time Geoff was taking to help him select the right shoe and with the fact that the Brooks GFS-105 shoe was on sale at a special price of $109. Peter declined Geoff's suggestion politely, explaining that he had decided on the Nike Air Stab.

Peter was wondering, as he left Sports-4, if he might be able to strike a deal at Sports Experts, considering he should probably think about buying a rainsuit anyway. After dinner, he walked back to the Rideau Centre, wandered into Sports Experts, and was met by Donna Williams, who had been so helpful earlier in the day. Peter requested the running shoes that he had asked her to hold for him, but expressed his dismay over the better deal offered by Sports-4. Peter asked if he might speak with the manager about the possibility of matching the Sports-4 price.

While Donna disappeared to get the manager, Peter spotted a Nike rainsuit that appealed to him and had been marked down in price. As he took the rainsuit off the display rack, he was greeted by the manager who had been directed to Peter by Donna Williams. Peter explained his dilemma and asked if Sports-4's sale price on the Nike Air Stab might be matched, provided that he purchase the rainsuit he had selected. The manager was eager for business and goodwill, especially since he considered Sports-4 to be Sports Experts' main competitor for running and triathlon equipment in the city. He nodded and offered to ring in the sale for him, all the while making conversation about running in Ottawa. Peter appreciated the concession that Sports Experts had made and thanked the manager and Donna Williams, telling them he would be sure to shop at Sports Experts stores in Toronto on a regular basis.

While running slowly along the Rideau Canal later that evening, Peter met Sheila Cambridge, who had just finished a 10 km run. The clean white of Peter's new shoes caught her eye and she commented that he had made an excellent choice. Peter continued on his run toward his apartment on the other side of the canal, feeling satisfied with his purchase. He could sense that he was going to enjoy running, and he was already thinking about entering his first road race later that summer.

Pertinent Web Sites

http://www.nike.com/
http://www.brookssports.com/

Questions

1. Identify the various factors that influenced Peter Taylor's behaviour in selecting a pair of running shoes. Why did he select the Nike brand?
2. What objectives do you feel Peter was trying to accomplish in the selection of running shoes? What motivated his final selection?
3. Why did he buy his shoes at Sports Experts? What could Geoff Wallace have done to persuade Peter to buy the Brooks shoe (or any other) at Sports-4?

Case 2-2

STARBUCKS POURING HOT IN CANADA

The battle in the Canadian specialty coffee market is heating up. The strength of this industry can be seen in the proliferation of coffee shops in recent years. Although only 4 percent of adult Canadians drank specialty coffees in 1994, this percentage doubled within a year, and the popularity of these premium-priced beverages remains quite strong. One of the new kids on the block is Seattle-based Starbucks. Since its entry into Canada in 1987, Starbucks has aggressively sought to increase its market share in large urban centres. Initially, Starbucks confined its operations to Vancouver, and the success there motivated entry into other Canadian cities. In 1996, when the company planned its entry into the Toronto market, it stirred up considerable controversy when it attempted to acquire prime locations for its corporate-owned stores adjacent to existing Second Cup franchises. The casualties in this confrontation were neighbourhood cafes, and this resulted in considerable negative press for Starbucks. Nevertheless, the company has continued its penetration of the Canadian market by opening stores in Edmonton and Calgary. Observers are questioning whether this success will continue. What is it that sets Starbucks apart from the competition? Are such differences sustainable, or are they merely part of some fad?

How is it that Starbucks has been able to penetrate a market served by such well-known brands as Tim Hortons, Second Cup, A.L. Van Houtte, and Timothy's Coffees of the World? The specialty coffee shops in Canada differentiate themselves according to various aspects of coffee drinking. Tim Hortons' president, Paul House, identifies his company as being in the "snack occasion" business and that the growth segments are lunches and bagels. The focus of Second Cup is on street-level stores — takeout coffee bars in commuter stations, hospitals, and shopping malls. Van Houtte, primarily a wholesale distributor to supermarkets and a supplier of coffee machines in offices and institutions, operates a number of retail outlets. Paul-Andre Guillotte, president of A.L. Van Houtte, says that his establishment caters to 18–25-year-olds who are increasingly using coffee shops as a meeting place. Van Houtte's customers view its coffee shops as a young, hip place serving high-quality coffee. The focus for Timothy's Coffees of the World is on the standard cup of fresh-brewed coffee. While Starbucks offers espresso-based products such as caffee latte, caffee mocha and cappuccino, some would argue that Starbucks' success is attributable to its ability to offer customers a total brand experience that extends beyond the consumption of a beverage. This process has involved a positioning of the company — its ideals and image — with various stakeholder groups: the community, its employees, and its customers.

Starbucks' ability to transform coffee into a lifestyle choice flows from its mission statement, which directs the company to a role of environmental leadership in all facets of its business. These words have been transformed into a variety of socially responsible actions, including sale of a reusable coffee tumbler designed to commemorate the one-hundredth anniversary in 1997 of the YWCA in Vancouver. In 1996, Starbucks and the Hospital for Sick Children in Toronto forged a long-term partnership that resulted in Starbucks making an annual contribution to the hospital foundation and opening a Starbucks location in the hospital's lobby. Starbucks actively supports organizations that benefit children's welfare, AIDS outreach, and environmental awareness; is involved in a variety of community cultural events; and supports a variety of programs in Guatemala, Indonesia, Kenya, and Ethiopia — all coffee-growing countries. This protection of the environment can be seen within the individual stores where "everything" that can be recycled is: from the cardboard butter patties to the used coffee grounds. Stale-dated coffee is donated to charitable organizations such as women's shelters.

This case was prepared by Judith A. Cumby, assistant professor, Faculty of Business Administration, Memorial University of Newfoundland, as a basis for class discussion and is not intended to reflect either an effective or an ineffective handling of management problems.

The positive press that the company receives from such community involvement extends to its internal marketing efforts. Despite the recent unionization of workers at some Canadian locations, Starbucks is known for its progressive personnel policies and generous compensation packages. In a proactive move, Starbucks offered all employees, or "partners," the same wages regardless of whether or not they were unionized. The company's claim that it is in the "people development" business as much as the coffee business is evidenced by its training programs, in which partners are encouraged to share their feelings about selling, about coffee, and about working for Starbucks. They are also encouraged to take personal responsibility for all aspects of their work, including the production of beverages to exact specifications and the encouragement of recycling and conservation wherever possible. Partners devote special attention to educating the consumer about the explanation for Starbucks' Italian drink names, the necessity to buy new beans weekly, and the requirement to never let coffee stand for more than twenty minutes. The relationship marketing efforts between Starbucks and its partners have translated into annual staff, or "barista," turnover of 60 percent, compared with 140 percent for hourly workers in the fast-food business.

This affinity toward Starbucks is also felt by customers, 10 percent of whom visit the store twice a day; the average customer visits eighteen times a month. The strength of such customer loyalty has provided the company with the luxury of using very little traditional advertising. Instead, the company has concentrated on creating an experience that customers are happy to promote. Starbucks devotees feel that the brand is defined as much by attitude as by products. It is Starbucks' treatment of its employees, the community, and the environment that has earned it respect with customers. This positive image is backed by premium products, including traditional specialty coffees and the new *Frappuccino*, a frozen coffee drink that is tremendously popular during the summer. Customers can buy Starbucks ice cream and bottled drinks in the supermarket. Some argue that the proliferation of brand extensions could serve to dilute the core concept.

What have other coffee companies been doing in the wake of Starbucks' aggressive marketing campaigns? Distribution is critical and has been extended beyond traditional retail outlets. There are Second Cup kiosks in all Borders bookstores in Canada, while Starbucks has opened outlets in Chapters bookshops. Second Cup coffee is served on all Air Canada flights, an alliance that accounts for 10 percent of the company's coffee sales in Canada. Second Cup and Tim Hortons operate franchises in hospitals. Tim Hortons coffee is available at over 1,100 company and franchise restaurants, many in rural locations, and through some Esso gas stations, and is promoted with the theme of "You've always got time for Tim Hortons." This is supplemented by the use of an emotional appeal in recent advertising campaigns in which the focus is on the unique role of Tim Hortons stores in the community. Lillian, age eighty-six, is shown walking through Lunenburg, Nova Scotia, on her way to enjoying her daily cup of Tim Hortons coffee. Customers have found Lillian to be warm and charming — just the image that the advertising creators were looking for. Another advertisement includes a spot on Sammi, a dog from Saint John, New Brunswick, who picks up her master's coffee from the local drive-through window. The use of such true stories is quite popular with customers in Atlantic Canada.

There are those who question whether the specialty coffee market will continue to grow or whether it is just a fad. Supporters maintain that the proliferation of coffee houses reflects changes in social views, particularly with young adults. Both Starbucks and Second Cup hope to capitalize on the profitability associated with catering to the time-strapped boomer by producing, selling, and playing CDs designed to attract people to the stores. Starbucks even maintains designers and architects in-house who adapt the mellow urban look to a given site and customer demographics. The creation of such a comfortable environment to complement the eclectic product offerings and corporate image is proving to be quite popular with Canadians in urban centres. Will this success continue in other parts of the country? Is it even sustainable over the long-run in existing centres? What changes will be necessary over the next few years?

Pertinent Web Site

http://www.secondcup.com

Questions

1. Who are the target markets for Starbucks? How do they differ from those of other coffee shops?
2. What is Starbucks' competitive advantage? Is it sustainable?
3. How is the company positioned? Illustrate this with a positioning map that reflects the major players in the coffee market.
4. Does the proliferation of Starbucks' brand extension dilute the core concept and negatively affect the company's positioning and competitive advantage?

Sources: "Brewing Up Stronger Sales for Specialty Coffee," *Canadian Grocer*, October 1996, p. 25; Simona Chiose, "A Little Jazz with Your Java?" *The Globe and Mail*, November 4, 1996, p. C1; Lesley Daw, "Tim Hortons Stars Pooch in True Story," *Marketing Magazine*, January 27, 1997, p. 4; "Dollars for Doughnuts," *Financial Post*, September 2/4, 1995, p. 7; Louise Gagnon, "Coffee Wars Perking Up in Quebec Market," *Marketing*, January 20, 1997, p. 3; Jo Marney, "Fresh-Brewed Data," *Marketing*, March 10, 1997, p. 21; Bill McDowell, "Starbucks Is Ground Zero in Today's Coffee Culture," *Advertising Age*, December 9, 1996; Jennifer Reese, "Starbucks: Inside the Coffee Culture," *Fortune*, December 9, 1996, pp.190–200; "Second Cup to Fly Air Canada with $2 Million Contract," *Financial Post Daily*, November 12, 1996, p. 11; "Starbucks and the Vancouver YWCA Announce Community Partnership," *The News Hook*, June 4, 1997; "Starbucks Coffee Company," *The Green Money Journal*, Spring/Summer 1995; "Starbucks Coffee Company Corporate Profile," *The News Hook*, September 24, 1996; "Starbucks Invades Toronto Market," *The Globe and Mail*, January 23, 1996, p. B19; "Starbucks Makes Long-Term Commitment to The Hospital For Sick Children," *Canada NewsWire*, July 2, 1996; Karen Van Hahn, "Brewing Up a Northwest Image," *The Globe and Mail*, April 10, 1996, pp. E5, E7; "Wendys Completes Tim Hortons Merger," *Canadian Press Newswire*, January 3, 1996.

Case 2-3

THE GAP: ADAPTING TO CHANGING CONSUMER PREFERENCES

By all accounts, The Gap is a marketing success story. The retail chain began by offering basic T-shirts and jeans that looked like designer clothes without the designer image or price. The Gap quickly grew into the most profitable specialty-clothing store chain in North America by positioning itself as offering "good style, good quality, good value." Its eight hundred stores do more than $3 billion in sales, and its divisions include GapKids, Banana Republic, and Old Navy stores.

The Gap's road to becoming a leader in specialty retailing was not without bumps. Donald Fisher started The Gap in 1969 out of frustration when a store refused to allow him to return a pair of Levi jeans that were too short. The first Gap store was located in San Francisco, and it stocked jeans in a wide range of sizes. The Gap soon expanded across the United States, supported by a fixed 50 percent markup that Levi Strauss required of all retailers selling its jeans. However, as a result of government regulatory changes and other factors in the mid-1970s, the price of jeans could no longer be set by manufacturers. This forced The Gap, which was totally dependent on jeans, to find a new position.

After a futile attempt to position itself as a retailer of higher-margin clothing carrying its own brand, a back-to-basics merchandise strategy was found to have the greatest appeal among The Gap's customers. Gap stores stocked all-cotton apparel items in a deep assortment of colours. The Gap's strong ties to manufacturers,

---

Adapted with permission by Judy Cumby, assistant professor at Memorial University of Newfoundland, from Michael J. Etzel, Bruce J. Walker, and William J. Stanton, *Marketing*, 11th ed. (New York: McGraw-Hill, 1997), pp. 186–187.

developed during its earlier efforts to sell its own store label, allowed the company to manage the quality of its products. Furthermore, the company was able to control costs by designing its clothes in-house.

Expansion into children's clothing followed the success of Gap stores in the 1980s. GapKids stores feature simple, basic apparel items (for example, dresses and overalls) for newborns to young children.

The Gap acquired Banana Republic in 1983. Banana Republic grew rapidly as safari fashion became very popular with the release of movies such as the *Indiana Jones* series, *Out of Africa*, and *Romancing the Stone*. However, the safari image waned by 1988, necessitating a change in position for the 150-store chain. The position that produced the best financial results was as an upscale Gap with more adventurous fashions.

The Gap's merchandise assortment allowed it to become the "uniform of the middle class and middle aged." However, two core customer groups, teens and Generation Xers, began to turn away from The Gap's staple clothing items. Leo Burnett Co.'s semiannual "What is hot among kids" market research survey indicated that a negative image of The Gap began developing among teens as early as 1992. In that year, over 90 percent of teens surveyed labelled Gap clothes as "cool." This rating slipped to 83 percent by the summer of 1993, 75 percent by the winter of 1993, and 66 percent by the end of 1994. The loss of interest by these important market segments forced The Gap to appeal to new customers by becoming more fashion-oriented and launching new products and retail store concepts.

The Gap shifted its emphasis in merchandise away from unisex items to clothing that is gender-specific and fashion-oriented. The effort worked, as the company's earnings increased by 23 percent from 1992 to 1993 despite a less favourable image among younger consumers. In addition, an effort was made to present a uniform picture of a Gap store by stocking all styles available in all Gap stores, whereas smaller stores previously received only a narrow selection of inventory.

Another attempt to expand The Gap's customer base resulted in its entry into discount retailing in the United States in 1993. Forty-eight low-performing Gap stores were converted into Gap Warehouse discount stores. This decision represented a radical departure from The Gap's success formula, which focused the company on being the leader in specialty clothing retailing. To prevent the cannibalization of sales at Gap stores, Gap Warehouses sold separate lines of clothes that were similar to the Gap's basic products — jeans, khaki pants, and T-shirts — but carried everyday low prices. In addition, the material used in Gap Warehouse clothes was different from those stocked at Gap stores. Jeans received fewer stone-washed treatments, and stitching was less detailed. And lighter-weight fabrics containing more polyester were used to control costs and keep retail prices low. Unlike The Gap, which targets only adults, Gap Warehouses targeted adults and children.

The following year, The Gap launched in the United States a second entry into discount retailing to compete with mass merchants. Its Old Navy Clothing Co. stores carry specially designed apparel and accessories for consumers with incomes of $20,000 to $50,000. The Old Navy stores offer a wide selection of casual apparel items priced 20 to 25 percent below The Gap's clothing lines. Old Navy stores are positioned as one-stop clothing outlets with department store-style assortments of clothing for men, women, boys, girls, and babies. In addition, the stores stock The Gap's non-clothing products (for example, picture frames, address books, and decorative shopping bags).

The Gap introduced a line of bath and body products in a further attempt to serve new market segments. Gap Scents includes a line of soaps, lotions, shampoos, conditioners, shower gels, bath salts, and scented candles. The bath and body products are designed to target a market estimated to be worth more than $1 billion annually and growing at 5 percent per year. In part, the development of Gap Scents was in response to the introduction of the Bath & Body Works chain by The Limited, The Gap's major competitor. The bath and body products are viewed by Gap management as the first step in making The Gap a lifestyle brand. If consumers begin to view The Gap as more than just a place for clothes, other product categories can be added.

Retailing also is undergoing radical changes. Data on North American shopping habits indicate that both the number of mall visits and the number of stores visited per shopping trip have dropped dramatically over the last twenty years. In addition, new technology is allowing retailers to control their costs as never before and devise new ways (for example, the Internet) to offer products to meet the needs of their customers. The face of specialty retailing will continue to be shaped in the 1990s as the echo boomer generation moves into its teens. These consumers switch brands easily and are comfortable with technology. One in three belongs to a minority group, compared with one in four in the general population. These teens have more purchasing power than previous generations and make many of their own purchase decisions, including those about clothes. The key to success for The Gap will be its ability to refine the position of its stores to meet the needs of its target markets while operating in an increasingly dynamic environment.

Pertinent Web Site

http://www.gap.com

Questions

1. What social influences will have an effect on The Gap's future marketing strategy?
2. Evaluate The Gap's entry into discount retailing in the United States with Gap Warehouse and Old Navy stores. Given the changes that have taken place over the last few years in discount retailing in Canada, where is The Gap positioned relative to the competition? Illustrate with use of a positioning map.
3. Given the changes taking place in retailing, what new products might The Gap offer? What changes to their marketing strategy can you suggest?
4. Visit The Gap's Web site and those of various competitors. How does The Gap's Web site compare with those of some of its competitors?
   http://www.dockers.com
   http://www.ebauer.com
   http://jcrew.com

Sources: Alice Cuneo, "Gap Floats Lower-Price Old Navy Stores," *Advertising Age*, July 25, 1994, p. 36; Christina Duff, "Bobby Short Wore Khakis — Who's He and Who Cares?" *The Wall Street Journal*, February 16, 1995, p. A1; Mary Kuntz, "Reinventing the Store: How Smart Retailers are Changing the Way We Shop," *Business Week*, November 27, 1995, p. 84; Russell Mitchell, "A Humbler Neighborhood for The Gap," *Business Week*, August 16, 1993, p. 29; Russell Mitchell, "A Bit of a Rut at The Gap," *Business Week*, November 30, 1992, p. 100; Russell Mitchell, "The Gap: Can the Nation's Hottest Retailer stay on Top?" *Business Week*, March 9, 1992, p. 58; Russell Mitchell, "The Gap Dolls Itself Up," *Business Week*, March 21, 1994, p. 46; Elaine Underwood, "Gap Sets Scent for November," *Brandweek*, August 22, 1994, p. 4; and Laura Zinn, "Teens Here Comes the Biggest Wave Yet," *Business Week*, April 11, 1994, p. 76.

Part Three

Products and Services

The planning, development, and management of the want-satisfying goods and services that are a company's products

Part Two focused on the selection and identification of target markets in accordance with the firm's marketing goals. The next step in the strategic marketing planning process is to develop a marketing mix that will achieve these goals in the selected target markets. The marketing mix is a strategic combination of four variables — the organization's products or services, pricing structure, distribution system, and promotional program. Each of these is closely interrelated with the other three variables in the mix.

Part Three, consisting of four chapters, is devoted to the product component of the marketing mix. In Chapter 9 we define the term product, consider the importance of product planning and innovation, and discuss the new-product development process. Chapter 10 deals mainly with product-mix strategies, the management of the product life cycle, and a consideration of style and fashion. Chapter 11 is concerned with branding, packaging, labelling, and other product features. Chapter 12 addresses the subject of services and how they are marketed to consumers.

CHAPTER 9 GOALS

After studying this chapter, you should have an understanding of:

- The meaning of the word *product* in its fullest sense.
- What a "new" product is.
- The classification of consumer and business products.
- The relevance of these product classifications to marketing strategy.
- The importance of product innovation.
- The steps in the product-development process.
- Criteria for adding a product to a company's line.
- Adoption and diffusion processes for new products.
- Organizational structures for product planning and development.

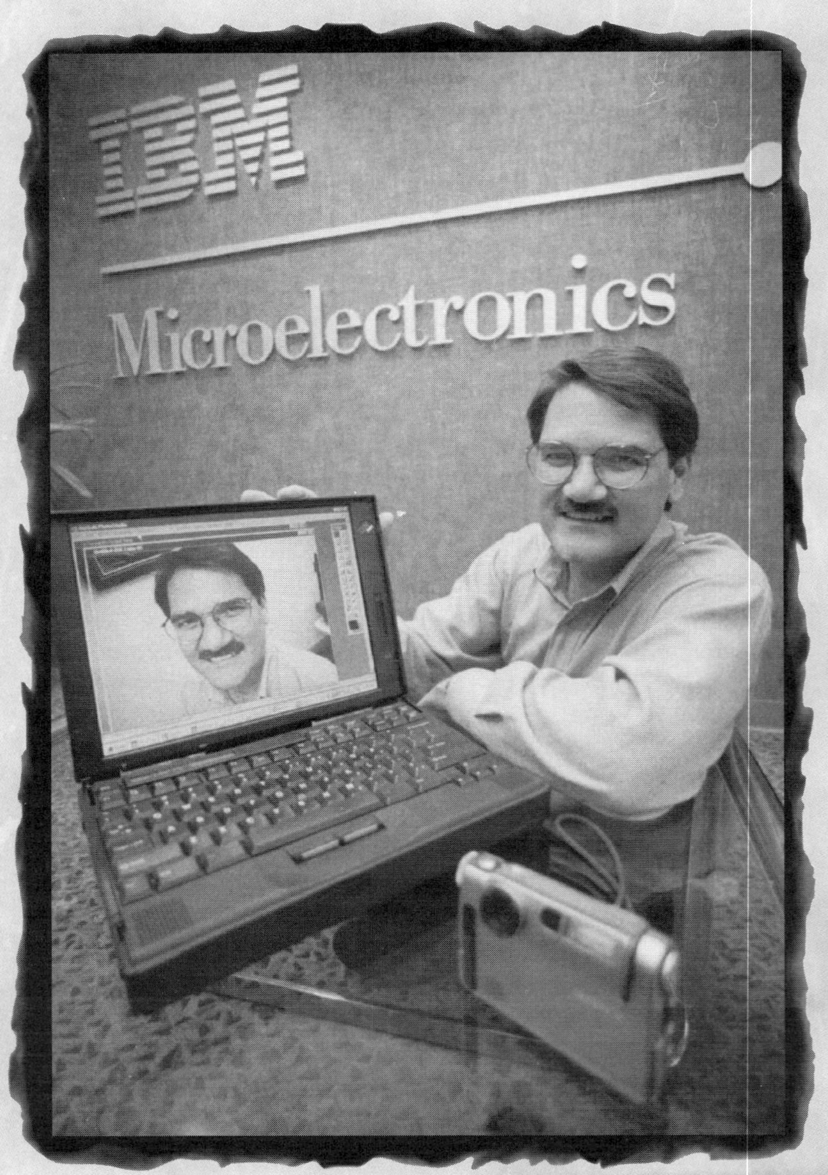

Chapter Nine

Product Planning and Development

INFRARED TECHNOLOGY PROMISES NEW FREEDOMS: THERE GOES THE WIRED WORLD

All around you are the marvels of communication and computer technology. Every day we get more. But aside from not necessarily knowing how to use a lot of these marvels, or finding out that they are sort of...well...boring, are some other problems. One of these has to do with the fact that frequently it takes up to three remote controls to watch a TV show or a video. That's because different manufacturers have been using different approaches to using infrared light — the invisible part of the light spectrum — to control such things as TVs, VCRs and CD players. Now we have new manufacturer-agreed-upon standards for a new generation of products that rely on a more sophisticated form of infrared technology. This means that one size fits all — well, maybe — and no more cables connecting everything to everything.

IBM's Markham, Ontario, Microelectronics Laboratory has the global mandate to develop infrared technology for IBM worldwide. Paul Belluz, director of the lab, says that the new-product development thrust is guided by "our vision [to have] in-room connectivity." Consumers won't have to fumble with cords to connect their devices, be they computers, pagers, telephones, electronic organizers, or personal digital assistants. The devices will make their own connections whenever they need to. Consumers won't know, or need to know, where and how all this is taking place. Infrared signal detection devices are under development and will be placed to operate so that when a person walks into a room or a building, any infrared-capable device that person is carrying will be automatically sensed and connected. If you are not interested in being detected by the network, or if you want to limit the access that others have to your network, you can do that.

www.holidayinn.com
www.travel.vancouver.bc.ca
www.cancer.ca

Who will likely be the first to take up these kinds of innovations? It's busy executives, managers and professionals who need to be in touch, as well as practitioners who buy computers and equipment for their home-based businesses (26 percent of PC sales), or to bring work home (16 percent), or to give their children a high-tech tutor (27 percent). These are the buyers — the consumer innovators and early adopters — who are willing to be the first to pay for wireless communication for voice and data, extra computing power, the latest portable computing, and the convenience of more specialized software. But for wireless products to really take off in the broader consumer market, cost is one problem, and useful applications, rather than technologically feasible ones, is another. While only 18 percent of current cellular phone users are interested in adding data services to their current wireless capability, more than 61 percent of notebook computer users are interested in adding wireless data services. All this new technology and product keeps rushing at us, but what happens if you stand between an infrared-equipped computer and a signal detector device — is it the same as standing between your remote TV controller and your TV set, hmmm?[1]

THE MEANING OF PRODUCT

In a narrow sense, a product is a set of attributes assembled in an identifiable form. Each product is identified by a commonly understood descriptive (or generic) name, such as steel, insurance, tennis racquets, or entertainment. Product attributes such as brand name and postsale service that appeal to consumer motivation or buying patterns play no part in this narrow interpretation. According to this interpretation, an Apple and a Compaq would be the same product — a personal computer. And Canada's Wonderland and Ontario Place would be an identical service — an amusement park.

In marketing, we need a broader definition of product to indicate that consumers are not really buying a set of attributes, but rather benefits that satisfy their needs. Thus consumers don't want sandpaper; they really want a smooth surface. To develop a sufficiently broad definition, let's start with *product* as an umbrella term covering goods, services, places, persons, and ideas. Throughout this book, when we speak of products, we are using this broad connotation.

Thus a product that provides benefits can be something other than a tangible good. The Holiday Inn's product is a service that provides the benefit of a comfortable night's rest at a reasonable price. The Vancouver Visitors Bureau's product is a place that provides romance, sun and sea, relaxation, cross-cultural experiences, and other benefits. In a political campaign, the New Democratic Party or Reform Party's product is a person (candidate) whom the party wants you to buy (vote for). The Canadian Cancer Society is selling an idea and the benefits of not smoking. In Chapter 12 we discuss in more detail the marketing of intangible products such as services and ideas.

To further expand our definition, we treat each brand as a separate product. In this sense, Kodacolor film and Fujicolor film are different products. Lantic sugar and St. Lawrence sugar are also separate products, even though the only physical difference may be the brand name on the package. But the brand name suggests a product difference to the consumer, and this brings the concept of consumer want satisfaction into the definition.

Any change in a feature (design, colour, size, packaging), however minor, creates another product. Each such change provides the seller with an opportunity to use a new set of appeals to reach what essentially may be a new market. Pain relievers (Tylenol, Anacin) in capsule and gelcap forms are different products from the same brand in tablet form, even though the chemical contents of the tablet and the other forms are identical. Seemingly minor product changes can be the key to success (or failure) in international markets. For example, to satisfy Japanese consumers, two modified versions of Oreo cookies were developed. One has less sugar in the cookie batter; the other omits the cream filling.[2]

We can broaden this interpretation still further. A Sony TV bought in a discount store on a cash-and-carry basis is a different product from the identical model purchased in a department store. In the department store, the customer may pay a higher price for the TV but buys it on credit, has it delivered free of charge, and receives other store services.

www.canadaswonderland.com • www.ontarioplace.com/

Our concept of a product now includes the services that accompany it when purchased. Occasionally, a seller's support and assurances may be extraordinary. For example, the new OnStar system that General Motors has included in some Cadillac models uses Global Positioning Systems to tell the vehicle's location at all times and link the car driver to a whole host of additional services. These include electronic route support, roadside assistance with location, remote door unlock, theft detection and notification, stolen vehicle tracking, emergency services, automatic notification of air bag deployment, and OnStar convenience services such as hotel reservations, the location of ATMs, and a hands-free, voice-activated cellular phone.[3]

We're now ready for a definition that is useful to marketers: A **product** is a set of tangible and intangible attributes, including packaging, colour, price, quality, and brand, plus the seller's services and reputation. A product may be a tangible product, service, place, person, or idea (see Figure 9-1). In essence, then, consumers are buying much more than a set of physical attributes when they buy a product. They are buying want satisfaction in the form of the benefits they expect to receive from the product. The physical product is only one aspect of the marketing relationship.

FIGURE 9-1 A Product Is Much More Than a Set of Physical Attributes

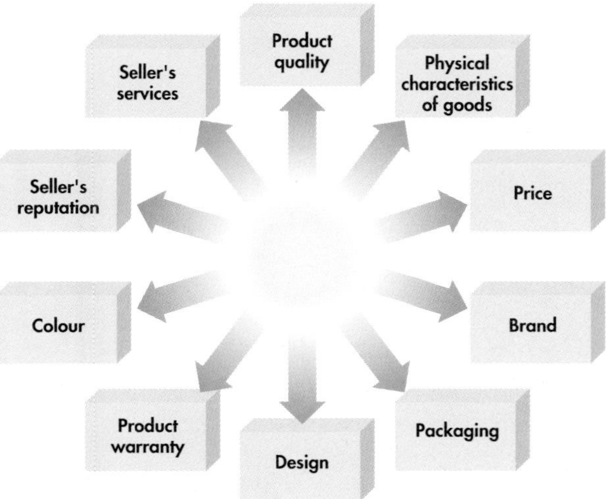

CLASSIFICATIONS OF PRODUCTS

To design effective marketing programs, organizations need to know what kinds of products they are offering to consumers. Thus it's helpful to separate products into homogeneous categories. First we will divide all products into two categories — consumer products and business products — that parallel our description of the market. Then we will subdivide each category still further.

Consumer and Business Products

Consumer products are intended for use by household consumers for nonbusiness purposes. **Business products** are intended for resale, for use in producing other products, or for providing services in an organization. Thus the two types of products are distinguished on the basis of who will use them and how they will be used.

The position of a product in its distribution channel has no bearing on its classification. Kellogg's Corn Flakes are categorized as consumer products, even if they are in the manufacturer's warehouses, in a freight line's trucks, or on retailers' shelves, if ultimately they will be used in their present form by household consumers. However, Kellogg's Corn Flakes sold to restaurants and other institutions are categorized as business products no matter where they are in the distribution system.

Often it is not possible to place a product in only one class or the other. Seats on an Air Canada flight from Toronto to Vancouver may be considered a consumer product if purchased by students or a family going on vacation. But a seat on the same flight bought by a sales representative for business use is categorized as a business product. Air Canada, or any other company in a similar situation, recognizes that its product falls into both categories and therefore develops separate marketing programs for each market.

These distinctions may seem like "splitting hairs," but they are necessary for the strategic planning of marketing programs. Each major category of products ultimately goes to a distinctive type of market and thus requires different marketing methods.[4]

Classification of Consumer Goods

For marketing purposes, distinguishing consumer goods from business goods is helpful but only a first step. The range of consumer goods is still too broad. Consequently, as shown in Table 9-1, they are further classified as convenience, shopping, specialty, and unsought goods. This classification is not based on intrinsic differences in the products themselves. Rather, it is based on how consumers go about buying a particular product. Depending on the buying behaviour of different consumers, a single product — such as wine or dress slacks — can fall into more than one of the four categories.

Convenience Goods A tangible product that the consumer knows enough about before going out to buy it and then actually buys it with a minimum of effort is termed a **convenience good**. Normally the advantages resulting from shopping around to compare price and quality are not considered worth the extra time and effort required to shop and compare. A consumer is willing to accept any of several

TABLE 9-1 Categories of Consumer Goods: Characteristics and Marketing Considerations

	Type of Product*		
	Convenience	**Shopping**	**Specialty**
EXAMPLES	Canned fruit	Furniture	Expensive suits
Characteristics			
Time and effort devoted by consumer to shopping	Very little	Considerable	Cannot generalize; consumer may go to nearby store and buy with minimum effort or may have to go to distant store and spend much time and effort
Time spent planning the purchase	Very little	Considerable	Considerable
How soon want is satisfied after it arises	Immediately	Relatively long time	Relatively long time
Are price and quality compared?	No	Yes	No
Price	Usually low	High	High
Purchase frequency	Usually frequent	Infrequent	Infrequent
Marketing Considerations			
Length of channel	Long	Short	Short to very short
Retailer	Relatively unimportant	Important	Very important
Number of outlets	As many as possible	Few	Few; often only one in a market
Stock turnover	High	Lower	Lower
Gross margin	Low	High	High
Responsibility for advertising	Producer's	Retailer's	Joint responsibility
Point-of-purchase display	Very important	Less important	Less important
Brand or store name important	Brand name	Store name	Both
Packaging	Very important	Less important	Less important

*Unsought products are not included. See text explanation.

brands and thus will buy the one that is most accessible. For most buyers, convenience goods include many food items, inexpensive candy, drug sundries such as shampoo and toothpaste, and staple hardware items such as light bulbs and batteries. Convenience services include such things as banking transactions, pay telephones, and photocopying.

Although for convenience goods the service expectation level is low, from time to time service is a requirement and poor service can cause a problem, while good service will not necessarily be an advantage on a product level, but will be in terms of the consumer's relationship with the store and the store personnel. The store personnel, if properly trained, and the retailer would both want a long-term relationship with consumers.

Shopping Goods A tangible product for which consumers want to compare quality, price, and perhaps style in several stores before making a purchase is considered a **shopping good**. Examples of shopping goods — at least for most consumers — are fashionable apparel, furniture, major appliances, and automobiles. The process of searching and comparing continues as long as the customer believes that the potential benefits from a better purchase more than offset the additional time and effort spent shopping. A better purchase might be saving several hundred dollars on the purchase of a new car or finally finding a software package that prepares financial statements in the manner desired by the buyer.

To buyers of a shopping good, the reputations of the stores carrying the product often are more important than the images of the manufacturers. For example, a consumer may be more loyal to a local Future Shop store than to various brands of audio and video equipment, such as JVC and Sanyo. The quality of store personnel and the way customer interaction is handled in the shopping process contribute to the store's reputation.

Specialty Goods A tangible product for which consumers have a strong brand preference and are willing to expend substantial time and effort in locating the desired brand is called a **specialty good**. The consumer is willing to forgo more accessible substitutes to search for and purchase the desired brand. Examples of products usually categorized as specialty goods include expensive men's suits, stereo sound equipment, health foods, photographic equipment, and, for many people, new automobiles and certain home appliances. Various brands, such as Armani, Nikon, and BMW, have achieved specialty-good status in the minds of some consumers.

Usually relatively few outlets carry such items, and since the product's brand name is important to buyers, both manufacturer and retailer advertise the product extensively. Often the manufacturer pays a portion of the retailer's advertising costs, and the name of the store carrying the specialty good frequently appears in the manufacturer's ads. Manufacturers are also prepared to provide training for store personnel because the information and service expectations of customers are high. Of course, specialized retailers have their own store reputation and image to consider, and the quality of service and manner in which the buying experience is handled can help trust and enable the selling of other stocked brands and repeat shopping.

Unsought Goods There's one more, quite different category of goods. In fact, it's so unlike the other three categories that we have not included it in Table 9-1. Nevertheless, because some firms sell unsought goods, this category deserves brief discussion.

An **unsought good** is a new product that the consumer is not yet aware of or a product that the consumer is aware of but does not want right now. For many people, unknown new products include computers that speak and video telephones. However, telephone companies are betting that new promotional programs will remove the latter product from the unsought category. As the name suggests, a firm faces a very difficult, perhaps impossible, advertising and personal-selling job when trying to market unsought goods. Having a good marketing relationship with customers allows buyers to more easily entertain unsought goods. The traditional approach would be to make consumers aware of the products so that they will buy the advertised brand when the need arises.

Classification of Business Goods

As with consumer goods, the general category of business goods is too broad to use in developing a marketing program. One factor, however, stands out, as shown in Table 9-2. For each of the five traditional categories of business goods displayed, the relationship between buyer and seller is of consequence and, in all but one case, very important.

We separate business goods into five categories: raw materials, manufactured parts and materials, installations, accessory equipment, and operating supplies. This classification is based on the product's

TABLE 9-2 Categories of Business Goods: Characteristics and Marketing Considerations

	Type of Product				
	Raw Materials	**Fabricating Parts and Materials**	**Installations**	**Accessory Equipment**	**Operating Supplies**
EXAMPLES	Iron ore	Engine blocks	Blast furnaces	Storage racks	Paper clips
Characteristics					
Unit price	Very low	Low	Very high	Medium	Low
Length of life	Very short	Depends on final product	Very long	Long	Short
Quantities purchased	Large	Large	Very small	Small	Small
Frequency of purchase	Frequent delivery; long-term purchase contract	Infrequent purchase, but frequent delivery	Very infrequent	Medium frequency	Frequent
Standardization of competitive products	Very much; grading is important	Very much	Very little; custom-made	Little	Much
Quantity of supply	Limited; supply can be increased slowly or not at all	Usually no problem	No problem	Usually no problem	Usually no problem
Marketing Considerations					
Nature of channel	Short; no intermediaries	Short; intermediaries only for small buyers	Short; no intermediaries	Intermediaries used	Intermediaries used
Negotiation period	Hard to generalize	Medium	Long	Medium	Short
Price competition	Important	Important	Varies in importance	Not main factor	Important
Presale/postsale service	Not important	Important	Very important	Important	Very little
Promotional activity	Very little	Moderate	Sales people very important	Important	Not too important
Brand preference	None	Generally low	High	High	Low
Advance buying contract	Important; long-term contracts	Important; long-term contracts	Not usual	Not usual	Not usual

broad uses. For example, a business good may be used in producing other products, in operating an organization, and in other ways we will discuss.

Raw Materials Business goods that become part of another tangible product before being processed in any way (except as necessary to assist in handling the product) are considered **raw materials**. Raw materials include:

- Goods found in their natural state, such as minerals, land, and products of the forests and the seas, and
- Agricultural products, such as cotton, fruits, livestock, and animal products, including eggs and raw milk.

Because of their distinctive attributes, these two groups of raw materials should be marketed differently. For instance, the supply of raw materials in their natural state is limited, cannot be substantially increased, and often involves only a few large producers. Further, such products generally are of a commodity nature, must be carefully graded, and, consequently, are highly standardized. Consider coal as an example; it is extracted in great quantities and then is graded by hardness and sulphur content.

The characteristics of raw materials in their natural state affect how they are marketed:

- Prices are normally set by supply and demand; thus producers have little or no control.
- Because of their bulk and low unit value, transportation costs are an important consideration; consider grain and fish as examples.
- Because of these same factors, natural raw materials frequently are marketed directly from producer to business user with a minimum of physical handling.
- There is very little branding or other product differentiation of this type of product. This puts the buyer–seller relationship in a pivotal position.
- It's also rare for marketers of natural raw materials to advertise or try to stimulate demand in other ways.

For raw materials in their natural state, competition is built around price and the assurance that a producer can deliver the product as specified.

Agricultural products are supplied by many small producers located some distance from their markets. The supply is largely controllable by producers — frequently through marketing boards — but it cannot be increased or decreased rapidly. The product is perishable and is not produced at a uniform rate throughout the year. Most Okanagan and Niagara soft fruits, for example, ripen in late summer and thus are readily available at that time of year and become less available in subsequent months. Standardization and grading are commonplace for agricultural products. Also, transportation costs are likely to be high relative to the product's unit value.

Close attention must be given to transportation and warehousing. Transportation costs are high relative to unit value, and standardization and grading are very important. Because producers are small and numerous, many producer co-operatives, intermediaries, and long channels of distribution are needed. Promotional activity is usually carried out by marketing boards.

Manufactured Parts and Materials Business products that become part of other finished products fit into the category of **manufactured parts and materials**. Some of these undergo further processing and may be referred to as **fabricating materials**; examples include yarn that is woven into cloth and flour used in making bread. What distinguishes them from raw materials is that they have already been processed and are bought by manufacturers for assembly into their final products. Some examples are the small motors that are bought by manufacturers of furnaces and lawnmowers, and the zippers used by clothing manufacturers.

Manufactured materials and parts are usually purchased in large quantities. Buying decisions are based on the price and the service provided by the seller. To ensure an adequate, timely supply, a buyer may place an order a year or more in advance. Because customers are concerned about price, service, and reliability of supply, most manufactured products are marketed directly from producer to user. Intermediaries are used most often when the buyers are small and/or when buyers have small fill-in orders (after the large initial order) requiring rapid delivery.

Branding manufactured materials and parts is generally unimportant. However, some firms have successfully pulled their business goods out of obscurity by branding them. Talon zippers and the NutraSweet brand of sweetener are examples.

Installations Manufactured products that are an organization's major, expensive, and long-lived equipment are termed **installations**. Examples are large generators in a dam, a factory building, diesel engines for a railway, and servers for an Internet service provider. The characteristic of installations that differentiates them from other categories of business goods is that they directly affect the scale of operations in an organization producing goods or services. Adding twelve new Steelcase desks will not affect the scale of operations at Air Canada, but adding twelve Airbus jet aircraft certainly will. Therefore, jet aircraft are categorized as installations, but desks normally are not.

The marketing of installations presents a real challenge, because each unit sold represents a large dollar amount. Often each unit is made to the buyer's detailed specifications and much presale and postsale servicing is essential, making buyer trust and confidence in the supplier essential. For example, a large printing press requires installation, maintenance, and — inevitably — repair service. Sales are usually made directly from producer to business user. Because installations are technical in nature, a high-calibre, well-trained sales force is needed to provide careful, detailed explanations, and quality service and personal selling. Promotion and advertising emphasizing service and expertise might be conducted using print media or through a Web page.

Accessory Equipment Tangible products that have substantial value and are used in an organization's operations are called **accessory equipment**. This category of business goods neither becomes an actual part of a finished product nor has a significant impact on the organization's scale of operations. The life of accessory equipment is shorter than that of installations but longer than that of operating supplies. Some examples are point-of-sale terminals in a retail store, small power tools, forklift trucks, and office desks.

It is difficult to generalize about how accessory equipment should be marketed. For example, direct sale is appropriate for some products in this category when an order is for several units or when each unit is worth a lot of money. Normally, however, manufacturers of accessory equipment use intermediaries — for example, office-equipment distributors. The reasons: typically, the market is geographically dispersed, there are many different types of potential users, and individual orders may be relatively small.

Operating Supplies Business goods that are characterized by low dollar value per unit and a short life and that aid in an organization's operations without becoming part of the finished product are called **operating supplies**. Examples are lubricating oils, pencils and stationery, and heating fuel. Purchasers want to buy operating supplies with fairly little effort. Thus operating supplies are the convenience goods of the business sector.

As with the other categories of goods, the characteristics of operating supplies influence how they should be marketed. Because they are low in unit value and are bought by many different organizations, operating supplies — like consumer convenience goods — are distributed widely. Thus the producing firm uses wholesaling intermediaries extensively. Also, because competing products are quite standardized and there is little brand insistence, price competition is normally stiff.

IMPORTANCE OF PRODUCT INNOVATION

A business exists to satisfy consumers while making a profit. Fundamentally, a company fulfils this dual purpose through its products. New-product planning and development are vital to an organization's success. A company cannot successfully sell a bad product over the long run.

Requirement for Growth

A guideline for management is "innovate or die." For many companies, a substantial portion of this year's sales volume and net profit will come from products that did not exist five to ten years ago. For example, innovation is credited for ING Canada's ability to move up in the financial services business. This company shot to number two among property and casualty insurers in Canada. Some of its innovations include setting up a national electronic banking

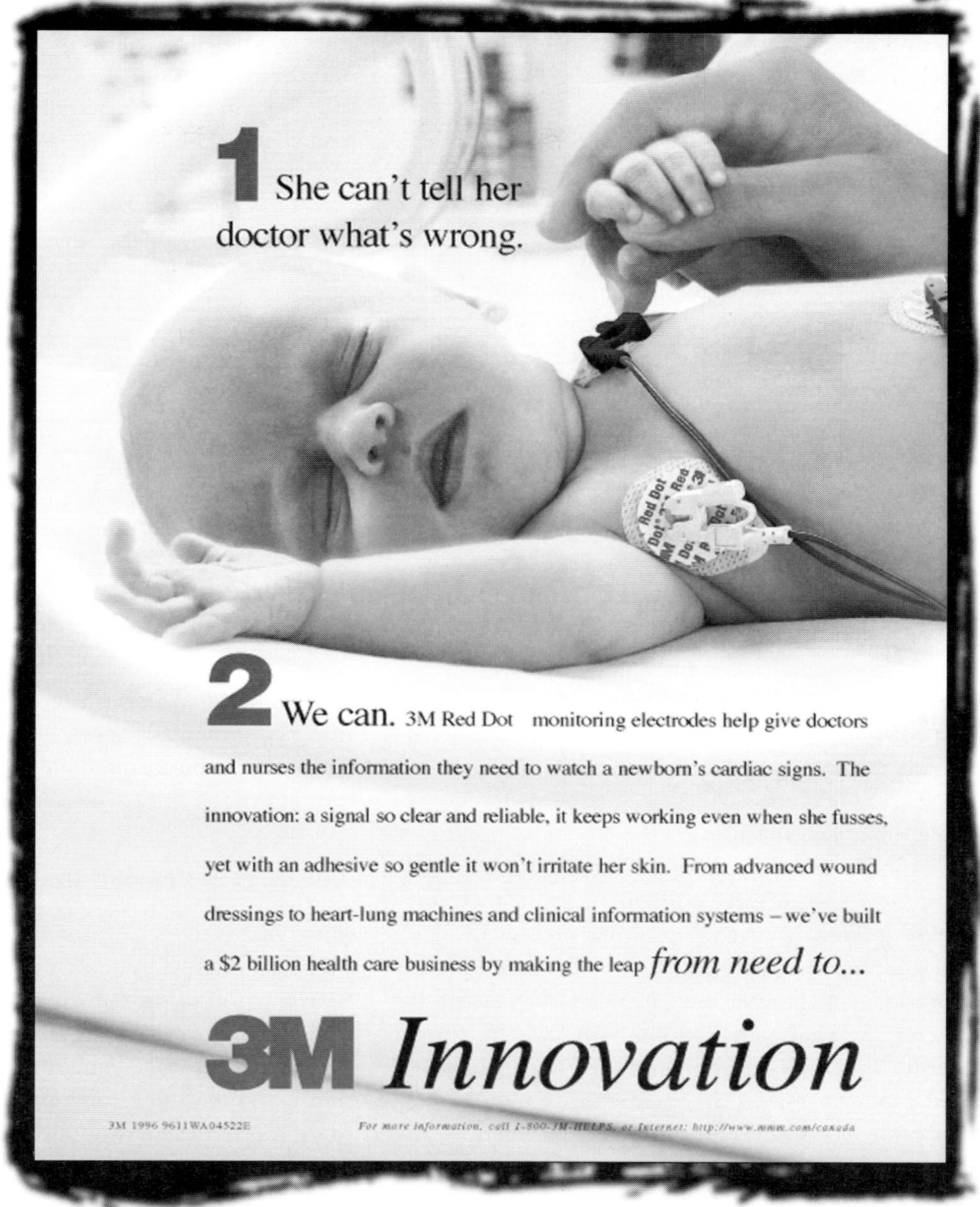

3M emphasizes how it built a large new business by working from needs to innovations.

service with no actual branches being opened and the introduction of a project in Quebec in which insurance brokers can sell residential mortgages, making ING one of the first insurance companies in Canada to move into this territory.[5]

Because products, like people, go through a life cycle, new products are essential for sustaining a company's revenues and profits. Sales of a product grow and then, almost inevitably, decline; eventually, most products are replaced. The concept of the product life cycle is discussed in more detail in Chapter 10, but we mention it here because it has two significant implications for product innovation:

- Every company's present products eventually become obsolete as their sales volume and market share are reduced by changing consumer desires and/or superior competing products.

- As a product ages, its profits generally decline. Introducing a new product at the right time can help maintain a company's profits.

Companies that develop innovative products can reap financial benefits. According to a research study in the United States, 39 percent of highly successful firms had introduced an innovative product during the previous five years, compared with only 23 percent of less successful firms.[6] Consider specific examples such as microwave popcorn, fibre optic cable, and Post-It notes. Each provided benefits that were not previously available.

Increased Consumer Selectivity

In recent years, consumers have become more selective in their choices of products. The economic environment of the early 1990s left consumers with reduced financial resources. Individuals, households, and organizations had to be very careful in their purchases. Even households and individuals who were not affected by economic downturns were selective in making additional purchases because they were already reasonably well fed, clothed, housed, transported, and equipped. The same can be said of companies that were not hurt by the recession.

Another reason for more selective buying is that consumers have to sort through an abundance (or, some would say, an excess) of similar products. Many new products are mere imitations of existing products and, as such, offer few if any added benefits. Is Procter & Gamble's introduction of HE (high energy) Tide really a new product?[7] This deluge of new products may lead to "product indigestion." The remedy is to develop truly new products — to innovate, not just imitate.

High Failure Rates

For many years, the "rule of thumb" had been that about 80 percent of new products fail. However, because of differing definitions of *new product* and *failure*, the statistics often vary from one study to another. One company that tracks new-product introductions placed the failure rate at even higher than 80 percent. According to another firm's annual survey, 72 percent of new products do not meet their primary business objectives.[8]

Why do new products fail? Most fail because they are not different from existing products. Other factors contributing to failures include poor positioning and lack of marketing support. Another reason a new product fails is that it is perceived as offering poor value in relation to its price.

Considering how vital new products are to a company's growth, the large number of new-product introductions, and the high failure rates, product innovation deserves special attention. Firms that are inattentive to their new products may face financial ruin due to the high cost of product failures. Companies that effectively manage product innovation can expect to reap a variety of benefits — differential advantage, higher sales and profits, and a solid foundation for the future.

DEVELOPMENT OF NEW PRODUCTS

It's often said that nothing happens until somebody sells something. This is not entirely true. First there must be something to sell — a product, service, person, place, or idea. And that "something" must be developed.

What Is a "New" Product?

Just what is a "new" product? Are the auto manufacturers' annual models new products? Was GM's introduction of the Saturn automobiles new? Or, in other product categories, is a new version of Corel's WordPerfect Office Suite software for word processing, communications, and spreadsheet work new? Or must a product be revolutionary, never before seen, before we can class it as new?

How new a product is affects how it should be marketed. There are numerous connotations of "new product," but we will focus our attention on three distinct categories of **new products**:

- Products that are really innovative — truly unique. A recent example is a security device that electronically compares the shape of a person's hand with the image of a hand encoded on an identification card. Another is a gadget developed by Hewlett-Packard that permits viewers to participate in "interactive" TV programs.[9] Still-to-be-

MARKETING AT WORK FILE 9–1

INNOVATING OF NECESSITY OR THE NECESSITY OF INNOVATING

The Canadian furniture industry lost half its manufacturing capacity in the early 1990s as hundreds of furniture makers "left the field" after the Canada–U.S. Free Trade Agreement gave producers in both countries equal access to each other's markets. American manufacturers made trendy, appealing sofas but, according to some, they fell apart after two years. Canadian manufacturers, on the other hand, did well on quality and durability but were stodgy about design.

When Cathy Carter began designing her own furniture in 1994, she couldn't get conservative manufacturers to produce what she felt customers really wanted. That being the case, she did what any self-respecting woman with ideas would do — she put them into practice herself with her new firm, C-Style International. Now she is doing quite well, thank you, by tapping into a trend that is away from matched sets of furniture. She is designing and producing innovative one-off pieces and creating a design and look that bridges antique and modern. She now has her designs on the floor at The Bay, Eaton's, and up-market boutiques. With the expected addition of Sears Canada, her Canadian business will grow even more.

Meanwhile, those of her compatriot designers and manufacturers who are part of the resurgence of the Canadian industry since the dark early 1990s are also doing well. Gerry Cockerill, of Toronto based Leda Furniture Ltd., believes that those who are successful have updated their designs, standardized their sizes, redesigned product, and focused on style and fashion. Shermag Inc. of Sherbrooke, Que., is taking advantage of the renewed interest in the arts and crafts style, a natural for Canadian producers because of its all-wood requirements.

Many Canadian furniture makers are boosting demand by working to shift consumers' perceptions of furniture from that of being a commodity to that of being a fashion item that needs to be replaced more frequently than in the past. The results are that Canadian business is growing, and exports are exploding. The Canadian industry experienced a revenue growth of 7 percent in 1996 and exports increased by 17 percent. As much as 95 percent of the exports are to the United States, but more distributors from France, England, Japan, and the United Arab Emirates are now shopping in Canada.

Source: Adapted from Carolyn Leitch, "Furniture Firms Sitting Pretty," *The Globe and Mail*, January 13, 1997, pp. B1, B3.

developed products in this category would be a cancer cure and easily and inexpensively repaired automobiles. Any new product in this category satisfies a real need that is not being satisfied at the time it is introduced.

- Replacements that are significantly different from existing products in form, function, and — most important — benefits provided. Johnson & Johnson's Acuvue disposable contact lenses and Sharp Corp.'s very thin (only 3 inches/7.5 cm deep) TV, which hangs on a wall like a picture, are replacing some traditional models. In some years, new fashions in clothing are different enough to fit into this category. Referring back to the earlier examples, probably GM's Saturn line falls into this category.
- Imitative products that are new to a particular company but not new to the market. Usually, annual models of autos and new versions of cereals are appropriately placed in this category. In another situation, a firm may simply want to capture part of an existing market with a "me too" product. To maximize company-wide sales, makers of cold and cough remedies routinely introduce imitative products, some of which compete

www.levi.com

with a nearly identical product from the same company. That's the case with Dristan Sinus and CoAdvil, both marketed in Canada by American Home Products. In a different field, following the early success of hotels featuring two-room suites rather than single rooms, Quality Inns added similar products.

Ultimately, of course, whether a product is new or not depends on how the intended market perceives it. If buyers consider it to be significantly different from competitive products in some relevant characteristic (such as appearance or performance), then it is indeed a new product. As in other situations, perception is reality!

New-Product Strategy

To achieve strong sales and healthy profits, every producer of business or consumer goods should have an explicit strategy with respect to developing and evaluating new products. This strategy should guide every step in the process.

A **new-product strategy** is a statement identifying the role a new product is expected to play in achieving corporate and marketing goals. For example, a new product might be designed to protect market share or maintain the company's reputation as an innovator. Or a new product's role might be to meet a specific return-on-investment goal or establish a position in a new market.

A new product's intended role also will influence the type of product to be developed. See the following box.

Only in recent years have many companies consciously identified new-product strategies. The process of developing new products has become more efficient and more effective for firms with strategies because they have a better idea of what they are trying to accomplish.

With the availability of new communication and information technology, firms are now beginning to orient their new-product strategies toward mass customization in order to provide increased product value. Individual consumer preferences can be built into new products either by requiring that a modular strategy be used for product design or by positioning the final step of individual product differentiation at the last minute in the product creation process, the delivery or consumer "try on" stage. Thus, Levi Strauss can deliver to your door, within two weeks of being electronically measured in a store and for an extra $10, tailor-made jeans, what 73 percent of jeans wearers would really like. Or Dell Computers can give you the system of your choice within forty-eight hours after your Internet order.[10]

Stages in the Development Process

Guided by a company's new-product strategy, a new product is best developed through a series of six stages, as shown in Figure 9-2. Compared with unstructured development, the formal development of new products provides benefits such as higher success rates, increased customer satisfaction, and greater achievement of time, quality, and cost objectives for new products.[11]

At each stage, management must decide whether to proceed to the next stage, abandon the

Company Goal		Product Strategy		Recent Examples
To defend market share.	→	Introduce an addition to an existing product line or revise an existing product.	→	Dairy desserts to complement other Healthy Choice "healthful" foods.
To strengthen a reputation as an innovator.	→	Introduce a really new product — not just an extension of an existing one.	→	Palmtop computers introduced by Hewlett-Packard.
To increase customer satisfaction.	→	Develop a mass customization system to improve service.	→	Paris Miki, world's largest eyewear retailer, developed an interactive fitting/styling system.

www.ahp.com

FIGURE 9-2 Major Stages in the New-Product Development Process

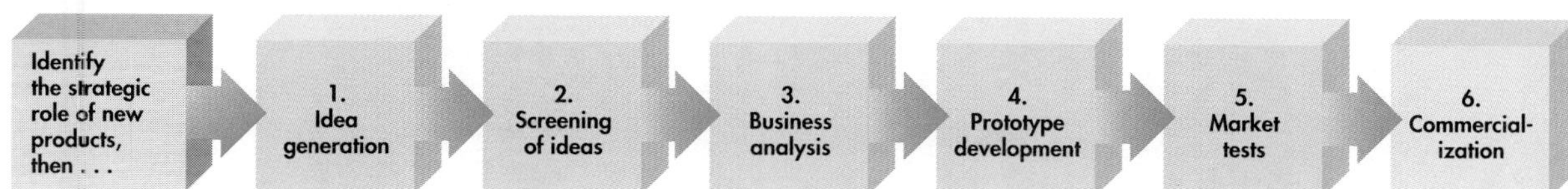

product, or seek additional information.[12] Here's a brief description of what should happen at each stage of the **new-product development process**:

1. *Generating new-product ideas.* New-product development starts with an idea or a concept. A system must be designed for stimulating new ideas within an organization and then acknowledging and reviewing them promptly. Customers should also be encouraged to propose innovations. In a research study, 80 percent of companies pointed to customers as their best source for new-product ideas.[13]
2. *Screening ideas.* At this stage, new-product ideas are evaluated to determine which ones warrant further study.[14] Typically, a management team screens the pool of ideas.
3. *Business analysis.* A surviving idea is expanded into a concrete business proposal. In the **business analysis**, management (a) identifies product features, (b) estimates market demand, competition, and the product's profitability, (c) establishes a program to develop the product, and (d) assigns responsibility for further study of the product's feasibility.
4. *Prototype development.* If the results of the business analysis are favourable, then a prototype (or trial model) of the product is developed. In the case of tangible products, a small quantity of the trial model is manufactured to designated specifications. Laboratory tests and other technical evaluations are carried out to determine whether it is practical to produce the product. A firm may be able to construct a prototype of a new type of cellular telephone but be unable to manufacture the new product in large quantities or at a cost low enough to stimulate sales and still yield a profit. In the case of services, the facilities and procedures necessary to produce and deliver the new product are designed and tested. That certainly is a necessary step in the development of a new rollercoaster ride at an amusement park!
5. *Market tests.* Unlike the internal tests conducted during prototype development, **market tests** involve actual consumers. A new tangible product may be given to a sample of people for use in their households (in the case of a consumer good) or their organizations (a business good). Following this trial, consumers are asked to evaluate the product. Consumer-use tests are less practical for services, due to their intangible nature.

   This stage in new-product development often entails **test marketing**, in which the product is placed on sale in a limited geographic area. Results, including sales and repeat purchases, are monitored by the company that developed the product and perhaps by competitors as well. In this stage, the product's design and production plans may have to be adjusted as a result of test findings. Following market tests, management must make a final "go–no go" decision about introducing the product.
6. *Commercialization.* In this stage, full-scale production and marketing programs are planned and, finally, implemented. Up to this point in development, management has virtually complete control over the product. Once the product is "born" and enters its life cycle, however, the external competitive environment becomes a major determinant of its destiny.

Note that the first two stages — idea generation and screening — are tied closely to the overall new-product strategy. This strategy can provide a focus for generating new-product ideas and a basis for evaluating them.

In the six-stage process, the first three stages are particularly critical because they deal with ideas and, as such, are the least expensive. More important, many products fail because the idea or the timing is wrong — and the first three stages are intended to identify

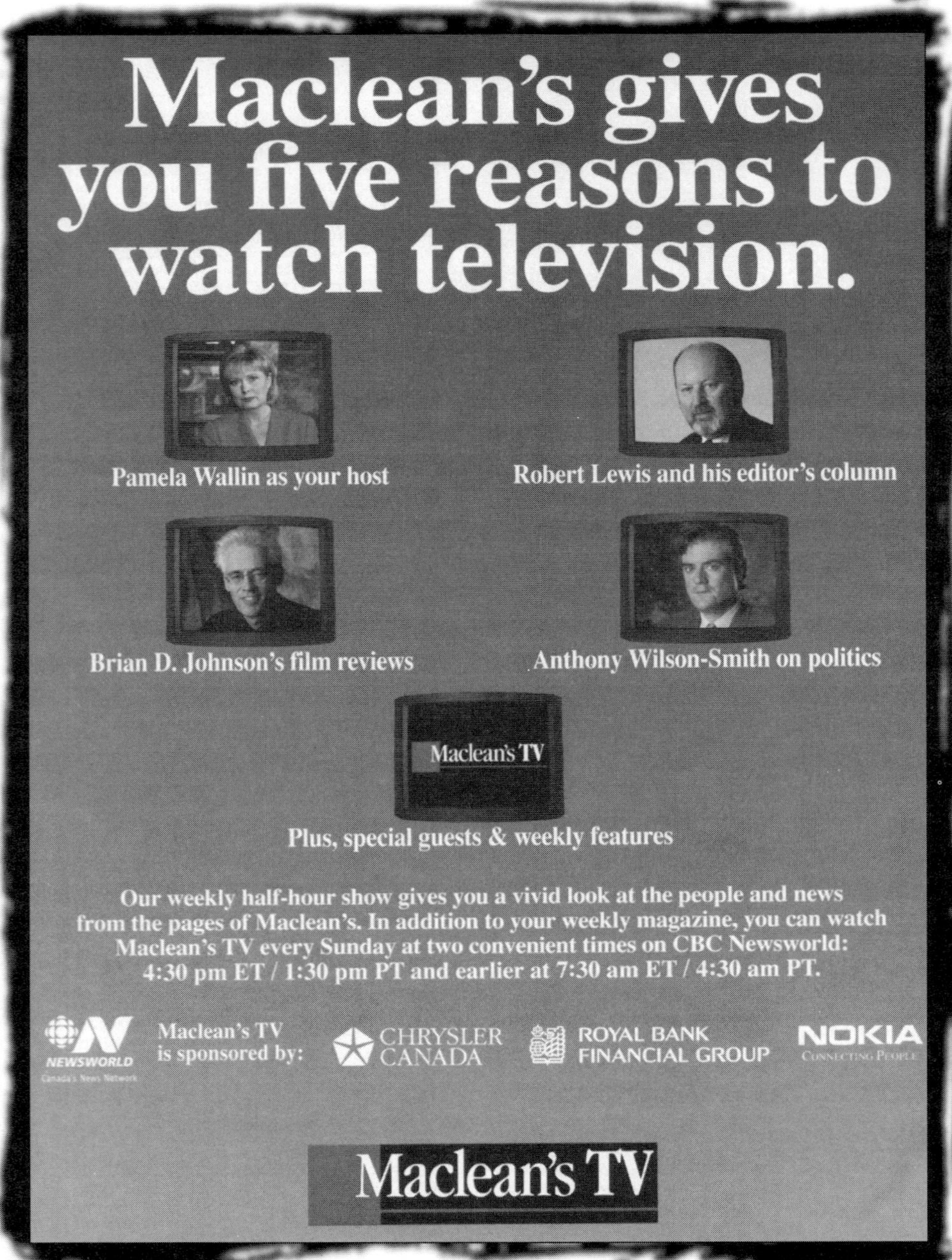

To increase market share and to make use of its reputation and expertise, *Maclean's* magazine now delivers an innovative product extension of interviews and reports in a new sponsored-television-program format.

such situations. Each subsequent stage becomes more costly in terms of the budget and human resources necessary to carry out the required tasks.

Some companies, trying to bring new products to market faster than their competitors, skip stages in the development process. The most common omission is the fifth stage, market tests. Without this stage, however, the company lacks consumer reactions to the proposed product.

Historically, the marketing of goods has received more attention than the marketing of services. Thus it is not surprising that the new-product development process is not as advanced in services fields as it is in goods industries. However, on the

MARKETING AT WORK FILE 9-2

PRODUCT TESTING

Have you ever wondered how the product manufacturer knows when the product will meet with consumer acceptance? Many times they don't know, and this is why so many products fail. Some product manufacturers are realizing, however, that better consumer input saves money in the long run.

Applied Consumer & Clinical Evaluations Inc. (ACCE) is in the business of providing consumers with the opportunity to bring their products to consumer groups. The company specializes in testing food products, primarily in the snack food category. ACCE draws its consumers from a database of more than six thousand families with all ages that have assorted product interests and uses. Small groups are chosen from this population. Each individual is placed in a separate, silent cubical with pumped-in, odourless air and identical lighting conditions and is given single samples, and told to fill in a short questionnaire rating his or her taste impressions.

Ellen Karp, president of Toronto market research firm Anerka International Inc., says that when you're close to a product you lose sight of it and start taking things for granted. Independent input into the product acceptability is essential in those circumstances.

Sometimes product developers are taken quite by surprise with the results they receive in the testing. In one situation identified by ACCE, a company wanted to find out why its sauce was not selling. It learned that when the sauce was poured on a hot plate, it slid right off. The problem wasn't thickness but chemical composition. A simple formula change to add more starch made the sauce work better, and sales improved.

Research into product acceptance by consumers gives manufacturers the opportunity to assess whether or not the products will sell before advertising and promotional expenses are incurred. Joan Berta, co-owner of ACCE, says that "companies can spend their money on an array of research areas, such as product positioning or the psychological impact of colour." She feels that they would be much better advised to gain an early understanding of what the customer really wants in the product.

Source: Adapted from Janet McFarland, "Testers Take Consumer Pulse," *The Globe and Mail*, September 23, 1996, p. B8.

positive side, that means services firms have more flexibility to devise a new-product development process that suits their distinctive circumstances.

Producer's Criteria for New Products

When should a company add a new product to its current assortment of products? Here are guidelines that some producers use in answering this question:

- *There must be adequate market demand.* Too often management begins with the wrong question, such as "Can we use our present sales force?" or "Will the new item fit into our production system?" The necessary first question is "Do enough people really want this product?"
- *The product must satisfy key financial criteria.* At least three questions should be asked: "Is adequate financing available?" "Will the new item reduce seasonal and cyclical fluctuations in the company's sales?" And, most critical, "Can we make sufficient profits with the product?"
- *The product must be compatible with environmental standards.* Key questions include: "Do the production processes avoid polluting the air or water?" "Will the finished product, including its packaging, be friendly to the environment?" And, "After being used, does the product have recycling potential?"

- *The product must fit into the company's present marketing structure.* Sherwin Williams Paint Company would probably find it quite difficult to add margarine to its line of paints. Specific questions related to whether a new product will fit the company's marketing expertise and experience include: "Can the existing sales force be used?" "Can the present channels of distribution be used?"

Besides these four issues, a proposed product must satisfy other criteria. For instance, it must be in keeping with the company's objectives and image. The product also must be compatible with the firm's production capabilities. And it must satisfy any pertinent legal requirements.

Intermediary's Criteria for New Products

Intermediaries, such as retailers and wholesalers, considering whether to buy a new product for resale should apply all the preceding criteria except those related to production. In addition, an intermediary should apply the following guidelines:

- The intermediary must have a good working relationship with the producer. By distributing a new product, an intermediary should stand to benefit from the producer's reputation, the possibility of getting the right to be the only company to sell the product in a given territory, and the promotional and financial help given by the producer.
- The producer and intermediary must have compatible distribution policies and practices. Pertinent questions include: "What kind of selling effort is required for the new product?" "How does the proposed product fit with the intermediary's policies regarding repair service, alterations (for clothing), credit, and delivery?"
- As in the case of producers, the product must satisfy key financial criteria. At least two questions should be asked: "If adding a new product necessitates eliminating another product due to a shortage of shelf or storage space, will the result be a net gain in sales?" And "Can we make sufficient profits with the product?"

NEW-PRODUCT ADOPTION AND DIFFUSION

The likelihood of achieving success with a new product, especially a really innovative product, is increased if management understands the adoption and diffusion processes for that product. Once again, we are stressing that organizations need to understand how consumers behave. The **adoption process** is the set of successive decisions an individual makes before accepting an innovation. **Diffusion** of a new product is the process by which an innovation spreads throughout a social system over time.[15]

By understanding these processes, an organization can gain insight into how a product is or is not accepted by consumers and which groups of consumers are likely to buy a product soon after it is introduced, later on, or never. This knowledge of consumer behaviour can be valuable in designing an effective marketing program.

Stages in Adoption Process

A prospective user goes through six **stages in the adoption process** — deciding whether to purchase something new. See the following box.

Stage	Activity in That Stage
Awareness	Individual is exposed to the innovation; becomes a prospect.
Interest	Prospect is interested enough to seek information.
Evaluation	Prospect judges the advantages and disadvantages of a product.
Trial	Prospect adopts the innovation on a limited basis. A consumer buys a sample, if the product can be sampled.
Adoption	Prospect decides whether to use the innovation on a full-scale basis.
Confirmation	After adopting the innovation, prospect becomes a user who immediately seeks assurances that decision to purchase the product was correct.

MARKETING AT WORK FILE 9-3

LUXURY TRAIN TRAVEL: THE DEVELOPMENT OF A SERVICE PRODUCT

The longest passenger train in Canadian history left Vancouver to travel to Kamloops on September 13, 1996. The thirty-seven cars were welcomed by flag-waving citizens of Kamloops. Travelling on the train were 1,100 guests invited by Rocky Mountaineer Railtours, the largest private passenger-rail operation in North America, owned and operated by Great Canadian Railtour Company Ltd. This promotional train journey was an opportunity for the company to showcase a tourism product that has been developing and growing since 1990.

Rocky Mountaineer Railtours offers to its customers luxury train travel through some of the most dramatic and beautiful scenery in North America. Billed as "The Most Spectacular Train Trip in the World," it provides travellers with the opportunity to see the full expanse of the mountainous terrain from a fully glassed upper deck as well as an observation platform. Passengers are pampered by three chefs and four onboard attendants who offer a complete menu that highlights indigenous ingredients, fresh produce, and wines from the local area. Travellers receive preferred baggage handling at train stations, escorted pre-boarding privileges, and memorabilia gifts along their journey.

According to Murray Atherton, vice-president, marketing and sales, train travel is one of the few modes of travel that combine comfort, service, and scenery. The development of this product had to take into consideration ways of ensuring that these elements came together in a marketable package. In June 1997, the company announced completion of three new "dome coaches," which enable the traveller to see the scenery. Over the years, Rocky Mountaineer Railtours has developed a series of attractive package tours with one-stop reservation service.

This product is best described as an "experience." It occurs over a period of two days and provides to the customer a combination of magnificent views, gourmet meals, an opportunity to feel pampered, and comfortable surroundings. All of these elements must combine in the right way to ensure the customer enjoys the experience.

Unlike the manufacturer of a chair, Rocky Mountaineer Railtours cannot produce the product and then send it to a retailer to be sold. Services products are developed in concept; then the components for completion are assembled, for example, the food ingredients for the meals; but the full production of the product occurs in association with the purchaser. Each traveller who uses the train experience has individual needs, preferences, and requirements that must be met from the point the reservation is made until the passenger disembarks. At all stages, the product is being developed on a continuous basis in concert with the buyer.

Sources: "Rocky Mountaineer Railtours Reinvents Luxury Train Travel," *Canada NewsWire*, June 1997, http://www.newswire.ca/releases/June 1997/25/c5428.html. "Rocky Mountaineer Railtours Announce the Longest Passenger Train in Canadian History," *Canada NewsWire*, September 1996, http://www.newswire.ca/releases/September 1996/13/c1924.html. "Rocky Mountaineer Railtours on Track and On-Line for 1997," *Rocky Mountaineer Home Page*, Press Release, January 14, 1997, http://www.rkymtnrail.com.

Adopter Categories

Some people will adopt an innovation soon after it is introduced. Others will delay before accepting a new product, and still others may never adopt it. Research has identified five **innovation adopter categories**, based on the point in time when individuals adopt a given innovation. Nonadopters are excluded from this categorization. Characteristics of early and late adopters are summarized in Table 9-3.

TABLE 9-3 Characteristics of Early and Late Adopters of Innovations

	Early Adopters	Late Adopters
Key Characteristics		
Venturesome	Innovators (3% of total adopters)	
Respected	Early adopters (13%)	
Deliberate	Early majority (34%)	
Sceptical		Late majority (34% of total adopters)
Tradition-bound		Laggards (16%)
Other Characteristics		
Age	Younger	Older
Education	Well educated	Less educated
Income	Higher	Lower
Social relationships: within or outside community	Innovators: outside Others: within	Totally local
Social status	Higher	Lower
Information sources	Wide variety; many media	Limited media exposure; limited reliance on outside media; reliance on local peer groups

Innovators Representing about 3 percent of the market, **innovators** are venturesome consumers who are the first to adopt an innovation. In relation to later adopters, innovators are likely to be younger, have higher social status, and be in better financial shape. Innovators also tend to have broad social relationships involving various groups of people in more than one community. They are likely to rely more on nonpersonal sources of information, such as advertising and the Internet, rather than on sales people or other personal sources.

Early Adopters Making up about 13 percent of the market, **early adopters** purchase a new product after innovators but sooner than other consumers. Unlike innovators, who have broad involvements outside a local community, early adopters tend to be involved socially within a local community. Early adopters are greatly respected in their social system; in fact, other people are interested in and influenced by their opinions. Thus the early-adopter category includes more opinion leaders than any other adopter group. Sales people are probably used more as information sources by early adopters than by any other category.

In the process of diffusion, a **change agent** is a person who seeks to accelerate the spread of a given innovation. In business, the person responsible for introducing an innovative new product must be a change agent. Consider the introduction of digital cameras. Sony's DSC-F1 and Epson's PhotoPC 500 camera are examples of this product that retail at a price substantially above the market price of more conventional technology.[16] The marketers of these products must be effective change agents, convincing consumers that it is worthwhile to pay the higher price. A change agent focuses the initial persuasive efforts on early adopters because other people respect their opinions and eventually will emulate their behaviour. If a firm can get early adopters to accept its innovative product, then the broader market eventually will accept the product as well.

Early Majority The **early majority**, representing about 34 percent of the market, includes more deliberate consumers who accept an innovation just before the "average" adopter in a social system. This group is a bit above average in social and economic measures. Consumers in the early-majority group rely quite a bit on ads, sales people, and contact with early adopters.

Late Majority The **late majority**, another 34 percent of the market, is a sceptical group of consumers who usually adopt an innovation to save money or in response to social pressure from their peers. They rely on their peers — late or early majority — as sources of information. Advertising and personal selling are less effective with this group than is word-of-mouth communication.

Laggards **Laggards** are consumers who are bound by tradition and, hence, are last to adopt an innovation. They make up about 16 percent of the market. Laggards are suspicious of innovations and innovators; they wonder why anyone would pay a lot more for a new kind of light bulb, for example. By the time laggards adopt something new, it may already have been discarded by the innovators in favour of a newer concept. Laggards are older and usually are at the low end of the social and economic scales.

We are discussing only adopters of an innovation. For most innovations, there are many people who are not included in our percentages. They are **nonadopters**; they never adopt the innovation.

Innovation Characteristics Affecting Adoption Rate

There are five **innovation characteristics that affect the adoption rate**:[17]

- *Relative advantage:* the degree to which an innovation is superior to currently available products. Relative advantage may be reflected in lower cost, greater safety, easier use, or some other relevant benefit. Safest Stripper, a paint and varnish remover introduced by 3M, scores high on this characteristic. The product contains no harmful chemicals, has no odour, and allows the user to refinish furniture indoors rather than having to work outdoors.
- *Compatibility:* the degree to which an innovation coincides with the cultural values and experiences of prospective adopters. Since many consumers want to save time and satisfy their desires now rather than later, microwave popcorn certainly satisfies this characteristic.
- *Complexity:* the degree of difficulty in understanding or using an innovation. The more complex an innovation is, the more slowly it will be adopted — if it is adopted at all. Combined shampoo-conditioners certainly are simple to use, so adoption of them was not impeded by complexity. However, many forms of insurance and some consumer-electronics products have problems with this characteristic.
- *Trialability:* the degree to which an innovation may be sampled on some limited basis. Setting aside the other characteristics, the greater the trialability, the faster will be the adoption rate. For instance, a central home air-conditioning system is likely to have a slower adoption rate than a new seed or fertilizer, which may be tried on a small plot of ground. In general, due to this characteristic, costly products will be adopted more slowly than will inexpensive products. Similarly, many services (such as insurance) are difficult to use on a trial basis, so they tend to be adopted rather slowly.
- *Observability:* the degree to which an innovation actually can be seen to be effective. In general, the greater the observability, the faster the adoption rate. For example, a new weed killer that works on existing weeds probably will be accepted sooner than a product that prevents weeds from sprouting. The reason? The latter product, even if highly effective, produces no dead weeds to show to prospective buyers!

A company would like an innovative product to satisfy all five characteristics discussed above. But few do. Kodak's camcorder video tape is a good example to assess these characteristics. Kodak sells this product as "backcoated," which it claims enables the video tape to perform better in a VCR, especially if it is an old VCR. The backcoating reduces the likelihood of losing images. This product comes prepacked in a cassette and is easy to use (reducing complexity), is a well-known brand name (contributing to trialability), and offers a feature that other film does not have — the backcoating that prevents damage to the film (representing relative advantage). The customer can observe the backcoating by checking the back of the film. A flat surface as opposed to a shiny one indicates that the product is backcoated. The product is widely distributed, which enhances compatibility with consumers' desire for convenient purchase.[18]

ORGANIZING FOR PRODUCT INNOVATION

If new-product programs are to be successful, they must be supported by a strong, long-term commitment from top management. This commitment must be maintained even when some new products fail. To implement this commitment to innovation effectively, new-product programs must be soundly organized.

Types of Organization

There is no "one best" organizational structure for product planning and development. Many companies use more than one structure to manage these activities. Some widely used organizational structures for planning and developing new products are:

- **Product-planning committee.** Members include executives from major departments — marketing, production, finance, engineering, and research — and, especially in small firms, the president and/or another top-level executive.
- **New-product department.** These units are small, consisting of five or fewer people. The department head reports to the president (which, in a large firm, may be the president of a division).
- **Venture team.** A small group, with representatives from engineering, production, finance, and marketing research, operates like a separate small business. Typically the team reports directly to top management.
- **Product manager.** This individual is responsible for planning new products as well as managing established products. Although still effective in some firms, we'll discuss in the next section why this structure is being displaced in many firms by one of the other structures discussed above.

Which organizational structure is chosen is not the key point here — each has strengths and weaknesses. What's critical is to make sure that some person or group has the specific responsibility for new-product development and is backed by top management. Product innovation is too important an activity to handle in an unorganized, nonchalant fashion, which presumes that somehow the job will get done. To maximize the chances for successful new-product development, it is vital that employees responsible for product planning have the right skills, particularly the ability to work well with other people and operate in a supportive environment.

As the new product is completed, responsibility for marketing it usually is shifted either to an existing department or a new department established just for this new product. In some cases the team that developed the product may continue as the management nucleus of the new unit.

Integrating new products into departments that are already marketing established products does carry at least two risks, however. First, executives who are involved with ongoing products may have a short-term outlook as they deal with day-to-day problems of existing products. Consequently, they may not recognize the long-term importance of new products and, as a result, neglect them. Second, managers of successful existing products often are reluctant to assume the risks inherent in marketing new products.

Product Manager

Beginning in the 1950s, many companies, such as Procter & Gamble and Kraft General Foods, assigned the responsibility for planning new products as well as co-ordinating the marketing efforts of existing ones to a product manager. Essentially, a product manager, sometimes called a brand manager, plans the complete marketing program for a brand or group of products. Specific tasks include setting marketing goals, preparing budgets, and developing plans for advertising and personal-selling and service activities. Developing new products along with improving established products may also be part of the job description.

Probably the biggest problem with this approach is that a company often saddles product managers with great responsibility but provides them with little authority. For instance, product managers are expected to develop the plan by which the sales force will market the product to wholesalers and retailers, but they have no real authority over the sales force. They are responsible for drafting advertising plans, but typically do not select the advertising agencies that will fully develop and execute them. Product managers have a profit responsibility for their brands, yet are often denied any control over product costs, prices, or advertising budgets. Their effectiveness depends largely on their ability to influence other executives to co-operate with their plans.

Many firms are relying on team efforts — such as the product-planning committees or venture teams previously discussed — to develop new products.[19] Typically, these are cross-functional teams consisting of representatives not only from marketing research and marketing but also product design, engineering, and manufacturing. Research has shown that a cross-functional team at Chrysler was able to reduce the time taken to design and build its LH line of sedans by 40 percent.

Summary

The first commandment in marketing is "Know thy customer," and the second is "Know thy product." The relative number and success of a company's new products are a prime determinant of its sales, growth rate, and profits. A firm can best serve its customers by producing and marketing want-satisfying goods or services. The scarcity of some natural resources and a growing concern for our environment make social responsibility a crucial aspect of product innovation.

To manage its products effectively, a firm's marketers must understand the full meaning of product, which stresses that consumers are buying want satisfaction. Products can be classified into two basic categories — consumer products and business products. Each category is then subdivided, because a different marketing program is required for each distinct group of products.

There are many views about what constitutes a new product. For marketing purposes, three categories of new products need to be recognized — innovative, significantly different, and imitative.

A clear statement of the firm's new-product strategy serves as a solid foundation for the six-stage development process for new products. The early stages in this process are especially important. If a firm can make an early and correct decision to stop the development of a proposed product, a lot of money and labour can be saved.

In deciding whether to add a new product, a producer or intermediary should consider whether there is adequate market demand for it. The product also should fit in with the firm's marketing, production, and financial resources. Management needs to understand the adoption and diffusion processes for a new product.

A prospective user goes through six stages in deciding whether to adopt a new product. Adopters of an innovation can be divided into five categories, depending on how quickly they accept an innovation such as a new product. These categories are innovators, early adopters, early majority, late majority, and laggards. In addition, there usually is a group of nonadopters.

Five characteristics of an innovation seem to influence the adoption rate: relative advantage, compatibility, complexity, trialability, and observability.

Successful product planning and development require long-term commitment and strong support from top management. Furthermore, new-product programs must be soundly organized. Most firms use one of four organizational structures for new-product development: product-planning committee, new-product department, venture team, or product manager. Recently, the trend has been away from product managers and toward team efforts for developing new products.

Key Terms and Concepts

Product (217)
Consumer products (217)
Business products (217)
Convenience good (218)
Shopping good (219)
Specialty good (219)
Unsought good (219)
Raw materials (221)
Manufactured parts and materials (221)
Fabricating materials (221)
Installations (222)
Accessory equipment (222)
Operating supplies (222)
New products (224)
New-product strategy (226)
New-product development process (227)
Business analysis (227)
Market tests (227)
Test marketing (227)
Adoption process (230)
Diffusion (230)
Stages in the adoption process (230)
Innovation adopter categories (231)
Innovators (232)
Early adopters (232)
Change agent (232)
Early majority (232)
Late majority (233)
Laggards (233)
Nonadopters (233)
Innovation characteristics that affect the adoption rate (233)
Product-planning committee (234)
New-product department (234)
Venture team (234)
Product manager (234)

Questions and Problems

1. In what respects are the products different in each of the following cases?
   a. A Whirlpool dishwasher sold at an appliance store and a similar dishwasher sold by Sears under its Kenmore brand name. Assume that Whirlpool makes both dishwashers.
   b. A Sunbeam Mixmaster sold by a leading department store and the same model sold by a discount house.
   c. An airline ticket purchased through a travel agent and an identical ticket purchased directly from the airline.
2. **a.** Explain the various interpretations of the term *new product*.
   b. Give some examples, other than those cited in this chapter, of products in each of the three new-product categories.
3. "Because brand preferences are well established with regard to many items of women's clothing, these items — traditionally considered shopping goods — will move into the specialty-goods category. At the same time, however, other items of women's clothing can be found in supermarkets and variety stores, thus indicating that some items are convenience goods."
   a. Explain the reasoning in these statements.
   b. Do you agree that women's clothing is shifting away from the shopping-goods classification? Explain.
4. Compare the elements of a producer's marketing mix for a convenience good with those of the mix for a specialty good.
5. In which of the five categories of business goods should each of the following be included? And which products may belong in more than one category?
   a. Trucks.
   b. Medical X-ray equipment.
   c. Printer paper.
   d. Copper wire.
   e. Printers.
   f. Nuts and bolts.
   g. Paper clips.
   h. Land.
6. In developing new products, how can a firm make sure that it is being socially responsible with regard to scarce resources and the environment?

7. Assume that the following organizations are considering additions to their product lines. In each case, does the proposed product meet the criteria for adding a new product? Explain your decisions.
   a. McDonald's — salad bar.
   b. Safeway — automobile tires.
   c. Esso — personal computers.
   d. Banks — life insurance.
   e. General Motors Canada — outboard motors for boats.
8. Describe the kinds of people who are most likely to be found in (a) the innovator category of adopters and (b) the late-majority category.
9. What are some of the problems typically connected with the product-manager organizational structure?

Hands-On Marketing

1. Arrange a meeting with the manager of a large retail outlet in your community. Discuss two topics with the manager:
   a. What recently introduced product has been a failure or appears destined to fail?
   b. Did this product, in retrospect, satisfy the criteria for adding a new product? (Remember to consider not just the intermediary's criteria but also applicable producer's criteria.)
2. Design (either in words or drawings) a new product that fits into one of the first two categories of new products — a really innovative product or a significant replacement, not just an imitative product. Then evaluate how your proposed product rates with respect to the five characteristics of an innovation that influence the adoption rate.

CHAPTER 10 GOALS

At any given time, a firm may be marketing some new products and some old ones, while others are being planned and developed. In this chapter we'll cover a number of strategic decisions pertaining to an organization's assortment of products and services. After studying this chapter, you should have an understanding of:

- The difference between product mix and product line.
- The major product-mix strategies:
  - Positioning
  - Expansion
  - Alteration
  - Contraction
- Trading up and trading down.
- Managing a product throughout a life cycle.
- Planned obsolescence.
- Style and fashion.
- The fashion-adoption process.

Chapter Ten

Product-Mix Strategies

www.molson.com
www.labatt.com

MEETING MARKET DEMANDS FOR CHANGE

In most industries, companies would not even consider keeping exactly the same products in their product lines year after year. The effective management of product lines demands that companies react quickly to changing customer needs and tastes and to the introduction of new products by competitors. The result is that marketers are constantly changing their lines in response to market pressures — introducing new products, modifying existing products, altering packages, repositioning. By examining how companies modify their product lines over time, we can gain considerable insight into their marketing strategies and how they approach the market.

The brewing industry presents an interesting example of how product lines are being adapted in response to changing consumer needs. The two principal competitors in the beer industry in Canada are Molson and Labatt. In recent years, changes in lifestyles and drinking behaviour, a growing interest in preservative-free beer, quality concerns, and new legislation had an impact on these major breweries and necessitated the introduction of a wide array of new products. Among these offerings are dry beers, nonalcoholic beers, no-preservative beers, and packaged draft beer. Labatt recently released a product called "The Blue Cooler Pack," which is a container holding twelve bottles of Labatt Blue with room for ice and water. This product is meant to offer a new twist on the cold-beer image that is used in the "ice" and "glacier" beer products. Labatt's newest beer, Labatt Select, has only 99 calories and an alcohol level of 4.2 percent, which is higher than the upper limit for light beers. This product is responding to the segment who are calorie conscious but who also wish to obtain more alcohol impact from a beer.[1] Molson's new release is Signature Cream Ale, which is being marketed as a premium product. Molson claims that this beer is a superior blend that uses high-quality ingredients and is aged a full twenty-eight days for a smoother, mellower taste.[2]

These new beer products are the result of a strategy designed to create variety in a stagnant market environment. Some of the recent products produced by the two large brewing companies in Canada are a direct response to competition from microbreweries. The growth of microbreweries has contributed to the niche products in this industry. Microbrews are seen by some market segments as being of better quality and taste. The popularity of these products, which have developed essentially over the last ten years, has forced the major brewing companies to expand their lines to include more "quality" products.

Reduced trade barriers in North America and Mexico have increased the availability of non-Canadian products. In addition, European beers are becoming quite popular and are being imported. These developments are seeing the two major breweries becoming more active in acquiring the rights to international brands and selling them in Canada. Labatt has introduced a Mexican beer to Canada — EL SOL. Molson markets several popular international brands, including Heineken, Kirin, Foster's, and Corona.

These examples illustrate how market pressures have forced these two major brewing companies to adapt product lines with changes that reflect customer demands and product competition.

PRODUCT MIX AND PRODUCT LINE

Very few firms rely on a single product or service; instead most sell many products. The set of all products offered for sale by a company is called a **product mix**. The structure of a product mix has both breadth and depth. Its **breadth** is measured by the number of product lines carried, its **depth** by the variety of sizes, colours, and models offered within each product line. A product-mix strategy is illustrated in Figure 10-1.

A broad group of products, intended for essentially similar uses and having similar physical characteristics, constitutes a **product line**. Firms may delineate a product line in different ways. Kimberley-Clark, a company that produces several lines of personal-care products, is the owner of the Huggies diaper brand. Diapers is but one of the product lines this company offers to the market. For the Huggies brand, pullup diapers, targeted to toddlers in toilet-training, is one of several varieties of diaper that represent a product line.

PLANNED PRODUCT-MIX STRATEGIES

Many large corporations, such as Kraft General Foods, Sony, and Procter & Gamble, offer a vast array of products to consumers. In service industries today, telecommunications companies such as Bell Canada and retail giants such as Sobey's and the Hudson's Bay Company offer customers many services and many ways to access them. Did these diverse assortments of products and services develop by accident? No — their existence reflects a planned strategy by the company. To be successful in marketing, producers and intermediaries need carefully planned strategies for managing their product mixes, as we'll see next.

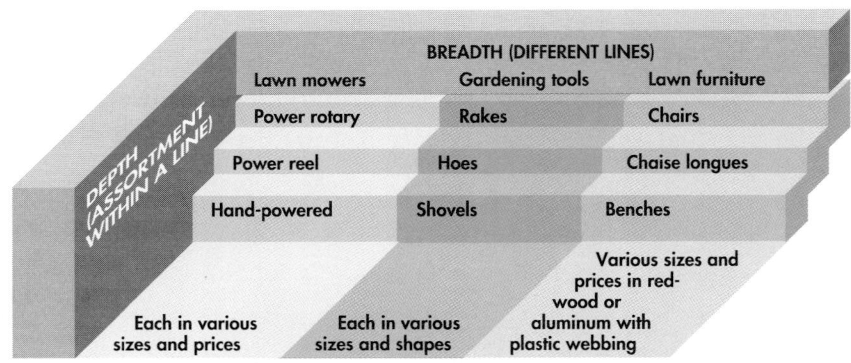

FIGURE 10-1

Product Mix — Breadth and Depth

Part of the product mix in a lawn and garden store.

www.cocacola.com
www.pepsi.com
www.vitasoy.com

Product Positioning

Management's ability to position a product appropriately in the market is a major determinant of company profit. A product's **position** is the image the product projects in the minds of consumers compared with competitive products and with other products marketed by the same company.

Marketing executives can choose from a variety of positioning strategies, in order to create the most useful meaning in the minds of consumers.[3]

Positioning in Relation to a Competitor For some products (Coca-Cola and Pepsi-Cola, for example), the best position is directly against the competition. For other products, head-to-head positioning is exactly what *not* to do, especially when a competitor has a strong market position. When Neilson Dairy decided to release its new soy beverage, it chose not to position the product directly against the soy beverages currently being sold by Sunrise Soya Foods, Eden Foods Inc., and Vitasoy International. Most other soy drinks are provided in tetrapacks. Neilson's product, on the other hand, is a fresh soy drink that has a slightly different taste. Soy Delight will compete nationally in the soy market, but will do so in a different niche than the others.[4]

Positioning in Relation to a Product Class or Attribute Sometimes a company's positioning strategy entails associating its product with (or dissociating it from) a product class or attribute. Some firms promote their wares as being in a desirable class, such as "Made in Canada," or having an attractive attribute, such as "low energy consumption" or "environmentally friendly."

Occasionally, a company or a province or region can position its products based on the fact that they are manufactured in the province or country of the target market, appealing to the consumer's sense of patriotism. A survey of consumers' opinions of manufactured goods made in various countries revealed that Canadians rate their own manufactured goods more favourably than products produced in Japan, Germany, and other countries.[5] These results are good news for Canadian firms that wish to position their products on a "made in Canada" basis.

The strategy of differentiating or positioning products on the basis of an attractive attribute is widely used in the food industry. Health attributes are very popular in differentiating products. In particular, low-fat varieties of food products are being seen in increasing numbers. In some cases, the low-fat and health-food attributes are very specific. For example, Quaker Oats Co. and General Mills are introducing cereal products with soluble fibre. These products are based on the claim that soluble fibre from oatmeal, when consumed as part of a low-fat diet, can help reduce the risk of heart disease.[6] Quaker and General Mills are positioning their cereals against breakfast products that do not provide oat bran. Low fat, as an attribute, is also showing up in traditionally high-fat areas to position these unhealthy products against more healthy ones. Haagen-Dazs Ice Cream, which established itself on the basis of its rich, high-fat products, has introduced low-fat varieties. It has recently rolled out ice-cream products that contain no more than three grams of fat per serving.[7] Low-fat products have also been showing up in fast-food chains. Their success has been minimal, however, and we are now seeing companies such as McDonald's, Taco Bell, and Kentucky Fried Chicken giving up on low-fat products. These companies are now introducing a new attribute and are promoting products with higher levels of taste-pleasing fat![8]

Positioning is a strategy that can work for services as well as for tangible products. The Mighty Ducks of Anaheim have been positioned as the "fun" team of the National Hockey League. The Disney-owned club chose teal and purple as the team colours, and Ducks merchandise is sold in retail stores throughout North America, including Disney stores. The team's logo and colour scheme were selected with merchandising in mind and to appeal not only to hockey's traditional audience, men, but to women and children as well.[9]

www.quakeroats.com
www.genmills.com
www.haagendazs.com
www.tacobell.com
www.kentuckyfriedchicken.com
www.mightyducks.com
www.disney.com

Some companies occupy very narrow niches.

Positioning in Relation to a Target Market Regardless of which positioning strategy is used, the needs of the target market always must be considered. This positioning strategy doesn't suggest that the other ones ignore target markets. Rather, with this strategy, the target market — rather than another factor, such as competition — is the focal point in positioning the product.

Day-Timers Inc., widely known for its organizing kits targeted at business persons, has recently released a product for the home. DayWatch is the result of a realization by the company that there was an untapped market of consumers looking for products to use in time-management in the home. The majority of this market is anticipated to be female. When researching the target market to design the product,

MARKETING AT WORK FILE 10–1

REPOSITIONING ONE COMPANY'S PRODUCTS — FROM FRILLY TO CLASSY

The international chain, Laura Ashley, is changing its image. Facing declining sales throughout the 1990s, this once very popular women's clothing and home furnishings chain is repositioning its product lines. The company is changing its clothing to reflect the needs of women who want feminine, not frumpy. It is also shifting its product mix away from women's clothing and more into home furnishings. This merchandiser became famous for small prints, which were used to make dresses, bedspreads, tablecloths and wallpapers. The women's clothing line had a reputation for being frilly and reflecting a very distinctive feminine image. According to the new CEO, Ann Iverson, sales dropped because the clothing products that were sold by Laura Ashley appeared to have gotten stuck in one mode and never moved on. To correct this situation, the firm has hired a new designer to change the look of the clothing and create a more fashionable and trendier look.

Laura Ashley has also changed its store layouts and increased floor space. These strategies are designed to position the store as a more current mechandiser — one that offers products and displays in less cramped environments that provide more inviting surroundings. The volume of home furnishing products offered can also be increased with greater floor space. The product mix will now be 35 percent clothing and 65 percent home furnishings, where previously it was evenly split.

In its repositioning, Laura Ashley did not want to lose its traditional values. It wanted to modernize the product line by changing the length of the skirt, the cut of the jacket, and the shape of the trousers, improving its display of home furnishings, and generally recapturing the target market that made it strong initially.

Source: Adapted from Sarah Lyall, "Resuscitating a Chintz Elephant," *The New York Times*, January 25, 1997, pp. 37–39.

the manufacturer learned that the proposed users wanted the planner to be basic, made of softer, leather-like material, with closures such as a zipper or a clasp. The product is being introduced in a variety of colours, designs, and sizes, and is being sold at very low prices in comparison with the business products.[10]

Positioning by Price and Quality Some retail stores are known for their high-quality merchandise and high prices (Harry Rosen, Holt-Renfrew). Positioned at the other end of the price and quality scale are discount stores such as WalMart and Zellers.

In the hotel industry, positioning by price and quality is common, particularly when it separates products in the high-end range from those in the middle or lower-end of the market. The Four Seasons Hotel chain in Canada and elsewhere is well known for its high standards in rooms and services. Luxurious furnishings and guest courtesies clearly differentiate this chain from others that target a lower-paying clientele.

Product-Mix Expansion

Product-mix expansion is accomplished by increasing the depth within a particular line and/or the number of lines a firm offers to consumers. Let's look at these options.

When a company adds a similar item to an existing product line with the same brand name, this is termed a **line extension**. For examples, pull the coupons out of your local newspaper or take a look at coupons that appear in your mailbox. You will probably see lots of examples of new products that are really line extensions. Dove soap, a product of the Lever Brothers Co., offers Dove Cares and Dove Skin Care products in addition to Dove bar soap. Dove added a liquid bath wash to its product mix

www.timhortons.com
www.pizzahut.com
www.ikea.dk

and markets it with the Dove body puff. Procter & Gamble, which manufactures Pringles Potato chips, has introduced a fat-free product as an extension to its regular chip products. Crest toothpaste, another Procter & Gamble brand, has just released Crest MultiCare, a toothpaste with special foaming action that is designed to deliver tartar protection in places that are hard to reach.[11]

The line-extension strategy is also used by organizations in services fields. For example, universities now offer programs to appeal to prospective older students, and municipalities are running garbage programs to collect recyclables. Many hospitals have added nutrition counselling clinics and even exercise classes to their product lines, acknowledging that an important part of their role is to keep people well.

There are many reasons for line extensions. The main one is that the firm wants to appeal to more market segments by offering a wider range of choices for a particular product. Another reason is that companies want to take advantage of the considerable value that resides in their established brands. There is often a much lower risk involved in introducing a new product as an extension to an existing line under a recognized brand than there would be to launch a completely separate line with a new brand name. To increase the success rate of new-product introductions, a line-extension strategy is a very obvious part of the marketing program of many companies.

Another way to expand the product mix, referred to as **mix extension**, is to add a new product line to the company's present assortment. To illustrate, when Johnson & Johnson introduced a line of Acuvue disposable contact lenses, that was mix extension because it added another product to the company's product mix. In contrast, line extension adds more items within the same product line. When J&J adds new versions of Tylenol pain reliever, that's line extension.

Under a mix-extension strategy, the new line may be related or unrelated to current products. Furthermore, it may carry one of the company's existing brand names or may be given an entirely new name. Here are examples of these four alternatives:

- *Related product, same brand:* To allow their customers to enjoy their favourite cup of coffee at home, Tim Hortons added canned ground coffee and then introduced a line of Tim Hortons coffee makers that customers could buy to take home; Kimberley-Clark added Kleenex toilet tissue to its long-established line of facial tissues; Nestlé added the Quik chocolate bar; and Crest added MultiClean toothbrushes to its toothpaste products.
- *Unrelated product, same brand:* Forschner Group, Inc., maker of the Original Swiss Army Knives, extended its mix by adding Swiss Army watches and sunglasses; and Swatch, a Swiss watch company, added a clothing line and then announced an even more, unlikely mix extension — small cars![12] 3M, the maker of Scotch Tape and other adhesive and abrasive products, expanded into audio and video tapes and then to computer discs, Scotch-Brite soap pads that never rust, and the famous Post-it notes.
- *Unrelated product, different brand:* This reflects a diversification strategy, such as when a company adds a new division in a different field. This strategy was very popular in the 1980s and early 1990s. Companies today are more likely to eliminate unrelated product lines. Pepsi-Cola, for example, amassed a number of diversified companies such as Pizza Hut and KFC. Recently it has announced its intention to spin-off these fast-food outlets.[13]
- *Related product, different brand:* Procter & Gamble introduced Luvs as a companion to its Pampers disposable diapers.

Most often, the new line is related to the existing product mix because the company wants to capitalize on its expertise and experience. For example, Ikea, which has been known for offering reasonably priced Scandinavian home furnishings, has expanded into a line of office furniture.[14] Thomson Minwax Ltd., of Richmond Hill, Ontario, is expanding beyond its line of wood stains and producing a new line of decorative paints. The Home Decor line includes bright colours, faux finishes, and blocking patterns.[15] In both cases, the new lines benefit from consumers' familiarity with and good feeling toward the brand. We'll consider this approach in more detail when we discuss brand equity in the next chapter.

www.jnj.com

Trading Up and Trading Down

The product strategies of trading up and trading down involve a change in product positioning and an expansion of product line. **Trading up** means adding a higher-priced product to a line to attract a broader market. Also, the seller intends that the new product's prestige will help the sale of its existing lower-priced products.

Consider some examples of trading up. Facing stiff competition in the middle-price market, Holiday Inns introduced the higher-price Crowne Plaza Hotels, with nicer surroundings and more amenities. To its line of inexpensive sport watches, Swatch added an $80 Chrono stopwatch and other upgraded watches. And even pet-food manufacturers have traded up to "superpremium" lines, as illustrated by Kal Kan's Pedigree and Quaker Oats' King Kuts.

A company is said to be **trading down** when it adds a lower-priced item to its line of prestige products. The company expects that people who cannot afford the original product will want to buy the new one because it carries some of the status of the higher-priced product. In line with this strategy, major manufacturers of 35 mm single-lens reflex (SLR) cameras, such as Pentax, Canon, and Minolta, have introduced smaller, simplified cameras for photography buffs who want to be seen to be using the major brands but who do not want to be bothered with the intricacies of 35 mm photography. Mont Blanc, the West German manufacturer of the "world's most famous fountain pen," introduced a lower-priced ballpoint pen, thereby allowing its purchasers to own a Mont Blanc without having to pay more than $300 for the top-of-the-line fountain pen.

Sometimes the effect of trading down can be achieved through advertising, without introducing new, lower-priced products. A manufacturer of fine crystal or chinaware might accomplish this by advertising some of the lower-priced items in its existing product lines.

Trading up and trading down are risky strategies because the new products may confuse buyers, resulting in negligible net gain. It is equally undesirable if sales of the new item or line are generated at the expense of the established products. When trading down, the new offering may permanently hurt the firm's reputation and that of its established high-quality product. To reduce this possibility, new lower-priced products may be given different brand names to distinguish them from the established brands.

In trading up, on the other hand, the problem depends on whether the new product or line carries the established brand name or is given a new name. If the same brand name is used, the firm must change its image enough so that new customers will accept the higher-priced product. At the same time, the seller does not want to lose its present customers. The new offering may present a cloudy image, not attracting new customers but driving away existing customers. If a different brand name is used, the company must create awareness for it and then stimulate consumers to buy the new product. This latter strategy means that the company will not be able to trade on the reputation of its existing brand.

Alteration of Existing Products

As an alternative to developing a completely new product, management should take a fresh look at the organization's existing products. Often, improving an established product — **product alteration** — can be more profitable and less risky than developing a completely new one. The substitution of NutraSweet for saccharin in diet soft drinks increased sales of those drinks. However, product alteration is not without risks. When Coca-Cola modified the formula for its leading product and changed its name to New Coke, sales suffered so much that the old formula was brought back three months later under the Coca-Cola Classic name.

For some products, redesigning is the key to their relaunching or repositioning. Many companies frequently redesign or reformulate their products to give them a fresh appeal. In recent years, disposable diapers have been redesigned to be less bulky and are now available in separate styles for girls and boys. Sometimes the redesign might simply involve the addition of a new flavour, in which case the product becomes more of a line extension, as when General Mills launched Apple Cinnamon Cheerios. Another example involves changing the shape or basic look of the product. This occurred when Hostess Frito-Lay introduced its new "flat" potato chip.

Alternatively, especially for consumer products, the product itself is not changed but its packaging is altered. This strategy is employed to gain a competitive advantage, as when Tylenol introduced its products in red-cap bottles with ridges for ease of opening or when Evian redesigned its bottle with mountain ridges to improve its ability to be crushed for recycling. Kraft began to package its cheese slices as Singles. Kraft, Black Diamond, and other manufacturers of cheese products are now offering their sliced and shredded cheeses in packages that reseal by using zipper-like closures. Thus, packages can be altered to enhance appearance or to improve the product's usability.

Product-Mix Contraction

Another product strategy, **product-mix contraction**, is carried out either by eliminating an entire line or by simplifying the assortment within a line. Thinner and/or shorter product lines or mixes can weed out low-profit and unprofitable products. The intended result of product-mix contraction is higher profits from fewer products. General Mills decided to concentrate on its food business and, consequently, sold its interest in Izod (the "alligator" apparel maker) and its lines of children's toys and games. In services fields, some travel agencies have shifted from selling all modes of travel to concentrate on specialized tours and trips to exotic places.

During the early 1990s, most companies expanded — rather than contracted — their product mixes. Numerous line extensions document this trend. As firms find that they have an unmanageable number of products or that various items or lines are unprofitable, or both, product-mix pruning is occurring. Procter & Gamble, for example, is currently engaged in a market research and development strategy to simplify its product lines. The company is looking to sell only products that have the best market impact and eliminate what they term the "flavours of the month."[16]

THE PRODUCT LIFE CYCLE

As we saw in Chapter 9, a product's life cycle can have a direct bearing on a company's survival. The life cycle of a product consists of four stages: introduction, growth, maturity, and decline. The concept of product life applies to a generic category of product (microwave ovens, for example) and not to specific brands (such as Sony or Braun). A **product life cycle** consists of the aggregate demand over an extended period of time for all brands making up a generic product category.

A life cycle can be graphed by plotting aggregate sales volume for a generic product category over time, usually years. It is also worthwhile to accompany the sales-volume curve with the corresponding profit curve for the product category, as shown in Figure 10-2. After all, we are interested ultimately in profitability, not just sales.

The shapes of these two curves vary from one product category to another. Still, for most categories, the basic shapes and the relationship between the sales and the profit curves are as illustrated in Figure 10-2. In this typical life cycle, the profit curve

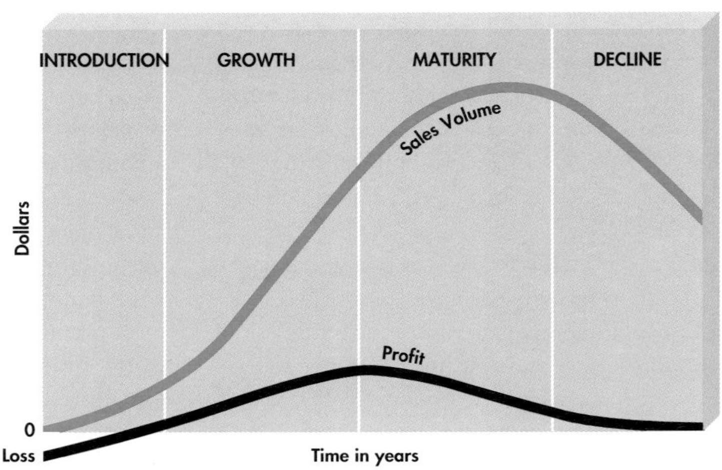

FIGURE 10-2

Typical Life Cycle of a Product Category

During the introduction stage of a life cycle, a product category — and virtually all brands within it — are unprofitable. Profits are healthy during the growth stage, but then start to decline while a product's sales volume is still increasing.

www.tylenol.com

for most new products is negative (signifying a loss) through much of the introductory stage. In the latter part of the growth stage, the profit curve starts to decline while sales volume is still rising. Profits decline because the companies in an industry usually must increase their advertising and selling efforts or cut their prices (or both) to sustain sales growth in the face of intensifying competition during the maturity stage. The length of time it takes a product to reach maturity varies considerably, depending on the nature of the product. Some products remain in the maturity stage much longer than others. Electronic equipment, such as computers, have a very short maturity stage. Continuous new developments in technology cause the life cycle of these products to be quite short.

Introducing a new product at the proper time will help maintain a company's desired level of profit. Building on its original product lines, Kraft is constantly extending product life cycles with innovations. Macaroni and cheese is a good example of a product that has been sustained in this way. Over the past fifteen years, the company has introduced spiral pasta, pasta shaped like cartoon characters, and different flavours of cheese. These products have all sold at premium prices.[17]

The product life cycle concept has been criticized as lacking empirical support and being too general to be useful in specific cases.[18] Although the concept is not perfect and must be adapted to fit different circumstances, this model is both straightforward and powerful. A company's marketing success can be affected considerably by its ability to determine and adapt to the life cycles for each of its product categories.

Characteristics of Each Stage

Management must be able to recognize what part of the life cycle its product is in at any given time. The competitive environment and marketing strategies that should be used ordinarily depend on the particular life cycle stage. Table 10-1 contains a synopsis of all four stages. Each stage is highlighted below.

TABLE 10-1 Characteristics and Implications of Different Product Life-Cycle Stages

Each stage of a product's life cycle has different characteristics; as a result, marketing must be modified over the course of the cycle.

	Stage			
	Introduction	**Growth**	**Maturity**	**Decline**
Characteristics				
Customers	Innovators	Mass market	Mass market	Loyal customers
Competition	Little, if any	Increasing	Intense	Decreasing
Sales	Low levels, then rising	Rapid growth	Slow/no annual growth	Declining
Profits	None	Strong, then at a peak	Declining annually	Low/none
Marketing Implications				
Overall strategy	Market development	Market penetration	Defensive positioning	Efficiency or exit
Costs	High per unit	Declining	Stable or increasing	Low
Product strategy	Undifferentiated	Improved Items	Differentiated	Pruned line
Pricing strategy	Most likely high	Lower over time	Lowest	Increasing
Distribution strategy	Scattered	Intensive	Intensive	Selective
Promotion strategy	Category awareness	Brand preference	Brand loyalty	Reinforcement

Source: Adapted from material provided by Professor David Appel, University of Notre Dame, Notre Dame, IN.

Introduction During the **introduction stage**, a product is launched into the market in a full-scale marketing program. It has gone through product development, including idea screening, prototype, and market tests. The entire product may be new, such as a substitute for fat in prepared foods. Or it may be well known but have a significant new feature that, in effect, creates a new product category; the fax machine and electronic mail are examples.

This introductory (sometimes called pioneering) stage is the most risky and expensive one, because substantial amounts of money must be spent in seeking consumer acceptance of the product. But many products are not accepted by a sufficient number of consumers and fail at this stage. For really new products, there is very little direct competition. Thus the promotional program is designed to stimulate demand for the entire product category rather than only the seller's brand.

Growth In the **growth stage**, or market-acceptance stage, sales and profits rise, often at a rapid rate. Competitors enter the market, often in large numbers if the profit outlook is particularly attractive. Mostly as a result of competition, profits start to decline near the end of the growth stage. Appropriate marketing strategies for this stage, as well as the other three, are summarized in Table 10-1.

Maturity During the first part of the **maturity stage**, sales continue to increase, but at a decreasing rate. When sales level off, profits of both producers and intermediaries decline. The primary reason: intense price competition. Seeking to differentiate themselves, some firms extend their product lines with new models. During the latter part of this stage, marginal producers, those with high costs or without a differential advantage, are forced to drop out of the market. They do so because they lack sufficient customers and/or profits.

Decline For most products, a **decline stage**, as gauged by sales volume for the total category, is inevitable for one of the following reasons:

- The need for the product disappears, as when frozen orange juice generally eliminated the market for juice squeezers.
- A better or less expensive product is developed to fill the same need. CDs have replaced vinyl records because the sound, durability, and storage capability of the new product is far superior to that of the old product. CDs require CD players, which have, of course, replaced turntables.
- People simply grow tired of a product (a clothing style, for instance), so it disappears from the market.

Seeing little opportunity for revitalized sales or profits, most competitors abandon the market during this stage. However, a few firms may be able to develop a small market niche and remain moderately successful in the decline stage. Some manufacturers of wood-burning stoves have been able to do this. Whether a product at this stage has to be abandoned or can be continued on a profitable basis often depends on the skills and creativity of the marketing manager responsible for the product.

Length of Product Life Cycle

The total length of the life cycle — from start of the introduction stage to the end of the decline stage — varies across product categories. It ranges from a few weeks or a short season (for a clothing fashion) to many decades (for autos or telephones). And it varies because of differences in the length of individual stages from one product category to the next. Furthermore, although Figure 10-2 suggests that all four life cycle stages cover nearly equal periods of time, the stages in any given product's life cycle usually last for different periods.

Three variations on the typical life cycle are shown in Figure 10-3:

- In one, the product gains widespread consumer acceptance only after an extended introductory period (see part a). The hand-held computer is an example of current product that, for this category, has experienced a long introductory period. Companies such as Apple, Sony, and AT&T have introduced versions of this product to limited success. Recently Casio, Compaq, Hewlett-Packard, and Philips, among others, have tried again to interest the market in paper-sized "personal digital assistants." It remains to be seen whether or not this product will reach the full market potential these companies anticipate.[19]

FIGURE 10-3

Product Life Cycle Variations

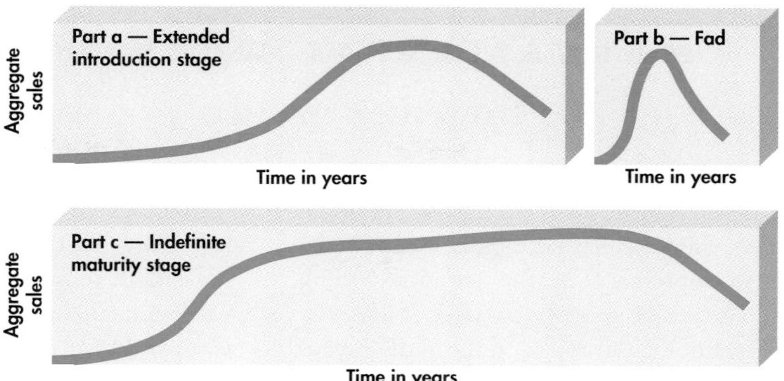

- In another variation, the entire life cycle begins and ends in a relatively short period of time (part b). This variation depicts the life cycle for a **fad**, a product or style that becomes immensely popular nearly overnight and then falls out of favour with consumers almost as quickly. Children's toys often fall into this category. Cabbage Patch dolls were immensely popular in the 1980s, but interest in the product died almost overnight, though there is some indication they may be gaining popularity through the introduction of video Cabbage Patch characters.
- In a third variation, the product's mature stage lasts almost indefinitely (part c). This life cycle is illustrated by canned, carbonated soft drinks and also by the automobile with a gasoline-powered, internal-combustion engine. Other forms, such as electric- and solar-powered cars, have been proposed, but the automobile as we know it remains dominant.

Setting aside fads, which represent a special case, product life cycles are getting shorter generally. If competitors can quickly introduce a "me too" version of a popular product, it may move swiftly into the maturity stage. Or rapid changes in technology can make a product obsolete virtually overnight. Could this happen in the audio field, as digital versatile discs (DVDs) are seen by some as a replacement for compact discs (CDs)? (See "Marketing at Work" File 10-2.)

Moreover, a number of product categories do not make it through all four stages of the life cycle. Some fail in the introductory stage.

Life Cycle Is Related to a Market

When we say that a product is in a specific stage of its life cycle, implicitly we are referring to a specific market. A product may be well accepted (growth or maturity stage) in some markets but still be striving for acceptance in other markets. At the time Ortho Pharmaceuticals introduced Retin-A as a treatment for acne, existing products already served this purpose. Thus the acne-treatment category probably was in the maturity stage. However, then it was discovered that Retin-A might be effective in reducing facial wrinkles. In effect, it created a new product category. Hence, Retin-A fit into both the acne-treatment category that was in the maturity stage among teenagers and into the wrinkle-remover category that was in the introductory or perhaps early-growth stage among the middle-aged.

Life Cycle Management

To a surprising extent, the shape of the sales and profit curves for a product category can be controlled. The collective actions of firms offering competing products in the same category shape the curves. But even single companies can have an impact. A giant firm may be able to shorten the introductory stage by broadening the distribution or increasing the promotional effort supporting the new product.

Most firms, however, cannot substantially affect the sales and profit curves for a product category. Thus their task is to determine how best to achieve success with their own brands within the life cycle for an entire product category. For an individual firm, successful life cycle management depends on (1) predicting the shape of the proposed product's cycle even before it is introduced and (2) successfully adapting marketing strategies at each stage of the life cycle.

MARKETING AT WORK FILE 10-2

FROM LPs TO CDs TO DVDs

The CD has seen a rapid growth stage in its life cycle. Introduced to the market in the early 1980s, this product has rapidly established a position of supremacy in the audio-recording industry. The vinyl record has passed into the annals of technology history, and the audio tape is rapidly following on its heels. It is interesting to examine the life cycles of the various forms in which recordings have appeared in recent years as technology has evolved.

It wasn't too many years ago that long-playing records (LPs) replaced the 78s and 45s that usually contained only one song per side. Then, we saw the rapid rise and fall of 8-track tapes, before the popular audio cassette came on the scene in the 1970s. But it was the CD that really sounded the death knell for the LP. In only seven or eight years after CDs became widely available, records were no longer produced.

A new technology is now beginning to emerge that shows potential for becoming the next step in entertainment products. The digital versatile disc, or DVD, has made its debut. This new technology enables seven times the storage capacity of the old CD and is ideally suited to storing full-length movies, music videos, and high-quality interactive multimedia programs. Sony of Canada Ltd. released hardware and software in the DVD format. New products include DVD video players, DVD-ROM drives, and DVD movie and music entertainment programs. Other companies are also involved in producing products using the DVD technology.

It is useful to think of the relative advantages that CDs and DVDs offer over LPs and cassettes, in an attempt to explain the rapid introductions. What will the future hold? Will DVD technology become as accepted as CDs? Changes in this field are occurring in shorter and shorter periods of time.

Source: "Sony to Introduce DVD Hardware and Software in April, 1997," *Canada News Wire*, January 8, 1997, http://www.newswire.ca. Reprinted with permission.

Entry Strategies A firm entering a new market must decide whether to plunge in during the introductory stage. Or it can wait and make its entry during the early part of the growth stage, after innovating companies have proven there is a viable market.

The strategy of entering during the introductory stage is prompted by the desire to build a dominant market position right away and thus lessen the interest of potential competitors and the effectiveness of actual competitors. This strategy worked for Sony with the Walkman; Perrier with bottled sparkling water; and Nike with running shoes. Evidently, there is benefit to getting a head start in marketing a new type of product. The hurdles may be insurmountable when you enter with a "me too" product and try to play catch-up.

However, delaying entry until the market is proven can sometimes pay off. Pioneering requires a large investment, and the risks are great — as demonstrated by the high failure rate among new products. Large companies with the marketing resources to overwhelm smaller innovating firms are most likely to be successful with a delayed-entry strategy. In one such case, Coca-Cola introduced Tab and Diet Coke, and Pepsi-Cola introduced Diet Pepsi — and the two giants surpassed Diet Rite Cola, an early pioneer.

It's not clear-cut which is the better entry strategy. Each has its advantages and disadvantages, its successes and failures. As with nearly all marketing decisions, sound managerial judgement is critical.[20]

Managing on the Rise When sales are growing strongly and profits are robust in a product category, you might think a marketing manager has little to do except tally up an anticipated bonus. Unfortunately, that's not the case. During the growth stage of the life cycle, a company has to devise the right strategies for its brand(s) in that product category. Promotion that will cause consumers to desire the company's brand of product must be considered. Distribution must be expanded. And product improvements must be considered. Decisions made during the growth stage influence (a) how many competitors enter the market and (b) how well the company's brand does within a product category both in the near and distant future.

Home video games were introduced in the 1970s, but the more captivating (perhaps addictive) Nintendo brand, in effect, created a new product category in the 1980s. As the 1990s began, this product appeared to be in the growth stage of its life cycle. However, in the mid-1990s, video games stagnated. Nintendo developed a two-part strategy to boost sales: (1) use advanced technology to add more graphics, video, and sound to its game cartridges; and (2) keep prices as low as possible, about $250 for its ultra 64-game player. In contrast, Sega, a potent competitor, is concentrating less on cartridges and more on CD-ROM discs.[21]

Managing during Maturity Various strategies may be effective in maintaining or boosting sales of a product during the maturity stage of its life cycle. Of course, what works magnificently for one product may perform dismally for another.[22] Common strategies during maturity include modifying the product, designing new promotion, and devising new uses for the product.[23] Campbell's Soups recently celebrated its one-hundredth birthday and used this event as an opportunity to redesign its labels, thus giving a new look to a mature product.[24] Such steps may lead to added purchases by present customers and/or may attract new customers. As sales in the North American cruise industry flattened out, some cruise lines modified their services by adding fitness programs and offering special theme cruises (sometimes in conjunction with a professional sports team).

Playskool, a division of Hasbro Canada Inc. of Longueuil, Quebec, has modified its mature product line of children's toys, equipment, and furniture. To make the products more competitive, the company has added an antibacterial agent to the plastic in the manufacturing stage.[25] Another example is CIGNA Life Insurance Company of Canada, which is marketing the Women's Health and Hope Plan. This plan provides financial aid to women diagnosed with a female-specific cancer, heart attack, stroke, or coronary artery surgery. This new twist on disability insurance is created to adapt an aging product line to a society of women with family responsibilities.[26]

Surviving the Decline Stage Perhaps it is in the decline stage that a company finds its greatest challenges in life cycle management. For instance, the advent of video camcorders and filmless cameras may hint at the decline of photographic film as a product category. Kodak Canada is trying to prevent the decline of this product while keeping pace with competitors in examining bold new products. With one such product, which Kodak calls Photo CD, consumers take pictures as they normally have; the big difference comes at the time of film processing, when the prints can be stored on a compact disc. Then they can be shown on a TV, if you have a new videodisc player![27] Kodak is also extending the life of the traditional film product by maintaining an aggressive research and development process to improve the overall performance of each roll. Film recently released offers improved colour accuracy, saturation, detail, and sharpness. A new product designed especially for "zoom" cameras improves light sensitivity and eliminates photographic problems with light reduction.[28]

When sales are declining, management has the following alternatives:

- Ensure that marketing and production programs are as efficient as possible.
- Prune unprofitable sizes and models. Frequently this tactic will decrease sales but increase profits.
- "Run out" the product; that is, cut all costs to the bare minimum to maximize profitability over the limited remaining life of the product.
- Best (and toughest) of all, improve the product in a functional sense, or revitalize it in some manner. Publishers of printed dictionaries may have done this. Other reference materials, including dictionaries on personal computers, seemed to have pushed the traditional dictionary into — or at

www.cigna.com

least toward — decline. However, some publishers are working hard to maintain the appeal of the dictionary. Houghton Mifflin, for instance, added sixteen thousand new words to its latest edition and backed it with $2 million in promotion.[29] Compact discs have had a similar effect on encyclopedias. This new technology offers an opportunity to revitalize this product in its declining stage.

If one of these alternatives doesn't work, management will have to consider product abandonment. The expense of carrying profitless products goes beyond what shows up on financial statements. For example, there is a very real cost to the managerial time and effort that is diverted to terminally ill products. Management often is reluctant to discard a product, however, partly because it is easy to become attached to the product over the years.

In the final analysis, the most compelling — but often painful — alternative may be **product abandonment**. Knowing when and how to abandon products successfully may be as important as knowing when and how to introduce new ones. Certainly management should develop systematic procedures for phasing out weak products.[30]

PLANNED OBSOLESCENCE AND FASHION

Consumers seem to be constantly searching for "what's new" but not "too new." They want newness — new products, new styles, new colours. However, they want to be moved gently out of their habitual patterns, not shocked out of them. Consequently, some manufacturers use a product strategy of planned obsolescence. The intent of this strategy is to make an existing product out of date and thus to increase the market for replacement products. Consumers often satisfy their thirst for newness through fashion. And producers of fashions rely heavily on planned obsolescence, as we'll now see.

Nature of Planned Obsolescence

Planned obsolescence may be interpreted in two ways:

- **Technological or functional obsolescence.** Significant technical improvements result in a more effective product. For instance, audio cassette tapes made phonograph records obsolete; and digital audio tapes threaten to make cassettes and compact discs obsolete. This type of obsolescence is generally considered to be socially and economically desirable, because the replacement product offers more benefits and/or a lower cost.
- **Style obsolescence.** Superficial characteristics of a product are altered so that the new model is easily differentiated from the previous model. Style obsolescence, sometimes called "psychological" or "fashion" obsolescence, is intended to make people feel out of date if they continue to use old models. Products subject to this type of obsolescence include clothing, furniture, and automobiles.

When people criticize planned obsolescence, they usually mean style obsolescence. In our discussion, when we refer to planned obsolescence, we will mean only style obsolescence, unless otherwise stated.

Nature of Style and Fashion

Although the words style and fashion are often used interchangeably, there is a clear distinction. A **style** is a distinctive manner of construction or presentation in any art, product, or endeavour (singing, playing, behaving). Thus we have styles in automobiles (sedans, station wagons), in bathing suits (one-piece, bikini), in furniture (Early American, French Provincial), and in dancing (waltz, "break").

A **fashion** is any style that is popularly accepted and purchased by successive groups of people over a reasonably long period of time. Not every style becomes a fashion. To be considered a fashion, or to be called "fashionable," a style must be accepted by many people. All of the styles listed in the preceding paragraph, except perhaps for break dancing, qualify as fashions. All societies, ranging from contemporary primitive groups to medieval European societies, have fashions.

Fashion is rooted in sociological and psychological factors. Basically, most of us are conformists. At the same time, we yearn to look and act a little different from others. We probably are not in revolt against custom; we simply wish to be a bit distinctive but not be accused of bad taste or disregard for norms. Fashion furnishes the opportunity for self-expression.

Fashion-Adoption Process

The **fashion-adoption process** reflects the concepts of (1) large-group and small-group influences on consumer buying behaviour and (2) the diffusion of innovation, as discussed in chapters 6 and 9. People usually try to imitate others at the same or the next higher socioeconomic level. One way people do that is purchasing a product that is fashionable in the group they want to be like.

Thus the fashion-adoption process is a series of buying waves that arise as a particular style is popularly accepted in one group, then another group and another, until it finally falls out of fashion. This movement, representing the introduction, rise, popular culmination, and decline of the market's acceptance of a style, is referred to as the **fashion cycle**. A case can be made that synthetic fibres, such as polyester, in clothing, and the convertible model of automobile are two products that have run the full fashion cycle.

There are three theories of fashion adoption (see Figure 10-4):

- **Trickle-down**, where a given fashion cycle flows downward through several socioeconomic levels.
- **Trickle-across**, where the cycle moves horizontally and simultaneously within several socioeconomic levels.
- **Trickle-up**, where a style first becomes popular at lower socioeconomic levels and then flows upward to become popular among higher levels.

Traditionally, the trickle-down theory has been used to explain the fashion-adoption process. As an example, designers of women's apparel first introduce a style to opinion leaders in the upper socioeconomic groups. If they accept the style, it quickly appears in leading fashion stores. Soon the middle-income and then the lower-income markets want to emulate the leaders, and the style is

Some clothing items seem never to go out of style.

FIGURE 10-4
Fashion-Adoption Processes

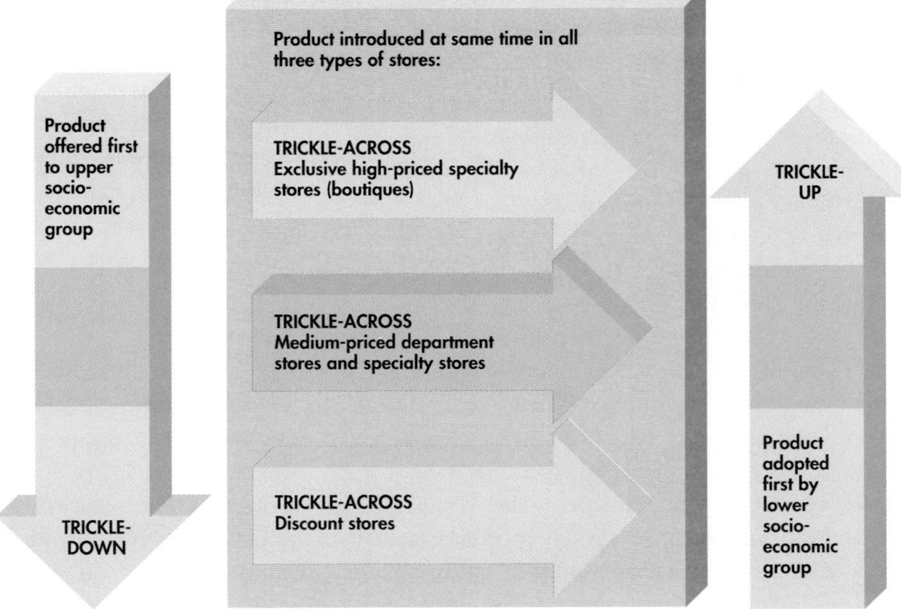

mass-marketed. As its popularity wanes, the style appears in bargain-price stores and finally is no longer considered fashionable.

Today the trickle-across theory best explains the adoption process for most fashions. It's true that there is some flow downward, and obviously there is an upward flow. But, by means of modern production, communication, and transportation, we can disseminate style information and products so rapidly that all social levels can be reached at about the same time. For example, within a few weeks of the beginning of the fall season, the same style of dress (but at different quality levels) appears (1) in small, exclusive dress shops appealing to the upper social class, (2) in large department stores appealing to the middle social class, and (3) in discount houses and low-price women's ready-to-wear chain stores, where the appeal is to the portion of the lower social class that has some disposable income.

Most apparel manufacturers produce a wide variety of essentially one style. They also produce different qualities of the same basic style so as to appeal to different income groups. When an entire cycle may last only one season, sellers cannot afford to wait for style acceptance to trickle down. They must introduce it to many social levels simultaneously.

Within each class, the dresses are purchased early in the season by the opinion leaders — the innovators. If the style is accepted, its sales curve rises as it becomes popular with the early adopters and then with the late adopters. Eventually, sales decline as the style loses popularity. This cycle is a horizontal movement, occurring virtually simultaneously within each of several socioeconomic levels.

The trickle-up process also explains some product-adoption processes. Consider how styles of music such as jazz and rap became popular. Also look at blue jeans, denim jackets, T-shirts, athletic footwear, and even pasta in the 1990s. They all have one thing in common: They were popular first with lower socioeconomic groups, and later their popularity "trickled up" to higher-income markets.

Marketing Considerations in Fashion

When a firm's products are subject to the fashion cycle, management must know what stage the cycle is in at all times. Managers must decide at what point to get into the cycle and when to get out.

Accurate forecasting is critical to success in fashion merchandising. This is extremely difficult, however, because the forecaster must deal with complex sociological and psychological factors. Frequently a retailer or manufacturer operates largely on intuition and inspiration, tempered by considerable experience.

MARKETING AT WORK FILE 10-3

EASY RIDERS AND HOG TALES

One product associated with myths of down-to-earth ruggedness and no-nonsense simplicity is the Harley-Davidson motorcycle. Once the symbol of the "Wild One" Brando rebel, the "Easy Rider" outcast, or the tough Hell's Angel, Harleys are becoming the new status symbol of fortysomething doctors, lawyers, agents, and film executives looking to drown out the noisy angst of their midlife crisis with the roar of their motorcycle. Rejecting the values conferred by past flashy status symbols, "rubbies" — rich urban bikers — are taking to the streets and rebelling, having missed out the first time because they were so busy getting into Harvard. Harley-Davidson says that close to 70 percent of its customers have college degrees and that their average age is forty. Accordingly, the company has moved to sell its product as not just a bike, but a lifestyle.

The popularity of the Harley-Davidson motorcycle has led the manufacturer to create the Harley Owners Group (H.O.G.). Designed to bring Harley-Davidson "closer to its customers," it is now the largest factory-sponsored motorcycle club in the world. About 35 percent of all Harley owners participate in the program — everyone from blue-collar workers to multimillionaires. At point of sale, a free one-year full membership, including a general list of benefits, is automatically issued to new owners of Harley-Davidson motorcycles. New owners as well as purchasers of used Harleys are eligible to join the H.O.G. program. The member magazine *Hog Tales* is but one of the benefits provided to members. Others include the H.O.G. *Touring Handbook*, the H.O.G. *World Atlas*, a mileage program, a touring contest, a fly and ride program for members who want to rent bicycles away from home...the list goes on. For women, the company tailors the membership program and calls it Ladies of Harley.

Another important element of Harley-Davidson ownership is rallies in which members "celebrate the Harley lifestyle." Members can participate in skill and customized-bike competitions, charity rides, demo rides, musical entertainment, and motorcycle seminars.

Through all of this, Harley-Davidson motorcycles are selling so fast that the manufacturer cannot keep up with the demand. One spokesman says, "Nothing feels or sounds like a Harley...You're buying into the Harley-Davidson family — the riding with friends, the rallies, the leather clothing." In catering to this vision, the manufacturer opened New York's Harley-Davidson Café, in which rubbies and their female counterparts — "frubbies" — can get together for a Harley Hogg sandwich and listen to tunes interspersed with the sound of revving bikes while fake exhaust pours from display motorcyles.

Sources: "Their Hearts Belong to Harley-Davidson," *The Times* (London), reprinted by *The Globe and Mail*, October 23, 1993, p. A2; Colloquy, "Harley Owners Journey to Meet their Maker...Again and Again," *(online)*, vol. 5, issue 4, 1997, http://www.colloquy.org/online/past_ issues/v5i4.

Ordinarily a retailer cannot participate successfully in all stages of the fashion cycle at the same time. Thus a specialty apparel store — whose stocks are displayed in limited numbers without price tags — should get in at the start of a fashion trend. And a department store appealing to the middle-income market should plan to enter the cycle in time to mass-market the style as it is climbing to its peak of popularity. Fundamentally, retail executives must keep in mind the product's target market in deciding at which stage(s) of the life cycle its stores should offer fashionable apparel.

Summary

Many strategic decisions must be made to manage a company's assortment of products effectively. To start, a firm must select strategies regarding its product mix. One decision is how to position the product relative to competing products and other products sold by the firm.

Another strategic decision is whether or how to expand the product mix by adding items to a line and/or introducing new lines. Alternatively, management may elect to trade up or trade down relative to existing products. Altering the design, packaging, or other features of existing products is still another option among the strategies of selecting the best mix. The product mix also can be changed by eliminating an entire line or by simplifying the assortment within a line.

Executives need to understand the concept of a product life cycle, which reflects the total sales volume for a generic product category. Each of the cycle's four stages — introduction, growth, maturity, and decline — has distinctive characteristics that have implications for marketing. Managing a product as it moves through its life cycle presents challenges and opportunities. Eventually, a product category may lack adequate acceptance from consumers; at that point, all or most companies will abandon their versions of this product.

Planned obsolescence is a controversial product strategy, built around the concepts of style, fashion, and the fashion cycle. Fashion — essentially a sociological and psychological phenomenon — follows a reasonably predictable pattern. With advances in communications and production, the fashion-adoption process has moved away from the traditional trickle-down pattern. Today the process is better described as trickle-across. There also are examples of fashions trickling up. Managing a product, such as expensive apparel, through a fashion cycle may be even more challenging than adjusting another type of product's strategies during its life cycle.

Key Terms and Concepts

Product mix (240)
Breadth (240)
Depth (240)
Product line (240)
Position (241)
Product-mix expansion (243)
Line extension (243)
Mix extension (244)
Trading up (245)
Trading down (245)
Product alteration (245)
Product-mix contraction (246)
Product life cycle (246)
Introduction stage (248)
Growth stage (248)
Maturity stage (248)
Decline stage (248)
Fad (249)
Product abandonment (252)
Planned obsolescence (252)
Technological (functional) obsolescence (252)
Style (fashion or psychological) obsolescence (252)
Style (252)
Fashion (252)
Fashion-adoption process (253)
Fashion cycle (253)
Trickle-down theory (253)
Trickle-across theory (253)
Trickle-up theory (253)

Questions and Problems

1. "It is inconsistent for management to follow concurrently the product-line strategies of expanding its product mix and contracting its product mix." Discuss.
2. "Trading up and trading down are product strategies closely related to the business cycle. Firms trade up during periods of prosperity and trade down during recessions." Do you agree? Why?
3. Name one category of tangible products and one category of services you believe are in the introductory stage of their life cycles. For each product, identify the market that considers your examples to be truly new.
4. What are two products that are in the decline stage of the life cycle? In each case, point out whether you think the decline is permanent. What recommendations do you have for rejuvenating the demand for either of these products?
5. How might a company's advertising strategies differ, depending on whether its brand of a product is in the introduction stage or the maturity stage of its life cycle?
6. What products, other than apparel and automobiles, stress fashion and style in marketing? Do styles exist among business products?
7. Is the trickle-across theory applicable to the fashion-adoption process in product lines other than women's apparel? Explain, using examples.
8. Planned obsolescence is criticized as a social and economic waste because we are urged to buy things we do not like and do not need. What is your opinion? If you object to planned obsolescence, what are your recommendations for correcting the situation?

Hands-On Marketing

1. Select a product category in which you are interested. Go to the library or search the Web and identify the national or provincial trade association for this product category. Then contact the association, requesting sales figures for this product over its history and other information that will allow you to plot the life cycle for this product. What stage of the life cycle is this product in? Explain.
2. Arrange a meeting with a supermarket manager or a department manager in a supermarket. Discuss how the manager handles the challenge of line extensions. In which product category are line extensions most common? When new items are added to the line, how does the manager find space for the new entries — by giving more space to this category, dropping other items carrying this same brand, pruning other brands in this category, or some other means?

CHAPTER 11 GOALS

As the Second Cup example that opens this chapter illustrates, the success of a product or service will depend to a very great extent on the image communicated by the brand name. Otherwise, how do you account for some people buying Bayer Aspirin, while others prefer to buy a private-label brand of ASA tablet, when both products are virtually identical? Consumer choice is influenced not only by the brand name, but also in the case of tangible products by the package, warranty, design, and other product features. Because these features of products and services are important elements in a marketing program, we devote this chapter to them. After studying this chapter, you should have an understanding of:

- The nature and importance of brands.
- The characteristics of a good brand name.
- The branding strategies of producers and intermediaries.
- Why and how a growing number of firms are building and using brand equity.
- The nature and importance of packaging and labelling.
- Major packaging strategies.
- The marketing implications of other product features — design, quality, warranty, and postsale service — that can satisfy consumers' wants.

Chapter Eleven

Brands, Packaging, and Other Product Features

www.secondcup.com

HOW ABOUT A SECOND CUP?

Did you know that coffee is a fruit? Or, that it takes five years of sun, shade, and rain for a shrub to produce the cherries that contain the green seeds we know as coffee? Second Cup makes those facts known in its promotional literature because it wants you to know it has a great deal of knowledge about coffee. It wants the consumer to believe that it makes the world's best cup of coffee. That is the image this corporation is trying to achieve in order to position itself as a premium, high-quality coffee producer and retailer.

The first Second Cup opened in Toronto in 1975. Since that time, the company has expanded its operations to include three hundred locations in Canada, coast to coast. The corporation also operates in the United States under the Gloria Jean and Coffee Plantation names, and it has recently opened a Second Cup outlet in Jerusalem. In 1996, its Canadian operations reported record results.

The image of Second Cup is based on the efficient provision of quality coffee. It establishes itself in shopping malls, airport terminals, busy street locations, and other sites where there are a lot of people who need a place to sit and relax for a brief time. The company's slogan is "Where The World Stops For Just A Second." The firm prides itself on its "uncompromising standards of customer service, quality, and freshness." The image of this company is so important to its success that it runs its own training college — Coffee College — where franchisees go to learn about coffee and customer service as well as the overall operation of the Second Cup store.

The only coffees sold in the Second Cup outlets are those prepared especially by the company and made from premium Arabica coffee beans. The company markets a signature blend known as Paradiso. Other exclusive blends have names (some of which are trademarked) such as Espresso Forte and Authentic Mocha Java. Exclusive Estate coffees from South America are also sold. To communicate the degree of roasting to its customers, Second Cup codes its beans and blends on a five-point scale, in which five is the longest roasting period. Through using only premium beans and communicating processing activities to the consumer, the company is signalling that its coffee is no ordinary supermarket blend but a very special variety that's the best you can buy.[1]

Second Cup is taking advantage of a lifestyle trend toward high-quality products. With advances in global trade, coffee products have taken on new meaning over the last decade. A proliferation of espresso bars and specialty coffee outlets has occurred throughout North America and Europe. Within Canada, this company is maintaining a position as a leading specialty coffee company. The image it has created is designed to enable it to continue to occupy that position.

When we think of brand names, most of us tend to think of products that we use often and that we have been using or at least have been familiar with for many years. Certainly, many well-established brands have been part of our consumer lives for fifty years. They include Tetley tea, Campbell's soup, Kodak film, Nabisco biscuits, and Wrigley chewing gum. But brand names are just as important in the marketing of services. A retail store name is really a brand, as are such names as Air Canada, Delta Hotels, and Canada's Wonderland, although these are not applied to tangible products. As we will see in this chapter, some retailer names have become so trusted and accepted by Canadians that they constitute widely regarded brand names in their own right.

The approach Second Cup is taking in differentiating itself from the competition is the equivalent of brand positioning, as was discussed in Chapter 10. If it is to remain on top of the ladder in specialty coffees, it must be seen by prospective customers to be able to offer more than its competitors, such as Starbucks and A.L. Van Houtte. For us to want to consume that second cup of coffee, it must be good! At least, that's the image of this brand.

BRANDS

The word *brand* is a comprehensive term, and it includes other, narrower terms. A **brand** is a name, term, symbol, or special design, or some combination of these elements, that is intended to identify the goods or services of one seller or a group of sellers. A brand differentiates one seller's products or services from those of competitors. A **brand name** consists of words, letters, and/or numbers that can be vocalized. A **brand mark** is the part of the brand that appears in the form of a symbol, design, or distinctive colouring or lettering. It is recognized by sight but may not be expressed when a person pronounces the brand name. Xerox, Bell Canada, Sega, and Canadian Airlines International are brand names. Brand marks are illustrated by the distinctive lettering of a name, for example, the bilingual spelling of Canadian in the Canadian Airlines International logo, the picture of the little girl with pigtails on the Wendy's sign, and the doughy character used by Pillsbury. These marks, logos, or designs are usually registered and may be used only by the company that owns the mark. In many cases the company name is the brand, and this is often the case for services companies such as Loblaws, Four Seasons, and Speedy Muffler.

A **trademark** is defined as a brand that is given legal protection because, under the law, it has been appropriated by one seller. Thus *trademark* is essentially a legal term. All trademarks are brands and thus include the words, letters, or numbers that can be pronounced. They may also include a pictorial design (brand mark). Some people erroneously believe that the trademark is only the pictorial part of the brand logo.

One major method of classifying brands is on the basis of who owns them — producers or retailers. Major brands such as Sony, Zenith, Lexus, Sunlight, GWG, and Ivory are producers' brands, while Motomaster, President's Choice, Viking, Kenmore, Body Shop, and Life are all brands that are owned by retailers.

The term *national* has been used for many years to describe producer-brand ownership, while brands owned by retailers are generally referred to as private brands or private labels. However, more acceptable terminology for many marketers would be the terms *producer* and *retailer* brands. To say that a brand of a small manufacturer of poultry feed in British Columbia that markets in only two or three Western provinces is a national brand, while those of Canadian Tire, Shoppers Drug Mart, Loblaws, and Sears are private brands, seems to be misusing these terms to some extent. Nevertheless, the brands of retailers generally continue to be referred to as private labels.

The issue of trademark protection arises quite often in marketing. In 1994, a Canadian retailer, Business Depot Limited, was granted a preliminary injunction by the Federal Court of Canada to prevent the largest office-supply warehouse chain in the United States, Office Depot Inc., from opening stores in Ontario. The court decided there was a serious legal question involved in the use of similar trademarks by competing companies in the same location, that Business Depot had established extensive goodwill with its trademark in Ontario, and that it could lose market share if customers were to go to an Office Depot store thinking it was a Business Depot outlet.[2] It is important to note that trademark protection under Canadian law extends not only to exact copies but to similar representations of brands as well.[3]

WHAT'S IN A NAME?

A history of brand marketing will tell us that once a brand establishes a position of leadership in a product category, this position is often maintained over a very long period of time. Many of the leading brands that we buy today were purchased regularly by our parents and even our grandparents. Brands that continue to dominate their consumer product categories include Kodak, General Electric, Kellogg, Levi, Kraft, Nabisco, Tide, and Campbell.

The development and protection of brand names has become a very important element of marketing management and one that demands increased attention all the time. Companies such as Colgate-Palmolive have made conscious decisions to manage their brand names in such a way as to dominate a product category. For example, this company has made a commitment to position Colgate as an all-purpose supplier of oral-health products. The importance of the Colgate name is summed up in a comment from Patrick Knight, former vice-president of marketing for Colgate-Palmolive: "We now consider the most valuable assets we have to be our trademarks."[4]

Such an attitude toward successful brands has led major companies to ensure that their brand names are assigned a value and are shown as assets on their balance sheets. Many of the leading brands have been the major targets in corporate takeovers as the purchasing companies have realized that the equity represented in successful brands is considerably more valuable than factories and distribution systems.[5] When Union Pacific Resources, an oil and gas exploration and production group, made a bid to take over Pennzoil's energy resources, it was seeking to acquire a brand name that was well known. The name of Union Pacific seemed to be equated by consumers with the railway business and was not felt to be easily associated, in the mind of customers, with oil and gas. Hence the company sought to achieve brand recognition through the Pennzoil name with its long association with motor oils.[6]

Equally important is the value of established brands in allowing their owners to apply the brand names to new products. As the cost of acquiring established brands increases, as does the cost and risk of introducing new products, many companies have been turning in recent years to the launching of brand extensions as a way of trading on the success of established brands and reducing the risk of new product failure. Hewlett-Packard, a company that has developed a strong reputation for printers, has now moved into selling personal computers. The company decided to do so because the brand was so highly regarded by individuals who had purchased printers to use with personal computers. The Hewlett-Packard LaserJet printers were noted for being headache-free. The brand popularity transferred to the introduction of the extension.[7]

Some companies have succeeded in keeping their brands successful and before the purchasing public for many years. Nabisco, maker of such cookies and crackers as Oreo, Ritz, Arrowroot, Chips

www.nabisco.ca

The owners of Roots have transformed a great idea into a national chain and a major brand name.

Ahoy, and Triscuit, has been making cookies in Canada since 1861. Triscuit Crackers date from 1895, Honey Maid Graham Wafers from 1900, and Ritz from 1935. Today, the success of the Nabisco brands is obvious, and many have spawned brand extensions.

By stretching the original successful brand name to cover a number of brand extension products, the marketer is trading on the success of the original brand but is running some risk at the same time. Clearly, there may be some new products to which the original brand should not be applied. This raises the question of how far the successful brand can be "extended" before the marketer is stretching the credibility of the link between the brand and the product. Colgate can with confidence launch a line of toothbrushes, dental floss, and mouthwash, but would consumers buy Colgate sunglasses or suntan lotion?

Brands make it easy for consumers to identify goods or services. Brands also help assure purchasers they are getting comparable quality when they reorder. For sellers, brands can be advertised and recognized when displayed on shelves in a store. Branding also helps sellers control their market because buyers will not confuse one branded product with another. Branding reduces price comparisons because it is hard to compare prices on two items with different brands. Finally, for sellers branding can add a measure of prestige to otherwise ordinary commodities (Sunkist oranges, Sifto salt, Lantic sugar, Highliner fish, Chiquita bananas).[8]

Reasons for Not Branding

The two major responsibilities inherent in brand ownership are (1) to promote the brand and (2) to maintain a consistent quality of output. Many firms do not brand their products because they are unable or unwilling to assume those responsibilities.

Some items are not branded because of the difficulty of differentiating the products of one firm from those of another. Clothespins, nails, and industrial raw materials (coal, cotton, wheat) are examples of goods for which product differentiation (including branding) is generally unknown. The physical nature of some items, such as fresh fruits and vegetables, may discourage branding. However, now that these products are often packaged in typically purchased quantities, brands are being applied to the packages.

Producers frequently do not brand the part of their output that is below their usual quality. Products graded as seconds or imperfects are sold at a cut price and are often distributed through channels different from those used for usual-quality goods.

Selecting a Good Brand Name

Some brand names are so good that they contribute to the sales success of the product or service; others appear to be so poor or inappropriate that they would appear to contribute little if anything to sales success and may even seem to be a factor in market failures. Some products seem to have been successful despite having names that may appear to add little to their appeal. Some brand names attain considerable value over time and remain consumer favourites for many years.

The Challenge Today, selecting a good name for a product or service is more challenging than ever. The reason is that we are running out of possibilities — and many of the good names have already been used. There are about ten thousand new products launched annually in North America, yet the standard desk-size dictionary contains only about fifty thousand words. When one considers that a new brand can't be labelled Panasonic, Oreo, Esso, or Timex because these brands have been used successfully for many years and that there are many other words one would not want to have associated with one's product or service, it is no surprise that companies often resort to words that aren't really words, or that they bring out the new product as an extension of an already-successful brand.

The need for names and brands that are likely to contribute to a product's success has led to the establishment of companies that specialize in coming up with attractive and appealing brand names. These firms will use database searches and will rely on unusual sources to identify likely names. Some even employ qualified linguists on staff. They often come up with names that aren't part of any language: Pentium (Intel's new microprocessor chip), Zoloft (a new pharmaceutical product), Lexus, Acura, and Compaq. The creation of a new brand name will often involve research to determine whether consumers will react positively to the brand being proposed. It also is not an inexpensive process, as some firms will charge $25,000 or more for a new brand name.[9]

Desirable Characteristics Five characteristics determine the desirability of a brand name for a product or service.[10] It is difficult to think of a brand that has all five. Still, a brand should possess as many of these characteristics as possible:

- *Suggest something about the product's characteristics* — its benefits, use, or action. Some names that suggest desirable benefits include Beautyrest, Motomaster, and — perhaps best of all — DieHard. Product use and action are suggested by Hi-Liter, Dustbuster, La-Z-Boy, Mr. Clean, Gleem, and Easy-Off.
- *Be easy to pronounce, spell, and remember.* Simple, short, one-syllable names such as Tide, Ban, Aim, and Raid are helpful. Top-cuts, Weedman, and Speedy are additional examples of brand names that are easy to remember. However, even some short names, such as NYNEX and Aetna, aren't easily pronounced by some customers.
- *Be distinctive.* Brands with names like National, Star, Ideal, or Standard fail on this point. Many services firms begin their brand names with adjectives connoting strength and then add a description of the business, creating brands such as Allied Van Lines and United Parcel Service. Some brand names play on patriotism as, for example, Maple Leaf food products, Air Canada, and Molson Canadian.
- *Be adaptable to new products that may be added to the product line.* An innocuous name such as Kellogg, Lipton, or Jelinek may serve the purpose better than a highly distinctive name suggestive of product benefits. Frigidaire is an excellent name for a refrigerator and other cold-image products. But when the producer expanded its line of home appliances and added Frigidaire kitchen ranges, the name lost some of its sales appeal.
- *Be capable of being registered and legally protected under the Trade Marks Act and other statutory or common laws.* Names that are generic and in common usage in the English language would not meet this criteria. For example, the word "water" used as a name could not by itself be registered and legally protected. Names must also not be registered or in usage by other firms.

Protecting a Brand Name

Over a period of years, some brands have become so well accepted that the brand name is substituted for the **generic name** of the particular product.

www.burgerking.com
www.hilton.com
www.kpmg.ca

Examples of brand names that legally have become generic are linoleum, celluloid, cellophane, kerosene, shredded wheat, and nylon. Originally, these were trademarks limited to use by the owner.

A brand name can become generic in several ways. Sometimes the patent on a product expires. There is no simple generic name available, so the public continues to use the brand name as a generic name. This happened with shredded wheat, nylon, and cellophane. Sometimes a firm just does too good an advertising and selling job with an outstanding brand name. While not yet legally generic, names such as Xerox, Band-Aid, Scotch Tape, Ski-Doo, and Kleenex are on the borderline.

It is the responsibility of the trademark owner to assert the company's rights in order to prevent the loss of the distinctive character of the trademark. A number of strategies are employed to prevent the brand name from falling into generic usage. The most common strategy is to ensure that the words "trade mark" or the letters "TM®" appear adjacent to the brand name wherever it appears. A second strategy is to use two names — the brand name together with either the company's name or the generic name of the product. Examples of this include Polariod Land camera and Dacron brand polyester. A third strategy for protecting a trademark involves the incorporation into the trademark of a distinctive signature or logo.

Finally, the owner of a registered trademark must be willing to prosecute any other companies attempting to market products under a brand name that is identical to or similar to the registered brand name. By prosecuting such infringements of the trademark protection, the company is demonstrating to the courts that it is actively protecting its right to use of the brand and is guarding against the brand falling into generic usage.

BRANDING STRATEGIES

Both producers and intermediaries face strategic decisions regarding the branding of their goods or services. Whether a firm is branding a product or a service, some fundamental things need to be kept in mind. Branding is a means of creating and maintaining a perception of customer value. There is an expectation on the part of the customer that the brand name stands for quality. Branding also provides the means of differentiating products and services from the competition. When consumers see the offerings as all being alike, there is a tendency to shop on the basis of price. Branding provides consumers with another reason to choose a product. When brands provide better quality in products and services, they tend to be remembered by the consumer.[11]

Product-branding strategies are often viewed differently than are services-branding strategies. Services branding is generally synonymous with the name of the company. The best example of services branding is franchising in which companies such as McDonald's, Burger King, and Tim Hortons sell the rights to their name and products. The brand or name has come to stand for a service encompassing recognizable features. For example, McDonald's represents fast service, a children's focus, and consistent products. Other examples of services branding include hotel chains like Westin or Hilton, and professional-service companies, including consulting firms like KPMG and Ernst and Young. Sometimes service products are licensed for sale by intermediaries. An example of this would be a training facility that delivers Microsoft training programs. The following strategies generally are used to brand tangible products. The strategic branding of services is dealt with later in the chapter.

Producers' Strategies

Producers must decide whether to brand their products and whether to sell any or all of their output under intermediaries' brands.

Marketing Entire Output under Producers' Own Brands Companies that market their entire output under their own brands usually are very large, well financed, and well managed. Polaroid, Maytag, and IBM are examples. They have broad product lines, well-established distribution systems, and large shares of the market. Only a small percentage of manufacturers follow this policy, and their number seems to be decreasing.

Some reasons for adopting this policy have already been covered in the section on the importance of branding to the seller. In addition, intermediaries often prefer to handle producers' brands, especially when the brands have high consumer acceptance.

Branding of Fabricating Parts and Materials Some producers of fabricating materials and parts (products used in the further manufacturing of other goods) will brand their product.[12] This strategy is used in the marketing of Fiberglas insulation, Pella windows, Acrilan fabrics, and many automotive parts — spark plugs, batteries, oil filters, and so on. DuPont has consistently and successfully used this strategy, notably with its Lycra spandex fiber and Stainmaster stain repellent for carpets.

Underlying this strategy is the seller's desire to develop a market preference for its branded part of material. For instance, G.D. Searle Ltd. wants to build a market situation in which customers will insist on food products sweetened with NutraSweet. In addition, the parts manufacturer wants to persuade the producer of the finished item that using the branded materials will help sell the end product. In our example, Searle hopes to convince food manufacturers that their sales will be increased if their products contain NutraSweet.

Certain product characteristics lend themselves to the effective use of this strategy. First, it helps if the product is also a consumer good that is bought for replacement purposes. This factor encourages the branding of Champion spark plugs, Atlas batteries, and Fram oil filters, for example. Second, the seller's situation is improved if the item is a major part of the finished product — a microprocessor within a personal computer, for instance. Intel Corp. developed the slogan "Intel Inside" to strengthen its product's position.[13]

Marketing under Intermediaries' Brands A widespread strategy is for producers to brand part or all of their output with the brands of their intermediary's customers. For example, a manufacturer of salad dressing makes products for Loblaw, and they are sold under the President's Choice label. For the manufacturer, this intermediary's brand business generates additional sales volume and profit dollars. Orders typically are large, payment is prompt, and a producer's working-capital position is improved. Also, manufacturers may use their production resources more effectively, including their plant capacities. Furthermore, refusing to sell under a retailer's or wholesaler's brand will not eliminate competition from this source. Many intermediaries want to market under their own brands, so if one manufacturer refuses their business, they will simply go to another.

Probably the most serious limitation to marketing under intermediaries' brands is that a producer may be at the mercy of the intermediaries. This problem grows as the proportion of that producer's output going to intermediaries' brands increases.

Intermediaries' Strategies

The question of whether or not to brand the products they may carry must also be answered by intermediaries. There are two usual strategies, as follows:

Carry Only Producers' Brands Most retailers and wholesalers follow this policy because they are not able to take on the dual burdens of promoting a brand and maintaining its quality.

Carry Intermediaries' Brands Alone or with Producers' Brands Many large retailers and some large wholesalers have their own brands. In fact, some of the most successful brands in recent years have been retailers' own brands, including President's Choice, St. Michael, and Life. Intermediaries may find it advantageous to market their own brands for several reasons. First, this strategy increases their control over their market. If customers prefer a given retailer's brand, they can get it only from that retailer's store. Furthermore, intermediaries can usually sell their brands at prices below those of producers' brands and still earn higher gross margins. This is possible because intermediaries can buy at lower costs. The costs may be lower because (1) manufacturers' advertising and selling costs are not included in their prices, or (2) producers are anxious to get the extra business to keep their plants running in slack seasons.

In addition to the two strategies mentioned above, some companies are carrying brands of other producers in association with their own. For example, Air Canada has entered into an agreement to provide Second Cup coffee on all of its flights.[14] McDonald's has an agreement with Wal-Mart to set up outlets inside their stores.

Intermediaries have more freedom in pricing products sold under their own labels. Products carrying a retailer's brand become differentiated products, and this hinders price comparisons that might be unfavourable to that retailer. Also, prices on manufacturers' brands can be cut drastically by competing retail stores. This last point is what has been happening in recent years in the marketing of clothing with designer labels such as Calvin Klein, Simon Chang, Ralph Lauren, and Alfred Sung. Some of the large retailers in their upper-priced clothing departments have increased their stocks of apparel carrying the store's own brand. These stores have cut back on products with designer brands such as Calvin Klein and others. The reason for this brand-switching is that some designer-labelled products are now available at much lower prices in stores such as K mart, Zellers, and other "off-price retailers."

The strategy of marketing as many products as possible under the retailer's own label has met with considerable success for such Canadian retailers as Loblaw and Canadian Tire. In fact, Loblaw is among the leading companies in the world in the private-label business, creating a situation where more than 30 percent of all Loblaw sales is accounted for by private-label products such as President's Choice Decadent chocolate chip cookies, Too Good To Be True cereals, and PC Cola. In fact, Loblaw has been so successful at developing the market for private-label products that the company has licensed the President's Choice brand to chains around the world. Loblaw is an excellent example of how private-label products can replace national brands in the consumer's mind when the retailer develops products and value in which the consumer can be confident.[15]

Strategies Common to Producers and Intermediaries

Producers and intermediaries alike must adopt some strategy with respect to branding their product mix and branding for market saturation.

Branding a Line of Products/Services At least four different strategies are widely used by firms that sell more than one product or service.

- The same "family" or "blanket" brand may be placed on all products. This policy is followed by Heinz, Catelli, Campbell's, McCain's, and others in the food field. Other examples include the YMCA and Pizza Hut.
- A separate name may be used for each product. This strategy is employed by Procter & Gamble and Lever Brothers. Pampers are produced by Procter & Gamble; Dove soap is a Lever product.
- A separate family brand may be applied to each grade of product or to each group of similar products or services. Sears groups its major home appliances under the Kenmore name, its paints and home furnishings under Harmony House, and its insurance under Allstate.
- The company trade name may be combined with an individual name for the product or service. Thus there is Johnson's Pledge, Microsoft's Excel, Kellogg's Rice Krispies, Molson Golden, Bank of Montreal's MasterCard, and Ford Mustang.

When used wisely, a **family-brand strategy** has considerable merit. This strategy makes it much simpler and less expensive to introduce new related products to a line. Also, the general prestige of a brand can be spread more easily if it appears on several products rather than on only one. A family brand is best suited for a marketing situation when the products are related in quality, in use, or in some other manner. When Black & Decker, a manufacturer of power tools, purchased General Electric's line of small appliances, the Black & Decker brand was put on those appliances, but not immediately. Because of the perceived differences between kitchen products and workroom products, Black & Decker realized it was a risky proposition to switch brands. Consequently, the company mounted a year-long brand-transition campaign before making the change. Also, during those years, Black & Decker introduced several other houseware products, and this helped in the General Electric–Black & Decker brand transition.

The success of major brands and families of brands certainly makes it easier for companies, whether manufacturers or intermediaries, to introduce new products under the established family brand or as brand extensions to well-established brands. This is obvious when one considers the number of varieties of Oreo cookies and Ritz

MARKETING AT WORK FILE 11-1

WHAT'S IN A BRAND?

Some of the greatest brands in the world include Coca-Cola, Procter & Gamble, Johnson & Johnson, and Nike. They have been able to successfully stand up to private labels as well as other branded-goods companies. These brands are a power to be reckoned with. They can command high "brand taxes," as is the case with Nike's $100-plus pricetags. They have the power, however, to go beyond adding price margins, to bestowing credibility and attracting instant attention.

According to George Stalk, Jr., senior vice-president in the Toronto office of Boston Consulting Group, branding is about the total experience in which products and services play a part. "It's about hooking customers into an experience they can trust and can be proud to tell others about."

Brands went through a period in the late 1980s and early 1990s when consumers balked at coughing up premiums for their purchase. Shoppers were beginning to wonder if brands were giving them value when they saw a proliferation of no-name brands hitting the market. There is an indication that the trend to devalue brands has switched and strong brands are again standing out as a beacon to the harried customer, a safe haven from the often confusing array of new products and sales pitches.

The way brands have been viewed by customers has changed dramatically over time. In the 1940s and 1950s, brands were revered as symbols of the good life. Disneyland, for example, opened as "the happiest place on earth." In the 1960s and early 1970s, brands developed an image of corporate magnanimity. Coca-Cola, for example, gathered people from all over the world to a hilltop in Italy in 1971 to sing "I'd like to teach the world to sing in perfect harmony." By the 1980s, brands had become symbols of one-up-manship. BMWs carried an image of success and achievement: Because I drive one, I'm better than you are. Through the 1980s, consumers began to demand more for their dollar than keeping up with the person down the street. Many of the big brands missed this point entirely and became quite arrogant, according to Roberto Goizueta, CEO of Coca-Cola. Brands began to be used to justify price differences without an increase in value. By the end of the decade, consumers were angry. They started to consider private labels. To compound the situation, some of the most trusted brands tripped up. Coca-Cola produced New Coke, a disastrous move; Perrier was caught with tainted mineral water; Intel sold faulty Pentium chips.

We are now seeing a realignment of brands and consumers. Brands are gaining popularity, and again this can be seen as a reflection of the times. The value demands of consumers are being met better by producers, and trust is being re-established. Consumers are viewing brands as ways of helping them to make choices. In technology, products change so rapidly that the only assurance of quality is the brand.

Trust, however, has to be earned. Stalk feels that companies need to analyze the buying, paying, getting, using or consuming, and after-sales servicing that a customer goes through in order to be able to transform all of these steps. He notes, for example, that the time intervals customers experience and are willing to accept change rapidly. "Only a few years ago, waiting half an hour to prepare food at home was considered normal for 'fast-food' offerings. Today, if a meal isn't on the table in five minutes or less, it's not fast. A two-week waiting period for vehicle servicing is about thirteen days too long!" People are less willing to have their feelings shaped by standard brand names. When consumers find a brand they can trust, they can significantly increase the value to the company through loyalty and word-of-mouth.

Source: Adapted from Betsy Morris, "The Brand's the Thing," *Fortune*, March 4, 1996, pp. 73–86; George Stalk, Jr., "What's in a Brand? It's the Experience," *The Globe and Mail*, May 23, 1997, p. B11.

crackers now produced by Nabisco and the wide array of products marketed under the Motomaster label by Canadian Tire. But the use of family brands and established brands to launch new products places a burden on the brand owner to maintain consistently high quality across all products marketed under that brand. One bad item can reflect unfavourably on other products that carry the brand and may even lead to the creation of a negative image for the overall brand.

Branding for Market Saturation Frequently, to increase its degree of market saturation, a firm will employ a **multiple-brand strategy**. Suppose, for example, that a company has built one type of sales appeal around a given brand. To reach other segments of the market, the company can use other appeals with other brands. For example, Procter & Gamble markets a line of detergents that includes Tide, Bold, Cheer, Oxydol, and Ivory Snow. There may be some consumers who feel that Tide, even with its many varieties (phosphate-free, with bleach, unscented, liquid, regular, and most recently, high-efficiency HE Tide), is not suitable for washing lingerie and other delicate clothing. For these people, Procter & Gamble offers Ivory Snow, a detergent whose image is gentler than that of Tide and trades on its association with the purity and gentleness of Ivory soap. With this brand line-up, Procter & Gamble is assured of having a brand or a brand variation to appeal to every segment of the detergent market.

Building and Using Brand Equity

Companies as diverse as GM, Microsoft, 3M, Kodak, and McCains recognize that the brands they own may be more valuable than their physical assets such as buildings and equipment. What we are talking about here is brand equity, one of the hottest topics in marketing over the past ten years. **Brand equity** is the value a brand adds to a product. In the minds of many consumers, just having a brand name such as Sony, Kenmore, or Reebok on a product adds value to it. Beyond a product's value in its potential to do what it's supposed to do, a brand adds value to that product through its name awareness and its connotations of favourable attributes (such as quality or economy).

If you're not convinced that a brand name by itself can have much value, consider the results of two studies. In one, the proportion of subjects choosing cornflakes cereal jumped from 47 percent when the brand was not known to 59 percent when the brand was identified as Kellogg's. In another study, conducted in 1993, when a sample of computer buyers were asked how much more or less they would pay for particular brands rather than the average computer brand, there was a range of $364. Consumers said they would pay $295 and $232 more for the IBM and Compaq brands, respectively. Other brands commanding a premium include Apple, Digital, and Dell.[16] According to a 1995 update of this study, IBM still commands the largest premium, followed by Compaq, Hewlett-Packard, and Dell. It's evident that Kellogg's, IBM, Compaq, and many other brands have substantial equity.

Today, creating brand equity is about more than positioning, packaging, and imagery. It involves developing a relationship with customers that they can trust and be proud to tell others about. Developing a brand is a process of creating loyal followers who provide word-of-mouth support and ultimately add value to the product.[17] Substantial brand equity provides many benefits to the firm that owns the brand:

- The brand itself can become a differential advantage, influencing consumers to buy a particular product. Examples include Volvo, Tetley tea, and Kenmore (Sears' brand of home appliances).
- Because it is expensive and time consuming to build brand equity, it creates a barrier for companies that want to enter the market with a similar product.
- Brand equity can help a product survive changes in the operating environment, such as a business crisis or a shift in consumer tastes. Tylenol seemed to fare better than Perrier when both products faced crises involving their purity.

Brand equity is most often used to expand a product line, especially to extend a brand into new varieties or even new products. In fact, it may be argued that brand extensions are not possible unless the brand has established considerable equity. Examples include Ocean Spray drinks in flavours other than the original cranberry, Tetley iced tea, and Ivory bath wash. The rationale for using an existing, strong brand name on a new item or line is that the brand's equity will convey a favourable impression of the product and increase the likelihood that consumers will at least try it.

If a brand has abundant equity, that does not necessarily mean it should be applied to other products. When it was developing a spaghetti sauce, Campbell determined that its popular brand name would not convey an Italian image, so it selected Prego as the name for its new sauce. Also, strong equity does not guarantee success for new items. Examples include Harley Davidson cigarettes, Levi's tailored men's clothing, and Swatch clothing, to name a few.

The issue of relative brand equity was most obvious in the early 1990s in the battle that arose between established national brands on the one hand and generally newer private-label or retailers' own brands on the other. In fact, this situation developed into one of the most important issues in marketing. This battle of the brands has been most obvious in grocery and personal-care products — the items that most households buy regularly from their neighbourhood supermarkets and drugstores. As consumer confidence in the quality of such private-label products has grown, so too has their share of the packaged-goods business.

The phenomenon of private-label products is international in scope and is attributed to three related causes. Research indicates that nearly two-thirds of consumers around the world believe there is no discernible difference between private-label and national-brand products; the proliferation of new products has led to fierce competition in some product categories; and consumers have gained greater confidence in the quality and value of private labels as they have developed. Many private-label products now occupy premium status. President's Choice illustrates this point.

There is some evidence that the battle between national and private-label brands has reached an equilibrium. Having seen a rapid rise in growth between 1989 and 1991, private-label goods as a percentage of supermarket spending then levelled off. Since 1993, the graph has been flat and increases in purchases of private-label goods have plateaued.[18]

Trademark Licensing

An effective branding strategy that has grown by leaps and bounds in recent years is **brand (or trademark) licensing**. Under this strategy, the owner of a trademark grants permission (a licence) to other firms to use the owner's brand name, logotype (distinctive lettering and colouring), and/or character on the licensee's products. In this case, Company A licenses its brand to be sold by Company B. The brand owner, Company A, collects royalties from the sale of its products and the second firm, Company B, capitalizes on the success of the established brand name. A recent example occurred at McCain Foods Ltd., which entered into a deal with Ore-Ida Foods to acquire its food-service frozen french fry and potato-specialties business. McCain did not, however, acquire the Ore-Ida name; it is retained by the original company. McCain has the right to market the products and pays royalties to Ore-Ida. Licensing is common practice among multinationals that are reluctant to give up ownership of a brand, especially when they are using the name for other products.[19] The owners of the trademark characters such as Spiderman, Batman, and the Simpsons have licensed the use of these characters on many different products and services. In particular, children's clothing use these trademarks all the time. The licensee typically pays a royalty of about 5 percent on the wholesale price of the product that carries the licensed trademark. However, this figure can vary on the basis of the perceived strength of the licenser's brand.

Strategy decisions must be made by both parties — the licenser and the licensee. Alfred Sung (a licenser) must ask, "Should we allow other firms to use our designer label?" A manufacturer of eyeglasses (a licensee) must ask, "Do we want to put out a line of high-fashion eyeglasses under the Alfred Sung name?"

Owners of well-known brands are interested in licensing their trademarks for various reasons. First, it can be very profitable because there is no expense involved on the part of the licenser. Second, there is a promotional benefit, because the licenser's name gets circulation far beyond the original trademarked article. Third, licensing can help protect the trademark. If Coca-Cola licenses its brand for use in a variety of product categories, it can block any other company from using that brand legally in those product categories.

For the company receiving the licence — the licensee — the strategy is a quick way to gain market recognition and to penetrate a new market. Today there is a high financial cost involved in establishing a new brand name. Even then there is no guarantee of success. It is a lot easier for an unknown firm to gain consumer acceptance of its product if that item carries a well-known brand.

Strategic Branding of Services

Throughout this chapter, we have discussed the competitive edge that a well-selected brand can give to a product. These advantages are equally applicable to tangible goods and intangible services. Furthermore, the marketers of services have to make many of the same strategic branding decisions as do the marketers of tangible products. Perhaps the first of these decisions is to select a good brand name for the service.[20] In services marketing, more so than in the marketing of tangible goods, the company name typically serves as the brand name.

The characteristics of an effective service brand are much the same as for tangible goods. Thus, a service brand should be:

- *Relevant to the service or its benefits.* Ticketron, the sales agency that sells tickets to sporting events, concerts, and other major attractions, conveys the nature of the service and the electronic speed with which it is delivered. Visa suggests an international activity and is relevant for a global financial service. Instant Teller is a good name for the automatic banking machines of the CIBC. Budget implies the best price for people who rent cars from that company. Four Seasons suggests a hotel chain that has something to offer year-round.
- *Distinctive.* This characteristic is difficult to communicate. The point is that companies should avoid branding their service with names that others could use. Thus, names like National, Canadian, and Royal should probably be avoided because, standing alone, they tell us nothing about the service or its benefits. When names such as these are used, the company will usually add words that tell us what service is being offered, such as Canadian Airlines International, Royal Trust, and National Life Insurance.

Some service marketers differentiate themselves from the competition by using a symbol (usually referred to as a logo) or a distinctive colour. We are all familiar with the golden arches of McDonald's, the lion of the Royal Bank of Canada, and Air Canada's maple leaf. For colour, we see the green of the Toronto-Dominion Bank, the red of Scotiabank, the claret of CIBC, and the blue of the Bank of Montreal. The use of a person's name such as Harvey's, Eaton's, and Tilden, or a coined word, such as Avis, Re/Max, and Amex, also offers distinctiveness, but it tells us little about the service being offered. This is the case until the name has been firmly established and it comes to mean something to the consumer. Certainly, many such names have become very well established in the marketplace.

- *Easy to pronounce and remember.* Simple, short names, such as Delta and A&W, usually meet this criterion. Others, such as Aetna and Overwaitea, pose pronunciation problems for some people. Sometimes, unusual spelling aids in having the consumer remember the name — the reverse R in Toys " Я " Us, for example.
- *Adaptable to additional services or regions.* Companies that change their mix of services and their geographical locations over time should be flexible enough to adapt to these extensions of their operations. Alberta Government Telephones (AGT) and Newfoundland Telephone changed their names to Telus and NewTel, respectively, as traditional telephone service became a smaller part of their business when they moved into Internet services and a range of other technology-based services. The Canadian Imperial Bank of Commerce has shortened its name to CIBC in anticipation of expanding its range of financial services beyond banking. Many successful companies (Bank of Montreal, London Life, Great-West Life) have been able to establish national reputations despite the fact that their names suggest a regional association, although it may be easier for companies with names like Canada Life and Canada Trust to do so.

www.royalbank.com
www.scotiabank.ca
www.cibc.com
www.bankofmontreal.com
www.tilden.com
www.avis.com
www.remax.com
www.americanexpress.com
www.londonlife.com
www.gwl.ca
www.canadatrust.com

MARKETING AT WORK FILE 11–2

CO-BRANDING — IS THERE MORE TO IT THAN SHARING A PACKAGE?

Unions of brands, or co-branding, is a very popular strategy, particularly with large companies. For example, the Pillsbury doughboy became very friendly with Oreo Cookies, and the Oreo Bars Baking Mix and Frosting was born! Similarly, Betty Crocker and Mars Inc. created the M&M's Cookie Bars baking mix. In theory this strategy is effective, because two brands offer double the recognition, double the endorsement power, and double the consumer confidence. Some marketers, such as Bryan Mattimore, president of the Mattimore Group consultants, feel this is the way branding will continue to go. Brand extensions, he feels, have been exhausted, and to gain additional mileage out of a brand, the only approach is to co-brand. Elinor Selame, president of BrandEquity International, suggests that introducing products in this way also offers opportunities for sharing expenses.

Some versions of co-branding are really ingredient marketing, such as can easily be seen in Betty Crocker's Super Moist Cake Mix with Sunkist Lemons. There are, however, some unusual combinations being seen on grocery shelves. Witness Hershey Foods Corp.'s Reese's Peanut Butter Puffs cereal and Nestle's Cheerios. Delicious Cookies markets its products with a number of different brand associations, such as Welch Foods Inc. and Chiquita Brands International Inc., and displays these brand names on its packages.

And then there is co-branding in the service sector. One of the most notable examples of services "unions" is the airline mileage programs. Air Miles, for example, is a union of 110 companies, including such brands as Bank of Montreal, Sears, Shell, Goodyear, Blockbuster Video, Canada Safeway, and National Tilden Interrent. American Express has recently joined forces with Air Miles to introduce the American Express Air Miles Credit Card. Consumers can collect travel miles faster by using this card with their collector card at participation companies.

But is co-branding only about sharing packages or dual logos? Alexander L. Biel, writing for *Marketing Magazine*, suggests that brand management is about image and personality. When researching brand perception, he suggests, researchers would do well to have respondents imagine the brand as a person and follow it around town all day. Researchers who have used this technique find that it poses no problems for consumers and it identifies images that are consistent across respondents. This personification technique is an interesting one to use in considering the brand unions discussed above. If one brand is more "frugal" than another, will they make a compatible couple? If one brand is too dominant, will it destroy the future independence of the other? Selame warns, "If the guest has a stronger trademark than the host, it can hold up the host as hostage." If the images that both brands present are not complementary, the consumer may also have difficulty envisioning their union and understanding the connection. The advertising business has long known that images associated with a brand have very significant consequences. Society may not be able to handle too many mixed marriages in the marketplace.

Source: Adapted from "Odd Couples on Store Shelves," *The Globe and Mail*, July 7, 1994, p. B4; Alexander L. Biel, "Making the Most of Metaphors," *Marketing Magazine*, January 15, 1996, p. 16; and "American Express and Air Miles (R) Reward Program Launch Co-branding Credit Card," *Canada NewsWire*, press release, http://www.newswire.ca/releases/January 1997/07/c0477.html.

When companies have names with geographic connotations, such as Canadian Pacific, they are often abbreviated when expansion takes place, as in CP Hotels. Airlines with names like Air BC and Air Atlantic are obviously regional carriers, while one named Air Nova may find it easier to expand beyond its original market area.

Another decision is whether to use family branding. Insurance companies and financial services firms often use the same brand name for the variety of services offered. On the other hand, the Canadian chartered banks generally operate their brokerage arms as separate entities.

Whether to get into trademark licensing is a strategic branding decision for many services firms. Companies, entertainers, and many professional sports teams, such as the Montreal Canadiens, Edmonton Oilers, and Toronto Blue Jays, license their names for use on many different products.

PACKAGING

Packaging may be defined as all the activities of designing and producing the container or wrapper for a product. Services can also be packaged even though they are not wrapped in cartons or displayed in containers. Examples of services packaging include travel tours or H & R Block personal income tax service. The customer purchases a package of services that are sold as one unit and that can include many elements. With services, the container is not the tangible package we associate with products; it is, nevertheless, a package of value for the consumer, and the process of packaging involves making the appearance of the collection of goods attractive to the consumer. There are three reasons for packaging:

www.hrblock.com

- *Packaging of products often serves several safety and utilitarian purposes.* It protects a product on its route from the producer to the final customer, and in some cases even while it is being used by the customer. Effective packaging can help prevent ill-intentioned persons from tampering with products. Some protection is provided by "child-proof" closures on containers of medicines and other products that are potentially harmful to children. Also, compared with bulk items, packaged goods generally are more convenient, cleaner, and less susceptible to losses from evaporation, spilling, and spoilage.
- *Packaging may be part of a company's marketing program.* Packaging helps identify a product and thus may prevent substitution of competitive products. At the point of purchase, the package can serve as a silent sales person. Furthermore, the advertising copy on the package will last as long as the product is used in its packaged form. A package may be the only significant way in which a firm can differentiate its product. In the case of convenience goods or business operating supplies, for example, most buyers feel that one well-known brand is about as good as another.

  Some feature of the package may add sales appeal — a no-drip spout, a reusable jar, or a self-applicator (a bottle of shoe polish or glue with an applicator top, for example). By packaging their toothpaste in a pump dispenser — a product long used in Europe — Colgate and Close-Up brands increased their sales considerably. Crest and Aim later adopted the same type of packaging.
- *A firm can package its product in a way that increases profit and sales volume.* A package that is easy to handle or minimizes damage losses will cut marketing costs, thus boosting profit. On the sales side, packaged goods typically are more attractive and therefore better than items sold in bulk. Many companies have increased the sales volume of an article simply by redesigning its package. Coca-Cola, for instance, launched its contour bottle to boost the image of the product.

Importance of Packaging in Marketing

Historically, packaging was a production-oriented activity in most companies, performed mainly to obtain the benefits of protection and convenience. Today, however, the marketing significance of packaging is fully recognized, and packaging is truly a major competitive force in the struggle for markets. The widespread use of self-service selling and automatic vending means that the package must do the selling job at the point of purchase. Shelf space is often at a premium, and it is no simple task for manufacturers even to get their products displayed in a retail outlet. Most retailers are inclined to cater to producers that have used effective packaging.

In addition, the increased use of branding and the public's rising standards in health and sanitation have contributed to a greater awareness of packaging. Safety in packaging has become a prominent marketing and social issue in recent years. Extensive consumer use of microwave ovens has had a significant impact on packaging. Many food products are now packaged so that they can go straight from the shelf or freezer into a microwave oven.

New developments in packaging, occurring rapidly and in a seemingly endless flow, require management's constant attention. We see new packaging materials replacing traditional ones, new shapes, new closures, and other new features (measured portions, metered flow). These all increase convenience for consumers and selling points for marketers.

To assist consumers in being able to browse through CD-ROM products, Ames Specialty Packaging has designed the CD BOOK PAK, a book-sized package with multiple configurations incorporating various tray, cover, and pocket options. This package enables customers to receive more information about the product and facilitates their ability to access that information before buying.[21]

Packaging is an important marketing tool for companies that operate in international markets. Most countries have regulations governing the packaging of products and the wording that must appear on labels. A company that wishes to export its product to another country must, therefore, be aware of the packaging laws of that country. For example, companies in other countries that export to Canada and the Canadian importers that represent them have to be aware of Canadian packaging regulations pertaining to metric package sizes, bilingual labelling, and the standard sizes of packages used in some industries. In addition to regulations, exporters must understand that packages that work in one country may not be accepted in another, because of design, illustration, or colour.

Packaging Strategies

Changing the Package In general, management has two reasons for considering a package change — to combat a decrease in sales and to expand a market by attracting new groups of customers. More specifically, a firm may want to correct a poor feature in the existing container, or it may want to take advantage of new materials. Some companies change their containers to aid in promotional programs. A new package may be used as a major appeal in advertising copy, or because the old container may not show up well in advertisements. A package change may be an important element in a brand repositioning strategy.

Packaging the Product Line A company must decide whether to develop a family resemblance in the packaging of its several products. **Family packaging** involves the use of identical packages for all products or the use of packaging with some common feature. Campbell's, for example, uses virtually identical packaging on its condensed soup products. Management's philosophy concerning family packaging generally parallels its feelings about family branding. When new products are added to a line, promotional values associated with old products extend to the new ones. On the other hand, family packaging should be used only when the products are related in use and are of similar quality.

Reuse Packaging Another strategy to be considered is **reuse packaging**. Should the company design and promote a package that can serve other purposes after the original contents have been consumed? Decorative biscuit tins can be used for any number of household functions, such as button boxes, containers for school supplies, or children's small-toy storage. Baby-food jars make great containers for small parts such as nuts, bolts, and screws. Reuse packaging also should stimulate repeat purchases as the consumer attempts to acquire a matching set of containers.

Multiple Packaging For many years there has been a trend toward **multiple packaging**, or the practice of placing several units in one container. Dehydrated soups, motor oil, beer, golf balls, building hardware, candy bars, towels, and countless other products are packaged in multiple units. Test after test has proved that multiple packaging increases total sales of a product.

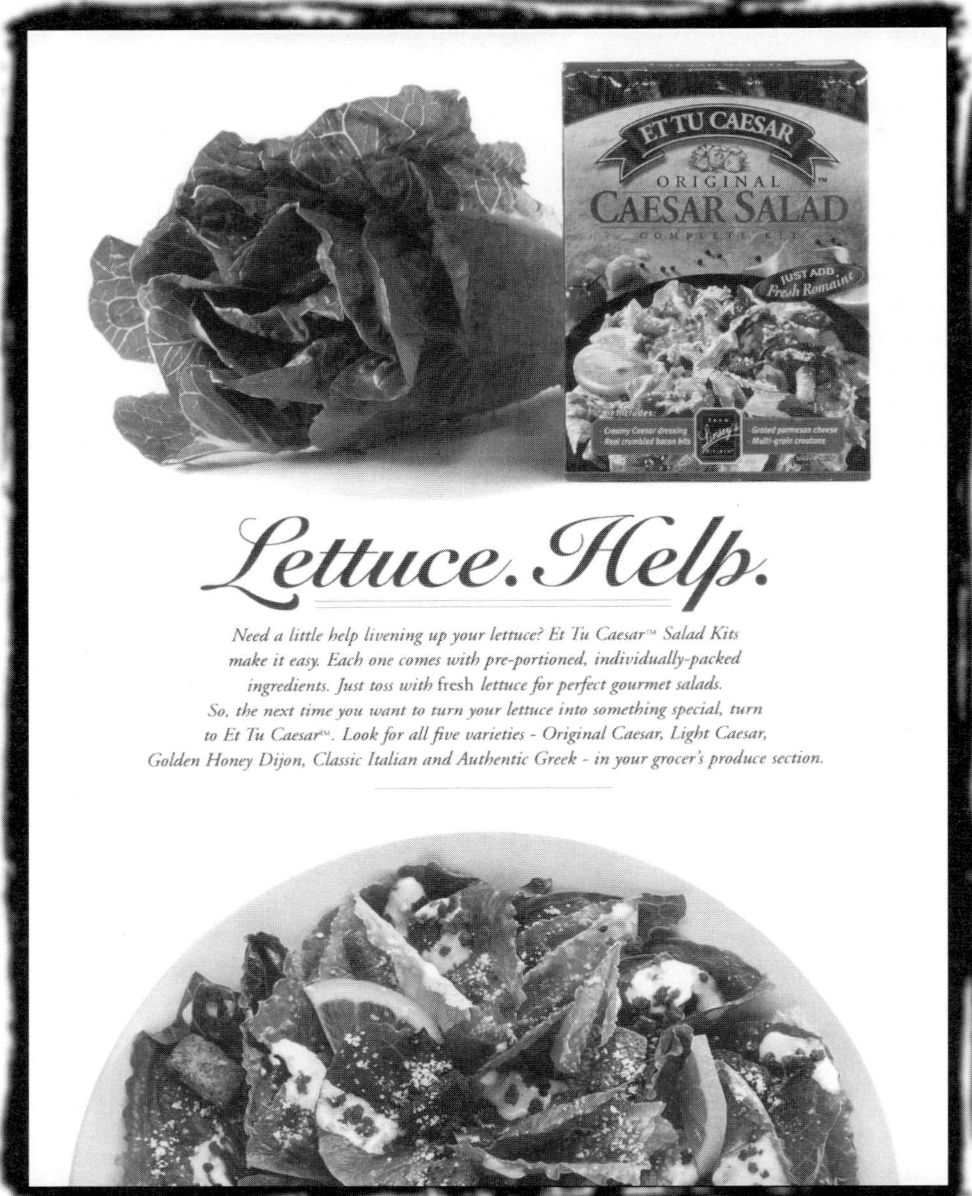

Salad in a box — just add lettuce.

Criticisms of Packaging

Packaging is in the forefront today because of its relationship to environmental pollution issues. Perhaps the biggest challenges facing packagers is how to dispose of used containers, which are a major contributor to the solid-waste disposal problem. Consumers' desire for convenience (in the form of throw-away containers) conflicts with their desire for a clean environment.

In many ways, the debate over the environmental impact of packaging often appears impossible to resolve, as the issue of the disposability of packaging is weighed against that of the use of energy and other effects associated with manufacturing it. Over the last decade the use of environmentally friendly containers has become common. LMG Reliance, a Winnipeg company, manufactures the Enviro-Chem agricultural chemical container, part of a closed-loop recycling system that involves the collection of used containers from landfill sites for recycling. Dow Canada produces its Fantastik cleaner in a stand-up pouch refill, as do many other makers of cleaners and detergents. The issue is, however, not a simple one. Environmentalists argue that companies should abandon disposable products, but the alternatives are often fraught with problems, as considerable energy may be required for their production and in recycling them for reuse.

Soft-drink and beer companies have moved toward a completely refillable packaging strategy, involving the exclusive use of glass bottles. The makers of the convenient aseptic containers are under pressure from environmentalists because the juice boxes are not recyclable and end up in municipal garbage dumps. Companies that have for years been supplying the restaurant industry and providing Canadians with convenient disposable products have been greatly affected by the environmental movement and have had to adopt strategies aimed at developing products that are less harmful to the environment.

Other criticisms of packaging are:

- *Packaging depletes our natural resources.* This criticism is offset to some extent by the use of recycled materials in the package and the fact that packaging reduces spoilage.
- *Packaging is excessively expensive.* In producing beer, for example, as much as half the production cost goes for the container. On the other hand, effective packaging reduces transportation costs and losses from product spoilage.
- *Health hazards occur from some forms of plastic packaging and some aerosol cans.* Government regulations have banned the use of several of these suspect packaging materials.
- *Packaging is deceptive.* Government regulation plus improvements in business practices regarding packaging have reduced the intensity of this criticism, although it is heard on occasion.

Truly, marketing executives face some real challenges in satisfying these complaints while at the same time retaining the marketing-effectiveness, consumer-convenience, and product-protection features of packaging.

LABELLING

Labelling is another product feature that requires managerial attention. The **label** is part of a product that carries information about the product or the seller. A label may be part of a package, or it may be a tag attached directly to the product. Obviously there is a close relationship among labelling, packaging, and branding.

Types of Labels

Typically, labels are classified as brand, grade, or descriptive. A **brand label** is simply the brand alone applied to the product or to the package. Thus, some oranges are brand-labelled (stamped) Sunkist or Jaffa, and some clothes carry the brand label Sanforized. A **grade label** identifies the quality with a letter, number, or word. Canadian beef is grade-labelled A, B, or C, and each grade is subdivided by number from 1 to 4, indicating an increasing fat content. **Descriptive labels** give objective information about the use, construction, care, performance, or other features of the product. On a descriptive label for a can of corn, there will be statements concerning the type of corn (golden sweet), the style (creamed or in niblet kernels), and the can size, number of servings, other ingredients, and nutritional content. There is also growing interest in **eco-labelling**, such as the Canadian government's Environmental Choice program, which encourages environmentally safe products through awarding seals of approval.[22] Many companies are now redesigning their products to qualify for environmental labels offered through such programs, which are now in operation in almost forty countries worldwide.[23]

Statutory Labelling Requirements

The importance of packaging and labelling in its potential for influencing the consumer's purchasing decision is reflected in the large number of federal and provincial laws that contain **statutory labelling requirements** to regulate this marketing activity. At the federal level, the Competition Act[24] regulates the area of misleading advertising, and a number of companies have been convicted of misleading advertising for the false or deceptive statements that have appeared on their packages. In this case, the information that appears on a package or label has been considered to constitute an advertisement.

The **Hazardous Products Act**[25] gives the federal government the power to regulate the sale, distribution, advertising, and labelling of certain consumer products that are considered dangerous. A number of products have been banned from sale under this Act, and all hazardous products, such as cleaning substances, chemicals, and aerosol products, must carry on their labels a series of symbols that indicate the danger associated with the product and the precautions that should be taken with its use.

Similarly the federal Food and Drugs Act regulates the sale of food, drugs, cosmetics, and medical devices. Under this Act, regulations deal with the manufacture, sale, advertising, packaging, and labelling of such products. Certain misleading and deceptive packaging and labelling practices are specifically prohibited. Without question, the strictest regulations applied to packaging in Canada pertain to the cigarette industry. Amendments to the Tobacco Products Control Act in 1993 required manufacturers to make a number of very detailed changes to their cigarette packages. Challenges to these amendments were made to the Supreme Court of Canada, and in 1995 it ruled that "the requirement to place unattributed health messages on tobacco packages infringed on the Charter."[26]

The Textile Labelling Act requires that manufacturers label their products, including wearing apparel, yard goods, and household textiles, according to the fibre content of the product. In the past, more than seven hundred fabric names have appeared on products, but most of these were brand names of individual companies. For example, the fibre known generically as polyester has been labelled as Terylene, Trevira, Dacron, Kodel, Fortrel, Tergal, Tetoron, and Crimplene, all of which are manufacturers' brand names for polyester. In order to reduce confusion among the buying public, products now have to be labelled according to the generic fibre content, with the percentage of each fibre in excess of 5 percent listed.

There also exist in Canada two government-sponsored consumer product-labelling schemes that are informative in nature. These programs are the Canada Standard Size program and the Textile Care Labelling program. The Textile Care Labelling program involves the labelling of all textile products with symbols that indicate instructions for washing and dry cleaning the product.

The **Consumer Packaging and Labelling Act** regulates all aspects of the packaging and labelling of consumer products in this country. The regulations that have been passed under this Act require that most products sold in Canada bear bilingual labels. The net quantity of the product must appear on the label in both metric and imperial units. The Act also makes provision for the standardization of container sizes. The first set of regulations to be passed under the Act set down the standard package sizes for toothpaste, shampoo, and skin-cream products, and it is in contravention of the regulations to manufacture these products in other than the package sizes approved.

The Consumer Packaging and Labelling Act requires that manufacturers of consumer products, especially in the food industry, incorporate the bilingual and metric requirements into the design of their labels.

The provinces have also moved into the field of regulating packaging and labelling. A number of provinces have passed legislation regarding misleading advertising, and any information that appears on a package or label is considered an advertisement.

We can expect to see further changes in the labels required on food and grocery items in the future, as consumers demand more information about the products they are consuming and using. The most likely changes relate to the listing of nutritional information on food products, brought about by the increasing interest of consumers in their health and nutrition.

OTHER IMAGE-BUILDING FEATURES

A well-rounded program for product planning and development will include a company policy on several additional product attributes: product design, colour, quality, warranty, and after-sale service.

Product Design and Colour

One way to satisfy customers and gain a competitive advantage is through skilful **product design**. In fact, a distinctive design may be the only feature that significantly differentiates a product. Many firms feel that there is considerable glamour and general promotional appeal in product design and the designer's name. In the field of business products, engineering design has long been recognized as extremely important. Today there is a realization of the marketing value of appearance design as well. Office machines and office furniture are examples of business products that reflect recent conscious attention to product design, often with good sales results. The marketing significance of design has been recognized for years in the field of consumer products, from big items like automobiles and refrigerators to small products like fountain pens and apparel.

Good design can improve the marketability of a product by making it easier to operate, upgrading its quality, improving its appearance, and/or reducing manufacturing costs. Recognizing the strategic importance of design, many companies have elevated the design function in the corporate hierarchy. In a number of firms, the director of design (sometimes called the director of human factors) participates in strategic planning and reports directly to top management.

Colour often is the determining factor in a customer's acceptance or rejection of a product, whether that product is a dress, a table, or an automobile. Colour by itself, however, is no selling advantage because many competing firms offer colour. The marketing advantage comes in knowing the right colour and in knowing when to change colours. If a garment manufacturer or a retail store's fashion co-ordinator guesses wrong on what will be the fashionable colour in this season's clothing, disaster may ensue.

Product Quality

The quality of a product is extremely significant, but it is probably the most difficult of all the image-building features to define. Users frequently disagree on what constitutes quality in a product, whether it be a cut of meat or a work of art or music. Personal tastes are deeply involved. One guideline in managing **product quality** is that the quality level should be compatible with the intended use of a product; the level need not be any higher. In fact, good and poor sometimes are misleading terms for quality. Correct and incorrect or right and wrong may be more appropriate. If a person is making a peach cobbler, grade B or C peaches are the correct quality. They are not necessarily the best quality, but they are right for the intended use. It is not necessary to pay grade A prices for large, well-formed peaches when these features are destroyed in making the cobbler. Another key to the successful management of quality is to maintain consistency of product output at the desired quality level.

In recent years, North American manufacturers have been increasingly concerned about the quality of their products.[27] For many years, consumers have complained about the poor quality of some products — both materials and workmanship. Foreign products — Japanese cars, for example — made serious inroads into the market because these products were perceived as being of better quality than their North American counterparts.

Quality of output also is a primary consideration in the production and marketing of services. The quality of its service can determine whether a firm will be successful. Yet it is virtually impossible for a firm to standardize performance quality among its units of service output. We frequently experience differences in performance quality from the same organization in appliance repairs, haircuts, medical exams, football games, or marketing courses.

To aid in determining and maintaining the desired level of quality in its goods and services, a company should establish a quality-improvement program. This should be an ongoing group effort of the design, production, marketing, and customer-service departments. One such program frequently implemented is **total quality management (TQM)**. A firm may then justifiably claim in its advertising that its product quality has improved. The problem is getting consumers to believe this fact.

Warranties

The purpose of a **warranty** is to assure buyers they will be compensated in case the product does not perform up to reasonable expectations. In years past, courts seemed to recognize only **express warranties** — those stated in written or spoken words.

Usually these were quite limited in their coverage and seemed mainly to protect the seller from buyers' claims. As a result, the following caution was appropriate: "Caveat emptor," which means "Let the buyer beware."

But times change! Consumer complaints led to a campaign to protect the consumer in many areas, including product warranties. Courts and government agencies have broadened the scope of warranty coverage by recognizing **implied warranty**. This means that a warranty was intended, although not actually stated, by the seller. Furthermore, producers are being held responsible even when the sales contract is between the retailer and the consumer. Now the caution is: "Caveat venditor," or "Let the seller beware."

In recent years manufacturers have responded to legislation and consumer complaints by broadening and simplifying their warranties. Many sellers are using their warranties as promotional devices to stimulate purchase by reducing consumers' risks. The effective handling of consumers' complaints related to warranties can be a significant factor in strengthening a company's marketing program.

The Hazardous Products Act indicates how the law has changed regarding **product liability** and injurious products. This law prohibits the sale of certain dangerous products and requires that other products that may be potentially dangerous carry an indication on their labels of the dangers inherent in their use. Some provinces have also passed Consumer Products Warranty Acts. These Acts sometimes provide for statutory warranties and the form written warranties must take.

Postsale Service

Many companies have to provide **postsale service**, notably repairs, to fulfil the terms of their warranties. Other firms offer postsale services such as maintenance and repairs not only to satisfy their customers but also to augment their revenues. Companies such as Otis and Montgomery, which sell elevators, rely on their service contracts for a substantial portion of their sales and profits. With more complex products and increasingly demanding and vocal consumers, postsale service has become essential. A constant consumer gripe is that manufacturers and retailers do not provide adequate repair service for the products they sell.

A manufacturer can shift the main burden for postsale service to intermediaries, compensate them for their efforts, and possibly even train their service people. This approach is evident in the automobile and personal-computer industries. Or a manufacturer can establish regional factory service centres, staff them with well-trained company employees, and strive to make product servicing a separate profit-generating activity. This is common in the appliance industry; for example, Black & Decker uses this approach.

Consumers become frustrated if they cannot voice their complaints and get their postsale-service problems solved. They want someone to listen and respond to their complaints. Many responsive companies have established toll-free 1-800 telephone numbers that connect the customer directly with a customer service representative. Many actually invite customers to complain, acting on the principle that if the customer doesn't complain, the company won't know there is a problem and can't take steps to correct it. Many companies post their 1-800 customer service numbers on the doors of their stores and feature them in their advertising. While it may not always be pleasant to listen to customer complaints, the alternative of customers taking their business elsewhere is much worse in the long run.

Like packaging and the other need-satisfying product features discussed in this chapter, postsale service can be either a differential advantage or a disadvantage for an organization. Thus it certainly should be on the list of matters managers need to heed constantly.

Summary

Effective product management involves developing and then monitoring the various features of a product — its brand, package, labelling, design, quality, warranty, and postsale service. A consumer's purchase decision may take into account not just the basic good or service but also the brand and perhaps one or more of the other want-satisfying product features.

A brand is a means of identifying and differentiating the products of an organization. Branding aids sellers in managing their promotional and pricing activities. The dual responsibilities of brand ownership are to promote the brand and to maintain a consistent level of quality. Selecting a good brand name — and there are relatively few really good ones — is difficult. Once a brand becomes well known, the owner may have to protect it from becoming a generic term.

Manufacturers must decide whether to brand their products and/or sell under an intermediary's brand. Intermediaries must decide whether to carry producers' brands alone or to establish their own brands as well. In addition, intermediaries must decide whether to carry generic products. Both producers and intermediaries must set policies regarding the branding of groups of products and branding for market saturation.

A growing number of companies are recognizing that the brands they own are — or can be — among their most valuable assets. They are building brand equity — the added value that a brand brings to a product. It's difficult to build brand equity but, if it can be done, it can be the basis for expanding a product mix. Products with abundant brand equity also lend themselves to trademark licensing, a marketing arrangement that is growing in popularity.

Packaging is becoming increasingly important as sellers recognize the problems, as well as the marketing opportunities, associated with it. Companies must choose among strategies such as family packaging, multiple packaging, and changing the package. Labelling, a related activity, provides information about the product and the seller. Many consumer criticisms of marketing target packaging and labelling. As a result, there are several laws regulating these activities.

Companies are now recognizing the marketing value of both product design and quality. Good design can improve the marketability of a product; it may be the only feature that differentiates a product. Projecting the appropriate quality image and then delivering the level of quality desired by customers are essential to marketing success. In many cases, firms need to enhance product quality to eliminate a differential disadvantage; in others, firms seek to build quality as a way of gaining a differential advantage.

Warranties and postsale service require considerable management attention these days because of consumer complaints and governmental regulations. Product liability is an issue of great consequence to companies because of the financial risk associated with consumers' claims of injuries caused by the firms' products.

Many companies provide postsale service, mainly repairs, to fulfil the terms of their warranties and/or to augment their revenues. To promote customer satisfaction, a number of firms are improving their methods of inviting and responding to consumer complaints.

Key Terms and Concepts

Brand (260)
Brand name (260)
Brand mark (260)
Trademark (260)
Generic name (263)
Family-brand strategy (266)
Multiple-brand strategy (268)
Brand equity (268)
Brand (trademark) licensing (269)
Packaging (272)
Family packaging (273)
Reuse packaging (273)
Multiple packaging (273)
Label (275)
Brand label (275)
Grade label (275)
Descriptive label (275)
Eco-labelling (275)
Statutory labelling requirements (275)
Hazardous Products Act (276)
Consumer Packaging and Labelling Act (276)
Product design (276)
Product colour (277)
Product quality (277)
Total quality management (TQM) (277)
Warranty (277)
Express warranty (277)
Implied warranty (278)
Product liability (278)
Postsale service (278)

Questions and Problems

1. List five brand names that you think are good ones and five you consider poor. Explain the reasoning behind your choices.
2. Evaluate each of the following brand names in light of the characteristics of a good brand, indicating the strong and weak points of each name.
   a. Xerox (office copiers).
   b. Tip Top (retailer).
   c. Holiday Inns (hotels).
   d. Dack's (shoes).
   e. Red Lobster (restaurant).
   f. Far West (clothing).
3. Suggest some brands that are on the verge of becoming generic. What course of action should a company take to protect the separate identity of its brands?
4. What are brand extensions? Why would a company launch a new product as a brand extension rather than as a completely new brand? What are the risks associated with such a strategy?
5. In which of the following cases should the company adopt the strategy of family branding?
   a. A manufacturer of men's underwear introduces essentially the same products for women.
   b. A manufacturer of women's cosmetics adds a line of men's cosmetics to its product assortment.
   c. A manufacturer of hair-care products introduces a line of portable electric hair dryers.
6. Suppose you are employed by the manufacturer of a well-known brand of skis. Your company is planning to add skates and water skis to its product line. It has no previous experience with either of these two new products. You are given the assignment of selecting a brand name for the skates and water skis. Your main problem is in deciding whether to adopt a family-brand policy. That is, should you use the snow-ski brand for either or both of the new products? Or should you develop separate names for each of the new items? You note that Campbell's (soups) and McCain (french fries) use family brands. You also note that Sears and Procter & Gamble generally do the opposite. They use different names for each group of products (Sears) or each separate product (P&G). What course of action would you recommend? Why?
7. A manufacturer of a well-known brand of ski boots acquired a division of a company that marketed a well-known brand of skis. What brand strategy should the new organization adopt? Should all products (skis and boots) now carry the boot brand? Should they carry the ski brand? Is there some other alternative that would be better?
8. Why do some firms sell an identical product under more than one of their own brands?
9. Assume that a large department-store chain proposed to Black & Decker that the latter company

supply the chain with a line of power tools carrying the store's own label. What factors should Black & Decker management consider in making such a decision? Would the situation be any different if a supermarket chain had approached Kraft General Foods with a request to supply a private-label jelly dessert similar to Jell-O?

10. A Canadian manufacturer of camping equipment (stoves, lanterns, tents, sleeping bags) plans to introduce its line into several Eastern European countries. Should management select the same brand name for all countries or market under the name that is used in Canada? Should they consider using a different name in each country? What factors should influence this decision?
11. What changes would you recommend in the typical packaging of these products?
    - **a.** Soft drinks.
    - **b.** Hairspray.
    - **c.** Adventure vacation.
    - **d.** Toothpaste.
12. If grade labelling is adopted, what factors should be used as bases for grading the following products or services?
    - **a.** Lipstick.
    - **b.** Hairdressers.
    - **c.** Diet-food products.
13. Give examples of products for which the careful use of the colour of the product has increased sales. Can you cite examples to show that poor use of colour may hurt a company's marketing program?
14. Explain the relationship between a product warranty on small electric appliances and the manufacturer's distribution system for these products.
15. How would the warranty policies set by a manufacturer of skis differ from those adopted by an automobile manufacturer?

Hands-On Marketing

1. Visit a large local supermarket and:
    - **a.** Obtain the store manager's opinions regarding which products are excellently packaged and which are poorly packaged. Ask the manager for reasons.
    - **b.** Walk around the store and compile your own list of excellent and poor packages. What factors did you use to judge quality of packaging?
2. Ask five students who are not taking this course to evaluate the following names for a proposed expensive perfume: Entice, Nitespark, At Risk, and Foreglow. For evaluation purposes, share with the students the characteristics of a good brand name. Also ask them to suggest a better name for the new perfume.

CHAPTER 12 GOALS

This chapter focuses on the marketing of services and the role of service in supporting marketing in all its forms. It discusses the changes in the field of marketing generated by the growth experienced in the services industries and through an increased emphasis on service provision across all industries. The concept of service quality and the connection between quality and profit, the linkage between human resource practices and marketing, and the development and implications of relationship marketing are key issues addressed in this chapter. After studying this chapter, you should have an understanding of:

- The nature of services.
- The importance of services in our economy.
- The characteristics of services, and the marketing implications of these characteristics.
- The issues related to the planning and marketing of services.
- The four Rs of services marketing.
- The relationship marketing approach.
- The impact of technology in the provision of services.

Chapter Twelve

Services Marketing and Customer Relationships

www.airmiles.ca

WHAT ELSE HAVE YOU GOT FOR ME TODAY?

Today, it's just not enough to offer customers a great product and an attractive price. While many customers are still looking for the lowest price, others are more satisfied if the companies with which they deal are able to offer something extra — something that will cause the customer to go back. Customers are saying, "Give me a reason to do business with you. Why should I buy your product or service or shop at your store?" This has led many companies to explore how they can add value for customers, so that they will want to come back again and again. While many companies and organizations are adding value through services (as we will discuss in this chapter), others have launched loyalty programs intended to reward loyal customers for their continued patronage.

One program designed to add value for customers is Air Miles, the brainchild of Craig Underwood, of The Loyalty Group, which now represents 121 sponsor companies by allowing infrequent fliers to accumulate points toward free air travel. There are now 5.6 million Canadians who are collecting Air Miles points when they buy from companies such as American Express, Bank of Montreal, Canada Safeway, Blockbuster Video, and Bell Canada. The system is simple and similar to those operated by many retailers, airlines, hotel chains, and other service companies. Customers build up points whenever they buy from participating companies, and when they accumulate enough points they qualify for free trips.

But the obvious rewards to customers are not the only benefit of a program such as Air Miles. Its greatest value lies in the detailed database that is developed on each of the participating customers. When customers first sign up with Air Miles, they are asked nine basic questions. Once they are enrolled, they are offered Air Miles as an incentive to complete a more detailed questionnaire. But, even without the questionnaire data, information on the purchasing patterns of the member is collected automatically whenever he or she uses the Air Miles card. The relational databases of The Loyalty Group can then sort the data to prepare lists of members for its clients — lists that can be used for direct marketing purposes. For example, a tire company might want a list of car drivers who regularly buy gas out of province (indicating that they drive a lot), or who have other expense patterns of interest. By knowing such information, the company can then tailor a specific marketing appeal toward a group of customers, because it already knows more about them.

Craig Underwood describes The Loyalty Group as an information company as much as a marketing company. The information that it can provide to its sponsor companies will help them develop closer relationships with their customers. Meanwhile, the customer benefits as he or she continues to buy from sponsor companies, thereby earning points toward that next holiday trip to Europe or Hawaii.[1]

NATURE AND IMPORTANCE OF SERVICES

Over the past twenty years, a major focus on the role of services in the Canadian economy has changed the thinking of marketers. In 1996, more than three-quarters of the 10.4 million working Canadians were employed in the services sector.[2] Many economists now see the services sector as holding the key to improved economic growth and job creation in the future, even though virtually all the growth in the number of jobs in Canada in recent years has been produced by the services sector.[3]

Some of the reasons for the rapid growth of this sector, which is undoubtedly the fastest-growing part of the Canadian economy, stem from the major environmental changes we discussed in Chapter 3. You will recall that these included such things as a more technologically oriented world and massive communication changes as well as changing work force demographics. Demands for and the ability to provide services have increased. For example, an entire industry has grown up around servicing the Internet. Other examples include increased requirements for eating out with both parents in the work force, more interest in time saving and convenience, as is acquired through home cleaning services and telephone banking, and the rapid growth in television networks and home entertainment products such as videos and direct-to-home television. All of these environmental changes have placed greater emphasis on services and increasing demands on the quality of service provision. Marketers have been required to change their focus from trying to sell tangible goods to identifying customer needs and wants in services, either to accompany those goods or on their own.

This discussion of the growth in the service sector tends to focus on the expansion of the economy in areas that have traditionally been classified as service industries. When we consider that the service sector includes transportation, entertainment, education, health care, government and public services, and financial services, it is no wonder that such a large portion of the Canadian economy is included. Advances in technology that have dramatically improved productivity in goods-producing industries have contributed to a decline in the percentage of jobs in manufacturing. While this is all very important, we should not lose sight of a very important aspect of this chapter — the need to remember that service is an integral component of the marketing of any product, whether tangible or intangible. Therefore, we will continue to refer to the provision of service and the importance of customer service in the achievement of customer satisfaction.

Traditionally, services marketing has been thought to be different from the marketing of tangible products. In concept, however, they are essentially the same. In each case, the marketer must select and analyze target markets. Then, a marketing program must be developed. There are characteristics of services that differentiate them from tangible products, and these must be considered in developing the marketing program. This section will identify these characteristics. Most tangible goods have a service element and, as consumers place more value on the services that accompany the purchase of tangible goods, the distinctions between services marketing and tangible-goods marketing become less significant.

Definition and Scope of Services

We are talking about the marketing of services, but do we have a clear understanding of what we mean by "services"? The term is difficult to define because, in addition to being the core product being sold in some instances (such as in banking or education, where the core is intangible), services are also marketed in conjunction with tangible products. Services require supporting products (you need an airplane to provide air transportation services), and products require supporting services (delivery, credit, and repair services accompany the sale of a refrigerator). Furthermore, a company may sell a combination of goods and services. Thus, along with repair service for your car, you might buy spark plugs or an oil filter. It may be helpful to think of every product as a mix of goods and services located on a continuum ranging from pure goods to pure services, as shown in Figure 12-1.

To move closer to a useful definition, we identify two classes of services. In the first group are services that are the main purpose or object of a transaction. These are what we have been referring to in this chapter as the **core services**. As an example, suppose you want to rent a car from Avis. The rental car company needs a car (tangible product) to provide the rental service. But you are buying the rental use of the car, not the car itself. The second group consists of **supplementary services** that support or facilitate the sale of a tangible good or another service. Thus, when you buy a compact disc player, you may want technical information and service from a sales person and the opportunity to pay with a credit card. Virtually every transaction that one can think of involves both tangible and intangible elements. It is useful to distinguish between situations where the core of what is being exchanged is intangible — this is the situation that we refer to as the marketing of services — and the supplementary services and general level of customer service that accompanies the sale of everything that we buy.

Consequently, our definition of services in this chapter is as follows: **Services** are identifiable, intangible activities that are sometimes the main object of a transaction and at other times support the sale of tangible products or other services. Although we are interested primarily in the marketing of services that are the principal objective of a transaction, as in financial services, entertainment, hotel accommodations, and car rentals, we must not overlook the very important services associated with the marketing of literally every product, whether tangible or intangible. Increasingly, marketers are realizing that one of the most effective ways to compete and to differentiate one's company from the competition is to offer excellent service. Thus, even to a company selling industrial supplies, there is a challenge to deliver the product on time and in good condition and to ensure that the customer is billed correctly and called on regularly.

We are concerned here primarily with the services marketed by business or professional firms with profit-making motives — commercial services. This is in contrast to services of not-for-profit organizations, such as churches, universities and colleges, arts and cultural organizations, and the government.

FIGURE 12-1 A Goods–Services Continuum

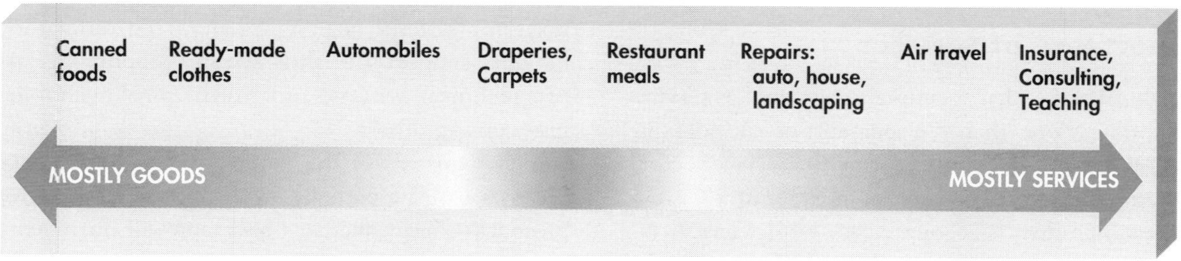

Canned foods
Ready-made clothes
Automobiles
Draperies, Carpets
Restaurant meals
Repairs: auto, house, landscaping
Air travel
Insurance, Consulting, Teaching

MOSTLY GOODS
MOSTLY SERVICES

A useful classification of commercial services by industry is as follows:

- Accommodations (includes rental of hotels, motels, apartments, houses, and farms).
- Household operations (includes utilities, house repairs, repairs of equipment in the house, landscaping, and household cleaning).
- Recreation and entertainment (includes rental and repair of equipment used to participate in recreation and entertainment activities; also admission to all entertainment, recreation, and amusement events).
- Food services (includes restaurants, fast-food outlets, and catering services).
- Personal care (includes laundry, dry cleaning, and beauty care).
- Medical and other health care (includes all medical services, dental, nursing, hospitalization, optometry, and other health care).
- Private education (courses taken at a community college, university, or private college).
- Business and other professional services (includes legal, accounting, management consulting, and computer services).
- Insurance, banking, and other financial services (includes personal and business insurance, credit and loan services, investment counselling, and tax services).
- Transportation (includes freight and passenger services on common carriers, automobile repairs and rentals).
- Communications (includes telephone, facsimile, computer, and specialized business communication services).

Note that no attempt was made to separate the above groups into consumer and business services, as we did with tangible products. In fact, most are purchased by both market groups.

Importance of Services

North America has genuinely become a service economy. More than 76 percent of all jobs in Canada are now accounted for by the service sector, and more than 70 percent of the country's gross domestic product is accounted for by services. Also, service jobs typically hold up better during a recession than do jobs in industries that produce tangible products. Canadians have become more dependent on the service sector for their jobs. Much of that employment, particularly in retail organizations, is now on a part-time basis.

While the share of total output accounted for by manufacturing has dropped to less than 20 percent in Canada, there is some evidence that even this value is overstated, as many of the activities that add value or contribute to final output in manufacturing companies are really services. *The Economist* has observed that the distinction between services and manufacturing is becoming less useful. Nevertheless, governments in particular continue to classify companies as manufacturing or services firms, despite the fact, for example, that the largest single supplier to General Motors is not a parts manufacturer, but Blue Cross–Blue Shield, a health-care provider. More than 20 percent of the value of final output of such "manufacturers" as Sony and General Motors is in the form of services.[4]

Jobs in the service sector pay either very well or very poorly. A Statistics Canada report issued in March 1996[5] found that when the salary ranges of service-sector jobs were divided into five percentiles, only 9 percent of employees were in the mid-range 20 percent of the work force. The highest percentile had 25 percent of the jobs; the lowest percentile had 20 percent of the jobs. The highest-paying jobs in the sector include a mixture of transportation, the public sector, and financial services. The absolute top dogs of the service sector work in brokerage houses and stock exchanges.[6] For several years the fastest-growing occupational category has been "professional, technical, and related work." The rapid growth of the technology industries has created a corresponding explosion in the number of technology jobs. For example, the Internet and other advances in computer systems have created a need for systems analysts, program co-ordinators, network support specialists, systems support specialists, technical writers, and instructional technologists, among others.

The growth in the market for **personal services** is at least partially explained by the relative prosperity that Canadians have enjoyed during the past forty years. As consumers became better able to satisfy their demand for tangible items, they turned to services either to provide things that they could not afford before or to do things for them that they no longer wished to do for themselves. It could be argued that many of the tangible products that we buy tend to be necessity purchases. People buy food, housing, clothing, and automobiles to meet essential needs. On the other hand, many services tend to be purchased, by end consumers at least, from discretionary spending. Such things as travel, entertainment, restaurant meals, and home cleaning services are usually purchased by the consumer after the essentials have been paid for.

The Canadian population that is approaching the millennium is more sophisticated than their parents and more active in leisure and entertainment activities. Increased global transportation systems have resulted in a high-growth travel industry, and advanced communications systems have stimulated increased awareness of travel destinations. Affluence and lifestyle changes have contributed significantly to this rapid growth in personal services.

The growth of **business services** may be attributed to the fact that business has become increasingly complex, specialized, and competitive. As a consequence, management has been forced to call in experts to provide services in marketing research, taxation, advertising, labour relations, and a host of other areas. Technology has also played a major role in the expansion of demand for business services. Many of the computer programming and services positions that exist in larger organizations in particular did not even exist ten years ago. Even amid relatively high rates of unemployment in parts of Canada, jobs in high-technology fields often go unfilled because of a shortage of trained individuals to fill existing vacancies.

Characteristics of Services

The special nature of services stems from a number of characteristics that distinguish services from tangible products. These features create special marketing challenges and opportunities. As a result, service firms often require strategic marketing programs that are substantially different from those found in the marketing of tangible goods. Also, these characteristics of services should cause us to consider certain implications for the provision of customer service in all industries.

Intangibility Because services are **intangible**, it is impossible for customers to sample — taste, feel, see, hear, or smell — a service before they buy it. Consequently, a company's promotional program must portray the benefits to be derived from the service, rather than emphasizing the service itself. Four promotional strategies that may be used to suggest service benefits are as follows.[7]

- *Visualization.* For example, Carnival Cruise Lines depicts the benefits of its cruises with ads that show people dancing, dining, playing deck games, and visiting exotic places.
- *Association.* Connect the service with a tangible object, person, or place. The Australian airline, Qantas, uses a cuddly koala bear in its advertising to project a warm, friendly image of Australia. Prudential Insurance suggests stability and security with its logo depicting the Rock of Gibraltar. Imperial Oil features its employees in its advertising to add a personal touch to retailing Esso gasoline.
- *Physical representation.* American Express uses colour — green, gold, or platinum — for its credit-card services to symbolize wealth and prestige. Fast-food chains, telephone companies, and many other firms dress their service representatives in clean, distinctive uniforms to stress visibility, cleanliness, and dependability.
- *Documentation.* Air Canada and other airlines cite facts and figures in their ads to support claims of dependability, performance, care for passengers, and safety.

Inseparability Services typically cannot be separated from the creator-seller of the service. Moreover, many services are created, dispensed, and consumed simultaneously. For example, dentists and hairstylists create and dispense almost all their services at the same time, and they require the presence of the consumer for the services to be performed. Because of this **inseparability** feature, many people are involved concurrently in the production operations and the marketing effort in services firms, and the customers

www.carnival.com • www.qantas.com.au • www.prudential.com • www.imperialoil.ca

receive and consume the services at the production site — in the firm's "factory," so to speak. Consequently, customers' opinions regarding a service frequently are formed through contacts with the production-marketing personnel and impressions of the physical surroundings in the "factory." Too often, contact personnel think of themselves as producers-creators of the service rather than as marketers.

From a marketing standpoint, inseparability frequently means that direct sale is the only possible channel of distribution, and a seller's services cannot be sold in very many markets. This characteristic limits the scale of operation in a firm. One person can repair only so many autos in a day or treat only so many medical patients.

As an exception to the inseparability feature, services may be sold by a person who is representing the creator-seller. A travel agent, insurance broker, or rental agent, for instance, may represent and help promote services that will be sold by the institutions producing them. Another way in which services are delivered by intermediaries is through franchising. Companies such as Swiss Chalet and National Tilden Rent-a-Car are in the service business, but their head offices deal with customers through franchise holders in various cities.

The inseparability of a service from the people providing it has important implications for companies that are operating in service-oriented businesses. This includes not only those companies in true "service" industries, such as financial services, entertainment, hotels, and restaurants, but also those who must pay particular attention to the services that support the marketing of their tangible products. For example, although Eastern Bakeries is technically a manufacturer of bakery products such as breads and cakes, it is also in the business of making sure that its products are delivered on time and in the quantity and condition the customer ordered.

For the most part, it is the employees of a company who have the greatest influence on the level of service provided to its customers. Eastern Bakeries may bake the most wholesome bread in Eastern Canada, but if employees cannot get it to the retail stores in time for consumers to buy it, then any product advantage Eastern may have had will be lost.

In fact, in many industries, particularly those where the products or services are technologically advanced or difficult for the consumer to understand, or where the customer cannot see important differences among the offerings of the various competitors, the ability to compete comes down to whether a company can deliver superior service. Most progressive companies have come to realize that their employees are extremely important in providing a level of service that will keep their customers happy.[8]

Mary Pascale, who runs a gourmet food and deli store with her husband, says loyalty is the most important thing she considers when selecting job applicants. This points to the importance of human resources matters that influence a company's performance in delivering service to its customers.

www.nationalcar.com

This applies to employees who come into direct contact with the customer — sales staff, repair technicians, and flight attendants — as well as to support personnel, who can damage a company's relationship with its customers even though they may never meet them directly. A clerk in the accounting department who fails to credit a customer's account correctly, or a baggage handler who sends a passenger's suitcase to Halifax when the passenger was travelling to Calgary, is just as responsible for service and customer relations as those staff members who meet and talk with customers.

Heterogeneity It is impossible for a service industry, or even an individual seller of services, to standardize output. Each "unit" of the service is somewhat different from other "units" of the same service. This is principally so because of the individualized approach that service providers take to the provision of a service. Because most services are delivered by people, service delivery is prone to the differences that exist across human beings. Because we are all different and our interaction with other people is affected by personality, mood, and a number of other factors, service delivery and quality are bound to vary considerably. For example, an airline does not give the same quality of service on each flight. All repair jobs an auto mechanic does are not of equal quality. An added complication is the fact that it is often difficult to judge the quality of a service. It is particularly difficult to forecast quality in advance of buying a service. A person pays to see a ball game without knowing whether it will be an exciting one (well worth the price of admission) or a dull performance. Some companies are able to address this by allowing customers to sample a service for a limited time — for example, cable television companies will give new subscribers a free trial month's service on new channels. However, it is difficult for most services companies to provide samples.

The **heterogeneity** of services is of concern to service providers, but the ability to deliver customer satisfaction is further complicated by the fact that customer expectations are not at all consistent. Although a student on a short lunch break may spend only fifteen minutes grabbing a quick meal at a restaurant near campus, the same student may take more than an hour to enjoy a pizza with a friend after a Saturday-night movie. In the first case, the customer wants to be served as quickly as possible; in the second, he or she is prepared to wait a little longer for service. Because service expectations differ across customers and even over time for the same customers, it is very difficult for service businesses to standardize their level of service.

In recent years, some service companies have turned to technology in an attempt to standardize the type and quality of service provided, but at the expense of losing personal contact and the ability to respond to customers' questions or concerns. Nevertheless, some services, such as those provided by automated banking machines, telephone banking, and self-service gas stations, can become standardized and are accepted by a large number of customers. Similarly, many companies and other organizations have installed telephone-answering and voice-mail systems that allow callers to leave messages for staff members who are out of the office or unable to answer their calls when the telephone rings. Canada's telephone companies have automated directory-assistance services and have introduced a voice-response system for handling third-party collect calls. To automate service even further, the telephone industry has encouraged customers to sign up for calling cards, which eliminate the need to contact an operator to place long-distance calls billed to a third number.

While such technology-based services achieve standardization of service, in part by delegating much of the service provision or delivery to the customers themselves, there are at least some risks inherent in their use. On the other hand, some customers may resent having to do all the work, especially when they are paying for the service. Also, some customers simply prefer to deal with real people and get confused or irritated when they encounter technology. Finally, in some industries management is faced with the dilemma of not being able to keep in touch with customers or to establish relationships with them, when the customers are dealing primarily with machines or computers.[9]

Service companies should pay special attention to the product-planning stage of their marketing programs. From the beginning, management must

MARKETING AT WORK FILE 12-1

WHERE DO YOU WANT TO EAT TONIGHT?

One thing is certain: There's lots of choice. More and more restaurants are opened in Canada each year. The total number reached almost sixty thousand in 1996, up 22 percent from 1991. But the fierce competition to lure customers has meant that sales per store have remained flat for the past six years, and the number of bankruptcies in the restaurant sector has increased to almost two thousand annually.

But there are shifts going on within the restaurant industry. Industry analysts indicate that the baby boomers, Canada's largest group of restaurant-goers, are turning away from fast-food establishments and are eating more at family-style restaurants like Swiss Chalet, Golden Griddle, and White Spot. Although the kids are likely to be clamouring for McDonald's, many parents are opting for restaurants where they can have their meals brought to their table in a sit-down environment. An improved economy, coupled with the fact that these customers have more money to spend and want better food for their money, have all contributed to the trend.

A step up is the casual-dining sector of the restaurant market, where customers can enjoy table service, alcoholic beverages, and a greater variety on the menu. This sector, which includes restaurants like East Side Mario's, Jack Astor's, and Milestone's, is expected to enjoy the greatest growth in the coming years.

A number of companies are well positioned to take advantage of the trend that will see more baby boomer families, with little time to prepare meals at home, seeking a comfortable environment that is less hurried than the fast-food outlets, yet offers good service and value for money. SIR Corporation of Toronto owns thirty-two restaurants, mostly in Toronto, including fourteen Jack Astor's outlets, and specialty restaurants like Alice Fazooli's and the Loose Moose. Vancouver's Spectra Group of Great Restaurants operates twenty-five restaurants in and around Vancouver and is planning to expand its Bread Garden and Milestone's franchises. Cara Operations planned to open thirty Swiss Chalet outlets in 1997.

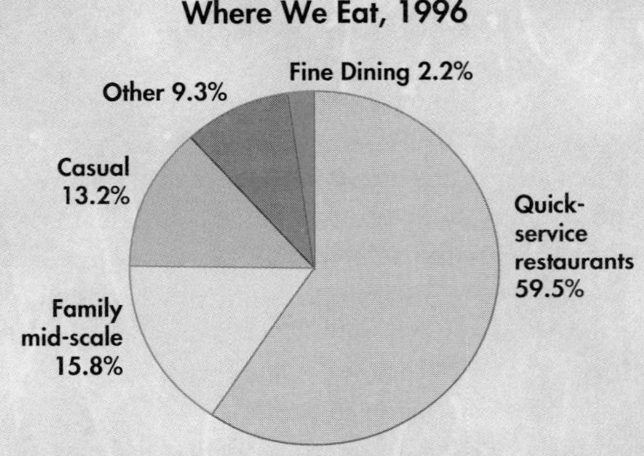

Although the fast-food industry is still the largest sector of the growing Canadian restaurant scene, we can expect to see continued growth in the family and casual dining sectors as the marketplace changes. What factors are contributing to these changes? How should McDonald's, Burger King, and Wendy's respond?

Source: Adapted from Andrew Poon and Dawn Walton, "Tables Turning on Fast Food," *The Globe and Mail*, July 5, 1997, pp. B1, B3. Reprinted with permission from *The Globe and Mail.*

do all it can to ensure consistency of quality and to maintain high levels of quality control. This important issue of service quality will be discussed in a later section of this chapter.

Perishability and Fluctuating Demand Services are highly perishable, and they cannot be stored. Unused telephone time, empty seats in a stadium, and idle mechanics in a garage all represent business that is lost forever. Furthermore, the market for services fluctuates considerably by season, by day of the week, and by hour of the day. Most ski lifts lie idle all summer, whereas golf courses go unused in the winter. The use of city buses fluctuates greatly during the day.

There are notable exceptions to this generalization regarding the **perishability** and storage of services. In health and life insurance, for example, the service is purchased by a person or a company. Then it is held by the insurance company (the seller) until needed by the buyer or the beneficiary. This holding constitutes a type of storage. Similarly, many services generally considered to be "public utilities" are able to store services until they are needed. For example, telephone and electricity services are available on demand. We can access them whenever we need them. Because of this, there is a very real probability that consumers will take such services for granted, simply because they are always there. This causes potential problems for companies that are marketing such services because it makes it difficult for them to interest their customers in buying more or in adopting new services.

The combination of perishability and **fluctuating demand** offers product-planning, pricing, and promotion challenges to services marketing managers. Some organizations have developed new uses for idle plant capacity during off-seasons. Thus, during the summer, several ski resorts operate their ski lifts for hikers and sightseers who want access to higher elevations. Advertising and creative pricing are also used to stimulate demand during slack periods. Hotels offer lower prices and family packages on weekends. Telephone companies offer lower rates at nights and on weekends.

THE FOUR Rs OF SERVICES MARKETING

The recent focus on marketing in services organizations has brought about an important change in how marketers view their dealings with customers and prospective customers. In short, there has been a realization on the part of many marketing managers that the provision of the four elements of the conventional marketing mix — product, price, advertising and promotion, and distribution channels — is not sufficient to ensure customer satisfaction. While we will devote much of the next four sections of this book to coverage of these four components of the marketing mix, it is important to do so in the context of a new view of marketing, one that focuses on services and how they are delivered. We have labelled the components of this new view the four Rs of marketing.

Retention Most successful marketing managers today have accepted the principle that long-term customers are more profitable and that their organizations should pay at least as much attention to keeping their existing customers (or, more correctly, some of them) as they do to trying to attract new ones. Recent studies have demonstrated quite clearly that customers become more profitable the longer they continue to do business with a firm.[10] This is the case because satisfied, long-term customers spend a larger portion of their total expenditure with the firm to which they are loyal. They also cost less to serve because they are generally more satisfied and don't need to be convinced to buy. They make fewer complaints and are less likely to quibble over price, often being prepared to pay more for good service. And they tell others how satisfied they are.

Referrals This last point leads to the second of our four Rs, referrals. One of the greatest benefits of satisfying customers is that they will refer their friends and associates to the firm providing them with superior service. This is one of the most important aspects of determining the benefits to be gained from satisfying customers. Through positive word-of-mouth, they can produce large volumes of new business. Conversely, a dissatisfied customer will either spread negative word-of-mouth or will disappear, never to return. Companies that provide a high level of customer service will always keep in mind the potential for existing customers to bring in new ones.

Relationships One of the most important developments in marketing in recent years has been the attention now being paid to the establishment of relationships between companies and their customers. This is an aspect of marketing that is gaining considerable attention and that is linked very closely to the notion that long-term customer satisfaction is a direct result of the provision of superior customer service.[11] The customer's definition of service very often extends to the establishment of a close relationship with a service provider. The idea of forming a relationship with customers makes considerable sense because it leads to the establishment of loyal customers who are likely to be very profitable. However, the establishment of a long-term customer relationship is not a simple task and is one that should be approached following much study of how the firm's customers define a relationship. Recent research has suggested that the customer must define the terms on which a relationship is to be formed with a company and that a company may feel a relationship is in place when the customer is of a quite different opinion.[12]

Many companies are now introducing relationship marketing programs to try to get closer to their customers so that they will feel more a part of the company. The most notable of these include examples like Saturn, the automaker, which holds picnics and barbeques for Saturn owners.[13] Many companies base their relationship marketing programs on the establishment of a detailed customer database that will allow them to know as much as possible about their customers so that they can direct tailored communications to each customer. For example, pharmaceutical companies have developed communications programs based upon databases that allow them to communicate with patients to ensure that they are taking their medication correctly.[14]

Recovery The final element in our four Rs of services marketing relates to service recovery — what a company can do to recover customer satisfaction when something has gone wrong. Inevitably, customers will encounter problems and poor service when dealing with service providers. Even the most meticulous companies cannot completely avoid delivering poor service on occasion. The issue is, what can and should the company do when something goes wrong? Certainly, the answer is not "do nothing." Particularly in services companies in recent years, managers have been paying increasing attention to the development of procedures to deal with service problems as they arise, with a view to solving the customer's problem before he or she decides to take his or her business elsewhere. Therefore, service recovery becomes an important component in a company's program to establish and maintain customer relationships. A company taking the necessary steps to deal with customers' problems efficiently and effectively will lead to those customers being satisfied, even to the point that they will be more loyal than they would have been if the service problem had never occurred![15]

Some companies are so intent on dealing with customer service problems that they openly encourage their customers to complain if they have a problem.[16] If the dissatisfied customer simply leaves, vowing never to return, the company has missed a chance to deal with the problem, management may never know that the problem exists, other customers may experience the same problem, and the exiting customer has the opportunity to spread the bad news about how he or she was treated. Complaints provide an opportunity to restore customer satisfaction and even to impress the customer.

STRATEGIC ASPECTS OF SERVICES MARKETING

Because of the characteristics of services (notably intangibility), the development of a total marketing program in a service industry is often uniquely challenging. This is also the case because many marketers, as they have advanced through their careers, seem to have focused principally on the marketing of tangible products. In addition, it may be said that strategic approaches to marketing have only recently been accepted in services organizations, and particularly in the not-for-profit sector. Nevertheless, as we have observed before, the fundamental principles of marketing are the same, regardless of what is being marketed. Ultimately, we are interested in achieving long-term customer satisfaction. Let's consider some developments that have been emerging in services marketing in recent years.

Selecting Target Markets

Marketers of services should understand the customers who buy their services. What are their buy-

www.saturncars.com

ing motives? Sellers must determine buying patterns for their services — when, where, and how do customers buy, who does the buying, and who makes the buying decisions? The psychological determinants of buying behaviour — attitudes, perceptions, and personality — become even more important when marketing services rather than tangible goods, because typically we cannot touch, smell, or taste a service offering. This has implications for how consumers buy and for the need to gain a complete understanding.

Some of the trends noted in chapters 4 to 6 are particularly worth watching because they carry considerable influence in the marketing of services. As an example, an aging population, increases in disposable income, and discretionary buying power mean a growing market for health care services, insurance, and transportation services. Shorter working hours result in increased leisure time. More leisure time plus greater income means larger markets for recreation and entertainment services.

Market segmentation strategies also can be adopted by services marketers. One of the most important issues arising from our discussion of the four Rs of services marketing relates to the question of **customer value**. Many services companies have begun to develop information systems to allow them to measure or estimate the value of a customer to their firms. The question of customer value is important when companies are trying to decide upon those customers they should retain and those with whom they should establish close relationships. The principle here is one that many firms and organizations often find difficult to accept — we may not want all the customers! Typically, companies earn as much as 80 percent of their profits from as few as 20 percent of their customers. The issue is to decide which are the most valuable ones. Some larger companies collect information on customers and their purchases and utilize this database information to assess the value of each customer. By categorizing customers, for example, into A, B, C, and D categories, based upon their value to the firm, a company can ensure that its best customers receive the highest levels of service and that attempts are made to address their problems immediately.[17]

Planning of Services

New services are just as important to a service company as new products are to a goods-marketing firm. Similarly, the improvement of existing services and elimination of unwanted, unprofitable services are also key goals.

Product planning and development has its counterpart in the marketing program of a service organization. Management must select appropriate strategies based on answers to these questions:

- What service products will be offered?
- What will be the breadth and depth of the service mix?
- How will the services be positioned?
- What attributes, such as branding, packaging, and service quality, will the service have?
- What support services are needed?
- What level of customer service should be offered?

Services Offering New services are just as important to a services company as new products are to a goods-producing company. Many firms have become successful by identifying a previously unsatisfied consumer need and then developing a service to address that need. A good example is the number of regional airlines that now serve smaller cities and towns in Canada, operating small aircraft and flying passengers to larger centres. The introduction of new services should involve a process very similar to that which may be used by manufacturers in introducing new tangible products. Attention must be paid to addressing customer needs and to knowing what will appeal to the customer. Failure to do so will lead to the same lack of success that manufacturers encounter when they do not follow these principles in launching new tangible products.[18]

Service-Mix Strategies Several of the product-mix strategies discussed in Chapter 10 can be employed effectively by services marketers. Consider the strategy of expanding or enhancing the line of services offered. This is often referred to as a process of adding value for the customer. In fact, one of the most effective ways of adding value to existing products and services is by adding new support services. Many hotel chains and even some

MARKETING AT WORK FILE 12-2

GROWING A SERVICE BUSINESS

Want to get into the lawn-care business, or set up a house-painting or window-cleaning operation, or move on to painting really big buildings? Maybe you should call Steve Rogers, president of Toronto-based The Franchise Company. Thousands of college and university students have gotten their start in business by painting houses for a summer with College ProPainters. The Franchise Company is a division of FirstService Corporation, and it specializes in establishing well-branded franchise operations.

The company's approach to expanding its business is based upon the philosophy of franchising set down when College Pro was founded in 1971, involving the recruitment of student supervisors who would recruit other students as house painters. The organization's success lies in the recruitment and training of franchisees and in the idea that it is possible for franchisees who start with College Pro to move into progressively larger franchises with The Franchise Company — possibly acquiring a Nutri-lawn Lawn Care franchise or one for Certa ProPainters.

Many service companies have chosen to go the franchise route to establish the distribution channel to reach their end customers. The Franchise Company has stepped up to the plate to deal with the issue of the low profile that is often associated with service franchises, a problem that many attribute to franchisor neglect. In other words, a franchised service operation begins with a flourish, but rapidly runs out of gas, often because the franchisors lose interest, for a variety of reasons:

- They have trouble maintaining consistency of product across a large number of outlets; consistency is essential, but everyone performs a service differently.
- Franchisees often see no need to continue to pay royalties to the franchisor after the business is up and running – many decide to go it alone once they have acquired the expertise.
- Franchisors often have difficulty monitoring sales volumes, and as a result some franchisees may work "under the table" to avoid paying royalties.

The Franchise Company has addressed these issues through its franchisee certification program, through which all franchisees achieve certification in a number of areas of management, including goal setting, coaching, time management, and interviewing. The company also provides superb marketing support for its franchisees, including the development of materials and programs that they would find impossible to produce on their own, and the operation of a centralized call centre that directs callers to the nearest franchise operation. Finally, it holds out the opportunity for franchisees to trade up to larger franchises with higher potential profits.

Source: Adapted from John Southerst, "Service Chain Develops Rare Brand Awareness," *The Globe and Mail*, July 7, 1997, p. B5.

"bed and breakfasts" have added fax machines, desks, and computer data ports to their rooms and provide photocopier and printer services on request for business guests.[19] Rental-car companies offer no-smoking cars and rent cellular telephones. Most now have computerized the process of returning rental cars at airports to speed travellers on their way. Many companies have chosen to add value for their loyal customers by establishing loyalty programs that reward them with free travel or gifts.[20]

Many firms have moved to alter their services offering in response to competition or to customer demands. To better serve customers who may have difficulty finding time to visit a conventional bank

President Steve Rogers views franchise owners as customers.

branch, the Bank of Montreal launched its mbanx service, which allows customers to access virtually all banking services through a 1-800 number, Internet, and ATMs. Some personal-care companies now offer in-home services, from foot care, to massages, to pet care for customers who are unable to get to their offices.[21]

Managing the life cycle of a service is another strategy that is being practised more and more by services marketers. Recognizing that the credit card industry is in its maturity stage, Canadian banks have explored new ways of getting their cards into the hands of new customers and of expanding use of the cards. The result in many cases is that consumers now carry several credit cards when they had only one previously. Variations on the Visa card include a deal between the Toronto Dominion Bank and General Motors, which sees 5 percent of all charges on the TD Visa held as a rebate that can be saved (up to a maximum of $500 per year for five years) and applied toward the purchase of a GM vehicle. CIBC offers a similar deal with Ford Motor Company of Canada, allowing for savings of up to $700 per year. This "co-branding" of credit cards has really extended the concept of the credit card as a means of savings toward a major purchase. The Bank of Montreal that has developed "affinity cards" on behalf of major universities, including McGill, Queen's, and Dalhousie; a percentage of cardholders' (usually alumni) purchases on Bank of Montreal's affinity MasterCard are donated to the participating university. Probably the most successful "new" credit card launch in recent years was the CIBC Aerogold Visa card, which allows holders to accumulate Air Canada Aeroplan points by using the card. Not to be outdone, The Royal Bank of Canada offers Visa card holders 30 percent off their long-distance telephone bills; Canada Trust offers a similar program to MasterCard holders.[22] The objective of all such programs is to extend the life of the credit card by developing new uses and increased usage.

Service Features In some respects, product planning is easier for services than for tangible goods. Packaging and labelling really are nonexistent in services marketing. However, other features — branding and quality management, for example — present greater challenges for services industries.

Branding of services is a problem because maintaining consistent quality (a responsibility of brand ownership) is difficult. Also, a brand cannot be physically attached to a label or to the service itself. A services marketer's goal should be to create an effective brand image. In most successful services companies, the company or organization name is the brand name. Thus, customers become loyal to Tim Hortons or to Air Canada or to Hilton. Although there are some exceptions, most services companies have not been successful in creating strong brands for their individual service products.

Most customers probably do not remember the brand that the bank has placed on their particular type of chequing account, or the various classes of service provided by a courier company.

The strategy to achieve a strong services brand image is to develop a total theme that includes more than just a good brand name. To implement this strategy, the following tactics may be used:[23]

- Include a tangible good as part of the brand image — like the umbrella of Travelers Insurance, Prudential's Rock of Gibraltar, or the koala bear of Qantas.
- Tie in a slogan with the brand — for instance, "You're in good hands with Allstate" or "Membership has its privileges" (American Express).
- Use a distinctive colour scheme — such as Avis's red or the green of the Toronto Dominion Bank.

Management of Service Quality In our brief discussion of product quality in Chapter 11, we noted the elusiveness of this important product feature. Quality is difficult to define, measure, control, and communicate. Yet in services marketing, the quality of the service is critical to a firm's success. Two airlines each fly a Boeing 747 for the same fare; two auto repair shops each use Ford or Chrysler parts and charge the same price; and two banks each offer the same investment accounts at identical interest rates. Assuming similar times and locations, quality of service is the only factor that differentiates the offerings in each of these paired situations.

However difficult it may be to define the concept of service quality, management must understand one thing: Quality is defined by the consumer and not by the producer-seller of a service. Your hairstylist may be delighted with the job she did on your hair. But if you think your hair looks terrible, then the service quality was poor. What counts is what consumers think about a service. **Service quality** that does not meet customer expectations can result in lost sales from present customers and a failure to attract new customers. Consequently, it is imperative that management strives to maintain consistent service quality at or above the level of consumer expectations. Yet it is sometimes virtually impossible to standardize service quality — that is, to maintain consistency in service output. Performance quality typically varies even within the same organization. This is true in such diverse fields as opera, legal services, landscaping, baseball, health care, and marketing courses.[24]

As part of managing service quality, an organization should design and operate an ongoing quality-improvement program that will monitor the level and consistency of service quality. A related, but also difficult, task is to evaluate service quality by measuring customer satisfaction — customers' perceptions of the quality of an organization's services.[25]

Most successful marketers of services and those responsible for the services associated with tangible products have begun to introduce programs that will allow them to measure the quality of the service they provide, as perceived by their customers. Many businesses have existed for years under the assumption that management knew what the customer wanted and how he or she wished to be treated. The most successful have now abandoned that way of thinking and have subscribed to the maxim that "good service is whatever the customer says it is." Thus, a program to measure the perceived quality of a business's service must start by defining the aspects of the contact with the company the customer considers to be most important.

Research with a number of Canadian and foreign companies in various industries has confirmed that consumers consider five components of service to be important: (1) the nature of the service itself (the core service); (2) the quality of services required to ensure that the core product performs to expectations; (3) the technical aspects of the process by which the product or service is delivered; (4) interaction with the people who deliver the service; and (5) affective dimensions of the interaction — literally, how the customer feels during his or her interaction with the company and its employees (see Figure 12-2). You will note that the components of service illustrated in Figure 12-2 correspond closely to the five "drivers of customer satisfaction" that were discussed in detail in Chapter 1.

Let's illustrate the components of service by considering customers of Bell Canada and other telephone companies who are interested, first of all, in ensuring that their telephone systems work properly, that calls go through, and that reception is clear (the "core product" aspects of the service). In fact, as technology has improved in the telecommunications industry, customers do not expect their telephone systems ever to fail — the core service in this industry is largely taken for granted by customers; they almost never think of it.

The next component of service relates to the processes and support services that the telephone company has in place to deliver and support the core service — telephone bills, installation of new lines, telephone directories, directory assistance services, and so-called vertical services such as voice mail and call forwarding. Thirdly, we raise the issue of the technical quality of the core service and of the support services — does the telephone work? Are the telephone bills accurate? Is installation done promptly?

Finally, we must also appreciate that the quality of service as perceived by customers is related to the way in which employees of the company interact with their customers — whether operators are courteous and polite, whether sales people know the technology, and how complaints are resolved. This not only relates to such aspects of personal service as courtesy, politeness, and general civility, but also to the final level of service, that relating to how the customer is made to feel by the service provider and by the company in general.[26]

FIGURE 12-2 The Domain of Customer Service

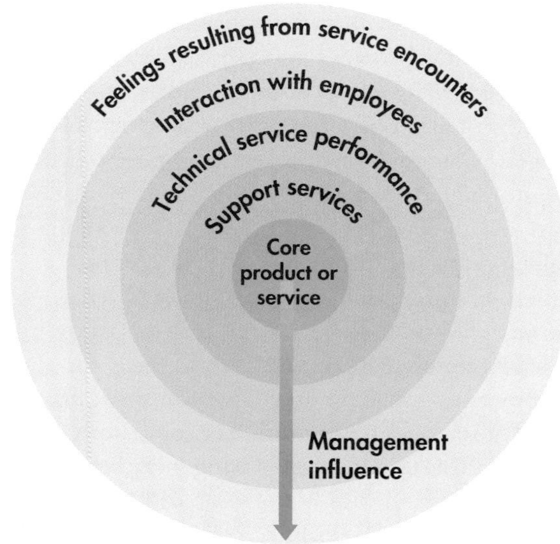

It may be suggested that as the nature of service moves farther away from the actual product or service and more toward the "people" aspects of service, the less control management has over the delivery, and therefore the quality, of the service offered. For example, an airline company can control the actual flight from Toronto to Vancouver (the core service, getting passengers from one city to another). Barring unforeseen circumstances management can control, to a greater or lesser extent, the services that support that core product: the frequency of flights, departure and arrival times, the number of ticket agents at the counter, baggage-handling systems, and type of meals served.

Management loses much more control over the details of the service provided at the interface between customer and employee — how the passenger agent greets the customer at the check-in counter, whether the baggage handler puts the suitcase on the right plane, whether the flight attendants are pleasant and helpful. In fact, it is in this latter component of service that many companies feel their greatest potential lies to differentiate themselves from the competition. Among international airlines, Air Canada, Singapore Airlines, and Cathay Pacific try to feature superior service and "cabin comfort" in their advertising.

It is this realization that employees have the potential to make or break a relationship with a customer that has led many companies to introduce programs of **internal marketing**. These are programs intended to ensure that employees "buy in" to the concept of customer service and appreciate that every satisfied customer means a returning customer. Again, the more progressive companies, and those that are most committed to exceptional levels of customer service, have developed elaborate training and motivation programs that emphasize excellence in treating the customer and reward those employees who treat customers well.[27]

Pricing of Services

In the marketing of services, nowhere is there a greater need for managerial creativity and skill than in the area of pricing. Earlier we noted that services are intangible, extremely perishable, and usually

www.singaporeair.com • www.cathaypacific-air.com

www.fabritec.com/sanitone/
www.computerland.com
www.mailposte.ca
www.purolator.ca
www.fedex.com

cannot be stored, and that demand for them often fluctuates considerably. All these features carry significant pricing implications. To further complicate the situation, customers may perform some services themselves (auto and household repairs, for example).

Because of the heterogeneity and difficulty of standardizing quality, most services are highly differentiated. Also, it is virtually impossible to have complete market information; customers often have considerable difficulty assessing the quality of the service and, therefore, the value for money that they have received. As an example, consider the issue of auto repairs. Many customers of auto dealers and repair shops do not understand how cars work, particularly with the on-board computer systems that are in most cars today. As a result, they are unable to assess whether or not they have received good value from the repair job. It's little wonder that auto repair businesses bear the brunt of large numbers of consumer complaints.

Many of the pricing strategies discussed in Chapter 13 are applicable to services marketing. Quantity discounts, for instance, are used by car-rental companies. Daily rates are lower if you rent the car for a week or a month at a time. Cash discounts are offered when insurance premiums are paid annually instead of quarterly. Mechanics will charge more if they must travel out of town, and engineers will usually command higher fees for work in foreign countries.

Channels of Distribution for Services

Traditionally, most services have been sold directly from producer to consumer or business user. No intermediaries are used when the service cannot be separated from the seller or when the service is created and marketed simultaneously. For example, medical care, repair services, and other personal services are typically sold without intermediaries, simply because the service could not exist without the people who are providing it. Not using intermediaries does limit the geographic markets that service providers can reach because they have to be there in person to provide the service. But it also enables sellers to personalize their services and get quick, detailed customer feedback.

The only other frequently used channel includes one agent intermediary. Some type of agent or broker is often used in the marketing of securities, travel arrangements, entertainment, and housing rentals. Sometimes dealers are trained in the production of the service and then are **franchised** to sell it. This is the case with Sanitone dry cleaning, Midas Muffler shops, Computerland, and similar franchises.

In recent years, some firms have realized that the characteristic of inseparability is not an insurmountable limitation to a seller's distribution system. With a little imagination, a services marketer can broaden distribution considerably. Let's look at some examples, starting with location.

The service provider or agent should be conveniently located for customers, because many services cannot be delivered. Many motels and restaurants have gone out of business when a new highway bypassed their locations, thereby drawing away customer traffic. On the other hand, banks have increased business by installing twenty-four-hour automated banking machines and by launching telephone and Internet banking, and allowing customers to access their accounts by computer from their homes or offices. Dental centres, chiropractors, and optometrists have opened offices in shopping-centre malls. They offer convenience of location, extended hours, and parking.

The use of intermediaries is another way to expand distribution of services. Some banks have arranged for companies to deposit employees' paycheques directly into their bank accounts. The employer thus becomes an intermediary in distributing the bank's service. Insurance firms have broadened distribution by setting up vending machines in airports. Canada Post now operates post offices in drugstores across Canada. Canada's lottery corporations sell their tickets through kiosks in shopping malls and through thousands of retail agents in convenience stores and gasoline stations across the country. Courier services such as Purolator and Federal Express have made it convenient for their customers by installing drop boxes on street corners in the downtown business districts of major cities.

The characteristic of intangibility essentially eliminates physical-distribution problems for most service producers. For example, other than office and other supplies, accountants have no physical inventory to store or handle. However, not all service producers are free from physical-distribution headaches. Those who are unable to deliver their service without the support of tangible products still have to address issues relating to physical storage and logistics. Retailing, for example, is considered a service industry, but retailers certainly have to deal with inventory issues and questions relating to location. Courier companies have to maintain fleets of truck and aircraft.

Many companies have succeeded in separating some services from the people who provide them by delegating the delivery of their services to vending machines. While we normally associate the concept of a vending machine with those that supply candy bars and soft drinks, much of the equipment and technology that now deliver services are essentially service-vending machines. When we make a telephone call from a pay phone — now virtually all converted from coin to card operated — we are using a vending machine of sorts. Similarly, ABMs supply financial services in much the same way that "Coke machines" supply soft drinks. When you use a coin-operated photocopying machine in your college library, you are buying a service. Two enterprising young Canadians even recently developed a joke-vending machine that will provide you with a minute of side-splitting entertainment — three or four jokes from professional comics — for fifty cents. They are marketing their invention to bars, restaurants, and clubs with the help of Yuk Yuk's Inc.[28]

Promotion of Services

Several forms of promotion are used extensively in services marketing, but because services are often inseparable from the people who provide them, personal selling plays the dominant role. Whether or not he or she realizes it, any employee of a service firm who comes in contact with a customer is, in effect, part of that firm's sales force. In addition to a regular sales force, customer contact personnel might include airline flight attendants, law-office receptionists, couriers, bank tellers, and ticket-takers and ushers at ballparks or theatres. We use the term **service encounter** to describe a customer's interaction with any service employee or with any tangible element such as a service's physical surroundings (bank, ballpark, law office). Customers often form opinions of a company and its service on the basis of service encounters. Consequently, it is essential that management recognize the strategic importance of service encounters and prepare contact personnel and physical surroundings accordingly. A key step in preparing to sell a service is to provide sales training and service information for contact personnel, impressing on them the importance of their role.[29]

For years, of course, advertising has been used extensively in many service fields — hotels, transportation, recreation, and insurance, for example. What is newer is the use of advertising by professional-services firms, including legal, accounting, and health services such as physiotherapists and chiropractors. Previously, professional associations in such fields prohibited advertising on the grounds that it was unethical. While some associations still control the type of advertising that may be done, the promotion of professional services is much more open and accepted than ever before.

In sales promotion, while point-of-purchase displays of services offered are often impossible, displays of the results of using a service can be effective. Many service firms, especially in the recreation and entertainment fields, benefit considerably from free publicity. Sports coverage by newspapers, radio, and television provides publicity, as do newspaper reviews of movies, plays, and concerts. Travel sections in newspapers have helped sell transportation, accommodation, and other services related to the travel industry.

As an indirect type of promotion, engineers, accountants, lawyers, and insurance agents may participate actively in community affairs as a means of getting their names before the public. Some professional firms are even offering guarantees. Service firms (banks, public utilities, lawyers) may advertise to attract new industry to the community. They know that anything that helps the community grow will automatically mean an expanded market for their services.

THE FUTURE OF SERVICES MARKETING

The boom in the services economy in recent years has been accompanied by a significant increase in competition in many service industries. This competition has been stimulated by several factors. One is the reduction in government regulation in many industries — airlines, telecommunications, and banking, for example. Relaxed regulations by professional organizations now permit advertising in the medical, legal, and other professions. New techniques have opened new service fields — in solar energy and information processing, for instance. Technological advances have also brought automation and other "industrial" features to service industries in which employees of organizations generally performed many manual tasks. Service chains and franchise systems are replacing the small-scale independent in many fields, including take-out food, auto repairs, beauty shops, and real estate brokerage.

Need for Increased Productivity

Throughout the 1990s, companies and other organizations in virtually every industry have been challenged to become more efficient and productive. The pressure on businesses is to deliver greater returns to shareholders, while in public-sector organizations, governments at all levels have been looking for new ways to produce better value for taxpayers. Because service industries are very labour-intensive compared with manufacturing, the pressure to become more efficient has led in many organizations to a phenomenon that has become known as "downsizing," reducing costs by reducing the number of employees. Also, since wages in the service sector of the economy have a major impact on prices, there has been pressure on labour unions and their employers to keep wage increases to a minimum in the interest of keeping inflation down. As a result of these forces, the forecast for the next few years is for continued growth in the service sector, but also for continued pressure to keep levels of productivity up.

Service firms are employing various strategies to improve productivity. One is to invest in education and training programs, not just to teach basic skills but also to improve employees' efficiency. Another strategy is to bring in new technology and adopt methods used in manufacturing. Machines have enhanced or even replaced labour in a wide range of service industries. The most widely adopted technology has been some form of computer-based system. Computers have increased the efficiency of operations in countless service firms. But the flip side is that computers (or computer users) have often fallen short of their potential. Sometimes the users are not properly trained, or existing systems are not adapted to make the most effective use of new technologies. A third productivity-improvement strategy is to restructure jobs so that each employee can accomplish a lot more in the same amount of time. Thus, auto repair shops have employees who specialize in brakes, transmissions, or mufflers. The introduction of assembly-line techniques at Burger King, Harvey's, and McDonald's has increased output per employee.

However, the basic premise of the manufacturing model is that machines and technology are the primary keys to increased productivity and successful operations. The people who deliver the services are less important — so goes the premise. But this premise simply no longer works in the competitive services environment of today. Instead, we need a model that puts customer-contact employees first and then designs the business operations around these people. Four key elements in this new model are:[30]

- Companies value investments in people at least as much as investments in machines.
- Firms use technology to support the work of customer-contact people, rather than using it to monitor or replace these workers.
- Companies make recruiting and training as important for sales people and other customer-contact employees as for executives.
- Management ties compensation to performance for employees at every level from bottom to top.

McDonald's, Taco Bell, and ServiceMaster are examples of firms working to implement this new services model. They would agree with Ron Zemke, president of Performance Research Associates, who said, "No amount of marketing money and moxie can wash away the effect of poor frontline service." Michael

Quinlan, McDonald's CEO, summed up the changing times when he said, "In the seventies, we focused on serving the customer; in the eighties, we emphasized satisfying the customer, and in the nineties, our goal is to exceed customer expectations."[31]

Impact of Technology

One of the most important issues facing services marketing relates to how technology affects the way services are delivered to customers and how it influences the quality of service provided to them. Certainly, we are unable to avoid technology today. Probably no other force has had the impact on service industries that technology has had in recent years and will continue to have in the future. Everywhere we turn there is evidence of technology-delivered service, from the myriad ways we can access financial services at our banks, to the 100-channel universe being delivered by direct-to-home television services such as StarChoice, to the Internet and all that it delivers.

Many advances in technology certainly make the life of the customer easier, even though the consumer may not even realize the role that technology is playing. Such is the case when Federal Express uses its sophisticated tracking system to allow customers to know exactly where a package is at all times, when it was delivered, and who signed for it. Companies that operate call centres to receive incoming calls from customers use sophisticated number-recognition software to direct a customer's call to the person to whom the customer last spoke, thereby helping in the building of a more personal relationship between an employee and the customer. Manufacturers like Caterpillar use on-board computers to measure the wear on parts and to send a signal to a satellite in order to inform the nearest Caterpillar dealer to contact the customer to replace the part *before* the customer's equipment fails.

Such use of technology to deliver improved levels of customer service is impressive. But, in service industries, particularly when one considers the quality of service delivered, technology has the potential to be a two-edged sword. The reason for this is simply that all consumers are not similarly comfortable and familiar with technology. Not everyone wants to use an ATM or bank through the Internet — some people don't even know what the Internet is! To people who are not technologically literate or who simply long for the "old days," technology often gets in the way of good service. They resent efforts by their banks to encourage them to use ATMs, because they are used to dealing with their favourite bank employee. They are uncomfortable with the interactive voice-response system they encounter when they want to place a collect call. They don't enjoy dealing with voice mail. Encountering technology may cause these customers not to want to do business with a company. This is an issue that some companies have begun to address, but many also seem to want to rush headlong into the implementation of more technology without giving much thought to its impact on customers and on their view of the firm.

Performance Measurement in Services Organizations

Profit-oriented service firms can evaluate their performance by using quantitative measures such as market share or return on investment, and then compare these figures with industry averages and trends. Unfortunately, many firms, particularly smaller businesses, do not have access to such comparative data and are unable to benchmark themselves against other companies. For many, it would be inappropriate to compare themselves with much larger firms or with those that operate in quite different markets. In any event, market share and return on investment are much too broad to serve as good measures of how the service company is performing.

To measure their performance, therefore, companies that operate in service industries must address the question of how consumers perceive the quality of the service provided and how well they are doing in meeting customers' expectations of service. One of the principal issues relates to how such measurement of perceived service quality is to be carried out; another deals with what should be measured. There are many ways to measure service quality, some of which have been mentioned in this chapter. But it is not a simple process, and it is made all the more difficult by the fact that we are dealing with intangibles and that every customer's definition of acceptable quality is different. This issue of developing a sound basis for measuring the quality of service is one that will continue to command the attention of services marketers in the future.

Another issue relating to measurement deals with the question of measuring payback on investment in service and with determining where such investment should be directed. For example, should a bank or airline or hotel chain spend much to provide superb service to a customer who may bring it little business and whose account may cost the company a great deal to service? Should a retail store invest in superior service if most of the customers it serves are passing traffic and if very few can be counted on for repeat business? These questions must be addressed by services marketers in deciding where to invest in the improvement of service. Dealing with this issue will also require improved cost-accounting systems in many companies so that they can track the effectiveness of investing in service improvements.[32]

Prospects for Growth

Services will continue to take an increasing share of the consumer dollar, just as they have done over the past forty years. This forecast seems reasonable even for periods of economic decline. History shows that the demand for services is less sensitive to economic fluctuations than is the demand for goods. The demand for business services should also continue to expand as business becomes more complex and as management further recognizes its need for business-service specialists. In professional services especially, the use of marketing programs is expected to increase considerably during the coming decade. This expansion will occur as more health-care organizations, lawyers, engineers, and other professionals come to understand the economic benefits they can derive from an effective marketing program.

Unfortunately, many service firms today still do not provide a satisfactory level of service quality. Most consumers undoubtedly would agree with this assessment by Leonard L. Berry, one of the leading researchers and authors in services marketing. Any prediction of profitable growth in services firms is based on senior management's raising their aspirations, learning from past mistakes, and providing effective leadership. More specifically, future profitability depends on a company's ability to correct the following basic mistakes related to service quality:[33]

- *Spending money on the wrong priorities.* A major hotel planned to install colour TV sets in some guest bathrooms when 66 percent of customer calls to the housekeeping department were requests for irons and ironing boards. The hotel later reversed these priorities.
- *Reducing quality by flaws in service design.* Computer-generated billing statements that are impossible for customers to understand; clothing-store dressing rooms that lack a minimum of two hooks — one for street clothes and one for try-on clothes.
- *Seeking easy solutions to quality problems.* Short-term, superficial, pep-talk solutions when the real need is an investment in managerial time, energy, and ego to change employee and management habits and attitudes regarding service quality.
- *Shortchanging fairness to customers.* Hotels and airlines that do not honour confirmed reservations; insurance companies that inadequately disclose important information.
- *Underinvesting in leadership development.* At all managerial levels, companies need leadership for employees faced with large numbers of demanding, sometimes rude, customers and other conditions that breed stress, fatigue, and discouragement.

Even manufacturers are taking an increasing interest in services as a basis for growth. Most tangible goods can be quickly and easily imitated. Consequently, manufacturers see their accompanying services as a key factor in giving a company a competitive advantage. The idea is to bundle services with goods to respond to a full range of customers' wants.

Summary

Most product offerings are a mix of tangible goods and intangible services, located on a spectrum ranging from pure goods to pure services. Services are separately identifiable, intangible activities that are the main object of a transaction designed to provide want-satisfaction for customers. Conceptually, tangible-goods marketing and services marketing are essentially the same. In reality, however, the characteristics that differentiate services from goods usually call for quite different marketing programs.

The scope of services marketing is enormous. About half of what we spend goes for services, and about two-thirds of nongovernmental jobs are in service industries. Not only are services of considerable significance in our economy today, but it is predicted that the services sector will continue to grow faster than the manufacturing sector of the economy. Services generally are intangible, inseparable from the seller, heterogeneous, and highly perishable, and they have a widely fluctuating demand. Each of these distinctive characteristics has several marketing implications.

The development of a program for the marketing of services parallels that for tangible goods, but takes into account the special characteristics of services. Management first identifies its target market and then designs a marketing mix to provide want-satisfaction for that market. In the product-planning stage, the element of service quality is critical to a company's success. Similar pricing strategies are used by services and goods producers, although is it often difficult to communicate value in services. In distribution, intermediaries are used less often, and location of the service marketer in relation to the market is important, particularly when the service is delivered in person. Personal selling is the dominant promotional method used in services marketing.

As we move into the next millennium, the service environment will continue to change. One of the biggest challenges for service industries today is to develop ways to improve efficiency and productivity without impairing the quality of the service provided. Productivity becomes more important as services account for a growing share of consumer expenditures and as organizations look for ways to provide better returns to their stakeholders. Service quality is often at risk in such situations, but it should remain a priority of service companies and not-for-profit organizations as consumers pay increasing attention to the quality of service that they receive.

Key Terms and Concepts

Core services (285)
Supplementary services (285)
Services (285)
Personal services (286)
Business services (287)
Intangibility (287)
Inseparability (287)
Heterogeneity (289)
Perishability (291)
Fluctuating demand (291)
Customer value (293)
Branding of services (295)
Service quality (296)
Internal marketing (297)
Services franchising (298)
Service encounter (299)

Questions and Problems

1. How do you explain the substantial increase in expenditures for services relative to expenditures for tangible products in the past forty years?
2. What are some marketing implications of the fact that services possess the characteristic of intangibility?
3. Why are intermediaries rarely used in the marketing programs of service firms?
4. Services are highly perishable and are often subject to fluctuations in demand. In marketing its services, how can a company offset these factors?
5. Cite some examples of service marketers that you feel are customer-oriented, and describe what these firms have done to make you feel this way about them.

6. Discuss how loyalty programs such as Air Miles and Club Z add value for customers.
7. Present a brief analysis of the market for each of the following service firms. Make use of the components of a market discussed in chapters 4 to 7.
   a. Canadian Airlines International.
   b. Toronto Airport Hilton hotel.
   c. Indoor tennis club.
   d. Credit union.
8. What are some of the ways in which each of the following service firms might expand its services mix?
   a. Chartered accountant.
   b. Hairstyling salon.
   c. Bank.
9. Explain the importance of demand elasticity in the pricing of services.
10. "Personal selling should be the main ingredient in the promotional mix for a marketer of services." Do you agree? Discuss.
11. Present in brief form a marketing program for each of the following services. Your presentation should start with a description of the target market you have selected for the service. Then explain how you would plan, price, promote, and distribute the service.
    a. A disc jockey for private parties in the community.
    b. Your electric company.
    c. Household cleaning.

Hands-On Marketing

1. Identify a company in your town that manufactures tangible products (a woodworking shop, a metal fabricating plant, or similar operation) and examine the services this company also must supply in supporting the sale of its tangible products.
2. Review a service encounter in which you have recently participated and in which you were not pleased with the outcome. Consider what went wrong, using the model shown in Figure 12-2. Was the problem with the "core" product or service, or in one of the outer rings? What could the service provider do to improve your experience next time?

Case 3-1

ACORN PARK HOTEL

The Acorn Park Hotel was opened in 1946 and is located in South Kensington, a quiet area of London, not far from Harrods and other fashionable shops, and very close to a number of museums and art galleries. With only eighty rooms, the Acorn Park was typical of the properties in the Redpath Group of Inns, who prided themselves as hotels that created a special atmosphere for their guests. It was Monday, July 18, and Geoffrey Thornton, guest relations manager, had just entered his office. The morning mail had arrived, and the first envelope Thornton opened contained the following letter.

Martha K. Stone, QC
Barrister and Solicitor
3265 Main Street
Fredericton, NB, Canada
E3B 4K6

July 13, 1998

Mr. Geoffrey Thornton
Guest Relations Manager
Acorn Park Hotel
100 Bromley Road, London

Dear Mr. Thornton:

My husband and I have just returned home, having spent the past ten days in London on a combined business and pleasure trip. We decided to end our trip with a short weekend stay at the Acorn Park before returning to Canada, as your hotel had been recommended by some good friends of ours who stayed there last summer. Our friends had nothing but good things to say about the Acorn Park Hotel. But, despite the hotel's excellent reputation, the service we received during our stay was quite the opposite. I have decided to write to you to describe the treatment my husband and I received from what can only be described as your tactless and unhelpful staff.

When we arrived last Friday, we were quite tired and were looking forward to relaxing in our room for a few hours before dinner. Upon checking in we were assigned room 216 which was, if I may say, not what one would expect in a four-star hotel. The room had not been cleaned, as items of clothing had been left by the previous guest. The window looked out on scaffolding and the room was unbearably hot. The person at the front desk, when I finally was able to get through, informed me that there was nothing she could do to find us an alternate room.

The next morning, we experienced totally unacceptable treatment when we ate breakfast in the dining room. The lady on the desk as we entered the dining room pointed out to us that, as we were not part of one of the tours staying at the hotel, our breakfast was not included in our room rate and we would have to pay for it! This was no surprise, as we had fully expected to pay.

We were quite surprised as we were leaving the dining room to be stopped again by this lady, who insisted that we pay either in cash or by credit card. Despite our protests that we were guests in the hotel and that she should simply put the charge on our room bill, she insisted that she had instructions to accept only cash or credit card payment from us, referring to the fact that our name was on a list that had been provided to her by the front office.

While I began the process of paying by credit card, my husband went looking for the front desk manager, who was most helpful and responded immediately. He accompanied my husband to the dining room where he ascertained that an error had been made and that the name opposite room 216 on the list which had been provided to the dining room staff was not ours. He apologized and the charge was allowed to go to our room bill. The dining room staff involved were totally unaccommodating and tactless in the manner in which they handled the matter. Needless to say, we did not eat breakfast at the hotel the following morning.

My second complaint refers to your telephone system. Shortly after arriving on Friday evening, I wanted to make an outside telephone call and dialled 9 to get an outside line. I did not get a second dial tone, but rather the line rang and rang for 15 or 20 rings with no answer. I tried two or three times before I could get an answer from the switchboard, only to be told that I should dial 9. Only when I explained that I had been dialling 9 was there an effort made to find out what had happened. Evidently, my line had been switched over in some way so that dialling 9 resulted in the telephone ringing at the front desk. Once this was rectified, I was able to make outside calls.

Checking out on Sunday morning was the final frustration. It was 9 o'clock; others were checking out, bus tours were leaving, guests were trying to have travellers' cheques cashed before their buses left, and the telephones were ringing constantly. The young lady who was working alone on the front desk was trying to deal with this confusion. Guests were becoming upset, the departure of the tours was being delayed, and your employee became so frustrated with the ringing telephones that she simply lifted them and placed them back down again, without answering them!

I do not blame the employee; she was doing her best under the circumstances. I find it totally unacceptable that a hotel would have one employee serving the front desk during what is one of the busiest periods of the day, and have her try to answer the telephones at the same time.

Despite the recommendation from our friends and the Acorn Park's excellent location, I would have to say that it is very unlikely that we will be back unless we have some assurance that the problems with customer service have been overcome. I would welcome your comments.

Sincerely

M.K. Stone

Martha K. Stone, QC

Questions

1. Why did Martha Stone write her letter?
2. What factors contributed to her dissatisfaction?
3. How important were the following factors in affecting the service the Stones had received?
   - Product
   - Process
   - Performance
   - People
4. What were the Stones' expectations when they arrived at the Acorn Park Hotel?
5. What does Martha Stone expect to happen now that she has written?
6. What could or should the front desk manager have done when he was called to the dining room on Saturday morning?
7. What should Geoffrey Thornton do now? What factors will influence how he responds?

Case 3-2

KAREN BROWNE'S ADVENTURE: A STUDY OF SERVICE FAILURE AND RECOVERY

It was a sunny Friday in early June, and Karen Browne was looking forward to her long weekend visiting friends near Niagara Falls, Ontario, just across the border from Buffalo, New York. Karen was a university student who was working in Boston for the summer, and she had been extremely busy for the past six weeks, working as part of a team overseeing the opening of a new French bistro on Newbury Street, in the heart of Boston's Back Bay area. Karen and her fellow team members had enjoyed little time off in recent weeks as the opening of the restaurant in mid-July drew nearer.

Karen was pleased that she had been able to obtain a discounted air fare for her weekend trip to Niagara Falls. The fare of $99 return seemed very reasonable, especially since she had booked with Alpha Airlines, one of the largest airlines in the United States. She was surprised, however, when she arrived at Logan Airport on Friday afternoon at 2:30 P.M. to find that she was, in fact, flying with Northern Express, a much smaller commuter airline that served as the connector airline for Alpha in the northeastern United States. She was also surprised to learn that she was to fly in a nineteen-seat propeller-driven airplane and that there was to be a stop in Syracuse, New York.

Karen's surprise concerning the identity of the connector airline and the size of the aircraft was quickly surpassed, however, when, at the end of the uneventful flight to Buffalo, her soft-sided suitcase failed to appear on the baggage carousel. Karen and her friends who had met her at the airport waited until all of the baggage had been claimed and the carousel had stopped revolving. They then made their way to the Northern Express customer service counter, where Karen was advised to complete a lost baggage report, which would then be used by the airline to trace the lost bag. The Northern Express employee with whom she spoke said that Karen would be telephoned as soon as the bag was located, and that it would probably be on the next flight from Boston, which was scheduled to arrive at 6:30 P.M. She and her friends then left to drive across the border to Niagara Falls, confident that the bag would be located and delivered.

Having heard nothing from Northern Express by noon on Saturday, Karen decided to telephone the airline's customer contact number at the Buffalo airport to determine if her bag had been located. It had not, and the employee with whom she spoke advised her that there was no news "in the system" concerning its whereabouts. She was advised to call back.

By Sunday afternoon, Karen had made four more telephone calls at her friends' expense to the Northern Express office at Buffalo airport and was advised each time that her bag had not been located. Feeling a little frustrated, she decided to call Alpha Airlines' "customer inquiries" in Toronto on its toll-free number to see if the "parent" airline might be able to help locate her bag. At that number, she talked with an Alpha employee named John who was able to check the same computer system and also advised her that her bag was still missing. However, John suggested that he would telephone the Alpha baggage people in Boston to see if they could help locate the bag and also advised Karen that she was entitled to claim up to $25 from Alpha for each day that her bag was missing. The next day, Monday, John telephoned Karen at her friends' home near Niagara Falls to tell her that her bag had not been found and that there was no trace of it in the system. He advised her that she should make a claim when she returned to Boston on Tuesday.

Upon landing in Boston the next morning, Karen located the Alpha Airlines customer service office in the baggage claim area and inquired about making a claim for her lost luggage. She was advised that, as she had not actually flown with Alpha Airlines, her claim should be directed to the Northern Express office. At that office, Karen was advised that she could not make a claim because the airline was still trying to locate her bag, and it had been only five days since it went missing. The employee took her name and address and the number on her baggage ticket stub and said that a claim form would be mailed to her if the bag had not been located by the end of the week.

Karen had spent five days away from her apartment without clothing and other items that were in

 This case is not intended to illustrate either correct or incorrect handling of a management situation. While the case is based on actual events, certain names have been changed.

Northern Express
The Alpha Connection

June 25, 1997

Ms. Karen Browne
Apartment 7, 2128 Lexington St.
Cambridge, MA 02138

Dear Ms. Browne:

We are sorry about the loss of your baggage and that our efforts to locate it have thus far been unsuccessful. Please accept our sincere apologies for the inconvenience this has caused you.

If your luggage has not been returned to you by another airline, we would appreciate your completing the attached form and returning it to us within 45 days from the date of this letter. If Northern Express does not receive the completed claim form and the proper documentation within the indicated time frame, search efforts will be hindered and your claim may be rejected. If more than one piece of luggage is involved, please list the contents of each bag separately. Include all items regardless of value, as this will help us to identify your property. Be sure to enclose the original or a copy of the Passenger's Coupon of your ticket and have the form notarized including the Notary Seal. Except for jewellery, cash, camera, and electronic equipment, for which we do not accept liability, we will also need purchase receipts, cancelled checks, credit slips, or invoices for all items. It is necessary for us to have these receipts and the notarized claim form in proper order before we can complete our investigation. If Northern Express does not receive the completed form and the proper documentation 45 days from the date of this letter, your claim may be rejected.

Just as soon as we hear from you, we will be able to finalize our search efforts. Please be advised that it will take 45–60 days to complete the claims process. I assure you that our people are diligently continuing their search for your lost property and will keep you informed of any progress we make.

Your early reply will help us bring the matter to a prompt conclusion. Thank you for your patience and co-operation.

Sincerely

Marvin Underwood

Marvin Underwood, Manager — Airport Customer Service

her suitcase, and she had spent over $150 purchasing T-shirts, jeans, and a number of personal items that she had needed. Her friends had refused her offer to pay for the long-distance telephone calls that she had made to Northern Express, trying to locate her missing bag. She arrived at her apartment in Cambridge rather frustrated and feeling that this had been a weekend that she would not soon forget.

Karen was met at the door of her apartment by her roommate, Heather, who informed her that she had received a telephone call that morning from an Alpha Airlines employee in Orlando, Florida, who was calling to see if Karen was missing a suitcase. It seems that the bag had been in the Orlando airport since Friday evening, but did not have an airline baggage tag on it. The Alpha employee told Heather that she had gotten Karen's name and telephone number from the address tag that she had attached to the bag when she had checked in for the flight to Buffalo on Friday. If Karen would call her back, she would send the bag to Boston on the next available Alpha flight, and it would be delivered to her apartment.

By Wednesday afternoon, Karen and her suitcase had been reunited. She was happy to have it back, because there were a few valuable items inside that she would not have wanted to lose. Two weeks later, the letter shown on p. 308 arrived in the mail.

Questions

1. Whose responsibility was it to address Karen's problem? Why do you feel the issue was not resolved by the airlines involved? Discuss the roles of the various employees with whom Karen came in contact.
2. Analyze the process through which Karen passed from her purchase of the airline ticket to the receipt of the letter from Northern Express. What went wrong? To what do you attribute the overall service failure?
3. Comment on the content of the letter that Karen received from Northern Express. Why do you feel it was written? What are the objectives of the airline in writing such a letter? How do you think Karen felt when she received it?
4. Comment on the approach of both Alpha Airlines and Northern Express to the challenge of service recovery.

Case 3-3

THE HAND GUARD

Alice Dicks was pondering the success of the hand guard that she had developed a number of years ago. As a nurse working for the Canadian Red Cross, she realized there was a need for a device to protect the hands of health-care workers responsible for transferring blood between syringes. Alice experimented with several prototypes of a hand guard before progressing to field trials. She hired patent lawyers in Ottawa to ensure that her trademark was legal. With assistance from the National Research Council, an injection mould was developed to produce a hand shield, which was imprinted with the product and corporate names. In response to an invitation, Alice displayed her hand shields at the Medi-Tech trade show in London, Ontario, and lined up a Canadian distributor. So far, Alice had "done everything by the book" and was quite encouraged by the headway she was making in Canada. She decided to attend another medical trade show, this time in Florida. That was when all the trouble started.

In the 1980s, Alice Dicks, RN, had been working at the Canadian Red Cross blood donor clinic in Grand Falls-Windsor, Newfoundland. In order to collect blood from donors, a 16-gauge needle is used. After collection, three samples must be transferred from the thick needle into 7-millilitre test tubes, each of which has rubber on the top. This process requires the health-care professional to hold the three test tubes in one hand and the 16-gauge needle in the other. The reason for the transfer to the test tubes was to allow the testing of donated blood for viruses and infections. The transfer to the three tests tubes must be made relatively quickly and consecutively. This requires considerable precision and caution by the health-care worker so as not to jab oneself in the process. With no protective guard between the 16-gauge needle and the tops of the three tests tubes, workers tended to prick themselves with the needle on occasion. Alice did this three times; the most recent stab was caused when she turned suddenly as she heard a donor yell out just before fainting!

Although the opportunity for infection associated with transferring blood had existed for many years, the consequences had suddenly become quite extreme. The prevalence of the HIV virus in the 1980s meant that such accidents could become a death sentence for those who had jabbed themselves with a donor's blood. Now that Alice had stabbed herself with a needle carrying someone else's blood, she had to undergo twelve months of testing to ensure that she had not been infected. In order to be considered safe, three months of negative HIV readings were required, and eventually they were received. During the testing process, Alice was quite worried about her health. She also kept thinking about the fact that there had to be some product out there that would prevent such a reoccurrence.

Alice knew that, in the blood bank setting in North America, there were thousands of needle pricks happening each year. She searched extensively and found only one apparatus designed to guard against such injuries. It was a very expensive intravenous (IV) line, which would necessitate a change to the clinic's entire blood collection system. Each IV line would have to be discarded after use, thus increasing the operating costs of the blood donor clinics and contributing to the problem of medical waste.

Alice was interested in a light-weight, economical device that she and other workers could carry in their pockets. Such a device should be simple to use, relatively inexpensive, and capable of being reused. That the protective unit should not be disposable was important to Alice, who felt that there is far too much damage being done to the environment through disposal of many items used in the health-care sector. She felt it was important that the hand shield be made of a material that could be sterilized after use. Other factors that influenced the product design included the fact that the guard needed to be transparent so that the person transferring the blood could see the test tubes below the protective shield.

This case was written by Judith A. Cumby, assistant professor, Faculty of Business Administration, Memorial University of Newfoundland, as a basis for class discussion and is not intended to reflect either an effective or an ineffective handling of a management problem. The author wishes to thank Alice Dicks for her support and assistance in the preparation of this case.

The material used in the guard needed to be impervious to needle scratches and cuts.

In the beginning, the hand shield was made from solid, opaque plastic. However, Alice soon realized that the guard had to be transparent and somewhat flexible. Initially, she worked with a local company that had designed a shield made from Plexiglas that did not have any rolled edges. However, it was quickly discovered that if you score Plexiglas with a needle, it could slip and puncture your wrist or crack the Plexiglas. Alice knew that there was a definite need for a hand guard, but was at a loss as to how to design a functional and safe product. She called the National Research Council and talked with a petroleum engineer and a specialist in Autocad design. Together, they developed a prototype for the hand guard, which Alice decided to call a Hema-Shield (the word *hema* means blood).

Field trials of the new product were conducted. Alice felt that this was a critical step to the development of any viable product because the actual users will offer suggestions for improvement. Through information obtained from the field trials and consultation with medical specialists, the Hema-Shield was altered again. The plastic was melted in order to provide rolled edges for the product. These edges would prevent the needle from sliding off the shield during use.

Supported by funding from the Industrial Research Assistance Program of the National Research Council, Alice had a firm in Ontario develop an injection mould that would be used to manufacture the hand guards. The manufacturers suggested a more pliable resin, which was ultimately used in the manufacture of the Hema-Shields. It took six months working with the manufacturers to finalize the design. The mould was imprinted with the product and corporate names, Hema-Shield: Med Search Corp, and these names then appeared on ten thousand hand shields. Alice said that she did not have to do any marketing research. She knew that the demand was there; there was an unfilled niche in the market. What was needed was a suitable product and a means by which to get it to the customers.

Alice hired patent lawyers in Ottawa to register her trademark, Hema-Shield, so that she would be protected from patent infringement. Her lawyers told her that there was no other product registered with the Patent Office of the federal government in Ottawa. She accepted an invitation to display her product at the Medi-Tech show in London, Ontario. Dicks also had brochures developed and displayed at the trade show. There she was approached by a lot of people who wanted to distribute the Hema-Shield. Eventually, she reached an agreement with a distributor in Etobicoke that would receive a commission based on the selling price of between $5.00 and $5.50 per shield.

Alice proceeded to Florida for a medical trade show, where her display generated considerable interest. Shortly after returning to Newfoundland, Alice received a letter from a company in New Jersey that said that she was being sued for patent infringement. The people in New Jersey had developed a silicon patch or graft that was used internally to repair aneurysms and veins. Many years ago, the company had applied to the Canadian government for a patent, but it was not registered in the patent database. As such, the Hema-Shield developed in the United States did not show when an initial patent search was done. Alice explained to the people in New Jersey that her Hema-Shield did not infringe on their product because the two shields served totally different functions. Alice hired new lawyers and was eventually convinced that she would have to change the name of her product. She feels that this infringement of the name was done through no fault of her own; it was the fault of the patent office and the lawyers. Still, Alice was the one incurring more costs and inconvenience.

Alice renamed her product the Med Search Hand Guard. However, with many of the original ten thousand products still in inventory and with the original Hema-Shield name imprinted in the manufacturing mould, Alice had to manually score through the original name before the products could be shipped.

Those who use the product find it quite convenient, almost too convenient from a business perspective. The reorders for the product have been slow because the health-care professionals are getting over a year's use from one hand guard. All health-care workers at the Canadian Red Cross have to use Alice's product; it is now part of the standard operating procedure in the organization's manual.

Her hand guard is also being used by all of the American Red Cross clinics that do not use the expensive and disposable IV line systems. Alice feels that she benefits from word-of-mouth promotion among health-care workers. However, she feels that the distributors are not even scratching the market for her hand guard. She says that there are many other markets where blood work is done and the hand guard should be used, such as veterinary clinics and police laboratories.

She realizes that the durable design of her product is not conducive to making a lot of money through repeat orders. However, Alice, a talented artist, is adamant that the environmental damage associated with more medical waste should be stopped. In retrospect, she feels that patents are a waste of money; there is nothing that cannot be copied. There are many examples of copycat products that sell quite well: CDs, Rolex watches, and Fendi bags. What is important, Alice feels, is developing a product that can serve a niche and sell for an attractive price. It is important to get one's trademark known. She feels that advertising is a waste of money in this regard; what is important is direct selling and making contacts through relationship marketing. There are still orders coming in for Alice's hand guard. As well, she is in the process of developing a digitized machine to be used for mixing red blood cells with anticoagulants. Still, Alice wonders what, if anything, she should be doing to increase sales of her hand guard.

Questions

1. Would formalized market research prior to the development of the hand guard have helped Alice in any way?
2. Evaluate Alice's decision to use distributors in Ontario in light of her feeling that there are many markets that have not yet been reached.
3. What could Alice have done differently to increase sales?
4. How have Alice's personal values and ethics influenced her business decisions?

Part Four

Price

The development of a pricing structure and its use as part of the marketing mix

We are in the process of developing a marketing mix to reach our target markets and achieve our marketing goals. Having completed product planning, we turn now to pricing, where we face two tasks. First, we must determine the base price for a product or service that is consistent with our pricing objectives; this endeavour is covered in Chapter 13. Second, we must decide on strategies (such as discounts and value pricing) to employ in modifying and applying the base price; these strategies are discussed in Chapter 14.

CHAPTER 13 GOALS

In this chapter we cover the role of price in the marketing mix — what price is, how it can be used, and how it is set relative to such factors as product costs, market demand, and competitors' prices. After studying this chapter, you should have an understanding of:

- The meaning of price.
- The significance of price in our economy, to an individual firm, and in a consumer's mind.
- The concept of value and how it relates to price.
- Major pricing objectives.
- Key factors influencing price.
- The types of costs incurred in producing and marketing a product.
- Approaches to determining prices, including cost-plus pricing, marginal analysis, and setting prices in relation only to other prices in the market.
- Break-even analysis.

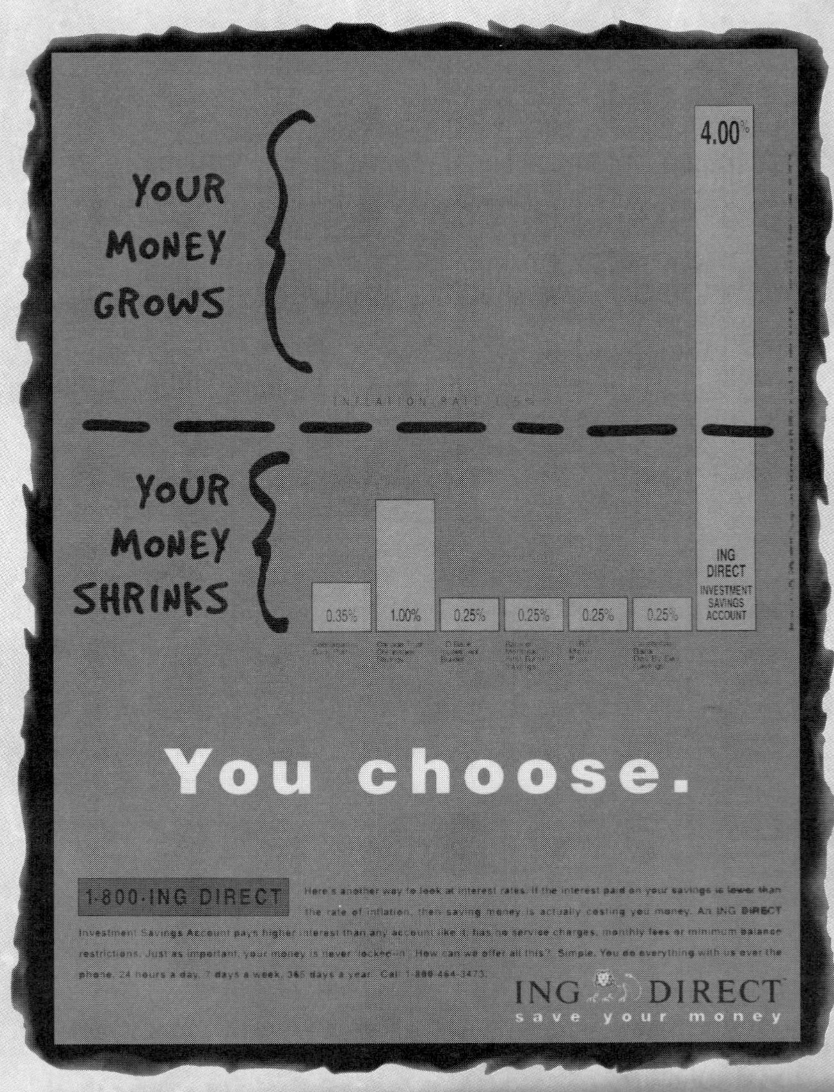

Chapter Thirteen

Price Determination

www.ingdirect.ca • www.belairdirect.com • www.pal.com/s0524.htm

VIRTUAL BANKING

Have you noticed the new bank on your block? You haven't? Thank goodness, because it's not there — physically, that is. It's not anywhere. Well, almost anywhere — it's a virtual bank. Do you need one? What can it do for you? How much will its services cost? Is it good value?

Ten years ago, Canada had seven pretty fair-sized banks, with lots of branches. Today, Canada still has seven fair-sized banks, with many more branches or potential branches. This is because in the interim, all the banks have been allowed to acquire trust companies and investment dealers and, shortly, insurance companies. You will really be able to engage in one-stop shopping for all financial services — if you want to. But large, full-service organizations with many units or branches cost money to manage and operate: personnel have to be trained again and again; expensive technology has to be maintained and reinvested in; branches have to be refurbished; and communicating with consumers and potential consumers is expensive. All these costs have to be paid for, and it is consumers, of course, who pay for them.

Into this technologically sophisticated and rapidly changing consumer financial services market, worth over $90 billion annually, comes ING Direct. ING Direct is owned by Amsterdam-based ING Groep NV, which has banking and insurance operations in over sixty countries and is larger than our biggest bank, the Royal. In Canada, ING owns such insurance companies as Belair, Halifax, Western Union, Groupe Commerce, and NN Life. ING Direct represents what Canadian financial services competitors have feared: the first entry into the retail banking market of a large foreign competitor.

ING Direct offers consumers no-fee, high-interest savings accounts and guaranteed investment certificates by telephone. The cost savings that result from operating electronically rather than with branches allow ING to offer customers interest on savings accounts that is more than twice as much as what competitors offer, as well as lines of credit and term loans that cost less. As soon as possible, ING will begin to sell low-cost insurance as well. According to Arkadi Kuhlmann, the chief executive of ING Direct, "We've hit the right chord with the marketplace and were getting very positive responses from customers." The first-year goal was set at 25,000 customers, and this will be exceeded. ING Direct promotes its services using billboards, television, and direct mail.

The Canadian experience will allow ING to enter the U.S. market, which is also mature and where the competitors are well established. Why Canada first? ING research showed that Canada would be a good pilot because consumers here are open to choice and alternatives. Success here means that this kind of a banking platform — low costs, low prices, and therefore high returns and value to consumers — can be used in other markets around the world.[1]

DETERMINING PRICE

The issue of how much a company should charge for its products and services will depend on many factors. As the ING Direct example shows, the actual costs of a product or service are always a factor influencing the price that can be charged. So, lowering costs generally will lead to lower prices. There are, of course, many other factors that must be taken into consideration, including the target segment for the product or service and the prices being charged by competitors. These factors must be considered when a company introduces a new product or service or considers changing the price of an existing one.

In this chapter we will discuss major methods used to determine the price to be charged. Before being concerned with actual price determination, however, executives — and you — should understand the meaning and importance of price.

MEANING OF PRICE

Some pricing difficulties occur because of confusion about the meaning of price, even though the concept is easy to define in familiar terms. Simply, **price** is the amount of money and/or other items with utility needed to acquire a product. Recall that **utility** is an attribute that has the potential to satisfy wants.

Generally, we tend to think of price in monetary terms; a sweater costs $100, a ticket to a movie $8, a visit to a doctor, how much? Because of our health-care system in Canada, very few of us have any idea what a visit to a doctor costs, because we don't pay for it, at least not directly. It may be useful to think of price as what it costs us to acquire something, whether that something is a tangible product or service.

What it costs to acquire that sweater is more than the $100 price; it involves shopping time and effort, and it may involve other nonmonetary considerations such as having to find a parking space, or arrange public transit, or having to visit several stores to find the size you need. Viewing price as a monetary factor only oversimplifies the buying process. When a customer decides whether he or she is satisfied with the sweater, or with the meal at the restaurant, he or she will implicitly think about the value received. As a result, we often hear customers say, "I'll never go back there. It's just not worth the __________." They may fill the blank with "money," but it is just as likely they will include words like "trouble" or "hassle."

Therefore, we need to consider **value** when we talk about price. A marketer who is interested in creating customer satisfaction will focus on creating value for the customer. There are many ways to create or add value, only one of which is to reduce price. But, because our economy utilizes money as the medium of exchange, we tend to state prices in monetary terms. But as you read this chapter, it may be useful to think of the effect that price has in communicating value to customers.

Practical problems also arise when we try to state simply the price of a product. Suppose you paid $325 for a desk, but your instructor paid only $175 for one of similar size. At first glance, it looks as if the instructor taught the student a lesson! Your desk — which has a beautiful finish — was delivered to your apartment, and you had a year to pay for it. Your instructor,

Price Is What You Pay for What You Get

Here are prices under various names:

- Tuition → Education.
- Interest → Use of money.
- Rent → Use of living quarters or a piece of equipment for a period of time.
- Fare → Taxi ride or airline flight.
- Fee → Services of an accountant or lawyer.
- Retainer → Lawyer's or consultant's services over a period of time.
- Toll → Long-distance phone call or travel on some highways.
- Salary → Services of an executive or other white-collar employee.
- Wage → Services of a blue-collar employee.
- Commission → Sales person's services.
- Dues → Membership in a union or a club.

And in socially undesirable situations, there are prices called blackmail, ransom, or bribery.

Source: Suggested in part by John T. Mentzer and David J. Schwartz, *Marketing Today*, 4th ed. (San Diego: Harcourt Brace Jovanovich, 1985), p. 599.

a do-it-yourself buff, bought a partially assembled desk with no finish on it. It had to be assembled and then stained and varnished. The seller provided neither delivery nor credit. Now who paid the higher price? The answer is not as easy as it first appeared.

This example indicates that the definition depends on determining exactly what is being sold. A seller usually is pricing a combination of (1) the specific product or service that is the object of the transaction, (2) several supplementary services (such as a warranty), and (3) in a very real sense, the want-satisfying benefits provided by the product. Sometimes it is difficult even to define the price of the predominant good or service itself. On one model of automobile, a stated price may include radio, power steering, and power brakes. For another model of the same brand of auto, these three items may be priced separately. So, to know the real price of a product, you need to look at the identifiable components that make up that product.

Also, it is often extremely difficult to determine what the actual price of a product or service is. How much does it cost to fly from Vancouver to Winnipeg on Air Canada? The answer will depend on many factors. You may find that a business person who has paid four or five times as much is seated next to a student who is visiting a friend in Winnipeg on a seat sale or stand-by ticket for which he or she has paid $249.

The price paid, therefore, will depend on circumstances; how much planning has gone into the purchase, how badly the customer needs the product, and how much he or she is prepared to put into the purchase: how much it is valued. If the business person absolutely has to attend a meeting in Winnipeg with a client, he or she may be prepared to pay a very high price. It all depends on how the customer is defining the value associated with the purchase.

Consider the case of CDs. This product is manufactured for roughly $2.50 and sold for anywhere from $14 to $25, depending on the product and the location of the vendor. The disc version of a recording costs roughly $4 more than the tape version. The price of this product has never come close to that of the vinyl album it replaced, which was anywhere from $8 to $12. Some consumer investigators who looked at this issue feel that it occurs because the consumer is willing to pay more. The music industry people say this is so because discs offer good value to the consumer.[2]

IMPORTANCE OF PRICE

Price is significant in our economy, to an individual firm, and in the consumer's mind. Let's consider each situation.[3]

"It seems like everybody's talking about price, when what really matters is value."

Kevin Stangeland, Ray Hueser, UFR Urban Forest Recyclers Inc.

UFR Urban Forest Recyclers Inc. Recycles paper products into molded fibre egg filler flats for customers throughout North America.

"We are not the lowest-price provider out there, and we don't want to be. We could make a cheaper product, but because of breakage, it'd end up costing our customers more. And costing us our customers. Having said that, there are more competitors entering the market every day, and we have to watch costs to keep our prices competitive. I admit, it's a bit of a juggling act."

Advantage Savings™ program and *Advantage Toll-free*™ service.

"Over the past year, Advantage has saved us over 55% on our long distance bill. And when you consider that most of our business is done with the U.S., that translates into some serious money – about $1200 a month. But in the end, it's not really about price, it's about value. It's about getting a solid, dependable product at a fair price. That's what we deliver, that's what Advantage delivers."

New solutions for business. From the new Bell.
1-888-783-1234

Bell deals with the question of the meaning of price in a competitive telecommunications environment by communicating what fair value means.

In the Economy

A product's price influences wages, rent, interest, and profits. Price is a basic regulator of the economic system because it influences the allocation of the factors of production. High wages attract labour, high interest rates attract capital, and so on. As an allocator of resources, price determines what will be produced (supply) and who will get the goods and services produced (demand).

Criticism of our system of reasonably free enterprise and, in turn, public demand for added restraints on the system are often triggered by negative reactions to prices or pricing policies. For example, concerns about rapidly rising prices (that is, inflation) may lead to a call for price controls. To reduce the risk of government intervention, businesses need to establish prices in a manner and at a level that consumers and government officials consider socially responsible.

In the Consumer's Mind

At the retail level, a small segment of shoppers is interested primarily in low prices. Another segment may be indifferent about price in making purchases. The majority of consumers are somewhat sensitive about price but are also concerned with other factors such as brand image, store location, quality, and value. Consumers' relative interest in price also can vary across demographic groups. Consumers with large families, single parents, and those on low incomes and/or fixed incomes are likely to be much more price sensitive. But even customers in these situations will, on occasion, be prepared to pay more to get what they consider better value.

Another consideration is that some consumers' perceptions of product quality varies directly with price.[4] Typically, the higher the price, the better the quality is perceived to be. Haven't you been concerned about product quality — such as when you are looking at ads for compact disc players — if the price is unexpectedly low? Or, at the other extreme, have you selected a restaurant for a special dinner because you heard it was fairly high priced, so you thought it would be very nice? Consumers' perceptions of quality are, of course, influenced by such other factors as store reputation, product colour or texture, advertising, or the nature of the service and sales encounter. Many consumers are prepared to pay more for good service.

Price is also important as a component of value. During the 1990s, more and more prospective buyers, in both consumer and business markets, have been demanding better value in the goods and services they purchase. Value is the ratio of perceived benefits to price and any other incurred costs. Time associated with shopping for the product, time and gasoline used in travelling to the place of purchase, and time and perhaps aggravation assembling the product are examples of these other incurred costs.

When we say a product has value, we don't necessarily mean it is inexpensive. Rather, good value indicates that a particular product has the kinds and amounts of potential benefits — such as product quality, image, and purchase convenience — that consumers expect from that product at a particular price level.

Many businesses are responding to consumers' calls for more value by devising new products and services. The intent is to improve value — essentially, the ratio of benefits to price. This can be accomplished by maintaining essential elements, adding a new element or two, dropping other elements to cut costs, and lowering prices.

Other businesses are striving for better value with existing products. Fast-food firms such as Harvey's and McDonald's have reduced prices on basic items by taking a "combination meals" approach, which bundles several items for a lower price than they would have if purchased separately. Industrial goods producers such as Asea Brown Boveri, makers of transformers and heavy equipment, have worked to increase quality and pare production costs. With lower costs, the urge to increase prices to maintain profits is lessened.

Attention to value is certainly heightened when an economy heads into a recession. However, don't expect concern about real value to dissipate even after a return to better times. According to market researchers, the increased emphasis on value reflects a more fundamental shift in consumer attitudes. At least in Canada and the United States, individuals, households, and organizations alike are now more interested in the ratio of benefits to price. This has created a new approach to pricing, not surprisingly called "value pricing," which we will discuss in Chapter 14.

In the Individual Firm

A product's price is an important determinant of the market demand for it. Price affects a firm's competitive position and its market share. But more than anything, price has a considerable bearing on a company's revenues and net profits. Through prices, money comes into an organization.

Some businesses use higher prices to convey an image of superior quality, but this would make sense only to consumers who consider quality to be important. Differentiated product features, a favourite brand, high quality, convenience, or some

www.randburg.com/no/asea.html

www.dupont.com/afs
www.sno.net/alcan
www.esso.ca

combination of these and other factors may be more important to consumers than price. As we saw in Chapter 11, one object of branding is to decrease the effect of price on the demand for a product.

Thus we see that prices are important to a company most of the time — but not always. To put the role of pricing in a company's marketing program in its proper perspective, it is only one of four marketing-mix elements that must be skilfully combined — and then adapted over time — to achieve business success.

PRICING OBJECTIVES

Every marketing activity — including pricing — should be directed toward a goal. Thus management should decide on its **pricing objective** before determining the price itself. Yet, as logical as this may sound, few firms consciously establish, or explicitly state, a pricing objective.[5]

To be useful, the pricing objective that management selects must be compatible with the overall goals set by the company and the goals for its marketing program. Let's assume that a company's goal is to increase return on investment from its present level of 15 percent to 20 percent within three years. It follows that the pricing goal during this period must be to achieve some stated percentage return on investment. It would not be logical, in this case, to adopt the pricing goal of maintaining the company's market share or of stabilizing prices. We shall discuss the following pricing objectives:

- Profit-oriented:
  - To achieve a target return.
  - To maximize profit.
- Sales-oriented:
  - To increase sales volume.
  - To maintain or increase market share.
- Status quo-oriented:
  - To stabilize prices.
  - To meet competition.

Recognize that all these objectives can be sought — and, it is to be hoped, attained — not just through pricing but also through other marketing activities such as product design and distribution channels. All these objectives are ultimately aimed at satisfactory performance over the long run. For a business, that requires ample profits.

Profit-Oriented Goals

Profit goals may be set for the short or long run. A company may select one of two profit-oriented goals for its pricing policy.

Achieve a Target Return A firm may price its product to **achieve a target return** — a specified percentage return on its sales or on its investment. Many retailers and wholesalers use a target return on sales as a pricing objective for short periods such as a year or a fashion season. They add an amount to the cost of the product, called a **markup**, to cover anticipated operating expenses and provide a desired profit for the period. Safeway or Loblaws, for example, may price to earn a net profit of 1.5 percent on a store's sales. A chain of men's clothing stores may have a target profit of 7 percent of sales, and price its products accordingly.

Achieving a target return on investment is measured in relation to a firm's net worth (its assets minus its liabilities). This pricing goal is often selected by the leading firm in an industry. Target-return pricing is used by industry leaders such as Du Pont, Alcan, and Esso because they can set their pricing goals more independently of competition than can smaller firms in the industry. The leaders may price so that they earn a net profit that is 15 or 20 percent of the firm's net worth.

Maximize Profits The pricing objective of making as much money as possible — using a "what the market will bear" approach — is probably followed more than any other goal. The trouble with this goal is that to some people, **profit maximization** has an ugly connotation, suggesting profiteering, high prices, and monopoly.

In both economic theory and business practice, and for most of us in pricing our own time, there is nothing wrong with profit maximization. Theoretically, if profits become high in an industry because supply is short in relation to demand, new capital will be attracted to increase production capacity. This will increase supply and eventually reduce profits to normal levels. In the marketplace where there is real competition, it is difficult to find many situations where profiteering has existed over an extended period of time. Substitute products are available, purchases are postponable, and competition can increase to keep prices at a reasonable level.

When prices are unduly high and entry into the field is severely limited, public outrage often is seen. For example, British Columbia hospitals have strongly objected to the price of Activase, a blood thinning drug used after heart attacks. The drug manufacturer, Hoffman La Roche, charges $2,700 a dose for this drug. This drug is generally considered the best "clot-buster" drug on the market, and hospitals want to be able to use it. The matter is being considered by the Patent Medicine Prices Review Board, which controls the prices of many medications in Canada.[6] If market conditions and public opinion do not bring about reasonable prices, agencies such as the review board are often set up to ensure equitable controls.

The goal should be to maximize profits on total output rather than on each single product. In fact, a company may maximize total profit by setting low, relatively unprofitable prices on some products in order to stimulate sales of others. In its advertising on televised athletic events, the Gillette Company frequently promotes razors at very low prices. The firm hopes that once customers acquire Gillette razors, they will become loyal customers for Gillette blades, which generate healthy profits for the company.

Sales-Oriented Goals

In some companies, management's pricing is focused on sales volume. The pricing goal may be to increase sales volume or to maintain or increase the firm's market share.

Increase Sales Volume The pricing goal of **increasing sales volume** is typically adopted to achieve rapid growth or to discourage potential competitors from entering a market. The goal is usually stated as a percentage increase in sales volume over some period, say, one year or three years. Management may seek higher sales volume by discounting or by some other aggressive pricing strategy, perhaps even incurring a loss in the short run. Thus, clothing stores run end-of-season sales, and auto dealers offer rebates and below-market financing rates on new cars to stimulate sales. Many vacation spots, such as golf courses and resorts, reduce prices during off-seasons to increase sales volume.

Maintain or Increase Market Share In some companies, both large and small, the pricing objective is to **maintain or increase market share**. Why is market share protected or pursued so vigorously? In growing fields such as computers, information technology, and communications, companies want large shares in order to gain leverage with vendors and to aid in driving down production and other costs that are sensitive to economies of scale.

Most other industries today are not growing much, if at all, and, if they have not yet rationalized their operations, have excess production and operations capacity. Since the size of the "pie" isn't growing in most cases, businesses that need added volume have to grab a bigger "slice of the pie" — that is, greater market share. The North American auto and airline industries illustrate these situations.

Other firms are intent on maintaining their market shares. For instance, when global organizations face currency fluctuations that result in price increases in various national markets, they must react if there is competition. When the Japanese yen rose considerably in relation to the Canadian and U.S. dollars, Japanese products — autos, for example — became more expensive in dollars and Japanese companies faced the prospect of losing market share. To maintain their shares, Toyota, Nissan, and Honda accepted smaller profit margins and reduced their costs so that they could lower their selling prices.

Status Quo Goals

Two closely related goals — **stabilizing prices** and **meeting competition** — are the least aggressive of all pricing goals. They are intended simply to maintain the firm's current situation — the status quo. With either of these goals, a firm seeks to avoid price competition.

Price stabilization often is the goal in industries in which the product is highly standardized (such as lumber products or bulk chemicals) and in which

MARKETING AT WORK FILE 13-1

RE-INTRODUCING OTTAWA TO THE NEW *CITIZEN*

The Ottawa *Citizen*, owned by Southam Inc., which in turn is controlled by Conrad Black's Hollinger Corporation, has been relaunched. In 1996, 5.2 million papers were sold daily in Canada — one for every 2.2 households, a decline of 2.2 percent from 1995. With the relaunch of the *Citizen* in early 1997, the national trend is being bucked in Ottawa, with daily circulation now on the increase — from 140,441 in February 1997 to 145,841 in May.

How is all of this happening? By improving product quality: The *Citizen* has increased its editorial staff by ten and its editorial budget by $2 million, runs six pages fatter than in 1996, has more business information, more national and international news, a bigger Sunday edition, and a revamped magazine. Experts see its upgrading as similar to what is occuring at the *Globe and Mail* — which is increasingly tailoring its product for a well-educated, high-income national audience. The new *Citizen* is now seen as a higher-quality newspaper than in the past. Readers seem to appreciate it in greater numbers, and, hopefully, so will advertisers.

What has happened to the *Citizen* in Ottawa has also happened to the Montreal *Gazette*, the *Daily Telegraph* in the United Kingdom, the *Times of London*, the *Los Angeles Times*, and the *Denver Post*. According to industry experts, each one has had its quality increased, the first two by Conrad Black's companies.

Now comes the question of consumer-perceived changes in value. There is one sure way of achieving a consumer-perceived increase and that is with an initial low-price policy. The *Los Angeles Times*, in its revamping, introduced just such a policy by cutting the daily cover price from 50 to 25 cents. Even if there were little or no increase in quality, the low-price policy should yield an increase in value. *Los Angeles Times* circulation increases demonstrate quite nicely that increasing quality and decreasing price can increase consumer-perceived value and sales quite rapidly. The *Times of London* used a similar approach — increasing quality, lowering price — and thereby increasing circulation. It did this in the face of the increased quality competition of Conrad Black's *Daily Telegraph*, which, unhappily, had to lower its cover price to meet the *Times*'s strong value challenge.

Should the Ottawa *Citizen*'s cover price be lowered? While readership may increase, what could happen to profits? At what point, if at all, should a low-initial-price policy be changed? Could changes in market share have anything to do with an answer?

Source: Adapted, in part, from Brenda Dalglish, "Southam Finds Serious Stuff Sells Papers," *The Financial Post*, July 4, 1997, p. 7. Reprinted with permission.

one large firm historically has acted as a leader in setting prices. Smaller firms in these industries tend to "follow the leader" when setting their prices. What is the reason for such pricing behaviour? A price cut by any one firm is likely to be matched by all other firms in order to remain competitive; therefore, no individual firm gains, but all may suffer smaller profits. Conversely, a price boost is unlikely to be matched, but the price-changing firm faces a differential disadvantage because other elements of a standardized product, such as gasoline, are perceived to be fairly similar.

Even in industries in which there are no price leaders, countless firms deliberately price their products

www.ottawacitizen.com
www.theglobeandmail.com
www.montrealgazette.com
www.telegraph.co.uk/home.html
www.the-times.co.uk
www.latimes.com
www.denverpost.com

to meet the prevailing market price. This pricing policy gives management an easy means of avoiding difficult pricing decisions.

Firms that adopt status quo pricing goals to avoid price competition are not necessarily passive in their marketing. Quite the contrary! Typically these companies compete aggressively using other marketing-mix elements — product, distribution, and especially promotion. This approach is called nonprice competition, and its objective is to provide the customer with other reasons for buying the firm's products or services.

FACTORS INFLUENCING PRICE DETERMINATION

Knowing the objective of its pricing, a company then can move to the heart of price management: determining the base price of a product. **Base price**, or list price, refers to the price of one unit of the product or service at its point of production, resale, or delivery. This price does not reflect discounts or special allowances, delivery or freight charges, or any other modifications (discussed in the next chapter), such as leader pricing and value pricing.

The same procedure is followed in pricing both new and established products. Pricing an established product usually is less difficult than pricing a new product, however, because the exact price or a narrow range of prices may be dictated by the market. Other factors, besides objectives, that influence price determination are discussed next.

Estimated Demand

In pricing, a company must estimate the total demand for the product. This is easier to do for an established product than for a new one. The steps in estimating demand are (1) determine whether there is a price the market expects and (2) estimate what the sales volume might be at different prices.

The **expected price** of a product is the price at which customers consciously or unconsciously value it — what they think the product is worth. Expected price usually is expressed as a **range of prices** rather than as a specific amount. Thus the expected price might be "between $250 and $300" or "not over $20."

A producer must also consider an intermediary's reaction to price. Intermediaries are more likely to promote a product if they approve of its price. Sometimes they don't approve, as Wal-Mart did not when Rubbermaid attempted to raise its prices on housewares not long ago. Rubbermaid was faced with a substantial cost increase for resin, a major ingredient in its housewares and toys. But since Wal-Mart was such an important reseller, Rubbermaid settled for a smaller increase (which hurt its profits) than it had originally planned for, thereby resulting in lower profits.

It's possible to set a price too low. If the price is much lower than what the market expects, sales may be lost. For example, it probably would be a mistake for L'Oreal, a well-known cosmetics maker, to put a $1.49 price tag on its lipstick or to price its imported perfume at $3.49 for 3 mL. In all likelihood, customers would be suspicious about product quality or their self-concept would not let them buy such low-priced products.

After raising a product's price, some organizations have experienced a considerable increase in sales. This situation is called **inverse demand** — the higher the price, the greater the unit sales. Inverse demand usually exists only within a given price range and only at low price levels. At some point inverse demand ends and the usual pattern — demand declines as prices rise — becomes evident.

How do sellers determine expected prices? They may submit products to experienced retailers or wholesalers for appraisal. A business-goods manufacturer might get price estimates by showing models or blueprints to engineers working for prospective customers. Another alternative is to ask a sample of consumers what they would expect to pay for the product or which item in a list of alternatives is most similar to the test product. Using such methods, a seller can determine a reasonable range of prices.

It is extremely helpful to estimate what the sales volume will be at several different prices. By doing this, the seller is, in effect, determining the demand curve for the product. Moreover, the seller is gauging **price elasticity of demand**, which refers to the responsiveness of quantity demanded to price changes. Estimates of sales at different prices also are useful in determining break-even points (we'll get to this topic shortly).

www.rubbermaid.com

Sellers can choose from several methods to estimate sales at various prices. Recall some of the demand-forecasting methods discussed in Chapter 5 — survey of buyer intentions, test marketing, and sales-force composite, for example. These methods can be used in this situation as well.

Competitive Reactions

Competition greatly influences base price. A new product is distinctive only until the inevitable arrival of competition. The threat of potential competition is greatest when the field is easy to enter and profit prospects are encouraging. Competition can come from these sources:

- *Directly similar products:* Nike versus Adidas or Reebok running shoes.
- *Available substitutes:* Air freight versus truck shipping or rail freight.
- *Unrelated products seeking the same consumer dollar:* Videocassette recorder (VCR) versus a bicycle or a weekend excursion.

In the case of directly similar products, a competitor may adjust its prices. In turn, other firms have to decide what price adjustments, if any, are necessary to retain their customers.

Other Marketing-Mix Elements

A product's base price is influenced considerably by the other ingredients in the marketing mix.

Product We have already observed that a product's price is affected by whether it is a new item or an established one. Over the course of the life of a product — its life cycle — price changes are necessary to keep the product competitive. The end use of the product must also be considered. For instance, there is little price competition among manufacturers of packaging materials or producers of industrial gases, so their price structure is stable. These business products are only an incidental part of the final article, so customers will buy the least expensive product consistent with the required quality. The price of a product is also influenced by whether (1) the product may be leased as well as purchased outright, (2) the product may be returned to the seller, and (3) a trade-in is involved.

The pricing of services is somewhat more difficult in that the customer has little or no opportunity to examine the service before buying. In many service industries, the "product" being sold is the expertise and experience of the employees of the firm. Thus a law firm may charge clients $400 per hour for the time that the senior partner spends on a file, but only $100 per hour for a junior lawyer.

Distribution Channels The channels and types of intermediaries selected will influence a producer's pricing. A firm selling both through wholesalers and directly to retailers often sets a different factory price for these two classes of customers. The price to wholesalers is lower because they perform services that the producer would have to perform — such as providing storage, granting credit to retailers, and selling to small retailers.

Also, in some cases, a more direct distribution channel may allow a firm to charge higher prices because customers are generally prepared to pay more for convenience and speedy delivery. The ING Direct example, which opened this chapter, is a good illustration of how a firm can pass on cost savings to customers because of a major change in its distribution channel.

Promotion The extent to which the product is promoted by the producer or intermediaries and the methods used are added considerations in pricing. If major promotional responsibility is placed on retailers, they ordinarily will be charged a lower price for a product than if the producer advertises it heavily. Even when a producer promotes heavily, it may want its retailers to use local advertising to tie in with national advertising. Such a decision must be reflected in the producer's price to these retailers.

Cost of a Product

The pricing of a product also should consider its cost. A product's total unit cost is made up of several types of costs, each reacting differently to changes in the quantity produced.

The cost concepts in the box "Various Kinds of Costs" are fundamental to our discussion of pricing. These concepts and their interrelationships are illustrated in Table 13-1 and Figure 13-1. The interrelationship among the various average costs per unit from the table is displayed graphically in the figure. It may be explained briefly as follows:

www.adidas.com • www.reebok.com

The **average fixed cost curve** declines as output increases, because the total of the fixed costs is spread over an increasing number of units.

The **average variable cost curve** usually is U-shaped. It starts high because average variable costs for the first few units of output are high. Variable costs per unit then decline as the company realizes efficiencies in production. Eventually the average variable cost curve reaches its lowest point, reflecting optimum output with respect to variable costs (not total costs). In Figure 13-1 this point is at three units of output. Beyond that point the average variable cost rises, reflecting the increase in unit variable costs caused by overcrowded facilities and other inefficiencies. If the variable costs per unit were constant, then the average variable cost curve would be a horizontal line at the level of the constant unit variable cost.

The **average total cost curve** is the sum of the first two curves — average fixed cost and average variable cost. It starts high, reflecting the fact that total fixed costs are spread over so few units of output. As output increases, the average total cost curve declines because unit fixed cost and unit variable cost are decreasing. Eventually the point of lowest total cost per unit is reached (four units of output in the figure). Beyond that optimum point, diminishing returns set in and average total cost rises.

The **marginal cost curve** has a more pronounced U-shape than the other curves in Figure 13-1. The marginal cost curve slopes downward until the second unit of output, at which point the marginal costs start to increase.

Various Kinds of Cost

- A **fixed cost**, such as rent, executive salaries, or property tax, remains constant regardless of how many items are produced. Such a cost continues even if production stops completely. It is called a fixed cost because it is difficult to change in the short run (but not in the long run).
- **Total fixed cost** is the sum of all fixed costs.
- **Average fixed cost** is the total fixed cost divided by the number of units produced.
- A **variable cost**, such as labour or materials, is directly related to production. Variable costs can be controlled in the short run simply by changing the level of production. When production stops, for example, all variable production costs become zero.
- **Total variable cost** is the sum of all variable costs. The more units produced, the higher is this cost.
- **Average variable cost** is the total variable cost divided by the number of units produced. Average variable cost is usually high for the first few units produced. It decreases as production increases, due to such things as quantity discounts on materials and more efficient use of labour. Beyond some optimum output, it increases due to such factors as crowding of production facilities and overtime pay.
- **Total cost** is the sum of total fixed cost and total variable cost for a specific quantity produced.
- **Average total cost** is total cost divided by number of units produced.
- **Marginal cost** is the cost of producing and selling one more unit. Usually the marginal cost of the last unit is the same as that unit's variable cost.

FIGURE 13-1

Unit Cost Curves for an Individual Firm

This figure is based on data in Table 13-1. Here we see how unit costs change as quantity increases. Using cost-plus pricing, two units of output would be priced at $184 each, whereas four units would sell for $120 each.

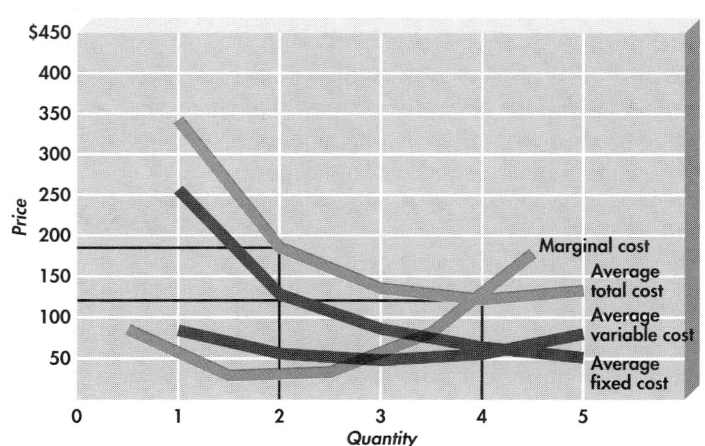

TABLE 13-1 An Example of Costs for an Individual Firm

Total fixed costs do not change in the short run, despite increases in quantity produced. Variable costs are the costs of inputs — materials and labour, for example. Total variable costs increase as production quantity rises. Total cost is the sum of all fixed and variable costs. The other measures in the table are simply methods of looking at costs per unit; they always involve dividing a cost by the number of units produced

(1) Quantity produced	(2) Total fixed costs	(3) Total variable costs	(4) Total costs (2) + (3)	(5) Marginal costs per unit	(6) Average fixed costs (2) ÷ (1)	(7) Average variable costs (3) ÷ (1)	(8) Average total costs (4) ÷ (1)
0	$256	$ 0	$256		Infinity	Infinity	Infinity
1	$256	84	340	$ 84	$256.00	$84	$340.00
2	$256	112	368	28	128.00	56	184.00
3	$256	144	400	32	85.33	48	133.33
4	$256	224	480	80	64.00	56	120.00
5	$256	400	656	176	51.20	80	131.20

Note the relationship between the marginal cost curve and the average total cost curve. The average total cost curve slopes downward as long as the marginal cost is less than the average total cost. Even though marginal cost increases after the second unit, the average total cost curve continues to slope downward until the fourth unit. This occurs because marginal cost — even when going up — is still less than average total cost.

The two curves — marginal cost and average total cost — intersect at the lowest point of the average total cost curve. Beyond that point (the fourth unit in the example), the cost of producing and selling the next unit is higher than the average cost of all units. The data in Table 13-1 show that producing the fifth unit reduces the average fixed cost by $12.80 (from $64 to $51.20), but causes the average variable cost to increase by $24. From then on, therefore, the average total cost rises. This occurs because the average variable cost is increasing faster than the average fixed cost is decreasing.

COST-PLUS PRICING

We now are at the point in price determination to talk about setting a specific selling price. Most companies establish their prices using one of the following methods:

- Prices are based on total cost plus a desired profit. (Break-even analysis is a variation of this method.)
- Prices are based on marginal analysis — a consideration of both market demand and supply.
- Prices are based only on competitive market conditions.

According to a survey that examined what approaches are used to price new as opposed to existing products:

- 9 percent of companies "guesstimate" what the base price for a new product should be.
- 37 percent match what competitors charge for similar items.
- 50 percent of firms charge what the market will bear.
- 52 percent, the most common approach, choose a price to cover costs and provide a fair profit.
- Since this totals 148 per cent, its clear that most firms use more than one approach — an important factor to keep in mind.[7]

Let's first discuss **cost-plus pricing**, which means setting the price of one unit of a product equal to the total cost of the unit plus the desired profit on the unit. Suppose that King's Kastles, a contractor, figures the labour and materials required to build and sell ten condominiums will cost $750,000, and other expenses (office rent, depreciation on equipment, management salaries, and so on) will be $150,000. The contractor wants to earn a profit of 10 percent on the total cost of $900,000. Cost plus desired profit is $990,000, so each of the 10 condos is priced at $99,000.

While it is an easily applied method, cost-plus pricing has limitations. One is that it does not recognize various types of costs or the fact that these costs are affected differently by changes in level of output. In our housing example, suppose that King's Kastles built and sold only eight condos at the cost-plus price of $99,000 each. As shown in Table 13-2, total sales would then be $792,000. Labour and materials chargeable to the eight condos would total $600,000 ($75,000 per house). Since the contractor would still incur the full $150,000 in overhead expenses, the total cost would be $750,000. This would leave a profit of only $42,000, or $5,250 per condominium instead of the anticipated $9,000. On a percentage basis, profit would be only 5.6 percent of total cost rather than the desired 10 percent.

A second limitation of this pricing approach is that market demand is ignored. That is, cost-plus pricing assumes that all the output will be produced and sold. If fewer units are produced, each would have to sell for a higher price to cover all costs and show a profit. But if business is slack and output must be cut, it is not wise to raise the unit price. Another limitation of this method is that is doesn't recognize that total unit cost changes as output expands or contracts. However, a more sophisticated approach to cost-plus pricing can take such changes into consideration.

Prices Based on Marginal Costs Only

Another approach to cost-plus pricing is to set **prices based on marginal costs only**, not total costs. Refer again to the cost schedules shown in Table 13-1 and Figure 13-1, and assume that a firm is operating at an output level of three units. Under marginal cost pricing, this firm could accept an order for one more unit at $80 or above, instead of the total unit cost of $120. The revenue from a unit sold at $80 would cover its variable costs. However, if the firm can sell for a price above $80 — say, $85 or $90 — the excess contributes to the payment of fixed costs.

Not all orders can be priced to cover only variable costs. Marginal cost pricing may be feasible, however, if management wants to keep its labour force employed during a slack season. It may also be used when one product is expected to attract business for another. Thus a department store may price meals in its café at a level that covers only the marginal costs. The reasoning is that this café will bring shoppers to the store, where they will buy other, more profitable products.

TABLE 13-2 King's Kastles: An Example of Cost-Plus Pricing

Actual results often differ from planned outcomes because various types of costs react differently to changes in output.

King's Kastles costs, selling price, and profit	Number of condominiums built and sold by King's Kastles: Planned = 10	Actual = 8
Labour and materials costs ($75,000 per condo)	$750,000	$600,000
Overhead (fixed) costs	150,000	150,000
Total costs	$900,000	$750,000
Total sales at $99,000 per condo	990,000	792,000
Profit: Total	$ 90,000	$ 42,000
Profit: Per condo	$ 9,000	$ 5,250
Profit: As percent of cost	10%	5.6%

Should the builder use the cost-plus method when pricing these condominiums?

Pricing by Middlemen

At first glance, cost-plus pricing appears to be widely used by retailing and wholesaling intermediaries. A retailer, for example, pays a given amount to buy products and have them delivered to the store. Then the retailer adds an amount, called a markup, to the acquisition cost. This markup is estimated to be sufficient to cover the store's expenses and provide a reasonable profit. Thus a building-materials outlet may buy a power drill for $30 including freight, and price the item at $50. The $50 price reflects a markup of 40 percent based on the selling price, or $66\frac{2}{3}$ percent based on the merchandise cost. Of course, in setting prices, intermediaries also should take into account the expectations of their customers.

Various types of retailers require different percentage markups because of the nature of the products handled and the services offered. A self-service supermarket has lower costs and thus can have a lower average markup than a full-service delicatessen. Figure 13-2 shows examples of markup pricing by intermediaries.

Is cost-plus pricing really used by intermediaries? For the following reasons, it's safe to say that cost-plus pricing is not widely used:

- *Most retail prices are really only offers.* If customers accept the offer, the price is fine. If they reject it, the price usually will be changed quickly, or the product may even be withdrawn from the market. Prices thus are always on trial.
- *Many retailers don't use the same markup on all the products they carry.* A supermarket will have a markup of 6 to 8 percent on sugar and soap products,

FIGURE 13-2 Examples of Markup Pricing by Retailers and Wholesalers

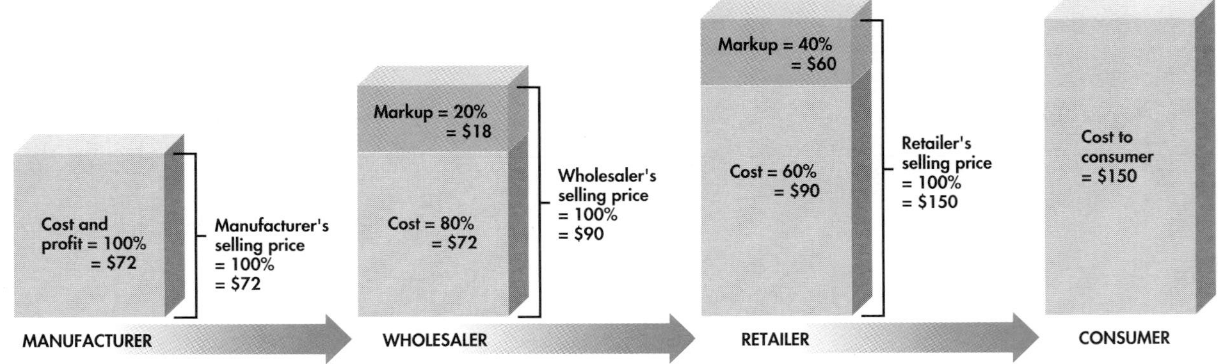

15 to 18 percent on canned fruit and vegetables, and 25 to 30 percent on fresh meats and produce. These different markups for distinctive products reflect competitive considerations and other aspects of market demand.

- The middleman usually doesn't actually set a base price but only adds a percentage to the price already set by the producer. The producer's price is set to allow each middleman to add a reasonable markup and still sell at a competitive retail price. The key price is set by the producer, with an eye on the final market.

Thus what seems to be cost-plus pricing by intermediaries is usually market-influenced pricing.

Evaluation of Cost-Plus Pricing

Since a firm should be market-oriented and cater to consumers' wants, why are we considering cost-plus pricing? Simply, cost-plus pricing must be understood because it is referred to often in business. Further, it is used by numerous industrial firms.[8]

The traditional perspective has been that costs should be a determinant of prices, but not the only one. Costs are a floor under a firm's prices. If goods are priced under this floor for a long time, the firm will be forced out of business. But when it is used by itself, cost-plus pricing is a weak and unrealistic method because it ignores competition and market demand.

In recent years, with low rates of inflation in our economy as well as in the United States, a consumer-oriented concept that price should determine costs has received great emphasis. Firms using this market-based perspective must re-engineer their production and operating systems to reduce costs wherever possible. The appropriate conclusion is that used by itself, cost-plus pricing is a weak and unrealistic method because it ignores market conditions, notably demand and competition.

BREAK-EVEN ANALYSIS

One way to consider both market demand and costs in price determination is to use **break-even analysis** to calculate break-even points. A break-even point is that quantity of output at which total revenue equals total costs, assuming a certain selling price. There is a different **break-even point** for each different selling price. Sales exceeding the break-even point result in a profit on each additional unit. The higher sales are above the break-even point, the higher will be the total and unit profits. Sales below the break-even point result in a loss to the seller.

Determining the Break-Even Point

The method of determining a break-even point is illustrated in Table 13-3 and Figure 13-3. In our example, the Futon Factory's fixed costs are $25,000 and variable costs are constant at $30 per unit. Recall that in our earlier example (Table 13-1 and Figure 13-1), we assumed that unit variable costs are not constant but fluctuate. To simplify our break-even analysis, we now assume that variable costs are constant.

TABLE 13-3 Futon Factory: Computation of Break-even Point

At each of several prices, we wish to find out how many units must be sold to cover all costs. At a unit price of $100, the sale of each unit contributes $70 to cover overhead expenses. The Futon Factory must sell about 357 units to cover its $25,000 in fixed costs. See Figure 13-4 for a depiction of the data in this table.

(1) Unit price	(2) Unit variable costs	(3) Contribution to overhead (1) − (2)	(4) Overhead (total fixed costs)	(5) Break-even point (rounded) (4) ÷ (3)
$60	$30	$30	$25,000	833 units
80	30	50	$25,000	500 units
100	30	70	$25,000	357 units
150	30	120	$25,000	208 units

FIGURE 13-3 Break-Even Chart for the Futon Factory with an $80 Selling Price

Here the break-even point is reached when the company sells 500 units. Fixed costs, regardless of quantity produced and sold, are $25,000. The variable cost per unit is $30. If this company sells 500 units, total costs are $40,000 (variable cost of 500 X $30, or $15,000, plus fixed costs of $25,000). At a selling price of $80, the sale of 500 units will yield $40,000 revenue, and costs and revenue will equal each other. At the same price, the sale of each unit above 500 will yield a profit.

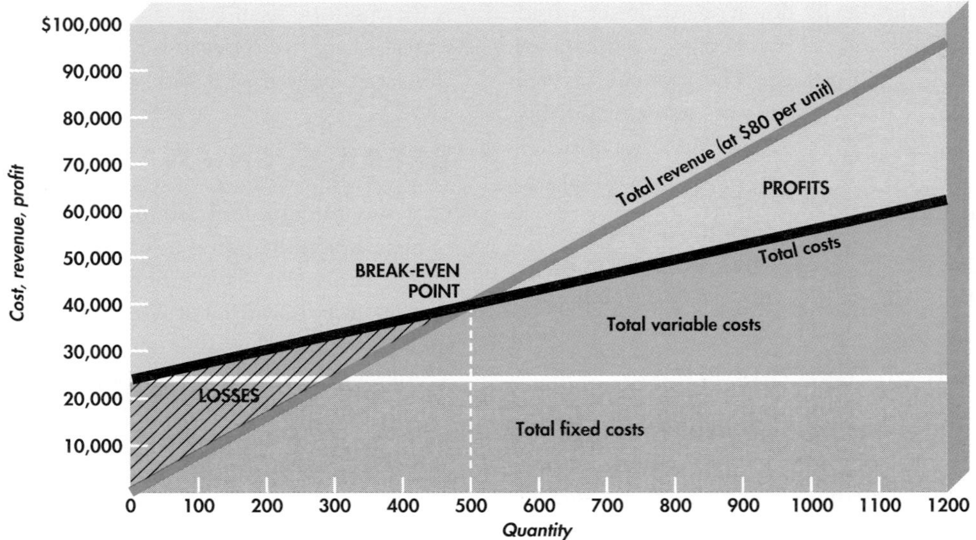

The total cost of producing one unit is $25,300 — the Futon Factory obviously needs more volume to absorb its fixed costs! For 400 units the total cost is $37,000 ($30 multiplied by 400, plus $25,000). In Figure 13-3 the selling price is $80 a unit, and variable costs of $30 per unit are incurred in producing each unit. Consequently, any revenue over $30 contributes to covering fixed costs (sometimes termed overhead). When the price is $80, that would be $50 per unit. At a price of $80, the break-even point is 500 units, because a $50 per-unit contribution will just cover overhead of $25,000.

Stated another way, variable costs for 500 units are $15,000 and fixed costs are $25,000, for a total cost of $40,000. This amount equals the revenue from 500 units sold at $80 each. So, at an $80 selling price, the break-even volume is 500 units. Figure 13-3 shows a break-even point for an $80 price, but it is highly desirable to calculate break-even points for several different selling prices.

The break-even point may be found with this formula:

$$\text{Break-even point in units} = \frac{\text{total fixed costs}}{\text{unit contribution to overhead}}$$

Because unit contribution to overhead equals selling price less the average variable cost, the working formula becomes:

$$\text{Break-even point in units} = \frac{\text{total fixed costs}}{\text{selling price} - \text{average variable cost}}$$

Two basic assumptions underlie these calculations:

- Total fixed costs are constant. In reality they may change, although usually not in the short run.
- Variable costs remain constant per unit of output. Actually, average variable costs usually fluctuate.

Evaluation of Break-Even Analysis

Two basic assumptions underlie break-even analysis: total fixed costs are constant; variable costs remain constant per unit of output. Actually, fixed costs may change, although not rapidly, and average variable costs normally fluctuate. Therefore, break-even analysis cannot be used conclusively in most companies. But it does provide some guidance.

TABLE 13-4 Limos for Lease: Demand Schedule for an Individual Firm

At each market price a certain quantity of the product — in this example, a two-hour rental of a limousine on a weekend night — will be demanded. Marginal revenue is simply the amount of additional money gained by selling one more unit. Limos for Lease gains no additional marginal revenue after it has rented its fourth limo at a price of $53.

Units sold (limos leased)	Unit price (average revenue)	Total revenue	Marginal revenue
1	$80	$ 80	
2	72	144	$64
3	63	189	45
4	53	212	23
5	42	210	−2
6	34	204	−6

Another drawback of break-even analysis is that it cannot tell us whether we can actually sell the break-even amount. Table 13-3, for example, shows what revenue will be at the different prices if the given number of units can be sold at these prices. The number the market will buy at a given price could well be below the break-even point. If that happens, the firm will not break even — it will show a loss.

Despite these limitations, management should not dismiss break-even analysis as a pricing tool. Even in its simplest form, break-even analysis is helpful because in the short run many firms experience reasonably stable cost and demand structures.[9]

PRICES BASED ON MARGINAL ANALYSIS

Another pricing method, marginal analysis, also takes account of both demand and costs to determine the best price for profit maximization. Firms with other pricing goals might use **prices based on marginal analysis** to compare prices determined by different means.

Determining the Price

To use marginal analysis, the price setter must understand the concepts of average and marginal revenue as well as average and marginal cost. **Marginal revenue** is the income derived from the sale of the last unit. **Average revenue** is the unit price at a given level of unit sales; it is calculated by dividing total revenue by the number of units sold.

Referring to the hypothetical demand schedule in Table 13-4, we see that Limos for Lease can sell one unit (that is, lease one limousine for a two-hour period on a weekend night) at $80. To attract a second customer and thereby lease two limos on the same night, it must reduce its price to $72 for each unit. Thus the company receives an additional $64 (marginal revenue) by selling a second unit. After the fourth unit, total revenue declines each time the unit price is lowered in order to sell an additional unit. Hence, there is a negative marginal revenue.

Marginal analysis is illustrated in Figure 13-4. We assume that a company — a services firm like Limos for Lease or a manufacturer — will continue to produce and sell its product as long as revenue from the last unit sold exceeds the cost of producing this last unit. That is, output continues to increase as long as marginal revenue exceeds marginal cost. At the point where they meet, production theoretically should cease. Ordinarily a company will not want to sell a unit at a price less than its out-of-pocket (variable) costs of producing a good or a service. The optimum volume of output is the quantity level at which marginal cost equals marginal revenue, or quantity Q in Figure 13-4a.

Thus the unit price is determined by locating the point on the average revenue curve that represents an output of quantity Q — the level at which marginal cost equals marginal revenue. Remember that average revenue represents the unit price. Referring to Figure 13-4b, in which the average revenue curve has been

FIGURE 13-4 **Price Setting and Profit Maximization Through Marginal Analysis**

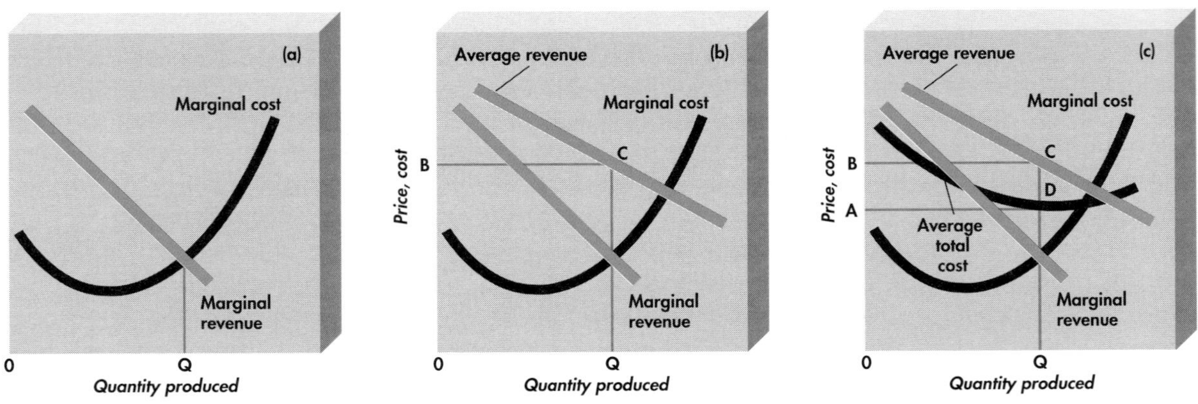

added, the unit price at which to sell quantity Q is represented by point C — that is, price B.

The average total cost curve has been added in Figure 13-4c. It shows that, for output quantity Q, the average unit cost is represented by point D — that is, unit cost A. Thus, with a price of B and an average unit cost of A, the company enjoys a unit profit given by B minus A in the figure. Total profit is quantity Q times the unit profit.

Evaluation of Marginal Analysis Pricing

Marginal analysis is not used often as a basis for price setting. According to business people, it can be used to study past price movements. However, many managers think that marginal analysis cannot serve as a practical basis for setting prices unless accurate, reliable data can be obtained for plotting the curves.

On the brighter side, management's knowledge of costs and demand is improving. Computerized data bases are bringing more complete and detailed information to management's attention all the time. And experienced management in many firms can do a fairly accurate job of estimating marginal and average costs and revenues.

PRICES SET IN RELATION TO MARKET ALONE

Cost-plus pricing is one extreme among pricing methods. At the other extreme are methods in which a firm's prices are set in relation only to the market price. The seller's price may be set right at the market price to meet the competition, or it may be set above or below the market price.

Pricing to Meet Competition

Pricing to meet competition is simple to carry out. A firm ascertains what the market price is and, after allowing for customary markups for intermediaries, arrives at its own selling price. To illustrate, a manufacturer of women's shoes knows that retailers want to sell the shoes for $70 a pair. The firm sells directly to retailers who want an average markup of 40 percent of their selling price. Consequently, after allowing $28 for the retailer's markup, the producer's price is $42. This manufacturer then has to decide whether $42 is enough to cover costs and provide a reasonable profit. Sometimes a producer faces a real squeeze if costs are rising but the market price is holding firm.

One situation in which management might price a product right at the market level is when competition is keen and the firm's product is not differentiated significantly from competing products. To some extent, this pricing method reflects the market conditions of **perfect competition**. That is, product differentiation is absent, buyers and sellers are well informed, and the seller has no discernible control over the selling price. Most producers of agricultural products and small firms marketing well-known, standardized products use this pricing method.

The sharp drop in revenue occurring when the price is raised above the prevailing market level indicates that the individual seller faces a **kinked demand**

MARKETING AT WORK FILE 13-2

AS THE MODEL YEAR CHANGES, SO DOES THE PRICING!

Pricing policies used in the automobile industry are not simple. General Motors of Canada, the market leader, with about one-third of the Canadian market, raised model-year total product-line base prices for 1997 by 3.9 percent and for 1998 by 2.5 percent. The 2.5 percent may not seem like very much, but within the industry it is viewed as quite aggressive, especially for GM Canada. Auto-trade experts anticipate Japan-based auto makers will undercut the 1998 model year prices just as they did those for 1997. While GM normally increases prices at the beginning of the calendar year as well as during the spring selling season when demand is high, for 1997 this was not done.

Make and model price increases varied from zero to 4.5 percent. Price increases on models carrying the same standard equipment as 1997 vehicles ranged from 1.5 percent on one version of the compact Chevrolet Cavalier to 4.5 percent on one of the Chevrolet Blazer/GMC Jimmy compact sport utility vehicles. Prices on one line, the Chevrolet Astro minivan, were not changed. It would appear that these increases are not unrelated to the market conditions GM Canada faces, in the sense that demand for compact sport utility vehicles is quite strong; compact demand is reasonable, but for the minivan, demand is weakening.

GM Canada spokesman, Greg Gibson, attributes the price increases to foreign-exchange considerations, safety enhancements such as depowered airbags, the addition of passenger side airbags to some models (the Blazer/Jimmy), and the improvement of emission systems. All of these represent additions to costs.

Nissan Motor Co., rather than increasing prices consistent with GM, announced significant price cuts for the newly redesigned Altima sedan 1998 model year and promises more. Industry analyst and consultant Dennis DesRosiers expressed some disappointment with the increases. GM Canada and its parent have been reducing costs by working with suppliers to reduce input prices, re-engineering their operations so that they are more efficient, and redesigning their vehicles so that they take less time to assemble and use fewer parts. Mr. DesRosiers said, "I'm waiting for some of that to translate itself down into lower prices." Studies report that GM now takes 3.47 workers to produce a car, compared with 3.64 a year earlier.

Honda Canada is expected to hold the line or cut prices. Both Nissan and Honda hold much smaller market shares than does GM. But Nissan is the most productive auto maker in North America, with 2.23 workers per vehicle in 1996. Honda is not far behind, with 2.38 workers per vehicle.

As we said, pricing in the auto industry is not simple. There are return on investment considerations, cost considerations, market position considerations, and a host of tactical matters — which we will discuss in the next chapter.

Source: Adapted from Greg Keenan, "GM Canada to Boost Prices by 2.5%," *The Globe and Mail*, June 27, 1997, p. B11; and Greg Keenan, "Big Three Closing Productivity Gap, Study Says," *The Globe and Mail*, June 12, 1997, p. B6.

(see Figure 13-5). The prevailing price is at A. Adjusting this price is not beneficial to the seller:

- Above the prevailing price, demand for the product drops sharply, as indicated by the fairly flat average revenue curve above point P. Above price A, demand is highly elastic and, as a result, total revenue declines.
- Below price A, demand for the product increases very little, as shown by the steeply sloping average revenue curve and the negative marginal revenue curve below point P. Demand is highly inelastic and, as a result, total revenue still declines.

www.ferrari.it
www.mercedes-net.com
www.waterford-usa.com
www.moda.iol.it/stilisti/fendi/e/default.htm

FIGURE 13-5 Kinked Demand Curve

This type of curve faces firms selling well-known, standardized products as well as individual firms in an oligopolistic market structure. The kink occurs at the point representing the prevailing price A. At prices above A, demand declines rapidly. A price set below A results in very little increase in volume, so revenue is lost; that is, marginal revenue is negative.

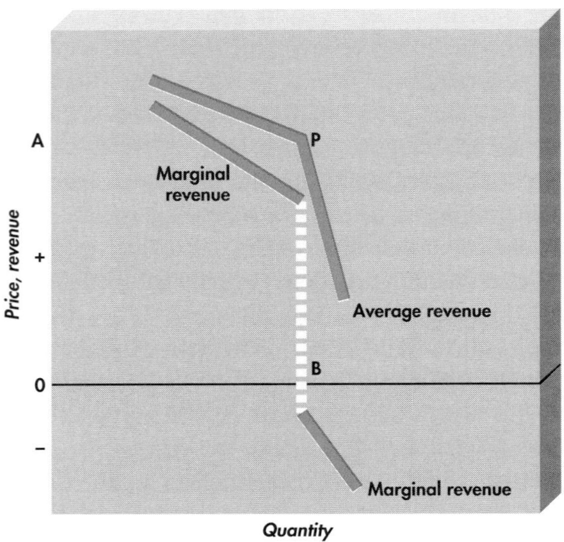

In the case of kinked demand, total revenue decreases each time the price is adjusted from the prevailing price, A in Figure 13-5. The prevailing price is strong. Consequently, when a single firm reduces its price, its unit sales will not increase very much — certainly not enough to offset the loss in average revenue.

So far in our discussion of pricing to meet competition, we have observed market situations that involve many sellers. Oddly enough, this same pricing method is often used when the market is dominated by a few firms, each marketing similar products. This type of market structure, called an **oligopoly**, exists in such industries as copper, aluminum, soft drinks, breakfast cereals, auto tires, and even among barber shops and grocery stores in a small community. When the demand curve is kinked, as in Figure 13-5, oligopolists should simply set prices at a competitive level and leave them there. Typically they do.

Pricing Below Competition

A variation of market-based pricing is to set a price below the level charged by your main competitors. **Pricing below competition** is done by discount retailers, such as Zellers and Wal-Mart, which stress low markup, high volume, and few customer services (including sales people). They price some heavily advertised, well-known brands 10 to 30 percent below the suggested list price, which is normally charged by full-service retailers. Even full-service retailers may price below the competitive level by eliminating specific services. Some gas stations offer a discount to customers who pay with cash instead of a credit card.

The risk in pricing below competition is that consumers begin to view the product as an undifferentiated commodity, such as coal and bulk salt, with all the focus on price differences. If that happens, and some would say it already has in fields such as personal computers, then consumers choose the brand with the lowest price. In turn, competing firms are likely to wind up in a price war that diminishes or eliminates profits.[10] One observer asked a question that applies to any industry in which firms rely on price as a way to gain an edge over competitors: "How can restaurant chains ever expect to charge top dollar again after relentlessly pushing value [low] prices?"[11]

Pricing Above Competition

Producers or retailers sometimes set their prices above the prevailing market level. Usually, **pricing above competition** works only when the product is distinctive or when the seller has acquired prestige in its field. Most communities have an elite clothing boutique and a prestigious jewellery store in which price tags are noticeably above the level set by other stores with seemingly similar products. However, a gas station that has a strong advantage based on a superior location (perhaps the only such station for many kilometres on the Trans-Canada Highway) may also be able to use above-market pricing.

Above-market pricing often is employed by manufacturers of prestige brands of high-cost products, such as automobiles (Ferrari, Mercedes), crystal (Waterford), leather products (Gucci, Fendi), and watches (Breguet, Rolex). Some retailers feel that luxury goods in Canada are doing better than ever. The lure of high-priced goods is felt to be quality and an image of elegance. In the mid-1990s, one retailer reported not being able to maintain stock on $2,300 cashmere jackets because they were selling so fast![12] Cartier Inc., the jewellers, is one example of a retailer that is thriving at the luxury end of the scale. This establishment feels that luxury and discount price outlets often thrive at the same time that the mid-range operations show limited growth. This is because the customers who frequent these establishments are often not affected by changes in economic situations.[13]

Above-market pricing is sometimes found even among relatively low-cost products — candies, for example. Godiva, a brand of imported Belgian chocolates, follows this practice in Canada and the United States.

The basic pricing methods covered in this chapter (cost-plus and marginal analysis, for instance) are equally applicable in the marketing of goods and services by businesses. Pricing of services was discussed in more detail in Chapter 12. Pricing in not-for-profit organizations, however, involves different considerations — discussed in Chapter 22.

www.godiva.com

Summary

In our economy, price influences the allocation of resources. In individual companies, price is one significant factor in achieving marketing success. And in many purchase situations, price can be of great importance to consumers. However, it is difficult to define price. A rather general definition is: Price is the amount of money and/or other items with utility needed to acquire a product.

Before setting a product's base price, management should identify its pricing goal. Major pricing objectives are to (1) earn a target return on investment or on net sales, (2) maximize profits, (3) increase sales, (4) hold or gain a target market share, (5) stabilize prices, and (6) meet competition's prices.

Besides the firm's pricing objective, other key factors that influence price setting are (1) demand for the product, (2) competitive reactions, (3) strategies planned for other marketing-mix elements, and (4) cost of the product. The concept of elasticity refers to the effect that unit-price changes have on the number of units sold and on total revenue.

Three major methods used to determine the base price are cost-plus pricing, marginal analysis, and setting the price in relation only to the market. For cost-plus pricing to be effective, a seller must consider several types of costs and their reactions to changes in the quantity produced. A producer usually sets a price to cover total cost. In some cases, however, the best policy may be to set a price that covers marginal cost only. The main weakness in cost-plus pricing is that it completely ignores market demand. To partially offset this weakness, a company may use break-even analysis as a tool in price setting.

In actual business situations, price setting is influenced by market conditions. Hence, marginal analysis, which takes into account both demand and costs to determine a suitable price for the product, is a useful price-determination method. Price and output level are set at the point where marginal cost equals marginal revenue. The effectiveness of marginal analysis in setting prices depends on obtaining reliable cost data.

For many products, price setting is relatively easy because management simply sets the price at the level of competition. Pricing at prevailing market levels makes sense for firms selling well-known, standardized products and sometimes for individual firms in an oligopoly. Two variations of market-level pricing are to price below or above the levels of primary competitors.

Key Terms and Concepts

Price (316)
Utility (316)
Value (316)
Pricing objective (320)
Achieve target return (320)
Markup (320)
Profit maximization (320)
Increase sales volume (321)
Maintain or increase market share (321)
Stabilize prices (321)
Meet competition (321)
Base price (list price) (323)
Expected price (323)
Range of prices (323)
Inverse demand (323)
Price elasticity of demand (323)
Fixed cost (325)
Total fixed cost (325)
Average fixed cost (325)
Variable cost (325)
Total variable cost (325)
Average variable cost (325)
Total cost (325)
Average total cost (325)
Marginal cost (325)
Average fixed cost curve (325)
Average variable cost curve (325)
Average total cost curve (325)
Marginal cost curve (325)
Cost-plus pricing (326)
Prices based on marginal costs only (327)
Break-even analysis (329)
Break-even point (329)
Prices based on marginal analysis (331)
Marginal revenue (331)
Average revenue (331)
Pricing to meet competition (332)
Perfect competition (332)
Kinked demand (332)
Oligopoly (334)
Pricing below competition (334)
Pricing above competition (334)

Questions and Problems

1. Explain how a firm's pricing objective may influence the promotional program for a product. Which of the six pricing goals involves the largest, most aggressive promotional campaign?
2. What marketing conditions might logically lead a company to set "meeting competition" as a pricing objective?
3. What is your expected price for each of the following articles? How did you arrive at your estimate in each instance?
   a. A new type of cola beverage that holds its carbonation long after it has been opened; packaged in 355-mL and 2-L bottles.
   b. A nuclear-powered 23-inch table-model television set, guaranteed to run for ten years without replacement of the original power-generating component; requires no battery or electric wires.
   c. An automatic garage-door opener for residential housing.
4. Name at least three products for which you think an inverse demand exists. For each product, within which price range does this inverse demand exist?
5. In Figure 13-1, what is the significance of the point where the marginal cost curve intersects the average total cost curve? Explain why the average total cost curve is declining to the left of the intersection point and rising beyond it. Explain how the marginal cost curve can be rising while the average total cost curve is still declining.
6. What are the merits and limitations of the cost-plus method of setting a base price?
7. In a break-even chart, is the total fixed cost line always horizontal? Is the total variable cost line always straight? Explain.
8. Referring to Table 13-3 and Figure 13-3, what would be the Futon Factory's break-even points at prices of $50 and $90, if variable costs are $40 per unit and fixed costs remain at $25,000?
9. A small manufacturer sold ballpoint pens to retailers at $8.40 per dozen. The manufacturing cost was 50 cents for each pen. Expenses, including all selling and administrative costs except advertising, were $19,200. How many dozen must the manufacturer sell to cover these expenses and pay for an advertising campaign costing $6,000?
10. In Figure 13-4, why would the firm normally stop producing at quantity Q? Why is the price set at B rather than at D or A?

Hands-On Marketing

1. Select ten items that college students purchase frequently at a supermarket. Be specific in describing the items (e.g., a six-pack of Diet Coke). Conduct separate interviews with five of your fellow students, asking them to indicate the price of each item at the supermarket closest to campus. Compare the students' answers with the actual prices charged by that supermarket. How many of the fifty answers were within 5 percent of the actual price? Within 10 percent? Do these results, admittedly from a small sample, suggest that consumers are knowledgeable and concerned about grocery prices?

2. Identify one store in your community that generally prices below the levels of most other firms and one that prices above prevailing market levels. Arrange an interview with the manager of each store. Ask both managers to explain the rationale and procedures associated with their pricing approaches. Also ask the manager of the store with below-market prices how profits are achieved with such low prices. Ask the manager of the store with above-market prices how customers are attracted and satisfied with such high prices.

CHAPTER 14 GOALS

In this chapter we discuss ways in which a firm adjusts a product's base price to coincide with its overall marketing program. After studying this chapter, you should have an understanding of:

- Price competition and value pricing.
- Pricing strategies for entering a market, notably market skimming and market penetration.
- Price discounts and allowances.
- Geographic pricing strategies.
- Special strategies, including one-price and flexible-price approaches, price lining, resale price maintenance, leader pricing, everyday low pricing, and odd pricing.
- Legal issues associated with pricing.

Chapter Fourteen

Pricing Strategies and Policies

www.challenger.bombardier.com

BOMBARDIER HOLDS THE PRICE LINE AND WINS

The regional jet market is now booming, and Bombardier is reaping the rewards after having been one of the pioneers in the business. Regional aircraft seat between fifteen and ninety people and are powered by turboprop or jet engines. The market for these aircraft has grown since the development of airline hubs in the United States and Europe in the 1980s. Small, short-range planes are used to ferry passengers into a central hub, where they are transferred to transcontinental or overseas flights on much larger aircraft. Regional planes are also cost-effective for carrying small passenger loads, either to smaller, non-hub cities or at off-peak hours. Regional traffic is growing at the rate of 10 percent annually in the United States and 13 percent in Europe.

In 1996 alone, Bombardier's regional aircraft division captured over 40 percent of the world market: seventy-one Dash 8 turboprops (35 percent share), and over sixty of the newer fifty-seat Canadair Regional Jets (52 percent). Three years ago, Bombardier's world market share was 22 percent. With two sales made to U.S. regional carriers in mid-1997, sales for the fifty-seat plane went past the target of 250 that Bombardier set in 1993. At that time, Bombardier said it would amortize its $250 million investment in the CRJ over the first 250 units. Now that the target has been achieved, the firm will make a higher profit on each additional unit sold.

The target of 250 planes was achieved with the important sale of thirty planes to U.S. regional carrier Comair Inc. of Cincinnati, Ohio. To get the sale, Bombardier was competing against Brazilian plane maker Embraer. Bombardier's plane was priced at $20 million, Embraer's at $16 million. But the market accepts that the CRJ flies faster and farther than the Embraer 145 and is technically superior where it counts.

Bombardier, in early 1997, launched the Canadian Regional Jet 700 series, a seventy-seat derivative of the fifty-seat CRJ. The plane is scheduled to fly in 1999, with first delivery in 2001. Within a few months of launch, American Eagle, the world's largest regional airline system, announced an unexpected initial purchase of twenty-five of the new CRJ 700s, with an option on another twenty-five. At time of delivery, the price is expected to be between $25 million and $28 million per unit. At the same time, American Eagle announced the purchase of forty-two Embraer fifty-seat planes from the Brazilian manufacturer.

American Eagle had initially been interested primarily in fifty-seat planes, and Bombardier and Embraer had both vied for sales. But while Bombardier impressed American Eagle with the seventy-seat CRJ 700 and landed an important sale for a plane still on paper, it lost the sale for the fifty-seat jets to Embraer. Bombardier's price was a firm $20 million per plane, and as Robert Brown, president of the aerospace division said, "We will not take on projects that do not meet our commercial requirements...It's very hard for people to meet certain pricing requirements and remain profitable." Embraer, noted for discounting to secure orders, had once priced its plane at $16 million. In this instance, it was listed at $14.5 million, and the final unit price was not disclosed. American Eagle President Dan Gorton told a journalist: "Anyone who tells you that price is not a critical factor in buying an airplane is not telling you the truth."[1]

PRICE COMPETITION

In developing a marketing program, a firm decides on the positioning of its offerings and then manages the elements of its marketing mix to achieve and maintain the position — or reposition if necessary. Some firms decide to compete primarily, but not exclusively, on price. Others use such nonprice approaches as concentrating on quality of product or service and/or distribution, advertising, and promotion, but always with a compatible pricing policy.

A firm engages in **price competition** by:

1. Regularly offering products priced as low as possible and accompanied by a minimum of services. Zellers, Wal-Mart, and other discount houses and off-price retailers compete in this way.
2. Instigating changes in price that change the consumer's perception of product value without relying on other marketing factors. Embraer's discounting of its airplanes is a good example of this approach.
3. Reacting to competitors' price changes with price changes of its own, for example, engaging in a price war. Bombardier's unwillingness to engage in a price war is a counter example to this reaction.

There is substantial price competition in North America today, and it has spread to other parts of the world as well. Price reductions became commonplace throughout Europe in the early 1990s as a result of the elimination of various trade barriers and, for a while, because of the continent's economic woes. All kinds of products — consumer electronics, computers, air travel, and autos — were available at discounted prices. Price competition has also travelled to Japan, where formerly it did not exist.

Value Pricing

In Chapter 13 and earlier, we discussed how more consumers are seeking better value in their purchases. In response, many companies in diverse industries are using what's called **value pricing**. This form of price competition aims to improve a product's value — the ratio of its benefits to its price and related costs (see "Marketing at Work" File 13-2). Using value pricing, a firm:

- offers products with lower prices but the same, or perhaps added, benefits; and
- at the same time seeks ways to slash expenses so that profits do not suffer.

www.embraer.com • www.americanair.com/aa_home/aeagle/index.html

During the 1990s, value pricing became a pivotal marketing trend in fields as diverse as air travel, groceries, personal computers, and fast food. For example, IBM reduced its price on its newest line of mobile products — ThinkPads 380, 560, and 760, all-in-one designs with integrated hard drive, floppy, and CD-ROM in one unit — to sell for nearly 25 percent less than the market price.[2]

Value pricing certainly emphasizes the price element of the marketing mix. But that's not enough. For the value buyer, if all that is offered is price, that is not going to guarantee the sale. People who are attracted to the value that a product or service offers make their purchases by weighing attributes and analyzing trade-offs. They ultimately purchase on the basis of what provides the highest utility for the lowest price.[3] Consequently, value pricing depends on creatively combining all the elements of the marketing mix in order to maximize benefits in relation to price and other costs. With a value-pricing strategy, products often have to be redesigned to expand benefits and/or shave costs. Relationships among channel members and customers have to be strengthened to generate repeat sales. Steps toward this end include frequent-buyer programs, toll-free customer-service lines, and hassle-free warranties. And advertising has to be revamped to provide more facts and fewer emotional appeals.

Relationship Pricing

Related to the concept of value pricing is that of **relationship pricing**. This strategy is one of the elements of relationship marketing discussed in Chapter 12. You will recall that relationship marketing is about developing long-term, ongoing relationships with customers, the benefits of which include loyalty and reduced costs of doing business. In relationship pricing, some of these benefits are shared with customers to ensure that they receive better value and have another incentive to remain loyal. In other words, the firm gives a better price to better customers. In relationship pricing, customers are given a price incentive to encourage them to do all or most of their business with one supplier. For example, if you maintain a chequing account, savings account, mortgage account, and retirement fund with one bank, you will very likely be offered reduced interest costs on any borrowing or invited to join a plan that provides no-cost transactions. The bank is establishing a relationship with you as a customer by offering you a preferred rate and is therefore encouraging you to do all of your business with them.[4]

MARKET-ENTRY PRICING STRATEGIES

In preparing to enter the market with a new product or service, management must decide whether to adopt a skimming or a penetration pricing **strategy**.

Market-Skimming Pricing

Setting a relatively high initial price for a new product is referred to as **market-skimming pricing**. Ordinarily the price is high in relation to the target market's range of expected prices. That is, the price

FIGURE 14-1
The Price-Determination Process

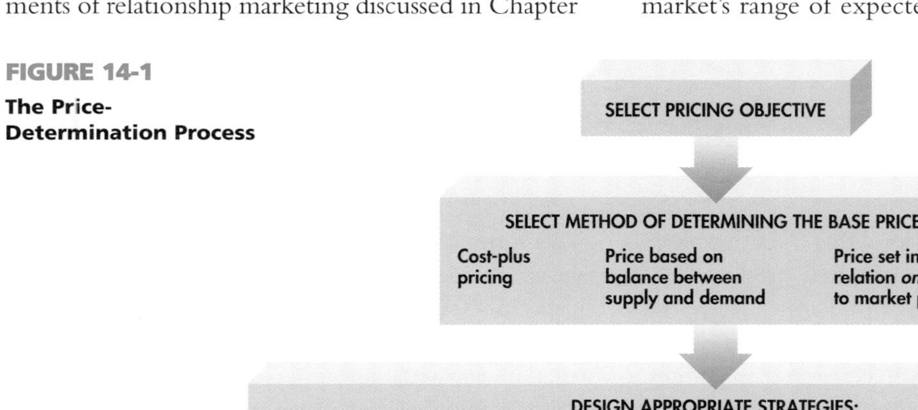

Hassle-free printing is priceless.

PrintPartner 10V
Value performer
$895.00*

PrintPartner 14V
Workgroup laser
$1,295.00*

PrintPartner 14ADV
Network versatility
$1,495.00*

PrintPartner 14ADV Duplex
Duplex workhorse
$1,995.00*

With Fujitsu, it's also priced-less.

Fujitsu's new PrintPartner laser printers make choosing and using a laser printer a hassle-free experience. For features and value, these printers offer unbeatable price-performance. When it comes to set-up, you'll appreciate the improved front panel LCD display, Quick Start installation guide and free Canada-wide tech support hotline. Fujitsu MarkVision™ by Lexmark administration software for network or stand-alone printers is included with each of these new PrintPartner models, enabling remote monitoring and control. PrintPartner laser printers also have one of the best warranties in the business, with an 18-month limited warranty and FREE first year Warranty Plus on-site replacement. From the economical 10V all the way up to the 14ADV duplex configuration, this new line of laser printers offers you the choice, value and peace of mind you could only expect from Fujitsu, the world's second largest computer company. Call Fujitsu Canada for more information. Because printing this easy is priceless.

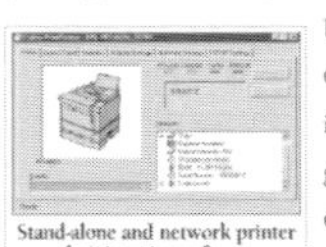

Stand-alone and network printer administration software.

HASSLE-FREE BONUS

For an extra $50, receive a multi-function feeder[†] or 16 MB extra RAM!

Limited time offer, direct from Fujitsu Canada, Inc.
Available April 15 - July 31, 1997.
See printer carton for redemption coupon.

[†] Multi-function feeder holds 100 sheets or 30 envelopes, and comes standard on the 14ADV.

COMPUTERS, COMMUNICATIONS, MICROELECTRONICS

Fujitsu Canada Inc.: 1-800-263-8716 Ext: 2719 **Quebec/Atlantic:** 1-800-663-0756 **Toronto:** (905) 602-5454 Ext: 2719 **Montreal:** (514) 685-6262

* Manufacturer's recommended special price; reseller may sell for less. PrintPartner and Warranty Plus are trademarks of Fujitsu. MarkVision is a trademark of Lexmark International, Inc.

Fujitsu offers new features, easy installation, support, warranty choice, value, and peace of mind — at very competitive prices.

is set at the highest possible level that the most interested consumers will pay for the new product.

The $25–$28 million Bombardier CRJ 700 price at time of delivery, 2001, is an example of this. Market-skimming pricing has several purposes. Since it should provide healthy profit margins, it is intended primarily to recover research and development costs as quickly as possible. Further, lofty prices can be used to connote high quality. Moreover, market-skimming pricing is likely to curtail demand to levels that do not outstrip the firm's production capacities. Finally, it provides the firm with flexibility, because it is much easier to lower an initial price that meets with consumer resistance than it is to raise an initial price that has proven to be too low to cover costs.

Market-skimming pricing is suitable under the following conditions:

- The new product has distinctive features strongly desired by consumers.
- Demand is fairly inelastic — most likely the case in the early stages of a product's life cycle. Under this condition, lower prices are unlikely to produce greater total revenues.
- The new product is protected from competition through one or more entry barriers, such as a patent.

Market skimming is often used in pricing new technological products such as cellular telephones and high-definition TVs. Over time, the initial price may be lowered gradually. Consider the introduction of digital cameras. Minolta manufactures a product called the Dimage V, which retails for approximately $1,000. A product of comparable photographic resolution in a film camera retails for under $500. It will be interesting to watch the price of digital cameras to observe whether this new technology will eventually become more affordable as it is introduced to a broader consumer base.[5]

Market-Penetration Pricing

In **market-penetration pricing**, a relatively low initial price is established for a new product. The price is low in relation to the target market's range of expected prices. The primary aim of this strategy is to penetrate the mass market immediately and, in so doing, generate substantial sales volume and a large market share. At the same time, it is intended to discourage other firms from introducing competing products.

Market-penetration pricing makes the most sense under the following conditions:

- A large mass market exists for the product.
- Demand is highly elastic, typically in the later stages of the life cycle for a product category.
- Substantial reductions in unit costs can be achieved through large-scale operations. In other words, economies of scale are possible.
- Fierce competition already exists in the market for this product or can be expected to materialize soon after the product is introduced.

When computer firms introduced clones that imitated IBM or Apple models a number of years ago, they were relying on market-penetration pricing by undercutting the prices of the large, well-known producers. Now, a number of years later, pricing approaches have changed again — see "Marketing at Work" File 14-2 for pricing computers in today's markets. When Sprint Canada, AT&T and others began entering the Canadian long-distance market, they introduced cut-rate savings on telephone charges in order to acquire customers and penetrate the market. These measures forced the local telephone companies to follow suit with their own savings plans. Undercutting actions by Sprint Canada have been viewed as escalating a price war in long-distance telephone service.[6]

DISCOUNTS AND ALLOWANCES

Discounts and allowances result in a deduction from the base (or list) price. The deduction may be in the form of a reduced price or some other concession, such as free merchandise or advertising allowances. Discounts and allowances are commonplace in business dealings.

Quantity Discounts

Quantity discounts are deductions from a seller's list price intended to encourage customers to buy in larger amounts or to buy most of what they need from the seller offering the deduction. Discounts are based on the size of the purchase, either in dollars or in units.

A **noncumulative discount** is based on the size of an individual order of one or more products. A retailer may sell golf balls at $2 each or at three for $5. A manufacturer or wholesaler may set up a quantity discount schedule such as the following, used by a manufacturer of industrial adhesives:

Boxes purchased in single order	Percent discount from list price
1–5	None
6–12	2.0
13–25	3.5
Over 25	5.0

Noncumulative quantity discounts are intended to encourage large orders. Many expenses, such as billing, order filling, and salaries of sales people, are about the same whether the seller receives an order totalling $10 or one totalling $500. Consequently, selling expense as a percentage of sales decreases as orders grow in size. With a noncumulative discount, a seller shares such savings with a purchaser of large quantities.

A **cumulative discount** is based on the total volume purchased over a specified period. This type of discount is advantageous to a seller because it ties customers more closely to that firm. The more total business a buyer gives a seller, the greater is the discount. Air Canada frequent-flyer and hotel frequent-guest programs are a form of cumulative discount. IBM offers an assortment of volume-over-time discounts. And Bell Canada competes with Sprint Canada and other telephone companies by offering discounts to two levels of high-volume users of long-distance telephone service.

Cumulative discounts also are common in selling perishable products. These discounts encourage customers to buy fresh supplies frequently, so that the buyer's merchandise will not become stale.

Quantity discounts can help a producer achieve real economies in production as well as in selling. On the one hand, large orders (motivated by a noncumulative discount) can result in lower production and transportation costs. On the other hand, frequent orders from a single customer (motivated by a cumulative discount) can enable the producer to make much more effective use of production capacity, even though individual orders are small and do not generate savings in marketing costs.

Trade Discounts

Trade discounts, sometimes called **functional discounts**, are reductions from the list price offered to buyers in payment for marketing functions the buyers will perform, such as storing, promoting, and selling the product. A manufacturer may quote a retail price of $400 with trade discounts of 40 percent and 10 percent. The retailer pays the wholesaler $240 ($400 less 40 percent), and the wholesaler pays the manufacturer $216 ($240 less 10 percent). The wholesaler is given the 40 and 10 percent discounts. The wholesaler is expected to keep the 10 percent to cover costs of the wholesaling functions and pass on the 40 percent discount to retailers. Sometimes, however, wholesalers keep more than the 10 percent — and it's not illegal for them to do so.

Note that the 40 and 10 percent discounts do not constitute a total discount of 50 percent off list price. They are not additive; rather, they are discounts on discounts. Each discount is computed on the amount remaining after the preceding discount has been deducted.

Cash Discounts

A **cash discount** is a deduction granted to buyers for paying their bills within a specified time. The discount is computed on the net amount due after first deducting trade and quantity discounts from the base price. Every cash discount includes three elements, as indicated in Figure 14-2:

- The percentage discount.
- The period during which the discount may be taken.
- The time when the bill becomes overdue.

Let's say a buyer owes $360 after other discounts have been granted and is offered terms of 2/10, n/30

FIGURE 14-2
Parts of a Cash Discount

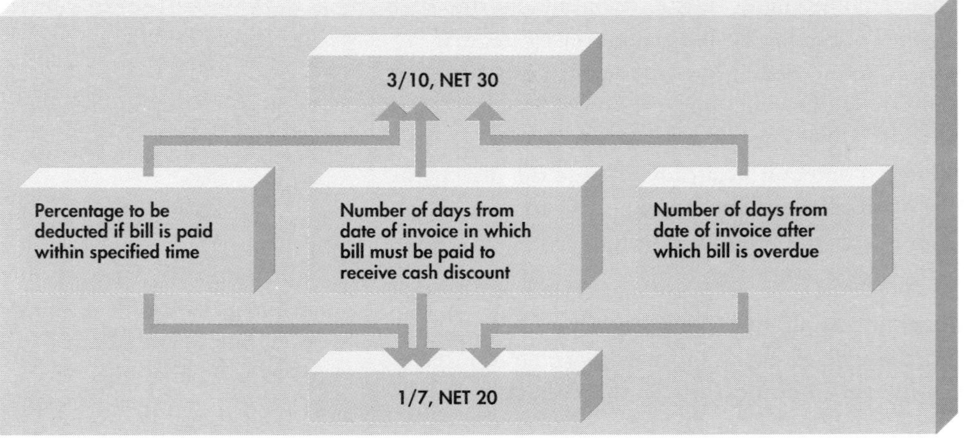

on an invoice dated November 8. This means the buyer may deduct a discount of 2 percent ($7.20) if the bill is paid within 10 days of the invoice date — by November 18. Otherwise the entire (net) bill of $360 must be paid in 30 days — by December 8.

There are almost as many different cash discounts as there are industries. For example, in women's fashions, large discounts and short payment periods have been common; thus a cash discount of 5/5, n/15 would not be surprising. Such differences persist not so much for business reasons but because of tradition in various industries.

Most buyers are eager to pay bills in time to earn cash discounts. The discount in a 2/10, n/30 situation may not seem like very much. But this 2 percent is earned just for paying 20 days in advance of the date the entire bill is due. If buyers fail to take the cash discount in a 2/10, n/30 situation, they are, in effect, borrowing money at a 36 percent annual rate of interest. Here's how we arrived at that interest rate: In a 360-day business year, there are 18 periods of 20 days. Paying 2 percent for one of these 20-day periods is equivalent to paying 36 percent for an entire year.

Other Discounts and Allowances

A manufacturer of goods such as air conditioners or toys purchased on a seasonal basis may consider granting a **seasonal discount**. This discount of, say, 5, 10, or 20 percent is given to a customer who places an order during the slack season. Off-season orders enable manufacturers to better use their production facilities and/or avoid inventory-carrying costs. Many services firms also offer seasonal discounts. For example, Club Med, other vacation resorts, and cruise lines lower their prices during the off-season.

Forward dating is a variation on both seasonal and cash discounts. A manufacturer of fishing tackle might seek and fill orders from wholesalers and retailers during the winter months. But the bills would be dated April 1, with terms of 2/10, n/30 offered as of that date. Orders filled in December and January help to maintain production during the slack season for more efficient operation. The forward-dated bills allow the wholesale or retail buyers to pay their bills after the season has started and they can generate some sales revenue from the products delivered earlier.

A **promotional allowance** is a price reduction granted by a seller as payment for promotional services performed by buyers. To illustrate, a producer of builders' hardware gives a certain quantity of free goods to dealers who prominently display its line. Or a clothing manufacturer pays one-half the cost of a retailer's ad featuring its product.

The Competition Act and Price Discrimination

The discounts and allowances discussed in this section may result in different prices for different customers. Whenever price differentials exist, there is **price discrimination**. The terms are synonymous. In certain situations, price discrimination is prohibited by the **Competition Act**. This is one of the most important federal laws affecting a company's marketing program. Below are some of the Act's implications for common pricing strategies.

Predatory Pricing

Section 50(1)(c) of the Competition Act states:

> Every one engaged in a business who...engages in a policy of selling products at prices unreasonably low, having the effect or tendency of substantially lessening competition or eliminating a competitor, or designed to have such effect, is guilty of an indictable offence and is liable to imprisonment for two years.

In order for a conviction to result under section 50(1)(c), it must be shown that prices are unreasonably low and that such prices have the effect, of reducing competition. The word "products" in the Competition Act includes articles and services.

Price Discrimination

Section 50(1)(a) of the Act regulates price discrimination:

> 50(1) Every one engaged in a business who (a) is a party or privy to, or assists in, any sale that discriminates to his knowledge, directly or indirectly, against competitors of a purchaser of articles from him in that any discount, rebate, allowance, price concession or other advantage

> that, at the time the articles are sold to such purchaser, is available to such competitors in respect of a sale of articles of like quality and quantity, ...is guilty of an indictable offence and is liable to imprisonment for two years.

This section goes on to state in section 50(2):

> It is not an offence under paragraph (1)(a) to be a party or privy to, or assist in any sale mentioned therein unless the discount, rebate, allowance, price concession or other advantage was granted as part of a practice of discriminating as described in that paragraph.

The following conditions must be met in order for a conviction to be registered for price discrimination: (1) a discount, rebate, allowance, price concession, or other advantage must be granted to one customer and not to another; (2) the two customers concerned must be competitors; (3) the price discrimination must occur in respect of articles of similar quality and quantity; (4) the act of discrimination must be part of a practice of discrimination. Not all price discrimination is, per se, an offence. It is lawful to discriminate in price on the basis of quantities of goods purchased.

It should be noted that the buyer is seen as being as liable as the seller in cases of discrimination. The legislation applies to those who are party to a sale, and this includes both buyer and seller. This wording was intended to restrain large-scale buyers from demanding discriminatory prices. In addition, the buyer (as well as the seller) must know that the price involved is discriminatory.

Granting Promotional Allowances as an Offence

The Act, in section 51, requires that promotional allowances be granted proportionately to all competing customers:

> 51(1) In this section, "allowance" means any discount, rebate, price concession or other advantage that is or purports to be offered or granted for advertising or display purposes and is collateral to a sale or sales of products but is not applied directly to the selling price...
>
> (3) For the purposes of this section, an allowance is offered on proportionate terms only if
>
> (a) the allowance offered to a purchaser is in approximately the same proportion to the value of sales to him as the allowance offered to each competing purchaser is to the total value of sales to such competing purchaser.
>
> (b) in any case where advertising or other expenditures or services are exacted in return therefor, the cost thereof required to be incurred by a purchaser is in approximately the same proportion to the value of sales to him as the cost of such advertising or other expenditures or services required to be incurred by each competing purchaser is the total value of sales to such competing purchaser, and
>
> (c) in any case where services are exacted in return therefor, the requirements thereof have regard to the kinds of services that competing purchasers at the same time or different levels of distribution are ordinarily able to perform or cause to be performed.

The provisions of section 51 apply to the sale of both articles and services. Discrimination in the granting of promotional allowances is a per se offence, not requiring proof of the existence of either a practice of discrimination or a lessening of competition. A company that wishes to discriminate among its customers may do so through the legal practice of granting quantity discounts.

GEOGRAPHIC PRICING STRATEGIES

In pricing, a seller must consider the costs of shipping goods to the buyer. These costs grow in importance as freight becomes a larger part of total variable costs. Pricing policies may be established where the buyer pays all the freight expense, the seller pays the entire cost, or the seller and buyer share this expense. The strategy chosen can influence the geographic limits of a firm's market, the locations of its production facilities, the sources of its raw materials, and its competitive strength in various geographic markets.

F.O.B. Point-of-Production Pricing

In one widely used geographic pricing strategy, the seller quotes the selling price at the factory or at some other point of production or origin. In this situation the buyer pays the entire cost of transportation. This is usually referred to as **f.o.b. factory pricing**. Of the four strategies discussed in this section, this is the only one in which the seller does not pay any of the transport costs. The seller pays only the cost of loading the shipment aboard the carrier — hence the term f.o.b., or free on board.

Under f.o.b. factory pricing strategy, the seller nets the same amount on each sale of similar quantities. The delivered price to the buyer varies according to the freight charge. However, this pricing strategy has serious economic and marketing implications. In effect, f.o.b. factory pricing tends to establish a geographic monopoly for a given seller, because transportation costs prevent distant competitors from entering the market. The seller, in turn, is increasingly priced out of more distant markets.

Uniform Delivered Pricing

Under the **uniform delivered pricing** strategy, the same delivered price is quoted to all buyers regardless of their locations. This strategy is sometimes referred to as "postage stamp pricing" because of its similarity to the pricing of first-class mail service. The net revenue to the seller varies, depending on the shipping cost involved in each sale.

A uniform delivered price is typically used where transportation costs are a small part of the seller's total costs. This strategy is also used by many retailers who feel that "free" delivery is an additional service that strengthens their market position.

Under a uniform delivered price system, buyers located near the seller's factory pay for some of the costs of shipping to more distant locations. Critics of f.o.b. factory pricing are usually in favour of a uniform delivered price. They feel that the transportaton expense should not be charged to individual customers any more than is any other single marketing or production expense.

Zone-Delivered Pricing

Under a **zone-delivered pricing** strategy, a seller would divide the Canadian market into a limited number of broad geographic zones. Then a uniform delivered price is set within each zone. Zone-delivered pricing is similar to the system used in pricing parcel post services and long-distance telephone service. A firm that quotes a price and then says "Slightly higher west of the Lakehead" is using a two-zone pricing system. The transportation charge built into the delivered price is an average of the charges at all points within a zone area.

When adopting this pricing strategy, the seller must walk a neat tightrope to avoid charges of illegal price discrimination. This means that the zone lines must be drawn so that all buyers who compete for a particular market are in the same zone. Such a condition is most easily met where markets are widely distributed.

Freight-Absorption Pricing

A **freight-absorption pricing** strategy may be adopted to offset some of the competitive disadvantages of f.o.b. factory pricing. With an f.o.b. factory price, a firm is at a price disadvantage when it tries to sell to buyers located in markets nearer to competitors' plants. To penetrate more deeply into such markets, a seller may be willing to absorb some of the transporation costs. Thus, seller A will quote to the customer a delivered price equal to (1) A's factory price plus (2) the freight costs that would be charged by the competitive seller located nearest to that customer.

A seller can continue to expand the geographic limits of its market as long as its net revenue after freight absorption is larger than its marginal cost for the units sold. Freight absorption is particularly useful to a firm with excess capacity whose fixed costs per unit of product are high and whose variable costs are low. In these cases, management must constantly seek ways to cover fixed costs, and freight absorption is one answer.

The legality of freight absorption is reasonably clear. The strategy is legal if it is used independently and not in collusion with other firms. Also, it must be used only to meet competition. In fact, if practised properly, freight absorption can have the effect of strengthening competition because it can break down geographic monopolies.

SPECIAL PRICING STRATEGIES

To set initial prices and evaluate existing prices, a firm needs to consider a number of distinctive strategies.

MARKETING AT WORK FILE 14-1

THE MODULAR APPROACH TO PRICING: BUNDLING AND UNBUNDLING

Bundling: Interleaf is a producer of high-end publishing software and uses price bundling as an important part of its marketing strategy. It sells its core Technical Publishing Software for $2,500. Then there are options that can be added, such as the Advanced Graphics module ($4,500) and the Book Catalogue module ($2,500). The full version of Technical Publishing Software, including other modules, sells for $15,000. Because its product is sold in optional parts, Interleaf is able to adopt a high-price strategy in its less-price-sensitive markets (where it has few rivals), while remaining competitive in lower-end markets, where competition is fierce and consumers are more price sensitive. With this strategy, Interleaf is able to standardize on one basic system while catering to the individual needs of specific customers — already it has designed add-on modules that appeal to the graphic arts, technical document, and newspaper market segments. Because potential and future modules can all be added to the core product, Interleaf is constantly able to expand its markets vertically.

Unbundling: Not long ago, the cost of providing many consumer banking services was invisible as far as most retail customers were concerned. Depending on the type of account you had, there were either no charges, or in a small number of cases a flat fee was levied. But as competition for customers increased, automatic banking machines spread in use, and telephone and electronic banking developed, things changed. The banks, faced with highly variable costs for different services, based mainly on the differential costs of delivering their services on a personal basis or electronically, resorted to a lot of unbundling. Costs were disaggregated and allocated to specific services; detailed schedules of service prices, ranging from $1.50 to $30.00, were made available to consumers. The charges appear to have both annoyed and confused many customers.

For example, TD Bank is cutting service costs and simplifying its fee schedule for electronic banking, which accounts for 80 percent of its transactions, to a flat rate of 40 cents per transaction, replacing fees that ranged from this level up to $1.50. While TD management believed it offered good value for the various previous fees, customers didn't — mainly because they couldn't understand the schedule. In the short run, this will cost the bank about a $6 million reduction in its $260 million service-charge revenue. It seems that when the bundle is a mystery for many, detailed unbundling is hazardous.

Source: Adapted, in part, from "TD to Cut Charges on Electronic Banking," *The Globe and Mail*, July 8, 1997, p. B6; and Denes Bartakovich, "Building Competitive Advantage Through Creative Pricing Strategies," *Business Quarterly*, Summer 1990, pp. 47–48.

It's likely that at least one, but probably not all, will apply to a particular pricing situation.

One-Price and Flexible-Price Strategies

Rather early in its pricing deliberations, management should decide whether to adopt a one-price strategy or a flexible-price strategy. Under a **one-price strategy**, a seller charges the same price to all similar customers who buy similar quantities of a product. Under a **flexible-price** (also called a **variable-price**) **strategy**, similar customers may each pay a different price when buying similar quantities of a product.

In Canada and the United States, a one-price strategy has been adopted more often than variable pricing. Most retailers, for example, typically follow a one-price policy — except in cases where trade-ins are involved, and then flexible pricing abounds. A one-price policy builds customer confidence in a seller, whether at the manufacturing, wholesaling, or retailing level. Weak bargainers need not feel that they are at a competitive disadvantage.

When a flexible pricing policy is followed, often the price is set as a result of buyer-seller bargaining. In automobile retailing — with or without a trade-in — price negotiating (bargaining) is quite common, even though window-sticker prices may suggest a one-price policy. Variable pricing may be used to meet a competitor's price. Canada's major airlines used aggressive flexible-price strategies to enter new markets in the United States after deregulation and to increase their market share on existing routes. Their new business comes from two sources — passengers now flying on other airlines and passengers who would not fly at higher prices. In the second group, especially, the demand for air travel is highly elastic. The trick is to keep the market segment of price-sensitive passengers separate from the business-traveller segment, whose demand is inelastic. The airlines keep these segments apart by placing restrictions on the lower-priced tickets — requiring advance purchases, over-the-weekend stays in destination cities, and so on.

A **single-price strategy** is an extreme variation of the one-price strategy. Not only are all customers charged the same price, but all items sold by the firm carry a single price! The origins of this approach may be traced to budget motels of thirty years ago. For instance, Motel 6 in the United States (where they "leave the light on" for you) originally priced all rooms at $6 a night for single occupancy.

Single-price stores, selling all goods at $1 or $2, were popular for a time but have now become more scarce. These stores typically purchase close-out and discontinued products as well as production overruns from a variety of sources at a small fraction of their original costs. Some analysts question whether single-price stores can be successful not just during a recession but during prosperous times as well.

Price Lining

Price lining involves selecting a limited number of prices at which a business will sell related products. It is used extensively by retailers of apparel. A sporting goods store, for instance, may sell several styles of running shoes at $69.95 a pair, another group at $89.95, and a third assortment at $119.95.

For the consumer, the main benefit of price lining is that it simplifies buying decisions. For the retailer, price lining helps in planning purchases. The buyer for the sporting goods store can go to market looking for shoes that can be retailed at one of its three prices.

Rising costs can put a real squeeze on price lines. That's because a company hesitates to change its price line every time its costs go up. But if costs rise and prices are not increased accordingly, profit margins shrink and the retailer may be forced to seek products with lower costs.

Odd Pricing

Earlier, we briefly discussed pricing strategies that might be called psychological pricing: pricing above competitive levels, raising an unsuitably low price to increase sales, and price lining. All these strategies are intended to convey desirable images about products. **Odd pricing**, another psychological strategy, is commonly used in retailing. Odd pricing sets prices at uneven (or odd) amounts, such as 49 cents or $19.95, rather than at even amounts. Autos are priced at $19,995 rather than $20,000, and houses sell for $189,500 instead of $190,000. Odd pricing is often avoided in prestige stores or on higher-priced items. Expensive men's suits, for example, are priced at $750, not $749.95.

The rationale for odd pricing is that it suggests lower prices and, as a result, yields greater sales than even pricing. According to this reasoning, a price of 98 cents will bring in greater revenue than a $1 price for the same product. Research indicates that odd pricing can be an effective strategy for a firm that emphasizes low prices.[7]

Resale Price Maintenance

Some manufacturers want control over the prices at which retailers resell the manufacturers' products. This is most often done in Canada by following a policy of providing manufacturers' suggested list prices, where the price is just a guide for retailers. It is a list price on which discounts may be computed. For others, the suggested price is "informally" enforced. Normally, enforcement of a suggested price, termed resale price maintenance, has been illegal in Canada since 1951. In this country, attempts on the part of the manufacturers to control or to influence upward the prices at which their products are sold by retailers have been considered akin to price fixing.

Section 50 of the Competition Act prohibits a manufacturer or supplier from requiring or inducing a retailer to sell a product at a particular price or not below a particular price. On occasion, a supplier may attempt to control retail prices through the use of a "suggested retail price." Under section 50, the use of "suggested retail prices" is permitted only if the supplier makes it clear to the retailer that the product may be sold at a price below the suggested price and that the retailer will not in any way be discriminated against if the product is sold at a lower price. Also, where a manufacturer advertises a product, and in the advertisement mentions a certain price, the manufacturer must make it clear in the advertisement that the product may be sold at a lower price. While retailers are free to sell a product at whatever price they deem appropriate, from time to time manufacturers attempt to exert pressure on retailers to sell at a particular price.

Leader Pricing and Unfair-Practices Acts

Many firms, primarily retailers, temporarily cut prices on a few items to attract customers. This price and promotional strategy is called **leader pricing**, and the items whose prices may be reduced below the retailer's cost are called **loss leaders**.

Leaders should be well-known heavily advertised articles that are purchased frequently. The idea is that customers will come to the store to buy the advertised leader items and then stay to buy other regularly priced merchandise. The net result, the firm hopes, will be increased total sales volume and net profit.

Three provinces — British Columbia, Alberta, and Manitoba — have had legislation dealing with loss-leader selling. The approach has been to prohibit a reseller from selling an item below invoice cost, including freight, plus a stated markup, which is usually 5 percent at retail. The general intent of these laws is commendable. They eliminate much of the predatory type of price-cutting; however, they permit firms to use loss leaders as a price and promotional strategy. That is, a retailer can offer an article below full cost but still sell above cost plus 5 percent markup. Under such Acts, low-cost, efficient businesses are not penalized, nor are high-cost operators protected. Differentials in retailers' purchase prices can be reflected in their selling prices, and savings resulting from the absence of services can be passed on to the customers.

On the other hand, the laws have some glaring weaknesses. In the first place, the provinces do not establish provisions or agencies for enforcement. It is the responsibility and burden of the injured party to seek satisfaction from the offender in a civil suit. Another limitation is that it is difficult or even impossible to determine the cost of doing business for each individual product. The third weakness is that the laws seem to disregard the fundamental idea that the purpose of a business is to make a profit on the total operation, and not necessarily on each sale of each product.

Everyday Low Pricing and High–Low Pricing

Everyday low pricing (EDLP) is "the hottest retailing price trend," according to one analyst.[8] While it may be trendy, it certainly is not new. Basically, it involves consistently low prices and few if any temporary price reductions. This strategy was used for a number of years by Eaton's, and not long ago, the company adandoned the practice. Analysts believed that Eaton's did not promote the policy either credibly or with enough effort in the face of competitors who were offering deep cut specials. Both Wal-Mart and Zellers have been extremely successful with this type of pricing, as have the various warehouse stores such as Price Club and Business Depot.

Many firms do not engage in EDLP but rather in **high-low pricing**. High-low pricing involves using relatively low prices on some products and higher prices on others. This strategy combines frequent price reductions and aggressive promotion to convey an image of very low prices. Many supermarkets, some department stores, and chain drugstores rely on this approach.

Which is better — EDLP or high-low pricing? A controlled experiment that compared the effects of the two pricing strategies on twenty-six product categories in a chain of eighty-six grocery stores provides an answer. EDLP increased sales somewhat, whereas high-low pricing resulted in slightly lower volume. More important, profits fell 18 percent with EDLP but jumped almost as much with high-low pricing.[9]

The use of EDLP has continued to expand because some manufacturers, notably Procter & Gamble, have replaced the special discounts, allowances, and other price deals they offered retailers with consistently lower prices. P&G did this to even out supermarket orders, which would allow them to control production more easily and reduce costs. As one of North America's largest advertisers, P&G has been very effective in this strategy.[10]

Proactive and Reactive Changes

After an initial price is set, a number of situations may prompt a firm to change its price. As costs increase, for instance, management may decide to raise its price rather than to maintain price, and either cut quality or promote the product aggressively. Larger firms tend to be less reluctant to raise prices than are smaller ones.

Temporary price cuts may be used to sell excess inventory or to introduce a new product. Also, if a company's market share is declining because of strong competition, its executives may react initially by reducing price. Cereal makers, faced with strong growth from private-label products, began aggressive pricing competition for a share of the market in 1996 and dropped the supermarket price of some cereals by as much as 20 per cent.[11] For many products, however, a better long-term alternative to a price reduction is improving the overall marketing program.

Any firm can safely assume that its competitors will change their prices — sooner or later. Consequently, every firm should have guidelines on how it will react. If a competitor raises its price, a short delay in reacting probably will not be perilous. However, if a

MARKETING AT WORK FILE 14-2

THE COMPUTER WARS CONTINUE

In the early 1990s, Compaq Computer Corp., currently the world's largest PC maker — just ahead of IBM — changed the competitive situation in the industry with new products and big price cuts. Later in the product life cycle, it's happening again. Compaq has again unveiled a new line of personal computers and cut prices.

Prices have been cut on the older corporate Deskpro models by up to 22 percent, and thirteen new models, at very aggressive prices, have been introduced. Compaq says that its new prices are 6 to 8 percent lower than those of its major competitor, Dell Computers. According to Compaq's president, his firm is making other manufacturers' models obsolete.

The new strategy is to build products based on customer orders — a complete focus on mass customization. Costs will be lowered by cutting out some distributors and reducing inventories. Some distributors will configure and build products for Compaq customers. The built-to-order strategy is aimed at competing with Dell Computers, Gateway 2000, and other firms that are being successfully competitive with lower prices and lower costs. Dell, Gateway, and other marketers sell directly over the telephone or the Internet, and provide machines to order. Dell is the fastest-growing of the major PC makers.

Compaq's chief financial officer said, "You are not going to see our margins going down because of our pricing on new products. It's not a price war, it's about passing on efficiences to our customers."

The Compaq announcement resulted in Hewlett-Packard, a major competitor in the corporate computer market, cutting prices by up to 24 percent. IBM said it planned to remain competitive but did not disclose details. Analysts believe many PC makers would not be able to win a price war with Compaq without hurting profits because their costs will not be as low.

Source: Adapted from "Compaq Unveils New Line of PCs, Chops Prices," *The Globe and Mail*, July 11, 1997, p. B6.

Land Rover plays on its reputation as an expensive vehicle by attracting humorous price attention and offsetting the price with a long list of features.

competing firm reduces price, a prompt response normally is required to avoid losing customers.

Occasional price reductions occur even in an oligopoly, because all sellers of the product cannot be controlled. In the absence of collusion, every so often some firm will cut its price. Then all others usually follow to maintain their respective market shares. However, vigorous short-term discount plans indicate that the major competitors are engaging in vigorous price competition at the initial stage of market and brand development.

From a seller's standpoint, the big disadvantage in price cutting is that competitors will retaliate — and not let up. A **price war** may begin when one firm decreases its price in an effort to increase its sales volume and/or market share. The battle is on if other firms retaliate, reducing price on their competing products. Additional price decreases by the original price cutter and/or its competitors are likely to follow until one of the firms decides it can endure no further damage to its profits. Most businesses would like to avoid price wars, but they always break out.

Always part of business, price wars seemed to be epidemic in the 1990s, breaking out in numerous fields: airlines, vacation packages, many grocery items, computers and computer software, gasoline on a local basis, long-distance telephone services, even bank service charges. Price wars can be extremely harmful to firms, particularly financially weak ones. One article summed up the damages of price wars as follows: "Customer loyalty? Dead! Profits? Imploding! Planning? Up in smoke!"[12]

In the short term, consumers benefit from price wars through sharply lower prices. But over the longer term, the net effects on consumers are not clear-cut. What is evident is that price wars can be harmful to many firms, especially the weaker ones, in an industry. Lower profits typically decrease the number of competitors and, over a longer period, possibly the vigour of competition. After extended price wars, some companies in industries as different as groceries and personal computers have gone out of business. Ultimately, a smaller number of competing firms might translate to fewer product choices and/or higher prices for consumers. Gaining sales and market share with price competition is only valid when it is managed as part of a longer-term marketing strategy for achieving, exploiting, or sustaining a longer-term competitive advantage.[13]

Summary

After deciding on pricing goals and setting the base (or list) price, marketers must establish pricing strategies that are compatible with the rest of the marketing mix. Another basic decision facing management is whether to engage primarily in price or nonprice competition. Although price competition was widespread in the 1990s, most firms prefer nonprice competition. Price competition establishes price as the primary, perhaps the sole, basis for attracting and retaining customers. A growing number of businesses are adopting value pricing to improve the ratio of benefits to price and, in turn, win customers from competitors.

When a firm is launching a new product, it must choose a market-skimming or a market-penetration pricing strategy. Market skimming uses a relatively high initial price, market penetration a low one.

Strategies also must be devised for discounts and allowances — deductions from the list price. Management has the option of offering quantity discounts, trade discounts, cash discounts, and/or other types of deductions.

Transportation costs must be considered in pricing. A producer can require the buyer to pay all freight costs (f.o.b. factory pricing), or a producer can absorb all freight costs (uniform delivered pricing). Or the two parties can share the freight costs (freight absorption). Decisions on discounts and allowances must conform to the Competition Act, a federal law regulating price discrimination.

Management also should decide whether to charge the same price to all similar buyers of identical quantities of a product (a one-price strategy) or to set different prices (a flexible-price strategy). Many organizations, especially retailers, use at least some of the following special strategies: price lining — selecting a limited number of prices at which to sell related products; odd pricing — setting prices at uneven (or odd) amounts; and leader pricing — temporarily cutting prices on a few items to attract customers.

Many manufacturers are concerned about resale price maintenance, which means controlling the prices at which intermediaries resell products. Some approaches to resale price maintenance are stronger than others; moreover, some methods may be illegal.

Market opportunities and/or competitive forces may motivate companies to initiate price changes or, in other situations, to react to other firms' price changes. A series of successive price cuts by competing firms creates a price war, which can harm the profits of all participating companies.

Key Terms and Concepts

Price competition (340)
Value pricing (340)
Relationship pricing (341)
Strategy (341)
Market-skimming pricing (341)
Market-penetration pricing (343)
Quantity discount (343)
Noncumulative discount (343)
Cumulative discount (344)
Trade (functional) discount (344)
Cash discount (344)
Seasonal discount (345)

Forward dating (345)
Promotional allowance (345)
Price discrimination (345)
Competition Act (345)
F.o.b. factory pricing (347)
Uniform delivered pricing (347)
Zone-delivered pricing (347)
Freight-absorption pricing (347)
One-price strategy (348)
Flexible-price (variable-price) strategy (348)
Single-price strategy (349)
Price lining (349)
Odd pricing (349)
Leader pricing (350)
Loss leaders (350)
Everyday low pricing (350)
High-low pricing (350)
Price war (352)

Questions and Problems

1. For each of the following products, should the seller adopt a market-skimming or a market-penetration pricing strategy? Support your decision in each instance.
   a. High-fashion dresses styled and manufactured by Yves St. Laurent.
   b. An exterior housepaint that wears twice as long as any competitive brand.
   c. A cigarette that is totally free of tar and nicotine.
   d. A tablet that converts a litre of water into a litre of automotive fuel.
2. Carefully distinguish between cumulative and noncumulative quantity discounts. Which type of quantity discount has the greater economic and social justification? Why?
3. A manufacturer of appliances quotes a list price of $800 per unit for a certain model of refrigerator and grants trade discounts of 35, 20, and 5 percent. What is the manufacturer's selling price? Who might get these various discounts?
4. The Craig Charles Company (CCC) sells to all its customers at the same published price. One of its sales managers discerns that Jamaican Enterprises is offering to sell to one of CCC's customers, Mountain Sports, at a lower price. CCC then cuts its price to Mountain Sports but maintains the original price for all other customers. Is CCC's price cut a violation of the Competition Act?
5. "An f.o.b. point-of-production price system is the only geographic price system that is fair to buyers." Discuss.
6. An eastern firm wants to compete in western markets, where it is at a significant disadvantage with respect to freight costs. What pricing alternatives can it adopt to overcome the freight differential?
7. Under what conditions is a company likely to use a variable-price strategy? Can you name firms that employ this strategy other than when a trade-in is involved?
8. On the basis of the topics covered in this chapter, establish a set of price strategies for the manufacturer of a new glass cleaner that is sold through an intermediary to supermarkets. The manufacturer sells the cleaner at $15 for a case of a dozen 482 mL bottles.

Hands-On Marketing

1. Talk to the owner or a top executive of a firm in your community regarding whether this company emphasizes price or nonprice competition and the reasons for following this course. Also ask whether its approach is similar to or dissimilar from the normal approach used by competitors to market the primary product sold by this firm.
2. Visit a local discount store such as Wal-Mart or Zellers. Note the prices of three products including a child's toy, a piece of electronic equipment such as a CD player, and a small appliance. Check these prices with other outlets that sell on the basis of high-low pricing, such as Sears, Eaton's, and the Bay. Determine whether there is a difference in price. Are the products selling at high or low prices in the nondiscount outlets?

Case 4-1

EJE TRANS-LITE INC.

In early 1994, Paul Edison, marketing director of EJE Trans-Lite Inc., was trying to decide what to do concerning the price of the Digi-Lite, the company's principal product. Paul had helped design the original Digi-Lite soon after he joined EJE in 1989. His technical background was in radio operations and electronic communications. He had completed a course in this at Red River College in Winnipeg before spending eight years in the offshore oil industry immediately prior to joining EJE.

When the Digi-Lite was introduced in 1990, it was the world's smallest rescue light; it measured 4.2 x 5.0 cm and weighed only 33 g. It could be tied to or sewn on any survival system (life jacket, survival suit, or life raft) by means of a plastic tie or specially designed patch. The light was visible for 1.2 nautical miles, and the lithium battery, when activated, would last 12 hours, 50 percent longer than competitive products. The Digi-Lite was the only product that operated automatically when in contact with water, a great advantage in marine applications where the user could be unconscious or seriously injured.

Sales growth was rapid, and by 1993, it was sold through approximately 45 independent distributors in 40 countries. EJE had a sales agent in the United States who sold to the distributors there. Ninety-seven percent of sales were outside Canada, with 60 percent going to the United States. Two of the largest distributors that EJE had were Unitor and Jotron, both Scandinavian-based companies that sold a broad range of products to the marine industry. Unitor advertised daily delivery to 837 ports throughout the world, and it had offices and warehouses in many of these ports. Jotron sold mainly to independent distributors throughout the world; EJE manufactured Digi-Lites for them with the Jotron brand name.

Besides using distributors, EJE sold direct to cruise lines and manufacturers of water survival clothing. Both were considered original equipment manufacturers (OEM) accounts, and the volume justified lower pricing. In fact, price was the major purchasing decision criterion among OEM accounts, followed by availability of inventory. For distributors, the decision criteria varied depending on the size of the distributor. The larger distributors placed more emphasis on price as they often sold to smaller distributors and sometimes to large user accounts. Smaller distributors generally sold in small quantities to final customers such as fishermen or recreational users, and price was less important as the final customer was not so price-sensitive. Availability was often the most important purchase criterion, along with the convenience of being able to purchase many items from a single source of supply. In some instances, for example, EJE and Jotron sold to the same distributors. EJE had the price advantage when large orders were involved, but Jotron had the advantage when smaller quantities were involved as it could offer the convenience of a broad range of items that could be bought at one time.

Paul estimated that his 1993 North American market share was 35 percent and market share in the rest of the world was 46 percent. There were two main competitors, ACR Electronics in the United States and McMurdo in the United Kingdom. Both had larger units that required manual operation and were slightly higher priced. ACR Electronics sold about the same number of units as EJE in North America, but its total annual sales were at least 10 times greater due to an expanded product line. It also sold strobe lights, buoy lights, search and rescue transponders, electronic positioning devices, and other electronic equipment.

The original unit, model A-12M, was for marine applications. In 1993, Paul introduced model A-12A, a similar model for aviation applications, and had sold one trial order of 500 units. Government approval for general sale was expected at any time, and Paul expected to sell 6,000 units in 1994. A final model was the A-12EWS, identical to model A-12M, but with a copper wire attached to it to ensure contact with the water in the event it was on an inflatable life jacket and was too high above the water to be activated automatically. The Canadian Coast Guard purchased 3,600 units in 1993 and was expected to buy another 4,800 in 1994. Paul also expected to sell 7,200 units of model A-12EWS to the United Kingdom in 1994.

Paul estimated the world market would grow by 20.4 percent in 1994, but his own sales should increase by 23 percent because of expected increases in sales of models A-12A and A-12EWS.

All Digi-Lites, while designed by EJE, were assembled by another firm in St. John's, Newfoundland, and were sold to EJE in lots of 10,000 units. Exhibit 1 shows the sales and profit data for 1993.

In January 1994, Paul was contacted by one of his major distributors and informed that unless he dropped his price by $12\frac{1}{2}$ percent, the distributor would have to buy elsewhere. Both competitors had dropped their prices, and although the distributor preferred to buy EJE Digi-Lites, the price differential was too great.

After a careful assessment, Paul determined that he stood to lose 27 percent of his 1994 projected sales. He thought that he would maintain proposed sales of model A-12A as these would be domestic sales, and there was no competitive product. He also thought he would maintain proposed sales of model A-12EWS in Canada, but would probably lose the U.K. order. Model A-12M would account for the balance of lost sales.

Paul was trying to decide what to do. This was the first major pricing decision he had to make. He really didn't want to lower his price as he worked on a 70 percent markup over cost and had used this markup for every product and every customer since the company started in business. EJE had just designed a unit with a slightly smaller, lighter lens that would be cheaper to produce, but, unfortunately, approval to design changes would take about a year, and production would delay introduction another six months.

Another alternative Paul had was to introduce units identical in size and appearance to the present units, only with flashing bulbs. These could be available in one month, would extend battery life to 40 hours, and would be the only flashing units on the market. It would cost about $15,000 for engineering and production set-up; otherwise, the additional cost per unit would be $0.60 to EJE. If they were introduced in 1994, and Paul kept his full markup on all models, he expected that his sales would still be 22 percent below his 1994 projections. He also anticipated sales for model A-12A would change totally to flashing units due to the extended battery life; sales of model A-12EWS would remain totally with regular bulbs as many users were uncomfortable with flashing bulbs because they believed they might be less visible due to wave action that could hide them at times. For model A-12M, Paul thought that 30 percent of his sales would be for flashing units.

Questions

1. What impact will the competitor's price reduction have on EJE?
2. What would be the financial impact on EJE if Paul decided to introduce the new models with flashing bulbs?
3. What should Paul Edison do?

EXHIBIT 2

EXHIBIT 1 EJE Sales and Profit Data, 1993

Model	Units Sold	Cost	Selling Price	Contribution/Unit	Contribution/Total
A-12M	90,871	7.74	13.16	5.42	492,520.82
A-12A	500	7.74	13.16	5.42	2,710.00
A-12EWS	3,600	8.94	15.20	6.26	22,536.00

Case 4-2

BREAK-EVEN EXERCISES

Case A: Karina's Pizza

Karina's Pizza produces two products, 12-inch pizzas and 16-inch pizzas, with the following characteristics:

	12-Inch Pizza	16-Inch Pizza
Selling Price	$500,000 ($5/unit)	$900,000 ($6/unit)
Variable Cost	$300,000	$300,000
Expected Sales (Units)	100,000	150,000

The total fixed costs for the company are $700,000.

Questions

1. What is the anticipated level of profits for the expected sales volumes?
2. Assuming that the product mix in units would be the same as above at the break-even point, compute the break-even point in terms of number of units of each of the products.
3. If the product sales mix were to change to four 12-inch pizzas for each 16-inch pizza, what would be the new break-even volume for each of the products? Comment on number of units required to break even for this sales mix, compared with the original sales mix.

Case B: Matthew's Mining Company

The following income statement represents Matthew's Mining Company's operating results for the fiscal year just ended. The company had sales of 1,600 tonnes during the current year. The manufacturing capacity of Matthew's facilities is 2,800 tonnes per year. (Ignore income taxes.)

Matthew's Mining Company
Income Statement
For the Year Ended December 31, Year One

Sales		$800,000
Variable costs:		
Manufacturing	$280,000	
Selling costs	160,000	
Total variable costs	$440,000	440,000
Contribution margin		360,000
Fixed costs:		
Manufacturing	$ 90,000	
Selling	112,500	
Administrative	45,000	
Total fixed costs	$247,500	247,500
Net income		$112,500

This case was prepared by Judith A. Cumby, assistant professor, Faculty of Business Administration, Memorial University of Newfoundland, as a basis for class discussion and is not intended to reflect either an effective or an ineffective handling of a management problem.

Questions

1. Calculate the company's break-even volume in tonnes for Year One.
2. If the sales volume is estimated to be 1,900 tonnes in the next year, and if the prices and costs stay at the same levels and amounts, what is the net income that management can expect for Year Two?
3. The company has a potential foreign customer that has offered to buy 1,700 tonnes at $450 per tonne. Assume that all of Matthew's costs would be at the same levels and rates as in Year One. What net income would the firm earn if it took this order and rejected some business from regular customers so as not to exceed capacity? Why might Matthew's consider accepting this order at a reduced selling price?
4. Matthew's plans to market its product in a new territory. Management estimates that an advertising and promotion program costing $42,000 annually would be needed for each of the next two or three years. In addition, a $15 per tonne sales commission to the sales force in the new territory, over and above the current commission, would be required. Assume that all of Matthew's costs would be at the same levels and rates as in Year One, with the only incremental costs being those related to advertising and promotion and the additional sales commission. How many extra tonnes would have to be sold in the new territory to maintain Matthew's current net income? (Ignore the information in question 3.)
5. Refer to the original data. Matthew's is considering replacing its labour-intensive process with an automated production system. This would result in an increase of $56,000 annually in fixed manufacturing costs. The variable manufacturing costs would decrease by $25 per tonne. Compute the new break-even volume in tonnes and in sales dollars.

Case 4-3

PRICING

A Great Deal on Heating Oil

The Maxwell Oil Company had been marketing home heating oil to homeowners in the Westville area for more than 50 years. This company operated an annual payment/purchase plan that offered customers a package that, for $99 per year, gave them regular maintenance, service and insurance on their furnaces, and the fuel at 34 cents per litre.

During the past year or so, the company had noticed it was receiving a number of telephone calls from customers who were calling to cancel their annual plan because a local competitor was offering them home heating oil at 30 cents per litre. Maxwell management agreed to match the deal for any customer who called in the future, thereby giving anyone who called a reduction of 4 cents per litre from the current contract price.

The net result was that many customers started to call, once it became generally known in certain Westville neighbourhoods that Maxwell was prepared to match the competitor's price. Then the company began to receive a number of calls from very angry customers who were upset at the fact that some of their neighbours, who apparently had signed up for the same contract, had been receiving their fuel at 4 cents per litre less — merely because they had called up and asked for it. Those who were still paying the higher price were not happy and threatened to leave. Some had been Maxwell customers for 30 years or more and felt "hurt" at being treated this way.

Questions

1. What obligation, if any, did the Maxwell company have to offer the same price reduction to all customers who were currently under contract with the annual plan?
2. What options did the company have when it first encountered the fact that the competition was offering fuel at 4 cents per litre less? Should it have let some of its customers go or tried to keep as many as possible?
3. Is there an ethical issue involved when prices are lowered for some customers and not for others?

SALE DAY AT THE BAY

Bob Jones was walking through the men's wear department of The Bay department store in downtown Westville, taking a shortcut to the restaurant where he was meeting Gail for lunch. As he neared the door, Bob noticed a rack of men's cotton slacks, above which was displayed a large sign announcing "SPECIAL! 50% OFF." Although Bob had not intended to buy slacks that day, he was attracted by the sign and stopped to look at the goods.

As Bob examined the slacks on the rack, he noticed that the brand was Ruff Hewn and that the original price was $80. He thought, "I could use a pair of slacks and this is a really good price." He had a couple of Ruff Hewn cotton shirts hanging in his closet, and he thought the sweater Gail had given him for his birthday was Ruff Hewn as well. He picked out a dark green pair, size 32 waist, and tried them on. They fitted perfectly, so he decided to buy them.

"Is that on your Bay account, sir?" asked the sales clerk. Bob replied that he would be paying cash and took a $50 bill from his wallet. The clerk then asked, "Do you have your Bay Day card?" Bob indicated that he wasn't familiar with a Bay Day card. The clerk explained that he should have picked up a Bay Day card as he entered the store and that, since this was Bay Day, he was entitled to scratch a certain part of the card to reveal the discount that he would receive on his purchase. As Bob didn't have a card, she reached under the counter and gave him one. Bob scratched the latex portion of the card and saw the words "30% OFF."

"Too bad I can't use this," Bob commented. "The pants are already 50 percent off." "Oh no," replied the sales clerk. "You get an additional 30 percent off the sale price. Let's see, that's another $12, so the price of the slacks will be $28." Bob was delighted. He really hadn't expected to get the pants for that low a price. He had thought he was getting a good deal at $40. He paid the $28, plus tax, thanked the sales clerk, and rushed off to apologize to Gail for being late.

Questions

1. What was the price of the pants that Bob bought?
2. What factors influenced his decision to buy?
3. What would Bob have done if he had seen a rack of pants at The Bay with a sign reading "COTTON SLACKS $28" or a sign that said "COTTON SLACKS $80"?

SANDSTROM STEREOTACTIC SYSTEM

Pia Sandstrom of Welland, Ontario, was studying medical technology at the University of Umea, Sweden, when her mother, Monica, came to see her and to visit her homeland. Monica, trained as a chemical engineer, was looking for a new career, having retired from her research job at a Hamilton chemical company. She decided to check out the possibility of importing Swedish medical devices to Canada. She and Pia came upon a revolutionary device that helps locate brain tumours. They decided to begin importing the product into North America, only to find that the product could not meet U.S. health standards.

They decided to begin manufacturing the device themselves and, three years later, having dipped into savings, sold off investments, and mortgaged the family home, the Sandstroms expected to sell forty of their Stereotactic Systems a year at $25,000 each. They rely on a chain of suppliers in the Hamilton area to make the components of the system and to assemble the final product.

Most North American hospitals have been using a device that is screwed into the patient's forehead with sheet-metal screws. These machines are heavy, painful, and expensive — at $60,000 to $100,000 each. The Sandstrom system attaches painlessly to the patient's ears and nose and can be worn all day without discomfort. And it sells for only $25,000.

Stereotactic systems work much like a sailor's sextant. A technician, working from X-rays or ultrasound, reads off the co-ordinates of the tumour and gives the information to the neurosurgeon. By pinpointing the location of the tumour, 85 percent of the cost of the surgery is saved. A professor of neurosurgery at the University of Saskatchewan observed, "The patient can go home the next day, instead of being hospitalized for three weeks. That makes the patient cheaper to look after."

The Sandstroms are a two-person company. They spend their time networking at medical trade shows where they meet doctors and academics and develop leads, which they then follow up. They have come to realize that it takes a considerable amount of time and effort to generate sales. It also took them some time to accept that a machine that costs only $1,700 to manufacture can be sold for 15 times that amount when it reaches the market.

Questions

1. What is the relationship between cost and price in the marketing of the Sandstrom Stereotactic System?
2. How would you explain to a professor of neurosurgery why the price of the device is $25,000?
3. How important is price to a senior hospital administrator who must justify the purchase of this device in an economic climate where hospital budgets are being severely cut by governments?

Part Five

Distribution

Channels of distribution from producer to user, wholesaling, and retailing institutions

We are in the process of developing a marketing program to reach the firm's target markets and achieve the goals established in strategic marketing planning. So far, we have considered the product and pricing structure in that marketing mix. Now we turn our attention to the distribution system — the means for getting products and services to the market.

The distribution ingredient in the marketing mix encompasses two broad topics: (1) strategies for selecting and operating channels of distribution — Chapter 15, and (2) the wholesaling and retailing institutions used in distribution — Chapters 16 and 17.

CHAPTER 15 GOALS

We will discuss distribution channels in this chapter from the point of view of the producer or the developer of the product or service. As you will see, however, the problems and opportunities that intermediaries face in managing their channels are similar to those faced by distributors. After studying this chapter, you should have an understanding of:

- The nature and importance of intermediaries.
- What a distribution channel is.
- The sequence of decisions involved in designing a channel.
- The major channels for consumer goods, business goods, and services.
- Vertical marketing systems.
- Intensity of distribution.
- How to choose individual intermediaries.
- The nature of conflicts and control within distribution channels.
- Legal considerations in channels management.

Chapter Fifteen

Channels of Distribution: Conflict, Co-operation, and Management

IS DISTRIBUTION ONLY ABOUT BEANS?

When marketers consider distribution they have traditionally thought of "how to get the beans on the supermarket shelf" and about the connections between the farmer, the wholesaler, the packager, the distributor, and the supermarket that make it possible to transfer the beans from the farmer's field to the consumer's table. Channels of distribution enable the consumer to access the product and consequently be in a position to purchase it. Often referred to as "place," this element of marketing considers most effective networks, how to reach the consumers when they are ready to buy, and issues of location and size of retail outlet. These questions are still very important in marketing — particularly in marketing beans. It would be very difficult to imagine how we would be able to produce Boston Browns in our ovens without these channels. But what of marketing products that are not as tangible as beans? For example, how does distribution apply in services? In particular, what about the distribution of financial services?

The Royal Bank of Canada is now accepting credit card applications via Internet.[1] Gord Kinkead, manager of the Eastern Card Centre of the bank, claims that the bank wants to give customers the convenience of applying directly to card processing centres through a personal computer. Using this route will speed up the application. American Express Canada Inc. gives its members advice on how to save money on travel and entertainment via its Internet site. On the same site it will assist you in making travel and vacation plans and finalize bookings made with your American Express credit card.[2] Visa, the Toronto Dominion Bank, and ScotiaBank provide an electronic cash card. This card was created to meet a consumer demand for convenience.[3]

What do all of these services provide? The obvious answer is access to money or the things money traditionally could buy. Are credit cards, Internet banking sites, and cash cards distribution channels? Can we think of these financial services as being distributed via this new technology? Most certainly. Services generally do not fit the conventional mode of distribution, in which the producer provides product to the wholesaler, who provides product to the distributor, who provides product to the retailer, who sells to the ultimate consumer. That model of distribution channel is valid for some tangible products. Services, however, do not fit this pattern. Services delivered through new technology, as is the case with financial services, fit the model less and less.

It is difficult to think of a credit card as being a distribution network, yet it is. Consumers avail themselves of credit cards for purposes of access to financial support. When a clerk in a department store swipes our credit card for that new pair of jeans, he or she is activating a distribution network that brings us money or its equivalent. Financial institutions are making the availability of credit as convenient as possible. When the Royal Bank provides credit application access via the Internet, it is distributing not only the use of the credit via this technology, but also the initial access to the service. In the case of Amex Canada Inc., the firm is linking its product — credit — to the ultimate product being considered by the consumer — travel. The credit service is, in effect, a distribution network for the travel product.

All of these variations on distribution of services and products are blurring the traditional model of distribution channels. As you read through this chapter, remember that distribution can occur in many ways and in many forms.

INTERMEDIARIES AND DISTRIBUTION CHANNELS

Ownership of a product has to be transferred somehow from the individual or organization that makes it to the consumer who needs and buys it. Goods also must be physically transported from where they are produced to where they are needed. The distribution channels for services can be viewed somewhat differently from those of goods. As we saw in Chapter 12, services are produced and consumed in the same place. To market services, those concerned with distribution must consider producing them in locations where they are wanted and accessible by the customer.[4]

Distribution's role within a firm's marketing program is getting the product or service efficiently and conveniently to its target market. The most important activity in getting a product to market is arranging for its sale (and the transfer of title) from producer to final customer. Other common activities (or functions) are promoting the goods or services, storing goods, ensuring that production capacity exists for services, and assuming some of the financial risk during the distribution process.

A producer can carry out these functions in exchange for an order (and, it is hoped, payment) from a customer. Or producer and consumer can share these activities. Typically, however, firms called intermediaries perform some of these activities on behalf of the producer or the consumer.

An **intermediary** is a business firm that renders services related directly to the sale and/or purchase of a product as it flows from producer to consumer. An intermediary either owns the product at some point or actively aids in the transfer of ownership. Often, but not always, an intermediary takes physical possession of the product. Most services don't involve the use of intermediaries because they are generally inseparable from the service provider. There are exceptions to that situation: The travel industry is an example of a situation in which services are transferred via intermediaries. Travel agents arrange flights, book hotels, purchase theatre tickets, and assist the traveller in many ways to plan a vacation or business trip.

Intermediaries are commonly classified on the basis of whether they take title to the products being distributed. **Merchant intermediaries** actually take title to the products they help to market. The two groups of merchant intermediaries are wholesalers and retailers. A distributor for Neilson chocolate bars is an example of a wholesale intermediary. Franchisee operators can be viewed as retail intermediaries in the service industry. **Agents** never actually own the products, but they do arrange the transfer of title. Real estate brokers, manufacturers' agents, and travel agents are examples of agents.

How Important Are Intermediaries?

Some critics say prices are high because there are too many intermediaries performing unnecessary or redundant functions. In recent years, some manufacturers also reached this conclusion and sought to cut costs by eliminating wholesaling intermediaries. While intermediaries can be eliminated from channels, lower costs may not always be achieved. The outcome is not predictable, because of a basic axiom of marketing: You can eliminate intermediaries, but you cannot eliminate the essential distribution activities that they perform. These activities — such as creating assortments and storing products — can be shifted from one party to another in an effort to improve efficiency. However, someone has to perform the various activities — if not an intermediary, then the producer or the final customers.[5]

Intermediaries may be able to carry out distribution activities better or more cheaply than either producers or consumers. Moreover, it is usually not practical for a producer to deal directly with ultimate consumers. Think for a moment how inconvenient your life would be if there were no retail intermediaries — no supermarkets, gas stations, post offices, or ticket sales outlets, for instance.

As illustrated in Figure 15-1, intermediaries serve as purchasing agents for their customers and as sales specialists for their suppliers. They provide financial services for both suppliers and customers. Intermediaries' storage services, their capability to divide large shipments into smaller ones for resale, and their market knowledge benefit suppliers and customers alike.

What Is a Distribution Channel?

A **distribution channel** consists of the set of people and firms involved in the transfer of title to a product as the product moves from producer to ultimate consumer or business user. A channel of distribution always includes both the producer and the final customer for the product in its present form, as well as any intermediaries such as retailers and wholesalers. In the case of services, the producer and the retailer are often one and the same.

The channel for a product extends only to the last person or organization that buys it without making any significant change in its form. When its form is altered and another product emerges, a new channel is started. When lumber is milled and then made into furniture, two separate channels are involved. The channel for the lumber might be lumber mill → broker → furniture manufacturer. The channel for the finished furniture might be furniture manufacturer → retail furniture store → consumer.

Besides the producer, intermediaries, and the final customer, other institutions aid the distribution process. Among these intermediaries are banks, insurance companies, storage firms, and transportation companies. However, because they do not take title to the products and are not actively involved in

FIGURE 15-1

Typical Activities of an Intermediary

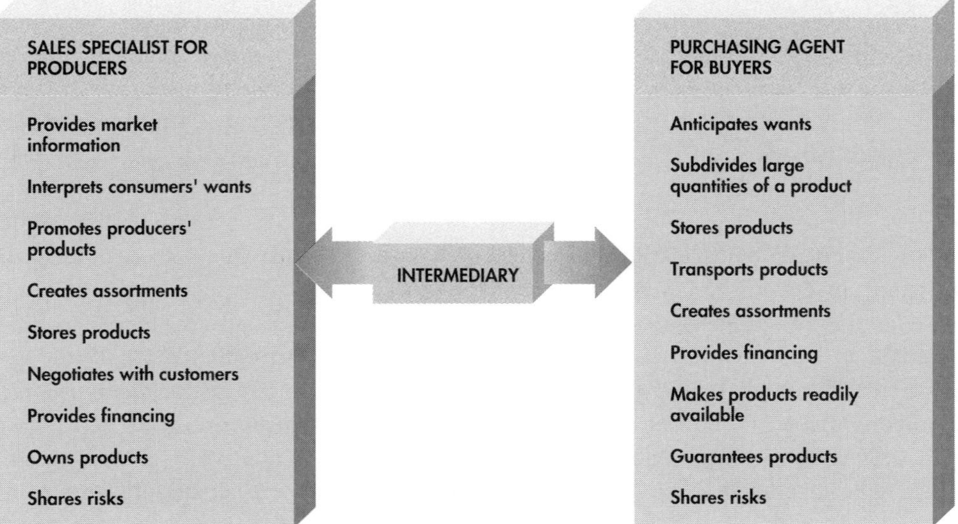

purchase or sales activities, these intermediaries are not formally included in the distribution channel.

This chapter focuses on the flow (or transfer) of ownership for a product, while part of Chapter 16 examines the physical flow of goods. These flows are distinct; consequently, different institutions may carry them out. For example, a contractor might order roofing shingles from a local building-materials distributor. To minimize freight and handling costs, the product might be shipped directly — for example, shingles manufacturer → contractor. But the channel for title (and ownership) would be manufacturer → distributor → contractor.

DESIGNING DISTRIBUTION CHANNELS

Companies that appear to be similar often have very dissimilar channels of distribution. For example, Tupperware sells its housewares primarily through a party-plan arrangement, in which customers buy products at Tupperware "parties" held in the homes of friends and neighbours. Rubbermaid, on the other hand, sells its similar line of housewares through conventional department and variety stores. Some companies use multiple channels of distribution. Hotels, such as the Westin Harbour Castle, for instance, sell their products and services directly to walk-in customers, through travel agents who make reservations and guarantee bookings with the customer, by mail, fax, or telephone, or through their homepage on the Internet.

Why do seemingly similar firms or the same firm wind up with such different channels? One reason is that there are numerous types of channels and intermediaries from which to choose. Also, a variety of factors related to the market, product, intermediaries, and company itself influence the choice of channels actually used by a firm.

A company wants a distribution channel that not only meets customers' needs but also provides an edge on the competition. Some firms gain a differential advantage with their distribution channels. Major corporations such as Caterpillar in construction equipment and John Deere in farm equipment use dealers to provide many important services, ranging from advice about financing programs to rapid filling of orders for repair parts. Gateway Computers has eliminated intermediaries in selling its products and is now dealing directly with customers via the Internet. Using this formula, Gateway is able to reap higher margins while selling computers at competitive prices.[6]

To design channels that satisfy customers and outdo competition, an organized approach is required.[7] As shown in Figure 15-2, we suggest a sequence of four decisions:

1. *Specifying the role of distribution.* A channel strategy should be designed within the context of the entire marketing mix. First the firm's marketing objectives are reviewed. Next the roles assigned to product, price, and promotion are specified. Each element may have a distinct role, or two elements may share an assignment. For example, a manufacturer of pressure gauges may use both intermediaries and direct-mail advertising to convince prospective customers that it is committed to servicing the product following the sale.

   In services marketing, the role of distribution is generally related to accessibility. Because the consumer is often involved in the provision of the service, as, for example, in legal services, the ability to access the service product directly is crucial to its saleability. Determining the role of distribution in the marketing plan includes consideration of the human resources that will be applied to the delivery of the service. Most services cannot be delivered by mail, stored on a shelf and passed over a counter by an intermediary, or delivered through indirect systems. The producer must be able to meet face-to-face with the buyer.

   A company must decide whether distribution will be used defensively or offensively. Under a defensive approach, a firm will strive for distribution that is as good as, but not necessarily better than, other firms' distribution. With an offensive strategy, a firm uses distribution to gain an advantage over competitors. Banks provide a good example of the use of offensive strategies. The major banks are moving rapidly to get the jump on their competitors with the use of online personal computer services, with telephone service options, and by sending employees to the

www.caterpillar.com • www.deere.com

FIGURE 15-2

Sequence of Decisions to Design a Distribution Channel

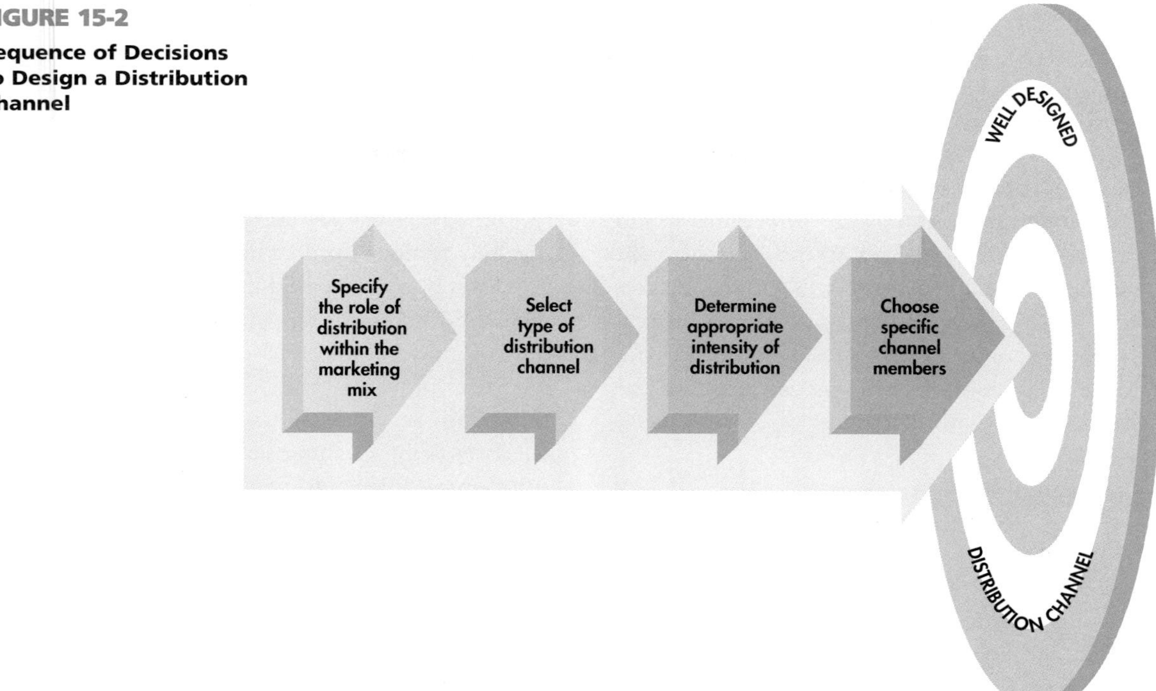

homes of customers to provide personal attention for banking needs. A British Columbia credit union recently announced that it offers "fully transactional Internet Banking service" where members can perform all their transactions using a Web site.[8]

2. *Selecting the type of channel.* Once distribution's role in the overall marketing program has been agreed on, the most suitable type of channel for the company's tangible product or service must be determined. At this point in the sequence, a firm needs to decide whether intermediaries will be used in its channel and, if so, which types of intermediaries will be used.[9]

   To illustrate the wide array of institutions available, as well as the difficulty of channel selection, consider a manufacturer of compact disc players. If the firm decides to use intermediaries, it must choose among many different types. At the retail level, the range of institutions includes specialty audio-video outlets, department stores, discount houses, mail-order firms, and Internet retail services. Which single type or combination of types would permit the manufacturer to achieve its distribution objectives? Another choice must be made if the firm decides to also use wholesaling intermediaries. In a subsequent section, this decision as well as the major types of channels for goods and services will be discussed in detail.

3. *Determining intensity of distribution.* The next decision relates to **intensity of distribution**, or the number of intermediaries used at the wholesale and retail levels in a particular territory. The target market's buying behaviour and the product's nature have a direct bearing on this decision, as we will see later.

4. *Choosing specific channel members.* The last decision is selecting specific firms to distribute the product. For each type of institution, there are usually numerous specific companies from which to choose.

   Recalling our CD player example, assume that the manufacturer prefers two types of intermediaries: department stores and specialty outlets. If the CD players will be sold in Toronto, the producer must decide which department stores and audio retail outlets — Sears, The Bay, Bay Bloor Radio, Toronto Music Super Store — will be asked to distribute its product line. Also one or more audio Internet distributors — including, among others, Sony Music Canada and World Records Ltd. — may need to be considered. Similar decisions must be made for each territory in the firm's market.

When selecting specific firms to be part of a channel, a producer should assess factors related to the market, the product, its own company, and intermediaries. Two additional factors are whether the intermediary sells to the market that the manufacturer wants to reach and whether the intermediary's product mix, pricing structure, promotion, and customer service are all compatible with the manufacturer's needs.

SELECTING THE TYPE OF CHANNEL

Firms may rely on existing channels, or they may use new channels to better serve current customers and reach prospective customers. In selecting its channels, a firm should seek to gain a differential advantage. For instance, besides selling through various types of retailers, Levi Strauss & Co. has started opening its own stores featuring, of course, Levi's apparel.[10] Alberto-Culver Canada Inc. of Toronto, which has been distributing its products — Alberto VO5 hair care, Alberto European toiletries — through drug store chains, is now moving into mass-market distribution and selling its products through supermarkets and mass-merchandise outlets.[11] L.L. Bean, the outdoor clothing distributor, who has distributed merchandise through a mail-order system since its creation, is now focusing on distributing via the Internet. This company is finding that this is the company's best source for new customers. Marketing through this channel also reduces costs for L.L. Bean by eliminating the need for paper usage in catalogue production.[12]

Most goods distribution channels include intermediaries, but some do not. A channel consisting only of producer and final customer, with no intermediaries providing assistance, is called **direct distribution**. ServiceMaster uses a direct approach to sell its building cleaning services to both residential and commercial customers. Services are generally distributed directly because production and consumption usually occur simultaneously. Red Lobster restaurants, for example, produce the food they sell and distribute it directly to the consumer.

In contrast, a channel of producer, final customer, and at least one level of intermediaries represents **indirect distribution**. Canadian Airlines International depends heavily on an indirect approach, involving travel agents, to market its air travel services to consumers. One level of intermediaries — retailers but no wholesaling intermediaries, for example — or multiple levels may participate in an indirect channel. (For consumer goods, sometimes a channel in which wholesalers are bypassed but retailers are used is termed *direct*,

MARKETING AT WORK FILE 15-1

THE DISTRIBUTION OF TRAVEL

Have you ever planned a vacation through a travel agent? Maybe you took that "good grades" trek through Europe or simply went home for spring break. In either case, if you used the services of a travel agent, or if you booked directly through airlines and hotels, you have been the beneficiary of the distribution channel of travel services. Think of what happens when you go into a travel agent's office. You speak with an agent and tell that individual you want to go, for example, to Europe for a vacation. The agent will very likely talk to you about what you hope to do on your vacation so that he or she can offer suggestions as to what countries to see and which sights to visit. The agent will show you brochures and travel guides for the countries and cities you are interested in visiting. Then together you will plan your vacation. The agent will make the bookings and eventually provide you with an itinerary. Now, let's think of the people who have been involved in bringing you that service.

Travel and tourism are sold through a number of different intermediaries. The airlines will determine the flights and seat prices that they make available. Through a computer network that connects the airlines and the travel agents, the information on flight availability and bookings is made available. The technology of the network is part of the distribution channel. Information on countries, hotels, and attractions is distributed, generally, in a much more complex manner. Many countries have tourism boards or agencies responsible for internationally marketing the country. The Canadian Tourism Commission maintains responsibility for promoting Canada in other locations around the world. In addition to the main tourism boards, cities, towns, or communities often have their own tourism bodies who co-ordinate the efforts of local tourism operators in marketing their location to potential travellers. These groups all produce literature and information on services and attractions that are of interest to the tourist. Individual hotels or attractions sometimes do their own international, as well as local, marketing. Tourism information is made available to travel agents, who then sell the products to travellers such as you when planning your vacation.

Another intermediary involved in marketing tourism is the wholesaler. This individual puts together tourism packages and sells them through the travel agent. Instead of planning your own vacation in Europe, you may wish to purchase a preplanned package that will take you to a number of countries in a two- or three-week vacation. The hotel arrangements and bus or train travel will be already taken care of, and you will join with a number of other people to visit the locations of the tour. To prepare this package, the tour wholesaler met with the hotel, bus, and attractions people and purchased their products, which were then made available for sale through the travel agents. The wholesaler may have met with the agents to promote the product that was being offered. In any case, promotional literature will have been developed and made available. Sometimes, travel agents will put together their own tours, thereby eliminating the need for a wholesaler.

Other avenues exist for distributing tourism products. The travel industry sets up trade shows and other venues to sell tour packages and promote destinations to any groups who may be interested in buying. For example, the various provinces and territories of Canada will often send representatives to European or Asian travel shows to sell this country to wholesalers and travel agents in those areas.

It is interesting to speculate what effect the advent of the Internet will have on this distribution network and whether or not travel agent services will continue to be used to the extent they have been in the past. Any traveller who wishes to purchase tours or arrange trips can do so through the Internet. Many, however, are not yet on-line and do not have the time required to research the Net and seek the information and services they desire. Debra Ward, president of the Tourism Industry Association of Canada, does not feel that travel agents are dead yet. "People whose time is more valuable than money will continue to use travel agents," she predicts.

Sources: "Canadian Tourism Information Network," *About the Canadian Tourism Commission,* July 18, 1997, http://zinfo.ic.gc.ca/Tourism/ctc.html; Catherine Mulrooney, "Don't Count Travel Agents Out Just Yet," The *Globe and Mail,* September 17, 1996, p. C1.

rather than indirect, distribution.) With indirect distribution, a producer must determine the type(s) of intermediaries that will best serve its needs. The range of options at the wholesale and retail levels will be described in the next two chapters.

Now we'll look at the major channels traditionally used by producers of tangible products and at two special channels. Then we can consider the factors that most influence a company's choice of channels.

Airline customers may eventually bypass travel agents like Alan Pink of Canplan Travel, Halifax, NS.

Major Channels of Distribution

Diverse distribution channels exist today. The most common channels for consumer goods, business goods, and services are described next and are summarized in Figure 15-3.

Distribution of Consumer Goods Five channels are widely used in marketing tangible products to ultimate consumers:

- *Producer → consumer.* The shortest, simplest distribution channel for consumer goods involves no intermediaries. The producer may sell from door to door, by mail, or on the Internet. For example, Arcuri Jewellers offers complete catalogue jewellery sales direct to the consumer through its Web page.
- *Producer → retailer → consumer.* Many large retailers buy directly from manufacturers and agricultural producers. Companies such as Loblaws and Wal-Mart maintain direct dealings with producers.
- *Producer → wholesaler → retailer → consumer.* If there is a traditional channel for consumer goods, this is it. Small retailers and manufacturers by the thousands find this channel the only economically feasible choice.
- *Producer → agent → retailer → consumer.* Instead of using wholesalers, many producers prefer to use agents to reach the retail market, especially large-scale retailers. For example, a manufacturer of a glass cleaner selected a food broker to reach the grocery store market, including large chains.
- *Producer → agent → wholesaler → retailer → consumer.* To reach small retailers, producers often use agents, who in turn call on wholesalers that sell to large retail chains and/or small retail stores.

Distribution of Business Products A variety of channels are available to reach organizations that incorporate the products into their manufacturing process or use them in their operations.[13] In the distribution of business products, the terms industrial distributor and merchant wholesaler are synonymous. The four common channels for business goods are:

- *Producer → user.* This direct channel accounts for a greater dollar volume of business products than does any other distribution structure. Manufacturers of large installations, such as airplanes, generators, and heating plants, usually sell directly to users.
- *Producer → industrial distributor → user.* Producers of operating supplies and small accessory equipment frequently use industrial distributors to reach their markets. Manufacturers of building materials and air-conditioning equipment are two examples of firms that make heavy use of industrial distributors.
- *Producer → agent → user.* Firms without their own sales departments find this a desirable channel. Also, a company that wants to introduce a new product or enter a new market may prefer to use agents rather than its own sales force.
- *Producer → agent → industrial distributor → user.* This channel is similar to the preceding one. It is used when, for some reason, it is not feasible to sell through agents directly to the business user.

FIGURE 15-3

Major Marketing Channels for Different Categories of Products

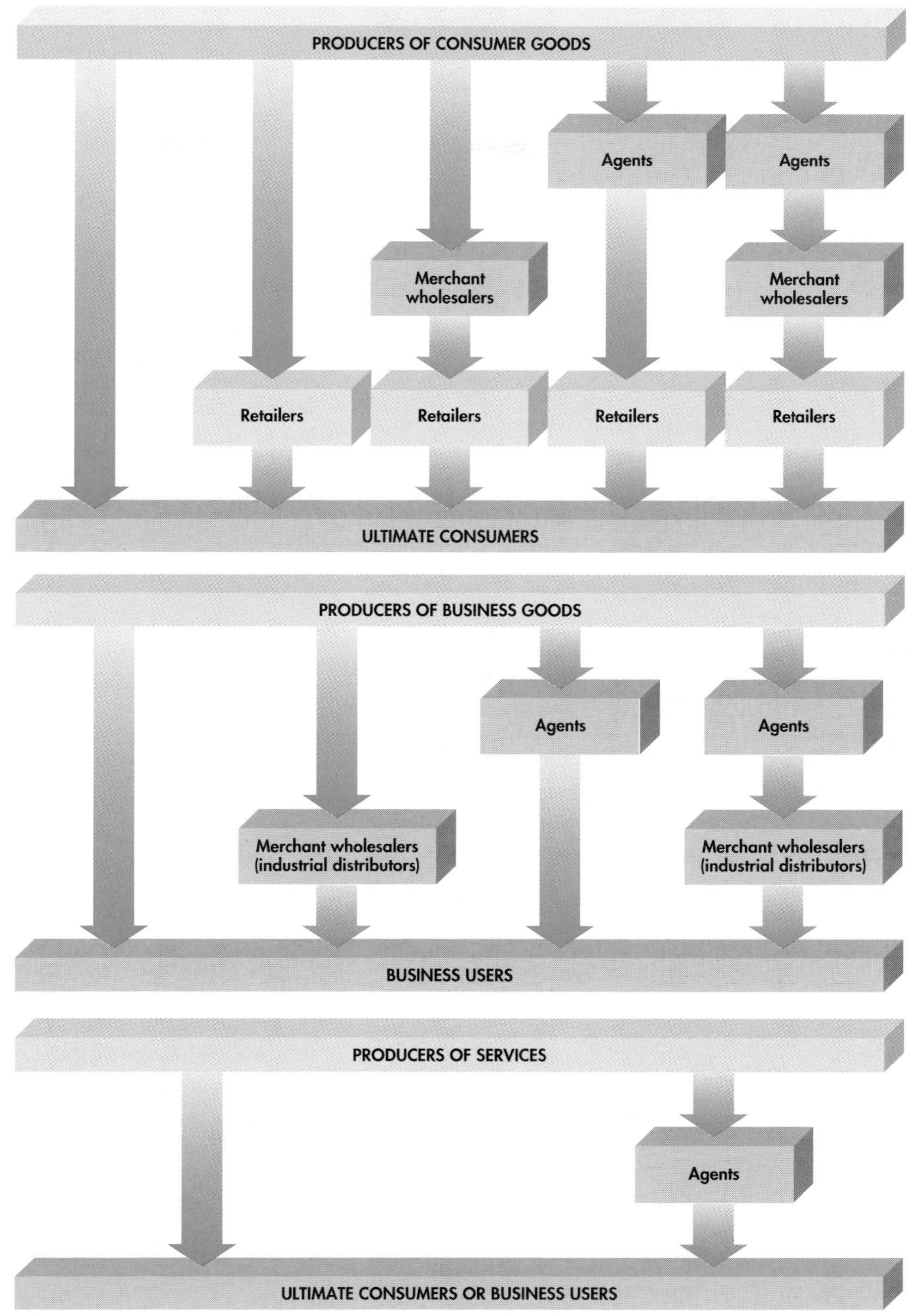

The unit sale may be too small for direct selling. Or decentralized inventory may be needed to supply users rapidly, in which case the storage services of an industrial distributor are required.

Distribution of Services The intangible nature of services creates special distribution requirements. There are only two common channels for services:[14]

www.goodyear.com

- *Producer → consumer.* Because a service is intangible, the production process and/or sales activity often require personal contact between producer and consumer. Thus a direct channel is used. Direct distribution is typical for many professional services, such as health care and legal advice, and personal services, such as haircutting and weight-loss counselling. However, other services, including travel, insurance, and entertainment, may also rely on direct distribution.
- *Producer → agent → consumer.* While direct distribution often is necessary for a service to be performed, producer–consumer contact may not be required for distribution activities. Agents frequently assist a services producer with transfer of ownership (the sales task) or related tasks. Many services, notably travel, lodging, advertising media, entertainment, and insurance, are sold through agents.

Multiple Distribution Channels

Many, perhaps most, producers are not content with only a single distribution channel. Instead, for reasons such as achieving broad market coverage or avoiding total dependence on a single arrangement, they employ **multiple distribution channels**. (Similarly, many companies establish multiple supply channels to ensure that they have products when needed.)

Use of multiple channels, sometimes called **dual distribution**, occurs in several distinct situations.[15] A manufacturer or producer is likely to use multiple channels to reach different types of markets when selling:

- The same product or service (for example, sporting goods or adventure tour packages) to both consumer and business markets.[16]
- Unrelated products (margarine and paint; rubber products and plastics).

Multiple channels are also used to reach different segments within a single market when:

- Size of the buyers varies greatly. An airline may sell directly to travel departments in large corporations but use travel agents to reach small businesses and end consumers.
- Geographic concentration differs across parts of the market. A manufacturer of industrial machinery may use its own sales force to sell directly to customers that are located close together, but may employ agents in sparsely populated markets.

A significant trend involves selling the same brand to a single market through channels that compete with each other. Nike shoes, Sherwin-Williams paints, and Goodyear tires are distributed through the manufacturers' own retail stores as well as through wholesalers, independent retailers, and large retail chains. Producers may open their own stores, thereby creating dual distribution, when they are not satisfied with the market coverage provided by existing retail outlets. Or they may establish their own stores primarily as testing grounds for new products and marketing techniques.

Although multiple distribution channels provide benefits to the producer, they can aggravate intermediaries. One approach, which is difficult to achieve, is to develop separate pricing and promotion strategies for each different channel.[17]

Vertical Marketing Systems

Historically, distribution channels stressed the independence of individual channel members. That is, a producer used various intermediaries to achieve its distribution objectives; however, the producer typically was not concerned with intermediaries' needs. Conversely, wholesalers and retailers were more interested in maintaining their freedom than in co-ordinating their activities with those of a producer. These priorities of conventional distribution channels provided an opportunity for a new type of channel.

During the past three decades, the vertical marketing system has become perhaps the dominant form of distribution channel. A **vertical marketing system** (VMS) is a tightly co-ordinated distribution channel designed specifically to improve operating efficiency and marketing effectiveness. A VMS illustrates the concept of function shifting discussed earlier. In a VMS no marketing function is sacred to a particular level or firm in the channel. Instead, each function is performed at the most advantageous position in the channel.

The high degree of co-ordination or control characterizing a VMS is achieved through one of three means: common ownership of successive levels of a channel, contracts between channel members, or the market power of one or more members. As shown in Table 15-1, there are three distinct forms of vertical marketing systems.

In a **corporate vertical marketing system**, a firm at one level of a channel owns the firms at the next level or owns the entire channel. Sherwin-Williams and Goodyear, for example, own retail outlets. Also, a growing number of apparel makers, such as Roots and Ralph Lauren, have opened retail stores to feature their brands of clothing.

Intermediaries may also engage in this type of vertical integration. For example, some grocery chains own food-processing facilities, such as dairies, which supply their stores. And some large retailers, including Sears, own all or part of manufacturing facilities that supply their stores with many products.

In a **contractual vertical marketing system**, independent producers, wholesalers, and retailers operate under contracts specifying how they will try to improve the effectiveness and efficiency of their distribution. Three kinds of contractual systems have developed: wholesaler-sponsored voluntary chains (for example, IGA grocery stores), retailer-owned co-operatives (Canadian Tire), and franchise systems (Pizza Delight pizza and Midas automotive maintenance and repairs). All will be discussed in Chapter 16.

An **administered vertical marketing system** co-ordinates distribution activities through the market and/or economic power of one channel member or the shared power of two channel members. This is illustrated by Corning in ovenware, Rolex in watches, and Kraft General Foods in food products. Sometimes a producer's brand equity and market position are strong enough to gain the voluntary co-operation of retailers in matters such as inventory levels, advertising, and store display. However, retailers — especially giant ones such as Loblaw and The Bay — are more likely to dominate channel relationships now than in prior years.

In the distant past, competition in distribution usually involved two different conventional channels. For instance, one Producer → Retailer → Consumer channel tended to compete with another Producer → Retailer → Consumer channel. More recently, competition pitted a conventional channel against some form of VMS. Thus a traditional Producer → Retailer → Consumer channel battled a contractual VMS for business. Increasingly, the most common competitive battles are between different forms of vertical marketing systems. For example, a corporate system (such as the stores owned by Goodyear) competes with a contractual system (such

TABLE 15-1 Types of Vertical Marketing Systems

Type of System	Control Maintained By	Examples
Corporate	Ownership	Singer (sewing machines), Goodyear (tires), Radio Shack (electronics), Bata (shoes)
Contractual:		
Wholesaler-sponsored voluntary chain	Contract	IDA and Guardian Drugs, IGA stores
Retailer-owned co-operative	Stock ownership by retailers	Canadian Tire stores
Franchise systems:	Contract	
Manufacturer-sponsored retailers		Ford, Chrysler, and other auto dealers
Manufacturer-sponsored wholesalers		Coca-Cola and other soft-drink bottlers
Marketers of services		Wendy's, Speedy Muffler, Harvey's, Holiday Inn, Tilden car rentals
Administered	Economic power	Samsonite luggage, General Electric, Labatt

as General Tire's franchised dealers). Considering the potential benefits of vertical marketing systems with respect to both marketing effectiveness and operating efficiencies, they should continue to grow in number and importance.

Factors Affecting Choice of Channels

If a firm is customer-oriented, its channels are determined by consumer buying patterns. The nature of the market should be the key factor in management's choice of channels. Other considerations are the product or service being marketed, the intermediaries, and the company itself.

Market Considerations A logical starting point is to consider the target market — its needs, structure, and buying behaviour:

- *Type of market.* Because ultimate consumers behave differently from business users, they are reached through different distribution channels. Retailers, by definition, serve ultimate consumers, so they are not in channels for business goods.
- *Number of potential customers.* A manufacturer with few potential customers (firms or industries) may use its own sales force to sell directly to ultimate consumers or business users. Canadair uses this approach in selling its jet aircraft. For a large number of customers, the manufacturer would likely use intermediaries. Tim Hortons relies on numerous franchisee outlets to reach the large number of consumers buying coffee. A firm using intermediaries does not need as large a sales force as a company selling directly to final consumers.
- *Geographic concentration of the market.* When most of a firm's prospective customers are concentrated in a few geographic areas, direct sale is practical. This is the situation in the textile and garment manufacturing industries. When customers are geographically dispersed, direct sale is likely to be impractical due to high travel costs. Sellers may establish sales branches in densely populated markets and use intermediaries in less concentrated markets.
- *Order size.* When either order size or total volume of business is large, direct distribution is economical. Thus a food-products manufacturer would sell directly to large grocery chains. The same manufacturer, however, would use wholesalers to reach small grocery stores, whose orders are usually too small to justify direct sale.[18]

Product Considerations While there are numerous product-related factors to consider, we will highlight three:

- *Unit value.* The price attached to each unit of a product affects the amount of funds available for distribution. For example, a company can afford to use its own employee to sell a large aircraft engine part that costs more than $10,000. But it would not make sense for a company sales person to call on a household or a business firm to sell a $2 ballpoint pen. Consequently, products with low unit value usually are distributed through indirect channels (that is, through one or more levels of intermediaries). There are exceptions, however. For instance, if order size is large because the customer buys many products at the same time from the company, then a direct channel may be economically feasible.
- *Perishability.* Some goods, including many agricultural products, physically deteriorate fairly quickly. Other products, such as services, can only be consumed in the presence of the producer. Legal advice, for example, is only available directly from a law firm. As was discussed in Chapter 12, services are perishable due to their intangible nature. Perishable products require direct or very short channels.
- *Technical nature of a product.* A business product that is highly technical is often distributed directly to business users. The producer's sales force must provide considerable presale and postsale service; wholesalers normally cannot do this. Consumer products of a technical nature provide a real distribution challenge for manufacturers. Ordinarily, manufacturers cannot sell the goods directly to the consumer. However, with the development of the Internet, it is becoming easier for products to be distributed directly from the manufacturer. Computers and electronic equipment are readily available on various Web sites.

Intermediaries Considerations Here we begin to see that a company may not be able to arrange exactly the channels it desires:

- *Services provided by intermediaries.* Each producer should select intermediaries that will provide those marketing services that the producer either is unable to provide or cannot economically perform.
- *Availability of desired intermediaries.* The intermediaries preferred by a producer may not be available. They may be carrying competitive products and may not want to add another line.
- *Attitude of intermediaries toward producers' policies.* Sometimes manufacturers' choices of channels are limited because their marketing policies are not acceptable to certain types of intermediaries. Some retailers or wholesalers, for example, are interested in carrying a line only if they receive assurance that no competing firms will carry the line in the same territory.
- *Channel or intermediary position.* In some cases, an intermediary has achieved such a strong or even dominant position in the market that a manufacturer cannot afford not to distribute through them. For example, Business Depot and Amazon.com occupy these types of positions.

Company Considerations Before choosing a distribution channel for a product, a company should consider its own situation:

- *Desire for channel control.* Some producers establish direct channels because they want to control their product's distribution, even though a direct channel may be more costly than an indirect channel. By controlling the channel, producers can achieve more aggressive promotion and can better control both the freshness of merchandise stocks and their products' and services' retail prices. In mid-1992, IBM started experimenting with mail-order sales of its personal computers. It experienced limited success with this move. Others, such as Dell computers, however, are having success with direct distribution systems via the Internet and mail-order.
- *Services provided by seller.* Some producers make decisions about their channels based on the distribution functions desired (and occasionally demanded) by intermediaries. For instance, numerous retail chains will not stock a product unless it is presold through heavy advertising by the producer.
- *Ability of management.* The marketing experience and managerial capabilities of a producer influence decisions about which channel to use. Many companies lacking marketing know-how turn the distribution job over to intermediaries.
- *Financial resources.* A business with adequate finances can establish its own sales force, grant credit to its customers, and/or warehouse its own products. A financially weak firm uses intermediaries to provide these services.

In a few cases, virtually all factors point to a particular length and type of channel. In most cases, however, the factors send mixed signals. Several factors may point to the desirability of direct channels, others to the use of wholesalers and/or retailers. Or the company may find the channel it wants is unavailable. If a company with an unproven product having low profit potential cannot place its product with intermediaries, it may have no other option but to try to distribute the product directly to its target market.

DETERMINING INTENSITY OF DISTRIBUTION

At this point in designing a channel, a firm knows: what role has been assigned to distribution within the marketing mix; whether direct or indirect distribution is better; and which types of intermediaries will be used (assuming indirect distribution is appropriate). Next the company must decide on the **intensity of distribution** — that is, how many intermediaries will be used at the wholesale and retail levels in a particular territory.

There are many possible degrees of intensity. As shown in Figure 15-4, we will consider the three major categories, ranging from intensive to selective to exclusive. Distribution intensity ordinarily is thought to be a single decision. However, if the channel has more than one level of intermediaries (wholesaler and retailer, for example), the appropriate intensity must be selected for each level.

Different degrees of intensity may be appropriate at successive levels of distribution. A manufacturer can often achieve intensive retail coverage with selective, rather than intensive, wholesale distribution. Or selective intensity at the retail level may be gained through exclusive intensity at the wholesale level. Of course, the wholesaling firm(s) will determine which retail outlets actually receive the product.

FIGURE 15-4
The Intensity-of-Distribution Continuum

INTENSIVE | SELECTIVE | EXCLUSIVE

Distribution through multiple, but not all, reasonable outlets in a market

Despite this lack of control, a producer should plan the levels of intensity needed at both the wholesale and retail levels. Making only one decision about distribution intensity is simplistic and can create serious problems.

Intensive Distribution

Under **intensive distribution**, a producer sells its product through every available outlet in a market where a consumer might reasonably look for it. Ultimate consumers demand immediate satisfaction from convenience goods and will not defer purchases to find a particular brand. Thus intensive distribution is often used by manufacturers of this category of product. Retailers often control whether a strategy of intensive distribution actually can be implemented. For example, a new manufacturer of toothpaste or a small producer of potato chips may want distribution in all supermarkets, but these retailers may limit their assortments to four fast-selling brands.

Retailers typically will not pay to advertise a product that is sold by competitors. Therefore, intensive distribution places most of the advertising and promotion burden on the producer.

Selective Distribution

In **selective distribution**, a producer sells its product through multiple, but not all possible, wholesalers and retailers in a market where a consumer might reasonably look for it. Selective distribution is appropriate for consumer shopping goods, such as various types of clothing and appliances, and for business accessory equipment, such as office equipment and handheld tools.

A company may shift to a selective distribution strategy after some experience with intensive distribution. The decision to change usually hinges on the high cost of intensive distribution or the unsatisfactory performance of intermediaries. Certain intermediaries perennially order in small, unprofitable amounts; others may be poor credit risks. Eliminating such marginal intermediaries may reduce the number of outlets but increase a company's sales volume. Many companies have found this to be the case simply because they were able to do a more thorough selling job with a smaller number of accounts.

A firm may move toward more selective distribution to enhance the image of its products, strengthen customer service, and/or improve quality control. For instance, the Italian firm of Guccio Gucci concluded that its brand was on too many leather goods and fashion accessories and that they were carried by too many retailers. Hence, as part of a new marketing strategy, Gucci slashed both its product line and the number of outlets carrying its goods.[19]

Exclusive Distribution

Under **exclusive distribution**, the supplier agrees to sell its product only to a single wholesaling intermediary and/or retailer in a given market. At the wholesale level, such an arrangement is normally termed an exclusive distributorship; at the retail level, an exclusive dealership. A manufacturer may prohibit an intermediary that holds an exclusive distributorship or dealership from handling a directly competing product line.

Producers often adopt an exclusive distribution strategy when it is essential that the retailer carry a large inventory. Thus exclusive dealerships are frequently used in marketing consumer specialty products such as expensive suits. This strategy is also desirable when the dealer or distributor must furnish installation and repair service. For this reason, manufacturers of farm machinery and large construction equipment grant exclusive distributorships.

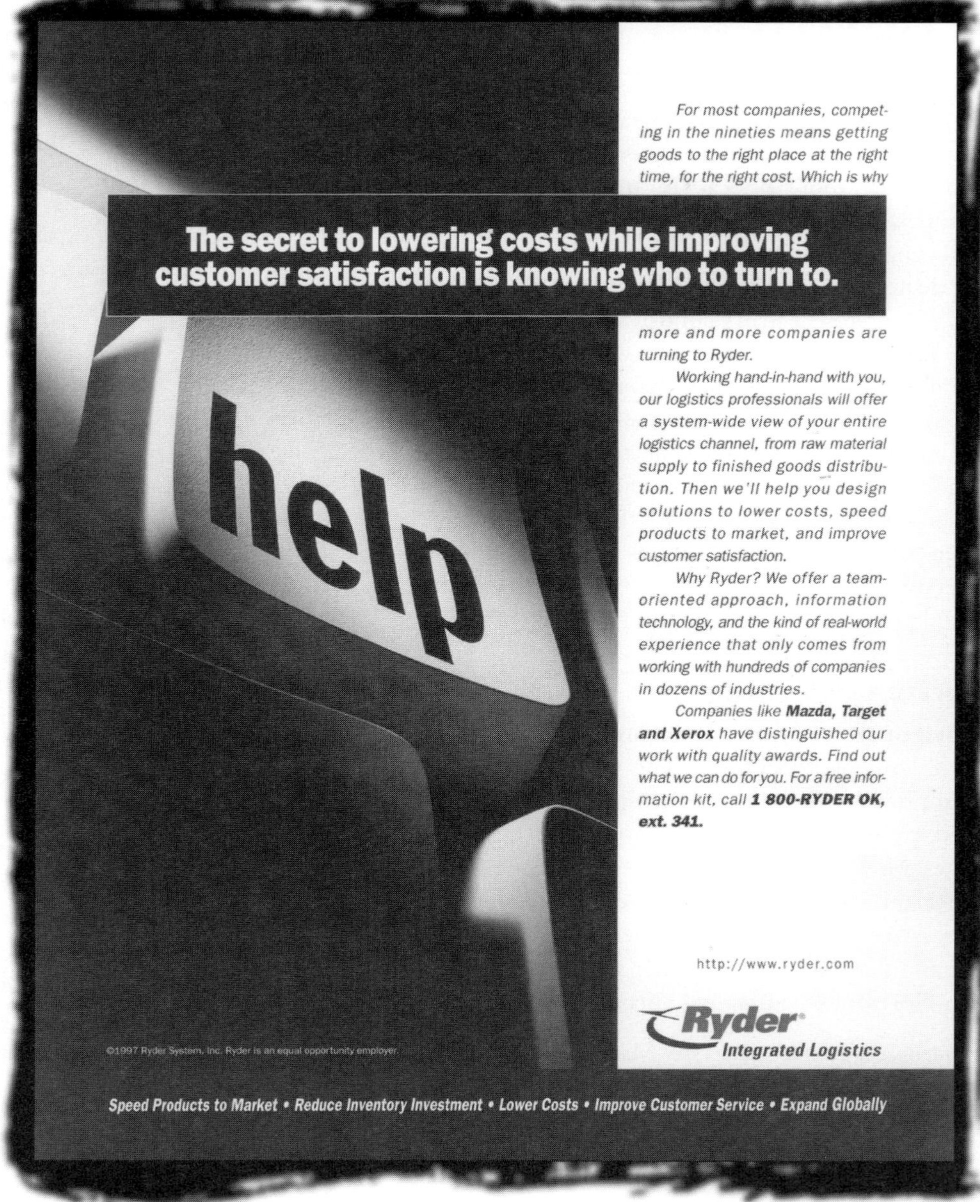

Effective management of the distribution channel requires that goods are in the right place at the right time.

Exclusive distribution helps a manufacturer control the last level of intermediary before the final customer. An intermediary with exclusive rights is usually willing to promote the product aggressively. Why? Interested customers will have to purchase the product from this intermediary because no other outlets in the area carry the same brand. However, a producer suffers if its exclusive intermediaries in various markets do not serve customers well. Essentially a manufacturer has "all its eggs in one basket."

An exclusive dealer or distributor has the opportunity to reap all the benefits of the producer's marketing activities in a particular area. However, under exclusive distribution, an intermediary may become too dependent on the manufacturer. If the manufacturer fails, the intermediary also fails (at least for that product). Another risk is that once sales volume has been built up in a market, the producer may add other dealers or, worse yet, drop all dealers and establish its own sales force.

CONFLICT AND CONTROL IN CHANNELS

Distribution occasionally is characterized by goals shared by suppliers and customers and by co-operative actions. But conflicts as well as struggles for control are more typical. To manage distribution channels effectively requires an understanding of both conflict and control, including techniques to (1) decrease conflict, or at least its negative effects, and (2) increase a firm's control within a channel.

Channel conflict exists when one channel member perceives another channel member to be acting in a way that prevents the first member from achieving its distribution objectives. Firms in one channel often compete vigorously with firms in other channels; this represents horizontal conflict. Even within the same channel, firms argue about operating practices and try to gain control over other members' actions; this illustrates vertical conflict.

Horizontal Conflict

Horizontal conflict occurs among firms on the same level of distribution. The personal-computer field provides an excellent example. Virtually all PCs used to be sold through conventional computer stores. Now PCs can be purchased at a multitude of other outlets — office-supply outlets, department stores, warehouse clubs, consumer-electronics retailers, and gigantic new computer superstores.

Horizontal conflict may occur between:

- *Intermediaries of the same type:* Maryvale Home Hardware versus Fred's Friendly Hardware, for example.
- *Different types of intermediaries on the same level:* Maryvale Home Hardware versus St. Clair Paint and Wallpaper versus K mart.

The main source of horizontal conflict is **scrambled merchandising**, in which intermediaries diversify by adding product lines not traditionally carried by their type of business. Supermarkets, for instance, expanded beyond groceries by adding health and beauty aids, small appliances, records, snack bars, and various services. Retailers that originally sold these product lines became irritated both at supermarkets for diversifying and at producers for using multiple distribution channels.

Scrambled merchandising and the resulting horizontal competition may stem from consumers, intermediaries, or producers. Many consumers prefer convenient, one-stop shopping, so stores broaden their assortments to satisfy this desire. Intermediaries constantly strive for higher gross margins and more customer traffic, so they increase the number of lines they carry. Producers seek to expand their market coverage and reduce unit production costs, so they add new outlets. Such diversification intensifies horizontal conflict.

Vertical Conflict

Perhaps the most severe conflicts in distribution involve firms at different levels of the same channel. **Vertical conflict** typically occurs between producer and wholesaler or producer and retailer.

Producer versus Wholesaler Tensions occasionally arise between producers and wholesalers. A producer and wholesaler may disagree about aspects of their business relationship. For instance, John Deere has argued with distributors about whether they should sell farm equipment made by other companies or should restrict their efforts to the Deere brand.

Why do conflicts arise? Manufacturers and wholesalers have differing points of view. On the one hand, manufacturers think that wholesalers neither promote products aggressively nor provide sufficient storage services. And wholesalers' services cost too much. On the other hand, wholesalers believe producers either expect too much or do not understand the wholesaler's primary obligation to customers.

Channel conflict typically stems from a manufacturer's attempts to bypass wholesalers and deal directly with retailers or consumers. Direct sale occurs because (1) producers are dissatisfied with wholesalers' services or (2) market conditions call for direct sale. Ordinarily battles about direct sale are fought in consumer goods channels. Such conflicts rarely arise in channels for business goods because there is a tradition of direct sale to ultimate customers in business markets.

To bypass wholesalers, a producer has two alternatives:

- *Sell directly to consumers.* Producers may employ house-to-house or mail-order selling. Since the

MARKETING AT WORK FILE 15-2

TRADE SHOWS: CONFLICTING APPROACHES

For years, trade shows have been popular ways for manufacturers and manufacturers' vendors to exhibit merchandise to retailers. Typically a trade show operates as follows: A group of vendors, often through some agency or private organization, bring samples of their merchandise to a venue where display booths or rooms are provided. The company sets up its display, and potential buyers, invited by the organizers, come to see the merchandise and place purchase orders. A furniture retailer, for instance, might attend several furniture shows and select the products desired for sale in the business. Of late, however, trade shows of this nature have met with some dissatisfaction, and companies are focusing their marketing strategies on private trade shows and travelling road shows.

A private trade show operates as follows: An organization, usually a retail chain, invites its store managers and key staff to attend a show at which the chain's vendors exhibit their wares. The event isn't open to the competition or the public. The private show allows vendors and dealers to conduct business without fear of the competition listening in. Organizers of these events feel that when people go to the conventional trade show they just look around. "The odd guy bangs out a deal, but attendees go mainly to source new items," according to Dan Logel, market chairman of Home Hardware Stores Ltd., of St. Jacobs, Ont. This feeling is shared by Paul Pappas, general manager of The Quality Tool Group of Pickering, Ont., who says that general trade shows are hit and miss because there's so much competition.

Shoppers Drug Mart holds annual one-day private shows in Vancouver and Toronto. It also puts on a show for its pharmaceutical suppliers, in which store pharmacists can discuss new drugs and various health issues. Companies like Revlon Canada Inc. can build a rapport with associate owners of the pharmacies and gain exposure for new products.

Travelling road shows are another way for manufacturers' vendors to reach the retail market and are used on a regular basis by the high-tech companies. They are typically multicity events that incorporate trade shows and educational and customer presentations. Xerox Canada Ltd., IBM Canada Ltd., and Microsoft Canada Inc. have all done travelling road shows. People who attend include end-users, resellers, and consultants. These companies use this method because they can control everything from content to choices of dates, speakers, and venues. It is also an opportunity to meet customers and potential customers in every market because the show is being brought to them.

This new breed of trade shows may be replacing the old traditional variety. For one thing, if all the large retailers are holding their own events, they will not be attending the general shows, and according to Scott Sillcox, owner of Maple Leaf Productions, an event management company in Ontario, there is no reason for vendors to pay thousands of dollars to exhibit in a trade show that just gets the Mom and Pop stores. A new era may be unfolding in this distribution chain.

Source: Adapted from Fawzia Sheikh, "Do Your Own Thing," *Marketing Magazine*, July 14, 1997, p. 13.

rise of the Internet, selling directly to consumers is becoming more prevalent via this technology. Essentially it is a form of mail-order where the contact is made electronically; however, unlike traditional mail-order, Internet purchases allow the buyer to view products on-line and often communicate more quickly with the seller via electronic mail. Producers may also establish their own distribution centres in different areas or even their own retail stores in major markets.

- *Sell directly to retailers.* Under certain market and product conditions, selling directly to retailers is feasible and advisable. An ideal retail market for this option consists of retailers that buy large quantities of a limited line of products.

Direct distribution — a short channel — is advantageous when the product (1) is subject to physical or fashion perishability, (2) carries a high unit price, (3) is custom-made, or (4) requires installation and technical service. Direct distribution, however, places a financial and managerial burden on the producer. Not only must the manufacturer operate its own sales force and handle physical distribution of its products, but a direct-selling manufacturer also faces competition from its former wholesalers, which no doubt now sell competitive products.

Wholesalers too can improve their competitive position and thereby reduce channel conflict. Their options include:

- *Improve internal management.* Many wholesalers have modernized their operations and upgraded the calibre of their management. Functional, single-store warehouses have been built outside congested downtown areas, and mechanized materials-handling equipment has been installed. Computers have improved order processing, inventory control, and billing.
- *Provide management assistance to retailers.* Wholesalers have realized that improving retailers' operations benefits all parties. Wholesalers help meet certain retailers' needs, such as store layout, merchandise selection, promotion, and inventory control.
- *Form voluntary chains.* In a voluntary chain (discussed in Chapter 16), a wholesaler enters into a contract with a group of retailers, agreeing to furnish them with management services and volume buying power. In turn, retailers promise to buy all, or almost all, of their merchandise from the wholesaler.
- *Develop private brands.* Some large wholesalers have successfully established their own brands. A voluntary chain of retailers provides a built-in market for the wholesaler's brand.

Producer versus Retailer Another struggle for channel control takes place between manufacturers and retailers. Conflict can arise over terms or conditions of the relationship between the two parties. Or producers may compete with retailers by selling direct via the Internet or catalogue or through producer-owned stores. A number of apparel makers — including Ralph Lauren, Levi Strauss, and Liz Claiborne — have opened retail outlets. In doing so, they have aggravated department stores and specialty retailers that also carry their brands.

Producer and retailer may also disagree about terms of sale or conditions of the relationship between the two parties. For example, some retailers demand a so-called **slotting allowance** to place a manufacturer's product on store shelves. This trend is most evident in the grocery-products field. In some cases, companies with new products are required to pay a fee of $100 to over $1,000 per store for each version of the product. Or payment may be in the form of free products. Of course, not all manufacturers are paying all of these fees. And some small producers cannot afford them. Manufacturers criticize slotting allowances, claiming they stifle the introduction of new products, particularly those developed by small companies. Retailers vigorously defend slotting allowances. Supermarkets contend they must find a way to recoup the costs of reviewing the flood of new products, stocking some of them, and removing failures.

Producers and retailers both have methods to gain more control. Manufacturers can:

- *Build strong consumer brand loyalty.* Creative and aggressive promotion is a key in creating such loyalty.
- *Establish one or more forms of vertical marketing system.*
- *Refuse to sell to unco-operative retailers.* This tactic has to be defensible from a legal standpoint.

Effective marketing weapons are also available to retailers. They can:

- *Develop store loyalty among consumers.* Skilful advertising and strong store brands are means of creating loyal customers.
- *Improve computerized information systems.* Information is power. Knowing what sells and how fast it sells is useful in negotiating with suppliers.
- *Form a retailer co-operative.* In this form of vertical marketing system, a group of retailers (usually fairly small ones) band together to establish and operate a wholesale warehouse. Their primary intent is to gain lower merchandise costs through volume buying power.[20]

Who Controls Channels?

Every firm would like to regulate the behaviour of the other companies in its distribution channel. When a channel member is able to do this, it has **channel control**. In many situations, including distribution channels, power is a prerequisite for control. **Channel power** is the ability to influence or determine the behaviour of another channel member. There are various sources of power in the context of channels. They include expertise (for example, possessing vital technical knowledge about the product), rewards (providing financial benefits to co-operative channel members), and sanctions (removing unco-operative members from the channel).

Traditionally, manufacturers have been viewed as controlling channels — that is, making the decisions regarding types and number of outlets, participation of individual intermediaries, and business practices to be followed by a channel. But this is a one-sided, outdated point of view.

Intermediaries often have considerable freedom to establish their own channels. Certainly the names Safeway, Loblaws, and Sears mean more to consumers than the names of most brands sold in these stores. Large retailers are challenging producers for channel control, just as many manufacturers seized control from wholesalers years ago. Even small retailers can be influential in local markets, because their prestige may be greater than their suppliers' prestige.

Manufacturers contend they should assume the leader's role in a channel because they create the new products and need greater sales volume to benefit from economics of scale. Conversely, retailers also stake a claim for leadership, because they are closest to final customers and, as a result, are best able to know customers' wants and to design and oversee channels to satisfy them. Various factors have contributed to retailers' growing ability to control channels. For instance, many retailers have implemented electronic scanning devices, which gives them access to more accurate, timely information about sales trends of individual products than producers have.[21]

A Channel Viewed as a Partnership

Sometimes, members see a channel as a fragmented collection of independent, competing firms. Suppliers and intermediaries should not think of channels as something they "command and control," but rather as partnerships aimed at satisfying end users' needs.[22] Thus co-ordination is needed throughout a distribution channel.

One possible reason for channel problems is that most producers do not have a person in the organization who is responsible for co-ordinating the firm's channel activities. While most producers have an advertising manager and a sales manager, few have a channels manager. Perhaps it is time for producers to create this position.

LEGAL CONSIDERATIONS IN CHANNEL MANAGEMENT

In various ways, organizations may try to exercise control over the distribution of their product as it moves through the channel. Generally speaking, any attempts to control distribution may be subject to legal constraints. In this section, we shall discuss briefly four control methods that are frequently considered by suppliers (usually manufacturers):

- **Dealer selection.** The manufacturer wants to select its customers and refuses to sell to some intermediaries.
- **Exclusive dealing.** The manufacturer prohibits its dealers from carrying products of the manufacturer's competitors.
- **Tying contracts.** The manufacturer sells a product to an intermediary only under the condition that this intermediary also buys another (possibly unwanted) product from the manufacturer. Or, at least, the intermediary agrees not to buy the other product from any other supplier.
- **Exclusive (closed) territories.** The manufacturer requires each intermediary to sell only to customers who are located within the intermediary's assigned territory.

None of these arrangements is automatically illegal. The Competition Act deals with such practices in Part VII, in which certain dealings between manufacturers and intermediaries are deemed illegal if they restrict competition.

Dealer Selection

Under section 75 of the Competition Act, it is illegal for a manufacturer or supplier to refuse to supply an intermediary with the supplier's products. Under certain circumstances, however, a supplier may refuse to deal with retailers or other intermediaries if they are unwilling or unable to meet the usual trade terms of the supplier. In other words, for example, if the intermediary engaged in selling the supplier's product as a loss leader, or failed to provide adequate postpurchase service, or in some other way failed to support the product, the supplier could refuse to deal with that company. Generally, it would be illegal to refuse to supply an intermediary if the company carried a competitor's product or resisted a tying contract.

Exclusive Dealing

Exclusive dealing contracts have been declared unlawful if the manufacturer's sales volume is a substantial part of the total volume in a market or if the volume done by the exclusive dealers is a significant percentage of the total business in an area. That is, the law is violated when the competitors of a manufacturer are essentially shut out from a substantial part of the market because of this manufacturer's exclusive dealing contract.

By inference, it is clear that exclusive dealing is not illegal in all situations. In fact, in cases where the seller is just getting started in a market or where its share of the total market is so small as to be negligible, its negotiation of exclusive dealing agreements may not only improve its competitive position but also strengthen competition in general.

Ordinarily there is no question of legality when a manufacturer agrees to sell to only one retailer or wholesaler in a given territory, provided there are no limitations on competitive products. Also, a manufacturer can sell to dealers who do not carry competitors' products, as long as this is a voluntary decision on the part of the franchise holder.

Tying Contracts

A supplier is likely to push for a tying agreement when:

- There are shortages of a desired product, and the supplier also wants to push products that are less in demand.
- The supplier grants a franchise (as in fast-food services) and wants the franchisee to purchase all necessary supplies and equipment from this supplier.
- The supplier has exclusive dealers or distributors (in appliances, for example) and wants them to carry a full line of the supplier's products.

With regard to tying contracts, apparently a dealer can be required to carry a manufacturer's full line as long as this does not impede competition in the market. The arrangement may be questionable, however, if a supplier forces a dealer or a distributor to take slow-moving, less attractive items in order to acquire the really desirable products.

Exclusive Territories

Traditionally, the strategy of exclusive (or closed) sales territories has been used by manufacturers in assigning market areas to retailing or wholesaling intermediaries. However, closed sales territories can create area monopolies, lessen competition, and restrict trade among intermediaries who carry the same brand. Exceptions are generally provided when a company is small or is a new entrant to the market, in order to facilitate market entry.

These limitations on closed sales territories are likely to foster vertical marketing systems, where the manufacturer retains ownership of the product until it reaches the final buyer. That is, the manufacturer could either (1) own the retail or wholesale outlet or (2) consign products on an agency basis to the intermediaries but retain ownership. In either of these situations, exclusive territories are quite legal.

THE CHANGING FACE OF DISTRIBUTION

Largely as a result of advancing technology and the changing balance of power within distribution channels, we are witnessing a change in the nature of distribution and in the means by which products and services reach the end consumer. It should be obvious from the examples in this chapter that many of the traditional channels by which products and services moved from their producers to consumers are under threat and may be expected to undergo considerable change in the years to come.

As we have seen earlier in this chapter, shopping from home is expected to be a major growth area in retailing in the future as systems become more sophisticated and as catalogue companies and other direct retailers become even better at serving their customers. We will see increased use of the Internet and direct-response television, which will involve customers ordering directly from the supplier's computer through touch-tone telephone, or by placing more conventional "voice" orders via 1-800 numbers.[23] As many consumers tire of the retail shopping-mall experience and have less time to indulge in it, more will turn to electronic shopping.

Finally, with the advances in technology today, it is not always clear what constitutes a distribution channel, as compared with an advertising or promotional tool. For example, many Canadian companies are using direct contact via the Internet to provide consumers with information about their products and make sales online. Amazon.com, which bills itself as "the world's largest bookstore," does all of its transactions on the Internet. This company provides services such as identifying new titles to match customer interests and preferences, gift wrapping when requested, locating books that are out of print, and recommending titles.[24] Kiosks that provide information on and direct links to hotels and tour companies are becoming very popular in airports and bus stations.

Do these examples represent new channels of distribution or merely variations on existing practices? Certainly, they will revolutionize the way in which many manufacturers, suppliers, and intermediaries conduct their business.

Summary

The role of distribution is getting a product to its target market. A distribution channel carries out this assignment with intermediaries performing some tasks. An intermediary is a business firm that renders services directly related to the purchase and/or sale of a product as it flows from producer to consumer. Intermediaries can be eliminated from a channel, but someone still has to carry out their essential functions.

A distribution channel is the set of people and firms involved in the flow of title to a product as it moves from producer to ultimate consumer or business user. A channel includes producer, final customer, and any intermediaries that participate in the process.

Designing a channel of distribution for a product occurs through a sequence of four decisions: (1) delineating the role of distribution within the marketing mix; (2) selecting the proper type of distribution channel; (3) determining the appropriate intensity of distribution; and (4) choosing specific channel members. A variety of channels are used to distribute consumer goods, business goods, and services. Firms often employ multiple channels to achieve broad market coverage, although this strategy can alienate some intermediaries. Because of deficiencies in conventional channels, vertical marketing systems have become a major force in distribution. There are three forms of vertical marketing systems: corporate, contractual, and administered.

Numerous factors need to be considered prior to selecting a distribution channel for a product. The primary consideration is the nature of the target market; other considerations relate to the product, the intermediaries, and the company itself.

Distribution intensity refers to the number of intermediaries used at the wholesale and retail levels in a particular territory. It ranges from intensive to selective to exclusive.

Firms distributing goods and services sometimes clash. There are two types of conflict: horizontal (between firms at the same level of distribution) and vertical (between firms at different levels of the same channel). Scrambled merchandising is a prime cause of horizontal conflict. Vertical conflict typically pits producer against wholesaler or retailer. Manufacturers' attempts to bypass intermediaries are a prime cause of vertical conflict.

Channel members frequently strive for some control over one another. Depending on the circumstances, either producers or intermediaries can achieve the dominant position in a channel. All parties may be served best by viewing channels as a system requiring co-ordination or distribution activities. Moreover, attempts to control distribution may be subject to legal constraints.

Key Terms and Concepts

Intermediary (364)
Merchant intermediary (364)
Agent (364)
Distribution channel (365)
Intensity of distribution (367)
Direct distribution (368)
Indirect distribution (368)
Multiple distribution channels (372)
Dual distribution (372)
Vertical marketing system (372)
Corporate vertical marketing system (373)
Contractual vertical marketing system (373)
Administered vertical marketing system (373)
Intensity of distribution (375)
Intensive distribution (376)
Selective distribution (376)
Exclusive distribution (376)
Channel conflict (378)
Horizontal conflict (378)
Scrambled merchandising (378)
Vertical conflict (378)
Slotting allowance (380)
Channel control (381)
Channel power (381)
Dealer selection (381)
Exclusive dealing (381)
Tying contracts (381)
Exclusive territory (381)

Questions and Problems

1. "You can eliminate intermediaries, but you cannot eliminate their functions." Discuss this statement.
2. Which of the following institutions are intermediaries? Explain.
   a. Avon sales person.
   b. Electrical wholesaler.
   c. Real estate broker.
   d. Railway.
   e. Auctioneer.
   f. Advertising agency.
   g. Grocery store.
   h. Stockbroker.
   i. Bank.
   j. Radio station.
3. Which of the channels illustrated in Figure 15-3 is most apt to be used for each of the following products? Defend your choice in each case.
   a. Fire insurance.
   b. Single-family residences.
   c. Farm hay balers.
   d. Washing machines.
   e. Hair spray.
   f. An ocean cruise.
4. "The great majority of business sales are made directly from producer to business user." Explain the reason for this first in relation to the nature of the market, and then in relation to the product.
5. Explain, using examples, the differences among the three major types of vertical systems — corporate, administered, contractual. Which is the best kind?
6. A small manufacturer of fishing lures is faced with the problem of selecting its channel of distribution. What reasonable alternatives does it have? Consider particularly the nature of its product and the nature of its market.
7. Is a policy of intensive distribution consistent with consumer buying habits for convenience goods? For shopping goods? Is intensive distribution normally used in the marketing of any type of business goods?
8. From a producer's viewpoint, what are the competitive advantages of exclusive distribution?
9. What are the drawbacks to exclusive distribution, from a retailer's point of view? To what extent are these alleviated if the retailer controls the channel for the particular brand?
10. A manufacturer of a well-known brand of men's clothing has been selling directly to one dealer in a small Canadian city for many years. For some time the market has been large enough to support two retailers very profitably. Yet the present dealer objects strongly when the manufacturer suggests adding another outlet. What alternatives does the manufacturer have in this situation? What course of action would you recommend?

11. "Manufacturers should always strive to select the lowest-cost channel of distribution." Do you agree? Should they always try to use the intermediaries with the lowest operating costs? Why or why not?
12. What role is the Internet playing in changing distribution networks? Provide examples to illustrate the changes that are occurring.
13. Why are full-service wholesalers relatively unimportant in the marketing of women's high-fashion wearing apparel, furniture, and large electrical equipment?

Hands-On Marketing

1. Arrange an interview with either the owner or a top-level manager of a small manufacturing firm. Inquire about (a) what distribution channel(s) the company uses for its primary product, (b) what factors were the greatest influences in arriving at the channel(s), and (c) whether the company would prefer some other channel(s).
2. Visit with either a supermarket manager or a buyer for a supermarket chain to learn more about slotting allowances and any other charges they levy on manufacturers. Inquire whether such charges have led to channel conflict and how the supermarket chain is handling this type of situation. Also ask whether any grocery-products manufacturers refuse to pay slotting allowances and whether the chain ever waives the fees.

CHAPTER 16 GOALS

This chapter will provide you with insight into how wholesale markets, wholesaling institutions, and physical-distribution activities relate to marketing. After studying this chapter, you should have an understanding of:

- The nature and economic justification of wholesaling and the role of wholesaling intermediaries.
- Differences across three categories of wholesaling intermediaries.
- Major types of merchant wholesalers, agent wholesalers, and manufacturers' sales facilities, and the services they render.
- What physical distribution is.
- The systems approach to physical distribution.
- How physical distribution is used to strengthen a marketing program and reduce marketing costs.
- The five subsystems within a physical distribution system: inventory location and warehousing; materials handling; inventory control; order processing; and transportation.
- Trends in wholesaling and physical distribution.

Chapter Sixteen

Wholesaling: Markets and Institutions

www.weber.com

GOING WITH THE FLOW MEANS BUCKING THE TREND

Every time there is a new piece of technology, someone somewhere says, "This will finally eliminate the middleman." The Internet is supposed to put wholesalers out of business. But David Weber, president of the 140-year-old company his family has owned since 1923, Weber Supply Company Inc., says, "We have that threat all the time; there is still a cost to bring that product to market."

Weber Supply Company Inc., of Kitchener, Ontario, is a wholesaler and distributor of hardware for eight hundred home building centres and of industrial maintenance, repair, and operating items for manufacturing, mining, and extraction operations. The firm has ten branches in Ontario and one in each of Manitoba and Saskatchewan, staffed with 175 employees; it carries thirty thousand items and generates annual sales of over $100 million.

David Ticoll, president of the Alliance for Converging Technologies in Toronto, believes that the Internet will cut the cost of distribution to the point where many retailers will simply deal directly with manufacturers — bypassing intermediaries. Weber, however, set up its own Web site in what can be called a pre-emptive strike. In building the Web site, David Weber aims to protect his core business. He has a head start in the sense that he has a large number of small-business customers who are the least likely to bypass the intermediary.

His accounts fall into two broad segments, both of which need prompt delivery of a wide range of products that are too expensive for them to stock themselves. The first consists of the eight hundred home-building centres that retail to do-it-yourself handymen. Weber supplies everything but appliances and lumber for these consumers. The second comprises manufacturing, mining, and extraction businesses who need various industrial maintenance, repair, and operating items.

With the launching of the Internet service, Weber now has a variety of customer ordering systems ranging from his direct-sales force to telephone, fax, custom EDI (electronic data interchange) for some large accounts, as well as a system that uses specialized software and modems connected to buyers' personal computers. All the electronic systems are designed to increase the productivity of the field sales force in Canada and the United States. The EDI systems, with private lines and specialized hardware and software, are expensive to operate, while the modem–PC systems are less expensive but sometimes less reliable. With the Web site, buyers tap into the Weber computerized inventory system and place orders from a 30,000-item catalogue. Customers with EDI systems are informed immediately about out-of-stock items; PC-based systems get the information when they access the system. The Web-based system is user friendly, has good technical detail, and contains product photos. One convert from fax orders says that he can do his ordering in two seconds. While never having used the Internet before, he was able to log on and navigate easily, and he believes he will save many hours of ordering time. Mr. Weber is waiting to see how things work, even though he is pleased to be one of the first wholesalers to make the technological leap. "Sometimes it's good to be at the bleeding edge — if it works."[1]

Although consumers shop regularly at the stores of retailing intermediaries, they rarely see the establishments of such wholesalers as Weber. Also, beyond noticing transportation carriers such as trucks and trains, consumers have little exposure to the way in which products actually are moved from the point of production to the point of final sale and consumption. As a result, wholesaling and physical distribution are often misunderstood — and occasionally criticized — by consumers. Nevertheless, wholesalers can be essential members of a distribution channel, and physical distribution is an integral aspect of marketing most goods. Therefore, it's critical that you understand the nature and managerial issues of both wholesaling and physical distribution.

NATURE AND IMPORTANCE OF WHOLESALING

Wholesaling and retailing enable what is produced to be purchased for consumption. We already know that retailing involves sales to ultimate consumers for their personal use. Now we'll see that wholesaling has a different role in the marketing system.

Wholesaling and Wholesaling Intermediaries

Wholesaling (or *wholesale trade*) is the sale, and all activities directly related to the sale, of goods and services to businesses and other organizations for (1) resale, (2) use in producing other goods or services, or (3) operating an organization. When a business firm sells shirts and blouses to a clothing store that intends to resell them to final consumers, this is wholesaling. When a mill sells flour to a large bakery for making bread and pastries, this is also a wholesale transaction. And when a firm sells uniforms to a business or another organization for its employees to wear in carrying out their duties, this is wholesaling as well.

Sales made by one producer to another are wholesale transactions, and the selling producer is engaged in wholesaling. Likewise, a discount house is involved in wholesaling when it sells calculators and office supplies to a business firm. Thus wholesaling includes sales by any firm to any customer *except* an ultimate consumer who is buying for personal, nonbusiness use. From this perspective, all sales are either wholesale or retail transactions — distinguished only by the purchaser's intended use of the good or service.

In this chapter we will focus on firms engaged *primarily* in wholesaling. This type of company is called a **wholesaling middleman or intermediary**. We will not be concerned with retailers involved in occasional wholesale transactions. And we will not focus on manufacturers and farmers because they are engaged primarily in production rather than wholesaling. Keep in mind, then, that *wholesaling* is a business *activity* that can be carried out by various types of firms, whereas a *wholesaling intermediary* is a business *institution* that concentrates on wholesaling.

Economic Justification for Wholesaling

Most manufacturing firms are small and specialized. They don't have the capital to maintain a sales force to contact the many retailers or final users that are (or could be) their customers. Even for manufacturers with sufficient capital, some of their products or lines generate such a small volume of sales that it would not be cost-effective to establish a sales force to sell them.

At the other end of the distribution channel, most retailers and final users buy in small quantities and have only a limited knowledge of the market and sources of supply. Thus there is often a gap between the seller (producer) and the buyer (retailer or final user).

A wholesaling intermediary can fill this gap by providing services of value to manufacturers and/or retailers. For example, a wholesaler can pool the orders of many retailers and/or final users, thereby creating a market for the small producer. At the same time, a wholesaling intermediary selects various items from among many alternatives to form its product mix, thereby acting as a buying service for small retailers and final users. Essentially, as we will see at various points in this chapter, the activities of a wholesaling intermediary create time, place, and/or possession utility.

From a broad point of view, wholesaling brings to the total distribution system the economies of skill, scale, and transactions:

- Wholesaling *skills* are efficiently concentrated in a relatively few hands. This saves the duplication of effort that would occur if many producers had to perform wholesaling functions themselves. For example, one wholesaler's warehouse in Winnipeg or Moncton saves many manufacturers from having to build their own warehouses to provide speedy service to customers in this area.
- Economies of *scale* result from the specialization of wholesaling intermediaries performing functions that might otherwise require several small departments run by producing firms. Wholesalers typically can perform wholesaling functions more efficiently than can most manufacturers.
- *Transaction* economies come into play when wholesaling or retailing intermediaries are introduced between producers and their customers. Let's assume that four manufacturers want to sell to six retailers. As shown in Figure 16-1, *without* an intermediary, there are 24 transactions; *with* one wholesaling intermediary, the number of transactions is cut to ten. Four transactions occur when all the producers sell to the intermediary, and another six occur when the intermediary sells to all the retailers.

Size of the Wholesale Market

In 1994, there were more than 56,000 wholesaling locations in Canada, with total annual operating revenue of about $282 billion. As is the case in retailing, the sales generated by wholesaling establishments have increased dramatically in recent years. Part of this increase is accounted for by increases in prices that have occurred during the past ten years or so, but even if sales were expressed in constant dollars, we would still see a substantial increase.

PROFILE OF WHOLESALING INTERMEDIARIES

A producer or retailer considering indirect distribution and the use of wholesaling intermediaries must know what alternatives are available, whom these intermediaries serve, and how they operate. Having this information increases the likelihood of establishing effective distribution arrangements.[2]

Four Major Categories

Classifying wholesaling intermediaries is difficult because they vary greatly in (1) products they carry, (2) markets to which they sell, and (3) methods of operation. To minimize the confusion, we will use the classification scheme shown in Figure 16-2. There, all wholesaling intermediaries are grouped into only four broad categories: wholesale merchants, manufacturers' sales branches and offices,

FIGURE 16-1 **The Economy of Transactions in Wholesaling**

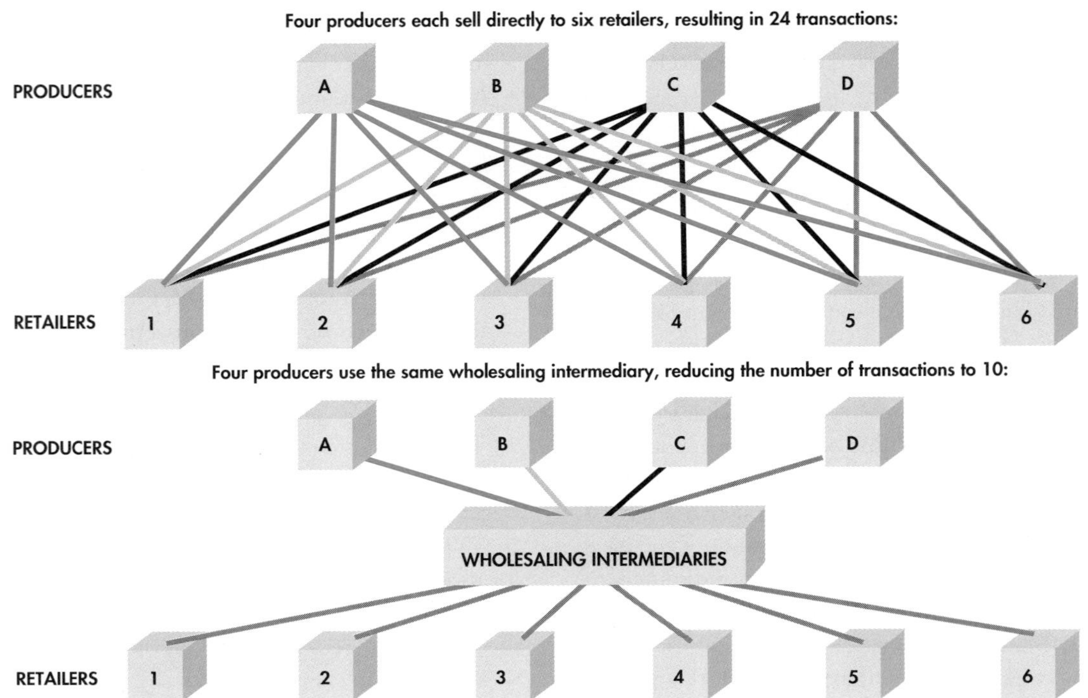

agents and brokers, and primary-product dealers. These four groups are the classifications used by Statistics Canada, which is the major source of quantitative data covering wholesaling institutions and markets. Later in this chapter we shall discuss merchant wholesalers, agents and brokers, and primary-products dealers in more detail.

- **Merchant wholesalers** are firms we usually refer to as wholesalers, jobbers, or industrial distributors. They typically are independently owned, and they take title to the merchandise they handle. They form the largest single segment of wholesaling firms when measured either by sales or by number of establishments. Statistics Canada reports that merchant wholesalers, along with manufacturers' sales branches and primary-product dealers discussed below, account for almost 85 percent of total wholesale trade.[3]
- **Manufacturers' sales branches and offices** are owned and operated by manufacturers, but they are physically separated from the manufacturing plants. The distinction between a sales branch and a sales office is that a branch carries merchandise stock and an office does not.
- **Agents and brokers** do *not* take title to the merchandise they handle, but they do actively negotiate the purchase or sale of products for their principals. The main types of agents are manufacturers' agents, commission merchants (in the marketing of agricultural products), and brokers. As a group, agents and brokers represent less than 20 percent of total wholesale trade.

TABLE 16-1 **Wholesale Trade in Canada, 1994**

Characteristics	Number of Locations	Total Operating Revenue ($millions)	Cost of Goods Sold ($millions)	Gross Margin ($millions)
Total	56,226	282,438	222,439	59,999

Source: Statistics Canada, *Wholesaling and Retailing in Canada*, cat. no. 63-236, 1994.

MARKETING AT WORK FILE 16-1

RAINCOAST UNDERSTANDS: IT PUBLISHES, WHOLESALES, AND DISTRIBUTES

A few years ago, Raincoast Books of Vancouver was an insignificant competitor in the Canadian book business. Today it is in the top twenty in Canadian publishing, with sales of over $21 million. What makes Raincoast notable is that it operates three different businesses. It is a book distributor, marketing books from thirty-six publishers located in Canada, the United States, Britain, and Japan. It is a book wholesaler, resupplying titles from Canadian publishers to western Canadian bookstores. It is a successful publisher of the Griffin and Sabine tales and a host of coffee table books, cookbooks, and other tomes. Many Canadian publishers, such as McClelland & Stewart, distribute other company's books, and the funds from distribution help to pay for their publishing operations. Wholesalers such as Toronto's Firefly and North49 Books are also publishers. But none operates in all three areas, and not on the West Coast.

Raincoast's owners started in the book business as publishers' representatives, selling books on commission and doing marketing and publicity for Canadian publishers. On their sales rounds, they would hear complaints from Vancouver booksellers about not being able to get reasonable delivery schedules — books just took too long to get from Toronto, where publishing and distribution is centred — to Vancouver. Book Express, the wholesale arm, can get books from Vancouver to Montreal faster than Toronto-based wholesalers can ship to Montreal, according to Nicholas Hoare, the Montreal-based wholesaler and retailer. Hoare says that "they handle all their orders like hot potatoes."

As soon as a bookstore places an order, it immediately goes into Raincoast's $500,000 computer system. Books ordered in the morning are shipped the same afternoon to Vancouver stores and the same afternoon or next day to booksellers in western Canada. An order will take six days to arrive in central Canada — considered record speed. When other distributors are closed for holidays — a time when books are selling — Book Express is shipping, and fast, and on time for the season. Book Express earns $11 million, the distribution business makes about $8 million, and publishing about $2 million. It turned its stock 6.1 times last year, compared with an average bookstore turn of three or four annually.

Running three businesses at different levels in the distribution chain gives Raincoast a deeper understanding of the total book business and of how the parts fit together. It also gains many cost economies, from sharing warehousing to accounting. Their attention to service has not only solidified their relationships with bookshops but also with foreign publishers such as Australia's famous Lonely Planet Publications, Bloomsbury Publishing of London, and Chronicle Books of San Francisco. Now — to be able to sign, publish, and distribute some first-rate fiction.

Source: Adapted from Jennifer Hunter, "Raincoast's Umbrella," *Report on Business Magazine*, June 1997, pp. 52–60.

- **Primary product dealers** are principally engaged in buying for resale primary products such as grain, livestock, furs, fish, fruit, and vegetables from the primary producers of these products. On occasion, they will act as agents of the producer. Co-operatives that market the primary products of their members are also included in this category.

Some other subcategories used in classifying the wholesaling business are reflected in Figure 16-2. For example, wholesaling intermediaries may be grouped by:

Ownership of products — merchant wholesalers versus agents.

Ownership of establishments — manufacturers' sales branches versus independent merchants and agents.

FIGURE 16-2

Types of Wholesaling Institutions

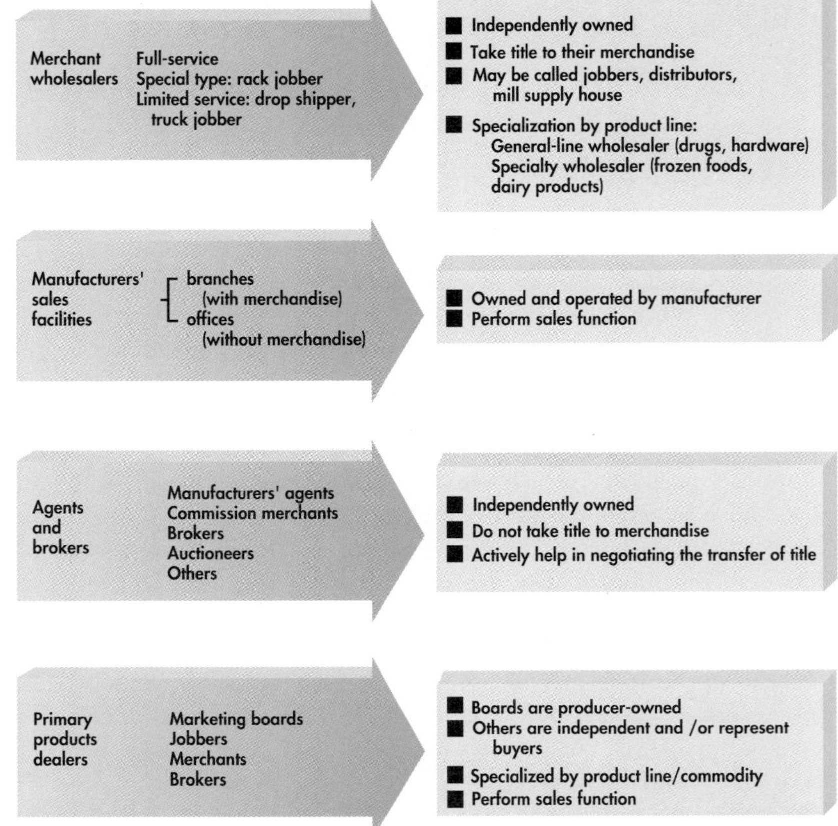

Range of services offered — full-service wholesalers versus limited-service firms.

Depth and breadth of the line carried — general-line wholesalers (drugs, hardware) versus specialty firms (frozen foods, dairy products).

Wholesalers' Customers

One might expect that total retail sales would be considerably higher than total wholesale trade, because the retail price of a given product is higher than the wholesale price. Also, many products sold at retail never pass through a wholesaler's establishment and so are excluded from total wholesale sales.

Total sales figures belie this particular line of reasoning (see Table 16-2). In each year, the volume of wholesale trade is considerably higher than total retail sales.

The explanation for this situation may be found in an analysis of the customers of wholesalers (see Figure 16-3).

Most merchant wholesalers' sales are made to customers other than retailers. That is, large quantities of business and industrial products are now sold through merchant wholesalers. Moreover, sales by the other types of wholesalers show this same pattern. Thus, overall, sales to retailers account for much less than total sales by merchant wholesalers.

Another trend that has become obvious in recent years is the increase in the percentage of consumer goods sold directly to retailers by manufacturers. Yet, in spite of this increased bypassing of the wholesaler, wholesaling is on the increase — an indication of the usefulness of wholesaling to the business world.

Operating Expenses and Profits of Wholesaling Intermediaries

The average total operating expenses for wholesaling combined has been estimated at about 16.7 percent of *wholesale* sales. It has also been estimated that

TABLE 16-2 Total Wholesale and Retail Trade, Selected Years

Year	Wholesale Trade ($millions)	Retail Trade ($millions)
1984	170,333	126,751
1986	188,236	152,880
1988	227,173	180,545
1990	255,081	192,555
1992	237,468	185,049
1994	282,438	208,856

Source: Statistics Canada, "Wholesale Trade-Historical Series, Canada, 1984–1994" and "Retail Trade — Historical Series, Canada, 1984–1994," *Wholesaling and Retailing in Canada, 1994*, p. 21.

operating expenses of retailers average about 34 percent of *retail* sales (omitting bars and restaurants, which do some processing of products).

Profit margins for the wholesaling industry are approximately equivalent to profit margins for retailing. In 1994, gross profit margins (before taxes) for the wholesale trade equalled 5.5 percent; corresponding profit margins for the retail trade equaled 5.05 percent.[4]

MERCHANT WHOLESALERS

Merchant wholesalers take title to the products they handle, and they account for the largest segment of wholesale trade.

Full-Service Wholesalers

An independent merchant wholesaler that performs a full range of wholesaling functions (from creating assortments to warehousing) is a **full-service wholesaler**. This type of intermediary may handle consumer and/or business products that may be manufactured or nonmanufactured (such as grown or extracted), and imported, exported, or made and sold domestically.

Full-service wholesalers comprise the majority of merchant wholesalers. They have held their own in competitive struggles with other forms of indirect distribution, including manufacturers' sales facilities and agent wholesalers. Actually, there has been an increase in full-service wholesalers' share of wholesale trade. But this trend may be a bit misleading. While full-service wholesalers have made gains in some industries, they have lost ground in others.

Individual manufacturers in some industries have begun to distribute their products directly, eliminating some or all of the wholesalers in their channels. Janes Family Foods, a major Ontario

FIGURE 16-3
Wholesale Trade Customers

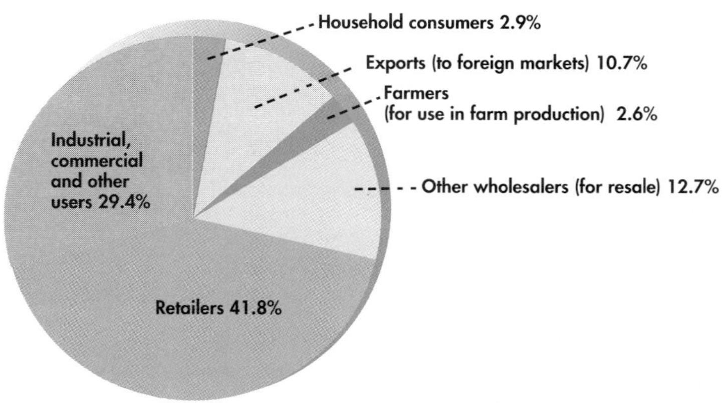

frozen-foods manufacturer, is now marketing directly to big restaurant chains, which follows its trend of selling directly to retail outlets.[5]

Full-service wholesalers survive and prosper by providing services needed by both their customers and producers. These services are summarized in Table 16-3. Large wholesalers use their clout to obtain good prices from producers. They also apply the latest technology to develop computerized inventory systems for their customers. By helping customers keep their inventories lean, a full-service intermediary can garner added loyalty.

Other Merchant Wholesalers

We should also consider two types of merchant wholesalers with distinctive operations:

- **Truck jobbers**, also called *truck distributors*, carry a selected line of perishable products and deliver them by truck to retail stores. Truck jobbers are common in the food-products field. Each jobber carries a nationally advertised brand of fast-moving, perishable or semiperishable goods, such as candies, dairy products, potato chips, and tobacco products. Truck jobbers furnish fresh products so frequently that retailers can buy perishable goods in small amounts to minimize the risk of loss. But truck jobbers are saddled with high operating costs, caused primarily by the small order size and inefficient use of their trucks (for example, only during parts of the day).
- **Drop shippers**, also known as *desk jobbers*, sell merchandise for delivery directly *from the producer to the customer*. Drop shippers do not physically handle the product. They are common in only several product categories, including coal, lumber, and building materials, that are typically sold in very large quantities and that have high freight costs in relation to their unit value.

AGENT WHOLESALERS

As distinguished from merchant wholesalers, agent wholesalers (1) do *not* take title to products and (2) typically perform fewer services. Agent wholesalers receive a commission intended to cover their expenses and to provide a profit. Commission rates vary greatly, ranging from about 3 to 10 percent, depending mainly on the nature of the product and the services performed.

Agent wholesalers have lost one-third of their wholesale trade since the late 1960s. In the case of agricultural products, agents are being replaced by merchant wholesalers or by direct sales to food-

TABLE 16-3 Full-Service Wholesalers' Typical Services to Customers and Producers

Service	Description
Buying	Act as purchasing agent for customers.
Creating assortments	Buy from many suppliers to develop an inventory matching needs of customers.
Subdividing	Buy in large quantities (such as a truckload) and then resell in smaller quantities (such as a dozen).
Selling	Provide a sales force for producers to reach small retailers and other businesses, at a lower cost than producers would incur by having their own sales forces.
Transportation	Make quick, frequent deliveries to customers, reducing customers' risks and investment in inventory.
Warehousing	Store products in facilities that are nearer customers' locations than are manufacturing plants.
Financing	Grant credit to customers, reducing their capital requirements. Aid producers by ordering and paying for products before purchase by customers.
Risk taking	Reduce a producer's risk by taking title to products.
Market information	Supply information to customers about new products and producers' special offers and to producer-suppliers about customers' needs and competitors' activities.
Management	Assist customers, especially small retailers, in areas such as inventory control, allocation assistance of shelf space, and financial management.

processing companies and grocery stores. Similarly, for manufactured goods, agents are being replaced by merchant wholesalers or direct distribution. As shown in Table 16-4, product characteristics and market conditions determine whether a distribution channel should include agent or merchant wholesalers.

On the basis of sales volume, the most significant types of agent wholesalers are manufacturers' agents, brokers, and commission merchants. These three types as well as several special types of agent wholesalers are described next.

Manufacturers' Agents

An independent agent wholesaler that sells part or all of a manufacturer's product mix in an assigned geographic territory is a **manufacturers' agent**, or *manufacturers' representative*. Agents are not employees of the manufacturers; they are independent business firms. Still, they have little or no control over prices and terms of sale, which are established by the manufacturers they represent.

Because a manufacturers' agent sells in a limited territory, each producer uses multiple agents for full coverage of its markets. Manufacturers' reps have continuing, year-round relationships with the companies (often called principals) they represent. Each agent usually serves several noncompeting manufacturers of related products. For example, a manufacturers' agent may specialize in toys and carry an assortment of noncompeting lines in board games, dolls, learning materials, and outdoor play equipment.

When a manufacturer finds it is not feasible to have its own sales force, a manufacturers' agent is often practical. An agent can be cost-effective because its major expenses (travel and lodging) are spread over a number of product lines. Also, producers pay agents a commission, which is a percentage of sales volume, so agents are paid only for what they actually sell.

Manufacturers' agents are used extensively in distributing many types of consumer and business goods, ranging from sporting goods to heating and air-conditioning vents and ductwork. Their main service to manufacturers is selling. Because a manufacturers' agent does not carry nearly as many lines as a full-service wholesaler, an agent can be expected to provide knowledgeable, aggressive selling.

Manufacturers' agents are most helpful to:

- A small firm that has a limited number of products and no sales force.
- A business that wants to add a new and possibly unrelated line to its existing product mix, but whose present sales force either is not experienced in the new line or cannot reach the new market. In this situation, a company's own sales force and its agents may cover the same geographic market, but for different product lines.

TABLE 16-4 Factors Suggesting Which Type of Wholesaling Middleman Should Be Used in a Channel

	Favouring Agent	Favouring Merchant
Nature of product	Nonstandard, perhaps made to order	Standard
Technicality of product	Simple	Complex
Product's gross margin	Small	Relatively large
Number of customers	Few	Many
Concentration of customers	Concentrated geographically and in a few industries	Dispersed geographically and in many industries
Frequency of ordering	Relatively infrequently	Frequently
Time between order and receipt of shipment	Customer satisfied with relatively long lead time	Customer requires/desires shorter lead time

Source: Adapted from Donald M. Jackson and Michael F. d'Amico, "Products and Markets Served by Distributors and Agents," *Industrial Marketing Management*, February 1989, pp. 27–33.

- A firm that wants to enter a new market that is not yet sufficiently developed to warrant the use of its own sales force.

There are limitations to what manufacturers' agents do. Agents do not carry an inventory of merchandise, usually do not install machinery and equipment, and typically are not equipped to furnish customers with extensive technical advice or repair service.

Depending on how difficult the product is to sell and whether it is stocked by the agent, operating expenses of manufacturers' agents can vary greatly. However, they average about 7 percent of sales. Some reps operate on a commission as low as 2 percent of net sales; others earn as much as 20 percent; the average is about 5.5 percent.

Brokers

Brokers ordinarily neither physically handle products being distributed nor work on a continuing basis with sellers or buyers. Instead, a **broker** is an independent agent wholesaler that brings buyers and sellers together and provides market information to either party. It furnishes information about many topics, including prices, products, and general market conditions. In recent years, manufacturers' agents and brokers have become more similar with respect to attributes and services.

Most brokers work for sellers, although some represent buyers. Brokers have no authority to set prices. They simply negotiate a sale and leave it up to the seller to accept or reject the buyer's offer.

Brokers are used in selling real estate and securities, but they are most prevalent in the food field. For example, a seafood broker handles the output from a salmon cannery, which operates only about three months each year. The canner employs a broker to find buyers among retail stores, wholesalers, and other outlets. When the entire output has been sold, the canner–broker relationship is discontinued — although it may be renewed the next year.

Brokers provide limited services and, as a result, incur fairly low expenses, about 3 percent of sales. Likewise, they receive relatively small commissions — normally less than 5 percent.

Other Agent Wholesalers

Four additional types of agent wholesalers account for smaller shares of wholesale trade than manufacturers' reps and brokers. Nevertheless, they provide valuable services for certain products and in specific markets. These intermediaries are:

- **Commission merchants**, common in the marketing of many agricultural products, set prices and terms of sale, sell the product, and perhaps physically handle it. (Despite the word *merchant*, a commission merchant is an *agent* wholesaler that normally does not take title to the products being handled and sold.)
- **Auction companies** help assembled buyers and sellers complete their transactions. They provide (1) auctioneers who do the selling and (2) physical facilities for displaying the sellers' products. Although they make up only about 1 percent of total wholesale trade, auction companies are extremely important in the wholesaling of used cars and certain agricultural products (such as tobacco, livestock, and fruit).
- **Selling agents** essentially substitute for a marketing department by marketing a manufacturer's entire output. Although selling agents transact only about 1 percent of wholesale trade, they play a key role in the distribution of textile products and coal and, to a lesser extent, apparel, food, lumber, and metal products.
- **Import-export agents** bring together sellers and buyers in different countries. Export agents work in the country in which the product is made; import agents are based in the country where the product will be sold.

NATURE AND IMPORTANCE OF PHYSICAL DISTRIBUTION

After a company establishes its channels of distribution, it must arrange for the physical distribution of its products through these channels. **Physical distribution**, which we use synonymously with *logistics*, consists of all the activities concerned with moving the right amount of the right products to the right place at the right time. In its full scope, physical distribution for manufacturers includes the flow of *raw*

MARKETING AT WORK FILE 16-2

GREY MARKETS GIVE PRODUCERS AND MIDDLEMEN GREY HAIR

Sometimes, products distributed by wholesalers don't end up where their manufacturers intended. And occasionally, items are sold through distribution channels that are not authorized by the manufacturer. This practice, called *grey marketing* or *export diversion*, usually involves products made in one country and destined for sale in another.

Cameras, computer disk drives, memory chips or even entire PCs, perfumes, cars, and liquor are among the diverse products that are sold through grey markets. Ordinarily, grey marketing arises when a product with a well-known brand name carries different prices under different circumstances. For example, a product's wholesale price may vary, depending on the country to which it is sold or the quantity purchased.

Grey marketing takes many forms. Usually, a wholesaling intermediary, such as an import or export agent, purchases a product made in one country and agrees to distribute it in a second country, but instead diverts the product to a third country (sometimes Canada). Because the product typically is sold at a discount in a reputable outlet, not on the "black market" or from the trunks of cars, it isn't apparent that normal distribution has not been used.

So what's wrong with grey marketing? After spending time and money to promote the product, authorized distributors lose sales to other distributors selling the same product through the grey market. Manufacturers then have to placate their authorized distributors. Grey marketing disrupts a producer's distribution and pricing strategies. And when consumers buy products through the grey market, they may wind up without warranties or service contracts valid in Canada.

Still, some parties (but definitely not authorized distributors) see benefits in grey marketing. Unauthorized distributors are able to sell products they normally cannot acquire. To sell excess output, some manufacturers quietly participate in, or at least do not discourage, grey marketing. Consumers pay lower prices for popular products and may also find them at more outlets.

Most manufacturers would like to eliminate grey marketing. However, some have concluded that it's too difficult and costly to fight. Other producers try to minimize grey marketing by revising price schedules and distribution policies and taking unauthorized distributors to court. Grey marketing represents one more challenge for both producers and wholesaling intermediaries.

One example of grey marketing being practised in Canada is in the automobile industry. Exporting vehicles is a lucrative business, but many automakers write clauses into their contracts with dealerships forbidding them from selling to exporters and setting out punitive fines if they do. The grey automobile marketers claim they are only exploiting a market niche by bringing hard-to-find autos to customers. Recently grey marketers of automobiles in Canada formed an association called The North American Automobile Trade Association to pool resources for legal cases and lobbying. This group is supported by the Canadian Automobile Dealers' Association, which is being caught in the middle between the grey marketers and the automobile manufacturers.

Source: Adapted from Amy Borrus, "Exports That Aren't Going Anywhere," *Business Week*, December 4, 1995, pp. 121–24; Fay Rice, "Closeout Sale on Grey Goods," *Fortune*, April 3, 1995, p. 17; Robert E. Weigand, "Parallel Import Channels — Options for Preserving Territorial Integrity," *Columbia Journal of World Business*, Spring 1991, pp. 53–60; Ian Jack, "Grey Marketers Unite for Fight," *The Financial Post*, September 21/23, 1996, p. 4.

www.challenger.com

materials from their sources of supply to the production line *and* the movement of *finished goods* from the end of the production line to the final users' locations. Intermediaries manage the flows of goods *onto* their shelves as well as *from* their shelves to customers' homes, stores, or other places of business.

The activities making up physical distribution are:

- Inventory location and warehousing.
- Materials handling.
- Inventory control.
- Order processing.
- Transportation.

A decision regarding any one of these activities affects all the others. Location of a warehouse influences the selection of transportation methods and carriers; the choice of a carrier influences the optimum size of shipments.

Increasing Attention to Physical Distribution

Through the years, management has made substantial progress in reducing production costs. Reductions have also been achieved in other costs of marketing. Physical distribution may be the last marketing area with substantial opportunities for cost cutting. And the potential savings are great. For certain products, such as furniture and building materials, the largest operating expenses are related to physical distribution. For other products, as much as one-half the wholesale cost is incurred in transportation and warehousing. For some businesses engaged in distribution, profits are small, so any savings are appreciated. A supermarket, for instance, may earn a net profit of 1 percent on sales. Thus every $1 a supermarket saves in physical distribution costs has the same effect on profit as a $100 increase in sales!

Effective physical distribution also can be the basis by which a firm gains and sustains a strong differential advantage. On-time delivery, which requires effective physical distribution, can provide a competitive edge. To accomplish this efficiency for their customers, many companies involved in distributing goods have streamlined their operations in recent years. PBB has three major distribution centres in Vancouver, Toronto, and Montreal. They offer specific services at every point along the supply chain. Customers receive software that permits them to dial into PBB's system and view orders being shipped, see which jobs have been completed and which are still open, and check a part number to see how much is in the warehouse.[6]

www.pbb.com

A business faces a problem (or maybe it's an opportunity) when it has a warehouse full of goods in Edmonton but unsatisfied customers in Calgary or too many ski parkas in Regina and too few in Winnipeg. These examples point up the importance of location in marketing, especially with respect to merchandise. That is, the appropriate assortment of products must be in the right place at the right time to maximize the opportunity for profitable sales. That's what physical distribution can help achieve.[7]

Since deregulation, transportation firms have been able to decide which rates (prices) and levels of service would best satisfy their target markets. For example, Challenger Motor Freight of Cambridge, Ontario, with 450 trucks operating in Canada and the United States, promises on-time deliveries and works hard to keep its promise. Toward this end, Challenger has equipped its trucks with satellite-tracking devices that allow the company to monitor their progress and to communicate with its drivers. From another perspective, companies that ship goods shop around for rates and service levels that best meet their needs.

Systems Approach to Physical Distribution

We have occasionally alluded to marketing as a *total system* of business action rather than a fragmented series of operations. Nowhere is this clearer than in physical distribution. But it has not always been this way. Traditionally, physical distribution activities were fragmented.

In many firms, physical distribution is still unco-ordinated. Managerial responsibility for it is delegated to various units that often have conflicting, perhaps opposite, goals. The production department, for instance, is interested primarily in long production runs to minimize unit manufacturing costs, even though the result may be high inventory costs. In contrast, the finance department wants a minimum of funds to be tied up in inventories. At the same time, the sales department wants to have a wide assortment of products available at locations near customers. Of course, there's always the temptation to select carriers with low rates, even though this may mean longer time in transit.

Unco-ordinated conditions like these make it impossible to achieve a flow of products that satisfies the firm's goals. However, the **systems approach to physical distribution** can bring together these individual activities in a unified way.

To implement a systems approach, some companies are contracting out, or outsourcing their physical distribution function. It's more and more common for logistics companies to manage firms' distribution processes under a multiyear contract. A large-scale example is Ryder, the company responsibile for overseeing the entire physical distribution for GM's Saturn division, from suppliers' shipments to delivery of new vehicles to auto dealerships. One Canadian survey found that most firms are already outsourcing at least part of their logistics work and expect that trend to increase.[8]

The growth of **contract logistics** reflects a broader trend whereby firms are outsourcing various business tasks, ranging from payroll to public relations. One outstanding example can be seen in Honda, which relies on outside suppliers for about 80 percent of the cost of its vehicles. The association between Honda and its suppliers is so strong that if they run into problems, Honda sends in its own experts to help them solve it.[9]

The Total Cost Concept

As part of the systems approach to physical distribution, executives should apply the **total cost concept**. That is, a company should determine the set of activities that produces the best relationship between costs and profit for the *entire* physical distribution system. This approach is superior to focusing strictly on the separate costs of individual distribution activities.

Too often, a company attempts to minimize the cost of only one aspect of physical distribution — transportation, for example. Management might be upset by the high cost of air freight. But the higher costs of air freight may be more than offset by savings from (1) lower inventory costs, (2) less insurance and interest expense, (3) lower crating costs, and (4) fewer lost sales due to out-of-stock conditions. The point is *not* that air freight is the best method of transportation. Rather, the key point is that physical distribution should be viewed as a *total* process, with all the related costs being analyzed.

Strategic Use of Physical Distribution

The strategic use of physical distribution may enable a company to strengthen its competitive position by providing more customer satisfaction and/or by reducing operating costs. The management of physical distribution can also affect a firm's marketing mix, particularly product planning, pricing, and distribution channels. Each opportunity is described below.

Improve Customer Service A well-run logistics system can improve the service a firm provides its customers, whether they are intermediaries or ultimate users. Furthermore, the level of customer service directly affects demand. This is true especially in marketing undifferentiated products (such as chemicals and most building materials), where effective service may be a company's only differential advantage.

To ensure reliable customer service, management should set standards of performance for each subsystem of physical distribution. These standards should be quantitatively measurable. Some examples:

- *Electronics manufacturer:* Make delivery within seven days after receiving an order, with no more than 20 percent of the shipment by air.
- *Sporting goods wholesaler:* Fill 98 percent of orders accurately without increasing the size of the order-fulfilment staff.
- *Industrial distributor:* Maintain inventory levels that enable fulfilment of at least 85 percent of orders received from inventory on hand, but maintain a stock turn of thirty days.

Reduce Distribution Costs Many avenues to cost reductions may be opened by effective physical distribution management. For example, eliminating unneeded warehouses will lower costs. Inventories — and their attendant carrying costs and capital investment — may be reduced by consolidating stocks at fewer locations.

Ryder offers a system-wide management view to handling logistics rather than providing a piecemeal approach.

Create Time and Location Value Storage, which is part of warehousing, creates *time value*. Storage is essential to correct imbalances in the timing of production and consumption. An imbalance can occur when there is *year-round consumption* but only *seasonal production*, as in the case of agricultural products. For instance, time value is added when bananas are picked green and allowed to ripen in storage. And skilful use of warehousing allows a producer to store a seasonal surplus so that it can be marketed long after the harvest has ended. In other instances warehousing helps adjust *year-round production to seasonal consumption*. A manufacturer may produce lawn mowers on a year-round basis; during the fall and winter, the mowers are stored for sale in the spring and summer.

Transportation adds value to products by creating *location value*. A fine suit hanging on a manufacturer's rack in Montreal has less value than an identical suit displayed in a retailer's store in Vancouver. Transporting the suit adds value to it.

Stabilize Prices Careful management of warehousing and transportation can help stabilize prices for an individual firm or for an entire industry. If a market is temporarily glutted with a product, sellers can store it until supply and demand conditions are better balanced. Such use of warehousing facilities is common in the marketing of agricultural products and other seasonally produced goods. Moreover, the judicious movement of products from one market to another may enable a seller to (1) avoid a market with depressed prices or (2) take advantage of a market that has a shorter supply and higher prices. If demand for heating oil is stronger in Kamloops than in Kelowna, a producer should be able to achieve greater revenues by shifting some shipments from Kelowna to Kamloops.

Influence Channel Decisions Decisions regarding inventory management have a direct bearing on a producer's selection of channels and the location of intermediaries. Logistical considerations may become paramount, for example, when a company decides to decentralize its inventory. In this case management must determine (1) how many sites to establish and (2) whether to use wholesalers, the company's own warehouses, or public warehouses. One producer may select merchant wholesalers that perform storage and other warehousing services. Another may prefer to use a combination of (1) manufacturers' agents to provide aggressive selling and (2) public warehouses to distribute the products ordered.

Minimize Shipping Costs Managers with shipping responsibilities need to ensure that their companies enjoy the fastest routes *and* the lowest rates for whatever methods of transportation they use. The pricing of transportation services is one of the most complicated parts of North American business. The rate, or tariff, schedule is the carrier's price list. Typically it is complex; to cite one example, shipping rates vary for many different types of goods, depending on many factors including not only distance to the destination but also the bulk and weight of the products. Therefore, being able to interpret a tariff schedule properly is a money-saving skill for a manager with shipping responsibilities.

TASKS IN PHYSICAL DISTRIBUTION MANAGEMENT

Physical distribution refers to the actual physical flow of products. In contrast, **physical distribution management** is the development and operation of processes resulting in the effective and efficient physical flow of products. An effective physical distribution system is built around five interdependent subsystems: inventory location and warehousing, materials handling, inventory control, order processing, and transportation. Each must be carefully co-ordinated with the others.

MARKETING AT WORK FILE 16-3

LOGISTICS LESSONS FROM WAL-MART

Wal-Mart, whatever else it might be, is a benchmark for logistics — other firms have watched it, have tried to do as well, and some have done even better. Wal-Mart's business vision was a complete dedication to fulfilling the needs of its customers that was to shape its goals: to provide customers with quality goods, to make these goods available where and when customers wanted them, to create a cost structure that would allow competitive pricing, and to develop a reputation for absolute trustworthiness. Of course, it is one thing to state such goals, and quite another to achieve them. Wal-Mart, however, hit on a valuable competitive strategy — "cross-docking." It was based on the way the company replenished its inventory, and it provided the nucleus for all its subsequent strategies.

"Cross-docking" refers to a system whereby goods are constantly delivered to Wal-Mart's warehouses, where they are selected, repacked, and then transported to stores, often without having to sit in inventory. The expensive warehouse costs saved by simply moving rapidly moving products from one loading dock to another proved significant. This means that while bypassing the usual inventory and handling costs, Wal-Mart is able to reap the full savings that result from buying trucks carrying large volumes of goods. While competitor K mart was able to run only 50 percent of its goods through its warehouse system, Wal-Mart can boast that almost 90 percent of its products avoid these costs. Such savings reduce Wal-Mart's costs of sales by 2 to 3 percent, a significant difference that makes possible its strategy of everyday low prices.

These low prices in turn lead to further savings by eliminating the cost of frequent promotions, as well as stabilizing prices so that sales are more predictable, thus reducing stockouts and excess inventory. And, of course, low prices attract more customers, which means more sales per retail square foot.

If "cross-docking" is so successful, why don't all retailers use it? The reason is that it's very difficult to manage.

In order to make cross-docking work, Wal-Mart had to make strategic investments in a variety of interlocking support systems far beyond what could be justified by usual return-on-investment criteria. For example, cross-docking demands constant contact between Wal-Mart's distribution centres, suppliers, and every checkout in every store so that orders can flow in, be consolidated, and executed within a matter of mere hours. This could be done only by investing in a private satellite communication system that daily sends point-of-sale data directly to Wal-Mart's four thousand vendors.

Wal-Mart maintains an information technology system that is totally integrated with its suppliers. Its system, developed in-house, openly shares information with its suppliers. The system is dubbed RetailLink and it puts each supplier roughly on an equal footing, in terms of the information available, with Wal-Mart's own internal buyers and financial analysts.

Another key investment was in the development of a rapid and responsive transportation system. Twenty distribution centres are serviced by a fleet of more than two thousand company-owned trucks, allowing Wal-Mart to ship goods from warehouses to stores in less than forty-eight hours and to replenish store shelves twice a week, compared with the industry average of twice a month.

Finally, however, all the logistical facets of the cross-docking strategy could never have functioned if it weren't for the fundamental changes made on the management level. Traditionally in retail, decisions about merchandising, pricing, and promotions have remained in the highly centralized hands of a few corporate executives, but the very nature of cross-docking turned this command-and-control logic upside-down. For, instead of the retailer pushing products into the system, cross-docking has customers "pulling" products when and where they need them. The upshot was a managerial style emphasizing frequent, informal co-operation between stores, distribution centres, and suppliers — with much less centralized control. Thus, instead of giving directives to individual store managers, senior managers at Wal-Mart are helping to create an environment where they can learn from the market — and from each other. In pursuing such goals, Wal-Mart has invested in information systems that provide store managers with detailed data about customer behaviour, while company airplanes regularly fly store managers to Wal-Mart's Bentonville, Arkansas, headquarters for conferences about market trends and merchandising.

Source: Adapted from George Stalk, Philip Evans, and Lawrence Shulman, "Competing on Capabilities," *Harvard Business Review*, 1992; and Charles B. Darling & J. William Semich, "Wal-Mart's IT Secret: Extreme Integration," *Datamation*, November 1996; www.datamation.com/Plugin/issues/1996/nov/11cover.html. (August 11, 1997).

Inventory Location and Warehousing

The name of the game in physical distribution is inventory management. One important consideration is **warehousing**, which embraces a range of functions, such as assembling, dividing (bulk-breaking), and storing products and preparing them for reshipping. Management must also consider the size, location, and transporting of inventories. These four areas are interrelated. The number and locations of inventory sites, for example, influence inventory size and transportation methods. These interrelationships are often quite complex.

Distribution Centres An effective inventory-location strategy may involve the establishment of one or more **distribution centres**. Such facilities are planned around markets rather than transportation requirements. The idea is to develop under one roof an efficient, fully integrated system for the flow of products — taking orders, filling them, and preparing them for delivery to customers.

Distribution centres have been established by many well-known firms. They can cut distribution costs by reducing the number of warehouses, pruning excessive inventories, and eliminating out-of-stock conditions. Storage and delivery time have been cut to a minimum, recognizing the adage that companies are in business to *sell* goods, not to *store* them. Ikea, the Scandinavian furniture retailer, expanded very slowly in Canada and the United States because the company wanted to find locations and facilities that met the needs of its distribution centres.[10]

Types of Warehouses Any producer, wholesaler, or retailer has the option of operating its own private warehouse or using the services of a public warehouse. A **private warehouse** is more likely to be an advantage if (1) a company moves a large volume of products through a warehouse and (2) there is very little, if any, seasonal fluctuation in this flow.

A **public warehouse** offers storage and handling facilities to individuals or companies. Public warehousing costs are a variable expense. Customers pay only for the space they use, and only when they use it. Public warehouses can also provide office and product display space, and accept and fill orders for sellers. Furthermore, warehouse receipts covering products stored in public warehouses may be used as collateral for bank loans.

Materials Handling

Selecting the proper equipment to physically handle products, including the warehouse building itself, is the **materials handling** subsystem of physical distribution management. Equipment that is well matched to the task can minimize losses from breakage, spoilage, and theft. Efficient equipment can reduce handling costs as well as time required for handling.

Distributors consider modern, efficient warehouses vital to their success.

Modern warehouses are often huge, one-storey structures located in outlying areas, where land is less expensive and loading platforms are easily accessed by trucks and trains. Conveyor belts, fork-lift trucks, and other mechanized equipment are used to move merchandise. In some warehouses the order fillers are even outfitted with in-line skates!

Containerization is a cargo-handling system that has become standard practice in physical distribution. Shipments of products are enclosed in large metal or wood containers. The containers are then transported unopened from the time they leave the customer's facilities (such as a manufacturer's plant) until they reach their destination (such as a wholesaler's warehouse). Containerization minimizes physical handling, thereby reducing damage, lessening the risk of theft, and allowing for more efficient transportation.

Inventory Control

Maintaining control over the size and composition of inventories, which represent a sizable investment for most companies, is essential to any physical distribution system. The goal of **inventory control** is to fill customers' orders promptly, completely, and accurately while minimizing both the investment and fluctuations in inventories.

Customer-Service Requirements Inventory size is determined by balancing costs and desired levels of customer service. That is, what percentage of orders does the company expect to fill promptly from inventory on hand? Out-of-stock conditions result in lost sales, loss of goodwill, even loss of customers. Yet to be able to fill 100 percent of orders promptly may require an excessively large and costly inventory. Generally speaking, about 80 percent *more* inventory is required to fill 95 percent of the orders than to fill only 80 percent. For example, if a firm now satisfies 80 percent of its requests by stocking 20,000 units, it would have to increase its inventory to 36,000 units to improve its rate of order fulfilment to 95 percent.

Perhaps the greatest boon to inventory control in recent years has been improvements in computer technology. These advancements have enabled management to shorten the order delivery time *and* substantially reduce the size of inventories. Canadian Tire is one of countless firms that has benefited from computer-based inventory control. Through its inventory-control system, goods reach the selling floor much more quickly when they are reordered electronically than they would under conventional inventory ordering systems.

Economic Order Quantity Management must establish the optimal quantity for reorder when it is time to replenish inventory stocks. The **economic order quantity (EOQ)** is the volume at which the sum of inventory-carrying costs and order-processing costs are at a minimum. Typically, as order size increases, (1) inventory-carrying cost goes up (because the average inventory is larger) and (2) order-processing cost declines (because there are fewer orders).

In Figure 16-4, point EOQ represents the order quantity having the lowest total cost. Actually, the order quantity that a firm considers best (or optimal) often is larger than the EOQ. That's because management must try to balance the sometimes conflicting goals of low inventory costs and responsive customer service. For various reasons, such as gaining a differential advantage, a firm may place a higher priority on customer service than inventory costs. To completely fill orders in a timely manner may well call for a larger order quantity than the EOQ — for example, quantity X in Figure 16-4.

FIGURE 16-4 Economic Order Quantity

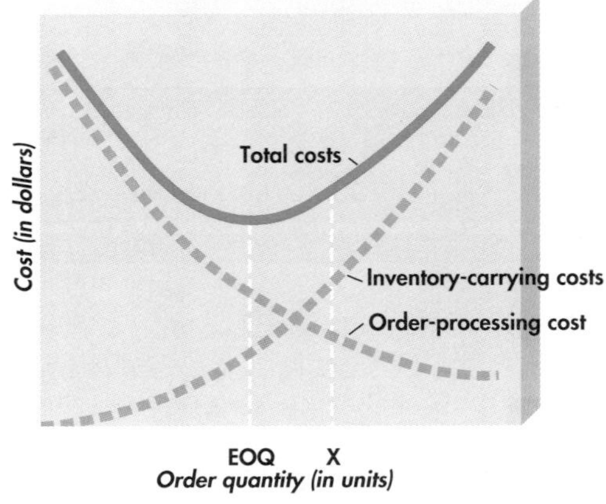

Just-in-Time A popular form of inventory control, purchasing, and production scheduling is the

just-in-time (JIT) concept. The idea of JIT is that you buy in small quantities that arrive *just in time* for production and then produce in quantities *just in time* for sale. JIT has commanded the attention of *top* management — not just marketing or physical distribution management — in many North American companies.

When effectively implemented, the just-in-time concept has many benefits. By purchasing in small quantities and maintaining low inventory levels of parts and finished goods, a company can achieve dramatic cost savings because fewer items are damaged or stolen, or otherwise become unusable. Production and delivery schedules can be shortened and made more flexible and reliable. The Japanese have found that quality improves with JIT purchasing. When order quantities are small and deliveries frequent, a company can more quickly spot and then correct a quality problem in the products received.[11]

In Canada and the United States, the JIT philosophy was first adopted in the auto industry. But the concept has been picked up by leading firms in other industries, such as IBM, Xerox, Apple, Black and Decker, and General Electric. For some firms the results have been quite positive. Xerox eliminated 4,700 suppliers in one year, and Black and Decker cut more than 50 percent of its suppliers in two years.[12] A producer that relies on JIT tends to use fewer suppliers because they must be close to the producer's facilities and also because there must be strong partnerships with suppliers, which is not feasible with large numbers of suppliers. Channel members — even entire channels — that employ JIT effectively can gain a differential advantage. As JIT becomes widespread, firms or channels that ignore it risk a differential disadvantage.[13] Ford of Canada's JIT strategy allows it to bring to St. Thomas, Ontario, 2,600 different types of auto parts from every continent except Africa to allow it to assemble the Crown Victoria and the Mercury Grand Marquis.

An updated version of JIT, labelled JIT II, stresses closer working relationships between manufacturers and suppliers. Under JIT II, a company provides a supplier with sales forecasts and other useful information, some of which may be confidential. This, obviously, can't be done unless there is a substantial relationship between the two firms with high levels of trust. Electronic data interchange (EDI) and company alliances in a channel allow for substantial cost savings and differential advantages to those involved.[14]

Market Response Systems JIT's focus tends to be on production and the relationship between the producer and its suppliers. A parallel trend involves producers or intermediaries of finished goods and their customers. We refer to this counterpart to JIT as **market response systems**; they are sometimes called quick response systems. The central idea is that a purchase by a final customer, one who intends to consume the product, should activate a process to produce and deliver a replacement item. In this way, a product is pulled through a channel on the basis of demand rather than being pushed through on the basis of short-term price reductions or other inducements that often result in excessive inventory costs.

The intent of a market response system is similar to that of JIT — to have the right volume of goods to satisfy consumers and to replenish exhausted stocks rapidly. By resulting in better inventory control, a market response system can both reduce stock carrying and operating costs. In the grocery industry, market response has been labelled efficient consumer response (ECR). Such systems are in the early stages of implementation.

Order Processing

Still another part of the physical distribution system is a set of procedures for receiving, handling, and filling orders. This **order processing** subsystem should include provisions for billing, granting credit, preparing invoices, and collecting past-due accounts.

Customer ill will results if a company makes mistakes or is slow in filling orders. That's why more and more firms have turned to computers to execute most of their order-processing activities. At the same time, some suppliers are providing retail stores with computer technology to use in placing orders. For example, a large distributor of drugs and health and beauty aids has equipped drugstores with hand-held electronic devices. Orders assembled using such devices are transmitted to the wholesaler by telephone and can usually be assembled and shipped within 24 hours.

There have been various computer-based advances in order processing such as EDI and automatic replenishment. Under EDI, orders, invoices and other business information are transmitted by computer rather than mail. EDI speeds up the process and reduces the paperwork. By providing customers with technology that assists them in placing orders, a supplier can gain in several ways. The orders are likely to be free of errors, increasing both the accuracy and efficiency of order processing. If better computer technology reduces the number of out-of-stock items at the next level of the distribution channel, then the supplier's sales should increase. Under automatic replenishment, for example, a wholesaler's computer system receives a retailer's stock position, say daily or weekly, and routinely ships to replenish the retailer's shelves. That contributes to greater sales at the retail level; manufacturers stand to gain through added sales from the wholesaler. Moreover, to the extent that improved technology produces time savings or other benefits for employees of the ordering firm, the customer is likely to exhibit loyalty to the supplier.

Transportation

A major function of the physical distribution system in many companies is **transportation** — shipping products to customers. Management must decide on both the **mode of transportation** and the particular carriers. In this discussion we will focus on *intercity* shipments.

Major Modes Railways, trucks, ships, and airplanes are the leading modes of transportation. In Table 16-5 these four methods are compared on the basis of criteria likely to be used by physical distribution managers in selecting a mode of transportation. Of course, the comparisons in the table are generalizations, and the ratings of alternative modes of transportation can vary from one manager to the next, even within the same buying centre in an organization.[15] Virtually all intracity freight movements are made by truck. The use of trucks has expanded greatly and accounts for roughly half the expenditures for transportation services, with rail accounting for between 25 and 30 percent.

Intermodal Transportation When two or more modes of transportation are used to move freight, this is termed **intermodal transportation**. The intent of intermodal transportation is to seize the advantages of multiple forms of transportation.

One type of intermodal transportation involves trucks and railways. So-called **piggyback service** involves carrying truck trailers on railway flatcars. This type of intermodal transportation provides (1) more flexibility than railways alone can offer, (2) lower freight costs than trucks alone, and (3) less handling of goods.

A similar type of intermodal transportation combines ships or barges with either railways or trucks, or both. One version of **fishyback service** transports loaded trailers on barges or ships. The trailers may be carried piggyback fashion by railway to the dock, where they are transferred to the ship. Then, at the other end of the water trip, the trailers are loaded back onto trains for completion of the haul. In an alternative use of the fishyback service, merchandise is trucked directly to ports, where the trailer vans are loaded on barges. At the end of the water journey, the vans are trucked to the receiving station.

Freight Forwarders A specialized marketing institution serving firms that ship in less-than-carload quantities is called a **freight forwarder**. Its main function is to consolidate less-than-carload or less-than-truckload shipments from several shippers into carload and truckload quantities. The freight forwarder picks up the merchandise at the shipper's place of business and arranges for delivery at the buyer's door. A small shipper benefits from the speed and minimum handling associated with large shipments. A freight forwarder also provides the small shipper with traffic management services, such as selecting the best transportation methods and routes.

Package-Delivery Firms A major development of the past thirty years has been the formation of companies that deliver small shipments of packages and high-priority mail. You certainly are familiar with United Parcel Service (UPS), Federal Express (FedEx), and Loomis. All these firms compete directly with Canada Post.

In many respects, these companies offer the same services as freight forwarders. However, whereas the typical freight forwarder does not have

TABLE 16-5 Comparison of Transportation Methods

	Transportation Method			
Selection Criteria	**Rail**	**Water**	**Highway**	**Air**
Speed (door-to-door time)	Medium	Slowest	Fast	Fastest
Cost of transportation	Medium	Lowest	High	Highest
Reliability in meeting delivery schedules	Medium	Poor	Good	Good
Variety of products carried	Widest	Widest	Medium	Somewhat limited
Number of geographic locations served	Very many	Limited	Unlimited	Many
Most suitable products	Long hauls of carload quantities of bulky products, when freight costs are high in relation to product's value	Bulky, low-value nonperishables	Short hauls of high-value goods	High-value perishables, where speed of delivery is all-important

its own transportation equipment, package-delivery firms do. Companies such as UPS and FedEx essentially are integrated as cargo airlines and trucking companies. Furthermore, package-delivery firms, in effect, use intermodal transportation. Consider FedEx, for example. A package is picked up by truck, shipped intercity or overseas by plane, and delivered locally by truck.

Summary

Wholesaling consists of the sale, and all activities directly related to the sale, of goods and services for resale, use in producing other goods or services, or operating an organization. Firms engaged primarily in wholesaling, called wholesaling intermediaries, provide economies of skill, scale, and transactions to other firms involved in distribution.

Three categories of wholesaling intermediaries are merchant wholesalers, agent wholesaling intermediaries, and manufacturers sales facilities. The first two are independent firms; the third is owned by a manufacturer. Merchant wholesalers take title to products being distributed; agent wholesaling intermediaries do not.

Merchant wholesalers, who account for the majority of wholesale trade, include both full- and limited-service firms. Of the three major categories of wholesaling intermediaries, merchant wholesalers offer the widest range of services and thus incur the highest operating expenses. The main types of agent wholesalers are manufacturers' agents and brokers. Because they perform more limited services, agent wholesalers' expenses tend to be lower than those of merchant wholesalers.

Physical distribution is the flow of products from supply sources to the firm and then from the firm to its customers. The goal of physical distribution is to move the right amount of the right products to the right place at the right time. Physical distribution costs are a substantial part of total operating costs in many firms. Moreover, physical distribution is probably the only remaining source of possible cost reductions in many companies.

Although physical distribution activities are still fragmented operationally and organizationally in many firms, they should be treated as a system. The total cost concept should be applied to physical distribution — that is, the focus should be on the cost of physical distribution in its entirety, rather than on the costs of individual elements. However, management should strive *not* for the lowest total cost of physical distribution, but for the best balance between customer service and total cost. Effective management of physical distribution can help a company gain an advantage over competitors through better customer service and/or lower operating costs. To improve their physical distribution, some firms are turning to contract logistics.

The operation of a physical distribution system requires management's attention and decision-making in five areas: (1) inventory location and warehousing, (2) materials handling, (3) inventory control, (4) order processing, and (5) transportation. They should not be treated as individual activities but as interrelated components within a physical distribution system. Effective management of these five activities requires an understanding of distribution centres, economic order quantity, just-in-time processes, and intermodal transportation.

Key Terms and Concepts

Wholesaling (388)
Wholesaling middleman or intermediary (388)
Merchant wholesaler (390)
Manufacturer's sales branch and office (390)
Agents and brokers (390)
Primary product dealers (391)
Full-service wholesaler (393)
Truck jobber (394)
Drop shipper (394)
Manufacturers' agent (manufacturers' representative) (395)
Broker (396)
Commission merchant (396)
Auction company (396)
Selling agent (396)
Import–export agents (396)
Physical distribution (logistics) (396)
Systems approach to physical distribution (399)
Contract logistics (399)
Total cost concept (399)
Physical distribution management (401)
Warehousing (403)
Distribution centre (403)
Private warehouse (403)
Public warehouse (403)
Materials handling (403)
Containerization (404)
Inventory control (404)
Economic order quantity (EOQ) (404)
"Just-in-time" (JIT) concept (405)
Market response systems (405)
Order processing (405)
Transportation (406)
Mode of transportation (406)
Intermodal transportation (406)
Piggyback service (406)
Fishyback service (406)
Freight forwarder (406)

Questions and Problems

1. Which of the following are wholesaling transactions?
   a. Colour Tile sells wallpaper to an apartment building contractor and also to the contractor's family for their home.
   b. General Electric sells motors to Whirlpool for its washing machines.
   c. A fish "farmer" sells fish to a local restaurant.
   d. A family orders carpet from a friend, who is a home decorating consultant, at 50 percent off the suggested retail price. The carpet is delivered directly to the home.
2. Why is it that manufacturers' agents often can penetrate a market faster and at a lower cost than a manufacturer's sales force can?
3. Which type of wholesaling intermediary, if any, is most likely to be used by each of the following firms? Explain your choice in each instance.
   a. A small manufacturer of a liquid glass cleaner to be sold through supermarkets.
   b. A small canner in Nova Scotia packing a high-quality, unbranded fruit product.
   c. A small-tools manufacturing firm that has its own sales force selling to the business market and now wants to add backyard barbecue equipment to its product mix.
   d. A Quebec textile mill producing unbranded towels, sheets, pillowcases, and blankets.

4. Looking to the future, which types of intermediaries do you think will increase in importance and which ones will decline? Explain.
5. "The goal of a modern physical distribution system in a firm should be to operate at the lowest possible *total* costs." Do you agree?
6. Name some products for which you think the cost of physical distribution constitutes at least one-half the total price of the goods at the wholesale level. Can you suggest ways of decreasing the physical distribution cost of these products?
7. "A manufacturer follows an inventory-location strategy of concentration rather than dispersion. This company's inventory size will be smaller, but its transportation and warehousing expenses will be larger than if its inventory were dispersed." Do you agree? Explain.
8. "The use of public warehouse facilities makes it possible for manufacturers to bypass wholesalers in their channels of distribution." Explain.
9. For each of the following products, determine the best transportation method for shipping them to a distribution centre in the community where your school is located. In each case the buyer (not the seller) will pay all freight charges, and, unless specifically noted, time is not important. The distribution centre has a rail siding and a loading/unloading dock for trucks.
   a. Disposable diapers from Ontario. Total shipment weight is 60 000 kg.
   b. A replacement memory card for your computer, which is now inoperative. The weight of the shipment is 1 kg, and you need this card in a hurry.
   c. Blank payroll cheques for your company. (There is a sufficient number of cheques on hand for the next two weekly paydays.) Shipment weight is 50 kg.
   d. Ice cream from London, Ontario. Total shipment weight is 21 000 kg.

Hands-On Marketing

1. Interview the owner or a manager at a firm that is a type of merchant wholesaler (such as a full-service wholesaler). Ask the owner or manager to describe the firm's activities, its differential advantage or disadvantage at the present time, and the company's prospects for the future. Conduct a similar interview with the owner or a manager at a firm that is a type of agent wholesaler (such as a broker). How do you explain any discrepancies between the interview results and the content of this chapter (other than saying that the chapter must be wrong)?
2. A manufacturer of precision lenses used in medical and hospital equipment wants to ship a 5 kg box of these lenses from your town to a laboratory in Stockholm, Sweden. The lab wants delivery in five days or less. The manufacturer wants to use a package-delivery service but is undecided as to which shipper to choose. Compile and compare the types of services provided and prices charged by Federal Express, United Parcel Service, and one other package-delivery firm.

CHAPTER 17 GOALS

You have abundant experience with retailing — as a consumer. And perhaps you also have worked in retailing. This chapter builds on that experience and provides insights about retail markets, different types of retailers, and key strategies and trends in retailing. After studying this chapter, you should have an understanding of:

- The nature of retailing.
- What a retailer is.
- Types of retailers, classified by form of ownership.
- Types of retailers, classified by marketing strategies.
- Forms of nonstore retailing.
- Trends in retailing.

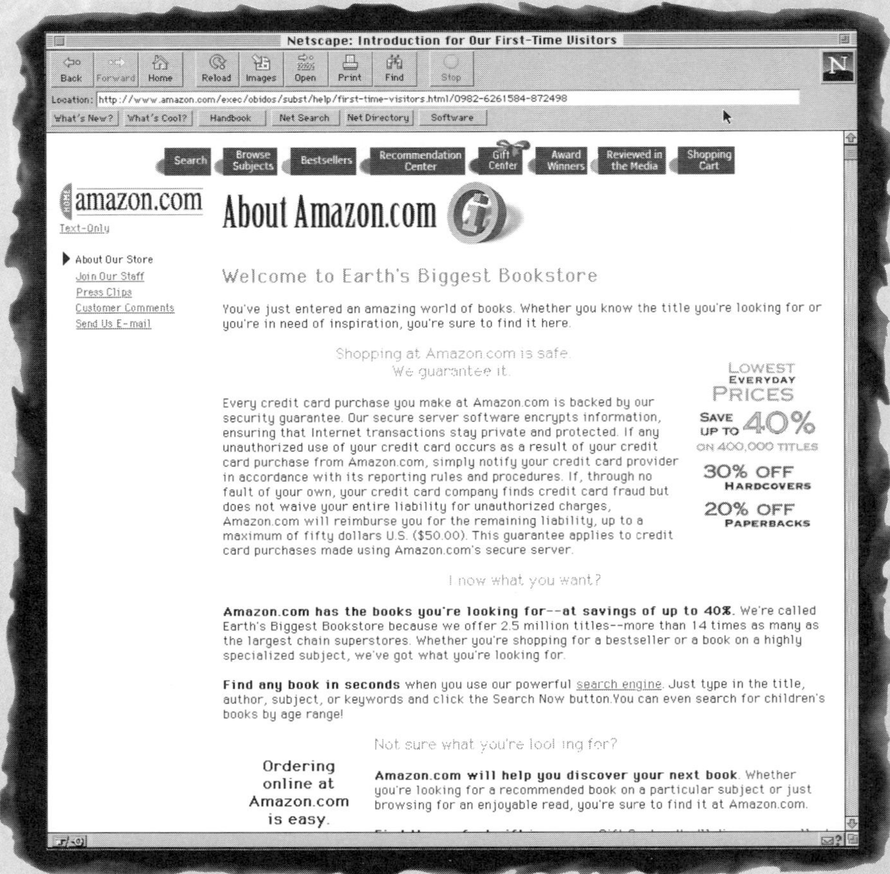

Chapter Seventeen

Retailing: Markets and Institutions

www.amazon.com

AMAZON.COM — THE EARTH'S BIGGEST BOOKSTORE IS ONLY A KEYSTROKE AWAY

Amazon.com, Earth's Biggest Booksore, cannot be found on the streets of Toronto, or Montreal, or New York, or Boston. In fact, Amazon.com cannot be found on any street, anywhere in the world — it does not have one physical location. The Earth's Biggest Bookstore operates on-line, offering 2.5 million books to its cyber-customers. That is truly a wide variety of books, considering the fact that some of the world's largest physical bookstores carry only about 175,000 books.

Amazon.com offers a lot more than a wide assortment of books; it also offers a number of services, such as "Eyes" and "Amazon.com Delivers," to make your cyber-purchase pleasurable. "Eyes" is a sophisticated, automated search agent that serves as a free personal notification service to the consumer. It is set up when the consumer informs Amazon.com about his or her preferred subjects and favourite authors and genres. The customer is notified via e-mail when publishers release books that match his or her described preferences. "Amazon.com Delivers" is a free personal review service that that will allow the customer to choose from more than fifty categories for reviews of books in the chosen areas.

Many people believe that the future of retailing lies in "cyber-stores," just like Amazon.com, and given the Net's rate of growth it is easy to see why this may be true — in 1993, there were only 130 Web sites; at last count in 1996, there were over 300,000 sites. In 1997, 29 percent of Canadians had access to the Internet at home or at work, and the penetration of the Internet was growing at a rate of 50 percent per year. More of these people are beginning to think of the Internet as a viable method of shopping. Data from A.C. Nielsen's annual Internet survey showed that 15 percent of adult Internet users in Canada in 1997 had completed at least one electronic commerce transaction on the Internet, up from 12 percent in 1996. Forresters research says that there will be $9 billion worth of e-cash transactions by the year 2000; by 2005 that figure is predicted to reach $30 billion, and by 2007, 20 percent of all household expenditures are expected to be funnelled through the Internet! Obviously, if these numbers prove accurate, the Internet is going to have a major effect on the retailing industry. IBM research projects that the Internet currently generates about $900 million in revenue; by the year 2000, that number will have increased to $200 billion, and by 2010, Net revenues are projected to reach $1 trillion. With these staggering projections, it seems that Amazon.com is just the tip of the iceberg for the future of retailing on-line.

Retailing is one of the distribution links between the producer and the ultimate consumer. As Amazon.com illustrates, the retailing industry is undergoing major changes with the development of the Internet. The many types of retailing institutions and their marketing activities are the subjects of this chapter.[1]

NATURE AND IMPORTANCE OF RETAILING

For every retail superstar like Wal-Mart, Amazon.com, or Loblaws, thousands of tiny retailers serve consumers only in very limited areas. Despite their differences, all these firms do have two common features: They link producers and ultimate consumers, and they perform valuable services for both parties. In all likelihood these firms are retailers, but all their activities may not qualify as retailing. How can that be? Explanations follow.

Retailing and Retailers

If Safeway or Sobey's sells some floor wax to a gift-shop operator to polish the shop floor, is this a retail sale? When a Shell or Petro-Canada service station advertises that tires are being sold at the wholesale price, is this retailing? Can a wholesaler or manufacturer engage in retailing? When a service such as hair styling or auto repair is sold to an ultimate consumer, is this retailing? Obviously we need to define some terms, particularly *retailing* and *retailer*, to avoid misunderstandings later.

Retailing (or **retail trade**) consists of the sale, and all activities directly related to the sale, of goods and services to ultimate consumers for personal, nonbusiness use. While most retailing occurs through retail stores, it may be done by any institution. A manufacturer selling brushes or cosmetics door to door is engaged in retailing, as is a farmer selling vegetables at a roadside stand.

Any firm — manufacturer, wholesaler, or retailer — that sells something to ultimate consumers for their own nonbusiness use is making a retail sale. This is true regardless of how the product is sold (in person or by telephone, mail, or vending machine) or where it is sold (in a store or at the consumer's home). However, a firm engaged primarily in retailing is called a **retailer**. In this chapter, we will concentrate on retailers rather than on other types of businesses that make only occasional retail sales.

While this chapter focuses primarily on retailers of goods, much of what is said — particularly regarding marketing strategies — applies equally well to retailers of services. As we discussed in Chapter 12, one of the characteristics of services relates to the inseparability of the service from the individual or company that provides it. Although this is certainly the case, the marketing of services is often delegated to retailers. For example, travel agents are really retailers who sell to end consumers the services offered by airlines, hotels, railways, and car rental companies. Banks and other financial services companies retail Canada Savings Bonds on behalf of the Government of Canada. Ticketmaster retails theatre and concert tickets.

Economic Justification for Retailing

All intermediaries basically serve as purchasing agents for their customers and as sales specialists for their suppliers. To carry out these roles, retailers perform many activities, including anticipating customers' wants, developing assortments of products, acquiring market information, and financing.

It is relatively easy to become a retailer. No large investment in production equipment is required, merchandise can often be purchased on credit, and store space can be leased with no "down payment." This ease of entry results in fierce competition and better value for consumers.

To get into retailing is easy but to be forced out is just as easy. To survive in retailing, a company must do a satisfactory job in its primary role — catering to consumers — as well as in its secondary role — serving producers and wholesalers. This dual responsibility is both the justification for retailing and the key to success in retailing.

Size of the Retail Market There were about 174,121 retail stores in Canada in 1994, and their total sales volume was more than $208 billion (see Figure 17-1). In spite of growth in total population and consumer incomes over the past thirty years, the total number of retail stores has not increased consistently. In fact, the volatility of the retail business is reflected in the fact that the total number of retail stores in Canada actually dropped from 227,200 in 1988 to 174,121 in 1994. Total sales dropped from $185.19 billion in 1991 to $184.90 billion in 1992, a level virtually unchanged from total retail sales in 1988. Subsequent to that recession period, sales increased to $208.80 billion in 1994.

Costs and Profits of Retailers

Information regarding the costs of retailing is very meagre. By gleaning data from several sources, however, we can make some rough generalizations.

Total Costs and Profits As nearly as can be estimated, the total average operating expense for all retailers combined is about 25 to 27 percent of retail sales. Wholesaling expenses are estimated at about 8 percent of the retail dollar, or about 10 to 11 percent of wholesaling sales. Thus, retailing costs are about $2\frac{1}{2}$ times the costs of wholesaling, when both are stated as a percentage of sales of the intermediaries in question (see Figure 17-2).

The proportionately higher retailing costs are generally related to the expense of dealing directly with the consumer. In comparison with wholesalers' customers, end consumers demand more services. The average retail sale is smaller, the rate of merchandise turnover is lower, merchandise is bought in smaller lots, rent is higher, and expenses for furniture and fixtures are greater. And retail sales people cannot be used efficiently because customers do not come into retail stores at a steady rate.

Costs and Profits by Kind of Business The expense ratios of retailers vary from one type of store to another. Table 17-1 shows average gross

FIGURE 17-1

Total Retail Trade in Canada, Selected Years

Sales volume has increased tremendously. However, note the reduction in number of stores since 1988.

Source: Statistics Canada

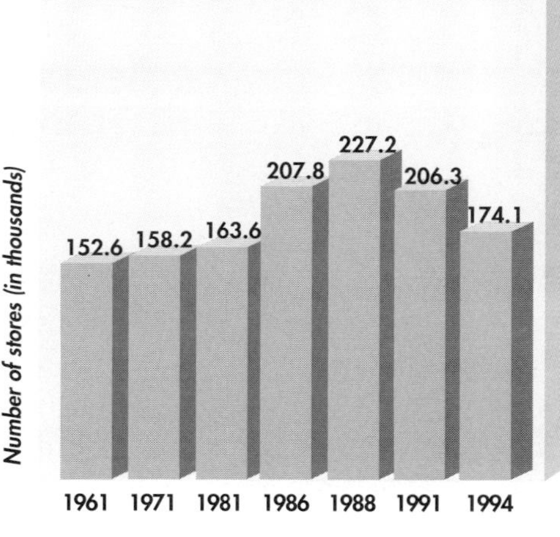

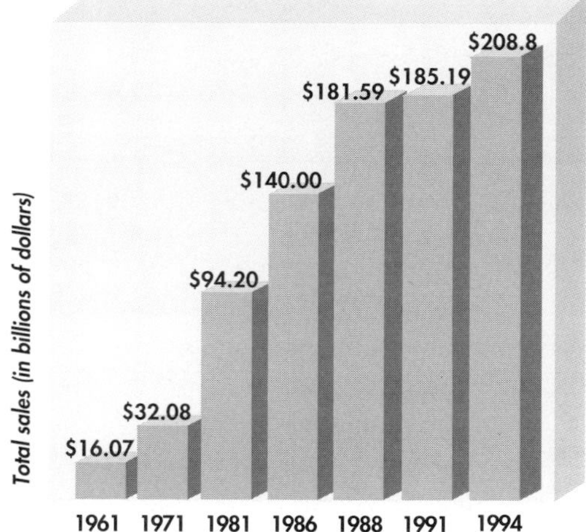

FIGURE 17-2
Average Costs of Retailing and Wholesaling

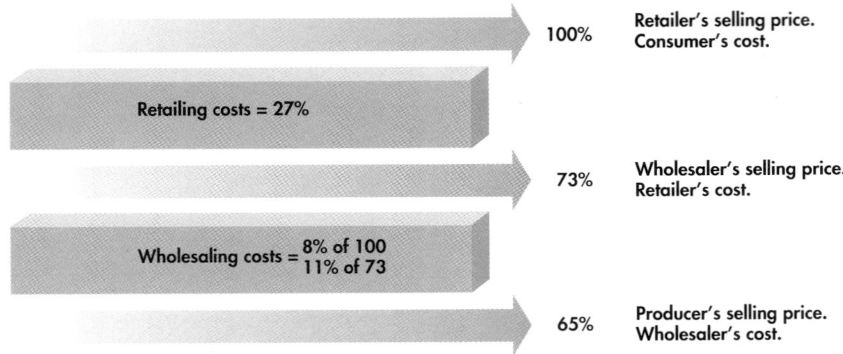

margins as a percentage of operating revenue for different kinds of stores. These margins range from 17.8 percent for motor vehicle dealers to 46.19 percent for women's clothing stores. Table 17-1 also shows average profit (before depreciation and income taxes) for each type of store. These figures range from 1.09 percent for general merchandise stores to 7.75 percent for gasoline service stations.

TABLE 17-1 Gross Margin and Net Profit as Percentage of Total Operating Revenue for Selected Types of Retailers

Gross margin (net sales minus cost of goods sold) is the amount needed to cover a company's operating expenses and still leave a profit. How do you account for the differences in operating expenses among the various types of retailers?

Line of Business	Gross Margin (%)	Operating Profit (%) (taxes and depreciation not included)
Supermarkets and grocery stores	21.98	2.66
All other food stores	35.43	6.14
Drug and patent medicine stores	28.27	4.40
Shoe stores	44.83	7.11
Men's clothing stores	42.87	3.19
Women's clothing stores	46.19	6.23
Other clothing stores	42.29	6.45
Household furniture and appliances	34.56	4.25
Household furnishings	39.61	6.55
Motor vehicle and RV	17.80	5.11
Gasoline service stations	21.71	7.75
Automotive parts and accessories	41.77	6.52
General merchandise	25.97	1.09
Semi-durable goods stores	39.77	6.05
Other durable goods stores	37.84	4.53
Other retail stores	41.14	17.41
TOTAL RETAIL TRADE	27.26	5.05

Source: Statistics Canada, "Wholesaling and Retailing in Canada, 1994," cat. no. 63-236-XPB, p. 54.

Store Size

Most retail establishments are very small; as many as 20 percent of all retailers have annual sales of $100,000 or less. However, despite their numbers, such stores account for a very small percentage of total retail sales.

At the same time, there is a high degree of concentration in retailing. A small number of companies account for a substantial share of total retail trade. These companies, such as Loblaws (part of the George Weston group of companies) and the Hudson's Bay Company (The Bay and Zellers), own many individual stores and account for the considerable degree of concentration in the industry. For example, the companies listed in Table 17-2, while numbering fewer than forty, probably account for close to half of all retail sales in Canada, particularly when one adds to the list some privately owned retail giants such as Eaton's.

Stores of different sizes present different management challenges and opportunities. Buying, promotion, personnel relations, and expense control are influenced significantly by whether a store's sales volume is large or small.

Size, or the lack thereof, brings with it certain advantages, several of which are evaluated in Table 17-3. This assessment suggests that relatively large stores have a competitive advantage over small stores. Small retailers do face many difficulties. The ones that cannot meet the challenges fail. If that's the case, how do so many small retailers succeed? The answer is twofold:

- Some small retailers have formed or joined contractual vertical marketing systems. These entities —

MARKETING AT WORK FILE 17-1

THE GAP WORKS HARDER

When The Gap opened in 1969 it was selling LPs and jeans — a far cry from the stores seen today! Over the last few decades, The Gap has ditched the records and has become an icon in the clothing industry. Everyone from Hollywood megastars (Sharon Stone wore a black Gap turtleneck sweater to the Oscars) to your next-door neighbour shops at The Gap. And now, with the trend moving toward a more casual workplace, The Gap is becoming even more popular, due to its well-earned reputation for good-quality, casual clothing at affordable prices.

The Gap is also well-known for its friendly and helpful sales team, and recently, Gap Canada decided to take its service to a new level. It launched a pilot project directed at western Canadians, in an attempt to extend The Gap's market penetration in this region. Popular Gap stores in Edmonton and Calgary now employ "client specialists" — employees who know the product and are willing to work one-on-one with customers. These client specialists will go to any length to please the customer. Kirsty Goodwin, a client specialist at The Gap in Edmonton's Eaton Centre, says that "if a client can only shop on Sunday mornings between, say, ten and eleven o'clock, we will open the store for her." This pilot has been extremely successful in Edmonton, and there are currently nine more stores across Canada (including Montreal, Victoria, and Toronto's Bloor Street) that will be introducing the new program.

In addition to this pilot program, The Gap has a 1-800 number that allows shoppers in western Canada to access The Gap's "charge/send" policy, under which a customer places an order and The Gap sends the desired items via courier to the customer's home, at no extra charge.

Katie Macdonald, The Gap's regional manager for western Canada, says that "clients are amazed at the extremes we will go to get their business — and at no charge to them. And it seems to be the best kind of relationship-building, since it is resulting in an increase in sales."

Source: Adapted from Jean Fraser, "Filling the Gap." *Montreal Gazette*, March 18, 1997, p. E2.

TABLE 17-2 Canada's Largest Retailers (1996–97 Sales and Profits)

Company	Revenue ($000)	Profit ($000)
Department Stores		
Hudson's Bay Co.	6,007,212	36,141
Sears Canada	3,959,300	8,800
Zellers Inc.	3,578,000	na
Price Costco Canada	2,702,000	na
K mart Canada	1,262,552	8,765
Clothing Stores		
Dylex Ltd.	1,243,308	22,855
Reitmans (Canada)	409,673	1,052
Suzy Shier	572,481	1,029
Château Stores of Canada	141,975	1,500
Mark's Work Wearhouse	225,868	3,923
Pantorama Industries	159,892	675
Specialty Stores		
Groupe Ro-na Dismat	656,850	9,130
Speedy Muffler King	775,150	6,053
Future Shop	1,303,828	17,235
Leon's Furniture	299,680	17,654
White Rose Crafts & Nursery	203,626	34,300
Food Distribution		
Loblaw Cos.	9,869,200	173,700
Oshawa Group	6,383,500	55,200
Canada Safeway	5,152,137	71,200
Métro-Richelieu Inc.	3,266,000	61,000
Great A&P Tea Co.	2,372,317	na
Sobey's Inc.	2,616,444	na
Hospitality Serices		
McDonald's Restaurants of Canada	1,740,301	na
Cara Operations	643,660	37,411
C.P. Hotels & Resorts	575,133	63,595
Groupe St-Hubert	183,780	na
A&W Food Services of Canada.	310,000	na
Four Seasons Hotels	125,447	29,866
Journey's End	58,433	3,051
Second Cup	63,902	−2,366
AFM Hospitality	20,137	−5,175
Scott's Restaurants	151,899	−5,730

Note: This list of Canadian retail chains is incomplete. Also, the reader may be unfamiliar with certain of the corporate names listed here: for example, Cara Operations operates Harvey's and Swiss Chalet restaurants; Dylex Limited operates a large number of clothing retailers, including Tip Top Tailors, Harry Rosen, Fairweather, and Braemar.

Source: "The Top 1000," *Report on Business Magazine*, July 1997. Reprinted with permission from *The Globe and Mail*.

TABLE 17-3 Competitive Positions of Large and Small Retail Stores

Selected Bases for Evaluation	Who Has the Advantage?
Division of labour and specialization of management	Large-scale retailers — their biggest advantage.
Flexibility of operations — merchandise selection, services offered, store design, reflection of owner's personality	Small retailers — their biggest advantage.
Buying power	Large retailers buy in bigger quantities and thus get lower costs.
Access to desirable merchandise	Large retailers promise suppliers access to large numbers of customers, whereas a single small retailer may be viewed as insignificant.
Development and promotion of retailer's own brand	Large retailers.
Efficient use of advertising, especially in citywide media	Large retailers' markets match better with media circulation.
Ability to provide top-quality personal service	Small retailers, if owners pay personal attention to customers and also to selecting and supervising sales staff.
Opportunity to experiment with new products and selling methods	Large retailers can better afford the risks.
Financial strength	Large retailers have resources to gain some of the advantages noted above (such as private brands and experimentation).
Public image	Small retailers enjoy public support and sympathy. However, this same public often votes with its wallet by shopping at big stores.

called retailer co-operatives, voluntary chains, or franchise systems — give individual members certain advantages of large stores, such as specialized management, buying power, and a well-known store name.

- Many consumers seek benefits that small stores can often provide better than large stores can. For instance, some people seek high levels of shopping convenience. Small outlets located near residential areas offer such convenience. Other consumers desire high levels of personal service. A small store's highly motivated owner-manager and well-supervised sales staff may surpass a large store on this important shopping dimension.

Many small stores take advantage of their comparative strengths and compete successfully against other retailers of varying sizes and types.

Physical Facilities

Later in this chapter we will classify retailers according to their product assortments, price strategies, and promotional methods. Here, we'll look at **physical facilities**, which represent the distribution element of a retailer's marketing mix.

Some firms engage in nonstore retailing — by selling through catalogues, the Internet, or door to door, for example — but many more firms rely on retail stores. Firms that operate retail stores must consider three aspects of physical facilities:

- *Location.* It is frequently stated that there are three keys to success in retailing: location, location, and location! Although overstated, this axiom does suggest the importance that retailers attach to location. Thus a store's site should be the first decision made about facilities. Considerations such as surrounding population, traffic, and cost determine where a store should be located.
- *Design.* This factor refers to a store's appearance, both exterior and interior.
- *Layout.* The amount of space allocated to various product lines, specific locations of products, and a floor plan of display tables and racks make up the store's layout.

As might be expected, retail locations tend to follow the population. Consequently, the bulk of retail sales take place in urban, rather than rural, areas. And suburban shopping areas have become more popular, while many downtown areas have declined.

Shopping centres have become the predominant type of retail location in most suburban areas. A **shopping centre** consists of a planned grouping of retail stores that lease space in a structure that is typically owned by a single organization and that can accommodate multiple tenants. Shopping centres can be classified by size and market served:

- **Convenience centre.** Usually consists of 5 to 10 outlets, such as a dry cleaner, branch bank, convenience grocery store, and video rental store.
- **Neighbourhood centre.** Has 10 to 25 tenants, including a large supermarket and perhaps a drugstore.
- **Community centre.** Includes 25 to 50 stores and features a discount house or junior department store. It may also include a supermarket. Given its composition of stores, a community centre draws shoppers from a larger area than does a neighbourhood centre.
- **Regional centre.** Anchored by one or more department stores and supermarkets and complemented by as many as 200 smaller retail outlets; typically an enclosed climate-controlled mall.

Many regional shopping centres are very large. They have become the hub of shopping and social activities in many communities; in fact they are "the meeting place" for many seniors and high school students. In the past twenty years, construction of new regional centres slowed considerably as the market became saturated. It is expected that relatively few shopping malls will be built in the future but that many existing ones will be renovated and modernized.

The growth of suburban shopping, especially in regional malls, led to decreased retail sales in many urban downtown areas. In recent years, therefore, some cities have worked to revitalize their downtown shopping districts. Often historical buildings or neighbourhoods are converted to shopping areas (for example, St. Lawrence Market in Toronto and the Cours de Mont Royal in Montreal). Enclosed shopping malls featuring distinctive designs have also been built in all major cities. Possibly the best known of these shopping centres is the West Edmonton Mall, which has become something of a tourist attraction in western Canada.

CLASSIFICATION OF RETAILERS

To understand how retailers serve both suppliers and customers, we will classify retailers on two bases:

1. Form of ownership.
2. Marketing strategies.

Any retail store can be classified according to both bases, as illustrated by the comparison below of The Bay and a neighbourhood paint store.

RETAILERS CLASSIFIED BY FORM OF OWNERSHIP

The major forms of ownership in retailing are corporate chain, independent, and vertical marketing system (VMS). Within the VMS category are several types of organizations: wholesaler-sponsored voluntary chains, retailer-owned co-operatives, and franchise systems.

Corporate Chains

A **corporate chain**, sometimes called a *chain-store system*, is an organization of two or more centrally owned and managed stores that generally handle the

Classification Bases

Sample Store	Form of Ownership	Marketing Strategies
The Bay	Corporate chain	Department store with broad, relatively deep assortments, moderate prices, and levels of personal service that vary across departments.
Neighbourhood paint store	Independent	Limited-line store that has narrow, relatively deep assortments, avoids price competition, and provides extensive personal service.

same lines of products. Three factors differentiate a chain from an independent store and contractual vertical marketing system:

- Technically, two or more units constitute a chain. Today, however, many small-scale merchants have opened two or three units in shopping centres and in newly populated areas. These retailers ordinarily do not think of themselves as chains. Having four or more units is a good definitional basis for discussing chain stores.
- Central ownership distinguishes corporate chains from contractual vertical marketing systems.
- Due to centralized management, individual units in a chain typically have little autonomy. Strategic decisions are made at headquarters, and there is considerable standardization of operating policies for all the units in a chain.

Corporate chains continue to play a major role in retail trade in Canada, as shown in Table 17-4. The predominance of chains varies considerably, however, depending on the kind of business. Organizations with four or more stores did almost 40 percent of all retail business in Canada in 1994. The importance of chains varies considerably from one type of business to another. Chains account for 70 percent or more of total sales in the general merchandise and variety stores categories and in family clothing and shoes. Among grocery stores, hardware stores, and pharmacies, however, chains account for 30 percent of sales or less. In the retail food business, there are several giant food chains (Loblaws, Steinberg, A&P, Provigo, Sobey's, Safeway, etc.). In 1994, chains made up 47.06 percent of supermarket and grocery stores and 11.74 percent of other food stores. There are still a large number of independent food retailers in small towns and neighbourhoods throughout Canada.

Competitive Strengths and Weaknesses Chain-store organizations are large-scale retailing institutions. As such, they are subject to the general advantages and limitations of all large retailers that we discussed earlier in this chapter. Let's look at a few of these points, especially as they relate to chain stores.

Lower Selling Prices Chain stores have traditionally been credited with selling at lower prices than independents. But the claim of lower prices needs careful scrutiny, because it can be misleading. It was probably more justified in the past than it is today. Many independents have pooled their buying power so that, in many instances, they can buy products at the same price as the chains can. However, it is almost certainly true that chains will have a cost advantage over independents.

It is very difficult to compare the prices of chains with those of independents. The merchandise is often not exactly comparable, because many chains sell items under their own brands. It is difficult to compare the prices of Del Monte peaches with Loblaws', Steinberg's, or Safeway's brand of peaches. Also, it is not accurate to compare the price of the product sold in a cash-and-carry, no-customer-service store with the price of an identically branded product in a full-service store. The value of services should be included in the comparison.

Multistore Feature of Chains Chain stores do not have all their eggs in one basket (or in one store). Even large-scale independent department stores or supermarkets cannot match this advantage of the chains. A multiunit operation has automatically spread its risks among many units. Losses in one store can be offset by profits in other units. Multistore organizations can experiment quite easily. They can try a new store layout or a new type of merchandise in one store without committing the entire firm.

A chain can make more effective use of advertising than even a giant single-unit independent store can. To illustrate, a grocery chain may have fifteen medium-sized stores blanketing a city. An independent competitor may have one huge supermarket doing three to four times the business of any single unit of the chain. Yet the chain can use the metropolitan daily newspaper as an advertising medium, with much less waste in circulation than the independent can. Many chains can also make effective use of national advertising media.

On the Negative Side Standardization, the hallmark of a chain-store system and a major factor in its success, is a mixed blessing. Standardization also means inflexibility. Often a chain cannot adjust rapidly to a local market situation. Chains are well

TABLE 17-4 Chains' Share of Total Retail Sales Volume (Operating Revenue for 1994 only) by Kind of Business, 1974–1994

Kind of Business	1974	1979	1986	1989	1994*
Total retail sales	41.1	41.5	41.5	39.3	37.28
Grocery and combination stores	57.5	60.4			
Combination stores (groceries and meats)			64.8	63.5	
Grocery, confectionery, and sundries			29.8	25.5	
Supermarkets and grocery stores‡					47.06
Other food stores	8.1	8.5	9.4	11.2	11.74
Department stores†	100.0	100.0	100.0	100.0	100.0
General merchandise	80.4	79.8	75.6	73.3	82.98
Variety stores	83.2	76.3	87.2	85.4	n/a
Men's clothing	18.6	34.3	54.9	58.8	57.48
Women's clothing	40.9	53.3	65.6	67.4	73.09
Family clothing	28.5	49.9	68.3	70.3	68.14
Shoe stores	51.8	66.0	71.7	73.5	72.31
Hardware stores	19.0	n/a	21.2	14.8	n/a
Furniture stores	19.2	19.5	50.9	58.3	47.55
Pharmacy stores	18.5	22.4	29.6	31.0	23.3
Jewellery stores	39.4	45.4	49.3	48.0	n/a

*Statistics Canada has revised its reporting methods and now presents data as a percentage of operating revenue as opposed to sales. Students should note that this is not directly comparable to sales percentages, since operating revenue often includes revenue generated from sources other than sales.

‡ Compilation of data in the grocery business has been changed on consecutive occasions, which results in the variation in data presented.

†All department stores are considered chains by Statistics Canada.

Source: Statistics Canada, *Market Research Handbook*, cat. no. 63-224, various years, and *Wholesaling and Retailing in Canada, 1994*, cat. no. 63-236-XPB.

aware of this weakness, however, and have consequently given local store managers somewhat greater freedom to act in various situations. Also, with improved information systems, chains can better tailor their merchandising efforts to local markets.

Independent Stores

An **independent retailer** is a company with a single retail store that is not affiliated with any type of contractual vertical marketing system. Most retailers are independents, and most independents are quite small. Of course, an independent department store or supermarket can have $10 million or more in annual sales, so it may have more economic power than small chains consisting of only a few stores. Still, independents usually have the characteristics of small retailers that were presented in Table 17-3.

Independents typically are viewed as having higher prices than chain stores. However, due to differences in merchandise and services, it is difficult to compare directly the prices of chains and independents. For instance, chains often have their own private brands that are not sold by independents. Also, the two types of retailers frequently provide customers with different levels — and perhaps quality — of services. Many customers are willing to pay extra for services that are valuable to them, such as credit, delivery, alterations, installation, a liberal return policy, and friendly, knowledgeable personal service.[2]

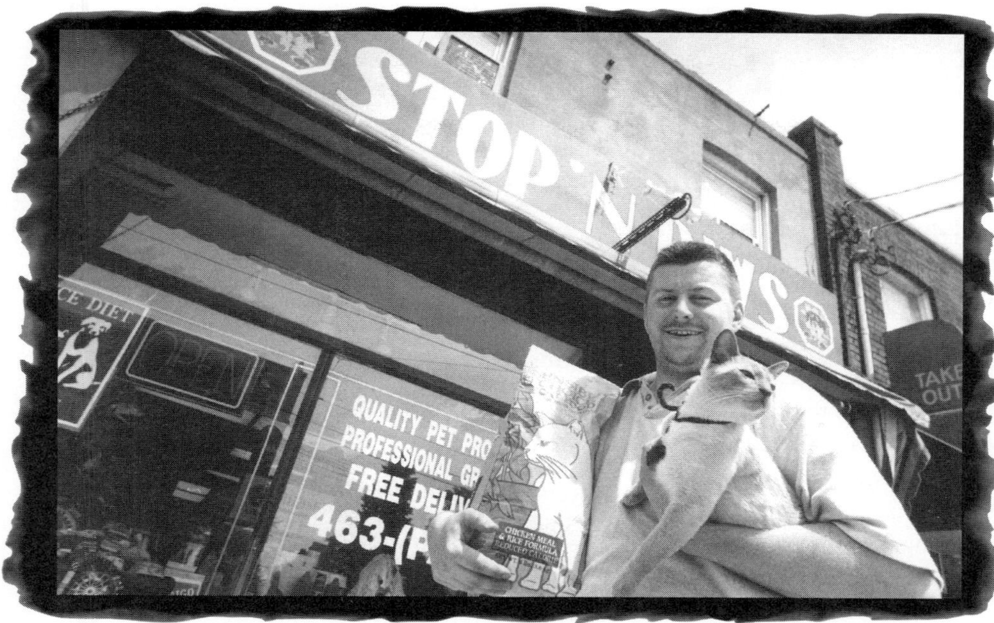

Some independent retailers are really small.

Contractual Vertical Marketing Systems

In a **contractual vertical marketing system**, independently owned firms join together under a contract specifying how they will operate. The three types of contractual VMS are discussed below.

Voluntary Retailer Co-operatives and Chains

Co-operatives and voluntary chains have the same basic purposes:

- To enable independent retailers to compete effectively with corporate chains through increased buying power.
- To provide members with management assistance in store layout, employee and management training programs, promotion, accounting, and inventory control systems.

The main difference between these two types of systems is who organizes them. A **voluntary chain** is sponsored by a wholesaler that enters into a contract with interested retailers. In contrast, a **retailer co-operative** is formed by a group of small retailers that agree to establish and operate a wholesale warehouse.

Historically these two forms of contractual VMS have been organized for defensive reasons — to maintain a competitive position against large, strong chains. Some differences between the two groups are as follows:

Voluntary Chain	Retailer Co-operative Chain
1. Sponsored by wholesalers, with a contract between wholesalers and independent retailer members.	1. Sponsored by retailers. They combine to form and operate a wholesale warehouse corporation.
2. Wholesaler provides a wide variety of management services — buying, advertising, store layout, accounting, and inventory control. Retailers agree to buy all (or almost all) their merchandise from wholesaler. Members agree to use common store name and design and to follow common managerial procedures.	2. Services to retailer members are primarily large-scale buying and warehousing operations. Members maintain their separate identities.
3. Most prevalent in grocery field (IGA). These chains also exist in hardware and building supplies (Castle), auto supplies (Western Auto), and variety stores.	3. Quite significant in grocery field in local areas, but not in other lines.

Franchise Systems **Franchising** involves a continuing relationship in which a franchiser (the parent company) provides the right to use a trademark and management assistance in return for financial considerations from a franchisee (the owner of the individual business unit). The combination of franchiser and franchisees is called a **franchise system**. This type of contractual VMS is growing rapidly.

There are two kinds of franchising:

- **Product and trade name franchising.** Historically the dominant kind, product and trade name franchising is most prevalent in the automobile (Ford, Honda) and petroleum (Esso, Ultramar, Petro-Canada) industries. It is a distribution agreement wherein a franchiser authorizes a franchisee-dealer to sell a product line, using the parent company's trade name for promotional purposes. The franchisee agrees to buy from the franchiser-supplier and also to abide by specified policies. The focus in product and trade name franchising is on what is sold.
- **Business-format franchising.** Much of franchising's growth and publicity over the past two decades has been associated with business-format franchising (including names such as Kentucky Fried Chicken, Harvey's, Midas, and H & R Block). (See Table 17–5.) This kind of franchising covers an entire format for operating a business. A firm with a successful retail business sells the right to operate the same business in different geographic areas. Quite simply, the franchisee expects to receive from the parent company a proven business format; in return, the franchiser receives from the individual business owner payments and conformance to policies and standards. The focus here is on how the business is run.

  In business-format franchising, the franchiser may be a manufacturer that provides franchisees with merchandise. More often, though, this is not the case. For example, some such franchisers do not sell products to their franchised stores; rather the stores buy their inventory from wholesalers. What the franchiser provides to franchisees in this case is management assistance, especially marketing expertise.

For a successful retail business that wants to expand, franchising provides critical advantages:

- Rapid expansion is facilitated, because franchisees provide capital when they purchase franchises.
- Because they have an investment at risk, franchisees typically are highly motivated to work hard and adhere to the parent company's proven format.

TABLE 17-5 Numerous Products Reach Consumer Markets through Business-Format Franchises

Product/Service Category	Sample Franchises
Fast food	McDonald's, Tim Hortons, A.L. Van Houtte, Harvey's, Druxy's, Pizza Hut, Second Cup, Grandma Lee's, Pizza Pizza, Treats
Auto rental	Avis, Hertz, Tilden, Thrifty, Budget
Auto repair	Midas, Speedy, Apple Auto Glass, Jiffy Lube, Thruway Muffler, Mister Transmission, Ziebart
Personal care/services	Magicuts, Body Shop, H & R Block, Faces, Money Concepts, Uniglobe Travel, Nautilus Fitness
Home decor/services	Color Your World, St. Clair, The Bathtub Doctor, College Pro Painters, Molly Maid, Weed Man, The Lawn Rangers
Printing/photography	Kwik-Kopy Printing, Japan Camera, U Frame It, The Frame UP, Direct Film, Kinko's
Clothing	Athlete's Foot, Benetton, Cotton Ginny, Kettle Creek Canvas, Mark's Work Wearhouse, Rodier
Computers and video	Compucentres, Computerland, Jumbo Video, Captain Video, Radio Shack
Health and personal care	Nutri/system, Shoppers Drug Mart, Optical Factory, Tridont Health Care, People's Drug Mart
Convenience stores	7-Eleven, Mac's, Beckers, Red & White

For an independent store facing stiff competition from chains and for a prospective new retail store, franchising offers advantages:

- Franchisees can use the parent company's well-known name, which should help attract customers.
- Various forms of management assistance are provided to franchisees prior to, as well as after, opening the store, including site selection and store-layout guidance, technical and management training, promotional programs, and inventory control systems.

Franchising is not without problems. Some franchises are based on poor products or unsound business practices and consequently fail. Further, a number of franchisees criticize franchisers for practices such as the following: enticing prospective franchisees by projecting unrealistically high revenues or unrealistically low operating costs; not providing franchisees with the promised and necessary levels of business support; locating too many of the company's outlets in the same market; or unjustifiably terminating or not renewing the franchise agreement. Conversely, franchisers have their own complaints, notably that some franchisees deviate from the system's policies and practices. As in most business fields, if self-regulation is ineffective, added regulation at the federal and provincial levels is likely.

Despite some challenges, continued growth in franchising is expected. Ambitious, successful retailers will exploit it as an offensive tool — for rapid expansion. Many small retailers will use it defensively — to achieve a viable competitive position against corporate chains. And prospective business owners will continue to buy franchises because of the two key attributes — a degree of independence and a variety of management assistance. In fact, many people with little or no business experience have purchased franchises for this reason.

A growing share of franchise buyers are people who were employed previously by large corporations. New franchisees include laid-off production and office employees as well as numerous managers and executives who were victims of corporate restructuring or who accepted early retirement. Such new entrants view franchising as a way of determining their own financial destiny.

RETAILERS CLASSIFIED BY MARKETING STRATEGIES

Whatever its form of ownership, a retailer must develop marketing-mix strategies to succeed in its chosen target markets. In retailing, the marketing mix emphasizes product assortment, price, location, promotion, and customer services. This last element consists of services designed to aid in the sale of a product. They include credit, delivery, gift wrapping, product installation, merchandise returns, store hours, parking, and — very importantly — personal service. (When personal service is intended to create a sale, then it is personal selling — a type of promotion.)

We will now describe the major types of retail stores, paying particular attention to three elements of their marketing mixes:

- Breadth and depth of product assortment.
- Price level.
- Number of customer services.

Table 17-6 classifies retail stores on the basis of these three elements.

Some types of retail stores, such as category-killer stores, are new and growing rapidly. Others, notably variety stores, are diminishing in importance. And still others, particularly department stores, are under competitive pressure to modify some strategies. We will see that certain retailers are similar to others because new or modified institutions have filled the "strategic gaps" that once separated different types of retail institutions.

Department Stores

A mainstay of retailing in Canada is the **department store**, a large-scale retailing institution that has a very broad and deep product assortment, tries not to compete on the basis of price, and provides a wide array of customer services. Familiar department store names include Eaton's, Sears, and The Bay.

Traditional department stores offer a greater variety of merchandise and services than any other type of retail stores. They feature both "soft goods" — such as apparel, sheets, towels, and bedding — and "hard goods" — including furniture, appliances, and consumer electronics. Department stores also attract — and satisfy — consumers by offering many customer services. The combination of distinctive, appealing merchandise and numerous customer services is designed to allow the stores to maintain the manufacturers' suggested retail prices. That is, department stores strive to charge "full" or "nondiscounted" prices.

Department stores face mounting problems, however. Largely due to their prime locations and customer services, their operating expenses are considerably higher than those of most other kinds of retail business. Many manufacturers' brands that used to be available exclusively through department stores are now widely distributed and often carry discounted prices in other outlets. And the quality of personal service, especially knowledgeable sales help, has deteriorated in some department stores.

Intense horizontal competition is also hurting department stores. Other types of retailers are aiming at consumers who have long supported department stores. Specialty stores, off-price retailers, and even some discount houses have been particularly aggressive in trying to lure shoppers away from department stores. To varying degrees, retail chains such as K mart, Wal-Mart, and Zellers compete directly against the department stores.

As a result of competitive pressures, primarily from large discount chains, some department stores have disappeared from the Canadian market in recent years. Simpson's, one of Canada's oldest retailing institutions, was closed by its parent company, Hudson's Bay Company, and some of its stores were converted to The Bay. Woodwards, a fixture in retailing in western Canada for generations, ran into difficulties in the early 1990s and closed many stores. The remainder were acquired by The Bay in early 1993. At the time of this writing, Eaton's was undergoing a major restructuring to avoid bankruptcy.

Seeking to gain a competitive advantage in a market increasingly dominated by the large discounters and category killers, the more conventional department stores have had to adopt new ways of doing business. For example, Sears, Canada's leading department store chain, is working on a strategy that involves creating a brand. Sears is striving to establish its trademark as a statement of quality and value. Following a major restructuring in the mid-1990s, this department store has been showing remarkable strength, with 7 to 8 percent annual growth figures.[3] Other strategies being used include redesigning stores, dropping or moving entire product lines, launching new ad campaigns, and stepping-up sales and promotions. Sears is trying to increase strength in products like apparel and home furnishings.[4]

TABLE 17-6 Retail Stores Classified by Key Marketing Strategies

Type of Store	Breadth and Depth of Assortment	Price Level	Number of Customer Services
Department store	Very broad, deep	Avoids price competition	Wide array
Discount house	Broad, shallow	Emphasizes low prices	Relatively few
Limited-line store	Narrow, deep	Traditional types avoid price competition; newer kinds emphasize low prices	Vary by type
Specialty store	Very narrow, deep	Avoids price competition	At least standard and extensive in some
Off-price retailer	Narrow, deep	Emphasizes low prices	Few
Category killer store	Narrow, very deep	Emphasizes low prices	Few to moderate
Supermarket	Broad, deep	Some emphasize low prices; others avoid price disadvantages	Few
Convenience store	Narrow, shallow	High prices	Few
Warehouse club	Very broad, very shallow	Emphasizes very low prices	Few (open only to members)
Hypermarket	Very broad, deep	Emphasizes low prices	Some

MARKETING AT WORK FILE 17–2

A TALE OF TWO FRANCHISES

The jury is still out on the relative success rate of franchises as compared with non-franchise start-ups. Success and failure depends on many factors. For example, it is much harder to come up with a fresh idea in the crowded restaurant industry than in areas such as home services, children's services, and Internet services. Geoff Wilson, a principal in the hospitality practice at KPMG in Toronto, believes that an original concept is critical in food-services franchising, due to the fact that there is limited market growth and that some concepts are nearing their saturation point.

Among the most recent trends in franchising is the idea of pairing two franchises at a single location. There are two methods: co-branding, in which one franchise carries products associated with another; and twinning, in which two franchises operate side by side and share an eating area. Examples of the twinning concept are Wendy's and Tim Hortons, both owned by Wendy's International Inc., and Harvey's and Church's Fried Chicken. The Tim Hortons/Wendy's twinning concept works especially well because Tim Hortons draws the morning coffee drinkers, both are strong for lunch, and Wendy's is popular in the evenings — the franchises complement each other. Sharing a location allows the franchisers to save on real estate and staff — two of their biggest costs.

Co-branding and twinning share many advantages, such as the cost savings, but many co-brandings occur in an attempt to give the consumer "more." Timothy's World News Cafés are now carrying Mrs. Field's cookies — a natural combination!

Another common alliance is those occurring between retail chains and franchises. McDonald's has become a common sight in Wal-Mart chains, and Starbucks (which is not a franchise) has set up shop in Chapters Inc. bookstores. These can make for profitable partnerships, as the food franchiser can help keep customers in the stores for longer periods of time and the retail outlets give the franchisers a broader market for expansion purposes.

Other franchising combinations have occurred between gas retailers and food franchisers. Esso has joined forces with Tim Hortons and several Irving outlets house Pizza Hut counters.

Franchising is entering the maturity stage in Canada, and these pairings are a method of growth. The Canadian Franchising Association estimates that the Canadian franchising business is growing at about 7 to 9 percent per year. Annual sales are about $90 billion, and there are approximately 65,000 franchised outlets in Canada.

Source: Adapted from Susan Nokes, "Creating Marriages of Convenience," *The Financial Post*, February 14, 1997, p. 16.

Despite the problems experienced by the department stores, many feel they still have a major role to play in retail sales.[5]

Discount Houses

Discount retailing uses price as a major selling point by combining comparatively low prices and reduced costs of doing business. Several institutions, including off-price retailers and warehouse clubs, rely on discount retailing as their main marketing strategy.

Not surprisingly, the prime example of discount retailing is the **discount house**, a large-scale retailing institution that has a broad, shallow product assortment, emphasizes low prices, and offers relatively few customer services. A discount house normally carries a broad assortment of soft goods (particularly apparel) and well-known brands of hard goods (including appliances and home furnishings). It also advertises extensively. K mart, Zellers, and Wal-Mart are leading discount-house chains.

The success of discount houses can be attributed to two factors. First, other types of retailers normally had large markups on appliances and other merchandise, thereby providing discount houses with the opportunity to set smaller margins and charge lower prices. Second, consumers were receptive to a low-price, limited-service format. Discount houses have had a major impact on retailing, prompting many retailers to lower their prices.

Wal-Mart has experienced tremendous success in Canada since it acquired the Woolco chain in 1994. That success has been built on the image of lowest prices, a position that has been promoted extensively by the chain. It also maintains a state-of-the-art distribution technology, which builds on strong supplier relationships, behind-the-scenes ordering, and inventory management systems. Wal-Mart also prides itself on an up-front emphasis on customer service.[6]

Zellers has felt the impact of the competition from Wal-Mart. To compete, it is amending its low-price strategy and complementing it with broader assortments, free giveaways with the Club Z loyalty card, and the merchant's own More credit card. It is also bringing in higher-priced merchandise.[7]

Limited-Line Stores

Much of the "action" in retailing in recent years has been in **limited-line stores**. This type of institution has a narrow but deep product assortment and customer services that vary from store to store. Traditionally, limited-line stores strived for full or nondiscounted prices. Currently, however, new types of limited-line retailers have gained a foothold by emphasizing low prices.

Breadth of assortment varies somewhat across limited-line stores. A store may choose to concentrate on:

- Several related product lines (shoes, sportswear, and accessories),
- A single product line (shoes), or
- Part of one product line (athletic footwear).

We identify limited-line stores by the name of the primary product line — furniture store, hardware store, clothing store, for example. Some retailers such as grocery stores and drugstores, which used to be limited-line stores, now carry much broader assortments because of scrambled merchandising.

Specialty Stores A very narrow and deep product assortment, often concentrating on a specialized product line (baked goods) or even part of a specialized product line (cookies), is offered to consumers by a **specialty store**. Examples of specialty stores are bake shops, furriers, athletic footwear stores, meat markets, and dress shops. (Specialty stores should not be confused with specialty goods. In a sense, specialty stores are misnamed because they may carry any category of consumer goods, not just specialty goods.)

Most specialty stores strive to maintain manufacturers' suggested prices and provide at least standard customer services. Some specialty stores, however, emphasize extensive customer services and particularly knowledgeable and friendly sales help. The success of specialty stores depends on their ability to attract and then serve well customers whose two primary concerns are deep assortments and extensive, top-quality services. In general, specialty stores in Canada are doing quite well. Some of their success can be attributed to clear strategies with a narrow focus, rather than the broad approach of department stores.[8]

Off-Price Retailers **Off-price retailers** position below discount houses with lower prices on selected product lines. These new discount retailers are most in evidence in the areas of clothing and consumer electronics; they offer a narrow, deep product assortment, emphasize low prices, and offer few customer services. Store names such as BiWay and Future Shop are now well known to consumers in many cities in Canada. A number of chains of off-price retailers now operate in various regions of the country.

Off-price retailers often buy manufacturers' excess output, inventory remaining at the end of a fashion season, or irregular merchandise at lower-than-normal wholesale costs. In turn, their retail prices are much lower than those for regular, in-season merchandise sold in other stores. Customers are attracted by the low prices and fairly current fashions.

Factory outlets are a special type of off-price retailer. They are owned by manufacturers and usually

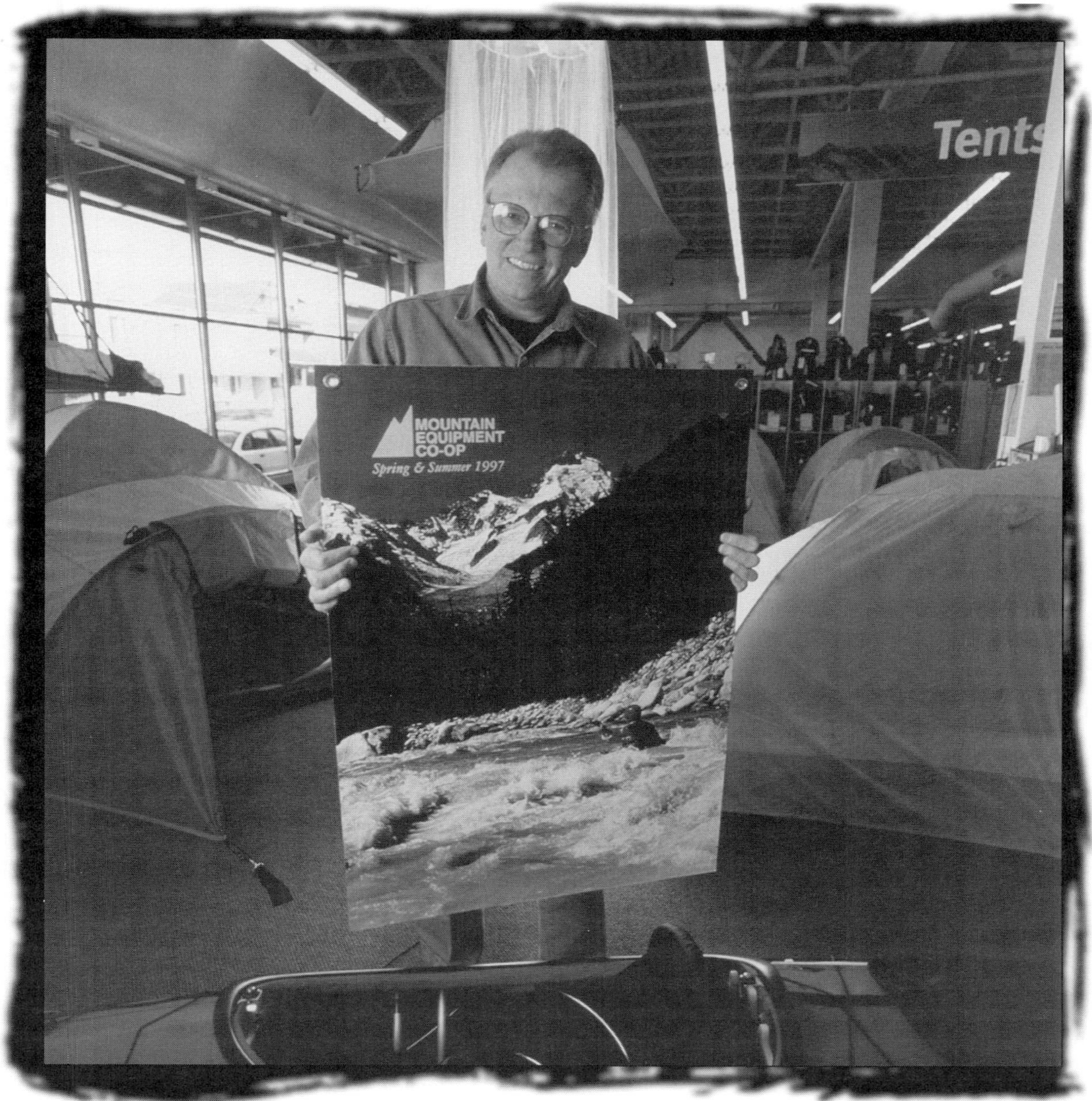

Mountain Equipment Co-op has found a very specific niche in Canadian retailing.

sell a single manufacturer's clearance items, regular merchandise, and perhaps even otherwise unavailable items. Many well-known and popular brands such as L.L. Bean, Esprit, Calvin Klein, Royal Doulton, and Wabasso can be found in factory outlets in the United States and occasionally in Canada. This is a retailing form that is well established south of the border but that has not yet made its presence felt in this country. As Canadian consumers become more familiar with shopping at factory outlets in the United States and as cross-border shopping continues to be part of the retailing scene in this country, we can expect the factory outlet to emerge here as well.

Category-Killer Stores These outlets have a narrow but very deep assortment, emphasize low prices, and have few to moderate customer services. They are so named because they are designed to destroy all competition in a specific product category. Highly successful category killers include Ikea in assemble-it-yourself furniture, Majestic and Future Shop in consumer electronics, and Toys "Я" Us. Other product areas where category killers tend to operate include office supplies, sporting goods, housewares, and records, tapes, and compact discs.

This relatively new form of retail institution concentrates on a single product line or several closely related lines. The distinguishing feature of a category killer is a combination of many different sizes, models, styles, and colours of the product, coupled with low prices. For example, Ikea stocks literally thousands of furniture and home furnishing items. Record retailers such as the major stores of Sam's and HMV carry such an assortment that the consumer needs to make only one stop to ensure that he or she can find a particular tape or compact disc.

That is the objective of the category killer in retailing: to dominate a category in such a way that the consumer believes this is the first store to visit and that the value will be better there. Although the major category killers tend to be found in large metropolitan markets, it is in fact easier for a major retailer to dominate a category in a smaller market, where the competition is not likely to be as fierce and where competitors tend to be smaller, local independents.

Sustained growth is forecast for category killers. However, most kinds of merchandise as well as many geographic areas will not generate the large sales levels that permit low prices through high-volume buying power. Furthermore, existing category killers are not without problems. In particular, they face a major challenge in maintaining inventories that are large enough to satisfy customer demand but not so large as to result in excess inventories, requiring significant markdowns.

Supermarkets

As was the case with discount, the word supermarket can be used to describe a method of retailing and a type of institution. As a method, **supermarket retailing** features several related product lines, a high degree of self-service, largely centralized checkouts, and competitive prices. The supermarket approach to retailing is used to sell various kinds of merchandise, including building materials, office products, and — of course — groceries.

The term *supermarket* usually refers to an institution in the grocery retailing field. In this context a **supermarket** is a retailing institution that has a moderately broad, moderately deep product assortment spanning groceries and some nonfood lines and offers relatively few customer services. Most supermarkets emphasize price. Some use price *offensively* by featuring low prices in order to attract customers. Other supermarkets use price more *defensively* by relying on leader pricing to avoid a price disadvantage. Since supermarkets typically have very thin gross margins, they need high levels of inventory turnover to achieve satisfactory returns on invested capital.

Supermarkets originated in the early 1930s. They were established by independents to compete with grocery chains. Supermarkets were an immediate success, and the innovation was soon adopted by chain stores. In recent decades, supermarkets have added various nonfood lines to provide customers with one-stop shopping convenience and to improve overall gross margins.

Today, stores using the supermarket method of retailing are dominant in grocery retailing. However, different names are used to distinguish these institutions by size and assortment:

- A *superstore* is a larger version of the supermarket. It offers more grocery and nonfood items than a conventional supermarket does. Many supermarket chains are emphasizing superstores in their new construction.
- *Combination stores* are usually even larger than superstores. They, too, offer more groceries and nonfoods than a supermarket but also most product lines found in a large drugstore.

For many years the supermarket has been under attack from numerous competitors. For example, a grocery shopper can choose among not only many brands of supermarkets (Loblaws, Safeway, A&P, Sobey's and Steinbergs) but also various types of institutions (warehouse clubs, gourmet shops, meat and fish markets, and convenience stores). Super-

www.hmv.ca

markets have reacted to competitive pressures primarily in one of two ways: Some cut costs and stressed low prices by offering more private brands and generic products and few customer services. Others expanded their store size and assortments by adding more nonfood lines (especially products found in drugstores), groceries attuned to a particular market area (foods that appeal to a specific ethnic group, for example), and various service departments (including video rentals, restaurants, delicatessens, financial institutions, and pharmacies). The trend to eating out has also cut into the profits of supermarkets. To fight this form of competition, supermarkets are offering a larger assortment of food products to address the needs of consumers in a variety of situations: eating quickly, easy preparation for the next day, and long-term meal planning.[9]

Convenience Stores

To satisfy the increasing consumer demand for convenience, particularly in suburban areas, the **convenience store** emerged several decades ago. This retailing institution concentrates on convenience groceries and nonfoods, has higher prices than most other grocery stores, and offers few customer services. Gasoline, fast foods, and selected services (such as car washes and automated teller machines) can also be found in many convenience stores.

The name *convenience store* reflects its main appeal and explains how the somewhat higher prices are justified. Convenience stores are typically located near residential areas and are open extended hours; some never close. Examples of convenience-store chains are 7-Eleven (originally open from 7 A.M. to 11 P.M. but now always open in most locations), Mac's, and Beckers.

Convenience stores compete to some extent with both supermarkets and fast-food restaurants. Furthermore, since the 1980s, gasoline companies have modified many service stations by phasing out auto repairs and adding a convenience store section.

Warehouse Clubs

Another institution that mushroomed during the 1980s is the **warehouse club**, sometimes called a **wholesale club**. A combined retailing and wholesaling institution, it has very broad but very shallow product assortments, extremely low prices, and few customer services, and is open only to members. This format originated in Europe many years ago and was first applied successfully in the United States in the mid-1970s by the Price Club. In this country, Price/Costco is the major warehouse club chain, although others also operate, primarily in Quebec, Alberta, and British Columbia. Price/Costco is the result of a merger of two U.S. warehouse giants, Price Co. and Costco Wholesale Corp. In Canada the two banners operate separately, with most Price Clubs in the East and Costcos in the western provinces.[10] Another warehouse club operating in Canada is Club Biz. Unlike the Price Club, anyone can join Club Biz, which carries a wider selection and provides service staff.[11]

Warehouse clubs' target markets are small businesses (some purchasing merchandise for resale) and select groups of employees (government workers and school personnel, for example), as well as members of credit unions. Prices paid by ultimate consumers are usually about 5 percent higher than those paid by business members.

A warehouse club carries about the same breadth of assortment as a large discount house but in much less depth. For each item, the club stocks only one or two brands and a limited number of sizes and models. It is housed in a warehouse-type building with tall metal racks that display merchandise at ground level and store it at higher levels. Customers pay cash (credit cards are not accepted) and handle their own merchandise — even bulky, heavy items.

Further growth of warehouse clubs is expected in the coming years. As with other retailing institutions, modifications and refinements can be anticipated as competition intensifies. Some warehouse clubs, for instance, are already experimenting with more service departments.

NONSTORE RETAILING

A large majority — perhaps 85 percent — of retail transactions are made in stores. However, a growing volume of sales is taking place away from stores. Retailing activities resulting in transactions that occur away from a retail store are termed nonstore retailing.

www.pricecostco.com

We will consider four types of **nonstore retailing**: direct selling, telemarketing, automatic vending, and direct marketing. (These names may be confusing, so don't worry about the names. Focus instead on the distinctive features and competitive standings of the four types.) Each type may be used by producers and/or retailers.

Direct Selling

Statistics Canada defines **direct selling** as the retail marketing of consumer goods to household consumers by other than the regular retail store outlet. This represents a major growth area in Canadian retailing, as consumers increasingly turn to nonstore retailers for the purchase of many products. In Canada, sales by direct selling total about $4 billion, a figure that does not include sales by foreign mail-order retailers, direct sales made to Canadians by the mail-order divisions of department stores (such as the Sears catalogue), or direct sales through vending machines or by wholesalers. We can expect the impact of nonstore retailers to increase in the future, as consumers demand the convenience of shopping from locations that are convenient to them and at times at which they are available.

The annual volume of direct selling in Canada has increased from approximately $772 million in 1969 to more than $3.4 billion in 1994. An increasing number of companies are turning to the direct-selling route to reach consumers in their own homes. There are many well-known direct-selling companies, including Avon, Tupperware, Mary Kay, Amway, Electrolux, and Encyclopedia Britannica. Many diverse products are sold through the direct-selling route, most of which require some form of testing or demonstration (cosmetics, water purifiers, vacuum cleaners). Essentially, the direct-selling approach involves a sales person contacting potential customers outside of a conventional retail store environment.

The two major kinds of direct selling are door-to-door and party plan. Sometimes **door-to-door selling** simply involves "cold canvassing" without any advance selection of prospects. The use of door-to-door techniques has declined considerably as both adult partners increasingly work outside the home. More often there is an initial contact in a store, by telephone, or by a mailed-in coupon. A relatively new form of direct selling has emerged in recent years, known as network marketing. This approach to nonstore retailing involves a series of levels of sales personnel, each of whom reports to an area or territory manager or captain. Sales are generated by sales people contacting prospects directly, usually in their homes. Commissions on sales are paid to each level in the sales hierarchy. Products currently sold by this method include cosmetics (Nu-Skin) and water purification systems (NSA).

With the **party-plan** approach, a host or hostess invites some friends to a party. These guests understand that a sales person — say, for a cosmetics or a housewares company — will make a sales presentation. The sales rep has a larger prospective market and more favourable selling conditions than if these people were approached individually, door to door. And the guests get to shop in a friendly, social atmosphere.

With such a large percentage of people now working outside the home, direct-selling firms have had to find new ways of making contact with prospective customers. For instance, Avon has moved in recent years to reach its target customers at their place of work by distributing catalogues at offices. Tupperware, possibly the best known of the party-plan retailers, continues to market its extensive range of plastic houseware products primarily through in-home parties, involving its 374,000 dealers in more than forty countries. However, because of the changing nature of the North American market, Tupperware is now also marketed through catalogues and Tupperware parties held at the office.

There are other drawbacks to direct selling. It is the most expensive form of retailing, with sales commissions as high as 40 to 50 percent of the retail price. Also, good sales people are extremely hard to recruit and retain. Some sales people have been too persistent or even fraudulent. As a result, a number of provinces have "cooling off" laws that permit consumers to nullify a door-to-door or party-plan sale during a period up to several days after the transaction.

Direct selling does give consumers the opportunity to buy at home or another convenient nonstore location. For the seller, direct selling provides the most aggressive form of retail promotion as well as the chance to demonstrate a product in the shopper's (rather than the seller's) environment.

www.avon.com • www.marykay.com • www.electrolux.se • www.eb.co.uk:195/

Telemarketing

Sometimes called *telephone selling*, **telemarketing** refers to a sales person initiating contact with a shopper and also closing a sale over the telephone. As with door-to-door selling, telemarketing may mean cold canvassing from the phone directory. Or it may rely on prospects who have requested information from the company or whose demographics match those of the firm's target market.

The telemarketing business has really developed only within the past ten years, as marketers found it increasingly difficult to reach consumers through conventional means. Also, the development of computerized mailing or calling lists and auto-dialling technology have meant that literally hundreds of calls can be made during a day by a single telemarketer. Many products that can be bought without being seen are sold over the telephone. Examples include home cleaning and pest-control services, magazine subscriptions, credit card and other financial services, and athletic club memberships.

Telemarketing's reputation has been damaged by the unethical sales practices of some firms. These firms tell consumers that they are conducting marketing research and "are not selling anything." Such unethical procedures hurt other telemarketing companies as well as legitimate research firms that conduct telephone surveys. Such practices are known as "sugging" — selling under the guise of research. The approaches used by some telemarketing companies, coupled with a desire on the part of many consumers not to be bothered at home, has led to a consumer backlash against telemarketing in some areas.[12]

Despite this problem, telemarketing sales have been increasing for several reasons. Certain consumers appreciate the convenience of making a purchase by phone. Also, the introduction of outgoing WATS lines about twenty-five years ago made telemarketing to consumers in distant locations more cost effective. Finally, computer systems today can automatically dial a telephone number or, going a step further, play a taped message and then record information that the consumer gives to complete the sale. Such systems reduce the normally high labour costs associated with telemarketing. These advances in technology, despite their obvious contribution to the efficiency of the process, contribute further to the negative feeling that many consumers have toward being sold products and services in such an intrusive manner. The truly effective telemarketing programs are being run by companies that have adopted an approach to telemarketing that involves doing a better job of targeting those customers who are likely to be interested in the products or service being offered (rather than the blanket calling of all households in a region) and conveying the message to the consumer in a polite and caring manner.

Direct Marketing

There is no consensus on the exact nature of direct marketing; in a sense, it comprises all types of nonstore retailing other than the three already discussed. We define **direct marketing** as the use of nonpersonal media to contact consumers who, in turn, purchase products without visiting a retail store. (Be sure to distinguish among the terms *direct marketing*, *direct selling*, and *direct distribution*.)

To contact consumers, direct marketers use one or more of the following media: radio, TV, newspapers, magazines, catalogues, and mailings (direct mail). Consumers typically place orders by telephone or mail. Direct marketing is big business. Everywhere we go today, we are exposed to direct-marketing efforts. We see advertisements on television from direct-marketing retailers of records and exercise aids, and we are encouraged to telephone a 1-800 number with our Visa or MasterCard number. We receive "bill stuffers" with our monthly gasoline bills, retail store bills, and credit card statements. We order clothing and other items from mail-order catalogues, by either mailing back an order form or more likely calling a toll-free long-distance telephone number. A large volume of direct-marketing effort is rarely seen by end consumers because it is directed at the business-to-business market, where direct marketers have relied on catalogues and mailing pieces for many years.

Given its broad definition, there are many forms of direct marketing. The major types are as follows:

- **Direct mail.** Companies mail consumers letters, brochures, and even product samples, and ask that orders be placed by mail or telephone, or through the Internet.

- **Catalogue retailing.** Companies mail catalogues to consumers and to businesses or make them available at retail stores. Examples of the latter include Tilley Endurables and Canadian Tire.
- **Television shopping.** There are basically two approaches to retailing through television. One we have mentioned above, in which individual products are advertised and the consumer places an order by telephoning a toll-free number and giving his or her credit card number. The second involves the use of a dedicated television channel such as the Canadian Home Shopping Network, which represents a continuous advertisement for a variety of products such as housewares, jewellery, and other items that can be sold without the need for demonstration or trial.
- **Internet shopping.** Through Internet home pages, many companies are selling products directly to the customer. By entering a home page, the customer can usually link to a "store" or catalogue display. With the use of a credit card, merchandise can be ordered directly, and it is then shipped to the consumer.

Some companies operate mail-order divisions as components of their department store operations — Sears is the best example. Others have launched catalogues as an additional vehicle for the distribution of their products. Others, such as The Added Touch, distribute only through their catalogues. Direct marketers can be classified as either general-merchandise firms, which offer a wide variety of product lines, or specialty firms, which carry merchandise in only one or two product categories.

Direct marketing represents a major growth area in retailing. Its advantages relate particularly to its ability to direct the marketing effort to those consumers who are most likely to respond positively. Also, it offers products and services in a way that is most convenient for the consumer. Companies that are using catalogues and direct mail to reach their target customers maximize the effectiveness of their marketing programs by having the most accurate and complete mailing list possible. In fact, the success of most direct-marketing programs lies to a very great extent in the preparation and maintenance of an accurate mailing list.

Technology has kept pace with (or even led) developments in the direct-marketing field as companies are now developing sophisticated computer databases of customers and prospective customers. These databases contain not only mailing addresses, but other data on the characteristics of the consumer and his or her household, and a history of purchases that the consumer has made. Companies such as American Express make very effective use of such databases to direct mailings to cardholders in their monthly statements. The types of advertisements that are sent to certain customers are determined to an extent by an analysis of their purchasing history using the American Express card.[13]

Like other types of nonstore retailing, direct marketing provides consumers with shopping convenience. Direct marketers often benefit from relatively low operating expenses because they do not have the overhead of retail stores. There are drawbacks to direct marketing, however. Consumers must place orders without seeing or trying on the actual merchandise (although they may see a picture of it). To offset this limitation, direct marketers must offer liberal return policies. Furthermore, catalogues and, to some extent, direct-mail pieces are costly and must be prepared long before they are issued. Price changes and new products can be announced only through supplementary catalogues or brochures.

In addition, some consumers have reacted negatively to receiving unsolicited mailing pieces at their homes, in much the same way that they are not exactly delighted to receive telemarketing solicitations. This negative reaction to direct-mail advertising in particular is exacerbated by the opinion shared by many that direct mail is "junk mail," in that much of it is wasted and represents a waste of paper at a time when more and more people are interested in conserving forest products. Some equate the receiving of "junk mail" to killing a tree and request that their names be taken off mailing lists to reduce the amount of unsolicited printed materials sent through the mail. The Canadian Direct Marketing Association has encouraged its 450 members to comply with these requests.

Automatic Vending

The sale of products through a machine with no personal contact between buyer and seller is called **automatic vending** (or *automated merchandising*). Most products sold by automatic vending are convenience-oriented or are purchased on impulse. They are usually well-known, presold brands with a high rate of turnover. For many years, the bulk of automatic vending sales has come from four main product categories: coffee, soft drinks, confectionery items, and cigarettes. In Canada, sales made through 203,758 vending machines in 1995 totalled $391 million, of which 34.4 percent was from coffee and 28 percent from soft drinks. Confectionery items, including ice cream, accounted for 17 percent of vending machine sales, while sales of cigarettes accounted for only 5.9 percent, down from 20.5 percent in 1989.

Vending machines can expand a firm's market by reaching customers where and when it is not feasible for stores to do so. Thus they are found virtually everywhere, particularly in schools, workplaces, and public facilities. Automatic vending has to overcome major challenges, however. Operating costs are high because of the need to continually replenish inventories. The machines also require occasional maintenance and repairs.

While sales through vending machines have been somewhat volatile in recent years, there is reason to believe that we can expect to see more products sold through this form of nonstore retailing in the future. The reason for this optimism relates to changes in vending machine technology. For example, DataWave Systems Inc. of Vancouver operates vending machines that dispense long-distance prepaid calling cards.[14] Developments such as these, which result from improved technology, make it possible to retail much more expensive items through vending machines, thereby expanding the base of this form of retailing beyond the small-beverage and confectionery items that have been its mainstay for years.

RETAILING MANAGEMENT

Fundamental to managing a retailing firm is the planning of sound strategies. Central to strategic planning are the selection of target markets and the development of customer relationships. Also, in the future, a factor called retail positioning will probably be even more critical. Let's briefly discuss these topics.

Positioning

Retailers are increasingly thinking about positioning as they develop marketing plans. **Positioning** refers to a retailer's strategies and actions designed to favourably distinguish itself from competitors in the minds (and hearts) of targeted groups of consumers. Positioning centres on the three variables we have stressed in this chapter: product assortment, price, and customer services.

Let's briefly examine several positioning strategies.[15] When only price and service levels are considered, two strategies that have potential value are *high price–high service* and *low price–low service*. The former is difficult to implement because it requires skilled, motivated employees (especially sales people); the latter necessitates careful management of operating expenses because gross margins are small.

When all three variables — product assortment, price, and customer services — are considered, two new options emerge. One is product differentiation, in which a retailer offers brands or styles different from those sold in competing stores. A second is service and personality augmentation, in which a retailer offers similar products but sets itself apart by providing special services and creating a distinctive personality or atmosphere for its stores.

A retailer's positioning strategy may include one or a combination of these options. Retail executives need to exhibit creativity and skill in selecting positioning strategies and implementing them.

Customer Retention

In recent years, marketers in many businesses, especially in retailing, have begun to subscribe in increasing numbers to the philosophy that it makes considerably greater sense to retain the customers they have than to compete vigorously in order to attract new ones. This viewpoint acknowledges what should have been obvious to all marketers — namely that a company's most valuable assets are loyal customers. While not denying the importance of going out to attract new customers, this approach to doing business places at least equal emphasis on keeping existing customers happy.

Two elements of a customer-retention strategy involve getting to know customers in as much detail as possible and rewarding those who are loyal and continue to give us their business. The former implies the development and maintenance of a customer database, and the latter often involves the establishment of a bonus program for frequent shoppers. Some of the most effective customer-retention programs combine these elements.

The best example of a customer-retention program (often called a *loyalty program*) in Canadian retailing is Club Z, operated by Zellers, the successful discount arm of the Hudson's Bay Company. Established in 1986 as a frequent-buyer program and modelled along the lines of the airlines' frequent-flyer programs, Club Z awards "points" to Zellers' shoppers based on the amount of their purchases. These points may be redeemed for premiums from a Club Z gift catalogue. The program has been wildly successful in differentiating Zellers from the competition and in creating a very loyal customer base — close to half of all Canadian households are Club Z members.[16]

Other retailers have had or have recently established similar programs to encourage shopper loyalty. Canadian Tire has issued its well-known "Canadian Tire money" for many years, essentially giving customers discounts of up to 5 percent on purchases made in the store. Sears Canada relaunched its Sears Club, a frequent-shopper program that rewards users of the Sears credit card with savings of up to 4 percent on purchases. These reward programs are really modern-day, electronic versions of trading stamps, which were distributed by many retailers primarily in the 1940s and 1950s.

RETAILING IN THE FUTURE

Retailers are facing challenges perhaps unequalled since the Great Depression of the 1930s. Many trends represent threats to retailers. But, as we know, a threat perceived and handled properly is really an opportunity. We will illustrate the dynamics of retailing by focusing on eight diverse, significant trends.

- *Changing demographics and industry structure.* The Canadian population is growing older, with proportional decreases in the 16-to-34 age group and increases in the 45-and-over age group. Real growth in retail sales is expected to be substantially less than in the 1970s and 1980s. Thus there may be too many shopping centres and retail stores, particularly as so many major chains entered the market in the mid-1990s.
- *Expanding computer technology.* Advancing technology dramatically affects both consumer behaviour and retail management. In particular, sophisticated computer systems that capture sales and inventory data influence the items retailers stock as well as what and when they reorder. Newer systems permit retailers to automatically place orders and reorders with suppliers that are linked to them via computer.[17]
- *Emphasis on lower prices and lower costs.* An expanding number of retailers are expected to stress value. For most of them, that strategy will dictate reducing prices and — if they intend to remain profitable — cutting costs. To pare their expenses over a period of years, more and more chains will need to take steps such as eliminating one or more layers of management, cutting advertising, and investing in labour-saving equipment such as computers that monitor inventory levels and automatically reorder merchandise as needed.
- *Accent on convenience and service.* Compared with the situation in past decades, consumers are busier, are older, and have more money to spend. They want products and ways to buy them that provide maximum convenience and service. Convenience means nearby locations, extended hours, short waiting times, and other factors that make shopping easier. Service also includes friendly, knowledgeable sales staff, easy credit, liberal return policies, and ample postsale service.
- *Experimentation.* Largely because of competitive pressures, many retailers are experimenting with new or modified formats and with nontraditional locations. For example, department stores are scaling back product assortments by eliminating "commodity" lines (such as fabrics and mattresses) and stressing fashion and quality. Discount houses are either trading up to become so-called promotional department stores or are digging in for price battles. Some retailers are expanding their markets through new types of locations, or by moving toward more nonstore retailing. Others are welcoming smaller, specialized retailers into their stores to operate specific departments as tenants or partners.

- *Internet.* Developments in this technology are enabling retailers to reach consumers through a new distribution network. The frequency of on-line shopping is increasing. One survey reveals that computer software, books, clothing, and airline tickets are the most common buys on the Internet. It is projected that the biggest growth in Internet buying will be in airline tickets and hotel reservations.[18] Retailing is seeing the development of on-line shopping malls. One Canadian project combines banking and shopping. Once an Internet access kit is purchased, consumers can make purchases from any number of cyber-stores using Paypro — Internet Payment Processing Inc.[19]
- *Emphasis on productivity.* Extremely small profits are forcing retailers to squeeze more revenues out of their resources (floor space, people, and inventories). Hence, virtually all products are being sold, at least to some extent, on a self-service basis. To boost motivation, some retailers have put sales people completely on commissions rather than on salaries plus commissions. Computer systems, as discussed above, can also help achieve greater productivity.
- *Continuing growth of nonstore retailing.* Retail stores will continue to be dominant. But more and more retailers are complementing their stores with one or more types of nonstore retailing. Many consumers prefer the novelty or convenience of nonstore retailing.

As consumers change, so do forms of retailing. Retail executives would like to anticipate changes in retailing before they occur. To some extent this is possible, as many of the evolutionary changes in retailing have followed a cyclical pattern called the **wheel of retailing**.[20] This theory states that a new type of retailer often enters the market as a low-cost, low-price store. Other retailers, as well as financial firms, do not take the new type seriously. However, consumers respond favourably to the low prices and shop at the new institution. Over time, this store takes business away from other retailers that initially ignored it and retained their old strategies.

Eventually, according to the wheel of retailing, the successful new institution trades up in order to attract a broader market, achieve higher margins, and/or gain more status. Trading up entails improving the quality of products sold and adding customer services. Sooner or later, high costs and, ultimately, high prices (at least as perceived by its target markets) make the institution vulnerable to new retail types as the wheel revolves. The next innovator enters as a low-cost, low-price form of retailing, and the evolutionary process continues.

There are many examples of the wheel of retailing. To mention a few, chain stores grew at the expense of independents during the 1920s, particularly in the grocery field. In the 1950s, discount houses placed tremendous pressure on department stores, which had become staid, stagnant institutions. The 1980s saw the expansion of warehouse clubs and off-price retailers, which have forced many institutions — supermarkets, specialty stores, and department stores — to modify their marketing strategies.

What will be the retailing innovations of the future? The 1990s have seen growth in nonstore retailing, direct marketing, and the use of the Internet. These trends will likely continue well into the future. The wheel of retailing can help retailers identify changes in retail institutions. Retail firms must identify and respond to significant trends that affect retailing, including institutional changes, by developing customer want-satisfying marketing strategies.

Summary

Retailing is the sale of goods and services to ultimate consumers for personal, nonbusiness use. Any institution (such as a manufacturer) may engage in retailing, but a firm engaged primarily in retailing is called a retailer.

Retailers serve as purchasing agents for consumers and as sales specialists for wholesaling intermediaries and producers. They perform many specific activities, such as anticipating customers' wants, developing product assortments, and financing.

More than 200,000 retail stores in Canada collectively generate almost $200 billion in annual sales. Retailers' operating expenses run about 27 percent of the retail selling price; profits are usually a very small percentage of sales.

Most retail firms are very small. However, small retailers can survive — and even prosper — if they remain flexible and pay careful attention to personally serving customers' needs.

Retailers can be classified in two ways: (1) by form of ownership, including corporate chain, independent store, and various kinds of contractual vertical marketing systems such as franchising; and (2) by key marketing strategies. Retailer types are distinguished according to product assortment, price levels, and customer service levels: department store, discount house, catalogue showroom, limited-line store (including specialty store, off-price retailer, and category-killer store), supermarket, convenience store, and warehouse club. Mature institutions such as department stores, discount houses, and supermarkets face strong challenges from new competitors, particularly different kinds of limited-line stores.

Although the large majority of retail sales are made in stores, an increasing percentage now occur away from stores. And this proportion is growing steadily. Four major forms of nonstore retailing are direct selling, telemarketing, automatic vending, and direct marketing. Each type has advantages as well as drawbacks.

Retailers need to carefully select markets and plan marketing mixes. Besides product, price, promotion, and customer services, executives also must make strategic decisions regarding physical facilities. Specific decisions concern location, design, and layout of the store. Downtown shopping areas have suffered, while suburban shopping centres have grown in number and importance. Retailers also should consider positioning — how to favourably distinguish their stores from competitors' stores in the minds of consumers.

Various trends present opportunities or pose threats for retailers. Institutional changes in retailing can frequently be explained by a theory called the wheel of retailing. To succeed, retailers need to identify significant trends and ensure that they develop marketing strategies to satisfy consumers.

Key Terms and Concepts

Retailing (retail trade) (412)
Retailer (412)
Physical facilities (417)
Shopping centre (418)
Convenience centre (418)
Neighbourhood centre (418)
Community centre (418)
Regional centre (418)
Corporate chain (418)
Independent retailer (420)
Contractual vertical marketing system (421)
Voluntary chain (421)
Retailer co-operative (421)
Franchising (422)
Franchise system (422)
Product and trade name franchising (422)
Business format franchising (422)
Department store (423)
Discount retailing (425)
Discount house (425)
Limited-line store (426)
Specialty store (426)
Off-price retailer (426)
Factory outlet (426)
Category-killer store (427)
Supermarket retailing (428)
Supermarket (428)
Convenience store (429)
Warehouse club (wholesale club) (429)
Nonstore retailing (430)
Direct selling (430)
Door-to-door selling (430)
Party-plan selling (430)
Telemarketing (431)
Direct marketing (431)
Direct mail (431)
Catalogue retailing (432)
Television shopping (432)
Internet shopping (432)
Automatic vending (432)
Positioning (433)
Wheel of retailing (435)

Questions and Problems

1. Explain the terms retailing, retail sale, and retailer in light of the following situations:
   a. Avon cosmetics sales person selling door to door.
   b. Farmer selling produce door to door.
   c. Farmer selling produce at a roadside stand.
   d. Sporting-goods store selling uniforms to a semi-professional baseball team.
2. How do you explain the wide differences in operating expenses among the various types of retailers shown in Table 17-1?
3. What recommendations do you have for reducing retailing costs?
4. Reconcile the following statements, using facts and statistics where appropriate:
   a. "Retailing is typically small-scale business."
   b. "There is a high degree of concentration in retailing today; the giants control the field."
5. Of the criteria given in this chapter for evaluating the competitive positions of large-scale and small-scale retailers, which ones show small stores to be in a stronger position than large-scale retailers? Do your findings conflict with the fact that most retail firms are quite small?
6. The ease of entry into retailing undoubtedly contributes to the high failure rate among retailers, which — in the view of some — creates economic waste. Should entry into retailing be restricted? If so, how could this be done?
7. What course of action might small retailers take to improve their competitive position?
8. In what ways does a corporate chain (Loblaws, Zellers, or Sears) differ from a voluntary chain such as IGA?
9. What can department stores do to strengthen their competitive positions?
10. "The supermarket, with its operating expense ratio of 20 percent, is the most efficient institution in retailing today." Do you agree with this statement? In what ways might supermarkets further reduce their expenses?
11. "Door-to-door selling is the most efficient form of retailing because it eliminates wholesalers and retail stores." Discuss.
12. What is the relationship between the growth and successful development of regional shopping centres in suburban areas and the material you studied in chapters 4, 5, and 6 regarding consumers?
13. Which of the retailing trends discussed in the last section of the chapter do you think represents the greatest opportunity for retailers? The greatest threat?
14. Do you agree with the axiom that there are three keys to success in retailing — location, location, and location? How do you reconcile this axiom with the fact that there is so much price competition in retailing at present?
15. Of the types of retail stores discussed in this chapter, which one(s) do you think have been or would be most successful in foreign countries? Which one(s) have been or would be unsuccessful in other countries? Explain your answers.

Hands-On Marketing

1. Arrange an interview with a small retailer. Discuss with this merchant the general positions of small and large retailers, as covered in this chapter. Which if any of these points does the small retailer disagree with, and why? Also ask what courses of action this merchant takes to achieve or maintain a viable competitive position. Interview a second small retailer, ask the same questions, and compare your answers.
2. Contact the headquarters of two retail franchise systems with which you are familiar and request information provided to prospective purchasers of a franchise. (Local units of the franchise systems should be able to supply you with the headquarters' mailing addresses.) Once you have received the information, evaluate whether you would like to own either of these franchises. What criteria did you use in making this evaluation?

Case 5-1

MURRAY INDUSTRIAL LIMITED

Murray Industrial Limited (MIL) was advertised as Newfoundland's most complete industrial supplier and sold to industrial accounts throughout Newfoundland and Labrador from three locations across the province. Products sold included hydraulic hose and fittings, bearings, conveyor products, hand power tools, fasteners (nuts, bolts, etc.), chain, packing, and general mill supply items.

According to Dave Rowe, general manager of MIL, "Our success has been largely due to our customer service strategy. We aim to provide superior service with a well-trained, motivated staff and a broad inventory of quality products. We have an ongoing commitment to in-house training and product seminars, and we have a 24-hour emergency service for all of our accounts."

Prior to 1991, MIL was subdistributor for Snowden Rubber, a Gates Rubber distributor located in Dartmouth, Nova Scotia. In 1991, an opportunity arose to become a distributor for one of North America's largest and best-known manufacturers of hydraulic hose and fittings when its Newfoundland distributor, Newfoundland Armature Works, became bankrupt.

Industrial distributors that sold hydraulic hose and fittings usually bought the more popular sizes and types of hose in full reel lengths and then cut it to fit particular customer applications. Frequently, distributors would attach hydraulic fittings or other special attachments to the shorter hose lengths as required by customers. When distributors bought full-length reels of hose (which varied in length, depending on the size of the hose) or full-box quantities of fittings (which also varied, depending on the size and style of fitting), they paid a standard distributor price for their inventory. If they desired to buy a cut-to-length piece of hose or a small quantity of fittings for special applications that might arise infrequently, they paid a 10 percent surcharge on the distributor price. For shipments that were needed urgently, manufacturers would often guarantee shipment within 24 hours but charged a $10 special-order handling charge.

At the time negotiations between MIL and the manufacturer began, the manufacturer had a distribution centre in Dartmouth, Nova Scotia, and prepaid shipments from there to distributors throughout Atlantic Canada. It offered a discount of 2 percent for payment by the twenty-fifth of the following month and co-op allowances to share promotion costs with distributors. Within a month (and before an agreement was signed), the Dartmouth warehouse was closed and the sales person was let go. Shipments were still prepaid but came from Toronto, and the sales person who serviced the Atlantic Provinces operated from Quebec. After about three months, the manufacturer's policy changed, and shipments became f.o.b. Toronto, and the prompt-payment discount was eliminated.

MIL increased sales by establishing subdistributors in remote regions; hydraulic hose eventually accounted for about 8 percent of the company's total sales and helped increase sales for complementary products. The largest customer MIL had was Royal Oak Mines, a gold mine located about one and a half hours from Port aux Basques and accessible only by air or water. It accounted for 35 percent of MIL's hydraulic hose sales.

Within a year, MIL began to have problems getting inventory. Back-order rates increased. The manufacturer closed its Toronto and Edmonton distribution centres in 1993 and decided to supply the Canadian market from the United States. The manufacturer's sales force was reduced from six to two representatives in Canada. Distributors were reduced from 140 to 40 (MIL was the twenty-second largest at the time). All co-op policies were eliminated, and the Canadian price sheets were removed so that Canadian distributors had to purchase from U.S. price sheets and add exchange, duty, brokerage, transportation, and whatever markup they needed.

"Our biggest problem," said Dave Rowe, "was that they didn't plan for the change to the distribution system. Service continued to worsen from

Toronto as inventory that was sold from there was not replaced, and we were told we couldn't order from the United States until July 1, 1993, when it would be organized to serve us. We haven't seen a sales person since early 1993, and any contact we have had with them since then has been initiated by us. Service started to affect our relationships with our customers. We eventually lost the Royal Oak Mines account, and they started buying Gates Rubber products. We were stuck with about $50,000 in inventory that we stocked specifically for them. When we approached the manufacturer, they refused to help us beyond their normal return goods policy. They were willing to take back up to 2 percent of our annual purchases as long as the material was still in new condition and was still a standard item listed in their catalogue. We had to pay return freight and a 15 percent restocking charge. It was also their policy not to accept return of any hose products after one year as hose quality deteriorated with time. While their pricing and inventory management practices were standard for the industry, we felt they had no obligation to help us as they were largely to blame for our lost customer."

Questions

1. What responsibility should the manufacturer have for the lost account (Royal Oak Mines)?
2. What can Dave Rowe do? What must he consider before taking any action?

Case 5-2

BOOKSTORES: VIRTUAL AND REAL

Amazon.com Inc.'s success in Internet retailing is legendary. Founded in July 1995 by Jeff Bezos, Amazon.com is selling $110-million-a-year worth of books after just two years of operations. The company lists over a million titles in its on-line catalogue, yet it keeps only four hundred or so titles in stock at its headquarters in Seattle. Customer orders are filled by purchasing from the nearby warehouse of one of America's largest book distributors, Ingram Book. More obscure books are obtained directly from the publishers. However, it is not just the availability of products that is contributing to the company's growth. Amazon.com's success seems to be attributable to its investment in customers, rather than inventory.

Amazon.com offers a variety of on-line features that make it easier for customers to find books that match their tastes and suit their needs. Although an Internet retailer cannot offer its customers the physical comforts of cozy furniture and specialty coffees, Amazon.com creates a special ambiance in other ways. Authors drop by electronically to post comments about their books. Customers are encouraged to do the same, regardless of their opinions on what they have read. Browsers find this type of openness refreshing. Value to the customer is enhanced by discount pricing and availability of shipping alternatives designed to meet customers' needs of timeliness and economy. Customers have the convenience of setting their own shopping hours.

This case was prepared by Judith A. Cumby, assistant professor, Faculty of Business Administration, Memorial University of Newfoundland, as a basis for class discussion and is not intended to reflect either an effective or an ineffective handling of a management problem.

Recognizing the value associated with loyal customers, Amazon.com has devoted considerable resources toward the development of a customer database, detailing customers' preferences and buying patterns. This information is linked to customers' postal and e-mail addresses, which are used to solicit customer feedback on changes to the Web site. The completion of these forms provides the company with valuable information for the building of good customer relationships. At the same time, it keeps the customer aware of, and involved in, Amazon.com's retail site. It is not surprising, then, to learn that 40 percent of Amazon.com's sales come from repeat customers. Despite the high percentage of repeat customers and a customer base of 180,000 in more than one hundred countries, the company is not profitable. The financial problems are attributable to too little Web traffic, which has forced the company to spend a lot of money on marketing and sales. Links to the Amazon.com site are available at a variety of other Internet locations, and the company has developed an "associates program" to encourage the promotion of these referrals. Associates at other Web sites, such as Yahoo, are offered a share of each sale they direct to the bookshop.

These results have not gone unnoticed by two of North America's largest booksellers: Borders Books and Barnes & Noble. In early 1997, these well-established retailers each decided to develop an Internet location. When Barnes & Noble first entered the cyber market, management of Amazon.com indicated that they had been expecting competition for a long time and did not intend to budge. However, by June 1997, Amazon.com indicated that it would slash prices at its site by up to 40 percent. Such actions are characteristic of an industry entering the growth stage of the product life cycle. New competitors entering the market are creating a downward pressure on prices. Despite these growing pains and the fragmentation of the book industry, many book retailers of all sizes are rushing to establish Internet store fronts. Estimates of online book sales range from 1 to 8 percent of the total market. What is not known is how many players the industry can sustain and whether it is possible to generate a profit by operating solely in cyberspace.

How are these Internet booksellers affecting retailers in Canada? Canada's largest bookseller, Chapters Inc., which was created in March 1995 by the merger of Coles Book Stores and SmithBooks, also operates Classic Bookstores, The Book Company, and World's Biggest Bookstore. In 1995, U.S. retail giant Borders was prevented from entering the Canadian market by a government ruling that indicated that a controlling interest of a Canadian bookstore by a U.S. retailer would be a threat to the Canadian publishing industry. However, in June 1996 the U.S. book retail giant, Barnes & Noble, was able to create a Canadian presence through acquisition of a 20 percent interest in Chapters Inc. At that time, Chapters operated 375 stores, located mostly in shopping malls, and had five superstores and annual sales in excess of $350 million. By September 1997, Chapters announced plans to continue its aggressive expansion in Canada. It intends to have seventeen stand-alone superstores in operation by April 1998 and to bring that total to seventy-five by the year 2000.

How is it that Chapters has identified a growth opportunity in the retail book market when Canadians have access to limitless choices of books from Internet retail locations? Traditionally, retailers have argued that location is the key to success. So why is it that Chapters' management thinks that it can be successful operating stand-alone stores? The answer lies in how the company positions itself. It is not just selling books; it is catering to the demands and lifestyles of its marketplace. The company locates its superstores in a market with between 15,000 and 18,000 university graduates and then attempts to create an atmosphere conducive to a sense of community among customers.

While Chapters stores have common design elements, with soft green and yellow colours with lots of wood accents, they also have features unique to their location. The superstore in Guelph, Ontario, has beautiful cathedral ceilings. The three-storey outlet in Victoria is located in a fully restored heritage building, and the front of the store is marble. The MacLeod Trail Chapters superstore in Calgary features one-of-a-kind western-themed decor, including rotating western art exhibits, a kids'-own corral, and a giant teepee in the children's department. The West Hills superstore in Calgary has hardwood floors and cherrywood fixtures, which give the store a warm atmosphere. Each store is equipped with cozy living-room furniture in which customers can relax and browse through a book or a selection from the large and eclectic assortment of magazines. Many locations have a Starbucks cafe. Within each superstore is a "My Books" children's section featuring CD-ROM terminals, colourful kid-sized seating, an assortment of books, and hopscotch. This combination of comforts is designed to encourage the customers to stay in the store as long as they wish.

The managers of many of the superstore locations have expressed their hopes of turning the store into a gathering place for the community. Many locations have a meeting room which is made available to community groups. There are a variety of events scheduled at the stores most weekends: live music, multimedia demonstrations, cooking demonstrations, and readings by Canadian authors. Chapters Inc. is a partner with Frontier College, an organization that has been teaching people to read since 1899. In October 1997, Chapters Inc. teamed up with Mordecai Richler and Peter Gzowski to present a benefit evening for Frontier College.

Chapters has created a college book division and will be running the bookstore at McGill University in Montreal. Company officials anticipate that the college division will have revenues of up to $100 million, but if history is to repeat itself, this will not happen without controversy. When Follett Corporation took over the management of the campus bookstore at Sheridan College in Oakville, Ontario, in 1996, it attracted the attention of many critics. Concerns included queries as to the propriety of diverting profits from operations at a tax-funded institution to corporate headquarters in the United States. Others were concerned that the sheer size of such companies might allow them to search outside of Canada for both new and used books. Despite such complaints to federal government ministers, an increasing number of Canadian colleges and bookstores are attempting to cut operating costs by contracting out the running of their bookstores. Some maintain that the real winners from such endeavours are the students, who benefit from lower prices.

Where does all this competition from Internet retailers, superstores, and foreign operators leave the small, independent Canadian book retailer? Some have recognized the need to establish a Web site to complement their physical location. However, there is the very real concern of how enough buyers can be attracted to their Internet location. If Amazon.com is having trouble generating sufficient traffic with its "associates programs," which encourages referrals, how then can a small entrepreneur hope to succeed in such a market? There are those who maintain that it is possible to carve out a niche through specialization. Such a strategy would require a total rethinking of the manner in which business is conducted: from the physical design of the store to the building and nurturing of customer relationships. Is it realistic to think that success can be achieved by independent operators who alter their way of business? Or should Canadians come to accept that their literary choices will be controlled by large corporations operating in exclusive locations or through the Internet?

Pertinent Web Sites

http://www.amazon.com
http://www.barnesandnoble.com
http://www.bookshelf.sympatico.ca
http://www.bookshop.co.uk
http://www.borders.com
http://www.cvbookstore.com
http://www.dillons.co.uk

Questions

1. How do bookstores operating on the Internet position themselves relative to competition operating from "traditional" stores? Illustrate this through use of a positioning map.
2. How do the superstore book retailers position themselves relative to stores operated by independent owners, those operated in shopping malls, and those operating solely through the Internet?
3. What role has store design played in the positioning of Chapters superstores?
4. What role should national and international book stores play in the operation of book stores on college and university campuses?
5. As book retailing via the Internet proceeds through the various stages of the product life cycle, what changes do you predict for the industry as a whole and for individual players?

Sources: "A River Runs Through It," *The Economist (Electronic Commerce Survey)*, May 10, 1997, pp. 9–10; "Barnes & Noble Buys 20 Percent of Chapters," *Financial Post Daily*, June 28, 1996, p. 8; "Calgarians Preview Their Second Chapters Book Superstore," *Canada News Wire*, June 18, 1997; "Chapters Book Superstore Opens in Victoria," *Canada News Wire*, July 28, 1997; "Chapters New Verse: A U.S. Giant Tiptoes into Canada's Book Market," *MacLeans*, July 8, 1996, p. 30; Anita Elash, "Follett, Barnes & Noble Make Inroads on Canadian Campuses: U.S. Lease Operators Now Run More Than 10 Stores South of the Border and Considering Further Expansion," *Quill & Quire*, November 1996, pp. 20–22; "Guelph Previews Chapters Book Superstore," *Canada News Wire*, July 29, 1997; "Hot on the Trail — New Chapters for Calgary," *Canada News Wire*, September 24, 1997; Matthew Ingram, "Starbucks Invades Toronto Market," *The Globe and Mail*, January 23, 1996, p. B19; Amanda Lang, "Still Searching for the Holy Grail," *Financial Post*, June 19, 1997, p. 17; "Large Format Independents Challenge Chapters at Its Own Game," *Quill & Quire*, October 1996, pp. 8–9; John Lorinc, "Chapters Unveils New Mall Design in Yorkdale Mall, Toronto," *Quill & Quire*, November 1996, p. B8; "Media Alert — Chapters Presents an Evening with Mordecai Richler and Peter Gzowski," *Canada News Wire*, October 2, 1997; Kurt Opprecht, "Barnes & Noble Undercuts Amazon.com Discount," *Wired News*, February 25, 1997; Kathy Rebello, "A Literary Hangout — Without the Latte," *Business Week*, September 23, 1996, p. 106; Randell E. Stross, "Why Barnes & Noble May Crush Amazon," *Fortune*, September 29, 1997, pp. 248, 250. "Tremble Everyone," *The Economist (Electronic Commerce Survey)*, May 10, 1997, pp. 11–13; Paul Waldie, "Chapters Speeds Up Superstore Expansion," *The Globe and Mail*, September 19, 1997, pp. B1, B6; "Web Site Looks to Wall Street," *Financial Post Daily*, April 1, 1997, p. 19.

Case 5-3

BANKING INNOVATIONS

Long gone are the days when customers were required to line up in front of bank tellers between the hours of 10 A.M. and 3 P.M. for the privilege of allowing an impersonal institution to handle their financial affairs. Customers now have many choices of how and when they may access information and transact their financial affairs. Many dealings can be initiated from the customer's telephone or personal computer at any hour. Automatic banking machines (ABMs) are located practically everywhere: outside bank branches, in stores, at airports, at universities and colleges, and even at some work locations. Customers who prefer not to handle cash have a variety of products at their disposal: cheques, credit cards, Interac cards, and electronic-cash cards. This combination of multiple access points and electronic products means that customers decide when, or even if, they wish to interact with bank personnel.

This case was prepared by Judith A. Cumby, assistant professor, Faculty of Business Administration, Memorial University of Newfoundland, as a basis for class discussion and is not intended to reflect either an effective or an ineffective handling of a management problem.

A pioneer in this virtual banking market was VanCity, a credit union in British Columbia. In June 1995, the VanCity Direct service was established, which provided customers with twenty-four hour phone service, banking software for PCs, and another version of the software for TV. However, it was the launching of Bank of Montreal's electronic banking service, mbanx, in October 1996 that generated considerable interest throughout the country. Some felt that the advertisements illustrating children wandering through wheat fields singing Bob Dylan's *The Times They Are A-changing* was a little extreme for the marketing of a financial institution. The focus of critics was on how, not what, mbanx was promoting.

This foray into home electronic banking has been motivated by a desire by banks and other financial institutions to cut their costs of distribution and by a desire by customers for more convenience and choice in how they manage their financial affairs. From the bank's perspective, a cash deposit made in a branch with a teller costs the bank $2.94; the same transaction costs 54 cents at an ABM and even less if the customer is using telephone or computer banking. Customers want to be able to bank when and where they wish. Software developed for home banking has to be compatible with personal-financial-management software such as Intuit's Quicken or Microsoft Money, which is used by some ten million people in the United States. In 1998, most of the larger Canadian banks had software that enabled customers to integrate their home financial programs with their records at the bank.

Electronic banking is not for everyone. Although use of ABMs is now taken for granted by many, some customers still prefer to deal with a person, not technology. There are risks to the bank of forcing customers to adopt a certain technology or way of doing business. Customers may resent this sort of attitude and decide to take their business elsewhere.

The use of proprietary bank software permits the customer to engage in a variety of exchanges, but only with his or her own bank. Advances in technology and the enhancement of security over the Internet could lead to the bridging of financial management software and the Web. If this happens, it will be easier for customers to switch from one financial institution to another, depending on the product or service sought. This will create a tremendous challenge to how bankers bundle their products and approach relationships with their customers. Although it appears high, one estimate is that the 10 percent of the population that currently use personal-financial-management software probably account for 75 percent of the profits of the banking system. What this means is that this segment of customers is significant to the success of banks. Management will have to carefully plan how it intends to keep these customers loyal to their banks.

Pertinent Web Sites

http://www.bankofmontreal.com
http://www.cibc.com
http://www.citizens.com
http://www.mbanx.com
http://www.royalbank.com
http://www.scotiabank.ca
http://www.tdbank.ca

Questions

1. How has product development influenced the changing operations of retail banking in Canada?
2. How is technology affecting the way that customer relationships with banks are established and developed?
3. Discuss whether the innovations discussed in this case (ABMs, Interac, telephone banking, credit cards, debit cards, on-line banking) are really new products or merely changes in the distribution channels for financial services. What are the implications?
4. How do Canadians measure the performance of their banks? What does it take to produce customer satisfaction with banks? Are the technological innovations discussed in this case likely to increase customer satisfaction?

Sources: Richard Blackwell, "CIBC and Royal Banking on \`Electronic Purses'," *Financial Post*, May 12, 1995, p. 1; Patrick Brethour, "Web Takes Business to a New Level," *The Globe and Mail*, July 7, 1997, p. B13; "CIBC Trims Electronic Fees," *Vancouver Sun*, August 1, 1996, pp. C1, D2; Philip B. Evans and Thomas S. Wurster, "Strategy and the New Economics of Information," *Harvard Business Review*, September–October, 1997, pp. 71–82; Jennifer Hunter, "Home Banking Changes the Face of Personal Finance," *The Globe and Mail*, April 9, 1996; "Introducing 24-hour Home Access," *Financial Post Daily*, November 15, 1996, p. 14; Valerie Lawtone, "Dawn of Cashless Society," *The Montreal Gazette*, February 13, 1997; Michael MacDonald, "Banks Help You Balance the Books with New Software," *The Evening Telegram*, July 12, 1997, p. 30; Katrina Onstad, "The Sound of One Clicking," *Canadian Business Technology*, Winter 1996, pp. 66–72.

Part Six

Marketing Communications

Designing and managing marketing communications to inform, persuade, and remind current and potential customers

We have examined product, price, and distribution — three of the four marketing-mix elements — to reach an organization's target markets and achieve its marketing goals. To complete the marketing mix, we now turn our attention to marketing communications.

In Chapter 18 we present an overview of marketing communications, including the nature of communications in a marketing context, types of marketing communications, the management of marketing communications, including the components of the promotional mix available to a marketer, the marketing communications budget, the campaign concept, and the regulation of marketing communications in Canada. Chapter 19 looks at the personal selling process and sales-force management. Advertising, sales promotion, public relations, and publicity are the subjects of Chapter 20.

CHAPTER 18 GOALS

This chapter will help you understand how marketing communications decisions are made by describing what marketing communications is and how it fits into a firm's total marketing program. After studying this chapter, you should have an understanding of:

- The components of a marketing communications strategy.
- The role marketing communications play in an organization and in the economy.
- How the process of communication applies in marketing.
- The concept and design of the marketing communications mix.
- The marketing communications campaign.
- Alternative marketing communications budgeting methods.
- Regulation of marketing communications.

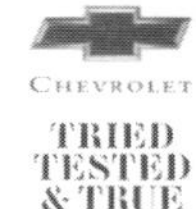

Chapter Eighteen

The Marketing Communications Program

www.gmcanada.com

GO FOR IT!

General Motors of Canada, the country's largest auto manufacturer, was faced with an interesting situation. While the Oshawa, Ontario-based company saw 1997 calendar year sales through November increase by 16.5 percent from the previous year, industry sales increased by almost the same amount. The question for GM Canada was: "How to increase sales more than the industry in order to gain market share?"

GM Canada has brought newly designed product to market, particularly in the mid-sized car market, with the Malibu, Pontiac Grand Prix, and Buick Century offerings. But these competed with a redesigned Camry from Toyota, a new Accord from Honda, and a redesigned Altima from Nissan, as well as Chrysler Canada's new mid-sized sedans. GM Canada felt its products were right for this market.

Having product available when buyers want to buy means not only getting the logistics right but also having the work force producing. GM in North America had a number of strikes, which prevented cars from getting to market when dealers were able to sell them. When this happened, marketing communications dollars invested in numerous programs were wasted in helping to create demand that could not be supplied. After two strikes that caused product-supply problems, labour difficulties seem to be minimal, new product is readily available, and dealer-stock positions are in good condition. Thus, the capacity seems to be in line to back up demand.

GM Canada's marketing programs were wide ranging and incorporated changes in the organization of marketing activities and advertising, as well as a special focus on dealer services. They included:

- Implementing a brand management strategy to identify the options and features that most customers want and, using economies of scale, package them together at a cost less than the sum of the individual items.
- Using its brands to provide a competitive advantage that no other manufacturer could match by developing and marketing products for the needs and wants of specific groups of customers.
- Introducing more effective timing for new product launches to provide a steady stream of new vehicles and increase the number of new models introduced annually.
- Launching an advertising campaign to support GM Canada's nationwide dealer sales and service network to help its dealers build relationships for future sales and increase after-sales service business.
- Utilizing co-operative dealer advertising and promotion of new products, programs, and services.
- Conducting thousands of detailed interviews with current and potential customers about their needs and expectations to enable GM to design and build products to satisfy customer requirements.
- Restructuring the marketing department at GM Canada by appointing segment brand managers, thus making each manager responsible for a single line, such as the Chevrolet Malibu or Lumina.
- Leveraging its worldwide product and engineering strengths to create different and distinctive vehicles, tailored and targeted for specific market segments around the world, consistent with the character and appeal of its individuals brands.
- Developing publicity programs aimed at auto magazines, newspaper automobile sections and their writers, and various interested groups and experts.

Was GM's strategy successful? The answer will only be determined in the months and years ahead. The auto business is one of the most competitive industries in the world today, so the task is a formidable one. But with a focused vision to be the leader in transportation products and services worldwide, GM feels equal to the challenge.[1]

NATURE OF MARKETING COMMUNICATIONS

The marketing-mix activities of product planning, pricing, and distribution are performed mainly within a business or between a business and the members of its distribution channels. However, through its marketing communications activities, a firm communicates directly with potential customers. And, as we will see, it is not a simple process.

Basically, **marketing communications** is an attempt to influence. More specifically, it is the element in an organization's marketing mix that serves to inform, persuade, and remind the market of a product or service and/or the organization selling it, in hopes of influencing the recipients' feelings, beliefs, or behaviour. As our opening example illustrates, GM Canada is clearly intent on doing this.

Marketing Communications Methods

There are five forms of marketing communications: personal selling, advertising, sales promotion, public relations, and publicity. Each has distinct features that determine in what situations it will be most effective.

- **Personal selling** is the direct presentation of a product or service to a prospective customer by a representative of the organization selling it. Personal selling takes place face-to-face, over the phone, or by means of an Internet "chat," and it may be directed to an intermediary or a final consumer. We list it first because, across all businesses, more money is spent on personal selling than on any other form of marketing communications. It is also that component of a company's marketing program that likely has the greatest impact on the firm's efforts to build long-term relationships with its customers, principally because it is a company's sales staff with whom the customer is most likely to come into contact.
- **Advertising** is impersonal mass communication that the sponsor has paid for and in which the sponsor is clearly identified. The most familiar forms of ads are found in the broadcast (TV and radio) and print (newspapers and magazines) media. However, there are many other advertising alternatives, from spots on heavily visited World Wide Web pages, to direct mail, billboards, and the Yellow Pages.

- **Sales promotion** is demand-stimulating activity designed to supplement advertising and facilitate personal selling. It is paid for by the sponsor and frequently involves a temporary incentive to encourage a purchase. Many sales promotions are directed at consumers, including the coupons that arrive in the mail and the contest that allows you to win tickets to a Blue Rodeo concert. Many sales promotions, however, are designed to encourage a company's sales force or other members of its distribution channel to sell its products more aggressively. This latter category is called trade promotion. Included in sales promotion are a wide spectrum of activities, such as contests, trade shows, in-store displays, rebates, samples, premiums, discounts, and coupons.
- **Public relations** encompasses a wide variety of communication efforts to contribute to generally favourable attitudes and opinions toward an organization and its products. Unlike most advertising and personal selling, it does not include a specific sales message. The targets may be customers, shareholders, a government agency, or a special-interest group. Public relations can take many forms, including newsletters, annual reports, lobbying, and sponsorship of charitable or civic events. The Labatt hot-air balloon is a familiar example of a public-relations device. Many large companies, such as the Royal Bank of Canada and Air Canada, gain national attention through their sponsorship of organizations and events such as symphony orchestras and the Special Olympics.
- **Publicity** is a special form of public relations that involves news stories about an organization or its products or services. Like advertising, it involves an impersonal message that reaches a mass audience through the media. But several things distinguish publicity from advertising: It is not paid for, the organization that is the subject of the publicity has little control over it, and it appears as news and therefore may have greater credibility than advertising. Organizations seek good publicity and frequently provide the material for it in the form of news releases, press conferences, and photographs. There is, of course, also bad publicity, which organizations try to avoid or deflect.

The Communication Process

Communication is the verbal or nonverbal transmission of information between someone wanting to express an idea and someone else expected or expecting to get that idea. Because the components of marketing communications are examples of communication between two or more parties, much can be learned about structuring effective marketing messages by examining the communication process.

Fundamentally, communication requires only four elements: a message, a source of the message, a communication channel, and a receiver. In practice, however, important additional components come into play:

- The information that the sending source wants to share must first be **encoded** into a transmittable form. In marketing, this means changing an idea into words, pictures, or some other form such as a product display in a supermarket, a coupon, or a "hot button" on a Web site.
- Once the message has been transmitted through some communication channel, the symbols must be **decoded**, or given meaning, by the receiver. The received message may be what the sender intended or something else, depending on the recipient's knowledge and experience.
- If the message has been transmitted successfully, there is some change in the receiver's knowledge, beliefs, or feelings. As a result of this change the receiver formulates a **response**. The response could be nonverbal (a positive reaction as indicated by a smile while watching an ad), verbal (suggesting to a friend that she try an advertised product), or behavioural (purchasing the advertised product).
- The response serves as **feedback**, telling the sender whether the message was received and how it was perceived by the recipient. Through feedback, the sender can learn why a communication failed and how to improve future communication.
- All stages of the process can be affected by **noise** — any external event or factor that interferes with successful communication, such as a competitive ad. Noise is occurring when a television viewer sees ads for both Speedy and Midas within a short time period.

Figure 18-1 illustrates these components of a communication process and relates them to marketing communications activities.

What does the communication process tell us about producing effective marketing communications programs? First, the act of encoding reminds us that messages can take many forms. Messages can be physical (a sample, a premium) or symbolic (verbal, visual), and there are a myriad of options within each of these categories. For example, a verbal message can be factual, humorous, or even threatening.

Second, the number of channels or methods of transmitting a message is limited only by the imagination and creativity of the sender. Most marketing communications messages are transmitted by familiar channels, such as the voice of a sales person, the airwaves of radio, the mail, the side of a bus, or the lead-in to a feature film in a movie theatre. Each channel has its own characteristics in terms of audience reach, flexibility, permanence, credibility, and cost. In selecting a channel, a marketer must have clearly defined objectives and a familiarity with the features of the many alternatives.

Third, how the message is decoded or interpreted depends on its form (encoding and transmission) and the capability and interest of the recipient. In designing and sending messages, marketers must be sensitive to the audience. What is their vocabulary and level of verbal sophistication? What other messages have they received? What experiences have they had? What will get and hold their attention?

Finally, every component of the marketing communications program should have a measurable objective that can be determined from the response and feedback provided by the recipients. Feedback may be collected in many forms — changes in sales, recall of advertising messages, more favourable attitudes, increased awareness of a brand or an organization — depending on the objective of the marketing communications message. For some promotional activities the objective may be modest, for example, an increase in the audience's awareness of a brand or stimulating trial of a new product. For others, such as a direct mail solicitation, the objective would be a particular level of sales. Without objectives, there is no way of evaluating the effectiveness of a message.

THE PURPOSES OF MARKETING COMMUNICATIONS

One of the attributes of a free-market system is the right to use communication as a tool to influence and inform consumers. In our system, from a business perspective, that freedom is reflected in the marketing communications efforts of firms to influence the feelings, beliefs, and behaviour of prospective customers. Let's examine how marketing

FIGURE 18-1 The Communication Process in Marketing Communications

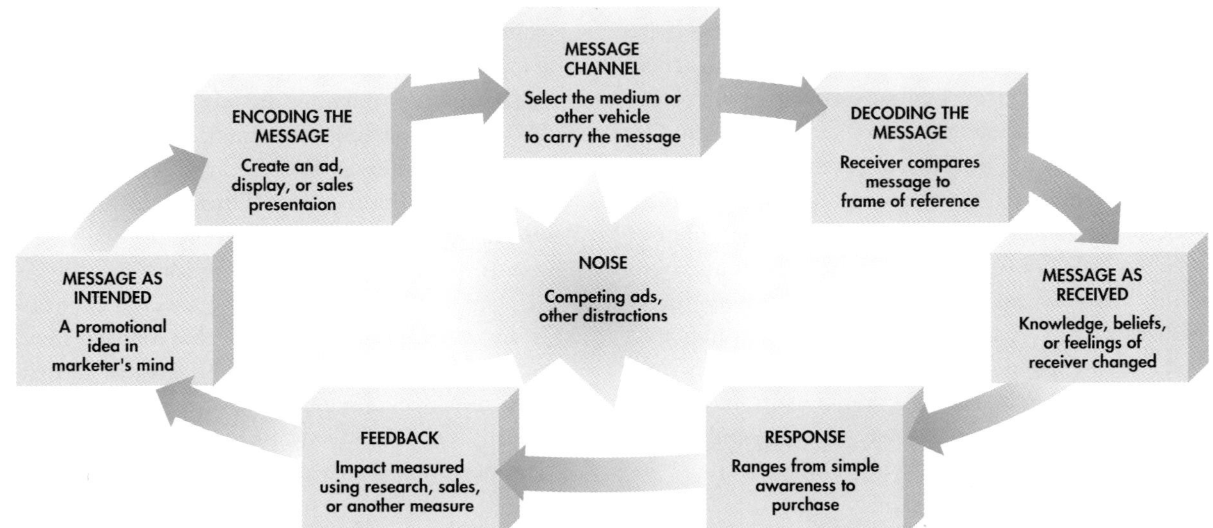

communications works from an economic perspective and from a marketing perspective.

Marketing Communications and Imperfect Competition

The North American marketplace operates under conditions of imperfect competition, characterized by product differentiation, emotional buying behaviour, and incomplete market information. A company uses marketing communications to provide more information for the decision-maker's buying-decision process, to assist in differentiating its product, and to persuade potential buyers.

Through marketing communications, a company strives to increase its sales volume at a given price (in economic terms, to shift its demand curve to the right). Simply stated, marketing communications is intended to make a product, service, or organization more attractive to prospective buyers or clients.

A firm also hopes that marketing communications will affect consumer responses to price increases and decreases. In other words, management wants marketing communications to create an image and to send certain messages that will give the consumer a number of nonprice reasons to buy. One of the main functions of marketing communications is to differentiate the offerings of a company from those of its competitors. In the absence of such differentiation, consumers are likely to conclude that there are no differences and will make their purchase decisions based largely on price. The marketing communications program of a company has the responsibility to convey the right messages that will lead the consumer to conclude that there are many nonprice reasons to buy from the firm.

Communications in the Context of Marketing

Marketing communications serves three essential roles: It informs, persuades, and reminds prospective customers about a company and its products. The relative importance of these roles varies according to the circumstances faced by a firm.

The most attractive product or brand will be a failure if no one knows it is available! Because distribution channels for tangible products are often long, a product may pass through many hands between its producer and consumers. Therefore, a producer must inform resellers as well as the ultimate consumers or business users about the product. Wholesalers, in turn, must inform retailers, and retailers must inform consumers. As the number of prospective customers grows and the geographic dimensions of a market expand, the problems and cost of informing target consumers increase.

Another purpose of marketing communications is persuasion. The intense competition among different industries, as well as among different firms in the same industry, puts tremendous pressure on the promotional programs of marketers. In our economy, even a product designed to satisfy a basic physiological need requires strong persuasive marketing communications, since consumers have many alternatives from which to choose. Campbell Soup Company has been selling soup for over 120 years and has annual soup sales of close to $2 billion. Studies show that 96 percent of Canadian households have some canned soup in the pantry. Yet the firm spends over $60 million a year advertising soup because there is still room to "win more stomachs for Campbell's." To remain competitive and to increase its share of the home-prepared soup market, Campbell's continues to innovate by launching new varieties of canned soup and fresh-frozen soups, all of which have to be advertised to make consumers aware of their existence.[2] In the case of a luxury product, for which demand depends on a seller's ability to convince consumers that the product's benefits exceed those of other luxuries, persuasion is even more important.

Consumers also must be reminded about the availability of a product or brand and its potential to satisfy. In addition, they need to be reminded on occasion of broader messages that are related to the corporate image of corporations and not-for-profit organizations. Advertisers bombard the marketplace with thousands of messages every day in the hope of attracting new consumers, leaving positive reinforcing messages with existing customers and establishing markets for new products and services. Given the intense competition for the attention of consumers, even an established firm must constantly remind people about its brand to retain a place in

www.campbellsoup.com

their minds. It is unlikely that a day goes by, for example, in which you don't see some form of communications (an ad, in-store display, counter sign, billboard, or imprinted T-shirt) for Coca-Cola. Thus, much of a firm's marketing communications activity may be intended simply to offset competitors' marketing efforts by keeping its brand in front of the market.

Marketing Communications and Strategic Marketing Planning

A company's personal selling, advertising, and other communications activities should form a co-ordinated marketing communications program within its total marketing plan. These activities are fragmented in many firms, with potentially damaging consequences. For example, advertising managers and sales managers may come into conflict over resources. But this wouldn't happen if the elements making up an integrated marketing communications program were a co-ordinated part of a firm's overall strategic marketing plan. Many authors and marketing managers are today advocating that firms take an integrated approach to marketing communications, based upon the belief that literally everything that a company does sends messages about it and its brands to customers and other stakeholders. By taking an integrated approach, management can ensure that the messages that are communicated are consistent with the image the company wishes to convey.[3]

To be effective, marketing communications activities must also be co-ordinated with product planning, pricing, and distribution, the other marketing-mix elements. Marketing communications are influenced, for instance, by how distinctive a product is and whether its price is above or below that of the competition. A manufacturer or middleman must also consider its marketing communications links with other firms in the distribution channel. For example, Chrysler Canada recognizes that its success is closely tied to the performance of its dealers. Therefore, in addition to advertising its automobiles directly to consumers, Chrysler offers cash incentives to dealers with high customer-satisfaction scores and trains the dealers' sales people in how to show a car and conduct a test drive.

Marketing communications should also contribute to a firm's overall strategic plan. Bausch & Lomb has achieved success with contact lenses by concentrating much of its promotional efforts on educating physicians. However, with the growing popularity of disposable lenses, the distribution of contact lenses has shifted from doctors' offices to optical retailers. To maintain its market position, Bausch & Lomb found it necessary to shift its marketing communications efforts from physicians to lens wearers and to focus its efforts on teenagers. To reach this market, the firm offered certificates for free-trial pairs of disposable lenses via a 1-800 number on MTV, advertised free-trial offers in teen magazines, and distributed book covers and gym bags in high schools. In Canada, major competitor Johnson & Johnson made the same "free trial pair" offer using a coupon in its advertising.

DETERMINING THE MARKETING COMMUNICATIONS MIX

A marketing communications mix is an organization's combination of personal selling, advertising, sales promotion, public relations, and publicity. An effective mix is a critical part of virtually all marketing communications strategies. Product differentiation, market segmentation, trading up and trading down, and branding all require effective communications with target audiences. Designing an effective marketing communications mix requires a number of strategic decisions, as we shall now see.

Factors Influencing the Marketing Communications Mix

These four factors should be taken into account when determining the marketing communications mix: (1) the target market, (2) the nature of the product or service being promoted, (3) the stage in the life cycle of the product or service, and (4) the amount of money available for marketing communications.

Target Market As in most areas of marketing, decisions on the marketing communications mix will be greatly influenced by the audience or target market. At least four variables affect the choice of an approach to communicating with a particular market segment:

MARKETING AT WORK FILE 18-1

AN INTERNATIONAL PERSPECTIVE ON ADVERTISING AND SALES PROMOTION

As more firms become multinational in their operations, it becomes less clear that there is one most effective way for them to promote their products. The question is, should their marketing communications approach be standardized for all countries, should they have a local program for each, or something in-between? Coca-Cola, for example, standardizes both its brand and its advertising; Volvo standardizes the brand but varies the advertising, and Procter & Gamble alters the brand names but maintains common advertising themes.

Research conducted with seventy-eight Canadian firms with international sales found that there was a high degree of brand standardization (78 percent) but little advertising standardization (18 percent). Of the firms engaged in some standardization, only 17 percent standardized both their brand and their advertising.

When it comes to sales promotion, there are a number of reasons why standardization is not necessarily possible:

- *Level of economic development.* Limited purchasing power, combined with low literacy rates, restricts the number of sales promotion options in developing countries. In the Philippines, most consumers buy in such small quantities (individual cigarettes and single portions of shampoo, for example) that in-package premiums are not possible. In developing countries, samples and demonstrations are the most common sales promotion tools, while coupons, common in developed countries, are seldom used.
- *Stage of market development.* The same product is frequently sold in mature markets, where there are numerous competitors and consumers are familiar with alternative brands, and in new markets, where not only is the brand unknown, but the product class is also new to consumers. In mature markets, greater emphasis is placed on increasing the number of stores that stock the product by using promotional tools such as trade allowances to intermediaries, while in new markets getting consumers to try the product through sampling and couponing is most appropriate.
- *Consumer values.* Sales promotion techniques are evaluated differently from culture to culture. In Japan, some consumers are embarrassed to be seen using them. Thus what might be seen as a valuable premium in one country may be viewed as an indication of poverty in another.
- *Government regulations.* Laws governing what is permissible and the manner in which promotions can be carried out differ across countries. In Japan, the value of a premium cannot exceed 10 percent of a product's price and cannot be more than 100 yen (about 80 cents). In Malaysia, marketing communications contests can be games of skill but not chance. The only sales promotions permitted by all member countries in the European Union are free samples, in-store demonstrations, and reusable packages.
- *Structure of retail trade.* The dominance of large and powerful chain stores versus small independent retailers in a market will influence the success of marketing communications. Chains prefer trade promotions that provide price discounts and in-store customer promotions. However, smaller stores do not buy in large enough quantities to benefit significantly from trade discounts. In Japan, where stores are very small, in-store displays take up too much space and create congestion.

Because the goal of advertising is to build awareness of and familiarity with a brand, the use of common themes around the world can be effective. But the objective of sales promotion is action — trial, purchase, repurchase, purchase of a larger quantity, and so forth. Thus, it must be adapted to the particular conditions of a market.

Source: Adapted from Dennis M. Sandler and David Shani, "Brand Globally but Advertise Locally," *Journal of Product and Brand Management*, no. 2, 1993, pp. 59–71; and Kamran Kashani and John A. Quelch, "Can Sales Promotion Go Global?" *Business Horizons*, May–June 1990, pp. 37–44.

www.sprintcanada.ca
www.apple.com
www.futureshop.com

- *Readiness to Buy.* A target segment may be in any one of six stages of buying readiness. These stages — awareness, knowledge, liking, preference, conviction, and purchase — are called the hierarchy of effects because they represent stages a buyer goes through in moving toward a purchase and each defines a possible goal or effect of marketing communications.

  At the awareness stage, the marketer's task is to let buyers know that the product or brand exists. Here the objective is to build familiarity with the product and the brand name. Recall the unconventional "shock" ads that Benetton used to attract attention. A controversial series of print ads depicted various forms of human suffering, including a dying AIDS victim, refugees jumping overboard from a ship, and a pool of blood from a war casualty. These ads attracted attention but were heavily criticized in some quarters, and some were banned in Germany.

  Knowledge goes beyond awareness to learning about a product's features. Goodyear and BF Goodrich are tire brands that are often confused simply because the founders had similar names. And the effectiveness of the Goodyear blimp as a corporate symbol led many consumers to confuse the two companies. For example, Goodrich introduced steel-belted radial tires to the North American market, but most consumers attribute the innovation to Goodyear. To establish itself as an industry leader in consumers' minds, Goodrich developed an information campaign to increase the knowledge of consumers about the company's innovations.

  Liking refers to how the market feels about the product or brand. Marketing communications can be used to move a knowledgeable audience from being indifferent to liking a brand. A common technique is to associate the item with an attractive symbol or person, which explains why Adidas Canada selected Olympic Gold Medal winner Donovan Bailey, "the world's fastest human," as a spokesman. But when Bailey made critical comments in public about his opponent in a key race and then apologized, the risk to Adidas had to be assessed by management. At the time, Adidas Canada stood by its spokesman, but critics felt he may have lost his credibility.[4]

  Creating preference involves distinguishing among brands such that the market prefers yours. It is not uncommon for consumers to like several brands of the same product, but the customer can't make a decision until one brand is preferred over the alternatives. Ads that make direct comparisons with the competition are intended to create a preference. In the vigorous competition for long-distance customers, Sprint Canada, frequently using spokesperson Candice Bergen, compares the simplicity of its rate structure with that of Canada's established telephone companies.

  Conviction entails the actual decision or commitment to purchase. A student may prefer an IBM PC over a clone, but not yet be convinced to buy a computer. The marketing communications objective here is to increase the strength of the buyer's need. Trying a product and experiencing the benefits that come from using it are very effective in strengthening the conviction to own it. Using Apple computers — promoted to schools at special prices — in a teaching laboratory or being allowed to play with a Nintendo in a store display are examples of this.

  Purchase can be delayed or postponed indefinitely, even for customers who are convinced that they should buy a product. The inhibitor might be a situational factor, such as not having enough money at the moment, or a natural resistance to change. Action may be triggered through a marketing communications price discount or offering additional incentives. The vast marketing communications behind Microsoft's Windows 95 was used by computer manufacturers as well as retailers such as Future Shop to speed purchases by providing the software free or at a special discount.
- *Geographic scope of the market.* Personal selling may be adequate in a small local market, but as the market broadens geographically, greater emphasis must be placed on advertising using a variety of media. The exception would be a firm that sells to concentrated pockets of customers scattered around the country. For example, the market for certain plastics is heaviest in Ontario and Quebec, because these plastics are used by component suppliers to the auto industry. In this case, emphasis on personal selling may be appropriate because spending on advertising that is widely distributed would be wasteful.

www.benneton.com • www.goodyear.com • www.bfgoodrich.com • www.adidas.com

Westin Hotels used an amusing testimonial approach that gained attention and did not require the Raptors basketball team actually to win.

- *Type of customer.* Marketing communications strategy depends in part on what level of the distribution channel the organization hopes to influence. Final consumers and resellers sometimes buy the same product, but they require different marketing communications. To illustrate, the 3M Company sells its computer diskettes to final consumers through computer and office supply stores. Marketing communications to dealers includes sharing the cost of Yellow Pages ads and advertising in specialized business magazines such as *Office Products Dealer*. Different ads aimed at final consumers are run in magazines such as *Personal Computing*. In many situations, intermediaries may significantly influence a manufacturer's marketing communications strategy. Large retail

www.bombardier.com
www.nba.com/grizzlies

chains may refuse to stock a product unless the manufacturer agrees to provide a certain amount of advertising or promotional support.

Another consideration is the variety among the target markets for a product. A market with only one type of customer will call for a different marketing communications mix than a market with many target markets. A firm selling large power saws used exclusively by lumber manufacturers may rely only on personal selling. In contrast, a company selling portable hand saws to consumers and to construction firms will probably include an ample portion of advertising in its mix. In this latter example, personal selling would be prohibitively expensive in reaching the firm's many customers.

- *Concentration of the market.* The total number of prospective buyers is another consideration. The fewer potential buyers there are, the more effective personal selling is, compared with advertising. For example, in Canada there are only a handful of manufacturers of household vacuum cleaners. Clearly, for a firm selling a component part for vacuum cleaners, personal selling would be the best way to reach this market.

Nature of the Product Several product attributes influence marketing communications strategy. The most important are:

- *Unit value.* A product with low unit value is usually relatively uncomplicated, involves little risk for the buyer, and must appeal to a mass market to survive. As a result, advertising would be the primary marketing communications tool. In contrast, high-unit-value products often are complex and expensive. These features suggest the need for personal selling. BMW dealers are being encouraged to have sales people get out of the showroom and call on prospects. By increasing the personal selling effort through techniques such as delivering cars to potential customers for test drives, BMW hopes to stimulate North American sales.
- *Degree of customization.* If a product must be adapted to the individual customer's needs, personal selling and service, or sometimes a technology-based equivalent, is necessary. Thus, you would expect to find an emphasis on personal selling for something like home remodelling or an expensive suit. However, the benefits of most standardized products can be effectively communicated in advertising. The increasing number of firms making use of advanced production techniques and information management have made it possible to customize some products for large markets without a great deal of personal service by relying on data warehousing and electronic communication.
- *Presale and postsale service.* Products that must be demonstrated, for which there are trade-ins, or that require frequent servicing to keep them in good working order lend themselves to personal selling, sometimes combined with Internet-based demonstrations and displays of product performance. Typical examples are riding lawn mowers, power boats, and personal computers. For example, Bombardier would want to show its Ski-doo and Sea-doo machines in action.

Stage of the Product Life Cycle Marketing communications strategies are influenced by a product's life-cycle stage. When a new product is introduced, prospective buyers must be informed about its existence and its benefits, and intermediaries must be convinced to carry it. Thus both advertising (to consumers) and personal selling (to intermediaries) are critical in a product's introductory stage. At introduction, a new product also may be something of a novelty, offering excellent opportunities for publicity. Later, if a product becomes successful, competition intensifies and more emphasis is placed on persuasive advertising. Table 18-1 shows how marketing communications strategies change as a product moves through its life cycle.

Funds Available Regardless of what may be the most desirable marketing communications mix, the amount of money available for marketing communications is the ultimate determinant of the mix. A business with ample funds can make more effective use of advertising than can a firm with limited financial resources. Small or regionally based companies are likely to rely on personal selling, dealer displays, or joint manufacturer–retailer promotions. For example, the Vancouver Grizzlies partner with corporate sponsors like Air Canada, BC Tel Mobility,

www.bmw.com

TABLE 18-1 Promotional Strategies for Different Product Life-Cycle Stages

Market Situation	Promotional Strategy
	Introduction Stage
Customers are not aware of the product's features, nor do they understand how it will benefit them.	Inform and educate potential customers that the product exists, how it might be used, and what want-satisfying benefits it provides. In this stage, a seller must stimulate *primary demand* — the demand for a type of product — as contrasted with *selective demand* — the demand for a particular brand. For example, producers had to sell consumers on the value of compact discs in general before it was feasible to promote a particular brand. Normally, heavy emphasis must be placed on personal selling. Exhibits at trade shows are also used extensively in the promotional mix. A trade show gives a new product broad exposure to many intermediaries. Manufacturers also rely heavily on personal selling to attract intermediaries to handle a new product.
	Growth Stage
Customers are aware of product's benefits. The product is selling well, and intermediaries want to handle it.	Stimulate selective (brand) demand as competition grows. Increase emphasis on advertising. Intermidiaries share more of the total promotional effort.
	Maturity Stage
Competition intensifies and sales level off.	Advertising is used more to persuade rather than only to provide information. Intense competition forces sellers to devote larger sums to advertising and thus contributes to the declining profits experienced in this stage.
	Decline Stage
Sales and profits are declining. New and better products are coming into the market.	All promotional efforts are cut back substantially. The focus becomes reminding remaining customers.

and IBM Canada to produce premiums like magnet game schedules, megaphones, and mouse pads, which add value for basketball fans and keep them coming back to the Grizzlies games.[5]

Lack of money may limit the options a firm has for its marketing communications effort. For example, television advertising can carry a particular message to far more people and at a lower cost per person than can most other media. Yet a firm may have to rely on less expensive media, such as Yellow Pages advertising, because it lacks the funds to take advantage of television's broad coverage.

Choosing a Push or a Pull Strategy

As we have seen, producers aim their marketing communications mix at both middlemen and end users. A communications program aimed primarily at intermediaries is called a **push strategy**, and a program directed primarily at end users is called a **pull strategy**. Figure 18-2 contrasts these two strategies.

When using a push strategy, a channel member directs its message primarily at the intermediaries who are the next link forward in the distribution channel. The product is "pushed" through the channel. Take the case of a hardware manufacturer like Stanley tools that sells its products to household consumers through wholesalers and retailers such as True Value and Home Hardware. The producer will promote heavily to wholesalers, which then also use a push strategy to retailers. In turn, the retailers promote to consumers. A push strategy usually involves a lot of personal selling and sales promotion, including contests for sales people and displays at trade

www.stanleyworks.com • www.truevalue.com • www.homehardwaredealers.com

www.loblaw.com
www.kodak.com
www.hallmark.com

FIGURE 18-2
Push and Pull Strategies of Marketing Communications

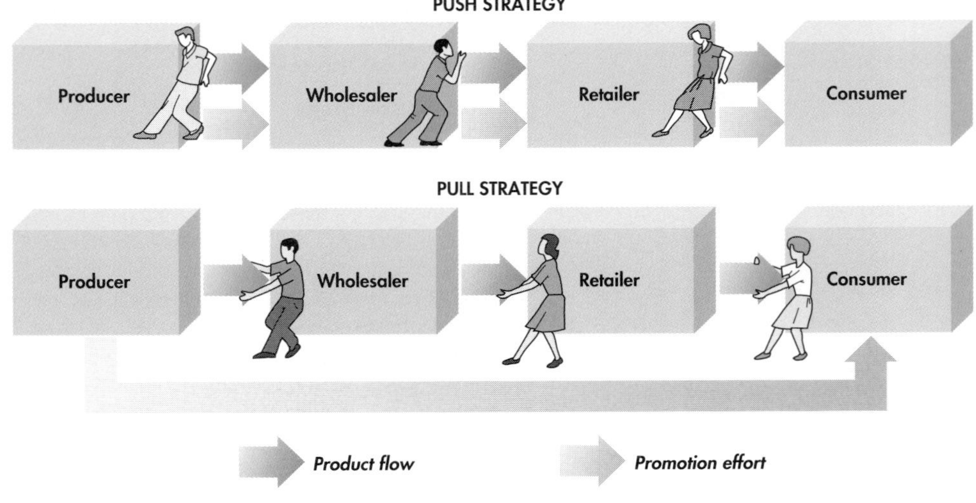

shows. This marketing communications strategy is appropriate for many manufacturers of business products, as well as for various consumer goods.

With a pull strategy, marketing communications messages are directed at end users — usually ultimate consumers. The intention is to motivate them to ask retailers for the product. The retailers, in turn, will request the product from wholesalers, and wholesalers will order it from the producer. In effect, marketing communications to consumers is designed to "pull" the product through the channel. This strategy relies on heavy advertising and various forms of consumer-directed sales promotion such as premiums, samples, or in-store demonstrations.

There is little incentive for retailers to provide shelf space for minor variations of existing brands unless they are confident that they will sell. So manufacturers of consumer packaged goods often use a pull strategy to get new products stocked on supermarket shelves. For example, Johnson & Johnson spent over $40 million on North American advertising and sales promotion to introduce Tylenol Extra Strength Headache Plus, a line extension. At this spending level, retailers had some assurance that the brand would sell.

WHAT MAKES A PRODUCT ADVERTISABLE?

Beyond the conditions mentioned in this section, advertising authority Neil Borden identified five product criteria that simply make certain products more "advertisable" than others. The criteria are:

- *Positive demand for the product.* Contrary to the opinion of many, advertising cannot successfully sell a product that people do not want. For example, despite the continuing efforts by an industry trade association, it is unlikely that advertising is going to produce a significant increase in the demand for Belgian endive, because some consumers dislike its bitter taste.
- *The presence of physical features that provide opportunities to differentiate the product.* A differentiated product gives the advertiser more things to say. For this reason, President's Choice cookies are easier to advertise than Sifto salt. Products that are not easy to differentiate by brand may still be advertised by a trade association. For example, beef and pork are products that are not usually purchased by brand name and that therefore are generally advertised by their respective trade associations as a means of stimulating primary demand.
- *Hidden qualities in the product.* This condition affords the seller opportunities for educating the market through advertising. Based on this criterion, a Kodak camera is simpler to advertise than are Hallmark greeting cards. Hallmark has embarked on a major television advertising campaign that does not feature individual card designs but is rather intended to create a certain image of Hallmark as the brand of choice in greeting cards.

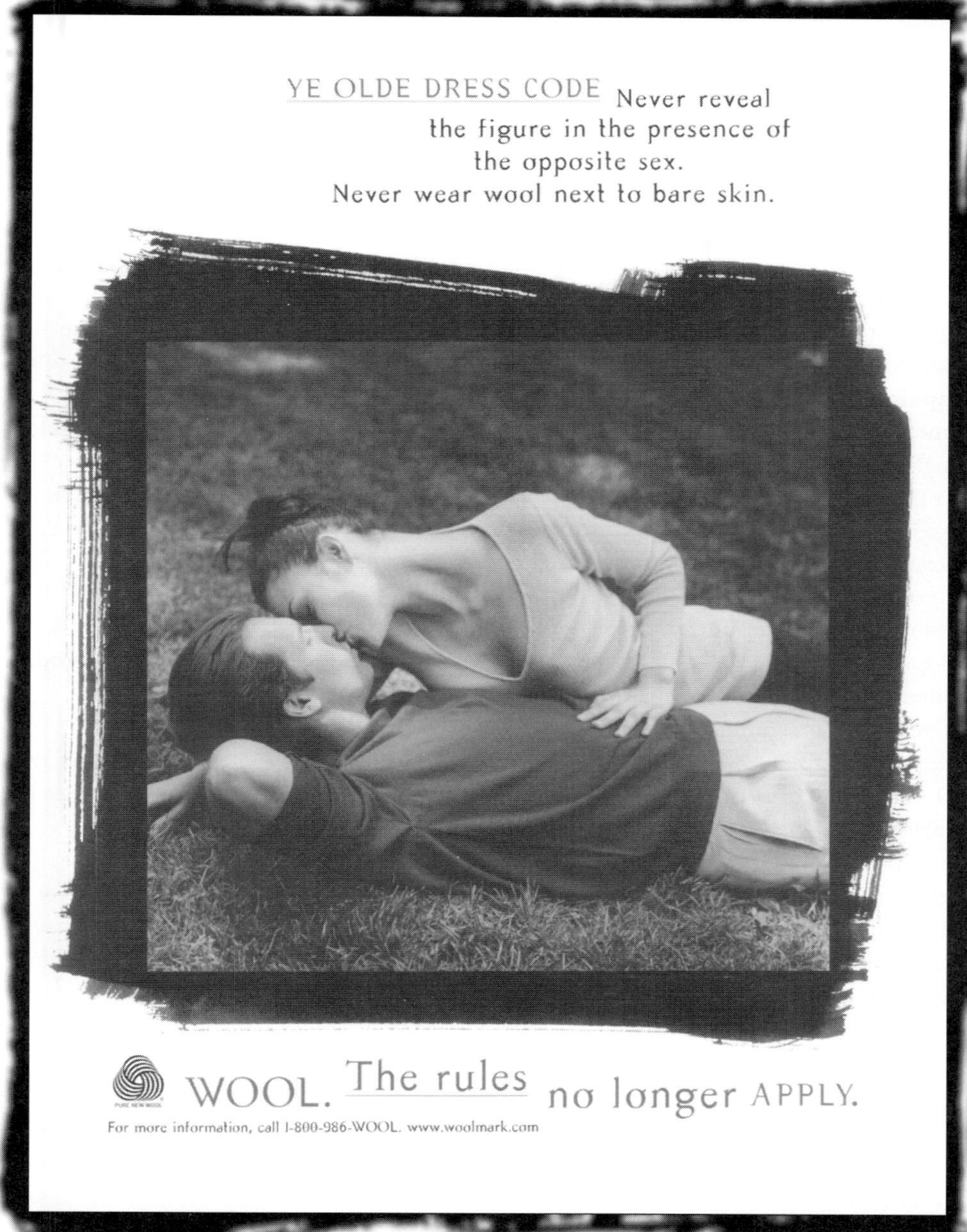

Emotional buying motives are matched by emotionally appealing imagery.

- *The existence of emotional buying motives.* Society has attached powerful emotional buying motives to some products. Buying action can be stimulated by appealing to these motives. It is easier to build an effective advertising campaign for Calvin Klein's Obsession perfume than for Sears' Craftsman socket wrenches.
- *Sufficient funds to support an advertising program adequately.* Gillette spent $100 million to launch the Sensor razor and $50 million to introduce a line of men's toiletries just in the North American market.

www.gillette.com

If all these criteria are met, there is an excellent opportunity to advertise. When a product or service meets some, but not all, of these conditions, advertising may be less effective.

THE CAMPAIGN CONCEPT

Having examined the factors that influence the marketing communications mix, we turn our attention to the concept of a communications campaign. In planning the marketing communications program for an organization, management should think in terms of creating a **campaign**, which is a co-ordinated series of communications activities and programs built around a single theme and designed to reach a specific goal in a defined period of time. In effect, a campaign is an exercise in strategic planning.

Although the term *campaign* is probably thought of most often in connection with advertising, it should embrace the entire marketing communications program. In developing a campaign, a company co-ordinates its advertising, personal selling, sales promotion, public relations, and publicity to accomplish an objective. For example, H. J. Heinz Co. of Canada set rapid sales growth as one of its objectives for 1993. To achieve the goal, Heinz cut its advertising budget by 43 percent and increased its sales promotion budget for activities such as coupons, contests, and in-store promotions by 100 percent, because sales promotion activity can provide a quicker increase in sales than advertising can. It was not until mid-1997 that Heinz changed its marketing communications approach to return to heavy brand advertising and reduced other promotions in order to strengthen the Heinz brand image for the longer run.[6] A company may conduct many types of marketing communications campaigns, and even run some concurrently. Depending on objectives and available funds, a firm may have local, regional, national, and international campaigns all running at the same time. Moreover, a firm may have one campaign aimed at consumers and another at wholesalers and retailers.

A marketing communications campaign begins with an objective. When it launched its new Buckley's Bedtime cough mixture, W.K. Buckley Ltd. set out to carve out a niche for the new product in the $24 million overnight-cold-remedies category, one dominated by the Procter & Gamble product Vick's Nyquil. In going head-to-head with Nyquil, Buckley had a clear strategy in mind. The new product was consistent with other Buckley cough remedies in that it is sugar-free and alcohol-free. It is targeted at adults and children older than twelve. And the new product is "symptom-focused," in that it is intended to work mainly on night-time coughs, while the Vick's product treats a variety of cold symptoms.

A television advertising campaign for the new Buckley's Bedtime was timed to begin in October, to coincide with the beginning of the cold and flu season. As with previous, award-winning Buckley's ads, the new product was pitched by Frank Buckley, the company's president, with lines like "The medicine may cause drowsiness. The taste may cause nightmares." The television advertising was supported with in-store displays, and an in-store sales promotion — a contest offering winners a Buckley's Winter Survival Kit; a supply of Buckley's product to get them through the winter season.[7]

With the **theme** established, each of the components of the **marketing communications mix** must be carefully co-ordinated to communicate the desired message. This means that:

- The advertising program consists of a series of related, well-timed, carefully placed ads that reinforce personal selling and sales promotion efforts.
- The personal selling effort is co-ordinated with the advertising program. The sales people must be fully informed about the advertising part of the campaign — the theme, the media used, and the schedule for the appearance of ads. The sales force should be prepared to explain and demonstrate the product benefits stressed in the ads. The sales people also should transmit the marketing communications message to middlemen so that they can take part in the campaign.
- The sales promotion devices, such as point-of-purchase display materials, are co-ordinated with other aspects of the campaign. New display materials must be prepared for each campaign. They should reflect the ads and appeals used in the current campaign to maximize the campaign's impact at the point of sale.

www.heinz.ca

- Publicity and public relations efforts are scheduled to coincide with the other mix components and to emphasize the same theme.

The last step in a campaign is to evaluate the results. The outcome is compared with the objective to determine if the marketing communications effort was successful. Unfortunately, in evaluating marketing communications, it is impossible to separate precisely the effects caused by a campaign from what would have occurred without it. As a result, it is impossible to determine exactly the value of a campaign. However, by comparing the cost of a campaign with the results, a firm can decide if the campaign was generally a success or a failure and identify ways of improving future efforts.

THE MARKETING COMMUNICATIONS BUDGET

Establishing marketing communications budgets is extremely challenging because management generally lacks reliable standards for determining how much to spend altogether on advertising or personal selling and determining how much of the total budget to allocate to each element of the marketing communications mix. A firm may have the alternative of adding seven sales people or increasing its trade show budget by $200,000 a year, but it cannot determine precisely what increase in sales or profits to expect from either expenditure. As a result, rather than one generally accepted approach to setting budgets, there are four common **marketing communications budgeting methods**: percentage of sales, all available funds, following the competition, and budgeting by task or objective. These methods are frequently discussed in connection with the advertising budget, but they may be applied to any communications activity as well as to determine the total marketing communications budget.

Percentage of Sales

The marketing communications budget may be related in some way to company income, as a percentage of either past or anticipated sales. A common approach for determining the sales base is to compute an average of the previous year's actual sales and expected sales for the coming year. Some businesses prefer to budget a fixed amount of money per unit of past or expected future sales. Manufacturers of products with a high unit value and a low rate of turnover (automobiles or appliances, for example) frequently use the *per unit* approach to setting budgets.

Because the percentage-of-sales method is simple to calculate, it is probably the most widely used budgeting method. Moreover, it sets the cost of marketing communications in relation to sales income, making it a variable rather than a fixed expense.

There are two things you need to realize about basing marketing communications expenditures on past sales. First, management is effectively making marketing communications a *result* of sales when, in fact, it is a *cause* of sales. Second, a percentage of past sales method reduces marketing communications expenditures when sales are declining — just when advertising and other forms of communications usually are most needed.

All Available Funds

A new company or a firm introducing a new product or service frequently ploughs all available funds into its marketing communications program. The objective is to build sales and market share as rapidly as possible during those early, critical years. After a time, management generally finds it necessary to invest in other things, such as new equipment or expanded production capacity, so the method of setting the marketing communications budget is changed.

Follow Competition

A weak method of determining the marketing communications budget, but one that is used occasionally, is to match the marketing communications expenditures of competitors or to spend in proportion to market share. Sometimes only one competitor is followed. In other cases, if management has access to industry average expenditures on marketing communications through a trade association, these become company benchmarks.

There are at least two problems with this approach. First, the firm's competitors may be just as much in the dark regarding how to set a marketing

MARKETING AT WORK FILE 18-2

THE BLUE MARKETING COMMUNICATIONS WARS OF SUMMER

It's a furious battle as Labatt pushes to reverse the market share decline of its leading brand, Labatt Blue. Analysts believe that Blue's share had moved from 18 percent to 15 percent in Ontario lately. It was still Canada's top-selling brand, with almost 50 percent of beer drinkers selecting it, but something had to be done, and the marketing manager for Blue felt that since most consumers already knew about the brand and many try it on a regular basis, "You say, what can you do to strengthen the relationship without going back to the same old, same old?"

Summer promotions have been standard beer marketing practice since there was summer. Blue's marketing manager says, "You have to do something to tangibly connect with people as opposed to just reaching them through electronic media or even print... I drive by the beer, I see the beer on TV, but does the brand actually interact with me in my life? When it does, it strengthens the brewer's relationship with consumers."

The Labatt Blue marketing team was assembled: ad agency Ammirati Puris Lintas; Marketing and Promotions Group; Echo Advertising and Promotion; and the internal customer marketing group. They set out to refresh their knowledge of the consumer; they spent time in bars, on Labatt's Web site talking to beer drinkers, and doing formal research through focus groups. The promotional program for Ontario was a series of events designed to make first-hand contact with Ontario drinkers and give them something to do during the hot, lazy, beer-drinking days of summer. The events were focused to be street level rather than the huge, fantasy types of marketing communications that rival Molson had launched.

The centrepiece of True Blue Summer was "Blue Jays Blue Hair Day." On a sunny Sunday, Labatt offered a free ticket to that day's Toronto Blue Jays game to those over eighteen who showed up and agreed to have their hair dyed blue. As a result, 1,500 blue-haired fans were put into one section of the stands — where, it so happens, TV cameras could provide some publicity as part of the baseball broadcast.

A "Blue Bus Escape" was run that ferried bar goers away to parties at unspecified destinations over three Fridays — bars were visited, patrons were given ninety seconds to decide whether or not to participate, and volunteers boarded the bus and were whisked off to mysterious northern destinations. And there was the Blue Bar Bonanza, which gave customers who filled out a ballot in over one thousand bars and restaurants across the province a chance to split $100,000. Patrons at the Dalby House in Elora were winners. And the Blue Urban Portage — twenty teams comprised of twenty members each, customers, licensee staff, Labatt staff, and other company staff — carried canoes through Toronto's downtown core, raising money for Tree Canada. And there was...the Blue Barge Bash.

The events not only attracted a good deal of consumer participation but also a surprising amount of media coverage — stories, front-page photos, TV and radio coverage. At the same time these events were taking place, there were transit, radio, and poster ads and the Blue hot air balloon covering southern Ontario.

The marketing communications ran for five weeks. It was six months in the planning, 60,000 people were touched directly, and 4,000 took part in events. Market share increased significantly...sorry, numbers were not made available.

Source: Adapted from Lara Mills, "Those Crazy Days of Summer," *Marketing*, January 27, 1997, p. 11.

communications budget. Second, a company's goals may be quite different from those of its competitors because of differences in the marketing strategies being followed.

www.labatt.com

Task or Objective

The best approach for establishing the marketing communications budget is to determine the tasks or objectives the communications program must accomplish and then decide what they will cost. The task method forces management to define realistically the goals of its marketing communications program.

Sometimes this is called the buildup method because of the way it is constructed. For example, a company may decide to enter a new geographic market. Management determines this venture will require ten additional sales people. The compensation and expenses of these people will cost a total of $520,000 per year. Salary for an additional sales supervisor and expenses for an extra office and administrative needs will cost $70,000. Thus in the personal selling component of the marketing communications mix, an extra $590,000 must be budgeted. Similar estimates can be made for the anticipated costs of advertising, sales promotion, and other communications tools. The budget is built up by adding up the costs of the individual marketing communications tasks needed to reach the goal of entering a new territory.

REGULATION OF MARKETING COMMUNICATIONS ACTIVITIES

Because the primary objective of marketing communications is to sell something by communicating with a market, marketing communications activities attract attention. Consequently, abuses by individual firms are easily and quickly noted by the public. This situation in turn soon leads to (1) public demand for correction of the abuses, (2) assurances that they will not be repeated, and (3) general restraints on marketing communications activities. To answer public demand, laws and regulations have been enacted by the federal government and by most provincial governments. In addition, many private business organizations have established voluntary codes of advertising standards to guide their own marketing communications activities. In addition, the advertising industry itself, through the Advertising Advisory Board and its Advertising Standards Councils, does a considerable amount of self-regulation.

The Federal Role

A number of departments of the federal government administer legislation aimed at controlling various aspects of marketing communications, particularly advertising. The **Broadcasting Act** established the Canadian Radio-television and Telecommunications Commission (CRTC) in 1968 and provided for sweeping powers of advertising regulation. Under section 16 of the Act, the CRTC may make regulations concerning the character of broadcast advertising and the amount of time that may be devoted to it. While the potential for substantial control exists, the CRTC does not in reality approve each radio and television commercial. What it has done is delegate authority in certain fields to other agencies such as the Health Protection Branch of Health Canada and the Combines Investigation Branch of Industry Canada.

The Health Protection Branch deals with advertising in the fields of drugs, cosmetics, and devices (officialese for birth-control products), and it has sweeping powers to limit, control, rewrite, or ban certain communications for the products under its authority. The authority itself is embodied in such Acts, and regulations associated with them, as the Health and Welfare Department Act, the Proprietary or Patent Medicine Act, the Food and Drug Act, the Criminal Code of Canada, and the Broadcasting Act. The various Acts and regulations result in general types of prohibition aimed at preventing the treatment, processing, packaging, labelling, advertising, and selling of foods, drugs, and devices in such a manner as to mislead or deceive, or even to be likely to create an erroneous impression concerning the nature of the products.

The Health Protection Branch also prohibits the advertising of whole classes of drugs. It has developed a list of diseases or conditions for which a cure may not be advertised under any circumstances. This prohibition stands even if a professionally accepted cure exists. The logic for the prohibition of advertising, in spite of the existence of a cure, is that the Health Protection Branch does not wish members of the general public to engage in self-diagnosis of the condition that can be treated.

By virtue of the powers delegated to it by the CRTC, the Health Protection Branch has absolute

www.crtc.gc.ca

control over radio and television advertisements for the products under its jurisdiction. All such advertisements must be submitted to it at least fifteen days prior to airing, and no radio or television station can air an ad without its having been approved by the branch and, thereby, the CRTC. In practical terms, the Health Protection Branch, even though an appeal route to the CRTC is available, has complete authority and advertisers have no recourse of any consequence.

In contrast to the delegated review powers the Health Protection Branch has over advertisements using the broadcast media, its position with reference to the print media is weak. Its formal control is over alleged Food and Drug violations, which must be prosecuted in court. Given the lack of jurisprudence in this area, the branch is loath to go to court in case it loses and thus sets a precedent or in case its regulations (many of which have not been tested in court) are found to be illegal. What the branch does is advise advertisers of its opinion of advertisements that are prepared for the print media. This opinion is not a ruling, and ads submitted, as well as those that are not, are still subject to the regulations for which the branch has responsibility. This does not mean that the branch does not monitor the print media. Newspapers and magazines are sampled and advertisements examined.

Industry Canada has substantial and major responsibility in the area of regulating marketing communications. The Bureau of Competition Policy of Industry Canada carries the major burden of marketing communications regulation. The Acts administered include: (1) the Hazardous Products Act (concerning poisonous compounds for household use), (2) the Precious Metals Marketing Act (i.e., definitions of sterling and carat weight), (3) the Trade Marks Act, (4) the Consumer Packaging and Labelling Act, and of greatest significance, (5) the **Competition Act**. Within the Competition Act, a number of sections pertain directly to the regulation of advertising and marketing communications activities. Section 35, for example, requires that manufacturers or wholesalers who offer marketing communications allowances to retailers must offer such allowances on proportionate terms to all competing purchasers. Section 36 of the Act regulates misleading advertising in general, while section 37 pertains specifically to "bait and switch" advertising.[8]

Section 36 of the Competition Act makes it illegal for an advertiser to make any false or misleading statement to the public in advertising or marketing communications materials or with respect to warranties. This section also regulates the use of false statements regarding the expected performance or length of life of a product and the use of testimonials in advertising. Section 36.2 of the Act regulates the use of "double ticketing" in retail selling and requires that, where a retailer promotes a product at two different prices or where two prices appear on a product or at the point of sale, the retailer must sell the product at the lower of the prices. Businesses or individuals who are convicted of violating section 36 are subject to fines as large as $25,000 or to imprisonment for up to one year.

Paragraph 36(1)(d) of the Competition Act regulates "sale" advertising and would apply particularly to retail advertisers. Section 37 requires that an advertiser who promotes a product at a "sale" price have sufficient quantities of the product on hand to satisfy reasonable market demand. Section 37.1 prohibits an advertiser from selling a "sale" item at a price higher than the advertised "sale" price. Finally, section 37.2 regulates the conduct of contests, lotteries, and games of chance. This section requires that advertisers who promote such contests disclose the number and value of prizes and the areas in which prizes are to be distributed, and further requires that prizes be distributed on a basis of skill or on a basis of random selection.

The provisions of the Competition Act relating to misleading advertising do not apply to publishers and broadcasters who actually distribute the advertising in question to the general public, provided that these publishers have accepted the contents of the advertising in good faith. In essence, this means that a newspaper cannot be prosecuted for misleading advertising if it accepted the advertising on the assumption that its contents were not misleading. Although no newspaper can be prosecuted for misleading advertising if it accepted the advertising in good faith, there is still some question concerning whether media production departments and advertising agencies, which actually participate with the

http://info.ic.gc.ca

advertiser in the production of misleading advertising, might not in the future be considered jointly responsible with the advertiser for the contents of the offending advertisement. This is a question with which Canadian courts may deal in the future.

The Provincial Role

In each of the provinces, a considerable variety of legislation exists that is aimed at controlling various marketing communications practices. For instance, in Ontario, various degrees of control are exercised by the Liquor Control Board of Ontario, the Ontario Board of Film Censors, the Ontario Superintendent of Insurance, the Ontario Human Rights Commission, the Ontario Securities Commission, the Ontario Police Commission, the Ontario Racing Commission, various ministries of the Ontario government responsible for financial, commercial, consumer, and transportation functions and services, and more. Most of the provinces have similar sets of legislation, regulatory bodies, and provincial departments. Each of the provinces, for example, regulates various aspects of the promotion of alcoholic beverages.[9] While much of the federal regulation must in the end result in argument and prosecution in a courtroom, the provincial machinery would appear to be much more flexible and potentially regulatory in nature, and if pursued, may have a more substantial effect on undesirable practices.

The powers of provincial governments in relation to the regulation of misleading advertising have been increased considerably in recent years. A number of provinces have legislation in place dealing with unfair and unconscionable trade practices. The "trade practices" Acts of British Columbia, Alberta, and Ontario, for example, contain "shopping lists" of practices that are made illegal by these Acts. In reality, these pieces of legislation write into law practices that have been considered illegal by federal prosecutors for a number of years. Relating to advertising, these Acts prohibit such practices as advertising a product as new when it is in fact used; advertising that fails to state a material fact, thereby deceiving the consumer; and advertising that gives greater prominence to low down payments or monthly payments rather than to the actual price of the product. The Alberta Unfair Trade Practices Act also contains a provision for corrective advertising. This provision means that a court, upon convicting an advertiser for misleading advertising, can order that advertiser to devote some or all of its advertising for a certain period to informing customers that the advertiser had been advertising falsely in the past and to correcting the misleading information that had been communicated in the offending advertisements.

The Province of Quebec has within its Consumer Protection Act a section that regulates advertising directed at children. This section forbids the use of exaggeration, endorsements, cartoon characters, and statements that urge children to buy. Quebec's Official Language Act also contains a number of sections that govern the use of French and English in advertising in that province.

Regulation by Private Organizations

Several kinds of private organizations also exert considerable control over the marketing communications practices of businesses. Magazines, newspapers, and radio and television stations regularly refuse to accept advertisements that they feel are false, misleading, or generally in bad taste, and in so doing they are being "reasonable" in the ordinary course of doing business. Some trade associations have established a "code of ethics" that includes points pertaining to sales-force and advertising activities. Some trade associations regularly censor advertising appearing in their trade or professional journals. Better Business Bureaus located in major cities across the country are working to control some very difficult situations. The Advertising Advisory Board administers the Canadian Code of Advertising Standards, a number of other advertising codes, including the Broadcast Code for Advertising to Children (on behalf of the Canadian Association of Broadcasters), and a code regulating the advertising of over-the-counter drugs, which was developed in co-operation with the Proprietary Association and Health Canada.

Summary

Marketing communications, the fourth component of a company's total marketing mix, is essential in modern marketing. The three primary methods of marketing communications are personal selling, advertising, and sales promotion. Other forms include public relations and publicity.

Fundamentally, the marketing communication process consists of a source sending a message through a channel to a receiver. The success of communication depends on how well the message is encoded, how easily and clearly it can be decoded, and whether any noise interferes with its transmission. Feedback, the response created by a message, is a measure of how effective communication has been.

The purposes of marketing communications are to inform, persuade, and remind customers. That means being able to make a product, service or organization attractive to potential customers at any given price. It also means that marketing communications aims to increase the attractiveness of a product or service by providing the customer with evidence that it is different from the competition, thereby offering a number of nonprice reasons for buying.

Marketing communications must be integrated into a firm's strategic planning because effective execution requires that all elements of the marketing mix — product, price, distribution, and marketing communications — be co-ordinated. When deciding on the communications mix (the combination of advertising, personal selling, and other marketing communications tools), management should consider: (1) the nature of the market, including the type of customer, the prospect's readiness to buy, and the geographic scope of the market; (2) the nature of the product or service, including unit value, the degree of customization required, and the amount of presale and postsale service; (3) the stage of the life cycle of the product or service; and (4) the funds available for all forms of marketing communications.

A basic decision is how much marketing communications effort should be focused on intermediaries and how much should be directed to end users. The options are a push strategy, which involves concentrating marketing communications efforts on the next link forward in the distribution channel, and a pull strategy, in which marketing communications is focused primarily on the final buyer.

A marketing communications campaign is a co-ordinated series of efforts built around a single theme and designed to reach a predetermined goal. The key to a successful campaign is to carefully plan and co-ordinate advertising, sales promotion, personal selling, public relations, and publicity.

Because the effects of communications are unpredictable, it is difficult to set a dollar figure for the total marketing communications budget. The most common method is to set the budget as a percentage of past or anticipated sales. A better approach is to establish the communications objectives and then estimate how much it will cost to achieve them.

As a result of criticism and concern regarding the use of advertising and marketing communications techniques, the federal government has enacted legislation that regulates marketing communications. The main federal laws are the Competition Act and the Broadcasting Act. Industry Canada and the Canadian Radio-television and Telecommunications Commission are charged with administering the legislation in this area. Marketing communications practices are also regulated at the provincial level through trade practices legislation, through voluntary codes of businesses and trade associations, and by the advertising industry itself.

Key Terms and Concepts

Marketing communications (448)
Personal selling (448)
Advertising (448)
Sales promotion (449)
Public relations (449)
Publicity (449)
Communication (449)
Encoding (449)
Decoding (449)
Response (449)
Feedback (449)
Noise (449)
Push strategy (457)
Pull strategy (457)
Campaign (460)

Campaign theme (460)
Marketing communications mix (460)
Marketing communications budgeting methods (461)
Broadcasting Act (463)
Competition Act (464)
Provincial role in regulating marketing communications (465)
Regulation by industry itself (466)

Questions and Problems

1. Describe and explain the components of the marketing communications process in the following situations:
   a. A college student trying to convince her parents to buy her a used car.
   b. A sales person trying to sell a car to a college student.
2. Explain how the nature of the market affects the marketing communications mix for the following products:
   a. Auto insurance.
   b. Golf balls.
   c. Plywood.
   d. Aircraft maintenance.
   e. Compact discs.
   f. Computers used as servers.
3. Describe how classifying consumer goods as convenience, shopping, or specialty goods helps determine the best marketing communications mix.
4. Evaluate each of the following products with respect to the criteria for advertisability. Assume that sufficient funds are available.
   a. Automobile tires.
   b. Calvin Klein fragrances.
   c. Light bulbs.
   d. Ten-minute oil changes.
   e. College or university education.
   f. Luggage.
5. Explain whether personal selling is likely to be the main ingredient in the marketing communications mix for each of the following products:
   a. Chequing accounts.
   b. Home swimming pools.
   c. Liquid laundry detergent.
   d. Large order of fries at McDonald's.
6. Explain whether retailer trade promotion efforts should be stressed in the marketing communications mix for the following:
   a. Levi's jeans.
   b. Sunkist oranges.
   c. Canada Saving Bonds.
   d. Visa card.
7. Identify the central idea — the theme — in three current marketing communications campaigns.
8. Assume you are marketing a liquid that removes creosote (and the danger of fire) from chimneys used for wood-burning stoves. Briefly describe the roles you would assign to advertising, personal selling, sales promotion, and publicity in your marketing communications campaign.
9. Do you think we need additional legislation to regulate advertising? To regulate personal selling? If so, explain what you would recommend.

Hands-On Marketing

1. An advertisement should have a particular objective that should be apparent to a careful observer. For each of the following marketing communications objectives, find an example of a print ad:
   a. Primarily designed to inform.
   b. Primarily designed to persuade.
   c. Primarily designed to remind.
2. A campaign is a co-ordinated series of marketing communications efforts built around a single theme and designed to reach a predetermined goal. A campaign often includes advertising, sales promotion, personal selling, public relations, and publicity. For an important event at your school (such as homecoming, recruiting new students, fund raising), describe the marketing communications tools used in the campaign and evaluate their appropriateness based on the criteria in the chapter for designing a marketing communications mix.

CHAPTER 19 GOALS

This chapter examines personal selling, directing a sales force, and evaluating a sales person's performance. After studying this chapter, you should have an understanding of:

- The part that personal selling plays in our economy and in an organization's marketing program.
- The variety of personal selling jobs.
- The changing patterns in personal selling.
- The major tasks in staffing and operating a sales force.
- Key issues in evaluating a sales person's performance.

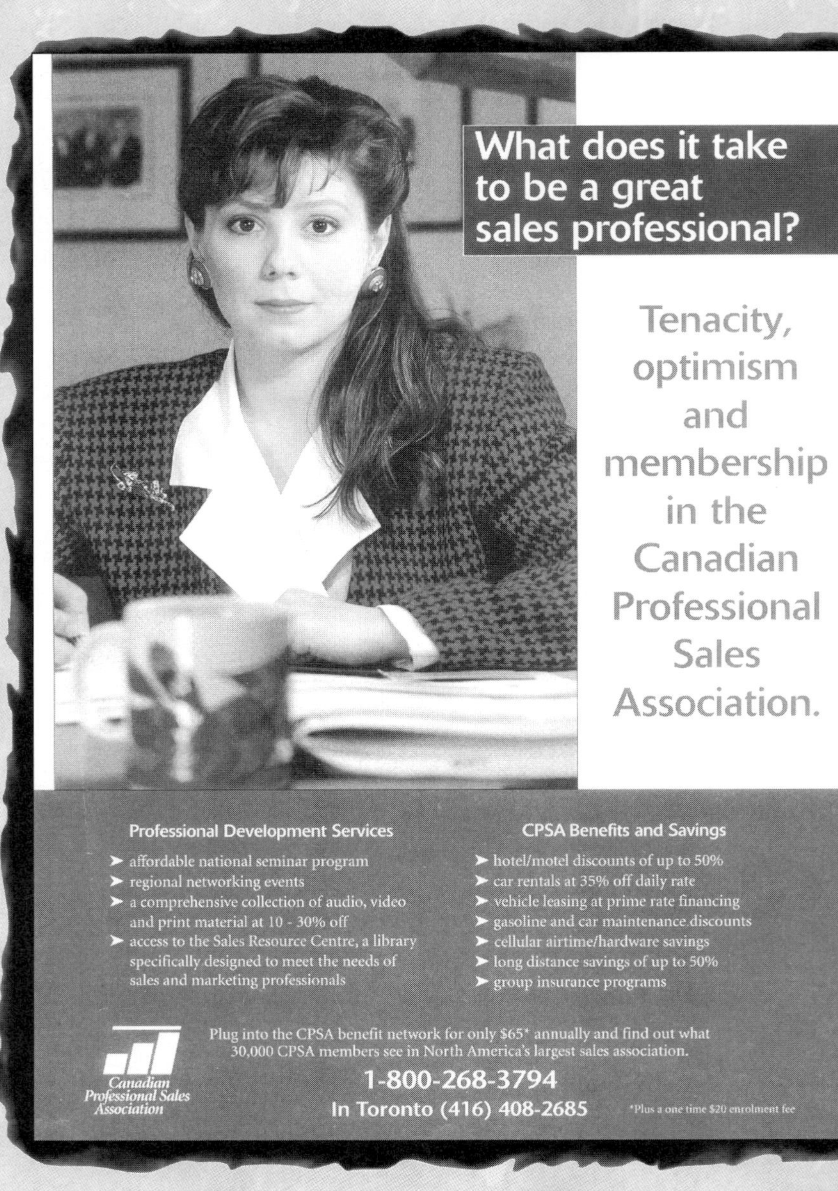

Chapter Nineteen

Management of Personal Selling

WHATEVER IT TAKES

What happens when somebody is selling? Let's say you're an advertising sales representative. You're not in downtown Edmonton, Toronto, or Winnipeg; you're not representing the *Edmonton Sun*, the *Toronto Star* or the *Winnipeg Free Press*; and your clients are not major department stores or corporate headquarters or provincial trade associations. No, you are Sharon Riley, and you're a sales rep for the Montague *Eastern Graphic*, in Montague, Prince Edward Island. Or you're Bernadette Jordan, a sales rep for three community weeklies owned by Lighthouse Publishing of Bridgewater, Nova Scotia.

When Sharon Riley dresses for work, she puts on a skirt, a blazer, and her three-inch heels — pretty straightforward, except that her clients could not only be in a shop or office building in Montague but also in a pig barn in the surrounding countryside or on a wharf at the equally near seaside. Sharon jokes about the range of accounts and the question of how to present "self" so as to use the "perceived similarity principle" to help clients feel comfortable with her. "I've thought of dressing down...but whenever I do, they ask me why I'm not working today." Riley's actions and comments reflect the nature of sales work at Canada's weekly newspapers from Port Hardy, British Columbia to Carbonear, Newfoundland. She is likely to be referred to by customers as the "ad girl," but "client sales and marketing consultant" would be more accurate. And she is as much educator, confidant, and friend as she is a sales person.

Being able to do a good job for clients also means understanding their business and even getting involved in it. For Riley, more than once it meant helping out when help was needed. "They told me, 'You want to sell something to us today, you'll have to help us find the time.' So I slapped on an apron and washed up the backlog of dishes in the diner's sink." She got the ad, and the small cafe is now a regular client.

Bernadette Jordan, who represents three weeklies and works in southern Nova Scotia, cites trust as the most important factor in the client–sales person relationship. "If they can't confide in me about how their children are doing in school, how can they trust me with the important financial details of their business?" And, of course, if you don't know the important details of their business, how can you really help them? "Most of my clients have never heard of Geographic Information Systems, but they sure want to know how I can bring more shoppers in their front door." That has a lot more to do with knowing how many boats are still fishing from the Lunenberg waterfront than any national buying trend. If Jordan doesn't meet her clients' expectations just once, they won't be interested in seeing her again.

Ad reps such as Riley and Jordan are constantly participating in training programs; they attend seminars and conventions sponsored by the Atlantic Community Newspapers Association. It's the information picked up from colleagues at "Ideas Exchanges" held at conferences that excites Jordan. "I sit there thinking, 'That's the perfect campaign for so and so.' I come home bursting with ideas, and that's good for my clients."

Remember, these people are involved, interested, trustworthy, persevering, helpful, and more. And they are paid on commission — they make money only when they are out there doing their jobs and clients can tell that they have been helped.[1]

NATURE OF PERSONAL SELLING

The goal of all marketing efforts is to increase profitable sales by offering want-satisfaction to consumers over the long run. Personal selling is by far the major communications method used to reach this goal. The number of people employed in advertising is a small fraction of the number employed in personal selling. In many companies, personal selling is the largest single operating expense, often equalling 8 to 15 percent of sales. In contrast, advertising costs average 1 to 3 percent of sales.

In Chapter 18 we discussed four factors that influence an organization's marketing communications mix — the market, the product, the product's life-cycle stage, and the budget available for promotion. Referring to those four factors, personal selling is likely to carry the bulk of the marketing communications load when:

- The market is concentrated either geographically or in a few industries, or in a few large customers.
- The product has a high unit value, is quite technical in nature, or requires a demonstration.
- The product must be fitted to an individual customer's need, as in the case of securities or insurance.
- The sale involves a trade-in.
- The product is in the introductory stage of its life cycle.
- The organization does not have enough money for an adequate advertising campaign.

Merits of Personal Selling

Personal selling is the individual, personal communication of information, in contrast to the impersonal communication of advertising, sales promotion, and other marketing communications tools. This means that personal selling can be more flexible than these other tools. Sales people can tailor their presentations to fit the needs and behaviour of individual customers. They can see their customers' reaction to a particular sales approach and make adjustments on the spot.

Also, personal selling usually can be focused or pinpointed on prospective customers, thus minimizing wasted effort. In contrast, much of the cost of advertising is spent on sending messages to people who would not consider themselves to be real prospects.

Another advantage of personal selling is that its goal is to make a sale. Other forms of promotion are designed to move a prospect closer to a sale. Advertising can attract attention, provide information, and arouse desire, but seldom does it stimulate buying action or complete the transfer of ownership from seller to buyer.

On the other hand, personal selling is costly. Even though personal selling can minimize wasted effort, the cost of developing and operating a sales force is high. Another disadvantage is that a company often is unable to attract the quality of sales people needed to do the job. At the retail level, many firms have abandoned their sales staff on the floor and have shifted to self-service selling for this very reason.

Scope of Personal Selling

There are two kinds of personal selling, as shown in Figure 19-1. In one, the customers come to the sales people. Sometimes called **inside selling**, it primarily involves retail-store selling. In this kind of selling, we also include the thousands of employees who work in call centres across the country and who take orders over the telephone. This, too, is retail selling because it involves sales to end consumers. By far, most sales people in Canada fall into this first category.

The other kind of personal selling, known as outside sales, involves sales people going to the customers. They make contact by mail, telephone, e-mail, or field selling. In these last cases, they sell in person at a customer's place of business or home. So-called "outbound" telephone sales calls also fall into this category.

Outside sales forces usually represent producers or wholesaling intermediaries, selling to business users and not to household consumers. However, in our definition of an outside sales force we also include (1) producers who sell directly to household consumers — for example, insurance companies such as Great-West Life, and in-home sellers such as Avon Products and Mary Kay Cosmetics; (2) representatives of retail organizations such as those from home heating, furniture and decorating, and insulation retailers; and (3) outside sales forces for not-for-profit organizations — for example, charity fund-raisers and workers for political candidates.

Today, some companies have a sales force that goes to the customers, but not in person. Instead, these reps are "going to the customers" by means of telephone, computer, and fax machines. In effect, some outside selling is becoming electronic, and the term **telemarketing** describes such communications systems. Many firms have used telephone selling for decades, and some sales reps regularly contact customers by mail or phone. What is different about telemarketing is the new telecommunications equipment used in "going to the customer." In addition, firms use telemarketing in a sales support function.

The insurance industry is one that has adopted a telemarketing approach to reaching clients in recent years. While many purchasers of various forms of insurance still want face-to-face service, others are quire accepting of the fact that they can buy home and auto insurance, and even life insurance, over the telephone. David Thibaudeau, president of the Life Underwriters Association of Canada, says that the more complex or personal the insurance product, the more likely the client will want to speak with someone in person.[2]

Telemarketing is becoming quite sophisticated as a result of the application of advanced information technology. Not only do telemarketing departments and companies today operate from advanced databases that allow the caller to tailor the sales presentation to the profile of the customer, but the technology ensures that the telemarketing employee is as informed as possible about the customer's history and characteristics. In the interest of building a closer relationship between the telemarketing employee and the customers he or she is calling, some companies have installed sophisticated caller-recognition software that identifies the telephone number of the inbound caller and routes the call to that employee who dealt with the customer last. When the employee picks up the call, the customer's detailed file and history are already on his or her computer screen.

Nature of Sales Jobs

The sales job of today is quite different from the stereotype of the past. The images of high pressure, false friendship, and glibness are largely outdated. Even the stereotype of the fast-talking salesman is outdated, as today we have women entering professional selling in greater numbers.

The Professional Sales Person A new type of sales rep is emerging: the **professional sales person**. Today these sales people are managers of a market

www.cphotels.ca
www.avon.com
www.aero.bombardier.com

FIGURE 19-1
Scope of Personal Selling

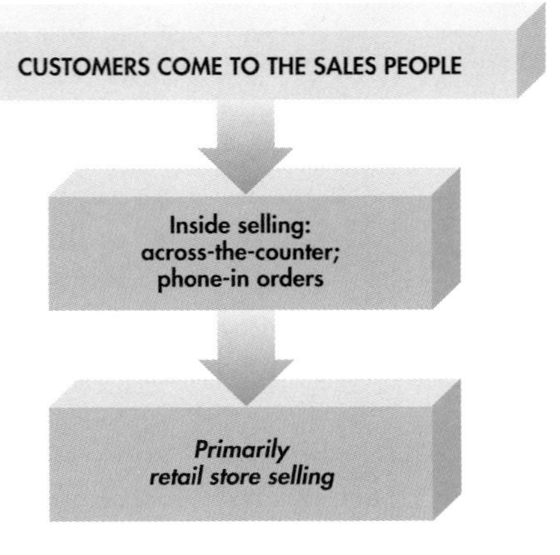

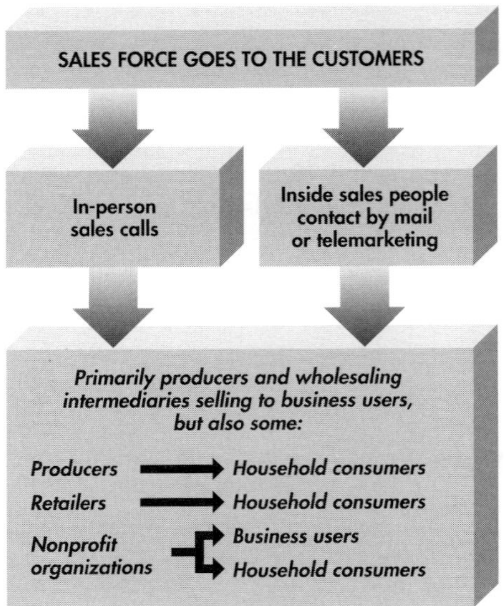

area — their territories. They engage in a total selling job — servicing their customers, building goodwill, selling their products, and training their customers' sales people. Today's reps act as a mirror of the market by relaying market information back to the firm. They organize much of their own time and effort. They often take part in recruiting new sales people, sales planning in their territories, and other managerial activities. *Sales and Marketing Management Magazine*, in its surveys among sales executives and customers concerning the factors that are considered in selecting good sales employees, point to the following criteria:[3]

- *Accuracy:* Do the sales people take care of details?
- *Availability:* Are the sales people responsive to customers' requests?
- *Credibility:* Do customers view the sales people as important resources?
- *Partnership:* Are the sales people sought out for advice?
- *Trust:* Are customers confident that the sales people will keep their word?
- *Discovery:* Do the sales people offer ideas that improve customers' businesses?

Wide Variety of Sales Jobs The types of selling jobs and the activities involved in them cover a wide range. Consider the job of a Humpty Dumpty potato chips driver–sales person who calls routinely on a group of retail stores. That job is in completely different from that of the IBM sales consultant who sells a computer system for managing hotel reservations to major chain like CP Hotels. Similarly, a sales rep for Avon selling door to door in Japan or China has a job only remotely related to that of a Challenger Aircraft sales engineer who leads the team that sells executive-type aircraft to large corporations around the world.

One way to classify sales jobs is on the basis of the creative selling skills required, from the simple to the complex. The classification that follows is adapted from one developed years ago by Robert McMurry, a noted industrial psychologist.

1. **Driver–sales person.** In this job the sales person primarily delivers the product — for example, soft drinks or fuel oil. The selling responsibilities are secondary; few of these people originate sales; they take and fill orders.
2. **Inside order taker.** This is a position in which the sales person takes orders at the seller's place of business — for example, a retail clerk standing behind the counter at an Eaton's store or a telephone representative at a catalogue retailer. Most customers have already decided to buy, and the sales person's job is to serve them efficiently.
3. **Outside order taker.** In this position, the sales person goes to the customer in the field and accepts an order. An example is a sales representative for

www.humptydumpty.com

An effective inside order taker can adjust to a customer's reactions and can build good customer relations.

Para Paints who calls on a building supplies store. The majority of sales made by outside order takers are repeat orders to established customers, although these sales people occasionally do introduce new products to customers.

4. **Missionary sales person.** This types of sales job is intended to build goodwill, perform promotional activities, and provide information and other services for the customers. This sales person is not expected to solicit an order. An example of this job is a missionary sales rep for Procter & Gamble, or a detail sales person for a pharmaceutical firm such as Merck or Eli Lilly.
5. **Sales engineer.** In this position the major emphasis is on the sales person's ability to explain the product to a prospective customer, and also to adapt the product to the customer's particular needs. The products involved here typically are complex, technically sophisticated items. A sales engineer usually provides technical support and works with another sales rep who calls regularly on a given account.
6. **Creative sales person** — an order getter. This involves the creative selling of goods and intangibles — primarily services, but also social causes and ideas (don't do drugs, stop smoking, don't drink and drive, as examples). This category contains the most complex, difficult selling jobs — especially the creative selling of intangibles, because you can't see, touch, taste, or smell them. Customers often are not aware of their need for a seller's product. Or they may not realize how that product can satisfy their wants better than the product they are now using. Creative selling often involves designing a system to fit the needs of a particular customer. For example, to make a sale, Nortel may design a communications system for a hospital, or Otis Elevator may develop a vertical lift system especially for a new office building.
7. **Professional business development.** We can add to this categorization the role of professional staff in many service firms whose responsibility it is to bring in new business. In law firms, chartered accountants, consulting engineers, advertising agencies, research firms, and other service organizations, some members of staff are often assigned the role of business development — essentially, selling the services of the firm. While this type of sales job may not involve the same sort of overt selling activity as do other sales roles, it nevertheless has to be done if new clients are to be attracted.

In summary, the above seven types of sales jobs fall into three groups: **order taker** (categories 1, 2, and 3), **sales-support personnel** (categories 4 and 5), and **order getter** (categories 6 and 7). One organization may have several different types of sales jobs. IBM, for instance, has sales people in all of the above categories except driver–sales person.

The Uniqueness of Sales Jobs The features that differentiate sales jobs from other jobs are:

- *The sales force is largely responsible for implementing a firm's marketing strategies.* And if the firm is practising relationship marketing, the sales person is crucial to establishing and maintaining relationships with customers or clients. Moreover, it's the sales reps who generate the revenues that are managed by the financial people and used by the production people.
- *Sales people represent their company to customers and to society in general.* Many sales jobs require the sales person to socialize with customers who frequently are upper-level managers in their companies. Opinions of the firm and its products are formed on the basis of impressions made by sales people in their work and outside activities. The

www.wal-mart.com
www.bell.ca
www.nestle.com
www.xerox.com
www.nortel.com
www.bombardier.com
www.magnaint.com

public ordinarily does not judge a company by its factory or office workers.

- *Sales people often operate with little or no direct supervision.* For success in selling, a sales rep must work hard physically and mentally, be creative and persistent, and show considerable initiative. This all requires a high degree of motivation.
- *Sales jobs often involve considerable travelling and time away from home.* Many companies have reduced sales travel time by redesigning sales territories, routing sales trips better, and relying more on telemarketing. Nevertheless, being in the field, sales people must deal with an endless stream of customers who may seem determined not to buy their products. These stresses, coupled with long hours and travelling, require a mental toughness and physical stamina rarely demanded in other jobs. Personal selling is hard work!

CHANGING PATTERNS IN PERSONAL SELLING

Traditionally, personal selling was a face-to-face, one-on-one situation between a sales person and a buyer. This situation existed both in retail sales involving ultimate consumers and in business-to-business transactions. In recent years, however, some very different selling patterns have emerged. These new patterns reflect a growing purchasing expertise among consumers and business buyers, which, in turn, has fostered a growing professionalism in personal selling. Let's discuss three of these patterns.

Selling Centres — Team Selling

To match the expertise on the buying side, especially in business markets, a growing number of firms on the selling side have adopted the organizational concept of a selling centre. This is sometimes called a sales team or team selling. A **selling centre** is a group of people representing a sales department as well as other functional areas in a firm such as finance, production, and research and development (R&D).

Team selling is expensive and is used only when there is a potential for high sales volume and profit. Procter & Gamble, for example, has selling teams comprising sales people and representatives from finance, distribution, and manufacturing. Each team is assigned to cover a large retailer such as Wal-Mart. When Bell Canada sells to a large multinational firm such as Nestlé, then it will send a separate selling team to deal with each of Nestlé's major divisions in Ontario and Quebec.

www.pg.com

Systems Selling

The concept of **systems selling** means selling a total package of related goods and services — a system — to solve a customer's problem. The idea is that the system — the total package of goods and services — will satisfy the buyer's needs more effectively than selling individual products separately. Xerox, for example, originally sold individual products, using a separate sales force for each major product line. Today, using a systems-selling approach, Xerox studies a customer's office information and operating problems, then provides a total automated system of machines and accompanying services to solve that customer's office problems.

Global Sales Teams

As companies expand their operations to various corners of the world, they expect their suppliers to do the same. Having products readily available and providing quick service became essential to maintaining global customers. Thus, many larger firms have established sales offices or distribution centres in some foreign locations to serve these customers. Now, to service their largest and most profitable customers, companies such as Nortel, Bombardier, Magna International and IBM Canada are forming global sales teams. A global sales team is responsible for all of a company's sales to an account anywhere in the world. The team manager may even be located close to the customer's headquarters, and the team members are prepared to deal with issues and opportunities wherever they may occur.

Telemarketing

Earlier we described telemarketing as the innovative use of telecommunications equipment and systems as part of the "going to the customer" category of personal selling. Telemarketing is growing because: (1) many buyers prefer it over personal sales calls in certain selling situations, and (2) many marketers find that it increases selling efficiency. Buyers placing routine reorders or new orders for standardized products by telephone or computer use less of their time than in-person sales calls. Sellers face increasingly high costs keeping sales people on the road; selling by telemarketing reduces that expense. Also, routine selling by telemarketing allows the field sales force to devote more time to creative selling, major account selling, and other more profitable selling activities. One important benefit of taking a telemarketing approach is that it allows a company to keep in touch with smaller customers in particular, many of whom may not generate sufficient sales revenue to warrant a visit by a sales representative. Smaller customers often appreciate the telemarketing contact because it allows them to maintain a relationship with the supplier.

Here are examples of selling activities that lend themselves nicely to a telemarketing program:

- Seeking leads to new accounts and identifying potentially good customers that sales reps can follow up with in-person calls.
- Processing orders for standardized products. In the case of Baxter International and some of the customers for its hospital supplies, for example, the buyer's computer talks with Baxter's computer to determine shipping dates and to place orders.
- Dealing with small-order customers, especially those with whom the seller would lose money if field sales calls were used.
- Improving relations with intermediaries. John Deere (farm equipment) "talks" via computers with its dealers about inventories, service, and financial management.
- Improving communications with intermediaries in foreign countries and competing better against manufacturers in those countries. In Europe, for example, the auto, chemical, steel, and shipbuilding industries have developed electronic communication systems involving manufacturers, suppliers, and even customs and shipping agents.

THE PERSONAL SELLING PROCESS

The personal selling process is a logical sequence of four steps that a sales person takes in dealing with a prospective buyer (see Figure 19-2). This process leads, hopefully, to some desired customer action and ends with a follow-up to ensure customer satisfaction. The desired action usually is to get the customer to buy a product or a service. However, the same four-step process may be used equally well in other selling situations. For example, Nabisco persuades Safeway and Sobey's to give Oreo cookies a good shelf location in a special promotion program; or Carleton University persuades alumni to contribute to a special fund-raising effort; or BMW wants its dealers to do some local advertising of their automobiles.

Prospecting

The first step in the personal selling process is called **prospecting**. It consists of first identifying prospective customers and then qualifying them — that is, determining whether they have the necessary purchasing power, authority, and willingness to buy.

Identifying Prospective Customers A sales representative may start the identification process by drawing up a profile of the ideal prospect. Records

FIGURE 19-2
The Personal Selling Process

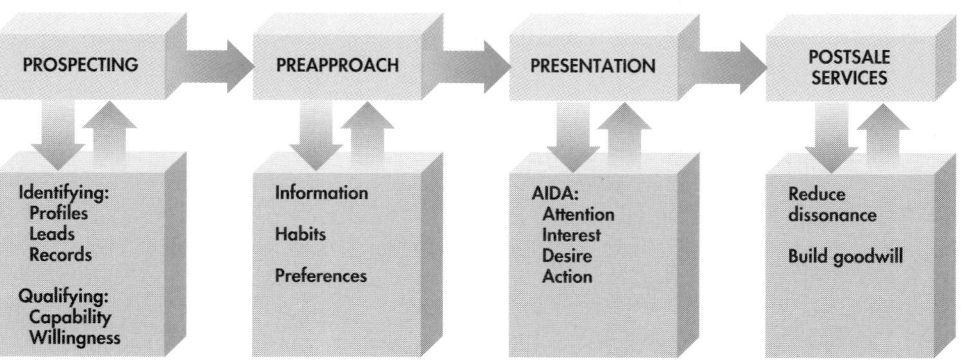

MARKETING AT WORK FILE 19–1

A COMMITMENT TO CUSTOMER SATISFACTION THROUGH SMART SELLING

Companies attract today's tougher customers through "smart selling" — focusing the entire company on customer service and on selling customers the products and services that will meet their needs, not what the firm thinks they need. In the past, businesses fought to improve their competitive position by improving quality and reducing costs. Many companies have gone a long way toward winning those battles. In fact, "These days, the product has to be great just to stay in the game," said an executive at Learning International, a sales training firm. Now, as we head into the next millennium, the competitive battleground has shifted to sales programs characterized by customer service and relationship building.

Forward-looking companies have identified six guidelines for reaching the goal of smarter selling:

1. *Focus the entire organization on sales and customer service.* Du Pont's flexible sales teams, drawn from sales reps, technicians, chemists, factory managers, and financial people, work together developing and selling new products. One such product — a herbicide that growers can apply less often — topped $57 million in North American sales during its first year.
2. *Involve top management in smart selling.* The founders and top executives of Home Depot stores regularly help prepare and participate in their sales training programs.
3. *Build deep, long-lasting relationships with customers.* Make frequent phone calls to customers, or write a note to frequent shoppers at a store. Use computerized technology to keep track of relations with customers, ensuring that the right products get to the right place at the right time. General Electric has engineers stationed full time at a customer's plant — Praxair, maker of industrial gases — to help improve that customer's productivity.
4. *Rethink the sales training program.* Forget the high-pressure selling and teach new skills to sales reps. New sales training firms emphasize new approaches such as teaching team selling, how to spot service problems, and ways to develop long-term relationships with customers.
5. *Change the motivation program — especially compensation.* Avoid traditional commission-based pay plans that encourage short-term, high-pressure selling. Reward sales people for working to retain customers and improving long-term customer satisfaction.
6. *Use sales people to solve customers' problems, not just take their orders.* Kraft General Foods sales people now offer research and tips for improving a store's profit. The reps no longer limit their efforts to designing in-store promotions.

Are these guidelines realistic, or are they just a bunch of nice, but meaningless, words?

Source: Adapted from Christopher Power, "Smart Selling," *Business Week*, August 3, 1992, p. 46.

of past and current customers can help determine characteristics of an ideal prospect. From this profile a seller can start a list of prospective customers.

Many other sources can be used to build the list of prospects. The representative's sales manager may prepare a list; current customers may suggest new leads; trade-association and industry directories can be a good source; and leads can come from people mailing in a coupon, phoning a 1-800 number stated in an advertisement, or responding to a Web site.

And a little thought often will suggest logical prospects. For example, the Brick (furniture store) can find prospects in lists of building permits issued. Toyota and Nissan auto dealers in Japan go door-to-door to seek prospects for new-car sales. Insurance companies, real estate firms, and even local diaper services use such sources as marriage and birth announcements in newspapers. Home and auto insurance companies, when making outbound telemarketing calls, will try to obtain the customer's policy renewal date.

Qualifying the Prospects After identifying prospective customers, a marketer should **qualify** them — that is, determine whether they have the necessary willingness, purchasing power, and authority to buy. To determine willingness to buy, a company can seek information about a prospect's relationship with its present suppliers. For example, a business firm or a household consumer may have had a long, satisfying relationship with Co-operators Insurance for auto insurance. In this case, there would seem to be little chance that an Allstate sales person could get that prospect's business, so he or she may be better advised to target other customers.

To determine a prospect's ability to pay, a marketer may refer to credit-rating services such as Dun & Bradstreet. For household consumers or small businesses in an area, a seller may obtain credit information from a local credit bureau. Identifying the person who has the authority to buy in a business or a household can be difficult, as we saw in chapters 6 and 7. In a business, the buying authority may rest with a committee or an senior manager in a distant location. Besides determining the buying authority, a seller also should identify the one or more persons who influence the buying decision. A purchasing agent may have buying authority, but what he or she buys may depend on the recommendation of office staff or factory engineers.

Preapproach to Individual Prospects

Before calling on prospects, sales people should learn all they can about the persons or companies to whom they hope to sell. This **preapproach in selling** might include finding out what products and services the prospects are now using and their reactions to these products. In business-to-business selling, a sales person or selling team should find out how buying decisions are made in the customer's organization. (Remember, in Chapter 7 we discussed the various roles played in the buying-decision process in business firms.) A sales representative can target the right people if he or she knows who the information gatekeeper is, who influences and/or makes the buying decision, and who actually makes the purchase.

Sales people also should try to find out the personal habits and preferences of a prospect. They should try to get all the information they can, so that they will be able to tailor their presentations to individual buyers. Today, this task is made much easier in many firms because of the use of customer and prospect databases.

Presenting the Sales Message

With the appropriate preapproach information, a sales person can design a **sales presentation** that will attract the prospect's attention. The sales person will then try to hold the prospect's interest while building a desire for the product; and, when the time is right, attempt to stimulate action by closing the sale. This approach, called **AIDA** (an acronym formed by the first letters of Attention, Interest, Desire, and Action), is used by many organizations.

Attract Attention — the Approach The first task in a sales presentation is to attract the prospect's attention and to generate curiosity. In cases where the prospect is aware of a need and is seeking a solution, simply stating the seller's company and product will be enough. However, more creativity often is required.

For instance, if the sales person was referred to the prospect by a customer, the right approach might be to start out by mentioning this common acquaintance. Or a sales person might suggest the product benefits by making some startling statement. One sales training consultant often greets a prospect with the question, "If I can cut your selling costs in half, and at the same time double your sales volume, are you interested?"

Hold Interest and Arouse Desire After attracting the prospect's attention, the sales representative can hold it and stimulate a desire for the product with a sales talk. There is no common pattern here. Usually, however, a product demonstration is invaluable. Whatever pattern is followed in the talk, the sales person must always show how the product will benefit the prospect.

Some companies train their sales people to use a "canned" sales talk — a memorized sales presentation designed to cover all points set by management. All sales people give the same presentation, verbatim or with minor changes. Many companies engaging in telephone selling or door-to-door selling often use canned sales talks or scripts. Although many people feel that this is a poor practice, canned talks have time and again proved to be effective. Nevertheless, they are used less and less today in face-to-face sales situations, because companies believe that flexible presentations can be more personal and tailored for individual customers' needs. Telemarketing companies, on the other hand, seem to continue to rely on scripted sales calls.

Meet Objections and Close the Sale After explaining the product and its benefits, a sales person should try **closing the sale** — obtaining the customer's agreement to buy. (This is the final A in AIDA — achieving the desired *action*.)

As part of the presentation, the sales person may periodically venture a **trial close** to test the prospect's willingness to buy. By posing some "either–or" questions, a sales person can bring the presentation to a head. For example, "Would you prefer the grey or the green model?" or "Shall I put this on your Visa?"

The trial close is important because it gives the sales person an indication of how near the prospect is to a decision. Sometimes sales are lost simply because the sales person fails to ask for the order.

The trial close also tends to bring out the buyer's objections. A sales person should encourage buyers to state their objections. Then the sales person has an opportunity to **meet the objections** and to bring out additional product benefits or re-emphasize previously stated points. The toughest objections to answer are those that are unspoken. A sales person must uncover the real objections before being able to close a sale.

Postsale Services

An effective selling job does not end when the order is written up. The final stage of a selling process is a series of **postsale activities** that can build customer goodwill and lay the groundwork for future business. An alert sales person will follow up sales to ensure that no problems occur in delivery, financing, installation, employee training, and other areas that are important to customer satisfaction.

Postsale service reduces the customer's postpurchase anxiety (cognitive dissonance, as discussed in Chapter 6) — the anxiety that usually occurs after a person makes a buying decision. In this final stage of the selling process, a sales person can minimize the customer's dissonance by (1) summarizing the product's benefits after the purchase, (2) repeating why the product is better than alternatives not chosen, and (3) emphasizing how satisfied the customer will be with the product.[4]

RELATIONSHIP MARKETING AND THE SALES PERSON

As we have emphasized in earlier chapters, the building of collaborative relationships with customers and suppliers is an important characteristic of progressive marketing firms in today's dynamic marketplace. While all relationships require that buyers receive the service and quality that they expect in order for customer satisfaction to result, high levels of trust are characteristic of those relationships that enhance competitiveness and reduce costs for both buyer and seller over extended periods of time.

In business marketing, we can most easily see how trust works and how buyers view trust in the seller's organization as distinct from trust in the seller's sales person. A long-term relationship with a trusted supplier is threatened if the supplier's sales person proves to be careless or dishonest. And highly trusted sales people can, in some cases, retain their buyer's commitment even when the selling organization has some policies and procedures that are not satisfactory to some of their customers. Since in all firms, and particularly in business marketing organizations, the sales force plays a key role in implementing the supplier's strategies and managing customer relationships, we should understand the customer's view of the nature of trust, the manner in which it can develop, and the role of the sales person in building it.

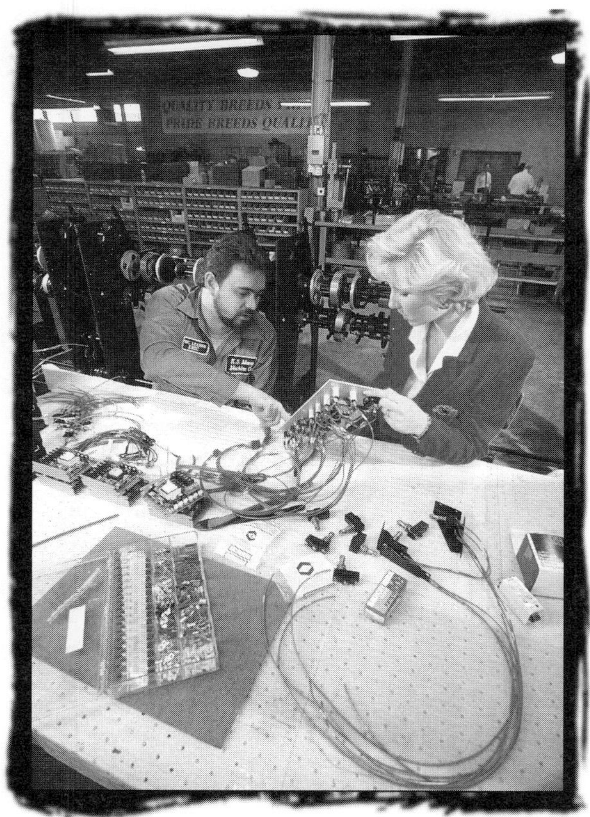

This sales representative works at developing buyer confidence as she travels to customers' factories to learn first-hand about their needs.

As shown in "Marketing at Work" File 19-2, the buyer relies on five **trust-building processes**: (1) assessing the relationship's value, (2) developing confidence in predicting the seller's behaviour, (3) assessing the seller's ability to meet commitments,(4) evaluating the seller's motivations, and (5) transferring outside proof of trust to the selling firm, to the sales person, or between the two.

For each of the five trust-building processes, a number of characteristics affect that process. Two are characteristics of the selling firm (F), that is, reputation and size; three represent the seller's approach to the relationship (FR), such as willingness to customize; another two are characteristic of the sales person (S); five are characteristics of the sales person's relationship with the buyer (SR); and two are external opinions made use of by the buyer. The characteristics of the supplying firm and its approach to the relationship affect the buyer's trust in the selling firm. The characteristics of the sales person and the sales person's approach to the relationship affect the buying firm's trust in the sales person. The external judgments provide independent confirmation.

The buyer's ultimate decision on a specific transaction then becomes a combination of trust in the supplying firm, trust in the sales person, external validation, and, finally, the specific details of the sale or exchange in question — that is, for the sale being negotiated, the delivery performance, prices and costs, product and service performance, and purchase experience with the supplier.

It's clear that the seller's marketing strategy must be effectively implemented throughout the organization and particularly through the sales force for relationship marketing to work. Among other things, the sales manager, whose responsibilities we next discuss, has important tasks to perform to ensure the success of a relationship marketing strategy.

STRATEGIC SALES-FORCE MANAGEMENT

Managing the personal selling function is a matter of applying the three-stage management process (planning, implementation, and evaluation) to a sales force and its activities. Sales executives begin by setting sales goals and planning sales-force activities within the context of the firm's strategic position. This involves forecasting sales, preparing sales budgets, establishing sales territories, and setting sales quotas.

Then a sales force must be organized, staffed, and operated to implement the strategic plans and reach the goals that were set. The final stage involves evaluating the performance of individual sales people as well as appraising the total sales performance.

Effective sales-force management starts with a qualified sales manager. Finding the right person for this job is not easy. In many organizations, the common practice when a sales management position becomes available is to reward the most productive sales person with a promotion. The assumption is that as a manager, an effective sales person will be able to impart the necessary wisdom to make others equally successful.

However, the qualities that lead to effective sales management are often not the same ones that help

MARKETING AT WORK FILE 19–2

TRUST IN THE BUYER–SELLER RELATIONSHIP: THE ROLE OF THE FIRM AND THE SALES PERSON IN BUSINESS MARKETING

We know that when a buying firm trusts its supplier, it is more co-operative and exerts more effort on the seller's behalf; conflict between the two is reduced, and buyer and seller satisfaction is increased. A buyer who trusts a supplier is more committed to and intends to stay in the existing marketing relationship. We also know that professional buyers can develop trust not only in the selling organization but also in the seller's sales people. What has not been too clear to date has been the process whereby trust is developed. Doney and Cannon have provided us with a framework for viewing the sales person's role in creating trust. Below are their five components of the trust-building process and five selling-company factors, seven sales person factors, and the two external trust-based factors that together affect the trust-building process. Some of these factors are managed by marketing strategists and operations managers, some by sales managers, some by sales persons on their own.

Trust-Building Process of Buyer	**Supplier Firm/Sales Person Influencers**
1. Assessing relationship's value: • gains if supplier is trustworthy • losses if supplier is not	Supplier firm reputation (F), size (F), willingness to customize (FR), to share confidential data (FR), duration of supplier relationship (FR), duration of sales person relationship (SR)
2. Confidence in seller's future behaviour: • learns more by repeated contacts • increases ability to predict	Duration of supplier relationship (FR), sales person likeability (S), similarity (S), frequency of social contact (SR)
3. Assessing seller's ability to perform: • credibility of sales person's promises	Sales person expertise(S), influence(S)
4. Evaluating seller's motivations: • helping or problem-solving intentions • interest primarily selfish	Supplier firm willingness to customize (FR), to share confidential data (FR), sales person likeability (SR)
5. Transferring external proof of trust: • finding trusted sources who know supplier and accepting their view	Supplier firm reputation (F), size (F), trust of supplier firm (external proof), trust of sales person (external proof)

Note how the influencing characteristics of the supplier firm (F), the supplier firm's approach to the relationship (FR), the sales person (S), the sales person's approach to the relationship (SR), and, finally, the external judgments of trust (external proof), are distributed across different phases of the trust-building process.

Source: Adapted from Patricia M. Doney and Joseph P. Cannon, "An Examination of the Nature of Trust in Buyer–Seller Relationships," *Journal of Marketing*, vol. 61, April 1997, pp. 35–61.

make a successful sales person. Probably the biggest difference in the positions is that sales people tend to be self-motivated and self-reliant. They often work independently, receiving all the credit or blame for their successes or failures. In contrast, sales managers must work through and depend on others and must be prepared to give recognition rather than receive it. Herein lies the dilemma. It is an unusual person who can be a successful sales manager without previous selling experience. To be effective, sales managers must understand customers, appreciate the role of the sales person and have the respect of the sales force. These attributes can only be acquired by spending time in a sales role.

The resolution to this dilemma may come in not using the sales management position as a reward for outstanding sales performance. Rather, the criteria for sales management should be respectable sales performance coupled with the necessary attributes of management.

STAFFING AND OPERATING A SALES FORCE

Most sales executives spend the bulk of their time in staffing and operating their sales forces. Hence, we now discuss what they do in these activities, as shown in Figure 19-3.

Recruitment and Selection

Staffing (personnel selection) is the most important management activity in any organization. This is true whether the organization is a business, an athletic team, or a university or college faculty. Consequently, the key to success in managing a sales force is selecting the right people. No matter what the calibre of sales management, if a sales force is distinctly inferior to that of a competitor, the competitor will win.

Sales-force selection includes three tasks:

1. Determine the type of people wanted, by preparing a written job description.
2. Recruit an adequate number of applicants.
3. Select the most qualified persons from among the applicants.

Determining Hiring Specifications The first step is to establish the proper hiring specifications, just as if the company were purchasing equipment or supplies rather than labour. To establish these specifications, management must first know what the particular sales job entails. This calls for a detailed review of the marketing strategy to determine the sales person's role. Then a detailed job analysis and a written job description can be developed. This description will later be invaluable in training, compensation, and supervision.

Determining the qualifications needed to fill the job is the most difficult part of the selection function. We still really do not know all the characteristics that make a good sales person. We cannot measure to what degree each quality should be present. Nor do we know to what extent an abundance of one can offset the lack of another.

The search for the qualities that make a good sales person continues. As one approach, some companies have analyzed the personal histories of their past sales representatives in an effort to determine the traits common to successful (and unsuccessful) performers.

Recruiting Applicants A planned system for recruiting a sufficient number of applicants is the next step in selection. A good recruiting system:

- Operates continuously, not only when sales-force vacancies occur.
- Is systematic in reaching all appropriate sources of applicants.
- Provides a flow of more qualified applicants than is needed.

To identify recruits, large organizations often use placement services on university and college campuses or professional employment agencies or

FIGURE 19-3 Staffing and Operating a Sales Force

"head-hunters," some of whom specialize in locating applicants for marketing and sales positions. Smaller firms that need fewer new sales people may place classified ads in trade publications and daily newspapers. Many firms solicit recommendations from company employees, customers, or suppliers. Sometimes, firms hire people away from their competitors because they believe the sales person has a special relationship with some accounts in which the hiring firm has an interest. While sometimes this approach works, frequently it causes internal and external problems of trust.

Matching Applicants with Hiring Specifications

Sales managers use a variety of techniques to determine which applicants possess the desired qualifications, including application forms, interviews, references, credit reports, psychological tests, aptitude tests, and physical examinations. Virtually all companies ask candidates to fill out application forms. In addition to providing basic screening information, the application indicates areas that should be explored in an interview.

No sales person should be hired without at least one personal interview. It is usually desirable to have several interviews conducted by different people in different physical settings. Pooling the opinions of a number of people increases the likelihood of discovering any undesirable characteristics and reduces the effects of one interviewer's possible bias. An interview helps an employer to determine (1) the applicant's degree of interest in the job, (2) the match between the requirements of the job and the applicant's skills, and (3) the applicant's motivation to work hard.

The individuals involved in the selection process should be aware of the various provincial laws against discrimination to avoid inadvertent violations. Testing for intelligence, attributes, or personality, while legal, is somewhat controversial. Some companies avoid testing for fear that they will be accused of discrimination. However, employment tests are legitimate selection tools as long as they can be shown to predict job performance accurately.

Assimilating New Sales People

After sales people are hired, management should ensure that they are integrated into the company family. Often this step is overlooked entirely. Prospective sales people are carefully selected and are often wined and dined to recruit them into the firm. Then, as soon as they are hired, the honeymoon is over and they are left to fend for themselves. In such cases, the new people often become discouraged and may even quit. A wise sales manager will recognize that the new sales people know very little about the details of the job, their fellow workers, or their status in the firm and must be informed and made comfortable if they are to become successful.

Training a Sales Force

Both new and experienced sales people need an effective training program to improve their selling skills, learn about new products, and improve their time and territory management practices. Management should answer the following questions in the course of designing a **sales training program**:

- *What are the goals of the program?* In very general terms, the aim of the program should be to increase productivity and stimulate the sales force. In addition, sales managers must determine what specific goals they want to reach. For instance, the goal may be to increase sales of high-profit items or to improve prospecting methods for generating new accounts.
- *Who should do the training?* The training program may be conducted by line sales managers, by a company training department, by outside training specialists, or by some combination of the three.
- *What should be the content of the program?* A well-rounded sales training program should cover three general topics: product knowledge, company policies, and selling techniques.
- *When and where should training be done?* Some companies believe in training new people before they go into the field. Others let new people first prove that they have the desire and ability to sell, and then bring them back into the office for intensive training. Firms may employ either centralized or decentralized training programs. A centralized program, usually at the home office, may take the form of a periodic meeting attended by all sales people. A decentralized program may be held in branch offices or during on-the-job training.

- *What instructional methods should be used?* The lecture method may be employed to inform trainees about company history and practices. Demonstrations may be used to impart product knowledge or selling techniques. Role playing is an excellent device for training a person in proper selling techniques. On-the-job training may be used in almost any phase of the program.

Motivating a Sales Force

Sales people, especially outside sales forces, require a high degree of motivation. Consider how a sales job is different from most other jobs. Sales people often work independently, without supervision and guidance from management. Outside sales people work most of the time away from the support and comfort of home-office surroundings.

Consequently, management faces a challenge in **motivating sales people**. One key is to determine what motivates the sales representatives — is it a need for status, control, accomplishment, or something else? People differ in what motivates them, and motivations change over time. A young person may be more motivated by monetary rewards alone, while older sales people may be more interested in receiving recognition for building long-term relationships with important buyers. This means, of course, that a motivational program, as much as possible, should reach the reps individually.

Sales executives can draw from a wide assortment of specific motivational tools.[5] Financial incentives — compensation plans, expense accounts, fringe benefits — usually are frequently effective. Nonfinancial awards — job enrichment, good consistent feedback from management, recognition and honour awards (pins, trophies, certificates) — may be appropriate. Sales meetings and sales contests are often-used and enjoyable alternatives. Many firms provide cruises, resort trips, and other travel incentives as rewards to sales reps who meet various qualitative and quantitative sales goals.[6]

Compensating a Sales Force

Financial rewards are still by far the most widely used tool for motivating sales people. Consequently, designing and administering an effective **sales compensation plan** is a big part of a sales manager's job. Financial rewards may be direct monetary payments (salary, commission) or indirect monetary compensation (paid vacations, pensions, insurance plans).

Establishing a compensation system calls for decisions concerning the level of compensation as well as the method of compensation. The level refers to the total dollar income that a sales person earns over a period of time. Level is influenced by the type of person required and the competitive rate of pay for similar positions. The method is the system or plan by which the sales person will reach the intended level.

Three widely used methods of compensating a sales force are straight salary, straight commission, and a combination plan. A **salary** is a fixed payment for a period of time during which the sales person is working. A salary-only plan (called a straight salary) provides security and stability of earnings for a sales person. This plan gives management control over the selling efforts of the sales person, and the sales representatives themselves are likely to cater to the customer's best interests. The main drawback of a straight salary is that it does not offer adequate incentive for sales people to increase their sales volume. Also, a straight salary is a fixed cost, unrelated to sales volume or gross margin.

Straight-salary plans typically are used when:

- Compensating new sales people or missionary sales people.
- Opening new territories.
- Selling a technical product with a lengthy period of negotiation.

A **commission** is a payment tied to a specific unit of accomplishment. Thus a sales representative may be paid 5 percent of sales or 8 percent of gross margin. A straight-commission plan (commission only) tends to have just the opposite merits and limitations of a straight salary. A straight commission provides considerable incentive for sales people, and it is a variable cost related directly to a representative's sales volume or gross margin. On the other hand, it is difficult to control straight-commission people. And it is especially difficult to get them to perform tasks for which no commission is paid.

Straight-commission plans may work well when:

- Great incentive is needed to get the sales.
- Very little nonselling work is required, such as setting up displays in retail stores.

- The company is financially weak and must relate its compensation expenses directly to sales or gross margins.
- The company is unable to supervise the sales force when they are outside the company's offices.

The ideal **combination compensation plan** has the best features of both the straight-salary and the straight-commission plans, with as few of their drawbacks as possible. To reach this ideal, a combination plan must be tailored to a particular firm, product, market, and type of selling. Today about three-quarters of firms in North America use some kind of a combination sales compensation plan.

Supervising a Sales Force

Supervising a sales force is difficult because sales people often work independently and where they cannot be observed. Yet supervision serves both as a means of continuing training and as a device to ensure that company policies are being carried out.

An issue that management must resolve is how closely to supervise. If too close, it can create a role conflict for the sales person. One of the attractions of selling is the freedom it affords sales people to develop creative solutions to customers' problems. Close supervision can stifle that sense of independence. Conversely, too little supervision can also cause problems. Sales people who are not closely supervised may lack an understanding of the expectations of their supervisors and companies. They may not know, for example, how much time should be spent in servicing existing accounts and how much in developing new business.

The most effective supervisory method is personal observation in the field. Typically, at least half of a sales manager's time is spent travelling with or spending time on the sales floor with sales people. Other supervisory tools are reports, correspondence, and sales meetings.

EVALUATING A SALES PERSON'S PERFORMANCE

Managing a sales force includes **evaluating the sales performance** of sales people. Sales executives must know what the sales force is doing in order to reward them or to make constructive proposals for improvement. By establishing performance standards and studying sales people's activities, management can develop new training programs for upgrading the sales force's efforts. And, of course, performance evaluation should be the basis for compensation decisions and other rewards.

Performance evaluation can also help sales people identify opportunities for improving their efforts. Employees with poor sales records know they are doing something wrong. However, they may not know what the problem is if they lack objective standards by which to measure their performance.

Both quantitative and qualitative factors should be used as bases for performance evaluation. **Quantitative evaluation bases** generally have the advantage of being specific and objective. **Qualitative evaluation factors**, although often reflecting broader dimensions of behaviour, are limited by the subjective judgment of the evaluators. For either type of appraisal, however, management faces the difficult task of setting standards against which a sales person's performance may be measured.

Quantitative Bases

Sales performance should be evaluated in terms of inputs (efforts) and outputs (results). Together, inputs such as number of sales calls per day or customer service activity, and outputs such as sales volume or gross margin over six months or even two years, with certain relationship marketing accounts, provide a measure of selling effectiveness.

Useful quantitative input measures include:

- Call rate — number of calls per day or week.
- Direct selling expenses — total dollars, or as a percentage of sales.
- Non-selling activities — promotion displays set up, training sessions held with distributors or dealers, client problem-solving sessions.

Some quantitative output measures useful as evaluation criteria are:

- Sales volume by product, customer group, and territory over different time periods, depending on the strategy for the category.
- Sales volume as a percentage of quota or territory potential.

- Gross margin by product line, customer group, and territory for different time periods.
- Orders — number and average dollar amount.
- Closing rate — number of orders divided by number of calls.
- Accounts — percentage of existing accounts sold, and number of new accounts opened.

An increasing number of firms, among them IBM and Hallmark, are using measures of customer satisfaction or of service quality as a performance indicator. In fact, a survey of two hundred firms in 1995 showed that 26 percent of them were using customer satisfaction as a component in their sales force evaluation process.[7]

Qualitative Bases

Performance evaluation would be much easier if it could be based only on quantitative criteria. It would minimize the subjectivity and personal bias of the evaluators. However, many qualitative factors must be considered because they influence a sales person's performance. Some of these factors are:

- Knowledge of products, company policies, and competitors.
- Time management and preparation for sales calls.
- Customer relations.
- Personal appearance.
- Personality and attitude — co-operation, creativity, resourcefulness.

A successful evaluation program will appraise a sales person's performance on as many different bases as possible. Otherwise management may be misled. A high daily call rate may look good, but it tells us nothing about how many orders are being written up. A high closing rate (orders divided by calls) may be camouflaging a low average order size or a high sales volume on low-profit items. Management must also be concerned about a sales person's ability to build long-term relationships with his or her customers. This is especially the case in service industries such as travel agencies and in professional service firms. Some sales representatives may be very good at "selling," that is, at moving products out the door, but not as good at getting close to the customer.

Summary

Personal selling is the main marketing communications tool used in North American business — whether measured by number of people employed, by total expenditures, or by expenses as a percentage of sales. The total field of personal selling comprises two broad categories. One covers selling activities where the customers come to the sales people — primarily retail-store or in-bound telephone-based selling. The other includes all selling situations where the sales people go to the customer — primarily outside sales forces.

The sales job today is not what it used to be. A new type of sales representative — a professional sales person — has been developing over the past few decades. Sales jobs today range from order takers through support sales people (missionary sellers, sales engineers) to order getters (creative sellers). Sales jobs differ from other jobs in several respects. Some changing patterns in personal selling have emerged in recent years — patterns such as selling centres (team selling), systems selling, relationship selling, and telemarketing.

The personal selling process consists of four steps, starting with prospecting for prospective buyers and then pre-approaching each prospect. The third step is the sales presentation, which includes attracting attention, arousing buyer interest and desire, meeting objections, and then hopefully closing the sale. Finally, postsale activities involve follow-up services to ensure customer satisfaction and reduce dissonance regarding the purchase.

The role of the sales person in relationship marketing can be viewed from the five-stage trust-building process. For each stage of the process, there is a combination of company and sales person characteristics, all amenable to management, which affect the particular stage of trust building. In the final analysis, a buyer's decision to buy is affected not only by the specific details of a transaction but also by his or her view of the amount of trust that can be placed on the supplying firm as well as in the salesperson.

The sales management process involves planning, implementing, and evaluating sales-force activities within the guidelines set by the company's strategic marketing planning. The tasks of staffing and operating a sales force present managerial challenges in several areas. The key to successful sales-force management is to do a good job in selecting sales people. Then plans must be made to assimilate these new people into the company and to train them. Management must set up programs to motivate, compensate, and supervise a sales force. The final stage in sales-force management is to evaluate the performance of the individual sales people.

Key Terms and Concepts

Personal selling (470)
Inside selling (471)
Outside sales forces (471)
Telemarketing (471)
Professional sales person (471)
Driver–sales person (472)
Inside order taker (472)
Outside order taker (472)
Missionary sales person (473)
Sales engineer (473)
Creative sales person (473)
Order taker (473)
Sales-support personnel (473)
Order getter (473)
Selling centre (474)
Systems selling (474)
Prospecting (475)
Qualify (477)
Preapproach in selling (477)
Sales presentation (477)
AIDA (477)
Closing a sale (478)
Trial close (478)
Meeting objections (478)
Postsale activities (478)
Trust-building process (479)
Sales-force selection (481)
Sales training program (482)
Motivating sales people (483)
Sales compensation plan (483)
Salary (483)
Commission (483)
Combination compensation plan (484)
Evaluating sales performance (484)
Quantitative evaluation bases (484)
Qualitative evaluation bases (484)

Questions and Problems

1. The cost of a full-page, four-colour advertisement in one issue of a national magazine is higher than the cost of employing two sales people for a full year. A sales manager is urging her company to eliminate a few of these ads and, instead, to hire a few more sales people. This executive believes that one good sales person working for an entire year can sell more than one ad in one issue of a magazine. How would you respond?
2. Refer to the classification of sales jobs from driver–sales person to creative seller, and answer the following questions:
   a. In which types of jobs are sales people most likely to be free from close supervision?
   b. Which types are likely to be the highest paid?
   c. For which types of jobs is the highest degree of motivation necessary?
3. What are some sources you might use to acquire a list of prospects for the following products and services?
   a. Bank accounts for new area residents.
   b. Dental X-ray equipment.
   c. Laptop computers.
   d. Contributors to the United Way.
   e. Baby furniture and clothes.
   f. Web page design services.
   g. House painting.
4. If you were preparing a sales presentation for the following products and services, what information about a prospect would you seek as part of your preparation?
   a. Two-bedroom condominium.
   b. New automobile.
   c. Carpeting for a home redecorating project.
   d. Marketing research project for a local department store.
   e. Building cleaning service.
5. What sources should be used for recruiting sales applicants in each of the following firms? Explain your choice in each case.
   a. The Delta Chelsea Inn hotel.
   b. IBM, for sales of mainframe (large) computers.
   c. Mount Pleasant Cemetery.

6. Compare the merits of straight-salary and straight-commission plans of sales compensation. What are two types of sales jobs in which each plan might be desirable?
7. How might a firm determine whether a sales person is using high-pressure selling tactics that might injure customer relations?
8. How can a sales manager evaluate the performance of sales people in getting new business?

Hands-On Marketing

1. Review your activities of the past few days and identify those in which:
   a. You did some personal selling.
   b. People tried to sell something to you.
   Select one situation in each category where you thought the selling was particularly effective, and tell why it was so.
2. Interview three students from your school who recently have gone through the job-interviewing process conducted by companies using your school's placement office. Ask the students to compare, contrast, and generally evaluate the recruiting practices of the companies they interviewed. Prepare a report covering your findings.

CHAPTER 20 GOALS

This chapter examines nonpersonal, mass communication promotional tools — advertising, sales promotion, and public relations. After studying this chapter, you should have an understanding of:

- The nature of advertising, what it means to the individual firm, and its importance in our economy.
- Characteristics of the major types of advertising.
- How advertising campaigns are developed and advertising media are selected.
- What sales promotion is, and how to manage it.
- The role of public relations and publicity in the marketing communications mix.

Chapter Twenty

Management of Advertising, Sales Promotion, and Public Relations

HITCHING OUR WAGON TO THE STARS

Everybody knows that Bill Cosby loves Jell-O, Michael Jordan and Tiger Woods wear Nike, and just about every Hollywood star, from Jennifer Aniston to Miss Piggy, drinks milk. Celebrity endorsements are used to enhance brand image largely through appearances in advertising or by wearing or appearing with the product or brand in the media, and if the celebrities chosen are suitable, this strategy can be quite successful. However, the consumer must identify with both the celebrity and the brand or product. Frequently, the consumer may recall the celebrity but not the brand, and this poses a major problem. The purpose of the celebrity endorsement is to encourage potential consumers to try the product — after that, the product stands alone.

The celebrity should be credible in his or her endorsement. Everyone knows that many celebrities get paid exorbitant amounts of money for their endorsements. This is a factor of celebrity endorsements that marketers aim to minimize through the choice of the perfect celebrity for their product. Ideally, marketers would like consumers to believe that the celebrity is endorsing the product because he or she simply loves the product. For example, people tend to believe that on occasion, Bill Cosby enjoys a big, cold, bowl of Jell-O. Why? Because Cosby has been endorsing Jell-O products for years, and he is not doing it because he needs the money! So he must really like Jell-O. And what about Michael Jordan and Nike? Michael Jordan, in the minds of many fans the best basketball player in the NBA, always wears Nike shoes. One would imagine that any number of the major athletic brands would have been only too happy to have Jordan on their team, but he chose Nike — so he must be a big Nike fan. This train of thought is what marketers strive to promote — a credible celebrity endorsement.

Companies also seek celebrities who possess characteristics that they would like associated with their brand. So, while products like Jell-O and milk may try to avoid controversy, edgier brands such as Nike or Miller Lite beer may not. Miller Lite once used former New York Yankees manager Billy Martin, who was notorious for his outrageous temper (and for repeatedly being fired) to promote their beer. Nike has used basketball's "bad boys," Dennis Rodman and Charles Barkley, to promote its products, and even contributed to figure skater Tanya Harding's legal fund to go to the Olympics. Many of these celebrities teeter on the edge of disrepute, bringing publicity, recognition, and a touch of notoriety to the brands they represent. However, there is a limit to what is deemed acceptable — what happens when a celebrity crosses the line between sensation and scandal?

Hertz is thankful that people are beginning to forget that their celebrity endorsement came from O.J. Simpson, who stood trial for the sensational murders of Nicole Simpson and Ron Goldman. Hertz quickly discontinued the advertisements featuring the ex–football star, after the infamous Bronco chase and the media coverage of the murder trial.

Celebrity endorsements are a time-worn advertising strategy that can work well if used carefully. Marketing consultant and author John Dalla Costa believes that it is a cheap way of marketing a product if you don't have an original idea. Dalla Costa states that "celebrity endorsements do work very, very well, but probably only in about 10 to 20 percent of the cases." Regardless, celebrity endorsements, as a marketing strategy, seem to be growing in popularity, and there is no shortage of superstars willing to lend their "star power" to almost any product imaginable.[1]

Advertising, sales promotion, and public relations are the mass communication tools available to marketers. As its name suggests, mass communication uses the same message for everyone in an audience. The mass communicator trades off the advantage of personal selling, the opportunity to tailor a message to each prospective customer, for the advantage of reaching many people at a lower cost per person. However, as the emergence of interactive television advertising and the use of the World Wide Web illustrates, mass communication is not indiscriminate. Advertisers are constantly seeking ways to present their messages to more clearly defined target audiences, and the use of new technology is making it increasingly possible to get a specific message into the hands of specific target customers.

NATURE AND SCOPE OF ADVERTISING

All advertisements have four features:

- A verbal and/or visual message.
- A sponsor who is identified.
- Delivery through one or more media.
- Payment by the sponsor to the media carrying the message.

Advertising, then, consists of all the activities involved in presenting to an audience a nonpersonal, sponsor-identified, paid-for message about a product or organization. Advertising in one form or another is used by most organizations. One of the most interesting changes taking place in advertising is the increasing ability of marketers to reach specific audiences with tailor-made messages. Thus, in the future, we will see advertising becoming less nonpersonal in nature.

Types of Advertising

Advertising can be classified according to (1) the target audience, either consumers or businesses; (2) what is being advertised, a product or service versus an organization or company; and (3) the objective sought, the stimulation of primary or selective demand. To fully appreciate the scope of advertising, it is essential to understand these three classifications.

Consumer and Business-to-Business Advertising

An ad is generally directed at either consumers or businesses — thus it is either **consumer advertising** or **business-to-business advertising**. Most retailers by definition sell only to end consumers, so they are generally organizations that are not faced with the choice of whether to target a consumer or a business audience. There are exceptions, such as Business Depot, which will target both.

The publishers of the *Financial Post* and similar newspapers and magazines must decide what portion of their advertising budget will be used to attract advertisers (called trade advertising), and what portion will go toward gaining subscribers and selling magazines and newspapers.

Product and Institutional Advertising All advertising may be classified as product (or service) or institutional (or corporate). Remember here that we are using the term "product" to include both tangible products and services. **Product advertising** focuses on a particular product or brand.

Product advertising is subdivided into direct-action and indirect-action advertising:

- **Direct-action advertising** seeks a quick response — for instance, a magazine ad containing a coupon or a 1-800 number may urge the reader to send or call immediately for a free sample, or a supermarket ad in a local newspaper may stress this week's specials. Many advertisements today include the advertiser's Internet address, inviting the consumer to "check us out on the Web."
- **Indirect-action advertising** is designed to stimulate demand over a longer period of time. It is intended to inform or remind consumers that the product exists and to point out its benefits. Most television advertising is of this type.

Institutional or corporate advertising presents information about the advertiser's business or tries to create a good attitude — build goodwill — toward the organization. This type of advertising is not intended to sell a specific product. Two forms of corporate advertising are:

- **Customer service advertising**, which presents information about the advertiser's operations. Advertisements describing the level of personal service available at Esso gas stations are an example.
- **Public service advertising**, which is designed to improve the quality of life and show that the advertiser is a responsible member of the community. Such ads may urge the audience to avoid drugs or to support a local anti-pollution campaign, or may show how the advertiser is making a contribution by supporting worthwhile projects and community activities.

Primary- and Selective-Demand Advertising **Primary-demand advertising** is designed to stimulate demand for a generic category of a product such as Colombian coffee, B.C. apples, or garments made from cotton. This is in contrast to **selective-demand advertising**, intended to stimulate demand for individual brands such as Nabob Coffee, Sunkist oranges, and clothing from The Gap.

Primary-demand advertising is used in either of two situations. The first is when the product is in the introductory stage of its life cycle. This is called **pioneering advertising**. A firm may run an ad about its new product, explaining the product's benefits, but not emphasizing the brand name. The objective of pioneering primary-demand advertising is to inform, not to persuade, the target market. The buying-decision-process model explains why such ads are limited to information. Recall from our discussion in Chapter 6 that a consumer must first be made aware of a product before becoming interested in or desiring it. Combine this with the fact that only so much information can be communicated in a single ad, and it becomes clear that only one objective can be accomplished at a time. In recent years, pioneering demand ads have been run for cellular telephones and video camcorders.

The second use of primary-demand advertising occurs throughout the product life cycle. It is usually done by trade associations trying to stimulate demand for their industry's product. Thus the Dairy Farmers of Canada's ads urge us to drink more milk. The bureau doesn't care what brand of milk and dairy products we buy, just that we use more of them.

Selective-demand advertising essentially is competitive advertising — it pits one brand against another. This type of advertising typically is employed when a product has gone beyond the introductory life-cycle stage. The product is reasonably well known and in competition for market share with several brands. The objective of selective-demand advertising is to increase the demand for a brand. To accomplish this goal, it emphasizes the particular benefits — the **differential competitive advantages** — of the brand being advertised.

Comparative advertising is an important kind of selective-demand advertising that is used for a wide variety of products. In comparative advertising, the advertiser either directly, by naming a rival brand, or indirectly, through inference, points out differences between the brands. We have all seen the comparative advertising for Coke and Pepsi, both of which show the competitor's brand. In some comparative advertising, the competitor's name is not mentioned, but it is obvious to the reader or viewer. In other cases, the competitor's product is named or even shown.

There is considerable ongoing debate in Canada concerning the use of comparative advertising techniques. In a series of court challenges in recent years, there have been a number of decisions that influence just how advertisers may make use of a rival's brand or images in advertising. Duracell was prohibited from using Eveready's Energizer bunny in its ads. The Duracell commercial had the pink bunny expiring on the dance floor, unable to keep up with a dancing doll powered by Duracell batteries. The judge in the case said that the commercial amounted to a "visual humiliation of a trademark at the hands of the other party."[2] Advertisers do not have to name a competitor explicitly to fall afoul of the law. Procter & Gamble, in advertising for its Bounty paper towels, referred to Scott products as "a national leading brand." In responding, Scott Paper actually named Procter & Gamble and the Bounty brand and made specific claims about the performance of its Clean Ultra brand of towels, as compared with Bounty.[3] In another case involving Procter & Gamble, a judge of the Ontario Court rejected claims from Unilever Canada and allowed P&G to continue to promote its new Oil of Olay beauty bar as superior to "a leading beauty bar" — a direct reference to Unilever's Dove. Judge Dunnet acknowledged that Dove was indeed the leading beauty bar "by both dollar and tonnage market share," but said she was satisfied that P&G had a reasonable basis for the claim of superiority.[4]

The Bureau of Competition Policy of Industry Canada has taken the position that truthful comparative advertising can be a pro-competitive force in the marketplace. In fact, the bureau has periodically published guidelines for the consideration of advertisers. The main point to be learned from the discussion of comparative advertising and its regulation is that a company planning to use the technique had better be very sure that what is being said in its advertising about the competition is completely accurate.

Co-operative Advertising **Co-operative advertising** promotes products of two or more firms that share the cost of the advertising. There are two types — vertical and horizontal. **Vertical co-operative advertising** involves firms on different levels of distribution. For example, a manufacturer and a retailer share the cost of the retailer's advertising of that manufacturer's product. Bombardier will share with its dealers across the country the cost of advertising Ski-doo and Sea-doo machines in local newspapers. Frequently, the manufacturer prepares the actual ad, leaving space for the retailer's name and location. Then the manufacturer and retailer share the media cost of placing the ad. Many retail ads in newspapers are co-operative ads.

Another type of vertical co-operative advertising uses an **advertising allowance**, or cash discount offered by a manufacturer to a retailer, to encourage the retailer to advertise or prominently display a product. The difference between co-operative advertising and allowances is the amount of control exerted by the manufacturer over how the money is actually spent. There is some question as to whether co-operative advertising allowances represent a form of advertising or a sales promotion activity. This illustrates the difficulty of classifying some forms of marketing communications as either advertising or sales promotions.

These co-op arrangements benefit retailers by providing them with extra funds for promotion. Manufacturers benefit from advertising at the local level. In addition, ad dollars go farther because rates for local media are typically lower for ads placed by local firms than for ads placed by national advertisers.

Horizontal co-operative advertising is undertaken by firms on the same level of distribution — such as a group of retailers — that share the costs of advertising. For example, all stores in a suburban shopping centre may run a joint newspaper ad. The principal benefit is that by pooling their funds, the firms can achieve much greater exposure than if they advertised individually.

www.duracellusa.com • www.eveready.com • www.unilever.com

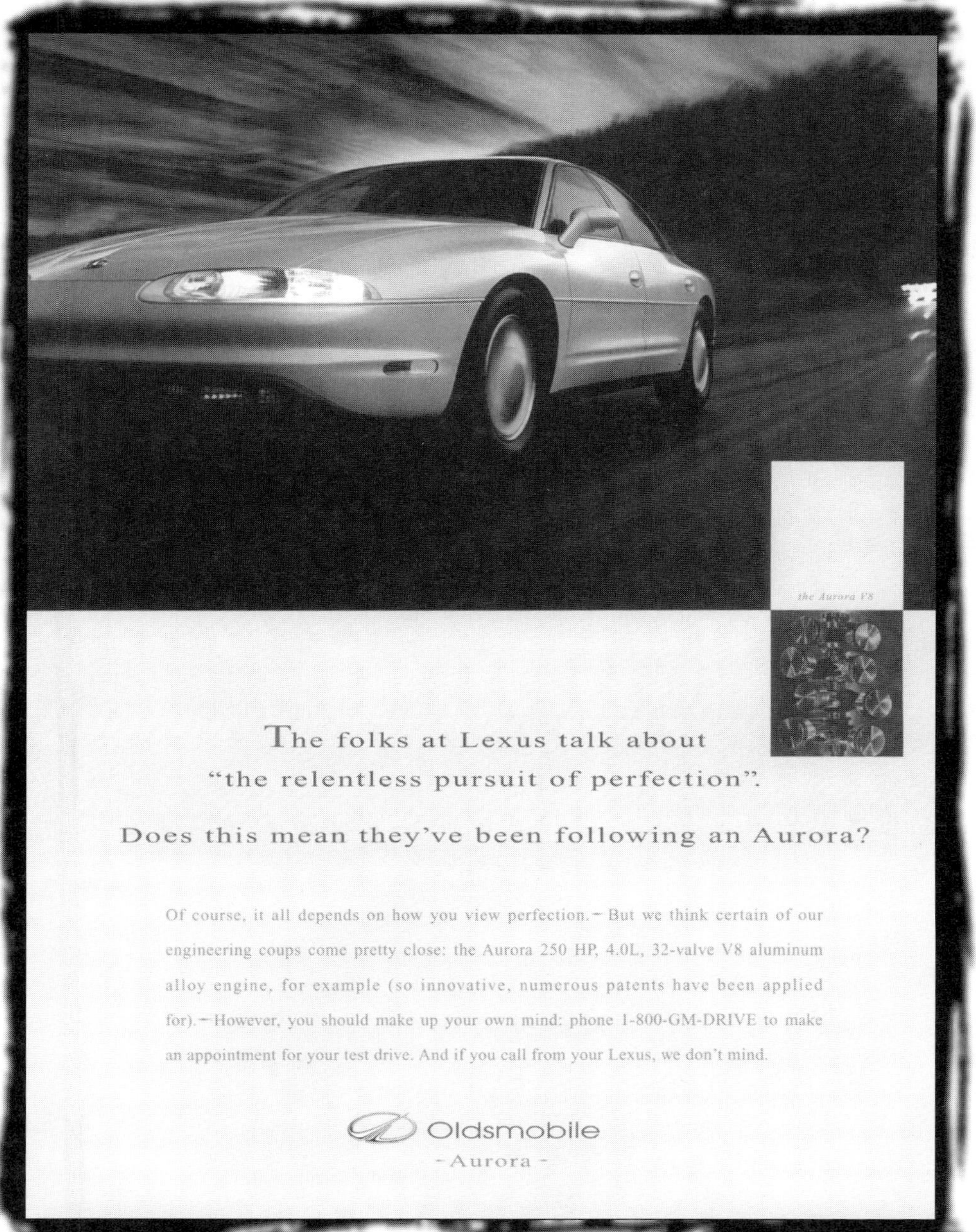

Some advertisers call the competition by name.

Companies that normally would not have a close association often co-operate in joint promotions. More and more companies are realizing that they can stretch their promotion dollars, benefit from the reputation of noncompeting successful brands, and open new markets with joint promotional programs. McCain Foods entered into a special promotion with Sony, with the hope that it would reposition the Pizza Pockets brand and draw teens to their nearest grocery store in search of the product. The food giant teamed up its snack brand with Sony's PlayStation, a video game player. Sony was receptive to the overture from McCain because it was in the process of launching its new video game Crash Bandicoot, its answer to Nintendo's Mario. It was a natural promotion, because both products appeal to a mostly male, pizza-eating, video-game-playing youth audience.[5] Other companies often decide to partner with appropriate firms or brands in other industries. Such partnerships are very popular in the travel and tourism industry.[6] Air Canada, Diners Club/en route, and Avis recently teamed up in a three-way promotion offering free membership in the Avis Preferred Renter program and 50 percent off a second ticket on Air Canada when the first ticket was purchased on the Diners Club/en route card.

Cost of Advertising

Advertising in one form or another is used by most marketers. The significance of advertising is indicated by the amount of money spent on it. In 1995, the gross expenditures on advertising in Canada totalled almost $10 billion. Table 20-1 shows the estimated total expenditure by medium.[7] For many years, daily newspapers have been the most widely used medium, but the percentage of total expenditures accounted for by newspapers has been declining steadily from approximately 30 percent in the mid-1970s to 19.8 percent in 1995. In fact, the percentage of total advertising expenditures going to the traditional mass media — radio, television, newspapers, and magazines — has been declining steadily, as many advertisers have been switching at least part of their advertising budgets to media such as direct mail, directories, and weekly papers, which can often do a better job of reaching targeted segments. What this table does not reflect, of course, is the use by Canadian advertisers of other forms of direct marketing that are discussed later in this chapter, including the World Wide Web.

Advertising Expenditures by Industry Some industries in Canada spend a lot more money than others on advertising. The information presented in Table 20-2 indicates that the retail industry spent almost $900 million on advertising in 1996 — much more than the $500 million spent by automobile manufacturers. The A.C. Nielsen Annual Summary of Expenditures indicates that there is relatively little change in the ranking of industries, in terms of

TABLE 20-1 Net Canadian Advertising Revenues by Medium, 1994–95

	Revenues ($millions)		%Change
Medium	**1995**	**1994**	**1994–95**
Catalogues, direct mail	2,319.0	2,203.6	+5.2
Daily newspapers	1,932.0	1,857.9	+4.0
Television[1]	1,843.5	1,767.7	+4.3
Yellow pages[2]	864.8	847.6	+2.0
Outdoor	820.0	796.0	+3.0
Radio	754.1	741.5	+1.7
Weeklies, semi-weeklies, tri-weeklies	584.0	578.6	+1.0
General magazines	336.7	317.6	+6.0
Business papers	187.5	183.8	+2.0
Other print[3]	98.0	97.6	+.04
Total Advertising	9,739.7	9,391.9	+4.0

1 Includes specialty services.

2 Excludes city directories.

3 Religious, farm, and school publications and weekend supplements.

Source: "A Report of Advertising Revenues in Canada," CARD Group, Maclean Hunter Publishing, Toronto. Printed with permission of Mclean Hunter Publishing Ltd.

what they spend on advertising. Retailers spend a lot more because there are many more of them, and some are very large.

It is important also to note that some of the advertisers who spend a large amount of money on advertising each year actually devote a very small percentage of their total sales to advertising. Data collected by Statistics Canada indicate that the largest percentage of sales spent on advertising is by companies that manufacture health and beauty aids and soaps and cleaning products. In general, companies in the consumer products field spend a higher percentage of sales on advertising than do manufacturers of industrial products. Major companies spend an average of about 2 percent of total sales on advertising, while companies that manufacture consumer products spend approximately 3 percent on average.

Advertising Cost Versus Personal Selling Cost

While we do not have accurate totals for the costs of personal selling, we do know they far surpass advertising expenditures. In manufacturing, only a few industries, such as drugs, toiletries, cleaning products, tobacco, and beverages, spend more on advertising than on personal selling. Advertising runs from 1 to 3 percent of net sales in many firms, whereas the expenses of recruiting and operating a sales force are typically 8 to 15 percent of sales.

TABLE 20-2 Top Twenty-five Advertising Categories, Canada, 1996

1996 Rank	Category	Number of Classes	Category Spending ($), 1996	1995 Rank	1994 Rank
1	Retail	65	892,410,700	1	1
2	Automotive: Cars, minivans, trucks, vans, dealer	15	508,390,700	2	2
3	Business equipment & services	57	445,323,400	4	4
4	Food	146	400,270,900	3	3
5	Entertainment	20	321,070,100	5	5
6	Financial services & insurance services	40	273,287,800	6	6
7	Travel & transportation	22	213,427,900	8	8
8	Restaurants, catering services, nightclubs	5	209,982,900	7	7
9	Local automotive dealer advertising	5	152,669,200	9	9
10	Cosmetics & toiletries	35	119,454,700	10	10
11	Drug products	36	108,897,300	12	13
12	Automotive: Oil companies & related services	28	105,693,100	13	12
13	Brewers & related products	8	102,738,500	11	11
14	Media: Television, radio, out of home	6	91,997,300	14	14
15	Home entertainment	13	61,767,300	18	19
16	Hair products	12	57,341,100	16	15
17	Publishing	4	48,283,600	22	22
18	Lotteries	1	43,431,700	17	17
19	Government	17	42,548,400	15	18
20	Household supplies	29	41,880,800	19	20
21	Sporting goods & recreational products	35	39,080,500	24	30
22	Schools, correspondence courses, seminars	5	37,912,800	25	28
23	Toys, games, dolls	6	36,827,200	20	16
24	Apparel	12	30,001,300	23	23
25	Mail order, direct mail	2	28,403,100	21	21
	Total All Classes	**851**	**4,800,373,600**		

Source: A.C. Nielsen Company Limited. Reprinted with permission.

At the wholesale level, advertising costs are very low. Personal selling expenses, however, may run ten to fifteen times as high. Even among retailers in total — and this includes those with self-service operations — the cost of personal selling is substantially higher than that of advertising.

DEVELOPING AN ADVERTISING CAMPAIGN

An **advertising campaign** consists of all the tasks involved in transforming a theme into a co-ordinated advertising program to accomplish a specific goal for a product or brand. For example, you have probably noticed the transit and television advertising campaign for Buckley's Mixture, the famous cough remedy from W.K. Buckley Limited, which uses the line, "It tastes awful. And it works." This campaign has been running successfully for several years and has now been extended to include recent additions to the Buckley's line. It relies on a blend of humour and trust in the grandfatherly figure of the company's president, Frank Buckley. An advertising campaign such as this is planned within the framework of the overall strategic marketing program and the promotional campaign. Before designing an advertising campaign, management must:

- Know who the target audience is.
- Establish the overall promotional goals.
- Set the total promotional budget.
- Determine the overall promotional theme.

With these tasks completed, the firm can begin formulating an advertising campaign. The steps in developing a campaign are: defining objectives, establishing a budget, creating a message, selecting media, and evaluating effectiveness.

Defining Objectives

The purpose of advertising is to sell something — product, service, idea, person, or place — either now or later. This goal is reached by setting specific objectives that can be expressed in individual ads that are incorporated into an advertising campaign. Recall again from the buying-decision process that buyers go through a series of stages from unawareness to purchase. Thus the immediate objective of an ad may be to move target customers to the next stage in the hierarchy — say, from awareness to interest. Note also that advertising seldom is the only promotional tool used by a firm. Rather, it is typically one part of a strategy that may also include personal selling, sales promotion, and other tools. Therefore, the objective of advertising may be to "open doors" for the sales force.

Specific advertising objectives will be dictated by the firm's overall marketing strategy. Typical objectives are:

- *Support personal selling.* Advertising may be used to acquaint prospects with the seller's company and products, easing the way for the sales force.
- *Improve dealer relations.* Wholesalers and retailers like to see a manufacturer support its products.
- *Introduce a new product.* Consumers need to be informed even about line extensions that make use of familiar brand names.
- *Expand the use of a product category.* Advertising may be used to lengthen the season for a product (as Lipton did for iced tea); increase the frequency of replacement (as Fram and Purolator did for oil filters); or increase the variety of product uses (as Arm & Hammer did for baking soda).
- *Counteract substitution.* Advertising reinforces the decisions of existing customers and reduces the likelihood that they will switch to alternative brands.

Establishing a Budget

Once a marketing communications budget has been established (discussed in Chapter 18), it must be allocated among the various activities making up the overall marketing communications program. In the case of a particular brand, a firm may wish to have several ads, as well as sales promotion and public relations activities, directed at different target audiences all under way at the same time. When Pepsi launched the "Taste it all" campaign for Diet Pepsi, it was the first totally new campaign for the soft drink since 1982. The theme of the $60-million-a-year campaign is that Diet Pepsi fits into the lifestyles of people who get the most out of life. It involves advertising, label changes, point-of-sale displays, and consumer sweepstakes with prizes of white-water rafting and dude-ranch vacations. Since all these efforts must be paid for from the marketing commu-

MARKETING AT WORK FILE 20–1

DISNEY GOES McHAPPY

Quick...name two of the world's best-known brand names. If this question were to be posed internationally, many people would undoubtedly respond "McDonald's and Disney." Given this, it is perfectly logical that these superstar brands have teamed up in a ten-year alliance, intending to combine their individual marketing power to promote each other around the globe.

The partnership is seen as a big victory for McDonald's, which has been competing with Burger King for the coveted Disney name, which in turn has been used by both hamburger chains for promotional tie-ins. Disney and McDonald's have partnered before, in the late 1980s, for the re-release of the Disney classic *Snow White and the Seven Dwarfs*, but the partnership came to an end in 1990 with a dispute over the film *Dick Tracy*. Disney then turned to McDonald's rival, Burger King, for the promotions for such movies as *Aladdin*, *Lion King*, and *Toy Story*.

However, as of 1997, McDonald's exclusive arrangement with Disney undoubtedly gives it an edge in the fast-food industry. Michael Ovitz stated, "It is the companies whose brands are best known and most trusted that will succeed in the world's marketplace of the future. McDonald's and Disney are two such brands. Our alliance will further enhance recognition of our pre-eminence in our respective industries."

McDonald's will be operating two restaurants in the Walt Disney World Resort, in Orlando, Florida, and one restaurant in Disneyland Paris. In addition, McDonald's will be sponsoring the Dinoland attraction in Florida's Walt Disney World Resort.

Coupling McDonald's 18,700 restaurants in ninety-three countries with Disney's unsurpassed popularity (and success) in movies, theme parks, and home videos is a marketing match made in heaven. Together they can capture the imaginations and appetites of the world's youth!

Source: Adapted from "Disney, McDonald's Form Global Advertising Alliance," *Vancouver Sun*, May 24, 1996, p. D3.

nications budget, the potential value of each must be weighed and allocations made accordingly.

One method that firms use to extend their advertising budgets is co-operative advertising, discussed earlier in this chapter. But not all firms are in a position to participate in co-operative advertising programs. Generally, such programs are available only to retailers and wholesalers who distribute the products of large manufacturers and who can take advantage of the co-operative budgets made available by those companies. This leaves many companies and other organizations who must plan and execute their own advertising programs and must pay the entire cost. Many firms, particularly smaller ones, find the establishment of an advertising budget to be a very difficult exercise. This is related to the fact that most business people find it equally difficult to measure the payback from advertising and, therefore, do not feel that they are in a position to decide where to place their advertising dollars to get the greatest return. The result is that a lot of advertising money is wasted, and many companies probably pay much more than they should for effective advertising.

Creating a Message

Whatever the objective of an advertising campaign, the individual ads must accomplish two things: get and hold the **attention** of the intended audience, and **influence** that audience in the desired way. Remember that the ultimate purpose of advertising is to sell something, and that the ad itself is a sales message. The ad may be a fast-paced sales talk, as in a direct-action TV ad by a car dealership. Or it may be a very long-range, low-key message, as are many institutional ads. Whatever the method, the goal is to sell something sooner or later.

Attention can be achieved in many ways (recall our discussion of perception in Chapter 6). The most common approach is to present the material in an unexpected manner or to use an unconventional technique to capture the attention of the audience. Thus a print ad may be mostly white space or a television commercial might show the product in an unusual setting or address a topic from a new perspective. American Express gets attention when it features well-known personalities in the advertising for its credit cards. Nike uses dramatic special effects (and personalities) in its television commercials. Some advertising for social programs, such as anti-smoking campaigns and appeals against drinking and driving, will use dramatic emotional content to shock viewers and to get their attention.

If the ad succeeds in getting the audience's attention, the advertiser has a few seconds to communicate a message intended to influence beliefs and/or behaviour. The message has two elements: the appeal and the execution. The **appeal** in an ad is the reason or justification for believing or behaving. It is the benefit that the individual will receive as a result of accepting the message.

Some advertisers mistakenly focus their appeal on product features or attributes. They either confuse attributes with benefits or assume that if they present the product's attributes, the audience will infer the correct benefits. Telling customers that a cereal contains fibre (an attribute) is much less meaningful than telling them that, because it contains fibre, consuming it reduces the likelihood of colon cancer (the benefit). Common appeals or benefits and examples of product categories in which they are frequently used include:

- Health (food, nonprescription drugs).
- Social acceptance (cosmetics, health and beauty aids).
- Material success (automobiles, investments).
- Recognition (clothing, jewellery).
- Sensory pleasure (movies, candy).
- Time savings (prepared foods, convenience stores).
- Peace of mind (insurance, tires).

Execution is combining in a convincing, compatible way the feature or device that gets attention with the appeal. An appeal can be executed in different ways. Consider the ways you could communicate the benefit of reliable performance in a home appliance — presenting operating statistics, obtaining the endorsement of a respected person or organization, collecting testimonials from satisfied owners, or describing the meticulous manufacturing process. Rather than doing any of these, Maytag opted for "the lonely repairman," an amusing and memorable execution that gets attention and conveys the benefit of reliability.

Creating an advertisement involves writing the copy, selecting the illustration (for visual media), preparing the visual or verbal layout, and reproducing the ad for the selected media. The **copy** in an ad is all the written or spoken material in it. Copy in a print ad includes the headline, coupons, advertiser's identification, and the main body of the message. In a broadcast ad the copy is the script.

For visual ads, the **illustration** is a powerful feature. The main points to consider about illustrations are (1) whether they are totally appropriate to the product advertised and (2) despite the adage "a picture is worth a thousand words," whether they are the best use of the space. The **layout** is the physical arrangement of all the elements in an advertisement. In print ads, it is the appearance of the page. For television, layout is the set as well as the positioning of actors and props. The layout of a radio ad is the sequence in which information is presented. A good layout can hold interest as well as attract attention. It should lead the audience through the entire ad in an orderly fashion.

The cost of creating an ad can vary from almost nothing for a local radio spot written by the staff at a radio station to as much as $500,000 for a complex television commercial. In recent years, production costs for network TV ads have escalated dramatically. As a result, fewer ads are being made, and they are kept on the air longer.

Selecting Media

In describing the steps in developing an advertising campaign, we have discussed creating an advertising message before describing the selection of **advertising media** in which to place the ad. In reality these decisions are made simultaneously. Both the message and the choice of media are determined by the appeal and the target audience. The following discussion focuses on selecting appropriate mass media in which to place advertising. As was suggested earlier in this chapter, advertisers are increasingly facing the decision of whether to use the mass media or to try to reach targeted audiences with more direct messages, using a number of alternatives to the traditional mass media that advertisers have been using for the past fifty years or more. Remember, media doesn't have to mean mass media.

Advertisers need to make decisions at each of three successive levels to determine which specific advertising medium to use:

1. Which type of medium will be used — newspaper, television, radio, magazine, or direct contact through mail or the Internet? What about the less prominent media of billboards, specialty items, and Yellow Pages?
2. Which category of the selected medium will be used? Television has network and cable; magazines include general-interest (*Maclean's*, *Time*) and special-interest (*Chatelaine*, *Canadian Business*) categories; and there are national as well as local newspapers.
3. Which specific media vehicles will be used? An advertiser who decides first on radio and then on local stations must determine which stations to use in each city.

Here are some general factors that will influence media choice:

- *Objectives of the ad.* The purpose of a particular ad and the goals of the entire campaign influence the choice of which media to use. For example, if the campaign goal is to generate appointments for sales people, the company may rely on direct mail or telephone contact. If an advertiser wants to induce quick action, newspaper or radio may be the medium to use.
- *Audience coverage.* The audience reached by the medium should match the geographic area in which the product is distributed. Furthermore, the selected medium should reach the desired types of prospects with a minimum of wasted coverage. Wasted coverage occurs when an ad reaches people who are not prospects for the product. Many media — even national and other large-market media — can be targeted at small, specialized market segments. For example, *Maclean's* magazine publishes regional editions with different ads in the Atlantic, Ontario, and Western editions, and a French-language edition for Quebec.
- *Requirements of the message.* The medium should fit the message. For example, food products, floor coverings, and apparel are best presented visually. If the advertiser can use a very brief message (the rule of thumb is six words or less), as is common with reminder advertising, billboards may be a suitable medium — provided, of course, that the audience includes people who are likely to drive or walk by the billboards.
- *Time and location of the buying decision.* The medium should reach prospective customers when and where they are about to make their buying decisions. Research shows that radio scores the highest in immediacy of exposure; over 50 percent of adults were last exposed to radio within one hour of making their largest purchase of the day. This factor highlights one of the strengths of place-based advertising. Likewise, in-store ads — for example, on shopping carts and in the aisles of supermarkets — reach consumers at the actual time of purchase.
- *Media cost.* The cost of each medium should be considered in relation to the budget available to pay for it and its reach or circulation. For example, the cost of network television exceeds the available funds of many advertisers.

Cost per thousand (CPM) persons reached (M is the Roman numeral for a thousand) is a standard measure routinely provided to prospective advertisers by all media. It allows an advertiser to compare costs across media. CPM is computed as follows:

$$\text{CPM} = \frac{\text{ad cost} \times 1{,}000}{\text{circulation}}$$

For example, let's assume that the advertising rate for a four-colour, one-page ad in *Holiday Getaways*, a magazine with an international circulation, is $42,000 and the circulation is 1,200,000. Therefore, CPM for the magazine is:

$$\text{CPM} = \frac{(\$42{,}000 \times 1{,}000)}{1{,}200{,}000} = \$35$$

Of course, it is essential to estimate what proportion of all persons reached are truly prospects for the advertiser's product. If an advertiser is interested only in females over fifty years of age, we might find that there are 650,000 *Holiday Getaways* readers in this category. Therefore, we would have to calculate a weighted CPM:

$$\text{Weighted CPM} = \frac{(\$42{,}000 \times 1{,}000)}{650{,}000} = \$64.62$$

Beyond these general factors, management must evaluate the advertising characteristics of each medium it is considering. We have carefully chosen the term characteristics instead of advantages and disadvantages because a medium that works well for one product is not necessarily the best choice for another product. To illustrate, a characteristic of radio is that it makes its impressions through sound and imagination. The roar of a crowd, running water, the rumbling of thunder, or screeching tires can be used to create mental images quickly and easily. But radio will not do the job for products that benefit from colour photography. Let's examine the characteristics of the major media.

Newspapers As an advertising medium, newspapers are flexible and timely. They account for the largest portion of total advertising dollars spent in Canada. They can be used to cover a single city or a number of urban centres. With the development of computer technology and regional printing in the publishing industry, once-local newspapers may now be printed in regional centres for distribution across the country. The daily *Financial Post* and *The Globe and Mail*, for example, are headquartered in Toronto but printed regionally and are now true national daily papers.

While newspapers are becoming more attractive to the national advertiser, they remain the principal advertising vehicle for the local advertiser, particularly when they are used as the distribution vehicle for advertising flyers. Ads can be cancelled on a few days' notice or inserted generally on one day's notice. Newspapers can give an advertiser an intense coverage of a local market because almost everybody reads newspapers. The local feature also helps in that the ads can be adapted to local audiences and to social and economic conditions. Circulation costs per prospect are low. On the other hand, the life of a newspaper advertisement is very short.

Television Television is probably the most versatile and the most rapidly changing of all media. It makes its appeal through both the eye and the ear; products can be demonstrated as well as explained. It offers considerable flexibility in the geographic market covered and the time of message presentation. By making part of its impression through the ear, television can take advantage of the personal, dramatic impact of the spoken word.

On the other hand, television can be an extremely expensive medium. The message is not permanently recorded for the message receiver. Thus the prospect who is not reached the first time is lost forever, as far as a particular message is concerned. Television does not lend itself to long advertising copy, nor does it present pictures as clearly as magazines do. As with direct mail and radio, television advertisers must create their own audiences.

Cable has also changed television as an advertising medium. Canada is among the most heavily "cabled" nations in the world, with 90 percent of homes in many urban areas wired for cable. In this country, having cable television has given Canadians access to fifty channels or more, many of which originate in the United States or carry specialized programming, including sports, weather, movies, youth programs, country music, arts and entertainment, and popular music videos. This increased access to television channels has resulted in a dramatic change in the nature and effect of television as an advertising medium.

In households with cable, television is now a much more focused medium, offering specialized television channels to people with particular interests. The sheer variety of channels has led to a situation described as **fragmentation**, where viewers regularly "zap" their way through the range of channels available, often when a commercial appears. This proliferation of channels through cable, coupled with the use of VCRs, remote control devices, video games, and the Internet, has meant that the audience likely to be exposed to a television commercial is reduced, thereby limiting the effectiveness of television in reaching a mass market. As a result, some advertisers have begun to use shorter, more attention-getting commercials, or have moved some of their advertising budgets away from television to other media.

In the cluttered world of television, advertisers are constantly looking for ways to reach targeted audiences and to make their advertising messages stand out. Some large advertisers are experimenting with interactive television, which many feel will become a major element in media advertising in the near future. Others are developing infomercials, which are intended to stand out from other forms of advertising on television. Finally, some companies have moved their advertising from the mainstream television networks to specialty channels in order to increase the likelihood of reaching their targeted audiences. Advertising on such specialty cable channels as CBC Newsworld, The Weather Network, MétéoMédia, TSN, RDS, MuchMusic, MusiquePlus, YTV, the Life Network, and Vision TV reach millions of viewers every day in Canada. The result is that television is fast becoming much more of a targeted medium and less of a mass medium to reach mass audiences.[8]

We can expect to see television become even more fragmented and more competitive in the future. With the introduction of two national direct-to-home satellite TV services, Star Choice and ExpressVu, Canadians who subscribe to these services can now have access to up to three hundred channels from all over the world and satisfying a multitude of interests.[9] Cable companies have responded by launching new cable channels, including the Comedy Channel, Teletoon, The History and Entertainment Channel, Home and Gardening, CTV all-news, and a science fiction channel. The result may be a confusing array of television-based options that lead some advertisers to rethink their use of the medium.[10]

Direct Mail Direct mail has probably become the most personal and selective of all the media. Because it reaches only the market that the advertiser wishes to contact, there is a minimum of waste circulation. Direct mail is not accompanied by articles or other editorial matter, however, unless the advertiser provides it. That is, most direct mail is pure advertising. As a result, a direct-mail ad creates its own circulation and attracts its own readers. The cost of direct mail per prospect reached is quite high compared with that of other media. But other media reach many people who are not real prospects and thus have higher waste-circulation costs. A severe limitation of direct mail is the difficulty of getting and maintaining good mailing lists. Direct-mail advertising also suffers from the stigma of being classed as "junk mail."

The effectiveness of direct mail has been increased in recent years through the application of technology to the process of identifying prospects to whom advertising materials are to be mailed. Highly specialized mailing lists can be purchased from mailing-list brokers, but many firms are now able to produce their own highly targeted mailing and contact lists from their own databases. Buying lists can be expensive, but they do offer the advertisers the ability to target precisely the group in which they are interested. Many companies have developed their own mailing lists through an effective design of their internal information systems. By capturing sales data in an appropriate way, for example, a travel agency can produce a list of all the clients who made a business trip to Europe in the past year, or took a vacation in the southern United States, or made more than fifteen business trips. These individuals then represent target segments for special-interest mailings. Wastage is dramatically reduced because the advertising reaches precisely those people who are most likely interested.

While direct mail is widely regarded as one of the most cost-effective of advertising media, it is also one that must be managed very carefully. In the first place, the effectiveness of a direct-mail advertising program is very heavily dependent on the accuracy of the mailing list being used. Some users of direct mail spend too little time on ensuring the accuracy of the mailing list, with the result that many people on the list may not be at all interested in the product or service, while some will receive two or three mailing pieces because their names appear on the list in a number of different forms. You have probably been mailed advertising material that you are not the least bit interested in. This contributes to the fact that many people have a low opinion of direct mail. In a study conducted for National Public Relations, seven out of ten respondents considered direct mail to be the least credible way for them to learn about a company's new product or service. However, many companies do use direct mail very effectively and in a manner that does not offend recipients. One good example is the direct-mail campaign that Oland's, the Labatt-owned brewing company in Nova Scotia, used to launch its Alexander Keith's Pale Ale in the Ontario market. The company targeted Nova Scotia university alumni living in Ontario and mailed each grad a personalized letter and a voucher for a six-pack of Keith's IPA, along with an invitation to the official launch of the beer aboard HMS *Bounty*, which had sailed from Halifax to Toronto.[11]

Radio Radio is enjoying a renaissance as an advertising and cultural medium and as a financial investment. When interest in television soared after World War II, radio audiences (especially for national network radio) declined so much that people were predicting radio's demise. But for the past ten years or so, this medium has been making a real comeback. Local radio (as contrasted with national networks) is especially strong. Radio accounts for just under 10 percent of all advertising revenues in Canada, attracting more than $780 million in sales annually.[12]

As an advertising medium, radio's big advantage is its relatively low cost. You can reach almost everybody with radio. At the same time, with special-interest, targeted programming, certain radio stations can do a very effective job of reaching specific target market segments. In recent years, for example, a number of Canadian radio stations began to pay more attention to the growing segment of the market in the 30-to-50 age group. As a result, the top three formats in Canadian radio stations are country and western, adult contemporary, and news/talk, all of which are likely to appeal to a more mature audience than are the rock music stations that were more popular in the 1970s and 1980s. Other specialty stations have emerged in many of the larger radio markets in Canada, ranging from The FAN, Toronto's all-sports station, to Vancouver's "The Bridge" (CKBD), which billed itself as Canada's first contemporary Christian music station.[13]

Although radio is one of the more targeted of the mass media and can deliver an audience at a fairly low CPM (cost per thousand), it does have its limitations. On the one hand, it makes only an audio impression, so it is of limited value where a visual impact is needed. On the other hand, some advertisers who believe in the value of radio consider this to be one of radio's strong points — it is able to stimulate the imagination of the listener. Radio also does not have a captive audience, in that many people listen to the radio for "background" entertainment while they are working around the house, driving in their cars, or doing homework! The exposure life of a radio commercial is quite short, resulting in a need to deliver multiple exposures to gain impact.

Magazines Magazines are an excellent medium when high-quality printing and colour are desired in an ad. Magazines can reach a national market at a relatively low cost per reader. Through special-interest or regional editions of general-interest magazines, an advertiser can reach a selected audience with a minimum of waste circulation. Magazines are usually read in a leisurely fashion, in contrast to the haste in which other print media are read. This feature is especially valuable to the advertiser with a lengthy or complicated message. Magazines have a relatively long life, anywhere from a week to a month, and a high pass-along readership.

With less flexible production schedules than newspapers, magazines require ads to be submitted several weeks before publication. In addition, because they are published weekly or monthly, it is more difficult to use topical messages. Magazines are often read at times or in places — on planes or in doctors' offices, for instance — far removed from the place where a buying impulse can be acted on.

Out-of-Home Advertising Out-of-home advertising, which includes billboards, posters, bus shelter ads, and the new electronic digital billboards, has a low cost per exposure. Because of the mobile nature of our society, outdoor ads reach a large percentage of the population. But, because it is typically seen by people "on the go," billboard advertising is appropriate only for brief messages. It is excellent for reminder advertising, and it carries the impact of large size and colour. Motion and three-dimensional figures can be incorporated in a billboard's design for increased attention-getting ability. Billboards provide flexibility in geographic coverage and

www.labatt.com

intensity of market coverage within an area. However, unless the advertised product or service is widely used, considerable waste circulation will occur. Although the cost of reaching an individual person is low, the total cost of a national billboard campaign can be quite high. Finally, the landscape-defacing aspect of outdoor advertising has aroused considerable public criticism. Another issue is that posters and billboards have to be maintained by the companies that erected them if they are going to have an appeal to passing consumers.[14]

Specialty Advertising An item of merchandise imprinted with the advertiser's name, message, or logo and given free is specialty advertising. According to the Specialty Advertising Association International, more than fifteen thousand different items, from pens and baseball caps to coffee cups and calendars, are used in specialty advertising, and annual expenditures are more than $5 billion in North America.

Specialty advertising is usually used in conjunction with other promotional activities, though it is sometimes used alone by firms with very small advertising budgets. Its greatest strength is its long life. Every time the specialty item is used, the advertising message is repeated.

Emerging Media Many advertisers consider several lesser-known media to be valuable, especially when used in conjunction with the better-known media:

- *Yellow Pages.* The traditional Yellow Pages are a directory of local businesses and their telephone numbers, organized by type of product or service. Although such advertising media have been around for many years, there are some new twists as "Yellow Pages" directories are being printed by companies in competition with the telephone companies, and directories of fax numbers are being issued. Tele-Direct, the national publisher of the Yellow Pages, now produces a CD-ROM version.
- *Infomercials.* These are the lengthy television advertisements that generally run for up to sixty minutes and combine information with entertainment and product promotions. They have been popular in the United States for many years, and many have been beamed into Canada on American channels, featuring such well-known presenters as Victoria Principal and Tony Robbins, promoting everything from diet plans and personal-improvement programs to baldness remedies and auto paint protectors. While infomercials are not as widely used in Canada as they are in the United States, a number of companies, including the Royal Bank of Canada and Cantel, have been experimenting with the concept in a variety of formats.[15]
- *Place-based media.* As we discussed earlier in this chapter, certain attractive target segments, such as young professionals, teenagers, and dual-career families, have become increasingly difficult to reach through traditional advertising media. The solution is to place the advertising where the people are. Consequently, we have seen an increase in advertising in airports, shopping malls, waiting rooms, supermarkets, phone booths, and even public washrooms. Brewers Retail in Ontario installed its own television network that beams programming to customers through its Beer Stores throughout the province.
- *Videos and CD-ROMs.* Bothered by the erosion of their network television audience by videos, some national advertisers have moved their advertising to reach the video watchers by placing ads on rental video movies or by co-sponsoring or co-producing them. Other companies are able to get their messages, especially complex messages, directly into the hands of prospective customers by having their own videos or CD-ROMs produced and then mailed directly to targeted customers.
- *World Wide Web.* Much has been written in recent years about the advertising potential of the World Wide Web. Many companies have had Web pages created and have begun to reach their target market utilizing this new medium. Canadian Tire, for example, developed an electronic flyer that allows consumers to receive selective promotional information at their individual e-mail addresses.[16]

Use of the Web is problematic at the moment because it is still (at least at the time this book was being written) an unproven medium. Many believe that advertising on the Web will become commonplace in a few years and that it will take the place of more conventional mass media. One of its obvious advantages is that it allows the customer to seek out

Bringing the ads to where the customers are.

the advertiser; in this regard it is like the Yellow Pages, in that whoever approaches a company's Web site is very likely interested in buying. A second feature of advertising on the Web is that it is easy. Many smaller companies in particular have turned to in-house personnel or to programmers who are not trained in advertising or marketing to develop their Web pages at very low cost. The result is often embarrassingly poor. Advertisers must realize that the Web will become an extremely important advertising medium in the future and that it has to be approached in the same way as other advertising media — with appropriate strategic planning and investment — if high-quality, effective communication is to be the result.

Evaluating the Advertising Effort

In managing its advertising program, a company should carefully evaluate the effectiveness of previous ads and use the results to improve the quality of future ads. Shrinking profit margins and increasing competition — both foreign and domestic — force management to appraise all expenditures. Top executives want proof that advertising is worthwhile. They want to know whether dollars spent on advertising are producing as many sales as could be reaped from the same dollars spent on other marketing activities.

Difficulty of Evaluation It is hard to measure the sales effectiveness of advertising. By the very nature of the marketing mix, all elements — including advertising — are so intertwined that it is nearly impossible to measure the effect of any one by itself. Factors that contribute to the difficulty of measuring the sales impact of advertising are:

- *Ads have different objectives.* Though all advertising is ultimately intended to increase sales, individual ads may not be aimed at producing immediate results. Some ads simply announce new store hours or service policies. Other ads build goodwill or contribute to a company's image.
- *Ads can have an effect over time.* Even an ad designed to have an immediate sales impact may produce results weeks or months after it appears. A consumer may be influenced by an ad but not be able to act on it immediately. Or an ad may plant in the consumer's mind a seed that doesn't blossom into a sale for several weeks. It is impossible to determine, with the exception of mail-order advertising, when a particular ad or campaign produced results.
- *Measurement problems.* Consumers cannot usually say when or if a specific ad influenced their behaviour, let alone if it caused them to buy. Human motivation is too complicated to be explained by a single factor.

In spite of these problems, advertisers try to measure advertising effectiveness because they must — and some knowledge is better than none. An ad's effectiveness may be tested before it is presented to the target audience, while it is being presented, or after it has completed its run.

Methods Used to Measure Effectiveness Ad effectiveness can be measured directly and indirectly. **Direct tests**, which measure or predict the sales volume attributable to an ad or a campaign, can be used only with a few types of ads. Tabulating the number of redemptions of a reduced-price coupon incorporated in an ad will indicate its effectiveness. Coupons frequently are coded so they can also be traced to the publications from which they came. Another direct test used to predict sales measures the number of inquiries received from an ad that offers additional information to prospects who call or write in.

Most other types of measures are **indirect tests** of effectiveness, or measures of something other than actual behaviour. One of the most frequently used measures is **advertising recall**. Recall tests are based on the premise that an ad can have an effect only if it is perceived and remembered. Three common recall tests are:

- *Recognition* — showing people an ad and asking if they have seen it before.
- *Aided recall* — asking people if they can recall seeing any ads for a particular brand.
- *Unaided recall* — asking people if they can remember seeing any ads within an identified product category.

For broadcast media this kind of testing can be conducted using a telephone survey, calling people at home within a few hours after an ad is aired, or after a campaign has been running for several weeks.

Television ads are often tested before they are presented to the general public in what are called **pretests**. Commercials in finished or nearly finished form (to save production costs) are presented to panels of consumers for their reactions. This is often done in theatre settings, with the test ad shown along with other ads in the context of a regular TV program. After viewing the program and the ads, the consumers are quizzed about the commercial being tested.

A criticism of pretests is that the situation is unrealistic. The ads often are not in the final forms that the actual target audience would see; the research respondents have been invited to a theatre to participate; and the respondents are usually given an incentive for their involvement. The testers argue that since these factors exist across all commercials tested, they in effect "wash out" and the scores provide useful comparative information.

Refinements are constantly being made in advertising testing. Developments in areas such as laboratory test markets and computer simulations hold promise for the future. However, the complexity of decision-making, combined with the multitude of influences on the buyer, will continue to make measuring the effectiveness of advertising a difficult task.

ORGANIZING FOR ADVERTISING

A firm can manage its advertising in three ways:

- Develop an internal advertising department.
- Use an outside advertising agency.
- Use a combination of an internal department and an outside advertising agency.

Regardless of which alternative is selected, generally the same specialized skills are necessary to do the advertising job. Creative people are needed to prepare the copy, generate illustrative material, and design the layouts. Media experts are required to select the appropriate media, buy the time or space, and arrange for the scheduled appearance of the ads. And managerial skills are essential to plan and administer the entire advertising program.

Internal Departments

All these advertising tasks, some of them, or just overall direction can be performed by an internal department. A company whose advertising is a substantial part of its marketing mix will usually have its own advertising department. Large retailers, for example, have their own advertising departments, and many do not use advertising agencies at all.

Advertising Agencies

Many companies, especially manufacturers of consumer products, use advertising agencies to carry out some or all of their advertising activities. An **advertising agency** is an independent company that provides specialized advertising services and may also offer more general marketing assistance, including public relations and media relations.

Advertising agencies plan and execute entire advertising and communications campaigns. They employ more advertising specialists than their clients do, because they spread the cost over many accounts. A client company can benefit from an agency's experience gained from other products and clients. Many large agencies have expanded the services they offer to include sales promotion and public relations, and they are frequently called upon to assist in new-product development, package design, and selecting product names. In fact, many of these firms have become integrated agencies, offering a full range of services from strategic planning to market research and Web page design that heretofore were performed by other outside specialists or by the advertisers themselves.

Inside Department and Outside Agency

Many firms have their own advertising department and also use an advertising agency. The internal advertising department acts as a liaison with the agency, giving the company greater control over this major expenditure. The advertising department approves the agency's plans and ads, is responsible for preparing and administering the advertising budget, and co-ordinates advertising with personal selling. It may also handle direct marketing, dealer displays, and other promotional activities if they are not handled by the agency.

SALES PROMOTION

Sales promotion is one of the most loosely used terms in the marketing vocabulary. We define **sales promotion** as demand-stimulating devices designed to supplement advertising and facilitate personal selling. Examples of sales promotion devices are coupons, premiums, in-store displays, trade shows, samples, in-store demonstrations, and contests.

Sales promotions are conducted by producers and intermediaries. The target for producers' sales promotions may be intermediaries, end users — households or business users — or the producer's own sales force. Intermediaries direct sales promotion at their sales people or prospects further down the channel of distribution.

Nature and Scope of Sales Promotion

Sales promotion is distinct from advertising or personal selling, but these three forms of promotion are often used together in a co-ordinated fashion. For example, an in-store display (sales promotion) furnished by Michelin to dealers selling its tires may feature a slogan and illustrations (including, of course, the Michelin Man) from Michelin's current advertising campaign. This display, which helps retailers sell tires, also makes them more receptive to talking with Michelin sales people. Or, as another example, prospective customers may be generated from people who enter a contest at the Canon copy machines exhibit at an office equipment trade show. These prospects might be sent some direct-mail advertising and then be contacted by a sales person.

There are two categories of sales promotion: **trade promotions**, directed to the members of the distribution channel; and **consumer promotions**, aimed at consumers. Manufacturers as a group spend about twice as much on trade promotion as they do on advertising, and an amount about equal to their advertising on consumer promotions.

The numbers attached to some sales promotion activities are mind-boggling. Almost 3.3 billion coupons were distributed directly to consumers in Canada in 1996 by packaged-goods manufacturers alone, an increase of 8 percent over 1995. These numbers do not even include coupons issued by restaurants, retailers, and other major users. In recent years, the face value of these coupons has increased to an average of seventy cents, and redemption rates actually went up.[17] This growth in the distribution of paper coupons to Canadian households continues despite an increasing acceptance of technology in the distribution of coupons, as some retailers use a system to distribute coupons selectively — for example, targeting them only to customers who purchase a competitor's product. Some supermarket chains, such as A&P, no longer issue paper coupons at all; rather, they use electronic couponing, which involves issuing discounts automatically to all purchasers who have a special card that scans for discounts as their purchases are checked in.[18]

Several factors in the marketing environment contribute to the surging popularity of sales promotion:

- *Short-term results.* Sales promotions such as couponing and trade allowances produce quicker, more measurable sales results. However, critics of this strategy argue that these immediate benefits come at the expense of building brand equity.

MARKETING AT WORK FILE 20-2

ALL PUMPED UP

Today's gas stations are slowly moving away from promotional "giveaways" or "collectables" and moving toward one-stop shopping stations and frequent-shopper programs, such as Petro-points. One-stop shopping has taken off, with Imperial Oil and Petro-Canada leading the way. Petro Canada has introduced Petrocan SuperStop stations, and Imperial Oil has opened Tiger Express convenience stores in its Esso stations. Petrocan SuperStops offer up to sixteen pumps, a high-tech car wash, fresh bread, gourmet coffee, the latest videos, ATMs, and even fast-food operators, such as Swiss Chalet and Harvey's. Tiger Express stores hold several of the same amenities but are often linked to fast-food chains such as Tim Hortons, Pizza Hut, and McDonald's.

In addition to these new convenience stores, many gas stations are trying to gain customer loyalty through the use of "frequent shopper" programs. Imperial Oil has joined forces with Zellers in an endeavour called Club Z Extra. Members of this club gain points by filling up at Esso stations and redeem the points for products in the Zellers Club Z program. Shell participates in the Air Miles travel reward program, and more recently, partnered with Sears to allow Canadians to use their Sears cards to pay for gas at any of Shell's 2,300 Canadian stations.

These reward programs carry more than the obvious benefits. While the initial desire is that these programs will build loyalty, there is also the bonus of gathering additional information on the spending habits of consumers.

The emergence of these new "convenience" stores and loyalty programs has come at a time of shrinkage in the gas and oil industry. The number of Canadian service stations has been steadily declining — there were 19,500 gas stations in 1990, but only 15,200 in 1995. Many believe this is an indication that the industry has acknowledged that success is not as straightforward as it was in the past. The additional services and amenities offered by the oil companies will allow for higher profit margins than those provided by gasoline alone. In addition, the stations will be better able to differentiate themselves from their competitors — through additional conveniences and better service.

Source: Brent Jang, "Gas Stations Pump Convenience," *The Globe and Mail*, September 2, 1996, p. B1. Reprinted with permission of *The Globe and Mail*.

They feel that an overemphasis on sales promotion may undermine a brand's future.

- *Competitive pressure.* If competitors are offering buyers price reductions, contests, or other incentives, a firm may feel forced to retaliate with its own sales promotions.
- *Buyers' expectations.* Once they are offered purchase incentives, consumers and channel members get used to them and soon begin expecting them.
- *Low quality of retail selling.* Many retailers use inadequately trained sales clerks or have switched to self-service. For these outlets, sales promotion devices such as product displays and samples often are the only effective promotional tools available at the point of purchase.

Management of Sales Promotion

Sales promotion should be included in a company's marketing communications plans, along with advertising and personal selling. This means setting sales promotion objectives and strategies, determining a sales promotion budget, selecting appropriate sales promotion techniques, and evaluating the performance of sales promotion activities.

One problem management faces is that many sales promotion techniques are short-run, tactical actions. Coupons, premiums, and contests, for example, are designed to produce immediate (but short-lived) responses. As a result, they tend to be used as stop-gap measures to reverse unexpected sales declines rather than as integrated parts of a marketing program.

Determining Objectives and Strategies We identified three broad objectives of sales promotion when we defined the term:

- Stimulating business-user or household demand for a product.
- Improving the marketing performance of intermediaries and sales people.
- Supplementing advertising and facilitating personal selling.

One sales promotion technique may accomplish one or two — but probably not all — of these objectives.

More specific objectives of sales promotion are much like those for advertising and personal selling. Examples are:

- *To gain trial for a new or improved product.* Tetley Tea or Neutrogena shampoo might send a free sample through the mail.
- *To disrupt existing buying habits.* A coupon offering a large discount might cause a consumer to switch brands of a product that is viewed as generic, such as orange juice or motor oil.
- *To attract new customers.* Financial institutions have offered small appliances and other premiums to encourage consumers to open accounts.
- *To encourage greater use by existing customers.* Air Canada and most other airlines have "frequent flyer" programs to encourage travellers to use their airlines more often. Other businesses have established similar "loyalty" programs, including the popular Air Miles program, to which a number of major retailers belong.
- *To combat a competitor's promotional activity.* One supermarket chain runs a lottery or game to attract shoppers, and a competitor retaliates by offering triple-value coupons.
- *To increase impulse buying.* End-of-aisle and island displays in supermarkets can increase sales of a product by as much as 50 percent.
- *To get greater retailer co-operation.* A sporting-goods manufacturer gets additional shelf space by setting up excellent point-of-purchase displays, training retailers' sales people, and providing tote bags to be given away with purchases.

The choice of sales promotion tools derives directly from the objectives of the total marketing program. Consider the following situations and the different strategies available:

- A firm's objective is to increase sales, which calls for entering new geographic markets using a pull strategy. To encourage product trial and attract consumers away from familiar brands, possible sales promotion tactics are coupons, cash rebates, free samples, and premiums.
- A firm's objective is to protect market share in the face of intense competition. This goal suggests a push strategy to improve retailer performance and goodwill. Training retailers' sales forces, supplying effective point-of-purchase displays, and granting advertising allowances would be appropriate sales promotion options.

Determining Budgets The sales promotion budget should be established as a specific part of the budget for the total marketing communications mix. Including sales promotion in an advertising or public relations budget is not likely to foster the development of a separate sales promotion strategy. And as a result, sales promotion may be overlooked or poorly integrated with the other components of marketing communications. Setting a separate budget for sales promotion forces a company to recognize and manage it.

Within the concept of developing an integrated marketing communications strategy, the amount budgeted for sales promotion should be determined by the task method. This forces management to consider specific objectives and the sales promotion techniques that will be used to accomplish them.

Selecting the Appropriate Techniques Common sales promotion techniques are shown in Table 20-3, where they are divided into three categories based on the target audience:

- *Sales promotion directed at final consumers.* Many of the tools in Table 20-3 probably are quite familiar to you, but a brief discussion of some of them will give you a better sense of their significance.

  "Advertising specialties" is a miscellaneous category of small, usually inexpensive items imprinted with a company's name or logo that are given or sold by producers or intermediaries to customers and prospects. Examples are pens, calendars, key rings, paperweights, coffee cups, hats, and jackets.

TABLE 20-3 Major Sales Promotional Tools, Grouped by Target Audience

End Users (Consumer or Business)	Intermediaries and Their Sales Forces	Producers' Own Sales Force
Coupons	Trade shows and exhibitions	Sales contests
Cash rebates	Point-of-purchase displays	Sales training manuals
Premiums (gifts)	Free goods	Sales meetings
Free samples	Advertising allowances	Packets with promotional materials
Contests and sweepstakes	Contests for sales people	Demonstration model of product
Point-of-purchase displays	Training intermediaries' sales force	
Product demonstrations	Product demonstrations	
Trade shows and exhibitions	Advertising specialties	
Advertising specialties		

- *Sales promotion directed at intermediaries.* Some of the tools just discussed may also be directed at intermediaries and their sales forces. In addition, trade associations in industries as diverse as shoes, travel, and furniture sponsor trade shows that are open only to wholesalers and retailers. Many producers also spend considerable time and money to train the sales forces of their wholesalers and retailers.
- *Sales promotion directed at a producer's own sales force.* Again, there is overlap between the tools directed at intermediaries and those designed for the producer's own sales force. Sales contests are probably the most significant of these tools, with many firms offering one kind or another. The most common incentive is cash, used in over half of all contests. Other incentives include merchandise, plaques, jewellery, and travel. Visual sales aids (flipcharts, slides) are prepared for sales people, and brochures are developed to reinforce sales presentations.

A key step in sales promotion management is deciding which devices will help the organization reach its promotional goals. Factors that influence the choice of promotional devices include:

- *Nature of the target audience.* Is the target group loyal to a competing brand? If so, a high-value coupon may be necessary to disrupt customers' purchase patterns. Is the product bought on impulse? If so, an eye-catching point-of-purchase display may be enough to generate sales.
- *The organization's marketing communications objectives.* Does a pull or a push strategy best complement the rest of the marketing communications program?
- *Nature of the product.* Does the product lend itself to sampling, demonstration, or multiple-item purchases?
- *Cost of the device.* Sampling to a large market may be prohibitively expensive.
- *Current economic conditions.* Coupons, premiums, and rebates are good options during periods of recession or inflation, when consumers are particularly price conscious.

Evaluating Sales Promotion Evaluating the effectiveness of sales promotions is much easier and the results are more accurate than is evaluating the effectiveness of advertising. For example, responses to a premium offer or a coupon with a specified closing date can be counted and compared with a similar period when no premiums or coupons were offered. It is easier to measure sales promotion because:

- *Most sales promotions have definite starting and ending points.* Coupons must be redeemed by a certain date. Contest entries must be submitted before a particular deadline. Contests for the sales force include only the sales made during a specified period. This is quite different from advertising, where there can be significant residual effects, and the results of one campaign may overlap with those of another.

- *Most sales promotions are designed to affect sales directly.* It is more difficult to measure a change in attitude or an increase in information about a product or brand than it is to count sales.

However, there are some pitfalls in measuring sales promotion effects. First, not all sales promotions meet the conditions just mentioned. For instance, training given to a distributor's sales force may be valuable but may not produce immediate results. Second, current sales promotion results may be inflated by sales "stolen" from the future. That is, a sales promotion may get buyers to act now but they may have bought the product in the future anyway. An indication of this "cannibalizing" effect is a lower level of sales after the promotion ends, compared with the level before the sales promotion began. Third, any attempt at measurement must take into consideration external conditions, such as the behaviour of competitors and the state of the economy. A firm's market share may not increase following an expensive sales promotion, for example, but the promotion may have offset the potentially damaging impact of a competitor's promotional activity.

PUBLIC RELATIONS[19]

Public relations is a management tool designed to favourably influence attitudes toward an organization, its products, and its policies. It is an often overlooked form of promotion. In most organizations this promotional tool is typically a stepchild, relegated far behind personal selling, advertising, and sales promotion. There are several reasons for management's lack of attention to public relations:

- *Organizational structure.* In most companies, public relations is not the responsibility of the marketing department. If there is an organized effort, it is usually handled by a small public relations department that reports directly to top management.
- *Inadequate definitions.* The term public relations is used loosely by both businesses and the public. There are no generally accepted definitions of the term. As a result, what actually constitutes an organized public relations effort often is not clearly defined.
- *Unrecognized benefits.* Only recently have many organizations come to appreciate the value of good public relations. As the cost of marketing communications has gone up, firms are realizing that positive exposure through the media or as a result of community involvement can produce a high return on the investment of time and effort.

Nature and Scope of Public Relations

Public relations activities typically are designed to build or maintain a favourable image for an organization and a favourable relationship with its various publics — customers, prospects, stockholders, employees, labour unions, the local community, and the government. Senior managers in a variety of industries are increasingly recognizing the importance of maintaining a positive reputation among the public.[20]

Unlike advertising, public relations need not use the media to communicate its message. Good public relations can be achieved by supporting charitable projects (by supplying volunteer labour or other resources), participating in community service events, sponsoring athletic teams, funding the arts, producing an employee or customer newsletter, and disseminating information through exhibits, displays, and tours. Major companies often sponsor public events or special programs on television as part of their public relations efforts. Cultural organizations such as ballet companies and symphony orchestras would not survive without the support they receive from major corporations.

Publicity as a Form of Public Relations

Publicity is any communication about an organization, its products, or policies through the media that is not paid for by the organization. Publicity usually takes the form of a news story appearing in a mass medium or an endorsement provided by an individual, either informally or in a speech or interview. This is good publicity.

There is also, of course, bad publicity — a negative story about a firm or its product appearing in the media. In a society that is increasingly sensitive about the environment and in which news media are quick to report mistakes, organizations tend to focus on this negative dimension of publicity. As a result, managers

MARKETING AT WORK FILE 20-3

WHEN THINGS GO AWRY

Although this chapter deals with the day-to-day issues of general public relations, it is also important to learn how to deal with bad publicity. The most common causes of crisis in the business world are as follows:

- white-collar crime — 20 percent
- mismanagement — 20 percent
- labour disputes — 12 percent
- business catastrophe — 7 percent
- environmental change — 6 percent
- financial damages — 5 percent

(Source: Institute for Crisis Management of Louisville, Ky.)

The question that automatically follows the consideration of such a list is often: What should companies do in times of trouble? This may be a difficult question to answer. John Lute, a public relations consultant, believes that companies must walk a very fine line in troublesome situations. Although managers in the organization many feel like disengaging themselves from the situation, more often than not, this is the worst possible reaction. In taking this approach, it is likely that top management will appear to be abandoning the company and its employees. This will not help the situation, nor the morale of the employees. The organization must show loyalty to its employees — both for their morale and to avoid future lawsuits.

Bob Irvine, of the Institute of Crisis Management, believes that the best way to deal with crisis situations is to try to prevent them from occurring in the first place. Mr. Irvine divides crises into two categories: sudden disasters and smouldering problems. Prevention of these problems will only occur with continuous monitoring of staff and careful observation of mistakes made by competitors.

All too frequently in a crisis situation, organizations withdraw and hope that the consumer will forget the mishap. However, in times of trouble, especially in high-publicity situations, the consumer will pay close attention to how the company reacts. Organizations must acknowledge the situation and devise a reasonable and comprehensive "solution." Perhaps most importantly, the company must learn from the situation and take steps to prevent the same thing from happening a second time.

Source: Elizabeth Church, "How Firms Should Handle Bad Publicity," *The Globe and Mail*, November 8, 1996, p. B9. Reprinted with permission of *The Globe and Mail*.

are so concerned with avoiding bad publicity that they overlook the potential of good publicity.

There are three means for gaining good publicity:

- *Prepare a story (called a news release) and circulate it to the media.* The intention is for the selected newspapers, television stations, or other media to report the information as news.
- *Communicate personally with a group.* A press conference will draw media representatives if they feel the subject or speaker has news value. Company tours and speeches to civic or professional groups are other forms of individual-to-group communications.
- *Engage in one-on-one personal communication, or lobbying.* Companies lobby legislators or other powerful people in an attempt to influence their opinions and, subsequently, their decisions.

Publicity can help to accomplish any communication objective. It can be used to announce new products, publicize new policies, recognize employees, describe research breakthroughs, or report financial performance — if the message, person, group, or event is viewed by the media as newsworthy. This is what distinguishes publicity from advertising — publicity is not "forced" on the audience. This is also the source of its primary benefit. The credibility of publicity typically is much higher than that of advertising. If we tell you our product is great, you may well be sceptical. But if an independent, objective third party says on the evening news that our product is great, you are more likely to believe it.

Other benefits of publicity are:

- *Lower cost than advertising or personal selling.* Publicity usually costs less because there are no media space or time costs for conveying the message and no sales people to support.
- *Increased readership.* Many consumers are conditioned to ignore advertising or at least pay it scant attention. Publicity is presented as editorial material or news, so it gets greater readership.
- *More information.* Because it is presented as editorial material, publicity can contain greater detail than the usual ad. More information and persuasive content can be included in the message.
- *Timeliness.* A company can put out a news release very quickly when some unexpected event occurs.

Of course, publicity also has limitations:

- *Loss of control over the message.* An organization has no guarantee that a news release will appear in the media. In fact, only a small proportion of all the news releases a firm prepares are ever used. In addition, there is no way to control how much or what portion of a publicity release the media will print or broadcast.
- *Limited exposure.* The media will typically use publicity material to fill space when there is a lack of other news and only use it once. If the target audience misses the message when it is presented, there is no second or third chance. There is no opportunity for repetition, as is the case in advertising.
- *Publicity is not free.* Even though there are no media time and space costs, there are expenses in staffing a public relations department and in preparing and disseminating news releases.

Recognizing the value of publicity, some organizations have special units or programs to generate information. For example, Campbell Soup Company sponsors a major national survey of the attitudes of Canadians toward health and nutrition; Christie's, the cookie company, sponsors the Christie Children's Book Awards; and The Body Shop actively supports the World Wildlife Fund and other environmental groups. All these activities are designed to link the companies involved with causes and activities that consumers believe to be important. Through their association, the companies intend to improve their corporate image. To fulfil its potential, however, publicity must be treated as part of the promotional strategy of the firm and be co-ordinated with the other promotional tools.

Evaluating Public Relations

Although few executives would argue that having a good image and staying in touch with an organization's publics are unimportant, evaluating public relations and publicity is difficult. In the past, evaluation usually involved a report of activities rather than results. Public relations departments maintained "scrapbooks" to show management how many stories were written and published, the number of employees who volunteered for civic projects, and the like. These days, to justify expenditures, more organizations are requiring publicity departments to provide specific public relations objectives and show measurable results. Because it is impossible to relate public relations and publicity directly to sales, other measures must be used. One is behavioural research to show, for example, increased awareness of a product or brand name, or changes in attitudes and beliefs about a firm.

Summary

Advertising is the nonpersonal, mass-communications component in a company's marketing communications mix. Advertising can be directed to consumers or businesses and can focus on products or institutions. Direct-action product ads call for immediate action, whereas indirect-action product ads are intended to stimulate demand over a longer time period. Product ads are also classified as primary-demand and selective-demand stimulating. Primary-demand ads are designed to introduce a new product, to stimulate demand for a generic product, or to sustain demand for an industry's products. Selective-demand ads, which include competitive and comparative advertising, are intended to increase the demand for a particular brand.

In vertical co-operative advertising, manufacturers and their retail dealers share the cost of advertising the manufacturers' product at the local level. Horizontal co-operative advertising involves joint sponsorship of ads by firms at the same level of distribution.

Advertising expenditures are large, but the average cost of advertising in a firm is typically 1 to 3 percent of sales. This is considerably less than the average cost of personal selling. Other frequently used advertising media are radio, magazines, Yellow Pages, and outdoor displays.

An advertising campaign should be part of a total marketing communications program. The steps in designing a campaign include defining specific objectives, establishing a budget, creating a message, selecting media, and evaluating the advertising effort. Objectives can range from creating awareness of a brand to generating sales. Vertical and horizontal co-operative arrangements can have a significant impact on advertising budgets. The advertising message — consisting of the appeal and the execution of the ad — is influenced by the target audience and the media used to deliver the message.

A major task in developing a campaign is to select the advertising media — the general type, the particular category, and the specific vehicle. The choice should be based on the characteristics of the medium, which determine how effectively it conveys the message, and its ability to reach the target audience.

A difficult task in advertising management is evaluating the effectiveness of the advertising effort — both the entire campaign and individual ads. Except for sales results tests, commonly used techniques measure only recall of an ad. To operate an advertising program, a firm may rely on its own advertising department, an advertising agency, or a combination of the two.

Sales promotion consists of demand-stimulating devices designed to supplement advertising and facilitate personal selling. The amount of sales promotion has increased considerably in recent years, as management has sought measurable, short-term sales results.

Sales promotion should receive the same strategic attention that a company gives to advertising and personal selling, including setting objectives and establishing a budget. Sales promotion can be directed toward final consumers, intermediaries, or a company's own employees. To implement its strategic plans, management can choose from a variety of sales promotion devices. Sales promotion performance also should be evaluated.

Public relations is a management tool designed to favourably influence attitudes toward an organization, its products, and its policies. It is a frequently overlooked form of promotion. Publicity, a part of public relations, is any communication about an organization, its products, or policies through the media that is not paid for by the organization. Typically these two activities are handled in a department separate from the marketing department in a firm. Nevertheless, the management process of planning, implementing, and evaluating should be applied to their performance in the same way it is applied to advertising, sales promotion, and personal selling.

Key Terms and Concepts

Advertising (490)
Consumer advertising (490)
Business-to-business advertising (490)
Product advertising (491)
Direct-action advertising (491)
Indirect-action advertising (491)
Institutional (corporate) advertising (491)
Customer service advertising (491)
Public service advertising (491)
Primary-demand advertising (491)
Selective-demand advertising (491)
Pioneering advertising (491)
Differential competitive advantage (491)
Comparative advertising (491)
Co-operative advertising (492)
Vertical co-operative advertising (492)
Advertising allowance (492)
Horizontal co-operative advertising (492)
Advertising campaign (496)
Attention (497)
Influence (497)
Appeal (498)
Execution (498)
Copy (498)
Illustration (498)
Layout (498)
Advertising media (498)
Cost per thousand (CPM) (499)
Fragmentation (500)
Direct tests (504)
Indirect tests (505)
Advertising recall (505)
Pretests (505)
Advertising agency (505)
Sales promotion (506)
Trade promotion (506)
Consumer promotion (506)
Public relations (510)
Publicity (510)

Questions and Problems

1. Businesses in different industries demonstrate quite different patterns in their advertising expenditures. Some are heavy advertisers on television, while others use no television at all. Some advertise heavily in daily newspapers, while others rely on magazines. Some firms, such as those in the consumer products field, spend as much as 15 percent of sales on advertising, while others, including many industrial marketers, spend less than 1 percent. How do you account for such variations in advertising expenditures?
2. Which advertising medium would you recommend as best for each of these products?
   - **a.** Wooden pallets.
   - **b.** Pantyhose.
   - **c.** Tax preparation service.
   - **d.** Funeral services.
   - **e.** Toys for young children.
   - **f.** Plastic clothespins.
3. Many grocery product and chocolate bar manufacturers earmark a good portion of their advertising budgets for use in magazines. Is this a wise choice of media for these firms? Explain.
4. Why do department stores use newspapers more than local radio stations as an advertising medium?
5. Why is it worthwhile to pretest advertisements before they appear in the media? How could a test market be used to pretest an ad? (You may want to refresh your memory with a review of test marketing in Chapter 8.)
6. What procedures can a firm use to determine the level of sales that resulted from a direct-mail ad? How would you determine whether any sales were cannibalized?
7. If a manufacturing firm finds a good ad agency, should it discontinue its own advertising department? Should it consider any changes?
8. Visit a supermarket, a hardware store, or a movie theatre and make a list of all the sales promotion tools that you observe. Which are particularly effective, and why?
9. Is sales promotion effective for selling expensive consumer products such as houses, automobiles, or cruise trips? Is your answer the same for expensive business products?
10. Explain how sales promotion might be used to offset weak personal selling in retail stores.
11. Describe a recent public relations event in your community. How did it benefit the sponsor?
12. How does publicity differ from advertising?
13. Bring to class an article from a daily newspaper that appears to be the result of a firm's publicity efforts. Summarize the points made in the article that may benefit the firm. Could the same benefits be obtained through advertising?
14. Give a recent example of a company or other organization with which you are familiar that encountered unfavourable publicity. How well do you feel the organization handled the situation? What public relations or publicity tools did it use?

Hands-On Marketing

1. Bring to class four print ads or describe four radio or television ads that illustrate at least four of the specific advertising objectives outlined early in the chapter. As an alternative, find and describe two ads for the same brand that appear to be directed at different objectives.
2. Visit a supermarket, drugstore, or hardware store, and make a list of all the sales promotion tools that you observe. Describe how each one relates to the sales promotion objectives described in the chapter. Which are particularly effective, and why?

Case 6-1

W.K. BUCKLEY LIMITED (A)

It was April 1985, and Frank Buckley was faced with an important decision concerning the advertising program for Buckley's Mixture for the 1985–86 advertising season. At the suggestion of his advertising agency, Mr. Buckley had done no advertising during 1984–85 for the principal product in the Buckley product line, using that year to conduct consumer research and to prepare an advertising strategy for the future. The research was now complete and Mr. Buckley had received the recommendations of the agency. The approach they were proposing would involve a major departure from the approach that had been used to advertise Buckley's Mixture in the past.

W.K. Buckley Limited

The over-the-counter drug industry is constantly changing. With continuous advances in the treatment of illness, many pharmaceutical products become outdated in a very short time. Continual success of a formula over any extended period in this industry would seem almost impossible. Apparently, W.K. Buckley discovered a product that has maintained its success even after more than seventy years of treating Canadians who suffer from coughs and colds. The product is Buckley's Mixture.

W.K. Buckley Limited is a privately owned, Toronto-based company, founded by William K. Buckley in 1920. The founder's son, Frank Buckley, joined the company in 1946 and is the current owner and president. It was 1919 when W.K. Buckley, the owner of a small Toronto drugstore, noticed the increasing popularity of one of his cough remedies. He decided to introduce the product to a wider market as Buckley's Mixture, a sugar-free, expectorant-type, non-prescription product, developed as an effective relief from coughs, colds, and bronchitis. The product was known for its distinctive taste and its effectiveness in combating coughs and colds. Among the ingredients that Mr. Buckley included and that are still found in Buckley's Mixture are ammonium carbonate, potassium bicarbonate, menthol, camphor, Canada Balsam, and pine needle oil. When other over-the-counter preparations were selling at 25 to 35 cents each, Mr. Buckley introduced Buckley's Mixture to the Toronto market at 75 cents. This higher price allowed him to advertise the product widely and gave him a better financial return. He continued this pricing policy when he expanded distribution to a network of retail drugstores in Toronto. Because it was so successful, he also priced Buckley's higher than competitive products when he began to distribute it throughout Ontario.

Although known primarily as the manufacturer of Buckley's Mixture, now available in 100 mL and 200 mL sizes, W.K. Buckley Limited today also produces and distributes a variety of other cough and cold remedies, as well as a veterinary line. Some of the company's other products include Jack and Jill cough syrup, Lemon Time, and Buckley's White Rub. A 1984 report indicated that 65 to 70 percent of Buckley's volume was sold through nonpharmacy outlets, including supermarkets and convenience stores. This was considerably different from sales patterns of cough medicines generally in Canada, as a recent Gallup study revealed that 84.5 percent of cough and cold remedies are sold through drugstores.

W.K. Buckley Limited distributes its products in Canada, the United States, and the Caribbean, and operates under licensing agreements in Australia, New Zealand, and the Netherlands. The company has remained small, employing only 20 people, all at the company's Toronto plant. Brokers and agents are employed on a regional basis across Canada, eliminating the requirement for the company to employ a sales force.

Numerous changes have taken place in the proprietary medicine industry since the introduction of

---

 This case was written by Leanne O'Leary and James G. Barnes of Memorial University of Newfoundland. The case was prepared with the co-operation and permission of W.K. Buckley Limited to illustrate the marketing initiatives of that company and not to indicate a correct or incorrect approach to the solution of marketing problems. The authors acknowledge the co-operation and support of Frank C. Buckley, president, John J. Meehan, vice-president, and David Rieger, manager of sales and marketing, of W.K. Buckley Limited, and Jackie Robertson of Ambrose Carr Linton Kelly, Inc., in the preparation of this case.

Buckley's Mixture. As the role of the independent drugstore began to decline in the 1960s, large drug supermarkets emerged as the principal outlet for health and personal care products. Another significant change occurred in the 1970s, when national and international pharmaceutical companies began to use some of the marketing and creative advertising strategies that had been employed successfully by W.K. Buckley. Fierce competition from large multinational companies and the introduction of many new products to the Canadian market caused a decline in popularity for Buckley's products during the 1970s and early 1980s.

Early Marketing Strategies

Always one to take advantage of every opportunity, the founder of the company realized the potential that advertising offered for increased sales. During an era when advertising was a relatively new and poorly understood business tool, W.K. Buckley invested in newspaper space and used radio extensively to promote his product. Efficient use of national radio helped establish Buckley's Mixture as a household name in the 1930s and 1940s. Radio spots were purchased adjacent to the news each morning at 8 o'clock, and just before the CBC Noon Farm Broadcast to reach rural areas. Mr. Buckley maintained that this timing and continuity were more economical, equalling more media buys, built market loyalty, and reached his audience. People in rural Canada may be too busy to listen to the radio, but W.K. Buckley knew they stopped everything to listen to the CBC Farm Broadcast. Even today, the sales of Buckley's Mixture in rural Canada reflect the loyalty established over fifty years ago.

The 1920s was a period of rapid growth at W.K. Buckley Limited, with new products introduced and distribution expanded into Quebec, the Maritimes, and the Prairies. With the Great Depression of the 1930s, the company consolidated its operations in what it did best, the manufacture of cold and cough preparations. By the end of that decade, W.K. Buckley had also recruited commission sales representatives, hand-picked and trained, to establish a sales force for the company's product line. A business graduate from the University of Toronto, Frank Buckley joined the company in 1946, about the same time his father was expanding its operations into international markets, and the domestic market began to pose increasing challenges. The growth of the nondrugstore market was an early indicator of major changes to come later in the decade. Two major changes swept the industry in the 1960s and 1970s: the transition from the small, independent drugstore to the larger drug supermarket, and the impact of marketing and creative advertising strategies on the promotion of the industry and its products. Frank Buckley believed that the 1980s represented an opportunity for his company to return to a "back to the basics" strategy.

The Market

The Canadian market for cough and cold remedies is highly competitive. In 1984, the industry generated approximately $70 million in sales. Within this total market, the over-the-counter category had remained relatively stable during the preceding ten years. However, this sector of the market was dominated by large multinational pharmaceutical companies who used their size to gain a lead in product development, media spending, and shelf positioning. The key competitive brands in this industry include Benylin (Parke Davis), Novahistine (Dow), Triaminic (Ancalab), Robitussin (A.H. Robins), Vicks (Procter & Gamble), and Buckley's Mixture (W.K. Buckley Ltd.).

Exhibit 1 presents some of the results of a 1984 research study of the liquid cough remedy market, carried out with the objective of defining the national market. The research, conducted by Butler Research Associates, using the data collection services of the Gallup National Omnibus, surveyed 2,100 adults across the country in their own homes. The exhibit presents market share and level of awareness data for the top seven brands in the market. Benylin was the leading brand in all five regions of Canada where data were collected. While Vicks had very high levels of awareness, it had considerably lower incidence of usage. The leading brands of cough and cold remedies listed in this exhibit must also compete with antihistamine and cold products, such as Tylenol, Hismanal, Sudafed, and Contac-C, for the same consumer dollar.

EXHIBIT 1 Research Results
Canadian Cough Remedy Market, 1984

	Top of Mind	Share of Mind	Total Awareness	Market Share*
Buckley's Mixture	5.4%	12.1%	64.6%	5.2%
Benylin	22.9	33.8	73.0	29.2
Vicks	19.5	36.8	86.8	14.3
Triaminic	6.4	12.9	42.1	13.6
Dimetapp	2.0	4.8	33.3	6.1
Robitussin	4.1	9.1	46.8	5.8
Novahistine	1.2	3.6	45.4	4.0

* brand bought most recently

Buckley's, with an estimated share of market of 5.2 percent nationally, was strongest on the Prairies and in Ontario. The brand held an 8.6 percent share of market among users aged 60 and older, 5.5 percent with those in the 45-to-59 age bracket, but only 3.6 percent among those aged 18 to 29. When asked what they liked most about the product, users of Buckley's Mixture most often referred to its effectiveness, the fact that it relieves cold symptoms and soothes a cough, that it relieves congestion and is fast-acting. When asked to list what they disliked about the product, users mentioned its taste and its bitter, menthol flavour.

Advertising campaigns in the liquid cough remedy industry are conducted primarily in the winter season, when most colds and coughs are likely to occur. Advertising for Buckley's Mixture in the early 1980s was focused on a "tastes strong" message. To a large extent, the advertising budget consisted of national radio spots aimed at the working person (both male and female) in the 39 and over bracket. The advertising was also directed to rural areas where it was thought that most frequent users of Buckley's Mixture lived. Advertisements were also placed in *Reader's Digest* and *TV Guide*. Exhibit 2 presents radio scripts of three commercials for Buckley's Mixture that were used in the early 1980s.

In April 1984, a new advertising agency was appointed to handle Buckley's advertising, replacing the previous agency, which had closed operations. The new agency, Ambrose, Carr, DeForest, and Linton, Ltd. of Toronto (later to become Ambrose Carr Linton Kelly, Inc.), determined that, although a specific target market had been defined for Buckley's products, there was no market research to confirm the accuracy of that definition. Considering the recent decline in the market share enjoyed by Buckley's Mixture, Ambrose Carr recommended that, before the $250,000 advertising budget was spent on promotion, it should be determined if the budget was being allocated effectively. Following the suggestion of his new advertising agency, Frank Buckley decided to do no advertising during the 1984–85 season; instead, the company commissioned marketing research to learn more about its market.

Research Results

The research project was conducted by Butler Research Associates, a Toronto marketing research company, using the data-collection capabilities of the Gallup National Omnibus service. The data were collected during a two-week period in November 1984. The project was a national survey and involved interviews with 2,100 adults, 18 years of age and over, in their own homes, in population centres of at least 1,000. A random block sampling procedure was used in urban centres, and a quota sample based on sex and age in rural areas. The research objectives established for this project included: (1) determining the level of awareness and share of market of Buckley's Mixture and of competitive brands; (2) determining the strengths and weaknesses of Buckley's Mixture; (3) examining the usage and purchase patterns of the users of liquid cough remedies; and (4) developing a profile of Buckley's users. Some of the significant findings were:

- The liquid-cough-remedy market was strongest in Ontario and Quebec, which together represented 63.1 percent of users.
- The largest user segments were 18 to 44 years of age (67.2 percent) and families with children (55.4 percent).
- 52 percent of respondents had a cold during the 1983–84 winter.
- 75 percent of cough sufferers decided on and bought their own remedy.
- 66 percent of cough and cold remedies were bought by an individual for his or her own use.
- Almost all purchases were made after a cough and/or cold had started.
- The market was not homogeneous nationally, and brand preferences differed across regions.
- Usage of and preference for Vicks was skewed toward the younger age segment (18 to 19).
- Benylin and Triaminic had the highest incidence of usage among families with children.
- Approximately 85 percent of liquid cough remedies are purchased in drugstores, and this statistic is even higher in urban centres.
- The most recent purchase was made by the female head of the household (73 percent).
- Consumers do not generally stock cough syrup, preferring to purchase it as required.

The research revealed some valuable information for the marketing of Buckley's Mixture. From the research, Frank Buckley and the creative staff of Ambrose Carr concluded that Buckley's Mixture was performing best in small communities (population fewer than 30,000), sales were skewed toward the less well educated, were strongest in the Prairies and Ontario, but were extremely weak in Quebec. Preference for Buckley's Mixture tended to be strongest among males and the oldest age segment. The research revealed that the total awareness of Buckley's was 64.6 percent, but the brand's market share was only 5.2 percent nationally. This invited the conclusion that Buckley's Mixture was either failing to elicit trial among consumers or failing to deliver after trial and was not being repurchased. Among current users, the strongest feature of Buckley's Mixture was its effectiveness in relieving coughs and congestion. This attribute was mentioned significantly more often by Buckley's users than by users of other liquid cough remedies. Buckley's sugar-free feature, however, was not particularly important to users in general or to Buckley's users.

In addition to the quantitative Gallup survey, W.K. Buckley Limited also commissioned a qualitative study of the market. A series of focus groups were conducted, two each in Montreal and Toronto. The principal objectives of the focus group discussions were to reveal usage and purchase patterns, identify key variables influencing brand selection, and determine the perceptions of and attitudes toward Buckley's Mixture in relation to competing brands. Consumers appeared to be loyal to a specific brand, with neither the price nor the ingredients of the product being particularly important in the selection of the brand. The discussions revealed that differences in usage patterns appeared not to be related to gender or culture. In most cases, consumers revealed that they used one brand for children and a different brand for adults. Heavy users of cough remedies were more likely than were light users to believe that the products were effective in dealing with a cold or cough. When the preferred brand could not be purchased, a pharmacist was consulted for recommendations. It was also noted that few consumers purchased liquid cough remedies on the basis of packaging.

The qualitative research revealed some key factors about Buckley's Mixture. Most of the participants recognized the brand, though few had tried the product recently. The focus group participants commented that the name had a connotation of old-fashioned reliability, trustworthiness, and security. Its major strengths, as indicated by focus group participants, included effective, old-fashioned strength, based on its sugar-free, natural ingredients. The participants commented that the product works well as a decongestant, coats the throat, and does not cause drowsiness. They also discussed the brand's weaknesses, which included its aroma, colour, taste, and consistency.

EXHIBIT 2 Radio Commercial Scripts — Buckley's Mixture

1: Sounds of Traffic in Background
Cab Driver:

"I drive a cab, and when I get a cough from a cold, I don't want to cough all over the customers.

"I take Buckley's Mixture, 'cause it works. It checks my coughing, but it doesn't stop me driving. Buckley's loosens congestion, helps me breathe easy, and clears that stuffy feeling; you know what I mean?

"Personally, I take it straight, but some people mix it with honey. Either way, when you take Buckley's Mixture, you know you've taken cough medicine.

"It tastes strong (HORN BLOWS) but it beats coughing."

2: Sound of Vacuum Cleaner in Background
Homemaker:

"When I get a cough from a cold, I take Buckley's Mixture, because it works and you can't let a cough stop you when there are meals to cook and children to worry about.

"Buckley's Mixture loosens congestion and helps clear that stuffy, chesty feeling. It helps during the day, and it helps at night.

"No point pretending I like the taste; I don't. So, I mix it with honey. Even so, you know you've taken cough medicine when you take Buckley's.

"It tastes strong, but it beats coughing."

3. Sounds of Factory Machinery operating in Background
Equipment Operator:

"When I get a cough from a cold, I take Buckley's Mixture; because it works and because you can't operate machinery if you are coughing all the time.

"Buckley's loosens congestion, helps me breathe without wheezing and spluttering. It checks my coughing, but it doesn't stop me working, and it's sugar-free, which is important to me.

"The thing is that when you've taken Buckley's Mixture, you know you've taken cough medicine.

"It tastes strong (WHISTLE BLOWS) but it sure beats coughing."

Conclusions

Once the research had been conducted and results analyzed, a strategy document presented to the Buckley management team by Ambrose Carr in March 1985 identified five key problems with Buckley's Mixture that were apparent from the consumer research:

1. Low top-of-mind awareness.
2. Low rate of trial.
3. Low awareness of its strength and effectiveness.
4. Perception of the product as being old-fashioned.
5. Negative perception of the taste, aroma, and texture.

After a comprehensive review of the results of both the national study and the qualitative focus groups, Peter Byrne, creative director of Ambrose Carr, presented several advertising campaign recommendations to Frank Buckley and his management team. One of the suggested campaigns involved Frank Buckley promoting his own product. This would continue the tradition of a face behind the name of W.K. Buckley Limited, a tradition that had been maintained over seven decades. The agency believed that Frank Buckley would portray the desired image of an honest businessman who believes in the effectiveness of his product and who promotes it on the basis of its true attributes. Another proposal was intended to turn the negative perceptions of the strong taste, aroma, and texture of Buckley's Mixture into positive aspects for the promotion efforts. The proposal from the agency involved the use of humorous phrases to illustrate the "awful" taste of Buckley's Mixture, simultaneously establishing it as an effective remedy.

Questions

1. What objectives should Frank Buckley and his management team have in determining the marketing program to support Buckley's Mixture in 1985–86?
2. As a fairly small company, operating in an industry where the competition consists primarily of large companies with many products in their product lines, what strategy would be most appropriate for Mr. Buckley to adopt for Buckley's Mixture?
3. Considering the recent slippage in the market share of Buckley's Mixture and the limited advertising budget available to W.K. Buckley Limited, would you recommend to Frank Buckley that he accept the recommendations of his advertising agency?
4. What are the implications for Mr. Buckley of appearing in his own advertising and of promoting negative aspects of the product? What consumer or market characteristics or trends would such an approach address?

Case 6-2

THE SALVATION ARMY RED SHIELD APPEAL (B)

As meetings between the senior public relations staff of the Salvation Army and its advertising agency, BBDO Canada, continued through 1993, it became obvious that a new approach to advertising the Red Shield Appeal would be necessary for 1994. The prolonged economic downturn being experienced in Canada had meant that the demands being placed upon the Salvation Army for assistance were increasing to the point where more resources were needed.

Finally, in late 1993, a decision was reached to depart somewhat from the slogans that had been used during the past nine years (see the Salvation Army Red Shield Appeal (A) case for background information on the Red Shield Appeal and earlier advertising campaigns). The overt reference to God that had been used in recent advertising was deleted in favour of a more straightforward, aggressive appeal for funds in light of the increased needs being addressed by the Salvation Army on behalf of these people who were being affected by the prolonged economic downturn in Canada. The slogan adopted for the 1994 campaign, which the Army and its agency expected to be used for two or three years, was "Help us help others."

The "Help us help others" slogan was arrived at after many other slogans and themes had been developed and screened by agency and Salvation Army personnel at various levels in the organizations. Elwes observed that "Help us help others" was found to be the most simple and direct communication, expressing a call to action that was in keeping with the strategic decision to be less subtle in asking for donations. While the slogan was direct and easily understood, much of what The Salvation Army stands for was to be communicated through the execution of the various advertising materials.

As Julian Elwes prepared to involve his creative people at BBDO Canada in the preparation of the 1994 Red Shield Appeal advertising, he issued to his staff the communications brief presented in Exhibit 1. This brief was intended to clarify the objectives and desired effect of the 1994 advertising campaign.

The 1994 Red Shield Appeal Campaign

Centred on the theme "Help us help others," the 1994 Red Shield Appeal campaign was launched in April 1994 to support the annual door-to-door canvass "Blitz Night" on May 2, 1994. The co-ordinated preparation of the various media materials included television and radio commercials, newspaper and magazine advertisements, and transit, outdoor, and mall posters. While the campaign focused on the six-week period leading up to "Blitz Night," BBDO Canada expected the materials to be used throughout the year as advertising media across Canada provided the Salvation Army with public service announcements and donated advertising time and space. The total budget for the development of the commercials and other advertising materials and for paid media time was set at less than $700,000 for 1994, with less than half that amount being devoted to production, an amount that could be amortized by the Salvation Army over three or four years. BBDO Canada expected that the total value of advertising the Salvation Army would obtain would total close to $1.4 million when the contributions of free time and space by the various media are taken into consideration.

Examples of print advertisements developed by BBDO Canada for the 1994 Red Shield Appeal campaign are presented in Exhibit 2.

Questions

1. Consider the decision to adopt "Help us help others" as the slogan for the 1994 Red Shield Appeal. Does this slogan accomplish the objectives of the Salvation Army and its advertising agency in light of the changing environment in which the Army is operating?

 The authors wish to thank Lt. Col. Mel Bond of the Salvation Army and Julian Elwes of BBDO Canada for their support and assistance in the preparation of this case.

2. Evaluate the execution of the print and television advertising materials against the objectives of both the Salvation Army and its advertising agency. How would you propose to evaluate the success of these advertising materials in accomplishing these objectives?

3. What aspects of the Red Shield Appeal advertising campaign make it different from most client–agency relationships and from situations that would likely apply in the marketing of most products and services in the private sector?

EXHIBIT 1

THE SALVATION ARMY "HELP US HELP OTHERS" RED SHIELD CAMPAIGN

COMMUNICATIONS BRIEF

PURPOSE: (Specifically, what do we want consumers to do as a result of seeing the advertising?)

To heighten awareness of the Salvation Army and solicit donations via its annual Red Shield Appeal. To persuade the target group to make generous financial contributions to the Red Shield Appeal. This is two-pronged in that we want existing donors to maintain/increase their contributions and we want to motivate new donors.

TARGET AUDIENCE: (Who are they — demographics? What are they like — psychographics, attitudes, values? What are their current beliefs about the category and the brand?)

All adults, with additional skew toward 18–34. Broad income and education base. English and French.

MEDIA: National — TV, radio, magazines, newspaper, transit, outdoor, mall posters. Campaign start date April 18. House-to-house canvass is "Blitz Night," Monday, May 2, 1994.

BACKGROUND: The Salvation Army develops a new Red Shield Appeal campaign every four or five years. The 1994 campaign is designed to be harder hitting, i.e., with greater emotional appeal, because:

1. Downturn in economy has led to higher unemployment, greater need for welfare, and therefore, overall, a significant increase in demands for Salvation Army services. Without a dramatic increase in contributions there will be a significant shortfall in public demand/Army services supply.
2. Competitive charities are proliferating.

PROMISE: (What is the single most important performance or emotional reward we are promising the target for buying/trying the product/service?)

Our target audience should feel that by making a financial donation they are significantly contributing to helping fulfil the needs of others less fortunate. Possibly, one day, it could be themselves or a relative/friend.

EXHIBIT 1 (continued)

SUPPORT: (Why should they believe what we say?)

The work of the Salvation Army is widely acknowledged, and oftentimes the caring support the Army provides has personally touched the lives of our target group. There is great credibility in the ministry of the Army.

DESIRED RESPONSE: (How do we want the consumer to respond or feel after seeing the advertising? How will it reinforce or alter his or her current beliefs?)

Existing donors should maintain/increase their annual contribution; new donors should be motivated to contribute. Make a difference — act now — make a donation and contribute to the caring of the less fortunate.

RED SHIELD PERSONALITY/ PROFILE: (What characteristics does the Red Shield Appeal have that distinguish it from competitors? Is there anything we need to modify?)

Unlike other fund-raising drives, charity appeals, etc., NRSA has a religious motivation, its workers are genuinely caring people, and the services provided have high visibility and extreme credibility. Funds raised by the appeal are used to legitimately reduce suffering and provide encouragement and care for those less fortunate in life.

COMMENTS: (What constraints, restrictions — legal or otherwise — do we need to consider?)

Funds for creative development and media placement are limited and traditionally have been bolstered by generous voluntary contributions of time by talent, production and recording studios, and the media (PSAs, bonus outdoor postings, etc.).

Creative materials requiring development include:

2 English and 2 French TV spots (minimum)
2 English and 2 French Radio spots (minimum)

Newspaper/magazine ads — English and French
Outdoor paper — English and French
Transit — Interior and Bus Shelters — English and French
Direct Mail — English and French

EXHIBIT 2

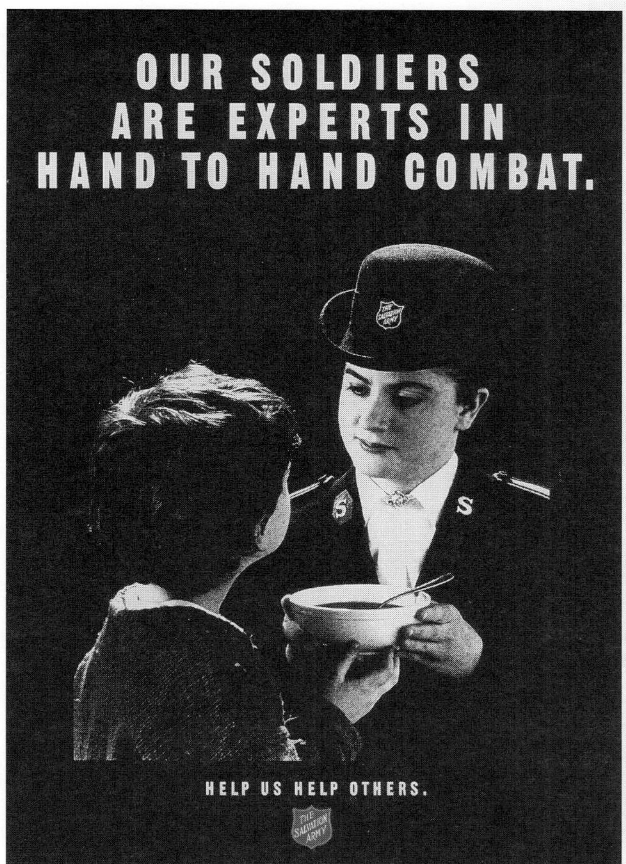

Case 6-3

NATURALLY YOURS

For the past decade, Naturally Yours has been the only company specializing in the distribution of organic produce in western Canada. By 1996, annual sales were over $5 million annually, profits were steady, dividends to members were significant and growing, and the Naturally Yours name was well known and respected in the food business in western Canada.

Naturally Yours has developed its market based on the production of organically grown (chemical-free) produce that appeals to health-conscious and environmentally conscious consumers. The organization is structured as a co-operative. The co-op buys produce from organic farmers, distributes it, and ploughs the profits back into the business. As a result, all members are committed to making the co-operative successful and realize the importance of producing good-quality produce. Naturally Yours has excellent relations with its suppliers, a good client list, and considerable credibility.

Organic farms in Canada tend to be small, are subject to stringent government regulation, and enjoy a relatively short growing season because of the length of the Canadian winter. Recently in Canada, the market for fresh fruit in general has been growing at the rate of about 12 percent per year. To date, all organic produce has been supplied

This case was prepared by Judith A. Cumby, assistant professor, Faculty of Business Administration, Memorial University of Newfoundland. The facts of this case are based on the *Wild West Organic Harvest Co-operative* case, written by Dr. Katherine Gallagher of Memorial University.

by Canadian producers, although there are no regulations preventing the import of such produce from the United States. There is little branding of organic foods in the Canadian market. Organically grown produce does not always have the "eye-appeal" that conventionally grown produce does. Some segments of the produce market see this difference as cosmetic only and are willing to pay more for produce that is healthier than the conventionally grown equivalent. The results of market research involving surveys of grocery shoppers in the greater Vancouver area indicated that 25 percent would be very or somewhat likely to buy organic produce. Ninety percent of those surveyed indicated that they were unhappy about the current pesticide and chemical practices of traditional producers.

Oregon Organics was a well-established distributor of organically grown fruits and vegetables in Oregon, Washington, and northern California. When Oregon Organics started producing organic apple juice, the members of Naturally Yours considered doing the same. Oregon Organics was generous in providing Naturally Yours with market information because the two organizations were not direct competitors.

Oregon Organics had tried both high prices and low prices, as well as high and low levels of advertising and promotion. They found that market shares varied, depending on the combination of price and advertising and promotion (see the table below).

Given the similarities of the produce markets in western Canada and the western United States, it is thought that these market shares would probably be about the same in Canada. Based on Statistics Canada data, Naturally Yours estimated the size of the apple juice market in western Canada to be 520,000 cases annually. The contribution per case would be $3.50 at the low price and $5.10 at the high price.

Oregon Organics had used only point-of-purchase materials in some areas; in others, it had supplemented point-of-purchase materials with personalized direct mail to a mailing list of known purchasers of organic produce. If Naturally Yours were to use similar advertising and promotion materials, point-of-purchase alone would cost approximately $5,000, while the mailing would cost $8,000. In addition, Naturally Yours would have to hire a part-time sales person to support the new apple juice. The sales person's compensation and expenses would amount to $15,000 annually. Product development costs would be minimal, mostly related to package design. They would total $5,000 in the first year only.

Some of the co-op members were hesitant to go ahead with the manufacture and distribution of apple juice. They thought it was too risky to get into manufacturing. In a meeting, the members of the co-op decided that they would only go ahead if there was a reasonable chance that the new product would produce a profit by the end of its first year.

Questions

1. Provide a financial analysis to support a decision regarding whether Naturally Yours should enter the apple juice market. Clearly indicate whether the numbers support entering the market and, if so, at what price and what level of promotion/advertising.
2. State your recommendation about whether Naturally Yours should introduce organic apple juice. What factors other than the quantitative ones in question 1 influenced your decision? Support your recommendation.
3. Suggest an advertising campaign for Naturally Yours. As part of your answer, identify the target audience, the advertising goals, and an advertising message and execution approach you would use.

Market Shares (%)

	Low Price	High Price
Low advertising and promotion	1.2	0.8
High advertising and promotion	2.0	1.0

Part Seven

Managing the Marketing Effort

Implementing a company's international marketing program, examining the issues involved in not-for-profit marketing, evaluating a company's total performance, appraising the role of marketing in our society today, and considering what it may be tomorrow

Up to this point, we have dealt separately with how a firm selects its target markets and then develops and manages the four elements of its marketing strategy for those markets. Now we bring those separate areas together as we present an overview of an organization's total marketing program.

We will apply the basic management process to a company's international marketing program in Chapter 21. In Chapter 22, we will examine not-for-profit marketing from a total marketing perspective. Following on the strategic planning stage introduced in Chapter 3, we will discuss the implementation and evaluation stages of the management process in Chapter 23. Then, in Chapter 24, we will appraise the current position of marketing in our socioeconomic system and consider where marketing is headed.

CHAPTER 21 GOALS

In selling abroad, a firm is often faced with cultural, economic, and legal systems that are quite different from those in its home country. Thus it must understand and adapt to a new and unfamiliar environment. Furthermore, for the firm interested in international marketing, its level of involvement can range from simply selling goods that will be exported to investing abroad. Thus we need to examine international marketing in some detail.

After studying this chapter, you should have an understanding of:

- The importance of international marketing to firms and countries.
- The impact of the macroenvironmental factors of culture, economics, and political/legal forces on international marketing.
- Alternative organizational structures for operating in foreign markets.
- Strategic considerations in formulating international marketing programs.
- The role of trade balances in international marketing.

Chapter Twenty-Two

Marketing in Not-for-Profit Organizations

www.coc.ca • www.culturenet.ca/vso/ • www.scouts.ca • www.bc.cancer.ca

FOR THE GREATER GOOD OF THE COMMUNITY

To attract members of the public to their concerts and performances, most Canadian performing arts groups engage in a series of activities that bear remarkable similarity to the marketing programs of companies such as The Bay, NorTel, and Bombardier. The difference is that the Canadian Opera Company, the Vancouver Symphony, and the Neptune Theatre are not marketing conventional products or services, but are trying to sell tickets and fill seats. They are examples of many types of not-for-profit organizations that rely on the general public to provide the funding and support that will allow them to accomplish their goals.

Universities and colleges conduct advertising campaigns and other promotional activities to attract students. Many museums, art galleries, zoos, and social agencies, such as Scouts Canada, the YM-YWCA, and the Canadian Cancer Society, use similar techniques to attract visitors, members, and donors (of money, time, and even sweat, if you participate in a fundraising fun run!) who contribute to their success and even to their very survival. Political candidates use advertising to attract voters and rely on "polling" and survey research to determine public opinion and voting preferences. Many religious organizations use television advertising, door-to-door visits, and other marketing techniques to put forth their message and to attract members and contributions. Symphony orchestras offer free lunch-time concerts to attract new patrons — a form of sampling. Universities offer evening programs and distance-education courses to broaden the market for their "products." Many social agencies mount sophisticated advertising and public awareness campaigns to warn the public of the dangers of smoking, unprotected sex, and drug abuse, and to encourage responsible behaviour, such as the use of bicycle helmets and automobile seat belts.

www.sallynet.org www.lions.org www.rotary.org www.kiwanis.org www.bc.cancer.ca www.hsf.ca

A number of common threads run through these examples. In the first place, all of the organizations mentioned are not-for-profit organizations; that is, profit is not an organizational objective, although breaking even is — the funds raised by most not-for-profit organizations are used to operate the organization and to provide needed services to its target clients. Second, all are engaged in the business of encouraging socially responsible behaviour or the support of programs and activities that are generally regarded as being good for the community and its residents. In all cases, such groups and organizations regularly rely on concepts and activities that represent a different application of marketing as we have been studying it.

While there are many similarities between the activities of not-for-profit organizations and those of "for-profit" businesses, there are dramatic differences as well. In the first place, very few of the organizations mentioned in this chapter are selling a tangible product; most are marketing cultural services, social causes and ideas, and "good works." Second — and this is a very important distinction — they are not marketing only to a single group of target customers. While most companies target their products and services at selected "consumers" who are in the market for breakfast cereal, a new car, or a trip to a holiday destination, many not-for-profit organizations are really targeting three groups: customers or patrons who will buy tickets to attend a performance of an orchestra or a theatre company or to visit a zoo or botanical garden, donors who will contribute to fund-raising activities, and volunteers who will perform the many activities necessary for the organization to succeed in its good work.

NATURE AND SCOPE OF NOT-FOR-PROFIT MARKETING

The marketing fundamentals for not-for-profit, nonbusiness organizations are the same as for the business sector. A marketing program should be strategically planned around a product or service that is effectively priced, promoted, and distributed to satisfy wants in a predetermined market. However, there are important differences in the implementation of the marketing program and in not-for-profit management's understanding of and attitudes toward marketing. These differences tend to limit the marketing activities of not-for-profit, nonbusiness organizations, even though these organizations need effective marketing.

Most not-for-profit companies market services, rather than tangible products. Consequently, many of the concepts discussed in Chapter 12 are relevant in this chapter.

Types of Not-for-Profit Organizations

Not-for-profit organizations number in the thousands and engage in a very wide range of activities. The following groupings will give you some idea of this broad spectrum:

- *Educational:* Private schools, high schools, colleges, universities.
- *Cultural:* Museums, zoos, symphony orchestras, opera and theatre groups.
- *Religious:* Churches, synagogues, temples, mosques.
- *Charitable and philanthropic:* Social welfare groups (Salvation Army, United Way, Canadian Red Cross Society), research foundations, fund-raising groups.
- *Social cause:* Organizations dealing with family planning, literacy, stopping smoking, preventing heart disease, environmental concerns, those for or against abortion, and those for or against nuclear energy.
- *Social:* Fraternal organizations, service clubs (Lions, Rotary, Kiwanis).
- *Health care:* Hospitals, nursing homes, health research organizations (Canadian Cancer Society, Heart and Stroke Foundation).
- *Political:* Political parties, individual politicians.

Although this list generally is a classification of not-for-profit organizations, note that there are some exceptions. A number of organizations within these groups — certain museums and performing-arts groups, for example — are profit-seeking (or surplus-seeking) organizations. They have to realize a surplus on their sales in order to stay in business.

The Exchange Concept and Not-For-Profit Marketing

In Chapter 1, marketing was broadly defined as an exchange intended to satisfy the wants of all parties

MARKETING AT WORK FILE 22-1

HARD-HITTING — GET THEIR ATTENTION

As governments are continuing to cut funding to public institutions and charities, competition for donations has been heating up in recent years. In 1995, there were almost 75,000 registered charities in Canada, competing for the goodwill of corporations and private citizens who are being asked to help finance their worthy causes. To separate themselves from the growing crowd, some charitable organizations are taking some radical approaches in their advertising.

In the first place, some have turned to advertising for the first time. Goodwill Industries of Toronto went to the advertising agency FCB to create a campaign that uses humour to explain how Goodwill sells donated clothing and household goods and uses the funds raised for employment training. It was the first time in its sixty-year history that Goodwill had turned to advertising. Its president, Jim Dreiling, observed, "We have to be more vocal now."

But not all charities are taking such a soft-sell approach. In an outdoor campaign for the Invest in Kids Foundation, a young boy, aged about six, frowns as he stares at the passing traffic. The headline reads, "By the time Jimmy grows up, it will cost well over $100,000 annually to keep him in prison. So let's invest in our children now, not in more prisons." The message is a direct plea for donations and an attempt to stand out from the crowd.

Another billboard for the Kids Help Phone has a stark white message on a black background, with the words "How do you do suicide?" The question was one received by the help line from a four-year-old caller. Such hard-hitting ads are a sign of the times. As Brian Featherstone, president of Ogilvy & Mather, observed, "The smart not-for-profits are being much more assertive." O&M and many other Canadian advertising agencies donate their time and creative talent to prepare campaigns for charities that normally do not have any money in their budgets for advertising. The result is some hard-hitting messages that will make Canadians stop and think.

Source: Ijeoma Ross, "Charities Take Direct Approach," *The Globe and Mail*, September 10, 1996. Reprinted with permission from *The Globe and Mail*.

involved in the exchange. And marketing consists of all activities designed to facilitate such exchanges. A discussion of marketing in not-for-profit organizations is certainly consistent with this broad, **exchange concept** definition of marketing, because not-for-profit organizations are also involved in exchanges.

As an example, Roots, a business organization, sells you a sweatshirt or jacket in exchange for a sum of money. In a similar vein, a local theatre company, a not-for-profit organization, may provide you with an evening's entertainment in exchange for money. A charitable or religious organization, such as the Salvation Army, provides you with a feeling of satisfaction and of having helped others, in exchange for a donation. The Canadian Cancer Society may provide you with a similar, intangible feeling when you participate in a fun run to raise funds to fight cancer. Finally, your university or college, another not-for-profit organization, offers you access to education and other experiences, in return for your money, time, and commitment.

Markets Involved in Not-for-Profit Marketing

A major difference between business and not-for-profit marketing is that not-for-profit organizations must reach more than one group with their marketing efforts. Business managers have traditionally defined their basic market as being made up of present and prospective customers. They have thus directed their marketing efforts primarily toward this one group. In contrast, most not-for-profit organizations are involved with three major markets. The

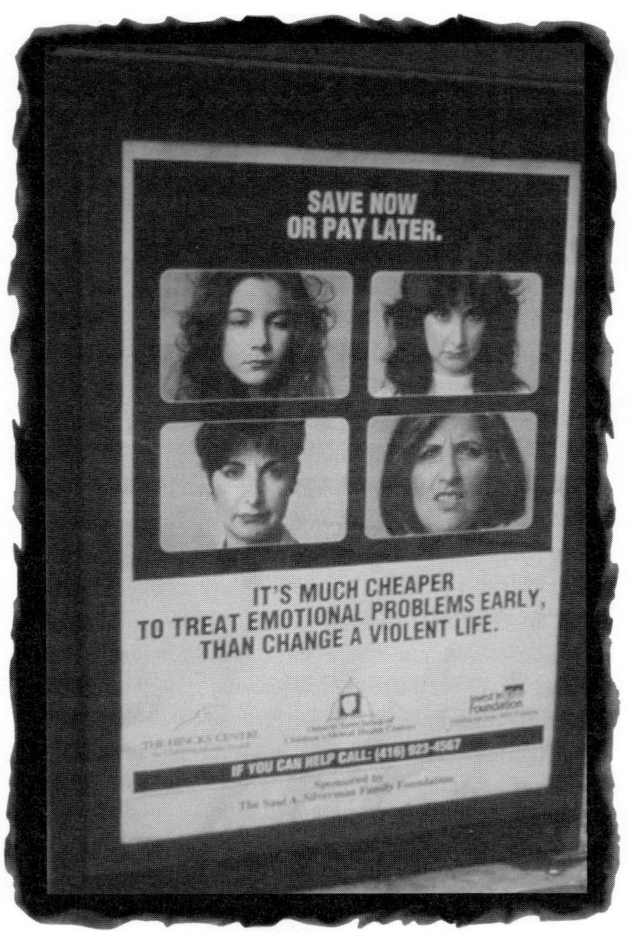

Some charities send hard-hitting messages.

first of these groups consists of the donors or **contributors** (of money, labour, services, or materials) to the organization. Here the not-for-profit organization's task is that of "resource attraction." To attract the resources it needs to operate, the organization must rely on donors and volunteers.

The second major target market is the organization's **clients** — the recipients of its money or services. This recipient market is much like that of the customers of a business company. However, not-for-profit organizations — such as churches, charities, nursing homes, symphony orchestras, and universities — are less likely to refer to their client–recipients as customers. Instead these organizations use such terms as parishioners, members, patients, audience, or students. Some social-welfare agencies refer to those to whom their services are directed as clients.

www.scouts.ca
www.girlguides.ca
www.bbbsa.org

A third very important group for most not-for-profit organizations is **volunteers**. Some writers may group them under contributors, but they are a special group of contributors who deserve special attention. They may also be donors of money, but they are for the most part people who devote their time and energy to ensuring that the organization operates successfully. They are the volunteer leaders of Scouts Canada and the Girl Guides, the Big Brothers and Big Sisters, the soccer coaches, the "candy stripers" at the local hospital, the "friends" of the botanical garden and the art gallery, and the behind-the-scenes people at the production of the summer theatre. They in many cases enable not-for-profit organizations to work. Without volunteers, most not-for-profits would not exist.

This distinction between business and not-for-profit marketing, based on the major markets involved, is significant for this reason: A not-for-profit organization must develop two separate marketing programs — one looking "back" to its contributors and volunteers, and the other looking "forward" to its clients. Moreover, like businesses, not-for-profit organizations also have relationships with several publics in addition to their main markets. A college or university, for example, must deal with government agencies, environmentalists, mass media, its faculty and staff, alumni, and the local community.

Importance of Not-for-Profit Marketing The attention that has been devoted to marketing by not-for-profit organizations in recent years is long overdue. Thousands of such organizations handle many millions of dollars each year and affect the lives of millions of people. Their work is extremely important in promoting behaviour and ideas that are in the broad public interest. Yet there are situations in which the operation of not-for-profit organizations is not as efficient as it might be, in part because these organizations do not have the resources to ensure efficiency. In some cases, we hear of a large portion of the money raised by some organizations going to cover administrative costs rather than being used to benefit the people for whom it was collected. When such events occur, there is a dual social and economic loss — donors' gifts are not directed as the donors intended, and clients are not served efficiently.

Marketing's significance also becomes apparent when not-for-profit organizations fail to do an effective marketing job. The result may be additional social and economic costs and waste. If the death rate from smoking rises because the Canadian Cancer Society and other similar organizations cannot persuade people of the harm of smoking, we all lose. When anti-litter organizations fail to convince people to control their solid-waste disposal, we all lose. When good museums or good symphony orchestras must cease operating because of a lack of contributions or lack of attendance, again there are social and economic losses.

By developing an effective marketing program, a not-for-profit organization can increase immeasurably its chance of (1) satisfactorily serving both its contributor and client markets and (2) improving the overall efficiency of its operations.

NOT-FOR-PROFIT ATTITUDE TOWARD MARKETING

Some managers of not-for-profit organizations often appear not to realize that they are "running a business" and should therefore employ business management techniques. It is true that making a profit is generally not the goal of these organizations. Nevertheless, they do need to identify goals, plan strategies and tactics to reach these goals, effectively execute their plans, and evaluate their performance. Above all, they must satisfy their major markets — contributors, clients, and volunteers — if they are to continue to operate successfully. Yet only very recently have many not-for-profit organizations started to employ information systems, financial controls, personnel management and labour relations, and other business management techniques.

Unfortunately, the acceptance of business management techniques often does not include planned marketing programs. Although the situation is changing rapidly, some not-for-profit organizations do not seem at all comfortable with the concepts of marketing. To many of these groups, marketing means some form of promotion, such as advertising or fundraising. These organizations often do not understand the concept of an integrated, strategic marketing program.

Many not-for-profit groups speak about marketing and even believe they are practising it. But in many cases they still have a strong production orientation or, at best, a selling orientation. These organizations tend to select — on their own — the goods, services, or ideas that they think their customers want (or should want). Then they decide how to distribute or sell these products. Only at the end of the process do these groups analyze their markets. This really is not a marketing orientation.

People working in not-for-profit organizations sometimes have a negative attitude toward marketing. They are apt to think that having a marketing program — and using the term "marketing" — is demeaning and in bad taste. They may even feel that it is unethical to use marketing in their organizations.

Perhaps the choice of words is important. The governing body in a church, for instance, will not object to "informational notices" (don't call it "advertising") in newspapers or in church bulletins regarding church activities. When church members go to foreign lands to bring new members into the fold, the churches don't call this activity "personal selling." It is "missionary work."

Not-for-profit groups seem to face a dilemma. On the one hand, they often are unaware of what marketing is all about or may have a negative attitude toward it. Yet, on the other hand, these organizations typically are in great need of effective marketing programs. However, as we move into the next century, the marketing climate in not-for-profit organizations is continually improving as the need for marketing is recognized. One of the problems faced by many not-for-profits is that they must rely for most of their human resources on volunteers, most of whom are completely committed to the organization but have no training in or knowledge of marketing.

While most not-for-profit organizations have been slower than their profit-oriented counterparts to employ modern marketing strategies and techniques, changing economic and social conditions have made many realize that they must do a better job of examining and understanding their "markets" and of marketing their operations. Not-for-profit organizations can no longer count on contributions from federal and provincial government sources, as they have in the past — health care and education organizations have been particularly hard hit as budgets are slashed. Changes to federal tax laws have made it less attractive to donate to charities as amounts that can be claimed as deductions have been reduced. Generally, in recent times, corporations and individuals have been less able and less willing to donate to charities. At the same time, competition for funds has been coming from a new generation of social causes, including public education about AIDS, Alzheimer's disease, child and sexual abuse, and drunk driving. Similarly, the demands being placed on many social agencies such as the Salvation Army, food banks, churches, and shelters, have never been greater. These changes have caused many not-for-profit organizations to realize that they must be professionally managed and adopt a marketing orientation if they are to survive.

DEVELOPING A STRATEGIC PROGRAM FOR NOT-FOR-PROFIT MARKETING

The basic procedure for planning and developing a marketing program is the same in any organization — profit or not-for-profit. That is, first we identify and analyze the target markets, and then we develop a

MARKETING AT WORK FILE 22-2

FILLING UP THOSE CLASSES

As the number of young Canadians in the age bracket that attends college and university declines, and as public funding for postsecondary education declines, many of Canada's universities are turning to conventional marketing programs to attract students to their campuses. Often, the competition takes the form of media advertising and the development of creative new programs and approaches intended to distinguish one university from another.

The University of Calgary targeted high school kids with a cheeky poster advertising campaign with the headline, "Call now and hold your seat!" The posters featured male and female models in ripped jeans clutching their butts while cradling a telephone. The campaign was a hit with the high school audience to which it was aimed. The university's director of public affairs, Rod Chapman, said, "We had to be fairly aggressive... The message had to be heard loudly and clearly."

Facing declines in enrolment, the University of Manitoba launched a multifaceted campaign to attract more students. The program included bus ads targeting prospective arts students, extending deadlines for admission applications, setting up a toll-free telephone number for the admissions office, using student ambassadors to recruit high school students, beefing up the scholarship program by $200,000, and faculty administrators writing successful applicants to encourage them to register, thereby addressing the "no-show" problem.

Wilfrid Laurier University has started even earlier, with a program aimed at students in grades 6, 7, and 8. These kids come to the university for a three-day program in which they live in residence, attend classes, participate in an archeological dig, act in a play, edit a newsletter, go swimming, and eat in the dining hall. The whole idea is to turn these future students on to the idea of attending university. In an observation that would have been quite foreign on university campuses only a few years ago, WLU geography professor Jerry Hall observed, "Down the road, we're looking at clients." Similar programs are in place at other universities across the country as campus tours, open houses, and high school visitation programs have been broadened to appeal to a wider and younger audience.

Source: Mike Dempster, "Ad Dicted," *Calgary Herald*, May 31, 1996, pp. B6; Allison Bray, "U of M Woos Student Bodies," *Winnipeg Free Press*, August 3, 1996, pp. A1, A3; and Jennifer Lewington, "Universities Try to Catch Them Young," *The Globe and Mail*, May 17, 1996, pp. A1, A6.

strategic marketing mix that will provide want-satisfaction to those markets. Throughout the process we use marketing research to help in our decision-making.

Target-Market Analysis

Not-for-profit organizations need two major marketing programs — one for the contributor market and one for the client market. It is important to pinpoint each market in some detail. Market pinpointing means using **market segmentation**. A broad (nonsegmented) appeal to the donor market is likely to result in a low return. Trying to be all things to all people in the recipient market is likely to result in being "nothing to nobody" and going broke in the process.

The possible bases for market segmentation for not-for-profit groups are generally the same as those discussed in chapters 4 and 5. In trying to reach its contributor market, for example, an organization may segment its appeals by age group, place of residence, record of past donations, or size of past donations. Recently, research has been devoted to segmenting donor markets on the basis of the benefits that donors derive from giving, their motivations, and the relationships that they establish with the not-for-profit organizations they support.[1] Segmentation analysis, involving examination of the demographic characteristics, needs, motivations, and lifestyles of donors, is critical to better understanding the segment of the market that supports charitable and social causes.

Many not-for-profit organizations segment their client markets, although they probably do not refer to this technique as market segmentation. For instance, political parties and major charities conduct fund-raising efforts that are directed at large corporate donors, smaller local businesses, professional groups such as lawyers and doctors, and former members or supporters. Country clubs develop different programs and membership categories for golfers, tennis players, swimmers, and curlers. Universities and colleges segment prospective students on the basis of age (current high school graduates and older people who are returning to university as "mature" students) and on their area of interest (engineering, science, business, and so on). When Wilfrid Laurier University is developing programs to appeal to junior high school students (see "Marketing at Work" File 22-2), it is really aiming at a new segment of the market, one that has generally not been targeted by universities, and one that Wilfrid Laurier University hopes will be a source of students in the future.

A decision to employ market segmentation means that a not-for-profit organization must tailor all or part of its marketing program to reach each segment, be it donor or client. Thus the product offering and the promotion may have to be adapted to each major segment. Universities are not the only not-for-profit organizations targeting the young. Many arts organizations have programs aimed at a young audience. The Toronto Symphony Orchestra offers eight different programs for students, including young people's concerts, attendance at TSO rehearsals, group masterclasses for high school bands and orchestras, adopt-a-player, and the TSO Youth Orchestra.

Careful market analysis requires sophisticated marketing research to identify the various markets. This poses a problem because many not-for-profit organizations are not familiar with marketing research. But there are encouraging prospects in this area. Political parties and individual politicians, for example, are frequent users of opinion polls to determine voters' preferences on candidates and issues. Segmentation research also has been used to identify the characteristics of various market segments attending art museums and presentations of the performing arts (opera, concerts, theatres).

Product Planning

Like a profit-seeking business firm, a not-for-profit organization must decide (1) what products it will offer, (2) what will be the nature of its product mix, and (3) what, if anything, it will do about product attributes such as branding and labelling. In not-for-profit marketing, again, an organization needs two sets of product strategies — one for its contributor market and one for its client market.

Product Offering In most not-for-profit organizations, the product offering to clients typically is a service, an idea, a person (in politics), or a cause. In the case of foundations and charitable organizations, the product offering often is a cash grant — a form of tangible product. Other organizations may offer

www.tso.on.ca

such tangible products as food and clothing, printed materials, or birth control devices. However, in such cases the tangible products are incidental to the main services provided by the organization.

The key to selecting a product offering is for an organization to decide (1) what "business" it is in and (2) what client markets it wants to reach. If a church views its mission only as providing religious services, its product offering will be relatively limited. On the other hand, if this church views its mission more broadly — as providing fellowship, spirituality, and personal development — it will offer more services to more markets. The church may then offer family counselling services, day-care services, religious education courses, and social activities for seniors.

Planning the product offering to the contributor market is more difficult. An organization asks people to donate their money or time to a cause. The money or time is the price that contributors pay for the organization's "product." But what are they getting for this price? What is the product that contributors are buying with their donations? The product is an assortment of benefits for donors and volunteers that includes:

- Making donors and volunteers feel good.
- Supporting their favourite organizations.
- Providing them with a tax deduction for donations.
- Contributing to their status in reference groups.
- Supporting their religious beliefs.

Management's task in product planning is to match a given benefit with the market segment that wants that benefit. Thus, the benefit of a tax deduction would be the product offering to one market segment, while another segment would be offered the benefit of furthering the organization's work. The difficulty lies in identifying the group of potential contributors (buyers) that want a particular benefit.

In order to broaden the appeal of the organization, managers in a not-for-profit setting must not only decide what actual products are to be offered (for example, the repertoire of a dance company or a symphony orchestra), but also must consider "what will sell" to the target audience. Often, arts organizations in particular consist of volunteers who give their time and talents to see that the orchestra or amateur theatre company succeeds. They may wish to perform a certain play or a certain piece of music, while the "marketplace" may want something quite different. Also, such organizations should consider strategic issues such as positioning and segmentation. Exactly what kind of organization does it wish to be? In addition to being known as a first-class symphony orchestra, the Toronto Symphony has recently begun to take on a new, more interesting positioning based largely on the personality and persona of its new conductor, Jukka-Pekka Saraste.[2]

Product-Mix Strategies Several of the product-mix strategies discussed in Chapter 8 can be employed in not-for-profit marketing. Consider, for instance, the strategy of expanding the product line. Theatre groups such as the Neptune Theatre of Halifax offer a range of products and distribution channels to reach a broader target audience. The Neptune not only offers a conventional season of performances in its new theatre but also performs tours of the province of Nova Scotia, offers a summer festival, and operates a Young Neptune Company.[3] Universities expanded their mix when they added adult night courses, off-campus extension programs, and concentrated between-semester courses. Many larger hospitals have added hostels for the families of long-stay patients, diet-counselling programs, and home-care programs.

The strategy of product differentiation is as important in not-for-profit organizations as it is in business. The principle is to set one's organization or program apart from the "competition" so as to encourage donations or support, or to attract clients. Many universities have differentiated their programs to attract students. Universities that serve populations scattered over wide geographic areas, such as Athabasca University and Memorial University of Newfoundland, deliver many courses and degree programs through distance education. Queen's University redesigned its MBA program so that it can be taken in cities across Canada through video-conferencing, or on the Kingston campus in a twelve-month format. Some Canadian universities, including Memorial, Queen's, and the University of Guelph, offer degree programs that give students an option to study at the universities' campuses in

Britain for a semester or more. Others offer exchange programs with overseas universities that allow students to spend semesters in another country.

The product life-cycle concept can be applied to not-for-profit marketing. Just as many business products and services become outdated and are replaced with new market entrants, so too do some not-for-profit organizations find that their entire reason for existence may no longer be relevant. This is especially the case in health-related organizations where (thankfully) progress is made in treating or even eradicating a particular disease. For example, organizations that were started many years ago to fight polio found that, particularly after the development of the Salk vaccine, they were headed into the decline stage of the life cycle. As a result, some health organizations alter their mandate to take in a broader range of health problems. Thus, the Canadian Heart Foundation became the Heart and Stroke Foundation, and the Canadian Tuberculosis Association became the Lung Association, as tuberculosis became much less prevalent in Canada. Unfortunately, such health issues as AIDS and Alzheimer's disease are looming as health issues that will continue to require attention from donors and volunteers for some time into the future.

Product Attributes Not-for-profit groups generally do not use product strategies such as branding and labelling. The little that has been done in this area, however, suggests that a not-for-profit organization can make its marketing more effective by emphasizing product attributes. For many years, colleges and universities have used nicknames (a form of brand name) primarily for their athletic teams, but also to identify their students and alumni. Most colleges and universities have school colours — another product attribute that helps increase the market's recognition and identification of the school.

Among health-research organizations, the Lung Association has registered as a trademark its double-barred Christmas-seal cross. The trademarks of the Girl Guides, the YM-YWCA, and Rotary International are recognized and remembered by many people.

Price Determination

Pricing in many not-for-profit organizations is quite different from pricing in a business firm. Pricing becomes less important when profit making is not an organizational goal. Also, many not-for-profit groups believe there are no client-market pricing considerations in their marketing because there is no charge to the client. The organization's basic function is to help those who cannot afford to pay.

Actually, the goods or services received by clients rarely are free — that is, without a price of some kind. True, the price may not be a monetary charge. Often, however, the client pays a price — in the form of travel and waiting time and, perhaps, degrading treatment — that a money-paying client-customer would not have to pay for the same service. Poor children who have to wear donated, secondhand clothes certainly are paying a price if their classmates ridicule these clothes. Alcoholics Anonymous and some drug rehabilitation organizations that provide "free" services do exact a price. They require active participation by their clients as well as a very strongly expressed resolve by clients to help themselves.

Some not-for-profit groups do face the same pricing problems as those discussed in chapters 13 and 14. Museums and opera companies must decide on admission prices; membership organizations must set a dues schedule; and colleges and universities must determine how much to charge for tuition. Not-for-profit organizations must (1) determine the base price for their product offering and (2) establish pricing strategies in several areas of their pricing structure.

Setting the Base Price Here again we are faced with two market situations — pricing in the contributor market and pricing in the client market.

When dealing with the contributor market, not-for-profit organizations really do not set the price of the donation. That price is set by contributors when they decide how much they are willing to pay for the benefits they expect to receive in return for their gifts. However, the organization may suggest a price. A charitable organization, for example, may suggest that you donate one day's pay or that you donate your time for one day a month.

Some of our discussion regarding the pricing of services (Chapter 12) is appropriate to the client market — for instance, in pricing admissions to museums, concerts, or theatre performances. But for

www.alcoholics.anonymous.org

www.ippf.org

most not-for-profit groups, the pricing methods used by business firms — cost-plus, balance of supply and demand, market alone — simply are not appropriate. Many organizations know they cannot cover their costs with prices charged to clients. The gap between anticipated revenues and costs must be made up by contributions.

As yet, there are no real guidelines — no methodology — for much not-for-profit pricing. A major problem here is that most not-for-profit organizations do not know the cost of the products and services they offer in their client markets.

Pricing Strategies Some of the pricing strategies discussed in Chapter 14 are also applicable in not-for-profit marketing. Discount strategies have widespread use, for example. Some museums offer discount prices to students and senior citizens. A season ticket for many theatre companies or symphony orchestras costs less per performance than do tickets purchased on an individual-performance basis. This is a form of quantity discount. The Montreal Symphony Orchestra allows subscribers to save 20 percent when they subscribe to a series. Subscribers also receive four coupons that are redeemable for savings and discounts on tickets to other theatre, opera, and ballet performances by other Montreal-based arts organizations and to area museums with which the symphony collaborates. This latter pricing strategy represents a form of cross-promotion.

Considerations regarding one price versus variable price also are strategies applicable in not-for-profit marketing. Some charities provide services according to the client's ability to pay — a variable-price strategy. A one-price strategy typically is followed by universities. That is, all students pay the same tuition for a full load of coursework in a particular degree program.

Distribution System

Setting up a distribution system in a not-for-profit organization involves two tasks. One is to establish channels of distribution back to contributors and forward to clients. The other task, usually the more important one, is to set up a physical distribution system to reach these two markets.

Channels of Distribution The channels of **distribution** used in not-for-profit marketing ordinarily are quite simple and short. The not-for-profit organization usually deals directly with its two major publics — no intermediaries are involved.

When an intermediary is used, it is an agent intermediary. For instance, to generate increased contributions, some charities and universities may employ an outside fund-raising organization to solicit contributions on their behalf. Not all donors welcome this approach to fund-raising, preferring that their entire donation go to the organization they wish to support, rather than a portion going to the professional fund-raiser as a commission. To reach potential customers, ballet companies, art galleries, and theatres may sell tickets through independent ticket agencies. In some cities, programs like Neighbourhood Watch and Crime Stoppers effectively use local police personnel as intermediaries. They distribute crime-prevention literature and programs to schools and to the general public.

Numerous not-for-profit organizations have established a separate marketing program whereby they serve as a retailer of goods that are related to the organization's primary service. Thus, we see art museums selling prints of paintings, colleges selling many items through the college bookstore, post offices selling stamps to collectors, and Planned Parenthood selling or giving away contraceptives. Over-the-counter and mail-order methods of retail selling may also be used in these situations. Most major museums, ballet companies, and symphony orchestras now operate "shops" that sell materials relating to the organization and to the branch of the arts it represents. These shops are operated by volunteers as a means of raising funds, and increasingly they are selling their wares through the World Wide Web.

Physical Distribution The primary goal in physical distribution is for a not-for-profit organization to locate where it can serve both contributors and clients most effectively. The organization should be as accessible as possible to its contributors so that giving is as easy and convenient as possible. Besides accepting cash and cheques, charities use payroll deductions, instalment plans, and credit cards. If the donor is contributing used goods, charities may col-

www.osm.ca

MARKETING AT WORK FILE 22-3

VIRTUALLY APPRECIATING ART

An obvious thing about art galleries is that one has to see the art to appreciate it. Increasingly, Canada's major art galleries are turning to technology to communicate with their visitors and patrons and to disseminate their "products" to the public. No longer does one have to visit Toronto to see the collection of the Art Gallery of Ontario. You can take a virtual tour on the World Wide Web.

The Web opens a line of communication between the AGO and people who are interested in its collection and programs, regardless of where they live. By accessing the AGO's Web site, one can learn about current exhibits, read about educational programs, or order merchandise from the extensive AGO bookstore. Eventually, children in art classes throughout Canada and beyond will be able to take a virtual tour of the collection, accompanied by a curator who will discuss new acquisitions and explaining the work of selected artists. The two-way channel will allow students and other interested "visitors" to ask questions and to send in comments.

The Montreal Museum of Fine Arts has also jumped on the WWW bandwagon. In addition to offering a virtual tour of the museum, the MMFA Web site offers visitors access to its extensive boutiques, including on-line ordering of books and other materials, information on current and coming exhibitions, and details on how to become a member of the MMFA's volunteer group, Friends of the Museum.

Source: Adapted from Christopher Hume, "AGO Revs Up to Join the Infobahn," *Toronto Star*, January 18, 1996, p. 65.

lect them at the donor's residence or at some other choice location instead of forcing the donor to haul the stuff across town to a central collection point.

Location is also critical in dealing with client markets. Thus, universities and colleges set up campuses in smaller cities and offer correspondence courses. Goodwill locates its stores in low-income neighbourhoods. Health-care organizations provide mobile units for lung X-rays, blood-pressure tests, and inoculations. City museums and art galleries arrange for portable exhibits to be taken to small towns. Theatre and ballet companies and symphony orchestras perform for younger audiences in their school auditoriums.

Marketing Communications Program

Marketing communications is the part of the marketing mix that many not-for-profit organizations are most familiar with and most adept at. They have regularly used advertising, personal selling, sales promotion, and publicity — often very aggressively and effectively — to communicate with both their contributors and their clients. However, many of these organizations have not integrated their marketing communications into a total marketing program. In fact, many not-for-profit groups believe that marketing communications and marketing are one and the same thing.

Advertising Advertising is used extensively to reach the donor market. Many not-for-profit organizations conduct annual fund-raising drives. Mass media (newspapers, magazines, television, radio) frequently are used in these efforts. Specific media also are used selectively to solicit funds. Direct mail can be especially effective in reaching segmented donor markets such as past contributors, religious or ethnic groups related to the organizations, or college alumni. Media such as alumni magazines and foreign-language newspapers can be used to pinpoint donor market segments.

Not-for-profit groups also can communicate with client markets through advertising. To offset declining enrolments, colleges and universities have run ads in a variety of media. A growing number of churches are advertising in print media and on radio and TV to increase their membership and attendance.

In some situations, a not-for-profit organization can reach both its contributor and its client markets with the same ad. The Heart and Stroke Association, the Canadian Cancer Society, or the Lung Association might advertise, asking you to contribute to its annual campaign. In the same ad, it might urge you to watch your diet, quit smoking, or get a medical checkup.

Most not-for-profit organizations, particularly those involved in social causes, find themselves in a dilemma when it comes to advertising. Food banks, shelters, youth groups, and others whose mandate is to serve clients who are in need face the criticism that much of the funds they raise is used for advertising, an expenditure that some supporters view as a waste and that reduces the amount of funding available for the organization's clients. Because they are not in a position to spend much on advertising, such social organizations and charities rely on the support of advertising agencies across the country who often donate their time and creative talents to prepare advertising campaigns for these not-for-profit organizations on a *pro bono* basis. Such advertising generally is placed particularly in the broadcast media as public service announcements, which broadcasters are required by the Canadian Radio-television and Telecommunications Commission (CRTC) to carry as a condition of receiving a broadcast licence.

Personal Selling Personal selling is often employed in fund-raising efforts. A door-to-door campaign may be used. At Christmastime, Salvation Army volunteers, standing by their red kettles, collect donations in the downtown areas of many cities. In addition, potential large donors may be approached by sales people.

Many not-for-profit organizations also use personal selling to reach their client public. These personal representatives may not be called sales people, but that is exactly what they are. For centuries, missionaries of countless religious groups have recruited new members by personal contact — personal selling. Personal selling also is employed to recruit new members for service organizations such as the YM-YWCA, Lions, Rotary, and Kiwanis. Colleges and universities send "sales people" — admission officers, alumni, current students — to talk to high school students, their parents, and their counsellors.

Using sales representatives to reach either contributors or clients poses some management problems for a not-for-profit organization. In effect, the organization has to manage a sales force, including recruiting, training, compensating, supervising, and evaluating performance. Not many not-for-profit organizations think in these terms, however, nor are they qualified to do this management job.

Sales Promotion Not-for-profit organizations have long recognized the value of sales promotion to reach their markets. Many organizations place exhibits (including donation boxes) in local stores and shopping centres and at sporting events. Usually there is no charge for this use of the space. Not-for-profit organizations are engaging in sales promotion when they conduct fund-raising events such as lotteries, fun runs, or bed races. Some operate booths or displays at summer fairs or conduct art auctions as fund-raisers.

IMPLEMENTATION OF MARKETING

In this final section, we discuss briefly three topics that will affect the future development of marketing in not-for-profit organizations.

Interest and Research in the Field

Marketing in not-for-profit organizations has a bright future. There is not only a growing interest in marketing among such organizations, but there is increasing evidence that volunteer leaders and full-time executives in the not-for-profit field really understand how the principles of marketing can be applied in a not-for-profit context and what marketing can contribute to their own organizations. Numerous books are being written on the subject, and journals with a specific interest in social and not-for profit marketing are being published.[4] Increasingly, marketing courses at universities and colleges are devoting time to the study of not-for-profit organizations and the application of marketing principles to their operations. There is considerable

www.hsf.ca • www.bc.cancer.ca • www.lung.ca • www.lions.org • www.rotary.org • www.kiwanis.org

research being carried out on the subject in Canadian universities, and special sessions on not-for-profit marketing are common at academic conferences.

Just a few years ago, research in not-for-profit marketing was initiated mainly by academics and other people outside the not-for-profit field. Now the marketing research is being generated by people working within various not-for-profit organizations. This is a healthy sign for the future.

Measuring Performance

A real managerial challenge is to establish some valid means of **measuring the marketing performance of not-for-profit organizations**. At present this is very difficult, if not impossible, for many of these organizations. A private business can evaluate its performance by using such quantitative measures as market share or return on investment, and then compare these figures with industry-wide averages and trends. For most not-for-profit organizations, however, there are no corresponding quantitative measures.

Not-for-profit organizations can quantify the contributions they receive, but the result reflects only their fund-raising abilities. It does not measure the services rendered to their clients. How do you quantitatively evaluate the performance of, say, the Lung Association? Perhaps by the number of people who make donations or the number who quit smoking?

Churches, museums, and YM-YWCAs can count their attendance, but how can they measure the services they provide for their clients? How does the Canadian Cancer Society assess its performance? By the decline in death rates from cancer? Perhaps, but such a decline may be due in part to factors other than the work of health-research organizations such as this. These are not easy questions to answer.

Increasingly, however, not-for-profit organizations are employing the same tools as marketers in businesses to assess the performance of their programs and of the organizations themselves. The Coalition for Head Injury Prevention carried out research on a program designed to promote increased use of bicycle helmets among children in Barrie, Ontario. The research showed that helmet use among elementary school children increased from 5.4 percent to 15.4 percent in one year.[5] Similarly, many hospitals are using patient-satisfaction and service-quality questionnaires to assess how well they are meeting the needs of their patients.[6] Some universities and colleges are even asking students whether they are satisfied with the way they are being served.

Managing the Marketing Effort

As stressed throughout this chapter, not-for-profit organizations are becoming increasingly familiar with the concepts of marketing. In fact, some have been practising marketing for some time, although they may not have been using marketing terminology. The marketing activities performed by not-for-profit organizations centre, in many cases, on advertising and promotion and are often not well co-ordinated. Typically, in many not-for-profit organizations, especially at the local and provincial levels, the organization of a marketing program depends on the availability of knowledgeable volunteers who are prepared to devote the time and effort needed to put a program together. In many situations, people who are given responsibility for **managing a marketing program in not-for-profit organizations** have no background in the field. Even in large organizations, like a university or a hospital, it is rare to find an individual with a marketing title, although this is becoming more common in not-for-profit organizations that actually market services directly to the general public, such as theatre groups, symphony orchestras, and public zoos.

Ideally, to establish a more formal marketing structure, a not-for-profit organization may select a group of people — both volunteer leaders and full-time staff — to decide what marketing objectives the organization wishes to accomplish. Such a group, in a series of marketing planning sessions, can define the organization's marketing goals and objectives and identify marketing strategies that will assist in reaching those goals. Decisions can even be made on the establishment of an internal marketing department. In smaller organizations, where there are few full-time staff, it generally falls to the executive director or senior full-time staff member to oversee marketing activities. In such a case, the organization may have to rely quite heavily on board members or other volunteers who have experience in marketing.

In larger not-for-profit organizations, as commitment to marketing activities increases and as a more formal structure develops, the organization may create a new middle-management position in marketing, with the title, for example, of director of marketing. In some cases, the marketing role is filled by individuals with titles such as patient relations manager or client services director. Eventually, as the function develops within the organization, a more senior marketing management position may be established at a level comparable with a vice-president of marketing in a business firm.

Summary

The marketing fundamentals apply to not-for-profit organizations as well as to firms in the business sector. But the development and implementation of a strategic marketing program are quite different in not-for-profit fields.

The not-for-profit field includes thousands of organizations spanning educational, cultural, religious, charitable, social, health-care, and political activities. Because of the large amounts of money and numbers of people involved in these organizations, marketing is quite important. Yet many people in not-for-profit organizations often seem opposed to marketing. Some do not understand what marketing is or what it can do for their organizations.

Most not-for-profit organizations must deal with two major groups (markets) — the contributors to the organization and the client-recipients of the organization's money or services. Consequently, a not-for-profit organization must develop two separate marketing programs — one to attract resources from contributors and one to serve its clients.

In developing its marketing programs, a not-for-profit organization first must identify and analyze its markets. Market segmentation is especially helpful at this stage. Then the organization is ready to develop its strategic marketing mix. The product offering will be determined largely by deciding what business the organization is in and what client markets it wants to reach. Product-mix strategies, such as expansion of mix or product differentiation, may well be used. Pricing in many not-for-profit organizations is quite different from the usual price determination in a business firm. Channels of distribution typically are quite simple in not-for-profit marketing. The main distribution challenge is to physically locate the organization where it can serve both contributors and clients. In promotion, many organizations have used advertising, personal selling, and other tools extensively, aggressively, and quite effectively.

Interest and research in not-for-profit marketing are growing. Both should be of help in implementing marketing programs in the future. Two important problems still to be solved are those of (1) measuring performance in a not-for-profit organization and (2) developing an internal structure to manage the marketing effort.

Key Terms and Concepts

- Exchange concept in not-for-profit marketing (549)
- Contributor (donor) markets (550)
- Client (recipient) markets (550)
- Volunteers (550)
- Importance of not-for-profit marketing (550)
- Market segmentation in not-for-profit organizations (553)
- Marketing mix in not-for-profit organizations:
  - Product offering (553)
  - Pricing (555)
  - Distribution (556)
  - Marketing communications (557)
- Measuring the marketing performance of not-for-profit organizations (559)
- Managing a marketing program in not-for-profit organizations (559)

Questions and Problems

1. Are nonbusiness organizations and not-for-profit organizations synonymous terms? If not,
   a. Name some nonbusiness organizations in which profit making is a major goal.
   b. Name some business organizations that are intentionally not-for-profit.
2. In this chapter it is noted that some people in not-for-profit organizations have a negative attitude toward marketing. What suggestions do you have for changing this attitude so that these people will appreciate the value of marketing for their organizations?
3. Identify the various segments of the contributor market for your college or university.
4. Identify the client markets for:
   a. Your college or university.
   b. The SPCA.
   c. Your church or other place of worship.
   d. The police department in your city.
5. What are some target markets (publics), other than contributors or clients, for each of the following organizations?
   a. YM-YWCA.
   b. Community hospital.
   c. Your school.
6. What benefits do contributors derive from gifts to each of the following?
   a. The Royal Winnipeg Ballet.
   b. The Boy Scouts.
   c. A symphony orchestra.
   d. A candidate for election to the House of Commons.
7. What is the product offering of each of the following?
   a. A political candidate.
   b. A family-planning organization.
   c. An organization opposed to nuclear energy.
8. A financial consultant for your university or college has suggested a change in the school's pricing methods. He recommended that the school discontinue its present one-price policy, under which all full-time students pay the same tuition. Instead he recommended that the tuition vary by department within the university. Thus students majoring in high-cost fields of study, such as engineering or a laboratory science, would pay higher tuition than students in lower-cost fields, such as English or history. Should the school adopt this recommendation?
9. Explain how the concept of the marketing mix (product, price, distribution, promotion) is applicable to the marketing of the following social causes:
   a. The use of returnable bottles, instead of the throwaway type.
   b. The prevention of heart ailments.
   c. A campaign against littering.
   d. Obeying the 100-km-per-hour speed limit.
10. How would you measure the marketing performance of each of the following?
   a. A local museum.
   b. Your school.
   c. The Liberal Party of Canada.
   d. A group in favour of animal rights.
11. The performance of a charitable organization may be measured by the percentage of contributions distributed among its clients. Explain why you think this is or isn't an effective measure of marketing performance.

Hands-On Marketing

1. Select a local arts organization or charity and arrange an interview with the executive director or senior person responsible for marketing. Identify the various elements of the marketing program of the organization that correspond to the elements of the marketing mix — product, price, marketing communications, and distribution. Also, try to identify the types of information that the organization relies on to make marketing decisions.
2. Assume that your college or university wants to hire a director of marketing. Prepare a job description for this position, indicating its scope, activities, location within the school's administration, and responsibilities.

CHAPTER 23 GOALS

In Chapter 3, we defined the management process in marketing as planning, implementing, and evaluating marketing in an organization. This process was illustrated in Figure 3-1. Most of this book has dealt with **planning** a marketing program. We discussed how to select target markets and how to design a strategic program to deliver want-satisfaction to those markets.

In this chapter, we discuss the implementation and evaluation of a marketing program. **Implementation** is the operational stage — the stage during which an organization attempts to carry out its strategic plan. At the end of an operating period (or even during the period), management should conduct an **evaluation** of the organization's performance — that is, determine how well the organization is achieving the goals set in its strategic planning.

After studying this chapter, you should have an understanding of:

- The role of implementation in the management process.
- Organizational structures used to implement marketing.
- The role of a marketing audit in evaluating a marketing program.
- The steps of the evaluation process in marketing.
- The meaning of misdirected marketing effort.
- Sales volume analysis.
- Marketing cost analysis.
- How findings from sales and cost analyses can be used by managers.

Chapter Twenty-Three

Marketing Implementation

www.canadiantire.ca • www.wal-mart.com • www.HomeDepot.com • www.sportsauthority.com

"GROWING OUT" OF A TIRE PROBLEM

Building trust: take a co-operative marketing audit, co-operatively produce a new plan, and you get co-operative implementation, which yields trust and, surprise, profits.

In 1993, Stephen Bachand took over as president of Canadian Tire. At that time, revenues were stagnant, many of the smaller stores were losing money, customers were annoyed by poor service, out-of-stock situations added to the consumer annoyance, and the company did not appear to care that it was being underpriced by domestic rivals as well as the new imports — Wal-Mart, Home Depot, and Sports Authority. And, not a trivial matter, Canadian Tire dealers were unhappy!

Canadian Tire had a unique relationship with its 390 dealers. The dealers owned the inventory and fixtures in their 429 stores and 20 percent of the parent company stock. During the 1980s, the dealers — having become quite well off (and complacent, say some) — tried to take over the company. When they failed, too many simply became inattentative to business.

Bachand started out his new presidency by concluding that pursuing a strategy of "growing out" of its problems — rather than, as other retailers were doing at the time, chopping branches and going into retreat — was the way to save and redevelop relationships with dealers, suppliers, and consumers.

Bachand believed that "unless we realized that we'd better figure out how to come to market with lower prices and still make money" — "we" meaning head office and the dealers together — "we would fall flat on (our) faces." He let it be known that Canadian Tire didn't need imported solutions from the United States or consultants: "People here were just waiting, ready to do the things they knew how to do." Bachand and the dealers jointly combed through the results of almost every known type of customer research from in-store surveys to focus groups. They learned that their customers wanted lower prices, greater assortments, an end to out-of-stock annoyance, better service, and a store that was easier to shop in.

Delivering on the demands uncovered in the evaluation and reappraisal of all this research meant massive overhaul. The overhaul plan that Bachand presented to dealers called on them to accept lower margins, invest their own money in bigger inventories, spend heavily on employee training, and pay a portion of the $8–14 million it would cost to overhaul or rebuild their stores. Head office suggested one hundred operating improvements that the dealers said wouldn't work; head office people turned down some of their suggestions. In the end, a plan was worked out, and the dealers consented partly because they helped Bachand draft the plan and because they had confidence in the outcomes.

Implementing the plan was another exercise in co-operation. The dealers and head office planners worked together to design the perfect Canadian Tire store for large and small communities, considering the size and type of market, the needed assortments, easy-to-navigate floor plans and layouts, colour-coded product location signs, impulse-shopping display space, the location of buttons to push for customer service, design of new carpeted and soundproofed waiting rooms for auto repair customers, and so on.

A committee made up of dealers and head office buyers had examined the performance of each of the 65,000 or so items carried by Canadian Tire. The results of this audit were accepted by Bachand and, in consultation with dealers, used to reorient assortments so that there was a big increase in the number of auto supplies carried and the reduction or elimination of slow-moving items such as ready to assemble furniture.

As part of restoring trust with suppliers, Bachand promised that Canadian Tire would do a better job of seeing to it that they got the shelf space they had been led to expect. He instructed his buyers to start sharing highly valued sales information with sellers so that they could see how their products were performing. By the time Bachand was able to report to suppliers that out-of-stock problems were a thing of the past, there was enough trust and goodwill that they were willing to cut Canadian Tire's marketing expenses by sharing more of the cost of advertising their goods.

What about the relationship with consumers? Bachand says that "when we started talking with customers about what was wrong, they didn't tell us 'I'm through with you, I'm never shopping there again.' They said, 'When are you going to do something about my Canadian Tire?' That's how they talked about it — people were rooting for us. You can't imagine what a great feeling it is to have a relationship like that with your customers."

There are still things to be done, but one of the biggest rebuilding programs in Canadian retailing — $1 billion worth — is much closer to being complete. Audit, plan, replan, build trust, build relationships — it's all at Canadian Tire.[1]

IMPLEMENTATION IN MARKETING MANAGEMENT

There should be a close relationship among planning, implementation, and evaluation. Without strategic planning, a company's operational activities — its implementation tactics — can go off in any direction, like an unguided missile. In the early 1980s, there was tremendous interest in strategic planning, sparked by management consulting firms. Then disenchantment set in, as many companies came to realize that strategic planning alone was not enough to ensure success. These plans had to be effectively implemented. Management began to realize that planners were great at telling them what to do — that is, designing a strategy. But planners often fell short when it came to telling management how to do it — how to implement the strategy.

Good planning cannot overcome poor implementation. But effective implementation often can overcome poor planning. Fortunately, in recent years considerably more attention is being devoted to implementing a company's strategies. For example, Holt Renfrew & Company is implementing a strong merchandising push toward private-label products. To assist in putting this strategy in place, the company uses its Club Select loyalty program, which rewards buyers who use the Holt Renfrew charge card. The retailer also sends customers a glossy magazine that touts its merchandise. Holt Renfrew has stepped up in-store events and susbscribes to the view that retail is entertainment. It also offers customers "comfort zones" to rest and make phone calls.[2]

Implementation comprises three activities:

1. *Organizing the marketing effort.* Once a company has developed its strategic marketing plan, an early activity is to organize the people who will implement it. The relationship between marketing and the other functional divisions of the firm must be defined. Then, within the marketing department, management must design an organization that will implement both strategies and tactics.
2. *Staffing the organization.* For plans to produce an intended result, an organization needs skilled, dedicated people to carry them out well. Thus, selection of people is very important. As we pointed out earlier, Four Seasons Hotels is very deliberate about selecting only those service personnel who have the "right" approach to treating people. A sales manager's success depends greatly on the people whom the manager selects. The success of relationship marketing programs rests substantially on the sales force as the key implementers of strategies and tactics.
3. *Directing the execution of marketing plans.* In this third phase of implementation, revenues are generated. To do so, management needs to direct the work of the people who have been selected and organized as the company's marketing team. Success in this phase depends on four important aspects of managing employees — delegation, co-ordination, motivation, and communication.

A detailed discussion of staffing and directing an organization is reserved for more specialized management courses, However, it is appropriate here to consider how organizational structures are used to implement marketing programs.

ORGANIZING FOR IMPLEMENTATION

After setting a company's strategic marketing plan, an early activity is to organize the people who will be implementing it. This involves first defining the relationship between marketing and the other functional divisions of the firm. Then, within the marketing department, management must design an organization that will implement the plans.

Organizational structures are receiving increasing attention in companies around the globe as management recognizes that yesterday's structures may hinder operations in today's dynamic environment. Satisfying customers profitably requires talking to them — and listening to them. Teamwork across functions such as marketing and production is also essential. Traditional organizational structures,

FIGURE 23-1

The Management Process in Marketing

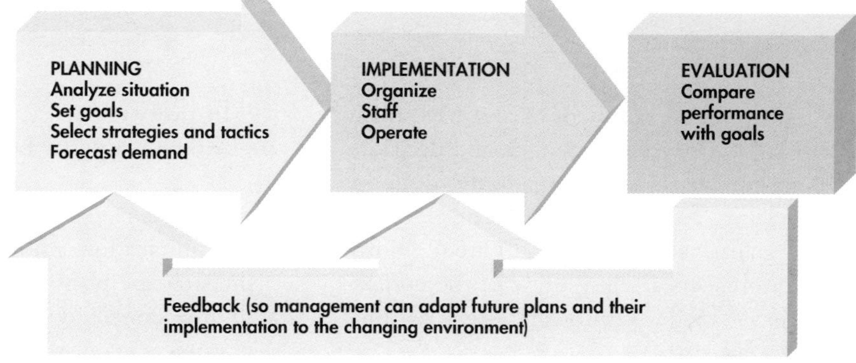

Getting the right person into a marketing job means getting people with the right people skills and personality. Drake offers the system to make the correct selections.

however, isolate different functions and have many managerial layers between customers and decision-makers. Recognizing this, large organizations such as Hewlett-Packard, Xerox, Siemens (the German electronics giant), and the "Big Three" North American automakers are just a few of the companies that have made significant organizational changes in recent years.

www.canada.hp.com • www.xerox.ca • www.siemens.com

In a very real sense, traditional vertical structures are being replaced by horizontal organizations.[3]

- *Fewer organizational levels.* The intent is to facilitate communication among executives who develop the strategic plans, the employees who have continuing contact with the market, and the firm's customers.

MARKETING AT WORK FILE 23-1

IMPLEMENTING A SHADY STRATEGY!

Ray-Ban is a cool company! Or at least that is how it sees itself, and judging by its success, that is apparently how others see it as well. It needs to be cool; its sells sunglasses. Check out *Men in Black*, *Top Gun*, *Risky Business*, *The Blues Brothers*, and *Jerry Maguire*. Ray-Ban sunglasses appear in all those movies.

The strategy of using movies to sell products is a relatively new one. Ray-Ban uses it well, but it also uses other strategies. These designer shades are now on display in a main-floor boutique at the The Bay on Queen Street in Toronto. This new approach is a shop-within-a-shop and is Ray-Ban's first such store in North America. The company intends it to be the first of many, however.

The decision to set up this boutique is part of a widespread effort to leverage a strong brand, in this case by attaching the sunglass brand to boutique clothing and accessories sold in The Bay. More and more brands are adding value to marketing strategies by associating with other products. Cosmetics and perfume makers have done it for years. Department stores lease space to Revlon, Clinique, Max Factor, and others who build on the associations shoppers make with other products as well as their own brands.

A lot of Ray-Ban's distribution has been done through Sunglass Hut, which can be found in most major regional shopping malls and some Eaton's stores. The strategy to open a boutique in The Bay is undertaken with a close eye on the relationship with Sunglass Hut and a determination not to erode that relationship in any way. You can be assured that Ray-Ban boutiques will not show up in areas in direct competion with Sunglass Hut. Often retailers must deal with the problem of one outlet or distribution system interfering with the implementation of its overall strategy in another area.

Scott Woodworth, director of global image for Ray-Ban eyewear, feels that sunglasses are an essential part of every outfit. Accordingly he promotes a strategy that would see the use of his sunglasses suit the occasion and the time of day. As he puts it, "You really need a pair for driving with the top up, another for top down, and a special pair for going out at night." No need to tell that to *Men in Black*!

Source: John Deverell, "Ray-Ban Puts a Shades Shop in Bay," *The Toronto Star*, April 25, 1997, p. E3; and www.ray-ban.com. Reprinted with permission — The Toronto Star Syndicate.

- *Cross-functional teams.* By having personnel from various departments work on a project, not only are barriers among functions broken down, but the best combination of expertise and experience can be focused on the assignment.
- *Employee empowerment.* Granting more authority to middle-level executives in decentralized locations can stimulate innovation and generate faster responses to market shifts.

These trends show that firms today demand an organizational flexibility to respond quickly in a dynamic, information-driven marketing environment characterized by diversity and turbulence. Undoubtedly, new organizational structures will continue to emerge in response to changing environments.

Company-Wide Organization

In Chapter 1, we stated that one of the three foundation stones of the marketing concept is to co-ordinate all marketing activities. In firms that are production-oriented or sales-oriented, typically we find that marketing activities are fragmented. The sales force is quite separate from advertising, and sales training may be under the human resources department.

In a marketing-oriented enterprise, all marketing activities are co-ordinated under one marketing executive, who usually is at the vice-presidential level. This executive reports directly to the president and is on an equal organizational footing with top executives in finance, production, and other major functions, as shown in Figure 23-2.

Another aspect of organizational co-ordination is to establish effective working relationships between marketing and each of the other major functional areas. Marketing can help production, for example, by providing accurate sales forecasts. Production can return the favour with desired-quality products precisely when they are needed to fill customers' orders. Marketing and finance people can work together to establish pricing and credit policies. Cross-functional teams, as described earlier, can break down organizational barriers, improve co-ordination across functional areas, and expedite work on major processes such as product development.

Organization within the Marketing Department

Within the marketing department — especially in medium-sized or large firms — the sales force frequently is specialized in some organizational fashion. This is done to effectively implement the company's strategic marketing plan. The sales force may be organized in one of these three forms of specialization: geographic territory, product line, or customer type.

Geographic Specialization Probably the most widely used method of specializing selling activities is on the basis of **geographic specialization**. Each sales person is assigned a specific geographic area — called a territory — in which to sell. Several sales people representing contiguous territories are placed under a territorial sales executive, who reports directly to the general sales manager. These territorial executives usually are called district or regional sales managers, as shown in Figure 23-3A.

A geographic organization usually ensures better implementation of sales strategies in each local market and better control over the sales force. Customers can be serviced quickly and effectively, and local sales reps can respond better to competitors' actions in a given territory. As its major drawback, a geographic organization does not provide the product expertise or other specialized knowledge that some customers may want. To address that problem, Kodak switched the professional imaging division from a geographic alignment of its sales force to one that takes into account sales people's expertise and customer needs. Rather than calling on all kinds of customers in an area, a Kodak rep now works with certain types of customers such as commercial laboratories and professional resellers in an expanded area.[4]

Product Specialization Another basis for organizing a sales force is **product specialization**, as illustrated in Figure 23-3B. A company such as a meat packer may divide all its products into two lines — meat products and fertilizers. One group of sales reps sells only the various meat products, while

FIGURE 23-2 Company Organization Embracing the Marketing Concept

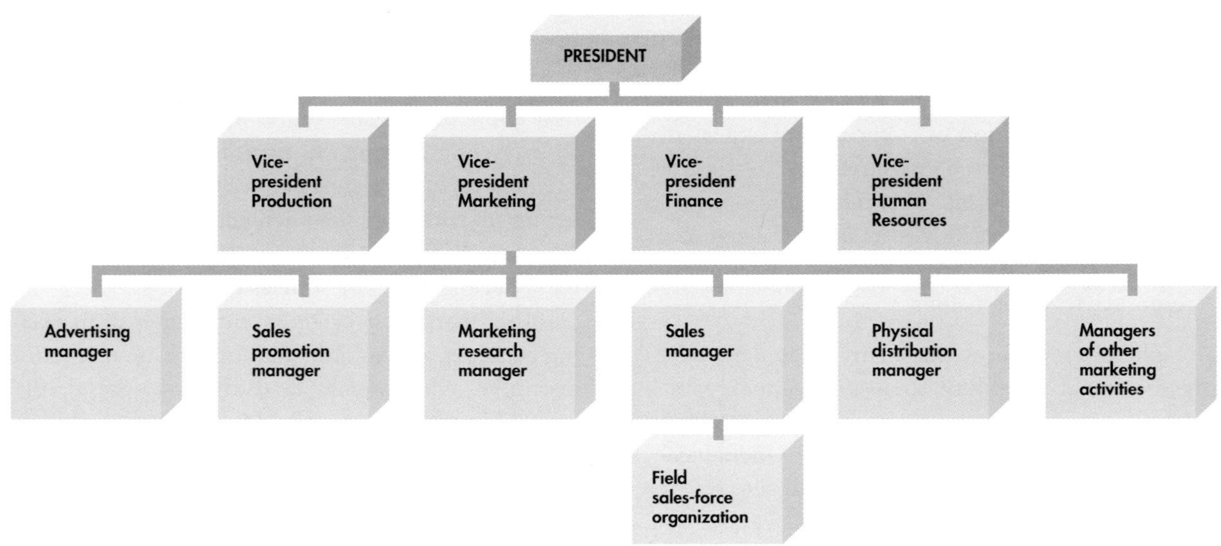

FIGURE 23-3

Major Forms of Sales Organization

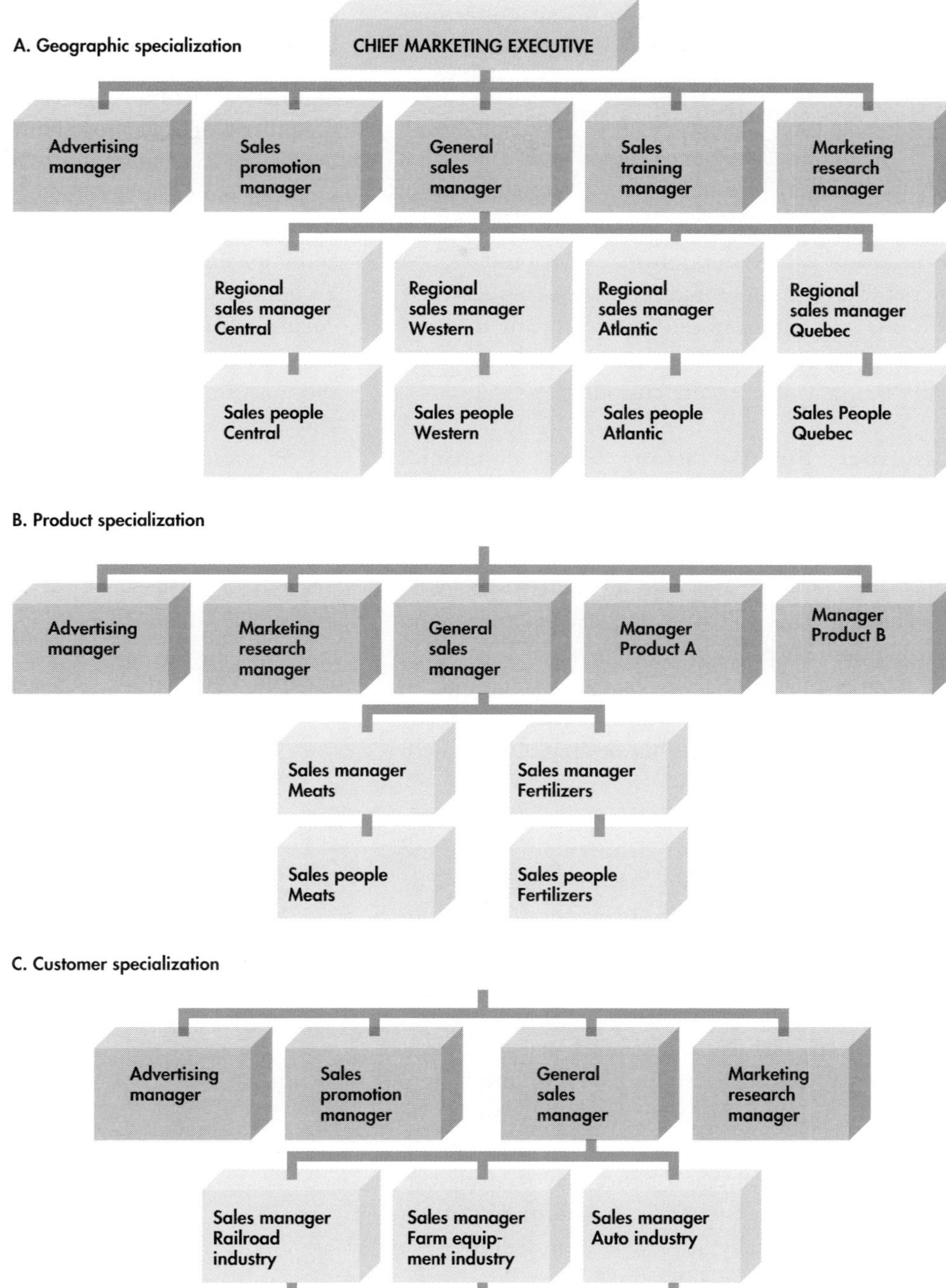

another group sells the fertilizer line. Each group reports to its own product sales manager, who in turn reports to the general sales manager.

This type of organization is especially well suited for companies that are marketing:

- *Complex technical products* — a manufacturer of a variety of electronic products.
- *Unrelated or dissimilar products* — a company marketing luggage, folding tables and chairs, and toy building blocks.
- *Thousands of items* — a hardware wholesaler.

The main advantage of a product-specialized sales organization is the attention that each product line can get from the sales force. A drawback is that more than one sales rep from the same company may call on the same customer. This duplication is not only costly, but may also irritate customers.

Customer Specialization Many companies today have divided their sales departments on the basis of **customer specialization**. Customers may be grouped by type of industry or channel of distribution. An oil company may divide its markets by industries, such as railroads, auto manufacturers, and farm equipment producers, as shown in Figure 23-3C. A firm that specializes its sales operations by channel of distribution may have one sales force selling to wholesalers and another dealing directly with large retailers.

As more companies fully implement the marketing concept and work to deliberately create and strengthen their marketing relationships, the customer-specialization type of organization is likely to increase. Certainly the basis of customer specialization is commensurate with the customer-oriented relationship philosophy that underlies the extended marketing concept. That is, the organizational emphasis is on customers and markets rather than on products.

A variation of customer specialization is the major-accounts organization. Many companies are adopting this structure as a better way to deal with large, important customers. A **major-accounts organization** usually involves team selling — a concept introduced in Chapter 19. A selling team, consisting perhaps of a sales rep, a sales engineer, a financial executive, and a manufacturing person, will negotiate with a buying team from the customer's organization. Procter & Gamble, for example, has established a series of selling teams, each specializing in a broad product category (for example, cleaning products or food products) to better service key accounts such as Zellers and Wal-Mart.

EVALUATING MARKETING PERFORMANCE

Soon after a firm's plans have been set in operation, the process of evaluation should begin. Without evaluation, management cannot tell whether a plan is working and what factors are contributing to its success or failure. Evaluation logically follows planning and implementation. Planning sets forth what should be done. Evaluation shows what really was done. A circular relationship exists, as illustrated in Figure 23-4. Plans are made, they are put into action, the results of those actions are evaluated, and new plans are prepared on the basis of this evaluation.

Previously we discussed evaluation as it relates to individual parts of a marketing program — the product-planning process, the performance of the sales force, and the effectiveness of the advertising program, for instance. Now let's look at the evaluation of the total marketing effort.

FIGURE 23-4 The Circular Relationship among Management Tasks

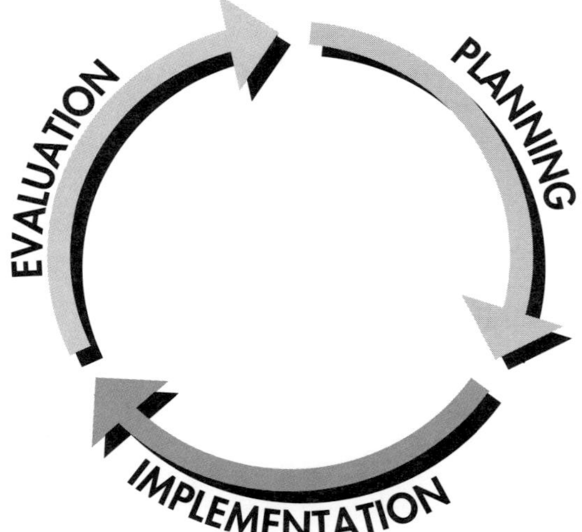

As we saw in Chapter 1, consumer satisfaction is driving marketing approaches.[5] In the product-focused marketing world, the emphasis was on the core product. There has been a shift away from focusing solely on the product and more to other elements that encompass customer service. You will recall from Figure 1-2, "Factors that Drive Customer Satisfaction," in Chapter 1, that the core product is the basic level provided by the organization. Generally, we tend to think of tangible products as the core because they are easy to visualize, but a service may be the core offering. Beyond the core are four other levels at which customer satisfaction can be provided — support services, technical performance, interaction between the customer and the employees, and the affective dimensions of the purchase experience.

Effective evaluation of the marketing program means consideration of all the factors that drive customer satisfaction. These factors will change in weighting depending on the nature of the exchange experience. In situations in which very little service is provided and there is almost no personal interaction, the customer's evaluation will be driven by the core product much more so than in situations in which the service component is much more prominent and important to the customer interaction. The significant point is that the evaluation of the marketing plan must reflect the elements that are important to the customer, and the evaluator must always keep in mind that a marketing initiative that doesn't reflect customer needs and wants is a poor one.[6]

A number of firms in various industries have developed approaches to measuring customer satisfaction as part of their relationship marketing strategies. In general, the customer-satisfaction measurement processes deal with understanding and measuring how well:

- a particular firm or organizational unit meets customer expectations,
- the firm responds to specific customer complaints,
- the firm manages the various components of the customer relationship, including transaction form and content; product, service, and process performance; service and processes quality,
- the firm improves processes and systems by analyzing customer feedback.

The customer satisfaction process starts with the identification of key customer segments and the strategies put in place to deal with them. The process ends with the communication of improvements and results to both customers and employees. A key aspect of most processes observed or discussed is designating a clear "owner" for the handling of satisfaction issues as they arose.

The marketing audit, discussed below, would include an evaluation of a customer satisfaction process as part of the total evaluation.

The Marketing Audit: A Total Evaluation Program

A **marketing audit** is an essential element in a total evaluation program. An audit implies a review and evaluation of some activity. Thus, a marketing audit is a comprehensive review and evaluation of the marketing function in an organization — its philosophy, environment, goals, strategies, organizational structure, human and financial resources, and performance.

It's true that a marketing audit involves evaluation. But it is much more than that. As suggested by Figure 23-4, the results of any evaluation — including a marketing audit — represent vital input to an organization's planning, as in the case of Canadian Tire. In advocating the value of marketing audits in the banking industry, one writer stressed, "Simply stated, a strategic marketing plan should only be written after completion of an intensive, objective, marketing audit."[7]

A complete marketing audit is an extensive and difficult project. That's why it is conducted infrequently — perhaps every two or three years. However, a company should not delay a marketing audit until a major crisis arises.

The rewards of a marketing audit can be great. Management can identify problem areas in marketing. By reviewing its strategies, the firm is likely to keep abreast of its changing marketing environment. Successes can also be analyzed so that the company can capitalize on its strong points. The audit can spot lack of co-ordination in the marketing program, outdated strategies, or unrealistic goals. Furthermore, an audit should anticipate future situations. It is intended for "prognosis as well as diagnosis. . . It is the practice of preventive as well as curative marketing medicine."[8]

Misdirected Marketing Effort

One of the benefits of evaluation is that it helps correct **misdirected** (or misplaced) marketing effort.

The 80–20 Principle In most firms, a large proportion of the total orders, customers, territories, or products accounts for only a small share of total sales or profit. Conversely, a small proportion produces a large share of sales or profit. This relationship has been characterized as the **80–20 principle**. That is, 80 percent of the orders, customers, territories, or products contribute only 20 percent of sales or profit. On the other hand, 20 percent of these selling units account for 80 percent of the volume or profit. We use the 80–20 figure simply to highlight the misplacement of marketing effort. In reality, of course, the percentage split varies from one situation to another.

The basic reason for the 80–20 split is that almost every marketing program includes some misdirected effort. Marketing efforts and costs are proportional to the number of territories, customers, or products, rather than to their actual sales volume or profit. For example, in a Sears Canada department store, approximately the same order-filling, billing, and delivery expenses are involved, whether a $500 suit or a $25 necktie is sold. Or a manufacturer such as Xerox may assign one sales person to each territory. Yet usually there are differences in the actual sales volume and profit among the territories. In each example, the marketing effort (cost) is not in line with the actual return.

Reasons for Misdirected Marketing Effort Frequently, executives cannot uncover their misdirected effort because they lack sufficient information. The **iceberg principle** is an analogy that illustrates this situation. Only a small part of an iceberg is visible above the surface of the water, and the submerged 90 percent is the dangerous part. The figures representing total sales or total costs on an operating statement are like the visible part of an iceberg. The detailed figures representing sales, costs, and other performance measures for each territory or product correspond to the dangerous submerged segment.

Total sales or cost figures are too general to be useful in evaluation; in fact, they often are misleading. A company may show satisfactory overall sales and profit figures. But when these totals are subdivided by territory or products, serious weaknesses often are discovered. A manufacturer of audio equipment showed an overall annual increase of 12 percent in sales and 9 percent in net profit on one product line one year. But management wasn't satisfied with this "tip of the iceberg." When it analyzed the figures more closely, it found that the sales change within territories ranged from an increase of 19 percent to a decrease of 3 percent. In some territories, profit increased as much as 14 percent, and in others it was down 20 percent.

A more basic cause of misplaced marketing effort is that executives must make decisions based on inadequate knowledge of the exact nature of marketing costs. In other words, management often lacks knowledge of: (a) the disproportionate spread of marketing effort; (b) reliable standards for determining what should be spent on marketing; and (c) what results should be expected from these expenditures.

As an illustration, a company may spend $250,000 more on advertising this year than last year. But management ordinarily cannot state what the resultant increase in sales volume or profit should be. Nor do the executives know what would have happened if they had spent the same amount on (a) new-product development, (b) management training seminars for sales staff or intermediaries, or (c) some other aspect of the marketing program.

The Evaluation Process

The evaluation process — whether a complete marketing audit or only an appraisal of individual components of the marketing program — is a three-step task:

1. *Find out what happened.* Get the facts, and compare actual results with budgeted goals to determine where they differ.
2. *Find out why it happened.* Determine what specific factors in the marketing program accounted for the results.
3. *Decide what to do about it.* Plan the next period's program so as to improve on unsatisfactory performance and capitalize on the things that were done well.

To evaluate a total marketing program we need to analyze performance results. To do this, two tools are available — sales volume analysis and marketing cost analysis. We'll discuss both of these tools using the Great Western Company (GW) — a firm that markets

www.sears.ca

office furniture. This company's market is divided into four sales districts, each with seven or eight sales people and a district sales manager. The company sells to office equipment wholesalers and directly to large business users. Great Western's product mix is divided into four groups — desks, chairs, filing equipment, and office accessories (wastebaskets and desk sets, for example). Some of these products are manufactured by GW, and some are purchased from other firms.

SALES VOLUME ANALYSIS

A **sales volume analysis** is a detailed study of the net sales section of a company's profit and loss statement (operating statement). Management should analyze its total sales volume, and its volume by product lines and market segments (territories and customer groups). These sales should be compared with company sales goals and industry sales.

We start with an analysis of Great Western's total sales volume, as shown in Table 23-1. Annual sales doubled from $18 million to $36 million during the ten-year period ending with 1997. Furthermore, sales increased each year, with the exception of 1994. In most years, planned sales goals were met or surpassed. Thus far in our analysis the company's situation is encouraging.

However, a study of total sales volume alone is usually insufficient and may even be misleading. Remember the iceberg principle! To learn what is going on in the "submerged" parts of the market, we need to analyze sales volume by market segments — sales territories, for example.

Table 23-2 is a summary of the planned sales goals and actual sales results in Great Western's four sales districts. A key measurement is the performance percentage for each district — that is, actual sales divided by sales goal. A performance percentage of 100 means that the district did exactly what was expected. From the table we see that districts B and C did just a little better than was expected. District A passed its goal by a wide margin. But district D was quite a disappointment.

So far in our evaluation, we know a little about what happened in GW's districts. Now management has to figure out why it happened and what should be done about it. These are the difficult steps in evaluation. Great Western's executives need to determine why district D did so poorly. The fault may lie in some aspect of the marketing program, or competition may be especially strong in that district. They also should find out the reasons for district A's success, and whether this information can be used in the other regions.

TABLE 23-1 Annual Sales Volume of Great Western Company, Industry Volume, and Company's Share in Market, 1988–1997

Year	Company Volume ($millions)	Industry Volume in Company's Market ($millions)	Company's Share of Market (percent)
1997	36.0	300	12.0
1996	34.7	275	12.6
1995	33.1	255	13.0
1994	30.4	220	13.8
1993	31.7	235	13.5
1992	28.0	200	14.0
1991	24.5	170	14.4
1990	22.5	155	14.5
1989	21.8	150	14.8
1988	18.0	120	15.0

TABLE 23-2 District Sales Volume in Great Western Company, 1997

District	Sales Goals ($millions)	Actual Sales ($millions)	Performance Percentage (actual ÷ goal)	Dollar Variation ($millions)
A	$10.8	$12.5	116	+1.7
B	9.0	9.6	107	+0.6
C	7.6	7.7	101	+0.1
D	8.6	6.2	72	−2.4
Total	$36.0	$36.0		

This brief examination of two aspects of sales volume analysis shows how this evaluation tool may be used. However, for a more useful evaluation, GW's executives should go much further. They should analyze their sales volume by individual territories within districts and by product lines. Then they should carry their territorial analysis further by examining volume by product line and customer group within each territory. For instance, even though district A did well overall, the iceberg principle may be at work within the district. The fine total performance in district A may be covering up weaknesses in an individual product line or territory.

Market-Share Analysis

Comparing a company's sales results with its goal is a useful evaluation, but it does not tell how the company is doing relative to its competitors. We need a **market-share analysis** to compare the company's sales with the industry's sales. We should analyze the company's share of the market in total, as well as by product line and market segment.

Probably the major obstacle encountered in market-share analysis is in obtaining industry sales information in total and in sufficient detail. Trade associations and government agencies are sources for industry sales volume statistics in many fields.

Great Western Company is a good example of the value of market-share analysis. Recall from Table 23-1 that GW's total sales doubled over a ten-year period, with annual increases in eight of those years. But during this decade the industry's annual sales increased from $120 million to $300 million (a 150 percent increase). Thus the company's share of this market actually declined from 15 to 12 percent. Although GW's annual sales increased 100 percent, its market share declined 20 percent.

The next step is to determine why Great Western's market position declined. The number of possible causes is quite large — and this is what makes management's task so difficult. A weakness in almost any aspect of GW's product line, distribution system, pricing structure, or promotional program may have contributed to the loss of market share. Or it may be that the culprit was competition. There may be new competitors in the market that were attracted by the rapid growth rates. Or competitors' marketing programs may be more effective than Great Western's.

MARKETING COST ANALYSIS

An analysis of sales volume is helpful in evaluating and controlling a company's marketing effort. A volume analysis, however, does not tell us anything about the profitability of this effort. Management needs to conduct a marketing cost analysis to determine the relative profitability of its territories, product lines, or other marketing units. A **marketing cost analysis** is a detailed study of the operating expenses section of a company's profit and loss statement. As part of this analysis, management may establish budgetary goals, and then study the variations between budgeted costs and actual expenses.

Types of Marketing Cost Analysis

A company's marketing costs may be analyzed:

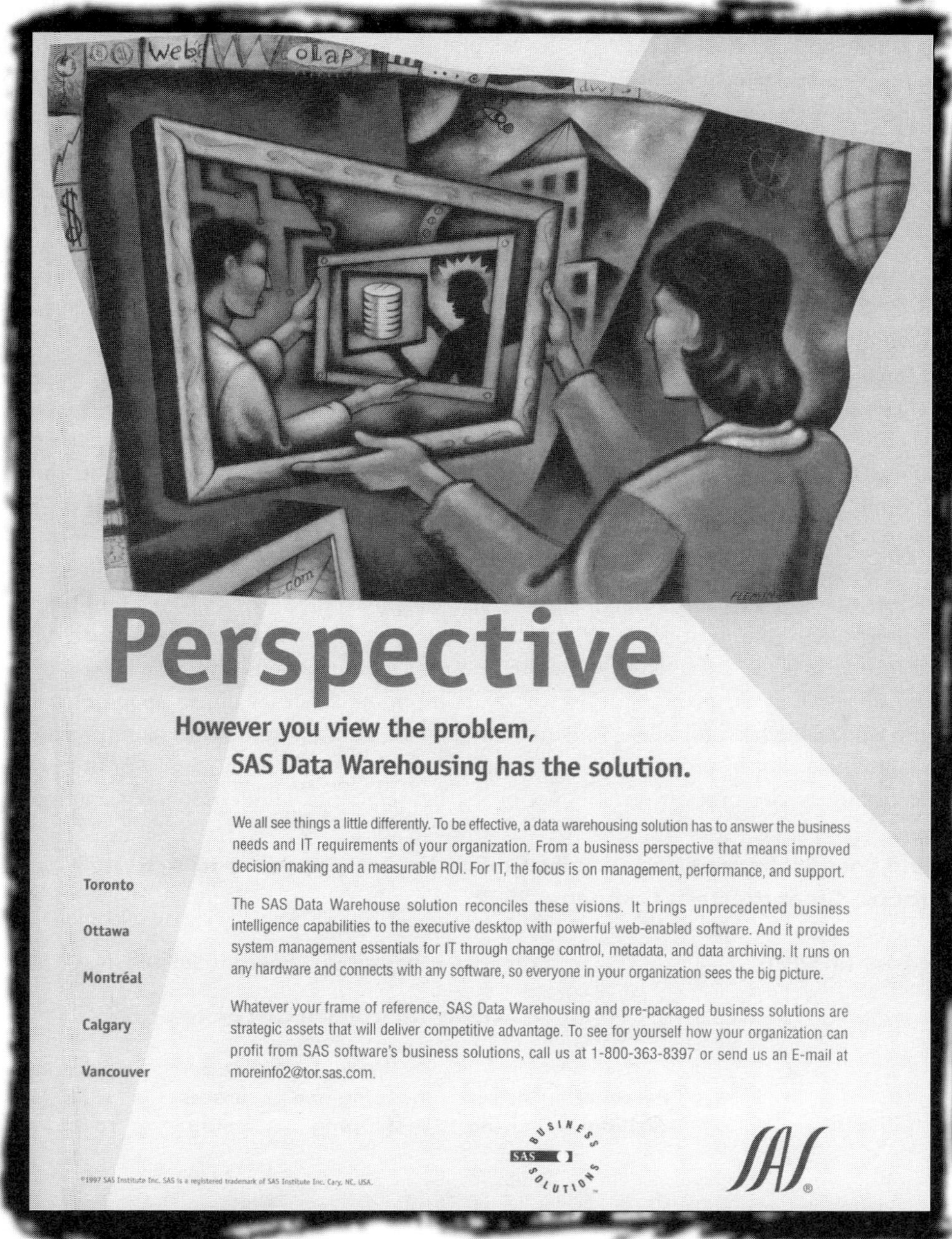

Evaluating marketing performance at any level of the organization, and in any region, requires the right data. Data Warehousing's solution to information-system design provides the software to manage, assess, and evaluate for decision-making purposes.

- As they appear in its ledger accounts and profit and loss statement.
- After they are grouped into activity classifications.
- After these activity costs have been allocated to territories, products, or other marketing units.

Analysis of Ledger Expenses The simplest and least expensive marketing cost analysis is a study of the "object of expenditure" costs as they appear in the firm's profit and loss statement. These figures come from the company's accounting ledger records. The simplified operating statement for the Great Western Company on the left side of Table 23-3 is the model we shall use in this discussion.

The procedure is to analyze each cost item (salaries and media space, for example) in detail. We can compare this period's total with the totals for similar periods in the past, and observe the trends. We can compare actual costs with budgeted expense goals. We should also compute each expense as a percentage of net sales. Then, we should compare these expense ratios with industry figures, which are often available through trade associations.

Analysis of Activity Expenses Marketing costs should be allocated among the various marketing activities, such as advertising or warehousing, for more effective control. Management can then analyze the cost of each of these activities.

The procedure here is first to identify the major activities, and then to allocate each ledger expense among those activities. As indicated in the expense distribution sheet on the right-hand side of Table 23-3, we have decided on five activity cost groups in our Great Western example. Some items, such as the cost of media space, can be apportioned entirely to one activity (advertising). For other expenses, the cost must be spread among several activities. So management must decide on some reasonable basis for allocation among these activities. For example, property taxes may be allocated according to the proportion of total floor space occupied by each activity. Thus the warehouse accounts for 46 percent of the total area (square metres) of floor space in the firm, so the warehousing and shipping activity is charged with $60,000 (46 percent) of the property taxes.

An analysis of the costs of the marketing activities gives executives more information than they can get from an analysis of ledger accounts alone. Also, an analysis of activity expenses in total provides a starting point for management to analyze costs by territories, products, or other marketing units.

Analysis of Activity Costs by Market Segments The third and most beneficial type of marketing cost analysis is a study of the costs and profitability of each segment of the market. This type of analysis divides the market by territories, products, customer groups, or order sizes. Cost analysis by market segment enables management to pinpoint trouble spots much more effectively than does an analysis of either ledger-account expenses or activity costs.

By combining a sales volume analysis with a marketing cost study, a researcher can prepare a complete operating statement for each of the product or market segments. These individual statements

TABLE 23-3 Profit and Loss Statement and Distribution of Natural Expenses to Activity Cost Groups, Great Western Company, 1997

Profit and loss statement (in $000)				**Expense distribution sheet (in $000)**				
				Activity (functional) cost groups				
				Personal selling	**Advertising**	**Warehousing and shipping**	**Order processing**	**Marketing administration**
Net sales		$36,000						
Cost of goods sold		23,400						
Gross margin		12,600						
Operating expenses:								
Salaries and commissions	$2,710		→	$1,200	$240	$420	$280	$570
Travel and entertainment	1,440		→	1,040				400
Media space	1,480		→		1,480			
Supplies	440		→	60	35	240	70	35
Property taxes	130		→	16	5	60	30	19
Freight out	3,500		→			3,500		
Total expenses		9,700						
Net profit		$2,900		$2,316	$1,760	$4,220	$380	$1,024

can then be analyzed to determine how they affect the total marketing program.

The procedure for a cost analysis by market segments is similar to that used to analyze activity expenses. The total of each activity cost (the right-hand part of Table 23-3) is allocated on some basis to each product or market segment being studied. Let's walk through an example of a cost analysis, by sales districts, for the Great Western Company, as shown in Tables 23-4 and 23-5.

First, for each of the five GW activities, we select an allocation basis for distributing the cost of that activity among the four districts. These bases are shown in the top part of Table 23-4. Then we determine the number of allocation "units" that make up each activity cost, and we find the cost per unit. This completes the allocation scheme, which tells us how to allocate costs to the four districts:

- Personal selling activity expenses pose no problem because they are direct expenses, chargeable to the district in which they are incurred.
- Advertising expenses are allocated on the basis of the number of pages of advertising run in each district. GW purchased the equivalent of 88 pages of advertising during the year, at an average cost of $20,000 per page ($1,760,000 ÷ 88).
- Warehousing and shipping expenses are allocated on the basis of the number of orders shipped. Since 10,550 orders were shipped during the year at a total activity cost of $4,220,000, the cost per order is $400.
- Order-processing expenses are allocated according to the number of invoice lines typed during the year. Since there were 126,667 lines, then the cost per line is $3.
- Marketing administration — a totally indirect expense — is divided equally among the four districts, with each district being allocated $256,000.

The final step is to calculate the amount of each activity cost to be allocated to each district. The results are shown in the bottom part of Table 23-4.

TABLE 23-4 Allocation of Activity Costs to Sales Districts, Great Western Company, 1997

Activity	Personal selling	Advertising	Warehousing and shipping	Order processing	Marketing administration
		Allocation basis			
Allocation basis	**Direct expense to each district**	**Number of pages of advertising**	**Number of orders shipped**	**Number of invoice lines**	**Equally among districts**
Total activity cost	$2,316,000	$1,760,000	$4,220,000	$380,000	$1,024,000
Number of allocation units		88 pages	10,550 orders	126,667 lines	4 districts
Cost per allocation unit		$20,000	$400	$3	$256,000
		Allocation of costs			
District A < units	—	27 pages	3,300 orders	46,000 lines	—
cost	$650,000	$540,000	$1,320,000	$138,000	$256,000
District B < units	—	19 pages	2,850 orders	33,000 lines	—
cost	$606,000	$380,000	$1,140,000	$99,000	$256,000
District C < units	—	22 pages	2,300 orders	26,667 lines	—
cost	$540,000	$440,000	$920,000	$80,000	$256,000
District D < units	—	20 pages	2,100 orders	21,000 lines	—
cost	$520,000	$400,000	$840,000	$63,000	$256,000

We see that $650,000 of personal selling expenses were charged directly to district A and $606,000 to district B, for example. Regarding advertising, the equivalent of 27 pages of advertising was run in district A, so that district is charged with $540,000 (27 pages × $20,000 per page). Similar calculations provide advertising activity cost allocations of $380,000 to district B; $440,000 to district C; and $400,000 to district D.

Regarding warehousing and shipping expenses, 3,300 orders were shipped to customers in district A, at a unit allocation cost of $400 per order, for a total allocated cost of $1,320,000. Warehousing and shipping charges are allocated to the other three districts as indicated in Table 23-4.

To allocate order-processing expenses, management determined that 46,000 invoice lines went to customers in district A. At $3 per line (the cost per allocation unit), district A is charged with $138,000. Each district is charged with $256,000 for marketing administration expenses.

After the activity costs have been allocated among the four districts, we can prepare a profit and loss statement for each district. These statements are shown in Table 23-5. Sales volume for each district is determined from the sales volume analysis (Table 23-2). Cost of goods sold and gross margin for each district are obtained by assuming that the company's gross margin of 35 percent ($12,600,000 ÷ $36,000,000) was maintained in each district.

Table 23-5 shows, for each district, what the firm's profit and loss statement shows for overall company operations. For example, we note that district A's net profit was 11.8 percent of sales ($1,471,000 ÷ $12,500,000). In sharp contrast, district D did rather poorly, earning a net profit of only 1.5 percent of net sales ($91,000 ÷ $6,200,000).

At this point in our performance evaluation, we have completed the "what happened" stage. The next stage is to determine why the results are as depicted in Table 23-5. As mentioned earlier, it is difficult to answer this question. In district D, for example, the sales force obtained only about two-thirds as many orders as in district A (2,100 versus 3,300). Was this because of poor selling, poor sales training, more severe competition in district D, or some other reason among a multitude of possibilities?

After a performance evaluation has determined why district results came out as they did, management can move to the third stage in its evaluation process. That final stage is, what should management do about the situation? This stage will be discussed briefly after we have reviewed major problem areas in marketing cost analysis.

TABLE 23-5 Profit and Loss Statements for Sales Districts (in $000), Great Western Company, 1997

	Total	District A	District B	District C	District D
Net sales	$36,000	$12,500	$9,600	$7,700	$6,200
Cost of goods sold	23,400	8,125	6,240	5,005	4,030
Gross margin	12,600	4,375	3,360	2,695	2,170
Operating expenses:					
Personal selling	2,316	650	606	540	520
Advertising	1,760	540	380	440	400
Warehousing and shipping	4,220	1,320	1,140	920	840
Order processing, billing	380	138	99	80	63
Marketing administration	1,024	256	256	56	256
Total expenses	9,700	2,904	2,481	2,236	2,079
Net profit (in dollars)	$ 2,900	$ 1,471	$ 879	$ 459	$ 91
Net profit (as percentage of sales)	8.1%	11.8%	9.2%	6.0%	1.5%

Problems in Cost Analysis

Marketing cost analysis can be expensive in time, money, and labour. In particular, the task of allocating costs is often quite difficult.

Allocating Costs The problem of allocating costs becomes evident when activity cost totals must be apportioned among individual territories, products, or other marketing units. Operating costs can be divided into direct and indirect expenses. **Direct costs**, also called separable expenses, are incurred totally in connection with one market segment or one unit of the sales organization. Thus salary and travel expenses of the sales representative in district A are direct expenses for that territory. The cost of newspaper space to advertise product C is a direct cost of marketing that product. Allocating direct expenses is easy. They can be charged entirely to the marketing unit that incurred them.

The allocation difficulty arises in connection with **indirect costs**, also called common costs. These expenses are incurred jointly for more than one marketing unit. Therefore, they cannot be charged totally to one market segment.

Within the category of indirect expenses, some costs are partially indirect and some are totally indirect. Order filling and shipping, for example, are partially indirect costs. They would decrease if some territories or products were eliminated. They would increase if new products or territories were added. On the other hand, marketing administrative expenses are totally indirect. The cost of the chief marketing executive's staff and office would remain about the same, whether or not the number of territories or product lines was changed.

Any method selected for allocating indirect expenses has obvious weaknesses that can distort the results and mislead management. Two commonly used allocation methods are to divide these costs (1) equally among the marketing units being studied (territories, for instance) or (2) in proportion to the sales volume in each marketing unit. But each method gives a different result for the total costs for each marketing unit.

Full-Cost versus Contribution-Margin Approach In a marketing cost analysis, two means of allocating indirect expenses are (1) the contribution-margin (also called contribution-to-overhead) method and (2) the full-cost method. A controversy exists regarding which of these two approaches is better for managerial control purposes.

In the **contribution-margin approach**, only direct expenses are allocated to each marketing unit being analyzed. These costs presumably would be eliminated if that marketing unit were eliminated. When direct expenses are deducted from the gross margin of the marketing unit, the remainder is the amount which that unit is contributing to cover total indirect expenses (or overhead).

All expenses — direct and indirect — are allocated among the marketing units under study in the **full-cost approach**. By allocating all costs, management can determine the net profit of each territory, product, or other marketing unit.

For any given marketing unit, these two methods can be summarized as follows:

Contribution margin	Full cost
Sales $	Sales $
less	*less*
Cost of goods sold	Cost of goods sold
equals	*equals*
Gross margin	Gross margin
less	*less*
Direct expenses	Direct expenses
equals	*less*
Contribution margin (the amount available to cover overhead expenses plus a profit)	Indirect expenses
	equals
	Net profit

Proponents of the full-cost approach contend that a marketing cost study is intended to determine the net profitability of the units being studied. They feel that the contribution-margin method does not fulfil this purpose and may be misleading. A given territory or product may be showing a contribution to overhead. Yet, after indirect costs are allocated, this product or territory may actually have a net loss. In effect, say the full-cost proponents, the contribution-margin approach is the iceberg principle in action. That is, the visible tip (the contribution margin) looks good, while the submerged part may be hiding a net loss.

Contribution-margin supporters contend that it is not possible to accurately allocate indirect costs among product or market segments. Furthermore, items such as administrative costs are not all related to any one territory or product. Therefore, the marketing units should not bear any of these costs. Advocates of the contribution-margin approach also say that a full-cost analysis may show that a product or territory has a net loss, but this unit may be contributing something to overhead. Some executives might recommend that the losing product or territory be eliminated. But they are overlooking the fact that the unit's contribution to overhead would then have to be borne by other units. With the contribution-margin approach, there would be no question about keeping this unit as long as there is no better alternative.

USE OF FINDINGS FROM VOLUME AND COST ANALYSES

So far we have been dealing with the first two stages of marketing performance evaluation — finding out what happened and why it happened. Now we're ready to see some examples of how management might use the results from a combined sales volume analysis and marketing cost analysis.

Territories

Knowing the net profit (or contribution to overhead) of territories in relation to their potential gives management several possibilities for action. It may decide to adjust (expand or contract) territories to bring them into line with current sales potential. Or territorial problems may stem from weaknesses in the distribution system, and changes in channels of distribution may be needed. Firms that use manufacturers' agents may find it advisable to establish their own sales forces in growing markets. Intense competition may be the cause of unprofitable volume in some districts, and changes in the promotional program may be necessary.

Of course, a losing territory might be abandoned completely. An abandoned region may have been contributing something to overhead, however, even though a net loss was shown. Management must recognize that this contribution must now be carried by the remaining territories.

Products

When the profitability of each product or group of products is known, unprofitable models, sizes, or colours can be eliminated. Sales people's compensation plans may be altered to encourage the sale of high-margin items. Channels of distribution may be changed. Instead of selling all of its products directly to business users, for instance, a machine tools manufacturer shifted to industrial distributors for standard products of low unit value. The company thereby improved the profitability of these products.

Management may decide to discontinue carrying a losing product. But it should not do so without first considering the effect this decision will have on other items sold by the company. Often a low-volume or unprofitable product must be carried simply to round out the product assortment. Supermarkets, for example, carry salt and sugar, even though these are profitless for a store. Customers expect a supermarket to carry those items. If they are not available at one store, that seller will lose business, because shoppers will go to other stores that do carry a full complement of grocery products.

Customer Classes and Order Sizes

By combining a sales volume analysis with a cost study, executives can determine the profitability of each group of customers. If one market segment generates an unsatisfactory net profit, then changes may be required in the pricing structure when selling to these customers. Or perhaps customers that have been sold directly by a producer's sales force should be turned over to wholesaling intermediaries. A manufacturer of air conditioners made just such a move when it found that direct sales to individual building contractors were not profitable.

A difficulty plaguing many firms today is the **small-order problem**. Many orders are below the break-even point. Revenue from each of these orders is actually less than allocated expenses. This problem occurs because several costs, such as billing or direct selling, are essentially the same whether the order amounts to $10 or $10,000. Management's immediate reaction may be that no order below the break-even point should be accepted. Or small-volume accounts should be dropped from the customer list. Such decisions may be harmful, however. Some of those small-order customers may, over time, grow into large, profitable accounts. Management should first determine why certain accounts are small-order problems and then figure out how to correct the situation. Proper handling can often turn a losing account into a satisfactory one. For example, a small-order handling charge, which customers would willingly pay, might change the profit picture entirely.

MARKETING AT WORK FILE 23-2

AUDIT, DOWNSIZE, RESTRUCTURE — AND THAT INCLUDES SALES!

Until recently, restructuring a sales department was considered taboo. Companies would rather redesign their factories — and reap the usually large and measurable cost savings — than tamper with their sales force. After all, selling was considered an art, and you couldn't analyze and then manipulate the efficiency of a sales person's art like you could that of machines. And besides, many firms argued, sellers were the ones who produce the revenue.

The problem with these views was that they fostered sales departments that were inefficient and technologically backward. Rick McCutcheon, a sales productivity consultant in Toronto, believes that Canadian sales departments are insufficiently automated because many sales managers have no computer experience and thus resist any efforts to computerize their operations. In such cases, it is no wonder that companies haven't a clue as to what exactly their sales force is up to all day. If they did, however, many would be shocked to discover that only 23.7 percent of sales people's time was spent actually selling to customers. As well, every time an industrial sales person walks through a customer's door, whether he gets a sale or not, he costs the company $227. And that's just averaging the direct selling costs — salary, car allowance, travel, and entertainment expenses. Then there are all the indirect expenses, too, from secretaries and managers to laptop computers and office space, all of which often adds up to triple what most companies spend on advertising and promotion combined.

Faced with such statistics, some Canadian companies have restructured their sales departments or are in the process. They are evaluating how sellers spend their time and they are ranking clients according to how much time they feel each needs, wants, or deserves. Then they cross-reference the two, trying to discover ways of offering the same service at reduced cost. Often, the answer is technology, which liberates sales people to spend more time actually selling. Another is to off-load tasks such as customer prospecting or after-sales service onto less expensive providers. This frequently results in a complete reorganization, applying a factory floor's productive discipline to the entire sales department. In this manner, according to Toronto-based consultant Dan Richards, "sales become much more a science and much less an art."

A major subscriber to this view is Kodak Canada. Surveys revealed that the firm's seventy-person sales force was spending only 50 percent of their time actually selling. The other 50 percent went to travel and administrative tasks. Call coverage — the number of personal calls per customer — was poor. And so was communication; although sales reps had laptop computers, they had no business-forms software and no way to file

www.kodak.com

electronic reports from the field, which resulted in thousands of pieces of paper being shifted from person to person, and from office to office. And how could sellers sell when they had to worry about rotating stock in retail outlets, verifying point-of-sale advertising, and replacing damaged or outdated products from sample kits in their cars?

Kodak introduced its "strategic sales plan." Sales reps now had their laptops loaded with sophisticated software, allowing them to file reports electronically from the field to company-wide data-bank networks where managers could cross-reference and analyze them.

There was also a new emphasis on telemarketing. With businesses in general discovering that the average telephone telemarketing contact call cost one-tenth that of a field sales call, and that the average telemarketer could contact as many clients in a day as a field sales rep could in a week — usually at half the cost — it is becoming *de rigueur* to hire telemarketers to handle time-consuming administrative tasks. Although at Kodak, telemarketing was formerly reserved exclusively for accounts that were either too small or remote for a sales rep to bother with, Kodak now encourages customers to take to their phones in order to acquire better ongoing services ranging from quicker inventory replenishment to more frequent updates on special offers. In order to keep the experience personal, Kodak sends clients pictures of its telesales reps accompanied by sales department flow charts. And in keeping with the changing nature of telemarketing itself, Kodak ceased hiring poorly educated part-timers who were simply punching out calls for minimum wage. Instead, the company recruited more experienced people whom they looked upon as *de facto* account managers, capable of screening calls, organizing information, and quickly linking field reps with any orders, requests, and complaints made by clients in their absence.

Furthermore, an independent merchandiser was hired to free sales people from having to visit retail outlets, rotate stock, check point-of-sale advertising, and take care of other merchandising distractions. With all these implementations — coupled with some slimming and trimming of the sales force itself — Kodak's sales department could finally devote itself unconditionally to the art of selling.

Ken Shaddock, manager of sales administration, says, "We are clearly reducing costs and saving people time. Call coverage has improved from terrible to excellent, with negligible complaints from customers." And sales people no longer have to push thousands of sheets of paper around the company. "We're down to hundreds," he laughed.

Source: Mark Stevenson, "The Lean, Mean Sales Machine," *Canadian Business*, January 1994, pp. 32–36. Reprinted by permission of Canadian Business Magazine © 1997.

Summary

The management process in marketing is the planning, implementation, and evaluation of the marketing effort in an organization. Implementation is the stage in which an organization attempts to carry out its strategic planning. Strategic planning is virtually useless if it is not implemented effectively.

Implementation includes three activities — organizing, staffing, and operating. In organizing, the company first should co-ordinate all marketing activities into one department whose top executive reports directly to the president. Then, within the marketing department, the company may utilize some form of organizational specialization based on geographic territories, products, or customer types.

The evaluation stage in the management process involves measuring performance results against predetermined goals. Evaluation enables management to determine the effectiveness of its implementation and to plan corrective action where necessary. A marketing audit is a key element in a total marketing evaluation program. Most companies are victims of at least some misdirected marketing effort. That is, the 80–20 and iceberg principles are at work in most firms because marketing costs are expended in relation to the number of marketing units (territories, products, customers), rather than to their profit potential. Too many companies do not know how much they should be spending for marketing activities, or what results they should get from these expenditures.

Two tools for identifying misdirected marketing efforts are a sales volume analysis and a marketing cost analysis. One problem in marketing cost analysis is allocating costs — especially indirect costs — to the marketing units. Given detailed analyses, management can study sales volume and marketing costs by product lines and market segments (sales territories, customer groups). The findings from these analyses can be helpful in shaping decisions regarding a company's marketing program.

Key Terms and Concepts

Planning (562)
Implementation (562)
Evaluation (562)
Organizational structures for implementing strategic planning:
- Geographic specialization (568)
- Product specialization (568)
- Customer specialization (570)
- Major-accounts organization (570)

Marketing audit (571)
Misdirected marketing effort (571)
80–20 principle (572)
Iceberg principle (572)
Sales volume analysis (572)
Market-share analysis (574)
Marketing cost analysis (574)
Direct costs (579)
Indirect costs (579)
Contribution-margin approach (579)
Full-cost approach (579)
Small-order problem (581)

Questions and Problems

1. "Good implementation in an organization can overcome poor planning, but good planning cannot overcome poor implementation." Explain, using examples.
2. Give some examples of companies that are likely to organize their sales force by product groups.
3. A manufacturer of small aircraft (Cessna, for example) designed for executive transportation has decided to implement the concept of a selling centre. Who should be on this company's selling teams? What problems might this manufacturer encounter when it uses team selling?
4. Give examples of how advertising and personal selling activities might be co-ordinated in a company's marketing department.
5. As a sales manager, how would you motivate these two sales reps?
   - **a.** An older salesman, who is satisfied with his present level of earnings. He intends to continue as a sales rep, with no promotion, until his retirement in five years.
   - **b.** An excellent sales rep whose morale is shot because she did not receive an expected promotion. She has been with the company for three years.
6. A sales volume analysis by territories indicates that the sales of a manufacturer of roofing materials have increased 12 percent a year for the past three years in the territory comprising Manitoba, Saskatchewan, and Alberta. Does this indicate conclusively that the company's sales volume performance is satisfactory in that territory?
7. A manufacturer found that one product accounted for 35 to 45 percent of the company's total sales in all but two of 10 territories across the country. In each of those two territories, this product accounted for only 14 percent of the company's volume. What factors might account for the relatively low sales of this article in the two districts?
8. What effects may a sales volume analysis by product have on training, supervising, and compensating the sales force?
9. "Firms should discontinue selling losing products." Discuss.
10. Should a company stop selling to an unprofitable customer? Why or why not? If not, then what steps might the company take to make the account a profitable one?

Hands-On Marketing

1. Interview a sales executive (a) in a manufacturing company and (b) in either a securities brokerage or a real estate brokerage firm to find out how they motivate their sales forces. As part of your report, give your evaluation of each motivational program.
2. Interview a marketing executive to find out how the total marketing performance is evaluated in his or her company. As part of your report, include your appraisal of this company's evaluation program.

CHAPTER 24 GOALS

Our discussion touched on the societal dimensions of marketing when we briefly examined marketing's role in the total economy in Chapter 1 and described the environment in Chapter 2. For the most part, however, we have approached marketing from the viewpoint of the firm, as we addressed the challenges facing an individual producer or intermediary in managing its marketing activity.

In this final chapter, we return to a broader perspective by identifying the major criticisms of marketing and responses to these criticisms. Then we conclude our discussion of marketing by looking into the crystal ball and considering some prospects for the future that are certain to provide the inspiration for responses such as those illustrated on the opening page of this chapter.

After studying this chapter, you should have an understanding of:

- A societal perspective for evaluating marketing performance.
- The major criticisms of marketing.
- Consumer, government, and business responses to consumer discontent.
- Consumerism and its effect on marketing.
- The ethical responsibilities of marketers.
- Trends influencing future marketing activity.
- Some strategic adjustments necessary to cope with change.

Chapter Twenty-Four

Marketing: Its Performance and Its Future

CHANGING WITH THE TIMES

All organizations, large and small, businesses and not-for-profits, manufacturers and retailers, must continue to change if they are to keep up to date with the changes that are going on around them, and if they are to remain relevant and attractive to the customers and clients they serve. An excellent example of a changing marketplace and the demands it is placing on companies that operate therein is the North American automobile industry.

Until recently, the auto industry was completely dominated by the "Big Three" — General Motors, Ford, and Chrysler. But, over the past ten years or more, the industry has had to face change like it had never seen in the past. The most obvious of these changes involves increasing competition from foreign automakers, most notably the Japanese, led by Honda, Toyota, Nissan, and Mazda. But, while the most obvious, the competition from imports was not necessarily the most important. Other, more subtle, changes were bringing about demands that required the Big Three to change completely the ways they do business.

The implications for product design, distribution, and customer service have been dramatic.

www.gmcanada.ca
www.ford.ca

Instead of making cars and then trying to sell them to a mass market, automobile manufacturers have discovered niche marketing and have begun to design vehicles that appeal to a specific segment of the market. While demographics is not the most sophisticated approach to segmentation, all three of the big automakers have begun to target college students with their presence on the Web and with on-campus promotions. While its Lincoln brand has been targeted to an upscale retired segment, Ford has launched the luxury sport/utility Navigator to appeal to well-off, over-forty-five baby boomers, with its attractive design and a direct-mail and video campaign. General Motors has done much the same with the launch of its Cadillac Catera line and has begun to reposition its older Buick and Oldsmobile brands in an attempt to make them more appealing to a younger audience. Ford has even taken the dramatic step of discontinuing its Thunderbird

Distribution has also been affected by changing consumer demands. In the United States, a consolidation of auto dealerships is under way. In a North American market that is widely considered to be "overdealered," we will see a move to restructure the distribution of cars and other vehicles. Already in the United States, fuelled by the attitude that consumers are tired of haggling over price in cramped, macho, high-pressure showrooms, massive dealers and auto malls are being established, housing several dealers who carry the vehicles of a number of manufacturers. These "superstores" also break from tradition in that they feature salaried sales people, no-haggle pricing, computer kiosks, and free coffee! Other new forms of auto retailing include car brokers who will work for a customer and find the car he or she wants at the lowest available price and in a way that avoids haggling. Chrysler has followed the lead of Saturn in launching its "Camp Jeep," an annual gathering of thousands of Jeep owners who assemble each year in Colorado for a week of mountain driving and fishing. Other auto retailers are springing up on the Internet, allowing customers to buy a car without ever talking to a conventional dealer.

Possibly one of the greatest changes in the automobile industry, however, is the way in which it is beginning to interact with women. Throughout its history, the industry has tended to be male-dominated, and it has been soundly criticized for the way in which women have generally been treated in dealer showrooms — many old-school sales people (i.e., salesmen) have been accused of either ignoring the female side of the family decision-making team, or of at least assuming that she was principally interested in the colour of the car and the seat fabrics. All of this is changing as automobile companies wake up to the fact that women now account for 50 percent of all vehicle purchases and influence another 25 percent.

Today the presidents and CEOs of both General Motors Canada and Ford Canada are women. Many product improvements have been made in response to changes requested by women in research conducted by the automakers. We are even seeing an increase in the number of women filling sales positions in dealerships — a role normally reserved for men. Notes Bobbie Gaunt, president and CEO at Ford, "If you plan to continue to grow the business, you really have to understand the segments that are driving growth — and that means women."

Gaunt is also credited with bringing a more strategic approach to marketing within the Canadian industry, particularly concerning issues like brand management and customer retention. She understands the importance, in an industry where the market share of North American automakers has been declining and where a share point is worth millions of dollars, of keeping the customers you already have. She makes the following observation: "If you are able to build that loyal base, it frees up some time to figure out those people who are coming out to your dealership and not buying. It frees up the company's time to figure out why those people are not buying your product, and what to do about it."[1]

What this example illustrates is that, even for the largest businesses and organizations, change and challenge are integral components of marketing. We see how companies are responding (or are being required to respond) to changes in the marketplace around them: to concern for the environment and for the prevention of illness, to consumer demands for safer, more healthy products, to competitive actions that seem to appeal to consumers, and to changes in consumers' values, including changing gender-role differences and changing expectations with respect to service.

www.chryslercorp.com • www.saturn.com

EVALUATING MARKETING

Before we can begin to appraise marketing, we have to agree on a **basis for evaluating performance** — what the objective of marketing should be. In our discussion of the marketing concept, we said that an organization's objective is to determine consumers' wants and satisfy them. Thus, from the point of view of the individual organization, if the firm's target market is satisfied and the organization's objectives are being met, then the marketing effort can be judged successful.

However, this standard makes no distinction between organizations whose behaviour is detrimental to society and those whose activities are socially acceptable. Firms that pollute the environment or stimulate demand for harmful products or services would qualify as good marketers right along with firms that behave responsibly. Therefore, we must take a broader, societal view that incorporates the best interests of others as well as the desires of a particular target market and the objectives of the marketer to satisfy that market. Marketing must balance the needs and wants of consumers, the objectives of the organization, and the welfare of society.

There is evidence all around us of the interrelationship of these three criteria. If a product does not meet the needs of consumers or if a firm is unable to provide the level of service customers want, the consumer will not buy that product or service. The business world is littered with companies that have gone out of business because they were unable to satisfy their customers. Likewise, if a firm behaves in a fashion that is viewed by consumers or the public to be detrimental to society, government will likely intervene, as it does in regulating the advertising of alcohol, tobacco, and other products judged to be potentially damaging to the health and safety of consumers. Finally, companies regularly change their advertising and promotional campaigns as their organizational objectives change.

CRITICISMS OF MARKETING

Criticisms of marketing focus on actions (or inaction) that relate to the balance between organizational objectives and the wants of customers and/or the well-being of society. These issues can be categorized as follows:

- *Exploitation.* Marketers are sometimes accused of taking unfair advantage of a consumer or of a situation. Examples of exploitation are price gouging during a shortage and misleading consumers with false or incomplete information. These behaviours may meet the organization's goal of sales and profits, but they are detrimental to consumers, society, or both, and are clearly in conflict with marketing's goal of long-term customer satisfaction.
- *Inefficiency.* Some critics feel that marketing uses more resources than necessary. Accusations include ineffective promotional activity, unnecessary distribution functions, and excessive numbers of brands in many product categories. Inefficiency results in higher costs to organizations, higher prices to consumers, and a waste of society's resources.
- *Stimulating unwholesome demand.* A number of marketers have been accused of encouraging consumers or businesses to purchase products that are harmful in some way to the individual or the organization. For example, debate has raged throughout the Western world for the past twenty years or more concerning the marketing of cigarettes. The issue tends to revolve around the fact that tobacco is a legal product; although there are regulations in most provinces and cities that prohibit the sale of tobacco products to teens and children, nevertheless, tobacco manufacturers have a legal right to sell their products and retailers have a right (although regulated) to sell those products to adults. Though the marketing of such products may meet the needs of some consumers and satisfy the objectives of organizations that produce and sell them, the marketing of tobacco products is controversial because society generally agrees that the product is detrimental to the health of Canadians.
- *Illegal behaviour.* Laws are passed to protect individuals, organizations, and society in general. Marketers are expected to abide by these laws, even when violating a law may benefit consumers or an organization. Price collusion, for instance, is likely to meet the needs of the organizations involved and might even result in lower prices for consumers than price competition. However, it is detrimental to competitors of the colluding firms. Therefore, since the behaviour is unfair to others in society, it is unacceptable.

- *Poor service.* Some of the most vocal criticisms of marketing in recent years have been reserved for the way service is delivered to customers when they come into contact with marketing organizations, particularly at the retail level. There is no doubt that some companies and organizations have made great strides and have developed well-deserved reputations for providing superior service. But, in many ways, this progress has made life difficult for those organizations who have not taken customer service seriously. Customer expectations with regard to how they want to be treated have increased, and many companies and other organizations have simply not stepped up to the challenge. The result is considerable consumer dissatisfaction with service.

Specific Criticisms

Another way of looking at the **nature of marketing criticisms** is through the components of the marketing mix — product, price, distribution, and marketing communications. Some specific examples are described below, but keep in mind that these are allegations. Some are unsubstantiated by facts; others apply only to specific situations.

Product Criticisms of products generally concentrate on how well they meet buyers' expectations. Critics charge that too many products are of poor quality or are unsafe. Examples cited include products that fail or break under normal use; food products that contain chemical preservatives, flavour enhancers, and colouring; commuter trains that run late; wash-and-wear clothing that needs ironing; products backed by confusing, inadequate warranties; and repair service that is unsatisfactory. Other examples include packages that appear to contain more of a product than they actually do; labels that provide insufficient or misleading information; and products advertised as "new & improved" that appear to offer only trivial improvements. Critics also argue that style obsolescence, particularly in clothing, encourages consumers to discard products before they are worn out, and that there is an unnecessary proliferation of brands in many food and household-product categories, such as breakfast cereal, detergent, and pet food. As a result, buyers are confused and production capacity is wasted.

Price It is probably the case that most consumers would like to pay less for the products and services that they buy, but most buyers are generally satisfied with what they consider a fair exchange, particularly when they feel that they have received good value. In fact, there are certainly situations when consumers would be perfectly willing to pay a *higher* price, if they would receive higher product and service quality as a result. Complaints about prices usually arise from the perception that the seller is making an excessive profit, or that the buyer has been misled about prices or the terms of sale, or simply because the consumer feels the product or service is simply not worth the price. We sometimes hear people say that prices are too high because they are controlled by large firms in an industry. Sellers are sometimes accused of building in hidden charges or advertising false markdowns. Critics feel that price competition has been largely replaced by non-price competition in the form of unnecessary product features that add more to the cost than to the value of a product. Finally, judging the acceptability of price is especially difficult in situations where the consumer is buying a service. Because of the intangibility of service, what one receives is often a matter of judgment. It is, therefore, particularly difficult in service industries for consumers to judge the value of what they receive.

Distribution Of the marketing-mix variables, the least understood and appreciated by consumers is distribution. This is probably because distribution channels can take so many forms. In addition, a consumer comes in direct contact with only one level of the distribution channel — retailers — so it is difficult to appreciate the functions performed at other levels. Criticisms related to channels reflect this lack of familiarity. For example, channels are sometimes seen as having too many levels of intermediaries, and channel members are accused of performing needless functions. These criticisms overlook the pressure that competition exerts on channels to be efficient. On the other hand, some criticisms are valid. For example, when a manufacturer pressures channel members to carry its less attractive products in order to get its more attractive ones, the channel members have higher capital and inventory costs, which are passed along to customers.

Marketing Communications The most frequent and vocal accusations against marketing tend to focus on marketing communications — especially personal selling and advertising. Most of the complaints about personal selling are aimed at the retail level and the allegedly poor quality of retail selling and service.

Criticisms of advertising fall into two categories — social and economic. From a social viewpoint, advertising is sometimes charged with overemphasizing material standards of living and underemphasizing cultural and moral values. Advertising is accused of manipulating impressionable people, especially children; making statements that are false, deceptive, or in bad taste; making exaggerated claims for products; and overusing fear and sexual appeals. Critics also argue there is simply too much advertising and that ad placement is often offensive. For example, some people resent promotional messages and advertisements on rental videos or in movie theatres.

The economic criticisms centre on the effect of advertising on prices and competition. The price argument goes like this. Advertising, particularly persuasive as opposed to informative ads, merely shifts demand from one brand to another. As a result, it only adds to the individual firms' marketing costs without increasing aggregate demand. Since the advertising must be paid for, the price of the product goes up. (There is a counterargument that advertising results in lower prices because it is an efficient method of reaching many people at a low cost per person. The mass market generated by the advertising results in economies of scale in purchasing, manufacturing, and distribution. These economies result in lower costs that more than offset the advertising expense, and the firm is able to charge lower prices than would be possible without the ads.)

The economic criticism of advertising is made from the perspective of competitive impact. It suggests that large firms can afford to differentiate their products through advertising. That is, through extensive advertising, they create the impression in consumers' minds that their brands are better than the brands of less-well-known rivals. In this way they create barriers to market entry for new or smaller firms. The result is an industry with a small number of firms, which leads to higher prices and higher profits. (The counterargument to this position is that advertising informs consumers about a product. If consumers find the information persuasive, they will try the product and return for more if they are satisfied. If they are not satisfied, no amount of advertising will bring them back. The fact that larger firms advertise more than smaller firms simply indicates that their products are valued by consumers.)

Right or wrong, marketers must take all allegations seriously because they reflect the perceptions of many people. We'll see next how marketers and society can deal with the allegations and the perceptions.

Understanding the Criticisms

To evaluate the charges against marketing, we must understand what actually is being criticized. Is the object of the complaint ultimately the economic system? An entire industry? A particular firm? If the criticism applies to a firm, is the marketing department or some other department the culprit?

The free-enterprise system encourages competition, and government regulatory bodies for many years have judged competition by the number of competitors in an industry. Thus when we complain about the number of toothpaste or cereal brands on the market, we are really criticizing the system. Within a particular firm, a faulty product may result from production mistakes, not from marketing problems. Clearly, a failure in manufacturing does not make consumers' complaints less valid. The point is that marketing is not to blame for every business mistake.

This possible confusion raises a very important question that has been implicit in several sections of this book — What exactly is "marketing"? Or, more correctly, what are the boundaries around the "marketing" function in an organization? We observed in Chapter 1 that the single most important objective of marketing is customer satisfaction. But a customer may become dissatisfied with a company for a variety of reasons, many of which have nothing to do directly with what would historically be considered the responsibility of the marketing function within a company.

If a customer is angry because of an error on his or her monthly statement, that has the same effect as if he or she had received poor service at the point of sale. But the error may have originated in the accounting department. Similarly, product failure may stem from problems in the production department. Some customer service problems, it may be argued, are not marketing problems *per se*, but rather result from the fact that the human resources department has not done a good job of staff selection or training.

Confused? The point we are making is that the responsibilities of marketing are difficult to define. If the marketing department in an organization actually "owns the customer," that is, has responsibility for customer satisfaction, then it is essential that it work closely with other departments within the organization. Also, this points out the need for other components of the firm to be "marketing oriented"; that is, they must have an appreciation for the fact that their functions have as much potential to influence long-term customer satisfaction and dissatisfaction as do those things that are traditionally considered be the responsibility of marketing.

We also need to consider the sources of criticism directed at marketing. Some critics are well intentioned and well informed. They point out real weaknesses or errors needing correction, such as deceptive packaging, misleading advertising, and irresponsible pricing. But some critics are simply ill informed. They do not understand the functions associated with distribution or are not aware of the costs of producing and selling a product. As a result, though their criticisms may have popular appeal, they cannot withstand careful scrutiny. There are other critics whose views do not reflect the sentiments of society. Nevertheless, they vociferously criticize behaviour they find objectional to serve their own interests. Some of the protests against the use of advertising in political campaigns is an example. We must examine criticism carefully to separate the legitimate from the erroneous and self-serving.

Operating in a socially undesirable manner is unacceptable. Fortunately, this kind of behaviour is only a small part of all the marketing that occurs, although it is widely publicized. More common, and more disturbing, are the situations that are not clear-cut. These are debatable issues such as full disclosure in advertising (What is the meaning of "full"?); planned obsolescence (How long should a product last?); and the cost of marketing (How much should it cost to develop, distribute, and promote a product?).

RESPONSES TO MARKETING ISSUES

Efforts to address the issues that arise from marketing activity have come from consumers, the government, and business organizations. In the following paragraphs we discuss some of these **responses to marketing issues**.

Consumer Responses

One response to marketing misdeeds, both actual and alleged, has come from consumer activists. The term **consumerism** was popularized thirty years ago when, in response to increasing consumer protests against a variety of business practices, Canada became the first country in the world to establish a government department at the federal level to be responsible for the rights of consumers. There had been earlier "consumer movements" in this country — in the early 1900s and again during the Great Depression of the 1930s. In these, the emphasis had been on protecting consumers from harmful products and from false and misleading advertising.

The movement that began in the 1960s, however, was different in three ways from earlier consumer movements. First, the most recent wave of consumerism occurred in a setting where consumer incomes are higher and the consumer's subsistence needs are largely met, in contrast to the harsher economic conditions that surrounded earlier movements. Second, the consumer-protection legislation enacted in Canada since the 1960s has been intended first and foremost to protect the consumer's interests. Emphasis in earlier legislation was placed on the protection of competition and competitors.

Third, the consumerism of the last half of the twentieth century is much more likely to endure, because it has become institutionalized and has led to

MARKETING AT WORK FILE 24-1

MARKETING THROUGH DOING GOOD WORKS

Social-cause marketing has become quite popular in recent years as more and more companies are identifying with various social and environmental organizations, with a view to gaining consumer support as a result. Companies that have taken this approach to marketing often forgo advertising in favour of gaining much lower-cost publicity from the media concerning how they conduct their business.

Good examples of firms that have adopted a social-cause stance are the Body Shop and Ben & Jerry's Ice Cream. The Body Shop is considered something of a pioneer in the field, having taken the same approach to business from its beginnings — supporting environmental and animal-rights groups, featuring social causes in its point-of-purchase materials and promotional items such as T-shirts, sourcing its raw materials in underdeveloped countries, and offering only "natural" products in reusable containers.

But some social-cause marketers have come in for media scrutiny in recent years, and criticism has been levelled at them for not being quite as "good" as they appear. Ben & Jerry's has been accused of causing arteriosclerosis in farm pigs, through their program of giving waste ice cream to local farmers to include in pig feed. The Body Shop has been criticized for not living up to its promises in that its products are not all-natural, and the real value of some its policies with regard to developing countries has been questioned.

Taking an ethical or social-cause approach to marketing is a tricky business. Although such an approach is commendable, it puts the firm in the public eye, where its every move is scrutinized. Also, who is to say what is or is not ethical? Some will argue that companies that take such an approach should not be criticized for at least trying to do the right thing. There is also the issue of whether social-cause marketing is good for business, and whether companies that take such an approach will outperform those that take a more conventional approach. What is clear is that a social-cause approach will only work for a company if a sufficient number of customers are willing to make purchase decisions based on their social preferences. What is also certain is that companies that take such an approach must ensure that they have a good product and prices that communicate good value if they are to get to first base with consumers.

Source: Based on Thomas W. Dunfee, "Marketing an Ethical Stance," *Financial Post*, November 2/4, 1996, pp. MM16–18; reprinted in *Financial Times Mastering Management* (London: Pitman Publishing, 1997), pp. 368–369. Reprinted with permission.

the creation of a structure to support it. Government agencies have been established to administer the consumer-oriented laws and to protect consumer interests. The social sensitivity of many businesses has increased, and various consumer- and environment-oriented organizations have developed.

However, through the 1990s, as governments have been hard-pressed to meet the increasing demands being placed on public finances, and as the economy grew and many companies and consumers prospered, consumer protection programs in some provinces and at the federal level fell victim to budget cuts. At the federal level, the Department of Consumer and Corporate Affairs was disbanded in 1993, as its function was assumed within Industry Canada. These developments were not only a result of government budget cuts, but also reflected the fact that consumers are now being protected in other ways, as many businesses and industry associations have adopted voluntary codes of behaviour to self-regulate their dealings with consumers and as legislation had been put in place at the federal and provincial level that affords a level of consumer protection that was not present before the 1970s.

Meaning and Scope of Consumerism

Consumerism includes three broad areas of dissatisfaction and remedial effort:

- *Discontent with direct buyer–seller exchange relationships between consumers and businesses.* This is the original and still the main focus of consumer complaints. Efforts to ban MSG, a flavour enhancer and preservative that can cause a severe allergic reaction in some people, would be an example.
- *Discontent with nonbusiness, not-for-profit organizations and governmental agencies.* Consumerism extends to all exchange relationships. The performance of such diverse organizations as schools (quality of education, performance of students on standardized tests, number of class days per year), hospitals (medical care costs, smoking in rooms, malpractice), and public utilities (rate increases, cutting service to people unable to pay their bills) has been scrutinized and subjected to organized and spirited consumer protests.
- *Discontent of those indirectly affected by the behaviour of others.* An exchange between two parties can sometimes have a negative impact on a third party. For example, farmers buy insecticides and pesticides from chemical companies. However, these products may pollute water supplies, rivers, and the air. Thus an exchange has created a problem for a third party or group. The effects of second-hand smoke is another example.

Consumer Actions Consumer reactions to marketing problems have ranged from complaints registered with offending organizations to boycotts (refusing to buy a particular product or shop at a certain store). Consumer groups over the past thirty years have recognized their potential power and became more active politically than ever. Some organized mass letter-writing campaigns to editors, politicians, and business executives. They supported consumer-oriented political candidates, conducted petition drives, and gained media attention through sit-ins and picketing.

More recently, many organized groups at both the local and national levels have become involved in a more broadly defined consumer movement. Some of these groups represent a variety of interests, dealing with the direct interaction of consumers with businesses as well as with broader issues such as environmentalism and animal rights. Others represent particular interest groups, including retired and elderly consumers, the urban poor, and victims of crime and fraud by businesses.

Consumerism in the Future Cultural conditions seem to have moved us away from brief periods of heightened consumerism to a more constant level of concern and individual activity. Consumers today are generally more sensitive to social and environmental issues, compared with the activities of businesses that affect them as consumers of specific products and sevices. Along with sources of dissatisfaction already described, the plight of the poor, air and water pollution, waste disposal, treatment of animals, and health and safety are other social and environmental causes that are receiving attention from organized consumer and social-action groups.

At the individual level, more people are willing and able to take an active role in their own activities as consumers. Compared with those of earlier generations, people are better educated, more articulate, and more inclined to speak out. People of all ages are generally less intimidated by large organizations and less willing to accept the status quo. Responding to this increased consumer sensitivity, many companies and other organizations have responded with their own programs to deal with consumer complaints — all in the interest of achieving the ultimate goal of marketing — customer satisfaction.

As we move into the next century, Canadian consumers are certainly better protected than they were thirty or more years ago. They are also more confident of their own rights and much more willing to speak out on their own behalf. Legislation and self-regulatory programs have made the Canadian marketplace one of the most "consumer-friendly" in the world. One important result of this change has been the sensitizing of the consumer to his or her rights to address consumer concerns. Most business have responded and now take consumer issues and complaints very seriously.

Some problems do remain, however, and it would be wrong to suggest that all is well with respect to consumer protection in Canada. There are still some firms that take advantage of consumers and that employ tactics that are unethical or even harmful. The new form of consumerism in the future will likely still focus on some of the same areas as in the past. For example, fair treatment for disadvantaged consumers and personal safety will be major concerns. But, in addition, broader social concerns such as waste management, the efficient use of resources, and the preservation of natural beauty are issues that will likely draw increased attention.

Government Responses

Interest in consumer issues is not likely to disappear. The main reason for this forecast is that today it is politically popular to support various consumer, social, and environmental causes. Since the 1960s, consumer-oriented activity at both the federal and provincial levels has been carried on at an unprecedented rate. All the provinces enacted legislation and put consumer protection programs in place.

A significant number of these laws were designed to protect the consumer's "right to safety" — especially in situations where consumers cannot judge for themselves the risk involved in the purchase and use of particular products. Legislation such as the Food and Drugs Act regulates and controls the manufacture, distribution, and sale of food, drugs, and cosmetic products. The Hazardous Products Act establishes standards for the manufacture of consumer products designed for household, garden, personal, recreational, or child use. Regulations under this Act require that dangerous products be packaged as safely as possible and labelled with clear and adequate warnings. This law also makes provision for the removal of dangerous products from the marketplace.

One controversial area of product safety legislation is the paternalistic type of law that is intended to protect the consumer, whether or not he or she wants that protection. Thus, it is mandatory to equip automobiles with seat belts, and it is illegal to operate an automobile unless the seat belts are fastened. In many cities, it is required that bicycle riders wear helmets. Toronto enacted a controversial by-law that prohibits smoking in any public building. In effect, somebody else is forcing a consumer to accept what the other person feels is in the consumer's best interests — truly a new and broadening approach to consumer legislation.

Another series of laws and government programs supports the consumer's "right to be informed." These measures help in such areas as reducing confusion and deception in packaging and labelling, identifying the ingredients and nutritional content in food products, advising consumers of the length of life of certain packaged food products, providing instructions and assistance in the care of various textile products, and determining the true rate of interest.

At the federal level, government has passed a number of pieces of legislation designed to provide consumers with more information. Possibly the most important of these is the Consumer Packaging and Labelling Act, which regulates the packaging, labelling, sale, and advertising of prepackaged products. The Textile Labelling Act requires manufacturers of textile products to place labels on most articles made from fabrics. These labels must name the fibres, show the amount of each fibre in the product by percentage, and identify the company for whom or by whom the article was made.

The consumer is also protected at both the federal and provincial levels in Canada in the area of misleading and dishonest advertising. The federal Competition Act contains a number of provisions dealing with misleading advertising; these have been discussed in Chapter 18.

One of the most significant responses to the consumer movement on the part of government has been a strengthened and expanded role of regulatory agencies involved in consumer affairs. At the provincial level, public utilities boards hold public hearings and receive briefs from concerned citizens and consumer groups whenever a hydro company is seeking a rate increase or a change in its services. It has become quite common for organized consumer associations and ratepayer groups to intervene at such hearings as representatives of consumer interests.

Federally, two major regulatory agencies have emerged as powerful arms of government in recent years. The Canadian Transport Commission (CTC) regulates all aspects of interprovincial travel and companies that operate nationally, such as railways and the major airlines. Applications for route changes and fare increases must be filed with the CTC, and opportunities are presented at public hearings for consumer groups to make representations. Similarly, the Canadian Radio-television and Telecommunications Commission (CRTC) regulates the broadcasting and telecommunications industries in this country. This regulatory body has become very much involved in marketing-related areas in recent years. It is responsible for awarding broadcasting licences to AM and FM radio stations, television stations, and cable and direct-to-home satellite television operators. The CRTC also regulates these broadcasters in the content of the programming they use and administers numerous codes of advertising standards in its role as the agency responsible for regulating broadcast advertising.

Finally, in all provinces and at the federal level in Canada there exist marketing boards that, to varying degrees, control the production, distribution, and pricing of products. These marketing boards, such as the Ontario Milk Marketing Board, the British Columbia Fruit Board, and the Canadian Egg Marketing Agency, wield considerable power over the marketing of the products that fall under their responsibility.[2] Most of these boards are involved in the distribution of agricultural products and were established to represent the interests of producers. However, through their efforts to promote marketing efficiency, marketing boards generally attempt to represent the best long-term interests of consumers.

It is difficult to judge the effectiveness of government effort, since it depends on one's perspective. From the point of view of some consumer advocates, government is too slow and too many issues are ignored or overlooked. Alternatively, some free-market spokespersons would prefer less regulation and view government activity as interference. In evaluating consumer protection, it is important to recognize that there are trade-offs. For example, there are costs involved in providing consumers with more information, designing and manufacturing products to eliminate all hazards, and keeping the environment clean. These must be weighed against the expected benefits. Often these are difficult comparisons; some, for instance, involve costs that will be incurred now for benefits that may not be realized until some time in the future.

One factor that is interesting and potentially important with regard to government response to consumer issues is that the regulatory thrust in recent decades has largely been focused on the regulation of manufacturing industries — companies that actually produce things, their content, their packages, and so on. While advertising is heavily regulated in Canada and may be considered a service industry, for the most part the legislative structure in service industries is less well-developed in this country and may well become a focus for government attention in the future.

Business Responses

An increasing number of businesses are making substantive responses to consumer problems. Here are a few examples:

- *Better communications with consumers.* Many firms have responded positively to the desire of consumers to be heard. Toll-free 1-800 phone numbers now appear on the packages of many manufacturers or in their advertising. They have become an integral part of customer service because they are easy to use and allow consumers to speak directly to a representative of the business. Increasingly, advertisers are including their Web site addresses in advertisements and are encouraging consumers to contact them via e-mail.
- *More and better information for consumers.* Point-of-sale information is constantly improving. Manufacturers' instruction manuals on the use and care of their products are more detailed and easier to read. In many instances, package labels are more informative than they were in the past. Many companies also have installed call-centre operations that are staffed twenty-four hours a day and allow consumers to call with questions or problems using the company's 1-800 toll-free number.
- *Product improvements.* More marketers are making a concerted effort to incorporate feedback from consumers in the designs of their products. As a result of consumer input or complaints, many companies have made improvements in their products. For example, detergent manufacturers have produced concentrated products that are more environmentally safe and scent-free products that

contain no perfumes that may irritate people with allergies. Soft-drink manufacturers have improved the design of the caps on their one- and two-litre bottles so that the product will retain its carbonation after opening.

- *Service quality measurement.* Many companies have realized that it is becoming increasingly difficult to gain a competitive advantage through product design and that the key to success is to offer the customer the best possible service. Realizing also that they need feedback so that they know how well they are doing, many have developed and introduced programs that allow them to measure consumers' perceptions of the level of service they are receiving.
- *More carefully prepared advertising.* Many advertisers are extremely cautious in approving ads prepared by their advertising agencies, in sharp contrast to past practices. Advertisers are involving their legal departments in the approval process. They are sensitive to the fact that the CRTC may reject a commercial or the Advertising Standards Council may find that the advertisement violates some particular code of advertising standards. The advertising industry and the media are doing a much more effective self-regulation job than ever before, especially through the Advertising Advisory Board and its Advertising Standards Councils.
- *Customer service departments.* A growing number of companies have established departments to handle consumer inquiries and complaints. Some even encourage customers to complain, or at least to provide feedback, by distributing short questionnaires in hotel rooms, airline seat pockets, and restaurants. In addition to dealing with complaints, customer service departments also gauge consumer tastes, act as sounding boards for new ideas, and often gain feedback on new products.

Some trade associations see themselves as defenders of their respective industry or profession. In that capacity, they try to moderate government anti-business legislation through lobbying and head off criticism with arguments to justify almost any behaviour. More enlightened associations have recognized the necessity for responsible corporate behaviour. Though they still engage in lobbying, these groups actively respond to consumer problems by setting industry ethical standards, conducting consumer education, and promoting research among association members.

ETHICS AND MARKETING

Ethics are standards of conduct. To act in an ethical fashion is to conform to an accepted standard of moral behaviour. Undoubtedly, virtually all people prefer to act ethically. It is easy to be ethical when no hardship is involved — when a person is winning and life is going well. The test comes when things are not going so well — when pressures build up. These pressures arise in all walks of life, and marketing is no exception.

Marketing executives face the challenge of balancing the best interests of consumers, the organization, and society into a workable guide for their daily activities. In any situation, they must be able to distinguish what is ethical from what is unethical and act accordingly, regardless of the possible consequences. However, there are many circumstances in which what constitutes ethical behaviour is far from straightforward.[3]

Setting Ethical Guidelines

Many organizations have formal codes of ethics that identify specific acts (bribery, accepting gifts) as unethical and describe the standards employees are expected to live up to. A large percentage of major corporations have ethics codes, as do many smaller businesses. These guidelines lessen the chance that an employee will knowingly or unknowingly violate a company's standards. In addition, ethics codes strengthen a company's hand in dealing with customers or prospects that encourage unethical behaviour. For young or inexperienced managers, these codes can be valuable guides, helping them to resist pressure to compromise personal ethics in order to move up in the firm.

However, every decision cannot be taken out of the hands of the manager. Furthermore, determining what is right and what is wrong can be extremely difficult. It is not realistic for an organization to construct a two-column list of all possible practices, one headed "ethical" and the other "unethical." Rather, a marketer must be able to evaluate a situation and formulate a response. Arthur Andersen and Co. has developed an ethical reasoning model that can be taught to current and future managers.[4] The model expands the traditional cost–benefit analysis to include all the individuals and groups affected, not just the decision-maker's organization, to help clarify the ethical dimensions of a decision. The procedure consists of:

1. Identifying the decision options and the likely consequences of each.
2. Identifying all individuals and organizations that will be positively or negatively affected by the consequences of each option.
3. Estimating the negative impact (costs) and positive impact (benefits) of each option from the point of view of each affected party, taking into consideration its particular interests and needs.
4. Ranking the costs and the benefits of each option and making a decision.

This approach is an attempt to be systematic and logical in ethical decisions. It will work only if the decision-maker can be objective and impartial. However, situations where ethics is an issue are also frequently charged with emotion. Thus, an alternative approach that attempts to personalize the situation may be more effective. When faced with an ethical problem, honest answers to the following questions should indicate which route to follow:

- Would I do this to a friend?
- Would I be willing to have this done to me?
- Would I be embarrassed if this action were publicized nationally?

Pragmatic Reasons for Behaving Ethically

Marketing executives should practise ethical behaviour because it is morally correct. While this is simple and attarctive in concept, it is not sufficient motivation for everyone. So let's consider four pragmatic **reasons for ethical behaviour**:

- *To reverse declining public confidence in marketing.* Occasionally, we hear about misleading package labels, false claims in ads, phony list prices, and infringements of well-established trademarks. Though such practices are limited to only a small proportion of all marketing organizations, the reputations of all marketers are damaged. To reverse this situation, business leaders must demonstrate convincingly that they are aware of their ethical responsibility and will fulfil it. Companies must set high ethical standards and enforce them. Moreover, it is in management's interest to be concerned with the well-being of consumers, since they are the lifeblood of a business.
- *To avoid increases in government regulation.* Our economic freedoms sometimes have a high price, just as our political freedoms do. Business apathy, resistance, or token responses to unethical behaviour simply increase the probability of more government regulation. Indeed, most of the governmental limitations on marketing are the result of management's failure to live up to its ethical responsibilities at one time or other. Moreover, once some form of government regulation has been introduced, it is rarely removed.
- *To retain the power granted by society.* Marketing executives wield a great deal of social power because they influence markets and speak out on economic issues. However, responsibility is tied to that power. If marketers do not use their power in a socially acceptable manner, that power will be lost in the long run.
- *To protect the image of the organization.* Buyers often form an impression of an entire organization based on their contact with one person. More often than not, that person represents the marketing function or is linked by the customer with marketing. You may base your opinion of a retail store on the behaviour of a single sales clerk. As Procter & Gamble put it in an annual report: "When a Procter & Gamble sales person walks into a customer's place of business . . . that sales person not only represents Procter & Gamble, but in a very real sense, that person is Procter & Gamble."

Socially Responsible Behaviour

Ethical behaviour goes beyond avoiding wrongdoing. The ethical marketer recognizes that the position he or she holds in society carries with it certain obligations. This **social responsibility** involves improving the well-being of society. Besides obeying the law and meeting the normal and reasonable expectations of the public, socially responsible organizations and individuals lead the way in setting standards of business and community performance. Some companies encourage their employees to join volunteer groups and will pay the fees for staff to join service clubs that get involved in community projects. Many large corporations sponsor television specials on environmental and other social issues and generally support public broadcasting. Publishers, such as McGraw-Hill Ryerson, donate scholarships to universities and colleges and support literacy programs. Many companies donate money raised from the sale of certain items to charitable organizations. Avon Canada raises about $1 million annually for breast cancer research through the sale of Avon Flame pink pens for $4 each. Avon is not only supporting a very worthwhile cause; it is able to identify with its female customer base.[5]

Protecting the Customer's Right to Privacy

One of the most troublesome issues facing marketers relates to behaviour that threatens the customer's right to privacy. This is especially important today because more and more companies are collecting information on customers from a number of sources and storing the data on databases to be used for marketing purposes. Some consumers object to businesses having the information in the first place and to their use of it to sell them things. The point is that the technology is available today to permit the integration of databases, making it possible to obtain information about the characteristics of consumers and their households and to match that information with data about purchases, credit card usage, and other consumption behaviour.

Nowhere is the issue of privacy more pertinent than in the area of telemarketing. As the use of the telephone has increased to contact people in their homes for the purpose of marketing products and services, so too has the public outcry against such practices. Some less-scrupulous marketers have used automated-dialling devices that continually dial telephone numbers selected at random and play a recorded sales pitch when the telephone is answered. While the use of such tactics is not at all widespread, many members of the public object to being telephoned at home. Consequently, many have turned to installing answering machines or a call management service provided by their telephone company that will allow them to screen calls, or they have paid for unlisted telephone numbers (although they will not be protected from random calling even with an unlisted number).

The direct marketing industry has taken steps to police itself with regard to offering protection to consumers against invasion of privacy. The industry association, the Canadian Direct Marketing Association, has adopted a code of standards that regulates its members, who account for about 80 percent of all direct marketers in Canada. The code, among other things, provides for the right of consumers to have their names deleted from mailing lists, provides for informing consumers of the source of their names appearing on any list, and ensures that data are protected against unauthorized use.

One consumer in Sudbury, Ontario, was so angry, having received persistent mailings from Columbia House, the mail-order video and record company, even after he had asked in writing that his name be removed from their list, that he started sending the company $10 for each piece of unwanted mail that he received, later increasing it to $100. When the mailings continued, he took Columbia House to small claims court to try to collect the $480 that he claimed they owed him. He won his case, thereby setting a legal precedent.[6]

Advertising and Social Responsibility

The issue of the social responsibility of marketing is also often related to the advertising that businesses present to their target consumers. For example, Benetton, the international Italian-owned clothing manufacturer and retailer, has in recent years employed rather controversial approaches in its advertising. Some consumers in many countries have been shocked by the content of Benetton ads, which have featured black and white people embracing, multicoloured condoms, a car burning in an urban

www.cdma.org • www.columbiahousecanada.com

ghetto, a group of refugees clambering up the side of a rusty ship, a black Queen Elizabeth, a photo of a dying AIDS patient with his anguished family looking on, and the blood-stained clothing of a recently killed Bosnian soldier. Benetton maintains that its ads are intended to force people to think of important social issues; however, many are offended by them.

Advertising is also criticized for the way in which certain groups in society are presented or for the effect that it may have on them. There has been considerable objection, for example, to the portrayal of ultra-thin young models in fashion advertising for such brands as Calvin Klein and Club Monaco. Critics suggest that such advertising promotes the view that thinness is glamorous and may contribute to eating disorders.[7] Similar public discussion surrounds such issues as whether or not manufacturers of prescription drugs should be allowed to advertise them to prospective consumers.[8] When Seagram Company Limited moved to begin advertising its liquor products on television in the United States, it set off a controversy involving government officials, health advocates, and rival liquor manufacturers.[9]

Other advertising is criticized as being socially irresponsible primarily because of the product being advertised. For example, Labatt Breweries encountered a stream of protest when the company introduced its Maximum Ice brand, a beer with a 7.1 percent alcohol content. The advertising, with its heavy-metal look, was said to appeal mostly to young, male beer drinkers. The introduction of the brand and its provocative advertising have been soundly criticized by organizations such as MADD (Mothers Against Drunk Driving) and is seen to be a threat to the efforts of many groups to curb excessive drinking and drunk driving in particular.[10]

Much advertising that appears in the mass media is controversial for a number of reasons. What is often interesting to observe is that the most violent criticism and the most strident demands for the removal of the offending advertising often come from people who are clearly not in the advertiser's intended target consumer segment.

PROSPECTS FOR THE FUTURE

Let's move now from looking at how marketers can and should behave to a description of what lies ahead for marketing. More specifically, in order to be more effective and efficient, and to increase levels of customer satisfaction, what do marketers need to know and what do they need to do?

Market Trends and Reactions

Many trends bear watching. To illustrate their significance, we will look at four areas: demographic changes, shifts in values, the impact of technology, and the growth of information.

Consumer Demographics Changes in demographics — the population's age distribution, income, education, ethnic composition, and household structure — all affect marketers' activities. For example, the population is getting older, and senior citizens are the fastest-growing age group. This shift creates expanded marketing opportunities in such areas as travel and tourism and health and medical care. Another demographic change is the greater ethnic diversity in Canada's cities, resulting primarily from increases in the level of immigration from Asia and other areas. These groups are large enough to attract the attention of marketers, but they present interesting challenges.[11]

Another important development is the decrease in household size. More people than ever live alone. Therefore, marketers of many consumer products must consider the impact of smaller households on meat preparation, the size of appliances, and package sizes, to cite several examples. Small households also mean fewer people to perform normal maintenance functions. Therefore, time has for many become an exceedingly important commodity in recent years.

What do these demographic changes tell us? They indicate that some markets will practically disappear and new ones will emerge. Marketers must remain abreast of these developments and adjust their strategies accordingly. For example, the aging population has created opportunities for products modified to accommodate the physical limitations of the elderly (labels and instructions in large print, easy-to-open containers), and time pressure has spawned firms that will do routine errands (getting the car serviced, picking up the dry cleaning, grocery shopping).

MARKETING AT WORK FILE 24-2

NOT IN MY CLASSROOM

One issue getting a lot of attention these days in education circles relates to the role of partnerships between schools and the private sector. In these times of reduced government support for education and other social programs, many school boards have to turn to alternative sources of funding. In many parts of the country, parents are exhausted by the number of fundraising initiatives in which they and their kids must participate, often simply to equip their schools with what were once considered essential supplies. The alternative is to strike a deal with local or national businesses that will lead to the achieving of objectives for both parties. The problem is that some deals are not exactly what some parents and teachers had in mind.

Generally, the most acceptable of the business-education partnerships involve broad-based collaboration between business, labour, and community groups that are aimed at achieving the learning objectives set out in the school curriculum. Other projects that are well-received involve an individual company adopting a school to donate equipment or the time of employees. Across Canada, the National Business and Education Centre of the Conference Board of Canada estimates that as many as 15,000 to 20,000 such projects are operating. But organizations like the Canadian Feder-ation of Teachers are concerned that business-education partnerships will lead to businesses getting more involved in curriculum matters.

Often criticized are projects in which a single company produces materials that give that company a presence in the classroom or that lead to exclusive business contracts to supply food items and other supplies. Hewlett-Packard (Canada) Limited produced a workbook on math and computers for use in grades 4 to 6, with a special focus on girls. TV Ontario and Spar Aerospace collaborated to produce a video, a teacher's guide, and a Web site to support Ontario curriculum on science and technology for grades 4 to 6. Somewhat more controversial are free classroom materials like the "Kernels of Knowledge" series from Hunt-Wesson Foods that saluted popcorn maker Orville Redenbacher as a great scientist who "made a difference." Organizations like the Canadian Centre for Policy Alternatives also criticize materials like those on the environment, supplied by Procter & Gamble, that defended the clear-cutting of trees.

Clearly, this is not an easy issue to address. Should school boards enter into partnership agreements with businesses? What guidelines should they follow?

Source: Jennifer Lewington, "Grappling with an Ethical Question," *The Globe and Mail, Guide to Education*, March 27, 1997, pp. C1, C3. Reprinted with permission from *The Globe and Mail.*

Values Values, the widely held beliefs in a society, change slowly. When they do, however, the impact on existing institutions and the opportunities for innovative marketers can be great. Value shifts often accompany demographic changes. As the Canadian population gets older and changes in other ways, we can expect some adjustments in values. For example, we are seeing:

- *Broadened perspectives.* Some forecasters see a shift away from a self-orientation to an "other-orientation." For example, volunteerism is on the upswing. Indications are that people may be disturbed by the materialism of the 1980s and early 1990s, a period in which self-gratification governed many choices.
- *Increased scepticism.* Education is at its highest level ever. Consumers have more confidence in their ability to make judgments and are less willing to accept unsubstantiated claims. Authority is subject to challenge. Consumers demand information and are willing to question traditions. The difficulty

North American automakers are having in winning back the confidence of consumers is an example of this development. The concerns of Canadians with regard to cuts in social programs, including health care and education, are causing considerable scepticism about the leadership of elected officials.

- *Balanced lifestyles.* From a society that focused on work to produce a richer lifestyle, we are moving to a society that wants to balance work and leisure to enjoy a lifestyle. This will mean an increasing concern with wellness in the form of nutrition and exercise, the allocation of more time to home, family, and leisure, and a desire to become involved in activities viewed as worthwhile and fulfilling. Younger Canadians, in particular, appear not to be driven to succeed nearly as much as were their parents.

What do these changes mean for marketing? We are likely to see all increasing emphasis on quality over quantity in consumption and a more careful evaluation of the value of product features that seem to add more to style than substance. One area in which values are evident is a heightened interest in the future quality of life. International concern over the dissipation of the atmosphere's ozone layer, the disappearance of rainforests, increases in acid rain, and the "greenhouse effect" is obvious. Other environmental issues of interest to consumers are waste disposal and landfills, air and water pollution, and biodegradability.

Environmentally sensitive product packaging, alternatives to fossil fuel, and energy conservation are excellent **green marketing** opportunities. Other prospects are not so obvious. One industry spawned by environmental interests and a desire to visit unspoiled, exotic locations is leisure travel to unusual destinations. But even this may have its downside. For example, there has been such an increase in the number of whale-watching tours in various parts of the world that some environmentalists are becoming concerned that the number of tourists may represent a threat to the animals they wish to protect.

The issues in the environmental debate are not at all clear. The complexity of the ecosystem means that it is possible for interest groups to argue that recyclable paper and cardboard containers are environmentally safer than polystyrene, while some scientists can make an equally rational case that the total use of energy is greater in the manufacture of the paper products. The net effect is that the consumer is probably confused. Inherently, however, the consumer is more likely to come down on the side of apparently "natural" products; therefore, cloth diapers are perceived to be less harmful to the environment than are disposables; cardboard fast-food containers are perceived to be less harmful than their "plastic" counterparts. Consequently, some companies have been accused of jumping on the bandwagon with respect to the environmental issue by labelling "green" some products that do not really offer an environmental advantage.[12]

- *Heightened interest in entertainment.* All signs in the first half of the 1990s pointed toward a lifestyle that had consumers focusing more on activities within the home. Stressful jobs and time constraints had led people to seek a place where they could relax in comfort and security. Consumers were spending more on their homes and on products that made their homes enjoyable. The ultimate definition of the lifestyle that would dominate the early 1990s was cocooning, epitomized by the views of trend-prophet Faith Popcorn that North Americans were so tired of the stresses of life that they were retreating to the security of their homes, settling in front of the television where they would be entertained by satellite television and all manner of computer games, and basically tuning out the world. But, by the late 1990s, Canadians were again emerging from their homes and spending more than ever on out-of-home entertainment, including movies, plays, opera and concerts. Officially, cocooning was dead.[13]
- *Demands for good service.* The success of businesses such as Four Seasons Hotels and Bell Canada makes it clear that consumers reward good service. It is also apparent that many firms recognize this opportunity. The effective "lonely Maytag repairman" ad campaign that has run for many years and airline ads emphasizing on-time arrival records are just two examples. Recognizing the need to offer good service is often easier than finding and training employees to provide it. A major challenge for organizations in the 1990s

A good hotel is a home away from home.

will be to design and implement systems that provide consumers with high-calibre service. There is every evidence that the offering of superior customer service represents a strategic competitive advantage for successful companies.[14]

Technology There can be little doubt that the practice of marketing has been revolutionized in recent years because of the impact of technology. The development of advanced technology has been so rapid that it has created both opportunities and problems that have serious implications for how marketing is carried out within just about every organization that you can think of. The developments in technology are so vast that we can only provide a brief overview here, but we will touch on a number of key areas where marketing has been affected.

- *Internet marketing.* One opportunity that is obvious from the advances in technology of recent years is the use of the Internet to market products and services to prospective customers around the world. Virtually every major company and many smaller ones have created Web sites, and many of these are designed to sell things. A number of issues should be considered when a company embarks upon a marketing program on the Internet. First, the Web is not like many other media, in that consumers actually seek out a marketer's site and are, therefore, likely to be in the market to buy. The Web allows a firm to reach consumers around the world and does not limit it to local or even national media. In theory, therefore, marketing on the Internet should be very cost-effective. But there are potential problems, not the least of which relates to the quality and visual appeal of the Web sites that are created.[15]
- *Fragmentation and customization of the electronic media.* Technology is revolutionizing the media to which consumers are exposed. Not only are there many more television stations, but there are numerous ways for consumers to access entertainment and educational programming. The result is

a mind-boggling array of alternatives, most of them delivered through electronic media and on the "Information Superhighway." There are stories of a 500-channel universe, where consumers could access the signals of hundreds of television stations around the world. We are seeing it in Canada with the launch of direct-to-home satellite television. While these developments result in a splitting of the electronic media into hundreds of options, it also creates an opportunity to allow advertisers to reach targeted niche consumers more directly.

- *Impact on service delivery.* Technology has had a very definite impact on the delivery of customer service. On the one hand, some would argue that the introduction of such technology as automated banking machines, interactive voice-response telephone systems, and call-management software has created an impenetrable barrier between some companies and their customers. This suggests that, at a time when companies are generally interested in establishing close relationships with customers, there is a very real danger that technology will get in the way of a company being able to establish personal relationships. On the other hand, this is a very good example of the "two-edged sword" nature of technology. At the same time that technology seems to be getting in the way of service delivery, there are many examples of how technology actually facilitates service delivery. We discussed earlier in this book the use of technology to analyze customer purchase data so that companies can put attractive promotions in front of the right customers. We also mentioned how sophisticated vehicles and equipment are being equipped with on-board computer chips that continually diagnose engine performance and notify the dealer or the owner when service is needed.
- *Customer monitoring.* Technology has made it possible for companies to get to know their customers far better than has ever been the case in the past. Supermarket scanners and other forms of technology essentially observe the purchase patterns and behaviour of customers and maintain a running record of what has been purchased, where, and when. The result is the comprehensive databases that we will discuss in the next section. But it is not only in a retail context that such information is captured. We are now seeing even more sophisticated applications of monitoring, using scanners and monitors. For example, the new Highway 407, which runs north of Toronto, is Canada's first electronic-toll highway, on which drivers will be monitored electronically and tolls paid automatically, thereby eliminating long queues at toll booths.[16]

Use of Customer Information Marketers have the ability to pinpoint customers as never before. Using scanner data that produces detailed purchase behaviour on a store-by-store basis, Statistics Canada data that provide demographic information down to the city block, and a variety of other sources such as warranty registration cards, contest entries, and rebate requests, firms can build detailed customer and prospect profiles. With this information, they are able to design products and assortments tailored specifically to a customer's needs. Consider the case of Black's Photo Corporation. In the past, the company would make a decision on where to locate a new store primarily "by the seat of its pants." Now it uses a software program from Toronto-based Compusearch Micromarketing to combine demographic and marketing data with mapping and topographical software to provide detailed information on the market potential of certain areas. The software, called Conquest/Canada, can provide the following: census data, consumer spending per household in more than eight hundred purchase categories, ownership data on household facilities and equipment, vehicle registrations, business activity in the area, and Compusearch's population and age-group projections ten years ahead. The result is that much of the guesswork is taken out of marketing decisions such as store location.[17]

Knowing more about the market has led to **market fragmentation** and to **niche marketing** — the identification of smaller and smaller market segments. There was a time when a packaged-goods manufacturer could develop a quality product, advertise it nationally using the national media, stock retailers' shelves, and have a reasonable chance of success. But the situation has changed. Marketers can no longer expect large numbers of consumers to compromise their needs and wants and buy standardized products. Rather, they must tailor goods and services to meet the needs of small market segments. The strategy of niche marketing significantly complicates the marketer's job. One version of a product is replaced by several. Different ads must be produced, and new media must be found to reach different consumers. Retailers must choose among many product variations, not all of which can be stocked. The added variety complicates inventory management, distribution, and personal selling.

Evidence of this fragmentation is everywhere. McDonald's, the king of hamburgers, not only has expanded its variety of burgers but has also test marketed fish-and-chips, lobster sandwiches, Mexican food, fried chicken, and pizza. From 1947 to 1984, Procter & Gamble had only one Tide. Today there are many versions, including Tide Ultra, Phosphate Free Tide, Liquid Tide, and Tide with bleach.

There are no indications that the trend to niche marketing will end. In fact, with more sophisticated electronic data-collection methods being developed and the diversity of the population increasing, all indications point to even greater fragmentation in the future. The reaching of smaller and smaller market segments is facilitated largely through advances in technology that make it possible to design a unique marketing program to address the needs of individual customers.

Strategic Marketing Adjustments

We have highlighted just four of the many changes taking place in the market — demographic changes, shifts in values, advances in technology, and the growth in information — and some of the implications they have for marketers. One common response to change, as illustrated by the examples, is simply to react as it occurs. However, realizing that change is always occurring, marketers should initiate strategic proactive efforts to improve performance. Six are described in this section.

Instilling a Market-Driven Orientation Describing the marketing concept and implementing it in an organization are two different things. The concept — combining a customer orientation with co-ordinated marketing and the organization's goals — certainly has intuitive appeal, yet many organizations seem unable to practise it consistently. Despite the fact that marketing has been taught in college and university business schools for over fifty years, the effective implementation of marketing is the exception rather than the rule. What does practising the marketing concept require?

- *The marketing concept involves a philosophy of business that focuses on the customer's needs.* However, when faced with the choice of putting the customer first or meeting their own needs, some employees often find it difficult to give the customer priority. Instilling this orientation requires top-management commitment. Lip service is not sufficient. Employees must see management putting the customer first.
- *There must be a reward system that encourages a customer orientation.* Employees must be empowered to make decisions that recognize the importance of customers and be publicly rewarded for those decisions. Take the case of the Federal Express driver who could not get a drop-box unlocked. Rather than give up and run the risk of not having the packages in the box delivered on time, he managed to load the 225 kg box in his truck and haul it back to the office where a mechanic could open it. For his decision (and his effort), he was given an award by the company.
- *Organizations must stay in close contact with the market.* This means having detailed, accurate market knowledge. Consumers are becoming less and less willing to compromise to satisfy their desires. Marketers must develop more marketing programs for smaller markets. Good information and decision-support systems are needed in making these decisions. In consumer marketing, this means conducting research on a continuous basis. In business-to-business marketing, it may mean creating new structures. For example, Procter & Gamble has a marketing team located permanently at Wal-Mart headquarters to ensure that this key customer is served adequately. Progressive research firms have helped their clients by developing research programs to measure the quality of service being delivered and to examine the state of customer relationships with service companies.

www.fedex.com

- *A sustainable differential advantage must be established by precisely matching the buyers' needs with the firm's capabilities.* This is an area where marketers are often guilty of narrow vision. Very few marketers, in fact, have a complete appreciation for the needs of their customers. Most have even less appreciation for the fact, as discussed in Chapter 1, that needs exist at a variety of levels for each customer. Thus, while we may feel that a customer needs a high-quality product at an attractive price, we often lose sight of the fact that he or she also needs to be made to feel welcome and needs attention, recognition, and appreciation.
- *Offer consumers the best value possible.* Many companies have realized that offering discounts and "specials" does little to build long-term customer loyalty and have instead turned to low everyday prices. The concept of adding value is of such importance that we will return to it later in this chapter.
- *Listen to the customer.* Successful companies no longer assume that they know what their customers want. Consequently, many are doing more marketing research than they have in the past. They have also learned that they can do nothing to improve the service to customers unless they know when customers are having problems or concerns. Consequently, many have implemented a program to encourage customers to complain and have then put in place a system that tracks every customer complaint and ensures that it is resolved to the customer's satisfaction.[18]
- *All exchange partners, not just customers, must be satisfied.* Exchange partners of an organization include its customers, suppliers, intermediaries, owners, regulators, and anyone else with whom it interacts. If suppliers, for example, feel their exchanges with an organization are unsatisfactory, they will not do everything in their power to ensure that the needs of end customers will be met. The same is true of employees. Essential to satisfying final customers are strong, positive relationships among all the parties who contribute to bringing a product or service to market.

Adopting a Global Orientation To be successful in the future, marketers must adopt a global orientation toward markets, products, and marketing activity. In the past, most firms could be successful by focusing on the domestic market and outperforming local rivals. However, that has changed. Now firms, both large and small, are going where the markets are the most attractive.

The cliché that we live in a "small world" is a reality for marketers. Virtually instantaneous communications have greatly increased global awareness. Economic, social, and political developments on one side of the world have an impact everywhere else. On the evening television news we are as likely to hear about developments on the Japanese stock market as we are about activity on Bay Street.

As a result, foreign firms are now major investors in Canada and Canadian firms in search of new mass markets have a renewed interest in opportunities overseas. Growing buying power in Asia, the elimination of trade restrictions in the European Union, and political changes in Eastern Europe have created interest among many Canadian businesses who are establishing their positions or launching initiatives to enter these markets. Canadian companies such as Northern Telecom and Bombardier now manufacture and export telecommunications and transportation equipment to many countries. McDonald's of Canada was responsible for that company's entry into Moscow. Canadian banks are major players in financing projects around the world and have long been among the leading domestic banks in regions such as the Caribbean. With the enormous potential established by the performance of the pioneering firms, many organizations are eagerly investigating global marketing. However, significant problems exist, and the risks may well exceed the benefits in some cases.

Despite problems, the trend toward global marketing will accelerate. The lure of millions of consumers, combined with an improved understanding of the markets and marketing practices necessary to be successful, will increase the attractiveness of such opportunities.

Understanding the Concept of Value and Its Relationship to Customer Needs One of the most talked-about but least understood concepts in marketing is value. We hear a great deal in marketing circles about adding value for customers. Presumably, this involves adding something over and above what the customer would normally get in order to make the offering more attractive than that of a competitor. What is often overlooked is the fact that, in order to add value, we must have a very good understanding of what it is that customers value in the first place. Few companies have invested sufficiently in research to be able to answer the question: What do customers value? This issue of adding value is very closely related to the concept of customer needs, as discussed above and in Chapter 1. Customers will value what allows them to better meet their needs. Thus, to add value for our clients, we must be able to understand their needs. Some companies presume to be adding value when they cut prices, but this is a dangerous strategy that often provokes price competition and a devaluing of what the firm offers. Others believe they are adding value when they add new features to tangible products; but customers often do not perceive any improvement or any added value. The most effective way of adding value is often to provide exceptional service.

Emphasizing Quality and Customer Satisfaction

In the 1970s, many businesses recognized that the quality of their products was significantly below the product quality of competitors from other countries. To correct the problem, they adopted a variety of quality-instilling techniques. One of the most popular was developed by W. Edwards Deming and Joseph Juran and has been practised by the Japanese since the 1950s. It is called Total Quality Management (TQM) and is the application of quality principles to all endeavours of an organization, not just manufacturing. It is a business philosophy that stresses a teamwork approach that involves every employee of a company. Advocates of TQM believe that it is as important to satisfy "internal customers" as it is to satisfy final consumers. So, for example, marketing managers are viewed as customers of the marketing research staff. TQM also involves changes in the way things are done, from manufacturing processes to record keeping.

The emphasis on quality in products and services that is sweeping business today requires a rethinking of the role of marketing and even of what marketing means. If marketing, as we have observed very early in this book, means an emphasis on customer satisfaction, then the goals of the quality movement are not at all removed from that. In fact, there may be some justification in arguing that marketing and quality really refer to the same thing — efforts to produce satisfied customers. They both refer to intrinsic values in organizations that are customer-focused: an attitude, an orientation toward doing whatever is necessary to satisfy the customer. Some companies have gone so far as to dismantle their marketing departments, instead assigning responsibility for customer relationships and satisfaction to senior strategy-makers and to the plants and field staff who actually make and deliver the products and services.[19]

Designing Environmentally Sound Strategies

Quality applies to more than making products that work better or longer. A broader issue is the general quality of everyday life and the way we treat the environment. In the past, commitments to single-issue efforts (for example, making a product biodegradable or eliminating chlorofluorocarbons) were enough to win consumer approval. However, in the future, environmental acceptance will be based on a product's entire life cycle, from design through disposal.

Firms will be forced to move away from looking for an exploitable or advertisable feature to making environmental concerns an integral part of the business system. This will require a new way of thinking about consumption. One example is to make products so that the materials, components, and packages can be used longer and reused either in part or whole, a process called **reconsumption**.[20] Forms of reconsumption include:

- *Refilling.* Rather than discarding a container when it is empty, if it is properly designed, it can be refilled. Over thirty million laser-printer cartridges are used and disposed of every year. Accutone has designed its cartridges so that they can be refilled. Similarly, Xerox produces a copier with a recyclable printing cartridge.
- *Repairing.* With proper maintenance, products can be used longer. Thus, rather than waiting to act until after a product fails, SKF, a Swedish bearing manufacturer, has developed a series of preventive support services and diagnostic techniques that its customers can use to greatly lengthen the life of its bearings.

www.skf.se

CHRYSLER IS A PROUD FOUNDING SPONSOR OF THE TRANS CANADA TRAIL.
AND WITH THE PURCHASE OR LEASE OF ANY NEW CHRYSLER VEHICLE THIS JULY, AUGUST OR SEPTEMBER, WE WILL BUY A METRE OF THE TRAIL ON YOUR BEHALF, PERMANENTLY DISPLAYING YOUR NAME IN A TRAIL PAVILION OF YOUR CHOICE.

CHRYSLER CANADA

AT CHRYSLER, WE'RE NOT JUST BUILDING CARS AND TRUCKS, WE'RE BUILDING CANADA.
1 800 361 3700

Companies like Chrysler Canada build upon their established brand image by supporting worthy projects like the Trans-Canada Trail.

- *Restoring.* Some products can be returned to their original condition by replacing parts and reconditioning others. Restoration requires that parts be designed in such a way that they can be economically removed from a product, and made from materials that can be reconditioned. BMW and Mercedes are now restoring damaged auto parts that in the past were simply discarded.
- *Reusing.* Packaging material is often discarded long before it is unusable. Lego, the Danish toy manufacturer, delivers its products to retailers in large, durable boxes that are returned to Lego for reuse.

The key to making reconsumption work is developing methods of manufacturing and marketing that make it profitable. This isn't easy. McDonald's has recently invested nearly 60 percent of its R&D budget in attempting to develop a soluble plastic for packaging. It also requires new ways of thinking. For years, manufacturers have focused on ways of assembling things efficiently. Now the focus must switch to developing technologies for separating materials. For example, finding a method to remove the ink from newspaper economically will be crucial to its recycling.

Marketing functions will also have to be rethought. Channels of distribution, for example, will have to flow both ways. For reconsumption, packages, products, and parts will have to be returned to the seller. Methods must be constructed to collect as well as distribute goods. To meet the needs of customers and gain their co-operation, these collection systems will have to be as easy to understand and operate as our existing one-way distribution methods.

Quality in many forms clearly is critical to customer satisfaction and therefore must have a high priority with management. The challenge for managers will be to identify or develop systems that can be successfully implemented and sustained within the existing business culture.

Building Relationships One of the most important aspects of the current new way of looking at marketing is the emphasis that many companies now have on the development of relationships with customers. There is a growing appreciation for the fact that it costs a company a great deal more to attract a new customer than it does to keep an existing customer happy. Therefore, we have seen a change in emphasis away from getting customers and toward keeping customers. In fact, some authors have suggested that in the future marketers must pay increasing attention to the "four Rs" of marketing: relationships, retention, referrals, and recovery.[21] In this new way of thinking, marketers will stress building relationships with customers who will generate long-term profits for the company, developing strategies that will keep them satisfied so that they will stay with the company, and creating strategies that will deal with recovering from problems and mistakes when they occur. As the following box reflects, there is a considerable difference between this new way of looking at marketing and what has been practised in the past.

Also pressured by the desire for short-term results, business-to-business marketers have emphasized immediate sales over the development of relationships. However, as in the examples above, the situation appears to be changing. Firms have discovered that it costs several times more to get a new customer than to keep an existing one. So, in both consumer and business-to-business marketing, there has been an increased recognition of the value of relationship building and customer retention. The question is, will it spread throughout all businesses?

One final issue that should be addressed concerns the type of relationship that a company should establish with its customers. There are some who believe that having a customer's name in a database and sending him or her regular mailings constitutes a relationship. But a genuine relationship that will last a long time requires the company to demonstrate a sincere interest in the customer and in his or her well-being — not really different from those factors that contribute to relationships between people.[22]

Old Marketing Model	New Marketing Model
• Focus on the product.	• Focus on process for serving customers.
• Define the target group.	• Feed and nourish the relationship.
• Set brand objectives.	• Extend respect and value to customers.
• Opportunity comes from analysis.	• Opportunity comes from synergy.
• Focus on brand benefit.	• Develop and refresh relevance.
• Create strategic advertising.	• Open the doors for dialogue.
• Operate against a brand plan.	• Improvise to sustain the relationship.
• Driven by a marketing group.	• A pervasive interdisciplinary attitude.

Source: John Dalla Costa, "Towards a Model Relationship," *Marketing*, June 27, 1994, p. 12. Reprinted with permission.

Summary

In addition to the financial analysis of marketing performance discussed in Chapter 23, a firm's marketing performance should also be appraised from a broad, societal perspective. Thus, evaluating an organization's marketing efforts must consider how well it satisfies the wants of its target customers, meets its own needs, and serves the best interests of society.

Marketing has been attacked for being exploitative, inefficient, and illegal, and for stimulating unwholesome demand. There are specific allegations of wrongdoing in all four areas of the marketing mix. Many criticisms of marketing are valid. However, the offensive behaviour is confined to a small minority of all marketers, and some of the criticism is based on issues that are more complicated than they first appear.

Efforts to address marketing abuses have come from consumers, government, and business. Consumerism — protests against perceived institutional injustices and efforts to remedy them — has had a significant impact on business behaviour. Consumer responses to marketing problems have included protests, political activism, and support of special-interest groups. Conditions that provide an impetus for widespread consumerism — sensitivity to social and environmental concerns, and the willingness to become actively involved — are present today. Government at the federal, provincial, and local levels enforces consumer-protection legislation. Businesses have responded to criticism by improving communications, providing more and better information, upgrading products, and producing more sensitive advertising.

Ethical behaviour is the best remedy for the charges against marketing. Many organizations have established codes of conduct to help employees behave ethically. However, it is not possible to have a rule for every situation. Managers can use a form of cost–benefit analysis to evaluate the ethics of alternatives. Another method of judging the ethics of a particular act is to ask three questions: Would I do this to a friend? Would I be willing to have this done to me? Would I be embarrassed if this action were publicized nationally? Besides being morally correct, ethical behaviour by organizations can restore public confidence, avoid government regulation, retain the power granted by society, and protect the image of the organization.

Prospects for the future of marketing are reflected in projected changes in consumer demographics, shifts in values, and the expansion of information. Marketers will react to these and other changes, but they will also have to make some basic strategic adjustments to compete in the twenty-first century. Among the needed adjustments are instilling a market-driven orientation, adopting a global orientation, better understanding key concepts like value, emphasizing quality and satisfaction, and retaining customers by building relationships.

Key Terms and Concepts

Basis for evaluating performance (587)
Nature of marketing criticisms (588)
Responses to marketing issues (590)
Consumerism (590)
Ethics (595)
Reasons for ethical behaviour (596)
Social responsibility (597)
Green marketing (600)
Market fragmentation (602)
Niche marketing (602)
Reconsumption (605)

Questions and Problems

1. Can all the criticisms of marketing be dismissed on the basis of critics' being poorly informed or acting in their own interest?
2. Some people believe there are too many fast-food outlets in their communities. Suggest a method for reducing the number of these outlets.
3. React to the following criticisms of advertising:
   a. It costs too much.
   b. It is in bad taste.
   c. It is false and deceptive.
   d. It creates monopolies.
4. What proposals do you have for regulating advertising to reduce the occurrence of false or misleading claims?
5. What specific recommendations do you have for reducing the cost of advertising?
6. What information do you think should be included in ads for each of the following goods or services?
   a. Snack foods.
   b. Basketball shoes.
   c. Nursing homes.
   d. Credit cards.
7. What are the social and economic justifications for "paternalistic" laws such as seat-belt regulations and warnings on cigarette packages and alcoholic beverage containers?
8. Discuss some ethical implications of the fact that many companies today are able to obtain considerable volumes of data about consumers and what they buy, and other information that some consumers may wish to keep confidential. What are reasonable boundaries on the use of such information for marketing purposes?
9. Describe a firm whose behaviour toward its customers reflects, in your opinion, the adoption of a customer-focused strategy.
10. Within the overall college and university student segment, describe a smaller or fragmented market segment that you believe exists.
11. What does global marketing have in common with domestic marketing?
12. Describe how you interact with a business or other organization with which you feel you have a positive relationship.

Hands-On Marketing

1. Examine the following items:
   a. A snack-food package.
   b. An owner's manual for a power tool.
   c. An apartment lease.
   d. A credit card application.
   What information does each contain that would be helpful to a consumer in making a purchase decision? How clearly is the information presented? What additional information would be useful?
2. Ask the managers of three firms in the same industry:
   a. What foreseeable developments will have the greatest impact on marketing in their industry over the next five years.
   b. How they think the industry should respond to the developments.

Case 7-1

W.K. BUCKLEY LIMITED (B)

It was the early summer of 1990, and a decision had to be made soon concerning the advertising approach to be used to promote Buckley's Mixture to the Canadian public during the 1990–91 "cough and cold" season. Frank Buckley and John Meehan realized that the advertising strategy adopted in 1985 had been very successful, contributing to dramatic increases in the sales of Buckley's Mixture. But the advertising that featured Frank Buckley and drew attention to the "awful" taste of the product had now been used for five seasons. While sales continued to increase, the management team at W.K. Buckley Limited wondered how much longer this advertising campaign would continue to work. Was 1990 the year when a new approach should be considered?

Buckley's Mixture Advertising

"It tastes awful. And it works." In 1984, Frank Buckley and his management team at W.K. Buckley Limited accepted the recommendation of its advertising agency and decided to use this simple yet honest advertising statement for their most important product, Buckley's Mixture. Since then, it has become a widely recognized and successful marketing slogan and has helped Buckley's Mixture increase its market share in the cough and cold remedy category. In the year ending February 1990, a time when the market for cold remedies had slipped by 2 percent, Buckley's Mixture had enjoyed a 16 percent increase in market share.

W.K. Buckley Limited is a privately owned Canadian company, founded in 1920 by William Buckley. The founder's son, Frank Buckley, joined the company in 1946 and is current owner and president. Primarily known for its flagship product, Buckley's Mixture, W.K. Buckley Limited also manufactures and distributes a variety of other cough and cold products, as well as a veterinary line. The Buckley product line includes Jack & Jill cough syrup, Buckley's White Rub, and Lemon Time. W.K. Buckley Limited operates in Canada, the United States, and the Caribbean and has products marketed under licensing agreements in the Netherlands, Australia, and New Zealand.

First introduced by William Buckley from his Toronto corner drugstore in 1919, Buckley's Mixture became a household name in the 1930s and 1940s, especially in rural areas of western Canada. Its sales were enhanced in the early years by the innovative use of advertising. Extensive promotion in the form of radio advertisements have been key to the success of Buckley's Mixture. Having realized the power of advertising in the consumer marketplace, major international pharmaceutical companies began using aggressive marketing and advertising strategies in the 1970s. This fierce competition contributed to a decline in the market share enjoyed by Buckley's flagship product.

The 1984-85 Advertising Decision

The peak season for the liquid cough remedy market is September to April. Before the beginning of the 1984–85 season, W.K. Buckley Limited appointed a new advertising agency, Ambrose, Carr, DeForest & Linton Limited (later to become Ambrose Carr Linton Kelly, Inc.) to co-ordinate the advertising programs for its products. Following its initial review of the W.K. Buckley account, the agency recommended marketing research to facilitate the definition of target market segments. For the 1984–85 season, on the advice of the new advertising agency, the company did not launch an advertising campaign, but undertook extensive research into the Canadian cough and cold remedy market.

From this research, five key problems became apparent. For Buckley's Mixture there was:

1. low top-of-mind awareness,
2. low rate of trial,

 This case was written by Leanne O'Leary and James G. Barnes of Memorial University of Newfoundland. The case was prepared with the co-operation and permission of W.K. Buckley Limited to illustrate the marketing initiatives of that company and not to indicate a correct or incorrect approach to the solution of marketing problems. The authors acknowledge the co-operation and support of Frank C. Buckley, president, John J. Meehan, vice-president, and David Rieger, manager of sales and marketing, of W.K. Buckley Limited, and Jackie Robertson of Ambrose Carr Linton Kelly, Inc., in the preparation of this case.

3. low awareness of its strength and effectiveness,
4. perception of it being old-fashioned,
5. negative perception of its taste, aroma, and texture.

Faced with a decreasing market share for Buckley's Mixture, the advertising agency decided that a different approach was required for the 1985–86 season. On the recommendation of Ambrose Carr, Frank Buckley took an unusual approach in promoting Buckley's Mixture. The agency recommended the use of radio and *Reader's Digest* as the chosen media for the season. The "It tastes awful. And it works" campaign actually drew attention to what some would consider a negative feature of Buckley's Mixture, its taste. The agency described this approach as an attempt to get away from the sameness of many ads that accentuate the positives and praise a product's good points. The objective was to draw attention to the advertisements and create a greater awareness of the product. Frank Buckley, the company's president, was to be featured in the advertisements to develop the concept of established effectiveness and trustworthiness. The agency proposed that Frank Buckley would represent an honest businessman who believed in his product and its attributes and was therefore willing to promote it straight, without gimmicks to hide its awful taste.

Traditionally, the market for Buckley's Mixture was in rural areas and in the lower-income segment (less than $30,000 annual household income). While the maintenance and development of this current market segment was important, its definition left a large nonuser market that could now be targeted. Based on market research conducted by the agency for W.K. Buckley Limited, the primary target group was redefined to be men aged 18 to 34 and, secondarily, women in the same age category, living in markets of more than 100,000 in Ontario only. The secondary target group remained adults aged 49 and older, living in markets with populations under 30,000. Although W.K. Buckley Limited was operating on a very limited advertising budget, both groups were targeted during the first year of the campaign. (See W.K. Buckley Limited [A] for a review of the 1984–85 marketing research and the recommended advertising strategy.)

Advertising Campaigns: 1985–86 to 1989–90

For the 1985–86 advertising season, two radio commercials were produced, featuring lyrics promoting Buckley's Mixture with accompanying music and sung to the tune of a popular song. These were tested with fifteen people from the target group (ages 18–34). Most liked the style of music (soft rock), found the lyrics interesting, and felt it was successful in encouraging listeners to try the product. The favourable reaction to these commercials was based on the appeal of using a song for advertising, rather than an announcer's voice. Respondents claimed that the terms "rot your socks," "strong taste," and "make you swoon" were creative in describing the taste of Buckley's Mixture and in catching the listener's attention. These commercials were subsequently launched in the Golden Horseshoe region of Toronto and southern Ontario.

Accompanying the product advertising campaign in the 1985–86 season was promotional support for new packaging for Buckley's Mixture. This represented the first package modification for the product in eight years. The new Buckley's Mixture package, although still available in 100 mL and 200 mL sizes, highlighted its sugar-free attribute. Advertisements ran in both English and French in *Reader's Digest* (see Exhibit 1).

During the 1986–87 season, transit advertisements were used extensively on a national basis. The transit campaign employed the same creative direction as the 1985–86 print campaign, with the reassurance that Buckley's Mixture is the same dependable product that Canadians had known since the 1920s. These advertisements featured Frank Buckley and used quotes such as, "I have recurring nightmares in which someone gives me a taste of my own medicine" and "I'm dedicated to ensuring that every new batch of Buckley's tastes as bad as the last" (see Exhibit 2). The main objectives for that season were to create consumer awareness of the Buckley's Mixture name, to increase awareness of the new package, and to retain trust in the brand as an effective, reliable product. National magazines *TV Guide* and *TV Hebdo* were used for the print component of the campaign (see Exhibit 3).

EXHIBIT 1 Buckley's Mixture Print Advertisement, 1985–86

WE'VE HAD A FACELIFT. BUT OUR PERSONALITY IS JUST AS NASTY AS EVER.

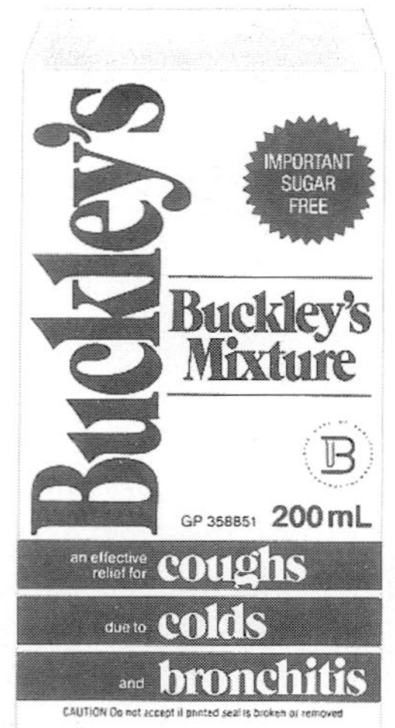

Most people who choose Buckley's Mixture will agree on two things. It tastes strong. It works hard. So the Buckley's Mixture you buy today is the same Buckley's Mixture that has been helping relieve coughs due to colds for 65 years.

The only thing we've changed is our package, so it will be easier to spot on the shelf. And that's good. Because the sooner you spot it, the sooner you can start to get rid of that nasty cough that comes with a cold.

W.K. Buckley Limited. A Canadian company.

EXHIBIT 3 Buckley's Mixture Print Advertisement, 1986–87

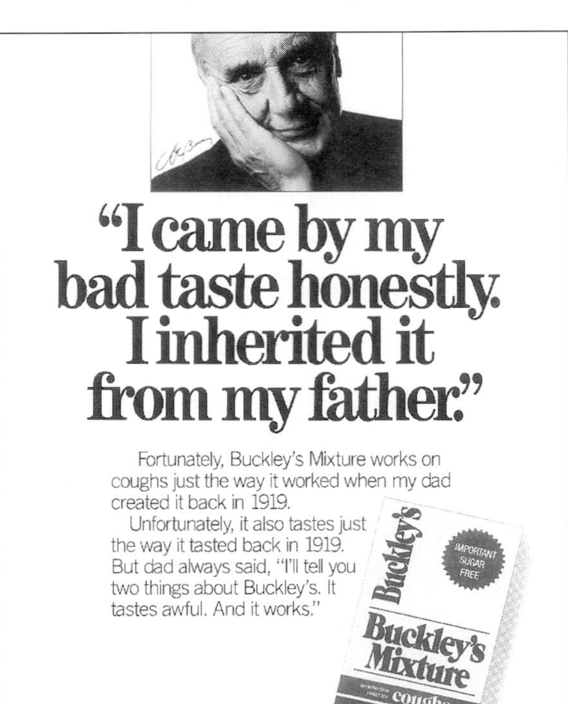

EXHIBIT 2 Buckley's Mixture Transit Advertisement, 1986–87

"I came by my bad taste honestly. I inherited it from my father."

Fortunately, Buckley's Mixture works on coughs just the way it worked when my dad created it back in 1919. Unfortunately, it also tastes just the way it tasted back in 1919. But dad always said, "I'll tell you two things about Buckley's. It tastes awful. And it works."

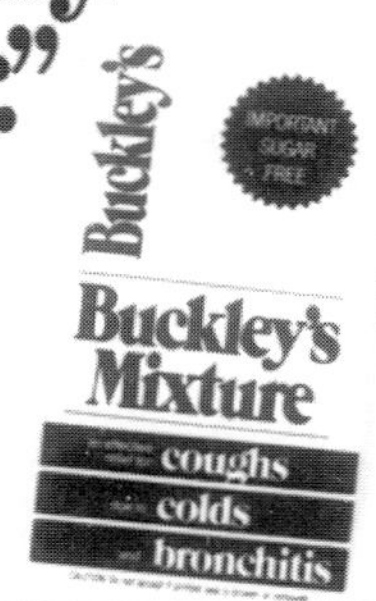

A television campaign was also initiated in Atlantic Canada in 1986–87, featuring a single commercial with a sea captain. It was felt that the association between the cold sea and coughs and colds would be appropriate to appeal to consumers in the Atlantic provinces.

This increased awareness also provided a foundation for the introduction of the "Buckley's DM" (Dextromethorphan) product. This addition to the Buckley's line was projected for a 1987–88 launch, but was postponed for a year because of product stability problems.

Transit advertising was continued for the 1987–88 season, as it provided good reach and high frequency with the target group and presented a strong visual advertising message. Preparing for the upcoming announcement of the DM product, Buckley's redefined the target market to include higher-income groups, as they were felt to represent the greatest sales opportunity for DM products. The 1987–88 transit ads were similar to those used during the previous year, with a picture of Frank Buckley and quotes such as "Four of the most dreaded words in the English language: Get out the Buckley's" and "Since 1919 we've been leaving Canadians with a bad taste in their mouths" (see Exhibit 4). The print advertising was continued in *TV Guide* and *TV Hebdo*, and the television campaign was used again in the Atlantic provinces.

In the 1988–89 season, Buckley's DM was introduced. This product was identical to the original Buckley's Mixture except it had added Dextromethorphan Hydrobromide (DM), an antitussive used for fast-acting suppression of a nonproductive cough. DM products, although new to the Buckley product line, had been on the market for several years and were well known to consumers. Transit ads were used, which now promoted the DM product (see Exhibit 5).

W.K. Buckley's advertising agency, Ambrose Carr Linton Kelly, believed that interior transit was an efficient, strategically correct medium for reaching the target group. During this season, radio was used for the first time in three years and television was introduced as a new medium for Buckley's advertising. Commercials on radio featured Frank Buckley describing the taste of Buckley's Mixture and referring to its effectiveness (see Exhibit 6). These were run in major urban markets across the country. The campaign also involved regional efforts that were customized for regional market segments. For example, the television campaign in Atlantic Canada was continued in 1988–89.

For the 1989–90 season, W.K. Buckley Limited expanded the advertising campaign by using television in the Toronto region for the first time. Commercials were aired nine times a week for four weeks on a Buffalo, N.Y., station that beamed its signal into the Toronto area. These commercials featured Frank Buckley, seated in a chair, holding a package of Buckley's Mixture. He explained in a lighthearted way how awful Buckley's tastes but

EXHIBIT 4 Buckley's Mixture Transit Advertisement 1987-88

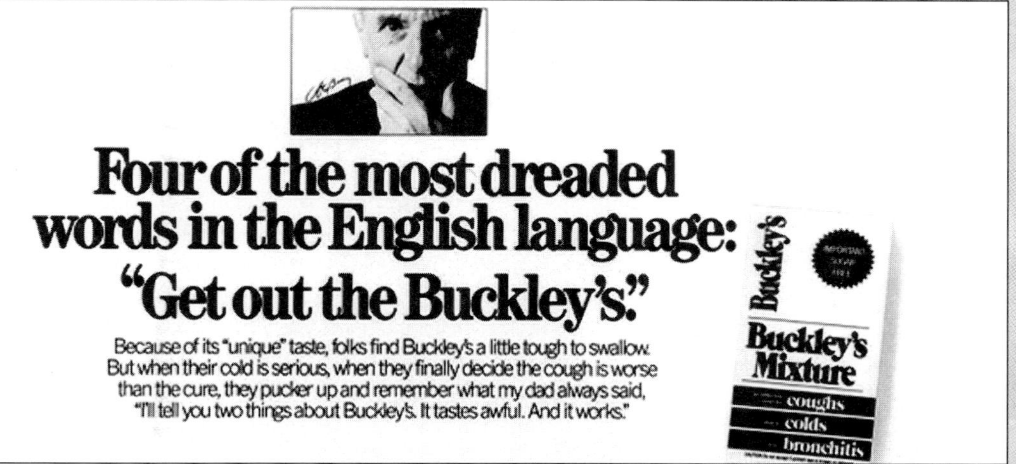

EXHIBIT 5 Buckley's DM Mixture Transit Advertisement, 1988–89

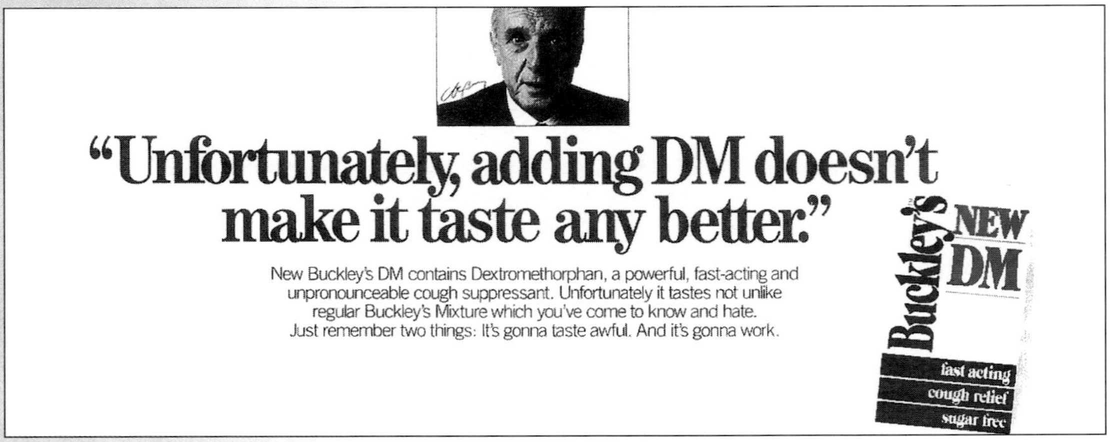

how effectively it works. These TV commercials were also aired in the Atlantic provinces and featured a similar dialogue to the radio commercials, which were run in major markets across the country. The budget allocated to transit advertising was increased and aimed at a better-educated group. "It contains oil of pine needles. What did you expect it to taste like?" was one of the advertising slogans created for the campaign that demonstrates the continued focus on the actual attributes of Buckley's Mixture (see Exhibit 7).

EXHIBIT 6 Buckley's Mixture Radio Commercial Scripts 1988–89 and 1989–90

Dedicated

Hi, I'm Frank Buckley, and I'm dedicated to ensuring that every batch of Buckley's Mixture tastes as bad as the last. You see, back in 1919 when my dad developed Buckley's Mixture, he used only ingredients that would make Buckley's Mixture provide fast, effective relief from coughs due to colds. He didn't particularly care how the stuff tasted. So just remember two things about Buckley's Mixture. It's going to taste awful and it's going to work.

Nightmares

Hi, I'm Frank Buckley, and I have recurring nightmares in which someone gives me a taste of my own medicine. That medicine is Buckley's Mixture. Now, I'd be the first one to admit Buckley's Mixture has a taste that will rot your socks. But when you've got a nasty cough due to a cold, close your eyes, brace yourself, and remember just two things. It's going to taste awful and it's going to work.

Honestly

My name is Frank Buckley and I came by my bad taste honestly. I inherited it from my father. Back in 1919 he developed Buckley's Mixture. Buckley's Mixture became known for two things, how well it worked and how badly it tasted. But 69 years later, when folks have a cough due to a cold or bronchitis, they pucker up and remember what Dad always said about Buckley's Mixture. It's going to taste awful and it's going to work.

1919

Hi, I'm Frank Buckley for Buckley's Mixture. My father came up with Buckley's Mixture back in 1919. About the same time my folks came up with me. Back then, people expected medicine to taste like . . . well, medicine. So, to be real honest, it tastes real bad. But if you do have a nasty hacking cough, but don't have time to pamper it, try Buckley's Mixture. Just remember two things. It tastes awful and it works.

Surprise

Hi, I'm Frank Buckley for Buckley's Mixture. If you've never tried Buckley's Mixture before, you're going to be very surprised, twice. You'll be surprised at how quickly and effectively Buckley's relieves the nastiest coughs due to colds, bronchitis, and even smoker's cough. But, just before you're surprised by how effective Buckley's Mixture is, you'll be very surprised by how it tastes. Buckley's Mixture, it tastes awful and it works.

EXHIBIT 7 Buckley's Mixture Transit Advertisement, 1989–90

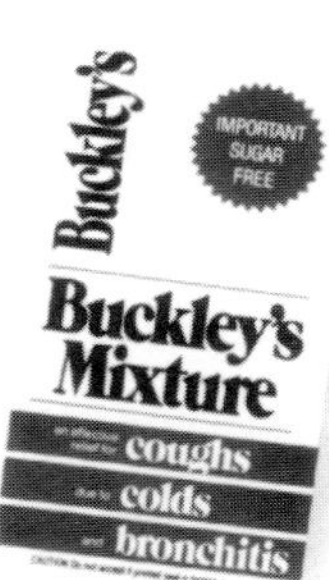

Exhibit 8 contains a detailed overview of the advertising budget allocations at W.K. Buckley Limited for the years from 1983 to 1990. The chart details the season, media used, market and target group, and the allocated budget.

Marketing Research

Marketing research remained an essential component of the marketing program at W.K. Buckley Limited. In 1988, with the objective of acquiring further information about the consumer of Buckley's Mixture, the company distributed 10,680 survey cards to purchasers in packages of Buckley's Mixture. Although the cards were distributed only in Ontario, among the 357 replies were some cards returned by purchasers from other provinces and two from the United States.

Some of the more significant information from this research came in the form of demographics. Fifty-five percent of purchasers who returned survey cards were aged over forty and 30 percent were over sixty. In addition, 26 percent were retired and 19 percent were homemakers, with only 8 percent at the white-collar or executive level. The most common annual household income mentioned by those who returned cards was $20,000 or less (36 percent), while 53 percent made less than $30,000.

Nearly half the respondents had been using Buckley's Mixture for more than ten years (49 percent) and only 22 percent had used it for two years or less. The "sugar-free" factor was important to 69 percent, while 14 percent were not aware of it. In addition, only 7 percent first became aware of Buckley's Mixture through advertisements (either bus, subway, or radio), while 61 percent learned of the product through friends or family. Ninety percent liked it most because of its effectiveness, 39 percent for its strength, and 7 percent actually liked the taste.

A qualitative study was conducted in 1989 to determine the public's attitudes toward Buckley's Mixture and the advertising approach for the brand. Three focus group interviews were conducted by Ambrose Carr Linton Kelly. Two extended groups were conducted, lasting two and one half hours. One of these groups contained current Buckley's users, the other nontriers of the brand. The third focus group consisted of one half triers and one half nontriers. This group discussion lasted three and one half hours.

Each group discussed exposure to other Buckley's products, the DM mixture, and price sensitivity in the market. The research concluded that a strong advertising foundation was being built on the message of honesty and efficacy, which is delivered in a humorous approach by Frank Buckley. In addition, it was found that Mr. Buckley successfully projects the strength of traditional values (honesty and sincerity) and also appears to be a contemporary businessman who understands today's needs. Participants concluded

EXHIBIT 8 Advertising Overview — Buckley's Mixture

Year	Media	Market	Target Group	Execution	Budget
1983/84	Radio	National excluding Atlantic Canada	Adult 39+, Rural	N/A	$228,000
	Television	Atlantic Canada	Adults 18–44	N/A	$22,000
1984/85	1 Year Advertising Hiatus for Market Research				
1985/86	Radio	Southern Ontario Ontario	Men 18–34 (Vicks users) (secondary: women 18-34) Urban 100M+ population Household income <$30M Education: high school or less	All I Want [:60] Feelin' Low [:60]	$172,000
	Magazine *Reader's Digest*	National Markets	Adults 49+ (Buckley's users) Under 30M population Household income <$30M High school and less	We've Had a Facelift (E&F)	$74,000
	Trade Brochure Developed for sales force and Shelf Talker				
1986/87	Interior Transit	National English only	Adults 18–44 (Triaminic DM users) Married, no children Urban 100M+ population Clerical or labourer	I have recurring nightmares. . . I'm dedicated to ensuring. . . I came by my bad taste. . .	$151,000
	Magazine *TV Guide/* *TV Hebdo*	National English/French		We've Had a Facelift I came by my bad taste. . .	$85,000
	Television	Atlantic Canada	Adults 18–44	Sea Captain	$19,000
1987/88*	Interior Transit	National English/French	Adults 18–44 Married, with/without children Urban 100M+ population Household income $30M+	Since 1919. . . Four of the Most. . .	$134,000
	Magazine	National		I came by my bad taste. . .	$77,000
	Trade Magazine	National — English	Pharmacists/ Drugstore owners	Here's Your Chance. . .	$10,000
	Television	Atlantic Canada		Sea Captain	$24,000
1988/89	Transit	National English/French	Adults 18–49 Household income $25M+ Average education Urban 100M+ population	Sometimes Just the Right. . . Unfortunately, adding DM. . .	$171,000
	Radio	Major Markets		Dedicated [:30] Nightmares [:30] Honesty [:30]	$186,000
	Television	Atlantic Canada		Sea Captain	$30,000
1989/90	Transit	National English/French	Adults 18+ Household income $25M+ High school education+ Professional	It contains oil of pine. . . How bad does it taste. . .	$193,000
	Radio	Major Markets		1919 [:30] Surprise [:30]	$223,000
	Television	Atlantic Canada Toronto spill (WUTV Buffalo)		1919 [:30] Surprise [:30]	$40,000 $5,000

* Buckley's Mint Flavour DM was scheduled for market introduction in 1987, but a decision was made not to launch because of problems with product instability.

Percentage of Total Sales of Buckley's Mixture

	Year to Date January 1989 (%)	Year to Date January 1988 (%)	Regional Change (%)
Atlantic Provinces	14.3	13.7	+22.6
Quebec	8.8	9.3	+13.0
Ontario	36.6	38.4	+13.0
Manitoba/Saskatchewan	11.9	12.5	+13.1
Alberta	17.8	13.9	+52.1
British Columbia	10.5	12.1	+ 2.8
Total	100.0	100.0	+18.5

that, as a brand spokesperson, he is an honest champion of a product he believes in. The discussions concluded that the message was delivered most strongly in the transit medium, as the consumer could visually fit Frank Buckley's style to their expectations. Participants felt that the image tended to lose a little of its impact on radio, as the advertisement moves faster and is filled with more detail than most feel was necessary. However, participants did believe that radio was a "logical" extension to the transit ads and the message was clearly understood by listeners.

Research participants were open to the idea of advertising for Buckley's Mixture on television and radio, expecting the same relaxed but confident presentation. They felt that future advertising, particularly on radio, should portray a softer-spoken, slower-paced, less professional voice. The message communicated should concentrate on heightened efficacy (i.e., bronchitis, serious coughs) and reference to the taste should be softened somewhat. The study revealed that the participants were also receptive to the use of other settings and new generations of the Buckley family.

When questioned about Buckley's DM, few participants in the group interviews were aware of it. Many did not understand the difference between the original Buckley's Mixture and the DM product. Others were concerned that an addition of another ingredient would take away Buckley's "natural" image and would contradict some of the advertising. However, some felt it showed that W.K. Buckley Limited was "keeping up with the times."

The sales of Buckley's Mixture have improved markedly since the launch of the "Tastes Awful" advertising campaign. Some areas of the country are more responsible for the sales increase than are others. Ontario, Alberta, and the Atlantic provinces account for almost 70 percent of the sales of Buckley's Mixture. Alberta and the Atlantic provinces have accounted for the largest sales increases in recent years. Consistent with historic results, Quebec has had very low sales compared with the size of its market.

Qualitative research conducted for Ambrose Carr by CRT Information Services involved creative testing of Buckley's Mixture transit advertisements. The research involved personal, in-depth interviews with thirteen English-speaking and thirteen French-speaking respondents. Among the French-speaking respondents, the "bad taste" emphasis and its communication were not perceived to be particularly humorous and had a negative effect on the desire to purchase. This response interfered with the perception of Buckley's Mixture as an efficient product. Also, the word "mixture" in French does not properly communicate the fact that the product is a cough syrup. These factors, as well as difficulty encountered in the consumers' ability to remember the name Buckley's, created very low stimulation to purchase in the Quebec market.

The 1990–91 Campaign

The time had come to decide on the advertising campaign for Buckley's Mixture for the 1990–91 season. Frank Buckley and vice-president John Meehan felt the company should give considerable thought to its future advertising efforts. The "Tastes Awful" campaign had been a great success, contributing to increased awareness of Buckley's Mixture and large increases in market share. Both Mr. Buckley and Mr.

Meehan agreed that some of the key points that must be conveyed in advertising include:

- Buckley's Mixture is a natural product with no artificial flavours or sugar, and
- the product has enjoyed a good established name since 1919.

In addition to the development of an advertising campaign for the upcoming season, the Buckley's management team had established several business objectives for the coming year. The company is aiming to build awareness and interest in Buckley's Mixture, to increase the trial of its products, while increasing sales by 5 percent real growth during the year and market share by 10 percent by 1991–92. The achievement of these marketing goals would occur while maintaining profitability at current levels.

Since Buckley's Mixture is W.K. Buckley's best-known product, it is expected to lead the way in meeting these objectives. Recognizing that users of Buckley's Mixture are very brand loyal, Frank Buckley and John Meehan agreed that the best way to increase sales would be to attract new users.

Questions

1. Evaluate the advertising strategy, use of budget, and media allocation used to promote Buckley's Mixture during the period from 1983 to 1990.
2. Recognizing the history of the Buckley's product line and the corporate goals established by W.K. Buckley Limited, what approach should be taken for promoting Buckley's Mixture in 1990–91?
3. Should Mr. Buckley and Mr. Meehan consider making a major change in the advertising strategy? Why?
4. What approach can W.K. Buckley Limited take to gain increased market share in Quebec?

Case 7-2

ETHICAL DILEMMAS IN BUSINESS-TO-BUSINESS SALES

The following were actual situations experienced by the case writer during more than fifteen years in business-to-business sales and sales management. The names of firms and individuals have been disguised due to the nature of the material in this case.

Halco Manufacturing

Dave MacDonald was excited when he got the unexpected phone call from Nicki Steele, a senior buyer from Halco Manufacturing.

"I know it's a year since we bought that prototype reel from you, but we just got a contract from the government to build ten more bear traps and we desperately need to hold our price on these units. Could you possibly sell us ten new reels at the same price you charged last year?" Nicki inquired.

"I'll see what I can do and call you back today," Dave replied.

Dave immediately retrieved the file from the previous year and saw that they had supplied the reel for $6,990 f.o.b. the customer's warehouse. There was a breakdown of the pricing on the file:

Manufacturer's list price	$4,000.00
Special engineering charge (25%)	1,000.00
Total list price	5,000.00
Distributor discount (20%)	1,000.00
Distributor net cost	4,000.00
Estimated currency exchange (8%)	320.00
Estimated duty ($22\frac{1}{2}$%)	972.00
Estimated freight	245.00
Estimated brokerage	55.00
Estimated distributor cost, f.o.b. destination	5,592.00
Mark-up (25%)	1,398.00
Selling Price, f.o.b. destination	$6,990.00

There were some notes on the file that Dave reviewed. The reel was designed as part of a "bear trap" on Canadian navy ships. These bear traps would hook onto helicopters in rough weather and haul them safely onto landing pads on the ship decks. The reel was really a model SM heavy-duty steel mill reel, except some of the exposed parts were to be made of stainless steel to provide longer life in the salt water atmosphere. There was a special engineering charge on the reel as it was a nonstandard item that had to be specially engineered. The manufacturer had suggested at the time it quoted that Dave could keep the full 20 percent discount as it thought there was only one other manufacturer capable of building this unit, and its price would likely be much higher.

When Dave got a price from the manufacturer on the 10 new units, he was surprised they quoted a price of only $3,200 each, less 40/10 percent instead of the 20 percent that was given on the original reel.

As Dave estimated his cost, things got better. The original reel was imported from the United States at $22\frac{1}{2}$ percent duty as "not otherwise provided for manufacturers of iron or steel, tariff item 44603-1." In the interim, the company Dave worked for got a duty remission on series SM steel mill reels as "machinery of a class or kind not manufactured in Canada, tariff item 42700-1" and the duty was remitted (and the savings supposedly passed on to the end customer). The currency exchange rate also improved in Dave's favour, and the estimated freight and brokerage charges per unit dropped considerably because of the increased shipment size. Dave estimated his new cost as follows:

Manufacturer's list price	$3,200.00
Distributor discount (40/10%)	1,472.00
Distributor net cost	1,728.00
Estimated currency exchange (2%)	35.00
Estimated duty (remitted)	0.00
Estimated freight	85.00
Estimated brokerage	14.50
Estimated distributor cost, f.o.b. destination	$1,862.50

Now that he had all the figures, Dave had to decide what the selling price should be to his customer.

Crown Pulp and Paper Ltd.

Bill Siddall had been promoted to the position of salesperson, and he was pleased when he received an order for nearly $10,000 for stainless steel fittings from the new pulp mill being built in his territory. Unfortunately, he quoted a price that was 40 percent below his cost.

"We have to honour the price quoted," Bill insisted.

"I know if you let me talk to Rory, he'll let us raise the price," replied Dave MacDonald, the sales manager. "Rory used to be the purchasing agent at one of my best accounts before he came to the mill."

"No. You gave me responsibility for this account, and I want to build a good relationship with Rory myself. He gave us the order over two weeks ago. He can't change suppliers now, because it would be unfair. Since this is our first order, I would like to supply it without any problems. We'll get back the money we lost on this order many times if we can get their future business. This material is needed for a small construction job, and they haven't even started to consider their stores inventory yet."

After much discussion, it was agreed that the order would stand, but Dave would call the fitting manufacturer's sales manager, Chuck Knowles, as the two men were good friends.

"We need some help on that last order we placed with you. Bill sold it at 40 percent below our cost," said Dave.

"How could that happen?" Chuck seemed amazed.

"Well," replied Dave, "you give us a 25 percent distributor discount and we gave 10 percent to the customer due to the size of the order. What we forgot was to double the list price because the customer wanted schedule 80 wall thickness on the fittings instead of standard schedule 40. This was Bill's first large inquiry and he made an honest mistake. He doesn't want me to get involved with the customer, and I don't want to force the issue with him, so I'm hoping you can help us on this one order. We expect to get a lot of business from this account over the next few years."

"I'll split the difference with you. What you're selling now for $0.90, you're paying $1.50 for, and if I give you an additional 20 percent discount, your cost will come down to $1.20. Can you live with that?" Chuck asked.

"It's a help. We appreciate it. We'll see you on your next trip to our territory, and I'll buy lunch."

"A deal. See you next month." The conversation ended.

When it was over, Dave went to the Brae Shore Golf Club. He was confident Rory would be there. Sure enough, at 8:00 A.M., Rory was scheduled to tee off. Dave sat on the bench at the first tee and waited for Rory to appear. Promptly, Rory arrived with Bob Arnold, one of his senior buyers. The three men greeted each other pleasantly, and Rory asked who Dave was waiting for.

"Just one of my neighbours. He was supposed to be here an hour ago, but I guess he won't show."

"Join us. We don't mind. Besides we might need a donation this fall when we have our company golf tournament. We'll invite you, of course, and we'll invite Bill if he plays golf."

"He doesn't play often, but he's pretty good. Beat me the last time we played. How is he doing at your mill? Is everything okay?" Dave asked.

"Checking up on him? Sure. He's fine. He made a mistake the other day when he went to see our millwright foreman without clearing it through my office first, but he'll learn. He'll do a lot of business with us because we want to buy locally where possible, and you have a lot of good product lines. I think he'll get along well with all of us as well. He seems a bit serious, but we'll break him in before long. We just gave him a big order for stainless fittings a few weeks ago, but we told him to visit at 10 o'clock next time and to bring the doughnuts."

"I know," replied Dave. "Unfortunately, we lost a lot of money on that order."

"Your price was very low. I couldn't understand it because I knew your material wasn't manufactured offshore. Did you quote the cheaper T304 grade of stainless instead of the T316 we use?"

"No. We quoted schedule 40 prices instead of schedule 80. The wall thickness for schedule 80 is twice as thick, and the price should have been double as well."

"Heck. Double the price. We'll pay it. I'll make a note on the file Monday. I know you're not trying to take us, and I can appreciate an honest mistake. At double the price, you might be a bit high, but you know we want to place the order with you anyway because you're local. Eventually we'll want you to carry some inventory for us, so we might just as well make sure we're both happy with this business."

Strait Structural Steel Ltd.

Dave MacDonald was sitting in the outer office waiting to see Stan Hope, the purchasing agent for Strait Structural Steel, a new account that had just begun operations in a remote, coastal location about 65 km from the nearest city. Stan had telephoned Dave the previous week and had an urgent request for four large exhaust fans that were required to exhaust welding fumes from enclosed spaces where welders were at work. The union had threatened to stop the project unless working conditions were improved quickly, and although Dave didn't sell fans at the time, he found a line of fans and negotiated a discount from the manufacturer, along with an agreement to discuss the further possibility of representing the fan manufacturer on a national basis.

When Stan gave the order to Dave for the fans, the two men discussed other products that Dave sold. Dave sold products for a company that was both a general-line and specialty-line industrial distributor. Included in the general-line products were such items as hand and power tools, cutting tools (drills, taps, dies), safety equipment, wire rope and slings, fasteners (nuts, bolts), and fittings (stainless steel, bronze, and carbon steel flanges, elbows, tees). Included in the specialty-line products were such items as electric motors and generators, motor controls, hydraulic and pneumatic valves and cylinders, rubber dock fenders, and overhead cranes. When the men finally met, they were almost instantly friends, and it was obvious that the opportunities for them to do further business were great. "One item that really interests me," said Stan, "is PTFE tape. We need some and we will be using a lot of it."

"We have the largest stock of PTFE tape in the country," replied Dave. "We import it directly from Italy, but it's high quality and is the same standard size as all others on the market — 1/20 wide, .0030 thick, and 4800 long. How much are you interested in?"

"Let's start with 400 rolls," Stan suggested.

PTFE tape was a white, nonadhesive tape that was used as a pipe thread sealant. It was wrapped around the threads of pipe or fittings before they were screwed together to make a leak-proof seal. The tape first came on the market in the late 1960s at prices as high as $3.60 per roll, but since then prices had dropped considerably. North American manufacturers were still selling the tape for list prices near $1.80 and were offering dealer discounts between 25 and 50 percent, depending on the quantities that dealers bought. Dave was importing the tape from Italy at a landed cost of $0.17 per roll.

"We have a standard price of $1 per roll as long as you buy 200 rolls," Dave offered.

"No question. You have an excellent price. How much would you charge M H Sales?"

"I don't know. Who is M H Sales?" asked Dave.

"A small industrial supply company located in my basement. The 'H' is for Hope. I share the company with Bruce Malcolm, the 'M,' and he's in purchasing at Central Power Corporation. M H Sales is a small company, and we are looking for additional products to sell. Between Strait Structural and Central Power, we could sell several thousand rolls of PTFE tape each year."

McCormick Gleason Limited

Dave MacDonald telephoned Clarey Stanley, a senior buyer at McCormick Gleason Limited. "Clarey, I'm calling about that quote we made on Lufkin tapes. Can we have your order?"

"Sorry. Your price was high. I gave the order to Ken Stafford. You need a sharper pencil."

"How much sharper?" Dave asked.

"I can't tell you that. But you were close," Clarey replied. "By the way, Kenny called me from the stores department this morning and he has a large shipment of electric relays that was delivered yesterday. They weren't properly marked, and he can't identify the ones with normally open contacts from the ones with normally closed contacts. Do you want them returned, or can someone see him and straighten it out here?"

"Tell him I'll see him immediately after lunch. I can tell them apart, and I'll see they get properly identified."

When the conversation ended, Dave made a note to see Clarey about the tapes. There was a problem somewhere. Dave knew his cost on Lufkin tapes was the lowest available, and he quoted 12 percent on cost because he really wanted the order. The order was less than $1,500, but it meant that Dave could place a multiple-case order on the manufacturer and get the lowest possible cost for all replacement inventory. That would increase the margin on sales to other customers who bought smaller quantities. There was no possibility that Stafford Industrial, a local, one-person, "out-of-the-basement" operation that bought Lufkin tapes as a jobber, not as a distributor, could match his price.

That afternoon, while waiting to see Ken MacKay, the stores manager, Dave noticed a carton from Stafford Industrial Sales being unloaded from a local delivery van. Although he knew that Stafford supplied quite a few maintenance, repair, and operating (MRO) supplies to this customer, Dave decided to play ignorant.

"What do you buy from Stafford Industrial?" he asked the young stores clerk who was handling the package.

Opening the carton, the clerk read the packing slip. "It says here we ordered 144 measuring tapes, 3/40 wide by 25 feet long."

"Are those things expensive?" Dave asked.

"Don't know. There's no price on the packing slip. Clarey Stanley in purchasing ordered them. You could talk to him." The clerk continued to unpack the shipment. As he did, Dave noticed the tapes were manufactured offshore and were of poor quality compared with the Lufkin tapes that he sold, and that he had quoted to Clarey Stanley the previous day.

"Aren't those supposed to be Lufkin tapes?" Dave asked.

"Not that I know. The packing slip just says tapes. Wait and I'll get our copy of the purchase order." The clerk went to a filing cabinet next to his desk and returned with a carbon copy of the purchase order. "No, it just says tapes. It doesn't specify any brand."

There was something wrong, and Dave was determined to get an answer.

Case 7-3

EVERDENE FOODS LIMITED

Introduction

"Well, based on all the analysis you have done to date, just what do you propose we do?" asked Beth Everdene, vice-president of marketing for Everdene Foods Limited, a company headquartered in Halifax. She was speaking to Dale Oake, Sandy Roberts, and Pat Densmore, senior consultants with J.D. Consulting Incorporated. Dale, Sandy, and Pat were about to deliver a major presentation to Ms. Everdene and three other senior managers of Everdene Foods. For the past three months, the consultants had been studying whether Everdene should launch a line of sweet goods in Atlantic Canada and, if so, how.

Company History

Everdene Foods Limited was established by Ezekiel Everdene (Beth's grandfather) in 1918. Mr. Everdene had been a chef in a large hotel, and at the age of twenty-seven had started to produce and market a line of bread products from his home. He offered his customers top-quality, always-fresh products, which were somewhat more expensive than similar products offered by competitors. But Mr. Everdene felt there was a segment of consumers who would always be willing to pay a premium for quality. He also invested considerable time and effort into building the family brand and creating distinctive packaging for his line of products. He was quoted as saying, "I want people to recognize the name and package of our products, and, regardless of whether they have previously purchased one of our products, associate the Everdene name with quality and freshness."

Between 1918 and 1959, Ezekiel Everdene served as president of Everdene Foods, cultivating the company into one of the top food products companies in Canada. In 1959, Ezekiel Everdene retired as president at the age of sixty-eight, passing the reins of the company to his daughter, Liddy, then twenty-six. In 1990, Liddy had hired her own daughter, Beth, as one of the company's four marketing managers. By 1994, Beth had risen to become vice-president of marketing for Everdene Foods.

Everdene Products and Branding Strategy

Since 1918, all Everdene product lines have proudly carried the Everdene name. Over the years, the consistently high quality and superior flavour found in all the company's products resulted in a high level of brand loyalty for Everdene. In fact, Everdene has become synonymous with premium-quality breads and bread products among adults all across Atlantic Canada. All Everdene products are quality guaranteed. Following are descriptions of the products Everdene produces and markets to supermarkets throughout Atlantic Canada. The company had 1995 revenues of approximately $120 million, with profits of approximately $25 million.

Everdene Breads Everdene's line of premium breads features rich, hearty, whole-grain bread varieties made from Ezekiel's original family recipes. This line of products is baked with care, using only the finest ingredients. Ongoing consumer and in-house testing ensures that each product lives up to the quality and freshness consumers have come to expect from Everdene Breads. Each product is made with no artificial preservatives and is cholesterol-free. The following bread varieties currently carry the Everdene Bread brand:

- Enriched White with Sesame Seeds
- Cracked Wheat with Honey
- Oatmeal with Molasses
- Raisin with Cinnamon
- Stone Ground 100% Whole Wheat
- Bran Bread

Everdene Rolls Everdene also carries a line of top-quality rolls. The major difference between Everdene rolls and some of the lower-end brands is their generous size and the use of the finest ingredients

---

This case is adapted from the original, which was written by Jennifer Hutchings and Darrin Howlett of Bristol Group, St. John's, Newfoundland. The company, characters, and figures in this case are fictional. The case is not meant to illustrate effective or ineffective handling of a management situation.

available, which produces a rich, home-made flavour. The following rolls are produced by Everdene:

- Pan Rolls (white pan and dinner rolls)
- Kaiser Buns
- Submarine Rolls (12" and 9")
- Deli Rolls

Everdene Buns The most recent addition to the Everdene family of products was Everdene buns — the company's line of hot dog and hamburger buns. As with Everdene rolls, these products are larger than regular buns, made to meet the size requirements of jumbo wieners, sausages, and hamburger patties. All products are topped with poppy seeds and enriched with the finest ingredients for superb flavour. The following items are carried in this line:

- Hamburger Buns (packages of 8 and 12)
- 60% Whole Wheat Hamburger Buns (8 per pack)
- Hot Dog Buns (packages of 8 and 12)
- 60% Whole Wheat Hot Dog Buns (8 per pack)

The Idea

In 1996, two of the marketing managers who worked under Beth — Ralph Foster and George LeGrow — had come to her with an idea for a new line* of products that Everdene might consider producing and marketing for the Atlantic Canadian marketplace: sweet goods (e.g., doughnuts, coffee cakes, pies). Both had told Beth of the success Canadian food manufacturers had been experiencing with sweet goods in the past ten years and that several signs indicated that there might be an opportunity for Everdene to market sweet goods in Atlantic Canada. They explained that there were twelve companies marketing sweet goods in Atlantic Canada, ten in the medium-quality segment and two in the premium segment. There had been three companies, all based in Ontario, serving the Atlantic region premium segment, but one company recently went bankrupt, owing to constant consumer complaints regarding product freshness.

"Beth, we both feel that this market might offer some potential for us, but Ralph's idea of how to best approach the market is quite different from mine, I'm afraid," said George. "Let each of us tell you our ideas and then we can discuss if and how we should pursue this opportunity," he continued. "Hold on a minute, George," interrupted Beth. "You know how things work around here. I'm not interested in hearing *opinions*. I have no problem with my managers coming to me to let me know of their ideas and the fact that they would like to investigate something further, but I don't like to make decisions based upon opinions and hunches. You both need to do some serious analysis before I decide on anything. I'm a little concerned that you both have different ideas on this market. In light of this, I suggest that you agree on an independent consulting firm who can do the analysis on each of your ideas. Then, early in the New Year, we'll have the consultants deliver their recommendations as to which, if either, of your ideas we should pursue."

The following day, Ralph and George hired J.D. Consulting Incorporated, one of the largest and most respected marketing consultancies in Atlantic Canada. During their first meeting with the consultants, Ralph and George explained their ideas. Ralph's proposal was that Everdene should launch a line of premium sweet goods in the region. George, on the other hand, was in favour of marketing a line of medium-quality sweet goods, for which he felt there was a large market.

The Task Ahead

"Well, we certainly have a lot of work ahead of us," said Sandy Roberts to the other J.D. consultants on October 2, 1996, the day after the company had been hired for the Everdene project. "Where do you propose we start?" asked Pat Densmore. "There's little doubt that we need to investigate how consumers view sweet goods," replied Dale Oake, "so I propose we organize some research to find out. While that is ongoing we also need to undertake secondary

* The term "line" denotes a group of products intended for essentially similar uses and possessing reasonably similar physical characteristics. In this case there are two product lines discussed: a premium line of sweet goods (comprised of strudels, coffee cakes, loaf cakes, pound cakes, muffins, biscuits, and sweet doughs), and a line of medium-quality sweet goods (comprised of cookies, pies, turnovers, and doughnuts).

research to get a thorough assessment of the sweet goods market, and speak with Everdene's employees to investigate the company's capabilities for sweet goods."

The Sweet Goods Market

One of the first tasks Dale, Sandy, and Pat had undertaken was to conduct some secondary research on the sweet goods market, paying particular attention to the Canadian market. They discovered that the sweet-goods market is quite developed in most parts of Canada. In 1995, sales of sweet goods in Canada totalled approximately $2.5 billion. The premium segment of the Canadian sweet goods market accounted for almost $400 million of these sales, the medium for over $800 million, and the low-quality segment accounted for the remainder. As shown in Table 1, there are many companies in the market, each with a different primary distribution channel.

In the past few years, Canadian sweet-goods manufacturers had been experiencing declining growth, owing to low growth in population, GDP, and inflation. (Atlantic Canada is faced with a similar population growth challenge. In 1996, there were 832,000 households in the region. This number is expected to grow by only 1 percent annually for each of the next five years.) Some Canadian industry experts felt that the best way for sweet-goods manufacturers to improve their performance was to increase market share and household consumption among the low- and medium-quality segments — to win more customers and encourage more sales per customer. Other insiders felt this to be an expensive strategy and had different ideas as to how such companies could ensure their profitability.

Focus Group Findings

Following their market review, the consultants had turned their attention to conducting research with consumers in the region. The qualitative component of the research took place in early November in the form of two focus groups in each of the Atlantic provinces. Between eight and twelve individuals who were the principal grocery shoppers in their household and were regular purchasers of sweet goods participated in each group. The main purpose of the sessions was to assist in the development of and to determine interest in a line of sweet goods in Atlantic Canada. This involved examining the frequency of sweet-goods consumption, how consumers view various sweet goods, branding issues, packaging issues, and what elements are important to sweet-goods consumers.

Who Eats Sweet Goods? What Products Do They Consume?

Focus group discussions had revolved around the most commonly consumed types of sweet goods: muffins, cookies, doughnuts, pies, biscuits, coffee cakes, sweet doughs, loaf cakes, pound cakes, strudels, and turnovers. The research concluded that

TABLE 1 Profile of Canadian Sweet-Goods Market

Segment	Number of Manufacturers Serving Canada	Number of Manufacturers Serving Atlantic Canada	Main Distribution Channel
Low-price/quality	35	18	• supermarkets • thrift stores • convenience stores
Medium-price/quality	20	10	• supermarkets • thrift stores • convenience stores • specialty stores
Premium	10	2*	• supermarkets • specialty stores

* Until recently, 3 manufacturers.

the sweet-goods market can be segmented into three major segments, as listed in Table 2.

In addition to the demographic differences, there are also some psychographic differences among the segments, as noted in Table 3.

From this analysis, it became obvious to Dale, Sandy, and Pat that Ralph's proposal was that Everdene should launch a line of sweet goods to market to Segment 1, the premium-quality-seeker segment, while George wished to launch a line of products that would cater to Segment 2, the value seekers: medium quality/price segment.

When Do People Purchase/ Consume Sweet Goods?

For most people, sweet goods are purchased on a weekly basis with their purchase of groceries, while some indicated they purchase certain items on a daily basis. The quantity of sweet goods purchased appears to be affected by seasonality. For example, some participants tend to buy more sweet goods during Christmas and the summer holidays.

The time of day at which sweet goods are consumed varies, depending on the type of sweet goods. Those products bought by Segment 1 are more likely to be consumed as breakfast foods, snacks during coffee breaks, or as dessert for special dinner occasions. Products appealing to Segment 2, however, are more likely to be packed in kids' lunch boxes or eaten as after-school snacks. They can also be enjoyed as after-dinner desserts for regular family meals.

The consumption of store-bought sweet goods is higher than that of home-made goods during the week because of a limited amount of preparation time available. These items are seen as being quick and easy snacks or meals because they are already prepared, making them easier to eat on the run. The incidence of baking the products at home is positively related to family size.

Where Do People Purchase Sweet Goods?

The type of outlet at which sweet goods are purchased depends on what people are planning to buy. For example, if the purchase is being made for family consumption, as is usually the case with the products bought by Segment 2, it is more likely to be bought at a grocery store or thrift store. Segment 2 products can also be purchased at convenience stores or at specialty stores. Research participants from Segment 1, however, indicated that if they were buying an item to serve to guests, they were more likely to buy it from stand-alone bakeries, since these stores have the image of being more expensive and providing more selection: places one would go for a treat. Segment 1 consumers indicated that they would primarily purchase at supermarkets.

Other Factors Influencing Sweet-Goods Consumption

In addition to the demographic and psychographic variables affecting the type of product people consume, several factors influence the specific products people buy. The choice of which specific sweet goods to purchase is an impulse decision. While most people plan to make a sweet-goods purchase, most do not decide specifically what they want until they are in the store. Therefore, in-store merchandising is very important. The purchase is less of an impulse decision for Segment 1 consumers, since they tend to look for specific brands.

Some of the factors influencing the brand of sweet goods that consumers buy include price, taste, freshness, flavour, moistness, abundance of ingredients, and the home-made look. The importance of each factor varies depending on occasion, type of product, and segment. For instance, the home-made look is important when serving a dessert to guests, which is more likely to occur with Segment 1 products. In fact, respondents indicated that they liked to see some slight imperfections in the product, or they liked to add a topping or sauce to a plain dessert to achieve the home-made look. The home-made look is most important to those interested in premium-quality products.

The research also concluded that Segment 1 consumers tend to be more brand loyal. They admitted that they were hesitant about trying a brand that they had never tried before. They would like to be assured of the quality before purchasing a product under a different brand name. Ways in which consumers can be ensured of a product's quality if it is an untried brand include being able to try the product and being able to touch, feel, or clearly view the product. While Segment 2 consumers also prefer

TABLE 2 Segment Profiles

Segment 1: Premium-Quality Seekers

- Purchaser: primary purchaser is adult females 25 +.
- Income: variety of household income categories with concentration in $45,000 – $59,999 range.
- Family Size: incidence of kids is low; mostly 2-person households.
- Age: primary consumer is male or female adults between 25 and 34 years of age.
- Sweet Goods Purchased Most Often: coffee cakes, biscuits, pound cakes, loaf cakes, strudels, muffins, sweet doughs.

Segment 2: Value Seekers: Medium Quality/Price

- Purchaser: primary purchaser is adult females 25 +.
- Income: variety of household income categories with concentration in $30,000 – $44,999 range.
- Family Size: incidence of kids is high; average family size is 3–4; also high incidence of families with over 5 people.
- Age: primary consumer is children (under 18 years).
- Sweet Goods Purchased Most Often: cookies, doughnuts, turnovers, pies.

Segment 3: Low-Price Seekers

- Purchaser: primary purchaser is adult females 25 +.
- Income: variety of household income categories with concentration in < $29,999 range.
- Family Size: incidence of kids is moderate: average family size of 2.5.
- Age: primary consumer is children (under 18 years); also consumed by more 65+ consumers than the general sweet-goods population.
- Sweet Goods Purchased Most Often: low-price cookies, doughnuts, turnovers, pies.

TABLE 3 Psychographics

Segment 1

- More interested in product quality; ensuring the product is fresh and uses the finest ingredients.
- More interested in making a positive impression on those around them; concerned about appearances.
- View sweet goods as a well-deserved treat.
- Tend to have more special occasions and group gatherings/dinners at which they serve sweet goods.

Segment 2

- Interested in product quality, but also interested in value for money. Will not spend the extra money to buy the finest if there is a good-quality product for less.
- Very interested in the amount of product being offered in each package.
- View sweet goods as a necessity to keep the family happy.
- Sweet-goods consumption is mostly a family event.

Segment 3

- Main concern is getting lowest price.
- Not interested in making a positive impression on those around them; little concern over product appearances.
- View sweet goods as a way to satisfy hunger.

buying familiar, trusted brands, they are more likely to take a chance and try something new than are the premium-quality seekers.

A Financial Assessment of the Opportunities

The Premium-Segment Opportunity

Following the focus groups, a telephone survey was conducted with 1,200 sweet-goods purchasers across the Atlantic region. The research explored consumption and purchase behaviour as well as brand and flavour preferences. Dale, Sandy, and Pat examined the survey results intently for indications of the premium-market size and potential. As shown in Appendix 7-3A and Appendix 7-3B, the research had revealed several important facts that the consultants would require when considering the merit of the idea of launching a line of sweet goods in Atlantic Canada. First, they had used the research to estimate the percentage of households in Atlantic Canada that eat at least one of each type of sweet good at home in an average month. For example, as shown in Appendix 7-3A, 48 percent of Atlantic Canadian households eat at least one strudel at home in an average month. The research had also revealed the average monthly consumption among each of these groups. For example, the average monthly strudel consumption among the 48 percent of households that eat at least one strudel per month is 12.64.

After conferring with several experts in the food industry, J.D. Consulting had determined that some sweet goods were predicted to be eaten by a higher percentage of households in the coming years, while other types of sweet goods were predicted to remain stable or experience decline. Based on this information, J.D. had created forecasts for each type of sweet good which Everdene was considering launching (see Appendix 7-3A).

As part of their analysis, Dale, Sandy, and Pat had conducted a pricing analysis for each type of sweet good that Everdene could offer (both medium and premium quality), and then prepared market-share forecasts for the company at each price. For premium sweet goods, J.D. Consulting had arrived at the conclusions outlined in Appendix 7-3B.

The consultants had also spoken with Elizabeth McDonald, manufacturing supervisor for all of Everdene's facilities. They had learned from Elizabeth that there was a major constraint under which premium sweet goods would have to be manufactured. She had explained that, owing to the factories' manufacturing design and setup/changeover costs, the only way premium muffins could be feasibly manufactured was if premium strudels were also made. Likewise, the only feasible way for premium coffee cakes to be made was if premium pound cakes were also manufactured. "We can outfit our operations to make any of the sweet goods that the company is considering marketing, but our marketing people have to realize the manufacturing realities under which we operate," said Elizabeth.

The Medium-Quality Segment Opportunity

The consultants had also used the information at their disposal to create forecasts for the idea of launching a medium-quality line of sweet goods. George LeGrow had informed them that he foresaw two opportunities in the medium segment. The first was to launch a medium-quality line of Everdene sweet goods (i.e., cookies, doughnuts, turnovers, and pies) through the company's traditional distribution channel — supermarkets. The consultants forecast that this option would garner Everdene a three-year profit of $9,500,000, and a projected profit margin of approximately 28 percent.*

George's second idea related to serving the large convenience-store market. George had been approached over the preceding few months by several representatives of independent, neighbourhood convenience stores, who were interested in having the company provide them with a medium-quality line of Everdene sweet goods they could offer their customers (who found the premium sweet goods carried by supermarkets and specialty food stores to be too expensive). He was particularly excited about this idea because convenience stores in Atlantic Canada outnumbered supermarkets and because

* All profit margin figures contained in this case are margins on revenues.

none of the manufacturing constraints that would apply to manufacturing premium sweet goods (as outlined previously) would apply (George envisioned Everdene outsourcing some of the manufacturing processes for medium-quality sweet goods, which would allow the company to realize a higher profit). J.D. Consulting estimated that this option would provide Everdene with a three-year profit of $15 million and a projected profit margin of approximately 35 percent.

APPENDIX 7-3A

Sweet-Good Type	Percentage of HHs That eat ≥1 at Home in an Average Month			Average Monthly Consumption	Percentage of Consumption That Is of Premium Products		
	Year 1	Year 2	Year 3		Year 1	Year 2	Year 3
Strudels	48	46	45	12.64	25	26	27
Coffee cakes	32	34	35	4.65	29	29	29
Loaf cakes	36	38	39	2.28	25	27	29
Pound cakes	15	17	18	1.89	50	51	52
Muffins	71	73	76	15.78	50	51	52
Buscuits	60	58	57	37.57	40	40	40
Sweet doughs	19	19	20	7.48	20	21	22

APPENDIX 7-3B Premium Segments: Projected Prices, Market Shares, and Costs, Years 1–3

Year 1	Projected Everdene Share	Price per Item	Projected Costs
Strudels	5%	$0.60	$1,000,000
Coffee cakes	6%	$4.49	$2,250,000
Loaf cakes	4%	$3.49	$ 750,000
Pound cakes	8%	$2.49	$ 350,000
Muffins	7%	$0.65	$2,500,000
Buscuits	6%	$0.15	$1,450,000
Sweet doughs	7%	$0.50	$ 275,000
Year 2	**Projected Everdene Share**	**Price per Item**	**Projected Costs**
Strudels	10%	$0.61	$ 950,000
Coffee cakes	11%	$4.55	$2,000,000
Loaf cakes	10%	$3.55	$ 650,000
Pound cakes	14%	$2.55	$ 325,000
Muffins	15%	$0.59	$2,000,000
Buscuits	12%	$0.17	$1,200,000
Sweet doughs	16%	$0.51	$ 175,000
Year 3	**Projected Everdene Share**	**Price per Item**	**Projected Costs**
Strudels	13%	$0.63	$ 950,000
Coffee cakes	11%	$4.59	$2,000,000
Loaf cakes	12%	$3.59	$ 650,000
Pound cakes	16%	$2.59	$ 325,000
Muffins	13%	$0.62	$2,000,000
Buscuits	12%	$0.19	$1,200,000
Sweet doughs	20%	$0.55	$ 175,000

The Decision

Before they could make a recommendation about if and how Everdene should market a line of sweet goods, Dale, Sandy, and Pat spoke with Beth Everdene regarding the company's objectives. "Well," said Beth to the consultants, "in order for us to launch a new line of products, that line must be projected to achieve at least a 20 percent profit margin within three years of launch, that is, 20 percent averaged over the first three years. The line must also further expand and/or strengthen our role in the food market."

Questions

1. What environmental trends and issues will influence Everdene's decision whether or not to launch a line of sweet goods?
2. What are the implications of the proposed launch for the equity of the Everdene brand?
3. Should Everdene launch the new line of sweet goods?
4. If so, how should the introduction of the new line be managed? Develop a plan to guide the launch.

Appendix

Planning Your Career in Marketing

After you graduate, then what? For most people it means looking for a job. But your goal should be more than just finding employment. Your first full-time job after graduation should serve as a springboard to a successful career. No matter how difficult or how easy the economic times are, setting goals and planning a job search will help get you where you want to go.

To get started in the right direction, you should begin your preparation for employment after graduation as early as possible and launch your job search at least one term, and preferably nine months, before graduation. In fact, you may want to get a head start on looking for employment in marketing, especially if you are enrolled in a co-op program, or if you consider working in a marketing position as a summer job. Both co-op placements and summer employment provide you with an opportunity to explore marketing positions even before you graduate. Much of what is presented in this appendix will be valuable as you seek co-op and summer positions.

To get you thinking about your employment ambitions and upcoming job search, this appendix first discusses choosing a career. Then a variety of career opportunities in marketing are described. Finally, in a section that is relevant to all students regardless of major, guidelines on obtaining a job after graduation are presented.

CHOOSING A CAREER

One of the most significant decisions you will ever make is choosing a career. This career decision will influence your future happiness, self-fulfilment, and well-being. Yet, unfortunately, career decisions often seem to be based on insufficient information, analysis, and evaluation of alternatives.

Early in the career-decision process, everyone should spend some time in introspection — the process of looking into yourself and honestly assessing what you want to do and what you have to offer. Let's look briefly at what this involves.

What Do You Want?

Perhaps this question would be better worded if we asked, "What is important to you in life?" To answer this broad question, you must answer several more specific ones, such as the following:

- How important are money and other financial rewards?
- Do you want your career to be the main event in your life? Or do you see a career principally as the means of financing leisure-time activities?
- How important are the social surroundings, climate, and other aspects of the environment in which you live?
- Would you prefer to work for a large company or a small organization?
- Would you prefer living and working in a small city or town, or in a major urban centre?
- Are you willing to relocate to another part of the country, or to another country? How often would you be willing to move?
- How important to you is the social prestige of a career?
- Do you prefer work that is evenly paced or occasionally hectic? How do you deal with the pressure of deadlines?
- Do you need tangible signs of results on a job to feel fulfilled?
- Do you prefer to work alone or as part of a team?

Another way to approach the question of what you want from a career is to identify in writing your goals in life. List both your intermediate-term goals (three to five years from now) and your long-term goals (ten years or more).

Still another approach is to simply describe yourself in some detail. By writing a description of your personality, likes and dislikes, hopes and aspirations, things you like and don't like to do, and things you feel you are good at doing, you may be able to identify various careers that would (or would not) fit your self-image.

What Can You Offer?

Next you need to identify in some detail your strong and weak points. Why would an employer want to hire you? What are your qualifications? What experience, work, education, and extracurricular activities do you have that might be attractive to prospective employers? Since these attributes aren't acquired overnight, you should start developing them early in your college program. However, keep in mind that prospective employers are much more interested in what a person accomplished in various roles than how many different titles he or she had. So be selective, and do a few things well.

Typically, employers will be looking for certain skill sets when hiring college and university graduates. The desired skills will differ according to the positions to be filled, but may be summarized under the following categories:

- *Communications Skills:* Practically all employers will want to hire individuals who can work well with others and who can communicate clearly and effectively, both in oral and written communications. Being able to work effectively as a member of a team is important in virtually every organization today; consequently, most employers will be looking for a good "fit" when hiring. Communications is also extremely important, as companies are looking to their employees to be able to represent them in dealing with customers and to make effective presentations in a number of situations. We cannot overemphasize the importance of your developing good interpersonal skills, as well as the ability to write clearly and without errors and to make effective presentations.
- *Leadership Skills:* Most employers will be looking to hire individuals who can move into progressively more senior positions and who can demonstrate leadership. As a result, they will be looking

for evidence that you have occupied positions in which you have had to function as a member of a team and were given responsibility. Employers will also want to ensure that you are motivated to assume such positions. Generally, you will need to show an employer that you really want the job and are equipped to handle it. Most companies and organizations are not interested in hiring people who want to work 9-to-5 and who are mainly motivated by a paycheque.

- *Facility with Technology:* It is difficult to think of a job in marketing today that does not involve the use of technology. Clearly, the use of technology will range from simple use of e-mail to the writing of software to drive electronic commerce. Regardless of the position, however, knowledge of the use of technology to gather information, to process it, and to support decision-making is a valuable asset in any marketing position.

WHAT ARE THE MARKETING JOBS?

In Chapter 1 we noted that about one-quarter to one-third of all jobs are in the field of marketing. These jobs cover a wide variety of activities and a great range of qualifications and aptitudes. For instance, jobs in personal selling call for a set of qualifications that are different from those in marketing research. A person who is likely to be successful in advertising may not be a good prospect in physical distribution. Consequently, the aptitudes and skills of different individuals make them candidates for different types of marketing jobs. In this section we briefly describe the major jobs in marketing, grouping them by title or activity.

Sales

Sales jobs are by far the most numerous of all the jobs in marketing. Personal selling spans a broad array of activities, organizations, and titles. Consider the following people: a driver–sales person for Coca-Cola, a sales clerk in a department store, a sales engineer providing technical assistance in sales of hydraulic valves, a representative for Canadair selling a fleet of airplanes, and a marketing consultant selling his or her services. All these people are engaged in personal selling, but each sales job is different from the others.

Sales jobs of one sort or another are available in virtually every locality. This means that you can pretty well pick the area where you would like to live and still get involved in a sales position.

There are opportunities to earn a very high income in sales. This is especially true when the compensation plan is straight commission or is a combination of salary plus a significant incentive element.

A sales job is the most common entry-level position in marketing. Furthermore, as illustrated in Figure A-1, a sales job is a widely used stepping stone to a management position. Many companies recruit people for sales jobs with the intention of promoting some of these people into management positions. Personal selling and sales management jobs are also a good route to the top in a firm because it is relatively easy to measure a person's performance and productivity in selling.

As we discussed in Chapter 19, a sales job is different from other jobs in several significant ways. Sales people represent their company to customers and to the public in general. The public ordinarily does not judge a firm by its factory or office personnel. Also, outside sales people (those who go to

FIGURE A-1 Typical Career Path Starting in Personal Selling

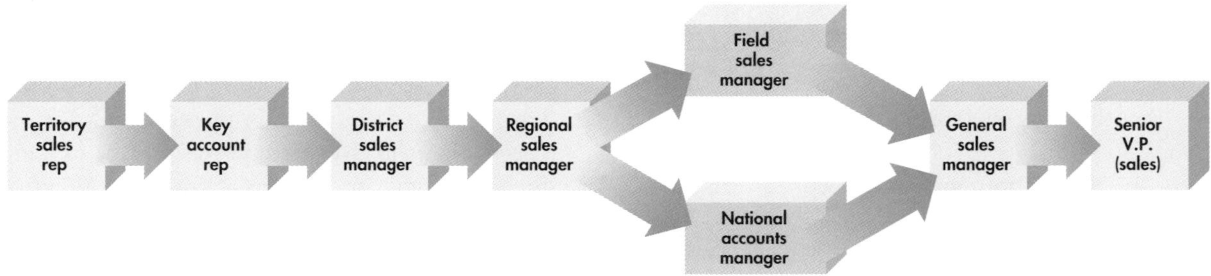

the customers) operate with very little or no direct personal supervision. They must have considerable creativity, persistence, and self-motivation. Furthermore, sales jobs often involve travelling and require much time away from home and family.

All in all, selling is hard work, but the potential rewards are immense. Certainly no other job contributes as much to the success of an organization. Remember, nothing happens until somebody sells something!

Retailing Management

Retailing is second only to sales in the number of job opportunities for new graduates. The two primary areas of opportunity in department store, specialty, and discount chains are in merchandising or buying (described in the next section) and store management.

Store managers have a great deal of responsibility and authority. A store manager's authority related to acquiring merchandise (the buying function) varies greatly from one firm to the next. However, once the merchandise arrives in the store, the manager has the responsibility and authority for displaying, selling, and controlling the inventory. Store managers in most companies, either directly or indirectly through department heads, oversee sales, promotion, credit, personnel management, and store security.

The entry-level position for store management typically is assistant department manager, department manager, or assistant store manager, depending on the size of the store. The performance of a store or department manager is directly measurable by sales or profits. Therefore, speed of advancement into higher positions is determined primarily by the results produced by the manager.

Buying and Purchasing

Most medium-size and larger organizations employ people who specialize in buying, rather than selling, goods and services. In one type of position, people select and acquire merchandise for resale. In another type of position, people purchase goods and services not for resale but for use in a manufacturing process or in operating an organization.

Every retail organization needs people to buy the merchandise that is to be resold. Frequently, the route to the top in retailing is through the buying (also called merchandising) division of the business. Large retailers have many positions for buyers and assistant buyers. Each merchandise department normally has a buyer. Consequently, you often have a chance to work with particular products that interest you.

A purchasing agent is the business-market counterpart of the retail store buyer. Virtually all large firms in the business market have purchasing departments. People in these departments buy for the production, office, and sales departments in their firms.

Retail buyers and purchasing agents need many of the same skills. They must be able to analyze markets, determine merchandise needs, and negotiate with sellers. It's also necessary to have some knowledge of credit, finance, and physical distribution.

Advertising

Opportunities in advertising can be found in many different jobs in various organizations. The primary areas of opportunity are:

- Advertisers, including manufacturers, retailers, and service firms. Some of these organizations (especially in retailing) prepare and place their own ads. In large manufacturing and services firms, the advertising department may be large, as they manage multimillion-dollar advertising budgets and work closely with advertising agencies.
- Various media (including newspapers, radio and TV stations, and magazines) that carry ads. In addition to the selling of advertising time and space, many of these media work closely with their advertisers to ensure that their expenditures in the media are as effective as possible.
- Advertising agencies that specialize in creating and producing individual ads and entire promotion campaigns.
- New media and electronic commerce. Many new companies have been established in recent years to take advantage of opportunities that have resulted from the availability of new technology. These include companies that are preparing advertising programs for the Internet, from the development of Web sites to the production of CD-ROMS.

Jobs in advertising encompass a number of aptitudes and interests: artistic, creative, managerial, research, and sales. The advertising field holds real opportunity for the artistic or creative person. Agencies and advertising departments need account executives, copywriters, artists, photographers, layout designers, programming experts, Web page developers, and others to create and produce ads.

The account executive is a key position in advertising agencies. People in this position provide the liaison between the agency and its clients (the advertisers). Account executives co-ordinate the agency's efforts with the clients' marketing programs.

Another group of advertising jobs involves buying and selling media time and space. Advertisers and agencies also often employ people who can conduct buyer-behaviour studies and other marketing research.

Internet and Electronic Commerce

The application of technology to marketing has led to the opening up of many new jobs that revolve around the Internet and electronic commerce. Technology has enabled marketers in a variety of businesses to interact with their customers through very different channels than they have been using in the past. This application of technology will increase dramatically in the coming years, creating many new jobs in this area of marketing.

The positions that will become available in increasing numbers range from the development of Web pages to the designing of interactive kiosks that allow customers to deal with companies at a distance. Internet-based commerce alone will require people who can write attractive copy for the Web, researchers who can measure the effectiveness of Web-based advertising, and artists and designers who can encourage users to visit their clients' sites. Generally, companies will be increasing their use of the Internet, telephone-based technology, and multimedia to interact with their customers and to deliver services to them.

Delivering services and selling products over the Internet and through telephone links will create many opportunities for careers in marketing. These include opportunities in direct marketing, such as the establishment and operation of call centres, involving both inbound customer ordering and service and outbound telemarketing. Database marketing opportunities also will increase in the future, as companies need to manage effectively the many databases that will be established to deal with customers in the new-technology environment.

Sales Promotion

The main function of sales promotion is to tie together the activities in sales and advertising. Effective sales promotion requires imagination and creativity, coupled with a sound foundation in marketing fundamentals.

One aspect of sales promotion is the design and creation of retailers' in-store displays and window displays. Another aspect deals with trade shows and other company exhibits. Sales promotion activities also include the development and management of premium giveaways, contests, product sampling, and other types of promotion.

Marketing Research

Marketing research jobs cover a broad range of activities outlined in Chapter 8. People are hired for marketing research jobs by manufacturers, retailers, services marketers, government agencies, and other organizations. There also are a large number of specialized marketing research companies. Generally, however, there are fewer jobs in marketing research than in personal selling or in retailing.

Marketing researchers are problem solvers. They collect and analyze masses of information. Thus they need an aptitude for precise, analytical work. Some quantitative skills are needed, particularly an understanding of statistics.

Product/Brand Management

In Chapter 9 we discussed briefly the position of product manager in connection with the organizational structure for new product planning and development. Product managers (sometimes called brand managers) are responsible for planning and directing the entire marketing program for a given product or group of products.

Early on, product managers make decisions about packaging, labelling, and other aspects of the product itself. Product managers also are responsible for the marketing research necessary to identify the market.

They plan advertising, personal selling, and sales promotional programs for their products. Product managers are concerned with pricing, physical distribution, and legal issues concerning the product.

In many respects, being a product manager is like running your own business. Product managers must have good analytical skills to keep abreast of what competitors are doing and what is happening in the market. They also need to be tactful and persuasive to gain the co-operation of functional areas such as manufacturing and sales.

Physical Distribution and Logistics

Many jobs exist in the field of physical distribution, and the prospects are even brighter as we look ahead. More and more firms are expected to adopt the systems approach in physical distribution to control the huge expenses involved in materials movement and warehousing.

Manufacturers, retailers, and all other goods-handling firms have jobs that involve two stages of physical distribution. First the product must be moved to the firm for processing or resale. Then the finished products must be distributed to the markets. These physical distribution tasks involve jobs in transportation management, warehousing, and inventory control. In addition, many transportation carriers and warehousing firms also provide a variety of jobs that may interest you.

Public Relations

The public relations department is a valuable connection between an organization and its various publics. The department must deal with, or go through, the news media to reach these publics. Public relations people must be especially good in communications. In fact, these people often have college degrees or diplomas in public relations, communications or journalism, rather than in marketing.

In essence, the job of public relations is to project the desired company image to the public. More specifically, public relations people are responsible for telling the public about the company, its products, community activities, social programs, environmental improvement activities, labour policies, and views regarding controversial issues. Public relations specialists are particularly important, and very visible, when a company responds to adverse publicity. Such publicity may come from a governmental investigation or a charge of unethical practices or unsafe products. Whether disseminating favourable publicity or responding to adverse publicity, the company's position must be stated in a clear, understandable, and, above all, believable fashion.

Customer Service

As more and more companies realize the importance of building customer relationships and accept that they can gain a competitive advantage through the provision of superior service, many are establishing customer service departments. They need employees who can identify with customer problems, who can be empathetic, and who have good communications skills. These employees deal with customer suggestions and complaints and with management programs to offer assistance to customers and to answer their questions, either by telephone or in person. Employees in customer service positions have to decide what action is needed to satisfy customers and must be able to work with others in the company to address customer service issues.

Consumer Affairs and Protection

The broad area of consumer affairs and protection encompasses several activities that provide job and career opportunities. Many of these jobs are an outgrowth of the consumer movement discussed in Chapter 24. Many companies have a consumer affairs department to handle consumer complaints. Several federal and provincial agencies keep watch on business firms and provide information and assistance to consumers. Grocery products manufacturers and gas and electric companies regularly hire graduates to aid consumers in product use. Government and private product-testing agencies hire people to test products for safety, durability, and other features.

Other Career Areas

In this appendix, it is not possible to list all the careers available to you in the wide field of marketing. We have, however, covered the major areas. You may get additional career ideas from the next section, which deals with organizations that provide these opportunities.

WHERE ARE THE MARKETING JOBS?

In this section we briefly describe the types of companies and other organizations that provide jobs in marketing. This section also includes comments on jobs in international marketing and a comparison of job opportunities in large versus small organizations.

Types of Organizations

Literally thousands of organizations provide jobs and career opportunities in marketing. The organizations can be grouped into the following categories.

Manufacturing Most manufacturing firms provide career opportunities in all the activities discussed in the previous section. In their promotional mix, some manufacturers stress selling, while others rely more on advertising. Even small companies offer job opportunities in most of the categories we have mentioned.

Because most manufacturers make products that are used by other businesses, their names are not familiar to the general public. Unfortunately, many college and university graduates overlook some of these potentially excellent employers just because they don't recognize their corporate names. Starting salaries are often higher in manufacturing firms than in retailing and the other organizations described next.

Retailing Retailers provide more marketing jobs by far than does any other organizational category, but many of these jobs are not intended for university and college graduates. Careers in retailing are not well understood by students, who may equate retailing with being a clerk in a department store or filling shelves in a supermarket. Students often perceive that retail pay is low and that retail work-hours include a lot of evenings and weekends.

Actually a career in retailing offers many attractive features for university and college graduates. There are opportunities for very rapid advancement for those who display real ability. Performance results, such as sales and profits, are quickly and highly visible. If you produce, management will generally note this fact in a hurry.

While the starting pay in many (but not all) retail companies is lower than in manufacturing, the compensation in higher-level retailing jobs typically is excellent. There are good retailing jobs in virtually every geographic area. Also, large retail chains generally have excellent management-training programs for recently hired college graduates.

Perhaps the main attractions in retailing are less tangible. Retailing can be an exciting field. You are involved constantly with people: customers, suppliers, and other workers. And there are challenges in merchandise buying, especially finding out what will sell well and what customers really want.

It is easier to start a career in retailing than in many other fields. In large stores there are jobs involving personnel management, accounting controls, and store operations (receiving, credit, and customer service departments). However, the lifeblood of retailing is the buying and selling of merchandise or services. Thus the more numerous and better-paying positions are in merchandising and store management. A typical career path is presented in Figure A-2. Note that after several years of experience in both areas, a retail manager often decides to concentrate on merchandising or store management.

Wholesaling Career opportunities in wholesaling generally are less well understood and appreciated than those in retailing or manufacturing. Wholesaling firms typically do not recruit on campuses, and they generally have a low profile among students.

Yet opportunities are there. Wholesalers of consumer products and industrial distributors provide many jobs in buying, personal selling, marketing research, and physical distribution. Manufacturers' agents, brokers, and the other intermediaries discussed in Chapter 16 also offer jobs and careers. Wholesaling intermediaries are increasing in numbers and in sales volume, and their future is promising.

Services Marketing The broad array of service industries discussed in Chapter 12 provides a bonanza of job and career opportunities in marketing. Many of these fields are expected to experience rapid growth in the future. The travel, hospitality,

FIGURE A-2 Typical Career Path in a Department Store Chain

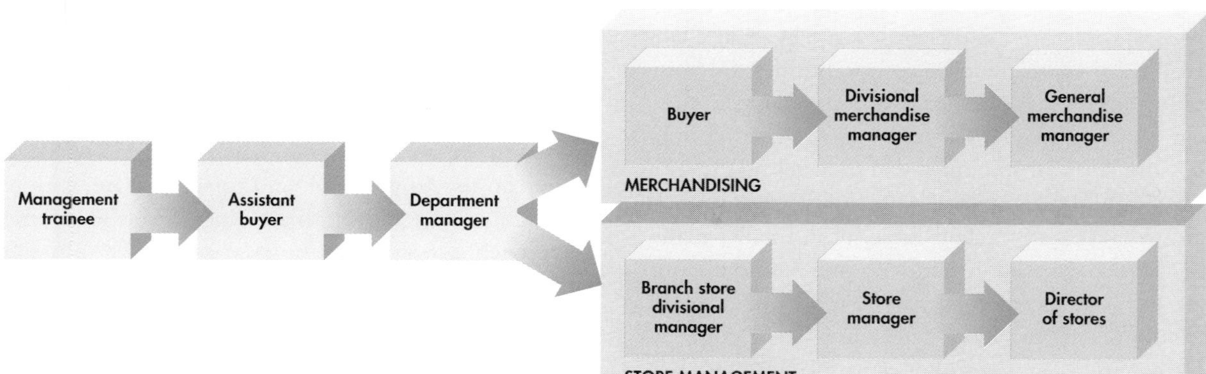

finance, entertainment, communications, and professional-services fields are prime examples. Recognizing the importance of marketing, many of these industries and organizations within them are now adding marketing-related personnel. Most of these firms really are retailers of services. Consequently, many of the statements we made earlier about retailing careers are relevant here.

Other Business Areas Besides the general types of organizations just described, more specialized business firms hire graduates for marketing-related positions. Entry-level opportunities can be found with communications media (such as TV stations), advertising agencies, franchise systems, participation and spectator sports organizations, public utilities, and transportation firms (such as truck lines). Many new marketing positions will be created in the coming years in technology-related industries. The development of new-media applications, electronic commerce, and direct and database marketing will provide many exciting opportunities in the near future.

Not-for-Profit Organizations As described in Chapter 22, not-for-profit organizations are realizing that marketing is key to their success. Consequently, it is likely that jobs and careers in many not-for-profit organizations will open up in large numbers as we enter the next century. Consider the wide variety of not-for-profit organizations: hospitals, museums, educational institutions, religious organizations, foundations, charities, and political parties, among others. Given this diversity, you can expect to find a wide range of marketing-related positions in not-for-profit organizations.

Government Countless federal and provincial government organizations hire people for marketing positions. Here we include the major government departments: agriculture, human services, and the others. We also include all the regulatory agencies. Government organizations employ people in purchasing, marketing research, public relations, physical distribution, consumer affairs and protection, and even advertising and sales promotion. Sometimes students tend to overlook the many marketing career opportunities in government.

Careers in International Marketing

Students who like to travel and experience different cultures may want to work at least part of the time in foreign countries. They may be interested in careers in international marketing, and they may even major in international business. Typically, however, companies do not hire graduates and immediately assign them to jobs in international marketing. People are normally hired for entry-level positions in the domestic divisions of a company's operations. Then, after some years of experience with the firm, an employee may have an opportunity to move into the firm's international divisions. If you have international aspirations, you would be wise to study a second language and take advantage of opportunities to learn about other cultures.

Large versus Small Companies

Should you go to work for a large company or a small firm? Or should you go into business for yourself upon graduation? For over a decade now, more and more students have been saying that they want to work for a small company. They feel that there is more freedom of action, more rapid advancement, and less restraint on their lifestyles in smaller firms.

Perhaps so. And certainly no one should discourage you from a career in small business. You may wish to consider starting your career in a larger company. Then, after a few years, you can move into a smaller firm. There are three reasons for this suggestion:

- A large firm is more likely to have a good training program in your chosen field. Many students have little or no practical marketing experience. The fine training programs provided by numerous large manufacturers, retailers, and major service marketers can be critical in launching a career.
- You can learn something about how a big company operates. After all, when you go into a smaller firm, large companies may be your competitors. So the more you know about them, the better able you will be to compete with them.
- After working for a while for a big company, you may change your mind and decide to stay with the larger firm after all. On the other hand, let's say that you want to go to a small company after you have worked a few years at a big firm. At that point it will be relatively easy to move from a large company to a smaller one. If you start in a small firm, however, and later want to move into big business, it is not so easy to move.

We have discussed various career fields and types of organizations that hire people in these fields. Now let's take a look at how you should go about getting a job with one of these organizations.

HOW DO YOU SEARCH FOR A JOB?

This book and your entire course are designed to teach you the fundamentals involved in developing and managing a marketing program. These fundamentals are applicable regardless of whether you are marketing a tangible product, service, idea, person, or place. They are equally applicable to (1) large and small organizations, (2) domestic and international marketing, and (3) business and nonbusiness organizations.

Now let's see whether we can apply these fundamentals to a program designed to market a person — you! We shall discuss a marketing approach that you can use to get a job and to start a career. Here we are talking about a marketing career. This same approach, however, can be used in seeking jobs and careers in any field.

Identify and Analyze the Market

The first step in building a marketing program is to identify and analyze the market. In this case the market consists of prospective jobs and employers. Right now you don't know exactly who comprises that target market. So you must research several possible markets and then eventually narrow down your choice. In effect, we are talking about "choosing a career." Much of what we discussed in the first section of this appendix is applicable here.

You should initially get as much information as you can about various career opportunities in marketing. For information sources you might start with one or two professors whom you know reasonably well. Then turn to the placement office in your school, or wherever postgraduation jobs are listed. Many companies prepare recruiting brochures for students, explaining the company and its career opportunities.

Newspapers and business journals are another good information source. Sometimes, looking carefully through a series of company annual reports can give you ideas of firms you might like to work for. You should exchange information with other students who also are in the job market. Possibly one of the best sources of information about careers in marketing and in other fields, and about employers, is the Internet. This source of information is so important today that we will devote the following section to it.

Job Search on the Internet

There are today literally hundreds of Web sites in Canada that will prove valuable to you in choosing a career and in finding job opportunities. With the expansion of the number of sites, the Internet has become the single most important source of career-related information available to you. Many of the Web sites not only provide information on careers and jobs, but also will allow you to apply for positions electronically, and to e-mail your résumé so that it can be accessed by interested employers. The challenge, in fact, lies in deciding where to start in using the Internet for your job search.

Mark Swartz, author of *Get Wired, You're Hired*, says you can avoid hours of being bogged down in following false leads if you start with what he considers to be the five best Web sites if you are looking for career information. These are all Canadian, and free![1]

- Canada WorkInfoNet (**www.workinfonet.ca**) lists hundreds of Canadian job-related Web sites, sorted by job category and province. This is probably the most comprehensive site, and a great place to start.
- You can attend a Career Fair (**www.hitechcareer.com**) where you can access dozens of employers at the same time. These are principally interested in technology-related jobs, but they are prepared to hire.
- If you are looking for jobs available right now, you can access the classified sections of daily newspapers (**www.worldchat.com/public/stcharle/jobform/html**) across Canada.
- The National Graduate Register (**http://ngr.schoolnet.ca/ngr/home**) is a free résumé posting service that will put your qualifications and interests in front of hundreds of prospective employers.
- If you are looking for employment outside Canada, you can identify job opportunities in many countries around the world through the CareerMosaic international gateway (**http://www.careermosaic.com**).

In our opinion, the best place to start your job search on the Internet is with a site created by Mark Swartz for Sympatico, the Internet Service Provider. By entering this site at **http://www1.sympatico.ca/Contents/Business/Careers/workplace** and clicking on "jobquest" and "guide," you will have access to a wealth of information on how to conduct your search. In addition to the Web sites listed above, you will be able to find more information about other valuable resources, including:

- One that Swartz considers "an electronic work-searcher's equivalent to the Bible" is *The Riley Guide* (**www.dmb.com/jobguide**). Swartz considers it to be the most "comprehensive instruction manual to finding work on the Net."
- The Canadian Association of Career Educators and Employers has a site where you can find out about employers and the opportunities they offer. It also has an on-line version of *Career Options* magazine. You can find it at **www.cacee.com**.
- If you are interested in jobs in a particular region of the country, or if you are going to school away from home and want to explore opportunities closer to home, there are sites that specialize in regional job opportunities. For example, a site devoted to positions in Atlantic Canada is **www.atl-can-careers.com**.

This section has been devoted to providing you with information that you can use to begin your search for a career in marketing. In summary, learn all you can about various firms and industries. Then, from this information search, zero in on the group of companies that are your leading choices. You will now be ready to develop your personal marketing mix that will be effective in marketing yourself to your target markets.

Product

In this case the "product" you are planning and developing is yourself and your services. You want to make yourself as attractive as possible to your market — prospective employers.

Start your product planning by listing in some detail your strong and weak points. These will lead into another list — your qualifications and achievements. This introspection is something we discussed in the first section of this appendix in connection with choosing a career.

When you are considering your qualifications, it may help to group them into broad categories such as these:

- Education — schools attended, degrees or diplomas earned, grade-point average, major, favourite subjects.
- Work experience — part-time and full-time, responsibilities.

- Honours and awards.
- Extracurricular activities and organizations — memberships, offices, committees, accomplishments.
- Hobbies.

Later, we will discuss the presentation of your qualifications in a personal data sheet or résumé.

An important aspect of product planning is product differentiation. How can you differentiate yourself from all the other students and graduates? What have you done that is different, unusual, or exceptional? This doesn't have to be earth-shaking; just something that shows a trait such as initiative, imagination, or perseverance.

Another part of product planning is packaging. When you go for an interview, be sure that the external package looks attractive. People do judge you by your appearance, just as you judge products by the way they look. This means paying attention to what you wear and how you are groomed. A good impression starts with the prospective employer's first meeting with you.

Price

"What salary do you expect?" "How much do you think we should pay you?" These are two of the questions a prospective employer might ask in a job interview. If you have not done some thinking in advance regarding the price you want for your services, these questions may throw you.

As part of your marketing program, find out what the market price is for people entering your field. Talk with placement officers, career counsellors, professors, and other students who are in the job market. From these sources you should get a pretty good idea of starting salaries in entry-level positions. Use this information to decide before the interview on a range of salaries for yourself. Remember that income can be stated in several different ways. For example, there may be a base salary, the possibility of a bonus, and fringe benefits such as the use of a company-supplied car.

Distribution Channel

There are only a few major channels you are likely to use in marketing yourself to prospective employers. The simplest channel is your placement office, assuming that there is one on your campus. Most colleges and universities, through their placement offices, host and assist companies that send job recruiters to do on-campus interviewing.

Another channel is the Internet and help-wanted ads in business journals, trade journals, and newspapers. Perhaps the most difficult, but often the most rewarding, channel is going directly to firms in which you are especially interested — knock on doors or write letters seeking a job interview. Many employers look favourably on people who display this kind of initiative in their job search.

Promotion

Other than planning and developing an excellent product, the most important ingredient in your marketing mix is a good promotion (or communications) program. Your promotion will consist primarily of written communications (a form of advertising) and interviewing (a form of personal selling).

To stand out from the crowd and be noticed, job applicants have tried everything from singing telegrams to skywriting. Most applicants use more conventional approaches. Frequently your first contact with a prospective employer is a cover letter in which you state briefly why you are writing to that company and what you have to offer. You enclose a personal résumé, and you request an appointment for an interview.

Cover Letter In the opening paragraph of your cover letter, you should indicate why you want to work for the firm. Mention a couple of key points regarding the firm — points you learned from your research. In the second paragraph, you can present a few highlights of your own experience or personality that make you an attractive prospect. In the third paragraph, state that you are enclosing your résumé, and request an appointment for an interview, even suggesting some dates and a time when you will telephone to arrange the meeting.

Résumé A résumé (also called a personal data sheet) is really a brief history of yourself. Personal computers make it possible to design a distinctive and very professional-appearing résumé. You can start with biographical information, including your name, address, and phone number. Then divide your résumé into sections, including education, work experience, and activities that were described in the product section.

At the end of your résumé, provide information about your references. One approach is simply to state, "References furnished upon request." The rationale for this approach is that interested employers will ask for names and addresses of references if or when they want to contact them. An alternative approach is to list your references by name (along with their titles, addresses, and phone numbers) at the bottom of your résumé or on a separate page. The thinking behind this approach is that you should make it as easy as possible for a prospective employer to check your references. Make sure you have obtained permission from those people you have listed as references!

It is difficult to overstate the value of a persuasive cover letter and a distinctive résumé. They are critically important elements in your job search. They certainly are two of the most important ads you will ever write.

Interview Rarely is anyone hired without one or more interviews. In some cases, as when recruiters visit your campus, the interview is your initial contact with the firm. In other situations the interviews come as a result of your letter of introduction and résumé.

The interview is an experience in personal selling; in this case, you are selling yourself. People are often uncomfortable and uptight in interviews, especially their first few, so don't be surprised or disappointed if you are. One way to reduce your anxiety and increase the likelihood of impressing the interviewer is to prepare yourself to answer tough questions that may be asked:

- Why should we hire you?
- What are your distinctive strengths?
- Do you have any weaknesses, and how do you plan to overcome them?
- What kind of job do you expect to have in five years?

Your performance in an interview often determines whether you get the job. So be on your toes, be honest in your answers, and try to look more relaxed and confident than you may feel!

After interviews with a company have been completed, it is worthwhile to write a letter to each of the interviewers. Thank them for the opportunity to learn about their company, and, if appropriate, restate your interest in the job.

Evaluating Job Offers You are likely to receive multiple job offers if:

- The economy is fairly healthy, and
- You have at least an acceptable academic record,
- You conduct an aggressive job search,
- You develop a persuasive cover letter and professional résumé, and
- You perform well in job interviews.

You should evaluate the suitability of a single job offer or compare multiple job offers against a set of criteria that are important to you. The criteria you select and the importance you place on them require some careful thought. Below are examples of criteria you might consider.

- Will you be happy in your work? It is no accident that we frequently hear about "Monday blues" (The weekend of freedom is finished and I have to go back to work) and "TGIF" (Thank God it's Friday). Many people are not happy with their jobs. Normally, half or more of your waking hours will be spent at work, commuting to and from work, or doing job-related work at home. So you should look for a job and career that you will enjoy.
- Does the career fit your self-image? Are the job and career in line with your goals, dreams, and aspirations? Will they satisfy you? Will you be proud to tell people about your job? Will your spouse (and someday your children) be proud of you in that career?
- What demands or pressures are associated with the career? Some people thrive on pressure. They constantly seek new challenges in their work. Other people look for a more tranquil work experience. They do not want a job with constant demands and deadlines to meet.
- Do the financial factors meet your needs? How does the starting salary compare with those of other jobs? Consider what the job is likely to pay after you have been there three to five years. Some

engineering jobs, for example, have high starting salaries, but soon hit a salary ceiling. In contrast, some marketing jobs have lower starting salaries but no upper limits.

- Are there opportunities for promotion? You should evaluate the promotion patterns in a job or in a firm. Try to find out how long it normally takes to reach a given executive level. Study the backgrounds of presidents of a number of large companies in the industry. Did they come up through engineering, the legal department, sales or marketing, accounting, or some other area?
- Are the travel considerations suitable? Some jobs involve a considerable amount of travel, whether you are an entry-level worker or an executive. Other jobs are strictly in-house, with no travel at all. You need to assess which situation would meet your needs.
- Is there job or career "transportability"? Are there similar jobs in many other geographic areas? If you and your spouse or partner are both career-oriented, what will happen to you if your spouse is transferred to another city? One nice thing about such careers as teaching, retailing, nursing, and sales is that generally these jobs exist in considerable numbers in many different locations.
- What is the supply-and-demand situation in this field? Determine generally how many job openings currently exist in a given field, as compared with the supply of qualified applicants. At the same time, study the future prospects regarding this supply-and-demand condition. Determine whether a present shortage or overcrowding of employees in a field is a temporary situation or is likely to exist for several years.

GOOD LUCK!

We encourage you to keep in mind the questions and guidelines presented in this appendix as you take this course and progress through your academic program. It's not too early to start thinking about and planning your search for a job, whether for your next work term, next summer, or after graduation!

Notes and References

CHAPTER 1

1. Adapted from Art Chamberlain, "Royal's Wooing Its Own Customers," *The Toronto Star*, October 26, 1996, pp. E1, E8; and Deborah Wilson, "Banks Face Task of Assuring Clients They're Served, Not Shadowed," *The Globe and Mail*, December 17, 1996, p. B27.
2. John Fialka, "Parents Love, Coaches Hate, a Safer Baseball," *The Wall Street Journal*, May 24, 1994, p. B1.
3. Geraldine Williams, "High Performance Marketing: An Interview With Nike's Philip Knight," *Harvard Business Review*, July–August 1992, p. 92.
4. "Meet the New Consumer," *Fortune*, Autumn–Winter, 1993, pp. 7–8.
5. James G. Barnes, "Customer Relationships: Drivers of Customer Satisfaction," presented at the 1997 Annual Conference of the Western Marketing Educators, Scottsdale, Arizona, April 1997.
6. James L. Heskett, Thomas O. Jones, Gary W. Loveman, W. Earl Sasser Jr., and Leonard A. Schlesinger, "Putting the Service-Profit Chain to Work," *Harvard Business Review*, 72 (March–April) 1994, pp. 164–174.
7. Frederick F. Reichheld, "Loyalty-Based Management," *Harvard Business Review*, 71 (March–April) 1993, pp. 64–73.
8. Robert Johnson, "In the Chips," *The Wall Street Journal*, March 22, 1991, p. B1.
9. Mark Nusca, "Hotels Roll Out Array of New Services," *The Globe and Mail*, September, 17, 1996, p. C22.
10. For a complete discussion of ethics in marketing, see Gene R. Lazniak and Patrick Murphy, *Ethical Marketing Decisions: The Higher Road* (New York: Allyn & Bacon, 1993).
11. Valarie Lawton, "Lying on the Job," *The Toronto Star*, June 11, 1997, pp. B1–B3.
12. Robert Walker and Susan Flanagan, "The Ethical Imperative," *The Financial Post 500*, 1997, pp. 28–36.
13. Richard Schoenberger, "Is Strategy Strategic? Impact of Total Quality Management on Strategy," *Academy of Management Executive*, August 1992, pp. 80–87.
14. Elizabeth Church, "Survivors Get It Right," *The Globe and Mail*, May 9, 1997, p. B9.

CHAPTER 2

1. McDonald's Corp., "McDonald's and Disney Announce Historic Marketing Alliance," Press Release, May 23, 1996, http://www.mcdonalds.com/a-syst...s-release/Press-Release13581784.
2. Mikala Folb, "McDonald's Pitches Happy Meal to Adults," *Marketing Magazine*, February 10, 1997, p. 1.
3. McDonald's Corp., "McDonald's Launches Campaign 55 with Eye-Opening Breakfast Event," Press Release, April 2, 1997, http://www.mcdonalds.com/a_syst...ss_release/Press_Release1350704.
4. For a detailed review of the demographics of the baby boomers and how demographics influence buying behaviour, see David K. Foot with Daniel Stoffman, *Boom, Bust & Echo* (Toronto: Macfarlane, Walter & Ross, 1996).
5. William R. Swinyard and Heikke J. Rinne, "The Six Shopping Worlds of Baby Boomers," *Business Horizons*, September–October 1994, pp. 64–69.
6. Cyndee Miller, "X-ers Know They're a Target Market, and They Hate That," *Marketing News*, vol. 27, no. 25, December 6, 1993, p. 2.
7. David K. Foot with Daniel Stoffman, *Boom, Bust & Echo* (Toronto: Macfarlane, Walter & Ross, 1996).
8. Bruce Little, "Demographics Overrated as Economic Influence, Study Says," *The Globe and Mail*, June 20, 1997, p. B4.
9. Milton Parissis and Michael Helfinger, "Ethnic Shoppers Share Certain Values," *Marketing*, January 11, 1993, p. 16.
10. Chad Skelton, "School Junk Hot Dogs, Hamburgers," *The Globe and Mail*, June 23, 1997, p. A6.
11. Keith McArthur, "Canadians Put Environment First," *The Globe and Mail*, June 23, 1997, p. A4.
12. IBM, "Internet Ascending," Advertising Supplement, *The Globe and Mail Report on Business*, November 1996, p. 105.
13. Ontario Transportation Capital Corporation, "Ontario Transportation Minister Registers for a Highway 407 Transponder," Press Release, Canada NewsWire, May 30, 1997, http://www.newswire.ca/releases/May1997/30/c6645.html.
14. Steve Ferley, "PMB'97 Reveals that Canadian Internet Usage Patterns Fall Along Both Language

and Demographic Lines," *Marketing Magazine*, May 5, 1997, p. 16.

15. Sympatico, "Why Should a Business go Online?" Sponsored Supplement, *Strategy*, May 26, 1997, p. 8.
16. The terms *middlemen* and *intermediaries* may be used interchangeably. We have chosen to use intermediaries throughout this book.

CHAPTER 3

1. Adapted from Val Ross and Marina Strauss, "Buy the Book," *The Globe and Mail*, January 11, 1997, pp. C1, C6.
2. Derek Abell, "Strategic Windows," *Journal of Marketing*, July 1978, pp. 21–26.
3. *Pulse of the Middle Market—1990* (New York: BDO Seidman, 1990), pp. 12–13.
4. See Emilio Cvitkovic, "Profiling Your Competitors," *Planning Review*, May–June 1989, pp. 28–30.
5. Malcolm H. B. McDonald, "Ten Barriers to Marketing Planning," *The Journal of Business and Industrial Marketing*, Winter 1992, p. 15.
6. Edward DiMingo, "The Fine Art of Positioning," *The Journal of Business Strategy*, March/April 1988, pp. 34–38.
7. Suein L. Hwang, "Its Big Brands Long Taunted as Fatty, CPC Tries a More 'Wholesome' Approach," *The Wall Street Journal*, April 20, 1992, pp. B1, B4.
8. Differential advantage in the context of services industries is examined in G. Bharadwj, P. J. Varadarajan, and John Fahy, "Sustainable Competitive Advantages in Service Industries," *Journal of Marketing*, October 1993, pp. 83–99. An excellent article stressing that strategy should focus on customer needs, not just on beating competition, is Kenichi Ohmae, "Getting Back to Strategy," *Harvard Business Review*, November–December 1988, pp. 149–156.
9. Barbara Buell, "Apple: New Team, New Strategy," *Business Week*, October 15, 1990, pp. 86–89.
10. An excellent source of information on how various companies prepare their marketing plans is Howard Sutton, *The Marketing Plan* (New York: The Conference Board, 1990).
11. *The Experience Curve Reviewed, IV. The Growth Share Matrix of the Product Portfolio* (Boston: Boston Consulting Group, 1973).
12. First proposed by H. Igor Ansoff, "Strategies for Diversification," *Harvard Business Review*, September–October 1957, pp. 113–124; see also Ansoff, *The New Corporate Strategy* (New York: John Wiley and Sons, 1988), pp. 82–85.
13. Eastman Kodak Company, "Kodak Provides a Hands-on View of What Digital Pictures Can Do," Press Release, June 2, 1997, http://www.kodak.com/aboutKodak...essReleases/pr19970602-05.shtml.

CHAPTER 4

1. YMCA Regina, "On-line Information on Programs at the Y," 1997, http://ymca.sask.com.
2. For an interesting and detailed discussion of the use of geodemographic clustering in marketing, see the December 1993 issue of *Research PLUS*, a magazine published by the Market Research Society, London, England.
3. *Market Research Handbook*, Statistics Canada, cat. no. 63-224. For additional information on the market represented by seniors in Canada, see *A Portrait of Seniors in Canada* (Ottawa: Statistics Canada, 1990), cat. no. 89-519.
4. For additional information on the market represented by children in Canada, see *A Portrait of Children in Canada* (Ottawa: Statistics Canada, 1990), cat. no. 89-520.
5. Elena Cherney, "Air Canada Bows to Kids' 'Pester Power'," *Montreal Gazette*, March 20, 1996, p. F1.
6. Eve Lazarus, "Making the Grade with Students," *Marketing Magazine*, November 25, 1996, pp. 22–24. For additional information on the buying power of the teen market in Canada, see *Youth in Canada* (Ottawa: Statistics Canada, 1989), cat. no. 89-511.
7. Jennifer Lewington, "Universities Give Recruitment Old College Try," *The Globe and Mail*, July 4, 1997, p. A1.
8. Andrew Trimble, "Feeding the Seniors' Market: A Food Company Is Developing a New Niche," *The Toronto Star*, March 31, 1997, p. E 3; Judy Creighton, "Gadgets for Seniors," *Winnipeg Free Press*, November 17, 1995, p. D3.
9. For an additional perspective on the changing segmentation of the women's market, see Michael Adams, *Sex in the Snow: Canadian Social Values at the End of the Millennium* (Toronto: Penguin, 1997).
10. For a view of the family life cycle that reflects the growing number of single adults, with or without dependent children, see Patrick E. Murphy and

William A. Staples, "A Modernized Family Life Cycle," *Journal of Consumer Research*, June 1979, pp. 12–22; and *New Trends in the Family: Demographic Facts and Features* (Ottawa: Statistics Canada, 1991), cat. no. 91-535E occasional.

11. For an excellent statistical overview of the modern Canadian family, see *A Portrait of Families in Canada* (Ottawa: Statistics Canada, 1993), cat. no. 89-523.
12. *Vancouver Sun*, September 29, 1995, p. C2.
13. Eve Lazarus, "Supermarket Chain Caters to Asian Shoppers," *Marketing News*, February 24, 1997, p. 2.

CHAPTER 5

1. Tom Incantalupo, "It Just Grows on You," *Calgary Herald*, December 6, 1996, p. E5.
2. Greg Goldin, "When Brand is Grand," *World Business*, November/December 1996, pp. 19–23.
3. Lesley Daw, "A Second Beer from B.C. Invades Ontario," *Marketing Magazine*, March 17, 1997.
4. Lynn R. Kahle, Sharon E. Beatty, and Pamela Homer, "Alternative Measurement Approaches to Consumer Values: The List of Values (LOV) and Values and Lifestyles (VAL)," *Journal of Consumer Research*, December 1986, pp. 405–409.
5. For a more complete discussion of VALS and VALS 2, see William L. Wilkie, *Consumer Behaviour*, 2nd ed. (New York: John Wiley & Sons, 1990).
6. Rebecca Piirto, "VALS the Second Time," *American Demographics*, July 1991, p. 6.
7. See Russell J. Haley, "Benefit Segmentation: A Decision Oriented Research Tool," *Journal of Marketing*, July 1968, pp. 30–35. For an update on this classic article and the concept of benefit segmentation, see Haley, "Benefit Segmentation — 20 years later," *Journal of Consumer Marketing*, vol. 1, no. 2, 1983, pp. 5–13.
8. Allanna Sullivan, "Mobil Bets Drivers Pick Cappuccino over Low Prices," *The Wall Street Journal*, January 30, 1995, p. B1.
9. Home page, "The Artful Cookie," 1997, http://www.vaxxine.com/cookie/.
10. Eve Lazarus, "The Bay 'Micro-Marketing' to Asians," *Marketing Magazine*, October 14, 1996, p. 5.
11. Gordon, Jaremko, "In Focus: Peter Jeune Launched the Camera Shop to Serve the Niche Photographic Market at the Top," *Calgary Herald*, December 16, 1996, p. C1.
12. Mark Maremont, "They're All Screaming for Häagen-Dazs," *Business Week*, October 14, 1991, p. 121.
13. Ann Kerr, "Service Is the Inn Thing as Prices Hit Floor," *The Globe and Mail*, September 14, 1993, p. C2.
14. Steven E. Prokesch, "Competing on Customer Service: An Interview with British Airways' Sir Colin Marshall," *Harvard Business Review*, November–December, 1995, pp. 101–112.
15. Mel Duvall, "Leap of Faith," *Calgary Herald*, July 15, 1996, p. C1.
16. Patrick Brethour, "Apple Taking Aim at Niche Markets," *The Globe and Mail*, November 1, 1996, p. B8.
17. Lara Mills, "Doc Martens Stepping Out to Reach an Older Market," *Marketing Magazine*, October 23, 1995, p. 2.
18. Eve Lazarus, "Sun-Rype Aims to Build Snack-Food Brands," *Marketing Online*, www.marketingmag.ca.
19. James Walker, "Designer Fries Find Niche," *The Financial Post*, September 3, 1996, p. 8.
20. Selkirk Tangiers home page, 1997, http://www.selkirk-tangiers.com/.
21. Toronto Dominion Bank home page, 1997, http://www.tdbank.ca/.
22. Allan J. Magrath, "Niche Marketing: Finding a Safe, Warm Cave," *Sales and Marketing Management in Canada*, May 1987, p. 40. The reader is also referred to Robert E. Linneman and John L. Stanton, Jr., "Mining for Niches," *Business Horizons*, vol. 35, no. 3, May/June 1992, pp. 43–51.
23. Philip Demont, "CBCI Telecom Inc.," *Financial Post*, December 11, 1996, p. 27.
24. Alex Taylor III, "Porsche Slices Up Its Buyers," *Fortune*, January 16, 1995, p. 24.
25. James Pollock, "Tales of Retail Turnaround Strategies," *Marketing Magazine*, February 3, 1997, p. 4.
26. James Pollock, "Pharma Plus Pushes New Health Store Formats," *Marketing Magazine*, September 23, 1996, p. 4.
27. Cyndee Miller, "Food Producers Appeal to Fat-Free Crowd," *Marketing News*, August 14, 1995, p. 3.
28. For more detail on the use of test markets and simulated test markets, see James G. Barnes, *Research for Marketing Decision Making* (Toronto: McGraw-Hill Ryerson, 1991), pp. 516–522.

CHAPTER 6

1. Adapted from Patrick Brethaur, "Is This the Year for Internet Commerce?" *The Globe and Mail*, January 15, 1997, p. B12; Christopher Anderson, "In Search of the Perfect Market: A Survey of Electronic Commerce," *The Economist*, May 10, 1997, pp. 2–18; and Amanda Lang, "Still Searching for the Holy Grail," *The Financial Post*, June 19, 1997, p. 17.
2. R. Craig Endicott, "Advertising Fact Book," *Advertising Age*, January 6, 1992, p. S-11.
3. Clyde Kluckhohn, "The Concept of Culture," in Richard Kluckhohn, ed., *Culture and Behaviour* (New York: Free Press, 1962), p. 26.
4. Dwight R. Thomas, "Culture and Consumption Behavior in English and French Canada," in Bent Stidsen, ed., *Marketing in the 1970s and Beyond* (Edmonton: Canadian Association of Administrative Sciences, Marketing Division, 1975), pp. 255–261.
5. S.B. Ashe, Carol Duhaime, and John A. Quelch, "Consumer Satisfaction: A Comparison of English- and French-Speaking Canadians," in Vernon Jones, *Marketing*, vol. 1, part 3, *Proceedings of the Administrative Sciences Association of Canada* (Montreal: Marketing Division, 1980), pp. 11–20.
6. Eve Lazarus, "The Bay 'Micro-Marketing' to Asians," *Marketing Magazine*, October 14, 1996, p. 5.
7. Mikala Folb, "Marketers Awaken to Ethnic Magazines' Promise," *Marketing Magazines*, July 15, 1996.
8. D.W. Greeno and W. F. Bennett, "Social Class and Income as Complementary Segmentation Bases: A Canadian Perspective," in *Proceedings of the Marketing Division, Administrative Sciences Association of Canada*, 1983, pp. 113–122.
9. W. Lloyd Warner and Paul Lunt, *The Social Life of a Modern Community* (New Haven: Yale University Press, 1941); and W. Lloyd Warner, Marchia Meeker, and Kenneth Eells, *Social Class in America*, (Chicago: Science Research Associates, 1949).
10. Anita Lahey, "Bauer Gets Boost at World Cup of Hockey," *Marketing Magazine*, September 2, 1996, p. 2.
11. See Elihu Katz and Paul Lazarsfeld, *Personal Influence*, (New York: Free Press, 1955), especially p. 325.
12. Sara Curtis, "Radio Show Targets Children 8 to 15," *Marketing Magazine*, October 7, 1996, p. 3.
13. Lara Mills, "Cadbury Spins Tale to Nab Easter Market," *Marketing Magazine*, March 10, 1997, p. 3.
14. A. H. Maslow, *Motivation and Personality* (New York: Harper & Row, 1954), pp. 80–106.
15. Edward M. Tauber, "Why Do People Shop?" *Journal of Marketing*, October 1972, pp. 46–49.
16. Other schools of thought on learning, principally the cognitive approach and gestalt learning, are discussed in books on consumer behaviour. See David Loudon and Albert J. Della Bitta, *Consumer Behavior*, 3rd ed. (New York: McGraw-Hill, 1988).
17. For an analytical review of self-concept studies, the research problems connected with these studies, and a comprehensive bibliography, see M. Joseph Sirgy, "Self-Concept in Consumer Behaviour: A Critical Review," *Journal of Consumer Research*, December 1982, pp. 287–300.
18. Gordon W. Allport, "Attitudes," in C. A. Murchinson, ed., *A Handbook of Social Psychology* (Worcester, MA: Clark University Press, 1935), pp. 798–844.
19. Andrew Poon and Dawn Walton, "Tables Turning on Fast Food," *The Globe and Mail Report on Business*, July 5, 1997, pp. B1, B3.
20. For a listing of Canadian companies found on Sympatico, check the Internet address http:\\maplesquare.sympatico.ca.

CHAPTER 7

1. Adapted from Elizabeth Church, "Family Firm Squares Off Against Giant U.S. Rival," *The Globe and Mail*, May 19, 1997, p. B5.
2. "Chrysler Pushes Quality Down the Supply Chain," *Purchasing*, July 13, 1995, pp. 125–128.
3. Joanne Lipmann, "Compaq Pushing New Line, New Images," *The Wall Street Journal*, June 2, 1992, p. B5; Michael Allen, "Developing New Lines of Low-Priced PCs Shakes Up Compaq," *The Wall Street Journal*, June 15, 1992, pp. A1, A4.
4. Some background on relationship building is described in F. Robert Dwyer, Paul H. Schurr, and Sejo Oh, "Developing Buyer–Seller Relationships," *Journal of Marketing*, April 1987, pp. 11–27. A simple approach to building relationships is described in Barry J. Farber and Joyce Wycoff, "Relationships: Six Steps to Success," *Sales & Marketing Management*, April 1992, pp. 50–58; see also Patricia Doney and Joseph Cannon, "An Examination of the Nature of Trust in Buyer–Seller Relationships," *Journal of Marketing*, vol. 61, April 1997, pp. 35–51.

5. An interesting description of value imaging, the psychological influences on business buying behaviour, can be found in Paul Sherlock, "The Irrationality of 'Rational' Business Buying Decisions," *Marketing Management*, Spring 1992, pp. 8–15.
6. Robert D. McWilliams, Earl Naumann, and Stan Scott, "Determining Buying Center Size," *Industrial Marketing Management*, February 1992, pp. 43–49.
7. Ken Yamada, "Apple to Unveil Mail Order Catalog and Sell Directly to Big Companies," *The Wall Street Journal*, September 17, 1992, p. B7.
8. For examples of benefit segmentation as used in the business market, see Mark L. Bennion, Jr., "Segmentation and Positioning in a Basic Industry," *Industrial Marketing Management*, February 1987, pp. 9–18; Susan A. Lynn, "Segmenting a Business Market for a Professional Service," *Industrial Marketing Management*, February 1986, pp. 13–21; Rowland T. Moriarty and David J. Reibstein, "Benefit Segmentation in Industrial Markets," *Journal of Business Research*, December 1986, pp. 483–486; and Cornelis A. de Kluyver and David B. Whitlark, "Benefit Segmentation for Industrial Products," *Industrial Marketing Management*, November 1986, pp. 273–286.
9. For some additional approaches to business marketing segmentation, see Benson P. Shapiro and Thomas V. Bonoma, "How to Segment Industrial Markets," *Harvard Business Review*, May/June 1984, pp. 104–110. See also James G. Barnes and Ronald McTavish, "Segmenting Industrial Markets by Buyer Sophistication," *European Journal of Marketing*, vol. 17, no. 6, 1983, pp. 16–33.
10. For an excellent review of the literature on industrial market segmentation — some thirty articles spanning twenty years — see Richard E. Plank, "A Critical Review of Industrial Market Segmentation," *Industrial Marketing Management*, May 1985, pp. 79–91. Also, a detailed coverage of the topic is contained in Thomas V. Bonoma and Benson P. Shapiro, *Segmenting the Industrial Market* (Lexington, MA: Lexington Books, 1983).

CHAPTER 8

1. Automatch, "Men vs. Women Car Buyers," June 9, 1997, http://www.automatch.com/.
2. Lesley Daw, "Success Insurance," *Marketing Magazine*, June 30, 1997, p. 21.
3. In "New Marketing Research Definition Approved," *Marketing News*, January 2, 1987, p. 1, the American Marketing Association defined marketing research as follows: "Marketing research links the consumer, customer, and public to the marketer through information — information used to identify and define marketing opportunities and problems; generate, refine, and evaluate marketing actions; monitor marketing performance; and improve understanding of marketing as a process. Marketing research specifies the information required to address these issues; designs the methods for collecting information; manages and implements the data collection process; analyzes the results; and communicates the findings and their implications."
4. Eva E. Kiess-Moser and James G. Barnes, "Emerging Trends in Marketing Research: The Link with Customer Satisfaction," Ottawa: The Conference Board of Canada, Report 82–92, 1992.
5. For an overview of the development of marketing information systems, the reader may wish to see Kimball P. Marshall and Stephen W. LaMotte, "Marketing Information Systems: A Marriage of Systems Analysis and Marketing Management," *Journal of Applied Business Research*, vol. 8, no. 3, Summer 1992, pp. 61–73.
6. For more information on the development of marketing decision support systems, see James G. Barnes, *Research for Marketing Decision Making* (Toronto: McGraw-Hill Ryerson, 1991), pp. 15–16; Louis A. Wallis, *Decision-Support Systems for Marketing*, Conference Board Research Report no. 923 (New York: The Conference Board, Inc., 1989); and Rajendra S. Sisodia, "Marketing Information Systems and Decision Support Systems for Services," *The Journal of Services Marketing*, vol. 6, no. 1, Winter 1992, pp. 51–64.
7. Gordon Arnaut, "The Best Is Still to Come, Data Base Analyst Says," *The Globe and Mail*, December 17, 1996, p. B29; Terrence Belford, "Air Mile Collectors Yield Wealth of Data," *The Globe and Mail*, December 17, 1996, p. B28.
8. Maurice Simms, "Retailers Pin Their Hope on Marketing Skill," *The Globe and Mail*, February 15, 1994, p. B28.
9. Mark Lurie, "Direct Mail Success Takes Sharp Aim," *The Globe and Mail*, December 17, 1996, p. B29.

10. For more information on the issue of privacy in the use of databases, see Joe Clark, "Privacy Issues Are Never Far from the Surface," *The Globe and Mail*, February 15, 1994, p. B28; and Deborah Wilson, "Banks Face Task of Assuring Clients They're Served, not Shadowed," *The Globe and Mail*, December 17, 1996, p. B27.
11. Robert C. Blattberg and John Deighton, "Interactive Marketing: Exploiting the Age of Addressability," *Sloan Management Review*, Fall 1991, pp. 5–14.
12. For a more detailed discussion of scanner panels and single-source data, see James G. Barnes, *Research for Marketing Decision Making* (Toronto: McGraw-Hill Ryerson, 1991), pp. 137–140.
13. Salem Alaton, "Mining the Internet," *The Globe and Mail*, December 17, 1996, p. B27.
14. For a discussion of the issue of the representativeness of the sample in mall-intercept surveys, compared with other approaches to data collection, see Alan J. Bush and A. Parasuraman, "Mall Intercept versus Telephone-Interviewing Environment," *Journal of Advertising Research*, vol. 25, no. 2, April/May 1985, pp. 36–43; and Thomas D. Dupont, "Do Frequent Mall Shoppers Distort Mall-Intercept Survey Results?" *Journal of Advertising Research*, vol. 27, August/September 1987, pp. 45–51.
15. See, for example, Srinivasan Ratneshwar and David W. Stewart, "Nonresponse in Mail Surveys: An Integrative Review," *Applied Marketing Research*, Summer 1989, pp. 37–46; Bruce J. Walker, Wayne Kirchmann, and Jeffery S. Conant, "A Method to Improve Response to Industrial Mad Surveys," *Industrial Marketing Management*, November 1987, pp. 305–314; and A.J. Faria and John R. Dickinson, "Mail Survey Response, Speed, and Cost," *Industrial Marketing Management*, February 1992, pp. 51–60.
16. For additional detail on the use of the individual depth interview and the focus group interview, see James G. Barnes, *Research for Marketing Decision Making* (Toronto: McGraw-Hill Ryerson, 1991), chapter 12; David Morgan, ed., *Successful Focus Groups* (Beverley Hills, CA: Sage Publications, 1993); Richard A. Krueger, *Focus Groups*, 2nd ed. (Beverley Hills, CA: Sage Publications, 1994); Thomas Greenbaum, *The Practical Handbook and Guide to Focus Group Research* (Boston: D.C. Heath and Co., 1988).
17. For two interesting articles on the use of focus group interviews by Canadian firms, see Suanne Kelman, "Consumers on the Couch," *Report on Business Magazine*, February 1991, pp. 50-53; and Jared Mitchell, "The Truth Is Not for the Squeamish," *Report on Business Magazine*, March 1987, pp. 75–76.
18. Robert Everett-Green, "The Great Canadian Hunt for Home-Grown Videos," *The Globe and Mail*, June 13, 1996, p. A13.
19. Howard Schlossberg, "Simulated vs. Traditional Test Marketing," *Marketing News*, October 23, 1989, pp. 1–2, 11.
20. Kathy Gardner Chadwick, "Some Caveats Regarding the Interpretation of Data from 800 Number Callers," *Journal of Services Marketing*, Summer 1991, pp. 55–61.

CHAPTER 9

1. Adapted from Geoffrey Rowan, "Infrared Connection Unshackles Wired World," *The Globe and Mail*, May 20, 1997, pp. B1, B8; Wendy Cukier, "Wireless Data's Delay," *The Globe and Mail*, April 8, 1997, p. C2; and, in part, Andrew Tausz, "Novelty Begins at Home," *The Globe and Mail*, January 14, 1994, p. B19.
2. Yumiko Ono, "Some Kids Won't Eat the Middle of an Oreo," *The Wall Street Journal*, November 20, 1991, p. B1.
3. "What's New for 1997," *Journey of Innovation*, Cadillac's home page, July 1997, http://www.cadillac.com/; Gerry Malloy, "TechByte Cadillac OnStar: Star Trek Technology for the Road," *The Globe & Mail*, October 10, 1996, p. E4.
4. For a different classification scheme that provides strategic guidelines for management by relating products and prices, along with an excellent bibliography on product classification, see Patrick E. Murphy and Ben M. Enis, "Classifying Products Strategically," *Journal of Marketing*, July 1986, pp. 24–42. Also see Ernest F. Cooke, "The Relationship Between a Product Classification System and Marketing Strategy," *Journal of Midwest Marketing*, Spring 1987, pp. 230–240.
5. Susan Yellin, "Innovation, Acquisition Catapulting to the Top," *The Financial Post*, February 12, 1997, p. 8.
6. "Study: Launching New Products Is Worth the Risk," *Marketing News*, January 20, 1992, p. 2.

7. "Procter & Gamble Unveils New Tide High Efficiency," *P&G Product News Releases*, P&G home page, March 1997, http://www.pg.com (March 20, 1997).
8. "1995 Innovation Survey," conducted by Group EFO Limited of Weston, CT.
9. Eugene Carlson, "Some Forms of Identification Can't Be Handily Faked," *The Wall Street Journal*, September 14, 1993, p. B2.
10. James Gillmore and Joseph Pine, "The Four Faces of Mass Customization," *Harvard Business Review*, January–February, 1997, pp. 91–101.
11. The benefits cited are from a study reported in Robert G. Cooper and Elko J. Kleinschmidt, "New Product Processes at Leading Industrial Firms," *Industrial Marketing Management*, May 1991, pp. 137–147. For an approach to improve the management of multiple new-product development projects, see Steven C. Wheelwright and Kim B. Clark, "Creating Project Plans to Focus Product Development," *Harvard Business Review*, March–April 1992, pp. 70–82.
12. For a report on the criteria used in making "go–no go" decisions in the product-development process, see Ilkka A. Ronkainen, "Criteria Changes across Product Development Stages," *Industrial Marketing Management*, August 1985, pp. 171–178.
13. "Study: Launching New Products Is Worth the Risk," loc. cit.
14. For more on the first two stages, termed opportunity identification, see Linda Rochford, "Generating and Screening New Product Ideas," *Industrial Marketing Management*, November 1991, pp. 287–296.
15. For foundations of diffusion theory and a review of landmark studies on diffusion of innovation, see Everett M. Rogers, *Diffusion of Innovations*, 3rd ed. (New York: Free Press, 1983).
16. Gerry Blackwell, "Digital Cameras Improving the Age" *Toronto Star*, February 27, 1997, pp. J1, J3.
17. Rogers, op. cit.
18. "Kodak Video Tape Feature Differentiation," Kodak home page, July 1997, http://www.kodak.com/ (July 14, 1997).
19. Various arrangements are discussed in Eric Olsen, Orville Walker, and Robert Reukert, "Organizing for Effective New Product Development," *Journal of Marketing*, January 1995, pp. 48–62.

CHAPTER 10

1. "Labatt Puts a New Twist on 'Ice' Beer," *Marketing Magazine*, August 12, 1996 p. 3; "Labatt Select in a Class of Its Own," May 10, 1996, news release, http:// www.labatt.com.
2. "Signature Cream Ale," May 26, 1997, news release, http://www.molson.com.
3. Adapted from David A. Aaker and J. Gary Shansby, "Positioning Your Product," *Business Horizons*, May/June 1982, pp. 56–58.
4. James Pollock, "Neilson Dives Into Soy Beverage Market," *Marketing Magazine*, March 3, 1997, p. 3.
5. Marina Strauss, "Canada Rated 6th in Quality of Its Manufactured Goods," *The Globe and Mail*, February 10, 1994, p. B6.
6. Judann Pollack and Ira Teinowitz, "Quaker, Gen'l Mills Start Oat Bran Ads," *Advertising Age*, January 27, 1997, p. 12.
7. Richard Gibson, "Haagen-Dazs' New Ice Creams Have Less Fat," *The Wall Street Journal*, January 10, 1997, p. B14.
8. Debra Sykes, "Low-Fat Market Proves Elusive for Fast-Food Chains," *Stores*, July 1996, pp. 50–53.
9. Kathy Tyrer, "Selling Hockey in the Land of La La and Disney," *Marketing*, November 8, 1993, p. 5.
10. Ginger Conlon, "A Brand New Day," *Sales and Marketing Management*, vol. 148, December 1996, pp. 58–63.
11. "New Crest Toothpaste, Toothbrush Introduced," news release, May 26, 1997, http:// www.pg.com.
12. Ariane Sains, "Swiss Army Swells Ranks," *Adweek's Marketing Week*, June 4, 1990, p. 24; Kathleen Deveny, "If Swatch Name Sells Watches, Why Not Cars?" *The Wall Street Journal*, September 20, 1990, p. B1.
13. Glenn Collins, "The Cola War Is Expected to Heat Up," *The New York Times*, January 25, 1997, pp. 37, 39.
14. James Pollock, "Ikea Puts Focus on Office Furniture Market," *Marketing Magazine*, November 4, 1996, p. 4.
15. Mikala Folb, "Minwax Makes Decorative Paint Entry," *Marketing Magazine*, October 14, 1996, p. 6.
16. "Proctor & Gamble Out to Simplify Its Product Lines," *Advertising Age*, September 30, 1996, p. 21.
17. Vijay Vishwanath and Jonathan Mark, "Your Brand's Best Strategy," *Harvard Business Review*, May–June, 1997, pp. 123–129.
18. The criticisms are summarized in Geoffrey L. Gordon, Roger J. Calantone, and C. Anthony di

Benedetto, "Mature Markets and Revitalization Strategies: An American Fable," *Business Horizons*, May–June 1991, pp. 39–50. Alternative life cycles are proposed in Edward D. Popper and Bruce D. Buskirk, "Technology Life Cycles in Industrial Markets," *Industrial Marketing Management*, February 1992, pp. 23–31; and C. Merle Crawford, "Business Took the Wrong Life Cycle from Biology," *The Journal of Product and Brand Management*, Winter 1992, pp. 51–57.

19. Laurence Zuckerman, "The Hand-Held Computer is Introduced Once Again," *The New York Times*, November 18, 1996, p. D8.
20. For more on this subject, see Steven P. Schnaars, "When Entering Growth Markets, Are Pioneers Better than Poachers?" *Business Horizons*, March–April 1986, pp. 27–36.
21. Jim Carlton, "Nintendo, Gambling with Its Technology, Faces a Crucial Delay," *The Wall Street Journal*, May 5, 1995, pp. A1, A4.
22. For a study examining business products, see Jorge Vasconcellos, "Key Success Factors in Marketing Mature Products," *Industrial Marketing Management*, November 1991, pp. 263–278.
23. For discussion of four strategies — recapture, redesign, refocus, and recast — that are particularly applicable to business products, see Paul C.N. Michell, Peter Quinn, and Edward Percival, "Marketing Strategies for Mature Industrial Products," *Industrial Marketing Management*, August 1991, pp. 201–206; for discussion of five strategies used by the Quaker Oats Company for consumer products, see James R. Tindall, "Marketing Established Brands," *The Journal of Consumer Marketing*, Fall 1991, pp. 5–10.
24. Lesley Daw, "How to Market a Milestone," *Marketing Magazine*, March 10, 1997, pp. 10–11.
25. Mikala Folb, "Playskool Beat Bacteria," *Marketing Magazine*, March 17, 1997.
26. Lesley Daw, "Cigna Markets Women's Health Insurance," *Marketing Magazine*, March 10, 1997, p. 4.
27. Joan E. Rigdon, "Kodak Tries to Prepare for Filmless Era without Inviting Demise of Core Business," *The Wall Street Journal*, April 18, 1991, p. B1.
28. "Kodak Is at the Heart of Photography with Its New Kodak Gold Film Portfolio," Kodak Limited, press releases, 1997, www.kodak.com.
29. Meg Cox, "Ad Blitz Turns Dictionary into Best Seller," *The Wall Street Journal*, October 23, 1992, p. A9A.
30. For suggestions on how to recognize the technological limits of an existing product — in effect, knowing when to get off the curve for an existing product and to jump on the curve for the next product — see Richard Foster, "When to Make Your Move to the Latest Innovation," *Across the Board*, October 1986, pp. 44–50.

CHAPTER 11

1. "Second Cup Facts," "Coffee Facts," *Second Cup Home Page*, April 1997, http://wwwsecondcup.com/2cup_facts.html (April 6, 1997).
2. Eric Swetsky, "The Naming of Names," *Marketing*, February 21, 1994, p. 30.
3. For an in-depth discussion of branding, the student is referred to Raymond Perrier, ed., *Brand Valuation*, 3rd ed. (London: Premier Books, 1997).
4. Howard Schlossberg, "Brand Value Can Be Worth More than Physical Assets," *Marketing News*, March 5, 1990, p. 6.
5. Larry Black, "What's in a Name?" *Report on Business Magazine*, November 1989, pp. 98–110.
6. "Marketing Energy: Name Games," *The Economist*, June 28–July 4, 1997, p. 65.
7. Betsy Morris, "The Brand's the Thing," *Fortune*, March 4, 1996, pp. 73–86.
8. For an in-depth discussion on the value of branding, see David Arnold, *The Handbook of Brand Management* (London: Pitman Publishing, 1992.
9. Jamie Beckett, "Inventing a Product Name Is Part Science, Part Art," *The Globe and Mail*, October 27, 1992, p. B4.
10. See also Kim Robertson, "Strategically Desirable Brand Name Characteristics," *The Journal of Product and Brand Management*, Summer 1992, pp. 62–72.
11. Kamran Kashani, "A New Future for Brands," *Financial Times, Mastering Management* (London: Pitman, 1997), pp. 171–174.
12. For an excellent discussion of the nature and benefits of this strategy, see Donald G. Norris, "Ingredient Branding: A Strategy Option with Multiple Beneficiaries," *The Journal of Consumer Marketing*, Summer 1992, pp. 19–31.

13. Russell Mitchell, "Intel Isn't Taking This Lying Down," *Business Week*, September 30, 1991, pp. 32–33.
14. Canada News Wire, "Air Canada and Second Cup Forge New Partnerships from the Grounds Up," press release, February 17, 1997, http://www.newswire.ca/releases/February 1997/17/c3272.html.
15. For a very interesting look at the success of Loblaw in the private-label business and at the developer of the program, Dave Nichol, see Mark Stevenson, "Global Gourmet," *Canadian Business*, July 1993, pp. 22–33; see also Anne Kingston, *The Edible Man: Dave Nichol, President's Choice and the Making of Popular Taste* (Toronto: Macfarlane, Walter & Ross, 1994).
16. The 1993 study of personal computers was summarized in Kyle Pope, "Computers: They're No Commodity," *The Wall Street Journal*, October 15, 1993, p. B1.
17. George Stalk, Jr. "What's in a Brand? It's the Experience," *The Globe and Mail*, May 23, 1997, p. B11.
18. Betsy Morris, "The Brand's the Thing," *Fortune*, March 4, 1996, pp. 73–86.
19. Fawzia Skeikh, "Borrowing Brands," *Marketing Magazine*, July 7, 1997, pp. 8–9.
20. For a good discussion of this topic, see Leonard L. Berry, Edwin F. Lefkowith, and Terry Clark, "In Services, What's in a Name?" *Harvard Business Review*, September/October 1988, pp. 38–40. Some of the examples in this section are drawn from this source.
21. Debbie Galante Block, "CD-ROM Packaging, Present and Future: The Drive Toward Automation and Alternative Casing," *CD-ROM Professional*, October 1996, pp. 69–79.
22. Information on this program can be obtained from Environment Canada's Web site: http://www.ns.ec.gc.ca/.
23. "Labeling Cooperation Urged," *Marketing News*, May 9, 1994, p. 17.
24. For information related to this Act, the Government of Canada has set up the Competition Bureau, which can answer any questions. You can write to Industry Canada, 50 Victoria Street, Hull, Quebec, K1A 0C9, or phone 1-800-348-5358. Industry Canada's web site is http://www.ic.gc.ca. All government departments can be reached on the Internet at http://www.gc.ca.
25. For further information on any federal Acts or regulations, contact the Government of Canada Web page at http://www.gc.ca.
26. Ann Gibbon, "Smoking's Labelling Perils," *The Globe and Mail*, May 5, 1994, p. B1; and "The Supreme Court of Canada Ruling on the Tobacco Products Control Act," Health Canada, 1997, http://www.hcsc.gc.ca/main.hc/web/datapcb/communc/home/news/85bk2e.html (December 1995).
27. For a list of reasons why product quality is so important and for a discussion of the marketing function's role in quality management, see Neil A. Morgan and Nigel F. Piercy, "Market-Led Quality," *Industrial Marketing Management*, May 1992, pp. 111–118.

CHAPTER 12

1. Adapted from Ijeoma Ross, "Loyalty Program Rewards Firm," *The Globe and Mail*, July 24, 1997, p. B10.
2. Brad Evenson, "For Better or Worse, Service Jobs Growing," *The Montreal Gazette*, March 13, 1996, pp. F1, F4.
3. Jacques Bughin, "Creating Jobs in the Service Sector," *Policy Options*, July–August, 1996, pp. 29–32.
4. "The Final Frontier," *The Economist*, February 20, 1993, p. 63.
5. Statistics Canada, "Are Services Jobs Low-paying," cat. no. 75-001-XPE, issue 96001, March 12, 1996.
6. "The Flip Side of Flipping Hamburgers," *The Globe and Mail*, April 8, 1996, p. A6.
7. Leonard L. Berry and Terry Clark, "Four Ways to Make Services More Tangible," *Business*, October/December 1986, p. 53. Also see Betsy D. Gelb, "How Marketers of Intangibles Can Raise the Odds for Consumer Satisfaction," *Journal of Services Marketing*, Summer 1987, pp. 11–17.
8. See Elizabeth Church, "Store Owners Struggle with Staffing," *The Globe and Mail*, November 25, 1996, p. B6; and "Service with a Smile," *The Economist*, July 12, 1997, p. 55.
9. William R. Pape, "Putting Customers on the Line," *Inc. Technology*, 1997, no. 1, pp. 23–24.
10. See for example, Frederick F. Reichheld and W. Earl Sasser, Jr., "Zero Defections: Quality Comes to Services," *Harvard Business Review*, September–October 1990, pp. 105-111; Barbara Ettorre, "The Bottom Line on Customer Loyalty," *Management Review*, March 1997, pp. 16–18; and Elizabeth Church, "How to Keep Customers," *The Globe and Mail*, February 27, 1996, p. B14.

11. James L. Heskett, Thomas O. Jones, Gary W. Loveman, W. Earl Sasser, Jr., and Leonard A. Schlesinger, "Putting the Service-Profit Chain to Work," *Harvard Business Review*, March–April 1994, pp. 164–174.
12. See for example, James G. Barnes, "Establishing Relationships: Getting Closer to the Customer May Be More Difficult Than You Think," *Irish Marketing Review*, May 1995, pp. 561–570; and James G. Barnes and Daphne A. Sheaves, "The Fundamentals of Relationships," in Teresa A. Swartz, David E. Bowen, and Stephen W. Brown, eds., *Advances in Services Marketing and Management*, vol. 5 (Greenwich, CT: JAI Press, 1996), pp. 215–245.
13. James Pollock, "Pumping Up the Relationship," *Marketing*, October 7, 1996, p. 10.
14. Tobi Swanwick-Billing, "Database Marketing Takes Off," *Marketing*, November 11, 1996, p. 23.
15. Christopher W. Hart, James L. Heskett, and W. Earl Sasser, Jr., "The Profitable Art of Service Recovery: How Best to Turn Complaining Customers Into Loyal Ones," *Harvard Business Review*, July–August 1990, pp. 148–156.
16. Oren Harari, "Thank Heavens for Complainers," *Management Review*, March 1997, pp. 25–29.
17. For a current discussion of the concept of customer value, see Robert B. Woodruff, "Customer Value: The Next Source for Competitive Advantage," *Journal of the Academy of Marketing Science*, vol. 25, no. 2, 1997, pp. 139–153; and A. Parasuraman, "Reflections on Gaining Competitive Advantage Through Customer Value," *Journal of the Academy of Marketing Science*, vol. 25, no. 2, 1997, pp. 154–161.
18. For a model of new-service development, see Eberhard E. Scheuing and Eugene M. Johnson, "A Proposed Model for New Service Development," *The Journal of Services Marketing*, Spring 1989, pp. 25–34. Also see G. Lynn Shostack, "Service Positioning through Structural Change," *Journal of Marketing*, January 1987, pp. 34–43. For an insight into the process for introducing new services to the business-to-business market, see Ulrike de Brentani, "Success and Failure in New Industrial Services," *Journal of Product Innovation Management*, vol. 6, 1989, pp. 238–258.
19. Douglas McArthur, "B&B's Join Cyberspace Bandwagon," *The Globe and Mail*, March 19, 1997, p. C2.
20. "Two Cheers for Loyalty," *The Economist*, January 6, 1996, p. 49.
21. Lisa Saunders, "House Calls," *Winnipeg Free Press*, February 4, 1996, p. B1.
22. Art Chamberlain, "Bank Offers Visa Holders Phone Break," *Toronto Star*, November 15, 1996, p. F3.
23. Leonard L. Berry, Edwin F. Lefkowith, and Terry Clark, "In Services, What's in a Name?" *Harvard Business Review*, September–October 1988, pp. 28–30. Also see Sak Onkvisit and John J. Shaw, "Service Marketing: Image, Branding, and Competition," *Business Horizons*, January/February 1989, pp. 13–18.
24. For an excellent overview of the subject of service quality, see Leonard L. Berry, *On Great Service: A Framework for Action* (New York: Free Press, 1995). Also, the topic of services and service quality is addressed from a number of different perspectives in a special issue of the *Journal of Retailing*, Spring 1993 (vol. 69, no. 1); finally, a rich collection of articles on the subject may be found in Roland T. Rust and Richard L. Oliver, eds., *Service Quality: New Directions in Theory and Practice* (Thousand Oaks, CA: Sage Publications, 1994).
25. For more on the measurement of customers' perceptions of service quality, see A. Parasuraman, Valarie A. Zeithaml, and Leonard L. Berry, "SERVQUAL: A Multiple-item Scale for Measuring Consumer Perceptions of Service Quality," *Journal of Retailing*, Spring 1988, pp. 12–40; V. A. Zeithaml, L.L. Berry, and A. Parasuraman, "The Behavioral Consequences of Service Quality," *Journal of Marketing*, vol. 60, April 1996, pp. 31–46; and L.L. Berry and A. Parasuraman, "Listening to the Customer — The Concept of a Service-Quality information System," *Sloan Management Review*, Spring 1997, pp. 65–76.
26. Judith A. Cumby and James G. Barnes, "How We Make Them Feel: A Discussion of the Reactions of Customers to Affective Dimensions of the Service Encounter," presented at the New and Evolving Paradigms: The Emerging Future of Marketing conference (Services Marketing Track), American Marketing Association, Dublin, Ireland, June 12–15, 1997.
27. "People, Not Tricks, Make Customer Service," *The Globe and Mail*, August 1, 1997, p. B8 (reprinted from *The Economist*).

28. Geoffrey Rowan, "Vending Machines Just Joking Around," *The Globe and Mail*, August 1, 1997, pp. B1, B4.
29. For further discussion of personal selling and service encounters, see William R. George, Patrick Kelly, and Claudia E. Marshall, "The Selling of Services: A Comprehensive Model," *Journal of Personal Selling & Sales Management*, August 1986, pp. 29–37; Mary Jo Bitner, Bernard H. Booms, and Mary Stanfield Tetreault, "The Service Encounter: Diagnosing Favorable and Unfavorable Incidents," *Journal of Marketing*, January 1990, pp. 71–84; and Mary Jo Bitner, "Evaluating Service Encounters: The Effects of Physical Surroundings and Employee Responses," *Journal of Marketing*, April 1990, pp. 69–82.
30. Leonard A. Schlesinger and James L. Heskett, "The Service-Driven Service Company," *Harvard Business Review*, September–October 1991, pp. 71–81.
31. Both quotations are from "How Does Service Drive the Service Company?" (letters to the editor regarding article in preceding note), *Harvard Business Review*, November–December 1991, pp. 146–147.
32. James G. Barnes and Judith A. Cumby, "The Cost of Quality in Service-oriented Companies: Making Better Customer Service Decisions Through Improved Cost Information," *Proceedings of the 23rd Annual Conference of the Atlantic Schools of Business*, Saint John, New Brunswick, November 4–6, 1993, pp. 241-250.
33. Leonard L. Berry, "Improving America's Service," *Marketing Management*, vol. 1, no. 3, pp. 28–38. For each of the five fundamental mistakes, the author discusses several examples, the reasons for the mistakes, and suggestions for correcting the situation.

CHAPTER 13

1. Adapted from Rob Carrick, "Dutch Insurer Makes Banking Beachead," *The Globe and Mail*, June 26, 1997, p. B15.
2. Simona Chiose, "The Not-So-Compact Price of CDs," *The Globe and Mail*, January 25, 1997, pp. C1, C19.
3. For a thorough review of pricing, see Thomas T. Nagle and Reed K. Holden, "Chapter 4: Customers: Understanding and Influencing the Purchase Decision," *The Strategy and Tactics of Pricing: A Guide to Profitable Decision Making* (Englewood Cliffs, NJ: Prentice-Hall, 1995), pp. 72–114.
4. Kimya Kamshad, "A Price for Every Customer," *The Financial Post*, February 13, 1997, pp. 12–13.
5. For a review of pricing strategy, see Nessim Hanna and H. Robert Dodge, *Pricing: Policies and Procedures* (London: McMillan Press, 1995).
6. Jane Coutts, "Drug Price 'Obscene,' Official Says," *The Globe and Mail*, March 26, 1997, p. A5.
7. "Pricing Gets Easier (Sort Of)," *Inc.*, Nov. 1993, p. 124.
8. Michael J. Morris and Roger Calantone, "Four Components of Effective Pricing," *Industrial Marketing Management*, November 1990, p. 323.
9. Thomas L. Powers, "Break-Even Analysis with Semi-Fixed Costs," *Industrial Marketing Management*, February, 1987, pp. 35–41.
10. For a discussion of price wars in fast food, see Gayle MacDonald, "High Stakes in Burger Bargains," *The Globe and Mail*, February 28, 1997, p. B11.
11. Dan Koeppel, "Fast Food's New Reality," *Adweek's Marketing Week*, March 30, 1992, pp. 22–23.
12. Jennifer Lanthier, "Luxury Retailers Enjoy Their Turn in the Spotlight," *The Financial Post*, December 2, 1995, p. 85.
13. Bruce Constantineau, "Cartier Defies B.C. Retail Trend," *Vancouver Sun*, March 29, 1997, pp. B1, B9.

CHAPTER 14

1. Adapted from Konrad Yakabuski, "Bombardier Lands $829-Million Deal," *The Globe and Mail*, May 31, 1997, pp. B1, B2; Konrad Yakabuski, "Bombardier's RJ Rules the Sky," *The Globe and Mail*, June 4, 1997, pp. B1, B6; Oliver Martin, "Regional Aircraft Market Flying High," *The Globe and Mail*, June 18, 1997, p. B6.
2. "IBM Reduces Cost of ThinkPads by Nearly 25 Per Cent," *Canada NewsWire*, July 1997, http://www.newswire.ca/releases/July1997/18/c2902.html.
3. For a discussion of value pricing, see Thomas T. Nagle and Reed K. Holden, "Chapter 8: Customer Negotiation, Pricing in the Trenches," *The Strategy and Tactics of Pricing*, 2nd ed. (Englewood Cliffs, NJ: Prentice-Hall, 1995).
4. Discussions on relationship pricing are included in Tony Cram, *The Power of Relationship Marketing: Keeping Customers for Life* (London: Pitman Publishing, 1994); and Leonard L. Berry, "Relationship Marketing," in Adrian Payne, Martin Christopher, Moira Clark, and Helen Peck, *Relationship Marketing for Competitive Advantage:*

Winning and Keeping Customers (Oxford: Butterworth–Heinemann, 1996), pp. 65–74.

5. Information on the Dimage V is available on Minolta's home page, http://www.minolta.com.
6. Robert Brehl, "Sprint Canada Heats Up Long Distance Price Wars," *The Toronto Star*, February 4, 1997, p. D24; "Sprint Canada Announces a Revolution in Long-Distance Savings," press release, *Canada News Wire*, February 3, 1997, http://www.newswire.ca/releases/February 1997/03/c0010html.
7. Robert M. Schindler and Lori S. Warren, "Effects of Odd Pricing on Price Recall," *Journal of Business*, June 1989, pp. 165–177; Robert Blattberg and Kenneth Wisniewski, "How Retail Price Promotions Work: Empirical Results," Marketing Working Paper No. 42 (Chicago: University of Chicago, 1987).
8. Gene Kaproski, "The Price is Right," *Marketing Tools*, September 1995, p. 56.
9. Stephen J. Hoch, Xavier Dreze, and Mary E. Purk, "EDLP, Hi-Lo and Marketing Arithmetic," *Journal of Marketing*, October 1994, pp. 16–27.
10. "Packaged Goods I: Watching Out for No. 1," *Advertising Age*, June 29, 1997, http://www.adage.com/ news_and_features/(June 29, 1997).
11. "Cereal Makers Face Pricing Crunch," *The Globe and Mail*, May 20, 1996, p. B5.
12. Andrew E. Serwer, "How to Escape a Price War," *Fortune*, June 13, 1994, pp. 82+.
13. Thomas T. Nagle and Reed K. Holden, *The Strategy and Tactics of Pricing: A Guide to Profitable Decision Making* (Englewood Cliffs, NJ: Prentice Hall, 1995). For an economic analysis of price wars, see Nessim Hanna and H. Robert Dodge, *Pricing: Policies and Procedures* (London: Macmillan, 1995).

CHAPTER 15

1. "Royal Bank of Canada Accepting Credit Card Application on the Internet," *Canada News Wire*, June 12, 1997, http://www.newswire.ca/releases/June 1997/12/c2426.html.
2. "Top Reasons to Visit American Express' New Web Site," *Canada News Wire*, July 17, 1997, http://www.newswire.ca/releases/July 1997/17/c2616.html.
3. "Visa, ScotiaBank and TD Announce Canadian Trial of Reloadable Visa Cash Card," *Canada News Wire*, April 15, 1997, http://www.newswire.ca/releases/April 1997/15/c3142.html.
4. For a discussion of services distribution, see Christopher Lovelock, *Services Marketing*, 3rd ed. (Englewood Cliffs, NJ: Prentice Hall, 1996).
5. The concept of shifting activities, the possibility of manufacturers shifting some functions away from their firms, and the opportunity for small wholesalers to perform added functions to maintain their economic viability are all discussed in Ronald D. Michman, "Managing Structural Changes in Marketing Channels," *The Journal of Business and Industrial Marketing*, Summer/Fall 1990, pp. 5–14.
6. Mark Evans, "Direct distribution Gives Dell, Gateway Competitive Edge," *Financial Post Daily*, August 6, 1996, p. 18.
7. An alternative approach that emphasizes market analysis is presented in Allan J. Magrath and Kenneth G. Hardy, "Six Steps to Distribution Network Design," *Business Horizons*, January–February 1991, pp. 48–52.
8. Michael McCullough, "B.C. Credit Union Launches Internet Service," *Marketing Online*, www.marketing-mag.ca/06/16/97.
9. Marshall Fisher, "What Is the Right Supply Chain for Your Product?" *Harvard Business Review*, March–April, 1997, pp. 105–116. For more on selecting channels for international markets, especially the decision of whether to use intermediaries, see Saul Klein, "Selection of International Marketing Channels," *Journal of Global Marketing*, vol. 4, 1991, pp. 21–37.
10. "Levi's Plans Own Stores," *Marketing News*, Jan. 30, 1995, p. 1.
11. "Alberto President Targets Mass Market," *Marketing Magazine*, July 8, 1996, p. 1.
12. "Now There Are 2 Great Ways to Shop On-line," *What's New*, L.L. Bean Home Page, June 16, 1997, http://www.llbean.com/new/; Christopher McCormick, "L.L. Bean," *Advertising Age's Marketing 100* (1996), June 1996, http://www.adage.com/news_and_features/ (July 30, 1997).
13. An excellent discussion of distribution channels for business goods and services is found in Michael D. Hutt and Thomas W. Speh, *Business Marketing and Management*, 4th ed. (Ft. Worth, TX: Dryden Press, 1992), pp. 359–392. For a review of emerging issues on business channels, see Al Magrath, "Managing Distribution Channels," *Business Quarterly*, Spring 1996, pp. 57–65.

14. For an admirable discussion of this topic, see Donald H. Light, "A Guide for New Distribution Channel Strategies for Service Firms," *The Journal of Business Strategy*, Summer 1986, pp. 56–64.
15. Rowland T. Moriarty and Ursula Moran, "Managing Hybrid Marketing Systems," *Harvard Business Review*, November–December 1990, pp. 146–155, use the term hybrid marketing system and stress the importance of analyzing basic marketing tasks to determine how many and what types of channels are needed.
16. For extensive discussion of this strategy, see John A. Quelch, "Why Not Exploit Dual Marketing?" *Business Horizons*, January–February 1987, pp. 52–60.
17. For further discussion of the advantages and disadvantages of multiple channels as well as ways to minimize conflict resulting from multiple channels, see Martin Everett, "When There's More Than One Route to the Customer," *Sales & Marketing Management*, August 1990, pp. 48–50.
18. For more on the idea that market considerations should determine a producer's channel structure, see Louis W. Stern and Frederick D. Sturdivant, "Customer-Driven Distribution Systems," *Harvard Business Review*, July–August 1987, pp. 34–41.
19. John Rossant, "Can Maurizio Gucci Bring the Glamour Back?" *Business Week*, February 5, 1990, pp. 83–84.
20. For further discussion of strategies that either create or offset conflict between manufacturers and retailers, see Allan J. Magrath and Kenneth G. Hardy, "Avoiding the Pitfalls in Managing Distribution Channels," *Business Horizons*, September–October 1987, pp. 29–33.
21. The emerging dominance of gigantic retailers and their dictates to manufacturers are described in Zachary Schiller and Wendy Zellner, "Clout!" *Business Week*, December 21, 1992, pp. 66–69. Customer market power in relation to channel control is covered in Gul Butaney and Lawrence H. Wortzel, "Distributor Power versus Manufacturer Power: The Customer Role," *Journal of Marketing*, January 1988, pp. 52–63.
22. Allan J. Magrath, "The Hidden Clout of Middlemen," *Journal of Business Strategy*, March/April 1990, pp. 38–41. For further ideas on how to build a good producer–intermediary relationship, see James A. Narus and James C. Anderson, "Distributor Contributions to Partnership with Manufacturers," *Business Horizons*, September– October 1987, pp. 34–42.
23. Dan Plashkes, "The Revolution in Television Shopping," *Marketing*, November 15, 1993, p. 53; Patrick Brethour, "Is This the Year For Internet Commerce," *The Globe and Mail*, January 15, 1997, p. B12.
24. "About Amazon.com," *Amazon.com home page*, http://www.amazon.com/exec/obid.

CHAPTER 16

1. Adapted from Patrick Brethaur, "Middleman Bucks Trend by Embracing the Web," *The Globe and Mail*, June 18, 1997, p. B9.
2. For a discussion on channels of distribution, see James A. Narus and James C. Anderson, "Rethinking Distribution: Adaptive Channels," *Harvard Business Review*, July–August, 1996, pp. 112–120.
3. The term *merchant wholesaler*, or *wholesaler*, is sometimes used synonymously with *wholesaling intermediary*. This is not accurate, however. *Wholesaling intermediary* is the all-inclusive term, covering the major categories of firms engaged in wholesale trade, whereas *wholesaler* is more restrictive, applying to only one category, namely, merchant wholesaling intermediaries.
4. Data relevant to the preceding two paragraphs is contained in "Wholesaling and Retailing in Canada, 1994" (Ottawa: Statistics Canada), cat. no. 63-236-XPB.
5. Lesley Daw, "Look! See Janes Build Frozen-Food Empire," *Marketing News*, March 24, 1997, p. 3.
6. Roger Morton, "How to Choose Between Public and Contract Warehousing," *Transportation & Distribution*, April 1997, pp. 107–109.
7. For a discussion of new directions in warehousing, see Tom Andel, "Get Your Warehouse Out of Storage," *Transportation & Distribution*, May 1997, pp. 84–105.
8. Janet McFarland, "Firms to Outsource More Functions: Survey," *The Globe and Mail*, July 30, 1996, p. B7.
9. Neville Nankivell, "Outsourcing Is Big and Growing," *Financial Post*, October 3, 1996, p. 21.
10. Janet Bamford, "Why Competitors Shop for Ideas at Ikea," *Business Week*, October 9, 1989, p. 88.

11. For further discussion of the JIT concept, see Claudia H. Deutsch, "Just in Time: The New Partnerships," *The New York Times*, October 28, 1990, section 3, p. 25; Gary L. Frazier, Robert E. Spekman, and Charles R. O'Neal, "Just-in-Time Exchange Relationships in Industrial Markets," *Journal of Marketing*, October 1988, pp. 52–67; William D. Presutti, Jr., "Just-in-Time Manufacturing and Marketing — Strategic Relationships for Competitive Advantage," *Journal of Business and Industrial Marketing*, Summer 1988, pp. 27–35.
12. Earnest C. Raia, "Journey to World Class (JIT in USA)," *Purchasing*, September 24, 1987, p. 48.
13. Steve McDaniel, Joseph G. Ormsby, and Alicia B. Gresham, "The Effect of JIT on Distributors," *Industrial Marketing Management*, May 1992, pp. 145–149.
14. Wal-Mart's information technology system, mentioned earlier, is a good example of an EDI.
15. For research results indicating that perceptions of different modes vary across members of the buying centre, see James H. Martin, James M. Daley, and Henry B. Burdg, "Buying Influences and Perceptions of Transportation Services," *Industrial Marketing Management*, November 1988, pp. 305–314.

CHAPTER 17

1. Adapted from: "About Amazon.com," home page, 1997, http://www.amazon.com (July 29, 1997); Ira Teich, "Design Is the Issue" and "The Future is Now for Net Retailing," *Marketing Magazine*, March 3, 1997, p. 14.
2. For an interesting insight into how a small family-owned kitchenware retailer in Calgary operates with an emphasis on personalized service, see Cathryn Motherwell, "Where the Business Is Cooking," *The Globe and Mail*, August 24, 1993, p. B28.
3. Lara Mills, "Sears Planning to 'Think Like a Brand'," *Marketing Magazine*, June 30, 1997, p. 2.
4. Anita Lahey, "Retail Renovations," *Marketing Magazine*, June 3, 1996, p. 15.
5. Marina Strauss, "Where Department Stores Fit in the Retail Future," *The Globe and Mail*, May 29, 1997, p. B15.
6. "Advertising Age — 1995 Power 50 — Retail," *Advertising Age*, http://adage.com (June 19, 1997).
7. Marina Strauss, "Zellers Amends its Price Law," *The Globe and Mail*, September 12, 1996, p. B14.
8. James Pollock, "Specialties Thrive on High-End Positioning," *Marketing News*, March 10, 1997, p. 3.
9. Donalee Moulton, "Canadians Eating Out More Often," *Marketing News*, May 12, 1997, p. 4.
10. Ann Gibbon, "Price Club Plans $200-Million Expansion," *The Globe and Mail*, August 31, 1995, p. B2; Marina Strauss, "Discounters Bite into Groceries," *The Globe and Mail*, September 16, 1993, p. B4; and Marina Strauss, "Supermarket Price War Flares Again," *The Globe and Mail*, May 5, 1994, p. B4.
11. Tamsen Tillson, "Edu-tainment Warehouse Planned for Toronto Area," *The Globe and Mail*, September 27, 1994, p. B12.
12. Michael W. Miller, "You're Selling What? Hold on, I'll Let You Speak to My Dog," *The Globe and Mail*, June 29, 1991, p. B18.
13. Statistics Canada, "Vending Machine Operators," cat. no. 63-213, annual; Mary Gooderham, "Your Supermarket Knows Who You Are," *The Globe and Mail*, August 17, 1993, pp. A1, A4.
14. "Datawave Announces Acquisition of Interurbain," *Canada NewsWire*, January 20, 1997, http://www.newswire.ca/releases/January 1997/20/c2737.html.
15. Positioning based on price and service is discussed in George H. Lucas, Jr., and Larry G. Gresham, "How to Position for Retail Success," *Business*, April–June 1988, pp. 3–13. Positioning that combines all three variables is presented in Lawrence H. Wortzel, "Retailing Strategies for Today's Mature Marketplace," *The Journal of Business Strategy*, Spring 1987, pp. 45–56.
16. For more on the use of frequent-shopper programs and other techniques designed to encourage customer retention, see Kenneth R. Wightman, "The Marriage of Retail Marketing and Information Systems Technology: The Zellers Club Z Experience," *MIS Quarterly*, December 1990, pp. 359–366; and Mark Evans, "Retailers in Battle for Frequent Buyer," *The Financial Post*, May 13, 1991, p. 8.
17. For an interesting insight into how Canadian retailers and their suppliers are using technology to make their operations more efficient, see James Pollock, "Faster, Cheaper, Better," *Marketing*, February 7, 1994, p. 11; and Gerald Levitch, "Mapping the Market," *Marketing*, February 7, 1994, p. 12.
18. Gayle MacDonald, "On-line Shopping Picks Up Steam," *The Globe and Mail*, July 25, 1997, p. B9.

19. Catherine Harris, "Shop till You Drop — from Home," *The Financial Post*, October 26, 1996, p. C5.
20. The wheel of retailing was first described in M.P. McNair, "Significant Trends and Developments in the Postwar Period," in A.B. Smith, ed., *Competitive Distribution in a Free, High-Level Economy and Its Implications for the University* (Pittsburgh: University of Pittsburgh Press, 1958), pp. 17–18.

CHAPTER 18

1. Based on information supplied by GM Canada.
2. See Glenn Collins, "Reinventing Plain Old Soup," *Montreal Gazette*, November 15, 1995, p. G2; "Campbell Introduces 19 New Soups," *The Financial Post*, June 19, 1996; and Wendy Cuthbert, "Campbell Debuts Frozen Soups," *Strategy*, August 18, 1997, pp. 1, 12.
3. See, for example, Tom Duncan and Sandra Moriarty, *Driving Brand Value* (New York: McGraw-Hill, 1997); Don E. Schultz, "The Inevitability of Integrated Communications," *Journal of Business Research*, vol. 37, 1996, pp. 139–146, and related articles in the same issue of this journal.
4. Marina Strauss, "Adidas Runs with Bailey Despite Trash Talk," *The Globe and Mail*, June 5, 1997, p. B13.
5. Fawzia Sheikh, "Power Premiums," *Marketing*, August 18–25, 1997, p. S4.
6. Joanne Lipman, "Food Companies Cut Ad Budgets While Beefing Up Promotion," *The Wall Street Journal*, April 2, 1992, p. B6; and Marina Strauss, "Coupon Craze Captures Canada," *The Globe and Mail*, June 21, 1997, p. B11.
7. Mark de Wolf, "Buckley Enters Nighttime Market with Buckley's Bedtime," *Strategy*, August 4, 1997, p. 2.
8. The Misleading Advertising Division of Industry Canada publishes a quarterly review of misleading advertising cases entitled the *Misleading Advertising Bulletin*. Individuals interested in receiving this bulletin can have their names placed on the mailing list simply by writing to Industry Canada.
9. See "Marketing's Guide to Liquor Advertising Regulations," *Marketing*, August 21–28, 1997, pp. 14–16.

CHAPTER 19

1. Adapted from Sheilah Allan, "Small Town Selling," *Marketing Magazine*, February 3, 1997, pp. 15-16.
2. Susan Yellin, "Making It Personal," *The Financial Post*, April 20/22, 1996, p. 6.
3. Geoffrey Brewer et al., "1995 Best Sales Force Awards," *Sales and Marketing Management*, October 1995, pp. 52–63.
4. For more on postsale activities, see A. Coskun Samli, Laurence W. Jacobs, and James Wills, "What Presale and Postsale Services Do You Need to Be Competitive?" *Industrial Marketing Management*, February 1992, pp. 33–41.
5. For a discussion of the importance of recognition in motivating a sales force, see Greg Cochrane, "Recognition Key to Sustaining Staff Passion," *Strategy*, August 18, 1997, pp. 16, 18.
6. See Mark de Wolf, "What Really Motivates the Salesperson Today," *Strategy*, August 18, 1997, pp. 19, 22; and Ann Kerr, "Incentive Travel Buoyed by Economic Recovery," *The Globe and Mail*, September 17, 1996, p. C11.
7. "More Sales Pay Linked To Satisfied Customers," *Sales & Marketing Management*, July 1995, p. 37.

CHAPTER 20

1. Jennifer Lanther, "Star Power," *The Financial Post*, January 27/29, 1996; p. 7; and Claudia H. Deutsch, "Duchess and Diet Firm a Good Fit," *The Globe and Mail*, February 6, 1997, p. B12.
2. Simon Israelson, "Court Drums Bunny Out of Rival Ad," *The Toronto Star*, November 21, 1995, pp. B1, B4.
3. Marina Strauss, "Towel War Turns to Name-Naming," *The Globe and Mail*, December 5, 1995, pp. B1, B10.
4. "Oil of Olay Creams Dove in Court," *The Globe and Mail*, February 24, 1996, p. B6.
5. Mikala Folb, "McCain Gets Hip In Fall Promotion with Sony," *Marketing*, July 8, 1996, p. 2.
6. Eve Lazarus, "Fellow Travellers," *Marketing*, December 2, 1996, p. 8.
7. Sara Curtis, "Media Groups' 1995 Ad Spend Data Differs," *Marketing*, September 16, 1996, p. 4.
8. Doug Sanders, "Advertisers Aim to Fracture TV Audience," *The Globe and Mail*, August 9, 1997, p. C3.
9. Harvey Enchin, "ExpressVu Launches Satellite TV Service," *The Globe and Mail*, September 11, 1997, p. B8.

10. Matthew Fraser, "Welcome to the Information Superhypeway," *The Globe and Mail*, September 13, 1997, pp. D1, D2.
11. 'Keith's Targets East Coast Expats," *Strategy*, July 7, 1997, p. 6.
12. Brenda Dalglish, "Canadians Listen to Less Radio but Industry Profit on Upswing," *The Financial Post*, February 7, 1997, p. 21.
13. Bob Mackin Jr., "Take Risks, Find a Niche, and Dare to Be Different," *Marketing*, March 7, 1994, pp. 20–21.
14. Doug Checkeris, "Leaner, Meaner and Better?" *Marketing*, November 18, 1996, p. 11.
15. "Powerful Pitches," *Marketing*, December 4, 1995, p. 14.
16. Marina Strauss, "Canadian Tire to Use E-mail to Promote Products," *The Globe and Mail*, September 11, 1997, p. B12.
17. Marina Strauss, "Coupon Craze Captures Canada," *The Globe and Mail*, May 22, 1997, p. B11.
18. See Terry Brodie, "A Renaissance in Coupon-Clipping," *Financial Times of Canada*, December 11, 1993, p. 8; and Wayne Mouland, "Coupon Dynamics," *Marketing*, February 14, 1994, p. 17.
19. For additional insight into the nature and management of public relations in Canada, you might wish to refer to a feature report on public relations that appeared in *Marketing*, February 24, 1997, pp. 11–18, and to a report on public relations in *Strategy*, May 12, 1997, pp. 25–37.
20. Ijeoma Ross, "Reputation Is a Depreciable Asset," *The Globe and Mail*, September 11, 1997, p. B17.

CHAPTER 21

1. Adapted from Gayle MacDonald, "Exports Drive Fast Growth Firms," *The Globe and Mail*, May 30, 1997, p. B10.
2. Anita Lahey, "Selling Molson Brew in the Land of Vodka," *Marketing Online*, http://www.marketing-mag.ca/cgi-...nk/marketing/search_footer.html. (September 6, 1997).
3. Laxmi Nakarmi and Igor Reichlin, "Daewoo, Samsung, and Goldstar: Made in Europe?" *Business Week*, August 24, 1992, p. 43.
4. Marion Stinton, "Apotex Venture Opens Door to French Market," *The Globe and Mail*, June 10, 1997, p. B9.
5. Greg Keenan, "Parts Makers Face Competitive Challenge," *The Globe and Mail*, July 14, 1997, p. B6.
6. Gayle MacDonald, "Bata Marches to a Loyal Foot Soldier," *The Globe and Mail*, June 26, 1997, p. B12.
7. Phil Davies, "Europe Unbound," *Express Magazine*, Spring 1992, pp. 16–19.
8. Joann S. Lublin, "Slim Pickings: U.S. Food Firms Find Europe's Huge Market Hardly a Piece of Cake," *The Wall Street Journal*, May 15, 1990, p. A1.
9. Rick Arons, *EuroMarketing* (Chicago: Probus, 1991), p. 186.
10. Laura Medcalf, "Is Canadian Marketing on the Line?" *Marketing Magazine*, July 1, 1996, pp. 1, 13.
11. James Pollock, "No Borders Here," *Marketing Magazine*, September 30, 1996, p. 10.
12. Michael Richardson, "ASEAN Admits Burma, Laos; Cambodia Waits," *The Globe and Mail*, July 24, 1997, p. A12.
13. Geoffrey York, "Canadians Aid Russia's Trade Bid," *The Globe and Mail*, May 9, 1997, p. B8.
14. Donald B. Pittenger, "Gathering Foreign Demographics Is No Easy Task," *Marketing News*, January 8, 1990, p. 23.
15. Lublin, loc. cit.
16. Cyndee Miller, "Not Quite Global, Marketers Discover the World but Still Have Much to Learn," *Marketing News*, July 3, 1995, p. 1–5.
17. Glenn Collins, "Coke Drops Domestic Concept in Favor of World Vision," *The Montreal Gazette*, January 13, 1996.
18. Ken Wells, "Selling to the World: Global Ad Campaigns, after Many Missteps, Finally Pay Dividends," *The Wall Street Journal*, August 27, 1992, p. A1.
19. Wells, loc. cit.

CHAPTER 22

1. Dianne S. P. Cermak, Karen Maru File, and Russ Alan Prince, "A Benefit Segmentation of the Major Donor Market," *Journal of Business Research*, vol. 29, no. 2, February 1994, pp. 121–130.
2. Tamara Bernstein, "Sex at the Symphony," *The Globe and Mail*, September 28, 1996, p. C20.
3. Elissa Barnard, "New Season at New Neptune Opens Sept. 28," Halifax *Chronicle Herald*, February 19, 1997, p. A21.
4. You might wish to refer to Siri Espy, *Marketing Strategies for Nonprofit Organizations* (Chicago: Lyceum Books); Alan R. Andreasen, *Marketing for*

Social Change (San Francisco: Jossey-Bass); and the *Journal of Public Policy and Marketing* (Chicago: American Marketing Association).

5. Brian A.P. Morris, Nancy E. Trimble, and Shawn J. Fendley, "Increasing Bicycle Helmet Use in the Community," *Canadian Family Physician*, vol. 40, June 1994, pp. 1126–1131.
6. Kevin Khayat and Brian Salter, "Patient Satisfaction Surveys as a Market Research Tool for General Practices," *British Journal of General Practice*, vol. 44, no. 382, 1994, pp. 215–219.

CHAPTER 23

1. Adapted from David Olive, "Tire on a Roll," *Report on Business Magazine*, July 1997, pp. 17–24.
2. Marina Strauss, "Holt Renfrew Brands a Strategy," *The Globe and Mail*, March 20, 1997, p. B13.
3. Gail E. Schares, "The New Generation at Siemens," *Business Week*, March 9, 1992, p. 46.
4. Melissa Campanelli, "A New Focus," *Sales & Marketing Management*, September 1995, pp. 56, 58.
5. For a detailed review of customer satisfaction, see Richard L. Oliver, *Satisfaction: A Behavioral Perspective on the Consumer* (New York: McGraw-Hill, 1997).
6. For further discussion on this point, see Ian Chaston, *Customer-focused Marketing* (Maidenhead: McGraw-Hill, 1993).
7. Dale Terry, "Does Your Bank's Marketing Size Up," *Bank Marketing*, January, 1995, pp. 55–58.
8. Abe Schuchman, "The Marketing Audit: Its Nature, Purpose, and Problems," in *Analyzing and Improving Marketing Performance: "Marketing Audits" in Theory and Practice* (New York: American Management Association, 1959), Management Report No. 32, p. 14. This article is the classic introduction to the marketing audit concept.

CHAPTER 24

1. See John Lorinc, "Now the Customer is Job 1," *Canadian Business*, July 1997, pp. 22–28; and Greg Keenan and Janet McFarland, "The Boys' Club," *The Globe and Mail Report on Business*, September 27, 1997, pp. B1, B5.
2. For an interesting insight into the efforts of the Ontario Milk Marketing Board to reverse the trend in the sales of milk in Canada, see Jared Mitchell, "Moving the Moo," *Report on Business Magazine*, March 1994, pp. 65–69.
3. For a very good overview of the ethical issues involved in marketing and advertising, see Jack Mahoney, "Buyer Beware: Are Marketing and Advertising Always Ethical?" *Financial Post*, December 14/16, 1996, pp. MM10–MM12; reprinted in *Financial Times Mastering Management* (London: Pitman Publishing, 1997), pp. 375–378.
4. Mary L. Nicastro, "Infuse Business Ethics into Marketing Curriculum," *Marketing Educator*, Winter 1992, p. 1.
5. John Deverell, "Fundraising Pitch Good for Business, Avon Says," *Toronto Star*, September 26, 1996, p. D3.
6. Eric Swetsky, "Consumer Wins Case Against Columbia House," *Direct Marketing News*, May 1993, p. 11.
7. Angela Kryhul, "'Waif' Ads under Fire," *Marketing*, November 22, 1993, p. 2.
8. Andrew Allentuck, "Drug Ads: A Prescription for Trouble?" *The Globe and Mail*, October 29, 1996, p. C7.
9. Sally Goll Beatty and Yumiko Ono, "Seagram Move to TV Stirs Controversy," *The Globe and Mail*, June 12, 1996, p. B8.
10. Laura Metcalf, "Labatt Strikes New Ice," *Marketing*, October 11, 1993, p. 2; and John Bates, "Point: Maximum Ice Undermines Responsible Use Efforts," *Marketing*, November 8, 1993, p. 8.
11. For a detailed overview of changes in Canada's population, see David K. Foot and Daniel Stoffman, *Boom, Bust and Echo: How to Profit from the Coming Demographic Shift* (Toronto: Macfarlane, Walter & Ross, 1996).
12. For an interesting discussion of the confusion caused by the environmental debate, see Arthur Johnson, "Ecohype — Consumer Beware: 'Green' Products May Not Be What They Seem," *The Financial Post Magazine*, May 1991, pp. 17–23; and Carey French, "'Smaller Is Better' Can Be a Tough Sell," *The Globe and Mail*, June 6, 1995, p. B29.
13. Explore the very interesting contrasts evident in these two articles that reflect very well how Canadian society changed through the 1990s: Michael Posner, "The Death of Leisure," *The Globe and Mail*, May 25, 1991, p. D1; and Doug Sanders and Alanna Mitchell, "It's Party Time Again," *The Globe and Mail*, September 13, 1997, pp. C1, C2.

14. Brian McGrory, "Happiness Is a Warm Hotel," *The Globe and Mail*, September 3, 1997, pp. D1, D2.
15. For additional insight into the complex world of Internet commerce, you might wish to read the following: "In Search of the Perfect Market — A Survey of Electronic Commerce," *The Economist*, May 10, 1997; Patrick Brethour, "Guru's Guide to On-Line Marketing," *The Globe and Mail*, May 14, 1997, p. B19; Patrick Brethour, "Is This the Year for Internet Commerce?" *The Globe and Mail*, January, 15, 1997, p. B12; Marina Strauss, "The Case for Advertising — On the Internet," *The Globe and Mail*, February 8, 1996, p. B12.
16. John Heinzl, "The Selling of a Highway," *The Globe and Mail*, September 26, 1996, p. B13.
17. Gerald Levitch, "Mapping the Market," *Marketing*, February 7, 1994, p. 12.
18. Jay Finegan, "The Rigorous Customer-Complaint Form," *Inc.*, March 1994, pp. 101–103.
19. John Dalla Costa, "A Commitment to Quality," *Marketing*, April 25, 1994, p. 8.
20. Sandra Vandermerwe and Michael Oliff, "Corporate Challenges for an Age of Reconsumption," *Columbia Journal of World Business*, Fall 1991, pp. 23–28.
21. James G. Barnes, "Close to the Customer: But Is It Really a Relationship," *Journal of Marketing Management*, 1994, vol. 10, pp. 561–570.
22. Daphne A. Sheaves and James G. Barnes, "The Fundamentals of Relationships," in Teresa A. Swartz, David E. Bowen, and Stephen W. Brown, eds., *Advances in Services Marketing and Management*, vol. 5 (Greenwich, CT: JAI Press, Inc., 1996); and James G. Barnes, "Closeness, Strength and Satisfaction: Examining the Nature of Relationships between Providers of Financial Services and their Retail Customers," *Psychology and Marketing*, Special Issue on Relationship Marketing, 1997.

APPENDIX

1. Lisa Wright, "Experts Help Avoid 'Cyber Surprises,'" *Toronto Star*, November 12, 1997, p. D1.

Glossary

accessory equipment In the business market, capital goods used in the operation of an industrial firm.

actual self The way you really see yourself. To be distinguished from *ideal self*.

ad See *advertisement*.

administered vertical marketing system A distribution system in which channel control is maintained through the economic power of one firm in the channel.

administration See *management*.

adoption process The stages that an individual goes through in deciding whether to accept an innovation.

advertisement A sponsor-identified message regarding a product or organization that can be verbal and/or visual, and that is disseminated through one or more media. Same as *ad*.

advertising All activities involved in presenting to a group a nonpersonal, sponsor-identified message regarding a product or organization.

advertising agency An independent company rendering specialized services in advertising in particular and in marketing in general.

advertising allowance A payment or cash discount offered by a manufacturer to a retailer to encourage the retailer to advertise or prominently display the manufacturer's product.

advertising campaign The total advertising program for a product or brand that involves coordination, central theme, and specific goals.

advertising media The communications vehicles (such as newspapers, radio, and television) that carry advertising.

advertising recall A measure of advertising effectiveness based on the premise that an ad can have an effect only if it is perceived and remembered.

agent A firm that never actually owns products that are being distributed but actively assists in the transfer of title.

agent wholesaler An independent firm that primarily engages in wholesaling and does not take title to the products being distributed but does actively negotiate their sale or purchase on behalf of other firms.

agents and brokers A broad category of wholesaling intermediaries that do not take title to products. The category includes manufacturers' agents, selling agents, commission merchants, auctioneers, brokers, and others.

agribusiness The business side of farming. Usually involves large, highly mechanized farming operations.

AIDA A sequence of steps in various forms of promotion, notably personal selling and advertising, consisting of attracting *A*ttention, holding *I*nterest, arousing *D*esire, and generating buyer *A*ction.

annual marketing plan A written document that details the planned marketing activities for the given business unit or product for the given year.

assumptive close In personal selling, the stage in the selling process when the sales person can often finalize the sale by asking questions that will settle the details of the purchase.

attitude A learned predisposition to respond to an object or class of objects in a consistently favourable or unfavourable way.

auction company An agent wholesaler that provides (1) auctioneers who do the selling and (2) physical facilities for displaying the sellers' products.

automated merchandising See *automatic vending*.

automatic vending A form of nonstore retailing where the products are sold through a machine with no personal contact between the buyer and seller. Same as *automated merchandising*.

average fixed cost The total fixed cost divided by the number of units produced.

average fixed cost curve A graph of average fixed cost levels, showing a decline as output increases, because the total of the fixed costs is spread over an increasing number of units.

average revenue The unit price at a given level of unit sales. It is calculated by dividing total revenue by the number of units sold.

average total cost The total cost divided by the number of units produced.

average variable cost The total variable cost divided by the number of units produced.

average variable cost curve A graph of average variable cost levels, which starts high, then declines to its lowest point, reflecting optimum output with respect to variable costs (not total costs), and then rises.

balance of trade In international business, the difference between the value of a nation's imports and the value of its exports.

barter The exchange of goods and/or services for other products.

base price The price of one unit of the product at its point of production or resale. Same as *list price*.

battle of the brands Market competition between producers' brands and intermediaries' brands. In recent years, generic products have entered this competitive struggle.

behavioural segmentation Market segmentation based on consumers' product-related behaviour, typically the benefits desired from a product and the rate at which the consumer uses the product.

benefit segmentation A basis for segmenting a market. A total market is divided into segments based on the customers' perceptions of the various benefits provided by a product.

Boston Consulting Group (BCG) matrix A strategic planning model that classifies strategic business units or major products according to market shares and growth rates.

brand A name, term, symbol, special design, or some combination of these elements that is intended to identify the products of one seller or a group of sellers.

brand competition Competition among marketers of branded products that are very similar and may be substituted for each other.

brand licensing See *trademark licensing*.

brand manager See *product manager*.

brand mark The part of a brand that appears in the form of a symbol, picture, design, or distinctive colour or type of lettering.

brand name The part of a brand that can be vocalized — words, letters, and/or numbers.

breadth of product mix The number of product lines offered for sale by a firm.

break-even point The level of output at which revenues equal costs, assuming a certain selling price.

broker An independent agent wholesaler that brings buyers and sellers together and provides market information to either party.

build-up method See *task method*.

business cycle The three recurring stages in an economy, typically prosperity, recession, and recovery.

business marketing The marketing of goods and services to business users.

business product A product that is intended for purchase and use in producing other products or in rendering services in a business.

business user An organization that buys goods or services to resell, use in its own business, or make other products.

buy classes Three typical buying situations in the business market — new-task buying, modified rebuy, and straight rebuy.

buyers The people in a buying centre who select the suppliers, arrange the terms of sale, and process the actual purchase orders.

buying centre All of the people in an organization who participate in the buying-decision process.

buying-decision process The series of logical stages a prospective purchaser goes through when faced with a buying problem. The stages differ for consumers and organizations.

buying motive The reason why a person buys a specific product or shops at a specific store.

campaign A co-ordinated series of promotional efforts built around a single theme and designed to reach a predetermined goal.

campaign theme In promotion, the central idea or focal point in a promotional campaign.

cartel A group of companies that produce similar products and combine to restrain competition in manufacturing and marketing.

cash cows According to the Boston Consulting Group matrix, strategic business units that are characterized by high market shares and do business in mature industries (those with low growth rates).

cash discount A deduction from list price for paying a bill within a specified period of time.

catalogue retailing One form of direct marketing, in which companies mail catalogues to consumers or make them available at retail stores and consumers make their purchases from the catalogues.

catalogue showroom A type of retail institution that offers a complete catalogue and some sample items in the showroom and the remaining inventory in an attached warehouse. It offers a broad but shallow assortment of merchandise, emphasizes low prices, and offers few customer services.

category killer store A type of retail institution that has a narrow but very deep assortment, emphasizes low prices, and offers few to moderate customer services. It is designed to "destroy" all competition in a specific product category.

category-management system A form of marketing organization in which an executive position called a category manager is established for each product category, and all the competing brand managers in each group report to this executive.

census metropolitan area The major population centres of Canada as defined by Statistics Canada; generally containing population centres of 100,000 or more.

chain store One in a group of retail stores that carry the same type of merchandise. Corporate chain stores are centrally owned and managed. Voluntary chains are an association of independently owned stores.

channel conflict A situation in which one channel member perceives another channel member to be acting in a way that prevents the first member from achieving its distribution objectives.

channel control The ability to influence the behaviour of other channel members.

client market Individuals and/or organizations that are the recipients of a not-for-profit organization's money and/or services. Same as *recipient market*.

closing In personal selling, the stage in the selling process when the sales person gets the buyer to agree to buy.

cognitive dissonance The anxiety created by the fact that in most purchases the alternative selected has some negative features and the alternatives not selected have some positive features.

combination salary plan The method of sales force compensation that combines a base salary with a commission related to some task(s).

commission Compensation tied to a specific unit of accomplishment.

commission merchant An independent agent wholesaler, used primarily in the marketing of agricultural products, that may physically handle the seller's products in central markets and has authority regarding prices and terms of sale.

communication process A system of verbal and/or nonverbal transmission of information between a sender and a receiver. The four elements are message, source, communication channel, and receiver.

community shopping centre A shopping centre that is larger than a neighbourhood centre but smaller than a regional centre. Usually includes one or two department stores or discount stores, along with a number of shopping-goods stores and specialty stores.

comparative advertising Selective demand advertising in which the advertiser either directly (by naming a rival brand) or indirectly (through inference) points out how the advertised brand is better.

Competition Act The major piece of federal legislation in Canada that governs the marketing and advertising activities of companies and organizations operating in Canada.

concept testing The first three stages in the new-product development process — pretesting of the product idea, in contrast to later pretesting of the product itself and the market.

consumer An individual or organizational unit that uses or consumes a product.

Consumer Packaging and Labelling Act Federal legislation that regulates the packaging and labelling of consumer products in Canada.

consumer product A product that is intended for purchase and use by household consumers for nonbusiness purposes.

consumerism Protests by consumers against perceived injustices in marketing, and the efforts to remedy these injustices.

containerization A cargo-handling system in which shipments of products are enclosed in large metal or wood receptacles that are then transported unopened from the time they leave the customer's facilities until they reach their destination.

contractual vertical market system An arrangement under which independent firms — producers, wholesalers, and retailers — operate under a contract specifying how they will try to improve their distribution efficiency and effectiveness.

contribution-margin allocation In marketing cost analysis, an accounting approach in which only direct expenses are allocated to the marketing units being studied. A unit's gross margin minus its direct cost equals that unit's contribution to covering the company's indirect expenses (overhead).

contributor market Individuals and/or organizations that donate money, labour, services, and/or materials to a not-for-profit organization. Also called *donor market*.

convenience goods A class of consumer products that the consumer has prior knowledge of and purchases with minimum time and effort.

convenience sample A sample that is selected in a nonrandom way such that every member of the universe does not have an equal chance of being included.

convenience store A type of retailing institution that concentrates on convenience-oriented groceries and nonfoods, has higher prices than found at most other grocery stores, and offers few customer services.

"cooling-off" laws Provincial or municipal laws that permit a consumer to cancel an order for a product — usually within a period of three days after signing the order.

co-operative advertising Advertising in which two or more firms share the cost.

copy The written or spoken material in an ad that makes up the primary message.

corporate chain An organization of two or more centrally owned and managed stores that generally handle the same lines of products.

corporate vertical marketing system An arrangement under which a firm at one level of a distribution channel owns the firms at the next level or owns the entire channel.

correlation analysis A method of sales forecasting that is a statistical refinement of the direct-derivation method.

cost per thousand (CPM) The media cost of gaining exposure to one thousand persons with an ad.

cost-plus pricing A major method of price determination in which the price of a unit of a product is set at a level equal to the unit's total cost plus a desired profit on the unit.

creative selling A selling job that often requires designing a system to fit the needs of the particular customer and may depend upon the expertise of several people who make up a sales team.

culture A complex of symbols and artifacts created by a given society and handed down from generation to generation as determinants and regulators of human behaviour.

cumulative discount A quantity discount based on the total volume purchased over a period of time.

customer An individual or organization that makes a purchase decision.

customer satisfaction The degree to which a customer's experience with a product meets or exceeds his or her expectations.

customer service advertising Advertising that presents information about the advertiser's operations.

database A set of related data that is organized, stored, and updated in a computer.

database marketing An approach to marketing that relies on the use of a data base of customers or prospective customers that is used to identify prospects for a direct marketing program.

deciders The people in a buying centre who make the actual buying decision regarding a product and/or supplier.

decision support system (DSS) A procedure that allows a manager to interact with data and methods of analysis to gather, analyze, and interpret information.

decline stage The fourth, and final, part of a product life cycle, during which the sales of a generic product category drop and most competitors abandon the market.

decoding The process of a receiver giving meaning to words, pictures, or both that have been transmitted by a sender.

Delphi method A forecasting technique, applicable to sales forecasting, in which a group of experts individually and anonymously assesses future sales and after which each member has the chance to offer a revised assessment as the group moves toward a consensus.

demand forecasting The process of estimating sales of a product during some future time period.

demography The statistical study of human population and its distribution.

department store A large-scale retailing institution that has a very broad and deep product assortment, prefers not to compete on the basis of price, and offers a wide array of customer services.

depth of product line The assortment within a product line.

derived demand A situation in which the demand for one product is dependent upon the demand for another product.

descriptive label A label that gives information regarding the use, care, performance, or other features of a product.

differential advantage Any feature of an organization or brand perceived by customers to be desirable and different from the competition.

diffusion of innovation A process by which an innovation is spread through a social system over time.

direct-action advertising Product advertising that seeks a quick response.

direct costs Separate expenses that are incurred totally in connection with one market segment or one unit of the sales organization.

direct-derivation method A sales forecasting method used to translate market-factor behaviour into an estimate of future sales.

direct distribution A channel consisting only of producer and final customer with no intermediaries providing assistance.

direct mail An advertising medium whereby the advertiser contacts prospective customers by sending some form of advertisement through the mail.

direct marketing A form of nonstore retailing that uses nonpersonal media to contact consumers, who, in turn, purchase products without visiting a retail store.

direct purchase A situation in which a customer makes a purchase directly from a producer.

direct selling A form of nonstore retailing in which personal contact between a sales person and a consumer occurs away from a retail store.

direct tests (in advertising) Measures of the sales volume produced by an ad or an entire advertising campaign.

discount house A large-scale retailing institution that has a broad and shallow product assortment, emphasizes low prices, and offers relatively few customer services.

discount retailing A retailing approach that uses price as a major selling point by combining comparatively low prices and reduced costs of doing business.

discretionary purchasing power The amount of disposable income remaining after fixed expenses and essential household needs are paid for.

dispersion In distribution, the intermediary's activities that distribute the correct amount of a product to its market.

disposable personal income Personal income remaining after all personal taxes are paid.

distribution centre A concept in warehousing that develops under one roof an efficient, fully integrated system for the flow of products — taking orders, filling them, and delivering them to customers.

distribution channel The set of people and firms involved in the flow of the title to a product as it moves from producer to ultimate consumer or business user.

diversification A product-market growth strategy in which a company develops new products to sell to new markets.

dogs According to the Boston Consulting Group matrix, strategic business units that are characterized by low market shares and operate in industries with low growth rates.

donor market See *contributor market.*

door-to-door selling A kind of direct selling in which the personal contact between a sales person and an individual prospect occurs at the prospective customer's residence or business.

driver sales person A selling job in which the job is primarily to deliver the product. Selling responsibilities, if any, are secondary to seeing that orders are filled correctly and on time.

drop shipper A limited-function merchant wholesaler that does not physically handle the product.

dual distribution The use by a producer of multiple and competing channels of distribution.

dumping The process of selling products in foreign markets at prices below the prices charged for these goods in their home market.

early adopters The second group (following the innovators) to adopt something new. This group includes the opinion leaders, is respected, and has much influence on its peers.

early majority A more deliberate group of innovation adopters that adopts just before the "average" adopter.

economic order quantity (EOQ) The optimal quantity for reorder when replenishing inventory stocks, as indicated by the volume at which the inventory-carrying cost plus the order-processing cost are at a minimum.

ego In Freudian psychology, the rational control centre in our minds that maintains a balance between (1) the uninhibited instincts of the id and (2) the socially oriented, constraining superego.

80–20 principle A situation in which a large proportion of a company's marketing units (products, territories, customers) accounts for a small share of the company's volume or profit, and vice versa.

elastic demand A price–volume relationship such that a change of one unit on the price scale results in a change of more than one unit on the volume scale.

encoding The process of translating an idea into a message in the form of words, pictures, or both in order that it can be transmitted from a sender to a receiver.

environmental monitoring The process of gathering information regarding a company's external environment, analyzing it, and forecasting the impact of whatever trends the analysis suggests.

ethics The rules and standards of moral behaviour that are generally accepted by a society.

ethnographic research The process of watching closely how consumers interact with a product and then deducing how it fits into their lives.

European Union A collection of countries in Western Europe and Scandinavia that have formed a political and economic alliance that has succeeded in liberalizing trade among its members. A number of Eastern European countries are expected to join in the future.

evaluation The process of determining what happened, why it happened, and what to do about it.

everyday low pricing (EDLP) A pricing strategy that involves consistently low prices and few, if any, temporary price reductions.

exchange The voluntary act of providing a person or organization something of value in order to acquire something else of value in return.

execution The step in creating an advertising message that tries to combine in a convincing, compatible way the feature or device that gets attention with the appeal.

exclusive dealing The practice by which a manufacturer prohibits its dealers from carrying products of competing manufacturers.

exclusive distribution A strategy in which a producer agrees to sell its product to only a single wholesaling intermediary and/or retailer in a given market.

exclusive territory The practice by which a manufacturer requires each intermediary to sell only to customers located within the intermediary's assigned territory.

executive judgment A method of sales forecasting that consists of obtaining opinions regarding future sales volume from one or more executives.

expected price The price at which customers consciously or unconsciously value a product — what they think the product is worth.

experimental method A method of gathering primary data in which the researcher is able to observe the results of changing one variable in a situation while holding all others constant.

exporting The activities by which a firm sells its product in another country, either directly to foreign importers or through import–export intermediaries.

express warranty A statement in written or spoken words regarding restitution from seller to customer if the seller's product does not perform up to reasonable expectations.

fabricating materials Business goods that have received some processing and will undergo further processing as they become part of another product.

fabricating parts Business goods that already have been processed to some extent and will be assembed in their present form (with no further change) as part of another product.

factory outlet A special type of off-price retail institution that is owned by a manufacturer and usually sells only that manufacturer's clearance items, regular merchandise, and perhaps even otherwise unavailable items.

fad A short-lived fashion that is usually based on some novelty feature.

family A group of two or more people related by blood, marriage, or adoption living together in a household.

family brands A branding strategy in which a group of products is given a single brand.

family life cycle The series of life stages that a family goes through, starting with young single people and progressing through married stages with young and then older children, and ending with older married and single people.

family packaging A strategy of using either highly similar packages for all products or packages with a common and clearly noticeable feature.

fashion A style that is popularly accepted by groups of people over a reasonably long period of time.

fashion-adoption process The process by which a style becomes popular in a market; similar to diffusion of an innovation.

fashion cycle Wavelike movements representing the introduction, rise, popular acceptance, and decline in popularity of a given style.

fashion obsolescence See *style obsolescence*.

feedback The component of communication that tells the sender whether the message was received and how it was perceived by the recipient.

field experiment An experiment in which the researcher has only limited control of the environment because the experiment is conducted in a real-world setting.

fixed cost A constant cost, regardless of how many items are produced or sold.

flexible-price strategy A pricing strategy in which a company sells similar quantities of merchandise to similar buyers at different prices. Same as variable-price strategy.

f.o.b. (free on board) factory price A geographic pricing strategy whereby the buyer pays all freight charges from the f.o.b. location to the destination. Same as *f.o.b. mill price*.

f.o.b. mill price See *f.o.b. factory price*.

focus group A preliminary data-gathering method involving an interactive interview of four to ten people.

form utility The utility that is created when a good is produced.

forward dating A combination of a seasonal discount and a cash discount under which a buyer places an order and receives shipment during the off-season but does not have to pay the bill until after the season has started and some sales revenue has been generated.

fragmented markets Small market segments that can be identified and isolated through increasingly sophisticated demographic, behavioural, and geographic data.

franchise system The combination of franchiser, franchisees, and franchiser-owned business units.

franchising A type of contractual vertical marketing system that involves a continuing relationship in which a franchiser (the parent company) provides the right to use a trademark plus various management assistance in opening and operating a business in return for financial considerations from a franchisee (the owner of the individual business unit).

freight absorption A geographic pricing strategy whereby the seller pays for (absorbs) some of the freight charges in order to penetrate more distant markets.

freight forwarder A specialized transportation agency that consolidates less-than-carload or less-than-truckload shipments into carload or truckload quantities and provides door-to-door shipping service.

fulfilment The process of filling orders as occurs, for example, when a catalogue company selects the items from its inventory to be sent to a customer who has ordered them.

full-cost allocation In a marketing cost analysis, an accounting approach wherein all expenses — direct and indirect — are allocated to the marketing units being analyzed.

full-service wholesaler An independent merchant wholesaler that normally performs a full range of wholesaling functions.

functional discount See *trade discount*.

gatekeepers The people in a buying centre who control the flow of purchasing information within the organization and between the buying firm and potential vendors.

generic product A product that is packaged in a plain label and is sold with no advertising and without a brand name. The product goes by its generic name, such as "tomatoes" or "paper towels."

generic use of brand names General reference to a product by its brand name — cellophane, kerosene, zipper, for example — rather than its generic name. The owners of these brands no longer have exclusive use of the brand name.

geodemographic clustering The use of statistical population data along with information on where people live, usually obtained from postal code data, to identify clusters of consumers or households with similar characteristics.

global marketing A strategy in which essentially the same marketing program is employed around the world.

goal See *objective*.

good A set of tangible physical attributes assembled in an identifiable form to provide want-satisfaction to customers.

government market The segment of the business market that includes federal, provincial, and local units buying for government institutions such as schools, offices, hospitals, and research facilities.

grade label Identification of the quality (grade) of a product by means of a letter, number, or word.

green marketing Any marketing activity of a firm that is intended to create a positive impact or lessen the negative impact of a product on the environment in order to capitalize on consumers' concerns about environmental issues.

growth stage The second part of a product life cycle, during which the sales and profits of a generic product category rise and competitors enter the market, after which profits start to decline near the end of this part of the cycle.

heterogeneity of a service A characteristic of a service indicating that each unit is somewhat different from other "units" of the same service.

hierarchy of effects The stages a buyer goes through in moving toward a purchase — awareness, knowledge, liking, preference, conviction, and purchase.

high involvement A purchase decision that involves all six stages of the buying decision process.

horizontal business market A situation in which a given product is usable in a wide variety of industries.

horizontal conflict A form of channel conflict occurring between firms on the same level of distribution — between intermediaries of the same type or between different types of intermediaries.

horizontal co-operative advertising Advertising that involves firms on the same level of distribution sharing the cost.

household A single person, a family, or any group of unrelated persons who occupy a housing unit.

hypermarket A type of exceedingly large-scale retailing institution that has a very broad and moderately deep product assortment, emphasizes low prices, and offers some customer services.

hypothesis A tentative supposition or a possible solution to a problem.

iceberg principle A concept related to performance evaluation stating that the summary data (tip of the iceberg) regarding an activity may hide significant variations among segments of this activity.

id In Freudian psychology, the part of the mind that houses the basic instinctive drives, many of which are antisocial.

ideal self The way you want to be seen or would like to see yourself. To be distinguished from *actual self*.

illustration The pictorial portion of an ad.

image utility The emotional or psychological value that a person attaches to a product or brand because of the reputation or social standing of that product or brand.

implementation The process of organizing for the marketing effort, staffing this organization, and directing the operational efforts of these people as they carry out the strategic plans.

implied warranty An intended but unstated assurance regarding restitution from seller to customer if the seller's product does not perform up to reasonable expectations.

import–export agent An agent wholesaler that arranges for distribution of goods in a foreign country.

impulse buying Low-involvement purchases made with little or no advance planning.

independent retailer A company with a single retail store that is not affiliated with any type of contractual vertical marketing system.

indirect-action advertising Product advertising that is intended to inform or remind consumers about a product and its benefits.

indirect costs Expenses that are incurred jointly for more than one marketing unit and therefore cannot be totally charged to one market segment.

indirect distribution A channel consisting of producer, final customer, and at least one level of intermediary.

indirect tests (in advertising) Measures of advertising effects that use something other than sales volume.

inelastic demand A price–volume relationship such that a change of one unit on the price scale results in a change of less than one unit on the volume scale.

influencers The people in a buying centre who set the specifications and aspects of buying decisions because of their technical expertise, financial position, or political power in the organization.

infomercials Television "programs" that may be thirty or sixty minutes or longer and that are paid commercials for businesses or other advertisers.

informal investigation The stage in a marketing research study at which information is gathered from people outside the company — intermediaries, competitors, advertising agencies, and consumers.

information utility The want-satisfying capability that is created by informing prospective buyers that a product exists.

in-home retailing Retail selling in the customer's home. A personal sales representative may or may not be involved. In-home retailing includes door-to-door selling, party-plan selling, and selling by television and computer.

innovators The first group — a venturesome group — of people to adopt something new (good, service).

inseparability A characteristic of a service indicating that it cannot be separated from the creator-seller of the service.

inside order taker A selling job in which the primary function of the sales person is to take orders in person or by phone inside a store or other type of business.

installations In the business market, long-lived, expensive, major industrial capital goods that directly affect the scale of operation of an industrial firm.

institutional advertising Advertising designed either to present information about the advertiser's business or to create a good attitude — build goodwill — toward the organization.

intangibility A characteristic of a service indicating that it has no physical attributes and, as a result, is impossible for customers to taste, feel, see, hear, or smell before buying.

intensity of distribution The number of intermediaries used by a producer at the retailing and wholesaling levels of distribution.

intensive distribution A strategy in which a producer sells its product in every available outlet where a consumer might reasonably look for it. Same as *mass distribution*.

interactive kiosks Computer terminals that are usually located in retail stores, shopping malls, or other public locations and that allow customers to order items or to obtain information.

intermediary A firm that renders services directly related to the purchase and/or sale of a product as it flows from producer to consumer.

internal marketing The process of directing programs to staff members with the intention of encouraging them to deliver superior service to customers and generally to adopt a customer focus in all that they do.

introduction stage The first part of a product life cycle, during which a generic product category is launched into the market in a full-scale marketing program.

inventory control The subsystem of physical distribution management that involves maintaining control over the size and composition of inventories in order to fill customers' orders promptly, completely, and accurately while minimizing both the investment and fluctuations in inventories.

inverse demand A price–volume relationship such that the higher the price, the greater the unit sales.

involvement level The amount of time and effort the consumer invests in a buying decision.

joint venture A partnership arrangement in which a foreign operation is owned in part by a Canadian company and in part by a foreign company.

"just-in-time" concept An inventory control system that involves buying parts and supplies in small quantities just in time for use in production and then producing in quantities just in time for sale.

label The part of a product that carries written information about the product or the seller.

laboratory experiment An experiment in which the researcher has complete control over the environment during the experiment.

laggards Tradition-bound people who are the last to adopt an innovation.

late majority The sceptical group of innovation adopters who adopt a new idea late in the game.

layout The physical arrangement of all of the elements of an ad.

leader pricing Temporary price cuts on well-known items. The price cut is made with the idea that these "specials" (loss leaders) will attract customers to the store.

learning Changes in behaviour resulting from previous experiences.

leasing A situation, found in both business and consumer markets, in which a good is rented rather than purchased outright.

licensing A business arrangement whereby one firm sells to another firm (for a fee or royalty) the right to use the first company's brand, patents, or manufacturing processes.

lifestyle A person's activities, interests, and opinions.

limited-function wholesaler A merchant wholesaler that performs only selected wholesaling functions.

limited-line store A type of retailing institution that has a narrow but deep product assortment. Its customer services tend to vary from store to store.

line extension One form of product-mix expansion in which a company adds a similar item to an existing product line with the same brand name.

list price See *base price*.

logistics See *physical distribution*.

loss leaders Products whose prices are cut with the idea that they will attract customers to the store.

low involvement A purchase decision in which the consumer moves directly from need recognition to purchase, skipping the stages in between.

loyalty programs Programs that reward loyal and frequent customers with points that can be redeemed for gifts, merchandise or services, such as the frequent-flyer programs operated by most airlines and the frequent-shopper programs of retailers such as Zellers and Sears. Same as *membership programs*.

mail-order selling A type of nonstore, nonpersonal retail or wholesale selling in which the customer mails in an order that is then delivered by mail or other parcel-delivery system.

mail survey The method of gathering data by means of a questionnaire mailed to respondents and, when completed, returned by mail.

mall-intercept interview Personal interview conducted in a shopping centre mall.

management The process of planning, implementing, and evaluating the efforts of a group of people working toward a common goal. Same as *administration*.

manufacturers' agent An independent agent wholesaler that sells part or all of a manufacturer's product mix in an assigned geographic territory.

manufacturer's sales facility An establishment that primarily engages in wholesaling and is owned and operated by a manufacturer but is physically separated from manufacturing plants.

manufacturer's sales office A manufacturer's sales facility that does not carry a stock of the product being sold.

marginal analysis A method of price setting that considers both demand and costs to determine the best price for profit maximization.

marginal cost The cost of producing and selling one more unit; that is, the cost of the last unit produced or sold.

marginal revenue The income derived from the sale of the last unit.

markdown A reduction from the original retailing selling price, usually made because the store was unable to sell the product at the original price.

market People or organizations with wants to satisfy, money to spend, and the willingness to spend it.

market aggregation A strategy whereby an organization treats its total market as a unit — as one mass market whose parts are considered to be alike in all major respects.

market development A product-market growth strategy in which a company continues to sell its present products, but to a new market.

market factor An item or element that (1) exists in a market, (2) may be measured quantitatively, and (3) is related to the demand for a good or service.

market-factor analysis A sales forecasting method based on the assumption that future demand for a product is related to the behaviour of certain market factors.

marketer Any person or organization that desires to make exchanges.

market fragmentation The identification of smaller and smaller market segments.

market index A market factor expressed as a percentage, or in another quantitative form, relative to some base figure.

market penetration A product-market growth strategy in which a company tries to sell more of its present products to its present markets.

market-penetration pricing See *penetration pricing*.

market potential The total sales volume that all organizations selling a product during a stated time period in a specific market could expect to achieve under ideal conditions.

market response system A form of inventory control in which a purchase by a final customer activates a process to produce and deliver a replacement item.

market segmentation The process of dividing the total market for a product into several parts, each of which tends to be homogeneous in all significant aspects.

market share The proportion of total sales of a product during a stated time period in a specific market that is captured by a single firm. Market share can refer to entire industries, narrow segments, or particular geographic areas and also can apply to past, present, or future time periods.

market-share analysis A detailed analysis of the company's share of the market in total as well as by product line and market segment.

market-skimming pricing See *skimming pricing*.

marketing A total system of business activities designed to plan, price, promote, and distribute want-satisfying products to target markets in order to achieve organizational objectives.

marketing audit A comprehensive review and evaluation of the marketing function in an organization — its philosophy, environment, goals, strategies, organizational structure, human and financial resources, and performance.

marketing communications All of the elements of an organization's marketing mix — usually advertising, publicity, public relations, personal sales, and sales promotion — that serve to inform actual and potential customers.

marketing communications budgeting methods The means used to determine the amount of dollars to be allocated to the marketing communications elements.

marketing communications mix The combination of personal selling, advertising, sales promotion, publicity, and public relations that is intended to help an organization achieve its marketing objectives.

marketing concept A philosophy of doing business that emphasizes customer orientation and co-ordination of marketing activities in order to achieve the organization's performance objectives.

marketing cost analysis A detailed study of the "operating expenses" section of a company's profit and loss statement.

marketing information system An ongoing organized set of procedures and methods designed to generate, analyze, disseminate, store, and retrieve information for use in making marketing decisions.

marketing intermediary An independent business organization that directly aids in the flow of products between a marketing organization and its markets.

marketing mix A combination of the four elements — product, pricing structure, distribution system, and promotional activities — that comprise a company's marketing program. Many marketers now consider service and the "people" side of marketing to be a fifth component of the marketing mix, especially in the marketing of services.

marketing-orientation stage The third stage in the evolution of marketing management, in which a company focuses on the needs of its customers and carries out a broad range of marketing activities.

marketing research The process of specifying, assembling, and analyzing information used to identify and define marketing opportunities and problems; generate, refine, and evaluate marketing actions; monitor marketing performance; and improve understanding of marketing as a process.

markup The dollar amount that is added to the acquisition cost of a product to determine the selling price.

Maslow's needs hierarchy A needs structure consisting of five levels and organized according to the order in which people seek need gratification.

mass distribution See *intensive distribution*.

materials handling The subsystem of physical distribution management that involves selecting and operating the equipment and warehouse building that is used in physically handling products.

maturity stage The third part of a product life cycle, during which the sales of a generic product category continue to increase (but at a decreasing rate), profits decline largely due to price competition, and some firms leave the market.

membership programs See *loyalty programs*.

merchant wholesaler An independently owned firm that primarily engages in wholesaling and ordinarily takes title to the products being distributed. Same as *wholesaler*.

missionary seller A selling job in which the sales people are not expected to solicit orders but are expected to influence decision-makers by building goodwill, performing promotional activities, and providing service to customers. In pharmaceuticals marketing, called "detail sales person."

modified rebuy In the business market, a purchasing situation between a new task and a straight rebuy in terms of time required, information needed, and alternatives considered.

motive A need sufficiently stimulated that an individual is moved to seek satisfaction.

multiple-brand strategy A strategy in which a firm has more than one brand of essentially the same product, aimed either at the same target market or at distinct target markets.

multiple packaging The practice of placing several units of the same product in one container.

multiple buying influences A situation in which a purchasing decision is influenced by more than one person in the buyer's organization.

multiple-segment strategy A strategy that involves two or more groups of potential customers selected as target markets.

national brand See producer's brand.

need recognition The stage in the buying decision process in which the consumer is moved to action by a need.

neighbourhood shopping centre A small group of stores situated around a supermarket and including other convenience-goods stores and specialty stores. Draws from a market located perhaps within ten minutes by car.

new product A vague term that may refer to (1) really innovative, truly unique products; (2) replacements for existing products that are significantly different from existing ones; or (3) imitative products that are new to the given firm.

new-product development process Developmental stages that a new product goes through, starting with idea generation and continuing through idea screening, business analysis, limited production, test-marketing, and eventually commercialization (full-scale production and marketing).

new-product strategy A plan as to what role new products are to play in helping the company achieve its corporate and marketing goals.

new-task buying In the business market, a purchasing situation in which a company for the first time considers buying a given item.

niche marketing A strategy in which goods and services are tailored to meet the needs of small market segments.

noise Any external factor that interferes with successful communication.

nonadopters Consumers who never adopt an innovation.

nonbusiness market Such diverse institutions as churches, colleges and universities, museums, hospitals and other health institutions, political parties, labour unions, and charitable organizations.

noncumulative discount A quantity discount based on the size of an individual order of products.

nonprice competition A strategy in which a firm tries to compete based on some factor other than price — for example, promotion, product differentiation, or variety of services.

nonstore retailing Retailing activities resulting in transactions that occur away from a retail store.

North American Free Trade Agreement (NAFTA) An agreement among Canada, the United States, and Mexico to eliminate tariffs between these countries.

not-for-profit organization An organization in which profit is not an intended organizational goal.

nutrition labelling The part of a product that provides information about the amount of calories, fat, cholesterol, sodium, carbohydrates, and protein contained in the package's contents.

objective A desired outcome. Same as *goal*.

observational method Gathering data by observing personally or mechanically the actions of a person.

odd pricing A form of psychological pricing that consists of setting prices at odd amounts ($4.99 rather than $5.00, for example) in the belief that these seemingly low prices will result in larger sales volume.

off-price retailer A type of retail institution, often found in the areas of apparel and shoes, that has a narrow and deep product assortment, emphasizes low prices, and offers few customer services.

off-price retailing A strategy of selling well-known brands below the manufacturer's recommended retail price.

one-price strategy A strategy under which a seller charges the same price to all customers of the same type who buy the same quantity of goods.

operating supplies The "convenience goods" of the business market — short-lived, low-priced items purchased with a minimum of time and effort.

opinion leader The member of a reference group who is the information source and who influences the decision-making of others in the group.

order processing The subsystem of physical distribution management that consists of the set of procedures for receiving, handling, and filling orders.

order taker One of three types of sales jobs, the others being sales-support personnel and order getter.

organizational mission The first step in strategic planning that defines the organization by asking the question "What business are we in?"

organizational portfolio analysis A key step in strategic planning that identifies the present status of each strategic business unit and determines its future role in the company.

organizational strategies Broad, basic plans of action by which an organization intends to achieve its goals and fulfil its mission. These plans are for (1) the total organization in a small, single-product company or (2) each SBU in a large multiproduct or multibusiness organization.

outside order taker A selling job in which sales people are primarily going to customers in the field.

outside sales force A group of sales reps engaged in field selling, that is, selling in person at a customer's place of business or home.

package The actual container or wrapper for a product.

packaging The activities in product planning that involve designing and producing the container or wrapper for a product.

party-plan selling A kind of direct selling in which a host or hostess invites some friends to a party at which a sales person makes a sales presentation.

past-sales analysis A method of sales forecasting that applies a flat percentage increase to the volume achieved last year, or to the average volume of the past few years, to predict future volume.

patronage buying motives The reasons why a consumer chooses to shop at a certain store.

penetration pricing A pricing strategy in which a low initial price is set to reach the mass market immediately. Same as *market-penetration pricing*.

percentage-of-sales method A method of determining the promotional budget in which the amount is set as a certain percentage of past or forecasted future sales.

perception Collecting and processing information from the environment in order to give meaning to the world around us.

perishability A characteristic of a service indicating that it is highly perishable and cannot be stored.

personal interview A face-to-face method of gathering data in a survey.

personal selling The personal communication of information to persuade a prospective customer to buy a good, service, idea, or other product.

positive reinforcement According to learning theory, receiving a desirable outcome as a result of behaviour.

personality An individual's pattern of traits that influences behavioural responses.

physical distribution Activities involved in the flow of products as they move physically from producer to consumer or industrial user. Same as *logistics*.

physical distribution management The development and operation of efficient flow systems for products.

piggyback freight service The service of transporting loaded truck trailers on railroad flatcars.

pioneering advertising Primary-demand advertising in the introductory stage of the product life cycle.

place utility The utility created when a product is made readily accessible to potential customers.

planned obsolescence A product strategy designed to make an existing product out of date and thus to increase the market for replacement products. There are two forms: technological and style.

planning The process of deciding now what one is going to do later, including when and how one is going to do it.

positioning A company's strategies and actions related to favourably distinguishing itself and its products from competitors in the minds (and hearts) of selected groups of consumers.

possession utility The utility created when a customer buys the product — when ownership is transferred to the buyer.

postage-stamp pricing See *uniform delivered price*.

postpurchase behaviour Efforts by the consumer to reduce the anxiety often accompanying purchase decisions.

postpurchase service The final stage of the selling process, including delivery, financing, installation, routine maintenance, employee training, billing, and other areas important to customer satisfaction.

pretest An activity in which commercials in finished or nearly finished form are presented to panels of consumers in order to gauge their reactions.

price The amount of money and/or products needed to acquire some combination of another product and its accompanying services.

price competition A strategy in which a firm regularly offers prices that are as low as possible, usually accompanied by a minimum of services.

price discrimination A situation in which different customers pay different prices for the same product.

price lining A retail pricing strategy whereby a store selects a limited number of prices and sells each item only at one of these selected prices.

price war A form of price competition that begins when one firm decreases its price in an effort to increase its sales volume and/or market share, the other firms retaliate by reducing prices on competing products, and additional price decreases by the original price cutter and/or its competitors usually follow.

pricing objective The goals that management tries to reach with its pricing structure and strategies.

primary data Original data gathered specifically for the project at hand.

primary demand The market demand for a general category of products (in contrast to the selective demand for a particular brand of the product).

primary-demand advertising Advertising designed to stimulate demand for a generic product.

private label A brand name that is owned by a retailer or wholesaler.

private warehouse A warehouse that is owned and operated by the firm whose products are being stored and handled at the facility.

producer's brand A brand that is owned by a manufacturer or other producer. Same as *national brand*.

product A set of tangible attributes, including packaging, colour, price, quality, and brand, plus the services and reputation of the seller. A product may be a good, service, place, person, or idea.

product advertising Advertising intended to inform or stimulate the market about an organization's products.

product development A product-market growth strategy that calls for a company to develop new products to sell to its existing markets.

product differentiation The strategy in which one firm promotes the features of its product over competitors' brands offered to the same market.

product-liability claim A legal action alleging that an illness, accident, or death resulted from the named product because it was harmful, faulty, or inadequately labelled.

product life cycle The stages a product goes through from its introduction, to its growth and maturity, to its eventual decline and death (withdrawal from the market or deletion from the company's offerings).

product line A broad group of products, intended for essentially similar uses and possessing reasonably similar physical characteristics.

product manager An executive responsible for planning the marketing program for a given product or group of products. Same as *brand manager*.

product-market growth matrix A planning model that consists of four alternative growth strategies, based on whether an organization will be selling its present products or new products to its present markets or new markets.

product mix All products offered for sale by a company.

product positioning The decisions and activities involved in developing the intended image (in the customer's mind) for a product in relation to competitive products and to other products marketed by the same company.

product-related segmentation Market segmentation based on product usage rate or product benefits desired by consumers.

production-orientation stage The first stage in the evolution of marketing management, in which the basic assumption is that making a good product will ensure business success.

promotion The element in an organization's marketing mix that is used to inform, persuade, and remind the market regarding the organization and/or its products.

promotional allowance A price reduction granted by the seller as payment for promotional services rendered by the buyer.

prospecting The stage in the personal selling process that involves developing a list of potential customers.

psychographic segmentation Market segmentation based on some aspect(s) of consumers' personality, lifestyle, or social class.

psychographics A concept in consumer behaviour that describes consumers in terms of a combination of psychological and sociological influences.

public relations A broad communications effort designed to build or maintain a favourable image for an organization with its various publics.

public-service advertising Advertising designed to improve the quality of life and indicate that the advertiser is a responsible member of the community.

public warehouse An independent firm that provides storage and handling facilities.

publicity A news presentation for a product or organization presented in any medium that is not paid for and has the credibility of editorial material.

"pull" promotional strategy Promotional effort directed primarily at intermediaries that are the next link forward in distribution channels.

qualifying The stage in the personal selling process in which the sales person determines if the prospect has both the willingness and capability to buy.

qualitative performance bases In sales force performance, judgmental indications of inputs and/or outputs.

qualitative research A form of marketing research that is usually employed for exploratory purposes that examines consumers' deeply held views, opinions, and feelings. Includes focus group interviews and one-on-one depth interviews.

quality How well a product or service meets the expectations of the customer.

quantitative performance bases In sales force performance, numerical measure of inputs and/or outputs.

quantitative research A form of marketing research that is intended to obtain statistical information about a sample of consumers or members of the public. Usually relies on surveys to collect the data.

quantity discount A reduction from list price when large quantities are purchased; offered to encourage buyers to purchase in large quantities.

questionnaire A data-gathering form used to collect the information in a personal, telephone, or mail survey.

rack jobber A merchant wholesaler that provides its customers with the display case or rack, stocks it, and price-marks the merchandise.

random sample A sample that is selected in such a way that every unit in the defined universe has an equal chance of being selected.

raw materials Business goods that have not been processed in any way and that will become part of another product.

recipient market See *client market.*

reciprocity The situation of "I'll buy from you if you'll buy from me."

recovery The process of correcting the situation when a customer is dissatisfied with service provided. A company may attempt to recover from a poor service experience by apologizing or by offering the customer a price reduction or other form of compensation.

reference group A group of people who influence a person's attitudes, values, and behaviour.

refusal to deal A situation in which a manufacturer desiring to select and perhaps control its channels may refuse to sell to some intermediaries.

regional shopping centre The largest type of planned suburban shopping centre (sometimes large enough to be a mini-downtown). Usually includes two or more department stores and many limited-line stores, along with service institutions such as banks, theatres, restaurants, hotels, and office buildings.

relationship marketing An attempt by a sales person or company to develop a deeper, longer-lasting relationship built on trust with key customers — usually larger accounts.

repositioning The process of moving a company or a store or a brand to a new position in the minds of target customers, usually by changing its image.

resale price maintenance A pricing policy whereby the manufacturer sets the retail price for a product.

reseller market Wholesaling and retailing intermediaries that buy products for resale to other business users or to consumers. A segment of the business market.

resident buyer An independent agent located in central market who buys for wholesalers and retailers located in outlying areas.

retail trade See *retailing.*

retailer A firm engaged primarily in retailing.

retailer co-operative A type of contractual vertical marketing system that is formed by a group of small retailers who agree to establish and operate a wholesale warehouse.

retailing The sale, and all activities directly related to the sale, of goods and services to ultimate consumers for personal, nonbusiness use. Same as *retail trade.*

retention The objective of keeping existing customers; the understanding being that the longer a customer continues to do business with a company, the more profitable the customer becomes.

sales engineer A selling job, often involving technically trained individuals selling some kind of sophisticated equipment, in which the emphasis is on the sales person's ability to explain the product to the prospect and perhaps to adapt it to the customer's particular needs.

sales-force composite A method of forecasting sales that consists of collecting from all sales people and intermediaries an estimate of sales in their territories during the forecasting period.

sales-force selection task The three steps in assembling a sales force, consisting of (1) determining the number and type of people wanted by preparing a written job description, (2) recruiting an adequate number of applicants, and (3) selecting the most qualified persons from among the applicants.

sales forecast An estimate of likely sales for one company's brand of a product during a stated time period in a specific market and assuming the use of a predetermined marketing plan.

sales-orientation stage The second stage in the evolution of marketing management, in which the emphasis is on selling whatever the organization produces.

sales potential The portion of market potential, applying only to one company's brand of a product, that a specific company could expect to achieve under ideal conditions.

sales promotion Activities, including contests for sales people and consumers, trade shows, in-store displays, samples, premiums, and coupons, that are designed to supplement advertising and co-ordinate personal selling.

sales-volume analysis A detailed study of the "net sales" section of a company's profit and loss statement.

satisfaction The consumer condition when experience with a product or service equals or exceeds expectations.

satisfaction utility A situation that exists when a customer is pleased with the product or service and it meets the individual's expectations about usefulness.

scrambled merchandising A strategy under which an intermediary diversifies its assortment by adding product lines not traditionally carried by its type of business.

seasonal discount A discount for placing an order during the seller's slow season.

secondary data Information already gathered by somebody else for some other purpose.

selective attention The process that limits our perceptions such that, of all the marketing stimuli our senses are exposed to, only those able to capture and hold our attention have the potential of being perceived.

selective demand The market demand for an individual brand of a product, in contrast to the primary demand for the broad product category.

selective-demand advertising Advertising that is intended to stimulate demand for individual brands.

selective distortion The process of mentally altering information that is inconsistent with one's own beliefs or attitudes.

selective distribution A strategy in which a producer sells its product through multiple, but not all, wholesalers and/or retailers in a market where a consumer might reasonably look for it.

selective retention The process of retaining in memory some portion of what is perceived.

self-concept A person's self-image.

self-image The idea or image one has of oneself.

selling agent A type of independent intermediary that essentially takes the place of a manufacturer's marketing department, marketing the manufacturer's entire output and often influencing the design and/or pricing of the products.

service An activity that is separately identifiable, intangible, and the main object of a transaction designed to provide want-satisfaction for customers.

service encounter In services marketing, a customer's interaction with any service employee or with any tangible element, such as a service's physical surroundings.

service quality The value that consumers perceive they are receiving from their purchase of services; generally very difficult to measure.

shopping centre A planned grouping of retail stores in a multiunit structure, with the physical structure usually owned by a single organization.

shopping goods A class of consumer products that are purchased after the buyer has spent some time and effort comparing the price, quality, colour, and/or other attributes of alternative products.

shopping-mall intercept A method of gathering data by conducting personal interviews in central locations, typically regional shopping centres.

simulated test market A confidential variation of test marketing in which consumers are shown advertising for a product and then are allowed to "shop" in a test store in order to measure their reactions to the advertising, the product, or both.

single-segment concentration strategy The selection of one homogeneous segment from within a total market to be the target market.

single-source data A data-gathering method in which exposure to television advertising and product purchases can be traced to individual households.

singles Households that consist of just one person.

situation analysis The stage in a marketing research study that involves obtaining information about the company and its business environment by means of library research and extensive interviewing of company officials.

situational influences Temporary forces, associated with the immediate purchase environment, that affect behaviour.

skimming pricing A pricing strategy in which the initial price is set high in the range of expected prices. Same as *market-skimming pricing*.

social and cultural forces A set of factors, including lifestyles, social values, and beliefs, that affect the marketing activities of an organization.

social class A division of society based on education, occupation, and type of residential neighbourhood.

social environment Family, friends, and acquaintances who directly or indirectly provide information about products.

social responsibility The commitment on the part of a company to improving the well-being of society.

societal marketing concept A revised version of the marketing concept under which a company recognizes that it should be concerned about not only the buyers of a firm's product but also other people directly affected by the firm's operations and not only with tomorrow but also with the long term.

specialty goods A class of consumer products with perceived unique characteristics such that consumers are willing to expend special effort to buy them.

specialty store A type of retail institution concentrating on a specialized product line, or even part of a specialized product line.

stabilizing prices A pricing goal designed to achieve steady, nonvolatile prices in an industry.

Standard Industrial Classification (SIC) system A coding system developed by the federal government that groups firms into similar types of businesses and thus enables a company to identify and analyze small segments of its market.

stars According to the Boston Consulting Group matrix, strategic business units that are characterized by high market shares and high industry growth rates.

stimulus-response theory The theory that learning occurs as a person responds to some stimuli and is rewarded with need satisfaction for a correct response or penalized for an incorrect one.

stockturn rate The number of times the average inventory is turned over, or sold, during the period under study.

storage An activity in physical distribution that creates time utility by holding and preserving products from the time of production until their sale.

straight commission compensation The method of sales force compensation in which payment is directly related to the tasks performed, usually the volume of the product(s) sold.

straight rebuy In the business market, a routine purchase with minimal information needs.

straight salary compensation The method of sales force compensation in which the sales person is paid a fixed amount, regardless of tasks performed or level of performance.

strategic business unit (SBU) A separate division for a major product or market in a multiproduct or multibusiness organization.

strategic company planning The level of planning that consists of (1) defining the organization's mission, (2) setting organizational objectives, (3) evaluating the firm's strategic business units, and (4) selecting appropriate strategies so as to achieve the organization's objectives.

strategic marketing planning The level of planning that consists of (1) conducting a situation analysis, (2) determining marketing objectives, (3) selecting target markets and measuring the market, and (4) designing a strategic marketing mix.

strategic planning The managerial process of matching a firm's resources with its market opportunities over the long run.

strategy A broad plan of action by which an organization intends to reach its objective(s).

style A distinctive presentation or construction in any art, product, or activity.

style obsolescence A product strategy in which superficial characteristics of a product are altered so that the new model is easily differentiated from the old one in order to make people dissatisfied with the old model. Same as *fashion obsolescence*.

subculture Groups that exhibit characteristic behaviour patterns sufficient to distinguish them from other groups within the same culture.

substitute products Two or more products that satisfy essentially the same need(s).

superego In Freudian psychology, the part of the mind that houses the conscience and directs instinctive drives into socially acceptable channels.

supermarket A type of retailing institution that has a moderately broad and moderately deep product assortment spanning groceries and some nonfood lines, that offers relatively few customer services, and that ordinarily emphasizes price in either an offensive or defensive way.

supermarket retailing A retailing method that features several related product lines, a high degree of self-service, largely centralized checkout, and competitive prices.

suppliers The people or firms that supply the goods or services that an organization needs to produce what it sells.

survey method A method of gathering data by interviewing a limited number of people (a sample) in person or by telephone or mail.

survey of buyer intentions A form of sales forecasting in which a firm asks a sample of current or potential customers how much of a particular product they would buy at a given price during a specified future time period.

SWOT analysis Identifying and evaluating an organization's most significant strengths, weaknesses, opportunities, and threats.

syndicated data Research information that is purchased from a research supplier on a shared-cost basis by a number of clients.

tactic An operational means by which a strategy is to be implemented or activated.

target market A group of customers (people or organizations) at whom a seller aims its marketing effort.

target return A pricing goal that involves setting prices so as to achieve a certain percentage return on investment or on net sales.

tariff A tax imposed on a product entering a country.

task method A method of determining the promotional appropriation under which the organization first decides what is to be accomplished and then calculates how much it will cost to reach this goal. Same as *build-up method.*

telemarketing A form of nonstore retailing in which a sales person initiates contact with a shopper and closes the sale over the telephone.

telephone survey A method of gathering data in a survey by interviewing people over the telephone.

televised shopping One form of direct marketing, in which TV channels and shows sell consumer electronics, jewellery, and other products at relatively low prices.

test marketing A marketing research technique in which a firm markets its product in a limited geographic area, measures the sales, and then — from this sample — projects (a) the company's sales over a larger area and/or (b) consumers' response to a strategy before committing to a major marketing effort.

time utility The utility created when a product is available to customers when they want it.

total cost The sum of total fixed costs and total variable costs, or the full cost of a specific quantity produced or sold.

total cost concept In physical distribution, the optimization of the cost-profit relationship for the entire physical distribution system, rather than for individual activities.

total quality management (TQM) A philosophy as well as specific procedures, policies, and practices that commit an organization to continuous quality improvement in all of its activities.

trade discount A reduction from the list price, offered by a seller to buyers in payment for marketing activities that they will perform. Same as *functional discount.*

trade promotion The type of sales promotion that is directed at members of a distribution channel.

trademark A brand that is legally protected.

trademark licensing A business arrangement in which the owner of a trademark grants permission to other firms to use the owner's brand name, logo-type, and/or character on the licensee's products in return for a royalty on sales of those products. Same as *brand licensing.*

trading down A product-line strategy wherein a company adds a lower-priced item to its line of prestige goods in order to reach a market that cannot afford the higher-priced items.

trading up A product-line strategy wherein a company adds a higher-priced, prestige product to its line in order to increase sales of the existing lower-priced products in that line and attract a higher-income market.

trend analysis A method of forecasting sales over the long term by using regression analysis, or over the short term by using a seasonal index of sales.

trial close The stage in the personal selling process when the sales person poses some "either–or" questions in such a way that the customer's answer is intended to close the sale.

trickle-across cycle In fashion adoption, a fashion cycle that moves horizontally within several social classes at the same time.

trickle-down cycle In fashion adoption, a fashion cycle that flows downward through several socioeconomic classes.

trickle-up cycle In fashion adoption, a fashion cycle by which a style becomes popular (fashionable) first with lower socioeconomic classes and then, later, with higher socioeconomic groups.

truck jobber A limited-function merchant wholesaler that carries a selected line of perishable products and delivers them by truck to retail stores.

trust-building processes A combination of sales person and selling-firm characteristics that combine to allow a buyer to have trust in the seller and its representative.

tying contract A contract under which a manufacturer sells a product to an intermediary only under the condition that this intermediary also buys another (possibly unwanted) product from the manufacturer.

ultimate consumers People who buy products for their personal, nonbusiness use.

uniform delivered price A geographic pricing strategy whereby the same delivered price is quoted to all buyers regardless of their location. Same as *postage-stamp pricing*.

unsought goods A type of consumer product that consists of new products the consumer is not yet aware of or products the consumer does not yet want.

unstructured interview In sales force selection, an interviewing procedure in which the interviewer is permitted the freedom to ask questions and explore issues as they develop in the flow of the interview.

users The people in a buying centre who actually use a particular product.

utility The attribute in an item that makes it capable of satisfying human wants.

VALS A psychographic segmentation tool, developed by a research firm, that divided adults into nine segments based on similarities in their values and life-styles.

value The quantitative measure of the worth of a product to attract other products in exchange.

variable cost A cost that varies of changes directly in relation to the number of units produced or sold.

variable-price strategy See *flexible-price strategy*.

vertical business market A situation in which a given product is usable by virtually all the firms in only one or two industries.

vertical conflict A form of channel conflict occurring between firms at different levels of the same channel, typically producer versus wholesaler or producer versus retailer.

vertical co-operative advertising Advertising in which firms at different levels of the distribution channel share the cost.

vertical marketing system (VMS) A tightly co-ordinated distribution channel designed to achieve operating efficiencies and marketing effectiveness.

voluntary chain A type of contractual vertical marketing system that is sponsored by a wholesaler who enters into a contract with interested retailers.

warehouse club A combined retailing and wholesaling institution that has a very broad but very shallow product assortment with very low prices and few customer services and is open only to members. Same as *wholesale club*.

warehousing A broad range of physical distribution activities that include storage, assembling, bulk breaking, and preparing products for shipping.

warning label The part of a product that tells consumers not to misuse the product and informs them of almost every conceivable danger associated with using it.

warranty An assurance given to buyers that they will be compensated in case the product does not perform up to reasonable expectations.

wheel of retailing The cyclical pattern of changes in retailing, whereby a new type of store enters the market as a low-cost, low-price store and over time takes business away from unchanging competitors; eventually, the successful new retailer trades up, incurring higher costs and higher prices and making the institution vulnerable to a new type of retailer.

wholesale club See *warehouse club*.

wholesaler See *merchant wholesaler*.

wholesaling All activities directly related to the sale of goods and services to parties for resale, use in producing other goods and services, or operating an organization.

wholesaling intermediary A firm engaged primarily in wholesaling.

wholly owned subsidiary A business arrangement in foreign markets in which a company owns the foreign operation in order to gain maximum control over its marketing program and production operations.

World Trade Organization An organization, formed in 1948 and now comprising over one hundred countries, that seeks to develop fair-trade practices among its members.

zone-delivered price A geographic pricing strategy whereby the same delivered price is charged at any location within each geographic zone.

Topical Index

Company and Brand Name Index

Credits

Statistics Canada information is used with the permission of the Minister of Industry, as Minister responsible for Statistics Canada. Information on the availability of the wide range of data from Statistics Canada can be obtained from Statistics Canada's Regional Offices, its World Wide Web site at http://www.statcan.ca, and its toll-free access number 1-800-263-1136.

CHAPTER 1

p. 2, Courtesy of Royal Bank of Canada.
p. 15, Courtesy of General Motors of Canada Limited, Goodwrench Service.
p. 20, Courtesy of Liberty Health, Canada.

CHAPTER 2

p. 24, Courtesy of McDonald's Restaurants of Canada Limited
p. 32, *The Globe and Mail,* Toronto.
p. 36, Courtesy of IBM Corporation.

CHAPTER 3

p. 44, Used by permission of Chapters Inc.
p. 49, Courtesy of mbanx.
p. 59, Courtesy of Chrysler Canada.

CHAPTER 4

p. 74, Courtesy of YMCA Canada.
p. 80, Courtesy of Chrysler Canada.
p. 89, Becel is a Registered Trade-mark owned by Lipton.

CHAPTER 5

p. 100, Courtesy of Saturn Canada.
p. 112, Courtesy of Rolex Watch Company of Canada Limited.
p. 115, Reproduced with permission of Labatt Brewing Company Limited.

CHAPTER 6

p. 124, Courtesy of Canadian Airlines.
p. 129, Courtesy of IBM Corporation.
p. 132, Advertisement courtesy of Ralston Purina Canada Inc.
p. 141, Courtesy of Lever Pond's, Toronto, Ontario.

CHAPTER 7

p. 152, *The Globe and Mail,* Toronto.
p. 164, Courtesy of Dell Canada.

CHAPTER 8

p. 174, Image Bank/J. Silverman.
p. 184, Courtesy of Zellers and Club Z.
p. 191, Courtesy of the Creative Research Group Limited.

CHAPTER 9

p. 215, *The Globe and Mail,* Toronto.
p. 223, Reprinted with permission of 3M Canada Company.
p. 228, Courtesy of *Maclean's* Magazine and Maclean's TV.

CHAPTER 10

p. 238, *Toronto Sun.*
p. 242, Courtesy of Just white shirts and black socks.
p. 253, Courtesy of Club Monaco. Photo by Walter Chin.

CHAPTER 11

p. 258, Courtesy of Second Cup Coffee Co.
p. 262, Courtesy of Roots Co-Founders, Michael Budman & Don Green.
p. 274, Courtesy of Linsey Foods Ltd. Creative by the Gencom Group. Photography by Michael Mahovlich.

CHAPTER 12

p. 282, Courtesy of The Loyalty Group.
p. 288, *The Globe and Mail,* Toronto.
p. 295, *The Globe and Mail,* Toronto.

CHAPTER 13

p. 314, Copyright © 1997, ING Bank of Canada.
p. 318, Courtesy of Bell Canada.
p. 328, Gruner/Light Images.

CHAPTER 14

p. 338, Courtesy of Bombardier.
p. 342, Courtesy of Fujitsu Canada, Inc.
p. 352, Ad created and produced by Grace & Rothschild, New York, New York. Courtesy of Land Rover Canada Inc. Mississauga, Ontario.

CHAPTER 15

p. 362, *The Globe and Mail,* Toronto.
p. 370, Alan Pink is President of Canplan Travel Halifax, NS, as well as President of the Association of Canadian Travel Agents (Atlantic Division).
p. 377, Printed with permission of Ryder Integrated Logistics.

CHAPTER 16

p. 386, Courtesy of Weber Supply Company Inc.
p. 400, Printed with permission of Ryder Integrated Logistics.
p. 403, Courtesy of Weber Supply Company Inc.

CHAPTER 17

p. 410, Courtesy of Amazon.com, Inc.
p. 421, *The Globe and Mail,* Toronto.
p. 427, Photo: Perry Zavitz.

CHAPTER 18

p. 446, Courtesy of General Motors of Canada Limited.
p. 455, Courtesy of Westin Hotels & Resorts.
p. 459, Courtesy of The Wool Bureau of Canada.

CHAPTER 19

p. 468, Courtesy of the Canadian Professional Sales Association.
p. 474, Courtesy of Radio Shack.
p. 479, Bruce Zake.

CHAPTER 20

p. 488, Courtesy of Omega®
p. 493, Courtesy of General Motors of Canada Limited.
p. 504, *The Globe and Mail,* Toronto.

CHAPTER 21

p. 526, *The Globe and Mail,* Toronto.
p. 531, Courtesy of Nortel (Northern Telecom).
p. 537, Courtesy of McCarthy Tétrault.

CHAPTER 22

p. 546, Courtesy of Sergiu Comissiona, Music Director, the Vancouver Symphony. Photography: David Cooper.
p. 550, Courtesy of Hincks Centre for Childrens Mental Health and Invest in Kids Foundation.

CHAPTER 23

p. 562, Wolf Kutnahovsky.
p. 566, Courtesy of Drake International.
p. 575, Courtesy of SAS Institute.

CHAPTER 24

p. 584, Courtesy of Ford of Canada.
p. 601, Courtesy of Canadian Pacific.
p. 606, Courtesy of Chrysler Canada.

CASE 1–1

p. 523, Courtesy of The Salvation Army and BBDO Canada.

CASE 7–1

pp. 612–15, With the permission of W.K. Buckley Limited.

cut here

STUDENT REPLY CARD

In order to improve future editions, we are seeking your comments on *Fundamentals of Marketing*, Eighth Canadian Edition, by Sommers, Barnes, and Stanton. Please answer the following questions and return this form via Business Reply Mail. Your opinions matter. Thank you in advance for sharing them with us!

Name of your college or university: ____________________

Major program of study: ____________________

Course title: ____________________

Were you required to buy this book? yes _______ no _______

Did you buy this book new or used? new _______ used _______ ($_______)

Do you plan to keep or sell this book? keep _______ sell _______

Is the order of topic coverage consistent with what was taught in your course?

cut here

fold here

Are there chapters or sections of this text that were not assigned for your course? Please specify:

Were there topics covered in your course that are not included in this text? Please specify:

What did you like most about this text?

What did you like least?

If you would like to say more, we'd love to hear from you. Please write to us at the address shown on the reverse of this card.

cut here

fold here

cut here

MAIL POSTE

Canada Post Corporation/Société des postes

Postage Paid — Port payé

if mailed in Canada — si posté au Canada

Business Reply — Réponse d'affaires

0183560299 01

Att.: Senior Sponsoring Editor
College Division
McGRAW-HILL RYERSON LIMITED
300 WATER STREET
WHITBY ON L1N 9Z9